The Encyclopedia of Public Choice

Volume II

The Encyclopedia
of
Public Choice

Editors

CHARLES K. ROWLEY

The Locke Institute, and
George Mason University

and

FRIEDRICH SCHNEIDER

Johannes Kepler University of Linz,
Institute of Economic Policy

Kluwer Academic Publishers

DORDRECHT / BOSTON / LONDON

Distributors for North, Central and South America:
Kluwer Academic Publishers
101 Philip Drive
Assinippi Park
Norwell, Massachusetts 02061 USA
Telephone (781) 871-6600
Fax (781) 871-6528
E-Mail <kluwer@wkap.com>

Distributors for all other countries:
Kluwer Academic Publishers Group
Post Office Box 322
3300 AH Dordrecht, THE NETHERLANDS
Telephone 31 78 6576 000
Fax 31 78 6576 474
E-Mail <orderdept@wkap.nl>

 Electronic Services <http://www.wkap.nl>

Library of Congress Cataloging-in-Publication

The encyclopedia of public choice / editors, Charles Rowley and Friedrich Schneider.
    p. cm.
  Includes bibliographical references and index.
  ISBN 0-7923-8607-8 (alk. paper)
  ISBN 0-306-47828-5 (electronic)
  ISBN 0-306-47830-7 (electronic plus print)
    1. Policy sciences–Encyclopedias. 2. Economic policy–Encyclopedias.
3. Social policy–Encyclopedias. 1. Rowley, Charles Kershaw. II. Schneider, Friedrich.

H41.E57 2004
320'.6'03–dc21   2003046109

We dedicate 'The Encyclopedia of Public Choice'
to the memory of

Duncan Black
23 May 1908 to 14 January 1991

The Founding Father of Public Choice

TABLE OF CONTENTS

CONCEPTS

PREFACE

The Encyclopedia provides a detailed and comprehensive account of the subject known as *public choice*. However, the title would not convey sufficiently the breadth of the Encyclopedia's contents which can be summarized better as the fruitful interchange of economics, political science and moral philosophy on the basis of an image of man as a purposive and responsible actor who pursues his own objectives as efficiently as possible.

This fruitful interchange between the fields outlined above existed during the late eighteenth century during the brief period of the Scottish Enlightenment when such great scholars as David Hume, Adam Ferguson and Adam Smith contributed to all these fields, and more. However, as intellectual specialization gradually replaced broad-based scholarship from the mid-nineteenth century onwards, it became increasingly rare to find a scholar making major contributions to more than one.

Once Alfred Marshall defined economics in neoclassical terms, as a narrow positive discipline, the link between economics, political science and moral philosophy was all but severed and economists redefined their role into that of 'the humble dentist' providing technical economic information as inputs to improve the performance of impartial, benevolent and omniscient governments in their attempts to promote the public interest. This indeed was the dominant view within an economics profession that had become besotted by the economics of John Maynard Keynes and Paul Samuelson immediately following the end of the Second World War.

Even during this 'dark age' for political economy, however, a little known Scot named Duncan Black was sowing the seeds for a *renaissance* that would once again provide for a reunion between economics and political science. Black launched the public choice research program in 1948 with a seminal paper on the rationale of group decision-making and in so doing earned later fame as the founding father of public choice.

Black's seminal contribution was extended in 1951 by Kenneth Arrow in his famous 1951 monograph entitled *Social Choice and Individual Values*. A further major extension occurred in 1957, when Anthony Downs published his seminal book entitled *An Economic Theory of Democracy*.

In 1962, James Buchanan and Gordon Tullock, in their famous book *The Calculus of Consent*, extended the perspective of public choice by shifting attention away from direct elections and parliamentary democracy, to outline a rational choice approach to the logical foundations of a constitutional republic. In 1965, Mancur Olson opened up the discussion of interest group behavior to rational choice analysis in his famous book entitled *The Logic of Collective Action*. In 1971 William A. Niskanen opened up the discussion of bureaucratic behavior to rational choice analysis in his book entitled *Bureaucracy and Representative Government*.

These six contributions constitute the foundations of the public choice research program. Two other books also contributed to the early public choice tradition, namely the 1951 monograph by Black and Newing entitled *Committee Decisions with Complementary Valuation* and the 1962 masterpiece by William Riker entitled *The Theory of Political Coalitions*. All these works are as relevant to scholars of public choice now as they were several decades ago when they were written.

Since public choice first emerged during the years of reconstruction from the devastation of the Second World War, the world's political environment has evolved and changed dramatically. The Marshall Plan enabled Western Europe to eliminate its dictatorships and to establish and/or to reinforce democracy. The European colonial powers eased themselves out of their imperial roles, releasing their former colonies into independence, albeit in many cases an independence that rapidly deteriorated into the one party state, outright dictatorship or even kleptocracy. Even Latin-America slowly has eased itself into democracy, albeit in many cases of a fragile and unstable nature.

The United States utilized its economic strength and its political resilience to confront and to contain the USSR throughout the Cold War and eventually to defeat it, thus opening up Eastern Europe and even Russia itself to varying forms of democratic or semi-democratic government. The remaining communist dictatorships, notably The People's Republic of China, Cuba and North Korea, clearly are endangered species, unlikely to survive the first decade of the new century. The last bastions of non-communist, non-sub-Saharan African dictatorship, mostly located in the Middle East, are finding it increasingly costly and difficult to fend off the democratic desires of their down-trodden and mostly impoverished subjects. For the first time in the history of the world, a majority of individuals now live under conditions of democracy, a state that public choice is uniquely qualified to analyze.

Given the enormity of the political changes outlined above, it is very reassuring to discover, not least through the contributions to this Encyclopedia, that public choice has retained its ability to explain and to predict the behavior of all actors in political markets — even the behavior of al-Qaeda terrorists — within the framework of the rational choice approach.

The Encyclopedia of Public Choice is a monumental offering. It consists of 306 entries each assigned to one of three headings, namely essays, concepts and biographies. The Encyclopedia is an entirely new work, all its contributions being newly commissioned. Drafts of the entries were received from the authors over the period October 2001 through September 2002, most of them arriving during the six months March 2002 through August 2002.

The essays are designed to be far-ranging discussions of central issues in the public choice literature, and evaluations of the lives and works of some of the founding fathers, each written by authors who have worked extensively in those fields. The authors were asked to avoid writing surveys, but rather to present their own views on the topic under review.

The concepts are designed to be more narrowly-focused contributions, offering up-to-date introductions and first-rate bibliographies. Once again, the authors were expected to explicate their own views and not to attempt to write a comprehensive survey. In several cases, where the issue was deemed to be sufficiently controversial, authors with differing viewpoints provide competing interpretations.

Every contributor to the essay and/or the concepts sections of the Encyclopedia was invited to contribute his or her own biography. The large majority complied. These are short outlines modeled on Mark Blaug's *Who's Who in Economics*. They provide interested readers with a short biography, a limited list of publications and a brief statement of the scholar's self-perceived career contribution to public choice.

The allocation of entries across these three categories is as follows: 28 essays, including two introductions, one by Charles K. Rowley and one by Dennis C. Mueller; 186 concepts; and 92 biographies. The Encyclopedia itself consists of well in excess of one million words. The contributors, and the editors, have taken care to make the language of the Encyclopedia as non-technical and comprehensible as possible. For this reason, the Encyclopedia should be accessible to all scholars, all graduate and undergraduate students of economics, political science, and public choice as well as to most scholars and students of such closely related disciplines as law, philosophy, sociology and psychology. The Encyclopedia should be an indispensable companion to all practitioners of public policy.

The editors have made every effort to present a well-balanced and comprehensive body of public choice scholarship from the early beginnings of the discipline to its current flourishing state. By and large, we believe that we have achieved this goal. However, as always, the proof of the pudding is in the eating. We trust that you will enjoy the rich banquet that is set before you.

CHARLES K. ROWLEY
Duncan Black Professor of Economics
George Mason University and
General Director
The Locke Institute

and

PROFESSOR DR. DR. h.c.mult. FRIEDRICH SCHNEIDER
Department of Economics
University of Linz

REFERENCES

Arrow, K.F. (1950). "A difficulty in the concept of social welfare." *Journal of Political Economy*, 58: 328–346.

Arrow, K.J. *Social Choice and Individual Values*. New York: Wiley.

Black, D. (1948). "On the rationale of group decision-making." *Journal of Political Economy*, 56: 23–34.

Black, D. and Newing, R.A. (1951). *Committee Decisions with Complementary Valuation*. London: W. Hodge.

Blaug, M. (2000). *Who's Who in Economics*. Cheltenham, UK and Northampton, USA: Edward Elgar Publishing.

Buchanan, J.M. and Tullock, G. (1962). *The Calculus of Consent*. Ann Arbor: University of Michigan Press.

Downs, A. (1957). *An Economic Theory of Democracy*. New York: Harper & Row.

Niskanen, W.A. (1971). *Bureaucracy and Representative Government*. New York: Aldine-Atherton.

Olson, M. *The Logic of Collective Action*. Cambridge: Harvard University Press.

Riker, W. (1962). *The Theory of Political Coalitions*. New Haven: Yale University Press.

ACKNOWLEDGMENTS

Our acknowledgments are due first to each scholar who has contributed to this Encyclopedia, and most especially to those who have made multiple contributions. Their enthusiasm and commitment to the project made our editorial task much easier than it would otherwise have been. We are especially indebted to the members of the distinguished Advisory Board (listed separately at the beginning of this volume) whose responses to our request for advice and help were always friendly and helpful. In particular we are indebted to William F. Shughart II and Robert D. Tollison whose help and intellectual support went far beyond anything that we could possibly expect.

We are also indebted to Marilea Polk Fried and Marian Scott at Kluwer Academic Publishers, both for their editorial help, and for their persistence in making sure that we adhered to deadlines.

The project was organized through the auspices of The Locke Institute in Fairfax, Virginia. The Locke Institute acknowledges with deep gratitude the financial support of the following individuals and foundations, without whose generosity, we could not successfully have completed this project: James T. Bennett; Robert S. Elgin; Daniel Oliver; Gordon Tullock; The Chase Foundation of Virginia and the Sunmark Foundation.

Charles Rowley is grateful to the James M. Buchanan Center for Political Economy for summer research support, and to Anne Rathbone for project support.

Concepts

A

ACADEMIA

In the history of the human race, the medieval university stands out as one of the great political institutions of all time. It drew Western Europe out of the Dark Ages and into the light. It invented cosmopolitan structures and norms that are still with us today.

Two archetypes emerged in 12th and 13th century France and Italy. Paris offered a free space for the theological debates that prepared the way for the Reformation. Bologna trained students in the legal statutes and reasoning that would come to support increasingly complex political and economic institutions all over Europe.

In both cases, a complex institution crystallized, the result of a decentralized process of annealing. Both Paris and Bologna were shaped by the conflict with their environment, and in similar ways, but they ended up at opposite ends of the governance spectrum, Paris controlled by its faculty, Bologna by its students.

Paris attracted students from all over Europe. They came to hear the charismatic Peter Abelard apply the scholastic method to questions of speculative theology, such as whether the bread and wine consumed during mass truly turn into the body and blood of Christ, or only in spirit. In an age permeated by religion, in which any position outside of the pale defined by the Church was considered heresy and heretics were burned at the stake, the *sic et non* (pro and con) exploration of a theological issue was nothing short of daring, and Abelard's students picked up on the fact that he was onto something big.

The University of Paris thus started out as an amorphous group of faculty and students collecting in and around the Cathedral School of Notre Dame, with few norms and no internal organizational structure in place. Over the years, the faculty fought with the Church over rights and entitlements, including in particular the right to appoint new faculty. The pope and the emperor were drawn into these fights, and the faculty played them off against each other.

Migration, boycott, and violence pushed forward the cause of the faculty. It helped that the medieval university had no physical plant — the faculty could threaten to leave for another city and take the university (themselves and their students) with them. On occasion, this threat was realized, in

which case it led to the founding of new universities in surrounding cities; mass migration turned out to be the mechanism by which the idea of the university, and its emerging structures, spread.

As each bitter conflict was resolved, some protective piece of structure fell into place — some right was awarded here, another entitlement there. Pieces of structure were negotiated to prevent future conflict, or to encourage non-violent conflict resolution, or for damage control purposes. In this way, over the course of a century, an extraordinarily complex institution emerged brick by protective brick. In a decentralized process planned by nobody, structures evolved that protected the inhabitants of the university from the outside world. Thus, in the midst of the Middle Ages, an era not known for its intellectual tolerance, the university carved out a safe space for intellectual inquiry.

Because it was the faculty who led the fight against the Church, Paris ended up with a governance structure dominated by the faculty: it was the faculty who voted on the issues of the day, staffed the administration, set the curriculum, and appointed new faculty.

As the university became increasingly differentiated into schools and departments, and factions within schools and departments, and factions within factions, it became internally conflicted. The members of a faction tend to reserve the most intense feelings of hatred for their intellectual neighbors rather than for the inhabitants of far-away worlds. This makes it very hard for faculty in the same, or closely related, fields to agree on appointments and curriculum design.

Protective structures followed faculty infighting: strong walls sprang up to separate the departments and schools, and federalist structures emerged. The voting procedures that aggregated the preferences within and across departments and schools became ever more complex. The university thus developed an intricate internal organization to protect the faculty from each other.

Meanwhile, students flocked from over the mountains (the northern and western parts of Western Europe) to study law in Bologna, and it was they who led the fight that created a university. Foreign students did not have the same rights and entitlements as the citizens of Bologna. They were vulnerable to exploitation by the local townspeople, especially landlords and tradesmen, with no legal recourse. If a drunken student got into a fight and killed a local, he would be judged by a jury consisting of local citizens, and the outcome would not generally be favorable — hence the students' demand to be judged by their student peers.

The foreign students banded together for reasons of protection. They formed nations, that is, groupings of students with shared geographic origins. Collectively, the students fought the Commune of Bologna for rights and entitlements. Here, too, the weapons of choice were migration, boycott, and violence. Once again, in the course of a century a complex institution emerged, loaded with rights and entitlements protecting its inhabitants from the outside world — but now, because it was the students who carried the water, the university ended up with a governance structure dominated by students: it was the students who voted on the issues of the day, staffed the administration, set the curriculum, and appointed the faculty.

The institutional structures that emerged in Paris and Bologna include bottom-up governance, representative assemblies, decentralized federalist structures, complex voting procedures, and institutionalized forms of conflict resolution (the latter snuffed out the violence that used to be an inevitable by-product of conflict).

The idea of the university emerged, manifesting itself in the norms of *ubique docendi* (the right to teach at any institution after graduating from one of the them), open access, open information, and free inquiry. These norms, powerful as they are, are ultimately derivative to the institutional structures of the university: a norm of free inquiry is not worth much without a structure in place that protects the inquirer from being imprisoned, killed, or (worst of all) excommunicated.

The Middle Ages saw the emergence of complex voting procedures in the Italian city state and of bottom-up governance in the medieval guild; but the politics of the city states remained violence-prone, and the guilds did not exactly embrace ideas of open access and open information. The university was unique in the astonishing combination of structures and norms it developed to let its inhabitants engage in peaceful intellectual inquiry and protect them from the outside world and from each other.

In its early fighting years, the medieval university was as intellectually vibrant as its structures were pliable. Once its structures, and the associated protections, got locked in, the university ossified intellectually. The scholastic method, wild and wonderful in its early years, matured and joined the establishment, finding its apotheosis in Thomas Aquinas' *Summa Theologica* (the title itself has an end-of-history quality, quite unlike Abelard's open-ended *Sic et Non*). The scholastic method degenerated into an ever more refined system of logic-chopping exercises applied in a mindless and mechanical way to questions of great irrelevance, as in, how many angels are there on a pinhead. As the society surrounding the university became more interested in history and language, and more empirically oriented, the scholastic method was doomed.

The medieval university missed the boat come the Renaissance. In Italy, some universities continued to teach the scholastic method for one hundreds years after the society around them had reinvented itself in full. The intellectual underpinnings of the Renaissance were developed in private academies outside of the university. Humanist ideas got picked up by newly founded universities, including universities in Northern Europe far away from the geographic center of Renaissance action.

During the religious wars of the 16th and 17th centuries, institutions of higher learning were established by local rulers seeking prestige and control (the principle of *cuius regio, eius religio* applied not only to countries, but also to universities). The university in Europe was in decline in the 17th century and moribund in the 18th century. It was missing in action during the Enlightenment and the Scientific Revolution, which largely took place outside of the university, in private academies, societies, and salons. Many of the leading scholars and scientists were independently wealthy, and it was their wealth that afforded them "a room of their own," and not the protective structures of the university.

After a steady decline lasting several centuries (and contradicting the idea of history as being an "ever upward-lifting" process), 19th century Germany entered the world stage with a couple of innovations that, together with the inventions of the medieval university, came to define the modern university.

Progressive reformers developed the norms of *Lehrfreiheit* (freedom to teach) and *Lernfreiheit* (freedom to learn). Wilhelm von Humboldt, in particular, promoted the idea that science is not a fixed body of knowledge that students can mechanically learn by heart. Our understanding of the world is necessarily incomplete, and the quest for knowledge is an ongoing enterprise which students must be an integral part of so they can partake in the emerging understanding, which is as much about process as it is about results. Even while Humboldt established the primacy of research over teaching, his humanist approach emphasized the unity of inquiry and learning. It was thus that Germany developed the idea and institution of the deeply specialized research professor who combines research and teaching on a single discipline-based subject.

Deep specialization had a powerful impact. Germany started out economically backward, and an intellectual backwater. It emerged as a leader in the industrial revolution in large part because of its universities. German science and industry flourished as a result of its path-breaking research and teaching in physics, chemistry, agriculture, forestry, and other disciplines of central importance to industrialization.

In the case of Germany, university reform was shaped by an element of design — Humboldt's brilliant ideas as they manifested themselves in the newly founded University of

Berlin. The vibrant German model was copied all over the world, including the United States (Johns Hopkins, Cornell, Chicago). In Germany, it ossified. Deep specialization, and its attendant narrow-mindedness, battled with the humanist desire for holistic understanding — and won. Lack of competition and inflexible bureaucracy contributed to the decline. Today, the German university is largely moribund.

The idea of the university, and its institutional manifestation, was refined over the course of eight centuries. The university is a hybrid mix of bottom-up elements, which were shaped by evolution, and top-down elements, which are the result of deliberate design. The structures and norms of the university allow human beings to conduct systematic and cumulative research and thereby gain a better understanding of the way the world works. The medieval university with its emphasis on speculative theology and law helped Western Europe shake off the yoke of religion and develop complex political and economic institutions, just as the German university contributed to the consolidation of the German nation and the industrialization of the German economy.

The history of the university gives us an idea of what the university is *for*. The university enables deep specialization, and it protects scholars from each other and the outside world.

There is a dark side to the university. Its history is largely a history of ossification punctuated by very occasional bursts of intellectual vibrancy and structural innovation, which typically occur in connection with the founding of new universities. Change occurs through replacement rather than existing scholars, departments, disciplines, and universities going with the times.

The tendency of the university to ossify is an integral part of its two positive functions, specialization and protection. As knowledge cumulates, it necessarily "moves on." Inevitably, areas of inquiry that are vibrant today will be explored to death by tomorrow and dead meat the day after. But a deeply specialized scholar cannot easily change his stripes. For many years, he has been tilling a minuscule plot of land in great depth, and his whole identity is wrapped up in the idea that this piece of land is the center of the universe. Similarly, departments and disciplines have a hard time accepting new ideas — it is precisely their function to protect the established lines of inquiry, and when those lines become obsolete, they keep right on protecting. And since institutions are ultimately made up of individual scholars, departments, and disciplines, institutions as a whole can easily get stuck in time.

History tells us that there is no easy solution to "the problem of the university." What makes the university strong is precisely what makes it weak.

At the level of the individual scholar, nothing can be done; ditto at the level of the departments and disciplines. These parts of the university enterprise are self-governed (for good reason) and self-perpetuating.

At the level of the institution, there is hope. A good leader can put into place structures that promote interdepartmental and cross-disciplinary efforts and thereby open the university to fresh ways of thinking. Though if the leader really wants to make a difference, he or she must penetrate recruiting and promotions, which is hard because the selection of academic personnel is controlled by the departments and disciplines. The best a leader can achieve is not to get rid of the departments and disciplines, but to leave them in peace and build new crosscutting structures on top of them.

At the level of the system of higher education, there, too, is hope, at least in the United States. Institutions of higher education are connected through intensely competitive markets for faculty, students, and administrators. At the same time, these institutions are a diverse lot, and their leaders are politically accountable to different sets of constituencies. Private institutions pander to their alumni, public institutions to their state legislatures; urban institutions care about the problem of the inner city, rural institutions promote agriculture; African-American Studies are powerful in the East, Asian-American Studies in the West; and so on and so forth. The combination of competition and diversity promotes experimentation and innovation — and the dissemination of successful experiments and innovations. It keeps the system as a whole open to change even while individual institutions within it ossify.

SUSANNE LOHMANN

REFERENCE

Lohmann, S. (2002). "How Universities Think," mimeograph. University of California, Los Angeles.

AL-QAEDA

1. Inception and Growth

al-Qaeda, referred to as '*the Base*' was founded in 1989 by Osama bin Laden and other like-thinking militant Muslims as the ultimate outcome of the 1979 invasion of Afghanistan by the USSR. Initially, al-Qaeda was created to record and track down the names of the *mujahideen* listed as missing during the guerrilla war against the USSR.

Bin Laden was born in 1957 as the seventeenth of fifty one children to a billionaire Saudi Arabian extended family and as an heir to its fortune accumulated in the construction industry from contracts negotiated with the Saudi Royal Family. In 1981, while studying at Jeddah's prestigious King Abdul-Aziz University, he first became associated with the Muslim Brotherhood and came under the spell of two prominent fundamentalist teachers of Islamic studies, Abdullah Azzam and Muhammad Qutb (Bergen, 2001, 47).

At the time of the Soviet invasion, Afghanistan lacked the necessary infrastructure, manpower and financial resources to fight an effective guerrilla war against a major super-power. Recognizing this, Abdallah Azzam, the spiritual leader and the head of the resistance group in Afghanistan during the period of Soviet occupation, inducted bin Laden into providing financial and personal support for the fragile resistance movement, known as the *Mujahideen*.

Together, Azzam and bin Laden in 1984 organized a recruiting office for resistance troops, known as the *Maktab al-Khidamat*, advertising world-wide for a war that was promoted as pitting the Muslim world against the oppressive, atheistic, communist regime of the USSR (www.ict.org). The recruits for the Afghan jihad became known as the Afghan Arabs, although none of them were Afghani and not all of them were Arabs. Most of them came from three countries, namely, Saudi Arabia, Yemen and Algeria (something that the newly-established U.S. Department of Homeland Security would do well to take into careful account in prescribing its immigration policies).

The United States, from the outset, eagerly and naively supported Bin Laden's resistance program, providing both financial and physical resources despite the fact that bin Laden was already voicing anti-American sentiments (Bergen, 2001, 50). For example, the Central Intelligence Agency funneled at least $500 million per annum to help to arm and to train the mujahideen guerrillas (www.ict.org). U.S. support also included a large number of "stinger" anti-aircraft missiles many of which are now under the control of al-Qaeda terrorists fanatically hostile to the United States.

The Afghan Arabs played a limited role in the ultimate defeat of the USSR in Afghanistan, numbering only in the low tens of thousands in comparison with the 250,000 annual strength of the Afghan mujahideen. The war was won 'primarily with the blood of Afghans and secondarily with the treasure of the United States and Saudi Arabia, who between them provided approximately $6 billion in support' (Bergen, 2001, 55).

In February 1989, the Soviet army withdrew from Afghanistan and bin Laden turned his attention to other struggles. By now, he was much more ambitious, harboring a vision for a radical Islamic empire that would extend well beyond the borders of Afghanistan. To this end, he conspired with Ayman Al-Zawahiri, an Egyptian physician located in Peshawar, where he himself had directed operations for much of the Afghan War, to merge al-Qaeda with Zawahiri's Jihad group, the organization that had been responsible for the 1981 assassination of Anwar Sadat.

The philosophic tenet of al-Qaeda is to purge the world of all heretical Muslim states and to replace them with *Sharia* (Islamic Law). It operates by declaring *fatwas*, religious rulings that call Muslims to take up arm in a Holy War to rid the world of its impurities. It also demands that its followers perform *bayat*, which is the 'quasi-medieval oath to an emir' (Bergen, 2001, 28).

Bin Laden returned to Saudi Arabia in 1989 intent on returning the country from heretical Islam to *Sharah*. To this end he embarrassed King Fahd and the Saudi Royal family by making popular anti-government speeches in the mosques. Although opposed to the invasion of the Gulf by Iraq, bin Laden became enraged when King Fahd invited the United States to use Saudi Arabia as a base for driving Iraqi forces out of Kuwait. King Fahd eventually removed bin Laden's citizenship and placed him under house arrest. In April 1991, bin Laden slipped out of Saudi Arabia, initially for Pakistan, then for Afghanistan, and finally in late 1991, he set up al-Qaeda operations in Sudan, where he was welcomed by Hassan al-Turabi, the leader of the country's National Islamic Front.

In Sudan, bin Laden built up a business empire, investing heavily from his own resources. At the same time, he built al-Qaeda, secretly paying members salaries ranging from $6,000 to $15,000 per annum. These were enormous sums for dirt-poor Arab refugees living in a very low cost, impoverished country. Bin Laden organized training camps in Sudan at which hundreds of his followers were trained in paramilitary tactics. During this period both bin Laden and al-Qaeda became increasingly radicalized by the influx of many angry young Arabs who faced persecution or death in their native Middle Eastern countries. By 1991, al-Qaeda had expanded to some 2000 members in Sudan and bin Laden had set up a number of military camps in the north.

Radicalization intensified in December 1992 when the United States moved troops into Somalia as part of a U.N. mission to feed starving Somalis. Bin Laden viewed such action as part of a new Crusade by the West against Islam. So the *fatwa* committee of al-Qaeda issued calls to attack U.S. troops in Somalia, calls that culminated in 1993 in the killing by al-Qaeda of more than a dozen U.S. troops stationed in Somalia. In 1997, bin Laden, unusually, claimed responsibility for this operation (Bergen, 2001, 81).

al-Qaeda has been indicted for a wide range of terrorist acts conducted during the six years that bin Laden was headquartered in Sudan. Among them are the bombing of the World Trade Center in 1993, the attempted assassination of Egyptian President, Mubarak in 1995, the truck-bomb attack on the Egyptian embassy in Islamabad in 1995 and conspiring to murder the Pope. By 1996, the United States and Egypt brought intense pressure to bear on Sudan to expel bin Laden.

For bin Laden this was good fortune indeed. He head-quartered al-Qaeda in Afghanistan, under the protection of the Taliban, attracting Arab militants to a country that was in the process of becoming the world's first jihadist state. The disastrous consequences of this shift of location for the United States would quickly become apparent. In February 1998, bin Laden founded the International Islamic front for Jihad Against the Americans and Israelis, translated as 'The World Front for the Struggle Against the Jews and Crusaders' (www.ict.org,3). The stage was now set for bin Laden's most spectacular terrorist attacks to date, namely the nearly simultaneous 1998 bombings of the American embassies in Tanzania and Kenya, to be followed early in 2001 by the bombing of U.S.S. Cole and then, on September 11, 2001 by the superbly organized, spectacular destruction both of the World Trade Center and of a significant part of the Pentagon. Al-Qaeda had evolved into a terrorist organization capable of terrifying the citizens of the world's only super-power and of provoking that sleeping giant into remorseless and ruthless revenge.

2. The Organization and Incentive Structure of al-Qaeda

Prior to the successful war against the Taliban, al-Qaeda was a multinational holding company, headquartered in Afghanistan, operating under the chairmanship of bin Laden (Bergen, 2001, 30). A holding company essentially comprises a core management group, controlling whole or partial interests in other companies. True to this model, al-Qaeda incorporated, in varying degree, subsidiary militant organizations in Egypt, Pakistan, Bangladesh, Algeria, Libya, Yemen, Syria, Kashmir, and Saudi Arabia. Only in the post-September 11, 2001 situation, and surely then only for political reasons, has al-Qaeda demonstrated any interest in Palestine.

al-Qaeda's training camps, in Afghanistan and elsewhere, had already attracted a 'rainbow coalition' 'of Turks, Palestinians, Iraqis, Saudis, Sudanese, Moroccans, Omanis, Tunisians, Tanzanians, Malaysians, Bangladeshis, Indians, Filipinos, Chechens, Uzbeks, Tajiks, Chinese, Uighurs,

Burmese, Germans, Swedes, French, Arab-Americans, and African-Americans' (Bergen, 2001, 30–31). With the collapse of its Afghanistan headquarters, and with the effective removal of its CEO, al-Qaeda metastasized like a malignant cancer, infecting at least 60 countries, including the leading nations in the 'war against terror', namely the United States and the United Kingdom.

Al-Qaeda is a very large, heterogeneous terrorist organization, with a membership that is widely dispersed across the globe. Its leaders expect members to put their lives at risk, even to commit suicide, for a cause — the dissemination of *Sharia* — that has strong publicness characteristics. Public choice analysis suggests that such an organization with such a goal is highly likely to under-achieve because of free-riding among the membership and the difficulty of establishing credible commitments within and across the terrorist network (Olson, 1965; Tullock, 1974).

The logic of collective action should be even more apparent since the victory of NATO over the Taliban, a victory that has left al-Qaeda headless, with its leaders hiding in caves and safe houses, and essentially unable to communicate with the network. Yet, al-Qaeda has continued in 2002 to sponsor successful terrorist acts, for example, in Pakistan, Kashmir and Bali, and to strike continuing fear among the citizens and governments of the advanced nations of the West.

There are several reasons for the continuing success of the highly decentralized al-Qaeda network, seemingly against all the public choice odds. First, during the early 1990s when al-Qaeda was emerging as an effective terrorist organization, its leaders prepared to educate the network by writing manuals that could be circulated throughout the organization.

The first manual was a multi-volume *Encyclopedia of the Afghan Jihad* that detailed everything that the Afghan Arabs had learned in the jihad against the Soviets. The *Encyclopedia* contains 800 pages on weaponry, including how to use the American stinger missiles, and 250 pages on how to mount terrorist and paramilitary attacks. A CD-ROM version of the *Encyclopedia* went on sale in the bazaars of Pakistan in the mid-1990s. A second, how-to terrorism book, *Military Studies in the Jihad Against the Tyrants*, was also prepared and similarly disseminated throughout al-Qaeda.

By the circulation of such volumes and the use of internet technology, the leaders of al-Qaeda were able to standardize the behavior of its many cells, much as American fast-food chains standardize the behavior of their many franchisees scattered throughout the world. By the use of satellite telephones, faxes and the internet, the leadership was also able to communicate with members without alerting the technology deficient and inefficiently-manned arms of U.S. 'intelligence', namely the Central Intelligence Agency and the Federal Bureau of Investigation, at least until September 11, 2001.

Second, the cell-like decentralized nature of al-Qaeda itself facilitates the making of credible commitments and works against free-riding among the membership. Each cell comprises a small number of al-Qaeda members, each cell with a distinct hierarchy, and each cell operating independently from all other cells. Because each cell is small, the problem of free-riding is greatly ameliorated, not least because the cell is able to mete out punishment to any individual who chooses to defect. Because each cell relies to some degree on central funding from the leadership, which can be adjusted according to its success or failure in mounting terrorist acts, selective incentives further reduce the likelihood of shirking behavior (Olson, 1965, 61).

Third, the leadership of al-Qaeda is able to facilitate its grip over the network because of its ability to move significant central funding across national borders without relying on bank transfers. It relies instead on a sophisticated mechanism of transfers through individuals and foundations loyal to its cause, moving monies obtained through the sale of heroin and other illegal drugs, laundered into relatively liquid commodities such as diamonds, to finance potentially successful terrorist cells. This mechanism has survived the weakening of the al-Qaeda leadership following the military victory of NATO in Afghanistan.

Fourth, the leadership of al-Qaeda takes advantage of fundamentalist Islam, *Sharia*, to motivate its members into suicidal terrorist attacks (Rathbone and Rowley, 2002). The tenets of *Sharia*, of course, do not seduce the leaders of al-Qaeda into laying down their lives in pursuit of Paradise. The 'leaders' flee from the field of battle and hide in caves while their ill-educated and heavily indoctrinated foot-soldiers eagerly seek out the promised joys of Paradise, including such Heavenly pleasures as rivers of sweet honey and holy wine, 72 virgin brides and 70 free passes to Paradise for each of their friends and relatives should they die in an attack on the Infidels.

Almost certainly, the tenets of *Sharia* do not motivate the 'relatively' well-educated leaders of each al-Qaeda cell, several of whom, for example, ignoring the strict tenets of their religion, consumed considerable quantities of alcohol in capitalist strip-tease and massage parlors immediately prior to the September 11, 2001 attacks. Envy and jealousy over the wealth that capitalism provides, compared with the poverty of their own basket-case economies, whose development is obstructed by the application of Islamic dogma, helps to motivate such individuals. Compensation promised to their families, in the case of their death, by such

rogue regimes as Iraq and Saudi Arabia, further enhances their willingness to die for *Sharia*. Fear of what might happen to themselves, or to their families, if they fail to act completes their rational choice to die quickly for the cause rather than slowly following humiliation and indescribable torture.

It is important to note that al-Qaeda, unlike such terrorist organizations as Fatah, Hamas and Hezbollah, is financed primarily from private sources and does not rely on large-scale funding by national governments. For this reason, it is much more flexible in response to changing environments and much less susceptible to bureaucratic inertia (Niskanen, 1971). It also implies that individual cells will vary in size and importance depending on access to private funding, which itself will be associated with relative success or failure in the terrorist market-place.

These circumstances give rise to a potential internal tensions within the al-Qaeda network. To avoid the logic of collective action problems, each cell must remain small. Yet, there are economies of scale in inflicting terror that are likely to encourage successful cells to expand in size and, in so doing, perhaps to find themselves in conflict with the primary goals of the organization (Iannaccone, 1992, 289). Moreover, as the Islamic world experiences economic growth, however feeble, the cells confront an increased opportunity cost in recruiting new members (Congleton, 2002). It is precisely at this point that the strength or weakness of the leadership in imposing its will on the cells becomes important, a factor that has yet to be tested in the post-Taliban era.

3. Undermining al-Qaeda Terrorism

To undermine the al-Qaeda terrorist network, threatened nations must pay careful attention to each of the above-listed characteristics of its organization and incentive structure. Whether or not their governments choose to do so, and select to take the appropriate actions, in large part, will be a result of the pressures, myopic or far-sighted, of their respective political markets, subject to the statesmanship of their leaders. By late 2002, only the United States and the United Kingdom have responded appropriately to the asymmetric war waged by al-Qaeda against those countries that do not practise *Sharia*.

In undermining al-Qaeda terrorism, governments should assume that all actors in the al-Qaeda network are rational and, as such, that they will respond predictably to changes in the cost-benefit calculus of terrorist acts. Nations that improve their intelligence networks, that improve their homeland security, that sequester al-Qaeda monies and shut down money laundering fronts, while responding aggressively to terrorist acts by systematically destroying the governments of those countries that give terrorists safe havens, and by killing, capturing, perhaps torturing, and ultimately executing convicted terrorists, predictably will reduce their exposure to al-Qaeda terrorism.

Nations that fail to do so increasingly will find that al-Qaeda diverts its acts to their territories. Bali is an excellent recent example of this diversionary phenomenon, a direct consequence of the unwillingness of the Indonesian government to root out and destroy al-Qaeda terrorist cells located within its territory. Germany, Italy, France, Spain, Belgium, the Netherlands, Canada and Australia predictably will follow the Bali example unless their governments find the will to adopt the Anglo-Saxon response model and to devote significant resources and resolve to dealing with the issue of asymmetric war.

ANNE RATHBONE
CHARLES K. ROWLEY

REFERENCES

Bergen, P. (2001). *Holy War, Inc.: Inside the Secret World of Osama bin Laden.* New York: Free Press.

Congleton, R.D. (2002). "Terrorism, interest-group politics, and public policy: curtailing criminal modes of political speech." *The Independent Review,* VII(1): 47–67.

Encyclopedia of the Afghan Jihad.

Iannaccone, L.R. (1992). "Sacrifice and stigma: reducing free riding in cults, communes and other collectives." *Journal of Political Economy,* 100(2): 271–291.

Military Studies in the Jihad Against the Tyrants.

Niskanen, W.A. (1971). *Bureaucracy and Representative Government.* Chicago: Aldine.

Olson, M. (1965). *The Logic of Collective Action.* Cambridge: Harvard University Press.

Rathbone, A. and Rowley, C.K. (2002). "Terrorism." *Public Choice,* 112(3–4): 215–224.

Sandler, T. and Lapan, H.E. (1988). "The calculus of dissent: an analysis of terrorists." *Synthese,* 76: 245–261.

Tullock, G. (1974). *The Social Dilemma.* Blacksburg: Center for Study of Public Choice.

www.ict.org.il

www.terrorism.org:Faces of al-Qaeda

ALTERNATIVE VOTING METHODS

In the British Parliament, and for elections to the national parliaments in almost all of Britain's larger former colonies, including Canada, India, the U.S., and until recently, New Zealand, most members have been elected from single seat constituencies under *plurality* voting. This method is known more commonly in Great Britain as *first-past-the-post* voting, because the election outcome is determined solely by the order of finish in terms of total votes received.

In contrast, throughout most of the rest of the world, elections to national parliaments are conducted using some form of proportional representation (PR), with the most common form of PR being *list PR,* in which political parties offer a list of candidates and winners are chosen in order of sequence from each of these lists (roughly) in proportion to the share of the vote received by each party. (For a listing of the electoral rules used for the various national parliaments, see Reynolds and Reilly, 1997: 139–142.) Although, in the past several years, with devolution, even the United Kingdom has chosen to use list PR methods for the election of its regional assemblies; and while the "Good Friday" accord provides that Northern Ireland use the *single transferable vote (STV)* form of PR (the form that has historically been used for parliamentary elections in Ireland as well as Northern Ireland), in the U.S. and elsewhere, the term *alternative voting method* is still most commonly used to refer to election methods other than simple plurality.

However, the degree of contrast between plurality and other methods depends upon the classification criteria of which we make use. While there is a long history of the study of election rules and their impact, the modern era can perhaps best be dated from the 1967 publication of Douglas Rae's seminal work, *The Political Consequences of Electoral Laws* (Rae, 1967). Other important work includes Taagepera and Shugart, *Seats and Votes* (1989), Lijphart, *Electoral Systems and Party Systems: A Study of Twenty-Seven Democracies* (1994), and Cox, *Making Votes Count* (1997). As perusal of the above works will demonstrate, there are a number of different aspects of electoral laws that are of relevance to Public Choice theory, and there are also a number of different dimensions along which electoral systems can be classified.

Perhaps the most important division is between majoritarian and minoritarian methods. Plurality is a *majoritarian method,* i.e., a majority of the voters, if they can agree on what ballot to submit, can determine the outcome of the election. Other majoritarian methods include the *alternative vote* (which is the application of the PR method the single transferable vote to a single-seat constituency), the *Coombs rule,* various forms of *runoff methods, approval voting,* and the *Borda rule. Minoritarian methods,* such as list PR, have the property that a minority of the voters can elect at least one candidate of their choice even over the opposition of the majority. Of necessity, minoritarian methods must be implemented in constituencies that elect more than a single candidate; but multi-seat constituencies (a.k.a. *multimember districts*) may also be used with majoritarian voting schemes such as *bloc voting* (the use of plurality in a multi-member constituency).

One natural way to think about plurality is in terms of the opposition between it and alternative methods that are of the minoritarian form. Those who advocate minoritarian methods most commonly argue for their use in terms of proportionality of vote share and seat share, since majoritarian methods such as plurality tend to lead to an overrepresentation of candidates favored by the majority/plurality bloc relative to that bloc's share of the electorate. For example, in the United States, in the second half of the 20th century, for two-party competition in the plurality based elections to the U.S. House of Representatives, the *swing ratio* (electoral responsiveness) has been estimated by various authors as falling between 1.5 and 2, i.e., for every percentage point of vote share above 50% it receives, the largest party will gain an additional 1.5% to 2% of House seats over a bare majority. Moreover, especially when we have party competition involving more than two parties, unlike what can be expected under most minoritarian methods, plurality can be expected to severely underrepresent the smaller parties relative to their vote share. For example, in the general election of 2001, the Liberal Party in Great Britain received 18.2% of the votes but less than 8% of the seats in the British House of Commons. Indeed, in multiparty settings, plurality may even result in outcomes in which the relationship between party vote share and party seat share is not monotonic.

Simple minoritarian methods, such as the *d'Hondt* form of list PR *cumulative voting*, and the *single non-transferable* vote, a.k.a. *SNTV* (*limited voting* in a multi-seat district in which voters are allowed only one vote), have the property that, if there are M winners to be chosen, any cohesive bloc of size slightly larger than $1/(M + 1)$ can guarantee electing a candidate of choice. When the *limited voting* rule used has more than one vote per voter but fewer votes per voter than there are seats to be filled, the size of the minority bloc needed to assure victory for at least one of its preferred candidates will be somewhere in between $1/(M + 1)$ and $1/2$. The properties of this class of rules were first systematically investigated by the 19th century mathematician Charles L. Dodgson (better known as Lewis Carroll).

From the perspective of the minimum vote share needed to guarantee a seat (known in the electoral systems literature as the *threshold of exclusion*), plurality can be taken to be a limiting case (M = 1) of both list PR and of limited voting. If we require vote allocations to be made in integer units, plurality can also be viewed as a limiting case (M = 1) of cumulative voting. But a limitation to integer allocations is not always found. For example, as cumulative voting was used in Illinois for elections to the lower chamber of the state legislature for most of the 20th century, voters had three votes to elect three candidates but, if they chose not to give one vote to each of three different candidates, they could choose to divide their vote either by cumulating all three votes on a single candidate or by splitting their vote among two candidates (one and a half votes to each).

In the past several decades, as a result of concerns over minority representation, both limited voting and (to a lesser extent) cumulative voting have been used for local elections in a number of southern jurisdictions in the U.S. as a (consent) remedy for a claimed violation of a federal anti-discrimination statute, Section 2 of the Voting Rights Act of 1965 (as amended in 1982). Authors such as Lani Guinier have advocated limited voting, as well as other minoritarian methods such as cumulative voting and STV, as mechanisms to improve the representation of both racial and partisan minorities over what is found under plurality or bloc voting.

A division that crosscuts the distinction between majoritarian and minoritarian methods is that between schemes that require voters to provide information only in the form of one or more X's on the ballot and those that require voters to rank order all (or at least some) of the candidates, or that require cardinal rankings. Both plurality in a single seat constituency and list PR in a multi-seat constituency are alike in that they require the voter to cast but a single X — for a candidate in the case of plurality, for a political party in the case of list PR. Similarly, both the Borda method in a single seat constituency and the single transferable vote in a multi-seat constituency require voters to provide a rank ordering of alternatives. However, the only method of which I am aware that requires voters to provide cardinal-level information about preferences, namely cumulative voting, is a minoritarian method. There are obvious advantages, especially in less developed democracies, for using "simple" methods.

In addition to looking at the amount of information about voter preferences provided in the ballot or the expected proportionality of electoral system results, there are other useful ways to determine the degree to which two different electoral systems are similar to one another. One of these is the extent to which an electoral system provides options to voters to choose among candidates as well as among parties (which affects the cohesiveness of political parties); another is in terms of the incentives for localism/particularism each system provides (which is relevant to understanding parliamentary budget choices: see e.g., the discussion of SNTV in Grofman et al., 1999). Each of these two methods of classification yield different conclusions about which alternative methods are most like plurality.

In the usual classification according to proportionality, STV and list PR are on one end of the continuum (most proportional) while bloc vote plurality is at the other end (least proportional), with SNTV toward the proportionality end, but not quite at the extreme because failure to run the optimum number of candidates can reduce that method's proportionality. However, if we classify systems according to the degree to which they are likely to give rise to strong and disciplined political parties, then, *ceteris paribus*, list PR is at one end, but now STV or SNTV may look a lot more like some instantiations of plurality (e.g., that in the U.S., with party primaries) than does list PR. Both STV and SNTV allow for intra-party competition when a party nominates more candidates within a constituency than its voting strength in the electorate will permit success to, and this normally gives rise to party factionalism. Moreover, under closed list PR, the party apparatus has control over candidate placement (and thus likelihood of electoral success) which gives the party a lot of clout in disciplining errant legislators by holding over them the threat of denying them renomination (or at least placing them so low on the list that their chances of victory are much reduced).

Similarly, if we classify systems according to the degree to which they foster localistically oriented representatives, then STV may look a lot more like plurality than it does list PR. In both STV in multi-seat elections and plurality in single member districts, running on the stronger party label may help, but it is not the whole story, and it is the local preferences among candidates that may prove decisive. If the success of a candidate depends on having enough personal support among voters in the local constituency this can be expected to sensitize the candidate to local concerns (see discussion in Bowler and Grofman, 2001).

We now turn from comparisons of plurality with minoritarian methods to comparisons of plurality with other majoritarian methods, focusing our attention on elections in constituencies that elect a single winner. Proportionality is usually the chief touchstone against which plurality elections are measured when we compare them to elections under minoritarian methods. When we compare plurality to other methods that may be used in single seat elections, then, from this perspective, the likelihood that a voting rule will select the *Condorcet winner*, a.k.a. the *majority winner* when there is one (i.e., that candidate, if any, who can receive a majority in paired contest against each and every

other alternative) becomes one natural standard of comparison. Measured against that standard, picking the Condorcet winner when one exists, plurality is generally found to be wanting.

For example, had the plurality rules in each state been replaced with the *alternative vote* (relabeled by its advocates in the U.S. as the *instant runoff*) then, *ceteris paribus*, we would have had a different outcome in the 2000 U.S. presidential election. Since most Nader supporters in Florida had Gore as their second choice, when the rank ordered ballots under the alternative vote would have been reallocated after Nader was eliminated from consideration, Gore would have been elected. Gore was the Condorcet winner in 2000 in Florida, and in the nation as a whole. *Ceteris paribus*, other runoff variants also would have increased the likelihood that the Condorcet winner, Gore, would have been chosen in Florida. In particular, if our concern is to increase the likelihood of picking a Condorcet winner when one exists (and, in real world elections, it is very likely that such an alternative will exist), then another form of runoff, the *Coombs rule*, has much to recommend it. The Coombs rule is almost the same as the alternative vote. The difference is that, that, when we eliminate candidates who have not received sufficient support, under the alternative vote, we drop the candidate with the fewest first place votes, while under Coombs, we drop the candidate with the most last place votes. It can be shown that, when voters have single peaked preferences (see Black's single-peakedness condition, this volume) the alternative vote will always select the Condorcet winner when there are four or fewer candidates; however, when preferences are single-peaked the Coombs rule will always select the Condorcet winner.

Of course, when we change electoral rules, we also can effect the number of parties/candidates who will choose to run. Thus, *ceteris paribus*, comparisons about outcomes under different voting rules must always be interpreted with care. Still, advocates of the use of the alternative vote (or of the Coombs rule) can plausibly argue that, unlike plurality, each permits supporters of minor parties to show support for their first place choice, without (significantly) increasing the likelihood that the major party candidate they least prefer will be elected.

However, not all supporters of rules such as the alternative vote would endorse choice of the Condorcet winner under all circumstances. From a political perspective, opponents of plurality are often most concerned about not inadvertently allowing an extremist candidate to emerge, in a crowded and competitive field, as the plurality winner. In a choice between two candidates with roughly equal and substantial levels of first place support, and a third candidate with little first place support who is the second choice of most voters and thus a Condorcet winner, some who would generally be sleptical about plurality might still argue that, in this instance, the Condorcet candidate might be politically weak/ unprepared for a leadership role and that it would actually be better to pick one of the candidates with substantial first place strength.

No discussion of alternative voting rules would be complete without at least some mention of both approval voting and the Borda rule. While each can be used to select more than one alternative, we will confine ourselves here to their use to select a single alternative.

Approval voting, is a rule under which voters indicate support for up to k −1 of the k alternatives: voters support those choices whose evaluations rise above some personally chosen threshold, so that the alternatives supported can be thought of as those of whom the voter is prepared to "approve." The alternative with the most approval votes is then chosen. This method has had an effective advocate in the political scientist Steven Brams, and largely due to his efforts it has been adopted for use in several professional organizations. Approval voting has much to recommend it, especially in terms of simplicity. For example, I view it as the ideal rule for a group of friends to use to decide which restaurant to go to. When used in elections in which the stakes are high(er), however, it creates incentives for voters to cast truncated ballots, making it look much like plurality than might otherwise appear to be the case.

The Borda rule is a member of the general class of positional methods known as *scoring rules*. Under the Borda rule, voters rank order the alternatives. If, for each voter, we assign to each alternative, i, one vote for each alternative that is ranked lower than alternative i by that voter, and then sum this tally across the set of voters, we get alternative i's *Borda score*. We then pick the alternative with the highest Borda score. The Borda winner and the Condorcet winner can both be thought of as mechanisms for selecting candidates who rank reasonably high, on average, in the preference orderings of most voters. While it is easy to construct examples in which the Borda winner and the Condorcet winner do not coincide, in practice, in most real-world political settings, they are likely to be the same. Moreover, if we are prepared to require votes to provide rankings, then the Borda rule has a number of desirable properties.

BERNARD GROFMAN

REFERENCES

Bowler, S. and Grofman, B. (2001). *The Single Transferable Vote in Ireland, Australia and Malta*. Ann Arbor, MI: University of Michigan Press.

Cox, G. (1997). *Making Votes Count: Strategic Coordination in the World's Electoral Systems*. Cambridge: Cambridge University Press.

Grofman, B., Lee, S-C., Winckler, E., and Woodall, B. (eds.) (1999). *Elections in Japan, Korea, and Taiwan Under the Single Non-Transferable Vote*. Ann Arbor, MI: University of Michigan Press.

Lijphart, A. (1994). *Electoral Systems and Party Systems: A Study of Twenty-Seven Democracies, 1945–1990*. Oxford: Oxford University Press.

Rae, D. (1967). *The Political Consequences of Electoral Laws*. New Haven, CT: Yale University Press.

Reynolds, A. and Reilly, B. (1997). *The International IDEA Handbook of Electoral System Design*. Stockholm: International Institute for Democracy and Electoral Systems.

Taagepera, R. and Shugart, M. (1989). *Seats and Votes: The Effects and Determinants of Electoral Systems*. New Haven, CT: Yale University Press.

ALTRUISM

Altruism is something of a puzzle to economists. While in theory the elements of the utility function are left unspecified, it is generally assumed that private goods consumed by the individual himself are the most important components. If not, then it becomes difficult to make falsifiable predictions and so scientific advance becomes impeded. Nonetheless, we observe that people do have altruistic elements in their behavior, and so the problem is to explain these elements and incorporate them in utility functions in ways that preserve testability. In this entry, I will mainly analyze altruistic acts towards non-relatives, with a brief discussion of altruism towards kin.

Altruism is said to exist when one individual's utility function contains elements of both the individual's own consumption (C_x) and also consumption of another individual (C_y):

$U_x = U_x(C_x, C_y)$, with $\partial U_x/\partial C_i > 0$, i = x,y.
(Spite exists when $\partial U_x/\partial C_y < 0$.)

The best general introduction to the public choice analysis of altruism is Tullock (1997). Tullock summarizes and extends many of the arguments here, and has a discussion of additional elements of redistribution as well. He points out that the major motive for redistribution is that the recipients desire to receive payments and have the political power to do so. This is obviously not related to altruism. The second most significant motive is altruism — a desire to help the poor. Third is envy, which is related to spite, as defined above. (Tullock, 1997, p. 6). He also indicates that insurance provides one non-altruistic motive for redistribution (p. 12).

Tullock also points out that although people are charitable (altruistic), they are not very charitable. He suggests that well under 5% of GNP is transferred to the poor, including both private and government transfers (p. 4).

There are three major themes in the literature analyzing altruism. Two of these begin with an assumption that utility functions contain elements of altruism, and are related to public choice analysis. First is the analysis of public goods issues in altruism. Second is the issue of the "Samaritan's dilemma." The third issue I discuss is the biological basis for altruistic utility functions. While this is only indirectly related to public choice issues, I believe that we must understand the basis for this element in utility functions for analysis to proceed usefully.

1. The Income Distribution as a Public Good

Hochman and Rodgers (1969) were the first to ask why government is involved in income redistribution. They began with utility functions of individuals, a classic public choice position. (Hochman was a faculty member and Rodgers a student at Virginia when this paper was written; among others, James Buchanan is thanked in the initial footnote.) Once they realized that everyone lives in the same society with the same income distribution, then the results are straightforward: each altruistic individual will benefit when any other such individual makes a contribution to the poor, and so each will have an incentive to free ride. Thus, as in the case of defense or any other public good, the only way to achieve optimality is for government to redistribute income.

A major addition to this analysis was in the work of Roberts (1984). Roberts pointed out that not only would altruists vote for transfers to the poor, but so would the poor themselves — a truly public choice insight. The result is that more would be transferred to the poor than altruists would desire. As a result, at the political equilibrium, even altruistic individuals would contribute nothing to private charity beyond what government would contribute. Roberts tested this model by examining private transfers after the 1930s, when government transfers became significant, and found evidence in support of his model. However, the strong prediction of no private transfers is obviously falsified.

Andreoni (1989, 1990) provided an answer to this puzzle. In his model, people desire to contribute for two reasons. One is the classic motive: to better the lot of the poor; this is "pure" altruism. The second reason is because the donor obtains a good feeling (a "warm glow" or "joy-of-giving") from the act of giving. This is "impure" altruism. This is a utility based argument, but the form of the utility function is arbitrary. These issues continue to inform research on altruism, both in mainstream economics and in public choice. For example Ribar and Wilhelm (2002) find that joy-of-giving motives dominate at the margin U.S. contributions to international relief organizations.

2. The Samaritan's Dilemma

The second set of theoretical concerns that motivate research on altruism is due to Buchanan (1975). The Samaritan's dilemma is that altruists cannot control the behavior of recipients. An altruist might want to condition giving on some behavior of the recipient, such as working or refraining from having excessive numbers of children. But once the action is taken (no money is earned, or the children are born) the altruist is unwilling to allow the recipient to starve. "He [the Samaritan] may find himself seriously injured by the necessity of watching the parasite starve himself while refusing work." (Buchanan, 1975, p. 76.) As a result, more will be given by government to the poor than the altruist would desire — a result that strengthens Roberts' conclusion, mentioned above. Coate (1995) uses this analysis to explain the form of government transfers: government provides insurance to try to avoid the Samaritan's dilemma.

3. Biology and Altruism

To the extent that altruism is an element of utility functions, then there must be an evolutionary basis for it. That is, we have those utility functions that served to make our ancestors survive to be our ancestors. We like sugar and fat and sex because our ancestors with those preferences did become our ancestors; those with other preferences were not our ancestors. Similarly, there must have been some survival value to altruistic preferences, or we would not have such preferences.

The biological problem of altruism is the same as the economic problem. Why did those with such preferences survive? Why were they not out-competed by more selfish individuals? Indeed, Wilson (1971, p. 3) has called altruism "the central theoretical problem of sociobiology." Several economists have recognized the relationship between the problem of altruism in economics and biology. Some examples: Bergstrom and Stark, 1993; Waldman and Bruce, 1990; Hirshleifer, 1999; and Samuelson, 1993. These papers deal with the existence of altruism. Rubin (2000, 2002) discusses the form of altruistic preferences that might survive.

I now discuss the biological explanations for altruism. (For a general introduction to the biological issues involved see Dawkins, 1989. This discussion is based in part on Rubin, 2002.)

4. Kin Selection

The first argument, due to William Hamilton (1964), is that there are evolutionary or fitness justifications for altruism to genetic relatives. The basic argument is this: we share genes with our relatives, so if a gene leads to behavior that improves the fitness of relatives it also increases its own chance for survival. Parents and children, and full siblings, are related by a factor of one half; half-siblings and grandchildren are related by one fourth; first cousins by one-eighth; and other relatives are related by lower percentages. This means that the probability of any given gene of an individual being found by common descent in the individual's parents or siblings is fifty percent. So if a gene for altruistic (helping) behavior should arise and lead to an individual helping a sibling, there is a fifty percent probability that the gene will also benefit itself.

Altruism towards kin is dependent on costs and benefits: as the cost to the altruist decreases or the benefit to the recipient increases, and as relatedness increases, such altruism becomes more likely. An altruistic act pays as long as $c < rb$ where c is the cost of the altruistic act, r is the degree of genetic relatedness between the actor and the beneficiary and b is the benefit to the recipient of the altruistic act. (This inequality is called "Hamilton's rule.") Of course, some kin benefits are obvious to anyone: parents spend large amounts of resources on their children. But Hamilton's point was much more general; many kinds of activities can be supported by kin selection, and it does not apply only to parental care.

Suicide bombings by terrorists are a form of kin altruism. First, it is well known that various governments provide substantial transfers to the families of suicide bombers, so that the act itself generates resources for kin. Second, such bombers are residents of polygynous societies. In such societies, some men have multiple wives, and so some men have none. The terrorists themselves might well not be able to marry. Thus, the fitness costs of suicide might be quite small. Therefore, although it does not appear altruistic, nonetheless, this class of activities is a perverted form of kin altruism.

5. Reciprocal Altruism

In a famous paper, Robert Trivers (1971) discovered contract in a biological setting and provided a biological basis for exchange. Essentially, it is a mechanism under which one party provides benefits today in return for benefits returned tomorrow. There are substantial requirements for reciprocity (or reciprocal altruism) to work. For one thing, animals have to be long lived, so that there is a reasonable expectation of receiving a return on an investment. For another, they have to be sufficiently intelligent both to identify specific other animals and to recall benefits received from such animals. Humans and some other advanced species (including apparently vampire bats) meet these requirements. Trivers also identified some mechanisms for enforcing reciprocity, including psychological mechanisms such as anger at being cheated and other forms of "moralistic aggression." The existence of reciprocal altruism means that the classical economists' arguments about the requirement of a "double coincidence of wants" as being necessary for barter is overdrawn; reciprocal altruism means that exchange can take place over time even without formal contracts. Current textbooks still provide this justification for money as opposed to barter, but it is not theoretically justifiable.

6. Additional Mechanisms

Other mechanisms that can generate some altruism, or reduce the amount of free riding, have been identified. One point is that the actual structure of interactions in real populations is not a "one-shot" prisoner's dilemma. Rather, long-lived animals (including humans) will interact with the same individuals many times over the course of a lifetime, particularly in small groups such as predominated during the evolutionary environment. This leads to the problem of the repeated game. The "folk theorem" tells us that essentially anything can happen in such games. That is, one equilibrium is cooperation; other equilibria include complete non-cooperation.

In one famous set of experiments, Axelrod (1984) showed that a strategy called "tit for tat" could be successful against many opposing strategies in a repeated prisoner's dilemma setting. In this strategy, I play this period whatever strategy you played last period. If you cheated last period, then I cheat this period. If you cooperated, then I also cooperate now. Thus, we can get a sequence started in which we both cooperate each period. Humans may be selected to play such strategies or variants of them because our predecessors who did were more likely to become our ancestors.

A mechanism that relies on intelligence is the possibility of punishment. Humans can punish those who violate rules, including free riders. De Waal (1996) has shown that chimpanzees also punish cheaters. Experimental evidence indicates that humans are quite willing to punish cheaters in public goods settings (see, for example, Fehr and Gachter, 2000). Second level punishment is even possible among humans, but not to my knowledge among other animals: humans can punish those who refuse to punish those who violate rules. It can be shown that second level punishment can generate almost any behavior among humans, whether efficient or inefficient (Axelrod, 1997;

Boyd and Richerson, 1992; Hirshleifer and Martinez-Coll, 1988; Gintis, 2000). In the evolutionary environment, punishment might have been relatively inexpensive, as it could have taken the form of banishment. Today, some forms of social punishment, such as social ostracism, are inexpensive; others, such as a trial and formal prison time, are rather expensive. Punishing wrongdoers is costly, and the willingness to engage in such punishment is a form of altruism, although not what is usually meant by this term. In a recent paper, Hirshleifer (1999) has discussed these and other pathways for the evolution of cooperation, and indicated that biologists err by emphasizing only kinship and reciprocity.

7. Group Selection

The strongest but most controversial force that could lead to altruistic behavior is what is called "group selection." With group selection, the unit of selection is the population rather than the individual or the gene. That is, we may think of several groups within a larger population competing with each other. Then the fittest group will survive. If individuals in one group are more cooperative than individuals in another, then the more cooperative group will survive, and so genes for cooperativeness will proliferate in the overall population. The theoretical problem with group selection is obvious: within a group, free riding would occur and eliminate the altruistic gene. For this reason, most biologists have argued that group selection is not possible.

Recently, Sober and Wilson (1998) have argued that group selection (or, more correctly, multilevel selection) is possible in some circumstances. (They also provide a history of the intellectual controversy over the issue.) Specifically, they argue that if groups periodically split up and reform then there is a possibility of group selection, in that groups with more cooperative or altruistic individuals will grow and when the split occurs the number of cooperative individuals in the population can then increase.

The possibility of group selection is the strongest case for altruistic preferences. Therefore, if some form of altruism cannot exist in this environment, then there cannot have been selection pressure for that form of altruism. We can use this argument to limit the possibilities of altruism in human preferences. Note that the Sober-Wilson mechanism depends on groups containing altruists to grow faster than others, so that the only possible forms of altruism are those that will lead to such growth. Such forms of altruism have been called "efficient altruism" (Rubin, 2000).

Then there are circumstances in which transfers to some individuals would have been in the group interest, and presumably in those circumstances the utility or well-being of the recipients would have become an element in the util-ity functions of the donors. In situations where a low cost transfer could save the life of the recipient and enable him to continue to participate in the group defense, or enable her to reproduce other defenders, then transfers would have been useful and so we might have preferences favoring such transfers. There are probably two situations that would have been relevant in the evolutionary environment, and moreover which are still relevant today (because we have tastes evolved in that environment). These are temporary income shortfalls, which could lead to starvation, and illness or injury, which could lead to death. Thus, we might have altruistic preferences favoring transfers in these circumstances. On the other hand, transfers to shirkers or permanently non-productive persons would not have been efficient. It is interesting that recent reforms in the US welfare system have emphasized work, and have been politically popular (Wax, 2000).

Also note that this form of altruism can justify some but not all ethical systems. Utilitarianism involves maximization of utility functions. To the extent that utility functions are based on fitness, then this ethical system is consistent with our evolved preferences. On the other hand, the Rawlsian system (Rawls, 1971) which entails making the worst-off person in society as well off as possible, would not be consistent. Consider: Group A does not adopt Rawls' principle. All active adult males have a nutritional level of 2500 calories per day except for one individual who obtains 2000 and is somewhat malnourished (but perhaps not in danger of immediate death). Group B begins with the same distribution but adopts the Rawlsian system and redistributes accordingly. The efficiency costs of redistribution (deadweight losses due to "taxation" in the form of forced transfers and shirking in the expectation of receiving the benefits of redistribution) are so high that once the redistributive process has run its course total income falls. As a result, at equilibrium, everyone in the group has a nutritional level of 2100 calories per day. According to Rawls, Group B is morally superior to Group A because the poorest person in B has 2100 calories and the poorest in A has only 2000. But even though Rawls and his disciples may prefer this outcome, it is not the outcome that would be selected in the evolutionary environment. Rather, members of Group A would translate their extra nutrition into increased strength or more hand axes and likely massacre the males (at least) in Group B. (Or, in a more benign scenario, all members of Group B except for the original poorest person would migrate to Group A.) In either case, group selection would not support the principles Rawls advocates, and so no evolutionary system would be consistent with these principles. Rawls claims that individuals behind a "veil of ignorance" would prefer his system, but human utility functions are not consistent with this argument.

Similarly, a Marxist principle of "from each according to his ability, to each according to his needs" would not be consistent with such evolved preferences because of the inefficiency of such a set of rules. Moreover, Marxism is itself a form of group selection (with class or, in modern variants, class, race and gender) as the defining elements of the group. Group selection of this sort is inconsistent with the Sober-Wilson analysis, and so is not consistent with evolutionary theory. (It is puzzling that some anthropologists who reject group selection nonetheless use Marxist analysis; see Roseberry, 1988 for a discussion of Marxism in anthropology.)

Public choice and economic analysis of altruism has proceeded based on arbitrary assumptions about utility functions and preferences. But if we realize that preferences have evolved, then we should be able to specify more carefully the form of utility functions and perhaps put more content into the analysis. For example, this can explain why voters favor some forms of transfers but not others.

One additional example: It was mentioned above that Andreoni's specification of a "warm glow" utility function is arbitrary. Here is an evolutionary argument that would lead to the same result but with additional implications: we evolved in small scale societies where each individual had an input into political decision making. As a result, we overestimate our influence in political situations. We therefore believe that our own contributions to the poor make more difference than is true. This same hypothesis can explain the puzzle of voting, and has other implications as well.

PAUL H. RUBIN

REFERENCES

Andreoni, James (1989). "Giving with impure altruism: applications to charity and ricardian equivalence." *The Journal of Political Economy*, 97(6): 1447–1458.

Andreoni, James (1990). "Impure altruism and donations to public goods: a theory of warm-glow giving." *The Economic Journal*, 100(401): 464–477.

Axelrod, Robert (1984). *The Evolution of Cooperation*. New York: Basic Books.

Axelrod, Robert (1997). *The Complexity of Cooperation: Agent-Based Models of Competition and Collaboration*. Princeton, NJ: Princeton University Press.

Bergstrom, Theodore and Oded Stark (1993). "How altruism can prevail in an evolutionary environment." *The American Economic Review*, 83(2): 149–155.

Boyd, Robert and Peter J. Richerson (1992). "Punishment allows the evolution of cooperation (or anything else) in sizeable groups." *Ethology and Sociobiology*, 13: 171–195.

Buchanan, James M. (1975). "The samaritan's dilemma," in Edmund Phelps (ed.) *Altruism, Morality and Economic Theory*. New York: Russell Sage Foundation.

Coate, Stephen (1995). "Altruism, the samaritan's dilemma, and government transfer policy." *The American Economic Review*, 85(1): 46–57.

Dawkins, Richard (1976; new edition, 1989). *The Selfish Gene*. Oxford: Oxford University Press.

De Waal, Frans (1996). *Good Natured: The Origins of Right and Wrong in Humans and Other Animals*. Cambridge: Harvard University Press.

Fehr, Ernst and Simon Simon Gachter (2000). "Cooperation and punishment in public goods experiments." *American Economic Review*, 90(4): 980–994.

Gintis, Herbert (2000). "Strong reciprocity and human sociality." *Journal of Theoretical Biology*, 211: 169–179.

Hamilton, William D. (1964). "The genetical evolution of social behavior I and II." *Journal of Theoretical Biology*, July: 1–16, 17–52.

Hirshleifer, Jack (1999). "There are many evolutionary pathways to cooperation." *Journal of Bioeconomics*, 1(1): 73–93.

Hirshleifer, Jack and J. Martinez-Coll (1988). "What strategies can support the evolutionary emergence of cooperation?" *Journal of Conflict Resolution*, 32: 367–398.

Hochman, Harold M. and James D. Rodgers (1969). "Pareto Optimal Redistribution". *American Economic Review*, 59 (4): 542–557.

Hochman, Harold M. and James D. Rodgers (1974). "Redistribution and the Pareto criterion." *The American Economic Review*, 64(4): 752–757.

Rawls, John (1971). *A Theory of Justice*. Cambridge: Belknap Press of Harvard University Press.

Ribar, David C. and Mark O. Wilhelm (2002). "Altruistic and joy-of-giving motivations in charitable behavior." *The Journal of Political Economy*, 119(2): 425–457.

Roseberry, William (1988). "Political economy." *Annual Review of Anthropology*, 17: 161–185.

Rubin, Paul H. (2000). "Group selection and the limits to altruism." *Journal of Bioeconomics*, 4: 9–23.

Rubin, Paul H. (2002). *Darwinian Politics: The Evolutionary Origin of Freedom*. New Brunswick: Rutgers University Press.

Samuelson, Paul A. (1993). "Altruism as a problem involving group versus individual selection in economics and biology." *The American Economic Review*, 83(2): 143–148.

Sober, Elliott and David Sloan Wilson (1998). *Unto Others: The Evolution and Psychology of Unselfish Behavior*. Cambridge: Harvard University Press.

Trivers, Robert L. (1971). "The evolution of reciprocal altruism." *Quarterly Review of Biology*, 46: 35–57.

Tullock, Gordon (1997). *Economics of Income Redistribution*, Second Edition. Boston: Kluwer Academic Publishers.

Waldman, Michael and Neil Bruce (1990). "The rotten-kid theorem meets the samaritan's dilemma." *The Quarterly Journal of Economics*, 105(1): 155–165.

Wax, Amy L. (2000). "Rethinking welfare rights: reciprocity norms, reactive attitudes, and the political economy of welfare reform." *Law and Contemporary Problems*, 63: 257.

Wilson, E.O. (1971). *The Insect Societies*. Cambridge: Harvard University Press.

THE ANATOMY OF POLITICAL REPRESENTATION

Representative government, whereby voters elect representatives to govern on their behalf, is a hallmark of modern democracies. However, the use of representatives to make collective decisions is far from universal. In many instances, such as referenda and ballot initiatives, individuals make collective decisions directly. When group decisions are assigned to representatives, the structure of representative governments can vary along several dimensions, creating a variety of forms of representative government. Differences in the structure of representative governments can potentially have significant impacts on the decisions made by representative bodies and the costs incurred in making those decisions.

1. The Choice of Representative Versus Direct Democracy

Formal analysis of the choice between direct democracy and representative government emanates from the seminal work of Buchanan and Tullock (1962). Buchanan and Tullock identify two costs associated with collective decision-making: external costs and decision-making costs. External costs include costs include costs imposed on an individual by the actions of others and decision-making costs are the costs one incurs as a result of his own participation in the process of making group decisions. Buchanan and Tullock hypothesize that rational individuals will select a decision-making mechanism that minimizes the sum of these two types of costs.

Barzel and Sass (1990) and Sass (1992) extend Buchanan and Tullock's model in two ways. First, they change the focus from the costs each individual incurs in the voting process to the total net costs borne by the group as a whole. They emphasize the deadweight costs associated with attempts to institute or prevent transfers of wealth within the group via voting, rather than the amount of the transfers themselves, which are often zero-sum. Second, they explicitly incorporate the costs to voters of acquiring information to make enlightened decisions into the concept of decision-making costs.

In representative governments there is an additional cost of voting, agency costs. Representative democracies can be viewed as an agency relationship where elected officials are the agents and the voters the principals. Representatives will seek to maximize their own utility, which may not coincide with maximizing the well-being of voters. Alternatively, representatives may simply be unaware of voters' preferences

(Matsusaka and McCarty (forthcoming)). Faced with the prospect of suffering losses from the decisions of representatives, voters will impose restrictions on the choices of representatives and will devote resources to monitoring the behavior of elected officials. Agency costs include the sum of the expenditures to monitor and constrain representative behavior plus the net cost of undesired representative actions that remain.

The choice between representative and direct democracy can be analyzed in terms of the tradeoffs between decision-making costs, wealth-transfer costs and agency costs. All else equal, representative government generally lessens decision-making costs by reducing the number of decision makers. However, differences in voting rules or other procedures between representative and direct democracies could create holdup problems that mitigate the savings in decision-making costs. By facilitating group decision making, representative democracy may also exacerbate the external and wealth-transfer costs of voting. For example, legislative logrolling may facilitate agreements that produce costly wealth transfers. Desires to clarify benefits to constituents, such as the use of in-kind rather than monetary welfare transfers, could add to the deadweight wealth-transfer costs of voting. In addition to these effects on decision-making and wealth-transfer/external costs, representative democracy obviously creates agency cost problems.

The few existing empirical studies of the choice of representative versus direct democracy offer somewhat mixed results, but generally support the economic model of constitutional choice. Sass (1991) and Fahy (1998) study the choice between open-town-meeting and representative governments in Connecticut and Massachusetts, respectively. Consistent with the notion that representative government economizes on decision-making costs, both Sass and Fahy find the likelihood of representative democracy increases with town population. Group heterogeneity, which increases decision-making costs and the potential for wealth transfers, is negatively correlated with representative government in Sass's data but Fahy finds that group diversity increases the probability of representative government. Hersch and McDougall (1997) obtain mixed results for the impact of constituent heterogeneity on the probability that Kansas legislators would vote to allow a form of direct democracy, the citizen initiative.

2. The Structure of Representative Government

Given that most political entities are organized as representative democracies, an interesting and important issue is the structure of representative government. Representative democracies can vary in many dimensions, including the ratio of representatives to voters, the rules for electing representatives, how representatives make decisions, the representatives' terms of office, and the extent of any constraints on representatives' decision-making authority.

Distinguishing the individual structural aspects of representative democracies is difficult. There are a multitude of components which can each affect the costs of voting, making the selection of each aspect of a representative government interrelated. Thus, with the exception of Sass' (1992) analysis of the tradeoffs in the structure of condominium associations, no one has attempted to investigate the simultaneous choice of multiple components of representative democracy. A generally more feasible approach is to consider institutions as a whole and compare distinct systems of representative government.

Within the universe of political representative democracies, a general distinction can be made between presidential (separation of powers) and parliamentary systems. In a two-party parliamentary system, like Great Britain, the executive and legislative branches of government are unified under the monopoly control of the majority party. Thus between elections the ruling party has virtually unchecked power to pass its legislative agenda. Monopoly power is weaker when the ruling party must rely on a coalition of parties to establish and maintain a majority, however. In contrast to parliamentary government, in the presidential system the executive and legislative branches may be controlled by different parties. Even when a single party controls both branches, weak party discipline can lead to conflicts between the executive and the legislature.

The differences in intragovernmental competition among parliamentary and presidential systems have important implications for the structure and performance of the two systems. A key aspect of the monopoly control associated with parliamentary government is the potential ease of reneging on past legislative deals. Given their monopoly control, a party could easily amend or nullify legislation they previously adopted. Similarly, subsequent governments could readily undue the deals made by their predecessors. Moe (1990) emphasizes two mechanisms that alleviate the commitment problem in parliamentary governments. First, parties can establish reputations for living up to commitments. The party's brand name capital acts as a bond that is forfeited if it reneges on legislative agreements. Second, ex-post opportunism can be limited by making interest group members a part of the bureaucracy. Co-opting interest groups serves to align incentives and gives interest groups inside information which can be used strategically to prevent reneging on prior commitments. Absorption of interest group representatives of course

comes at the cost of reducing the majority party's power to implement its own agenda.

The ability of interest groups to entrench themselves in the bureaucracy of a parliamentary government can also serve to insulate themselves from policy shifts brought about when control of the government shifts from one party to another. Further, the repeated-game nature of party competition across multiple elections may also serve to limit one party from wholesale abrogation of the other party's previous commitments.

Another important distinction between the presidential and parliamentary systems is the organization of administrative agencies. Moe and Caldwell (1994) argue that competition between the executive and the legislature in the separation-of-powers system leads to formalized bureaucratic structures and limitations on agency discretion which have negative effects on agency performance. In contrast, single-party monopoly over the executive and legislative branches in the parliamentary system produces greater control of the bureaucracy by political leaders and less reliance on externally imposed rules.

3. The Impact of Government Structure on Policy Outcomes

The choice of government structure can have significant effects on policy outcomes and the efficiency of government performance. Theory suggests that agency problems associated with representative government should produce policies that deviate to some degree from the preferences of voters. In particular, the self-interest of representatives could lead to higher governmental spending either because representatives directly value a larger bureaucracy or simply because representatives consume perquisites at government expense.

Numerous empirical studies have analyzed the relationship between government form and governmental expenditure. The majority of studies fail to find a strong link between representative democracy and either the absolute level of government expenditure or deviations from the expenditure level desired by the median voter. For example, Wheeler (1967) does not find significant differences between school expenditures in open-town meetings and representative governments in Maine. Pommerehne and Schneider (1978) analyze aggregate expenditures across Swiss municipalities and find only modest differences in the fit of the median voter model between direct democracies with referenda and representative democracies with no referenda. Santerre (1989) finds that representative-government township governments in Connecticut are associated with marginally significant higher per-capita municipal expenditures but *lower* per pupil school expenditures. These differences are not significant, however, when government form is treated as endogenous (Sass, 1991). Pommerehne (1978) is the only study to find strong positive effects of representative government on expenditures. Using data for a single year he finds the fit of the median voter model much better in Swiss municipalities with direct democracies than in representative democracies without referenda. These findings suggest that either the structure of representative governments is sufficient to keep agency costs low, that agency problems occur in dimensions other than budget maximization or that neither direct or representative democracy yield decisions reflecting the median voter's preferences.

Another empirical approach is to analyze the fiscal effects of more limited forms of direct democracy, initiatives and referenda. Initiatives allow citizens to directly propose and adopt new legislation while referenda give voters the opportunity to pass judgment on laws initiated by the legislature. Though the evidence is somewhat mixed, research on the impact of referenda and initiatives tends to support the predicted agency-cost reducing effects of direct democracy.

Pommerehne (1978), Pommerehne and Frey (1978) and Pommerehne and Schneider (1978), measure the marginal impact of referenda on expenditure in representative democracies in Switzerland. They find that the median voter model of expenditures produces a better fit in municipalities with referenda than those without, though the differences are not always statistically significant. They also find that time until the next election (which should increase agency costs) is positively correlated with the level of public expenditure in cities without referenda, but uncorrelated with expenditure in cities with referenda. In a more recent study of municipalities in Switzerland, Feld and Kirchgassner (1999) find that budget referenda are associated with both lower total expenditures per capita and reduced per capita debt. Similarly, Feld and Matsusaka (2001) find that both referenda and initiatives lead to lower per capita spending in Swiss cantons, with the two forms of direct democracy acting as partial substitutes.

In contrast to the Swiss studies, evidence on the impact of initiatives and referenda in the United States is mixed. At the local level, McEachern (1978) finds no significant effect of referenda on per capita debt. Similarly, Megdal (1983) finds no significant impact of referenda on local school expenditures, suggesting agency problems are minimal. At the state level, there is conflicting evidence on the fiscal effects of initiatives and referenda. Matsusaka (1995) compares the 27 states that allow voter initiatives with the 23 states where laws must be drafted by the legislature.

Using annual data for 1960–1990 Matsusaka finds that in initiative states state-level governmental expenditures per capita are lower but local government per capita expenditures are higher. Using a similar panel, Kiewiet and Szakaly (1996) find that states which require referenda for debt approval have lower relative levels of guaranteed and total debt than states without a referendum requirement. A more recent study by Matsusaka (2000) suggests that effect of initiatives on expenditures may vary over time, however. Matsusaka essentially replicates his previous study for an earlier time period, 1900–1950, and finds initiatives are associated with both higher per capita state-level and local spending.

In addition to constraining bureaucratic incentives to increase expenditures, improved monitoring through direct democracy could improve the efficiency of government. Pommerehne (1983) finds that the threat of referendum significantly lowers the cost of refuse collection in Swiss municipalities. Costs of production are the lowest in municipalities with direct voter control and a private supplier. Pommerehne and Weck-Hannemann (1996) present evidence that direct democracies are more efficient at tax collection; less income is concealed by residents of Swiss municipalities with budget and tax referenda than in municipalities without such direct voter controls.

TIM R. SASS

REFERENCES

Barzel, Y. and Sass, T.R. (1990). "The allocation of resources by voting." *Quarterly Journal of Economics*, 105: 745–771.

Buchanan, J.M. and Tullock, G. (1962). *The Calculus of Consent.* Ann Arbor: The University of Michigan Press.

Fahy, C.A. (1998). "The choice of local government structure in Massachusetts: a historical public choice perspective." *Social Science Quarterly*, 79: 433–444.

Feld, L.P. and Kirchgassner, G. (1999). "Public debt and budgetary expenditures: top down or bottom up? Evidence from Swiss municipalities," in J. Porterba and J. von Hagen (eds.) *Fiscal Institutions and Fiscal Performance.* Chicago: University of Chicago Press.

Feld, L.P. and Matsusaka, J.G. (2001). "Budget referendums and government spending: evidence from Swiss cantons" (unpublished manuscript).

Hersch, P.L. and McDougall, G.S. (1997). "Direct legislation: determinants of legislator support for voter initiatives." *Public Finance Review*, 25: 327–343.

Kiewiet, D.R. and Szakaly, K. (1996). "Constitutional limitations on borrowing: an analysis of state bonded indebtedness." *Journal of Law, Economics and Organization*, 12: 62–97.

Matsusaka, J.G. and McCarty, N.M. "Political resource allocation: benefits and costs of voter initiatives." *Journal of Law, Economics and Organization* (forthcoming).

Matsusaka, J.G. (1995). "Fiscal effects of the voter initiative: evidence from the last 30 years." *Journal of Political Economy*, 103: 587–623.

Matsusaka, J.G. (2000). "Fiscal effects of the voter initiative in the first half of the twentieth century." *Journal of Law and Economics*, 43: 619–650.

McEachern, W.A. (1978). "Collective decision rules and local debt choice: a test of the median voter hypothesis." *National Tax Journal*, 31: 129–136.

Megdal, S.B. (1983). "The determination of local public expenditures and the principal and agent relation: a case study." *Public Choice*, 40(1): 71–87.

Moe, T.M. (1990). "Political institutions: the neglected side of the story." *Journal of Law Economics and Organization*, 6: 213–253.

Moe, T.M. and Caldwell, C. (1994). "The institutional foundations of democratic government: a comparison of presidential and parliamentary systems." *Journal of Institutional and Theoretical Economics*, 150: 171–195.

Pommerehne, W.W. (1978). "Institutional approaches to public expenditure: empirical evidence from Swiss municipalities." *Journal of Public Economics*, 9: 255–280.

Pommerehne, W.W. (1983). "Private versus öffentliche Müllabfuhr — nochmals betrachtet." *Finanzarchiv*, 41: 466–475.

Pommerehne, W.W. and Frey, B.S. (1978). "Bureaucratic behavior in democracy: a case study." *Public Finance*, 33(1–2): 98–111.

Pommerehne, W.W. and Schneider, F. (1978). "Fiscal illusion, political institutions, and local public spending." *Kyklos*, 31(3): 381–408.

Pommerehne, W.W. and Weck-Hannemann, H. (1996). "Tax rates, tax administration and income tax evasion in Switzerland." *Public Choice*, 88: 161–170.

Santerre, R.E. (1989). "Representative versus direct democracy: are there any expenditure differences?" *Public Choice*, 60(2): 145–154.

Sass, T.R. (1991). "The choice of municipal government structure and public expenditures." *Public Choice*, 71: 71–87.

Sass, T.R. (1992). "Constitutional choice in representative democracies." *Public Choice*, 74: 405–424.

Wheeler, H.J. (1967). "Alternative voting rules and local expenditure: the town-meeting vs. city." *Papers on Non-Market Decisionmaking*, 2: 61–70.

APPROVAL VOTING

Proposed independently by several analysts in the 1970s (Brams and Fishburn, 1983), *approval voting* (AV) is a voting procedure in which voters can vote for, or approve of, as many candidates as they wish in multicandidate elections — that is, elections with more than two candidates. Each candidate approved of receives one vote, and the candidate with the most votes wins. In the United States, the case for AV seems particularly strong in primary and nonpartisan elections, which often draw large fields of candidates.

Supporters of AV argue that it has several compelling advantages over other voting procedures:

1. *It gives voters more flexible options*. They can do everything they can under plurality voting (PV) — vote for a single favorite — but if they have no strong preference for one candidate, they can express this fact by voting for all candidates they find acceptable. In addition, if a voter's most preferred candidate has little chance of winning, that voter can vote for both a first choice *and* a more viable candidate without worrying about wasting his or her vote on the less popular candidate.

2. *It helps elect the strongest candidate*. Today the candidate supported by the largest minority often wins, or at least makes the runoff if there is one. Under AV, by contrast, the candidate with the greatest overall support will generally win. In particular, *Condorcet candidates*, who can defeat every other candidate in separate pairwise contests, almost always win under AV, whereas under PV they often lose because they split the vote with one or more other centrist candidates.

3. *It will reduce negative campaigning*. AV induces candidates to try to mirror the views of a majority of voters, not just cater to minorities whose voters could give them a slight edge in a crowded plurality contest. It is thus likely to cut down on negative campaigning, because candidates will have an incentive to try to broaden their appeals by reaching out for approval to voters who might have a different first choice. Lambasting such a choice would risk alienating this candidate's supporters and losing their approval.

4. *It will increase voter turnout*. By being better able to express their preferences, voters are more likely to vote in the first place. Voters who think they might be wasting their votes, or who cannot decide which of several candidates best represents their views, will not have to despair about making a choice. By not being forced to make a single — perhaps arbitrary — choice, they will feel that the election system allows them to be more honest, which will make voting more meaningful and encourage greater participation in elections.

5. *It will give minority candidates their proper due*. Minority candidates will not suffer under AV: their supporters will not be torn away simply because there is another candidate who, though less appealing to them, is generally considered a stronger contender. Because AV allows these supporters to vote for *both* candidates, they will not be tempted to desert the one who is weak in the polls, as under PV. Hence, minority

candidates will receive their true level of support under AV, even if they cannot win. This will make election returns a better reflection of the overall acceptability of candidates, relatively undistorted by strategic voting, which is important information often denied to voters today.

6. *It is eminently practicable.* Unlike more complicated ranking systems, which suffer from a variety of theoretical as well as practical defects, AV is simple for voters to understand and use. Although more votes must be tallied under AV than under PV, AV can readily be implemented on existing voting machines. Because AV does not violate any state constitutions in the United States (or, for that matter, the constitutions of most countries in the world), it requires only an ordinary statute to enact.

Probably the best-known official elected by AV today is the secretary-general of the United Nations. AV has been used in internal elections by the political parties in some states, such as Pennsylvania, where a presidential straw poll using AV was conducted by the Democratic State Committee in 1983. Bills to implement AV have been introduced in several state legislatures. In 1987, a bill to enact AV in certain statewide elections passed the Senate but not the House in North Dakota. In 1990, Oregon used AV in a statewide advisory referendum on school financing, which presented voters with five different options and allowed them to vote for as many as they wished.

Since 1987, AV was used in some competitive elections in countries in Eastern Europe and the Soviet Union, where it was effectively "disapproval voting" because voters were permitted to cross off names on ballots but not to vote for candidates. But this procedure is logically equivalent to AV: candidates not crossed off are, in effect, approved of, although psychologically there is almost surely a difference between approving and disapproving of candidates.

Beginning in 1987, several scientific and engineering societies inaugurated the use of AV (Brams and Fishburn, 1992). It has worked well in finding consensus candidates; all these societies continue to use it today and include the following:

- Mathematical Association of America (MAA), with about 32,000 members;
- American Mathematical Society (AMS), with about 30,000 members;
- Institute for Operations Research and Management Sciences (INFORMS), with about 15,000 members;
- American Statistical Association (ASA), with about 15,000 members;

- Institute of Electrical and Electronics Engineers (IEEE), with about 377,000 members.

Smaller societies that use AV include the Society for Judgment and Decision Making, the Social Choice and Welfare Society, the International Joint Conference on Artificial Intelligence, and the European Association for Logic, Language and Information.

Additionally, the Econometric Society has used AV (with certain emendations) to elect fellows since 1980; likewise, since 1981 the selection of members of the National Academy of Sciences at the final stage of balloting has been based on AV. Coupled with many colleges and universities that now use AV — from the departmental level to the school-wide level — it is no exaggeration to say that several hundred thousand individuals have had direct experience with AV.

As cherished a principle as "one person, one vote" is in single-winner elections, such as for president, supporters of AV consider it somewhat of an anachronism today. Democracies, they contend, could benefit from the alternative principle of "one candidate, one vote," whereby voters are able to make a judgment about whether each candidate on the ballot is acceptable or not.

The latter principle makes the tie-in of a vote not to the voter but rather to the candidates, which is arguably more egalitarian than artificially restricting voters to casting only one vote in multicandidate races. This principle also affords voters an opportunity to express their intensities of preference by approving, for example, of all except the one candidate they may despise.

Although AV encourages sincere voting, it does not altogether eliminate strategic calculations. Because approval of a less-preferred candidate could hurt a more-preferred approved candidate, the voter is still faced with the decision of where to draw the line between acceptable and nonacceptable candidates. A rational voter will vote for a second choice if his or her first choice appears to be a long shot — as indicated, for example, by polls — but the voter's calculus and its effects on outcomes is not yet well understood for either AV or other voting procedures (Nurmi, 1987; Merrill, 1988).

While AV is a strikingly simple election reform for finding consensus choices in single-winner elections, in elections with more than one winner — such as for a council or a legislature — AV would not be desirable if the goal is to mirror a diversity of views, especially of minorities; for this purposes, other voting systems need to be considered (Brams and Fishburn, 2002). On the other hand, minorities may derive indirect benefit from AV in single-winner elections, because mainstream candidates, in order to win, will be forced to reach out to minority voters for the approval *they* (the mainstream candidates) need to win. While promoting majoritarian candidates, therefore, AV induces them to be responsive to minority views.

STEVEN J. BRAMS

REFERENCES

Brams, Steven J. and Peter C. Fishburn (1983). *Approval Voting*. Cambridge, MA: Birkhäuser Boston.

Brams, Steven J. and Peter C. Fishburn (1992). "Approval voting in scientific and engineering societies." *Group Decision and Negotiation*, 1: 41–55.

Brams, Steven J. and Peter C. Fishburn (2002). "Voting procedures," in Kenneth Arrow, Amartya Sen, and Kotaro Suzumura (eds.) *Handbook of Social Choice and Welfare*, Volume I. Amsterdam: Elsevier Science, pp. 175–236.

Merrill, Samuel, III (1988). *Making Multicandidate Elections More Democratic*. Princeton, NJ: Princeton University Press.

Nurmi, Hannu (1987). *Comparing Voting Systems*. Dordrecht, Holland: D. Reidel.

ARBITRATION AND BARGAINING

Arbitration provides a private sector alternative to the civil court system. In addition, it may serve as a substitute for the strike in labor management bargaining. This is particularly important for workers in the public sector who may not have the legal right to strike. Under conventional arbitration (CA), the arbitrator may impose whatever settlement he sees fit. Many have argued that if arbitrators in labor disputes merely split the difference between the positions of labor and management, arbitration would have a chilling effect on negotiations. That is, each party would be reluctant to make bargaining concessions, because these concessions would lead to a worse outcome at the arbitration hearing. In response to this perceived problem, Stevens (1966) argued for the use of what came to be know as final offer arbitration (FOA). Under this procedure, each party submits a final offer and the arbitrator is forced to choose one of these two offers as the final outcome of arbitration.

In the wake of Stevens' article, final offer arbitration was adopted by a variety of jurisdictions to govern the outcome of public sector labor disputes. A voluminous academic literature has followed. This literature has focused on comparing the two arbitration procedures, either to each other or to the strike mechanism. Some of the issues addressed in this literature include the previously mentioned chilling effect, the frequency of arbitration usage, and the quality of the settlements achieved through the arbitration process. There is a strong presumption in the literature that negotiated settlements are superior to settlements imposed by an arbitrator on the bargaining parties.

Farber (1981) pointed out that if arbitrators under CA really split the difference in a simplistic way, then parties would adopt very extreme positions in the arbitration hearing. Since this is counterfactual, he argues that arbitrators adopt a decision rule which places less weight on unreasonable offers. As a result, the offers of the parties will not diverge to extreme values. This suggests that the chilling effect of CA is not as serious as earlier commentators had claimed.

Farber and Bazerman (1986) and Bloom (1986) sent hypothetical wage disputes to actual arbitrators. This research is designed to understand arbitrator behavior under CA. Do the final positions of the parties matter, or do arbitrator's ignore these final offers and make a decision based solely on the facts in question? Though the two studies differ in important details, both agree that the final positions of the parties to the dispute do affect the outcome of CA.

Uncertainty plays a big role in discussions of arbitration schemes. In the absence of any uncertainty about the value of the arbitrator's most preferred settlement, FOA and CA lead to the same certain outcome. This outcome is equal to the arbitrator's most preferred settlement (Crawford, 1979). If the arbitrator's most preferred settlement is described by a symmetric distribution, which is common knowledge, then the final offers under FOA will be distributed symmetrically about the mean of this distribution (Farber, 1980).

Stevens argued that FOA was a strike like mechanism, due to the uncertainty it generated about the final outcome. In the presence of risk aversion and identical beliefs about the expected arbitration outcome, this uncertainty would lead to the establishment of a contract zone. Of course uncertainty about the arbitrator's preferred settlement would also generate a contract zone under CA. Farber and Katz (1979) and Bloom (1981) analyze the effects of risk aversion and uncertainty on negotiated settlements under CA.

As Farber and Bazerman (1989) point out, under CA risk averse bargainers are exposed to the entire distribution of preferred settlements, while under FOA, they are exposed to two points, which are the offers each party submits to the arbitrator. Early discussions of the issue to the contrary, there should be no a priori expectation that FOA is riskier than CA. For a constant absolute risk aversion utility function, Farber and Bazerman report that the contract zone under CA is larger for most of the parameter combinations used in their numerical simulations. This calls into question the belief that FOA is riskier than CA.

Based on field data, Ashenfelter and Bloom (1984) report that police salaries in New Jersey have a lower variance under FOA than under CA. Though there are selection issues (the choice of procedure is endogenous), this casts further doubt on the notion that FOA is inherently riskier than CA.

There seems to be some tension in the literature regarding the quality of arbitration awards and the effects of arbitration procedures on bargaining. Most authors view it as important that the arbitration procedure lead to the creation of a sizable contract zone. If the contract zone is a single point, then there is no real bargaining; the outcome merely reflects an imposition of the arbitrator's preferred settlement. If parties are risk averse, a large contract zone is generated through an uncertain arbitration outcome. However, a large degree of uncertainty in the arbitration outcome suggests that some of the imposed outcomes will be of low quality, i.e., very different from what the parties would negotiated in the absence of the arbitration procedure.

It is generally thought that a good arbitration procedure is one which is not used very often. As a result, comparisons of CA and FOA often focus on the expected dispute rates under the two procedures. This requires having a theory of disputes, and there is not a total consensus on what causes bargaining failure. The early literature on arbitration relied on exogenous divergent expectations about the arbitration outcome as an explanation of bargaining failure. Typically in this approach, each party to the dispute has exogenous beliefs about the likely outcome at trial which may differ from one another. If expectations diverge sufficiently, then a contract zone may fail to exist and a dispute results. As discussed above, based on simulation analysis, Farber and Bazerman (1989) find larger contract zones for CA than FOA. These contract zones are computed under the assumption of identical expectations. Farber and Bazerman's results suggest that if divergent expectations are the cause of disputes, there will be more disputes under FOA.

An alternative approach is to assume that disputes are caused by asymmetric information. Bebchuk (1984) is an important early example from the literature on civil litigation of a model in which asymmetric information leads to bargaining failure. While this paper led to an explosion of papers on civil litigation analyzing the role of asymmetric information, only a few papers have analyzed this issue in the arbitration context. Gibbons (1988) constructs a model in which the arbitrator learns about the state of the world from the offers submitted by the parties to the dispute. Samuelson (1991) derives optimal offers in the presence of asymmetric information. Neither of these papers is

attempting to explain the cause of disputes. Risk preferences are not directly observable, and Curry and Pecorino (1993) argue that asymmetric information on risk preferences can be a cause of bargaining failure. While they develop this in a model of FOA, a similar mechanism would lead to disputes under CA as well.

An interesting aspect of FOA is that negotiations can take place after potentially binding offers have been submitted to the arbitrator. These offers have the potential to transmit privately held information held by the parties to the dispute. This in turn may lower the dispute rate. Farmer and Pecorino (1998) analyze a model of FOA with asymmetric information. In the absence of a pooling equilibrium, they find that allowing for negotiation after the submission of offers to the arbitrator lowers the dispute rate. However, the ability to negotiate after submission of offers to the arbitrator makes the existence of the pooling equilibrium, in which all cases settle, less likely. Pecorino and Van Boening (2001) conduct an experiment based on this model. The experiment is calibrated so that a pooling equilibrium is not predicted. They find that allowing for negotiation after the submission of offers to the arbitrator results in a substantial reduction in the dispute rate.

Experimental analysis is one important branch of the literature on arbitration. Farber et al. (1990) conduct an experimental analysis of CA in which they simulate labor-management wage negotiations. They find, as predicted by almost all theories of bargaining failure, that settlement is increasing in the cost of a dispute. They also induce risk aversion in some bargainers, by manipulating the relationship between the settlement and the participant's cash payoff. Risk aversion increases the size of the contract zone, but the authors only find a weak positive relationship between induced risk aversion and the propensity to settle. They also report some settlement when no contract zone exists and some settlement outside of the contract zone when it does exist. These results are typical of experimental bargaining research in a certain sense; theory generates stark predictions on behavior, while the actual behavior of experimental subjects often generates anomalous results relative to these predictions.

Ashenfelter et al. (1992) conduct an experimental comparison of FOA and CA. In contrast to some earlier research on arbitration, participants were given considerable information about the arbitrator's preferred settlement. Among their findings are that the dispute rate is inversely related to the cost of disputes and that disputes are more likely under CA when the variance of the arbitrated outcome is lower. The authors also report that dispute rates are higher in FOA than in the comparable treatment for CA. This work contrasts with some earlier experimental research (e.g., Neale and Bazerman, 1983) which had reported lower dispute rates under FOA.

There has also been a great deal of research which analyzes arbitration using field data. Delaney (1983) finds for teacher salaries that the ability to strike and the availability of arbitration have similar positive effects on teacher salaries. They each raise salaries by about 10%. On the other hand, he does not find a systematic relationship between the use of the strike or arbitration mechanisms and teacher salary. Using a large Canadian data set, Currie and McConnell (1991) find that the right to strike raises public sector wages 2% and that a switch to compulsory arbitration raises wages an additional 1–2%. Thus, in contrast to Delaney, they find that wages are higher under an arbitration mechanism than under the strike mechanism. They also report that the probability of a bargaining impasse is 13 percentage points lower in right to strike jurisdictions than in jurisdictions covered by mandatory arbitration. However, because the cost of a dispute is so much lower under arbitration, they conclude that total dispute costs are lower under the arbitration mechanism.

Using data on Canadian teachers, Currie (1994) finds that negotiated and arbitrated wages have a similar mean. This agrees with the findings of Delaney. However, she also finds that the variance of arbitrated wages are lower than the variance of negotiated wages. She interprets this to mean that negotiated wages reflect information held by the bargaining parties, but not known to the arbitrator. These results call into question the quality of arbitrated outcomes.

Olson and Rau (1997) examine how the bargaining parties learn about arbitrator preferences from a prior experience of having proceeded to arbitration. They find that the variance of the subsequent negotiated settlement falls by 30%. They attribute this to learning by the parties to the dispute. In addition, subsequent to an arbitrated outcome, negotiated settlements more closely reflect the decision criteria of the arbitrator.

Arbitration continues to be a rich area for both theoretical and empirical research. In addition, it is an area where academic writings, in particular Stevens (1966), have had a major impact on actual practice. While not as influential as Stevens' call for the use of FOA, the literature has produced several other proposals for new arbitration procedures (e.g., Brams and Merrill, 1986).

PAUL PECORINO

REFERENCES

Ashenfelter, Orley and Bloom, David E. (1984). "Models of arbitrator behavior: theory and evidence." *American Economic Review*, 74: 111–124.

Ashenfelter, Orley, Currie, Janet, Farber, Henry S., and Spiegel, Matthew (1992). "An experimental comparison of dispute rates in alternative arbitration systems." *Econometrica*, 60: 1407–1433.

Bebchuk, Lucian A. (1984). "Litigation and settlement under imperfect information." *Rand Journal of Economics*, 15: 404–414.

Bloom, David E. (1981). "Is arbitration really compatible with bargaining?" *Industrial Relations*, 20: 233–244.

Bloom, David E. (1986). "Empirical models of arbitrator behavior under conventional arbitration." *Review of Economics and Statistics*, 68: 578–585.

Brams, Steven, J. and Merrill, Samuel (1986). "Binding verses final-offer arbitration: a combination is best." *Management Science*, 32: 1346–1355.

Crawford, Vincent P. (1979). "On compulsory-arbitration schemes." *Journal of Political Economy*, 87: 131–159.

Currie, Janet (1994). "Arbitrator behavior and the variances of arbitrated and negotiated wage settlements." *Journal of Labor Economics*, 12: 29–40.

Currie, Janet and McConnell, Sheena (1991). "Collective bargaining in the public sector: the effect of legal structure on dispute costs and wages." *American Economic Review*, 81: 693–718.

Curry, Amy Farmer and Pecorino, Paul (1993). "The use of final offer arbitration as a screening device." *Journal of Conflict Resolution*, 37: 655–669.

Delaney, John T. (1983). "Strikes, arbitration, and teacher salaries: a behavioral analysis." *Industrial and Labor Relations Review*, 36: 431–446.

Farber, Henry S. (1980). "An analysis of final offer arbitration." *Journal of Conflict Resolution*, 24: 683–705.

Farber, Henry S. (1981). "Splitting the difference in interest arbitration." *Industrial and Labor Relations Review*, 35: 70–77.

Farber, Henry S. and Bazerman, Max H. (1986). "The general basis of arbitrator behavior: an empirical analysis of conventional and final offer arbitration." *Econometrica*, 54: 819–854.

Farber, Henry S. and Bazerman, Max H. (1989). "Divergent expectations as a cause of disagreement in bargaining: evidence from a comparison of arbitration schemes." *Quarterly Journal of Economics*, 104: 99–120.

Farber, Henry S. and Katz, Harry C. (1979). "Interest arbitration, outcomes and the incentive to bargain." *Industrial and Labor Relations Review*, 33: 55–63.

Farber, Henry S., Neale, Margaret A. and Bazerman, Max H. (1990.) "The role of arbitration costs and risk aversion in dispute outcomes." *Industrial Relations* (Fall): 361–384.

Farmer, Amy, and Pecorino, Paul (1998). "Bargaining with informative offers: an analysis of final offer arbitration." *Journal of Legal Studies*, 27: 415–432.

Gibbons, Robert (1988). "Learning in equilibrium models of arbitration." *American Economic Review*, 78: 896–912.

Neale, Margaret A. and Bazerman, Max H. (1983). "The role of perspective taking ability in negotiating under different forms of arbitration." *Industrial and Labor Relations Review*, 36: 378–388.

Olson, Craig, A. and Rau, Barbara (1997). "Learning from interest arbitration: the next round." *Industrial and Labor Relations Review*, 50: 237–251.

Pecorino, Paul and Mark Van Boening (2001). "Bargaining and information: an empirical analysis of a multistage arbitration game." *Journal of Labor Economics*, 19: 922–948.

Samuelson, William F. (1991). "Final offer arbitration under incomplete information." *Management Science*, 37: 1234–1247.

Stevens, Carl M. (1966). "Is compulsory arbitration compatible with bargaining?" *Industrial Relations*, 5: 38–52.

ARROW'S IMPOSSIBILITY THEOREM

Kenneth Arrow's *Social Choice and Individual Values* (1951, 1963), one of the five "founding books" of the Public Choice movement, is a seminal work in social science. It reformulates the theory of social welfare in ordinal rather than cardinal terms; it demonstrates the power of an axiomatic approach to economic modeling; and it offers a new approach to traditional issues in democratic theory having to do with the nature of collective choice that has had enormous impact in political science, presaging later aspects of "economic imperialism" vis-à-vis the other social sciences. The key result in the book, Arrow's Impossibility Theorem, is arguably the best known purely mathematical result in the social sciences. Directly inspiring a huge literature, including numerous axiomatic formulations that were more in the nature of characterization or existence results than impossibility theorems, Arrow's work laid the reinvigorated foundations for the subfield of social choice and welfare that came to be exemplified in the journal of that same name. The impossibility theorem is also perhaps the most important of the many contributions which earned Arrow his Nobel Prize in Economics in 1972.

The Impossibility Theorem is deceptively simple. Arrow begins by insisting, seemingly incontrovertibly, that any social welfare ordering, R, be a (weakly) *transitive* collective preference ordering among the set of feasible alternatives; i.e., such that xRy and yRz together imply that xRz, thus requiring that the social welfare function be *acyclic*. Arrow then identifies a number of features of mechanisms for aggregating individual preference orderings into a collective preference that appear, on their face, noncontroversial and/or trivial. He then shows that no function that always generates a transitive social welfare ordering can simultaneously satisfy this set of seemingly reasonable and desirable features unless we are prepared to let a single individual, a dictator, make at least some of the choices for the society.

Arrow's original four conditions are: *unrestricted domain* (every possible combination of individual preference orderings over the feasible set of alternatives is permitted); *weak positive responsiveness* (if individual preferences change so that some alternative is higher ranked than it used to be, then the collective ranking should place that alternative no lower than it used to be); *independence of irrelevant alternatives* (if some individual preferences change, but no individual changes the relative ordering of two alternatives, x and y, then the collective ordering of x and y also should not change); *citizen sovereignty* (choices over any pair, x and y, should not be externally imposed; i.e., there must be some sets of individual preference orderings for which x is collectively ranked ahead of y and some other sets of individual preference orderings for which y is collectively ranked ahead of x). The Impossibility Theorem states that these four seemingly minor conditions are not compatible with *nondictatorship* (an individual is said to be a *dictator* with respect to the relative ranking of x and y if his preferences govern that ranking regardless of the preferences of the rest of the collectivity; the nondictatorship condition requires that there be no pair of alternatives for which any individual, i, is a dictator). Thus, the horns of Arrow's dilemma: either give up on transitivity, or give up on "democratic" procedures for aggregating preferences and embrace dictatorship.

In the decades after Arrow's Theorem was announced, numerous variants of his theorem were propounded. For example, William Vickrey showed that we could replace weak positive responsiveness and citizen sovereignty with *unanimity* (if every individual has xRy, then so must the social welfare ordering), while still preserving the result that dictatorship was unavoidable. However, most of the energy of scholars has gone into attempts to escape the horns of the Arrowian dilemma.

There are five basic avenue of "escape" that can be pursued:

(1) Seize the horns of the dilemma and either claim that transitivity is overrated, since collectivities are not individuals and thus need not be expected to generate a transitive social welfare ordering, or that dictatorship need not be so bad (e.g., by permitting dictators as long as they are *representative dictators*).

(2) Seek to modify the fundamental framework in order to avoid an impossibility result, e.g., by weakening the requirement of transitivity (by replacing it with *quasi-transivity* or with the requirement that the social welfare ordering only be a *semi-order*); or by requiring only that a unique best choice be selected but not that preferences be transitively ordered; or by shifting from an ordinal to a cardinal framework; or by introducing a lottery or other probabilistic elements.

(3) Reject the implications of the result for the infeasibility of meaningful collective choice and for democratic theory, e.g., by emphasizing that Arrow's Theorem is about possibilities rather than probabilities and claiming that the theorem is generally irrelevant in that, in most *real-world* settings, there are a range of social welfare functions that can be expected to yield transitive orderings; or by claiming that, even though cycles occur, they will largely or entirely be among alternatives that are virtually indistinguishable from one another; or that the cycles that are present can be viewed as of little moment because collectivities do not even notice when they are there; or that we can cheerfully go on about our business even in the presence of cycles as long as outcomes are generated by rules that "legitimate" social choices.

(4) Reject the appropriateness/desirability of one or more of the basic postulates of the Theorem other than domain restriction, and argue that once we remove the unsatisfactory postulates, aggregation methods exist that are quite satisfactory

(5) Consider the possibility of domain restriction and search for plausible ways to limit feasible preference orderings in such a fashion that the impossibility result does not hold.

Trying to reject transitivity does not get us very far. The problem with this first line of attack is that the existence of cycling makes it hard to see what choices to make when the mechanism that is used to specify collective preferences does not yield a clear ordering among alternatives. Although we can simply choose a preferred alternative (perhaps at random) from among the elements in the *top cycle set* (each of whose elements is undominated by any element not in the set), often the top cycle set can be very large, perhaps even encompassing the entire set of feasible alternatives. Thus this line of approach will often not help us very much. Still, there has been considerable progress in understanding the structure of collective preference (especially for the case of majority rule) and in identifying the alternatives that lie in particular subsets of the top cycle set (such as the *uncovered set* or the *Banks set*) which have claims to be considered as "reasonable" choices.

The second of these approaches, the attempt to reformulate either the transitivity condition or dictatorship in a way that will make the impossibility result go away, has led to numerous mathematically sophisticated approaches that have greatly enhanced our understanding of the nature of preference aggregation mechanisms but that, in my view, have all turned out to be dead ends vis-à-vis being ways to

plausibly avoid the horns of the Arrowian dilemma (see the excellent review in Plott, 1976).

The third approach, arguing for the practical irrelevance of Arrow's Theorem, is found in many of my own relatively recent works in social choice theory [see e.g., Uhlaner and Grofman, 1985; Feld and Grofman, 1992; Regenwetter et al. (forthcoming)]. Suffice it to say that I regard this work as an important strand of the debate over the meaning/ importance of Arrow's Theorem.

The fourth approach, rejecting one of the axioms used to establish the impossibility result other than domain restriction, often chooses the criterion of independence of Irrelevant Alternatives (CIIA) as the axiom to reject. For example, Donald Saari (1994) argues that CIIA is an undesirable property for social welfare functions/voting rules to have in that it forces the decision process to throw away information. Furthermore, Saari has emphasized that, if we limit the social welfare function to only using information on pairwise choices, it will not distinguish between transitive and intransitive individual preference inputs.

In the context of majority rule processes, the criterion of independence of irrelevant alternatives, when combined with the other elements of Arrow's Theorem, implies that the only feasible decision rules are those that can be thought of as *Condorcet extension methods*, i.e., rules that will always pick the *Condorcet winner* (a.k.a. the *majority winner*), that alternative, if any, that is undefeated against each and every other alternative in paired contest. Saari's views about CIIA and Arrow's Theorem can in many ways be thought of as resuscitating the debate between the two eighteenth century figures who are key progenitors of modern social choice theory, the Marquis Nicolas Caritat de Condorcet and John Charles Borda — with Arrow in the role of Condorcet, emphasizing how things can go wrong, and Saari as the defender of the Borda method.

The *Borda method* is a *scoring rule* assigning points to alternatives based on how far up in each individual ranking they are found, as a reasonable way to generate social welfare orderings/social choices. We can use each alternative's Borda scores to rank order the alternatives in a transitive fashion, and the Borda method can also be given a variety of plausible axiomatic underpinnings. However, the Borda rule is not a Condorcet extension method. In the context of democratic processes, the logic of choosing a majority winner is quite compelling if we are fortunate enough to have a Condorcet winner that could be chosen. Indeed, arguably, this is what majority rule is all about. By dropping independence of irrelevant alternatives we are giving up on rules that guarantee that we will pick majority winners when such exist. (For the history of the Condorcet-Borda debate see Black, 1958.)

The fifth approach seeks to avoid the impossibility result by imposing constraints on admissible preferences. One way to do this is to imagine that individual preferences are based on some common, but imperfectly understood, evaluative criterion, such as a notion of the public good (Grofman and Feld, 1988). Another way is to limit the number of alternatives. If there are only two alternatives then Arrowian impossibility results do not apply. Similarly, if voters are limited to classifying alternatives into two categories (say, satisfactory and unsatisfactory), then we can also avoid impossibility results. However, the most common way in which constraints on preferences are imposed is by limiting preferences over each triple of alternatives in some way, such as by the Black *single-peakedness condition* (referred to by Amartya Sen as *the NW condition*). Arrow (1963) states a possibility theorem for single-peaked preferences, showing that we can create a transitive social welfare function while avoiding dictatorship and satisfying positive responsiveness, CIIA, and citizen sovereignty, if we restrict ourselves to single-peaked preferences. In particular, the single-peakedness restriction guarantees that majority rule will be transitive. (We will discuss domain restriction conditions in more detail in the essay in this volume on Black's single-peakedness condition.)

We would offer one final observation on Arrow's Theorem. Arrow does not explicitly make use of a game-theoretic framework, nor connect his work to considerations of strategic misrepresentation of preferences (see, however, pp. 20–21). Nonetheless, as Craven (1992) observes, there is a deep mathematical connection between the impossibility result and later results on manipulability of social choice processes, such as the Gibberd-Satterthwaite Theorem.

BERNARD GROFMAN

REFERENCES

Arrow, K. (1963). *Social Choice and Individual Values*. New York: Wiley, First Edition, 1951; Second Edition, 1963.

Black, D. (1958). *The Theory of Committees and Elections*. Cambridge: Cambridge University Press.

John Craven, John (1992). *Social Choice: A Framework for Collective Decisions and Individual Judgements*. New York: Cambridge University Press.

Grofman, B. and Feld, S. (1988). "Rousseau's general will: a condorcetian perspective." *American Political Science Review*, 82(2): 567–576. (Reprinted in J.P. Johnston and H. Pasis (eds.) *Representation and Electoral Systems: Canadian Perspectives*. NJ: Prentice Hall of Canada, 1990. Translated and reprinted in abridged form as La volonte generale de Rousseau: perspective Condorceene. In P. Crepel and C. Gilain (eds.), *des Actes du Colloque International Condorcet*. Paris: Editions Minerve, 1989.)

Feld, S.L. and Grofman, B. (1992). "Who's afraid of the big bad cycle?" *Journal of Theoretical Politics*, (2): 231–237.

Plott, C. (1976). "Axiomatic social choice theory: an overview and interpretation (in the workshop)." *American Journal of Political Science*, 20(3): 511–596.

Regenwetter, M., Adams, J., and Grofman, B. "On the condorcet efficiency of majority rule: an alternative view of majority cycles and social homogeneity." *Theory and Decision* (forthcoming).

Saari, D. (1994). *Geometry of Voting*. New York: Springer-Verlag.

Uhlaner, C. and Grofman, B. (1985). "Metapreferences and reasons for stability in social choice: thoughts on broadening and clarifying the debate." *Theory and Decision*, 19: 31–50.

AN 'AUSTRIAN' PERSPECTIVE ON PUBLIC CHOICE

[F]rom the economic viewpoint, such 'goods' as family, church, love and the like are merely linguistic devices for a totality of concretely useful renditions of services. (Bohm-Bawerk, 1881, 133)

It is impossible to draw a clear-cut boundary around the sphere or domain of human action to be included in economic science. (Knight, 1934, 110)

The Austrian school of economics and the Virginia school of political economy have a long history of interdependence — methodological, analytically, and ideologically. While Austrians typically focus on an analysis of market processes, Virginia Political economists analyze the dynamics of the political realm. Despite their seemingly disparate fields of interest both Austrians and members of the Virginia school share a commitment to methodological individualism and the development of a rational choice paradigm in the human sciences; a commitment to a catallactic or exchange based model of social phenomena that emphasizes the dynamic processes of adjustment by individuals within the process and not exclusively the static efficiency of equilibrium states; and a deep appreciation of the classical liberal tradition and its teachings about the necessary institutional pre-requisites for a society of free and responsible individuals.

1. The Domain of Economic Explanation

Both the Austrian and Virginia schools consider the discipline of political economy a subset of the larger, more general science of human action called *praxeology* (see Buchanan and Tullock, 1962, 16–30). By employing the praxeological approach, Austrians and public choice economists are able to apply the "economic way of thinking" to a wide variety of social phenomena, including areas like politics, that for many years were considered by economists to lie outside the scope of rational choice theory. From the Austrian perspective, the purpose of economics is to understand/elucidate purposive behavior in the context of the actor's intent and to bring into relief the unintended consequences of human action. Public choice, as a discipline operating in the same praxeological framework as Austrians, has the same mission but with regard to political activity.

The praxeological approach represents the culmination of the economic way of thinking. The fullest, most consistent application of this approach belongs to the Austrian school, particularly the work of Ludwig von Mises. According to Mises, what distinguishes economics from other sciences is that it deals with *conscious* action. Unlike the unmotivated subject matter of the physical sciences, the subjects of economics' study are rational, conscious agents with certain desires and beliefs about how to achieve them. In the physical sciences, the ultimate causes of matter's "behavior" can never be known. But the science of economics is a science of human action. And its praxeological status is what allows economic scientists, who are themselves human, to thus begin with knowledge of the ultimate causes driving man's behavior. Man engages in purposeful action and his purpose, his ends are what drive him. For Mises and the rest of the Austrian school, this understanding of man's action as purposeful serves as the foundation for all of economic science. The radical philosophy of science implications of the Austrian stance are explored in various writings by Mises and Hayek (see, e.g., Hayek, 1952). Because Austrians viewed themselves as working within the broader field of human action, their application of the "economic way of thinking" to political problems came naturally, and in doing so they anticipated several of the contributions later made by public choice.

2. 'Austrian' Contributions to the Economics of Politics

Mises is often credited by public choice scholars as one of the first scholars to approach the problems of bureaucracy from an economic point of view (see Niskanen, 1994, 3, 7). Mises's *Bureaucracy* contrasted economic organization on the basis of the profit-motive in the market, with the organization of public administration outside the context of the market economy. Mises argued that "Bureaucratic management is the method applied in the conduct of administrative affairs the result of which has no cash value on the market. ... Bureaucratic management is management of affairs which cannot be checked by economic calculation"

(1944, 47–48). In the absence of profit and loss, bureaucratic organizations must rely on rules and monitoring of subordinates. These rules and monitoring devices impede the economic performance of these organizations and their adaptability to changing economic conditions.

Mises' 1945 essay, "The Clash of Group Interests" provides another excellent example of how scholars in the Austrian school tradition addressed topics such as the logic of concentrated benefits and dispersed costs and special interest politics. As its title suggests, this essay constitutes an early analysis of the causes and consequences of special interest group formation in the vein of public choice. Mises begins by pointing out the growing trend of special interest group emergence and battle for political privilege. Popular opinion holds that different groups have different interests that can only be served at the expense of one another. As a result, "[o]ur age," Mises tells us, "is full of serious conflicts of economic group interests." The emergence of these special interests in the first place is the result of government intervention that favors one group over another. Consequently, it should come as no surprise that these groups see each other as enemies and the struggle for survival as a zero-sum game. One of the first implications of special group formation, Mises says, is the formation of even more special interest groups. So-called "producers policy" (whereby government aims to support floundering businesses) begets group conflict as interests vie for government privilege, and group proliferation, as new interests organize to get their piece of the pie. Mises not only anticipates the growth and influence that special interest groups will increasingly have over economic policy but also traces this fact to the economic ignorance of the voting masses. He ends by correctly predicting the continuation of this trend in the future but believes one thing may have the power to thwart special interest group domination — the Constitution. In making this remark Mises foreshadows the later public choice development that stresses the importance of constitutional constraints in tieing the hands of self-interested government.

Hayek's *The Road to Serfdom* also provides an excellent example of early Austrian contributions to public choice theory. Here, Hayek is concerned with how socialism changes the demands on a democratic systems and how through this process socialism transforms the institutions of democracy into institutions of tyranny. This effect of socialism is evident in the growth of special interest groups. With the acceptance of socialist ideology, Hayek points out, comes the erosion of liberal constraints on intervention favoring particular groups. Consequently, as socialism's popularity grew, the number of special interests pleading for privilege ballooned (Hayek, 1945, 40). Like public choice theorists, Hayek understood the danger of interest groups in the context of the logic of concentrated benefits and dispersed costs. While these "innumerable interests ... could show that particular measures would confer immediate and obvious benefits on some, the harm they caused [on others] was much more indirect and difficult to see" (Hayek, 1945, 17–18). Hayek not only understood the logic of concentrated benefits and dispersed costs, but also understood the importance of rules over discretion and federalism in binding government power (Hayek, 1945, 73).

Another recurrent theme in Hayek's *The Road to Serfdom* is an analysis of the organizational logic of socialism, particularly the incentives motivating the planners and the shape they caused collective planning to take. Without market-generated information, socialism requires the exercise of political power to make it work. The best planners will therefore be the most power hungry and ruthless. The system thus selects the most unsavory characters to take its helm, who in turn have an incentive to extend their use of power as far as possible to enforce the plan and prevent others from taking their place. But power vested in the hands of the most devilish individuals is not the cause of socialism's problems, Hayek tells us. Rather it is the necessary consequence of the incentive structure created by planning in the first place, and the type of behavior required to make the plan feasible. In order for planning to work at all, discretionary rather than rule-bound power is requisite (Hayek, 1945, 56–87). In exploring the dynamics of democracy under socialism and the organizational logic of collective planning, Hayek was applying the "economic way of thinking" to political problems.

Joseph Schumpeter's work in *Capitalism, Socialism and Democracy* represents another example of an 'Austrian' contribution to public choice. In this book, Schumpeter's section on democracy not only offers an "inquiry" into the "nature of democracy," but also explodes the myths of the "Classical Doctrine of Democracy" and collective action (Schumpeter, 1942, 240). The classical doctrine is somewhat akin the pre-public choice approach to politics. Via majority votes, the "will of the people" is expressed and then carried out by public-spirited, benevolent politicians. In contrast to this, Schumpeter points out that it is also "possible to frame a theory of the democratic process that takes account of all the realities of group-wise action" (Schumpeter, 1942, 249). Schumpeter uses this account of the democratic process to dismantle the myths of the classical doctrine of democracy and paint a more realistic portrait of the democratic process.

Schumpeter's analysis anticipates the public choice concept of the rationally ignorant voter. He begins by pointing out that within the small sphere of his own private affairs,

the individual has very specialized knowledge of circumstances and behaves quite rationally because in these areas the individual not only has a great degree of control over things but also the effects of his decisions will be felt strongly due to his closeness to the issues upon which he is deciding. However, "when we move still farther away from the private concerns of the family and the business office into those regions of national and international affairs that lack a direct and unmistakable link to those private affairs, individual volition, command of facts and method of inference" cease to exist. When it comes to politics, becoming informed is costly and the perceived benefit very small due to the individual voter's inability to affect change. As a result, Schumpeter says, the average citizen "expends less disciplined effort on mastering a political problem than he expends on a game of bridge." Due to this pervasive problem, Schumpeter tells us, voter "ignorance will persist" (Schumpeter, 1942, 258–262).

Schumpeter also anticipated the public choice implications of such rational voter ignorance. Because obtaining and using credible information and reason to inform their decisions is too costly and yields no perceptible difference to the outcome, voters act on "irrational prejudice and impulse." This in turn, he points out, generates opportunities for politician-special interest group interaction to exert tremendous influence over political decisions. Politicians prey on the cost/benefit circumstance facing voters by offering "personal pecuniary profit to individual voters and groups of voters" in the form of "direct payments, protective duties, silver policies and so on" and spreading the costs across the ill-informed (Schumpeter, 1942, 260). Schumpeter's analysis gets at a central concern of public choice — the logic of concentrated benefits and dispersed costs.

Politician-special interest group dynamics, which form part of the logic of democracy, Schumpeter says, lead to the creation of *professional* politics. "[P]olitics will unavoidably be a career. This in turn spells recognition of a distinct professional interest in the individual politician and a distinct group interest in the political profession as such" (Schumpeter, 1942, 285). Contrary to the classical theory of democracy, Schumpeter suggests an approach in which politicians are viewed as engaged in a "competitive struggle for the people's vote," and politics is viewed as a business "dealing in votes" (Schumpeter, 1942, 269, 287).

3. The Constitutional Moment in Political Economy

The rebirth of political economy in modern economics is largely due to the scholarly output of James Buchanan.

Along with Gordon Tullock, he helped in the creation of research and teaching centers for political economy at University of Virginia, Virginia Polytechnic Institute, and George Mason University. Buchanan and Tullock's *The Calculus of Consent* (1962) is considered the *locus classicus* in constitutional political economy. Buchanan and Tullock's unique contribution to political economy was their emphasis on the 'constitutional moment'. In subsequent work, Buchanan has continually argued that one of the most important distinctions in political and economic analysis is the distinction between games *over* the rules, and games *within* the rules. In addition to his emphasis on the different levels of analysis, Buchanan has championed the use of the consistent use of the *homoeconomicus* postulate at both levels of analysis. The reason for this is rather straightforward — by making a "worst case" move at the pre-constitutional (game over the rules) and post-constitutional level (game within the rules), Buchanan is able to provide a *robust* theory of political economy. The rules of the game determine optimal strategies players will choose within the game, but the examination of those strategies and their impact can provide feedback in our judgment on whether the chosen rules are "good" rules for social order.

Buchanan's unique research program for political economy is well-known (if not always well understood), as is his intellectual connection to his 'teacher' Frank Knight. But, it is little known that Buchanan's position is one anticipated by the Austrian economics, and in particular F.A. Hayek. Buchanan's emphasis on rules and strategies is unique to him and Knight, but the intellectual strategy for building a robust set of rules for the economic game is not. Mises and Hayek explicitly sought to address the question of robustness in political economy.

Mid-century public interest theories assumed both benevolence and omniscience on the part of policy makers, and thus promoted a Romantic conception of the state. Ludwig Mises pointed out that whenever intellectual and moral perfection is attributed to the state the logically inescapable conclusion is that the state should be in direct control of all decision-making (Mises, 1949, 692). Because of the mid-century prevailing wisdom that in the social sciences questions of incentives were questions about motivation, and because of Mises's own style of value-free, he chose to question the assumption of intellectual perfection while leaving the assumption of moral perfection in place. Even if good spirited public officials wanted to allocate resources in an effective manner, they would not have the requisite information/knowledge to make rational economic calculations about the alternative use of scarce resources. This is the crux of Mises's famous "impossibility" thesis with regard to rational economic calculation under socialism.

Public choice economics as developed in the 1950s and 1960s, took a different analytical path. Public choice theorists adopted a hard-headed economics which challenged the benevolence assumption, but left the omniscient assumption alone. Political agents (voter, bureaucrat, politician) act in their own interest with perfect information. Hence, by ignoring the structural uncertainty of the future and the diffuseness and subjectivity of knowledge, public choice analysis, one could argue, is methodologically inconsistent with Austrian economics. On the other hand, Austrian political economy, challenges the omniscience assumption, but continues to be reluctant to relax benevolence (Kirzner, 1985; Ikeda, 1997) and is therefore inconsistent with public choice. In simplest terms, a combined Austrian-public choice approach to political economy would relax both assumptions, and many contributions to the broader literature in Virginia Political Economy fit within this category. This hybrid market process and public choice paradigm for political economy analysis was, in fact, championed by Hayek, and it was argued by him that this approach was indeed a crucial aspect of the great contribution which Hume and Smith made to human knowledge in the 18th century. As Hayek put it:

> [T]he main point about which there can be little doubt is that Smith's chief concern was not so much with what man might occasionally achieve when he was at his best but that he should have as little opportunity as possible to do harm when he was at his worst. It would scarcely be too much to claim that the main merit of the individualism which he and his contemporaries advocated is that it is a system under which bad men can do least harm. It is a social system which does not depend for its functioning on our finding good men for running it, or on all men becoming better than they now are, but which makes use of men in all their given variety and complexity, sometimes good and sometimes bad, sometimes intelligent and more often stupid. (1948, 11–12)

Hayek devoted his intellectual energies post-1950 to exploring the Smithian research program in political economy, and in particular the institutional design of a free society. *The Constitution of Liberty* (1960) and *Law, Legislation and Liberty* (1973–1979) sought to examine in detail the requisite institutional constraints in politics and law to maintain a free economy and a peaceful social order. Hayek, like Buchanan after him, argued that the state was both coercive and necessary for large-scale human society to emerge, but for that human society to flourish both argued that the coercive powers of the state must be severely restricted through constitutional design.

A particular concern in Hayek's writings is the consequences of the social system when one group is permitted to benefit at the expense of other groups. Special interest politics will undermine the legal and political order of a free people by diluting the 'generality' principle that underlies the rule of law. *Leges*, the Latin for the law, is to be contrasted with *privi-leges*. As we saw earlier with regard to the rule of law, Hayek was particularly concerned with the fixed features aspects of the institutional environment that a constitutionally limited government provides. As he wrote:

> The conception of freedom under the law that is the chief concern of this book rest on the contention that when we obey laws, in the sense of general abstract rules laid down irrespective of their application to us, we are not subject to another man's will and are therefore free. It is because the lawgiver does not know the particular cases to which his rules will apply, and it is because the judge who applies them has no choice in drawing the conclusions of the case, that it can be said that laws and not men rule. Because the rule is laid down in ignorance of the particular case and no man's will decides the coercion used to enforce it, the law is not arbitrary. This, however, is true only if by 'law' we mean the general rules that apply equally to everybody. This generality is probably the most important aspect of that attribute of law which we have called its 'abstractness.' (1960, 153)

Hayek further argues that the chief safeguard against abuse in a constitutionally limited government is that the rules must apply equally to everybody — the government as well as the governed — and that nobody be granted exceptions from the general rule. Buchanan and Roger Congleton attempt to tease out the full implications of the generality norm for the operation of democracy in *Politics By Principle, Not Interest* (1998).

In *Law, Legislation and Liberty*, Hayek pursued his critique of special interest politics from the point of view of generality even more forcefully. Hayek acknowledged the noble and inspiring constitutional project of the American founders, but concluded that "The first attempt to secure individual liberty by constitutions has evidently failed" (1973–1979, 1). Whereas in *The Constitution of Liberty* Hayek confined his discussion mainly to a restatement of the general principles of law in a liberal society, *Law, Legislation and Liberty* devotes considerably more time to institutional construction. Hayek tells his readers that his project can be usefully seen as an attempt to do what the founders would do if they had the benefit of the knowledge we have gained in the meantime since their time in terms of the institutional weaknesses of their own design to constrain the growth of government that threatens the preservation of individual freedom. In particular, Hayek had since the 1940s advocated various forms of federalism as a means of providing a competitive check (e.g., 1948, 255–71), but starting with *The Constitution of Liberty* (1960, 206, fn. 12)

and *Law, Legislation and Liberty* (1973–1979), Hayek presented arguments for alternative institutional structures — bi-cameralism, fixed term limits, and age requirements for legislators — that would curtail special interest politics from undermining the constitutional order.

It is not our intent to critically examine Hayek's institutional remedies to the problems of the democratic fetish (his term) and special interest politics. Instead, for our purposes we just wanted to point out how Hayek's work in constitutional political economy touched upon themes later developed in the work of James M. Buchanan. Buchanan is clearly one of the leading thinking in constitutional political economy, but Hayek's leading role in exploring the constitutional moment in political economy must be acknowledged as well.

4. Conclusion

We have argued that Austrian economists have made contributions to the economic analysis from politics that anticipated many of the major developments. Austrians were among the first economists that recognized that the economic way of thinking was not limited to market exchange, but was generally applicable across social settings. We have concentrated our survey on the work of Mises, Hayek and Schumpeter and pointed out how various key concepts in public choice analysis — for example, special interest manipulation; the logic of concentrated benefits and dispersed costs in political decision making; voter ignorance; the bundled nature of political decisions; bureaucratic incentives; and the constitutional moment — are deployed by these Austrian economists in their political economy scholarship dating from the 1940s. The Austrian economists, in short, possess deep methodological, analytical and ideological affinities with their public choice brethren — especially of the Virginia School tradition.

PETER BOETTKE
PETER LEESON

REFERENCES

Bohm-Bawerk, E. (1881). "Are Legal Rights Economic Goods." Reprinted in *Shorter Classics*. South Holland: Libertarian Press.

Buchanan, J.M. (1969). *Cost and Choice*. Chicago: The University of Chicago Press.

Buchanan, J.M. (1977). *The Limits of Liberty*. Chicago: The University of Chicago Press.

Buchanan, J.M. (1978). *What Should Economists Do?* Indianapolis: Liberty Press.

Buchanan, J.M. and Congleton, R.D. (1998). *Politics By Principle, Not Interest*. New York: Cambridge University Press.

Buchanan, J.M. and Tullock, G. (1962). *The Calculus of Consent: Logical Foundations of Constitutional Democracy*. Ann Arbor: University of Michigan Press.

Hayek, F.A. (1945). *The Road to Serfdom*. Chicago: The University of Chicago Press.

Hayek, F.A. (1948). *Individualism and Economic Order*. Chicago: The University of Chicago Press.

Hayek, F.A. (1952). *The Counter-Revolution of Science*. Indianapolis: Liberty Classics, 1979.

Hayek, F.A. (1960). *The Constitution of Liberty*. Chicago: The University of Chicago Press.

Hayek, F.A. (1973–1979). *Law, Legislation and Liberty*, 3 volumes. Chicago: The University of Chicago Press.

Ikeda, S. (1997). *The Dynamics of the Mixed Economy*. London: Routledge.

Kirzner, I. (1976). *The Economic Point of View*. Kansas City: Sheed, Andrews, McMeel.

Kirzner, I. (1985). "The perils of regulation," in ibid., *Capitalism and the Discovery Process*. Chicago: The University of Chicago Press.

Knight, F. (1934). "The common sense of political economy (Wicksteed Reprinted)." Reprinted in F. Knight (ed.), *On the History and Method of Economics*. Chicago: The University of Chicago Press, 1956, pp. 104–118.

Mises, L. (1944). *Bureaucracy*. New Haven: Yale University Press.

Mises, L. (1945). "The clash of group interests," in Richard Ebeling (ed.) *Money, Method and Market Process*. Boston: Kluwer Academic Publishers, 1990, pp. 202–214.

Mises, L. (1949). *Human Action: A Treatise on Economics*. New Haven: Yale University Press.

Niskanen W.A. (1994). *Bureaucracy and Public Economics*. Aldershot, UK and Brookfield, VT: Edward Elgar Publishing.

Schumpeter, J.A. (1942). *Capitalism, Socialism and Democracy*. New York: Harper & Row, 1950.

AUTOCRACY

Historically democracy has been a rather unusual form of government. At the moment about half of the human race lives under a democratic government with the poverty stricken citizens of India making up almost half of that half. This is historically unusual, but not unique. Many of the Greek city states, Rome in its early years, and most of the Phoenician city states were democracies with sharply restricted franchises. In addition, of the current non-democratic nations, almost all are dictatorships. This is also unusual. Mainly, autocratic governments have been hereditary monarchies. It seems likely that the existing dictatorships if they do not become democracies, will shift to hereditary monarchies in time. At the moment the rulers of North Korea, the area which used to be the Belgian Congo, and Syria are relatives of the previous autocrat. Libya, Iraq and Cuba show signs of moving in the same direction.

Since most of the existing autocracies are not hereditary, I will start by discussing them and then turn to hereditary monarchies later. The first thing to be said about non-hereditary dictators is that they have obtained their position by climbing the slippery pole. They are normally highly intelligent, personally brave, because the contest for dictatorships is dangerous, and rather unscrupulous. They have proven their mastery of intrigue and battle, albeit the battle is mainly within the bureaucracy. Still a number of them have engaged in the kind of battle in the bureaucracy which sometimes is fatal. Almost all of them have been efficient in disposing of their rivals by deadly or less than deadly means.

In all this is hardly a selection process that will lead to the noble and just reaching ultimate control. Still there is no reason to believe that the winners have bad motives. They are unusually ambitious, but not necessarily wicked in any other respect. They are as likely to choose a government policy that will benefit those subjected to the dictatorship as is a democratically elected president. In both cases intelligence, energy, ambition, and a lack of too many scruples are necessary. Once he has achieved power the autocrat will realize that the higher officials in his government would like to replace him. They are the instruments that he must use in governing but they are also his rivals. Keeping the system balanced so that he makes use of their talents while preventing one of them from making use of him as a stepping stone to ultimate power for himself is a difficult task, and one which he must master if he is to stay in power. Of course any knowledge of the history of such autocracies will show that not all of them succeed in that task.

Normally such a dictator has the best interest of his country and his citizens in mind, but it must necessarily take second-place to protecting his power. In this sense he is like a democratic president. The president normally aims at the good of his country, but he normally is more concerned with winning the next election. The two objectives do not necessarily conflict, but when they do, the president is apt to give winning election priority. Similarly a dictator will give preventing a coup or revolution priority over simply benefiting his subjects.

One thing that should be kept in mind dealing with either hereditary or non-hereditary autocrats is that their attitude to what are commonly called public goods is radically different than that of the ordinary person. For them many public goods are actually private goods. An improved road can be regarded as a public good from the standpoint of the citizens or the economic analysis, but it may increase the wealth or security of the autocrat and hence is a private good from his standpoint. This is of course one of the reasons why autocrats in fact provide so much in the way of public goods.

This should not be oversimplified, however. The autocrat like a democratic politician is aware of the fact that the road will benefit the country as a whole but also special-interest groups in it. Thus like a democratic politician he selects the public goods in part in terms of what they will do in benefiting influential individuals and groups who may repay that benefit by support. It is doubtful that by simply examining the road network or other collections of government expenditures on public goods one would be able to tell whether the government was a dictatorship or a democracy. If the democracy is not particularly corrupt, one could tell by examining such things as the Swiss bank accounts of the "President."

Examining the personal life of the ruler is usually one way of telling whether he is a president or dictator. The dictator has far more facilities to keep things secret than does an elected president. He can have a spectacular mistress or even a harem, palaces much more elaborate than the White House, and take long vacations without the public finding out about them. Of course if he wishes to stay in power he will find that leaving his government to take care of itself for any length of time is likely to lead to his being replaced by one of his high-ranking subordinates.

The Oriental myth in which the ruler sits under a bare sword supported only by a thread is not a bad description of the life of such an autocrat. Many autocrats, Stalin and Mao Sze Dung are examples, have died naturally. Many others have died either by assassination or as the result of a successful coup. Finding it necessary to retire and live on their illicit gains in some place safer than their own country is also quite common. Trying to arrange a peaceful succession followed by a luxurious retirement is difficult.

The conventional wisdom assumes that dictators provide bad government. In the earlier part of my life, particularly during the 1960s, however, the orthodoxy held that certain dictators; specifically Stalin and Mao Sze Dung provided very much better governments than capitalist democracies. Many intellectuals genuinely believed that Ho Chi Min would give a better government than would any elected alternative. Yet, all such favored autocrats were mass murderers and all of them favored an economic system which, if at the time was fashionable, is now realized to be seriously defective. Ho's rivals in the South were victimized by street riots in the United States, that eventually led successive American governments to abandon them. In the case of one of them, Diem, President Kennedy actually organized a coup to get rid of him. Altogether uneasy lies the head that wears the crown.

We now turn to the more common type autocracy, the hereditary monarchy. It should be kept in mind that hereditary monarchies, if more stable than dictatorships, are by no means free of risk. Most of the readers of this encyclopedia will be more familiar with English history than other monarchies, and, as it happens, the English throne was one of the least stable in Europe. It was decidedly uncommon in England for a great-grandson to succeed to the throne peacefully. Most monarchies have been able to pass on their power with less difficulty so that three generations after the founder are reasonably common.

The hereditary king is in personality and ability quite different from the man who was fought his way up the slippery pole to dictatorship. In the first place the accidents of human heredity mean that the son of extraordinarily capable and ambitious person may well be quite stupid and lazy. Louis XVI seems to have been not very much above a moron in intellectual ability. He used to fall asleep at cabinet meetings. Since the United States was given its independence by his support, I suppose we should refrain from criticisms, though he was quickly abandoned by Thomas Jefferson once his purpose had been served. From the standpoint of France, however, Louis XVI was a disaster.

Of course, some hereditary monarchs are of outstanding capacity. Alexander the Great is an excellent example. But on the average hereditary monarchs do not have intellectual or character capacity greater than that of the average citizen. Typically, they receive special training as children intended to prepare them for royal careers. Unfortunately, this special training may educate them in expensive and entertaining ways of spending leisure time as well as in how to govern. In some cases, in fact training in luxury takes full priority over training intended to increase the competence of the future monarch. All this is rather similar to the training of the only son of a wealthy and powerful man in an open society. Altogether the hereditary monarch is quite a different person from the dictator who has achieved power by competition. It is not obvious which of them is better from the standpoint of the average citizen.

"The Prince" is largely devoted to advice to a sovereign ruler on how to retain power. Napoleon liked to keep his generals quarreling. Machiaveli would surely have approved. Mussolini moved his higher officials around and put some of them out of government for lengthy periods. He called this "changing the guard". Once again he would have met the approval of the author of "The Prince". Indeed most rulers do rotate the armed men who provide physical security. In Stalin's time the secret police officers who guarded him and his higher officials would not know where they were to serve on a given day nor with whom they would be serving. These two things were determined by random draws so that they could not conspire in advance to admit dangerous persons.

Precautions like these are more frequently encountered among non-hereditary autocracies than among hereditary monarchies. Nevertheless, crown princes have killed their fathers and dynasties have been overthrown. So at least some precautions are always necessary. It is not obvious that the cost of guarding an autocrat is greater than the cost of guarding presidents and legislatures. Indeed it seems likely that the total cost in terms of office space, living space when that is provided, and guards in Washington is greater than the equivalent cost in Berlin during the Third Reich. The guards serve a different purpose of course. The president does not fear assassination by a senator but by a conspiracy of low ranking people. Nevertheless he requires guards and so do the Senators, Congressman, and high civil servants.

The decision processes in democracies and in autocracies are quite different. In general, policy debates are conducted rather quietly in autocracies whereas they make a lot of noise in democracies. Further although autocrats sometimes tell their cabinet to vote on policies, the final decision is theirs. There is a myth that when Lincoln proposed the emancipation proclamation his cabinet all voted against. Lincoln then said, "Passed unanimously." This is a myth but it does show the power that a central single person can have even in so-called democracies.

That the common man has little influence on policies in autocracies is normally regarded as a disadvantage of that form of government. There are, however, a number of cases in which democracies have been overthrown by autocrats with popular support. Both of the Napoleon's carried off such an operation. So did Mussolini. Normally however autocracies are established by well entrenched and armed minorities that displace democracies by means of *coups d'etat*.

The view that democracy is better than autocracy is a current orthodoxy. There are cases where everyone favors the autocracy. The citizens of Rome and modern historians think that Augustus Caesar provide a better government than the late Republic. Gibbon lists the period of the adoptive emperors as the happiest time in the history of the human race. Not everyone is as enthusiastic, but it must be admitted that they gave very good government. One of them was also a philosopher of such importance that his work is still taught in modern universities.

There appear to have been three comparatively short periods in which democracy was common before modern times. It is not clear but it looks as if the first civilization, Sumer, had democratic aspects; but these were quickly extinguished. The second was a classical period of Greece Rome and Phoenicia. This ended when the Roman Republic conquered the bulk of the other democratic systems. It itself was replaced by emperors. The third case is a large collection of democratically governed city-states in the Middle Ages. Most but not all of these were replaced by 1600 or earlier. Altogether autocracies were the dominant to form of government until very recently. Whether they will continue to account for about half of all governments, or rise to complete dominance or fall back to a minority form of government is uncertain. I have my own preferences; but there is no evidence that these preferences will prevail.

GORDON TULLOCK

REFERENCES

Tullock, G. (1974). *The Social Dilemma: The Economics of War and Revolution*. Blacksburg: Center for Study of Public Choice.
Tullock, G. (1987). *Autocracy*. Dordrecht: Kluwer Academic Publishers.

AUTOCRATIC SUCCESSION

In autocracies a "succession" takes place, when one autocrat replaces another. In practice, this happens in one of three ways: An autocrat may live out his term of office, or he may retire peacefully (e.g., voluntarily or when his term expires), or he may be forced out. Obviously some of these options are not exclusively at the discretion of the autocrat alone, and his future will depend on his foresight and his ability to protect himself, and among these are his ability to nominate his own successor or change the succession rules. Seen from the perspective of a potential contender for the role as autocrat, the choices are, in a way, more simple: He can do nothing and hope to become the autocrat himself some day or he can try to improve his own career prospects by forcing the autocrat out of office. Either way, the situation is one of strategic interaction and with institutions playing an important role.

This is not a trivial problem. Historically all states, including existing democracies, have begun as autocracies of some form and moved through a long process of state building, including — among many other things — a constitutionalization of the regime, whereby its procedures have been formalized, either through written and explicit constitutions, or through agreements and implicit and gradually evolved common law rules (cf. De Long and Shleifer, 1993; Congleton, 2001). Accordingly, the succession of one autocrat to another is probably the most frequent type of regime change in world history. Nonetheless, except for anecdotal studies the question of autocratic succession has only received little attention. The first scholar to investigate the issue theoretically was Gordon Tullock in his public choice analyses of autocracy (Tullock, 1974, 1987a,b, 2001), and this has recently been formalized and empirically applied (Kurrild-Klitgaard, 2000; cf. Anderson and Boettke, 1993).

In order to analyze the strategic considerations facing autocrats and contenders, we may distinguish between two different elements typically found in the succession rules of autocracies: eligibility rules and selection rules. Eligibility rules regulate who may come into consideration as possible new autocrats in terms of, e.g., sex, family, caste, class, or political party. Selection rules stipulate the proper procedures for how to select the autocrat from among those eligible and may range from the simple and informal to the complex and formal; they may stipulate, e.g., that the successor is appointed by the autocrat, or that he is elected by some body, or that there is some combination of appointment and approval. Finally, an autocracy may be strictly hereditary, as the vast majority of European autocracies have been over the last — at least — 2000 years, but even hereditary autocracies exhibit a wide range of different selection rules.

For analytical purposes we will distinguish between three ideal typical forms of succession rules: "Open" succession where no individual is pre-selected as the autocrat's automatic successor and two forms of "closed" succession: one where the successor is appointed and one hereditary. The strategic choices of autocrats and contenders may obviously be very different under such alternative rules. To see this, let us assume that there are two relevant positions: That of autocrat and that of potential successor, i.e., a contender who aspires to succeed the autocrat, and who may or may not be a relative. Let us further assume that the potential successor is faced with a simple choice of either trying to overthrow the autocrat or remaining passive and not attempt a coup. The variables to be considered include the benefits of being autocrat, the probability of becoming the next autocrat if he himself puts the present autocrat out of office, but also the direct costs associated with the coup and the potential costs of an unsuccessful overthrow and the probability of incurring these. All these must be compared with those of remaining passive, first and foremost the benefits from being a potential successor and the probability of remaining so. The requirement for a potential successor to attempt to overthrow is accordingly that his expected payoff from doing so must exceed his expected payoff from remaining in his current position. If this is not the case, then the rational course of action for the potential successor will be to remain passive.

Obviously, the autocrat himself has a say in the process. We should expect an autocrat to try to maximize his expected payoff, i.e., his benefits of being an autocrat as well as the probability of maintaining this position, which we for the present purposes will assume is a function of the constitutional rule governing succession; this is, of course, an extreme simplification, but one which for the present purposes may be defensible. Thus, if an autocrat is faced with a choice between the two or more constitutional rules, we may assume that he will favor the one that will minimize the danger of coups. Constitutional rules can, however, never be changed without costs, and he must therefore also consider these transaction costs when considering his expected payoff from alternative rules. In other words, if the costs of changing a constitutional rule of succession are low or non-existent, the ruling autocrat will prefer that rule which he believes will maximize his probability of remaining so. And if he has the power to do so, he will change the constitutional rule from one he prefers less to one he prefers more.

Under a constitutional rule of open succession, there will typically be several individuals contending for the place as the successor, and they may have much to gain. On the other hand, it is often a relatively low-cost enterprise to depose autocrats; the direct costs are quite small (often just the investment, e.g., in some poison, a knife, or a gun). Furthermore, a contender in an autocracy with open succession will not know for certain that he will end up succeeding, and so he must do something about the situation himself. There may even be some element of self-defense in doing so, since other contenders may have an interest in improving their own chances by worsening his. This will clearly negatively affect his expected benefits from passivity, and hence increase his expected payoff of attempting an overthrow relatively. If there are several contenders in an autocracy with no constitutional rules of succession at all, any equilibrium may turn out to be extremely fragile, and the situation one of continuously shifting coalitions, coups, and counter-coups. On the other hand, the uncertainty may also work in exactly the opposite direction, if the expected costs of an unsuccessful coup attempt are considerable, in which case the equilibrium may be that nobody dares move first. An autocracy with open succession may accordingly exhibit either extreme instability or a considerable stability, depending on whether institutions may be developed that will induce and support equilibria and increase the costs of attempting a coup.

In a regime with appointed succession the autocrat's challenge is to choose someone who is unlikely to pose a serious threat against himself. For while an appointed successor may be relatively better off than one who is merely one out of several contenders, the latter's expected benefits of overthrowing the autocrat are considerable, especially if he is certain that he will become the new autocrat and the direct costs of attempting a coup are likely to be negligible. Finally, since he is the appointed successor the probabilities of getting away with it are quite favorable. The appointed successor must also consider the risk that the autocrat may change his mind and appoint another heir as well as the risk that some other hopeful will try to eliminate the appointed successor in order for him to take this place. Both possibilities will affect the appointed successor's expected benefits negatively and increase his expected payoff of a coup attempt relatively.

If we compare these considerations with those of a system with hereditary succession, there are important differences. The differential in gains between the current position and that of an autocrat may be smaller for an heir-apparent than for a remote contender, while the risk of being removed by the autocrat or others, or dying before succeeding, are quite small. Furthermore, an heir-apparent in a hereditary monarchy is often a relatively young person, whereas an appointed successor in a non-hereditary autocracy (or a contender in an autocracy with open succession) may be more resourceful individuals in their own right and of an age and experience comparable to that of the autocrat himself. The high certainty of succession, which may create the incentive for an appointed successor to kill off the autocrat, thus works in exactly the opposite direction under hereditary succession.

Some simples games may illustrate the evolution of constitutional rules of succession in autocracies. Let us assume that we have two players, the Autocrat (A) and the potential Successor (S), and that each has a choice between two different strategies. The Autocrat may choose between two succession rules (R_o or R_h), where the former is maintaining a status quo of open succession and the latter is a new rule of hereditary succession, while the potential Successor may choose between either attempting an overthrow (O) or remaining passive (P). Let us further assume that it indeed is the case that hereditary autocracies exhibit more stability and fewer coups than non-hereditary autocracies, and that the costs of changing succession rules are negligible.

Given these assumptions, it follows that the Autocrat favors the new rule (hereditary succession) over the present rule (open succession), and we may assume that the Autocrat's preference ordering over the outcomes is a given by the lower left numbers in the cells of the matrix in Figure 1. Let us furthermore assume that potential Successors may come in one of two forms: Those who may be personally benefiting from a change in the rules (e.g., because they will come closer to the position as Autocrat) and those who will not benefit. In that case we may have two types of games. Let us, for example, assume that the potential Successor, is someone who would benefit directly from this new rule, an Heir-Apparent (S_h), and that the difference between the benefits of remaining a potential successor and becoming autocrat faster and with greater certainty is small, and that the costs involved in attempting a coup are insignificant. In that case we may give his preference ordering over the outcomes as in the upper right corners of the cells of the matrix in Figure 1. This game has a unique Nash equilibrium, namely the outcome (R_h, P), i.e., that the Autocrat will change the rules from open succession to hereditary

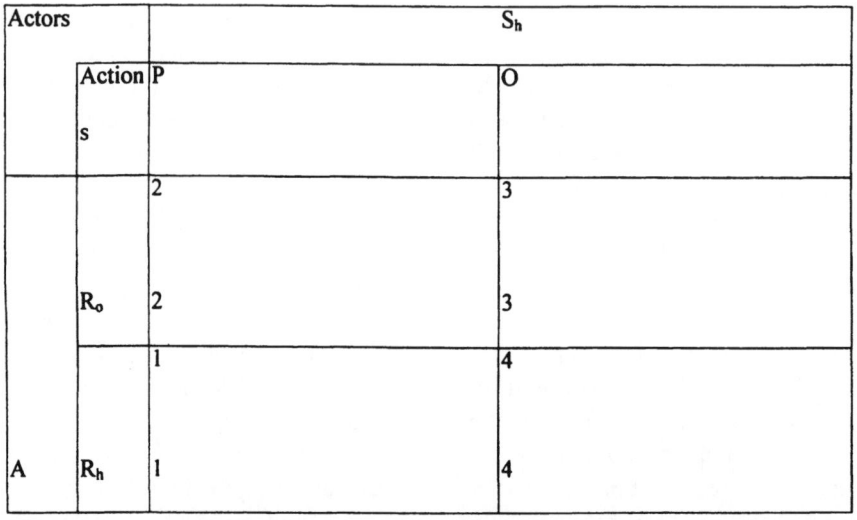

Actors			S_h
	Action s	P	O
		2	3
	R_o	2	3
		1	4
A	R_h	1	4

Figure 1: Interaction between autocrat and heir-apparent.

succession, while his Heir-Apparent will not attempt a coup but remain passive.

A slightly different situation is where the potential Successor is someone who would not benefit directly from this new rule, i.e., a more remote contender (S_c). Let us assume that the difference between the benefits of remaining a potential successor and becoming autocrat faster and with greater certainty are considerable, but that the costs involved in attempting a coup vary depending on whether the succession is open or hereditary. In that case the interaction may have the structure of the game in Figure 2, which has two Nash equilibria, (R_h, P) and (R_o, O), and thus resembles the game called Chicken. In this game, one player will give in, if the other gets his will.

These games illustrate that given certain assumptions one should expect an autocrat to attempt to move from open succession to hereditary, and that this will coincide with potential successors generally not attempting coups. They are of course extremely stylized, and in the real world the situation is far less simple; most fundamentally, we are here only considering two types of succession, and the evolution of constitutional rules are rarely the outcome of the decisions of a single individual, not even succession rules in autocracies. An important point to note is that if the costs of changing the succession rules are considerable, the autocrat's preference ordering over the outcomes may likely be: (R_o, P) (tm) (R_h, P) (tm) (R_o, O) (tm) (R_h, O). The game between Autocrat and Heir-Apparent now has the unique Nash equilibrium (R_o, P), i.e., the Heir-Apparent will still not attempt a coup and the Autocrat will not attempt to change the rules. In contrast, the game between Autocrat and Contender now has a unique Nash equilibrium (R_o, O),

i.e., the latter will attempt a coup, while the Autocrat still will stick with the rules.

This analysis highlights the importance of the costs of changing rules: If the autocrat's costs of doing so are negligible, he will try to move towards hereditary rules. We should thus expect that autocracies over time will move from open succession to hereditary succession; appointed succession will, in contrast, generally only occur as a proxy for hereditary succession. Another implication is that simultaneous with such a process, we should expect that there would be a decline in the number of coups against autocrats undertaken by potential successors. In this way the introduction of hereditary succession may be seen as a rational form of self-defense.

The empirical applicability of these results may be illustrated with data from two of the European states with the longest periods of unbroken autocratic regimes, Denmark ca. 935–1849 and Sweden ca. 970–1844. In the period under consideration, Denmark had approximately 54 autocratic "reigns," and of these 13 monarchs (24 pct.) may be said to have been deposed by their successors. The observations include periods with open succession (935–1165 and 1326–1340), appointed succession combined with election (1165–1326 and 1340–1536), and more or less formalized hereditary succession (1536–1849). In the periods with open succession, almost every second monarch was deposed by his successor, while more or less formalized hereditary succession guaranteed an extraordinary degree of stability. The periods with a combination of appointed succession and subsequent election were relatively stable, at least when compared with those of open succession. In Table 1 the data have been submitted to a simple χ^2 statistical test, which

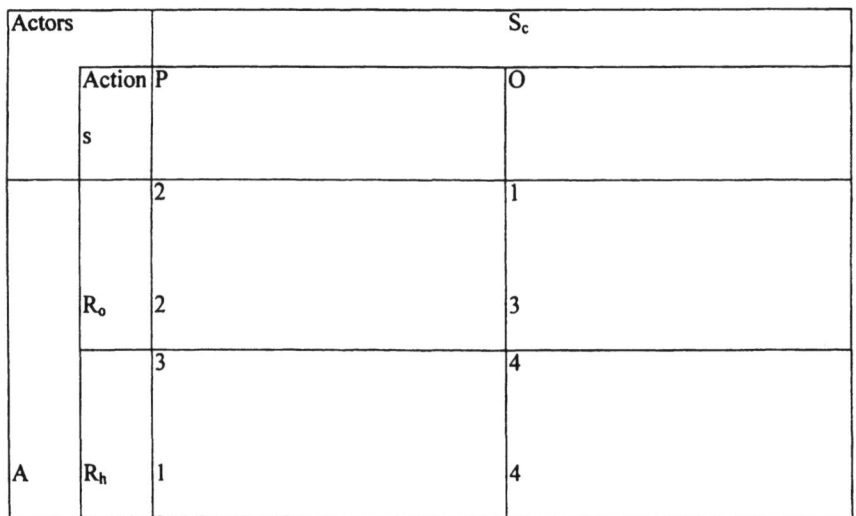

Actors			S_c
	Action s	P	O
		2	1
	R_o	2	3
		3	4
A	R_h	1	4

Figure 2: Interaction between autocrat and contender.

Table 1: Coups and constitutional rules of succession, Denmark ca. 935–1849

Constitutional rule	Non-coups	Coups	Total
Open succession	13	10	23
Appointed succession	16	3	19
Hereditary succession	12	0	12
Total	41	13	54

χ^2 (Pearson): 9.256; P: 0.010.
χ^2 (Likelihood ratio): 11.542; P: 0.003.

Table 2: Coups and constitutional rules of succession, Sweden ca. 970–1844

Constitutional rule	Non-coups	Coups	Total
Open/app. succession	23	31	54
Hereditary succession	15	2	17
Total	38	33	71

χ^2 (Pearson): 10.828; P: 0.001.
χ^2 (Likelihood ratio): 12.089; P: 0.001.

shows that a null hypothesis of the number of coups against monarchs being independent of the constitutional rules of succession must be rejected at a high level of significance.

In the period considered Sweden experienced approximately 71 monarchical "reigns," of which 33 monarchs are known to have been deposed by their successors (46 pct.). The amount and quality of information about the early medieval period is not perfect, but with some reservations the observations may be divided into two periods: more or less open succession, i.e., with election or appointment (ca. 970–1544) and hereditary succession (1544–1844). In the former period 31 out of 54 monarchs were deposed by their immediate successors (57 pct.), while in the latter only two of 17 monarchs were (12 pct.). Table 2 summarizes the

statistical data and shows that the null hypothesis again must be rejected at a very high level of significance.

The empirical evidence, such as it is, thus overwhelmingly suggests that there is truth to Tullock's claims that autocracies with hereditary succession will have less coups than those with some form of open succession, and that autocracies over time tend to move from non-hereditary to hereditary succession rules. Furthermore, the suggestion by Tullock (1987a: 162) that on average approximately one in five monarchs are deposed by their successors comes quite close to the over-all ratio of coups/monarchs in the Danish case (24 pct.), while it underestimates the frequency of coups in Sweden (46 pct.). As an interesting perspective we may mention that one study has summarized the English succession 1066–1702 as containing 31 monarchs of which 18 were deposed or whose reign otherwise resulted in a disputed succession (De Long and Shleifer, 1993); if we extend this period to include the other British monarchs up to Queen Victoria, the result is 18 out of 43 (42 pct.).

PETER KURRILD-KLITGAARD

REFERENCES

Anderson, G. and Boettke, P.J. (1993). "Perestroika and public choice: the economics of autocratic succession in a rent-seeking society." *Public Choice*, 75(2): 101–118.

Congleton, R.D. (2001). "On the durability of king and council: the continuum between dictatorship and democracy." *Constitutional Political Economy*, 12(3): 193–215.

De Long, J.B. and Shleifer, A. (1993). "Princes and merchants: European city growth before the industrial revolution." *Journal of Law and Economics*, 36(2): 671–702.

Kurrild-Klitgaard, P. (2000). "The constitutional economics of autocratic succession." *Public Choice*, 103(1–2): 63–84.

Tullock, G. (1974). *The Social Dilemma: The Economics of War and Revolution*. Blacksburg: Center for Study of Public Choice.

Tullock, G. (1987a). *Autocracy*. Dordrecht: Kluwer.

Tullock, G. (1987b). "Autocracy," in G. Radnitzky and P. Bernholz (eds.) *Economic Imperialism: The Economic Approach Applied Outside the Field of Economics*. New York: Paragon, pp. 365–381.

Tullock, G. (2001). "Monarchies, hereditary and non-hereditary," in W.F. Shugart and L. Razzolini (eds.) *The Elgar Companion to Public Choice*. Cheltenham: Edward Elgar, pp. 140–156.

B

BICAMERALISM

A bicameral structure divides members of the legislative branch into two separate decision-making bodies, or chambers. This structure requires each legislative proposal to be approved at least twice, obtaining a majority vote in each chamber before it can become law. Montesquieu first put forth the idea of separate legislative chambers as an institution to limit the ability of one group to use its majority status to dominate the minority, and the first experiment with bicameralism appears to be in 14th Century England. Since then bicameralism has been widely praised as the best possible compromise between constituents of "common people," typically, best represented in the lower chamber, and aristocrats, represented in the upper chamber, to prevent each organized interest from plundering the other (Tsebelis and Rasch, 1995; Tsebelis and Money, 1997). In James Madison's words, "the improbability of sinister combinations will be in proportion to the dissimilarity of the two bodies" (*Federalist* No. 62).

In the early Twenty-first Century roughly one-third of the world's democracies employ a dual-chambered legislative branch; however, among more developed democracies the bicameral legislature is the dominant institutional choice. Bicameralism has not always been the norm, even in the United States where all but one of the states have bicameral legislatures; instead, it evolved from unicameral systems used in the pre-Revolutionary war era. Initially, most American colonies had single chamber legislatures whose members represented different coalitions of citizens. These coalitions ultimately grew and then separated into distinct chambers for passing laws. By the time of the founding of the United States in 1789 only Pennsylvania and Georgia still operated under unicameral systems. At the national level, the United States' first legislature under the Articles of Confederation was unicameral, a contentious element with the Articles. Drawing on this experience, the Framers feared that assigning legislative power only to states or to the population as a whole would result in the tyranny of majority by small population states or large population states. The eventual compromise over constituent representation was deemed so important to the constitutional convention that it was dubbed the "Great Compromise." The adoption of a bicameral system under the new Constitution,

with two legislative bodies differently composed, was considered a progressive step to alleviate many of the problems with the former system.

Modern scholars who have analyzed bicameralism using formal techniques generally reach a common conclusion, one that reinforces the Framers' intuitive logic (Hammond and Miller, 1987; Brennan and Hamlin, 1992; Riker, 1992; Perrson et al., 1997; Tsebelis and Money, 1997; Diermeir and Myerson, 1999). A bicameral structure predictably protects minority interests through two channels, which we label *constituent homogeneity* and *legislative stability*. We describe each channel, discuss empirical measures of bicameralism, and conclude with a summary of studies that examine the effects of bicameralism on policy making and fiscal outcomes.

1. Constituent Homogeneity

Seminal works in modern political economy posit that the major effect of bicameralism stems from different bases of representation in the two chambers. Tullock (1959) first noted that a second legislative chamber dampens the inherent problem of tyranny of the majority much like the adoption of inclusive voting rules (for example, a rule that requires a two-thirds majority to approve legislation). The requirement to satisfy legislative preferences in two differently composed chambers decreases the likelihood that a minority's interests will be ignored in the final agreement (Buchanan and Tullock, 1962; Stigler, 1976; Crain, 1979; Hayek, 1979; Tsebelis and Money, 1997; Bradbury and Crain, 2001, 2002).

If the composition of chambers leads to differing policy preferences for the median representative in each chamber, these differences predictably affect legislative outcomes. Consider the extreme case in which the districts in the two chambers hold no constituents in common. As Gilligan et al. (1989) note, in that case "when different interests dominate different houses, each interest, in effect, holds a veto over legislation." However, as the difference shrinks between the median voters in the chambers, it becomes increasingly easy for the two chambers to reach consensus on policy. More similarity across the two chambers facilitates inter-cameral trade, because as constituencies across chambers become more similar, bicameral chambers will be more likely to agree on which constituents to tax or to subsidize.

The homogeneity of constituencies raises potentially observable implications. First, two chambers with quite different constituencies should experience less spending on redistributive projects than two chambers with similar preferences. Second, spending on public goods should increase as constituent diversity across chambers increases. As redistribution becomes difficult, and therefore relatively less likely to occur, constituents will be more willing to bear higher tax burdens because revenues will be devoted to expenditures on public goods.

2. Legislative Stability

Riker (1992) and Levmore (1992) tout the second virtue of bicameralism: the use of dual legislative chambers to reduce the feasible set of policy outcomes, which in turn produces stability in legislative outcomes. If preferences are multi-dimensional and unstable, fiscal policy may cycle with changes in the majority coalition over time. A bicameral structure may reduce cyclical majority problems by excluding many non-Condorcet-winning majorities from the legislative choice set. If the legislature enacts a law that can be defeated by the formation of a new coalition, a change in legislative preferences, or legislative turnover, policy outcomes will change frequently. This can impose costs on the economy through the instability of laws and by encouraging legislators to act strategically to maximize profit from short-run majority tyranny in response to cycles. A dual chamber legislature induces legislative stability similar to a supermajority rule, yet it has the advantage of allowing majority agreement on single-dimension policy issues that do not cause policy cycles. For instance, spending decisions regarding public goods, on which there is likely to be stable majority agreement, will pass under a simple majority rule. However, under a supermajority requirement these projects might not pass even though they would not increase budget swings. Bicameralism uniquely reduces the passage of non-Condorcet winners on multi-dimensional issues while allowing majority agreement on single-dimensional issues.

Dixit et al. (2000) provide a related argument for why a bicameral legislature is superior to a unicameral chamber operating under a supermajority rule. In the model, two interests vie for the power to make political decisions. The party in power may use its status to exploit the minority or adopt general rules. Because this is a repeated game parties may decide to enter into agreements so that the ruling party will not exploit the minority. The current party knows that in the future the minority party may come to power and punish the current party for wealth reducing policies. Under a simple majority rule, party dominance is more likely to change than under supermajority rule where the defecting party cannot be punished until the exploited party gains the necessary representation. A party changeover in power is less likely under a supermajority rule, because the minority power must obtain a larger vote-share than it would under

simple majority rule. Thus, the ruling party will be more willing to renege than it would be under a simple majority rule, because of the reduced chance of retaliation or the retaliation is far in the future.

Thus, bicameralism offers a second advantage in protecting minority interests relative to a unicameral chamber with a supermajority rule. Bicameral chambers composed of opposing interests can continually enforce legislative agreements rather than relying on the threat of retaliation to enforce legislative bargains over time, which is the only enforcement option in unicameral legislatures. If different interests control the chambers then the parties do not have to enforce legislative agreements through retaliation over time. A veto player limits the likelihood of minority exploitation in each period.

3. Measures of Bicameralism and Empirical Studies

Several empirical papers stress the many variations in bicameralism, even among the American States. Early empirical studies of American state bicameral chambers, such as Crain (1979) and McCormick and Tollison (1981) observed differences in chamber size affect legislative output. Crain (1979) finds as chamber sizes become more equal legislative output, measured in terms of legislation passed, increases. McCormick and Tollison (1981) find that more equal chamber size leads to economies of scale in redistributive lobbying, and thus increases redistributive activity. More recently Bradbury and Crain (2002) examine bicameral differences using proxies of constituent preferences. The empirical model measures bicameralism not a discrete structure, but rather a continuous institutional arrangement based on the degree of constituent homogeneity across chambers. This ranges from identically composed chambers to totally different bases of representation across the chambers. In this perspective, as the chambers' demographic characteristics become more diverse the legislature becomes increasingly "bicameral." Changes in the identity of the median legislator within each chamber alters the degree of bicameralism, and determines the similarity of the dominant coalitions between the two chambers. To reiterate, the impact of bicameralism on policy comes principally from the different bases of representation across the two chambers. Moreover, measured in this way, the degree of bicameralism, at least in American legislatures, changes regularly as a consequence of the redistricting process.

The theoretical analysis predicts that bicameralism should make spending more efficient — not simply limit the spending level — by limiting agreement to the set of policies agreed upon by the median constituents of both chambers. This suggests that increased bicameralism may increase spending in some areas of the state budget but not others. As legislators become less able to seek transfers, they may devote more spending to efficient public goods where they agree. Results for the American States indicate that bicameralism is positively related to education expenditures, highway expenditures, and total expenditures, in other words programs that might be considered public goods. In contrast, bicameralism is negatively related to expenditures on welfare and other redistributive programs.

Internationally, Bradbury and Crain (2001) examine the discrete difference between bicameral and unicameral systems in different countries. Specifically, this study examines the effect of the bicameral institution on redistributive spending due to the "Law of $1/n$," which is pork-barrel spending fueled by an increase in elected representatives. The study finds that countries with bicameral legislatures experience less $1/n$ spending than unicameral countries, which is consistent with the hypothesis that adding a second legislative chamber limits redistributive spending.

In summary, modern analysis and empirical evidence indicate that bicameral chambers serve the intended purpose of the Founding Fathers to limit government to the protection of the "general welfare." This has particularly strong policy implications for new and developing countries that seek to design constitutions that restrict the government from engaging in harmful redistributive activities.

JOHN CHARLES BRADBURY
W. MARK CRAIN

REFERENCES

Bradbury, John Charles and Crain, W. Mark (2001). "Legislative organization and government spending: cross-country evidence." *Journal of Public Economics*, 82(3): 309–325.

Bradbury, John Charles and Crain, W. Mark (2002). "Bicameral legislatures and political compromise." *Southern Economic Journal*, 68(3): 646–659.

Brennan, Geoffrey and Hamlin, Alan (1992). "Bicameralism and majoritarian equilibrium." *Public Choice*, 74: 169–179.

Buchanan, James M. and Tullock, Gordon (1962). *The Calculus of Consent*. Ann Arbor: University of Michigan Press.

Crain, W. Mark (1979). "Cost and output in the legislative firm." *Journal of Legal Studies*, 8: 607–621.

Diermeir, Daniel and Myerson, Roger B. (1999). "Bicameralism and its consequences for the internal organization of legislatures." *American Economic Review*, 89: 1182–1196.

Dixit, Avinish, Grossman, Gene, and Gul, Faruk (2000). "The dynamics of political compromise." *Journal Political Economy*, 108: 531–568.

Gilligan, Thomas W., Marshall, William J., and Weingast, Barry R. (1989). "Regulation and the theory of legislative choice: the interstate commerce act of 1887." *Journal of Law and Economics*, 32: 35–61.

Hamilton, Alexander, Madison, James, and Jay, John (1992). *The Federalist Papers*. Cutchogue, NY: Buccaneer Books.

Hammond, Thomas H. and Miller, Gary J. (1987). "The core of the constitution." *American Political Science Review*, 81: 1155–1174.

Hayek, F.A. (1979). *Law, Legislation, and Liberty: The Political Order of a Free People*, Volume 3. University of Chicago Press.

Levmore, Saul (1992). "Bicameralism: when are two decisions better than one?" *International Review of Law and Economics*, 12: 145–162.

McCormick, Robert E. and Tollison, Robert D. (1981). *Politics, Legislation, and the Economy*. Boston: Martinus Nijhoff Publishing.

Perrson, Torsten, Roland, Gerard, and Tabellini, Guido (1997). "Separation of powers and political accountability." *Quarterly Journal of Economics*, 112: 1163–1203.

Riker, William (1992). "The justification of bicameralism." *International Political Science Review*, 13: 101–116.

Stigler, George J. (1976). "The sizes of legislatures." *Journal of Legal Studies*, 5: 17–34.

Tsebelis, George and Money, Jeanette (1997). *Bicameralism*. Cambridge: Cambridge University Press.

Tsebelis, George and Rasch, Bjornerick (1995). "Patterns of bicameralism," in Doering, Herbert (ed.) *Parliaments and Majority Rule in Western Europe*. New York: St. Martin's.

Tullock, Gordon (1959). "Problems of majority voting." *Journal of Political Economy*, 67: 571–579.

BLACKMAIL

The term blackmail first entered the English language in the 1500s. It referred to tribute exacted by families or clans along the Scottish — English border in return for immunity from raids by Scottish or English bands. One way to make a living during that era was to steal sheep and horses from the English or Scots and others not paying protection money. This process of midnight "acquisitions" became known as *reiving*, from which we get the name bereavement. Blackmail was a term used as well to refer to this activity. (www.mercyseat.com) Scottish — English border tribute continued until the 18th century.

Today blackmail is legally defined as the criminal offense of attempting to extort money or property by threats of exposure of a crime or disreputable conduct. Blackmail is distinguished from extortion in its broadest sense, which is the use of any means of illegal compulsion or oppressive exaction. As a rule defense to the charge of blackmail cannot include the claim that the person threatened with exposure of criminal or shameful conduct is in fact guilty of the offenses charged or that the attempt at extortion was not successful (MicroSoft: 2000).

Blackmail prosecutions are not common, for a simple reason: the person being blackmailed is not likely to report it and thereby publicly to expose a shameful or criminal act. A widely publicized case was prosecuted in the New York Federal District Court. On January 20, 1997, Autumn Jackson, a woman claiming to be comedian Bill Cosby's illegitimate daughter, was arrested and charged with attempting to extort $40 million in exchange for her not going to a tabloid with the story. On December 12, 1997, Autumn Jackson was found guilty of threatening to injure another person's reputation with the intent to extort money in violation of 18 U.S.C. §875(d) and 2 (1994), traveling across state lines to promote extortion in violation of the Travel Act, 18 U.S.C. §1952(a)(3) and 2 (1994) and conspiring to commit extortion, in violation of 18 U.S.C. §371 (1994). A New York judge sentenced her to 26 months in prison. Granting her leniency, U.S. District Judge Barbara Jones gave Miss Jackson the option of reducing her sentence by completing a six-month rehabilitation program of physical wellness, education and counseling. Afterward, Jackson could become eligible for home confinement and community service.

The term extortion is frequently used in connection with blackmail. However, extortion is variously defined as "declaration of intent to injure another by doing an unlawful act, with a view to restraining his freedom of action" or "the offense of obtaining from a person money or property not legally owed, through the use of fear, force or authority of office."

More specifically, the Hobbs Act (18 U.S.C. 1951(b)(2)) defines extortion as "the obtaining of property from another, with his consent, induced by wrongful use of actual or threatened force, violence, or fear, or under color of official right."

Whether blackmail is deemed to be a criminal act or not, the question can be raised: is blackmail an exchange not dissimilar to other exchanges not deemed criminal? I think we can preliminarily at least answer that question in the affirmative.

Let us return to the Bill Cosby/Jackson case and examine several possible scenarios. Let us begin by assuming that Autumn Jackson's paternity allegations are true and that Bill Cosby is in fact her father. For Bill Cosby, it would appear that the preferable state of affairs is for Miss Jackson not to release that information to a tabloid and thereby to harm his reputation and suffer whatever economic consequences or marital problems that might ensue.

Constitutional guarantees of free speech protect Miss Jackson's right to tell her story to a tabloid, other news sources, and the world. Let us pose the welfare economics question, Bill Cosby would be better off under which scenario — being able to pay for her silence regarding her paternity or not being able to pay her (make blackmail payments) and have her publicize her story? Because of the inherent subjectivity of the expected costs and evaluation of personal preferences, a third party cannot answer that question. We can say that people are more likely to achieve preferred levels of satisfaction the wider the choice set they confront. Were we to observe Cosby voluntarily making a blackmail payment, the most we are qualified to say is that Cosby deemed himself better off as a result of making the payment than his next alternative, that could also be freely chosen, that of not making a blackmail payment.

Thus, a blackmail offer fits the description of the standard win — win exchange i.e., "I will do something good for you if you do something good for me." A typical example of a win — win exchange is when one offers a grocer $3 for a gallon of milk. The essence of the transaction is: "I hold the property rights to this $3 and you, the grocer, hold the property rights to the gallon of milk. I will transfer my title to the $3 to you if you transfer your title to the gallon of milk." If the offer is accepted, it is a positive — sum game where both parties better off in their own estimations.

The blackmailer's offer is identical. He owns information about the observed immoral personal conduct. He has a right recognized and protected by law to divulge that information to whomever he pleases. He violates no law publicizing the information. When he propositions the miscreant that he will give up his clear right to publicize his information in exchange for money, he does not do anything that differs from any other kind of peaceable, voluntary exchange.

There is another way to think about whether blackmail should be a criminal act. It is clearly unlawful for a person to murder or rob another. Therefore, it is clearly unlawful for a person to threaten another that unless he is paid money he will rob or murder him. On the other hand, it is not unlawful for a person to publicly expose the moral indiscretions of another. Therefore, why should it be unlawful for a person to offer not to expose those indiscretions in exchange for money? Generally, if to do act A is lawful then the threat not to do act A in exchange for money should also be lawful.

There is also the question: are there benefits of blackmail? Examination of some of the possible effects of blackmail might help us with the normative question of whether blackmail should be criminal. The blackmailer and the person being blackmailed (blackmailee) are seldom the only parties involved. There is a third party. That party might be the blackmailee's wife or fiancee, friend, business partner or some other associate. This recognition suggests that blackmail has some of the characteristics of social sanctions that promote socially acceptable behavior. If blackmail were legal, there would be a monetary inducement for people to spy on others in an effort to detect, say in the case of marriage, adultery. If a person knew that his adulterous affairs were more likely be detected, and he would have to pay a price for concealment, it is reasonable to suggest there would be a reduced likelihood of persons engaging in adultery. In other words, blackmail acts as a tax on behavior that the blackmail victim does not want exposed. (Palgrave: 107) If blackmail were to produce that result, then a clear beneficiary would be spouses and other associates. In this case the blackmailer might be seen as a private enforcer of moral conduct and marital oaths of fidelity. Criminalization of blackmail eliminates the tax and reduces the incentive for people to search for discrediting information about others.

Blackmailers are often held in violation of 18 U.S.C. §875(d): "Whoever, with intent to extort from any person, firm, association, or corporation, any money or other thing of value, transmits in interstate or foreign commerce any communication containing any threat to injure the property or reputation of the addressee or of another or the reputation of a deceased person or any threat to accuse the addressee or any other person of a crime, shall be fined under this title or imprisoned not more than two years, or both."

In the Cosby case, the threat was to injure the "reputation of the addressee." The question might be asked: is one's reputation his property? Reputation is defined as: "estimation in which a person or thing is commonly held, whether favorable or not; character in the view of the public, the community, etc." (Webster's: 1998) In other words, one's reputation is what others think of him. While reputation is an asset created by investments in honesty and other forms of socially accepted behavior, it is difficult to make an argument that the thoughts of others are in fact his property.

To the extent that the information the blackmailer threatens to reveal is true, the blackmailer threatens to perform a socially valuable function of informing others that the blackmailee is undeserving of the esteem placed upon him. By accepting money in return for his silence, the blackmailer converts this social value to private gain for himself and continued misrepresentation by the blackmailee.

Before the 19th century, blackmail was a crime only if it involved extortion such as threatening to do bodily or property injury if payment were not made. It was not a crime to threaten to expose a person's criminal or immoral behavior in exchange for a payment. Posner says that this was a period in the nation's history when there was more private enforcement of laws, including criminal laws.

It was with the rise of public enforcement of laws that blackmail became criminal (Posner: 1983, pp. 284–285).

What constitutes a crime can be divided into two classes *mala in se* and *mala prohibita*. Homicide and robbery are wrong in themselves (*mala in se*). They involve the initiation of force against another. By contrast blackmail, drug abuse, and gambling re *mala prohibita* offenses, and considered criminal, not because they violate the property or person of another, but because society seeks to regulate such behavior. *Mala prohibita* offenses such as alcohol consumption drift in and out of criminal codes according to changes in public opinion, tastes, customs or religious standards.

WALTER E. WILLIAMS

REFERENCES

Microsoft Encarta Online Encyclopedia (2000).

The New Palgrave Dictionary of Economics and the Law (P–2) Edition. Peter Newman, Macmillan Reference Limited, 1998.

Posner, R. (1983) *The Economics of Justice*. Cambridge, MA: Harvard University Press.

Webster's New World Dictionary & Thesaurus. Accent Software International Ltd., Macmillan Publishers Version 1.0, 1998.

See *http://www.mercyseat.com/little2.htm* and also, *http://www. electricscotland.com/history/social/sh16.html*.

BLACK'S SINGLE-PEAKEDNESS CONDITION

Like Kekulé's vision about the ring structure of the carbon molecule, the notion of single-peaked preferences came to Duncan Black as a sudden flash of insight. In the 1940s, Black had independently rediscovered the concept of cyclical preferences and was looking for a way to avoid majority rule cycles (Black, 1958). In single-peakedness he found one.

While single-peaked preferences can be defined in more than one way, Black's definition has a simple elegance: a *single-peaked curve* is one that changes its direction at most once, from up to down. A set of preference orderings is said to be *single-peaked* with respect to some continuum (sequencing of the alternatives) if every voter's utility function over the set of alternatives can be graphed as a single-peaked curve with respect to that continuum. Black's *median voter theorem* states that, when preferences are single-peaked, majority rule preferences are transitive and the feasible alternative which lies highest on the preferences of the median voter is a *majority winner* (a.k.a. a *Condorcet winner*), i.e., can (for an odd number of voters) receive a majority against each and every other alternative in paired contest.

Black's Theorem is important because the notion of single-peaked preferences provides a useful idealization of a variety of real-world decision-making processes over a single-dimension of choice, and because the theorem is directly linked to important bodies of economic and political theory, including Arrow's Possibility Theorem for Single-Peaked Preferences, Anthony Down's *median voter* (Downs, 1957), *Duverger's Law* (Duverger, 1957), and Amartya Sen's *value restriction* condition (Sen, 1970).

Moreover, the concept of the median voter on a line can be generalized beyond a single dimension (Black and Newing, 1951), and turns out to be critical in understanding the conditions for the existence of core outcomes in multidimensional issue spaces. A natural generalization of Black's Theorem is the result (for *Euclidean preferences*) that a majority rule core exists in a multidimensional voting game if and only if all median lines intersect at a point. Also, the idea of single-peakedness is directly analogous to the ideas that form the basis of the scaling models of mathematical psychologists (Coombs, 1964) which have been used to study the underlying dimensions of choice in legislatures and multi-judge courts (see e.g., Grofman and Brazill, forthcoming).

In the second edition of Arrow's *Social Choice and Individual Values* (1963) Arrow incorporates Black's work on single peakedness, although he defines single-peaked preferences differently, making use of the *betweeness* relation. In Arrow's Possibility Theorem for Single-Peaked Preferences, Arrow replaces his unrestricted domain condition (see Arrow's Theorem, this volume) with the requirement that preference orderings be single-peaked over a single dimension. However, in doing so, he has dramatically restricted the set of feasible preference orderings. For k alternatives, there are k! (k factorial) possible strict preference orderings; but only 2^{k-1} of these are single-peaked with respect to any pre-specified continuum. It is easy to see that the ratio of k! $/2^{k-1}$ approaches zero as k approaches infinity. (However, as I argue below, even when not all preferences are single-peaked, single-peakedness can still be a very powerful explanatory concept.)

Black's median voter theorem can also be linked to the median voter theorem of Anthony Downs. Downs is dealing with voter preferences which are proximity based, i.e., voters are posited to have ideal points (issue preferences) on a line or in a multidimensional issue space, such that, in a choice between any two alternatives, each voter prefers

that alternative which lies closest to her own ideal point. Proximity-based preferences along alternatives that can be characterized as points on a line imply single-peaked utility curves over that line. Thus, in the context of Down's analysis, when alternatives and voter ideal points can be viewed as points on a line, Black's median voter theorem says that the alternative closest to the ideal point of the median will be able (for an odd number of voters) to defeat any other alternative on the line that might be proposed. However, the two median voter theorems should not be confused.

Downs' median voter theorem is about the structure of competition between political parties. Downs' theorem says that, when voters have proximity based preferences along a line, and when voting is by simple plurality, and when there are only two political parties, and when a variety of other quite specific "institutional" and "behavioral" assumptions are satisfied (see Grofman, 1993), competition creates incentives that lead to party platforms that converge to the ideal point of the median voter.

Thus, while Black's Theorem tells us that the median voter's preferences are potentially influential because her ideal point is a majority winner, Downs states conditions under which that potential influence will be realized when we have two-party competition in a single dimension. Black's result is about the structure of preferences; Down's theorem is (at least implicitly) a game-theoretic model about the results of strategic interactions.

Black's median voter result also can be viewed as a potential foundation for Duverger's Law, the claim that political party competition in single member districts using plurality to select the winner will result in the reduction of the number of (effective) competing parties to two. (Recall that Downs posited two-party competition; he did not derive it endogenously from an explicit model.) Theorists who have attempted to provide a precise game-theoretic basis for Duverger's Law have usually done so in expectational terms, i.e., arguing that voters will not choose to waste votes on candidates who have no chance of winning (and candidates with no choice of winning will be discouraged from running), and observing that, in a plurality-based system with a single winner, in a repeated game framework, there will usually be at most two candidates who have any realistic chance of victory. However, if we posit that party competition is over a one-dimensional issue space, then we can argue that, if there are two relatively centrist parties already in place, third parties will be deterred from entry because a party that locates between the two existing parties will receive few votes, and a party that locates toward one end of the issue space, away from the median voter also will be unlikely to do well (cf. Taagepera and Grofman, 1985). Of course, other non-Duvergerian equilibria may also exist.

Amartya Sen (1970) has generalized Black's single-peakedness condition by recognizing that there are three parallel ways to avoid cycles, of which single-peakedness is only one. Since cycles are based on triples, it is sufficient to examine conditions for cyclicity on triples. For simplicity of exposition we restrict ourselves to strict orders (no ties). Sen's condition on triples that is equivalent to single-peakedness is the NW (not worst) condition, the requirement that of the strict orders we find among any three alternatives, there be one alternative among the three that is never found to be worst in the preference ordering of any voter (i.e., at the bottom of the voter's ordering). A second conditions is NB (not best), which is equivalent to what Black calls *single-troughedness*, involving curves that change their direction at most once, from down to up. The third condition is the NM (not middle) condition, which has no clear spatial analogue, and no clear intuitive underpinning either.

A well-known (and frequently misinterpreted) result due to Sen is that the combination of these three conditions (referred to as *value restriction*) is, for strict orders, both sufficient and necessary for transitivity. Here, however, Sen is using the term necessary in a way that is different from common practice (Sen, 1970, p. 183). Sen uses necessity to refer to a condition that guarantees transitivity no matter what frequency (or probability) distribution we assign to the orderings that are allowed to be feasible. But, in actuality, we will always have a particular distribution of preference orderings. It is easy to show that that we can find a set of preference orderings that simultaneously violates NW, NB and NM, yet generates transitive majority rule. Consider, for example, two voters each with preference ordering abc, plus one voter each with orderings acb, bac, bca, cab, and cba respectively. All six possible strict orderings are present, and value restriction is thus clearly violated, yet the majority rule order is abc (Regenwetter et al., forthcoming).

Similarly, when Feld and Grofman (1988) studied voter preferences in 1980 among four potential candidates for president of the U.S., they found that all 24 of the possible strict orders were present among the electorate, yet there was a transitive majority ordering among the four alternatives which was single-peaked with respect to the left-right political spectrum on which the candidates would be placed by expert observers. Moreover, when they looked at subsets of the electorate, they also found transitive majority preferences that were single-peaked with respect to that left-right dimension, even though the specific ordering could vary depending upon the characteristics of the subset being examined.

Indeed, the work of a number of scholars, and not just my own, has demonstrated that, while single-peakedness may not characterize all (or even most) voters, in real world polities, political choices often tend toward single-peakedness at an aggregate level, when we allow opposite preferences to cancel out. (*Opposite preferences* are pairs of orderings which run in reverse order, e.g., abc and cba.) We can account for this empirical phenomenon of the prevalence of single-peaked orderings at the aggregate level either in terms of general tendencies toward single-peakedness at the individual level that are coupled with a probabilistic error structure that "hides" the underlying pattern, or in terms of a (small) subset of the electorate being characterized by single-peaked preferences and the rest of the electorate having preferences shaped by numerous and diverse considerations that in the aggregate tend to cancel each other out (Regenwetter et al., forthcoming).

BERNARD GROFMAN

REFERENCES

Arrow, K. (1963). *Social Choice and Individual Values*, Second Edition. New York: Wiley.

Black, D. (1958). *The Theory of Committees and Elections*. New York: Cambridge University Press.

Black, D. and Newing, R.A. (1951). *Committee Decisions with Complementary Valuation*. Edinburgh: William Hodge and Co.

Coombs, C. (1964). *A Theory of Data*. New York: Wiley.

Downs, A. (1957). *An Economic Theory of Democracy*. New York: Harper and Row.

Duverger, M. (1957). *Political Parties*. New York: Wiley.

Feld, S.L. and Grofman, B. (1988). "Ideological consistency as a collective phenomenon." *American Political Science Review*, 82(3): 64–75.

Grofman, B. (1993). "Toward an institution-rich theory of political competition with a supply side component," in B. Grofman (ed.) *Information, Participation and Choice*. Ann Arbor: University of Michigan Press, pp. 179–193.

Grofman, B. and Brazill, T. (1953–1991). "Identifying the median justice on the supreme court through multidimensional scaling: analysis of 'natural courts'." *Public Choice* (forthcoming).

Regenwetter, M., Adams, J., and Grofman, B. "On the condorcet efficiency of majority rule: an alternative view of majority cycles and social homogeneity." *Theory and Decision* (forthcoming).

Regenwetter, M., Marley, A.A.J., and Grofman, B. "General concept of value restriction and preference majority." *Social Choice and Welfare* (forthcoming).

Sen, Amartya (1970). *Collective Choice and Social Welfare*. New York: Holden-Day.

Taagepera, Rein and Bernard Grofman (1985). "Rethinking Duverger's law: predicting the effective number of parties in plurality and PR systems — parties minus issues equals one." *European Journal of Political Research*, 13: 341–352.

BUDGETARY PROCESSES

A government budget is a formal agreement that stipulates how much revenue will be raised, the sources of this revenue, and how the revenue will be spent. In most polities, "the budget" is actually a collection of policy agreements that stipulate tax laws and spending levels for specific programs, rather than a comprehensive, all-inclusive document. The budgetary process thus refers to the set of rules and procedures that policy makers use to formulate, enact, and enforce these revenue and spending agreements.

The process used by American state governments and the United States federal government to create budgets is relatively easy to describe in a stylized fashion. In general, revenue and spending proposals follow the same path through the legislative and executive branches as all measures that get signed into law. Legislators introduce formal revenue and spending proposals; hearings and debates are held on the proposals; votes are taken in oversight committees and then by the full legislative membership; and finally bills are sent to the chief executive for consideration. At the last stage, as with other types of legislation, budget bills can become law in two ways: the chief executive either "signs" the bill into law or, if he or she refuses, the bill can become law with the approval of a super-majority vote of both houses of the legislature.

The periodic or repetitive nature of budget legislation, combined with the relative imperative that it be approved, means that some specialized rules and procedures will emerge that apply solely to budget making. In this sense there is a "budgetary process," as distinguished from the rules and procedures that generally apply to the "legislative process." Within this stylized overview for how budgetary policies move through the political system in the United States, we find key institutional divergences in the budgetary processes employed. Naturally, such differences invite empirical scrutiny, and numerous scholars have exploited the cross-sectional and time-series variation among American states to analyze how specific budgetary institutions affect fiscal outcomes.

In his 1997 comprehensive survey of the studies of state budgetary institutions James Poterba concludes that while the evidence is not conclusive, the preponderance of studies suggest that institutions are not simply veils pierced by voters but are important constraints on the nature of political bargaining. In essence, the demand for public spending and taxation is mediated through a set of fiscal and budget rules. In Poterba's succinct assessment: "fiscal institutions matter."

The remainder of this essay summarizes major findings in the literature on how specific rules that define the budgetary process affect fiscal outcomes.

1. Balanced Budget Rules

Every state except Vermont has a balanced budget requirement. However, the details of these 49 state requirements differ in an important respect, namely the stage in the budget process at which balance is required. A survey of past research points to four categories. The weakest standard requires the governor to submit a balanced budget. A stricter standard requires the legislature to pass a balanced budget. Under these two categories actual expenditures may exceed revenues, if end-of-year realizations happen to diverge from the enacted budget. The third standard requires the state to acknowledge its deficit, but allows the deficit to be carried over into the next budget with no consequences. Bohn and Inman (1996) aptly label these three categories "prospective budget constraints." The fourth and strictest form of balanced budget rule combines the practice of enacting a balanced budget with a prohibition on a deficit carry-forward. Bohn and Inman label this strictest form a "retrospective budget constraint." While numerous studies have examined state balanced budget rules, four studies convincingly advance the idea that the "retrospective" standard has a significant impact on budgetary outcomes, whereas the other three do not.

Bohn and Inman find that balanced budget rules that prohibit the carry-over of end-of-year budget deficits have a statistically significant effect, reducing state general fund deficits by $100 per person. In contrast, soft or "prospective" budget constraints on proposed budgets do not affect deficits. Importantly, the deficit reduction in retrospective budget constraint states comes through lower levels of spending and not through higher tax revenues.

Poterba (1994) examines the fiscal responses in states to unexpected deficits or surpluses. He compares the adjustments to fiscal shocks under "weak" versus "strict" anti-deficit rules, categories that closely resemble the Bohn-Inman division. Poterba's results suggest that states with weak anti-deficit rules adjust less to shocks than states with strict rules. A $100 deficit overrun leads to only a $17 expenditure cut in a state with a weak rule and to a $44 cut in states with strict rules. Poterba also finds no evidence that anti-deficit rules affect the magnitude of tax changes in the aftermath of an unexpected deficit.

Alt and Lowry (1994) focus on the role of political partisanship in fiscal policy. They examine reactions to disparities between revenues and expenditures that can exist even in states with balanced budget requirements. In states that prohibit deficit carryovers, the party in control matters. In Republican-controlled states, they find a one-dollar state deficit triggers a 77-cent response through tax increases or spending reduction. In Democrat-controlled states a one-dollar deficit triggers a 34-cent reaction. In states that do not prohibit carryovers, the adjustments are 31 cents (Republicans) and 40 cents (Democrats). In other words, the Alt-Lowry evidence suggests that state politics plays an important role, and that anti-deficit rules affect fiscal actions.

Crain (2003) examines panel data for the years 1969 through 1998 and finds that states with a strict balanced budget requirement spend on average 3.2 percent less than other states. Crain also re-examines the often-voiced concern over a balanced budget requirement, namely its potential to force tax increases in response to a fiscal imbalance. Consistent with Bohn and Inman (1996) and Poterba (1994), the updated results suggest that strict budget balance rules influence fiscal policy largely through expenditure adjustments and not through increases in taxes or other revenue sources.

2. The Item Reduction Veto

Governors in all but five states have the ability to veto a particular item in an appropriations bill (a rule known as an item veto), in addition to their normal authority to veto an entire bill. Several studies on the fiscal impact of the item veto provide mixed and inconclusive results. Bohn and Inman (1996) find that the item veto generally has no statistically significant relationship to state general fund surpluses or deficits. Similarly, Carter and Schap (1990) find no systematic effect of the item veto on state spending. Holtz-Eakin (1988) finds that when government power is divided between the two parties, one controlling the executive branch, the other controlling the legislative branch, the item veto helps the governor reduce spending and raise taxes. Under political conditions of non-divided government, Holtz-Eakin finds that the item veto yields little, if any effect on budget outcomes.

The Holtz-Eakin study stresses that the item veto powers differ among states, and Crain and Miller (1990) examine these different powers in further detail. Of the 45 states that have an item veto, 10 give their governors the authority to either write in a lower spending level or to veto the entire item, the so-called item reduction veto. Crain and Miller argue that the item reduction veto differs from the standard item veto because it provides the governor with superior agenda setting authority. For example, a governor faced with excessive funding for a remedial reading program is unlikely to veto the measure, but likely would consider a marginal reduction in the amount of funding for that type of program. In contrast to a generic classification of the item veto, Crain and Miller find that the item reduction veto significantly reduces state spending growth. In a subsequent

analysis, Crain (2003) again finds that the item reduction veto authority has major budget consequences. An item reduction veto predictably lowers per capita spending by about 13 percent relative to the mean in state spending per capita.

3. Tax and Expenditure Limitations (TELs)

The earliest studies of TELs concluded that they have virtually no affect on state fiscal policy (for example Abrams and Dougan, 1986). Elder (1992) was among the first studies to examine TELs using an empirical model that controlled for other factors (such as income and population) that influence spending. With this improved specification Elder finds evidence that TELs reduce the growth of state government.

Eichengreen (1992) estimates regression models for both the level and growth rate in state spending as a function of the presence of tax and expenditure limits and the interaction between these limits and the state's personal income growth rate. He finds that the interaction term is particularly important because limits are typically specified as a fraction of personal income. In states with slow income growth rates, limitation laws have had a more restrictive effect on government growth than in states with fast income grow rates. Shadbegian (1996) specifies an almost identical empirical model, again taking into consideration the interaction between income and TELs.

Reuben (1995) develops an empirical specification that controls for the potential endogeneity problem that the passage of tax limits may be related to a state's fiscal conditions. Reuben finds that when these institutions are treated as endogenous the explanatory power of the institutional variables rises markedly; the estimated effects indicate that TELs significantly reduce state spending.

Crain (2003) updates the analysis using panel data for the 1969–1998 period based on the methodology in Eichengreen (1992) and Shadbegian (1996). Evaluating the effect at the mean of per capita income, Crain's projections indicate that if a state's income were one standard deviation below the mean, a TEL would reduce per capita spending by 3 percent in relation to mean spending. Alternatively, if a state's income were one standard deviation above the mean, a TEL would increase spending by 16 percent. As Shadbegian (1996) points out, one interpretation of these results is that TELs may provide political cover for state policymakers. Legislators can claim that the government is not growing too fast because a TEL law designed specifically to curtail government is in force. In effect, under some conditions (high state income) the TEL guidelines may become a floor for spending increases rather than a ceiling.

4. Super-Majority Voting Requirement for Tax Increases

Knight (2000) points out that in addition to the 12 states that have enacted super-majority requirements, 16 states in the 1990s introduced proposals to enact such requirements. Adding a super-majority voting requirement to the U.S. federal budget process is also a popular reform measure. Three empirical studies have analyzed the effect of super-majority requirements on state fiscal outcomes. Crain and Miller (1990) find that such rules reduce the growth in state spending by about 2 percent based on a relatively short sample period, 1980–1986. The study by Knight (2000) expands the sample period, employs pooled time-series, cross-sectional data, and uses state and year fixed effects variables. He finds that supermajority requirements decrease the level of taxes by about eight percent relative to the mean level of state taxes. Crain (2003) estimates that the super-majority voting requirement for a tax increase lowers per capita spending by about four percent evaluated at the sample mean.

5. Budget Cycles

Since 1977 a number of proposals have been introduced in the U.S. Congress to lengthen the federal budget cycle from an annual to a biennial process. The perception behind these proposals is that a federal biennial budget would help curtail the growth of federal expenditures. Motivated by these federal proposals, the U.S. General Accounting Office (1987) conducted a study of the state experiences. That study reports a positive correlation between state spending and annual budget cycles.

Kearns (1994) lays out the theoretical issues and provides a comprehensive empirical study of state budget cycles. Kearns presents two competing hypotheses. On the one hand, a biennial budget transfers power over fiscal decisions from the legislative branch to the governor. This power transfer reduces spending activities associated with logrolling and pork barrel politics because legislators favor programs that benefit their narrow, geograhically-based constituencies. The main costs of such geographically targeted programs may be exported to non-constituents. By comparison, the governor makes fiscal decisions based on more inclusive benefit-cost calculations because he or she represents a broader, statewide constituency. In other words, at-large representation mitigates the fiscal commons problem. As an alternative hypothesis, Kearns posits that a biennial budget cycle imparts durability to spending decisions and thereby encourages political pressure groups to seek government programs. Empirically Kearns finds that states with biennial budgets have higher spending per capita than states with annual budgets. Crain (2003) finds evidence that coincides with Kearns, in at least some model specifications; spending per capita is three percent higher in biennial budgeting states relative to annual budgeting states, other things equal.

6. Budgetary Baselines

Crain and Crain (1998) analyze alternative budget baseline rules. The two main choices for a budget baseline are the dollar amounts spent the year before or the level of services that those dollars bought, which is labeled a 'current services' baseline. For example, the U.S. federal budget procedure for computing the current services level takes what was spent in the year before, adjusts it for inflation and, in the case of programs like Social Security or unemployment compensation, for the number of people projected to be eligible in the year ahead, and that becomes the spending baseline. Any amount in excess of that level is defined as a spending increase, lesser amounts a spending cut. A current services baseline and a last year's budget baseline create different reference points, and based on prospect theory and experimental evidence, Crain and Crain posit that legislators may exhibit loss averting behavior in voting on budgetary proposals (for example, see Tversky and Kahneman, 1986). This means that future spending levels on programs enacted under a current services baseline are more secure than spending levels on programs enacted under a budgetary rule that uses last year's spending as a baseline. The present value of programs enacted under a current services regime is thus higher than under the latter budgetary regime. This increase in present value in turn raises the expected return to investments in lobbying by pressure groups to secure wealth transfers and thereby fuels an expansion in public sector spending. Controlling for a host of institutional, economic, and demographic factors, the findings in Crain and Crain show that over the course of the 1980s a current services baseline rule added about five percentage points to the growth in real state government spending.

7. Fiscal Volatility

Crain (2003) develops the argument that fiscal uncertainty impairs efficiency and raises the cost of government programs. Empirically, a 10 percent increase in expenditure volatility increases per capita spending by 3.5 percent relative to the state mean. This link between budget volatility and spending levels can be framed in a constructive manner: a state may reap substantial budgetary savings by reducing fiscal volatility. Importantly, the trade-off between budget volatility and government efficiency means that the role of budgetary institutions is more complex than previous analysis has generally assumed. Some institutions appear to carry a duel role, exerting not only a direct influence on spending, but also an indirect influence on the size of state budgets via their impact on fiscal stability.

The wide array of budgetary processes among American states provides a rich empirical laboratory to analyze the impact of specific institutions on spending and revenue policy. A growing body of work indicates that the design of budgetary processes conveys major fiscal consequences. Models of fiscal policy that treat institutions as relatively transparent and neutral communicators of voter preferences have severely limited explanatory power.

W. MARK CRAIN

REFERENCES

Abrams, Burton and William Dougan (1986). "The effects of constitutional restraints on government spending." *Public Choice*, 49: 101–116.

Alt, J.E. and Lowry, R.C. (1994) "Divided government, fiscal institutions, and budget deficits: evidence from the states." *American Political Science Review*, 88: 811–828.

Bohn, Henning and Robert P. Inman (1996). "Balanced budget rules and public deficits: evidence from the US states." *Carnegie-Rochester Conference Series on Public Policy*, 45: 13–76.

Carter, John and David Schap (1990). "Line-item veto: where is thy sting?" *Journal of Economic Perspectives*, 4: 103–118.

Crain, W. Mark (2003). *Volatile States: Institutions, Policy, and the Performance of American State Economies*. Ann Arbor: University of Michigan Press.

Crain, W. Mark and Nicole V. Crain (1998). "Fiscal consequences of budget baselines." *Journal of Public Economics*, 67: 421–436.

Crain, W. Mark and James C. Miller III (1990). "Budget process and spending growth." *William and Mary Law Review*, 31(4): 1021–1046.

Eichengreen, Barry J. (1992). "Should the Maastrict treaty be saved?" International Finance Section Working Paper 74. Princeton: Princeton University.

Elder, Harold E. (1992). "Exploring the tax revolt: an analysis of the effectiveness of state tax and expenditure limitation laws." *Public Finance Quarterly*, 20(1): 47–63.

Garrett, Elizabeth (1999). "Accountability and restraint: the federal budget process and the line item veto act." *Cardozo Law Review*, 20(3): 871–937.

Holtz-Eakin, Douglas (1988). "The line item veto and public sector budgets: evidence from the states." *Journal of Public Economics*, 36: 269–292.

Inman, Robert (1996). "Do balanced budget rules work? US experience and possible lessons for the EMU." NBER Working Paper No. 5838.

Inman, Robert and Henning Bohn (1996). "Balanced-budget rules and public deficits: evidence from the US states." *Carnegie-Rochester Conference Series on Public Policy*, 45: 13–76.

Kearns, Paula S. (1994). "State budget periodicity: an analysis of the determinants and the effect on state spending." *Journal of Policy Analysis and Management*, 13(2): 331–362.

Knight, Brian G. (2000). "Supermajority voting requirements for tax increases: evidence from the States." *Journal of Public Economics*, 76(1): 41–67.

Poterba, James M. (1994). "State responses to fiscal crises: the effects of budgetary institutions and politics." *Journal of Political Economy*, 102: 799–821.

Poterba, James M. (1996). "Budget institutions and fiscal policy in the US states." *American Economic Review*, 86(2): 395–400.

Poterba, James M. (1997). "Do budget rules work?" in Alan J. Auerbach (ed.) *Fiscal Policy: Lessons from Economic Research*. Cambridge, MA: The MIT Press, pp. 53–86; reprinted as NBER No. 2152.

Rueben, Kim (1995). "Tax limitation and government growth: the effect of state tax and expenditure limits on state and local government," mimeo, MIT Department of Economics.

Shadbegian, Ronald J. (1996). "Do tax and expenditure limitations affect the size and growth of state government." *Contemporary Economic Policy*, 14: 22–35.

Tversky, A. and D. Kahneman (1986). "Rational choice and the framing of decisions." *Journal of Business*, 59: 251–284.

U.S. General Accounting Office (1987). *Budget Issues, Current Status and Recent Trends of State Biennial and Annual Budgeting*. Washington, DC: GAO.

BUDGET DEFICITS

[I]f [government] cannot raise its revenue in proportion to its expence, it ought, at least, accommodate its expence to its revenue. (Smith [1776] 1976: 946)

Pyramid-building, earthquakes, even wars may serve to increase wealth, if the education of our statesmen on the principles of the classical economics stands in the way of anything better. (Keynes, 1936: 129)

Public spending may be financed in one of three ways: by levying taxes on the private sector, by printing money, or by borrowing. In the United States and much of the industrialized world, the last of these tools was used sparingly prior to roughly 1970. Only wars and other national emergencies prompted governments to resort to the bond market; the public sector otherwise operated on a balanced-budget, pay-as-you-go basis. Furthermore, the issuance of public debt to finance wartime spending was simply an unavoidable expedient: "An immediate and great expence must be incurred in that moment of immediate danger, which will not wait for the gradual and slow returns of the new taxes. In this exigency government can have no other resource but in borrowing" (Smith [1776] 1976: 909). Once the hostilities had ended, the accumulated debt customarily was retired, often through the establishment of a 'sinking fund', consisting of revenues earmarked specifically for that purpose. In most times and places, the restoration of peace brought a return to public budget balance. The normative principle that, except for periods of 'hard necessity', government should live within its means was rarely questioned and widely practiced.

For reasons not yet well understood, that pattern was broken in the last third of the twentieth century (Anderson, 1986). Chronic budget deficits became the peacetime norm in the United States until 1998, when, owing to dramatic cuts in defense spending and to the robust economic expansion of the 1990s, the federal government's receipts exceeded its outlays for the first time since 1969 (Alesina, 2000). The proximate cause of this period of persistent budget imbalance was massive growth in so-called entitlement programs, especially Medicare and Medicaid, established to help pay the health care bills of elderly and poor Americans. Such programs, which are open-ended in the sense of providing benefits to everyone who meets predetermined eligibility criteria, ensured that spending would rise continuously with increases in the populations of qualified recipients, even with no changes in benefit levels or eligibility requirements. And, indeed, if the future liabilities of these programs are added to those of the social security system, the ostensible budget 'surpluses' of the late twentieth and early twenty-first centuries quickly sink in a sea of red ink.

In fact, because governments generally do not follow the standard accounting practices accepted for use in the private sector, the magnitude of the public budget's net balance (and even its algebraic sign) is a matter of considerable scholarly controversy. Whether or not the public budget is in surplus or deficit at any point in time — and by how much — depends on the treatment of items such as the financing of long-lived capital projects, the future obligations accrued by social insurance and other entitlement programs, the revenues and expenses of state-owned enterprises (and the disposition of the proceeds realized from the sale of such properties), the assets and liabilities of government loan programs, publicly owned lands and mineral rights, and many other public sector activities, both off-budget and on, having important fiscal consequences. Because accounting conventions differ widely across nations, as do the sizes and scopes of their public sectors, cross-country comparisons of fiscal stance are even more problematic (Blejer and Cheasty, 1991).

Whether one assesses the government's budget conventionally as the simple difference between current revenues and current expenses, or adjusts it to include the present values of the public sector's most significant future obligations, it seems clear that the last third of the twentieth century witnessed a unique period in the history of public finance. Why did budget deficits appear suddenly in the late 1960s and why did they persist for 30 years (or more)?

'Ideas matter' is one answer to that question. The norm of governmental fiscal responsibility rested for 160 years on the intellectual foundations laid by the classical economists, who for the most part viewed public debt as inimical to economic growth. With the exception of Thomas Malthus, the classicals thought that, by competing for scarce loanable funds and, hence, by diverting wealth from relatively productive private investment projects to relatively unproductive public spending programs, government borrowing impairs capital formation and, in so doing, makes a nation poorer than otherwise. That is true even if all of the public's debt is 'internal' (i.e., held domestically). Adam Smith, for one, recognized that, while the government's creditors have a general regard for the national welfare, insofar as their interest income is contingent on continued prosperity, the holders of the public debt do not have the same incentives for deploying resources to their highest valued uses as the owners of those resources, who are taxed to service the debt. An income transfer between these two groups therefore 'must, in the long-run, occasion both the neglect of land, and the waste or removal of capital stock' (Smith [1776] 1976: 928).

Smith's reasoning explodes the hoary myth — hoary apparently even in 1776 — that the payment of interest on the public debt has no real economic consequences because "it is the right hand which pays the left" or because "we owe it to ourselves" (ibid.: 926). That "apology for the public debt", founded on the "sophistry of the mercantile system" that Smith exposed so ably, was also wrong as a factual matter then, as it is now, "the Dutch, as well as several foreign nations, having a considerable share of our publick funds" (ibid.: 927).

The classical analysis of budget deficits and public debt was swept away by the Keynesian revolution. Writing at a time when the global economy seemed to be in freefall and the private market economy seemed incapable of self-correction, John Maynard Keynes (1936) argued forcefully that full employment would be restored only if governments intervened aggressively, using their fiscal policy tools to offset the calamitous and apparently permanent decline in private investment spending that began in 1929. Keynes prescribed increases in government spending, on useful public works if possible, but on pyramids if need be, in order to inject purchasing power into the economy and put people back to work. Every new dollar spent by the public sector would increase national income many times over through the operation of a 'multiplier effect' as consumption spending by the initial recipients passed into the hands of merchants, who in turn spent a portion of their now higher incomes, enriching others who increased their own expenditures, and so on and so on. If, in addition, the increase in government spending was financed by debt (what Keynes called 'loan expenditure'), the holders of the bonds would experience a 'wealth effect' that would generate further increases in private consumption and investment spending. Using its considerable resources to augment aggregate demand, the public sector is thus able, in the Keynesian system, to jump-start a stagnant economy, setting it on the return path to full-employment equilibrium.

In imparting intellectual respectability to deficit spending, Keynes destroyed the norm of public budget balance (Buchanan and Wagner, 1977). Indeed, the relationship between public revenues and expenditures became an unimportant byproduct of government's Keynesian responsibility of actively countering the peaks and troughs of the business cycle so as to maintain the economy at full employment. These ideas were taken to their logical extreme by Keynes's disciple, Abba Lerner (1943), who rejected totally the classical orthodoxy in favor of a doctrine of 'functional finance', which judges fiscal policy, not by its impact on budget balance, but by its impact on the economy. Lerner went to great lengths in attempting to dispel the 'fairy tales of terrible consequences' from undertaking a prolonged program of deficit spending, if that was what was needed to deal with chronic economic stagnation. He clung tenaciously to the view that, because "we owe it ourselves" (or "to our children or grandchildren and to nobody else"), internal debt's possible adverse effects are largely "imaginary". Government can therefore borrow freely, even for the purpose of paying interest on its outstanding debt, without imposing any untoward burden on the economy.

Public choice scholars entered the fray at a time when post-Keynesian macroeconomists were in the process of reexamining the effects of public debt and concluding that government borrowing does in fact impair private capital formation as the classicals had taught. Analyzing the public debt problem from the perspective of the individual economic actors who, as citizens of a democratic polity, collectively must choose methods of financing the expenditures of government, James Buchanan ([1958] 1999: 26–37, [1964] 1982) observed that the decision to borrow involves a tradeoff between present and future taxes. The fact that the national debt must be serviced and retired in the future implies a future tax liability. Accordingly, it is future taxpayers who shoulder the burden when government borrows to finance current spending.

The debate became livelier following Robert Barro's (1974) reformulation of what has since erroneously been called the doctrine of 'Ricardian equivalence' (O'Driscoll, 1977). Barro's theoretical model starts with the assumption that the members of each generation care about the welfare of the next (more precisely, that the utility attained by one generation depends partly on its own consumption and partly on the utility attainable by that generation's immediate descendants). If, in addition, there exists a "chain of operative intergenerational transfers" (private bequests) that connects the current generation to future generations, individuals will behave as if they live forever. Under these assumptions, the issuance or retirement of public debt has no differential impact (relative to the tax alternative) on personal wealth, on aggregate demand, or on capital formation because current taxpayers will alter their bequests to offset the implied change in future tax liabilities. Bequests will be increased to compensate future generations fully for the heavier tax burden otherwise imposed on them by increases in public indebtedness and, when debt is retired, bequests will be lowered by the full amount of the reduction in the future tax burden. Changes in future tax liabilities, in other words, are fully capitalized in intergenerational wealth transfers, thereby neutralizing completely the effects of changes in the government's budget balance. Debt and taxes are equivalent tools of public finance.

Buchanan (1976) replied that such equivalence is illusory because rational taxpayers will predictably respond to an increase in the public debt, which implies a corresponding increase in future tax liabilities, by shifting income from the future to the present. The attempt on the part of current taxpayers to lower their future tax bills by reallocating their incomes intertemporally means that individuals will save less under deficit finance than they would under the revenue-equivalent current period tax, thereby impairing capital formation. It also means that, at prevailing tax rates, future tax collections will not be adequate for meeting debt service and amortization obligations.

Buchanan's broader point was that, even if future tax obligations are fully anticipated, taxpayers are placed in a prisoners' dilemma situation with respect to public debt issues. In particular, future tax liabilities in the Barro model are contingent because each individual is required to make spending plans for himself (and for his immediate descendents) under the assumption that everyone else will likewise plan to discharge his pro rata share of the community's deferred tax liabilities. However, if any one taxpayer fails to do so, the other members of the community will find their future tax bills to be larger than expected even though they themselves acted responsibly. Moreover, if one taxpayer has incentive opportunistically to shift some (or all) of his future tax burden to others, everyone does.

Under a pay-as-you-go system of public finance in which current spending is financed by current taxes, a steady stream of public revenue is more or less assured because fluctuations in individuals' incomes tend to cancel out. No such offsets occur with loan-financed expenditure, however, because all individuals must accumulate sufficient funds to pay their shares of the community's future tax bill. Under circumstances where it is costly to monitor the spending plans of fellow taxpayers and, moreover, where individuals can shift their future tax liabilities to others by acting irresponsibly from the community's perspective, tax-financed expenditure will be preferred to debt-financed expenditure. Once again, 'equivalence' does not hold as a theoretical proposition. Nor does the weight of the evidence seem to support it (Evans, 1993; Stanley, 1998).

In any case, the historical record of the past 30 years, a period distinguished in much of the West by persistent government spending in excess of current revenues and ever-growing public debt, seems inconsistent with the neo-Keynesian orthodoxy, which calls for budget balance over the business cycle. One explanation for the theory's failure to fit the facts is that the political institutions governing fiscal policy choices and the political actors who formulate and implement the chosen policies are absent from the analysis. Neo-Keynesians assume that government is exogenous to the economy and portray its fiscal policymakers as being guided by some version of the public's interest, selflessly pursuing broad social objectives such as economic stabilization or 'tax smoothing' (i.e., acting to prevent volatile changes in tax rates over the business cycle). Fiscal policy thus responds mechanistically, predictably, and impartially to given economic conditions.

The neo-Keynesian gap between theory and political reality is filled by public choice, which brings government within the ambit of the macro economy. Public choice is essentially an exercise in modeling the behavior of self-interested political agents in a given institutional setting and, as such, offers a rich set of testable hypotheses about why democratic political processes might produce a bias toward budget deficits, a bias reinforced by the electorally foreshortened time horizons of politicians and by the 'fiscal illusion' of rationally ignorant voters, who underestimate their future tax liabilities. The literature proceeds on several levels (Buchanan et al., 1986; Rowley et al., 2002).

At one level there is a consideration of the base-line incentives for politicians to prefer spending to taxes, and so to be driven by their self-interest to a policy of deficits. Deficits involve easy choices and budget balance hard choices for politicians. By deferring tax obligations to the future, loan-financed expenditures afford politicians the opportunity to shift the responsibility of paying for current government spending programs to voter-taxpayers, some yet unborn, living beyond the end of the incumbents' electoral time horizons. A balanced-budget increase in public spending financed by higher current taxes, on the other hand, threatens incumbents with an immediate loss of political support. Hence, there is a natural tendency, grounded in the vote motive, for democratic governments to run deficits.

At a deeper level the various institutional features of representative democracies can influence the incentives of political agents to run deficits. Here, we encounter issues of dynamic policy consistency and the durability of public spending as aspects of political behavior that can tip the balance in favor of deficit finance (Persson and Svensson, 1989; Alesina and Tabellini, 1990). For example, a fiscally conservative administration may run deficits to tie the hands of a successor liberal administration. By forcing a larger fraction of future tax revenues to be used for servicing the public debt, a roadblock is placed in the way of the next regime's plans for launching major new spending initiatives. Alternatively, a liberal government may systematically underestimate the future spending requirements of a policy proposal to get the camel's nose under the tent, thereafter depending on the program's beneficiaries or the fallacy of sunk costs to sustain a steady stream of funding.

The voters themselves play decisive roles in public choice analyses of fiscal policy choice. Simple majority voting rules afford opportunities for taxpayers who benefit disproportionately from public spending programs to shift the burden of financing those benefits to others (Browning, 1975; Tabellini and Alesina, 1990). Because voters in the present period cannot make binding contracts with voters in the next period, incentives likewise exist for supporting second-best policy options in order to avoid even worse outcomes in the future (Glaszer, 1989; Crain and Oakley, 1995). Because the configuration of costs and benefits facing individuals differs when choices are made collectively than when they are made privately, the rational behavior of self-interested voters may cause public spending to grow more rapidly than otherwise, requiring corresponding increases in the amounts that government borrows and taxes.

Bringing public choice principles to bear also suggests that popular ideas like term limits affect the fiscal behavior of politicians. The behavior of term-limited governors ('lame ducks') differs markedly during their last terms in office compared with earlier terms, for example. Taxes and public expenditures tend to be higher when the chief executive cannot run for reelection and, because of this, the time series of fiscal variables (taxes, spending, and debt) tends to be more volatile in states that impose gubernatorial terms limits than states that do not (Crain and Tollison, 1993; Besley and Case, 1995).

Emphasizing that institutions matter, public choice analyses of fiscal choices have shown that constitutional limits on taxing and spending can effectively constrain deficit finance and the growth of government (Porterba, 1997). Certain features of legislative organization and of public budgetary processes and procedures have likewise been found to be significant in maintaining fiscal discipline (Crain and Miller, 1990; Crain and Muris, 1995; Crain and Crain, 1998). Such rules and institutions are as important at a time of ostensible budget surpluses as they may have been during the era of high deficits. In the period since 1950, new spending has absorbed 73 cents of every surplus US budget dollar, on the average, whereas 21 cents was used to reduce the public debt and only a nickel was returned to the tax-payers (Vedder and Gallaway, 1998). The public choice lesson is that discussions of the appropriate size and scope of government cannot be separated from discussions of the appropriate mix of debt and taxes used to finance it.

WILLIAM F. SHUGHART II

REFERENCES

Alesina, A. (2000). "The political economy of the budget surplus in the United States." *Journal of Economic Perspectives*, 14: 3–19.

Alesina, A. and Tabellini, G. (1990). "A positive theory of fiscal deficits and government debt." *Review of Economic Studies*, 57: 402–414.

Anderson, G.M. (1986). "The US federal deficit and the national debt: a political and economic history," in J.M. Buchanan, C.K. Rowley, and R.D. Tollison (eds.) *Deficits*. Oxford: Basil Blackwell, pp. 9–46.

Barro, R.J. (1974). "Are government bonds net wealth?" *Journal of Political Economy*, 82: 1095–1117.

Besley, T.J. and Case, A. (1995). "Does electoral accountability affect economic policy choices? Evidence from gubernatorial term limits." *Quarterly Journal of Economics*, 110: 769–798.

Blejer, M.L. and Cheasty, A. (1991). "The measurement of fiscal deficits: analytical and methodological issues." *Journal of Economic Literature*, 29: 1644–1678.

Browning, E.K. (1975). "Why the social insurance budget is too large in a democracy." *Economic Inquiry*, 13: 373–388.

Buchanan, J.M. ([1958] 1999). "Public principles of public debt: a defense and restatement," in H.G. Brennan, H. Kleimt, and R.D. Tollison (eds.) *The Collected Works of James M. Buchanan*, Volume 2. Indianapolis, IN: Liberty Fund.

Buchanan, J.M. ([1964] 1982). "Public debt, cost theory and fiscal illusion," in J.M. Ferguson (ed.) *Public Debt and Future Generations*. Westport, CT: Greenwood Press, pp. 150–163.

Buchanan, J.M. (1976). "Barro on the Ricardian equivalence theorem." *Journal of Political Economy*, 84: 337–342.

Buchanan, J.M., Rowley, C.K., and Tollison, R.D. (eds.) (1986). *Deficits*. Oxford: Basil Blackwell.

Buchanan, J.M. and Wagner, R.E. (1977). *Democracy in Deficit: The Political Legacy of Lord Keynes*. New York: Academic Press.

Crain, W.M. and Crain, N.V. (1998). "Fiscal consequences of budget baselines." *Journal of Public Economics*, 67: 421–436.

Crain. W.M. and Miller, J.C. III (1990). "Budget process and spending growth." *William and Mary Law Review*, 31: 1021–1046.

Crain, W.M. and Muris, T.J. (1995). "Legislative organization of fiscal policy." *Journal of Law and Economics*, 38: 311–333.

Crain, W.M. and Oakley, L.K. (1995). "The politics of infrastructure." *Journal of Law and Economics*, 38: 1–17.

Crain, W.M. and Tollison, R.D. (1993). "Time inconsistency and fiscal policy: empirical analysis of U.S. states, 1969–89." *Journal of Public Economics*, 51: 153–159.

Evans, P. (1993). "Consumers are not Ricardian: evidence from nineteen countries." *Economic Inquiry*, 31: 534–548.

Glazer, A. (1989). "Politics and the choice of durability." *American Economic Review*, 79: 1207–1213.

Keynes, J.M. (1936). *The General Theory of Employment, Interest, and Money*. New York: Harcourt, Brace & World.

Lerner, A.P. (1943). "Functional finance and the federal debt." *Social Research*, 10: 38–51.

O'Driscoll, G.P. Jr (1977). "The Ricardian nonequivalence theorem." *Journal of Political Economy*, 87: 940–971.

Persson, T. and Svensson, L.E.O. (1989). "Why a stubborn conservative would run a deficit: policy with time-inconsistent preferences." *Quarterly Journal of Economics*, 104: 325–345.

Porterba, J.M. (1997). "Do budget rules work?" in A.J. Auerbach (ed.) *Fiscal Policy: Lessons From Economic Research*. Cambridge: MIT Press, pp. 53–86.

Rowley, C.K., Shughart, W.F. II, and Tollison, R.D. (eds.) (2002). *The Economics of Budget Deficits*, 2 volumes. The International Library of Critical Writings in Economics, (ed. by M. Blaug). Cheltenham, UK and Northampton, MA, USA: Edward Elgar.

Smith, A. ([1776] 1976). "An inquiry into the nature and causes of the wealth of nations," in R.H. Campbell, A.S. Skinner, and W.B. Todd (eds.) The *Glasgow Edition of the Works and Correspondence of Adam Smith*, Volume II. Oxford: Oxford University Press.

Stanley, T.D. (1998). "New wine in old bottles: a meta-analysis of Ricardian equivalence." *Southern Economic Journal*, 65: 713–727.

Tabellini, G. and Alesina, A. (1990). "Voting on the budget deficit." *American Economic Review*, 80: 37–49.

Vedder, R.K. and Gallaway, L.E. (1998). "Budget surpluses, deficits and government spending." Joint Economic Committee, US Congress.

BUREAUCRATIC DISCRETION

1. Introduction

This paper reviews the individual choice literature about the causes of the collective decision by legislators to delegate decision-making authority to executive agencies, and about the consequences of agency discretion. Discretion is the power or the right of deciding according to one's own judgement. If the legislature decides to delegate to the executive rather than to decide for itself, the legislature is cast as a principal, the bureau as an agent. When legislatures are bicameral and executive power is separate, the bureau is an agent with multiple principals. The first part of this paper examines what we know about why such legislatures sometimes delegate to bureaus.

The second part of this paper examines the consequences of agency discretion. The main concern is that the principal-agent problem of moral hazard and adverse selection characterizes agency discretion, especially since there are multiple principals. Others contend that felicitous selection of agency personnel can counterbalance the problem of moral hazard. Another complication is that the causes of agency discretion may affect its consequences.

2. Theories of Delegation

Delegation is often thought to increase when multiple principals disagree; faced with competing signals among multiple principals, agents can choose to implement policy within a policy space set by the diversity of the principals' preferences. This argument is set forth formally by Hammond and Knott (1996) and by many others as well. The formal arguments pertain to discretion in public bureaus that have multiple principals — the President, the House, and the Senate. Each principal has an effective veto over the other. The President can overturn what the House and Senate agree on, and the House and Senate can reject what the other body or what the President proposes. The formal argument also applies to the case of internal controls within a public bureaucracy when tasks are complex and where multiple principals have an effective veto over one another. The agency is free to pursue any policy within (or on) a space outlined by the intersection of contract lines between each pair of agents in, say, a 2-dimensional space. For example, if there are 3 principals whose preferences the agent knows with certainty, then the agent is free to pursue any policy in the triangle outlined by their preferences. As the distance between the preferences of the principals increases (i.e., the more they disagree), the greater the agent's zone of discretion. Now suppose the preferences of the principals are close together. In this case, the core has shrunk and so has the discretion of the agent.

There is another version of the same argument. Epstein and O'Halloran (1999) and many others argue that when principals disagree, the time and political costs of deciding increase accordingly. Politicians reduce these transactions costs by agreeing on a vague policy, delegating the details to the agents, who then have more discretion.

Moe (1990), McCubbins et al. (1987), and others disagree with this result. Each using somewhat different arguments, they conclude that disagreement among multiple principals reduces rather than expands agents' discretion. There are two versions of the argument. One version contends that agencies are structured, in part, by their enemies, and will consequently be designed to fail. The dominant coalition wants to ensure that its preferred policies are carried out effectively by the bureau agent, while opponents will seek to undermine effective performance by the governing coalition. The enacting coalition anticipates that it has neither permanent nor complete property rights to the exercise of authority. It protects the agency from the current or future exercise of political authority by the opposition by specifying exactly what the agency is to do, and how it is to do it. The empirical expectation is that political conflict among principals engenders more rules, reducing agents' discretion, and ultimately reducing the effectiveness of their activities. Scholz (1991) adds that, in the context of enforcing regulations, the principals who sponsor the regulatory legislation (usually Democrats) anticipate their eventual replacement by principals with different principles. They respond by crafting legislation that mandates enforcement "by the book" rather than flexible enforcement, where agency officials in the field have discretion to negotiate the terms and timing of compliance by regulated entities. Scholz shows that flexible enforcement will be more effective in bringing about eventual compliance than maximum enforcement that goes by the book.

Uncertainty may be another source of regulations and administrative procedures designed to reduce discretion. Principals may be uncertain not only about the precise location of agents' preferences but also about eventual outcomes. They reduce their uncertainty by structuring agencies to facilitate both ex ante and ex post monitoring of agency decisions by interest or other outside groups. They do so by writing regulations with cumbersome administrative procedures for oversight, review, hearings and appeals designed to maximize the revelation of information by the agents. Detailed administrative procedures regarding rule writing, rule implementation and rule enforcement have two effects: they reduce agents' discretion as well as the principals' uncertainty (Calvert et al., 1989).

These two arguments can be restated within the context of the alternative theory that disagreement among principals increases agents' discretion. Doing so points out some of the limits of that theory, which is silent on two issues. One is that of agency effectiveness (Scholz, 1991). The other is that of monitoring costs, which are endogenous to disagreement among principals. As the disagreement among principals increases, the gains to each principal from monitoring exactly what the agent does increase and the less discretion the agent will have. Rules not only constrain discretion; they also reduce an organization's productivity or effectiveness, no matter what its definition. Instead of producing output, employees spend time complying with rules (Moe, 1990; Thompson, 1998; Fehr and Gachter, 2000).

Monitoring, however, can take a variety of forms (Horn, 1995; Moe, 1990; Langbein, 2000). One type of ex ante monitoring requires agents to adhere to numerous rules and regulations and other administrative procedures ("red tape") before taking any action. These additional steps are designed to alert the principals about the agent's intended decision before any action is taken and will reduce agents' discretion. Another type of ex ante monitoring is direct oversight by important and attentive principals, whose approval is needed before the next step can be taken. Ex ante monitoring by direct supervision may expand or reduce agents' discretion. If it reduces agents' discretion, more time is spent supervising and checking up, and being checked up, waiting for instructions and approval. The end result is a less effective, productive organization (Milgrom and Roberts, 1992). The opposite may be true if the supervision expands discretion.

Monitoring can also be ex post. Ex post monitoring (e.g., monitoring by performance standards) is believed to be compatible with more discretion and greater effectiveness (Thompson, 1998).

Discretion is also thought to vary with the complexity of the task to be undertaken; the usual assumption is that there is more discretion when tasks are complex (McCubbins and Page, 1987). Discretion also varies positively with the amount of monitoring by customers or clients, when they are important; their monitoring is always ex post (Brehm and Gates, 1997: ch. 9).

While discretion is somewhat manipulable, many of its putative causes, including especially disagreement among principals and task complexity, are not. An implication is that there may be limits to the efficacy of "reinventing" government by giving employees more discretion, since disagreement among principals and task complexity are themselves not readily malleable.

When principals disagree, not only does the incentive to monitor agents increase, but uncertainty also enters among principals and sometimes between principals and agents. As disagreement among principals increases, so also do the decision-making costs of reaching an agreement among principals on what the agent(s) is (are) to do, and on what rules they are to follow. One way to reduce these decision making costs is to be vague concerning agents' tasks and even about the rules, introducing uncertainty into agents'

conceptions of what the principals preferences are (Bawn, 1995; Spence, 1997). The risk averse agent will then act within the veto-proof set of what the agent sees as the principals' fuzzy goals. For a given amount of expected disagreement among principals, as the variance in the expectation increases, the zone of discretion for the risk-averse agent decreases. In the face of uncertainty about principals' preferences, the risk-averse employee does what everyone else around him is doing, which is the same thing that was done yesterday, as long as those actions evoked no adverse reaction by any of the principals. The usual characterization of such an organization is that it is stagnant, inefficient, and unresponsive (Warwick, 1975; Light, 1995).

The importance of uncertainty depends partly on the amount of fuzziness in agents' perception of disagreement among principals. It also increases with the distance between principal and agent (Langbein, 2000). Distant principals lack information about what the agent is doing, and the agent does not know what each distant principal wants. Further, the higher up on the organizational hierarchy the principal is, the easier it is for principals to resort to vagueness to reduce their decision-making costs, which contributes to uncertainty on the part of agents. The expectation is that when distant principals are important, attentive, and disagree, agents become uncertain regarding principals' expectations, and their zone of discretion decreases. By contrast, when proximate principals are important, attentive, and disagree, they cannot resort to vagueness to resolve disagreements. Agents know a lot about these principal's preferences. In the relative absence of uncertainty, disagreement among relatively proximate principals, such as mid-level managers, increases agents' discretion.

Uncertainty and disagreement, together, are important for understanding discretion. but uncertainty and disagreement are themselves reflective of other contextual characteristics. Uncertainty and disagreement among high level principals are both more likely in public than private sector organizations (Dixit, 1997). Even when they disagree, there is probably more certainty among agents about what principals want in the private than in the public sector, where tasks are less well defined and where there is a mix of often incommensurate goals (e.g., responsiveness, equity, and x-efficiency). However, many private firms are directly affected by political decisions, especially if they are directly regulated by government (e.g., communications; power), or if the government is a primary client (e.g., defense, aerospace, and some firms in industries like computers and software that supply items primarily to the government). Thus, when relatively distant political principals are important and attentive, no matter what the sector of the firm, their disagreement is likely to reduce agents' discretion. Political control may matter more than sector (Bozeman, 1992).

3. Theories About the Consequences of Discretion

The usual assumption in the context of the dominant principal-agent model is that agents, left to their own discretion, will either shirk (i.e., do nothing), or do something that the principals do not want (sabotage or bureaucratic drift) (Brehm and Gates, 1997). In other words, no matter what the reason for delegation, principals who delegate to agents lose control, and must balance that against the decision-making and other costs of not delegating. Congress not only faces that delegation dilemma with respect to executive agencies; the same dilemma exists within each executive agency (Miller, 2000). Thus, "solving" the legislative-executive principal-agent problem only pushes it down to another level within the executive.

In theory, opportunities for agents' moral hazard can be constrained with persistent monitoring by principals and by the design of information-revealing agency procedures and efficient reward systems. However, even when agency procedures produce information at no cost to the principals, it is costly for principals to make use of that information and to otherwise monitor agents' behavior. Nonetheless, some forms of monitoring may be cheaper and more effective. Ex post monitoring, while not foolproof, may be more productive than ex ante monitoring (McCubbins and Schwartz, 1984). With respect to rewards, optimal incentive systems appear impossible when the work product requires joint effort. There is no ex ante incentive system that simultaneously motivates agents to take actions that are Pareto optimal for the principal(s), does not waste money, and meets a budget constraint (Miller, 1992).

In light of the recognition that the moral hazard problem between agents and principals may be intractable, growing theoretical and empirical evidence suggests that selection can reduce the moral hazard dilemma in a repeated principal-agent game (Brehm and Gates, 1997; Miller, 2000). First, even in non-repeated games, many players cooperate even when the dominant solution is to defect (i.e., do nothing or maximize individual rather than group gains) (Ostrom, 1998) Second, workforce games are repeated, and cooperation increases in repeated games (Fehr and Gachter, 2000). Third, non-cooperators are more likely to cooperate when others do. Fourth, there is evidence that people work not only for instrumental ends (e.g., to make money) but also to pursue consumption values (Frey, 1997; Kreps, 1997; Gibbons, 1998). Fifth, when people work for intrinsic values, they are more likely to cooperate with others who share those values. When such a cooperative "heuristic"

prevails, it appears that primary reliance on extrinsic rewards and sanctions (such as performance pay, ex ante monitoring, and ex ante and ex post sanctions) actually crowds out intrinsic values (Scholz and Lubell, 1998). The implication is that careful selection of agents who generally share the preferences of principals (even when they are conflicting) can reduce the moral hazard dilemma (Frank, 1991; Baker, 2000; Miller, 2000).

However, this implication is better supported with respect to reduced shirking than with respect to reduced sabotage. Investigators can model and observe the amount of work. It is far more difficult to model and observe whether that work reflects the preferences of multiple principals in that it minimizes the sum of (possibly squared) distances between the agents' final policy choice or act and the preferences of each of the multiple principals. In the absence of data on principals' preferences and policy outcomes, much of the empirical work on discretion or responsiveness in public bureaus may in fact indicate the opposite (Hammond and Knott, 1996; Chaney and Saltzstein, 1998; Keiser and Soss, 1998; Soss et al., 2001; Scholz and Wei, 1986; Scholz et al., 1996; Wood and Waterman, 1991, 1993). (See Scholz and Wood, 1999, for an exception.)

Dixit (1997) adds that, when multiple principles disagree, and, by extension, when their conflicting preferences are unclear, employees have weak performance incentives; they are answerable to different constituencies with conflicting and often unclear preferences. In being beholden to everyone, they are beholden to no one. The consequence is not only less discretion, but also a less effective organization.

La Porta et al. (1997) also argue that, without trust, there is less cooperation in large organizations. Size means that production is often joint. Consequently, employees need to cooperate with many others (including possibly clients and customers, as well as other employees) who they see rarely. The larger the organization, the fewer the repeated interactions between any two employees, or between employee and customer. In the absence of trust, these one-shot contacts become non-cooperative games, whose equilibrium is not optimal for the organization (Miller, 1992). Further, without trust, managers in large organizations are likely to invoke rules and active ex ante monitoring of employees. They are also likely to be more distant from agents, which promotes uncertainty among agents about principals' preferences. All of these factors constrain employee discretion.

By contrast, monitoring by professional peers, however, regardless of organizational size, signals the presence of "trust." Professionals in the same field share similar values and have repeated contacts; they have an incentive to cooperate because they know that professional peers are a source of future assistance in securing a better job

(Frank, 1991; Kreps, 1997). Thus, a large organization governed by the norms of a single profession compared to one governed by a more diverse set of principals is not as likely to be encumbered with rules and squabbling, distant principals that are likely to reduce both discretion and effectiveness.

Customers or clients may be another important monitoring group. The usual assumption is that monitoring by this set of principals is more prevalent in the private than the public sector. Further, as these external, proximate principals become increasingly important, agents will have correspondingly more discretion to figure out how best to respond to these external principals, enhancing organizational effectiveness. Once again, the expectation is that it is the importance of the customer/client that is relevant, and not just the sector (Thompson, 1998).

The dominant principals-agent models that frame the issue of discretion as a moral hazard dilemma assume that principals' preferences are exogenous with respect to agents. However, agent discretion may come entirely or partly from their ability to influence the preferences of their principals, and thereby to control their own agenda (Wood and Waterman, 1994; Krause, 1996). The ability of agents to control their own agenda may be greater when tasks are highly technical and when there are few competing sources of supply. This may be particularly likely in the case of public supply of national defense and in some areas of economic regulation.

The consequence is that it is important to examine differences in discretion both within and between the public and private sector, but it is equally important to determine why these sector differences exist. Understanding the reasons for differences in discretion and output between and within public and private sector organizations is essential in order to find whether discretion enhances or retards effectiveness in the eyes of the organization's principals. Delegation by external principals to bureaucratic agencies may or may not wind up as discretion in the hands of employees within the agencies. Further, the ultimate impact of discretion on the allocative and technical efficiency of bureau performance remains an open question.

LAURA LANGBEIN

REFERENCES

Baker, G. (2000). "The use of performance measures in incentive contracting." *American Economic Review*, 90(2): 415–420.

Bawn, K. (1995). "Political control versus expertise: congressional choices about administrative procedures." *American Political Science Review*, 89(1), 62–73.

Bozeman, B. (1992). "Red tape and task delays in public and private organizations." *Administration and Society*, 24: 290–322.

Brehm, J. and Gates, S. (1997). *Working, Shirking, and Sabotage: Bureaucratic Response to a Democratic Public*. Ann Arbor: University of Michigan Press.

Calvert, R.L., McCubbins, M.D., and Weingast, B.R. (1989). "A theory of political control and agency discretion." *American Journal of Political Science*, 33: 588–611.

Chaney, C.K. and Saltzstein, G.H. (1998). "Democratic control and bureaucratic responsiveness: the police and domestic violence." *American Journal of Political Science*, 42(3), 745–768.

Dixit, A. (1997). "Power of incentives in private versus public organizations." *American Economic Association Papers and Proceedings*, May: 378–382.

Epstein, D. and O'Halloran, S. (1999). *Delegating Powers: A Transaction Cost Politics Approach to Policy Making Under Separate Powers*. Cambridge. Cambridge University Press.

Fehr, E. and Gachter, S. (2000). "Fairness and retaliation: the economics of reciprocity." *Journal of Economic Perspectives*, 14(3): 159–181.

Frank, R. (1991). "Social forces in the workplace," in K.J. Koford, and J.B. Miller (eds.) *Social Norms and Economic Institutions*. Ann Arbor: University of Michigan Press, pp. 151–179.

Frey, B.S. (1997). *Not Just For the Money: An Economic Theory of Personal Motivation*. Cheltenham, UK: Elgar.

Gibbons, R. (1998). "Incentives in organizations." *Journal of Economic Perspectives*, 12(4) (Fall): 115–132.

Hammond, T.H. and Knott, J.H. (1996). "Who controls the bureaucracy: presidential power, congressional dominance, legal constraints, and bureaucratic autonomy in a model of multi-institutional policymaking." *Journal of Law, Economics and Organization*, 12(1): 119–166.

Horn, M. (1995). *The Political Economy of Public Administration: Institutional Choice in the Public Sector*. New York: Cambridge University Press.

Keiser, L. and Soss, J. (1998). "With good cause: bureaucratic discretion and the politics of child support enforcement." *American Journal of Political Science*, 42(4): 1133–1156.

Krause, G.A. (1996). "The institutional dynamics of policy administration: bureaucratic influence over securities regulation." *American Journal of Political Science*, 40(4): 1083–1121.

Kreps, D.M. (1997). "The interaction between norms and economic incentives: intrinsic motivation and extrinsic incentives." *American Economic Review*, May: 359–364.

Langbein, L.I. (2000). "Ownership, empowerment and productivity: some empirical evidence on the causes and consequences of employee discretion." *Journal of Policy Analysis and Management*, 19(3): 427–449.

La Porta, R., Lopes-de-Silanes, F., Schleifer, A., and Vishny, R.W. (1997). "Trust in large organizations." *American Economic Association Papers and Proceedings*, May: 333–338.

Light, P. (1995). *Thickening Government: Federal Hierarchy and the Diffusion of Accountability*. Washington, DC: Brookings.

McCubbins, M.D., Noll, Roger G., and Weingast, Barry R. (1987). "Administrative Procedures as Instruments of Political Control." *Journal of Law, Economics and Organization*, (3): 243–277.

McCubbins, M.D. and Page, T. (1987). "A theory of congressional delegation," *in Congress: Structure and Policy.*

M.D. McCubbins and T. Sullivan, (eds.) Cambridge: Cambridge University Press, pp. 409–425.

McCubbins, M.D. and Schwartz, T. (1984). "Congressional oversight overlooked: police patrols versus fire alarms." *American Journal of Political Science*, 28: 165–179.

Milgrom, P. and Roberts, J. (1992). *Economics, Organization and Management*. Englewood Cliffs, NJ: Prentice-Hall.

Miller, G. (1992). *Managerial Dilemmas: The Political Economy of Hierarchy*. New York: Cambridge University Press.

Miller, G. (2000). "Above politics: credible commitment and efficiency in the design of public agencies." *Journal of Public Administration Research and Theory*, 10: 289–328.

Moe, T. (1990). "Political institutions: the neglected side of the story." *Journal of Law, Economics and Organization*, 6(Special Issue): 213–253.

Ostrom, E. (1998). "A behavioral approach to the rational choice theory of collective action." *American Political Science Review*, 92(1): 1–22.

Scholz, J.T. (1991). "Cooperative regulatory enforcement and the politics of administrative effectiveness." *American Political Science Review*, 85(1): 115–136.

Scholz, J.T. and Lubell, M. (1998). "Trust and taxpaying: testing the heuristic approach to collective action." *American Journal of Political Science*, 42(2): 398–417.

Scholz, J.T., Twombly, J., and Headrick, B. (1991). "Street-level political controls over federal bureaucracy." *American Political Science Review*, 85(3): 829–850.

Scholz, J.T. and Wei, H.F. (1986). "Regulatory enforcement in a federalist system." *American Political Science Review*, 80(4): 1249–1270.

Scholz, J.T. and Wood, B.D. (1999). "Efficiency, equality, and politics: democratic controls over the tax collector." *American Journal of Political Science*, 43(4): 1166–1188.

Soss, J., Schram, S., Vartanian, T.P., and O'Brien, E. (2001). "Setting the terms of relief: explaining state policy choices in the devolution revolution." *American Journal of Political Science*, 45(2): 378–395.

Spence, D.B. (1997). "Administrative law and agency policymaking: rethinking the positive theory of political control." *Yale Journal on Regulation*, 14(2): 407–450.

Thompson, F. (1998). "Public economics and public administration," in J. Rabin, B. Hildreth, and G. Miller (eds.) *Handbook of Public Administration*, Second Edition. New York: Marcel Dekker, pp. 995–1063.

Warwick, D.P. (1975). *A Theory of Public Bureaucracy*. Cambridge, MA: Harvard University Press.

Wood, B.D. and Waterman, R.W. (1991). "The dynamics of political control of the bureaucracy." *American Political Science Review*, 85(3): 801–828.

Wood, B.D. and Waterman, R.W. (1993). "The dynamics of political-bureaucratic adaptation." *American Journal of Political Science*, 37(2): 497–528.

Wood, B.D. and Waterman, R.W. (1994). *Bureaucratic Dynamics: The Role of Bureaucracy in a Democracy*. Boulder, CO: Westview Press.

C

CAMPAIGN CONTRIBUTIONS AND CAMPAIGN FINANCE

As a great deal of work has been done in the area of campaign finance, I have chosen to focus on four areas in this essay. They are 1) the effect of contributions on congressional votes, 2) inferences from contribution patterns about the structure of the U.S. Congress or about the strategies of players, 3) the effects of campaign spending on electoral outcomes, and 4) the effects of campaign finance laws on electoral outcomes.

One research question is whether campaign contributions are effective in altering politicians' voting behavior. The best test of whether contributions influence legislators' voting behavior will examine roll call votes where legislators' votes have a clear economic payoff to contributors, and benefits of those votes are concentrated and accrue to the contributor, and costs are distributed throughout the electorate. When costs of the proposed legislation are distributed throughout the electorate, often no serious opposition exists and the potential impact of the contribution is largest for this type of legislation. Further, the best test occurs when votes are not well publicized, as is often the case for amendments to particular bills.

Stratmann (1991, 1995) analyzes a total of fifteen roll call votes in the U.S. House of Representatives in 1981 and 1985 that satisfy these criteria. Some of these votes increase government farm subsidies, others decrease farm subsidies. Controlling for the simultaneous determination fo contributions and votes, he finds that campaign contributions increase the probability that a legislator is voting in contributors' interests. Other studies find similar results (for example, Welch, 1980; Durden et al., 1991) while others find mixed, little or no evidence for the hypothesis (for example, Kau et al., 1982; Evans, 1986; Chappel, 1981; Vesenka, 1989).

Research examining the effects of campaign contributions on voting behavior, and wanting to establish a causal effect going from contributions to voting behavior, has to recognize that contributors may give to their friends. This implies that it would be incorrect to assume that every vote favoring a contributor has been purchased. However, it is difficult to sign the bias if one does not control for endogeneity, as the direction of the bias depends on the strategies of

Political Action Committees (PACs). In the previous example, the effect of contributions is overstated. However, it is possible for the effect of contributions to be understated if PAC give to those who tend to oppose them, as those are the legislators whose votes have to be swayed. While some of the previously mentioned work controls for the endogeneity of contributions in the vote equation in a variety of ways, recent work takes a different approach. This recent work examines changes in contribution patterns over time. While examining broad aggregates Bronars and Lott (1997) find no evidence of vote buying. Stratmann (2002), in contrast, looks at a specific financial services regulation and finds evidence that contributions change legislators' votes. Other work on the influence of contributions does not study the effects of contributions on outcomes, i.e., votes, but the effect of contributions on inputs, namely time spent by the legislator. This work indicates that contributions make legislators spend more time on legislation of interest to the donor (Hall and Wayman, 1990).

Another line of research examines the timing of contributions relative to the timing of congressional votes. There is evidence of a significant increase in contributions at the time that congressional votes are taken. This is consistent with the hypothesis that the contribution-for-vote exchange occurs, in part, at the time the legislation is voted on (Stratmann, 1998).

Other work on campaign finance has examined PACs' strategies. Work by Grier and Munger (1991) examines the patterns of PAC giving, and they study the distribution of monies across committees. Using a natural experiment approach Milyo (1997) identifies the value of having a seat on the House Budget committee. A great deal of work examines which legislator characteristics and which committee assignments are associated with larger contributions. Some of the early work includes the study by Poole et al. (1987). They examine which legislator characteristics may influence the pattern of PAC contributions. Their findings indicate that highly rated incumbents receive more money from PACs when they are in close races. More recent work typically includes legislators' committee assignments, their seniority and constituency interests, party affiliation, and an ideological rating when explaining the distribution of funds. Snyder (1992) argues that special interests engage in long-term investment in politicians who favor their positions. Kroszner and Stratmann (1998) argue that legislators structure Congress in such a way as to assist themselves in building a clear and credible reputations with special interest contributors. Romer and Snyder (1994) examine the effect of changes in committee assignments on changes in PAC contribution patterns. They find that PACs increase contributions when the legislators become members of important committees. Kroszner and Stratmann (2002) examine the role of contributions for legislator reputation building and find support for the hypothesis that legislators do not follow a strategy of ambiguity, but develop relationships with PACs that are based on firm reputations in favor or opposed.

One issue is how PACs would behave if their objective were to influence legislators' voting decisions. Rational allocation of funds implies that PACs do not contribute to those legislators who will vote in their favor regardless of whether or not they receive contributions, but to legislators who are likely to be opposed to their interests. The more a legislator is opposed to PAC interests, the more the PAC is going to have to contribute to swing his or her voting decision. Moreover, given that Congress uses a simple majority rule to decide on issues such as, tariffs, subsidies, and price supports, PACs have an incentive to give contributions in order to secure a majority, not unanimity. Therefore, if PACs could rank legislators in terms of how likely they are to oppose PACs' interest, most contributions would have to be given to the median legislator, i.e., the legislator with the median level of opposition to the PACs' interests. Legislators with declining opposition would receive fewer contributions, in line with their level of opposition.

Stratmann (1992) examines farm PACs and argues that the smaller the farm constituency size the less likely the legislator will support farm PAC interests, and thus the larger the necessary contribution required to change his or her voting behavior, where legislators with more than the median amount of opposition do not need to receive any contributions. He finds support for this hypothesis and finds, for example, that legislators with virtually no farm constituency, such as Representatives from New York City and Los Angeles, receive little or no farm contributions. Most contributions are received by legislators with a median farm constituency (for example, legislators from Maryland), and, the larger the farm constituency beyond the median (legislators from Montana, and the Dakotas), the lower the amount contributed by farm PACs. In related works, Stratmann (1996) finds that labor PACs contribute more to conservative Democrats than they do to liberal Democrats, and that corporate PACs give more to liberal Republicans than they do to conservative Republicans. This finding provides further support for the hypothesis that PACs try to sway the votes of those legislators who are likely to oppose them, instead of focussing their contributions on those who are likely to suport them regardless of whether they received contributions.

The academic debate on the effect of campaign spending on vote shares goes back at least to Jacobson (1978). Jacobson found that incumbent spending has no effect on his or her vote share, but that challenger spending had a large and statistically significant effect. One challenge when estimating this relationship is that the incumbent may be of high quality (an omitted variable in the regression), and thus he receives little contributions because potential contributors know that he is likely to win. An alternative omitted variable is brand name recognition (Lott, 1987). In these cases contributions are endogenous. Since Jacobson, scholars who have analyzed this relationship have tried to control for this omitted variable in one way or another or have attempted a different empirical specification which allows the marginal impact of spending to differ across incumbents. Some of the recent literature on campaign spending that has a richer empirical specification than earlier empirical work has found a positive effect of campaign spending for challengers and a smaller, but positive effect for incumbents (Grier, 1989; Green and Krasno, 1988), while others have not (Coates, 1998). In an innovative study Levitt (1994) examines repeat challengers, thus reducing the omitted variable bias by being able to control for challenger quality. He finds that money has little or no effect on vote shares.

Recently a theoretical and empirical literature has emerged on the effect of campaign finance laws (Coate, 2002; Prat, 2002; Wittman, 2002). Assuming that contributions solely inform voters about candidate's position, the theoretical work suggests that contribution limits lead to closer elections. In these models high quality candidates have a higher likelihood of winning the election because contributions allow them to advertise that they are better than the other candidate. Without contributions, the high quality candidate does not have this option and both candidates win with equal probability. With contributions voters do not know who is the better candidate, thus reducing the high quality candidate's chances of winning and thus contribution limits are predicted to lead to lower margins of victories. In the U.S. campaign finance regulation have changed very little until recently, thus there is little variation in the law to test this hypothesis. However U.S. states differ widely in their regulations. Empirical work on campaign finance laws finds that restrictions are binding, meaning that states with stricter limits have fewer contributions (Hogan, 2000). The previously mentioned prediction regarding the margin of victory finds support in recent empirical work. Stratmann (2002) examines campaign finance restrictions for individuals, corporations, unions, PACs, and parties, and finds that contribution limits lead to closer elections. Stricter limits are also associated with increase in incumbent defeats and with a larger number of candidates entering the race.

THOMAS STRATMANN

REFERENCES

Bronars, Stephen G. and John R. Lott, Jr. (1997). "Do campaign donations alter how a politician votes? Or, do donors support candidates who value the same things they do"? *Journal of Law and Economics*, 40: 317–350.

Chappel, Henry W., Jr. (1981). "Campaign contributions and voting on the cargo preference bill: a comparison of simultaneous models." *Public Choice*, 36: 301–312.

Coate, Stephen (2002). "On the desirability of campaign contribution limits," mimeo, Cornell University.

Coates, Dennis (1998). "Additional incumbent spending really can harm (at least some) incumbents: an analysis of vote share maximization." *Public Choice*, 95(1–2): 63–87.

Daniel, Kermit and John R. Lott (1997). "Term limits and electoral competitiveness: evidence from California's state legislative races." *Public Choice*, 90: 165–184.

Durden, Garey C., Jason F. Shogren, and Jonathan I. Silberman (1991). "The effects of interest groups pressure on coal-strip-mining legislation." *Social Science Quarterly*, 72: 237–250.

Epstein, David and Peter Zemsky (1995). "Money talks: deterring quality challengers in congressional elections." *American Political Science Review*, 89: 295–308.

Evans, Diana M. (1986). "PAC contributions and roll-call voting: conditional power," in A.J. Cigler and B.A. Loomis (eds.) *Interest Group Politics*, Second Edition. Washington, DC: Congressional Quarterly.

Green, D. and Krasno, J. (1988). "Salvation of the spendthrift incumbent: reestimating the effects of campaign spending in house elections." *American Journal of Political Science*, 32: 363–372.

Grier, Kevin B. (1989). "Campaign spending and senate elections, 1978–84." *Public Choice*, 63(3): 201–220.

Grier, Kevin B. and Michael C. Munger (1991). "Committee assignments, constituent preferences, and campaign contributions." *Economic Inquiry*, 29: 24–43.

Hall, Richard and Wayman, Frank (1990). "Buying time: moneyed interests and the mobilization of bias in congressional Committees." *American Political Science Review*, 84: 797–820.

Hogan, Robert (2000). "The costs of representation in state legislatures: explaining variations in campaign spending." *Social Science Quarterly*, December.

Jacobson, Gary C. (1978). "The Effects of Campaign Spending in Congressional Elections." *American Political Science Review* 72: 469–491.

Kau, James B., Donald Keenan, and Paul H. Rubin (1982). "A general equilibrium model of congressional voting." *Quarterly Journal of Economics*, 97: 271–293.

Kroszner, Randall S. and Thomas Stratmann (1998). "Interest group competition and the organization of congress: theory and evidence from financial services' political action committees." *American Economic Review*, 88: 1163–1187.

Kroszner, Randall S. and Thomas Stratmann (2002). "Corporate campaign contributions, repeat giving, and the rewards to legislator reputation," mimeo, University of Chicago.

Levitt, Steven (1994). "Using repeat challengers to estimate the effect of campaign spending on election outcomes in the U.S. House." *Journal of Political Economy*, 103: 777–798.

Lott, John R. (1987). "The effect of nontransferable property rights on the efficiency of political markets." *Journal of Public Economics*, 31(2): 231–246.

Milyo, Jeffrey (1997). "The economics of campaign finance: FECA and the puzzle of the not very greedy grandfathers." *Public Choice*, 93: 245–270.

Milyo, Jeffrey (1997). "Electoral and financial effects of changes in committee power: the Gramm-Rudman-Hollings budget reform, the tax reform act of 1986, and the money committees in the house." *Journal of Law and Economics*, 40(1): 93–112.

Ortuno-Ortin, Ignacio and Christian Schultz (2000). "Public funding for political parties." CESifo Working Paper No. 368.

Potters, Jan, Randolph Sloof, and Frans van Winden (1997). "Campaign expenditures, contributions, and direct endorsements: the strategic use of information and money to influence voter behavior." *European Journal of Political Economy*, 13: 1–31.

Poole, Keith, Thomas Romer, and Howard Rosenthal (1987). "The revealed preferences of political action committees." *American Economic Review*, 77: 298–302.

Prat, Andrea (2002). "Campaign spending with office-seeking politicians, rational voters, and multiple lobbies." *Journal of Economic Theory*, 103(1): 162–189.

Romer, Thomas and James M. Snyder (1994). "An empirical investigation of the dynamics of PAC contributions." *American Journal of Political Science*, 38: 745–769.

Snyder, James M., Jr. (1992). "Long-term investing in politicians: or, give early, give often." *Journal of Law and Economics*, 35: 15–43.

Stratmann, Thomas (1991). "What do campaign contributions buy? Deciphering causal effects of money and votes." *Southern Economic Journal*, 57, 606–664.

Stratmann, Thomas (1992). "Are contributions rational? Untangling strategies of political action committees." *Journal of Political Economy*, 100(3): 647–664.

Stratmann, Thomas (1995). "Campaign contributions and congressional voting: does the timing of contributions matter?" *Review of Economics and Statistics*, 77(1): 127–136.

Stratmann, Thomas (1996). "How reelection constituencies matter: evidence from political action committees' contributions and congressional Voting." *Journal of Law and Economics*, 39(2): 603–635.

Stratmann, Thomas (1998). "The market for congressional votes: is the timing of contributions everything?" *Journal of Law and Economics*, 41: 85–114.

Stratmann, Thomas and Francisco J. Aparicio-Castillo (2002). "Competition policy for elections: do campaign contribution limits matter?" mimeo, George Mason University.

Stratmann, Thomas (2002). "Can special interests buy congressional votes? Evidence from financial services legislation." *Journal of Law and Economics*, October 45(2): 345–373.

Vesenka, Mary H. (1989). "Economic interests and ideological convication, a note on PACs and agriculature acts." *Journal of Economic Behavior and Organization*, 12: 259–263.

Welch, William P. (1980). "Allocation of political monies: economic interst groups." *Public Choice*, 20: 83–97.

Wittman, Donald (2002). "Candidate quality, pressure group endorsements, and uninformed voters," mimeo, University of California, Santa Cruz, CA.

CAMPAIGN FINANCE 1

Total expenditures by the United States federal government in 2001were $1.8 trillion, or 18 percent of GDP. Candidates for congressional office spent $1.01 billion in the 2000 election cycle; for presidential office the sum was $354 million. On top of this, national parties spent an additional $495 million in soft money. Both candidate spending and soft money have risen sharply in recent years: in comparison to the 2000 figures, congressional spending and soft money averaged $730 million and $169 million respectively over the previous four election cycles (FEC, 2001; CRP, 2002). Most political commentators and politicians have decried these sums and trends as too high. Consider, however, that private sector advertising was $240 billion in 2000 (Census, 2001), which was 3.2 percent of the private sector share of GDP. In contrast, advertising in the 2000 national elections was 0.001 percent of the federal government's share of GDP. The latter figure would be even lower if I included the non-budget roles of the federal government (such as tax expenditures, loans and loan guarantees, mandates, and regulations). This comparison should provide some perspective in demonstrating the relatively small amount of money devoted to campaign finance. Despite this fact, campaign finance has been, and with recent reforms will continue to be, a major and contentious political issue to which political economists can contribute.

1. What does Campaign Finance do?

To better understand the role of campaign finance I begin with a general distinction: campaign contributions are not equivalent to campaign expenditures. In an accounting sense, the distinction is trivial. In an economic sense, however, the distinction draws attention to the functions that campaign finance serve and the various incentives that these functions create. What do campaign contributions do? And what do campaign expenditures do?

One view maintains that campaign contributions are intended to promote the electoral chances of the contributor's favored candidate. In this electoral view of contributions, individuals and PACs donate to the candidate whose policies would best serve their interests, but they are not intended to shift the candidate's policy position. This view is troubled because the election outcome is unaffected by the marginal contribution and, as a result, contributing solely on this motive would be irrational: free riding would dominate as a strategy in ways similar to the voting

paradox. Another view suggests that groups make contributions with the intention of increasing their relative influence over the eventual winner. Those who have donated to a legislator's (re)election campaign will, ceteris paribus, have greater access to the candidate once in office. With greater access, the group can then persuade the legislator through conventional lobbying (Austen-Smith, 1987; Austen-Smith and Wright, 1994). A more instrumental view maintains that contributions are made in exchange for legislators' votes on issues that are important to the donor. In other words, PAC donations directly shift legislators' policy positions. I will discuss the plausibility of these latter views in the section on vote-buying below.

Turning to the expenditures side, these can be informative, persuasive, or both — a distinction I borrow from Mueller and Stratmann (1994). In the informative view, campaign expenditures are simply a means for the candidates to announce their policy positions. This is analogous to a firm that says "here is our product; take it or leave it." Of course, the firm will maximize profits by making a product that consumers will purchase. Likewise, with informative campaigning, candidates will have the incentive to alter their policy positions to maximize the probability of winning the election. Very little of the literature takes the view that expenditures are informative. In the persuasive view, campaign expenditures are intended to convince voters to vote for the candidate without necessarily regarding the candidate's policy position. This is analogous to a firm saying "our product will enhance the quality of your life; you should buy it." In this case, the firm may be more concerned with image than the quality of the good. Likewise, with persuasive campaigning, relatively extreme candidates, or candidates who have deviated from voters' interests and/or campaign promises, may win votes despite their actual policy positions. In House elections during the 1990s, incumbents who had deviated more from constituents also spent more in their re-election bids (Campbell and López, 2002). Most of the literature has taken the view, at least implicitly, that campaign expenditures are primarily persuasive.

These views that I have listed are not mutually exclusive. Indeed, evidence suggests that contributions and expenditures play different roles depending on specific circumstances. The campaign finance literature has much to show for delineating these circumstances and adding to our understanding of how campaign finance shapes the incentives of the involved political agents — including candidates, lawmakers, interest groups, firms, and voters. I will illustrate this progress by discussing two areas in which scholars have quite fruitfully debated the functions of campaign finance.

2. Do contributions buy votes?

When a PAC donates to a successful candidate, will the candidate qua lawmaker then be more likely to vote in the PAC's interest? The correct answer depends partly on the form of the empirical estimation. For example, in a single-equation, cross-sectional model, Wright (1985) shows that contributions in the 97th House are not significant, even for powerful PACs on the votes that are most important to them. But the structure of the problem is conditional. Contributions may first influence the election prospects of the candidate and then influence floor voting. Also, if contributions flow to candidates with higher election probabilities, the marginal effect of contributions on voting will be upwardly biased in a single equation because it will capture both the donors' expectation of the candidate's election probabilities as well as any vote-buying motive that may be present. In contrast, simultaneous equations models indicate that contributions have little to no influence on general or omnibus votes (Chappell, 1982). On narrower votes (e.g., commodity-specific agricultural policies) the same type of estimation has revealed floor voting to be far more sensitive to PAC contributions (Stratmann, 1991; Brooks, 1997). The influence also depends on the timing of the contributions; there is a stronger relationship on votes that come very soon after contributions are made (Stratmann, 1995). So contributions appear to buy votes in certain circumstances. The issue is not that simple because contributions are made to candidates who, when elected, would have voted in the PAC's interest anyway. It has been shown theoretically and empirically that these donations can be understood as intending to affect the outcome of the election, either by influencing the candidates' positions or their election probabilities (Bronars and Lott, 1997; Stratmann, 1991; Ball, 1999). In addition, many PACs make large donations over several election periods to win legislators over, which implies a long term investment approach in which contributions help to buy relationships, not necessarily votes (Snyder, 1990, 1992). In some models, legislators allocate access to lobbyists according to whether their associated PAC had contributed to previous campaigns (Austen-Smith, 1995, 1998) — a view that enjoys support from several empirical studies.

Based on this debate, the views on contribution motives would appear to be conflated: contributions reflect partly vote-buying and partly access-buying motives. Hence, it should be expected that a strong correlation between contributions and votes would only sometimes be revealed in the data, or only in certain circumstances. Furthermore, contributions data is muddled by the fact that PACs donate to candidates of opposing policy positions (or at least want to lobby them as in Austen-Smith and Wright, 1994), and tend to give more to moderates in general (Stratmann, 1992).

3. Are Incumbent and Challenger Expenditures Equally Effective?

Around the work of Jacobson (1978, 1980, 1985) a conventional wisdom developed that marginal incumbent expenditures were far less effective at acquiring votes than were marginal challenger expenditures. The basis of this view is an argument that campaigning in general exhibits diminishing returns: since incumbents possess more reputation and typically spend more, their marginal expenditure is less valuable in terms of producing votes. In a series of studies that used two-stage least squares to control for endogeny with challenger spending, Jacobson (1978, 1980, 1985) showed this result. While founded on plausible microeconomic grounds, these results suggested some political puzzles. First, they contradicted the extant conventional wisdom that campaign spending is the main source of incumbent advantage. Instead, the infrastructure of the office itself (staff, accumulated parliamentary rights, reputation, etc.) would have to account for most or all of incumbent advantage. Second, if true, why would incumbents raise and expend money in their re-election campaigns? These puzzles and others fueled a debate in the literature, and more recent contributions may be turning Jacobson's conventional view on its ear because they exercise statistically superior models to control for endogeneity in the data. The first type of statistical advance came in the quality of instrumental variables (IVs) used. Jacobson (1978) use poor instruments based on exclusion restrictions such as incumbent tenure that will affect the election outcome. In contrast, Gerber (1998) used IVs based on exclusions like incumbent wealth and state population, which affect the ability to raise funds but do not affect the election outcome. The use of quality IVs resulted in roughly equal estimates of the effectiveness of incumbent and challenger spending. A second advance came in controlling for endogeny of the expected closeness of the election (Gerber, 1998), and again the earlier result was overturned. This undermined the diminishing returns argument because incumbent campaigns are typically much larger than challengers. New theories have emerged in the recent literature to explain the relationships between incumbent spending, challenger spending, and election returns. In one example — a formal game in which incumbent spending, challenger spending, and election probability are all interdependent — candidates' equilibrium spending levels increase in races that are expected to be close (Erickson and Palfrey, 2000). This is not so surprising. But the authors extend the game to a formal empirical system in which they derive and sign the asymptotic bias of a linear estimator (e.g., OLS) to the system. If the incumbent is expected to be safely re-elected, the estimate of incumbent spending is deflated while the estimate of challenger spending is inflated. Given that most races reflect this kind of incumbent advantage, this result explains why earlier results showed incumbent spending was relatively ineffective. In races that are expected to be close, however, there is no bias to OLS estimates. In short, the simultaneity problem varies with the expected closeness of the race or, equivalently, with the degree of a given incumbent's advantage. This presents a problem for empirical studies that pool races of varying expected closeness (essentially all empirical studies on the subject to date) even if IV estimation is used, because there is more than one true coefficient. In fact, there is a true coefficient for each level of closeness, and each coefficient must be estimated for an accurate assessment of the electoral effectiveness of incumbent vs. challenger spending.

4. Specification Issues

Both of the above questions necessitate grappling with multiple simultaneously determined variables. Incumbent spending, challenger spending, and closeness of the election are all endogenous, and for intuitive reasons: both incumbent and challenger spending decisions jointly affect, and are jointly affected by, the expected probability of re-election. Incumbent spending would tend to increase in the presence of a serious challenger — a challenger whose campaign expenditures are high. An incumbent who spends more will increase the margin of victory, while a challenger who spends more will decrease the margin of victory. Until recently, results found in the journals did not satisfactorily address the identification problem of this multiple simultaneity.

Consider the literature with legislator voting as dependent variable. Even while controlling for the effect of contributions on election probabilities, these contributions did not control for endogeny with challenger spending nor the fact that PACs contribute to challengers and legislators of policy positions opposed to their own. It may be time to reconsider these results, and redraw the lines around circumstances in which contributions appear to buy votes.

With the endogeneity being dependent on the expected closeness of the race, the same could be true for models that place incumbent spending as a dependent variable (Campbell and López, 2002) and models that explain challenger spending (Lott, 1987). In the latter case, for example, Lott showed that challenger spending increases

with current incumbent spending, but decreases with incumbent's cumulative prior spending. This suggests that spending contains an investment component that carries benefits over time — a candidate's reputation is partly a function of his or her prior campaign expenditures. But this result failed to control for the multiple simultaneity problem at hand. Revisiting this result with a model that accounts for possible non-linear simultaneity would be worthwhile.

5. Understanding Political Economy through Campaign Finance

This kind of progress in the literature is central to our understanding of campaign finance and to our properly conceiving the incentives faced by political agents. Clearly if contributions are vote-buying and expenditures are persuasive, we have simple exchange motives among interest groups and lawmakers. This would tend to be contrary to preferences of voters, whom lawmakers must subsequently win back with persuasive advertising — as appears to have been the case with House election in the 1990s (Campbell and Lopez, 2002). But there are important incentive effects even if contributions are electoral and expenditures are informative; here we have no exchange between lawmakers and contributors, but lawmakers know that contributions depend on their policy positions, and will change their positions in response. Understanding the influence of interest groups, the constraining power of constituent interests, and the policy positions that lawmakers will take implies understanding the role of campaign finance. Is campaigning primarily informative for blowout races but primarily persuasive for close races? What are the lessons for reform? For example, if campaigning is primarily informative, is it likely that contribution limits enhance welfare? Is there evidence for this? Addressing these types of questions would produce valuable future research.

6. Reform

Reform of campaign finance is inextricably tied to incumbent advantage. Incumbent advantage is the battle cry for reformers, while the effect of nearly every reform since the 1974 FECA amendments has been to increase incumbent advantage. It is no surprise that the rules would favor incumbents because they are better suited to collusion as a group than challengers are, and they are the first movers in setting the rules of the game (Baron, 1989). Congress (or the FEC under Congressional oversight) makes its own rules, subject to judicial review.

As evidenced by the passage of the Shays-Meehan campaign reform bill in March 2002, the actual reform instruments being used include outright bans and pre-set limits on certain types of fundraising, and more resources devoted to enforcement. In contrast, reforms that might legitimately diminish incumbent advantage have sat unlegislated on the sidelines for decades. Current examples of such proposals include full public financing, complete deregulation (i.e., laissez-faire), tying public funding to voluntary spending limits, and anonymous donations. Space limitations prevent my evaluation of these proposals. (I do not mean to suggest that these proposals would necessarily reduce incumbent advantage.) But why are they all neglected? Consider that the objectives of reform differ for each role player in the reform process. Among economists and political scientists the objective tends toward enhancing the efficiency of political markets — to make elections more competitive. Among judges and legal scholars the objective is to protect free speech. Among the public and political commentators, the objectives are to increase fairness and decrease corruption. But among lawmakers, the objective is some amalgamation of these various objectives into an overriding concern to maintain high re-election probabilities over their time horizon. The time horizon is key to understanding the success of Shays-Meehan. In the short run contribution limits may improve electoral competition, as apparently evidenced at the state level (Stratmann and Aparicio, 2002). But like stamping out weeds, prohibitions on various types of financing will only engender the emergence of new types of financing in the future. The current marriage of soft-money with issue-advocacy was provided for by the legal infrastructure that developed in the 1970s (the 1974 FECA amendments, *Buckley v. Valeo*, and FEC regulatory rules). But this marriage took over a decade to form. The long-term consequence of 1970s reform was to redirect campaign finance and probably to significantly increase its growth profile as well. Similarly, the long-term effects of Shays-Meehan will be to redirect, and perhaps increase, campaign finance in the future. A legal framework that prohibits campaign finance will, to paraphrase Thomas E. Mann, eventually become little more than an annoyance to incumbents establishing electoral advantage. As Mann (1999: 454) writes:

> The architects of the Federal Election Campaign Act did not envision soft money — funds raised by the parties for purposes other than directly influencing federal election campaigns — and such funds have no official standing in federal election law.

Similarly, Shays-Meehan does not envision the next major innovation — the next marriage of soft-money and issue-advocacy — that will come from market experimentation.

Efficiency requires a more general reform than bans and pre-set limits, a reform that alters the underlying incentives of the political agents involved, particularly lawmakers.

The legal and political institutional structure, including the election market, *contains* the campaign finance structure. Reforming the latter can only insignificantly affect reform of the former. In contrast, reforming the former can significantly affect the latter. Efficacious reform would recognize that the size of the campaign sector is tied to the size of the public sector overall (Lott, 2000). And campaign finance is a market that helps the overall political market clear. It is because of the underlying preferences of voters and interest groups for using the government sector as a means of acquiring wealth, and of competition among politicians for fulfilling these preferences, that we see a campaign finance system occupying so many resources. If anything, it is surprising that the campaign sector is not drastically bigger than it is. As such, rather than attempt to stamp out this weed, efficacious reform would find its roots and pull it out by them.

EDWARD J. LÓPEZ

REFERENCES

Austen-Smith, D. (1998). "Allocating access for information and contributions." *Journal of Law Economics and Organization*, 14(2): 277–303.

Austen-Smith, D. (1995). "Campaign contributions and access." *American Political Science Review*, 89(3): 566–581.

Austen-Smith, D. (1987). "Interest groups, campaign contributions, and probabilistic voting." *Public Choice*, 54: 123–139.

Austen-Smith, D. and Wright, J.R. (1994). "Counteractive lobbying." *American Journal of Political Science*, 38(1): 24–44.

Ball, Richard J. (1999). "Opposition Backlash and Platform Convergence in a Spatial Voting Model with Campaign Contributions," *Public Choice*, 98(3/4): 269–286.

Baron, D.P. (1989). "Service-induced campaign contributions and the electoral equilibrium." *Quarterly Journal of Economics*, 104(1): 45–72.

Bronars, S.G. and Lott, J.R., Jr. (1997). "Do campaign donations alter how a politician votes? or, do donors support candidates who value the same things that they do?" *Journal of Law and Economics*, 40: 317–350.

Brooks, J. (1997). "Congressional voting on farm payment limitations: Political pressure or ideological conviction?" *Journal of Agricultural and Resource Economics*, 22(2): 281–295.

Campbell, N.D. and López, E.J. (2002). Legislator vote records and campaign expenditures in a price theoretic model of congressional seats. University of North Texas Working Paper 00-07 (under second review at *Eastern Economic Journal*).

Cantor, J.E. (2001). Campaign Financing. *CRS Issue Brief for Congress* IB87020, Congressional Research Service (May 21).

Census, U.S. Bureau of (2001). Statistical abstract of the United States. Table 1271. *www.census.gov/statab/www/*.

Chappell, H.W., Jr. (1982). "Campaign contributions and congressional voting: A simultaneous probit-tobit model." *Review of Economics and Statistics*, 64: 77–83.

CRP (2002). Soft money's impact at a glance. Center for Responsive Politics. *www.opensecrets.org*.

Erikson, R.S. and Palfrey, T.R. (2000). "Equilibria in campaign spending games: Theory and data." *American Political Science Review*, 94(3): 595–609.

FEC (Federal Election Commission) (2001). "FEC Reports on Congressional Financial Activity for 2000," Press release dated May 15, 2001. *www.fec.gov*.

Gerber, A. (1998). "Estimating the effect of campaign spending on Senate election outcomes using instrumental variables." *American Political Science Review*, 92(2): 401–411.

Jacobson, G.C. (1985). "Money and votes reconsidered: Congressional elections, 1972–1982." *Public Choice*, 47: 7–62.

Jacobson, G.C. (1980). *Money in Congressional Elections*. New Haven: Yale University Press.

Jacobson, G.C. (1978). "The effects of campaign spending in Congressional elections." *American Political Science Review*, 72: 469–491.

Lott, J.R., Jr. (2000). "A simple explanation for why campaign expenditures are increasing: The government is getting bigger." *Journal of Law and Economics*, 43(2): 359–393.

Lott, J.R., Jr. (1987). "The effect of nontransferable property rights on the efficiency of political markets: some evidence." *Journal of Public Economics*, 32: 231–246.

Mann, T. E. (1999). "The U.S. campaign finance system under strain," in *Setting National Priorities: The 2000 Elections and Beyond*. Washington: Brookings Press, pp. 449–478.

Mueller, D.C. and Stratmann, T. (1994). "Informative and persuasive campaigning." *Public Choice*, 81: 55–77.

Snyder, J.M., Jr. (1990). "Campaign contributions as investments: The U.S. House of Representatives 1980–1986." *Journal of Political Economy*, 98(6): 1193–1227.

Snyder, J.M., Jr. (1992). "Long-term investing in politicians; or, give early, give often." *Journal of Law and Economics*, 35: 15–43.

Stratmann, T. (1995). "Campaign contributions and congressional voting: Does the timing of contributions matter?" *Review of Economics and Statistics*, 77(1): 127–136.

Stratmann, T. (1992). "Are contributors rational? Untangling strategies of political action committees." *Journal of Political Economy*, 100(3): 647–664.

Stratmann, T. (1991). "What do campaign contributions buy? Deciphering causal effects of money and votes." *Southern Economic Journal*, 57(3): 606–620.

Stratmann, T. and Aparicio, F.J. (2002). Competition policy for elections: Do campaign contribution limits matter? Unpublished Manuscript.

Wright, J.R. (1985). "PACs, contributions, and roll calls: An organizational perspective." *American Political Science Review*, 79: 400–414.

CAMPAIGN FINANCE 2

In 1903 Lenin along with Julius Martov founded the newspaper Iskra, which was later to become Pravda. At the time, Lenin was a ferocious advocate of a free press and free political discourse. After coming to power we find Lenin addressing a Moscow crowd in 1920 with the words "Why should any man be allowed to buy a printing press and disseminate pernicious opinions calculated to embarrass the government?" Lenin is not alone in the frenzied attention he paid to controlling speech. In 1971 and 1974 the US Congress passed limits on campaign spending by candidates to the House and Senate and outlawed spending by private citizens wishing to express their private views during elections. In its 1976 Buckley v. Valeo ruling the Supreme Court ruled that campaign spending limits violated the First Amendment's protection of free speech, but ever since some congressmen and senators, and activist groups such as Common Cause, have sought to amend the constitution to limit campaign spending and replace private funding of elections by state funding.

The huge attention campaign finances have won from the media and politicians is due to the fear that money can buy elections and that money can buy political favours. Research on campaign spending and contributions has as a result focused on the effect of spending on votes, and on asking what determines how much money a candidate has to spend.

1. Effect of Campaign Spending on Votes

As in almost any field of social and physical sciences, empirical work precedes theory. The question on the lips of early researchers was how to estimate the effect of campaign spending on political success. The natural approach was to run a regression of vote-share on campaign spending and other control variables such as whether a candidate was an incumbent or a challenger on the candidate's share of votes in an election. The first to exploit datasets on campaign spending made available by campaign spending laws was Kristian Palda (1973) who used simple OLS to show that for Quebec provincial elections campaign spending was more powerful at the margin for challengers than for incumbents and that incumbents seem to start their races with a committed bloc of voters. Using US House of Representatives data from the 1974 elections Gary Jacobson (1978) found the seemingly extreme result that incumbent spending had almost no effect at all at the margin. This result has provoked disbelief among political scientists, but it is not a mystery if we take it that incumbents have low to zero marginal costs of raising extra dollars, as Coates (1998) has pointed out. In such a case they will spend money until the marginal return, as measured by votes, falls to zero.

A string of papers throughout the 1980s from different countries (summarized in Palda, 2000) seemed to confirm the Jacobson findings. These papers are cross-sectional, focus mainly on district level data and are almost completely divorced from time-series regressions that seek to explain votes by cycles in government spending (such as those in the tradition of Kramer, 1971). These findings became the most investigated and contested "stylized facts" about campaign spending. At issue were the claims of politicians that campaign spending limits were in the public interest and the doubts raised by public choice scholars that these limits served as artificial barriers to entry in the political market. As Abrams and Settle (1978) write

> Rational, self-interested individuals, groups, or industries seek regulation as a means of serving their own private interests... When regulation has the potential for directly affecting the legislators themselves (e.g. political campaign regulations), the economic approach [to regulation] suggests that the regulation would be designed to serve the legislators' interest rather than some vaguely defined 'public interest'.

Jacobson and others (Palda and Palda, 1985) wove a story to explain why, if true, these results could help understand incumbents' universal eagerness to pass a spending limit. An incumbent during his or her tenure in office uses the government frank and paid research and support staff to run a continuous election campaign. Come election time the incumbent may have exhausted the potential of money to enlighten voters on his or her performance and policy views. Challengers are usually less well known, and a long tradition of empirical studies summarized in Jacobson (1990) suggests that challenger spending at the margin is more potent than incumbent spending in getting votes. The reason is that voters, even though they may not wish to elect the challenger, demand to know their alternatives to the incumbent, and may give some support to the challenger, provided the challenger is not too unacceptable, in order to discipline the incumbent. A spending limit thus may not harm the incumbent, but may prevent the challenger from dispelling basic doubts in voter minds about his or her integrity and policy positions.

The lack of any study that could tie the political profits from campaign spending limits to how legislators vote on those limits does not allow public choice scholars to make conclusive pronouncements on the motives for such limits. We must depend on an unproved model to mediate between data on marginal productivity of spending and conclusions about candidate motives for passing spending limits. In this tradition Bender (1988) showed that candidates who voted for the 1974 spending limits in Congress were also those with the lowest marginal products of campaign spending. In countries that impose spending limits it is hard to find any sudden rise in the votes of incumbents. The problem with this conclusion, as I explained in Palda (1996), is that

spending limits may give incumbents a potential advantage in votes which they choose to "spend" by giving favours to special interest groups. They will give such favours until their voteshares fall back to where they were before the limits. In other words, spending limits may influence policy more than they influence votes. Palda's theory suggests that spending limits will have an effect on policy. In what is perhaps the first empirical study that seeks to find how spending limits influence policy Crain et al. (1990) concluded that US states which have spending limits in state elections are more likely to pass regulations (off budget spending) than are states without spending limits. These latter states are likelier than spending limit states to have higher on-budget spending.

The dispute over whether incumbent or challenger marginal products are greater and whether money has any effect on electoral outcomes has put money into the pockets of some scholars preoccupied with this question. Dozens of court cases challenging or seeking to enforce spending limits have called on these scholars as experts. There is perhaps no area of public choice which feels a greater demand for its expert services than the campaign spending area. What guarantees employment for the experts is that few can agree on what is the effect of spending on votes. As early as the 1970s researchers felt that OLS was not an appropriate way to estimate vote production functions. Money may get votes, but anticipated votes get money from contributors. Research on the simultaneity between campaign spending and votes has gone through two phases. The first phase, launched by Palda (1975) and carried on by the work of Jacobson (1980, 1985, 1990) and Green and Krasno (1988) has sought different instruments for campaign spending that would allow identification of the voters equation. Depending on the use of instrument one could find, as Jacobson has that challenger spending is roughly twice as powerful at the margin as incumbent spending. Green and Krasno (1988) used past expenditures as an instrument for current expenditures and found that in general incumbent and challenger spending have equal marginal productivity. The second phase of research as exemplified by Levitt (1994) and Milyo (1998) warns that instrumental variables used in the first-phase studies of simultaneity are likely to be correlated with omitted variables and provide what is perhaps the best critique of empirical work in the field to date. The omission of forces correlated with instrumented variable may exaggerate the importance of those variables.

The magnitude of campaign spending may not be the only factor that influences votes. The diversity and concentration of the campaign contributions that give rise to campaign spending may also influence votes.

Theoretical support for this idea goes back to Madison and Montesquieu, but has more recently been elaborated by Potters et al. (1997) and Dharmapalla and Palda (2002). Palda and Palda (1998) found that in French parliamentary elections candidates who relied on their own funds to finance their campaigns tended to receive fewer votes. Dharmapalla and Palda found that the greater was the concentration of contributions to challengers or open seat candidates in US House elections, the fewer votes those candidates tended to receive. The significance of this research is that it contradicts the 1976 US Supreme Court Buckley v. Valeo ruling that contributions are not a form of speech and therefore may be limited by law.

2. The Sources of Spending

Campaign spending is not possible without a contributor. In the US, private contributors dominate government contributions to campaigns. A booming branch of public choice is to show the link between contributions to candidates and the types of votes they make in Congress. US data is perhaps the most suited to finding whether contributions buy political favours. In most European countries (Gunlicks, 1993) government subsidies dominate elections. In those countries where private contributions are tolerated, party discipline prevails and it is difficult to hold that the individual representative has much say of his own in the legislature. In the US Congress, representatives have great independence from their party and it is reasonable to seek a link between how they vote on legislation and the contributions they receive.

In a study representative of many in the field, Snyder (1990) has found that an interest group has to give money over many years before it can influence policy. The meaning though of this influence is not clear. If environmentalists support a candidate through several elections in return for his support in the legislature, does this mean the candidate has been corrupted? Or has he perhaps been won over by the arguments and the persistence of the lobby group? No one can really answer this question with authority. Public Choice scholars have perhaps focused too much on the potentially harmful effects of campaign finances and the manner in which government regulations can restrain these harmful effects.

Studies that try to relate roll-call voting to contributions by particular groups have recently been joined by more macro studies such as those of Palda (1992) and later of Lott (2000). Both using statewide data sought to tie the size of campaign spending to the size of government. The idea behind these researches is that a large government is a prize over which interest groups will fight. Part of the resources spent in this fight are campaign advertising dollars. These studies suggest that campaign spending grows with the size of government.

3. The Value of Campaign Spending

Not all research into campaign spending is concerned purely with the links between spending and voters. A less well known branch of research into campaign spending has sought to determine whether campaign spending is simply rent-seeking expense or whether it contributes to educated debate on issues of public interest. Complicated theoretical models exist to support either position. Campaign spending may be harmful if politicians can consistently mislead voters, and if one believes that election campaigns are battles over a fixed pie of government resources rather than debates from which useful suggestions and ideas emerge for reforming government. In summarizing a large literature of laboratory studies and surveys, Crête (1991) concluded that

1. Election advertising increases voters' knowledge of issues and candidates.
2. Message repetition (frequency) is an important factor in familiarizing voters with candidates and issues.
3. There is a connection between the issues candidates propose in their advertising and the issues the electorate cares about.
4. Candidates who take a position on the issues in their advertising rate higher with the electorate than those who do not.

Coleman and Manna (2000) round out Crête's summary in their study of 1994 and 1996 House elections. Using survey data they find that "Campaign spending increases knowledge of and affect toward candidates, improves the public's ability to place candidates on ideology and issue scales, and encourages certainty about those placements... Spending neither enhances nor erodes trust and efficacy in politics or attention and interest in campaigns."

If public choice scholars wish to conclusively pronounce themselves on the need for regulation of campaign finances they should understand that by closing one avenue to power such regulations will force electoral contestants to shift their efforts at influencing government to other avenues, such as back-room lobbying. The advantage may then go to those who are good at backroom lobbying rather than to those who are good at making a case directly to the public. This shift in regulated funds to less regulated uses is what Issacharoff and Karlan (1999) have called a "hydraulic effect" which could exacerbate the pathologies it was intended to correct.

FILIP PALDA

REFERENCES

Abrams, Burton A. and Settle, Russell F. (1978). "The economic theory of regulation and the public financing of presidential elections." *Journal of Political Economy*, 86(April): 245–257.

Bender, Bruce, (1988). "An analysis of congressional voting on legislation limiting congressional campaign expenditures." *Journal of Political Economy*, 96: 1005–1021.

James L. Buckley et al. *v.* Francis R. Valeo, Secretary of the United States Senate, 424 U.S. 1, (1976).

Coates, Dennis (1998). "Additional incumbent spending really can harm (at least some) incumbents: An analysis of vote share maximization." *Public Choice*, 95: 63–87.

Coleman, John J. and Paul F. Manna (2000). "Congressional campaign spending and the quality of democracy." *The Journal of Politics*, 62: 757–789.

Crain, Mark W., Robert D. Tollison, and Donald R. Leavens (1990). "Laissez-faire in campaign finance" in W. Mark Crain and Robert D. Tollison (eds.) *Predicting Politics: Essays in Empirical Public Choice*. Ann Arbor: The University of Michigan Press, pp. 257–270.

Crête, Jean (1991). "Television, advertising and Canadian elections," in Frederick J. Fletcher (ed.) *Media and Voters in Canadian Election Campaigns*, Dundurn Press, Toronto, pp. 3–44.

Dharmapalla, Dhammika and Filip Palda (2002). "Campaign contributions as information: The case of recent US House elections." *Public Choice* (forthcoming 2003).

Green, Donald Philip and Krasno, Jonathan S. (1988). "Salvation for the spendthrift incumbent: Reestimating the effects of campaign spending in House elections." *American Journal of Political Science*, 32: 884–907.

Gunlicks, Arthur B. (ed.) (1993). *Campaign and Party Finance in North America and Western Europe*. San Francisco: Westview Press.

Issacharaoff, Samuel and Pamela S. Karlan (1999). "The hydraulics of campaign finance reform." *Texas Law Review*, 77: 1674–1749.

Jacobson, Gary C. (1978). "The effects of electoral campaign spending in congressional elections." *American Political Science Review*, 72: 469–491.

Jacobson, Gary C. (1980). *Money in Congressional Elections*. New Haven, Conn: Yale University Press.

Jacobson, Gary C. (1985). "Money and votes reconsidered: congressional elections, 1972–1982." *Public Choice*, 47: 7–62.

Jacobson, Gary C. (1990). "The effects of campaign spending in House elections: New evidence for old arguments." *American Journal of Political Science*, 34: 334–362.

Kramer, G.H. (1971). "Short run fluctuations in U.S. voting behavior, 1896–1964." *American Political Science Review*, 65: 131–143.

Levitt, Steven (1994). "Using repeat challengers to estimate the effect of campaign spending on election outcomes in the U.S. House." *Journal of Political Economy*, 102: 777–798.

Lott, John R. (2000). "A simple explanation for why campaign expenditures are increasing: The government is getting bigger." *Journal of Law and Economics*, 43: 359–393.

Milyo, Jeff (1998). "The electoral effects of campaign spending in House elections: A natural experiment approach." Department of Economics working paper, Tufts University.

Palda, Filip (1992). "The determinants of campaign spending: The role of the government jackpot." *Economic Inquiry* 30: 627–638.

Palda, Filip (1994). *How Much is Your Vote Worth? The Unfairness of Campaign Spending Limits*. San Francisco: The Institute for Contemporary Studies Press.

Palda, Filip (1996). "The economics of election campaign spending limits." *Economia delle scelte pubbliche*, 2–3: 113–137.

Palda, Filip (2000). "Regulacion del Financimiento Electoral: Lecciones de Canada y los Estados Unidos," in Prieto, Salvador Valdés (éd.). *Reforma del Estado. Volumen I, Financimiento Politico*. Santiago, Centro de Estudios Publicos, pp. 215–274.

Palda, Filip and Kristian S. Palda (1985). "Ceilings on campaign spending: Hypothesis and partial test with Canadian data." *Public Choice*, 5: 313–331.

Palda, Filip and Kristian S. Palda (1998). "The impact of regulated campaign expenditures on political competition in the French legislative elections of 1993." *Public Choice*, 94: 157–174.

Palda, Kristian S. (1973). "Does advertising influence votes?' An analysis of the 1966 and 1970 Quebec elections." *Canadian Journal of Political Science*, 6: 638–655.

Palda, Kristian S. (1975). "The effect of expenditure on political success." *Journal of Law and Economics*, 18: 745–771.

Potter, Jan, Sloof, Randolph, and Frans van Winden (1997). "Campaign expenditures, contributions and direct endorsements: The strategic use of information and money to influence voter behavior." *European Journal of Political Economy*, 13: 1–31.

Snyder, James M., Jr. (1990). "Campaign contributions as investments: The U.S. house of representatives, 1980–1986." *Journal of Political Economy*, 98: 1195–1227.

CENTRAL BANKS

There have been three great inventions since the beginning of time: fire, the wheel, and central banking. (Will Rogers, American humorist)

For much of human history, people lived in small groups counting a few hundred at most. They lived at subsistence level, their self-preservation regularly threatened by starvation, disease, sexual rivalry, extreme cold, and war. Starting around 3200 BC, people organized themselves in larger units counting thousands and later hundreds of thousands and millions, and formal structures of government came into being. The modern state emerged in the last couple of centuries, mass democracy, in the last one hundred years. The Bank of Sweden and the Bank of England are the oldest central banks, having been founded in 1668 and 1694, respectively, but most central banks in existence, like most democracies, are creatures of the twentieth century.

How do the modern state, democracy, and central banking relate to the wealth of nations? DeLong (1998) reports the average world GDP per capita, measured in 1990 international dollars, for the period one million BC to AD 2000. In the pre-government period, around one million to 3000 BC, average world GDP per capita increased from 92 to 113. In the pre-modern period with government, around 3000 BC to AD 1600, GDP fluctuated between 89 and 143, and most of the time its values were well above those of the pre-government period. Starting in the Middle Ages from an all-time low of 89 in 1300, GDP steadily increased, to 109 in 1400, 138 in 1500, 141 in 1600, 164 in 1700, and 195 in 1800. With the Scientific and Industrial Revolutions in place, GDP exploded in the 19th and 20th century, taking on the values 679 in 1900 and 6539 in 2000. These are per capita numbers that control for the increase in population.

The number for the year 2000 is a world average that hides extreme inequalities across countries: GDP per capita in the richest countries in the world (most of them in Western Europe and North America) is on the order of 1,000 times as large as the GDP per capita of the poorest countries in the world (most of them in Africa). The latter compares to the GDP per capita of the pre-government era of the human race.

What caused the enormous rise in GDP in the last two centuries, and what explains the enormous differences across countries today? The countries that have improved their lot are precisely those that have developed well-functioning economic and political institutions, or "capitalism and democracy" for short.

Fiat money is one of the wealth generators. It implies low transaction costs of exchange and thereby enables specialization. Fiat money has no inherent value. Its exchange value depends on a vast system of iterated beliefs: today a person is willing to accept dollars for a cow because she believes that tomorrow she can use those dollars to buy a pig because she believes that the owner of the pig believes that he in turn can use the dollars he gets for the pig to purchase a bunch of chickens because she believes that he believes that the owner of the chickens believes ... For fiat money to work, it must be common knowledge (everybody believes that everybody believes ... *ad infinitum*) that little green pieces of paper are a store of value.

This system of beliefs is fragile. Whoever controls the money printing press can flood the economy with little green pieces of paper and thereby devalue the existing stock of little green pieces of paper (as measured by how many cows and pigs and chickens it is worth). For people to believe that money is a store of value, and for them to believe that other people believe that other people believe ... that money is a store of value, the person or institution that controls the money printing press must be visibly and credibly committed not to inflate the money supply. This is where central banking enters the picture. A well-functioning central bank is credibly committed not to inflate the money supply, and it coordinates people's beliefs accordingly.

It would appear, however, that the introduction of a central bank merely shifts the problem without solving it. For fiat money to work its wonders, it must be common knowledge that it is credible, and a central bank can give it credibility, but where does the credibility of the central bank come from (a.k.a. *quis custodiet ipsos custodes*)? Modern central banks are fiat institutions, meaning: they are created by political fiat and can be done away with by political fiat. If the government wants to use the money printing press, and the central bank stands in the way, surely the government that created the central bank can get rid of it when the central bank refuses to do the government's bidding. And the public, knowing that this is the case, won't get snookered by the existence of a central bank in the first place.

A fiat institution can be credible only if something stands in the way of the government getting rid of it by political fiat. That something can be a physical barrier or a political cost.

To understand the concept of a political cost, it is useful to contemplate an alternative solution to the problem of credible commitment — the establishment of a physical barrier.

Consider the general who commits his army to fight by destroying a bridge and who thereby makes it physically impossible for his soldiers to flee in the face of the enemy. Hostage-taking is another physical commitment mechanism that enjoyed considerable popularity in the history of warfare.

Historically, coin producers devalued the currency by shaving the edges of coins to collect the silver and gold. Over time, "credible coins" came into being, with ridges on their edges. Destroyed ridges made currency manipulations visible to the casual user of coins.

Dollarization can be thought of as a fixed exchange rate regime that creates a physical barrier to government manipulations of the money supply. If the private sector in a country outside of the United States uses the U.S. dollar as its currency of choice, it is practically impossible for the domestic government to expand the money supply. True, the government could create a new currency along with a central bank and pass laws prohibiting foreign currency holdings, and then it could proceed to inflate its newly created currency. But as a practical matter the government cannot do all of this in a couple of weeks or in complete secrecy, and by the time it is done, the private sector will have adjusted to the new regime — people will have demonetized some of their exchanges, added appropriate inflation markups to nominal prices and contracts, and shifted their capital out of the country.

Alternatively, institutional commitment can be backed up by a political cost. If a left-wing government with a credibility problem appoints a charismatic conservative figure to head the central bank, it is true there is nothing in principle preventing the government from dismissing the central banker if he refuses to do the government's bidding. Nothing, that is, except for the political fall-out: dismissed central bankers have an awkward way of making front-page news. The government pays a political cost, which is potentially huge. Voters lose confidence in the government and vote it out of office; wagesetters write high inflation markups into nominal wage contracts; financial markets engage in destabilizing speculation or shift investment capital to other countries; cooperative understandings with foreign governments break down because of the domestic government's "loss of political capital." It is precisely because everybody understands that the government will pay a political price for dismissing the central banker that the appointment of the central banker generates credibility in the first place.

Creating an institution draws a line in the sand that focuses the expectations of an audience: voters, wagesetters, financial markets, and other political and economic actors. The line in the sand is a public focal point that allows hundreds, thousands, or even millions of people to coordinate their beliefs about the punishment strategies that will be executed in the event of an institutional "defection." The dismissal of a central banker; a devaluation; the failure to achieve a monetary target — all of these are institutional defections that generate an audience cost (Lohmann 2003).

To understand the concept of an audience cost, compare two situations. First, a man and a woman sit together in a restaurant, and the man asks the woman how she would feel about marrying him. Second, a man and a woman stand together in a church in front of an audience of relatives, and a priest asks each of them in turn whether they want to marry the other. In the first situation, there is no audience, and it is easy for the man and the woman to disagree on the question of what exactly, if anything, was promised. In the second situation, there is an audience, and there is a line in the sand, and these two ingredients explain why the degree of commitment is higher in the second situation than in the first.

In sum, an institution enjoys credibility if the act of institutional creation publicly attaches the institution to an audience that can and will monitor the integrity of the institution and impose audience costs on the government if it messes with the institution.

Economists often discuss the pros and cons of various monetary institutions on narrow technocratic grounds. Such discussions miss an important point: the defining characteristic of an institution is its audience. Different institutions invoke different audiences. By selecting a monetary institution, the policymaker selects an audience and thereby fixes the political cost of an institutional defection.

Let us compare an inflation target with a monetary target. Voters collectively observe inflation (they experience rising prices in the supermarket); in a country like Germany, they get upset about it; and a government that presides over high inflation rates loses popularity and eventually gets run out of office. In contrast, a monetary target does not generally trigger strong emotions: it is hard for voters to get excited about M3, in part because they have no idea that their central bank is tracking M3, in other part because they have no idea what M3 is. The audience for a monetary target is necessarily a relatively small and specialized elite audience of central bank watchers (including academic economists). If this elite audience loses faith in the government, it can communicate its disaffection to the financial markets. These two audiences, the mass electorate and a specialized elite, can both impose a political cost, but the size and nature of the political cost is audience-specific.

Next, consider an exchange rate target. In a small and very open economy such as Belgium, anything having to do with exchange rates makes front-page news. Here, an exchange rate peg offers itself as a commitment mechanism because it comes with an informed mass audience that can impose significant political costs. An exchange rate peg will not work in the same way in a large closed economy such as the United States, with its inward-looking voters who don't know what an exchange rate is and who can barely place Europe on a world map (and all they know about Belgium is that it must be Tuesday).

Audiences differ in the size and nature of the political costs they can impose. They also differ in the kinds of defections they can identify and care about; they differ in their definition of justified defections (which are excused) and unjustified defections (which are punished); in the probability that the punishment is executed "in equilibrium"; in the quality and severity of the punishments they can dole out; and in the distribution of the punishment burden (who pays).

Consider once again our two audiences — the mass electorate and the specialized elite — that are in charge of monitoring an inflation target and a monetary target, respectively. These two audiences differ in the degree to which they are attentive and informed and can understand and excuse defections that are justified by the circumstances.

Voters can impose the ultimate political cost: they can vote a government out of office. They experience how well off they are, and they can observe big events that make front-page news, like the dismissal of a central banker. But voters are generally inattentive and ill-informed about the details of monetary policy. As a result, their punishment strategies tend to be simple (not state-contingent). The simplicity comes about because voters don't have the expertise to distinguish a large number of states of the world; it also arises because voters face a coordination problem — voters are large in number, and in practice it is impossible for millions of people to coordinate their beliefs on a complex (highly state-contingent) punishment strategy.

Elite audiences are different. Trade union and employer organizations who negotiate wage contracts; banks and other big players in financial markets; academic economists — these are political actors who can monitor the fulfillment of a monetary target even while they can assess the central bank's excuses when the central bank misses its target. The audience knows that the target exists, it has the expertise to understand the economic implications of the target, it has an interest in tracking whether the central bank is on target, it observes economic and political developments that justify deviations from the target, and in the case of justified defections the audience can waive the punishment. In short, an elite audience can execute a state-contingent punishment strategy.

A well-functioning monetary institution typically consists of a messy collection of sub-institutions that are monitored by audiences with different stakes, attention cues, and information sets. Collectively, these differentiated audiences create a complex menu of audience costs. As a result, the monetary institution can accommodate political pressures at zero cost — up to a point; deviate from a rigid decision rule at a political price that is just low enough that it is sometimes worthwhile paying the price and just high enough that it doesn't always pay; and change when its audiences insist that it has become dysfunctional and obsolete, and do so forgivingly and at low social cost rather than breaking down violently and ripping the fabric of beliefs that holds together the society.

On this count, it is useful to compare two historical monetary regimes, on the one hand the gold standard and on the other hand the Deutsche Bundesbank in its full glory before it got folded into the European Central Bank (Lohmann, 1998).

The gold standard credibly committed countries not to inflate, and it did offer some flexibility (countries could and did go on and off the gold standard). But the very simplicity of the gold standard implied that the exercise of flexibility was extraordinarily costly for the economies involved.

By way of comparison, the Bundesbank in its heyday was very much credibly committed to a low inflation monetary policy, but it was also an extraordinarily complex institution monitored by multiple audiences. For starters, the Bundesbank had a mass audience — the general public — that served as a referee of sorts in the event of a public conflict between the Bundesbank and the federal government. German voters were ready to impose political costs on the federal government in the event that inflation ran out of control, which provided a low-inflation anchor to the German central banking system. But this mass audience had its limitations. The general public was not involved at all in the two historical debates about degree of centralization and independence of the German central banking system, 1955–1957 and 1990–1992 — these debates were carried by an elite audience.

The regional state governments, on the other hand, were quite inattentive in matters of inflation but hyper-attentive whenever the federal government threatened to mess with the Bundesbank institution. The reason is simple. To this day, the Bundesbank is embedded in the federalist structure of the German political system. Its central bank council consists of a minority of federal government appointees and a majority of regional state appointees. Changes to the Bundesbank Law, which defines the scope of the Bundesbank's legal independence, require the acquiesence of the second house of parliament, which is controlled by the regional state governments. For both reasons, the regional state governments served as political veto players in the event of federal government threats to the Bundesbank institution or the independent status of the Bundesbank. It has always been possible for the federal government to change the structure or legal status of the Bundesbank, and still is, but the presence of federalist veto players generates delay, transaction costs, and political costs.

Starting in 1973, the Bundesbank announced a monetary target to "discipline" the inflation expectations of German wage setters. Astonishingly, the Bundesbank missed its target about half the time — and when it missed, it usually erred on the side of having expanded the money supply too much. One might think that the Bundesbank's reputation as a committed inflation fighter would have taken a hit. In fact, whenever the Bundesbank missed its target, it explained why to an understanding audience of Bundesbank watchers, with the result that its reputation didn't suffer at all. Even so, it would be an error to infer that the monetary target had no bite. On the contrary, the Bundesbank's announcements helped to coordinate the expectations of wagesetting elites and convinced them to write low inflation markups into nominal wage contracts.

In sum, the historical Bundesbank was an exceptionally well-functioning central bank, and not because it was a simple, transparent, or apolitical institution. On the contrary, the Bundesbank "worked" because it was complex, messy, and political. The institution spoke to informationally segmented audiences, with the result that some aspects of its operations were transparent to some audiences and opaque to others. Audience scrutiny generated credibility; but not everything the Bundesbank did was scrutinized by everybody all the time, which is what generated flexibility.

Over recent decades, with the emergence and refinement of mass democracy, governments have shifted from employing physical and charismatic mechanisms of commitment to fiat and impersonal mechanisms, apparently because the former are relatively rigid, the latter, more flexible (cf. Lohmann, 1992).

The gold standard is an example of a commitment mechanism with a physical component (hostage-taking is another example). Appointing a well-known public figure to head the central bank, with the idea that his personal reputation will back up the commitment to a sound monetary policy, is an example of a charismatic commitment mechanism.

Monetary institutions in advanced democracies are mostly fiat institutions; if they are credible, it is because everybody believes everybody else believes... that they are credible. And they tend to be run by faceless, interchangeable bureaucrats: even if the occasional bureaucrat becomes a public figure, the credibility of the institutions does not stand and fall with him. The historical Bundesbank is a prominent example.

Not only has the nature of commitment mechanisms changed over time; their quality has increased over time. Indeed, some of the best-performing monetary institutions — best-performing in historical and contemporary perspective — are located in modern mass democracies. This poses a puzzle. After all, to many economists, mass democracy, or the electoral and partisan politics that are an inevitable by-product of regular free elections in a regime characterized by mass suffrage, is seen as the devil who has a hard time keeping his paws off monetary policy.

More specifically, we find sound monetary policies and great central banks in mass democracies that come attached to developed economies and mature political systems. In contrast, less developed economies and non-democracies have an uneven record when it comes to supporting sound monetary policies or well-functioning institutions (Cukierman, 1992). If one set of countries — the highly developed democracies — has figured out how to isolate monetary policy from popular pressures and government interference, why can't another set of countries — the less developed democracies and non-democracies — simply follow their example?

The reason is, quite simply, that sound monetary policies and well-functioning monetary institutions are politically embedded. Institutional commitment requires policymakers who are politically accountable to multiple heterogeneous audiences consisting of people with different stakes, attention cues, and information sets. This is where mass democracy, in its institutionally mature variant, enters. Highly developed and institutionally dense economic and political systems deliver audiences. A developed economy is highly specialized: people do different things and as a consequence they have different stakes, they pay attention to different cues, they know different things. An institutionally dense political system contains a highly structured network of overlapping and partially independent centers of power that are accountable to different constituencies, have access to different resources, and make decisions in different ways.

An institutionally thick democracy can enter a complex institutional commitment (the Bundesbank) where an institutionally thin tinpot dictatorship must resort to primitive commitment mechanisms (machine guns). Mature democracies have more, and more powerful, and more varied, audiences. This is why they have well-functioning central banks, and this is why they are rich.

SUSANNE LOHMANN

REFERENCES

Cukierman, Alex. (1992). *Central Bank Strategy, Credibility and Independence*. Cambridge: MIT Press.

DeLong, J.B. (1998). Estimating world GDP, one million B.C. — present. Department of Economics, University of California, Berkeley (*http://www.j-bradford-delong.net/TCEH/1998_Draft/World_GDP/Estimating_World_GDP.html*).

Lohmann, S. (1992). "Optimal commitment in monetary policy: Credibility versus flexibility." *American Economic Review*, 82: 273–286.

Lohmann, S. (1998). "Federalism and central bank independence: The politics of German monetary policy, 1957–1992." *World Politics*, 50: 401–446.

Lohmann, S. (2003). "Why do institutions matter? An audience cost theory of institutional commitment." *Governance*, (forthcoming).

CHICAGO POLITICAL ECONOMY

Chicago Political Economy (CPE) is a body of literature which analyzes government from the perspective of price theory and positive economics. It is essentially the Chicago version of the modern development of public choice theory. In CPE the state is a mechanism which is used by rational economic agents to redistribute wealth. Wealth transfers are the essence of regulatory and governmental behavior in this approach. Government may, in fact, produce some real goods and services, but these are by-products of effective schemes for wealth transfers.

George J. Stigler is the key architect of CPE. The thrust of the CPE research program derives from Stigler's (1971) paper on economic regulation. Other key contributors to CPE have been Peltzman (1976) and Becker (1983). Stigler (1988) offers a collection of papers reflecting contributions to CPE. Other Chicagoians should not be confused with those who work in the tradition of CPE as defined in this paper. These include Friedman, Coase, Harberger, and Lucas, each of whom have distinct contributions and traditions of their own, not to be confused with CPE. In a word, there are presently (and historically) several Chicago Schools.

CPE is based on the principles and practice of positive economics. Not only is the formulation of testable implications emphasized, but so too is the actual testing of theories.

CPE began (Stigler, 1971; Peltzman, 1976) as a theory of economic regulation, that is, as a theory of a limited subset of off-budget government. Becker (1976) proposed including all regulation under the rubric of the theory, and that has been a very fruitful suggestion. Other writers on CPE, including Landes and Posner (1975) and Becker (1983), have generalized the wealth-transfer theory into a theory of all government, appropriately called the interest-group theory of government.

CPE theories of political and regulatory processes are equilibrium theories. If the politician/regulatory transfer too much (or too little) wealth, he will be disciplined in the next election. Equilibrium Now! Moreover, wealth-transfer processes such as economic regulation are typically long-lived. The Interstate Commerce Commission, for example, has been around for over 100 years, a tenure nurtured by its ability to direct and sustain a predictable wealth-transfer process.

Political agents in CPE are analyzed in politically neutral terms. The personal preferences of politicians do not enter into political decisions; ideology does not impact on political outcomes. Politicians are driven by constraints, not by preferences, and their role is to broker wealth transfers among relevant "suppliers" and demanders of the same. Subject to the relevant electoral constraints, the CPE approach is that markets for representation are perfect in that controlling coalitions obtain their political objectives at least cost.

CPE theory focuses on how politics impacts on resource allocation and other broad theoretical areas of inquiry. Less attention has been paid to the role and evaluation of specific political institutions (though see Stigler, 1976). Becker (1983), for example, focuses on the allocative consequences of lobbying and obtains the result that lobbying minimizes the deadweight costs of government intervention in the economy. In Becker, there are no voting rules, no legislature, no bureaucracy, and so forth. These processes, as it were, are all perfect agents of interest groups which facilitate Becker's result. The transactional nature of politics has been largely ignored by CPE writers.

As stressed, CPE is primarily concerned with positive economic issues. Where welfare results are derived, as in Becker (1983, 1985), activities such as rent-seeking are not taken into account. Becker's result can be interpreted as an efficiency hypothesis. Deadweight costs are minimized by lobbying, and, in general, government is not free. There are incentives in the competitive process for governmental influence that lead the social costs of wealth transfers to be minimized. The world is efficient, or it would be reordered by competing interest groups to minimize social costs.

The efficiency hypothesis has been further elaborated and propounded by Wittman (1989, 1995), who seeks to explain why democracies and their associated political markets are in accord with efficient outcomes. Needless to say, this strong point of view has attracted critics (Rowley and Vachris, 1995; Rowley, 1997), as well as supporters (Lott, 1997). The critics weigh in heavily against the idea that political markets are efficient, while supporters suggest that the efficiency hypothesis is testable. Thus far, however, there has been little progress in formulating a generally acceptable way to test the hypothesis.

This is a quite different world than that envisaged in Gordon Tullock's (1967) rent-seeking paper. In Tullock's world, one theorizes and measures social costs so as to compare them to something; that something must logically be a better way to organize society so that government and regulation will cost less. The Tullock approach is potentially reformist/utilitarian; the CPE approach says that the social costs of government are minimized in the transfer society.

Another strand of argument in CPE, mostly associated with Stigler (1979, 1982), is that ideas do not matter. By this something like the following is meant. A great economist like Adam Smith or Keynes writes a book.

Intellectuals then arrogate the power of these ideas by writing intellectual histories in which Adam Smith caused free enterprise in England and Keynes rescued the world from depression. Stigler, in particular, would take issue with such procedures. His reasoning is that this approach is hard to test, and causal evidence suggests that it is wrong. Keynes wrote a book in 1936; perennial deficits in the U.S. began in the 1960s. This emphasis on the secondary role of ideas in CPE is related to the positive economics emphasis on understanding the world and not changing it. Moreover, ideas carry little or no weight just like ideological values in relation to the basic economic forces which drive the redistribution process.

In 1971, the primary alternative to Stigler's theory of economic regulation was the Pigovian or public-interest theory of government, which was already under heavy assault from earlier contributions to public choice theory. Today, virtually no one thinks in such terms. The interest-group theory of government has accumulated widespread recognition as a valuable theory of government. The interest-group theory has shown its explanatory power in a remarkably wide range of areas of governmental activity in both a contemporary and historical context (Ekelund and Tollison, 2001).

The fundamental point is that CPE is founded and pursued on the grounds of positive economics and price theory and not only is *testability* a key criterion of theories, but *actual testing* is tantamount to being taken seriously by CPE scholars. Other traditions in public choice embody certain elements of the CPE approach, but none are so rigorously empirical as CPE.

ROBERT D. TOLLISON

REFERENCES

Becker, G.S. (1985). "Public policies, pressure groups and deadweight costs." *Journal of Public Economics*, 28: 329–347.

Becker, G.S. (1983). "A theory of competition among pressure groups for political influence." *Quarterly Journal of Economics*, 98: 371–400.

Becker, G.S. (1976). "Comment." *Journal of Law and Economics*, 19: 245–248.

Ekelund, R.B. and Tollison, R.D. (2001). "The interest-group theory of government," in W.F. Shughart and L. Razzolini (eds.) *The Elgar Companion to Public Choice*, Northampton: Edward Elgar, pp. 357–378.

Keynes, J.M. (1936). *The General Theory of Employment, Interest and Money*. London: Macmillan.

Landes, W.M. and Posner, R.A. (1975). "The independent judiciary in an interest-group perspective." *Journal of Law and Economics*, 18: 875–901.

Lott, J.R. (1997). "Donald Wittman's *The Myth of Democratic Failure*." *Public Choice*, 92: 1–13.

Peltzman, S. (1976). "Toward a more general theory of regulation." *Journal of Law and Economics*, 19(August): 211–40.

Rowley, C.K. (1997). "Donald Wittman's *The Myth of Democratic Failure*." *Public Choice*, 92: 15–26.

Rowley, C.K. and Vachris, M.A. (1995). "Why democracy does not necessarily produce efficient results." *Journal of Public Finance and Public Choice*, (December): 97–111.

Stigler, G.S. (ed.) (1988). *Chicago Studies in Political Economy*. Chicago: University of Chicago Press.

Stigler, G.J. (1982). *The Economist as Preacher and Other Essays*. Chicago: University of Chicago Press.

Stigler, G.J. (1976). "The sizes of legislatures." *Journal of Legal Studies*, V(January): 17–34.

Stigler, G.J. (1971). "The theory of economic regulation." *Bell Journal of Economics and Management Science*, 2(Spring): 3–21.

Stigler, G.J. (1979). "Why have the socialists been winning?" *Ordo*, 13: 61–68.

Tullock, G. (1967). "The welfare costs of tariffs, monopolies, and theft." *Western Economic Journal*, 5: 224–232.

Wittman, D. (1995). *The Myth of Democratic Failure*. Chicago: University of Chicago Press.

Wittman, D. (1989). "Why democracies produce efficient results." *Journal of Political Economy*, 97: 1395–1424.

THE CLAYTON ACT

The Clayton Act of 1914 was one of the major pieces of legislation of the Progressive Era in American history. It prohibited four specific types of monopolistic practices: (1) price discrimination; (2) exclusive-dealing contracts and tying agreements; (3) the acquisition of competing companies through stock purchases; and (4) interlocking directorates among companies with a market value of at least $1 million, and in the same industry. Its main objective was to prevent business practices that may tend "to substantially lessen competition or tend to create a monopoly." It underwent several amendments in subsequent years partly because of lax judicial interpretations. The most important ones include the Robison–Patman Act of 1936, which strengthened price discrimination prohibition, and the Celler–Kefauver Act of 1950, which prohibited corporate mergers that would tend to reduce competition or promote monopolies (Shughart, 1990; Shenefield and Stelzer, 2001).

The theoretical foundations justifying the existence of antitrust laws in general, and the Clayton Act in particular, rely on analytical models of industrial organization and microeconomic theory. These models show that the economic paradigm of competitive markets, in which economic decisions are freely made by firms and individuals, each looking out for its own interest, deliver the highest possible level of social welfare. The system of prices and the allocation of resources in such an environment is the most efficient one in the sense that a reallocation of resources cannot make someone better off without making someone else worse off. The reason such an outcome obtains is because in a purely competitive environment equilibrium prices of goods and services reflect exactly the cost of the inputs used in the production of these goods or the provision of these services.

This result has two socially desirable implications. First, only the correct quantity of goods and services is produced. This follows from the fact that in equilibrium the extra revenue the firm receives from selling one more unit of the good is its price, which exactly equals its production cost. Increasing the level of production of this good further will result in a price decline, and hence, in a negative profit for the firm. Analogously, a decrease in this level of production will result in a price increase, and hence, positive profit for the firm. A positive profit, in turn, will encourage firms to increase their output levels. The price level will consequently decline until it finally reaches its production costs.

This well-known result of microeconomic theory was understood even as early as the 18th century. Adam Smith ([1776] 1981), for example, made the following observation:

> When the quantity of any commodity which is brought to markets falls short of the effectual demand, all those who are willing to pay the whole value of rents, wages, and profit, which must be paid in order to bring it thither, cannot be supplied with the quantity which they want. Rather than want it altogether, some of them will be willing to give more. A competition will immediately begin among them, and the market price will rise ... When the quantity brought to market exceeds the effectual demand, it cannot be sold to those who are willing to pay the whole value of the rent, wages, and profit, which must be paid in order to bring it thither. Some part must be sold to those who are willing to pay less ... The market price will sink more or less below the natural price. (Smith, 1776 [1981]: 73–74)

A second socially desirable implication is that only the correct number of firms prevails in the industry. This follows from the fact that in equilibrium there are no economic profits because positive profits will attract new entrants, while negative ones will force some firms to leave the industry.

These two results obtain when there are a large number of firms in an industry, or when there are no entry barriers to keep new entrants from exploiting profitable opportunities. When there are only a few firms participating in the market, these results may no longer hold. The extreme case would be when there is only one firm, a monopolist, operating in the market. As the only participant, the monopolist has the ability to control the market price of its product, as well as its production level. Because the monopolist's objective is to maximize its profit, not society's welfare, the equilibrium price of the good or service that the monopolist charges will be higher than the cost of the inputs necessary to produce the good or service. In addition, the resulting level of output is lower than what obtains under competition. As a result, a market structure in which there is only one firm is seen, in general, as a socially undesirable outcome.

There are instances in which a monopoly delivers the most efficient output level in an industry. This may happen when production costs decline as the size of the firm increases due to, for example, very high initial fixed costs. Public utilities are classic examples of these industries. However, even in these instances, the monopolist will choose to produce below the social's optimal level, since it has full control of prices and production.

Thus, when the effect of a monopolist on society's welfare is likely to be severe, public policy is seen as necessary to correct or prevent such outcomes (Blair and Kaserman, 1985). Although this is a highly simplified description of how markets operate in reality, it forms an integral part of the economic rationale for government intervention (Singer, 1981; Shenefield and Stelzer, 2001).

Few would dispute the validity of these theoretical arguments. However, the notion that government intervention will result in an improvement of social welfare by "correcting" the deficiencies associated with large deviations from the competitive equilibrium paradigm is not well founded theoretically or empirically. One of the major tenets of public choice theory is that governments and regulatory agencies are composed of individuals who, just as other market participants, seek to maximize their own well-being, and not necessarily social welfare (McChesney and Shughart, 1995). When the objective of regulators and politicians is changed from the hypothetical maximization of social welfare to the maximization of their own well-being, there are profound implications, many of which can result in outcomes that, from a social welfare point of view, are worse than simply not intervening at all. Consider, as an example, the arguably sensible proposition that one of the most important objectives of a politician is to maximize his or her probability of re-election. Because this probability is an increasing function of campaign expenditures among other factors, politicians may have an incentive to vote strategically on bills in order to maximize contributions from constituents and corporate supporters who stand to gain (or lose) disproportionately from a bill being considered in congress. As a result, legislation debated, and ultimately passed or rejected in congress is subject to the influence of contributors as well as constituents. It is no longer clear that the enactment of a law will necessarily result in an enhancement of society's welfare.

The Clayton Act of 1914 is no exception to this. Because of the way it was drafted and ultimately enacted, it ended up redistributing wealth among economic agents, necessarily creating winners and losers. The historical exposition provided in the next section helps to illustrate this point. Recent research on the public choice interpretation of the Clayton Act also presents convincing evidence that interest groups affected the outcome of the legislation. This research is reviewed further below.

1. Historical Origins of the Clayton Act

As industrial capitalism emerged in the late 1870s, large amounts of capital were required for its growth, necessitating a rapid transformation in the banking and financial services industry. This transformation in finance facilitated the extent to which business could grow and expand in order to exploit economies of scale. But this expansion raised concerns over the extent to which corporations could dominate or control interstate commerce and prices. Businessmen and financiers allegedly made collusive agreements frequently in order to increase prices and maintain dominant market shares, not just in the railroad industry, but in other industries as well. In 1890, Congress passed the Sherman Antitrust Act as a response to the populist outcry that the trusts were choking American consumers through their monopolistic practices.

Despite the enactment of this legislation, populist concerns over the dealings of large businesses and financiers continued well into the beginning of the twentieth century. The Great Merger Wave of 1898–1904, arguably one of the greatest merger movements in U.S. history, the financial panics of 1902–03 and 1907, and the ostensibly illegal financial arrangements of many large corporations such as Standard Oil, American Tobacco, and the New York, New Haven, and Hartford Railroad renewed the trusts issue in political platforms throughout the 1908 and 1912 election cycles. When Woodrow Wilson won the presidential election in 1912, trust legislation aimed at strengthening its legislative predecessor, the Sherman Antitrust Act, was all but imminent.

Although there was strong pressure in Congress to pass antitrust legislation to correct the perceived deficiencies of the Sherman Act, the House of Representatives and the Senate had different perspectives regarding how to amend it.

The House version listed specific actions by corporations that were to be considered illegal, and proposed to make violations criminal offenses. The Senate version, however, intended to delegate the determination of illegal business practices to the newly created Federal Trade Commission. The House and the Senate settled these differences by including in the final version of Clayton Act a list of specific business practices that were deemed to be illegal, but not offenses subject to criminal penalties. The Federal Trade Commission was given the mandate to enforce the new law (McAllister, 1953; Neale and Goyder, 1980; Shughart, 1990).

2. Public Laws–Private Interests

Public choice analyses of the Clayton Act include the work of Benson et al. (1987), Ekelund et al. (1995), Ramírez and Eigen-Zucchi (2001), and Shughart (1990). This research identifies the most important interest groups at stake: (1) agriculture; (2) large manufacturing companies; and (3) small manufacturing companies. Agricultural interests were benefited by this Act because of its partial exemptions to agricultural organizations to form cooperatives (section 6). This exemption is not trivial because by allowing the formation of cooperatives, the Act implicitly permitted collusive behavior in the agricultural sector. Benson et al. (1987) argue that the inclusion of this provision in the bill was probably the result of the influence of agricultural interests. Further work by Ramírez and Eigen-Zucchi (2001) confirm this suspicion. Their research provides evidence showing that agricultural interest groups indeed influenced the outcome of the vote on the Clayton bill when it was under consideration in the Senate.

The "holding company" section of the Act (section 7) intended to prohibit the acquisition of companies through stock purchases. The idea was, of course, to prevent the creation of monopolistic conglomerates at the industry level. However, as Shughart (1990) and Ekelund et al. (1995) point out, this section had an obvious loophole: although mergers or acquisitions through stock purchases were banned, they could be accomplished through the purchase of physical assets. This loophole necessarily affected companies of different size asymmetrically. In particular, because of better access to credit markets, it was easier for larger and well-established companies to circumvent this limitation. Thus, according to this interpretation, companies that, for one reason or another, did not have full access to credit markets were at a disadvantage.

Although section 7 appeared to favor large companies over small ones (which tend to have more difficulty raising funds from external markets), it does not follow that the

Act, in its entirety, benefited large companies at the expense of small ones. As Stigler (1985) points out, the overall effect of the Act may have been more beneficial to small companies than to large ones. After all, an acquisition of a company would have likely attract more attention from regulators and perhaps the public, if the acquirer was a large company with dominant market share than if the acquirer was a small firm with control over a limited market. Hence, from this perspective, one could argue that small companies benefited relatively more from this legislation than large ones. Ramírez and Eigen-Zucchi (2001), using stock market evidence, find that this was indeed the case. The evidence presented in their work consists of comparing the cumulative returns of two portfolios: one consisting of large, well-established companies, and the other one of small firms with limited market shares in their industries. The results indicate that during the Act's gestation period (which they argue, started in November 1912, when Woodrow Wilson won the presidential elections, and finished in January 1914, when news about the impending legislation appeared in the press) the portfolio of small companies outperformed that of the large ones by almost 9 percent. This suggests that the market viewed the Clayton Act as being more beneficial to small companies than to large companies with dominant market shares.

Following Ekelund et al. (1995), Ramírez and Eigen-Zucchi (2001) also examine empirically the pattern of the Senate vote by states, and find that economic interests explain a great deal of the variation in the vote. In particular, their evidence shows that the proportion of state wealth in agriculture, which measures agricultural interests at the state level, had a positive and significant influence on the vote: senators representing states where agriculture was relatively more important tended to vote in favor of the bill. In addition, their evidence indicates that the probability of a senator voting in favor of the bill increased with variables measuring the influence of small manufacturing interests and interests representing large companies in the state. However, they find that the magnitude of the effect was larger for small manufacturing interests, a result consistent with the hypothesis that the Act was more beneficial to small companies than to large ones. It is also consistent with their stock portfolio evidence using stock market returns.

Given all of this evidence, it is difficult to dismiss the notion that private interests played a pivotal role in determining the outcome of this legislation. This conclusion carries important public policy implications. Since interest groups influenced the enactment of this law, it no longer follows that its imposition was beneficial to society in general. In fact, it is very likely that it has resulted in

a reallocation of resources that was far from optimal from a social welfare perspective. The long-term effect of this legislation may have consequently resulted in a cost to society far larger than the alternative of not intervening at all.

CARLOS D. RAMÍREZ

REFERENCES

Benson, B.L., Greenhut, M.L., and Holcombe, R.G. (1987). "Interest groups and the antitrust paradox." *Cato Journal*, 6(3): 801–817.

Blair, R.D. and Kaserman, D.L. (1985). *Antitrust Economics*. Homewood, IL: Richard D. Irwin, Inc.

Ekelund, Robert B., McDonald, Michael J., and Tollison, Robert D. (1995). "Business restraints and the Clayton Act of 1914: Public- or private-interest legislation?" in F.S. McChesney and W.F. Shughart (eds.) *The Causes and Consequences of Antitrust: The Public-Choice Perspective*. Chicago and London: University of Chicago Press, pp. 271–286.

McAllister, B.P. (1953). "Where the effect may be to substantially lessen competition or tend to create a monopoly." *American Bar Association, Section of Antitrust Law, Proceedings at the Annual Meeting*, 3: 124–148.

McChesney, Fred S. and Shughart, William F. (1995). "Introduction and overview," in Fred S. McChesney and William F. Shughart (eds.) *The Causes and Consequences of Antitrust: The Public-Choice Perspective*. Chicago and London: University of Chicago Press, pp. 1–6.

Neale, A.D. and Goyder, D.G. (1980). *The Antitrust Laws of the United States of America*. Cambridge: Cambridge University Press.

Ramírez, Carlos D. and Eigen-Zucchi, Christian (2001). Understanding the Clayton Act of 1914: An analysis of the interest group hypothesis." *Public Choice*, 106(1–2) (January): 157–181.

Shenefield, John H. and Stelzer, Irwin M. (2001). *The Antitrust Laws: A Premier*. Washington, DC: The AEI Press.

Shughart, William F. (1990). *Antitrust Policy and Interest-Group Politics*. Westport, CT: Quorum Books.

Singer, Eugene M. (1981). *Antitrust Economics and Legal Analysis*. Columbus, OH: Grid Publishing, Inc.

Smith, Adam ([1776] 1981). *An Inquiry into the Nature and Causes of the Wealth of Nations. Volumes I and II*. Indianapolis, IN: Liberty Press.

Stigler, G.J. (1985). "The origin of the Sherman Act." *Journal of Legal Studies*, 14(1): 1–12.

COALITIONS AND POWER INDICES

Assume that there are three parties, A, B and C, which share the seats in parliament by 45%, 35% and 20%. Given that decisions are made by simple majority it seems not very likely that the distribution of power, however defined, coincides with the distribution of seats (votes). Power indices have been developed to discuss issues of assigning power values to the resources (e.g., votes) of decision makers and to explain how these values change if the (vote) distribution changes or a new decision rule is applied. They seem to be valuable instruments to analyze institutional changes and effects of alternative institutional design. The two volumes, "Power, Voting, and Voting Power" (Holler, 1982a) and "Power indices and Coalition Formation" (Holler and Owen, 2001) not only contain original contributions to this discussion but also illustrate the development in this field over the last twenty years. A recent monograph by Felsenthal and Machover (1998), "The Measurement of Voting Power," contains a formal treatment of problem.

There is a growing interest in power measures such as the Shapley-Shubik index and the Banzhaf index, to name the two most popular measures, and the application of power indices to political institutions and, in particular, to the analysis of the European Union. There are, however, also new theoretical instruments and perspectives that support these applications. Of prime importance is the probabilistic model of coalition formation which is made operational by the multilinear extension of the characteristic function form of coalition games. This instrument triggered off a probabilistic reinterpretation of existing power indices and the formulation of new ones. This development has been accompanied by an intensive discussion of the concept of power in general — what do we measure when we apply power measures? — and the properties that an adequate measure of power has to satisfy.

More recent research tries to relate power measures to non-cooperative game theory, making use of Nash equilibrium and its refinements as solution concepts, to give further justification for the application of traditional measures as well as to develop measures for cases when the capacity of binding agreements and exogenous enforceability is not prominent. However, here we will focus on situations were the enforceability of agreements is not an issue; it is either guaranteed (e.g., by law or self-interest) or not relevant (e.g., ballot). For an illustration, we will briefly introduce four power measures. Each of the four measures is supported by a different set of axioms, which we will, due to space constraints, not discuss here.

The Shapley–Shubik index (SSI) is not only the pioneer in the history of power indices, but also serves as a point of reference for the great variety of measures which have been since developed. It derived from the *Shapley value* which had been proposed in Shapley (1953) as a solution concept for cooperative games. Shapley and Shubik (1954) applied this concept to voting games.

The SSI is based on the concept of a *pivot player*. Given a simple game (N, v), where N is the set of players and v is the characteristic function which assigns the values $v(S) = 1$, if S is a winning coalition, and $v(S) = 0$, if S is a losing coalition. Player i is *pivotal* if i turns a losing coalition S\{i}, which consists of the first $s - 1$ elements of an ordering, into a winning coalition S by joining coalition S\{i} such that i is the sth element of coalition S.

The expression #pivots(i) counts the number of orderings for which i is a pivotal member (i.e., permutations of the elements of the set of payers N). The contribution of a pivotal player to the winning of a coalition S is measured by $v(S) - v(S\setminus\{i\}) = 1$. Then SSI is a vector $\Phi(v) = (\Phi_1(v), ..., \Phi_n(v))$ with components defined as the ratio #pivots(i)/Σ#pivots(i) where the summing is over all players i in N. Obviously, the SSI values sum up to 1 and a probability interpretation is straightforward.

In order to calculate $\Phi_i(v)$ we look at all subsets S of N which have i as an element and ask, for each such S, (i) whether S is a winning coalition and, if *yes*, (ii) whether i can turn a winning coalition into a losing coalition by defecting from S. If the answer is *yes* again then we get $v(S) - v(S\setminus\{i\}) = 1$ for the specific S. Next, we take into account that the SSI is based on orderings and ask how likely it is that i is in the pivot position if coalition S forms: it is $(s - 1)!(n - s)!/n!$, where s and n are the numbers of players in S and N, respectively, and n! is the number of total orderings which can be formed by n players. Finally, we sum the resulting product (of the probability that i is pivotal and the value of i being pivotal) over all subsets S of N which have i as an element. For instance, consider a weighted voting game $v^* = (d; w) = (55; 50, 30, 20)$ where $d = 55$ is the decision (i.e., majority) rule and $w = (50, 30, 20)$ represents the vote distribution. The set of permutations has n! = 6 elements. Player 1, characterized by voting weight $w_1 = 50$, is the pivot element of 4 permutations while players 2 and 3 are pivot elements of only one permutation each. The SSI of (N, v^*) therefore is: $\Phi(v^*) = (2/3, 1/6, 1/6)$.

It is not easy to justify the application of orderings intuitively when only coalitions, i.e., unordered sets seem to matter. This is all the more because the fact that each permutation is taken into account with equal probability gives unequal weights to coalitions which have different numbers of members. There are 2^n coalitions which correspond to a set of players of n members, including the null coalition and the grand coalition, while only n! permutations can be derived from this set. The classical story to justify the focus on permutations, given in Shapley and Shubik (1954), assumes that those players with stronger preferences to form a winning coalition S enter the coalition formation process first, followed by players with weaker preferences. Therefore, the pivotal player i, the last player in the sequence who turns a losing coalition S\{i} into a winning coalition S is the member of S with the weakest preferences concerning this coalition: it is assumed that i will get the undivided coalition value $[v(S) - v(S\setminus\{i\})] = 1$ because the members of S\{i} will get "nothing" if i does not join them. However, since no specific information on preferences is given with respect to the various winning coalitions S, all n! permutations of n players are considered. This amounts to saying that i is only with a certain probability in the pivotal position with respect to coalition S in which i is a member.

Alternative and perhaps more convincing stories could be told to justify the SSI, e.g., the probabilistic approach in Straffin (1977). Shapley and Shubik (1954, p. 790) themselves considered the arranging of the voters in all possible orderings to be "just a convenient conceptual device."

The *Banzhaf index (BI)* is credited to Banzhaf (1965), however, its basic idea has already be introduced by Penrose (see Felsenthal and Machover, 1998, pp. 6–10). It derives from the concept of swing players. Player i has a *swing* for coalition S if i can turn S from a winning coalition into a losing one by leaving S, i.e., $v(S) = 1$ and $v(S\setminus\{i\}) = 0$.

The *non-normalized* (or absolute) Banzhaf index of player i, β_i', is defined by the number of i's swings, #swings(i), divided by the number of coalitions which have i as a member, #coalitions(i). The latter number is 2^{n-1} if the number of players is n. Thus, we have $\beta_i'(v) = $ #swings(i)/2^{n-1}. Because the sum of the $\beta_i'(v)$ values do, in general, not sum up to 1, some authors call this measure Banzhaf value. The *normalized* version of the Banzhaf index is $\beta_i(v) = \beta_i'(v)/\Sigma \beta_i'(v)$, where the summation is over all players in N. Obviously, $\Sigma\beta_i(v) = 1$.

Applying the normalized BI to the above weighted voting game $v^* = (d; w) = (55; 50,30,20)$ we get $\beta(v^*) = $ (3/5, 1/5, 1/5). These values are different from the SSI, which indicates that the choice of index is not trivial. In this example, players 1, 2 and 3 (labeled by their voting weights 50, 30 and 20), have the following *sets of swing sets*: $W_{50}(v) = \{\{50, 30\}, \{50, 20\}, \{50, 30, 20\}\}$ for player 1; $W_{30}(v) = \{\{50, 30\}\}$ for player 2; and $W_{20}(v) = \{\{50, 20\}\}$ for player 3. This demonstrates that coalitions enter the calculation of the $\beta(v)$ with *different weights* although it is assumed that they are formed with equal probabilities. Coalitions {50, 30} and {50, 20} each enter the calculation twice while {50, 30, 20} is only considered once.

The *Deegan-Packel index (DPI)*, $\rho(v)$, introduced in Deegan and Packel (1979), is based on $M(v)$, the set of *minimal decisive coalitions* (MDC): if S is a winning coalition and any coalition T, which is a true subset of S, is

a losing coalition, then S is an MDC and thus an element of $M(v)$. That is, all members of coalition S are crucial for S to be a winning coalition. S does not contain *surplus players*. Coalitions in $M(v)$ are also called *(strict) minimal decisive coalitions*.

The DPI assumes that the members of a MDC S *share* the coalition value $v(S)$ such that each member of S receives a value $v(S)/s$ where, again, s is the number of members of S. The shares $v(S)/s$ of player i will be summed up for all S, which have i as a member, and divided by $1/|M(v)|$, where $|M(v)|$ is the total number of MDCs. If v is a simple game and thus $v(S) = 1$, and we get $\rho_i(v) = (\Sigma 1/s)/|M(v)|$. The multiplier $1/|M(v)|$ assures us that $\Sigma\rho_i(v) = 1$ holds. A probabilistic interpretation of $\rho_i(v)$ is straightforward. If each S in $M(v)$ forms equal probability and the payoff of i in S is 1/s, then the expected value of i equals $\rho_i(v)$.

The DPI is *not* monotonic in voting weights (i.e., violates *local monotonicity*). This can be easily demonstrated by the example of the weighted voting game $v' = (d; w) = (51; 35,20,15,15,15)$ which results in $\rho(v') = (18/60, 9/60, 11/60, 11/60, 11/60)$. Although the second player has the second largest voting weight it has a smaller power value than the three players with smaller votes.

The *Holler-Packel Index (HPI)*, also called *Public Good Index*, has been introduced in Holler (1978, 1982b) and axiomatized in Holler and Packel (1983). It is based, like DPI, on MDCs. This specification is supported by the fact that the coalition value is considered to be a public good. If players in a winning coalition consider the value $v(S) = 1$ as a public good then there should be no *rivalry in consumption* and each member of S will enjoy this value if S is formed. Further, if there are no entry costs or transaction costs of coalition formation, S will be formed: since S is a coalition in $M(v)$ and all players in S are crucial, no possibility of *free-riding* exists. If S is not an MDC then, because of the potential of free-riding, it will be only formed by "luck," and not because of the power of its members — or because the outcome of S is *identical* with the outcome of T and T is an MDC and a true subset of S. In the latter case, S is not a MDC and double counting results if, in addition to T, S is taken into consideration. By its restriction to MDCs, the HPI avoids these problems.

Let $c_i(v)$ express the *decisiveness* of player i, i.e., the number of coalitions S so that S is an element of $M(v)$ and i is in S, then the value of the HPI for player i in the simple game (N, v) is defined by $h_i = c_i(v)/\Sigma c_i(v)$. Again the summation is over all n players in N so that $\Sigma h_i(v) = 1$. The larger the number c_i of MDCs of which i is a member, the larger will be i's power in the game. However, this number is not monotonic in the size of voting weights as the application of HPI to the weighted voting game $v' = (d; w) = (51; 35,20,15,15,15)$ illustrates. The corresponding values are $h_i(v') = (16/60, 8/60, 12/60, 12/60, 12/60)$. That is, HPI is *not* monotonic in voting weights. The HPI shares this property with the DPI (see above), however, the indices give different values for the same game as the numerical example illustrates.

There is a large number of indices which are either variants of the four discussed measures index or are even identical with one of the four but give a different interpretation. Because of this variety, it seems appropriate to ask "what is the right index?". To answer this question, we might follow various strategies: (a) to take up the discussion of the meaning of power; (b) to discuss the various measures with respect to selected properties such as monotonicity; (c) to apply the index to well-defined decision situations; and (d) to accept the measures as a source of arguments for a more general discussion of social institutions and collective decision making.

A popular view of power indices, applied to voting games, is that these measures "represent a reasonable expectation of the share of voting power given by the ability to contribute to the formation of winning configurations" (Turnovec, 1997). That is, (i) there is an "ability" called "voting power", which we cannot measure directly; but (ii) we can calculate indices which represent "reasonable expectations" of this ability. Related is the definition of power as the *probability* of influencing the outcome of collective decision problem. SSI seems to be an appropriate measure in the light of this interpretation. Note that the values add up to one without normalization.

Alternative probabilistic interpretations of power indices are based on the multilinear extension of the characteristic function form of coalition games (introduced in Owen, 1972). Loosely speaking, the multilinear extension of the characteristic function of a cooperative game assumes that players are members of coalitions with a probability that is assumed to be randomly distributed. The standard result with respect to voting power (see Straffin, 1977) says that SSI results if voters are homogeneous and vote "yes" with equal probabilities which are uniformly distributed on the interval [0,1]; and the (non-normalized) BI results if voters are independent and each has an expected value of 0.5 to vote "yes." If some voters are homogeneous and others are independent, then we have a case of partial homogeneity and the application of a *partial homogeneity index*, which is a combination of SSI and BI. Brueckner (2001) derives a similar probabilistic model of HPI. However, it is not always obvious whether the conformity of the probabilistic results and power measures are justified by conceptual agreement or merely by formal identity.

Widgrén (2001) analyzes the probabilistic relationship of the HPI (h_i) and the normalized BI (β_i). He demonstrates that the normalized BI can be written as a linear function of the HPI such that $\beta_i = (1 - \pi)h_i + \pi\varepsilon_i$. Here $(1 - \pi)$ represents the share of MDCs, compared to all minimum winning coalitions (MWC), i.e., coalitions that contain at least one swinger; and ε_i expresses the share of minimum winning coalitions which have i as a member, but are not strict and thus are not in $M(v)$, compared to the number of *all* MWCs which are not strict. Obviously, the larger these two shares the more β_i and h_i deviate from each other.

Widgrén interprets $\pi\varepsilon_i$ as an expression of "luck" in the sense of Barry (1980). If the institutional setting is such that MWC which are not in $M(v)$, and the corresponding coalition goods are produced, then the normalized BI seems an appropriate measure and, at least, local monotonicity is guaranteed with respect to the power to influence the outcome. This implies that the institutions are such that the fundamental free-rider problem (of which the HPI takes account of) does not apply.

If power is interpreted as an expectation over outcomes, then it seems straightforward to take the probability into consideration that specific coalitions will form. These probabilities can depend on a non-cooperative bargaining setting of the decision problem (see Napel and Widgrén, 2002) or on the preferences of the individual decision makers. For instance, whether voters are homogeneous and or independent depends on the preferences of the voters. On the other hand, preferences are dependent on the issues to be decided on.

Owen (1977, 1982) has developed a formal apparatus to consider "*a priori* unions" in a modified SSI and BI "so as to take into account the possibility that some players ... may be more likely to act together than others" (1977, p. 76). However, a power measure which depends on preferences becomes dependent on specific decision situations: this seems appropriate if we use power measures as instruments of forecasting but causes problems if we apply them for the analysis of institutions with a long-term perspective and membership that changes over time. In addition, the preferences of members are also subject to changes over time. Garrett and Tsebelis (1999) have repeatedly argued that the use of power indices in evaluating power in the European Union is inappropriate on the grounds that they ignore preferences. (See Holler and Widgrén (1999) for a comment and Nurmi (2000) for further discussion.) If we look, however, at the EU Council of Ministers, which consists of representatives of 15 member states, then it is far from clear as to (i) what their preferences are and (ii) what their preferences will be in the future. These preferences may depend on national factors such as government popularity and election results. If we recall the 1957 *Treaty of Rome*, on the one hand, and consider the expected extension of the EU in the not-too-far-off future, on the other, it remains uncertain who are members playing the EU voting game. The assumptions of specific preferences appears rather dubious. In this and other cases of analyses of *institutional design*, it seems more natural to rely on power measure that abstracts from specific preferences in order to distill some general results on power relations *behind a veil of ignorance.*

Allingham (1975, p. 293) proposes that "power is interpreted as ability to influence outcomes — irrespective of the desirability of these; the concept of power should therefore be independent of any concept of utility." This brings us back to the alternative view that power indices express voting power, *and not* expectations of it. In this case, the measure has to be directly related to the ability to contribute to form winning coalitions and the type of winning coalition will be decided by the quality of the outcome and strategic considerations. For instance, HPI seems appropriate to use if coalition values can be considered public goods. Because of its underlying principles of *non-rivalry in consumption* and *exclusion of free-riding* only MDCs are to be considered; all other coalitions are either nonwinning or contain at least one surplus player. If winning coalitions of the second type are formed, then it is by luck, similarity of preferences, tradition, etc. — *but not because of power.*

Note that the HPI does not maintain that only MDCs will be formed. It maintains that these and only these are relevant for measuring power if the outcome of a winning coalition is a public good. In many decision situations there might be good reason why the winning coalition contains surplus players. For instance, the surplus player could be an agenda setter who decides through his proposal which coalition is likely to form. In these cases, the HPI will be a poor instrument for forecasting.

It is often argued that expectations are considered reasonable if the index measure, which is used to quantify these *expectations*, satisfies *monotonicity* "to some degree" (see, e.g., Freixas and Gambarelli, 1997). However, if a measure which, like the HPI, builds in a reasonable way on the *accepted decision principles* suffers from nonmonotonicity then we have to conclude that power is nonmonotonic.

When it comes to monotonicity of power with respect to voting weights, it is important to note that none of the existing measures guarantees that the power measure of a player i will *not* decrease if the voting weight of i increases. Fischer and Schotter (1978) demonstrate this result (i.e., the *paradox of redistribution*) for SSI and the normalized BI.

The paradox stresses the fact that power is a social concept: if we discuss the power of an individual member of a group in isolation from his or her social context, we may experience all sorts of paradoxical results. It seems that sociologists are quite aware of this problem and nonmonotonicity of an individual's power with respect to his or her resources does not come as a surprise to them (see, e.g., Caplow, 1968). Political scientists, however, often see the nonmonotonicity of power as a threat to the principle of democracy. It is hard for them to accept the idea that increasing the number of votes a group has could decrease its power, although it seems that there is ample empirical evidence of it. (See Brams and Fishburn (1995) for references.) In general, economists also assume that more resources is more likely to mean more power than less. However, they also deal with concepts like monopoly power, bargaining, and exploitation which stress the social context of power and the social value of resources (assets, money, property, etc.). Note that in the discussion of power indices voting weights are often proxies for resources.

Needless to say, the power measures are not always suitable to express our *expectations* if our intuition, which is at the heart of these expectations, implies monotonicity. However, if we could trust our intuition, then power indices in general would be rather useless. The number of paradoxes related to the application of these measures, which are the result of deviations from intuition, indicate that our intuition most likely needs help when it comes to evaluating power — or to forming "reasonable expectations" with respect to power.

MANFRED J. HOLLER

REFERENCES

Allingham, M.G. (1975). "Economic power and values of games." *Zeitschrift für Nationalökonomie (Journal of Economics)*, 35: 293–299.

Barry, B. (1980). "Is it better to be powerful or lucky: Part I and Part II." *Political Studies*, 28: 183–194 and 338–352.

Brams, S.J. and Fishburn, P.C. (1995). "When is size a liability? Bargaining power in minimal winning coalitions." *Journal of Theoretical Politics*, 7: 301–316.

Brueckner, M. (2001). "Extended probabilistic characterization of power," in M.J. Holler and G. Owen (eds.) *Power Indices and Coalition Formation*. Boston, Dordrecht and London: Kluwer, pp. 29–43.

Caplow, T. (1968). *Two Against One: Coalitions in Triads*. Englewood Cliffs, NJ: Prentice-Hall.

Felsenthal, D. and Machover, M. (1998). *The Measurement of Voting Power. Theory and Practice, Problems and Paradoxes*. Cheltenham: Edward Elgar.

Fischer, D. and Schotter, A. (1980). "The Inevitability of the paradox of redistribution in the allocation of voting weights." *Public Choice*, 33: 49–67.

Freixas, J. and Gambarelli, G. (1997). "Common Internal Properties Among Power Indices." *Control and Cybernetics*, 26: 591–603.

Garrett, G. and Tsebelis, G. (1999). "Why resist the temptation to apply power indices to the EU." *Journal of Theoretical Politics*, 11: 321–331.

Holler, M.J. (1978). "A priori party power and government formation." *Munich Social Science Review*, 1: 25–41. (*Reprinted in* M.J. Holler (ed.) (1982). *Power, Voting, and Voting Power*, Würzburg and Vienna: Physica-Verlag, pp. 273–282.)

Holler, M.J. (ed.) (1982a). *Power, Voting, and Voting Power*. Würzburg and Vienna: Physica-Verlag.

Holler, M.J. (1982b). "Forming coalitions and measuring voting power." *Political Studies*, 30: 262–271.

Holler, M.J. and Owen, G. (eds.) (2001), *Power Indices and Coalition Formation*. Boston, Dordrecht and London: Kluwer.

Holler, M.J. and Packel, E.W. (1983). "Power, luck and the right index." *Zeitschrift für Nationalökonomie (Journal of Economics)*, 43: 21–29.

Holler, M.J. and Widgrén, M. (1999). "Why power indices for assessing EU decision making?" *Journal of Theoretical Politics*, 11: 291–308.

Napel, S. and Widgrén, M. (2002). "The power of an inferior player," in M.J. Holler, H. Kliemt, D. Schmidtchen and M. Streit (eds.) *Power and Fairness (Jahrbuch für Neue Politische Ökonomie*, Vol. 20). Tübingen: Mohr-Siebeck (forthcoming).

Nurmi, H. (2000). "Game theoretical approaches to the EU institutions: an overview and evaluation." *Homo Oeconomicus*, 16: 363–391.

Owen, G. (1972). "Multilinear extensions of games." *Management Science*, 18: 64–79.

Owen, G. (1977). "Values of games with a priori unions," in R. Henn and O. Moeschlin (eds.) *Essays in Mathematical Economics and Game Theory*. Berlin and New York: Springer-Verlag, pp. 76–88.

Owen, G. (1982). "Modification of the Banzhaf-Coleman index for games with a priori unions," in M.J. Holler (ed.) *Power, Voting, and Voting Power*. Würzburg and Wien: Physica-Verlag, pp. 232–238.

Shapley, L.S. (1953). "A value for n-person games," in H. Kuhn and A.W. Tucker (eds.) *Contributions to the Theory of Games II*, Princeton: Princeton University Press, pp. 307–317.

Shapley, L.S. and Shubik, M. (1954). "A method of evaluating the distribution of power in a committee system." *American Political Science Review*, 48: 787–792.

Straffin, P.D. (1977). "Homogeneity, independence, and power indices." *Public Choice*, 30: 107–118.

Turnovec, F. (1997). "Power, power indices and intuition." *Control and Cybernetics*, 26: 613–615.

Widgrén, M. (2001). "On the probabilistic relationship between public good index and normalized banzhaf index," in M.J. Holler and G. Owen (eds.) *Power Indices and Coalition Formation*. Boston, Dordrecht and London: Kluwer, pp. 127–142.

COALITIONS AND SOCIAL CHOICE

A central aspect of any social life is the way in which society goes about aggregating individual preferences into social choices. The difficulty involved with any such process was known for centuries and stands at the heart of any effort at social organization as such. More than two centuries ago, Condorcet (1785) alluded to this problem in the following simple terms: Suppose three individuals $\{i,j,k\}$ have to choose between three outcomes $\{a,b,c\}$. i prefers a to b to c, j prefers b to c to a, k prefers c to a to b. Using majority rule, a is preferred to b by i and k, b is preferred to c by i and j, but c is preferred to a by j and k. Majority rule leads to *cyclical preferences*. This means that, by majority rule, each outcome has another outcome preferred to it by some coalition of two.

Arrow (1951) generalized this insight to any social choice mechanism. He started from the insight that any social choice mechanism can be characterized by the set of decisive coalitions it defines. He then imposed basic restrictions on social choice mechanisms to make sure that they actually aggregate individual preferences in some sensible way. He then tried to see if any such mechanism can be guaranteed to yield, as an output, a 'weak' order of social preferences that satisfies 'completeness,' 'transitivity' and 'reflexivity.' Arrow's *Impossibility Theorem* states that any mechanism that satisfies some basic requirements of consistency and substantive reliance on the preferences of individuals to determine the preferences of society as a collective, may lead to *cyclical preference orders*, given some *preference profiles*. A *preference profile* specifies the preferences of all individuals in society. A *preference order* states the preferences of society as a whole, as aggregated by a social choice mechanism such as majority rule. A preference order is *cyclical* if it violates the condition of transitivity.

Condorcet's paradox (1785) makes clear the difficulty raised by *cyclical* preferences orders. If outcome a is preferred to another outcome b but, by the same preference order, outcome b is preferred to a it is difficult to make use of this preference order to guide societal decision. Arrow (1951) proved that any social choice mechanism that tries to aggregate individual preferences into societal preference orders will lead to cyclical preference orders, given some preferences profile of the individuals in society. Later research has established that majority rule almost always leads to *cyclical preference orders* (McKelvey and Schofield, 1987).

Coalitions are crucial to the process of social choice. Social decision making is far from trivial, as demonstrated by Condorcet (1785), Arrow (1951), McKelvey and Schofield (1987). Thus, coalitions become the centerpiece of social decision making as such.

This observation motivated Riker's seminal work on *The Theory of Political Coalitions* (1962). His *size principle* states that in n-person constant-sum games agents would form coalitions just as large as necessary to obtain the prize (Riker, 1962: 32–33). Following the publication of Riker's (1962) work the study of coalitions became a focal point of the social sciences. It lead to two important insights that motivate this study to this day. On the one hand only minimum winning coalitions (MWC) should form but, on the other hand any MWC is readily defeated by another MWC.

Liberal democracies often rely on majority to aggregate preferences of legislators into legislation. The theoretical prevalence of majority cycles and the generic emptiness of majority *core* in *constant sum games* suggest that majority rule leads to coalition instability. But in the real world coalitions are often stable, or else no legislation would ever see the light of day. How, then, can we expect coalitions to be stable? What coalitions are likely to form? Finally, what kind of legislation should we expect coalitions to implement?

Baron and Ferejohn (1989) suggest that the key to stability is risk aversion and discount factors that diminish the value of the 'pie' to members as time passes by. Given this incentive structure, the first legislator who gets to propose an allocation will propose shares of the divisible 'pie' of the budget to be allocated to a MWC of legislators. Each selected member of this MWC of legislators is uncertain about who will get to propose the next allocation. S/he realizes that the value of the 'pie' diminishes with time and that the next legislator to propose an allocation may not include him or her in the coalition at all. Therefore, s/he will approve this allocation if s/he receives a big enough share of the 'pie' to make it worth while to forgo the uncertain and diminishing payoff that may come his or her way in any future proposed allocation.

Neo-institutionalism was founded on the observation that institutions mediate between individuals and social choices (Shepsle, 1986: 51–55). Agenda setting, procedural rules and committee structures reduce the prevalence of majority cycling. Laver and Shepsle (1996) applied this insight to the study of coalitions. In their model, after each election, parties 'scan' all decisive coalitions to derive the policy that each coalition will implement based on ministries allocations to coalition members, assuming that each department implements the policy of the party to which it is allocated. Each coalition is associated with a unique multi-dimensional policy point. A MWC associated with a policy point preferred by its members to any policy point

that may be implemented by any other decisive coalition will eventually form.

Duverger's (1954) Law emphasized the importance of electoral rules in this context. It states that plurality rule tends to reduce the set of significant parties to two. Instead of wasting their vote on small parties, voters vote for their preferred party between the two large parties. In the English parliament one of two parties controls a majority after each election. In this case, the majority party is the 'ruling coalition.' Party organization and common ideology serve as the cohesive forces behind such 'majority party coalitions.'

But in parliamentary systems that use electoral rules such as proportional rule, many parties pass the minimum requirement threshold and get seat in parliamensts allocated to them. Unlike the British parliament, in multiparty parliamentary systems a single party rarely wins the majority of the seats in parliament. The formation of a majority coalition becomes a sine qua non for the establishment of viable and effective majority governments. Schofield (1993) studied multiparty parliamentary politics as *weighted voting games*. He found that a large central party establishes a *core* point in in the policy space of parliament. This gives any such central large party a relative advantage in the bargaining process that follows each election and leads, eventually to the formation of a viable ruling cabinet. This insight allowed Schofield (1993) to solve the puzzle of *dominant* parties like the *Christian Democrats* in Italy between 1948 and 1987. Such parties puzzled researchers in that they were part of each coalition during long periods of time. Schofield (1993) found that *Dominant* parties are simply *core* parties.

Sened (1996) extended Schofield's analysis to predict probable coalitions. Parties maximize policy-related payoffs and utility from government perquisites (Laver and Schofield, 1998). Schofield's analysis implies that structures of parliaments and not the composition of coalitions (cf. Laver and Shepsle, 1996, discussed above) determine the set of feasible policies. Parties are concerned with the cost of endorsing these policies that may be distant from their declared policy positions. They bargain for government perquisites to offset this cost. Given the advantage of the *core* party in this game, it forms a MWC with parties close to it. Such parties are 'cheaper' to lure into coalition agreements, as they demand less to join because their policy preferences are more in line with those of the central party that forms the coalition. When the *core* of the parliament is empty, central parties lose some of their bargaining power. Future coalition partners must take into account that in the absence of a *core* party in parliament, policy decisions will *cycle* in some larger set of feasible outcomes, as determined by the structure of parliament (Schofield and Sened, 1998, 2002). Still, according to Sened (1996) the logic of coalition formation will follow the same logic. Taking into account the uncertainty associated with the uncertain final policy outcomes, parties will bargain over government perquisites to offset the larger cost of joining a coalition with uncertain policy goals. Eventually, the 'cheapest' coalition will form in the sense that some close by parties will find it in their best interest to coalesce and form a government, pay the cost of endorsing uncertain policy directives, but allow themselves to share the 'pie' of government perquisites.

The discussion above focused on theory. But the most exciting current research on coalition is using new tools of statistical analysis that allow careful empirical studies of coalition formation and the incentives of voters, parties and legislators in multiparty parliamentary political processes (e.g., Schofield et al., 1998).

ITAI SENED

REFERENCES

Arrow, Kenneth (1951). *Social Choice and Individual Values*. New York: John Wiley.

Baron, David P. and Ferejohn John (1989). "Bargaining in legislatures." *American Political Science Review*, 83: 1181–1206.

Condorcet, Marquise De N. (1785). *Essay sur l'application de l'analyse à la probabilité des decisions rendues à la pluralité des voix*. Paris: L'Imprimerie Royale.

Duverger, Maurice (1954). *Political Parties: Their Organization and Activity in the Modern State*. New York: Wiley.

Laver, Michael and Shepsle, Kenneth (1996). *Making and Breaking Governments*. New York: Cambridge University Press.

Laver, Michael and Schofield, Norman (1998). *Multiparty Governments*. Ann Arbor: The University of Michigan Press.

McKelvey, Richard D. and Schofield, Norman (1987). "Generalized symmetry conditions at a core." *Econometrica*, 55: 923–933.

Riker, W.H. (1962). *The Theory of Political Coalitions*. New Haven: Yale University Press.

Schofield, Norman (1993). "Political competition and multiparty coalition governments." *European Journal of Political Research*, 23: 1–33.

Schofield, Norman, Martin, Andrew, Quinn, Kevin and Whitford, Andrew (1998) Multiparty electoral competition in the Netherlands and Germany: a model based on multinomial probit." *Public Choice*, 97: 257–293.

Schofield, Norman and Sened, Itai (2002) "Local Nash equilibrium in multiparty politics." *The Annals of Operation Research*, (forthcoming).

Sened, Itai (1996). "A model of coalition formation: Theory and evidence." *Journal of Politics*, 58(2): 350–372.

Shepsle, Kenneth (1986). "Institutional equilibrium and equilibrium institutions," in H.F. Weisberg (ed.) *Political Science: The Science of Politics*, New York: Agathon Press.

COASE THEOREM AND POLITICAL MARKETS

During the nineteenth century, the enlightened ideals of democratic decision-making and the dynamics of political governance fostered a change in the conception of statutory law. Ideals of democratic legislation gradually replaced the historic conception of statutory law as a written articulation of laws of a higher and older origin. Laws were no longer considered the expression of preexisting natural or fundamental rights, but became rather the primary, if not the only, source of individual rights. Rights were derived from laws, rather than laws being derived from the protection of individual rights. Legislative bodies created law as opposed to recognizing preexisting values and legal norms. Such a paradigmatic shift gave new importance to the "process" for collective decision-making in that the outcome in the legislative bodies was strictly conditioned by the chosen procedural rules. With the exception of some minimal constitutional constraints on lawmaking, national legislatures act as sovereign lawmakers that set their own procedural rules. Such unbounded legislative powers are constitutionally and politically justified by the alleged function of legislative organs as faithful agents and political representatives of the people, ideals that persist in spite of the observed shortcomings of democratic decision-making and political representation in lawmaking.

1. Political Bargaining and Politics-like-Markets Metaphors

Through the lens of public choice theory, scholars have been able to draw attention to the limits of the representation mechanisms in the political process. Two specific limitations have emerged in the public choice and social choice literature (Riker, 1982). First, within the public choice tradition, we learn that political representatives are agents of their constituents. Such political representation is often affected by pervasive agency problems. The correction of these problems requires the choice of collective decision-making procedures promoting the alignment of the incentives of political representatives with those of the represented citizens, or else an effective monitoring and accountability of political agents. Agency problems of this type do not affect political representation if incentives are effectively aligned. Much of the public choice and constitutional design literature addresses the alignment of incentives and agency problems.

Second, even in the absence of agency problems in representation, politics can be viewed as a framework for bargaining among the various political agents in society. Inherent in this view of the political markets is the selection of appropriate criteria for aggregating individual preferences. The question in that context is whether political bargaining can successfully yield a consensus among the various political groups such that political outcomes can be legitimately and unambiguously identified with "the will of the people." As the social choice literature has often pointed out, even if we contemplate a world of perfect incentive alignment between political representatives and represented citizens (i.e., even if we assume away agency problems in political representation), there is no assurance that the mechanisms of law making are responsive to the underlying preferences of individuals in society.

1.1. Collective Decision-Making and the Political Coase Theorem

Other limits to open political markets become apparent in the study of public and social choice theory. One of the main insights from social choice theory is that the correlation between preference and choice is weaker for groups than for individuals (Shubik, 1982, p. 124). According to Arrow's (1951) possibility theorem, it may indeed be too much to expect methods of collective decision-making to be both rational and egalitarian. Arrow's theorem shows that social decisions — that is, policies and practices adopted by a given society — must by definition violate at least one of six self-evident axioms of normative political theory, commonly described as: range, universal domain, unanimity, non-dictatorship, independence of irrelevant alternatives, and rationality. Arrow's conclusion poses a dramatic threat to the legitimacy of political decisions. Observing that the likelihood of cycling majorities decreases when the number of decision-makers exceeds the number of choices does not affect the practical relevance of Arrow's analysis, at least when it is applied to the political process with large numbers of decision-makers concentrated into a restricted number of interest groups with group votes.

The heart of Arrow's theorem states that there are no non-dictatorial rules or procedures for collective decision-making that reflect the combined preferences of voters for a consistent collective outcome (Arrow, 1951). The implications of the theorem concern the existence of cyclical majorities which are capable of repealing any resolution that has been previously adopted. Parisi (1998) suggests that if all voters are allowed to enter into binding agreements over the policy outcome to be adopted by the majority coalition, collective preferences in a multi-dimensional policy space will be transitive as long as individual

preferences are single-peaked. This intuition runs contrary to conventional wisdom in public and social choice theory (Bernholz, 1973; Miller, 1977; Schwartz, 1977). Most of the literature on the stability implications of logrolling and vote-trading considers bargaining for the formation of coalitions where side-payments are only instruments for entering the majority coalition (and no side payments are made by those outside the majority). The political reality, however, is often different than what is contemplated by scholars. Bargaining is certainly permitted even between minority and majority voters, with exchanges taking place among all coalitions. If we allow for a broader role for bargaining and side-payments, and if we contemplate binding and enforceable political bargains across different coalitions, the results would be quite different (Parisi, 2003).

1.2. One Man, One Vote and the Role of Logrolling

Intransitivity may result in situations in which no strong political consensus is reached on a given issue. Intransitivity implies that a different order in the decision-making process may affect the outcome. Any winning coalition may be undermined by the reintroduction of an alternative it previously defeated. The structure of the voting process does not allow the cycle to be broken by examining the intensity of voters' preferences. The outcome is arbitrarily determined by the order of motions, with no guarantee that the ultimate result will yield a higher level of social welfare than that potentially afforded by any other defeated policy alternative. The inability of the democratic process to capture the intensity of the voters' preferences is a by-product of the generally espoused principle that every individual is entitled to one vote only. The one man, one vote rule is further explained by the fact that individual voters do not face the opportunity cost of casting their vote. Whether their preference is strong or weak, voters will cast their vote in favor of their preferred option. Even if voting were specifically designed to allow voters to indicate the intensity of their preferences, the voting ballot could not possibly capture such intensity. Absent a mechanism to extract the true intensity of their preferences, individual voters would tend to overstate their preference in order to maximize the impact of their votes.

Democracy gives equal weight to all votes regardless of how strongly voters feel about an issue. Consequently, numerically equal groups have an equal political voice in the process. However, if the distribution of sentiments on an issue is asymmetrical, and the minority holds strong preferences, the outcome will be inefficient. By introducing the possibility of bargaining and vote-trading in the process, the intensity of preferences will be reflected in the decision-making process. With bargaining and side-payments, the one man, one vote rule would provide the initial entitlement for each voter-trader. The exchange mechanism would then reveal the relative strength of individual preferences. Political bargaining may provide a solution to the intensity problem, while at the same time correcting the cyclicality problem.

Logrolling and political bargaining in many ways increase the internal predictability of the outcome for those who are involved in the process and are fully informed of it. Logrolling allows for bargaining and political exchange to foster stable political arrangements. To the extent to which political exchange is supported by enforcement mechanisms (e.g., reputation of political players), legislators sharing similar information about their respective prospects will have an opportunity to bargain under conditions of symmetric information, trading votes for issues on which they hold weak preferences in exchange for votes on issues on which they hold strong preferences. Economic theory teaches that bargaining between politicians will continue until the marginal utility of gaining one vote on a certain issue equals the marginal cost of giving up one vote for another issue. The outcome selected by majorities in such an environment of costless and enforceable political bargaining improves the combined welfare of the platforms. These results confirm Buchanan and Tullock's (1962, p. 153) important observation that with all side payments prohibited, there is no assurance that collective action will be taken in the most productive way. Both stability and efficiency will be obtained through bargaining, as long as the exchanges are enforceable and relatively costless to carry out. These conclusions also provide a conjectural solution to Tullock's (1981) puzzle as to why there is so much stability in the political process.

The implications of this line of thought are far-reaching and can be articulated in the following two propositions: (1) If the conditions for the Coase theorem (Coase 1960) are present for all voters (i.e., if political agents can enter into enforceable coalition contracts with other agents), the composition of the initial majority coalition is irrelevant for the policy outcome; and (2) If the Coase theorem holds, voters' preferences are strictly concave, and if vote exchange agreements are enforceable, then cycling in a multi-dimensional policy space is excluded (Parisi, 1998). Thus, if political bargains are attainable at no cost and political agreements are enforceable, the resulting political equilibrium will be unique and will occur at a point of social maximum. Any point other than the global maximum will be unstable, as there will always be enough surplus to allow for side payments to voters in exchange for policy concessions.

Once the socially optimal point is reached, there will be no opportunity to destabilize the policy arrangement.

2. The Limits of Political Markets

The politics-like-markets metaphors create a foundation for the work in public choice and political economy. Stigler (1971), Becker (1983) and Peltzman (1990), among others, have provided seminal formulations of the efficiency hypothesis of politics. The trust of this foundational hypothesis is that political markets are generally clearing, at least in the sense that, in equilibrium, no individual can improve his wealth (or utility) without reducing the wealth (or utility) of at least one other individual. For an outsider's review essay on the Chicago perspective on political markets, see Rowley (1993, pp. 11–14).

In real politics, however, legislative and political bodies seldom work like markets. A full analysis of the politics-like-markets analogy cannot be accomplished in a vacuum, but rather must be exposed to the reality of democratic politics. Cooter (2000) points out several flaws in the politics-like-markets analogy. First, political agents are limited to the extent to which they can enter into enforceable political contracts. Second, the value of a legislator's vote often depends upon how other legislators vote. There are pervasive externalities and resulting free riding incentives in political action. Third, real life politics has too many political actors for each one to bargain with everyone else. Unlike the atomistic marketplace of traditional economics, bilateral negotiations would be prohibitively expensive in real life politics. Fourth, there is a diffuse hostility to a rationalization of politics as a market for consensus. Ordinary citizens with little information about legislative bargains would resist any institutionalization of political bargaining, objecting to their representatives participating in open logrolling.

Parisi (2003) introduces four corollaries to further establish why politics-like-markets analogies are imprecise: (1) limited enforceability of political contracts; (2) issue bundling; (3) free riding and bargaining failures; and (4) agency problems and the political dilemma.

2.1. Enforcing Political Bargains

The viability of political markets with Coasian constructs such as logrolling or vote-trading rests on the condition that all political agreements contain effective enforcement mechanisms. For the purpose of our analysis, the enforcement mechanism can be legal, institutional or informal in nature. Indeed, regardless of whether the stability of political agreements is effectuated by judicial bodies, as in traditional contract adjudication in the courts, or is spontaneously achieved through other means, as in the informal enforcement mechanisms considered in Kronman (1985), the Coasian bargaining results holds in politics like in markets.

The enforceability condition further requires that any attempt to modify the policy choice bargained for by a coalition of voters would have to be accepted by all parties — contracts can be resolved only with the consent of the contracting parties. In this setting, minority voters can join the coalition and have a marginal effect on the policy outcome by out-bidding or "bribing" all members of the preexisting majority. With enforceable contracts, members of a majority coalition cannot secede unilaterally by joining with a minority group. Rather, they will collectively entertain offers made by minority voters who will influence the status quo with their side payments, but they will not be able to break away from an existing coalition, since such coalition agreements can be modified only with the consent of all parties.

These ideal conditions, however, are rarely met in real life politics. As pointed out by Cooter (2000), in real politics, bargaining is afflicted by a special problem usually absent in private contracts. Political agents are limited to the extent to which they can enter into enforceable political bargains. For example, coalition agreements are only good until a new coalition is formed. Likewise, there is no way to bind future voting decisions in a logrolling context, or to constrain the choices of future office-holders.

In a traditional contract setting, a contractual agreement can be undone only with the consent of all original contracting parties. Conversely, in informal political agreements, any political agent can betray the original agreement and destabilize the original coalition. There are no direct legal remedies to render such agreements enforceable.

In general, no agreement between current legislators regarding future voting is enforceable under the law. For example, majority deliberations cannot prohibit future amendments altogether or require that such amendments be carried out with a super-majority vote. Legislators sometimes have to be creative to make contracts enforceable in the real world market for votes. In several occasions political actors attempt to signal the enforceability of their bargains (and ensure its influence against the status quo) in a future vote by publicly stating that they would not "go back and undo the things that they pledged that they would do." In other situations, the repeat interaction among politicians may induce the fulfillment of some political bargains, thus facilitating political cooperation. Finally, as well known in the collective action literature (e.g., Olson, 1965), groups with lower collective action costs can be more effective in gathering the most effective bribe, as

public choice theory has extensively demonstrated in a variety of rent-seeking contexts (Kahn, 1990; Dixit and Olson, 1997). However, the general non-enforceability of political bargains limits the deals that can be struck among political representatives and among the various branches of government.

2.2. Issue Bundling and the Reduced Domains of Political Bargaining

Transaction costs exist in the real world of politics. To minimize the effect of transaction costs, policy "packages" are traded and voted upon in the usual course of dealing. Political deals are indeed characterized by a bundling of different issues. Voting on legislation normally requires a binomial vote, supplying a bundle of bargained-for provisions. Most legislative bodies permit amendments that are unrelated to the subject matter of the bill at issue (Dixon, 1985; Riggs, 1973).

From an efficiency perspective, bundling, like tying in a commodity market, may generate suboptimal outcomes. In order for a vote exchange process to work at its best, all dimensions of the policy space should be the potential object of bargaining and trade. Bundling reduces the dimensions of the bargaining space. At the limit, all policy dimensions may collapse into a two-dimensional policy space, limiting the domain of the bargaining process.

In an ideal world with no transaction costs, no bundling should exist in order to maximize the beneficial functioning of the political market. In the real world with positive transaction costs, a positive amount of bundling is to be expected and is part of the global optimization process. Elhauge (1991, p. 31) has noted that where there is issue bundling, "diffuse interests can be systematically underrepresented even if voters face no collective action problem." However, the market will adjust to reach the optimal tradeoffs between the savings on transaction costs and the inefficiencies of tying.

2.3. Collective Action Problems and Political Bargaining Failures

One further consideration should be made on the issue of transaction costs. A costless transaction requires the absence of strategic behavior in the bargaining process. This condition is highly problematic in the context of multi-party voting. The opportunity for individual strategic behavior is elevated where two polar groups seek compromise. In the real-world market for votes, the term "triangulation" has been used to describe the result of efforts to legislate in the middle ground between ideological extremes, where vote-trading transaction costs are high (Broder, 1997, attributing the "triangulation" concept to former Clinton advisor Dick Morris).

All cyclicality problems require the presence of at least three voters. Bargaining among three voters in a two dimensional space is highly sensitive to free riding and other forms of strategic preference revelation. If we think of this triangular situation in a spatial voting setting, we can realize that any movement in the policy space will generate benefits or losses for at least two parties. In the great majority of cases, all three parties will be affected by a potential policy change. Under such conditions, any bargaining carried out by one voter has the potential of creating side benefits for another voter. Any policy change "purchased" by one voter is potentially a free good (or a free bad) for another voter. In a three-party bargain, the voters are thus faced with a collective action problem. The problem is exacerbated by an increase in the number of voters. In a multi-voter setting, strategic behavior may indeed plague the bargaining process.

The collective action problem described above is not different from any other free riding problem in a Coasian setting. Olson (1997) has discussed the collective action problem in the context of Coasian bargaining, questioning the practical validity of the Coasian proposition in a multi-party context. If the object of one individual's bargaining generates a benefit to other individuals who are not involved in the bargain, what is obtained through the bargaining of one individual creates a positive externality to other individuals. Thus the incentives to undertake the bargaining may be seriously undermined. Every individual wishes to be the free rider, having somebody else pay for the common good. Thus, similar to any public good situation, there will be a sub-optimal level of bargaining for the common interest.

2.4. Agency Problems and the Political Accountability Dilemma

Public law scholars suggest that logrolling and other implicit or explicit political exchanges should be discouraged because they undermine political accountability and because imperfections in the market for votes are likely to engender costs that outweigh their benefits (Karlan, 1999). The analysis of the hypothetical market for votes discussed here considers the voters' will as a given. If bargaining is carried out in the absence of agency problems, the bargaining result maximizes the voters' utility. But where the bargaining is carried out by interested representatives, there is an opportunity to depart from the optimality outcome

described above. Further analysis should consider the effect of agency problems in the bargaining mechanism. In the real world of politics, most collective decisions are carried out by political representatives who undertake the decision-making process as agents of the represented individuals. Public choice theory provides ample analysis of the factors of such incentive misalignment, including (a) rational abstention; (b) rational ignorance; and (c) regulatory capture and consequent special interest legislation. Such discrepancies are most visible when an agency problem in political representation occurs at the margin of a crucial vote.

In general terms, if market mechanisms are allowed to operate in political contexts, the collective decision-making mechanism is lubricated. In the absence of representation failures, the collective outcome will approximate the allocative outcome of a competitive market. If bargaining is carried out by agents whose underlying incentives differ from those of their principals, the market mechanism may generate greater discrepancies between the ideal and the real political outcomes, including the fact that agents may be induced to abandon their principals' core values.

3. Conclusion

The absence of legal enforcement mechanisms in political contracts increases transaction costs and often represents an insurmountable obstacle to political cooperation. In this respect, modern public law theory presents a striking paradox, noting that many public law systems invite "wholesale" vote buying, but prohibit vote buying at the "retail" level (Levinson, 1999, 1749). The exchange of campaign contributions for favorable governmental policy outcomes from political office-holders, is an uncontested reality of the political market, yet there is a substantial intellectual hostility in the recognition, let alone the enforcement, of explicit transactions for political consensus. Such hostility is often the result of the belief that logrolling favors organized pressure groups. Most recently, Karlan (1999, 1711) provided an explanation of this commonly observed public law dogma, suggesting that the legal system denies legal enforcement to political agreements to discourage political deals. The buying of votes is prevented and, at the same time, implicit vote-buying through campaign promises is permitted because the wholesale campaigns "serve an informational role that enables voters generally to choose more intelligently among candidates."

From a law and economics perspective, the lack of institutions for favoring political bargaining in the procedures of political democratic assemblies reflects the belief that logrolling would be impeding proper democratic representation. The belief that the enforcement of political deals would be detrimental to society at large — often crystallized into public law dogmas — has prevented a coherent theoretical treatment of this legal and political issue.

To the extent that political bargaining may be instrumental to improving upon the limitations of majoritarian democracy, the institutional design of lawmaking should promote arrangements that minimize the transaction costs of political bargaining. This can be done with the full awareness that the existence of effective exchange mechanisms within politics accentuates the features of the underlying political system. In a world of "good" politics, exchange mechanisms allow for better outcomes. Conversely, in a world of political failures, they may exacerbate the existing problems.

In a political reality already characterized by implicit bargaining under the form of logrolling, the existence of enforcement mechanisms within politics would promote stability and reduce costly intransitivity in the bargaining process or, worse yet, in the policy outcomes. The legal and institutional recognition of this practical reality, far from exacerbating the agency problems in political representation, would increase the political accountability of political actors. A transparent and tractable market for political consensus, such as a recorded system of vote-trading, supported by means of institutional enforcement, would give full visibility to the opaque system of implicit logrolling. This would unquestionably augment the political accountability of political actors in cases of representative democracy. Furthermore, the application of the most basic principles of contract law in the enforcement of political contracts would alone generate the necessary safeguards for the stability of political coalitions without reducing the ability of minority groups to bargain with majority coalitions to change the chosen policy agenda.

The enforceability of political bargains delivers more than mere stability. Institutions may be designed in order to give an opportunity to political actors to reveal the true intensity of the preferences of their voters (or their own preferences, in the event of direct democracy) by entering into binding vote exchanges and facing the true opportunity cost of casting their vote, rather than transferring it to higher valuing political actors. Supporting such exchanges with institutional enforcement would yield the dual benefit of minimizing the welfare costs of voting intransitivity and allowing the political outcome to reflect the cardinal preferences of the voters. The existence of institutions to facilitate political exchange may be a valuable instrument of stability and political efficiency.

The true benefit of having enforceable political bargains, however, should not be solely measured by the stability of the political outcomes. Stability cannot be used as a proxy for efficiency. It is postulated in social and public choice literature that where a "Condorcet winner" can at times be inefficient, it can always at least be trusted to satisfy the preferences of the majority of voting individuals. Absent mechanisms to induce voters to reveal the true intensity of their preferences, democratic legislative systems cannot improve on Condorcet winners and should maintain rules that allow such alternatives to prevail when they exist. If Condorcet winners do not exist, the method and sequence of voting (e.g., agenda setting) determine the political outcome. In these cases, as Cooter (2000) aptly observes, politics becomes a contest among alternative competing coalitions, where procedural rules and agenda-setting will influence which majority's preferences will be satisfied, rather than satisfying the preferences of a unique majority.

FRANCESCO PARISI

REFERENCES

Arrow, K.J. (1951). *Social Choice and Individual Values*. New Haven: Yale University Press.

Becker, Gary S. (1983). "A theory of competition among pressure groups for political influence." *Quarterly Journal of Economics*, 98: 371–400.

Bernholz, P. (1973). "Logrolling, Arrow-paradox and cyclical majorities." *Public Choice*, 15: 87–95.

Broder, David S. (1997). "Catatonic politics," *Washington Post*, Nov. 11, at A19.

Buchanan, J.M. and Tullock, G. (1962). *The Calculus of Consent. Logical Foundations of Constitutional Democracy*. Ann Arbor: University of Michigan Press.

Coase, R.H. (1960). "The problem of social cost." *Journal of Law and Economics*, 3: 1–44.

Cooter, R.D. (2000). *The Strategic Constitution*. Princeton: Princeton University Press.

Dixit, Avinash and Olson, Mancur, Jr. (1997). Does voluntary participation undermine the Coase theorem? Unpublished manuscript on file with the *George Mason Law Review*, August 6.

Dixon, Alan J. (1985). "Line-item veto controversy." *Congressional Digest*, 64: 259, 282.

Elhauge, Einer R. (1991). "Does interest group theory justify more intrusive judicial review?" *Yale Law Journal*, 101: 31.

Kahn, Peter L. (1990). "The politics of unregulation: public choice and limits on government." *Cornell Law Review*, 75: 280, 312, n. 101.

Karlan, P. (1999). "Symposium commentary: politics by other means." *Virginia Law Review*, 85: 1697.

Kronman, A. (1985). "Contract law and state of nature." *Journal of Law, Economics & Organization*, 1: 5.

Levine and Plott (1977). "Agenda influence and its implications." *Virginia Law Review*, 63: 561.

Levinson, D. (1999). "Symposium Commentary: Market Failures and Failures of Markets." *Virginia Law Review*, 85: 1745.

Miller, N.R. (1977). "Logrolling, vote trading and the paradox of voting: a game theoretical overview." *Public Choice*, 30: 51.

Olson, Mancur (1965). *The Logic of Collective Action*. Cambridge: Harvard University Press.

Olson, Mancur (1997). The Coase theorem is false? Paper presented at the 1997 American Law and Economics Association annual conference held in Toronto, Canada.

Parisi, F. (1998). "The market for votes: Coasian bargaining in an Arrovian setting." *George Mason University Law Review*, 6: 745.

Parisi, F. (2002). "Votes and outcomes: rethinking the politics-like-markets metaphor." *European Journal of Law and Economics*, 13: __.

Parisi, F. (2003). Political coase theorem. *Public Choice*. Vol. 115: 1–36.

Pelzman, Sam (1990). "How efficient is the voting market?" *Journal of Law and Economics*, 33: 27–63.

Riggs, Richard A. (1973). "Separation of powers: congressional riders and the veto power." *University of Michigan Journal of Law Reform*, 6: 735, 743–745.

Riker, W.H. (1982). *Liberalism Against Populism: A Confrontation Between the Theory of Democracy and the Theory of Social Choice*. San Francisco: Freeman Publishing.

Rowley, C.K. (1993). *Public Choice*, 3 Volumes. Brookfield: Edward Elgar Publishing.

Schwartz, T. (1977). "Collective choice, separation of issues and vote trading." *American Political Science Review*, 72.

Shubik, M. (1982). *Game Theory in the Social Sciences: Concepts and Solutions*, First Edition. Boston: M.I.T. Press.

Stigler, George J. (1971). "Economic competition and political competition." *Public Choice*, 13: 91–106.

Tullock, G. (1981). "Why so much stability?" *Public Choice*, 37(2): 189–202.

COERCION

Though choices are always constrained, the analysis of coercion is concerned with a particular kind of constraint, namely that which vitiates the chooser's volition in such a guise that her consent in an agreement cannot be considered as voluntary. Embedded within such a general framework, issues of coercion emerge in many contexts ranging from the philosophical problem of providing necessary and sufficient conditions for lack of voluntariness, to the legal doctrines of duress and unconscionability, to the economic analysis of inequality in bargaining power, to international relations.

1. Section 1

Our focus in this entry shall be limited to the analysis of the conditions for coercive agreements. As Trebilcock (1993) has argued, two theories compete in the provision of these conditions. Rights theorists, among which the most prominent are Nozick (1969), Fried (1981), Feinberg (1986) and Wertheimer (1987), draw a distinction between threats and offers. Welfare theorists such as Kronman (1980) and Epstein (1993), argue that voluntary consent entails a theory of distributive justice. To elicit the general character of both camps we focus on Epstein (1993) and on Wertheimer (1987).

The next section will set out certain preliminary issues. A review of the two approaches shall be conducted in the third (welfare-based) and fourth (rights-based) sections of the entry.

2. Section 2

To start with, we wish to clear the way from a related but analytically irrelevant issue. It is fair to say that there are two kinds of involuntary agreements. The first arises when physical strength or psychological pressure are applied to impose a behavior on an individual. Those cases can be straightforwardly classified as cases of coercion. But, since voluntariness is absent, the ensuing acts do not reflect the will of the actor but that of the coercer and, therefore, they turn out to be of little analytical interest. They shall not be analyzed any further in this essay. The second case includes instances of 'constrained volition' where both parties express their will in the adoption of a certain conduct. Since consent is voluntary, coercion is *dispositional* and its detection is not straightforward. Analytically, these cases are of particular interest given the consequences that ethics and law attach to blameworthy in the presence of coercion. They are the object of this study.

Since dispositional coercion requires voluntary agreement, then it takes place within a bargaining game in which an agent (the sender) makes a *proposal* to another (the target). Proposals in a bargaining game may be regarded as either *offers* or *threats*, depending on whether society's welfare (welfare-based theories) or the possibilities for choice of the target (rights-based theories) are increased by the proposal. Note that voluntariness is forced into consent only by threats which then lie at the core of coercion.

3. Section 3

In general, welfare-based theories of coercion are outcome oriented: they detect coercive constraints on volition on the basis of the outcome of the bargaining game that the parties are playing. In Epstein (1993) coercion stems from the parties' agreement whenever it has a negative impact on social welfare. To make such an assessment, Epstein needs a theory of distributive justice. In his view, resources should be assigned to the use which "generate the greatest social benefit" and such an assignment can only be attained thru a mechanism that directs resources to their higher value uses and keeps transaction costs to a minimum. Such a mechanism is the smooth functioning of competitive markets.

When consent to a transaction is given under threat, though the terms of the agreement may be mutually beneficial, society's welfare (i.e., the welfare sum of the two parties involved in the transaction minus costs) is decreased by the exchange. The deadweight loss imposed by their high transaction costs on coercive exchanges is the first and most straightforward instance. In the 'your money or your life' example, if the target has a right to both money and physical integrity, then, under the assumption that the marginal return of money for both agents is equal, the exchange does not create value since the original welfare of both the sender and the target could be restored by re-transferring the money back to the latter. The coercive exchange is then a 'wash' in Epstein's terminology and society's welfare is negatively affected because, as the parties gain nothing, transaction costs cannot be compensated.

Coercion may also arise in other, more subtle, circumstances. Suppose that Sean agrees to sell a good to Terry for X dollars, including delivery, that she dutyfully pays. If after reaching the agreement Sean claims compensation for the delivery, his proposal can be legitimately considered as coercive since, though Terry gains from paying the extra charge, society's welfare has been reduced by the exchange. Note that transaction costs can be compensated in this case. The welfare loss stems from the disruptive consequences for trading and social relationships of allowing the kind of exchange depicted in the example. Social calculus considerations move beyond transaction costs and extend to the dynamics of interactions. Parties' agreements cannot be seen in isolation but are nested in their larger context where exchanges are bundled together and the story of how they have been brought about matters. The distinction between threats and offers "cannot be located in the mutually beneficial nature of the [...] exchange [...]. Instead, the distinction must rest in the way in which this immediate transaction nests into the overall social outcomes of the result in question" (Epstein, 1993, p. 47).

4. Section 4

Rights-based theories of coercion follow quite a different argumentative strategy. In a nut, they claim that:

(a) threats involve making the target worse-off with respect to some baseline;

(b) given certain assumptions on the parties' intentionality, threats coerce whereas offers do not.

Consider again Sean and Terry example. Is he making an offer or a threat? The normal (or expected) course of events (*statistical* baseline) is that the good shall be delivered to Terry at no extra charge. As the proposal alters such a course against her interests, then it is a threat. Things do not change if the baseline is what *should* be expected (*moral* baseline). Since the original agreement is backed by the view about how business relationships should go, Sean cannot ask for an extra charge and his proposal is a threat. Things are seldom so smooth, however.

Consider Nozick's case of the drug dealer.

> *The drug dealer case.* S is the normal supplier to T of illegal drugs at price X. One day S proposes to supply T only if he beats another person A.

Though the question is similar to that in Sean and Terry's example (is S making a threat or, as Harry Frankfurt would say, just a less attractive offer?), yet the answer differs. Consider what it is expected. In this case, S is making a threat since he is worsening T's position with respect to the normal course of events. Now take the moral baseline. Then, S is making an offer to T since he is not morally required to supply drugs for money at all.

The drug dealer example raises two issues. First, the moral baseline's answer presupposes a specific view of the way in which economic interactions (and, in particular, the marketplace) work, according to which sellers charge at the prevailing market rate and this is morally acceptable. This applies to competitive markets but it leaves open the issue of coercion in monopolistic settings, when a party may exploit his own position to extract all the rent from the other. Though we do not deal with this problem, it is worth noting that the underlying logic used by rights-based theories to solve the problem does not change.

In more general terms, the distinction made by rights-based theories of coercion between threats and offers hinges on some view of the just allocation of property rights or, as Trebilcock says, on "whether it is possible to fix a conception of what is right and what is wrong, of what rights people have in contractual relations independent of whether their contracts should be enforced" (1993, p. 80). In this respect, rights-based theories come close to welfare-based.

Second, when the statistical and the moral baselines conflict, does a right answer exists? In Nozick's view the baseline which takes precedence should be that most favorable to the target. Wertheimer takes a different stance: there is no right answer to identifying baselines for detecting coercion and each conclusion backed by each different baseline may be supported.

SEBASTIANO BAVETTA
ANTONIO COGNATA

REFERENCES

Baldwin, D.A. (1989). *Paradoxes of Power*. New York: Basil Blackwell.

Brams, S.J. (1990). *Negotiation Games*. New York: Routledge.

Cooter, R. (1984). "Prices and sanctions." *Columbia Law Review*, 84: 1523–1560.

Culyer, A.J. (1971). "Merit goods and the welfare economics of coercion." *Public Finance/Finances Publiques*, 26: 546–572.

Eaton, J. and Engers, M. (1992). "Sanctions." *Journal of Political Economy*, 100: 899–928.

Eaton, J. and Engers, M. (1999). "Sanctions: some simple analytics." *American Economic Review*, 89: 409–414.

Epstein, R.A. (1993). *Bargaining with the State*. Princeton: Princeton University Press.

Feinberg, J. (1986). *Harm to Self*. Oxford: Oxford University Press.

Fried, C. (1981). *Contract as Promise. A Theory of Contractual Obligation*. Cambridge: Harvard University Press.

Kronman, A. (1980). "Contract law and distributive justice." *Yale Law Journal*, 89: 472.

Miller, D. (1983). "Constraints on freedom." *Ethics*, 94: 66–86.

Muthoo, A. (1999). *Bargaining Theory with Applications*. Cambridge: Cambridge University Press.

Nozick, R. (1969). "Coercion," in S. Morgenbesser, P. Suppes, and M. White (eds.) *Philosophy, Science and Method*. New York: St. Martin's Press.

Trebilcock, M.J. (1993). *The Limits of Freedom of Contract*. Cambridge: Harvard University Press.

Wertheimer, A. (1987). *Coercion*. Princeton: Princeton University Press.

COLLECTIVE ACTION UNDER THE ARTICLES OF CONFEDERATION

The American confederation faced several collective action problems between 1775 and 1789. The confederation could not enforce a unified response to trade barriers imposed by foreign nations (McGillivray, 2001), it had problems coordinating attendance at the confederation congress (Riker, 1987), and it could not enforce judicial decisions over the states. But perhaps the most obvious collective action problem was associated with the system of requisitions. Requisitions were a request for state resources, similar to an unenforced tax upon the states. The confederation requisitioned the states for soldiers, money, and supplies and used these resources primarily for defense and the reduction of war debts.

When Congress requisitioned the states, it first voted on the amount of money (or soldiers) needed for the ensuing year, by an affirmative vote from nine of the thirteen state delegations. It then asked each state to contribute a fixed proportion of the total by a particular due date. Article VIII and article IX provided Congress with the clear constitutional authority to requisition the states for money and men, but they did not provide Congress with an enforcement mechanism. To preserve state sovereignty, states were supposed to enforce these edicts on their own. Since Congress spent almost all of its revenue on traditional public goods (national defense and debt reduction), one might expect that the states faced a pure public goods problem with summation technology and income effects (Sandler, 1992).

Although this may or may not be the case, evidence suggests that the states clearly faced some type of collective action problem. States frequently ignored requisitions. When they did comply, their compliance was almost always partial and incomplete. Take the requisition in response to Shays' Rebellion, for example (Cain and Dougherty, 1999). In October 1786, Congress requisitioned 1,340 men and $530,000 from the states for the army needed to subdue the insurgents in western Massachusetts. These resolutions were unanimously agreed to by all the states in attendance.

But despite the fact that Shays Rebellion was spilling into other states, despite the possibility of losing a federal arsenal to Shays' men, and despite the unanimous decision to raise resources, Virginia was the only state to comply. Massachusetts and Connecticut passed laws to raise their quotas in soldiers, but never gave their recruiting officers enough money to enlist soldiers. And neither state paid any of the money requested by Congress. Other states made no attempt. After receiving a motion to adjourn from the Maryland house of delegates, the Maryland Senate wrote back, "you have not taken any measures to comply with raising a troop of horse" or "passed an assessment bill to bring any money into the state or continental treasury." The house then replied, "We shall only say in reply that we have paid every possible attention to the public affairs of the union, and the interest and happiness of our people ... we repeat our request to close this session this evening" (quoted in Dougherty, 2001, 120).

Connecticut was not so bold. Rather than simply ignoring the monetary requisition, Connecticut claimed it had no money. James Davenport, a member of the Connecticut General Assembly, responded that Connecticut's claim was ridiculous and "chided" the house for its declaration (Dougherty, 2001, 116, n. 30). By the time Congress received reports that Connecticut would not reply, James Madison bemoaned, "In fact payments to the treas[ury] are ceasing every where, and the minds of the people are losing all confidence in our political system" (ibid.).

Similar problems occurred throughout the confederation. According to Alexander Hamilton, the New York assembly described a Congressional funding program as "wise and indispensable but a majority thought it would be unwise in one state to contribute this way alone" (Morris, 1975, 6: 504–505).

Such observations led Hamilton and Madison to develop their own theories of free-riding behavior (Dougherty, 2002a). Madison proclaimed at the Virginia ratifying convention:

> One reason to prevent the concurrent exertions of all the States will arise from the suspicion, in some States, of delinquency in others. ...were it known that the citizens of one district were not performing their duty, and it was left to the policy of the Government to make them come up with [their own payment], the citizens of other districts would be quite supine and careless in making provisions for payment. (Jensen, 1976, 9: 144–146)

According to Madison, the anticipated actions of others discouraged states from contributing. Early Americans observed free-riding behavior and they developed theories to explain it. Clearly, some type of collective action problem existed during the confederation.

The exact type is not as clear. States did not entirely free-ride, as one might expect from a pure public good model (Luenberger, 1995). States contributed 53 percent of the soldiers requisitioned from 1777 to 1782 (roughly 144,000 men), and 40 percent of the money requisitioned from 1782 to 1789 (roughly 6.4 million dollars). No fewer than eight states contributed money every year from 1782 to 1789. And the confederation received enough resources to reduce domestic debts by one fifth within six years of the war. These contributions appear to be larger and more frequent than predicted by the traditional theory of public goods (Dougherty, 2001).

The pattern of contribution might be explained in several different ways. First, Gordon Wood (1969) claimed that early Americans viewed republican government as one that required sacrifice of individual interests for collective needs.

The structure of the confederation was predicated on the idea. It is possible that state politicians tried to act virtuously and this is why they contributed to the confederation. Inadequate resources explain why the states contributed only part (Brown, 1993).

Although state resources were clearly limited, the civic virtue explanation does not explain the decision to withhold resources when resources were available. Arguably, the economy rebounded by the end of the confederation (Perkins, 1994), yet compliance with requisitions did not. For example, many of the states that did not comply with the Shays requisition seemed to have adequate resources. Pennsylvania appeared to have adequate resources and Massachusetts raised a larger force than the federal army requested in the eleventh hour (Dougherty, 2001, 119). Clearly Massachusetts had adequate funds. Moreover, the claim that state's acted solely out of civic virtue is inconsistent with standard economic theory, and inconsistent with the data (Dougherty, 2002b). Civic virtue may have had minor effects on state behavior, but it does not appear to be the primary reason why states contributed.

Second, state contributions might have been the result of iterative play. As Bendor and Swistak (1997) show, cooperative equilibria exist in iterative prisoners' dilemmas when the prospect of future rounds is sufficiently high. As long as state politicians thought that the confederation would continue, reciprocity might have encouraged them to cooperate as well.

Although an iterative argument seems reasonable, there are at least three obstacles that any such a conjecture must face. First, most of the formal theoretic results on iterative play are based on tournaments of pair-wise prisoners' dilemmas. The decision to contribute under the confederation was a n-player game and may not be amenable to these models. Second, there were empirical reasons to believe that states would highly discount future contributions. George Washington regularly noted that states anticipated the war's end from its inception to its conclusion. He believed this was why the states did not send more recruits (Risch, 1981). When the war was finally over, Congress made several attempts to amend the Articles of Confederation and end its dependence on requisitions (Dougherty, 2001, 60–62, 131–140). Both would lead to discounting of future play and cause less cooperation. Third, the trend in state compliance with requisitions resembled the behavior observed in experiments on finite prisoners' dilemmas more than it resembled expected outcomes from infinite play. When indents are set aside, cooperation unraveled as the confederation progressed. This might suggest that states were learning the nature of their one-shot game rather than reciprocating cooperation with cooperation as an iterative explanation might suggest.

Finally, state contributions might be explained by the presence of joint products. Joint products are goods that produce multiple aspects of publicness — in this case both private benefits and public benefits. Although the public aspects of confederation goods would not give the states incentive to contribute, the private aspects might. For example, national defense produced public aspects, like expelling the British from American soil or deterring the Spanish from invasion, and it produced private aspects, like preventing the British army from quartering in American homes and limiting damage to local property and persons. A state would have incentive to contribute to obtain the private aspects of continental defense but it would not have incentive to contribute public aspects of continental defense. This conjecture is supported empirical analysis of state contributions using direct (Dougherty, 2001) and indirect (Dougherty, 2002b) measures of joint products. It should be noted, however, that such an explanation does not preclude other factors.

Although state behavior under the Articles of Confederation may exemplify the collective action problem, it should *not* be characterized as one of complete free-riding. States contributed sizable portions of their requisitions, they regularly sent delegates to Congress (at least at first), and some states attempted to support the confederation's trade policy. The period may be accurately characterized as the American era of collective action problems, but complete free-riding was not its norm.

KEITH DOUGHERTY

REFERENCES

Bendor, Jonathan and Piotr Swistak (1997). "The evolutionary stability of cooperation." *American Political Science Review*, 91: 290–307.

Brown, Roger H. (1993). *Redeeming the Republic*. Baltimore: John Hopkins University Press.

Cain, Michael, J.G. and Dougherty Keith L. (1999). "Suppressing Shays' rebellion: collective action and constitutional design under the articles of confederation." *Journal of Theoretical Politics*, 11(2): 233–260.

Dougherty, Keith L. (2001). *Collective Action under the Articles of Confederation*. New York: Cambridge University Press.

Dougherty, Keith L. (2002a). "Madison's theory of public goods," in Samuel Kernell (ed.) *James Madison: The Theory and Practice of Government*. Stanford: Stanford University Press (forthcoming).

Dougherty, Keith L. (2002b). "State interest or national unity? a test of federalist and anti-federalist theories of state behavior, 1775–1782," mimeo.

Jensen, Merrill (ed.) (1976). *The Documentary History of the Ratification of the Constitution*. Madison: State Historical Society of Wisconsin.

Luenberger, David G. (1995). *Microeconomic Theory*. New York: McGraw-Hill.

McGillivrary, F. (2001). "Trading free and opening markets: US trade under the Articles of Confederation." in McGillivrary, McClain, Pahre, and Schonardt-Baily (eds.) *International Trade and Political Institutions*. Cheltenham: Edward Elgar.

Morris, Robert (1975). *The Papers of Robert Morris*. James Ferguson et al. (eds.) Pittsburgh: University of Pittsburgh.

Perkins, Edwin J. (1994). *American Public Finance and Financial Services, 1700–1815*. Columbus: Ohio State University Press.

Riker, William (1987). "The lessons of 1787." *Public Choice*, 55: 5–34.

Risch, Erna (1981). *Supplying Washington's Army*. Washington, DC: Center of Military History.

Sandler, Todd (1992). *Collective Action: Theory and Applications*. Ann Arbor: University of Michigan Press.

Wood, Gordon S. (1969). *The Creation of the American Republic, 1776–1787*. New York: W.W. Norton.

COMMITTEE ASSIGNMENTS

> When [a bill] goes from the clerk's desk to a committee-room it crosses a parliamentary bridge of sighs to dim dungeons of silence whence it will never return. (Wilson, 1885, p. 58)
>
> [Congressional government is] a government by the chairmen of the Standing Committees of Congress.... (Wilson, 1885, p. 58)

The idea of using a committee, or subset of the entire membership of an organization, to carry out various functions is as old as the idea of collective organization itself. In Athens before 400 B.C.E., the democratic government maintained "committee chambers," or *prytaneion*, where small groups could caucus and deliberate. The Roman Senate delegated experts to advise the nation in a *Senatus Consultum* signed by a "committee" five members in the period of the Republic. Later, Caesar Augustus used a committee of the *Senatus Populusque* as an advisory and legitimating body in Imperial Rome. This "committee" (consisting of the consuls, certain other magistrates, and 15 senators chosen by lot) was much closer to the modern "cabinet" than what we think of as committees, however.

Today, most legislatures use some procedure to divide up the tasks of writing, discussing, assessing, and amending legislation into "committees." *Ad hoc* or *Select* committees are temporary, exist only to address a single issue, and often serve at the pleasure of the presiding officer of the assembly. *Standing* committees are permanent bodies that deal with specialized matters (defined by their "jurisdiction") throughout the term of the legislature. Standing committees may have membership that extends beyond legislative terms or sessions, and membership may be regarded as a formal property right by those who have served on the committee in the previous session.

Joint committees are a feature of multicameral systems, and as the name suggests joint committees have members that represent all of the legislative bodies involved. *Conference* committees likewise have members from all (usually both) chambers. But they might better be called "joint select" committees, since they exist only for the purpose of negotiating changes in legislation already passed by each house, in order to reconcile discrepancies in the competing versions. The amended legislation must be passed in identical form in each of the two houses.

The explanations for the creation and survival of committee structures can be divided into three large categories. (1) Saving of time through division of labor. (2) Delegation to smaller group, members chosen for their expertise. (3) Division of benefits for claiming the benefits of membership, to advantage the incumbent members who occupy the committee seats and positions of leadership. Each of these three will be considered in turn.

1. Division of Labor

"Committee" has an archaic meaning, deriving from Anglo-Norman and Latin roots. This meaning is simply a person who can be trusted with a charge or task. The modern meaning of a collective noun referring to a group delegated by a larger group to perform a function is fairly recent. Yet its origins are logical: divide the group up into committees, and have every committee work at the same time on different matters, bringing back to the next large group meeting a fully developed proposal that we can act on. If the larger group really can trust the committees, in fact, the group can get nearly n times as much work done, in terms of issues decided, where n is the number of disjoint groups working simultaneously.

The delegation and division of labor model of committee work gave rise to the nonpartisan, "delegation of the median member" model of Gilligan and Krehbiel (1990) and Krehbiel (1990). For the division of labor to work, each committee must literally represent the larger chamber in every important respect. This rules out two possible selection mechanisms, self-selection and lottery. Committees cannot be exclusively self-selected (except possibly by expertise), since this would result in membership being "outliers." (For a contrasting view, see Hall and Grofman, 1990.) The consequence would be that committee actions such as bills would contain no information about the correct course of action, because floor members know committees are biased "high demanders." Similarly, if membership is

chosen by lot there is no reason to believe that the *ex post* draw of members (at least for small committees) would be a truly representative sample.

2. Delegation to Expertise

Another possibility is that committee membership might be granted on the basis of expertise, or expertise might be acquired through long experience if there is a system of standing committees. A reading of the historical literature on the evolution of committees in the American system (e.g., Baumgartner et al., 2000; Canon and Stewart, 2001; Cooper, 1970; Fenno, 1978; Gamm and Shepsle, 1989; Price, 1977; Stewart, 1992; Westefield, 1974) shows that this rationale for committee function is often invoked, both by committees and the floor.

The first standing committee in the U.S. House of Representatives was the Committee on Enrolled Bills, established in 1789. By 1810, the House had 10 standing committees. The Senate, smaller and (like the Roman Senate) composed *entirely* of "experts," established fewer standing committees, and relied on them less for guidance on legislative questions. One reason for this is the Senate practice of allowing unlimited free debate (again, like the Roman Senate). The right to filibuster, and the capacity of Senators to attach "riders," ignoring germaneness rules that bind their House counterparts, make Senate committees much less important.

3. Division of Benefits to Incumbency

David Mayhew famously, though controversially, observed that "the organization of Congress meets remarkably well the electoral needs of it members ... If a group of planners sat down and tried to design a pair of American national assemblies with the goal of serving members' electoral needs year in and year out, they would be hard pressed to improve on what exists." (Mayhew, 1974, pp. 81–82). Mayhew's claim is that members' need to get reelected induces a preference to achieve three categories of activity in the assembly: credit-claiming, increased name recognition, and position-taking.

Though there are other features of congressional organization that are salient to Mayhew's argument, the key feature is the committee system. The committee system is organized to minimize "zero-sum conflict" (Mayhew, 1974, p. 82), and allow members to claim credit credibly for policy actions within their committees jurisdiction (the organizational development of this view is beyond the scope of this essay; see Crain and Muris, 1995; Rohde and Shepsle, 1973; Shepsle, 1975, 1978; Shepsle and Weingast, 1981, 1987;

Weingast and Marshall, 1988; for an overview of the controversy, see Krehbiel et al., 1987).

What conditions would have to be met for this view of committee organization and function to work? To simplify greatly, the argument works as follows: Members of Congress all have electoral needs, and if those needs are not met those members do not survive in Congress. So, all members have an interest in designing or accepting an institutional structure that advantages incumbents. Districts differ in what they need and want, so members have different derived demands for legislative jurisdictions. Over time, the leadership of the chambers, but most particularly the House of Representatives, has designed a stable and institutionalized log-roll. Each member receives, or can expect to receive for loyalty, a committee assignment that allows him or her plausibly to claim credit for legislation that matters to that particular district.

The problem would appear to come at the point of voting on final legislation. After all, if my committee has reported out the bill I want, and yours has reported the one you want, what is there to say that we won't defect at the point of final passage and vote down each other's bill? There are two factors that mitigate against this outcome. First, members care more about their own committee's bills. So, they are quite satisfied to let other bills pass as long as their own bills also get through. More simply, the cost of "bad" legislation from other committees is much less than the electoral benefits that accrue to the "good" legislation from my own committee bill passing the full House. Second, since this process is repeated a large number of times, given the high median seniority of the House, the norm of "reciprocity" and deference to committees is well-established.

There is another part of the "benefits of incumbency" view of committees to emphasize. The problem of the absence of equilibria in majority voting processes in either sincere or strategic settings may potentially be solved by the "partition" of the policy space into disjoint and exhaustive committee jurisdictions. This point (Shepsle, 1979; Shepsle and Weingast, 1981; Enelow and Hinich, 1983) is discussed in greater detail in Hinich and Munger (1997).

4. Applications in Public Choice: Committees as "Loyalty Filters"

There is a wide variety of applications of the theories on committees in the public choice literature. Some of the most important work is that which has grown up around research by Mark Crain. Coker and Crain (1994), building on Crain (1990), point out that, if committee assignments are valuable and if party and chamber leaders have power to give or

withhold choice assignments, the standard agency literature on member behavior may be underspecified. In particular, leadership may have considerable hold over members as "agents." This view is also discussed in some earlier work (Munger, 1988; Weingast and Marshall, 1988), but Crain deserves significant credit for most fully developing the insight and exploring its empirical implications.

If members shirk, then, by voting in ways other than that desired by the leadership, they are less likely to be awarded their most desired assignments. Conversely, members who do get the best assignments are expected to show less variance in voting patterns, and have a mean voting pattern that matches the leadership's desires quite closely. Consequently, committees function institutionally as "loyalty filters" (Akerlof, 1983).

Mixon and Ressler (2001) develop Crain's idea of a "loyalty filter" further for committees, in the specific instance of the "Congressional Black Caucus" (CBC). These authors point out that, since CBC members vote as a solid bloc, and have more internal consistency than nearly any other group in Congress, their behavior approximates a successful cartel quite well. As a result, according to Mixon and Ressler, members of the CBC are disproportionately awarded membership on key committees. The net result is that representation for the districts represented by CBC members may have more actual power to influence policy than would be obvious from simply considering the number of black members as a proportion of the overall House population.

MICHAEL MUNGER

REFERENCES

Akerlof, G. (1983). "Loyalty filters." *American Economic Review*, 73: 54–63.

Baumgartner, Frank, Bryan D. Jones, and Michael C. MacLeod, (2000). "The evolution of legislative jurisdictions." *Journal of Politics*, 62: 321–349.

Coker, David and W. Mark Crain (1994). "Legislative committees as loyalty-generating institutions." *Public Choice*, 81: 195–221.

Crain, W. Mark, (1990). "Committees as loyalty filters," in Crain and Tollison (eds.) *Predicting Politics*, Ann Arbor, MI: University of Michigan Press.

Crain, W. Mark and Timothy J. Muris (1995). "Legislative organization of fiscal policy." *Journal of Law and Economics*, 38: 311–333.

Crain, W. Mark and John T. Sullivan, (1997). "Committee characteristics and re-election margins: an empirical investigation of the US House." *Public Choice*, 93: 271–285.

Canon, David and Charles Stewart (2001). "The evolution of the committee system in Congress," in Lawrence Dodd and Bruce

Oppenheimer (eds.) *Congress Reconsidered*, Seventh, Edition. pp. 163–191.

Cooper, Joseph (1970). "The origins of the standing committees and the development of the modern house," *Rice University Studies*, 56(Summer): 1–90.

Enelow, James and Melvin Hinich (1983). "Voting one issue at a time: the question of voter forecasts." *American Political Science Review*, 77: 435–445.

Fenno, Richard (1978). *Congressmen in Committees*, Boston: Little, Brown.

Gamm, Gerald and Kenneth Shepsle (1989). "Emergence of legislative institutions: standing committees in the House and Senate, 1810–1825." *Legislative Studies Quarterly*, 14: 39–66.

Gilligan, Thomas, and Keith Krehbiel (1990). "Organization of informative committees by a rational legislature." *American Journal of Political Science*, 34: 531–564.

Hall, Richard and Bernard Grofman (1990). "The committee assignment process and the conditional nature of committee bias." *American Political Science Review*, 84: 1149–1166.

Hinich, Melvin and Michael C. Munger (1997). *Analytical Politics*. New York: Cambridge University Press.

Krehbiel, Keith (1990). "Are Congressional committees composed of preference outliers?" *American Political Science Review*, 84: 149–163.

Krehbiel, Keith, Kenneth A. Shepsle, and Barry R. Weingast (1987). "Why are Congressional committees powerful?" *American Political Science Review*, 81: 929–945.

Leibowitz, A.A. and Robert Tollison D. (1980). "A theory of legislative organization: making the most of your majority." *Quarterly Journal of Economics*, 46: 261–248.

Mayhew, David (1974). *Congress: The Electoral Connection*. New Haven, CT: Yale University Press.

Mixon, Franklin and Rand Ressler (2001). "Loyal political cartels and committee assignments in Congress: evidence from the Congressional Black Caucus." *Public Choice*, 108: 313–330.

Munger, Michael (1988). "Allocation of desirable committee assignments: extended queues vs. committee expansion." *American Journal of Political Science*, 32: 317–344.

Price, Douglas (1977). "Careers and committees in the American Congress," in William Aydelotte (ed.) *The History of Parliamentary Behavior*. pp. 28–62.

Rohde, David and Kenneth Shepsle (1973). "Democratic committee assignments in the House of Representatives: strategic aspects of a social choice process." *American Political Science Review*, 67: 889–905.

Shepsle, Kenneth A. (1975). "Congressional committee assignments: an optimization model with institutional constraints." *Public Choice*, 22: 55–78.

Shepsle, Kenneth A. (1978). *The Giant Jigsaw Puzzle: Democratic Committee Assignments in the Modern House*. Chicago: University of Chicago Press.

Shepsle, Kenneth A. (1979). "Institutional arrangements and equilibrium in multidimensional voting models." *American Journal of Political Science*, 23: 27–60.

Shepsle, Kenneth, A. and Weingast Barry, R. (1987). "The institutional foundations of committee power." *American Political Science Review*, 81: 85–104.

Shepsle, Kenneth A. and Barry Weingast (1981). "Structure induced equilibrium and legislative choice." *Public Choice*, 37(3): 503–519.

Stewart, Charles (1992). "Committee hierarchies in the modernizing House, 1875–1947." *American Journal of Political Science*, 36: 835–856.

Weingast, Barry, R. and William Marshall (1988). "The industrial organization of Congress." *Journal of Political Economy*, 96: 132–163.

Westefield, L.P. (1974). "Majority party leadership and the committee system in the House of Representatives." *American Political Science Review*, 68: 1593–1604.

Wilson, Woodrow (1885). *Congressional Government: A Study in American Politics*. Boston: Houghton, Mifflin.

COMMITTEE JURISDICTIONS AND PAC CONTRIBUTIONS

It is his jooty to rigorously enforce th' rules iv th' Sinit. There ar-re none. Th' Sinit is rule be courtesy, like th' longshoreman's union. (Finley Peter Dunne, *Dissertations by Mr. Dooley*, 1906)

The "institution" of long-term membership on disjoint committee jurisdictions that span the entire set of policy dimensions is a rare one. In fact, it exists only (if then) in the U.S. House of Representatives. But because this is the textbook example of legislative organization in so many public choice models, it has been widely studied and argued about.

Committee jurisdictions figure prominently in such classic accounts as Niskanen (1971), Mayhew (1974), Shepsle and Weingast (1981), and Weingast (1984). For Niskanen, the institution of committees transformed the oversight process into a "stylized farce." The reason is that review committees, composed of "high demanders" of the policies within each committee's jurisdiction, simply checked to see whether the bureaucratic agency had correctly gauged the maximum budget likely to pass the full legislature.

Mayhew saw committees as fulfilling the needs of members for forms of organization that facilitated the "credit-claiming, position-taking, and advertising" activities on which successful reelection efforts depend. For Shepsle and Weingast, committees' gatekeeping role and agenda control meant that all members, and the legislative leadership, depend on the committee system to maintain order and predictability in the process of legislation. As Weingast further argued, the policy direction of federal agencies appears to follow changes in composition of committees, making access to and influence on committee members of disproportionate importance to those industries whose activities are within the committee's jurisdiction.

These theoretical accounts gave rise to a wave of scholarship, focusing on the data made available under the U.S. "Freedom of Information Act" (FOIA) on campaign contributions. The Federal Election Campaign Act of 1974, amended in 1975 and again 1976, after the Supreme Court decision on Buckley v. Valeo (1976), required disclosure of many details about the identity of contributors, and the recipients of those contributions. The first election where the data are available in electronic (i.e., machine-readable) format was the 1977–1978 cycle. The tapes containing the contribution data became available under FOIA request requirements in 1982, and by 1985 contribution data for both challengers and incumbents in U.S. elections was freely available from the ICPSR (Interuniversity Consortium for Political Science Research) and other data archiving organizations.

The first published public choice paper using the new data was Poole and Romer (1985) (see also Poole et al., 1987). The view taken here was that committee assignments had no impact on campaign contributions. Instead, Poole and Romer argued that the primary determinant of contributions was the voting record, or "ideology," of the legislator.

A contrasting view was offered by Munger (1984). The model underlying this work was Denzau and Munger (1986), and the argument was quite different from the Poole and Romer work. If legislators differ in their productivity in policy work, by virtue of committee assignments and experience, then the pattern of contributions from interest groups should be shaped by these productivity differences.

Poole and Romer argue that the "committee" assignments simply signal collections of ideologically similar members. Consequently, the statistical significance of dummy variables denoting committee membership would be spurious, because it is really ideology, not membership, that drives contributions. The truth is that the process of self-selection onto committees may prevent researchers from disentangling the separate effects of membership and ideology. What is clear is that, at both the aggregate (Munger, 1984; Grier and Munger, 1986, 1991, 1993; Grier et al., 1990) and industry (Munger, 1989) levels, PACs appear to target members of committees whose substantive legislative and regulatory jurisdictions are of interest to them.

A wide variety of published papers have followed up, amended, and extended the view advanced in Grier and Munger (1986), and the theoretical model described in Denzau and Munger (1986). One of the most important

was Hall and Wayman (1990), who showed that the pattern of time expenditure by members of Congress very closely tracks the pattern of campaign contributions by PACs. This study appears to answer the question, "what is being purchased by PACs?" Over and over, it has been difficult to show any direct effect on policy. But Hall and Wayman found that there is a significant correlation between "effort" (to use the Denzau and Munger term) and contributions.

Endersby and Munger (1992) extend the Grier and Munger findings to contributions by labor unions. Bennet and Loucks (1994) showed that House members of the Banking and Finance Committee received far more contributions than nonmembers from the financial services industry. Loucks (1996) followed up with a similar finding for the Senate. Dow et al. (1998) collect an innovative data set from the California assembly, and test a variety of hypotheses on those data. The advantage of the California setting is that both PAC and organization (i.e., corporations and labor unions themselves) can make contributions.

Regens et al. (1991) extend the basic Grier and Munger results in several important ways, but confirm the basic result that the pattern of committee jurisdictions appear to cause a corresponding pattern in campaign contributions. Stratmann (1992), and Kroszner and Stratman (1998) present a very sophisticated analysis of both time series and cross sectional variation in contributions, conditioned on committee membership and seniority. This is probably the most carefully conducted empirical study yet published.

There are still other views, about which the literature on PAC contributions has not reached any firm conclusions. Briefly, these other views include:

- Krehbiel (1991), who argued that committees are not composed of "high demanders," but rather represent the both the mean and variance of the larger chamber. This argument is interesting, but then how are we to rationalize the observed pattern of campaign contributions? Shouldn't committees be unimportant as attractors of campaign funds?

- Cox and McCubbins (1993) argue that control by party leadership in the legislature is paramount. Committee members provide services, as well as receive benefits. Consequently, even though committee members may in fact receive disproportionate contributions from PACs within their jurisdictions, the members must act in accordance with the wishes of the leadership "cartel," and the freedom members appear to enjoy is not real.

- Romer and Snyder (1994) argue (quite rightly) that the association of committees with "relevant" industries, unions, and PACs is ad hoc. Their claim is that the most telling context for research is the result of a *change* in committee assignment, and looking for a *change* in the consequent pattern of PAC contributions. This design clearly has a number of advantages. Their results confirm that there are systematic relationships between particular industry or union sectors and specific committees. But they also show that other factors, such as seniority on a committee or voting record, may swamp the individual committee effect.

MICHAEL C. MUNGER

REFERENCES

Bennett, Randall, W. and Christine Loucks (1994). "Savings and loan and finance industry PAC contributions to incumbent members of the House Banking Committee." *Public Choice*, 79: 83–104.

Cox, Gary and Mathew D. McCubbins (1993). *Legislative Leviathan: Party Government in the U.S. House.* Berkeley, CA: University of California Press.

Denzau, Arthur T. and Michael C. Munger (1986). "Legislators and interest groups: how unorganized interests get represented." *American Political Science Review*, 80: 84–106.

Dow, Jay, James Endersby, and James Menifield (1998). "The industrial structure of the California Assembly: committee assignments, economic interests, and campaign contributions." *Public Choice*, 94: 67–83.

Endersby, James, and Michael Munger (1992). "The impact of legislator attributes on Union PAC contributions" (with James Endersby). *Journal of Labor Research*, 12: 79–97.

Grier, Kevin B. and Michael Munger (1986). "The impact of legislative attributes on interest group contributions." *Journal of Labor Research*, 7: 349–361.

Grier, Kevin and Michael Munger (1991). "Committee assignments, constituent preferences, and campaign contributions." *Economic Inquiry*, 29: 24–43.

Grier, Kevin and Michael Munger (1993). "Corporate, labor, and trade association contributions to the U.S. House and Senate, 1978–1986." *Journal of Politics*, 55: 615–644.

Grier, Kevin, Michael Munger, and Gary Torrent (1990). "Allocation patterns of PAC monies: the U.S. Senate." *Public Choice*, 67: 111–128.

Hall, Richard and Frank Wayman (1990). "Buying time: moneyed interests and the mobilization of bias in congressional committees." *American Political Science Review*, 84(3): 797–820.

Krehbiel, Keith (1991). *Information and Legislative Organization.* Ann Arbor, MI: University of Michigan Press.

Kroszner, Randall, S. and Thomas Stratmann (1998). "Interest-group competition and the organization of Congress: theory and evidence from financial services' political action committees." *American Economic Review*, 88: 1163–1187.

Loucks, Christine (1996). "Finance industry PAC contributions to U.S. Senators, 1983–88." *Public Choice*, 89: 219–229.

Mayhew, David (1974). *Congress: The Electoral Connection.* New Haven, CT: Yale University Press.

Munger, Michael (1984). "Institutions and outcomes," Ph.D. Thesis, Washington University, St. Louis.

Munger, Michael (1989). "A simple test of the thesis that committee assignments shape the pattern of corporate PAC contributions." *Public Choice*, 62: 181–186.

Munger, Michael C. and Gary M. Torrent, (1993). "Committee power and value in the U.S. Senate: implications for policy." *Journal of Public Administration Research and Theory*, 3: 46–65.

Niskanen, William (1971). *Bureaucracy and Representative Government.* Chicago, IL: Aldine-Atherton.

Poole, Keith, and Thomas Romer (1985). "Patterns of political action committee contributions to the 1980 campaigns for U.S. House of Representatives." *Public Choice*, 47: 63–112.

Poole, Keith T., Thomas Romer, and Howard Rosenthal (1987). "The Revealed Preferences of Political Action Committees." *American Economic Review*, 77(2): 298–302.

Regens, James, Euel Elliot, and Ronald Keith Gaddie (1991). "Regulatory costs, committee jurisdictions, and corporate PAC contributions." *Social Science Quarterly*, 72: 751–760.

Romer, Thomas and James Snyder (1994). "An empirical investigation of the dynamics of PAC contributions." *American Journal of Political Science*, 38: 745–769.

Shepsle, Kenneth and Barry Weingast (1981). "Structure-induced equilibrium and legislative choice." *Public Choice*, 37: 503–519.

Stratmann, Thomas (1992). "Are contributors rational? Disentangling strategies of political action committees." *Journal of Political Economy*, 100: 647–664.

Weingast, Barry, R. (1984). "The congressional-bureaucratic system: a principal-agent perspective (with applications to the SEC)." *Public Choice*, 44: 147–191.

COMMITTEES IN LEGISLATURES

The committee system is a part of the institutional structure of Congress that enables the members of legislatures to achieve their goals more efficiently by creating a formal division of labor, and by assigning property rights to components of the legislative agenda. There is no legal requirement that legislatures be organized into committees, and the U.S. Constitution that created the nation's Congress makes no mention of committees. The system evolved over time, designed by legislators for their own benefit.

The most obvious function of the committee system is to allow a division of labor so that legislators can specialize in particular issues, allowing the legislature as a whole to accomplish more. One well-recognized aspect of this division of labor is that it allows committee members some power of agenda control over areas their committees oversee (Niskanen, 1971; Shepsle and Weingast, 1987). Less obvious is that in the absence of an institutional structure, the legislative agenda is a non-exclusive resource, with the associated inefficiencies (Cheung, 1970). Without institutional constraints, every legislator would have access to every part of the legislative agenda, resulting in an inefficient overuse of the legislative agenda. All legislators would have an incentive to bring to the floor all issues for which they had an interest, regardless in the merits of the issues or their likelihood of approval. This would result in the legislative agenda being clogged with issues of questionable value, crowding out more valuable issues. Because of the common pool nature of the legislative agenda, its overuse would lower its value to every legislator.

The committee system privatizes the legislative agenda by assigning committees property rights to components of it. Much as when over-used common grazing grounds are enclosed and given to private owners, this gives committee members the incentive to maximize the value of their portion of the agenda, and only bring to the floor proposed legislation that has the highest value to the committee members. The committee system is a method of assigning private property rights to the legislative agenda that would otherwise be an over-used communal resource (Holcombe and Parker, 1991).

By creating a more efficient system of property rights, the committee system allows a legislature to accomplish much more than could be accomplished in its absence. The committee system may be viewed as specialization and division of labor necessitated by an increasingly complex government, but the causation goes both ways, and an increasingly large and complex government also has been the result of the committee system that has enabled the legislature to do more.

Committees were a part of Congress from the beginning, but the creation of standing committees in the U.S. Congress was controversial in the 19th century, and their importance rose and fell over that century (Polsby, 1968). Prior to 1911 all committee assignments in the House of Representatives were made by the Speaker of the House, giving the Speaker considerable power over representatives in the House. A revolt among House members in 1911 created the modern committee system, and committee assignments were made by a committee on committees which took into account the seniority of members. After 1946 assignments have almost always been made based on seniority, and once a committee assignment is made or a committee chairmanship is assigned, it is almost impossible to take away. Deering and Smith (1997) provide a great deal of institutional detail on the workings of committees in the U.S. Congress.

The seniority system as a legislative institution is complementary to the committee system (Holcombe, 1989). The committee system divides up and assigns private property rights to the legislative agenda, and the seniority system protects legislators' property rights in their portion of the agenda. Without the seniority system, legislators would have

to continually work to protect their right to their committee membership, in a manner analogous to ranchers who must spend their time guarding their herds against thieves. Any time and effort legislators must devote to protecting their rights to committee assignments takes away from the time and effort they will be able to devote to getting legislation passed. Because the seniority system protects those rights, legislators can devote more effort to achieving their legislative goals, making all legislators better off. One might object to the seniority system by arguing that the most qualified and competent legislators on a committee should hold the leadership positions rather than giving irrevocable rights to those positions to those who now hold them, but the system is designed to create a secure right, so legislators can use their efforts to achieve their legislative goals rather than to preserve their committee assignments and leadership positions. The committee system creates a property right to a portion of the legislative agenda, alleviating the common resource problem, and the seniority system protects that property right from being taken by others.

Committee assignments are valuable because committees are able to control the legislative agenda over the issues their committees oversee, giving them a bargaining advantage over other members of the legislature. Legislators seek assignments on committees overseeing those areas in which they have the most interest, and committee members tend to be high-demand members of the legislature (Niskanen, 1971). By controlling their subset of the legislative agenda, committees tend to propose more government activity in the areas they oversee than the median member of the legislature might prefer, and the legislature tends to favor the committee's recommendations over any challenges that might come from legislatures not on the committee (Fenno, 1973, 197). The process of legislative bargaining is designed to give each participant special interest benefits, favoring recommendations from the participants' committees, resulting in more government than would be preferred by the median legislator (Weingast et al., 1981; Holcombe, 1985). In addition to the agenda-setting power committees have, after bills are passed, committee members get a second chance to mold legislation to their liking in the conference committees that reconcile the House and Senate versions of bills (Shepsle and Weingast, 1987).

One consequence of this institutionalization of the legislature through the committee system and the seniority system is that legislators are serving more terms. Until about 1875 about half of the members of the U.S. House of Representatives were serving their first terms. This fell to about thirty percent in the early 20th century, and to less than twenty percent by 1950. The average number of terms served by representatives prior to 1875 was about two, and by 1950 the average representative served more than five terms (Polsby, 1968). Undoubtedly causation is bi-directional. Seniority and the committee system makes seats held by more senior members relatively more valuable, encouraging legislators to run for reelection, and because more senior members are more powerful, constituents have an incentive to vote for incumbents, who always have more seniority than their challengers (Fiorina, 1989).

As Fenno (1973) notes, congressional committees do differ from one another in their goals and in the details of their operation, and there are differences between committee institutions in the House and Senate (Deering and Smith, 1997), but general principles apply despite specific differences. While most of this discussion (and most academic research) has been on committees in the U.S. Congress, state legislatures tend to have similar committee structures, and tend to operate in similar ways. Because the committee system was designed by legislators themselves, and because the institutional details are similar among legislatures, the conclusion that these institutions benefit legislators is reasonable, and there are strong theoretical arguments that lean this way.

RANDALL G. HOLCOMBE

REFERENCES

Cheung, S.N.S. (1970). "The structure of a contract and the theory of a non-exclusive resource." *Journal of Law & Economics*, 13(1): 49–70.

Deering, C.J. and Smith, S.S. (1997). *Committees in Congress*, Third Edition. Washington, DC: Congressional Quarterly.

Fenno, R.F. Jr. (1973). *Congressmen in Committees*. Boston: Little, Brown, and Company.

Fiorina, M.P. (1989). *Congress: Keystone of the Washington Establishment*, Second Edition. New Haven: Yale University Press.

Holcombe, R.G. (1985). *An Economic Analysis of Democracy*. Carbondale: Southern Illinois University Press.

Holcombe, R.G. (1989). "A note on seniority and political competition." *Public Choice*, 61(3): 285–288.

Holcombe, R.G. and Parker, G.R. (1991). "Committees in legislatures: a property rights perspective." *Public Choice*, 70: 11–20.

Niskanen, W.A. (1971). *Bureaucracy and Representative Government*. Chicago: Aldine-Atherton.

Polsby, N.W. (1968). "The institutionalization of the U.S. House of Representatives." *American Political Science Review*, 52(1): 144–168.

Shepsle, K.A. and Weingast, B.R. (1987). "The institutional foundations of committee power." *American Political Science Review*, 81(1): 85–104.

Weingast, B.R., Shepsle, K.A. and Johnsen, C. (1981). "The political economy of benefits and costs: a neoclassical approach to distributive politics." *Journal of Political Economy*, 89(4): 642–664.

COMMONS AND ANTICOMMONS

Commons and anticommons problems are the consequence of symmetric structural departures from a unified conception of property. Commons and anticommons problems have been shown to be the consequence of a lack of conformity between use and exclusion rights (Parisi et al., 2001).

1. Commons and Anticommons: Two Tragedies on Common Grounds

Recently, a new term of art has gained acceptance among law and economics scholars of property law: the anticommons. The concept, first introduced by Michelman (1982) and then made popular by Heller (1998, 1999), mirror-images in name and in fact Hardin's (1968) well known tragedy of the commons.

In situations where multiple individuals are endowed with the privilege to use a given resource, without a cost effective way to monitor and constrain each other's use, the resource is vulnerable to overuse, leading to a problem known as the tragedy of the commons. Symmetrically, when multiple owners hold effective rights to exclude others from a scarce resource, and no one has an effective privilege of use, the resource might be prone to underuse, leading to a problem known as the tragedy of the anticommons. As pointed out by Buchanan and Yoon (2000), the effects of the two problems are in many respects symmetrical.

1.1. The Commons Problem

If a depletable resource is open to access by more than one individual, incentives for overutilization will emerge. As the number of individuals that enjoys free access grows larger relative to the capacity of the common resource, overutilization will approach unsustainable levels and the utilizers will risk the complete destruction of the common good. Although Hardin (1968) terms this destruction the "tragedy of the anticommons," he credits a mathematical amateur named William Forster Lloyd (1794–1852) for formalizing it in a little-known pamphlet published in 1833 on population growth.

Since Lloyd, other economists have identified the problems associated with the common ownership of resources exploited under conditions of individualistic competition. Most notably, Gordon (1954) pointed out that, absent controls on entry, common resources will be exploited even at levels of negative marginal productivity. This is because external effects are not fully internalized within the choice of each individual decision-maker. The sources of externalities in a commons problem are twofold. First, there are static (or current) externalities, in that the use of the resource reduces the benefit from usage to others. Secondly, there are possible dynamic (or future) externalities because the use of a renewable resource today bears its consequences into the future. Due to the lack of conformity between use and exclusion rights, individuals do not have to consider the full social costs of their activities. Private and social returns diverge and total use by all parties exceeds the social wealth maximizing point.

1.2. The Anticommons Problem

The term "anticommons" was coined by Michelman (1982) in an article on ethics, economics and the law of property (Michelman, 1982). Michelman defined the anticommons as "a type of property in which everyone always has rights respecting the objects in regime, and no one, consequently, is ever privileged to use any of them except as particularly authorized by others" (Michelman, 1982), which had almost no counterpart in real-world property relations. The hypothetical example would be that of a wilderness preserve where any person has standing to enforce the wilderness conservation laws and regulations.

Heller (1998) revitalized the concept in an article on the transition to market institutions in contemporary Russia, where he discusses the intriguing prevalence of empty storefronts in Moscow. Storefronts in Moscow are subject to underuse because there are too many owners (local, regional and federal government agencies, mafia, etc.) holding the right to exclude. The definition of the anticommons as employed by Heller is "a property regime in which multiple owners hold effective rights of exclusion in a scarce resource" (Heller, 1998, 668).

In the "tragedy of the anticommons," the coexistence of multiple exclusion rights creates conditions for suboptimal use of the common resource. If the common resource is subject to multiple exclusion rights held by two or more individuals, each co-owner will have incentives to withhold resources from other users to an inefficient level. In the presence of concurrent controls on entry exercised by individual co-owners acting under conditions of individualistic competition, exclusion rights will be exercised even when the use of the common resource by one party could yield net social benefits. To put it differently, some common resources will remain idle even in the economic region of positive marginal productivity. Again, this is because the multiple holders of exclusion rights do not fully internalize the cost created by the enforcement of their right to exclude others.

As with the commons problem, the sources of externalities in an anticommons problem are also twofold. First, there are static (or current) externalities, in that the exercise of a right of exclusion by one member reduces or eliminates the value of similar rights held by other individuals. In price theory terms, one can think of this externality as the cross price effect of the various exclusion rights. Second, the withholding of productive resources may create dynamic (or future) externalities, because the underuse of productive inputs today bears its consequences into the future, as standard growth theory suggests.

2. In Search for a Common Ground: A Unified Conception of Property

The symmetrical features of commons and anticommons cases are the result of the same underlying problem. In both situations there is a misalignment of the private and social incentives of multiple owners in the use of a common resource. The misalignment is due to the presence of externalities that are not captured in the calculus of interests of the users (commons situations) and excluders (anticommons situations).

The unitary basis of the problem can be understood in terms of the traditional structure of a property right. According to the traditional conception of property, owners enjoy a bundle of rights over their property which include, among other things, the right to use their property and the right to exclude others from it. In such a framework, the owner's rights of use and exclusion are exercised over a similar domain. Right to use and right to exclude are, in this sense, complementary attributes of a unified bundle of property rights.

The commons and anticommons problems can be seen as deviations in symmetric directions. In commons situations, the right to use is stretched beyond the effective right (or power) to exclude others. Conversely, in anticommons situations, the co-owners' rights of use are compressed, and potentially eliminated, by overshadowing rights of exclusion held by other co-owners. In both commons and anticommons cases, rights of use and rights of exclusion have non-conforming boundaries. Such lack of conformity causes a welfare loss due to the forgone synergies between those complementary features of a unified property right.

This conceptualization of the commons and anticommons suggests a link between the welfare losses of the two cases and a dual model of property. As noted above, welfare losses are produced by a discrepancy between the rights of use and the rights of exclusion held by the various owners. The problem is in this way detached from the usual understanding of the tragedy of the commons as a consequence of poorly defined or absent property rights (Cheung, 1987). Common and anticommons problems are not confined to situations of insufficient or excessive fragmentation of ownership, but result from the dismemberment and resulting non-conformity between the internal entitlements of the property right.

It follows that the qualitative results of the commons and anticommons models represent limit points along a continuum, each characterized by different levels of discrepancy between use and exclusion rights, with varying welfare losses from commons or anticommons problems.

FRANCESCO PARISI
BEN DEPOORTER

REFERENCES

Buchanan, James M. and Yoon, Yong J. (2000). "Symmetric tragedies: Commons and Anticommons," *Journal of Law and Economics*, 43(1): 1–13.

Cheung, S.N.S. (1987). "Common property rights." *New Palgrave Dictionary of Economics*, 1: 504–505.

Gordon, H.S. (1954). "The Economic Theory of a Common Property Resource: The Fishery," *Journal of Political Economy*, 62: (April) 124–142.

Hardin, G. (1968). "The tragedy of the Commons." *Science*, 162: 1243–1248.

Heller, M.A. (1998). "The tragedy of the Anticommons: property in the transition from Marx to markets." *Harvard Law Review*, 111: 621.

Heller, M.A. (1999). "The boundaries of private property." *Yale Law Review*, 108: 1163–1223.

Michelman, F.I. (1968). "Property, utility and fairness: comments on the ethical foundations of Just Compensation Law." *Harvard Law Review*, 80(6): 1165–1258.

Michaelman, F.I. (1982). "Ethics, economics and the law of property." *Nomos*, 24(3): 9.

Parisi, F., Schulz, N., and Depoorter, B. (2001). "Fragmentation in property: vertical and horizontal Anticommons." *Journal of Institutional and Theoretical Economics*, (forthcoming).

CONSTITUTION

The word "Constitution" has two distinct although intermixed meanings. In the first place it can simply be a set of rules for the functioning of the government. It establishes for example a two chamber Legislature and an independent executive branch in the case of the United States, but parliamentary supremacy in England. It should be said that England can be argued not to have a true Constitution even in this sense. The gradual reduction and power of the House of Lords for example proceeded through a sequence of simple parliamentary acts.

It is possible for non-democratic governments to have a set of internal rules that can be called "Constitutions," mainly for administrative convenience. The current dictator of Pakistan has revised the Constitution several times for the apparent purpose of solidifying his power. Needless to say under the circumstances, the Constitution is of only minor importance.

The other meaning of Constitution, that is perhaps best exemplified by the United States, involves restrictions on the functioning of the government mainly in order to protect certain liberties of the citizenry or to prevent government organs from expanding their power by trenching on the powers of other organs. It is frequently said that the American Constitution was deliberately designed to provide conflict between the three principal branches of the federal government — the legislature, the executive and the judiciary — and between the federal government as a whole and the states. If this was the intent it clearly has not succeeded, since the United States has experienced significant conflicts of both kinds, conflicts that on balance have restricted the growth of government.

Unfortunately although this has restricted the growth of government, it has not prevented it. Large-scale transfers from the federal to the state governments have greatly reduced the potential for conflict between the states and federal government. The conflict in the federal government, however, has continued. It is far from clear which of the three main branches, Executive, Legislative and Judicial is winning the power struggle.

The Supreme Court has recently assumed an essentially legislative role. Cheered on by the large majority of U.S. law professors, it has recently taken the position that it is the body that should take the lead in changing the ethical code. The recent decisions about death penalties included, for example, language about public opinion on the subject with the apparent view that the Supreme Court should follow the views of the public rather than leaving these to elected officials. But this is only a more overt expression of a policy position that has been gradually growing in legal decisions.

To take a quite different example, the United Kingdom is an example of a country without a written constitution and yet, that possesses an informal constitution enforced through a slowly evolving common law system. The common law system itself has been eroded by legislation. For example, civil cases are no longer tried with juries. Further, the English equivalent of the American Fifth Amendment is now largely in abeyance. Further, the Home Secretary of the British Labour Government is attempting to remove trial by jury even in criminal cases. The development of separate quasi governments in Scotland and Wales is also an example of changes which are politically feasible in the absence a written Constitution and with a general acceptance of the supremacy of Parliament. Nevertheless, the British government is far from tyrannical.

Needless to say these are not the only two countries that have Constitutions, but they are examples of the two extremes. The American Constitution is formally strong and the British Constitution is formally weak. Most other democracies lie between these two extremes. For undemocratic governments, the Constitution is normally merely a convenience for the ruling dictators rather than a constraint on their actions.

GORDON TULLOCK

REFERENCES

Buchanan, J.M. and Tullock, G. (1962). *The Calculus of* Consent. Ann Arbor: University of Michigan Press.
Mueller, D.C. (1996). *Constitutional Democracy.* Oxford: Oxford University Press.
Tullock, G. (1987). *Autocracy.* Boston: Kluwer Acacemic Publishers.

CONSTITUTIONAL FRAMEWORKS AND ECONOMIC PROGRESS

1. Introduction

After a century of neglect, economists returned in the mid-twentieth century to the subject of economic growth. The theory of economic growth developed in the 1950s linked economic growth to capital accumulation and technical progress. Growth theory is devoid of an institutional framework. Nevertheless, an institutional framework for transforming the less developed world needed to be put in place as Europe abandoned its colonies, in the 1960s.

The Western industrial nations had achieved a high standard of living through the adoption of the institutions of capitalism, representative government, and rule of law. After the second world war, the nationalists of the less developed world favored socialism, central planning, and dictatorship as the route to transformation. Since socialism was fashionable in Western intellectual circles, few warned that this choice of a development model would doom the less developed world to poverty and dependency.

By the mid-1980s, some asked whether freedom mattered for economic growth. It does, as will be discussed momentarily. But, the thinking in many of the international agencies and in numerous Western nations that were providing foreign aid to the less developed world was that government control of resources and government intervention in markets was necessary to break the vicious cycle of poverty. Men, markets, and private property could not be trusted to bring prosperity. As a result, a generation of government-led economic development programs has been catastrophic. The failure is most egregious in Africa, where many nations have a lower living standard than they had at independence, and where life expectancy in some cases has fallen to where it was at the end of the Roman Empire.

2. The Effect of the Constitutional Framework on Economic Growth

People can use their resources productively and earn a return or they can use the political market to employ them in the directly unproductive or rent-seeking activities of redistributing income from someone else to themselves. The resources employed in these rent-seeking activities have an opportunity cost equal to their return in the privately productive economy, and, their withdrawal into directly unproductive activities affects economic growth.

Institutions or rules arise from many sources (custom, religion, law, constitutions, and so on), and many of these rules have wealth effects. Some institutions or rules (e.g., private property, market allocation) are efficient or wealth-promoting and some (e.g., licensing, price control) are inefficient or wealth-reducing. A rule is efficient in the Hicks-Kaldor sense, if the total wealth gain (benefit) to society is greater than the total wealth loss (cost). Government policy can be evaluated on the same criteria.

An economy is described by an aggregate production function. The production function is a concept that describes the way in which inputs such as capital and labor, combined with technology, are transformed into national output. The constitutional framework is the political, social, legal, and economic framework in which economic decisions are made. Different rights structures affect resource allocation and hence the efficiency of economies. To the extent that differences in the constitutional framework affect the efficiency of these economies, the growth rates of these economies will be affected by the choice of the rights structure.

3. Stylized Facts about Economic Progress and Constitutional Frameworks

Economic growth has remained high in the mature capitalist nations, since the end of the second world war. Real per capita income has grown above 3 percent for 50 years. Aside from the Asian Tigers, with their rapid capital accumulation and export-led growth, economic growth in the Third World has been low (about 1 percent per annum for Africa, about 1.8 percent for Latin America). And, it is not low capital accumulation, per se, that is the problem. The growth rate of real gross per capita investment actually is higher in Africa than it is in Europe/North America.

Capital formation (both physical and human) and technical progress are the main engines of growth. But, not all nations are equally adept at transforming increases in capital and technology into increases in output. Plainly, some are miserably inefficient. The lion's share of that inefficiency arises from poor choices of rules and policy.

If we classify nations on the basis of how much political, civil, and economic freedom they have, here is what we find. Europe/North America and Oceania have the freest constitutional frameworks; Africa is the least free. Asia and Latin America/Caribbean are in between. Africa has the highest incidence of dictatorship, with 90 percent of its nations fully authoritarian. The rule of law is not widely admired in Africa. By classification of their economies, more than 60 percent of African nations are restricted market economies or statist economies. Only 5 of 50 African nations are economically free. The picture is more promising in Asia and in Latin America, but there are pockets of statism and authoritarianism.

If we examine certain aspects of economic policy (money growth and inflation, freedom of international trade, and freedom of capital markets), here is what we find. Measured on a scale of A (best) to F (worst), 30 of 35 African nations score D or F, and no nation scores an A. In Latin America/Caribbean, 14 countries get a B or C and 8 a D or F. Asian nations are about equally divided across the A to F scale. In Europe/North America the modal grade is C, but 11 countries got an A or a B, and only 3 flunked. Oceania has had uniformly bad economic policy.

4. How Important is the Constitutional Framework for Economic Growth?

How much does bad choice in the constitutional framework and in economic policy matter for economic progress? Actually, it matters a great deal. If one considers only the constitutional framework, holding the growth rate of real capital formation constant, the spread in the rate of economic growth of real gross domestic product per capita between the least free and the most free nations is 2.5 percentage points (3.25 versus 0.8 percent). That means it takes four times longer (roughly 88 years versus 22 years) to double per capita income in the poor, unfree nations than it does in the free and rich countries. Economic policy matters, also. Nations with the best policies grow about 2 percent more per annum than nations with the worst policies.

If one objects that per capita income and the growth rate are not the only standard by which human progress is to be judged, consider life expectancy. If one looks at the Third World and compares the free and the unfree nations with real per capita gross domestic product of $1,000 and $5,000, respectively, one finds the following. The predicted life expectancies in the poor but free nation is 57 years compared to 52 years in the poor but unfree nation. In the $5,000 per capita income comparison, it is 73 versus 67 years.

The poor economic performance of the Third World has less to do with capital accumulation and technology transfer, although these do matter, than it has to do with poor choices made in the economic, legal, and political framework and in the economic policies pursued. One is tempted to conclude that a modern standard of living is beyond the grasp of many of these nations without the installation of free institutions and classically liberal policies.

GERALD W. SCULLY

REFERENCES

Barro, R.J. (1991). "Economic growth in a cross section of countries." *Quarterly Journal of Economics*, 106: 407–443.

Rowley, C.K. (2000). "Political culture and economic performance in sub-Saharan Africa." *European Journal of Political Economy*, 16 (March): 133–158.

Scully, G.W. (1988). "The institutional framework and economic development." *Journal of Political Economy*, 96: 652–662.

Scully, G.W. (1992). *Constitutional Environments and Economic Growth*. Princeton: Princeton University Press.

Solow, R.M. (1956). "A contribution to the theory of economic growth." *Quarterly Journal of Economics*, 70: 65–94.

THE CONSTITUTION OF THE EUROPEAN UNION

1. Constitutional Elements in the Law of the European Union

1.1. Introduction

Since the creation of the European Union (EU) with the Maastricht Treaty in 1992, both politicians and legal scholars have often stressed the necessity to create a constitution for the EU. The debate on the constitutional question has recently reached its peak when the "Convention on the Future of Europe" began work in 2002. Among other issues, the Convention is expected to propose a "constitution" for the European Union, or at least some comprehensive document which simplifies and unifies the existing treaty law.

The Constitutional Law of the EU consists of four fundamental treaties. The core is the original Treaty Establishing the European Community (EC; before 1992: European Economic Community EEC) of 1957, which has been amended by the Treaty on European Union (Maastricht Treaty of 1992), the Treaty of Amsterdam (1997), and the Treaty of Nice (2001). The Treaties combined with the judiciary on human rights which the European Court of Justice (ECJ) has developed over the years can be considered to be the constitution of the EU. They contain the classic elements of constitutional law as known from national constitutions: rules on mechanisms of governance, rules on the relation between individuals and the state, and rules for changing the constitution. In particular, the EU Treaties contain some elements which stress the constitutional character of the Union, and which are in contrast to traditional international treaty law, such as the doctrines of direct effect and of supremacy of Community Law, the doctrine of implied powers, and the Community system of judicial review on both Community and Member State level (e.g., Craig and de Burca, 1998; Weiler, 1999).

Public Choice theory may contribute important economic insight to the European constitution in two ways. First, Constitutional Economics, as a subfield of Public Choice, takes constitutional law as *explanandum*. In its normative, contractarian branch, it addresses the process of constitution making and amending, and questions of legitimacy of a European Constitution (Buchanan, 1991; Vibert, 1995). A positive branch of Constitutional Economics (Constitutional Public Choice) analyzes which institutions are likely to be chosen, given the procedural rules as well as the interests of the actors involved in the constitution making process (Mueller, 1996b, 1997). Second, in a view which sees constitutional rules as *explanans*, we can analyze the impact of a given set of constitutional rules (institutions and decision making procedures), and of given interests of the agents involved (Mueller, 1996a; Cooter 2000; for the EU, Mueller, 1997; Schmidtchen and Cooter, 1997). The focus of this article is on the consequences of the rules given by the Treaties. In the concluding sections, we also discuss current problems and concrete reform proposals for the European Constitution, as well as the process of further constitutional change.

1.2. EC and EU, institutions of the EC

The EU is often described as the institutional "roof" over three separate "pillars" of European economic and political cooperation. The most important one is the supranational pillar of the EC, which has evolved starting from the original Treaties of Rome which in 1957 founded the European Economic Community (EEC) and the European Atomic Energy Community (EAEC) (besides the European Community of Steel and Coal (ECSC) founded in 1951). Important policy fields in the EC have been above all market integration, in addition the Common Agricultural Policy, Regional Policy, and since 1992 the European Monetary Union.

The *executive* branch of government in the EC is the Commission. It proposes legislation and, together with Member State administrations, implements EC law. The *legislative* branch of the EU consists of the Council (Council of Ministers or Council of chiefs of national governments) on one side, and the directly elected European Parliament (EP) on the other side. The *judiciary* of the EU is the European Court of Justice (ECJ), which interprets EC law and rules on matters of treaty enforcement.

In addition to the traditional first pillar of the EC, the Maastricht Treaty of 1992 has created two additional pillars of the European Union the Common Foreign and Security Policy (second pillar), and the Cooperation in the Fields of Justice and Home Affairs (third pillar). While in the EC as the first pillar of the EU the traditional, supranational institutions become effective, policy making in the second and third pillars is by intergovernmental cooperation.

2. Institutional Interaction in the Legislative Process

2.1. Voting Rules in the Council

2.1.1. Unanimous Decision Making

In the first decades of European Integration, before the number of Member States significantly increased in the 1980s, the predominant rule for legislation in the Council had been unanimity. Even though it had never been formally part of the EC Treaties, the "Luxembourg compromise" agreement, which demands a rule of unanimity on all matters of "vital national interest," dominated EC politics before the Single European Act of 1986. Unanimous decision making in the Council implies that only Coasean agreements can become Community policies. Since every single Member State government has a right to veto, only policy outcomes within the Pareto set of Member State governments are possible. It is always the least integrationist government which determines policy outcomes, and thus the system is biased towards the status-quo. The predominant procedure of lawmaking is bargaining, which, as opposed to voting, takes the intensity of preferences into account and may thus lead to more efficient outcomes as long as transaction costs are low. Here, mechanisms which can overcome the opposition of single governments while bargaining in the Council are issue linkage, threats, or financial offers.

2.1.2. Qualified Majority Voting

The Single European Act of 1986, which had the aim of facilitating decision making in order to allow for the completion of the internal market, put aside the Luxembourg compromise by promoting decisions by qualified majorities and by giving the commission significant agenda setting power. Qualified majority rule means that larger Member States are given more votes, and it requires the number of votes to exceed a certain level (usually about 72 percent) for decisions to pass. The rule can be seen as a compromise between the idea of giving each state the same number of votes (Senate model), and giving each state the voting power which corresponds with its share in population. Since the number of votes for a Member State is not directly proportional to the share in population, the rule is biased in favor of small states. In order to prepare the decision making procedure for further EU enlargement, the Treaty of Nice signed in 2001 has significantly changed the qualified majority rules: It adjusted the weights of the votes of national governments in a way to decrease the bias toward small states (e.g., the largest states, Germany, France, United Kingdom and Italy, now have 29 votes instead of formerly 10; Luxembourg as the smallest state now has 4 votes as compared to 2 pre-Nice). In addition, the Nice Treaty created two more decision criteria which have to be met simultaneously: Proposals have to be approved by at least half of the Member States — a rule which was included as a response to the fear of small states to lose power. Furthermore, in reaction to the concerns of larger states, proposals have to be supported by as many Member State governments as to represent at least 62 percent of the population of the Union. The Nice Treaty also set the number of votes for the 12 new states expected to join the EU with Eastern enlargement.

If we consider also strategic interaction of governments in Council decision making, it is not only the relative number of votes for a single Member State which determines voting power, but the probability that the votes of that State will be decisive for a specific decision. This aspect of majority voting has been analyzed using power indices, which relate the number of possible voting situations in which a state can change a losing coalition to a winning one, or vice versa, to the total number of possible voting situations (for the EU see e.g., Laruelle and Widgren (1998); Sutter (2000), Felsenthal and Machover (2001)). Table 1 gives an overview on voting power according to the rules of the Treaty of Nice before and after Eastern enlargement using the Banzhaf power index.

Even though, in the course of European integration, qualified majority voting has been extended to an increasing number of policy fields, most of them concerning market integration, unanimous decisions are still required not only for Treaty amendments, but also for policy making in a number of important fields, such as taxation and economic and social cohesion policies, as well as for decision making in the framework of the Common Foreign and Security Policy, and the Cooperation in the Fields of Justice and Home Affairs. In conclusion, while under the unanimity rule the crucial determinant of policy outcomes is the right to veto, with majority voting the important determinant becomes which institutions have agenda setting power, which we will discuss in the following section.

2.2. Strategic Interaction of Institutions and the Horizontal Division of Power

Power indices analysis for the EU has been criticized as focusing too narrowly on decision making within the Council, but as neglecting the strategic interaction of the different institution of the Union (Garret and Tsebelis, 1999; Steunenberg et al., 1999). In the process of European integration, EC Treaty amendments have brought new procedural rules with a systematically increasing degree of involvement of the European Parliament into lawmaking — from the assent procedure via the consultation and cooperation procedures to the co-decision procedure which was introduced by the Maastricht Treaty and further extended by the Amsterdam Treaty (see e.g., Tsebelis and Garrett, 1996).

The two crucial changes in legislative procedure in the EC have been the shift from the unanimity rule to decisions with qualified majority in the Council (as seen in Section 2), and the increasing involvement of the EP in lawmaking. It can be analyzed in game-theoretic settings what impact these developments have on the balance of power between the European institutions, particularly on the discretionary power of the Commission when proposing legislation, and of the European Court of Justice. In most policy fields, the Commission has the power to propose legislation, which the legislative institutions (Council, or Council and EP) can enact, amend or reject. Therefore, the easier it is to enact new legislation for the legislative bodies, the more likely the Commission's proposal is to become law, thus the more discretionary power the Commission has. The ECJ has the ultimate power to interpret EC law. However, judicial interpretation by the ECJ can be repealed by new legislation. Therefore, the easier the legislative bodies can enact new legislation, the less power remains with the ECJ.

Table 1: Voting power before and after Eastern enlargement using Banzhaf power index

| Country | EU of 15 Member States | | | | EU of 27 Member States | | | |
| | • 169 out of 237 votes, and
• 8 Member States, and
• qualified majority represents
62 percent of population | | | | • 258 out of 345 votes, and
• 14 Member States, and
• qualified majority represents
62 percent of population | | | |
Voting rules	No. of votes	Share in votes (percent)	Banzhaf power index	Share in population (percent in 2001)	No. of votes	Share in votes (percent)	Banzhaf power index	Share in population (percent in 2001)
Germany	29	12.2	12.1	21.8	29	8.4	7.7	17.0
United Kingdom	29	12.2	12.0	15.8	29	8.4	7.7	12.4
France	29	12.2	12.0	15.8	29	8.4	7.7	12.3
Italy	29	12.2	11.95	15.3	29	8.4	7.7	12.0
Spain	27	11.4	11.1	10.5	27	7.8	7.4	8.2
Poland	—	—	—	—	27	7.8	7.4	8
Romania	—	—	—	—	14	4.1	4.3	4.6
Netherlands	13	5.5	5.5	4.2	13	3.8	4	3.3
Greece	12	5.1	5.2	2.8	12	3.5	3.7	2.2
Czech Rep.	—	—	—	—	12	3.5	3.7	2.1
Belgium	12	5.1	5.2	2.7	12	3.5	3.7	2.1
Hungary	—	—	—	—	12	3.5	3.7	2.1
Portugal	12	5.1	5.2	2.7	12	3.5	3.7	2.1
Sweden	10	4.2	4.3	2.4	10	2.9	3.1	1.8
Bulgaria	—	—	—	—	10	2.9	3.1	1.7
Austria	10	4.2	4.3	2.2	10	2.9	3.1	1.7
Slovakia	—	—	—	—	7	2.0	2.2	1.1
Denmark	7	3.0	3.1	1.4	7	2.0	2.2	1.1
Finland	7	3.0	3.1	1.4	7	2.0	2.2	1.1
Ireland	7	3.0	3.1	1	7	2.0	2.2	0.8
Lithuania	—	—	—	—	7	2.0	2.2	0.8
Latvia	—	—	—	—	4	1.2	1.3	0.5
Slovenia	—	—	—	—	4	1.2	1.3	0.4
Estonia	—	—	—	—	4	1.2	1.3	0.3
Cyprus	—	—	—	—	4	1.2	1.3	0.1
Luxembourg	4	1.7	2.0	0.1	4	1.2	1.3	0.1
Malta	—	—	—	—	3	0.9	1	0.1
	237				345			

Source: Eurostat yearbook 2002; http://www.ruhr-uni-bochum.de/mathphys/politics/.

2.2.1. Impact of Voting Rules in Council on Power of Commission and ECJ

If the Council has to decide under the unanimity rule, new legislation, which may repeal ECJ adjudication, is difficult and therefore less likely to be passed. Thus, the ECJ has more power of interpretation as compared to decision making by qualified majority (Cooter and Ginsburg, 1997). In fact, unanimous decision making in the years of the Luxembourg compromise has given the ECJ additional discretionary power, which it has in fact made use of, as we can see from the pro-integrationist adjudication promoting market integration during these years. However, if the Council decides with qualified majority, transaction costs of decision making are lower than under unanimity, and new legislation to repeal adjudication by the ECJ is more likely to be passed. Thus, the ECJ loses power of interpretation with an increasing number of decisions taken under a qualified majority rule.

With changes in the procedural rules for enacting proposals made by the Commission, the discretionary powers of the Commission and the ECJ always change in opposite directions. These findings are supported by the observation that in the late 1980s, when, after the dominance of the unanimity rule had been weakened, the Commission became the dominant actor in enhancing market and monetary integration, and successfully put further market integration (implementation of free movement of goods, persons, services and capital) as well as monetary integration (European Monetary Union created by Maastricht Treaty of 1992) on the agenda.

2.2.2. Impact of Parliament Involvement on Power of Commission and ECJ

It has been shown in a similar game-theoretic setting that an increasing degree of participation of the EP in lawmaking has the same effect on the likelihood of ECJ adjudication to be repealed by new legislation as the shift from unanimity to majority decisions in the Council. Thus, as explained above, with an increase in power of the European Parliament, the power of interpretation of the ECJ increases, while the discretionary power of the Commission decreases (Cooter and Drexl, 1994). In this light, the gradually increasing involvement of the EP in lawmaking with the Treaties of Maastricht, Amsterdam and Nice could be one explanation for the relative reduction in influence of the Commission in the 1990s as compared to its dominant position pre-Maastricht.

3. Division of Power between Member States and the EU

In accordance with the Community's primary goal of creating a Common Market, the original EC Treaty gives the Council the necessary powers to achieve that goal (functional definition of competences). As a response to a growing fear of over-centralization, the Maastricht Treaty has introduced the subsidiarity principle as an additional rule of competence assignment. It seeks to allocate policy responsibilities to the lowest level of government at which the objectives of that policy can best be achieved. The subsidiarity principle has often been criticized as being vague and difficult to implement. In addition, it is unlikely to be effective in counteracting excessive policy centralization, since the ultimate power of interpretation remains with the ECJ, whose ruling in the past has been significantly biased towards a centralization of powers in Brussels (Kirchner, 1998; Van den Bergh, 2000). For a more balanced interpretation of the subsidiarity principle, and in order to control the gradual shift of powers related to market integration away from the Member States, it has been proposed to create a special subsidiarity Court of high judges from the Member States (Kirchner, 1998).

4. Relation Between Individual Citizens and the EU: Fundamental Rights

While until the early 1990s the traditional fields of Community policies have all been related to the ultimate goal of market integration, the Maastricht Treaty has created Union Citizenship, a constitutional element until then unknown in supranational law, which, even though not yet filled with significant legal consequences, adds a new element of a direct relationship between individuals and the Union to the Treaties. With respect to the protection of human rights, the ECJ has judicially developed an (unwritten) charter of rights. Although this has gradually enhanced the status of human rights within EU law, this is not (yet) part of Treaty law. An important further step towards the protection of individual rights by the EU is the Charter of Fundamental Rights of the European Union, which was officially proclaimed by the Council of Nice. There is an ongoing discussion about whether the Charter should be integrated into the Treaties of the EU, and, more importantly, whether these fundamental rights will be justiciable for individuals at all, either with the ECJ or with national courts. It has to be seen to what extend the ECJ will apply the charter in its jurisdiction in addition, or even in place of, the existing case law on human rights.

5. Towards "United States of Europe"? Future Challenges for the Constitution of the European Union

5.1. Overcoming the Democratic Deficit

While the shift from unanimity to majority decisions in the Council enhanced political efficiency by lowering the transaction costs of decision making, this development is often criticized as reinforcing the "democratic deficit" of the EU: Single Member State governments, which are directly democratically legitimized by their citizens, can easily be overruled by a majority in the Council. In response to this problem, EC Treaty amendments since the 1980s have gradually strengthened the EP as the only directly elected institution of the EU, most recently by the creation of a co-decision procedure with the Maastricht Treaty, and by applying the co-decision procedure to additional policy fields with the Amsterdam Treaty. However, despite the gradual increase in the power of the EP, it is factually still far from being a second chamber of legislation equal to the Council. For example, even under the co-decision procedure, the Council can still overrule a veto of the European Parliament by unanimity.

Alternative proposals to overcome a potential democratic deficit are an increased involvement of national Parliaments into EC legislation. Also, the election of the President of the Commission by an electoral committee of both members of the EP and members of national Parliaments, or even by Europe-wide direct election is expected to significantly increase the degree of democratic legitimization of the Commission.

5.2. Demarcation of Competences Between Member States and the Union Level

Apart from the interpretation of the subsidiarity principle, which is often seen to primarily refer to issues of market integration, the question of the constitutional demarcation of responsibilities between the EU level and the member will be a crucial controversial issue in further constitutional development. There is an ongoing discussion on whether a catalogue of competences for EU and Member States codified in the Treaties would better serve to protect the remaining power for Member States than more flexible constitutional mechanisms of competence assignment, which have lead to a gradual erosion of state powers in other federal systems.

Another important issue is the future of the second and third pillars of the EU, where further "communitization" may significantly erode Member State sovereignty in foreign policy and justice and home affairs. A further important economic question is whether the European Monetary Union will imply the need for a common fiscal policy, or even a system of transfer payment in cases of asymmetric shocks in the monetary union.

5.3. EU institutions Facing Eastern Enlargement

During the next decade, the EU expects the most extensive enlargement of its history. However, for given institutions, a larger number of Member States increases the transaction costs of decision making in the Council (see Section 2.1 above), as well as the workability of an increasingly bureaucratic Commission. Thus, the Nice Treaty has reduced the number of Commissioners per country. However, since not every Member State will be able to send a Commissioner to Brussels any longer, this may decrease the perception of democratic legitimacy of the Commission in these states.

5.4. The Discussion about the Codification of a "European Constitution"

Since at present, the constitutional law of the EU is spread over four separate treaties, it is often argued that simplification and the reorganization of the basic provisions into one single constitutional document would significantly contribute to making the Union more transparent and more accessible for citizens. Also, integrationists bring forward the argument that a (codified) European constitution would lead to the emergence of Europe-wide constitutional values, which would be a necessary precondition for legitimising the present institutional structure of the EU, as well as provide a necessary basis for further economic and political integration. On the other hand, it has to be questioned whether such common values should be enhanced by a written constitution as long as a common European identity is still missing in the constitutional policy making process. For example, political parties as the crucial institutions for interest aggregation are still organized along national borders rather than pursue common European goals.

6. Conclusion: The Future of the Constitution Making Process

Whether the evolution of the EU towards an "ever closer Union" will continue, even with Eastern enlargement, depends crucially on the way in which constitutional amendments are negotiated, in particular on how national interest are taken account of in that process. So far the procedure of constitutional change has been by Treaty amendments negotiated at European summit meetings, where, besides the Commission preparing documents, the primary actors are Member State governments, and where the decision rule is unanimity. National Parliaments are only asked to ratify a Treaty as a whole, and only some Member States, such as Denmark or the UK, require popular referenda for European Treaty amendments. As an alternative to intergovernmental conferences as the traditional procedure for changing the constitution of the EU, a convention model has recently been tested successfully with the EU Convention for a Charter of Fundamental Rights. In such a convention, not only national governments and EU institutions are represented, but also e.g. national parliaments, or lower level governments. In addition, hearings of NGOs and interest groups can take place in a formalized way, and due to the publication of detailed records the procedure is more transparent for citizens. Thus, the convention model can be expected to increase the degree of representation of citizens' preferences in the constitution making process.

STEPHANIE SCHMID-LUBBERT
HANS-BERND SCHAFER

NOTES

1. For that reason and for simplicity, we will use the terms EC and EU as synonymous, even though, strictly speaking, the EC is only part of the EU, and the European Institutions (Council, Commission, European Parliament, European Court of Justice) are only effective in the EC framework.

REFERENCES

Buchanan, J.M. (1991). "An American perspective on Europe's constitutional opportunity." *Cato Journal*, 10(3): 619–629.

Cooter, R.D. (2000). *The Strategic Constitution*. Princeton: Princeton University Press.

Cooter, R.D. and Drexl, J. (1994). "The logic of power in the emerging European Constitution: game Theory and the division of powers." *International Review of Law and Economics*, 14: 307–326.

Cooter, R.D. and Ginsburg, T. (1997). "Comparative judicial discretion: an empirical test of economic models," in D. Schmidtchen and R.D. Cooter (eds.) *Constitutional Law and Economics of the European Union*. Cheltenham: pp. 108–131.

Craig, P. and de Burca G. (1998). "*EU Law. Text, Cases, and Materials*, Second Edition. Oxford.

Felsenthal, D.S. and Machover, M. (2001). "The Treaty of Nice and Qualified Majority Voting." *Social Choice and Welfare*, 18: 431–464.

Garret, G. and Tsebelis, G. (1999). "Why resist the temptation to apply power indices to the European Union." *Journal of Theoretical Politics*, 11(3): 291–308.

Inman, R.P. and Rubinfeld, D.L. (1994). "The EMU and fiscal policy in the new European Community: an issue for economic federalism." *International Review of Law and Economics*, 14: 147–161.

Inman, R.P. and Rubinfeld, D.L. (1998). "Subsidiarity and the European Union," in P. Newman (ed.) *The New Palgrave Dictionary of Economics and the Law*. London: Macmillan pp. 545–551.

Kirchner, C. (1998). "Competence catalogues and the principle of subsidiarity in a European Constitution Union." *Constitutional Political Economy*, 8: 71–87.

Laruelle, A., and Widgren, M. (1998). "Is the allocation of voting power among EU States fair." *Public Choice*, 94: 317–339.

Mueller, D.C. (1996a). *Constitutional Democracy*. Oxford: Oxford University Press.

Mueller, D.C. (1996b). "Constitutional quandaries in Europe." *Constitutional Political Economy*, 7: 293–302.

Mueller, D.C. (1997). "Federalism and the European Union: a constitutional perspective." *Public Choice*, 90: 255–280.

Schmidtchen, D. and Cooter, R.D. (eds.) (1997). "*Constitutional Law and Economics of the European Union*. Cheltenham: Edward Elgar Publishing.

Sutter, M. (2000). "Fair allocation and re-weighting of votes and voting power in the EU before and after the next enlargement." *Journal of Theoretical Politics*, 12(4): 433–449.

Steunenberg, B., Schmidtchen, D., and Koboldt C. (1999). "Strategic power in the European Union. Evaluation the distribution of power in policy games." *Journal of Theoretical Politics*, 11(3): 339–366.

Treaty of Nice (2001). "*Official Journal*, C 80 (10.03.2001) (see http://europa.eu.int/eur-lex/en/treaties).

Treaty on European Union (1992). Maastricht Treaty. Consolidated version incorporating the changes made by the Treaty of Amsterdam in 1997. *Official Journal*, C 340 (10.11.1997): 145–172 (see http://europa.eu.int/eur-lex/en/treaties).

Treaty establishing the European Community (1957). (consolidated version incorporating the changes made by the Treaty of Amsterdam in 1997), *Official Journal*, C 340 (10.11.1997): 173–308 (see http://europa.eu.int/eur-lex/en/treaties).

Tsebelis and Garrett (1996). "Agenda setting power, power indices, and decision making in the European Union." *International Review of Law and Economics*, 16: 345–361.

Van den Bergh, R. (2000). "Towards an institutional legal framework for regulatory competition in Europe." *Kyklos*, 53(4): 435–466.

Vibert, F. (1995). *Europe: A Constitution for the Millenium*. Aldershot: Edward Elgar Publishing.

Weiler, J.H.H. (1999). *The Constitution of Europe*. Cambridge: Cambridge University Press.

CONSTITUTIONAL POLITICAL ECONOMY

1. Introduction

Representatives of Constitutional Political Economy (CPE) are primarily interested in the analysis of the choice of rules as opposed to the analysis of choices within rules. Buchanan and Tullock (1962, vii) define a constitution as "... a set of rules that is agreed upon in advance and within which subsequent action will be conducted." Defined as such, quite a few rule systems would qualify as constitutions: a firm's partnership agreement as well as the statute of a church. Constitutional economics could thus be conceived of as not primarily interested in a specific subject matter but rather as a specific approach for analyzing a broad number of rule sets. In this contribution, we will restrict ourselves to those rule sets that are to constrain and to enable the representatives of nation-states. On the other hand, we will broaden the scope of CPE by also asking for the (economic) consequences of various constitutional arrangements.

Two broad avenues in the economic analysis of constitutions can be distinguished: (1) The normative branch of the research program whose representatives are interested in legitimizing the provision of public goods by forced contributions (such as taxes) of the citizens. (2) The positive branch of the research program whose representatives are interested in explaining (a) the emergence and modification of constitutional rules (the constitution as *explanandum*) and (b) the outcomes that are the consequence of (alternative) constitutional rules (the constitution as *explanans*).

In the remainder of this entry, we will focus exclusively on the positive branch of CPE. The two branches are complimentary and the normative one is covered by Buchanan's entry "Constitutional Political Economy" in this encyclopedia. Book-length treatments of the topic that deal with both aspects are Mueller (1996) and Cooter (2000). The positive branch is a more recent development. At times, the entry will therefore appear more like the description of a research program than a fully established theory. Voigt (1999) is a book length treatment.

2. Constitutional Rules as *Explanandum*

Constitutional rules can be analyzed as the outcome of certain procedures used to bring them about. Elster (1991, 30) inquires into the consequences of time-limits for constitutional conventions, about how constitutional conventions that simultaneously serve as legislature allocate their time between the two functions, about which effects the regular information of the public concerning the progress of the constitutional negotiations has and about how certain supermajorities and election rules can determine the outcome of conventions. Riker (1984, 2) calls for an extension of traditional rational choice-theory pointing to the fact that in its traditional form it is incapable of taking into account dynamic and creative processes which structure the decision room of the actors.

Procedures are a modus of aggregating preferences. It is hence only a logical step to ask whether and to what extent the preferences of (1) the members of constitutional conventions will directly enter into the deliberations and whether and to what extent the preferences of (2) all the citizens concerned will be recognized in the final document. If the preferences of different groups are reflected in the constitution to different degrees, this indicates that individual utility maximization plays a role even on the constitutional level, a conjecture sometimes denied by representatives of normative constitutional economics.

McGuire and Ohsfeldt (1986, 1989a,b) have tried to explain the voting behavior of the Philadelphia-delegates as well as that of the delegates to the 13 state ratifying conventions that led to the US-constitution in 1787. They show that merchants, western landowners, financiers, and large public-securities holders, *c.p.*, supported the new constitution, whereas debtors and slave owners, *c.p.*, opposed it (1989a, 175). Similar studies for other states are not available but are surely a desideratum for future research.

Procedures and preferences can be used to explain the passing of constitutions. But constitutions get modified over time. Constitutional change that results in a modified document will be called explicit constitutional change here whereas constitutional change that does not result in a modified document — i.e., change that is due to a different interpretation of formally unaltered rules — will be called implicit constitutional change.

One approach towards explaining long run explicit constitutional change focuses on changes of the relative bargaining power of organized groups. If an (organized) group is convinced that its own importance for maintaining order and the surplus accruing from it have increased, it will demand constitutional renegotiation with the aim of securing a higher share of the surplus. In this approach, bargaining power is defined as the capability to inflict costs on one's opponent. Change in (relative) bargaining power will lead to modified constitutional rules (Voigt, 1999, ch. 6).

Boudreaux and Pritchard (1993) analyze the hitherto 27 amendments to the U.S.-Constitution from an economic perspective. They begin with the conjecture that a lobby-group interested in constitutional change principally has two possibilities of seeking its realization: It can either lobby for a simple law or it can lobby for constitutional change. The second option is, however, more expensive. The trivial prediction of rational choice theory is that the group will choose the option with the higher expected utility. In order to be able to have in bringing about implicit constitutional change. Cooter and Ginsburg (1996) show that it depends on the number of chambers whose consent is needed to pass fresh legislation. The higher its number, the more difficult it will be for the other branches to correct implicit constitutional change by changing the constitutional document explicitly. Other variables that influence the amount of implicit constitutional change include the following: (1) If implicit constitutional change can only be corrected by members of the other branches if they change the document explicitly, the necessary majority becomes a factor. The more inclusive it is, the more difficult it will be to correct such change. (2) The possibility of constitutional referenda should be another explanatory variable. If the population at large can overturn the justices, they have an incentive not to deviate too drastically from the preferences of the median voter in their decisions. (3) The extent of implicit constitutional change should be higher in common law-systems than in continental law-systems because in the first group, decisions by justices become directly applicable law (see also Voigt, 1999, ch. 7); whereas in civil law systems they do not, at least in principle.

3. Constitutional Rules as *Explanans*

In the previous section of this entry, constitutional rules have been analyzed as *explananda*. Such an analysis is only of interest if it can be shown that constitutional rules are themselves relevant to bringing about certain results or patterns that concern economists or social scientists in general, or, in other words: if constitutions matter at least some of the time. Possible *explananda* include per capita income, its growth rate, but also income distribution, the stability of a constitutional system, the degree to which human rights are respected etc. (Pummerehne, 1990).

The analysis of economically relevant consequences of the separation of powers has long been neglected almost entirely. In a survey, Posner (1987) writes that the separation of powers increases the transaction costs of governing. This would hold for welfare-enhancing as well as for redistributive or even exploitative measures. North and Weingast (1989) use the British case of the 17th century to demonstrate that the separation of powers can secure property rights because it is one way for the governing to credibly commit themselves. This aspect is also stressed by Barzel (1997) and Sutter (1999) (other recent treatments of the separation of powers include Alesina and Rosenthal, 1996 and Persson et al., 1997; these are critically discussed in Brennan and Hamlin, 2000).

The meaning of the notion of separation of powers has recently been extended beyond the traditional separation between legislature, executive, and judiciary. Now, decisions of the "traditional" government branches to delegate powers to domestic agencies — such as central banks — or to international organizations — such as the WTO or the European Union — are also analyzed under that heading. Epstein and O'Halloran (1999) focus on the U.S. and are interested in identifying the issues that are subject to delegation. Voigt and Salzberger (2002) deal with the question under what circumstances legislatures prefer international over domestic legislation if both are feasible and derive a number of hypotheses in which kind and extent of delegation are a function of the given constitutional structure.

A first attempt to compare the differential effects of unicameral and bicameral legislatures dates back to Buchanan and Tullock (1962, ch. 16). In their analytical frame, that decision-rule is optimal which leads to a minimum of interdependence costs which are defined as the sum of decision-making costs and those external costs an actor has to bear in case his individually most preferred outcome is not the outcome of the collective choice. They conjecture that in comparison with unicameral systems bicameral systems have higher decision costs and continue: "On the other hand, if the basis of representation can be made significantly different in the two houses, the institutions of the bicameral legislature may prove to be an effective means of securing a substantial reduction in the expected external costs of collective action without incurring as much added decision-making costs as a more inclusive rule would involve in

a single house" (ibid., 235f.). The larger the majority required to reach a certain decision, the lower the external costs connected with that decision because the number of opponents to a decision is negatively correlated with the required majority. On the other hand, it will become increasingly difficult to get proposals passed because the decision costs are positively correlated with the required majority. One possibility of keeping the external costs down is to require a supermajority (say of 3/4 or 5/6) in the single house system. Supermajorities in a single house system and simple majorities in a two house system can thus be considered as alternatives. Buchanan and Tullock now conjecture that — given identical external costs — the decision costs would be lower in a bicameral than in a unicameral system.

Miller and Hammond (1989) inquire into the effects of bicameralism and the executive veto — which is sometimes simply considered the third chamber — on stability in the sense that it reduces the probability of cycling majorities à la Condorcet or Arrow (1951). They conclude that bicameralism and the executive veto increase stability. The stability-enhancing effect of bicameralism depends on some preference-difference between the two chambers. Levmore (1992) somewhat changes the focus of the analysis when he conjectures that a bicameral system might be better suited than a corresponding qualified majority in a unicameral system to reduce the power of the agenda setter.

Based on a simple spatial voting model, Feld and Kirchgässner (2001) show how various institutions of direct democracy (mandatory referendum, optional referendum, initiative) can result in an outcome closer to the ideal point of the median voter than in the absence of direct-democratic institutions. They test the model empirically by estimating the effects of direct-democratic institutions on fiscal policy (more specifically public expenditure, public revenue, budget deficits, and public debt) in the cantons of Switzerland. Their model can explain the variance of cantonal public spending, revenue, and deficits quite well. The authors (ibid., 329) conclude that "elements of direct democracy are associated with sounder public finance, better economic performance and higher satisfaction of citizens."

Frey and Bohnet (1994, 73) count the number of times in which the preferences expressed by referendum have deviated from those expressed by Parliament. Between 1848 and 1990, this was the case in 39% of the referenda and the authors interpret this number as a proof of the hypothesis of a better reflection of voters preferences via referenda. Keep in mind that from a rational choice perspective, these cases constitute "accidents" if one assumes that politicians aim at not to be voted against by their citizens and (try to) formulate policies accordingly.

The question of whether societies whose constitutions grant individual rights to their citizens grow faster than societies that do not has received considerable attention over the last couple of years. The most comprehensive study on the relationship between individual economic liberties and growth is due to Gwartney et al. (2000) For the period between 1975 and 1997, 103 countries are evaluated on an index comprising 21 components that puts special emphasis on the security of property rights and the freedom to contract. Two results are of special interest: (1) There is a clear-cut positive relation between individual economic liberty and per-capita income. There is reason to hypothesize that this not merely a correlation but also a causality: Countries scoring best on the index of economic liberties first carried out liberalization and became wealthy only later on. (2) Economic liberties are also significantly correlated with a society's rates of economic growth. Countries that liberalized most between 1975 and 1995 without exception secured positive growth rates. (Pommerehne and Frey, 1992).

Feld and Voigt (2002) inquire into the growth effect of the independent judiciary which they assume to be crucial for the credibility of the basic rights formally granted in the Constitution. They distinguish between *de iure* and *de facto* judicial independence, *de iure* being the degree found in the formal law, and *de facto* being the degree to which it is factually implemented. They find that *de iure* judicial independence is not correlated with economic growth, whereas *de facto* judicial independence is conducive to economic growth. It is thus important to look at the factual implementation of constitutional rules rather than at the constitutional document when inquiring into the economic effects of constitutions.

To sum up — Economic liberties seem to enhance economic growth. Direct-democratic rights tend to make sure that citizen preferences are better reflected in policy outcomes. A federal structure might help to tame Leviathan and make the economic liberties more secure. Some normative conclusions thus almost seem to suggest themselves. Before drawing them, one needs, however, to clarify the conditions that have to be fulfilled in order to implement any of the above institutions successfully.

4. Outlook

As early as 1981, McCormick and Tollison were quite critical concerning the relevance of the normative approach to constitutional choice, writing that "... it is extremely doubtful whether such analysis will make a perceptible difference in the character of prevailing institutions. Normative theory is useful in helping us clarify our norms, but it is another question whether such analysis will impact on the pattern of real institutional development" (ibid., 126). Over the last

couple of years, an increasing number of papers has dealt with positive constitutional economics, and ever more of them appear in leading journals. For the future, an even closer cooperation between scholars of public choice, law & economics as well as the New Institutional Economics promises additional gains from trade. New trends often originate in the U.S., constitutional political economy is no exception to this general observation. This is why the number of empirical studies dealing with U.S. law is so much higher than those dealing with non-U.S. law. But this, too, is changing.

STEFAN VOIGT

REFERENCES

Alesina, Alberto and Rosenthal Howard (1996). "A theory of divided government." *Econometrica*, 64(6): 1311–1341.

Barzel, Yoram (1997). "Parliament as a wealth-maximizing institution: the right to the residual and the right to vote." *International Review of Law and Economics*, 17: 455–474.

Boudreaux, Donald J. and Pritchard, A.C. (1993). "Rewriting the constitution: an economic analysis of the constitutional amendment process." *Fordham Law Review*, 62: 111–162.

Brennan, Geoffrey and Hamlin Alan (2000). *Democratic Devices and Desires*. Cambridge: CUP.

Buchanan, James M. and Tullock Gordon (1962). *The Calculus of Consent — Logical Foundations of Constitutional Democracy*, Ann Arbor: University of Michigan Press.

Cooter, Robert D. (2000). *The Strategic Constitution*, Princeton: PUP.

Cooter, Robert D. and Ginsburg Tom (1996). "Comparative judicial discretion: an empirical test of economic model." *International Review of Law and Economics*, 16(3): 295–313.

Elster, Jon (1991). "Arguing and bargaining in two constituent assemblies," The Storrs Lectures.

Epstein, David and Sharyn O'Halloran (1999). *Delegating Powers — A Transaction Cost Politics Approach to Policy Making under Separate Powers*. Cambridge: CUP.

Feld, Lars and Gebhard Kirchgässner (2001). "Local fiscal referenda — the dampening effect on taxes and spending." *Economic Policy*, (October): 329–367.

Feld Lars and Stefan Voigt (2002): "Economic growth and judicial independence: cross country evidence using a new set of indicators," mimeo (downloadable from: http://www.ruhr-uni-bochum.de/agvwp2/.

Frey, Bruno, S. and Bohnet Iris (1994). Democracy by Competition: Referenda and Federalism in Switzerland.

Gwartney, J., Lawson, R., Park, W., and Skipton, Ch. (2001). *Economic Freedom of the World 2001 — Annual Report*. Vancouver: Fraser Institute.

Levmore Saul (1992); "Bicameralism: when are two decisions better than one?." *International Review of Law and Economics*, 12: 145–162.

McCormicky, R. and Tollison, R. (1981). *Politicians, Legislation, and the Economy — An Inquiry into the Interest-Group Theory of Government*. Boston: Nijhoff.

McGuire, Robert A. and Ohsfeldt, Robert L. (1986). "An economic model of voting behavior over specific issues at the constitutional convention of 1787." *Journal of Economic History*, 46(1): 79–111.

McGuire, Robert A. and Ohsfeldt, Robert L. (1989a). "Self-interest, agency theory, and political voting behavior: the ratification of the United States constitution." *American Economic Review*, 79(1): 219–234.

McGuire, Robert A. and Ohsfeldt, Robert L. (1989b). "Public choice analysis and the ratification of the constitution," in Grofman, Bernard and Donald Wittman (Hrsg.) *The Federalist Papers and the New Institutionalism*. New York: Agathon, pp. 175–204.

Miller, Gary J. and Hammond, Thomas H. (1989). "Stability and efficiency in a separation-of-powers constitutional system," in B. Grofman and D. Wittman (eds.) *The Federalist Papers and the New Institutionalism*. New York: Agathon Press, pp. 85–99.

Mueller, D. (1996). *Constitutional Democracy*. Oxford: Oxford University Press.

North, Douglass C. and Weingast, Barry W. (1989). "The evolution of institutions governing public choice in 17th century England." *Journal of Economic History*, 49: 803–832.

Persson, T., Roland, G., and Tabellini, G. (1997). "Separation of Powers and Political Accountability." *Quarterly Journal of Economics*, 115: 1163–1202.

Pommerehne, Werner W. (1990). "The empirical relevance of comparative institutional analysis." *European Economic Review*, 34: 458–468.

Pommerehne, Werner W. and Frey, Bruno S. (1992). "The effects of tax administration on tax morale," paper presented at the Conference on Tax Administration and Tax Evasion of the International Seminar in Public Economics (ISPE); El Escorial, June.

Posner, Richard A. (1987). "The constitution as an economic document." *George Washington Law Review*, 56(1): 4–38.

Riker, William H. (1984). "The heresthetics of constitution-making: the presidency in 1787, with comments on determinism and rational choice." *American Political Science Review*, 78: 1–16.

Sutter, Daniel (1999). "*Divide and constrain: dividing power to control government*," mimeo, Department of Economics, University of Oklahoma.

Voigt, Stefan (1999). *Explaining Constitutional Change — A Positive Economics Approach*. Cheltenham: Edward Elgar.

Voigt, Stefan and Eli Salzberger (2002). "Choosing not to choose: when politicians choose to delegate powers." *Kyklos*, 55(2): 247–268.

THE CONTEMPORARY POLITICAL ECONOMY APPROACH TO BUREAUCRACY

> *Bureaucracy*: The support staff that is responsible for developing plans, collecting and processing information, operationalizing and implementing executive decisions, auditing performance, and, more generally, providing direction to the operating parts of a hierarchical enterprise. Bureaucracy is attended by low powered incentives (due to the impossibility of *selective interventions*) and is given to *subgoal* pursuit (which is a manifestation of opportunism). Oliver Williamson (1994, 102)

The government may chose to engage in public production, though a preponderance of evidence suggests that public bureau's production costs are higher than private firm's (Bennett and Johnson, 1980; Borcherding et al., 1982). By critically analyzing the theories developed to explain the connection between the behavior of bureaucrats and the costs of producing public sector output, we attempt to elucidate two reasons why this is so. There may be comparative advantages to public supply depending on the nature of the output being produced, and the ease of bargaining, monitoring and enforcing production quality and quantity. In addition, given the goal of politicians is not just to arrange for the production of government goods and services, but also to generate political transfers, the government may, in fact, be choosing the lowest cost producer of public sector output when it chooses the public bureaucracy over contracting out with private firms.

Past theories or "paradigms" formulate several explanations for the divergence between private and public enterprises in production costs. Broadly speaking, three of these key paradigms are Niskanen's budget-maximizing bureaucrat, Alchian and the UCLA School's property rights approach, and Stigler and the Chicago School's regulatory capture theory. The current political economy paradigm integrates these important behavioral approaches with newer political insights into a comprehensive theory of government bureaucracy. Further, the latter also enriches them with notions from sociological economics such as commitment, culture, social capital, and trust. With this in mind, a good theory of public bureaucracy, in our opinion, must account for three elements: bureaucratic self-interest, the effect of competition on bureaucratic behavior, and the role of political institutions. Past paradigms have captured one or even two elements; none of these theories has satisfactorily combined all three into a coherent explanation of bureaucratic behavior. We hope to show that contemporary theory has successfully combined these elements into a coherent approach, though it is still short of complete.

1. The Three Traditional Approaches

Niskanen (1971) identifies a classic principal–agent problem and describes the conditions leading to its existence. His hypothesis asserts that bureaucrats are interested in more of the "3 Ps" — pay, power, and prestige. By maximizing their agencies' budgets, bureaucrats raise their 3 Ps, since each P is positively related to budget size. Niskanen's theory of budget maximization describes the bureaucrat as a self-interested, rational actor whose action is to benefit himself at the expense of voters and taxpayers. This approach captures the element of self-interest, but does not account for observed competition or the institutional oversight structure. Niskanen assumes that the bureaucracy is an effective all-or-nothing monopolist, possessing full knowledge of the legislature's preferences. There is no control of bureaucratic behavior by the legislature through the application of its potential monpsonistic power. Extensions of Niskanen's model attempt to rectify the exclusion of competition and bureaucratic control, but they never develop this element as strongly as they do the idea of unfettered bureaucratic self-interest.

Armen Alchian, his students and followers — loosely termed the UCLA School (Khursheed and Borcherding, 1998) — in the 1960s and 1970s argued that the distinction between public and private firms lies in the structure of property rights, and attribute the higher costs of publicly produced output to the lack of ownership transferability (Alchian, 1965; Alchian and Kessel, 1962). Because voters, the "owners" of the public firm, are so diffuse and unable to buy and sell public firm shares, they have little incentives to monitor the behavior of self-interested bureaucrats. Further, since output is generally not sold in the marketplace, competitive pressures from very close substitutes are absent. This property rights approach concentrates heavily on the effect of institutions, but pays little attention to the actual behavior of bureaucrats and leaves unexplained why such an institution would ever be selected to produce public sector goods and services. Extensions of the work of Alchian et al. account for competition that bureaucrats face. Both Wittman (1989, 1995) and Wintrobe (1987, 1997) published highly optimistic studies that view political instruments, particularly free elections, as able to discipline bureaucrats as effectively as takeover bids discipline private firm managers. DeAlessi (1976) and Demsetz (1982) disagreed with these sanguinary views, stating that political elections only discipline behavior close to election time, and then only imperfectly.

The Chicago School approach, initially described by Stigler (1971) and later modeled by Peltzman (1976) and Becker (1983), describes bureaucratic behavior as wholly controlled by outside interests, and examines political outcomes as emerging from competition between opposing political forces. Politically influential interest groups exert considerable control over public agency policies in an attempt to redistribute income toward themselves, though diminishing returns and transactions costs insure that no

one interest group entirely dominates. Although a theory of political pluralism, the Chicago School ignores not only the role of political institutions, but also the role bureaucratic influences on competition. First, the Chicago group treats political institutions as a detail of no theoretical concern to the analyst (Moe, 1990, 1997). Second, they do not look at bureaucracies as either alternative source of public supply or as control devices used by the legislature. Third, they disregard the power bureaucrats (and public employee unions) have as an interest group to influence the demand for public goods. Among public choice scholars, the Becker–Peltzman–Stigler model is jocularly known as "the theory of politics without the politics." The current political economy approach

Current theory argues that public bureaucracy has particular advantages and disadvantages relative to market contract-out alternatives, based on various economic, political, and social factors which enhance productivity and/or the redistribution of income. The decision to "make-or-buy" goods and services involves evaluating costs, transactions as well as production costs. The former are associated with bargaining, monitoring, and enforcing contracts. The existence of public firms provides evidence that the government finds it less costly to produce certain goods and services itself instead of contracting out production to private firms. Given this insight, the "so-called inefficient" public firm may actually be the least-cost alternative when all motivations, including income transfers, are considered (Borcherding, 1983, 1988; Borcherding et al., 1982). McCubbins et al. (1987, 1989), Milgrom and Roberts (1992), Moe (1990, 1997), and Weingast and Moran (1983), have developed a current paradigm that integrated the three aspects of bureaucratic behavior mentioned above.

Unlike the previous approaches, today's political economy modeling of bureaucracy focuses on the legislature as the monitor of bureaucratic behavior and on the various control techniques it imposes to prevent bureaucratic misconduct and to minimize transactions costs. The key scholars here take as given bureaucratic self-interest, as well as non-minimizing production cost behavior due to the costliness of governance mechanisms. The legislature recognizes this agency problem, however, and attempts to redirect bureaucratic behavior toward desired legislative goals. Two approaches within this current political economy paradigm have attempted to model the legislature as an authoritative monitor of bureaucratic behavior. The first, using legislative supremacy assumptions, accepts bureaucratic self-interest, but does not explicitly include the strategic interaction between principal and agent. The second includes all sorts of strategic interaction between the legislature and bureaucrats, including bureaucratic resistance to legislative control.

The agency literature examines the development of incentive structures in private firms to control the behavior of private firm managers. Alchian and Demsetz (1972) and Jensen and Meckling (1976) see control devices — profit sharing, monitoring, reputational effects and other enforcement techniques incorporated into the governance structure — as specifically designed (or evolved) to align managers self-interest with the interests of the firm. Carrying this idea into the public sector, Milgrom and Roberts (1992) devote their paper to this neo-institutional view of government. The legislature uses control devices such as sunset legislation, agenda control, encouragement of "professionalism" in the bureaucracy, and its own oversight to ensure compliance with implicit contracts and to put itself in a dominant position over the bureaucracy in an effort to reduce waste associated with realizing its policies.

While Weingast and Moran (1983) demonstrated that direct monitoring of bureaucratic action is not necessarily the most economic or effective system of control, indirect methods such as political control of bureaucratic appointments are often less costly and at least as effective. By controlling key appointments at the upper ranks of bureaucracy, Weingast and Moran argued, Congress is able to exert effective indirect control over agency discretion. As a result, the costlier methods of direct oversight and congressional investigations of bureaucratic behavior are less frequently employed. In effect, Congress implicitly steers the bureaucracy from straying off the path it has set, regardless of its seemingly lax monitoring. The public agency behaves as the legislature chooses, since the legislature appoints individuals with similar political motivations to run the bureaucracy, a modern equivalent of the "spoils system," which Wilson (1961) found to be quite effective. In this modern view of bureaucracy, higher public firm costs are not remedial, but reflect political transfers desired by members of the legislature. Weingast and Moran concur that the legislature makes bureaucratic appointments that crucially affect the form and direction these transfers take.

Reversing Niskanen's conclusions, legislative supremacy models maintain an extreme view of congressional dominance where bureaucrats are treated as passive actors. Legislative supremacy models do not wholly answer, however, why bureaucracies produce inefficient public output, since they assume legislature controls them (Weingast and Moran, 1983). Paying little attention to whether and how bureaucrats respond to the actions taken by legislators, these models imply that legislators' control with certainty bureaucratic behavior. A more sophisticated principle-agent model of government supply predicts, however, that self-seeking bureaucrats will search for "loopholes" in the common rules and control devices adopted by the legislature, even if those interests are aligned through key bureaucratic appointments.

In response to this criticism, McCubbins et al. (1987, 1989) known collectively as McNollGast, formulated a second, rather descriptive, but exceeding useful model in which bureaucrats are treated as strategic actors in relation to legislators. Realizing the high transactions costs associated with the use of ex post controls such as monitoring and enforcement, the legislature opts instead to control the bureau ex ante. In order to reduce transactions costs from monitoring and asymmetric information, McNollGast argue that legislatures deliberately design administrative procedures to avoid ex ante agency problems, and to control bureaucratic action without constant legislative supervision. Instead, the legislature requires public agencies to disclose information following specific and often cumbersome procedures identifying the quantity, quality, and completeness of bureaucratic information. This ex ante governance allows the legislature to learn the bureaucracy's plans before they are put into place. This structure and process also slows the speed of bureaucratic action, providing the legislature an opportunity to intervene.

The McNollGast paradigm captures all the important elements required for a complete theory of bureaucratic behavior — bureaucratic self-interest, the effect of competition on bureaucratic behavior, and the role of political institutions. Absent these indirect controls Niskanen's monopoly assumption has merit, but by using "structure and process," the legislature restrains the behavior and aligns the goals of the bureau with their own. According to the property rights view, competition for bureaucratic positions disciplines bureaucrats through fear of replacement and reduces the legislature need to exert control over them. The legislators' participation in the structure and process assures their influence on bureaucratic decision-making and supports the Chicago School focus on the potency of special interests. A signal that public firms could be the low-cost producer of certain goods and services, especially transfers, is seen in the evolution of these disciplinary devices. Therefore, synergies must exist between the legislature and the bureaucracy, which is not present between the legislature and the private industry suppliers.

Unlike McNollGast, Moe (1997) concentrated on the behavior of bureaucrats as opposed to legislators, including a more defined role for interest groups, since they add uncertainty to political outcomes. Since legislators do not own property rights to their current positions, they cannot be sure that the agencies, programs, and rules they created will survive the next political cycle. As Moe (1997, 469) puts it: "Political uncertainty leads legislators to lock in bias to protect the bureaucracy from changes in group power and public authority." He argues that political authorities currently in office make decisions that favor certain special interest in exchange for their political support and ensure that targeted interests continue to benefit from the political system, then and in the future. Thus, biases are built into the system so they cannot be easily altered or dismantled by others in the future. This necessarily provides the bureaucracy with greater autonomy, but in highly constrained ways. Moe concludes that the bureaucracy is rationally conceived by the legislature as a semi-autonomous decision-making entity and political uncertainty leads to a structure of power sharing between legislature and bureaucracy. He attributes the relative high cost of public production to the legislature rationally granting bureaucratic independence, since it anticipates "wasteful" acts by its agents. While in Niskanen's model the legislature is duped by the asymmetric information, in Moe's model the legislature fully consents to the "inefficiencies" of asymmetric information, since it gains in control over other margins which its special-interest clients particularly value. Yet, unresolved is how the current legislature actually locks its biases into the decision-making structure of the bureaucracy.

2. What is to be Done?

Notions of agency costs and deadweight losses along with the neo-institutional methodology expose the logic of bureaucratic contractual forms that have developed within the constraints imposed by political structures. To many economists, society's control devices are only two — markets and polities — yet, there may be a third and possibly powerful constraint: social controls which emanate from customs and morals. The pressure of social values in enforcing contacts, which we will simply term norms, has been much discussed in recent years by economists and others, particularly Coleman (1990), Elster (1989), Frank (1988), Fukiyama (1995), Granovetter (1985), and Kreps (1990). These scholars hold that social capital — the fourth factor of production after the Ricardian triad of labor, land, and capital — reduces free-riding and opportunism and causes individuals to internalize at least some external costs in a Ronald Coase-cum-Talcott Parsons functionalist fashion. This shift towards a new "moral sentiments" analysis is due to the realization that formal markets, common law, statutes, and politically driven policy would not work nearly as well as they do given self-interest fettered only by market and political constraints. Social capital theory with its concentration on customs, morals, reputation, and trust, makes sense of what otherwise would be mysterious deviations from strict self-interest within public agencies (as well as for-profit firms).

Breton and Wintrobe (1982) treated trust relationships as key in understanding the logic of public bureaucracy. They noted that human relationships of a vertical nature within an organization — between superiors and subordinates — when fortified with trust lower transactions costs. Preferences shown certain groups in hiring, attention to education, class, and ideological convictions, care in examining recommendations, encouragement of professional association memberships, are predicted to increase the level of trust in an organization. Horizontal trust relationships among equals and co-workers, on the other hand, can raise the level of opportunism and deadweight costs, since these can act as devices to disguise or cover up chiseling and malfeasance.

Consider political and social environments where a group has a great deal of social capital embeddedness (Granovetter, 1985) which lowers the political cost of formal political contracting. Here social capital is complementary with political action as vertical trust relationships lower the transactions costs of political interaction, while shaping organizational structures and process behavior accordingly. Setting aside whether the notions of social capital theory are yet operational, introducing trust norms into the theory of public supply seems a useful addition to rational choice politics. Courts and legal services, education, the military, fire and police services, and social work all come to mind as activities characterized by deep horizontal and vertical relationships well beyond the links of formal contracting. Can anyone explain the behavior of the fire and police forces in response to the "September 11" incident of the World Trade Center and Pentagon bombing without this element?

3. Conclusion

Our general theme has been that institutions play important roles in channeling behavior in public sector supply and that their shape reflects to some significant degree differential transactions costs. Knowing how institutions condition relative transaction costs at the margin of exchange to the various parties, at least in some first-order sense, is important if one is to understand why some bureaucratic structures have survival value over others. Bureaucratic structures and processes adjust to the private benefits and costs as these costs are internalized by the various individuals and groups that bear them. One key characteristic that varies among the different supply arrangements is the ease of making political transfers. We believe that a more thorough understanding of the positive political economics of bureaucracy must proceed before any serious normative speculations about the bureaucratic invisible hand are undertaken. Finally, we would like to reiterate the major theme that public sector supply mechanisms have many margins of choice beyond the neoclassical price–quality dyad, including the constraining force of social values in enforcing contracts.

THOMAS E. BORCHERDING
PORTIA D. BESOCKE

REFERENCES

Alchian, A. (1965). "Some economics of property rights." *Il Politico*, 30: 816–829.

Alchian, A. and Demsetz, H. (1972). "Production, information costs, and economic organization." *American Economic Review*, 62: 77–95.

Alchian, A. and Kessel, R. (1962). "Competition, monopoly, and the pursuit of money," in NBER, *Aspects of Labor Economics*. Princeton: Princeton University Press.

Becker, G.S. (1983). "A Theory of Competition Among Pressure Groups for Political Influence". *Quarterly Journal of Economics*, 98(3): 371–400.

Bennett, J. and Johnson, M. (1980). "Tax reduction without sacrifice: private sector production of public services." *Public Finance Quarterly*, 8: 363–396.

Borcherding, T. (1983). "Toward a positive theory of public sector supply arrangements." in J.R.S. Pritchard (ed.) *Crown Corporations in Canada*. Toronto: Butterworths, pp. 99–184.

Borcherding, T. (1988). "Some revisionist thoughts on the theory of public bureaucracy." *European Journal of Political Economy*, 4: 47–64.

Borcherding, T., Pommerehne, W., and Schneider, F. (1982). "Comparing the efficiency of private and public production: the evidence from five countries." *Zeitschraft fuer Nationaloekonomie*, 2(Suppl.): 127–156.

Breton, A. (1996). *Competitive Governments: An Economic Theory of Politics and Public Finance*. New York: Cambridge University Press.

Breton, A. and Wintrobe, R. (1982). *Logic of Bureaucratic Conduct: An Economic Analysis of Competition, Exchange, and Efficiency in Private and Public Organization*. New York: Cambridge University Press.

Coleman, J. (1990). *Foundations of Social Theory*. Cambridge: Belknap Press.

De Alessi, D. (1974). "Managerial tenure under private and government ownership in the electric industry." *Journal of Political Economy*, 82: 645–653.

Demsetz, H. (1982). *Economic, Legal and Poltical Dimension of Competition*. Amsterdam: North-Holland Publishers.

Denzau, A. and Munger, M. (1986). "Legislators and interest groups: how unorganized interests get represented." *American Political Science Review*, 80: 89–106.

Downs, A. (1957). *An Economic Theory of Democracy*. New York: Harper and Row.

Fama, E. (1980). "Agency problems and the theory of the firm." *Journal of Political Economy*, 88: 288–307.

Frank, R. (1988). *Passions within Reason: The Strategic Role of the Emotions*. New York: W.W. Norton and Co.

Granovetter, M. (1985). "Economic action, social structure, and embeddedness." *American Journal of Sociology*, 91: 481–510.

Hayek, F. (1945). "The use of knowledge in society." *American Economic Review*, 35: 519–530.

Hirschman, A. (1970). *Exit, Voice, and Loyalty: Responses to Declines in Firms, Organizations, and States*. Cambridge, MA: Harvard University Press.

Jensen, M. and Meckling, M. (1976). "Theory of the firm: managerial behavior, agency costs and ownership structure." *Journal of Financial Economics*, 4: 305–360.

Khursheed, A. and Borcherding, T. (1998). "Organizing government supply: the role of bureaucracy," in F. Thompson and M. Green (eds.) *Handbook of Public Finance*. New York: Marcel Dekker, pp. 43–91.

Kreps, T. (1990). "Corporate culture and economic theory," in J. Alt and K. Shepsle (eds.) *Perspectives on Positive Poltical Economy*. New York: Cambridge University Press, pp. 90–143.

Milgrom, P. and Roberts, J. (1992). *Economics, Organization and Management*. New Jersey: Prentice Hall.

McCubbins, M., Noll, R., and Weingast, B. (1987). "Administrative procedures as instruments of political control." *Journal of Law, Economics and Organization*, 3: 243–277.

McCubbins, M., Noll, R., and Weingast, B. (1989). "Structure and process, politics and policy: administrative arrangements and the poltical control of agencies." *Virginia Law Review*, 75: 431–482.

Moe, T. (1990). "The politics of structural choice: toward a theory of public bureaucracy," in O. Williamson (ed.) *Organization Theory: From Chester Barnard to the Present and Beyond*. New York: Oxford University Press, pp. 116–153.

Moe, T. (1997). "The positive theory of public bureaucracy," in D. Mueller (ed.) *Perspectives on Public Choice: A Handbook*. Cambridge: Cambridge University Press, pp. 455–480.

Niskanen, W. (1971). *Bureaucracy and Representative Government*. New York: Aldine-Atherton.

Olson, M. Jr. (1965). *The Logic of Collective Action: Public Goods and the Theory of Groups*. Cambridge: Harvard University Press.

Peltzman, S. (1976). "Toward a more general theory of regulation." *Journal of Law and Economics*, 19: 211–240.

Stigler, G. (1971). "The theory of economic regulation." *Bell Journal of Economics and Management Science*, 2: 3–21.

Stigler, G. and Becker, G. (1977). "De gustibus non est disputandum." *American Economic Review*, 67: 76–90.

Tiebout, C. (1956). "A pure theory of local expenditure." *Journal of Political Economy*, 64: 416–424.

Weingast, B. and Moran, M. (1983). "Bureaucratic discretion or congressional control? regulatory policy-making by the federal trade commission." *Journal of Political Economy*, 96: 132–163.

Williamson, O. (1994). "Transaction cost economics and organization theory," in N. Smelser and R. Swedberg (eds.) *The*

Handbook of Economic Sociology. Princeton, New Jersey: Princeton University Press, pp. 97–107.

Wilson, J. (1961). "The Economy of patronage." *Journal of Political Economy*, (August): 369–380

Wilson, J. (1989). *Bureaucracy: What Government Agencies Do and Why They Do It.* New York: Basic Books.

Wintrobe, R. (1987). "The market for corporate control and the market for political control." *Journal of Law, Economics and Organization*, 3: 435–448.

Wintrobe, R. (1997). "Modern bureaucratic theory," in D. Mueller (ed.) *Perspectives in Public Choice.* Cambridge: Cambridge University Press, pp. 429–454.

Wittman, D. (1989). "Why democracies produce efficient results." *Journal of Political Economy*, 97:1395–1424.

Wittman, D. (1995). *The Myth of Democratic Failure: Why Political Institutions are Efficient.* Chicago: University of Chicago Press.

CONTRACTARIANISM

Public choice, considered either as an inclusively defined research program or as a subdiscipline that combines elements from economics and political science, emerged in the second half of the twentieth century. The early contributors were, with few exceptions (Riker, Tullock), drawn from the ranks of academic economists (Arrow, Black, Bowen, Buchanan, Downs, Olson, Schumpeter). It is not, therefore, surprising that precursory ideas in political theory, if such ideas were to be found at all, might be located in those works that embodied the same set of hard core propositions that informed economists' whole explanatory enterprise. In particular, methodological individualism, rational choice, and voluntary exchange, which are treated as parameters for scientific inquiry in economics are also incorporated, in both positive and normative application, in contractarian political philosophy, or as sometimes called, social contract theory (Gough, 1957; Buchanan and Tullock, 1962, esp. Appendix I; Buchanan, 1978, 1987).

Methodological clarification is achieved if economics, defined as a scientific discipline, is replaced terminologically by catallaxy, the "science of exchange." In this approach, the elementary starting point is the voluntary exchange relationship between two parties, each one of whom enters into the exchange or contract with the expectation of securing some gain. The mutuality of gains from exchange is the essential attribute of the institutional structure inclusively referred to as "the market."

The exchange or contract theory of the state involves the extension of the explanatory logic of market relationships to collective action, that is, to the realm of politics, generally considered. The contract theory offers an alternative to either the organic model of the state, in which separated individual interests are subsumed into some supra-individualistic and independent collective entity, or the pure conflict model, in which the political interaction among persons is analyzed as one of offsetting gains and losses (zero sum in game theoretic terms).

In a genuine sense, the contract or exchange theory of politics may be interpreted as the view through the economist's window. This Nietzschean metaphor suggests that few would, or could, claim exclusive domain for the contract theory or model, either as positive explanation or as normative justification. Some of the politics that is observed is surely conflictual in nature, and for purposes of discussion it is also often useful to model collective entities as if these have an independent existence.

The relative advantage of the contractarian model lies in the ethical justification that it offers. How can the coercion that necessarily characterizes political action be justified in the absence of some explanatory structure that identifies the mutuality of benefits from such action to all constituents? Neither of the alternative models offers any explanation as to why an individual should not remain, philosophically, always a potential revolutionary. Neither of these models offers a compelling logic for political obligation, for loyalty to the collectivity.

What is the nature of the "contract" or "exchange" that may describe the political relationship? There are two quite distinct exchanges, abstractly considered, that must be discussed. First, consider individuals in some stylized initial setting, some state of nature, that is described by an imputation of generally respected natural rights or boundaries. They recognize, however, that there exist mutually desired "goods" that must necessarily be shared among many or all users (these are collective consumption or public goods in modern terminology; Samuelson, 1954). These goods are not, however, being produced and provided, either at all or in sufficient quantities, because no single person finds it advantageous to make the required outlay. In this setting, each person finds it advantageous to give up some of her own value, measured in private goods, in *exchange* for agreement on the part of others to do likewise. Each person gives up value, measured in tax payments, to secure the greater benefits promised by access to the shared goods (including the protective legal order) that can be financed by the tax payments of all persons in the relevant collective unit (for elaboration, see Buchanan, 1968).

This contract or exchange is strictly confined to the several individuals, each of whom shares both in the payments or contributions for and in the benefits from the shared goods. Ideally, this exchange is voluntary; each person agrees to and abides by the terms of the contract; and all persons secure net benefits. The only difference between this contract and that among the separate contracting parties in the market lies in the number of parties that must be included in the nexus. Ideally, the complex exchange in the shared-goods setting must include all persons in the collective unit, as compared with the simple exchange in the market in which single buyers contract with single sellers. The early contribution of Knut Wicksell (1896) was to point out that the criterion for efficiency, or the signal for mutuality of gains, was the observed agreement among all parties, or, in a political context, the rule of unanimity.

Note that this "logic of collective action" (Olson, 1965) offers the basis for understanding why and how separate persons (families) might join with others in political organization. And, in the stylized or limiting model here, they reach agreement on the terms of exchange. Each person gives up something which she values, measured in taxes, for something she values more, measured in benefits from the shared goods. She does so, however, only when and if others make like commitments.

In this basic logic for collective action, or for politics, there is, in the stylized model, no coercion, as such. Each person enters into the complex exchange process, and each secures net gains from participation. Coercion enters only upon the recognition that persons, in a collective-choice setting, will not necessarily agree upon terms of exchange, even though this exchange may, in net, offer mutual gains. There will exist differential distributional gains promised to those in the group who can succeed in getting the relatively best terms in the exchange. These prospects offer incentives for persons to hold out, to make generalized agreement or consensus almost impossible to achieve.

To secure the mutual gains that collective action promises, persons must enter into a second sort of exchange or contract. They must, both individually and collectively, contract with someone or some group, either chosen from their own ranks or from outside, who will agree, for compensation, to enforce the terms of the more basic contract of collective action. This basic contract involves persons giving up some of their own liberties, which they value, to the "sovereign" in exchange for the services involved in enforcing orderly adherence to the rules of collective action. This second contract, which we may call "Hobbesian" (Hobbes, 1651), essentially brings something that can be called "the state" into being. It is not clear how the "sovereign" can be made to comply with this bargain in the post-constitutional environment.

This conceptual explanation for the origin of the state is perhaps the most important element in the whole contractarian construction. The state, as such, does not exist independently from its establishment by persons who recognize the need for political authority. The familiar illustration is that of the group of workmen who, by separate ropes, are pulling a barge along a canal. They recognize that each member of the group has a private incentive to slack, to free ride, on the work of others, despite the fact that all want to move the barge along. They agree to select one from among their number, to give him a whip or lash, and authorize this person, who now personifies a state, to police against free riding. In this stylized setting, each and every participant gains from the two complex exchanges involved.

In this construction, note that, at least conceptually, the coercion or potential coercion exercised by the state emerges from the agreement among persons. In this sense, the coercion may be brought within the logic of voluntary exchange, which carries with it an obligation on the part of individuals to adhere to the terms, or, in political terms, to think of themselves as citizens rather than subjects.

As Hobbes himself so well recognized, however, the contractarian logic, although useful in explaining the conceptual origins of the state, cannot readily be extended to offer a logic for controlling the state authority, once it is established. How is the sovereign, to whom or to which enforcing authority is granted, to be constrained to remain within the limits of the contractual agreement of establishment? How are the controllers to be themselves controlled (Buchanan, 1975)? This problem has plagued political societies throughout history, and without permanent solution.

Constitutionalism and interjurisdictional competition have in part and on occasion worked to keep the state, once established, within some reasonable bounds. Constitutionalism is based on the notion that political authority, as exercised by the state, remains legitimate only if this authority remains within the limits laid down, explicitly or implicitly, in the set of rules that make up the contract of continuing establishment. The implication is that the state itself must abide by the terms of the contract if it is to command loyalty. In various historical circumstances, constitutions seem to have effectively controlled the state (Gordon, 1999).

Interjurisdictional competition among separate political units may offer another means through which these units may be kept more or less within the terms of the contract of establishment. To the extent that persons, goods, resources, and information can move freely among separate polities, the ability of any one of these units to exploit those persons within its jurisdiction is limited.

Contractarianism, as an analytical window through which the complex reality of politics and the state may be assessed, has been criticized from several perspectives. The approach has, first of all, been widely misinterpreted to be a proffered explanation for the historical origins of states.

As noted previously, however, such explanation has never been the purpose of the enterprise. Second, politics as observed seems to be dominated by conflictual elements rather than by the cooperative elements that contractarianism emphasizes. In part this reality stems from a breakdown in constitutional barriers to state expansion, which, in turn, may itself be traced to failures to understand and to appreciate the logic of contractarianism itself. Third, idealist strands have not been eliminated from political thinking, despite revolutions in both events and ideas during the last century. If politics is viewed, ultimately as a search for some supraindividualistic "truth," out there to be discovered, any relation to individual values becomes nonexistent. Contractarianism is, at base, individualistic; it seems difficult for those to whom individual values count to reject this approach unless all politics is to be deemed illegitimate.

JAMES M. BUCHANAN

REFERENCES

Buchanan, J.M. (1968). *The Demand and Supply of Public Goods*. Chicago: Rand McNally.

Buchanan, J.M. (1975). *The Limits of Liberty: Between Anarchy and Leviathan*. Chicago: University of Chicago Press.

Buchanan, J.M. (1978). *Freedom in Constitutional Contract: Perspectives of a Political Economist*. College Station: Texas A&M University Press.

Buchanan, J.M. (1987). "The constitution of economic policy." *American Economic Review*, 77(3): 243–250.

Buchanan, J.M. and Tullock, G. (1962). *The Calculus of Consent: Logical Foundations of Constitutional Democracy*. Ann Arbor: University of Michigan Press.

Gordon, H. (1999). *Controlling the State: Constitutionalism from Ancient Athens to Today*. Cambridge: Harvard University Press.

Gough, J. (1957). *The Social Contract*, Second Edition. Oxford: Clarendon Press.

Hobbes, T. ([1651] 1962). *Leviathan*. New York: Collier.

Olson, M. (1965). *The Logic of Collective Action*. Cambridge: Harvard University Press.

Samuelson, P. (1954). "The pure theory of public expenditure." *Review of Economics and Statistics*, 36(November): 387–389.

Wicksell, K. (1896). *Finanztheoretische untersuchungen*. Jena: Gustav Fischer.

CORRUPTION 1

Government corruption, from an economic point of view may be defined as the sale by government officials of government goods and services (properties) for personal gain (Shleifer and Vishny, 1993). This sale needs not to be directly beneficial to the corrupted public official. Gains from corruption may go primarily to organisations to which he is affiliated.

The legal concept of corruption may not coincide with the economic one. Some practices that, in an economic view, appear corruptive, may not be unlawful. On the other hand, both the legal and the economic concepts of corruption include sale of lawful acts by public government official for personal gain as granting a visa to persons entitled to it. Corrupters may pay simply to avoid a delay. Thus the concept of corruption includes heterogeneous phenomena.

The empirical research on the extent of corruption in different areas has related it to the most diverse factors of the economic system and of the political, economic, social institutions and even to the type of religion (Paldam, 2000). Yet the "size" of corruption is *per se* an ambiguous concept because it may be referred to the number of corruptive "practices" or/and to their aggregate economic value or/and to the aggregate amount of benefits obtained by the corrupted. These benefits, in turn, have a different economic meaning in countries with different income levels. Indicators of degree of corruption often avoid these definitional questions, because they rely on the "perception of corruption" (Lambsdorff, 1998, 2000) by the business community or by other observers. These subjective judgements normally under-assess the most refined ways of corruption as, for instance, the revolving doors system. Thus the evidence that there is more corruption in underdeveloped than in developed economies, with the same degree of public interventions, if based on "perception" indices, is likely to be misleading. Somebody relies on the amount of crimes of corruption discovered. But countries and regions where police and courts are more efficient and less corrupted detect a greater number of *crimes* of corruption.

The economic effects of corruption are questionable too. In an economy with arbitrary public interventions corruptive practices may improve the allocation of resources. This is normally not the case, with public aids conceived in an orthodox market economy perspective, to promote economic growth. Corruption may result in a waste of resources. Bigger governments and more discretionary public interventions giving room to more corruption, therefore, may result in perverse allocation effects, in spite of their good intentions. Corruption thus, for market economies, may be listed among government failures to be weighed against market failures, when considering the case for or against public intervention.

But public choice analysis combined with modern theory of contracts may offer much help in developing a theory of why, how and when corruption develops and of the proper remedies.

Corruption of politicians may be related to the cost of being elected and to the private component of these costs. The higher these costs, the higher the incentive to corruption and the higher the likelihood that the population of elected politicians consists of corrupted persons or rich people or both. Limits to the private costs of political campaigns have been appropriately suggested to combat these results. As for the electoral systems it may be argued with Myerson (1993) that those, as the proportional system, that promote the entry of new parties and allow a multiplicity of candidates in the same list, defend voters against corruption more than plural systems. Persson et al. (2000), however, argue that single-member constituencies are better than large district in containing corruption, because reduce the costs of the electoral campaign. The greater the magnitude of the district on which candidates make their campaign and the higher the thresholds of the representation, the bigger the spur to corruption. (Polo, 1999; Svensson, 1998; Persson and Tabellini, 1999; Persson et al., 2002) also predict that rent seeking and hence corruption increases if there is political instability which implies shorter legislatures.

The public officials' choice of being corrupt may be analysed as one form of opportunistic behaviour under the principal agent paradigm. It has been argued that a reason why public investment expenditure is often preferred to current public expenditures it is that it allows more corruption. Tanzi and Daawood (1998), by an elaborated cross-country analysis, have shown a positive relation between public investments and corruption. Yet the mere inference that "the more the corruption the higher the amount of public investments" as in Ades and Di Tella (1997) and of Tanzi (2000) might be simplistic. Likely there is an "interdependence" between the extent of public expenditure for investments and corruption. Generally speaking public expenditures for goods and services and for transfers to firms whether for investment or current purposes, offer more room for corruption than personnel expenditures and money transfers to families. But this is not sufficient to infer a systematic distortion against these expenditures. Public bureaucrats may be an electoral clientele and transfers to families increase the politicians popularity. Corruption thus may be one of the causes of the tendency to excessive public spending and deficit. Incentive contracts may reduce the convenience of the bureaucrats of being corrupted, provided that controls are done on their conduct. Thus Becker and Stigler (1974) suggest to pay to public bureaucrats higher than market clearing wages and to periodically control their activities. Ades and Di Tella (1999) use an efficiency wage model of corruption to focus on the effects of rents on wage contracts.

It is maintained that corruption has lesser room where competition prevails amongst public officials (Susan Rose-Ackerman, 1978). Referring to the club theory, a multiplicity of governments seems apt to reduce the extent of corruption, if they are allowed to compete among them and transparency about their results is granted (Fedeli and Forte, 2003). According to Wade (1997), India's central governments because too centralised has originated great corruption in infrastructure policy. But Brueckner (1999) has claimed that corruption is more likely amongst local governments because private local entrepreneurs may have closer ties with local politicians. Fisman and Gatti (1999), by an extensive empirical research conducted by a cross-country analysis, showed a strong, significant relationship between fiscal decentralisation and corruption, because there are more cases of corruption in US states transfer policy than at federal level. One might argue that the states of a federal system, like the US, are more effective in detecting corruption because closer to taxpayers and therefore more stimulated and more efficient in promoting a correct use of public funds. Generally transparency may reduce corruption, via competition among governments.

It has been argued that increasing competition in the market for public procurement may be a way to reduce corruption. The basic idea is that in a perfect competitive market, which implies no excess profits with which to pay the bribe, bribes have no basis. This theory implies that no firm has rents unless it is a monopoly, that the bribes are paid with the rents and that bribes to corrupted officials cannot be shifted in extra government costs. Bliss and di Tella (1997) state that, in spite of the expectations of the beneficial effects of competition on reducing corruption, "countries that have increased levels of competition in the economy have sometimes experienced upsurges in corruption" (p. 1001).

Rent seeking theory seems to us to be the proper place in which to develop the theory of corruption as a chapter of monopolistic/oligopolistic competition (Lerner, 1933–34; Rotschild, 1947; Stigler, 1947; Chamberlin, 1948; Shubik, 1959; Tirole, 1988). The model of rent dissipation introduced by Krueger (1974) and Posner (1975) and then developed with variations by Tullock and Buchanan implies that competition among rent seekers increases the amount that they are ready to pay to get the rents, up to the point of full dissipation is reached. The bidding for Government rents, has been connected with the bidding by advertising for the consumers demand in market economy imperfect competition games (Tollison, 1982). Corruption, then, may be considered as a "selling cost" (as in Butters, 1977) adopted by the firms competing for Government procurement and for public subsidies, to capture the demand for their "services." Obviously the assumption is that this type of selling cost is effective, i.e., that public officials like to be corrupted, being ethically neutral and considering the cost of being discovered as a minor one. In this context, it is possible to analyse corruption with the tools of the oligopolistic/monopolistic competition in market games. Therefore, for a given size of the government's demand for private procurement or for projects to be subsidised, the more the competitors in that market, the bigger the corruption-selling expenses. And *conversely* the bigger the potential demand for procurement and/or of private projects to be financed, the higher the corruption-selling costs, i.e., the amount of bribes. This is necessarily so, because a market in which corruption is allowed to enter as selling costs, is not a perfect competitive market where the demand curves are given and the quantities demanded are only affected by the prices, but a Chamberlinian market where the demand is manipulated, at any given price, by the suppliers. And as in the case of combative promotional practices, in ordinary private economy markets, the effort of any supplier may be balanced by similar efforts by the others. At the end, for each supplier, the demand for his goods (in our case either the procurement of goods and services to government or the forms to be financed by public transfers as providing quasi public good), net of (corruption) selling costs, might be the same. But the (corruption) selling costs have substantially increased.

In the case of the consumers in a private market economy, they may get the benefits of the extra costs for selling expenses, if these expenses translate in better information and consumers services. In the case of governments corrupted by private firms the bribes appear generally a dead weight loss, as the benefits to public officials in rent seeking. The model may be complicated introducing price competition (in the case of transfers to private firms a lower public subsidy for unit of investment or output or unit of employment). But still under product differentiation on the supply side, corruption selling costs may be decisive. Similarly, rent seekers manipulate the political or bureaucratic market for rents. But while in the rent seeking context the maximum to be undergo for these costs for each private competitor is given by the dissipation of the rent obtainable, in the case analysed here of private supply to governments the maximum is determined by the possibility of the private agents of shifting forward the cost of bribes, in extra public expenditures. Government officials may feel that a too high extra cost due to bribes may be too risky. On the other hand private firms, ethically indifferent, but more efficient than the average, may accept the competition by these peculiar selling costs if they have no other alternative place where to compete by reduction of price and no way to demonstrate that their "prices" after due consideration of

the different products, are the best. In other words the market is contestable. In turn, this requires the assumption of transparency, effective controls, freedom of entry of any form in that market. The argument that under transparent markets and free entry there are no margins for corruption has a degree of circularity. If the seller may avail policies to influence the demand curve (corruption being one of them) they may also try to render the market non transparent and to reduce the freedom of entry, by manipulating the decision makers behaviours. The markets may be made both transparent and contestable by appropriate institutions if free trade and multiplicity of governments whose behaviours may be compared.

In spite of the abundance of literature on economics of corruption, public choice has yet much to tell in this area. Particularly important questions to be developed include the case of repeated games, the relations between bureaucrats and politicians, and the diffusion of the ethical norms in society (see Forte, 1995).

FRANCESCO FORTE

REFERENCES

Ades, A. and di Tella, R. (1997). "National champions and corruption: some unpleasant interventionist arithmetic." *The Economic Journal*, 107(July): 1023–1042.

Ades, A. and di Tella, R. (1999). "Rents competition and corruption." *The American Economic Review*, 80(4)(September): 982–993.

Becker, G. and Stigler, G. (1974). "Law enforcement, malfeasance and the compensation of enforcers." *Journal of Legal Studies*, 3(1)(January): 1–19.

Bliss C. and di Tella R. (1997). "Does competition kill corruption?" *Journal of Political Economy*, 105(5): 1001–1023.

Brueckner, J. (1999). "Fiscal decentralization in LDCs: the effects of local corruption and tax evasion," mimeo, Department of Economics, University of Illinois at Urbana-Champaign.

Butters, G. (1977). "Equilibrium distribution of prices with advertising." *Review of Economic Studies*, 44: 465–492.

Chamberlin (1948). *The Theory of Monopolistic Competition, A Re-orientation of the Theory of Value*, Sixth Edition, Cambridge: Harvard University Press (First Edition, 1932).

Fedeli, S. and Forte, F. (2003). "Public co-financing of private sector's investments. Subsidiarity and corruption." *Public Choice*.

Fisman, R. and Gatti, R., (1999). "Decentralization and corruption: cross-country and cross-state evidence," mimeo, World Bank.

Forte, F. (1995). *Etica Pubblica e Regole del Gioco*. Napoli: Liguori.

Krueger, A.O. (1974). "The political economy of the rent-seeking society." *American Economic Review*, 44: 291–303.

Lambsdorff, J.G. (1998). "Corruption in comparative perception," in A.K. Jain (ed.) *The Economics of Corruption*. Kluwer Academic Publishers.

Lambsdorff, J.G. (2000). "The transparency international corruption perceptions index. 5th edition 1999," in *Transparency International Source Book*.

Lerner, A.P. (1933–34). "The concept of monopoly and the measurement of monopoly power," *Review of Economic Studies*, I: 157–175.

Myerson, R.B. (1993). "Effectiveness of the electoral system for reducing government corruption: a game theoretic analysis." *Games and Economic Behaviour*, 5: 118–132.

Paldam, M. (2000). "The big pattern of corruption. Economics, culture and the seesaw dynamics," mimeo, Aarhus University, Denmark.

Persson T., Roland, G., and Tabellini, G. (2000). "Comparative politics and public finance." *Journal of Political Economy*, 108: 1121–1141.

Persson T., Tabellini, G., and Trebbi, F. (2002). "Electoral rules and corruption," NBER Working Paper, 8154.

Persson, T. and Tabellini, G. (1999). "The size and scope of government: comparative politics with rational politicians, 1998 Alfred Marshall lecture," *European Economic Review*, 43: 699–735.

Polo, M. (1999). "Electoral competition and political rent," IGIER Working Paper, 144.

Posner R.A. (1975). "The social cost of monopoly and regulation." *Journal of Political Economy*, 83: 807–827.

Rose-Ackerman, S. (1978). *Corruption: A Study of Political Economy*. New York: Academic Press.

Rotschild K.W. (1947). "Price theory and oligopoly." *The Economic Journal*, LVII: 299–320.

Shleifer, A. and Vishny, R. (1993). "Corruption." *Quarterly Journal of Economics*, 108(August): 599–617.

Shubik, M. (1959). "A Theory of Oligopoly, (Part 1)." *Strategy and Market Structure Competition, Oligopoly and the Theory of Games*. New York: Wiley and Sons, Ch. 10; "Monopolistic competition revisited." ibid., Ch. 8.

Stigler, G. (1947). "The kink oligopoly demand curve and rigid prices," *Journal of Political Economy*, LV: 432–449.

Svensson, J. (1998). "The control of public policy: electoral competition, polarization and primary election," mimeo, The World Bank.

Tanzi, V. and Daawood H. (1998). "Roads to nowhere: how corruption in public investments hurts growth," IMF Staff Papers, IMF, Washington DC.

Tanzi, V. (2000). "Governance, corruption and public finance: an overview," in S. Schiavo Campo (ed.) *Governance, Corruption and Public Financial Management*. Asian Development Bank.

Tirole, J. (1988). *The Theory of Industrial Organization*. Cambridge, Massachusetts: The MIT Press.

Tollison, R.D. (1982). "Rent seeking: a survey." *Kiklos*, 35: 575–602.

Wade, R. (1997). "How infrastructure agencies motivate staff: canal irrigation in India and the Republic of Korea," in Ashoka Mody (ed.) *Infrastructure Strategies in East Asia*. Washington DC: World Bank.

CORRUPTION 2

1. Introduction and Definition

Corruption has been defined by Robert Klitgaard (2000) as "the abuse of office for personal gain." Corruption is an ancient phenomenon (Noonan, 1984 offers an excellent historical account of corruption). Today it appears to be widespread in many developed and most under-developed nations (Susan Rose-Ackerman, 1978, 1999; Klitgaard, 1988; are excellent accounts of the causes, consequences and cures for corruption). Indeed, it can reasonably be conjectured that corruption is one of the primary causes of the continued under-development in South Asia, Latin America and Africa and an important cause of the disappointing performance of the post-communist transition in the former Soviet Union.

Corruption takes many forms. Grand corruption refers to the capture of high offices of government by elites and the use of these offices for private gain. Sometimes this is done by illegal means when it is clearly corrupt. At other times, as in the continued campaign finance scandals in many countries, this form of state capture may be legal, but perhaps insisting that political quid pro quos resulting from campaign finance are not a form of corruption is to use too narrow a definition of corruption. Petty corruption refers to the "tips" and bribes demanded by low-level officials, sometimes to provide services they're supposed to provide for free, and sometimes to bend or break the law in favor of the supplicant. Nor is corruption entirely a public sector phenomenon. Teachers and professors reportedly take bribes for both admitting students and for giving them better grades in both public and private institutions. The senior managers and directors of firms sometimes collude to inflate CEO salaries and occasionally conspire to transfer assets to firms owned by the managers and directors below market prices.

The boundaries of the term "corruption" are not always clear. There is behavior that some would consider corrupt and others not. For instance an informal payment can be regarded as a tip in some societies and a bribe in others. But these disagreements tend to be about relatively inconsequential actions like a patient giving a present to his doctor after the fact. There is little disagreement across societies on whether a judge deliberately making an unfair decision on the basis of a bribe, or a doctor diluting vaccinations to the detriment of public health, are corrupt acts. Few would disagree with the statement that "a doctor in public service who provides sub-standard care to a patient who won't give him a present," is corrupt.

Data on corruption often combines petty and grand corruption, which may in fact be functionally related by the sale of jobs. The data set with the broadest coverage across time and countries is the International Country Risk Guide (ICRG) from Political Risk Services. This is data produced for potential investors interested in the socio-political conditions in the countries where they are considering new investments. The data is based on surveys of international businessmen and is available for many countries from the mid-1980s to the present (Knack and Keefer, 1995 contains an excellent description of this data set). Since the mid-1990s Transparency International has produced annual corruption rankings of countries. This ranking is produced by combining data from at least three sources, hence Transparency International only provides data on countries for which there are at least three independent sources of data (the ICRG data is one of the many sources used by Transparency International). The data is therefore thought to be the most reliable and the annual rankings get considerable press across the world. The data with the widest country coverage is produced by the World Bank (Kauffmann et al., 2000). They use largely the same sources as Transparency International but present data on all countries for which data exists. Most of the studies reviewed below use one of these three data sets- exceptions are the early work of Mauro (1995) who used data from Business International, and Azfar et al. (2001) who use data based on their surveys of the Philippines.

2. Consequences of Corruption

It was once fashionable to argue that in the presence of inefficient regulations, corruption might improve welfare by greasing the wheels of commerce (Huntingdon, 1968; Leff, 1964 however provided an early dissent from this position). It has since been shown that corruption leads to lower growth, poor investment decisions, and worse health and education outcomes. Today, corruption is widely believed to hamper economic development.

First of all, corruption, which was once thought of as just another tax, is now thought to be a particularly inefficient tax. Because public officials often have overlapping jurisdictions over the same economic activity, they often increase rent extraction to extremely inefficient levels much as vertically differentiated monopolies raise prices to extremely inefficient levels (Shleifer and Vishny, 1993). Corruption may also have adverse effects on the allocation of talent, tempting the most talented people to move from production to predation (Murphy et al., 1993).

Second, and perhaps more importantly, when corruption becomes endemic, it can threaten the basic rule of law, property rights, and enforcement of contracts. As Olson (1996), North (1981, 1990), and others have argued, the

benefits of markets can be realized only if they are supported by the appropriate institutions. The development of markets, especially the development of sophisticated markets like the market for capital, needs social peace and the enactment and enforcement of sensible laws. Corruption, which weakens the state, and lowers the enforcement of all laws good and bad, may thus be more likely to retard than augment commerce. Furthermore, corruption may contribute to the very existence of poor laws.

The serious empirical study of the effect of corruption-and more generally misgovernance — on economic outcomes, began in the mid-1990s with the concurrent work of Mauro (1995) and Knack and Keefer (1995) who showed that corruption and misgovernance reduced the levels of investment and economic growth. A large number of subsequent studies have corroborated these findings.

Corruption has also been shown to distort public expenditure priorities, diverting resources away from health and education — where senior officials may find it difficult to capture rents- to military and infrastructure investments — where kickbacks can more easily be demanded and received by corrupt senior officials (Mauro, 1998). Corruption has also been shown to have a negative effect on health and education outcomes. This has been show both at the cross-national level by Gupta et al. and at the cross-district level by Azfar et al. (2001). Rajkumar et al. (2001) have shown that corruption undermines the productivity of public expenditures on health and education by showing that the interaction term of health and education expenditures and corruption is negative and significant in regressions of health and education outcomes.

Yet, might it not be the case that in some sectors like international trade, where there are evidently inefficient laws, corruption may grease the wheels of commerce? It appears that even this defense of corruption is flawed because corruption may contribute to the persistence of restrictions on trade. For instance, Lee and Azfar (2001) have shown that countries with higher initial levels of corruption have slower subsequent reductions in tariffs.

There are however a couple of important methodological caveats. First causality is not always easy to resolve in cross-country regressions and more analytic narratives in the tradition of Bates et al. (1998) that helped identify that corruption was in fact the cause of worse outcomes in a few specific instances would help. Indeed such evidence probably exists in newspaper articles and magazines across the world, but a systematization of this knowledge would be helpful. Some papers (like Gupta et al., 2000 on health and education outcomes) do in fact present such anecdotes, and in those cases the concerns about causality are less serious.

Micro-level evidence can also help identify the consequences of corruption. For instance, the time costs of dealing with government officials are positively correlated with bribes paid (Kauffman and Wei, 1999), and businessmen routinely state they are willing to pay to reduce corruption. Businessmen report they do not use the courts because of unfair decisions by corrupt judges and that they spend a fair amount of money on private security forces because the police is corrupt. Businessmen also state they don't participate in bids for government contracts because they think the auction process is corrupt. All these pieces of micro-evidence suggest that corruption is sand rather than grease in the wheels of commerce and a drain on public revenues (see Anderson et al., 1999 for micro-evidence and Azfar et al., 2001b for a review).

The second important caveat is that corruption ratings are highly correlated with other measures of misgovernance, and it's generally impossible to disentangle the effect of corruption from the effect of some other aspect of misgovernance on the relevant outcome variable. Again micro-level evidence provides some reason to think that corruption is one of the culprits by showing functional links between corruption and other forms of misgovernance. For instance, the sale of jobs undermines meritocracy in the civil service and thus the quality of the bureaucracy (Azfar et al., 2001b). Thus even if many aspects of misgovernance affect the outcome variable, this may not invalidate the cross-country findings on the harmful consequences of corruption.

The sum of evidence on the consequences of corruption, suggests that corruption is in fact harmful to economic development. This evidence shows that corruption is related to lower investment, lower growth, the diversion of resources away from health and education, and worse health and education outcomes, and, finally, that corruption in fact contributes to the very restrictions its apologists say it helps people avoid.

3. Causes and Remedies

According to the economic theory of crime (Becker, 1968), we would expect the level of corruption to be high when the probability of being caught was low, the costs of being caught inconsequential and the benefits from corruption were high. We might think that the level of education in society and the freedom of the press were related to the probability of being caught (transparency); the degree of democracy and government wages related to the costs of being caught (accountability and wages); and the amount of natural resources, the share of the economy controlled by the government, and the number of regulations over which public officials had discretion related to the benefits of being corrupt (discretion). We might also expect that if government officials did not have a monopoly of force over parts of the economy, for instance if the economy was open to international markets, then the level of corruption would be lower (monopoly). The resulting formula for the level of corruption adapted from Klitgaard (1988) is

Corruption = Monopoly + Discretion − Transparency − Accountability − Wages.

Treisman (2000) shows that corruption rates are lower in countries which have been consistently democratic. Lederman et al. (2001) using a large panel data set of many countries over many years have corroborated this finding. They show that that both being democratic and the number of years of being a stable democracy have strong effects on the level of corruption. Besides being democratic, the form of democracy may also matter. The separation of powers for instance may reduce corruption. The problem with an empirical assessment of this claim is deciding whether presidential or parliamentary systems have a more effective separation of powers. Parliamentary systems have an executive more directly accountable to the legislature but also — perhaps as a consequence — have much closer ties between the executive and the legislature. In fact parliamentary systems appear to have less corruption than presidential systems. The effectiveness of political disciplines may also be related to voting turnouts and the reasons for voting. Azfar et al. (2001) have shown that voting in local elections is correlated with lower levels of corruption across Philippine municipalities.

Weder and van Rijkehem (2001) have shown that government wages are related to lower levels of corruption. However, Lederman et al., and Rauch and Evans (2000) state this result is not robust. Similarly, the freedom of press does not have a robust relationship with corruption.

The results on the links between decentralization and corruption are mixed. Fisman and Gatti (2000) find that countries where sub-national governments control a larger share of expenditure are less corrupt, but they acknowledge this could be driven by reverse causality, as the central governments in highly corrupt countries are unlikely to devolve expenditure authority to local governments. Treisman (1999), using a typology created by political scientists, which ranks some states as federal and others as unitary, finds that federal states are more corrupt.

The openness of an economy might increase the costs of being corrupt as the country would lose internationally mobile resources. Ades and Di Tella (1999) and Shang Jin Wei (2000) have argued that more open economies have lower levels of corruption. However, Knack and Azfar (2002) have demonstrated that the results of Wei and Ades and di Tella are driven by a sampling bias. Smaller countries trade more, and data sets on corruption tend to include all large countries but only well-governed small countries (there is typically data on Luxembourg but not Equatorial Guinea), which creates an artificial relationship between small — hence open — states and good governance. The international mobility of factors therefore does not appear to have a strong effect on the quality of governance. The mobility of labor within the Philippines also appears to have no effect on the level of corruption (Azfar et al., 2001a).

Besides economic determinants, aspects of social structure may also affect the level of corruption. Treisman (2000) has shown that countries with predominantly Protestant populations have lower levels of corruption. Swamy et al. (2001) have shown using both micro and macro evidence that women disapprove more of bribery, that firms managed by women are less likely to pay bribes — in the former Soviet Republic of Georgia — and that countries with more women in public life have lower levels of corruption. The degree of ethno-linguistic fractionalization also appears to increase corruption (Easterly and Levine, 1997).

In broad terms the remedies of corruption consist of reducing monopoly and discretion, and increasing transparency and accountability. In terms of specifics, there are many different kinds of corruption and each needs its own tailored remedy (Klitgaard et al., 2000) is an excellent text on remedies for corruption. An anti-corruption reform can start with a major public announcement (a big splash) followed by the arrest and conviction of some important public figures who have been blatantly corrupt (fry a big fish), but very soon after must move to a reform of incentives that public officials are faced with. There needs to be a reduction and simplification of licensing procedures, a physical separation of supplicants and officials, public statements about the transfer of funds from the government to service providers (Ablo and Reinika, 1998), publicly accessible registries of the assets of public officials, spot checks, legislation allowing private citizens to charge officials with corruption, an increase in civil service pay and a reduction in the size of the civil service. At the political level there needs to be democratization and an end to press censorship. A country that followed this advice may still not eliminate corruption, but might be able to reduce corruption to manageable levels.

OMAR AZFAR

REFERENCES

Ablo, Emmanuel and Ritva Reinikka (1998). "Do budgets really matter? evidence from public spending on education and health in Uganda," Policy Research Working Paper 1926, Africa Region, Macroeconomics 2, The World Bank.

Ades, Alberto and Rafael Di Tella (1999). "Rents, competition, and corruption." *American Economic Review*, 89(4): 982–993.

James Anderson, Omar Azfar, Daniel Kaufmann, Young Lee, Amitabha Mukherjee, and Randi Ryterman (1999). "Corruption in Georgia: survey evidence," mimeo, World Bank.

Azfar, Omar, Satu Kähkönen, and Patrick Meagher (2001). "Conditions for effective decentralized governance: a synthesis of research findings," mimeo, IRIS Center, University of Maryland.

Azfar, Omar, Young Lee, and Anand Swamy (2001b). "The causes and consequences of corruption." *Annals of the American Association of Political and Social Science*, 573: 42–57.

Bates, Robert, Avner Greif, Margaret Levi, Jean-Laurent Rosenthal, and Barry Weingast (1998). *Analytic Narratives*. Princeton.

Becker, Gary (1968). "Crime and punishment: an economic approach." *Journal of Political Economy*, 76: 169–217.

Easterly, William and Ross Levine (1997). "Africa's growth tragedy: policies and ethnic divisions." *Quarterly Journal of Economics*, 112(4): 1203–1250.

Fisman, Ray and Roberta Gatti (2000). "Decentralization and corruption: evidence across countries," World Bank Policy Research Working Paper 2290.

Gupta, Sanjeev, Hamid Davoodi, and Erwin Tiongson (2000). "Corruption and the provision of health care and education services," IMF Staff papers.

Huntingdon, Samuel (1968). *Political Order in Changing Societies*. New Haven: Yale University Press.

Kaufmann, Daniel, Aart Kraay, and Paolo Zoido-Lobaton (1999). "Aggregating governance indicators," World Bank Policy Research Working Paper 2195.

Kaufman, Daniel and Shang-Jin Wei (1999). "Does 'Grease Money' speed up the wheels of commerce?," NBER Working Paper 7093.

Klitgaard, Robert (1988). *Controlling Corruption*. Berkeley: University of California Press.

Knack, Stephen and Omar Azfar (2003). "Country size, trade intensity and corruption," *Economics of Governance* (forthcoming).

Knack, Stephen and Philip Keefer (1995). "Institutions and economic performance: cross-country tests using alternative institutional measures." *Economics and Politics*, 7(3): 207–227.

Lee, Young and Omar Azfar (2000). "Does corruption delay trade reform?" IRIS Center, University of Maryland.

Leff, Nathaniel (1964). "Economic development through bureaucratic corruption." *American Behavioral Scientist*, 8: 8–14.

Mauro, Paolo (1995). "Corruption and growth." *Quarterly Journal of Economics*, 110: 681–712.

Mauro, Paolo (1998). "Corruption and the composition of government expenditure." *Journal of Public Economics*, 69: 263–279.

Murphy, Kevin, Andrei Shleifer, and Robert Vishny (1993). "Why is rent seeking so costly for growth?" *American Economic Review*, 83: 409–414.

Noonan, John T. (1984). *Bribes*. New York: Macmillan.

North, Douglas (1981). *Structure and Change in Economic History*. Cambridge: Cambridge University Press.

North, Douglas (1990). *Institutions, Institutional Change and Economic Performance*. Cambridge, Mass: Cambridge University Press.

Olson, Mancur (1996). "Big bills left on the sidewalk: why some nations are rich and others poor?" *Journal of Economics Perspectives*, 10: 3–24.

Rauch, James and Peter Evans (2000). "Bureaucratic structure and bureaucratic performance in less developed countries." *Journal of Public Economics*, 75: 49–71.

Rajkumar, A. Sunil, and Vinaya Swaroop (2001). "Public spending and outcomes: does governance matter?" mimeo, The World Bank.

Rose-Ackerman, Susan (1978). *Corruption: A Study in Political Economy*. New York: Academic Press.

Rose-Ackerman, Susan (1999). *Corruption and Government: Causes, Consequences, and Reform*. Cambridge, Mass: Cambridge University Press.

Shleifer, Andrei and Robert W. Vishny (1993). "Corruption." *Quarterly Journal of Economics*. 108(3): 599–617.

Swamy, Anand, Stephen Knack, Young Lee, and Omar Azfar (1999). "Gender and corruption." *Journal of Development Economics*, 64(1, February 2001): 25–55(31).

Treisman, Daniel (2000). "The causes of corruption: a cross-national study." *Journal of Public Economics*, 76(3): 399–457.

Wei, Shang-jin (2000). "Natural openness and good government," World Bank Policy Research Working Paper 2411 and NBER Working Paper 7765.

COST AND CHOICE

In the summer of 1954, CE (Ed.) Lindblom and I were invited as guest scholars to the then-flourishing Rand Corporation in Santa Monica, California. Our assignment was to carry out a generalized overview of Rand's research, particularly that done by its economists. It was soon apparent that these economists considered that their primary contribution was simply to elaborate, variously, the elementary notion of opportunity cost. TANSTAAFL (there ain't no such thing as a free lunch) was, and remains, as a first principle to be mastered on the way toward rudimentary economic understanding. Something of value can only be secured if something else of value that could be produced does not come into being. Naive and utopian notions that good things can be created from nothing must be dispelled.

It soon became apparent to us, however, that Rand's economists were often, themselves, naive in their implicit presumption that the decision authorities to whom the research findings were addressed were guided by relative "social" value of the alternatives within the relevant choice sets. Rand's clients, the military authorities, and primarily the United States Air Force, did not choose among their weapons systems options on the basis of comparative nationwide or even systemwide objectives; these authorities chose among such options on the basis of *their own* objectives which may not have coincided with those aggregate efficiency norms, as measured by the economists.

This example suggests that the simple version of opportunity cost, although possibly valuable as a first step, is not sufficiently sophisticated to be of much explanatory use. It is necessary to examine the words "opportunity" and "cost" more carefully. My small book, *Cost and Choice: An Inquiry in Economic Theory* (1969), was an exploratory inquiry.

The word *opportunity* suggests the presence of alternatives as they are confronted by a chooser or decision maker. When we say that someone has an opportunity, say, to go to university, we imply that the person in question could, if she so chooses, reject this opportunity and do something else other than go to university. For the person without financial means, we say that she does not have such an opportunity, by which we mean that she has no choice along this dimension.

Opportunity is, therefore, intimately related to choice, and it has little or no meaning outside of some context of choice. Recognition of this point implies, in turn, that "cost" also when used with "opportunity" must be related directly to the choice setting. "Cost" becomes, quite straightforwardly, the value of the next best alternative that is sacrificed or given up in order to secure that which is chosen.

It follows from this elementary logical relationship that a choice, as confronted by a decision maker, cannot be informed by any scale of comparative values that are external to this decision maker. Opportunity cost, therefore, must necessarily be reckoned in a subjective utility dimension; it cannot be represented in some objectively measurable commodity or resource dimension.

Once this point is accepted, the elementary TANSTAAFL principle seems to be in jeopardy. Suppose that the money or numeraire value of a lunch is, say, five dollars. This principle correctly implies that something that is worth five dollars in the economy that might have been produced has not been produced. "Society" has, somehow, given up the "opportunity" to use five dollars' worth of resources in some way other than providing the lunch.

Well and good. But whose choice has been involved here? Whose evaluation on resources has been determining in making the lunch available? For the person to whom the lunch is offered without charge, TISTAAFL (there is such thing as a free lunch) rather than TANSTAAFL applies. The foregone opportunity involved in choosing to take the free lunch is at least close to zero and is in no way connected to the resource value embodied in the lunch as provided. But who, then, has suffered the opportunity cost that might be reflected somehow in this latter value? Suppose that the free lunch was financed by a tax levied on the citizenry generally. Who chose to impose the tax?

Consider a familiar democratic process. The tax is imposed by a majority of the members of an elected legislature. We may examine the calculus of a decisive member of the majority coalition that makes the fiscal choice here. Such a person does not face the opportunity cost of the lunch financed from tax revenues in any sense remotely related to the measured objective economic value of the lunch itself. There is, of course, an opportunity cost involved in this legislator's choice measured either by her evaluation of some alternative item of collective outlay or by her evaluation of taxpayers' disposition of the five dollars.

The choice calculus just discussed depends critically, however, on the presumption that the legislator is decisive in determining the collective outcome. Consider, however, the setting where a single legislator is one among many in a large body. This person is now called upon to vote for the imposition of the tax necessary to finance the free lunch program. What is the opportunity cost of a vote for the free lunch? It is obvious that this choice may involve little or no reckoning that is even remotely related to the resource value actually involved in making the lunch available collectively from tax sources. That which is sacrificed in a vote for the lunch is, quite simply, a vote against the free lunch. And, in a large group, the value placed on either side of the account may be negligible. In such a setting, as for the final recipient of the lunch, TISTAAFL rather than TANSTAAFL may be more descriptive of the setting. The member of a large-number group who is asked to participate in a collective choice, whether this be a large-number legislative body or a referendum among all voters, finds that the opportunity cost of voting expressively is low indeed (Brennan and Buchanan, 1984; Brennan and Lomasky, 1993). The voter may find that the utility loss involved in giving up a negative vote is almost nonexistent, and if she is moved at all by considerations for the potential recipient of the free lunch, a positive vote may emerge with little or no reckoning of the ultimate resource value that the lunch embodies.

Although the emphasis is seldom expressed in this way, the differences in the opportunity-cost setting offers an effective means of distinguishing "public choice" from "private choice." In the latter, that is, in private choice, as exemplified in the stylized market setting, the individual chooser, whether this be a buyer or seller, bears the total incidence of the choice. The person who pays five dollars for her own lunch bears the full opportunity cost, as measured by the anticipated utility loss from having to forego the enjoyment of that which is given up when the outlay on the lunch is chosen. In the idealized market setting, in which there are no externalities or spillover effects on those who are not direct parties to exchange, there is no value or utility loss suffered by others, just as there is no value or utility gain or benefit. Indeed, this is precisely what is conveyed by the adjective "private" when appended to "choice." In this idealized market setting, TANSTAAFL applies fully and without qualification.

The linkage between the two sides of the choice account, so to speak, is broken once the incidence of any decision extends outside the direct exchange between contracting parties. In this setting, any choice becomes "public" to some degree. But the existence of external or spillover effects does not, at least directly, have implications for the opportunity cost of the choice alternatives. The setting is modified in the sense that the person confronted with choice does not secure either the full utility gains or the anticipated utility losses of the decision to be made. On the other hand, precisely because two sides of the choice calculus are reckoned in utility terms, the decision maker may well include her own evaluation of others' utility losses. The breakdown of the effective linkage between the two sides of the choice account, as introduced by the presence of external or spillover effects, can be used to generate predictions about behavioral changes only under the postulate that choosers are, in fact, more influenced by their own experienced utility benefits and losses, as anticipated, than they are by the benefits and losses that their choices might impose on others. In other, and familiar, terms, if incentives matter, any attenuation of the effective incidence of choice must have predictable behavioral consequences.

As analysis moves beyond the effects of externalities on choice behavior in market-like exchanges and to the institutional structures that explicitly involve "public choices," that is decisions to be made on behalf of, and applicable to, all members of a collective unit, the attenuation of incidence becomes the central feature. A person, no matter what her role, who explicitly chooses for others cannot internalize the benefit and loss utility flows enjoyed or suffered by those person who actually experience the effects of choices made. At best, such a public choosing agent can base her calculus on a translation of these utility flows into her own utility dimensions.

In sum, the degree of "publicness" in any choice may be measured by the attenuation of the incidence of the effects of the decision taken, with idealized market choice at the one extreme of the imagined spectrum here and externally imposed collective choice at the other. Returning to the simple lunch illustration, the person who buys her own lunch is identified as being at the one limit, while the person who pays no taxes at all but is the effective decision maker that imposes taxes on others to finance the free lunch program is located at the other limit.

The subject matter of public choice, inclusively defined, as a research program or subdiscipline, concentrates attention on the choice calculus of persons who are located between these limits, and more specifically on this calculus within those institutional settings where the alternatives are explicitly public or collective. In any such choice calculus, it is immediately evident that TANSTAAFL is not fully applicable, if the two sides of the choice account are understood to be chooser-experienced ex ante utility gains and losses.

The opportunity cost faced by an agent choosing for the whole collectivity, or participating in such choice in any capacity, cannot, by definition, include the anticipated utility losses suffered by others from failure to choose the relevant alternative to that which is chosen. This agent can always, to an extent, if she is so inclined, enjoy the equivalent to the free lunch, with no reckoning for the utility losses suffered by others.

The "market failure" logic that was central to the welfare economics of the mid-twentieth century decades was based on the Pigovian distinction between private cost and social cost. Departures from the idealized limit of market exchanges with no external or spillover effects were identified to warrant politicized correction. Contributors to this strand of literature failed to recognize that any proposed politicized correction, based on the same behavioral models as those allowing for the identification of market failure, would itself embody attenuation of the incidence of the effects of any action (Buchanan, 1962). Public choosers, or choosers for the public, in any capacities (as voters, elected representatives, bureaucrats) cannot, by definition, choose among options on other than calculations of their own anticipated utility gains and losses. The effective scalar cannot, again by definition, be equivalent either to the utility gains and losses experienced by those affected by the actions, or to some imagined dimension measured by economists' reckoning of "social" cost.

Many of the contributions from the related subdisciplines or research programs variously described under public choice may be reinterpreted as applications of the basic principle of opportunity cost, properly understood, to varying choice settings. The commonly encountered statement that "institutions matter" says little more than that differing settings for choice present choosers with differing opportunities. The anticipated value of that which is foregone when a choice is made, which is the proper meaning of opportunity cost, can never be objectified and quantified in such fashion as to make specification of the parameters of choice unnecessary.

JAMES M. BUCHANAN

REFERENCES

Brennan, G. and Buchanan, J.M. (1984). "Voter choice: evaluating political alternatives." *American Behavioral Scientist* 28 (November–December): 185–201.

Brennan, G. and Lomasky, L. (1993). *Democracy and Decision: The Pure Theory of Electoral Preference*. Cambridge: Cambridge University Press.

Buchanan, J.M. (1962). "Politics, policy, and the pigovian margins." *Economica*, 29 (February): 17–28.

Buchanan, J.M. (1969). *Cost and Choice: An Inquiry in Economic Theory*. Chicago: Markham Publishing Co.

Buchanan, J.M. and Thirlby, G.F. (eds). (1973). *L.S.E. Essays on Cost*. London: Weidenfeld and Nicolson.

THE COST DISEASE OF THE PERSONAL SERVICES[1]

The cost disease of the personal services, sometimes called "Baumol's disease," refers to the tendency of costs and prices in a number of services, notably healthcare, education, legal services and live artistic performance, to rise persistently and cumulatively faster than the rate of inflation. This phenomenon has led to pressing social and political problems. Where the activities are provided via the market, less-affluent individuals have been deprived of such services, many of which are generally considered essential for their welfare. Where government finances the services in question, their rising cost has led to dramatic fiscal pressures and has engendered great political controversy. The data show unambiguously that such cost and price behavior of the affected services has persisted with little or no hiatus for as long as the statistical data are available, in some cases well over a century. The evidence also indicates that none of the many different programs various countries have adopted to counteract the cost disease has succeeded. Yet, as will be shown below, the cost disease is not a threat to the general welfare unless the measures taken to counteract it turn out to conflict with the public interest. Unfortunately, socially damaging policy responses are a very real possibility.

The evidence that the cost disease pervades all the industrialized countries seems incontrovertible, though there is often the illusion in any particular country that it alone is infected. Popular attempts at explanation usually entail a search for wrongdoers and the disease is frequently attributed to greed on the part of the suppliers of the services, notably "greedy lawyers and greedy doctors." Where this hypothesis is patently indefensible, as in education, the explanation often offered is incompetence and inefficiency. Yet, while there may indeed be instances of greed and inefficiency, there is reason to conclude that these are peripheral influences, and the fundamental explanation is to be found in the special technology of the affected services and the implications of such technology for the relative rate of productivity growth in those sectors. Their technology tends to make productivity in the pertinent services grow more slowly than it does elsewhere in the economy and that, in turn, makes relative increases in their costs and prices unavoidable.

1. What Types of Service are Affected by the Cost Disease?

The cost disease generally affects only services, not manufacturing or agriculture. But there are also many services, such as telecommunications, that are immune. Only those services whose production is highly labor intensive and *in which it is very difficult to reduce the labor content* have experienced the problem. Besides, as will be shown, they have experienced it with little let up and for very long periods. Because the affected services are characterized by substantial direct labor content it is convenient to refer to them as the "personal services," that is, services whose supply entails direct personal labor. The reasons why just these outputs are affected will be explained below, as the key to the analysis of the cost disease.

2. Significance of the Issue

Over the years, many communities have experienced a decline in the quality of a variety of public and private services. Not just in the United States, but throughout the world, streets have grown increasingly dirty. Bus, train, and postal services have all been reduced. For example, in the 1800s in suburban London, there were twelve mail deliveries per day on weekdays and one on Sundays (Kapp, 1972,

p. 48n). Today, British postal services are held up as an extreme example of breakdown in performance. Parallel cutbacks have occurred in the quality of private services. Doctors now virtually never visit patients at home, though 50 years ago it was commonplace. Today, even some of the most elegant and expensive restaurants serve frozen and reheated meals — charging high prices for what amounts to little more than TV dinners. Overall, the result has been a threat to the affordability and quality of some of the services many associate most closely with quality of life.

3. Illustrative Data on Cost Trends of Personal Services

In the half century between 1948 and 1999 the Consumer Price Index increased at an average rate of about 3.8 percent per year, whereas the price of physicians' services rose 5.4 percent per year. Compounded over those 51 years it increased the price of a doctor visit 125 percent, in dollars of constant purchasing power. An example that is even more extreme is the price of a hospital room, that during this same period increased at an annual rate of 8.2 percent compounded, amounting to an almost 900 percent increase since 1948, in constant dollars (U.S. Department of Labor, 2001). The available data for the real cost of a doctor visit and the real cost of a day in the hospital also indicate that the pattern of sharply rising real costs of these services had virtually no let up, compounding and accumulating throughout the second half of the 20th century.

Virtually every major industrial nation has tried to prevent health-care costs from rising faster than its economy's rate of inflation, but none has succeeded, as Table 1 shows. The table reports for 9 leading OECD economies for the more than quarter century 1970–1998 that real health-care cost per person has grown at an annual compounded rate between 0.8 percent (United Kingdom, Italy) and 7.3 percent (Japan). In the Netherlands, Germany, and Japan real health-care cost has grown even faster than in the United States, with its absence of price controls (OECD, 1998).

The cost of education has a similar record — real cost per pupil in the United States has increased an average of 2.7 percent per year, compounded, between 1965 and 1994. The corresponding figures are 3.4 percent for Canada, 4.3 percent for Germany, 7.25 percent for Japan and 9.7 percent for France. Only in the United Kingdom have these costs not kept up with the economy's rate of inflation (UNESCO, 1999).

These increases in costs occurred despite the fact that doctors' earnings barely kept up with the economy's overall inflation rate during this period (Noether, 1986), and teachers' salaries actually fell behind. Persistent cost

Table 1: Growth rates, real per-capita healthcare costs, 1960–1998

Country	U.K.	Italy	Sweden	France	Canada	U.S.	Netherlands	Germany	Japan
Growth Rate (%/Yr)	0.8	0.8	1.4	3.2	3.5	4.6	4.7	5.2	7.3

increases have also plagued other services such as postal delivery, police and fire protection, libraries, and theater tickets.[2]

4. Why do Personal Service Costs Consistently Outpace Inflation?

These ever-increasing costs may sometimes be attributable partly to inefficiencies in government management or to political corruption. But there is also another reason — one that cannot be avoided by any government administration, no matter how pure and efficient — and one that affects the private service industry just as severely as it does the public sector. The common influence underlying all of these problems of rising cost and deterioration in service quality, which is *economic* in character and expected to grow even more serious with time, is the cost disease.

The problem stems, ultimately, from differences in rates of productivity growth in the different sectors of the economy. It is hardly surprising that productivity growth rates should differ among industries, sometimes substantially. But what is perhaps less widely recognized is the persistence of the pattern. Industries whose productivity growth is relatively slow today are largely the same industries as those for which this was true many decades ago and even longer. This persistence phenomenon is not accidental, and is critical for the analysis.

The cost disease stems from the inherent technology of the personal services and the resulting slow growth in their productivity. Most such services have *handicraft attributes*. They often require slight or large differences in the work done, from one unit of output to another, as when one hospital patient requires different treatment from another. Others unavoidably entail direct contact between those who provide the service and those who consume it. Doctors, teachers, and librarians all engage in activities that require direct, person-to-person contact. Moreover, the quality of their service deteriorates if less time is provided by doctors, teachers, and librarians to each user of their activities.

In contrast, in other parts of the economy such as manufacturing, products and the production processes are uniform for all units of a given product and no direct personal contact between the consumer and the producer is required. For instance, an automobile comes off an assembly line and its buyer usually has no idea who worked on it and could not care less how much labor time went into its production. A labor-saving innovation in auto production need not imply a reduction in product quality. As a result, over the years it has proved far easier for technological change to save labor in manufacturing than to save labor in providing the personal services. Labor productivity (output per worker) in U.S. manufacturing and agriculture has increased at an average rate of something like 2 percent a year since World War II, but the productivity of college teaching (crudely measured by number of students taught per teacher) has increased at a rate of only 1 percent per year during that period. And, in elementary and secondary education labor productivity has actually *declined* — the average number of pupils per teacher has fallen from about 27 pupils per teacher in 1955 to 17 pupils per teacher in 1994, partly because classes have become smaller.[3]

5. Consequences for Costs and Prices

These disparate productivity performances have direct consequences for prices. When manufacturing wages rise 2 percent, the cost of manufactured products need not rise because increased output per worker can make up for the rise in wages. But as we have just seen, the nature of many services makes it very difficult to introduce labor-saving changes. A 2 percent wage increase for teachers or police officers is not offset by comparable increases in productivity and must lead to a substantial rise in municipal budgets. In the long run, wages for all workers throughout the economy tend to go up and down together, for otherwise the activity whose wage rate falls seriously behind will tend to lose its labor force. So autoworkers and police officers will see their wages rise at roughly the same rate in the long run. But if productivity on the assembly line advances, but productivity in the patrol car does not, then police protection must grow ever more expensive, relative to manufacturing, as time goes on.[4]

Because productivity improvements are very difficult for most personal services, their costs and prices can be expected to rise faster, year in and year out, than those of manufactured products. Over a period of several decades, this difference in the growth rate of costs of the two sectors adds up. In this way, personal services have grown steadily more costly compared to manufactured goods, and they are likely to continue to do so.[5]

6. A Future of More Goods but Fewer Services: Is it Inevitable?

If some services continue to become ever more expensive in comparison to goods they can significantly affect patterns of consumption. With continued growth in general productivity in the economy the typical household may well enjoy an abundance of goods that is difficult to imagine. But it may suffer from great deterioration in public services such as garbage removal. The services of doctors, teachers, and police officers may, to the extent feasible, be increasingly mass produced and impersonal, and the arts and crafts may be increasingly supplied only by amateurs, because the cost of professional work in these fields is too high. Many will undoubtedly question whether the quality of life has really increased.

But the cost disease does not make this future inevitable. To see why, one must first recognize that the problem's source, paradoxically, is the growth in our economy's productivity — or rather, the *unevenness* of that growth. Trash removal costs go up, *not* because garbage collectors become less efficient but because labor in automobile manufacturing becomes *still more* efficient, thus enhancing the sanitation worker's potential value on the automotive assembly line. The sanitation worker's wages must go up to keep him at his garbage removal job.

But increasing productivity in goods manufacturing makes an economy wealthier, not poorer. It does *not* make it unable to afford things that could be afforded in the past. Increasing productivity means that a society can afford more of *all* things — televisions, electric toothbrushes, cell phones, *and* medical care, education, and other services (Bradford, 1969).

The role of services in the future depends on how the community orders its priorities. If it values the personal services sufficiently, it can have more and better services — at some sacrifice in the rate at which manufacturing output grows. Society *does* have a choice, and if it fails to take steps to exercise it, plausibly the economy will continue to drift toward a world in which material goods are abundant and many things that most people now consider primary requisites for a high quality of life are scarce.

The problem is that the *relative* prices of the personal services can be expected to rise as a consequence of the cost disease, and this creates the illusion that they are no longer affordable. But the rising real incomes that stem from near-universally growing productivity means that the public need only reallocate some of its purchasing power from the relatively lower priced outputs to those that will grow comparatively more expensive, and it will receive more of both types of output.

7. Government Intervention may Make the Problem Worse

The cost disease is not correctly interpreted as an example of market failure. The market *does* give the appropriate price signals, indicating correctly that the input cost of the personal services, though perhaps even declining slightly in absolute terms, is rising relatively, that is, in comparison to the real input cost of other outputs. But the general public, and government along with it, is likely to misunderstand these signals. The numbers are startling. If current trends continue for half a century, outlays on healthcare and education may well approach half of GDP. Such frightening numbers, along with their current budgetary manifestations, may well lead governments to make decisions that do not really promote the public interest.

For example, because the cost disease drives health-care costs to rise faster than the economy's rate of inflation, if we want to maintain standards of care in public hospitals, it is obviously not enough to keep health-care budgets growing at the economy's prevailing inflation rate. Those budgets must actually grow *faster* if a decline in quality is to be prevented.

Thus, suppose the current inflation rate is 4 percent, but hospital costs are rising at a rate of 6 percent. Then it is to be expected that a political body that increases its hospitals' budgets by 5 percent per year will feel that something is wrong. For, despite the fact that the budget steadily outpaces the inflation rate, standards of quality at the hospitals are condemned to be constantly slipping in this scenario. If the legislators do not realize that the cost disease is causing the problem, they will look for explanations such as corrupt or inefficient hospital administrators. The net result can be a set of wasteful rules that hamper the freedom of action of hospitals and doctors inappropriately or that tighten hospital budgets below the levels that demands and costs would yield if they were determined by the market mechanism rather than by government.

In many cases, *price controls* are proposed for sectors of the economy affected by the cost disease — for medical services, insurance services, and the like. But price controls can only eliminate the symptoms of the disease, and they often create problems that are more serious than the disease itself. These, then, are examples of government failure, the public sector counterpart of market failure. But the resulting damage to the public welfare is self-inflicted, and by no means unavoidable.

WILLIAM J. BAUMOL

NOTES

1. For further materials on the subject see Towse (1997) and Moynihan (1993). For the origins of the analysis see Fourastié (1963) and Baumol and Bowen (1966).
2. On the case of the arts see Frey and Pommerehne (1989); Throsby (1994); Towse (1997); and Blaug (2001).
3. On the educational issues see Ryan (1992). On healthcare see Hay (1992) and Scheiber and Poullier (1987).
4. This must be true of relative *real* input costs even if wages in the different economic sectors change at different rates. It must be true by definition that if product A's labor productivity is rising faster than B's, then the labor cost of B will rise relative to that of A.
5. For further analysis see Baumol et al. (1989).

REFERENCES

Baumol, William J. and William Bowen, G. (1966). *Performing Arts: The Economic Dilemma*, New York: Twentieth Century Fund.

Baumol, William, J., Sue Anne Batey Blackman, and Edward Wolff, N. (1989). *Productivity and American Leadership: The Long View*. Cambridge, Mass.: MIT Press.

Blaug, Mark (2001). "Where are we now on cultural economics?" *Journal of Economic Surveys*, 15 (April).

Bradford, David (1969). "Balance on unbalanced growth." *Zeitschrift für National Ökonomie*, 29: 291–304.

Fourastié, Jean (1963). *Le Grand Espoir du XXᵉ Siécle*, Paris: PUF, 1949, Gallimard.

Frey, B.S. and Pommerehne, W.W. (1989). *Muses and Markets. Explorations in the Economics of the Arts*. Oxford, U.K.: Blackwell.

Hay, Ian (1992). *Money, Medicine, and Malpractice in American Society*, New York: Praeger.

Kapp, Yovonne (1972). *Eleanor Marx*. New York: Pantheon.

Moynihan, D.P. (1993). *Baumol's Disease, New York State and the Federal Fisc: XVII, Fiscal Year 1992*. Taubman Center for State and Local Government, John F. Kennedy School of Government, Harvard University, July 29.

Noether, Monica (1986). "The growing supply of physicians: Has the market become more competitive?" *Journal of Labor Economics*, 4: 503–537.

Organization for Economic Cooperation and Development (OECD) (1998). *Health Data 1995*. Paris: OECD.

Ryan, Paul (1992). "Unbalanced growth and fiscal restriction: public spending on higher education in advanced economies since 1970." *Structural Change and Economic Dynamics*, 3: 261–288.

Scheiber, G.J. and Poullier, J.-P. (1987). "Trends in international health care spending." *Health Affairs*, 6(Fall): 105–112.

Throsby, D.C. (1994). "The production and consumption of the arts: a view of cultural economics." *Journal of Economic Literature*, 32 (March), 1–29.

Towse, Ruth (ed.) (1997). *Baumol's Cost Disease: The Arts and Other Victims*. Cheltenham, UK and Northampton, Mass.: Edward Elgar.

United Nations Educational, Scientific and Cultural Organization (UNESCO) (1999). *Statistical Yearbook*. Paris: UNESCO.

U.S. Department of Labor, Bureau of Labor Statistics (2001). *CPI Detailed Report*. (January). Washington, DC: U.S. Government Printing Office.

CUSTOMARY LAW

A fundamental insight of the economic analysis of law is the notion that legal sanctions are "prices" set for given categories of legally relevant behavior. This idea develops around the positive conception of law as a command backed by an enforceable sanction. Law and economics uses the well-developed tool of price theory to predict the effect of changes in sanctions on individual behavior. One essential question, however, remains unanswered: how can the legal system set efficient prices if there is no market process that generates them? In other words, how can legal rules reflect the level of social undesirability of the conduct being sanctioned?

Although the legal system sometimes borrows a price from the actual market (e.g., when the sanction is linked to the compensatory function of the rule of law), there is a wide range of situations in which legislative and judicial bodies set prices in the absence of a proper market mechanism. From a law and economics perspective, customary law can be viewed as a process for generating legal rules that is analogous to a price mechanism in a partial equilibrium framework.

Both the emergence of custom from repeated contractual practice and the role of custom as a non-contractual solution to game inefficiencies have been the object of study in both the economic and philosophical literature. Law and economics has revisited this familiar theme, considering the spontaneous emergence of customary law, and, more recently, emphasizing the issue of legal and institutional change in an evolutionary setting (Cooter, 1994; Parisi, 1995, 1998; Posner, 1996; Bernstein, 1996).

One important discussion in customary law centers on the domain of custom among the spontaneous sources of legal order. This discussion explores the formative elements of customary rules and their legal effects. Game-theoretic models become useful tools to evaluate the sufficiency of customary law as an exclusive source of social order (Parisi, 2000a,b). In addition to considering the commonly criticized problems of inaccessibility and inelegant fragmentation, this study attempts to characterize the institutional settings that remain outside the reach of spontaneous cooperation and the situations in which inefficient customary rules may develop. Further, this discussion must address the public choice dimension of the process of customary law formation, considering the potential for norm manipulation.

1. Theory of Customary Law

In the "social contract" framework, customary rules can be regarded as an implied and often non-verbalized exercise of direct legislation by the members of society. Those legal systems that grant direct legal force to customary rules regard custom as a primary, although not exclusive, source of law. In such legal traditions, courts enforce customary rules as if they had been enacted by the proper legislative authority. Custom thus amounts to a spontaneous norm that is recognized by the legal system and granted enforcement as a proper legal rule.

Judicial recognition of spontaneous norms amounts to a declaratory, as opposed to a constitutive, function that treats custom as a legal fact. The legal system finds the law by recognizing social norms, but does not create the law. The most notable illustration is the system of international law, where, absent a central legislative authority, custom stands next to treaties as a primary source of law. Specifically, Article 38(1) of the Statute of the International Court of Justice and the Restatement 102 of the Foreign Relations Law of the United States support this notion.

Whenever they are granted legitimate status in a legal system, customary rules are usually given the same effect as other primary sources of law. Although often subordinated to formal legislation, customary rules derive their force from the concurrence of a uniform practice and a subjective belief that adherence to them is obligatory (*opinio iuris*), without necessarily being formally incorporated into any written body of law. In this setting, they are usually classified as "immaterial" sources of law (Brownlie, 1990). This notion implies that custom remains the actual source of law even after its judicial recognition. For this reason, the judicial decisions that recognize a custom offer only persuasive evidence of its existence and do not themselves become sources of law. In turn, this prevents the principle of *stare decisis* from crystallizing customary law.

Modern legal systems generally recognize customary rules that have emerged either within the confines of positive legislation (*consuetudo secundum legem*) or in areas that are not disciplined by positive law (*consuetudo praeter legem*). Where custom is in direct conflict with legislation (*custom contra legem*), the latter normally prevails. In some instances, however, a custom supersedes prior legislation (*abrogative custom*), and some arguments have been made in support of emerging practices that conflict with obsolete provisions of public international law (*desuetudo*, or abrogative practice).

2. Anatomy of Customary Law

The theory of customary law defines custom as a practice that emerges outside of legal constraints and which individuals and organizations spontaneously follow in the course of their interactions, out of a sense of legal obligation. Gradually, individual actors embrace norms that they view as requisite to their collective well-being. An enforceable custom emerges from two formative elements: (a) a quantitative element consisting of a general or emerging practice; and (b) a qualitative element reflected in the belief that the norm generates a desired social outcome.

> (A) *The Quantitative Element.* The quantitative requirements for the formation of customary law concern both the length of time and the universality of the emerging practice. Regarding the time element, there is generally no universally established minimum duration for the emergence of customary rules. Customary rules have evolved from both immemorial practice and single acts. Still, French jurisprudence has traditionally required the passage of forty years for the emergence of an international custom, while German doctrine has generally required thirty years. (Tunkin, 1961). Naturally, the longer the time required to form a valid practice, the less likely it is for custom to effectively anticipate the intervention of formal legislation, and to adapt to changing circumstances over time.

Regarding the condition of universality, international legal theory is ambivalent. The system of international relations is analogous to a world of individuals in the state of nature, rather than a system of unanimous consent by all participants as required before binding customary law is formed. Rather than universality, recent restatements of international law refer to consistency and generality (D'Amato, 1971). Where it is impossible to identify a general practice because of fluctuations in behavior, the consistency requirement is not met. Similarly, more recent cases in international law restate the universality requirement in terms of increasing and widespread acceptance, allowing special consideration for emerging general norms (or local clusters of spontaneous default rules) that are expected to become evolutionarily stable over time.

With regard to rules at the national or local level, the varying pace with which social norms are transformed suggests that no general time or consistency requirement can be established as an across-the-board condition for the validity of a custom. Some variance in individual observation of the practice should be expected because of the stochastic origin of social norms. A flexible time requirement is particularly necessary in situations of rapid flux, where exogenous changes are likely to affect the incentive structure of the underlying relationship.

> (B) *The Qualitative Element.* The second formative element of a customary rule is generally identified by the phrase *opinio iuris ac necessitatis*, which describes a widespread belief in the desirability of the norm and the general conviction that the practice represents an essential norm of social conduct. This element is often defined in terms of necessary and obligatory convention. (Kelsen, 1939, 1945; D'Amato, 1971; Walden, 1977). The traditional formulation of *opinio iuris ac necessitates* is problematic because of its circularity. It is quite difficult to conceptualize that law can be born from a practice which is already believed to be required by law.

The practical significance of this requirement is that it narrows the range of enforceable customs: only those practices recognized as socially desirable or necessary will eventually ripen into enforceable customary law. Once there is a general consensus that members of a group ought to conform to a given rule of conduct, a legal custom can be said to have emerged when some level of spontaneous compliance with the rule is obtained. As a result, observable equilibria that are regarded by society as either undesirable (e.g., a prisoner's dilemma or an uncooperative outcome) or unnecessary (e.g., a common practice of greeting neighbors cordially) will lack the subjective and qualitative element of legal obligation and therefore will not generate enforceable legal rules.

As discussed above, two elements are generally required for the finding of customary law: (1) the practice should emerge out of the spontaneous and uncoerced behavior of various members of a group and (2) the parties involved must subjectively believe in the obligatory or necessary nature of the emerging practice (*opinio iuris*). To an economist, the first element corresponds to the rather standard assumption of rational choice. The second element may be appraised as a belief of social obligation, emerging in response to game inefficiencies, to support behavioral rules that avoid aggregate losses from strategic behavior.

3. Terminology Compared

The concept of *opinio iuris* introduces a distinction between mere behavioral regularities and internalized obligations. This distinction may be related to the parties' awareness of the expected aggregate payoffs from the game, a distinction that is crucially important in the normative setting. Two categories of social rules are generally distinguished: (a) those that reflect mere behavioral patterns that are not essential to the legal order and (b) those that reflect an internalized belief that the practice is necessary or socially desirable. A mere behavioral regularity, lacking the qualitative element of *opinio iuris*, does not generate a customary rule. In legal jargon, such behavior is a mere usage; in economic terms it simply represents an equilibrium convention. On the other hand, norms considered necessary for social well-being are treated as proper legal customs and can enter the legal system as primary sources of law.

Finally, the terminology used in the legal and economic literature should be contrasted with the terminology employed in sociological literature (Weber, 1978, 319–320). What is legally termed a mere usage is defined in sociological literature as a custom (*sitte*), in the sense of a typically uniform activity that is not considered to be socially necessary. Convention, the sociological notion closest to the legal concept of custom, amounts to conduct manipulated by express approval or disapproval by other members of the group, but it lacks the enforceability that characterizes a legal custom.

FRANCESCO PARISI

REFERENCES

Bernstein, L. (1996). "Merchant law in a merchant court: rethinking the code's search for immanent business norms." *University of Pennsylvania Law Review*, 144: 1765.

Brownlie, I. (1990). *Principles of Public International Law.* Oxford: Clarendon Press.

Cooter, R.D. (1994). "Structural adjudication and the new law merchant: a model of decentralized law." *International Review of Law & Economics*, 14: 215–227.

D'Amato, A. (1971). *The Concept of Custom in International Law.* Ithaca: Cornell University Press.

Parisi, F. (1995). "Toward a theory of spontaneous law." *Constitutional Political Economy*, 6: 211–231.

Parisi, F. (1998). "Customary law." P. Newman (ed) *The New Palgrave Dictionary of Economics and the Law.* Macmillan, pp. 572–578.

Parisi, F. (2000a). "The cost of the game: a taxonomy of social interactions." *European Journal of Law and Economics*, 9: 99–114.

Parisi, F. (2000b). "Spontaneous emergence of law: customary law." *Encyclopedia of Law & Economics* 5: 603–630 Aldershot: Edward Elgar Publishing.

Posner, E. (1996). "Law, economics, and inefficient norms." *University of Pennsylvania Law Review*, 144: 1697.

Tunkin, G.I. (1961). "Remarks on the juridical nature of customary norms in international law." *California Law Review*, 49: 419.

Walden, R.M. (1977). "The subjective element in the formation of customary international law." *Israel Law Review*, 12: 344.

Weber, M. (1978). *Economy and Society*. Berkeley: University of California Press.

D

THE DEMAND-REVEALING PROCESS

The demand-revealing process (DR) is a way of making collective decisions that is designed to choose the option with the greatest aggregate value, which option is identified by giving participants incentives to report the intensities of their preferences honestly. That is, DR is designed to achieve 'individual incentive compatibility.'

DR was first described in print by Edward Clarke (1971, 1972). Groves and Loeb (1975) developed it independently as a variation on Groves' (1973) work on incentives in teams. Tideman and Tullock (1976) is frequently used to explain DR to students. Bailey (2001) is the most elaborate development of the idea. Many economists see Vickrey's (1961) work on second-price auctions as a harbinger of DR's incentive compatibility. DR is sometimes called the pivotal mechanism.

DR can be understood as an application of the principle of marginal cost pricing. Each participant in the decision-making process, i, is charged a fee for participation (a 'Clarke tax'), equal to the sum over all other participants of the cost of moving from the outcome that would be chosen if i reported a 'standard preference' to the outcome that is chosen in view of the preference that i actually reports. In the same way that marginal cost pricing motivates people to make efficient consumption decisions, it can also motivate them to purchase efficient amounts of influence over collective decisions.

The mechanics of DR can be explained most easily in terms of an example. Suppose that seven persons have agreed to use DR to decide whether to have their picnic on Saturday or Sunday. To proceed, they must agree on a numeraire in which their preferences will be aggregated. Economists think of money as the natural numeraire, but anything that is measurable, addable, and that the participants would regard as a sacrifice, can be used for the demand revealing process. A good numeraire would have the same subjective cost to all participants; unfortunately, there is no objective test of whether this criterion is met. Two possible alternatives to money are time spent in an activity that people would prefer to avoid, such as picking up roadside trash, and 'estimated utility,' estimated as the product of preferences in money and an agreed estimate of the individual's marginal utility of money (Good, 1977).

For simplicity, assume that preferences are measured in money.

Suppose the reported preferences of the seven picnickers are:

Saturday		Sunday	
Albert	£4	Doris	£2
Betty	£12	Ellen	£5
Charles	£9	Fred	£6
		Grace	£7
Total	£25	Total	£20

Those who favor Saturday report a greater total value for their preferences than those who favor Sunday, so the picnic is held on Saturday. In the simplest version of DR, each person's standard preference is indifference between the two options. Those who are pivotal, and therefore owe a Clarke tax, are those on the winning side who voted more than the winning margin, namely Betty and Charles. The amount of each Clarke tax (the net cost to all others of changing the outcome in response to a pivotal preference) is the winning margin in the opposite direction when the voter is removed (when the voter's standard preference is substituted). This can also be computed as what that person offered minus the winning margin. Thus Betty is charged £7 and Charles is charged £4.

Betty has an incentive to report her preference honestly despite the tax because any increase in her reported preference or any decrease that leaves Saturday still winning has no effect on her tax, and a decrease to a figure less than £7 causes Sunday to win, depriving her of the chance to get something worth £12 to her at a cost of just £7. A similar analysis holds for Charles. Albert has no incentive to misstate his preference because the outcome he favors is chosen at no cost to him. Doris has no incentive to misstate her preferences because the cost to other voters of accommodating her preference would be £7. Any increase in her stated preference that changed the outcome would give her a Clarke tax of this magnitude, which she would find not worth paying to change the outcome. A similar analysis holds for the other voters on the losing side. Thus all participants have incentives to report their preferences honestly.

While DR provides incentives for individuals acting alone to report their preferences honestly, it is vulnerable to coalitions. If Fred and Grace both increased their reported preferences by £15, then Sunday would win and neither one would be charged a Clarke tax. Thus to make DR workable, such coalitions must be deterred. It would presumably suffice to require secret voting and make it impossible for voters to prove afterward how they had voted. Then self interest would motivate voters to ignore any coalition agreements they had made and vote their true preferences.

Like other applications of marginal cost pricing, DR generally does not achieve budget balance. It usually produces a surplus (the Clarke taxes), although there are some variants for which the sign of the budget imbalance is uncertain (Bailey, 2001: 192–195, 214–246). Since budgets must balance in the end, DR must be augmented by a device for achieving budget balance. If the budget surplus is distributed among the participants, the prospect of receiving a share of it distorts incentives, although this distortion is arguably imperceptible when there are more than a few dozen participants. It is possible to reduce the imbalance by an order of magnitude, at a cost of making its sign uncertain (Bailey, loc cit.), and it is possible to dispose of the surplus without distortion or waste, either by having two collectivities exchange their surpluses or by holding an auction before the decision, among people outside the collectivity, for the right to receive the surplus.

DR is assured of achieving full individual incentive compatibility only in the case of a choice between just two options. For choices over more than two options, income effects produce a possibility of cycles in the comparison of options, leading to difficulty in applying the principle of marginal cost pricing. For example, suppose that the picnic could be held on any of the days of a three-day weekend. Suppose that Albert would be willing to pay £4 to have the picnic on Saturday rather than Sunday, and £6 to have it on Sunday rather than Monday. He would presumably find it worth less than £10 (the sum of these two amounts) to have the picnic on Saturday rather than Monday, because he is poorer if he must pay £4 to move the picnic from Saturday to Sunday than if he is offered the chance to move the picnic from Sunday to Monday without that prior step. Suppose he is willing to pay just £9 to have the picnic on Saturday rather than Monday. It could happen that Betty's preferences were £4 for Sunday rather than Monday, £6 for Monday rather than Saturday, and £9 for Sunday rather than Saturday, while Charles preferences were £4 for Monday rather than Saturday, £6 for Saturday rather than Sunday, and £9 for Monday rather than Sunday. In this case, summing the three preferences leads to the cycle that Saturday is preferred to Sunday by £1, Sunday is preferred to Monday by £1, and Monday is preferred to Saturday by £1.

To select an outcome when there is such a cycle, a collectivity must have a rule for cutting through the cycle. The case presented is completely symmetric and would most reasonably be decided by a random process. When the result is not symmetric one might apply a rule such as the minimax loss rule: The winner is the option whose worse loss in paired comparisons is least bad.

When there are cycles, it is possible for the measured cost of responding to a voter's reported preference to be greater than what the voter has offered to pay. In the example above, suppose that Saturday is selected at random as the winner. If Albert had been indifferent among the options, Monday would have won. The loss to the other two voters from Albert's participation is £10, although it is worth only £9 to Albert to have the picnic on Saturday rather than Monday. To avoid charging voters more than they are willing to pay, the Clarke tax can be defined as what the voter offered for the effect of the vote, minus the 'generalized winning margin,' defined as the difference between the worst loss of the winner and the worst loss of the option that would have won if the voter had been indifferent among the options. This reduces to the standard Clarke tax in the case of two options.

While this Clarke tax ensures that voters are not charged more than they are willing to pay, it creates opportunities for voters to profit from strategic misstatements of their preferences (Tideman, 1997). Still, it is unlikely that people could guess what strategic misstatements of their preferences would profit them, so that DR is still potentially valuable as a mechanism for making a collective decision among more than two options. Furthermore, for many collective decisions it can reasonably be expected that income effects will be minute, so they would be unlikely to pose practical problems.

So far, DR has been discussed in the contest of choices that have no budgetary cost. If there are budgetary costs, allocations of the costs among the participants must be incorporated into the specification of the options. DR can be used only to choose among fully financed options. It loses its incentive compatibility completely if reported preferences are used to assign cost shares to participants.

The examples discussed have been discrete choices. When DR is used to make continuous choices (such as quantities of public goods) and income effects are inconsequential, it is convenient to have voters report their preferences as marginal valuation schedules. Efficiency in the choice of a continuous parameter occurs where the aggregate marginal value of an increase in the parameter (net of any costs) is zero. If each voter's standard preference is indifference with respect to the parameter (given assigned costs), then each voter's Clarke tax is the aggregate loss to all other voters of moving from the level of the parameter that would be chosen if the voter were indifferent with respect to the parameter, to the level actually chosen. Ignoring income effects, this is the integral of the sum of the other voters' net marginal valuations schedules, from the actual outcome to the outcome that would be chosen if the voter reported the standard preference.

While for discrete choices the probability that a voter will be decisive approaches zero as the number of voters increases, in the case of continuous choices, a positive Clarke tax for every participant is a virtual certainty, but the expected magnitude of each Clarke tax approaches zero as the number of participants increases. Margolis (1982) has argued that in this circumstance, people would not vote in terms of their personal preferences as we ordinarily understand them, but would rather seek to cast votes that would give them Clarke taxes with magnitudes representing what they were prepared to spend to see that a good public decision was made. Tideman (1983a) responded that we should understand value to mean whatever people are willing to pay, for whatever reason.

If Clarke taxes are inconsequentially small, then there is no need to take account of income effects. But if Margolis is right about how people would behave, then it would be essential to take account of them, because the value to a person of a marginal change in a continuous parameter would then depend significantly on how much the person had already spent to affect it. To take account of income effects, voters would need to report their preferences in enough detail that the vote processors could determine the voter's valuation of the change from any level of the parameter to any other level. The vote processors could then use a discrete approximation of a continuous decision to estimate the level of the continuous parameter that beat all other levels in paired comparisons, or failing that, the level whose worst loss in paired comparisons was least bad.

Tideman (1983b) reports the results of an experiment in which university fraternities made decisions in their regular meetings by DR. Over 96 decisions, DR produced an apparent increase in efficiency of 2.25%. Total Clarke taxes came to 3.04% of the net value of all decisions.

T. NICOLAUS TIDEMAN

REFERENCES

Bailey, M.J. (2001). *Constitution for a Future Country*. Basingstoke, Hampshire, UK and New York: Palgrave.

Clarke, E.H. (1971). "Multipart pricing of public goods." *Public Choice*, 11(Spring): 17–33.

Clarke, E.H. (1972). "Multipart pricing of public goods: an example," in Selma Mushkin (ed.) *Public Prices for Public Products*. Washington: The Urban Institute, pp. 125–130.

Good, I.J. (1977). "Justice in voting by demand revelation." *Public Choice*, 29(2) (Spring): 65–70.

Groves, T. (1973). "Incentives in teams." *Econometrica*, 41(July): 617–631.

Groves, T. and Loeb M. (1975). "Incentives and public inputs." *Journal of Public Economics*, 4(3): 211–226.

Margolis, H. (1982). "A thought experiment on demand-revealing mechanisms." *Public Choice*, 38: 87–92.

Tideman, T.N. (1983a). "A collective conception of collective value." *Perspectives on Local Public Finance and Public Policy*, 1: 3–22.

Tideman, T.N. (1983b). "An experiment in the demand-revealing process." *Public Choice*, 41: 387–401.

Tideman, T.N. (1997). "Voting and the revelation of preferences," in Dennis Mueller (ed.) *Perspectives on Public Choice*, Cambridge: Cambridge University Press, pp. 226–244.

Tideman, T.N. and Tullock, G. (1976). "A new and superior process for making social choices." *Journal of Political Economy*, 84(December): 1145–1160.

Vickrey, W. (1961). "Counterspeculation, auctions, and competitive sealed tenders." *Journal of Finance*, 16(March): 8–37.

DEREGULATION OF POSTAL SERVICE

Although deregulation is a relatively recent innovation, it already has had profound effects on network industries. While its impact on the postal sector has been even more recent and its full effect has yet to be felt, this should be seen as an opportunity for the postal sector to learn from some of the lessons of the other industries. A key issue in all of these industries is who should provide and pay for the default service obligation, which in postal service is known as the Universal Service Obligation (USO). We will see that the USO is the central focus of the deregulation debate in the postal sector.

The USO assures ubiquitous service at a uniform price, and therefore implies some level of cross subsidies from low-cost delivery areas to high-cost areas. Under liberalization or deregulation, these cross subsidies send a signal to entrants by inflating the potential profits of entry into the low-cost areas. It is thus possible for entrants with higher costs to undercut the incumbent and even to undermine completely the financial viability of the incumbent faced with a USO. This has led incumbent postal operators to claim the need for entry restrictions to maintain financial viability under the USO (e.g., Crew and Kleindorfer, 2001). Opponents of the postal monopoly (e.g., Cohen et al., 2000) have attacked the USO on a number of grounds, notably that it is unnecessary and is little more than a device to enable incumbents to hang on to their monopoly.

Following the public choice literature, we argue that rent seeking offers some insights in explaining the process of deregulation and understanding the implications for the USO. One major problem with the term deregulation is that it is used and applied in a very loose manner. The "de" prefix itself is open to considerable interpretation. In postal services, deregulation has come in several forms. First have come changes such as price-caps and other forms of incentive regulation designed to encourage internal (or X-) efficiency. Second has come liberalization of access in upstream operation such as collection and barcoding of mail. The logic of such access is to promote competition from entrants who can perform these upstream operations more efficiently than the incumbent postal operator. Third have been more radical proposals to allow entry and competition anywhere in the postal value chain.

Each of these deregulation proposals has faced real problems in the postal sector. Incentive regulation in the postal sector has typically not confronted the problem of labor costs, which in some proposals remain completely outside the realm of regulatory purview. The application of incentive regulation in public enterprises, the dominant form in postal services, is problematical owing to the absence of residual claimants so central to effective incentive regulation (Crew and Kleindorfer, 2001).

The second form of deregulation, increased entry and competition in upstream operations, has also generated considerable controversy in the literature (Mitchell, 1999; Crew and Kleindorfer, 2002). The central point of the debate has been, as in telecommunications, the appropriate pricing for access, or equivalently the appropriate discount offered to competitors for the upstream operations they perform in lieu of the postal operator. The controversies surrounding avoided cost approaches and efficient component pricing rules have not been spared the postal service deregulation debate.

The third form of deregulation, complete liberalization of entry, is of more recent vintage. Some countries have taken away completely the letter monopoly (e.g., New Zealand and Sweden), allowing any qualified entrant to provide end-to-end postal and delivery service. Other countries (e.g., the United Kingdom) are actively considering proposals to allow such entry or at least significantly less restrictive policies on services that entrants can offer in competition with the postal incumbent. Some of these proposals have been accompanied by granting considerably greater commercial freedoms to the postal operator, including privatization of the postal operator (e.g., the Netherlands and Germany). The key issue in the debate surrounding these cases has been balancing the objective of commercializing the postal service against the desire to maintain the wherewithal to fund the USO. This is no small challenge, given the uniformity in letter-mail pricing, and there is no clear resolution in sight as to the appropriate mix of regulatory incentives and governance structures to promote or achieve the desired balance (Crew and Kleindorfer, 2000, 2001).

In the eyes of economists, the objectives of deregulation are generally laudable if the idea is to obtain the benefits of competitive entry and in the process avoid some of the inefficiencies of monopoly and the transactions costs and other inefficiencies of the associated regulation. Ideally, we would like to believe that deregulation implies reducing regulation. However, given its history, even this low standard is difficult to attain. The practice of deregulation is such that almost any regulatory change can be passed off as deregulation. Add to the mix that regulation is now generally considered undesirable and deregulation desirable, we have a fertile ground for the creation of all sorts of mischief in the name of deregulation.

If deregulation were only striving for the benefits of competitive entry, it would at least be well defined and consistent. It would amount to abolishing regulation. It would amount to a realization that regulation had had its day for the industry concerned and that superior governance structures existed, namely, competition. In practice, deregulation is rarely interpreted in this manner because politicians, pressure groups and regulators are not willing to abandon certain features that have become the very essence of regulation. In particular, cross subsidy and consumer protection are often seen as the distinguishing features of regulation. Yet, it is these features of regulation that make deregulation so problematical or even unattainable.

The original rationale for regulation in the minds of economists was the desire to avoid monopoly inefficiency. From a societal point of view the original objective was to protect the consumer from monopoly exploitation. The notion of *justum pretium* or "just price" has a long history in the common law and underlies much statute law including statutes governing monopoly. However, the practice of regulation became more than this as elected representatives realized its considerable potential for providing them with opportunities of taxation and subsidization that had distinct advantages relative to the usual taxes and subsidies. Redistribution by regulation lacked the transparency and therefore the accountability of traditional methods of taxation and subsidy. From the government's point of view, this was a huge advantage and provides a potentially convincing explanation of why deregulation is often a failure. Politicians preach deregulation while simultaneously retaining the redistribution mechanism that regulation provides.

For politicians, regulation is first and foremost about redistribution. The avowed objective of regulation is to protect consumers from price gouging by a firm with monopoly power. This in itself is a form of redistribution in that it redistributes the monopolist's profits to the consumers. This notion is *prima facie* reasonable and is not likely to be generally unacceptable to economists. The problem is that achieving this apparently simple objective of redistribution of monopoly rents by government sets in motion a number of forces. Given that government in a democracy is subject to the will of people, some of the people will attempt to influence government to make the redistribution work in their favor. Indeed, the act of monopoly regulation sets in motion the rent seeking process, a term first coined in Tullock's (1967) path breaking paper. Rent seekers will devote considerable resources to obtaining a share of the monopoly rents of which government now has taken control through the regulatory process. Thus, it is not difficult to see that regulation goes much further than this in terms of redistribution than just returning the monopoly rents to the consumers. It redistributes from one class of customers to another. Typically, this redistribution takes the form of subsidizing small customers at the expense of large customers, presumably in the service of generating electoral support for regulators or their political sponsors.

The cross subsidy of large customers to small customers also applies in the case of postal service although the connection is a little less obvious. In postal service the redistribution takes place through the USO. Ostensibly, this implies subsidizing isolated or rural locations at the expense of urban or congested locations. It involves urban mailers paying the same stamp price as rural mailers. This implies that not only small urban mailers subsidize rural mailers but also that large mailers subsidize small rural customers. While the large mailers obviously receive a benefit from getting mail to rural locations, they receive a larger benefit from delivering it to urban locations. The extra expenses large mailers incur as a result of this subsidy flow are presumably significantly greater than the benefit they receive from reaching the subsidized locations. The other effect of the cross subsidy is to attract entrants by the artificially high profit margin on low costs routes resulting from the uniform pricing policy.

The dilemma created by deregulation would still remain even if a mechanism were devised such that politicians were to forego the potential for opaque redistribution that has been a hallmark of regulation. This dilemma would arise from what we characterize as *Residual Monopoly* and what might generally be described as *Default Service Obligation*.

Residual Monopoly is a problem that might always occur after deregulation. There is some remaining element of natural monopoly that cannot be eliminated. One approach to this might be just to ignore it as argued by Posner (1969, 1974). There have been few takers. The problem is that the residual monopoly affects classes of consumers very differently. Large industrial and commercial customers are usually not going to face much risk of monopoly exploitation because they have significant alternatives. They can

generate their own electricity. They can connect directly to the gas pipeline; they do not need the local gas distribution company. Similarly, they have alternatives to the local phone company and would have no difficulty obtaining mail service in the absence of a postal monopoly. The situation for small customers is, however, very different. They have few alternatives. Indeed, for most of them the reality of natural monopoly is obvious. The only way that they can be supplied economically is by a single producer with the ability to spread large fixed costs across many small customers and the ability to recover customer specific sunk costs. Regulation provided rough and ready consumer protection for these small customers. Even if the potential for cross subsidy that regulation provided could be abandoned, the problem of monopoly exploitation of small customers would remain as a serious issue to be addressed.

The *Default Service Obligation* might be considered an extension of the protection from monopoly exploitation that regulation offered to small customers. However, it turns out to be a major obstacle to deregulation, especially in the postal sector. The USO may be considered a special case of the default service obligation. Generally, the default service obligation may be considered the right of any customer, in practice normally only a constraint in the case of small customers, to receive service of some defined quality at a "reasonable" price. This notion was rather easily achievable under monopoly. The regulator, in effect, guaranteed that the profitable large customers could not be picked off by entrants, in return for which the monopolist faced the obligation to provide service to customers large and small at the rate set by the regulator. As Goldberg (1976) argued, an "administered" contract existed between the regulator and the monopolist. The regulator, in determining "reasonable" prices, had considerable potential to cross subsidize and even this did not overly concern the monopolist as long as the regulator barricaded the market against entry. All this changed under deregulation. The regulator started to allow entry into the profitable parts of the incumbent's business while at the same time continuing to require the incumbent to provide default service. In short, the regulator retained the obligation to serve while simultaneously removing the wherewithal to finance it.

We argue that deregulation must address these twin issues of residual monopoly and default service. One approach is the Posnerian one. This would essentially say, "Let 'er rip". If these residual problems remain as a result of deregulation, so be it. The difficulties of fixing them are just too great. At the other extreme there is tight regulation of the cost-of-service variety that addressed these twin issues in a rigorous manner. Many economists would find the Posnerian view attractive. However, most of them would recognize that the Posnerian approach is not feasible politically. Indeed, there is considerable evidence that consumers and politicians desire the redistribution made available by regulation.

The framework we have just sketched enables us to understand better the nature of deregulation. It explains why deregulation can mean almost any change in the regulatory process. The monopoly rents that are being redistributed by the regulatory process are what drive deregulation. This also explains why deregulation is such an ill-defined concept. The change planned depends upon what form of redistribution of the monopoly rents is being sought. Much current deregulation can be based upon the attempt by big business to seek a greater share of the pie. The attempts to protect small users from monopoly exploitation and to maintain the USO provide a means for small customers to fight back in an attempt to hold on to their share of the rents.

Addressing the twin challenges of curbing monopoly exploitation for the residual monopoly and maintaining default service are critical if deregulation is to succeed. These problems are so serious as to threaten deregulation entirely. The lesson we should draw is that deregulation is likely to have many different consequences than intended and therefore economists need to improve their ability to analyze proposals. One consequence of all of this might be that the gains from deregulation are likely to be much less than originally anticipated and there may be significant transactions costs of regulation in the face of increased complexity resulting from the interaction of competition and regulation. One potentially significant problem that could result is that universal service itself may be endangered.

By refocusing on rent seeking attempts to redistribute the monopoly rents our approach implies that the battle lines of deregulation will be drawn within the requirements to provide default service and the problem of providing protection from residual monopoly power. The requirement to provide default service without a regulated monopoly to finance it inevitably leads to major problems that are not easily fixed. The discussion, in our minds at least, does yield a clearer understanding of regulation and the problems of deregulation than heretofore enunciated. In the case of postal service deregulation and the attempts to capture a share of the monopoly rents underlines the tension between large and small customers with a high likelihood of the USO being lost in the process.

Postal service faces a significantly different situation from that faced by the other industries in that irrevocable decisions have not yet been made on the deregulation front anywhere near to the extent that they have in telecommunications and in electricity. Thus, this presents opportunities in postal

service that are not available in the other industries. On the negative side postal service faces problems that may be more significant than those in the other industries. Postal service has none of the advantages of technological change that telecommunications is enjoying today. Indeed, technologies like the Internet mean that postal revenues are under attack with declines in letter mail volume rather likely in the near future. Technology is not helping much in reducing costs with over 80% of cost consisting of labor. Given the current situation, postal service may be very vulnerable if major changes are now made in the name of deregulation particularly if they are of a piecemeal nature and still retain strong default service provisions in the USO. California electricity deregulation has amply demonstrated the impact piecemeal deregulation can have on a vulnerable system.

All of these ideas require significant development. One lesson, however, is clear. Piecemeal deregulation can have severe consequences as the California electricity crisis demonstrates. In the postal sector, ill-conceived piecemeal deregulation is likely to have very bad consequences because of slow technological change, severe competition from e-Commerce and the need for POs to become increasingly commercial. What is required is a balanced and deliberate approach to deregulation that promotes internal efficiency of the national postal operator while preserving the financial viability of this operator to meet an agreed USO. This is no easy task.

MICHAEL A. CREW
PAUL R. KLEINDORFER

REFERENCES

Cohen, Robert H., William W. Ferguson, John D. Waller, and Spyros S. Xenakis (2000). "Universal service without a monopoly," in Michael A. Crew and Paul R. Kleindorfer (eds.) *Current Directions in Postal Reform*. Boston, MA: Kluwer Academic Publishers.

Crew, Michael A. and Paul R. Kleindorfer (2001). "Whither the USO under competitive entry: a microstructure approach," in M.A. Crew and P.R. Kleindorfer (eds.) *Future Directions in Postal Reform*. Boston: Kluwer Academic Publishers.

Crew, Michael A. and Paul R. Kleindorfer (2001). "A critique of the theory of incentive regulation," in M.A. Crew and P.R. Kleindorfer (eds.) *Future Directions in Postal Reform*. Boston: Kluwer Academic Publishers.

Crew, Michael A. and Paul R. Kleindorfer (2002). "Putty-putty, putty-clay or humpty-dumpty?" in M.A. Crew and P.R. Kleindorfer (eds.) *Postal and Delivery Services: Pricing, Productivity, Regulation and Strategy*. Boston: Kluwer Academic Publishers.

Goldberg, Victor P. (1976). "Regulation and administered contracts." *The Bell Journal of Economics*, 7(2)(Autumn): 426–448.

Mitchell, Robert W. (1999). "Postal worksharing: welfare, technical efficiency, and pareto optimality," in M.A. Crew and P.R. Kleindorfer (eds.), *Emerging Competition in Postal and Delivery Services: Pricing, Productivity, Regulation and Strategy*. Boston: Kluwer Academic Publishers.

Posner, Richard A. (1969). "Natural monopoly and its regulation." *Stanford Law Review*, 21(February): 548–643.

Posner, Richard A. (1974). "Theories of economic regulation." *Bell Journal of Economics*, 5(Autumn): 335–358.

Tullock Gordon (1967). "The welfare costs of tariffs, monopolies and theft." *Western Economic Journal*, 5(June): 224–232.

DICTATORS AND SOCIAL CONTRACTS

1. Introduction

The systematic analysis of government structures beyond democracy has long been neglected by economists. This negligence was in no way confined to representatives of public choice, but was common in almost the entire discipline. Modern public choice evolved predominantly in the U.S., so the primordial focus on incentive structures induced by democratic systems can be made plausible easily. Yet it is very likely that during the history of mankind, only a minority of the world population lived in countries with a democratic government structure at any period. Viewed like this, democracy is a rather marginal phenomenon both historically and geographically.

Gordon Tullock (1974, 1987) was the first — and for a long time probably also the only — economist working on a comprehensive theory of autocracy or dictatorship. Ronald Wintrobe (1990, 1998) proposed a taxonomy of dictators distinguishing (inter alia) between tinpots and totalitarians. According to his model, dictators generally have at their disposal two instruments in order to reach their goals, namely repression and loyalty. Whereas totalitarians derive utility from power as such and thus try to maximize it, tinpots choose the level of power that secures their remaining in office. Their utility is rather derived from (1990, 849) "palaces, Mercedes-Benzes, (and) Swiss bank accounts." Wintrobe's model constitutes an important step toward a more theoretical foundation of the economic theory of dictatorship. Even though, his approach of attributing different preference-functions to different kinds of dictators is problematic as long as the model does not provide for the conditions under which a particular type will make it to power. The ex post evaluation that a certain dictator belongs to one of the categories lacks predictive power.

Mancur Olson (1991) and McGuire and Olson, (1996) deal with the incentives of "roving bandits" to turn into "stationary bandits" — or dictators in the terminology used here. Olson's papers have led to an increased interest in the topic and spawned other papers, e.g., by Niskanen (1997). In the meantime, interest in the economics of dictatorship as well as the economics of transition from one kind of government structure to another has burgeoned. The *Economics of Governance*, a new journal in which quite a few papers are devoted to these issues started to appear, and more and more papers in mainstream journals, such as the *American Economic Review*, allocate space to this topic (see, e.g., Acemoglu and Robinson, 2001).

The topic "dictators and social contracts" seems to imply a contradiction. According to Webster's Dictionary, a dictator can be defined as "one ruling absolutely, typically with brutality, oppression, and ruthless suppression of opposition." A social contract, in turn, is defined as "an agreement between the community and the ruler that defines and limits the rights and duties of each." In this entry, we are interested in the conditions under which even dictators have incentives to be bound by certain constraints and to factually observe them in their behavior. If these constraints are subsumed under the label "social contract," the topic might not have to imply a contradiction. But it might imply a somewhat modified notion of social contracts. This will be taken up in section III below.

Due to space restrictions, this entry does not deal with a number of closely related and highly interesting topics such as

- the economics of anarchy; here the question is for the conditions that have to be met in order for anarchy to be a stable regime (Taylor, 1987 is a masterly treatment of the topic; Bush, 1972 and Bush and Mayer, 1973 heavily influenced the notion of anarchic equilibrium in Buchanan, 1975; Hirshleifer, 1998 contains a brief overview).

- the transition from anarchy to dictatorship; if anarchy is not stable, one option is the emergence of dictatorship (Usher, 1989 explains cycles between anarchy and despotism — in our terminology: dictatorships — by changes in population growth that change the relative payoffs between bandits and farmers; Konrad and Skaperdas, 1999 are interested in identifying the conditions under which anarchy turns into a dictatorship ("Leviathan" in their terminology) or, alternatively, into self-governance on the one hand and competing lords on the other).

- the transition from dictatorship to the rule of law and/or democracy; here the questions are (i) under what conditions an explicit set of constraints that places government members under the law will be established and enforced and (ii) under what conditions universal suffrage as a method to exchange governments will be implemented.

- the conditions under which democracy and the rule of law are stable equilibria (recently, the degree of inequality observed in societies has figured prominently as an explanatory variable for the stability of democratic regimes, see, e.g., Acemoglu and Robinson, 2001 and Boix and Garicano, 2001 who, albeit identifying common explanatory variables, fundamentally disagree concerning the details of their explanations).

The rest of the entry is organized as follows: the next section is devoted to some shortcoming of the standard notion of social contract theory. Section 3 introduces a modified version of the social contract and section 4 introduces the dilemma of the strong state. Section 5 concludes.

2. Some Shortcomings of Social Contract Theory

Social contract theory has been severely criticized many a time (see, e.g., the critique by Hume, 1777/1987, 465ff.). Yet, it still plays an important role in constitutional political economy. Often, the interaction structure that the actors find themselves in is conceptualized as a Prisoners' Dilemma whose Pareto-inferior consequences they could only overcome by founding a state via a social contract. This approach seems to be incoherent for at least two reasons (see also Voigt, 1999):

(1) Suppose that the players establish a social contract to solve their dilemma. This is the attempt to overcome the inability to comply with a mutually beneficial (private) contract by entering into yet another (now social) contract. Compliance with the social contract, i.e., enforcement of the private contract, would make all parties better off. However, non-cooperation is still the dominant strategy. The social contract needs to be enforced in order to be able to enforce the private contract. This would require yet another contract — and so forth, which leads to an infinite regress.

(2) The notion of a third-party enforcer does not solve the problem: suppose that the parties who failed to solve the Prisoners' Dilemma enter into a social contract and found the state with the intention of establishing an impartial arbitrator and an enforcement agency. The parties to the private contract then disarm themselves and pay a fee to a third party for its services instead. They endow this third-party enforcer with the monopoly on using force. However, what incentives does the third party then have to stick to its role of

impartial arbitrator instead of expropriating the two parties who originally founded it? Again, the social contract between the parties of the private contract and the third party needs to be enforced, which again leads to an infinite regress.

3. Modifying the Concept of Social Contract

Kirstein and Voigt (2001) propose to modify the concept of social contract so that it can be used to explain the emergence of certain governmental structures. If constitutional rules are assumed to be the most basic layer of rules, they cannot be seen as a contract to be enforced exogenously, since this would require a more basic layer of rules according to which the enforcement takes place. The social contract thus needs to be self-enforcing. If a contract is self-enforcing, one can also do without the third party which is miraculously introduced to solve a (two person) Prisoners' Dilemma. In such a notion of the social contract, it is analyzed whether the contracting parties have incentives to stick to its provisions in the post-constitutional stage, i.e., the stage following the one in which the terms of the contract get fixed. Rather than admitting, as Brennan and Buchanan (1980, 10) do that "our whole construction is based on the belief, or faith, that constitutions can work, and that tax rules imposed within a constitution will prevail", a modified version of the social contract would ask for the conditions under which the contents of such a contract are self-enforcing in the sense that no actor can make himself better off by unilaterally reneging from its constraints.

A social contract can be understood as an exchange between a limited number of actors. One actor might, e.g., offer security both against external aggressors and internally, other actors might promise to produce a private consumption good with a high level of effort which the security-producing actor might tax up to a certain amount. The security-providing actor — or dictator — faces a number of constraints he needs to take into account when solving his optimization problem. Among these are (i) competing would-be dictators from the same territory, (ii) potential invaders from elsewhere, (iii) the possibility that the subjects choose to exit from the territory (Hirschman, 1970), and (iv) tax evasion.

In their model, Kirstein and Voigt (2001) assume society to consist of two (groups of) individuals one of which has a comparative advantage in producing security, whereas the other one has a comparative advantage in producing a private good. The dictator chooses a certain tax level, the weak chooses a level of effort that he uses in order to produce the private consumption good. He also chooses whether he wants to challenge government subsequent to its choice of tax level. Three different types of equilibria are introduced: (i) compliance with the social contract ("cooperation"), (ii) exploitation that, however, avoids the dictators' risk of being overthrown ("moderate exploitation"), and (iii) exploitation followed by a revolution ("maximum exploitation"). Here, the parameter constellations that make a dictator comply with the social contract are of special interest. It is shown that its self-enforceability increases (i) with the productivity of the effort that is displayed for the production of the consumption good, (ii) with high exploitation cost on the dictator's side, and (iii) with low revolution costs.

Grossman and Noh (1990, 1994) identify the conditions under which the survival probability of a government is the decisive paramter for an income maximizing government to behave (almost) as if it were an agent of its citizens.

4. The Dictator's Dilemma

If dictatorship is defined as having absolute power without effective constitutional limitations, then it has definite advantages to be the dictator. But it has also been pointed out (Weingast, 1993) that the strength of the dictator to make and enforce rules as he pleases is also his great weakness: in order to make his subjects invest in long-term projects which would increase total output, the dictator has incentives to promise his subjects that he will refrain from ex post opportunism, i.e., the attenuation of property rights or outright expropriation. But if the dictator has the power to make and enforce rules as he wishes, his promise will not be credible. Rational dictators thus have an interest in establishing institutional mechanisms that would allow them to make credible promises.

Breaking promises must be costly for the dictator. As long as the expected utility from carrying out one's promises is higher than that from breaking one's promises, a rational dictator can be expected to stick to his promises. He could thus create institutions that allow his subjects to depose of him in case he has broken his promises. One step could be to publish a constitution which creates clear-cut duties and obligations and allows his subjects to identify trespasses unequivocally. That being the case, the subjects might still not be able to solve their collective action problem. A rational dictator could reduce this problem by intentionally establishing focal points (Schelling, 1960) as, e.g., conventional meeting points.

Barzel (1997) discusses the role of parliament as a device for dictators to credibly bind themselves. He argues that secure kings deliberately gave up some of their power. This enabled them to credibly commit themselves to their promise not to confiscate the property of their subjects. Barzel's approach thus contradicts the more conventional one that conceptualizes the emergence of parliament as the consequence of a shift in the relative power between a dictator and its subjects. Ex post, the functional separation of powers can be explained as an attempt to reduce the self-commitment problem of government. Other devices include the vertical separation of powers (i.e., federalism) and the delegation of competence to international organizations (Levy and Spiller, 1994; Voigt and Salzberger, 2002).

Grossman and Noh (1990, 1994) show that the credibility of a government is a precondition for its acting as if it were an agent of the citizens. The credibility is shown to be positively correlated with the survival probability of a particular government.

5. Conclusion

The economics of dictatorship is still in its infancy. A better understanding of the working properties of dictatorship seems to be a precondition for understanding transitions from anarchy to dictatorship on the one hand and transitions from dictatorship to democracy on the other. As the recent transition processes of Central and Eastern Europe, but also of some Latin American countries prove, this is not only of academic interest but also empirically highly relevant. Supposedly, the most interesting discussion will take place between those who believe that institutional factors explain the government structures on the one hand and those who stress other factors (resource endowment, climate, geography etc.) on the other (see, e.g., Engerman and Sokoloff, 1997; Moselle and Polak, 2001).

STEFAN VOIGT

REFERENCES

Acemoglu, D. and Robinson, J. (2001). "A theory of political transitions." *American Economic Review*, 91(4): 938–963.

Barzel, Y. (1997). "Parliament as a wealth-maximizing institution: the right to the residual and the right to vote." *International Review of Law and Economics*, 17: 455–474.

Boix, Ch. and Garicano, L. (2001). "Democracy, inequality and country specific wealth." mimeo.

Brennan, G. and Buchanan, J. (1980). *The Power to Tax: Analytical Foundations of a Fiscal Constitution*. Cambridge: Cambridge University Press.

Buchanan, J. (1975). *The Limits of Liberty — Between Anarchy and Leviathan*. Chicago: University of Chicago Press.

Bush, W. (1972). "Individual welfare in anarchy." in G. Tullock (ed.) *Explorations in the Theory of Anarchy*. Blacksburg: Center for Study of Public Choice, pp. 5–18.

Bush, W. and Mayer, L. (1973). "Some implications of anarchy for the distribution of property," mimeo, Blacksburg, Center for Study of Public Choice.

Engerman, S. and Sokoloff, K. (1997). "Factor endowments, institutions, and differential paths of growth among new world economies: a view from economic historians of the United States," in Stephen Haber (ed.) *How Latin America Fell Behind – Essays on the Economic Histories of Brazil and Mexico, 1800–1914*. Stanford: Stanford University Press, pp. 260–306.

Grossman, H. and Noh, S. (1990). "A theory of kleptocracy with probabilistic survival and reputation." *Economics & Politics*, 2(2): 157–171.

Grossman, H. and Noh, S. (1994). "Proprietary public finance and economic welfare." *Journal of Public Economics*, 53(1): 187–204.

Hirschman, A. (1970). *Exit, Voice and Loyalty — Responses to Decline in Firms, Organizations, and States*. Cambridge, MA: Harvard University Press.

Hirshleifer, J. (1998). "Stability of anarchic societies," in P. Newman (ed.) *The New Palgrave Dictionary of Economics and the Law*, Volume 3. London: Macmillan, pp. 495–502.

Hume, D. (1777/1987). *Essays — Moral, Political, and Literary* (edited and with a Foreword, Notes, and Glossary by Eugene F. Miller). Indianapolis: Liberty Classics.

Kirstein, R. and Voigt, S. (2001). "The violent and the weak: when dictators care about social contracts." mimeo.

Konrad, K. and Skaperdas, S. (1999). "The market for protection and the origin of the state," Centre for Economic Policy Research, Research Paper No. 2173.

Levy, B. and Spiller, P. (1994). "The institutional foundations of regulatory commitment: a comparative analysis of telecommunications regulation." *Journal of Law, Economics, and Organization*, 10(2): 201–246.

McGuire, M. and Olson, M. (1996). "The economics of autocracy and majority rule: the invisible hand and the use of force." *Journal of Economic Literature*, 35:72–96.

Moselle, B. and Polak, B. (2001). "A model of the predatory state." *Journal of Law, Economics, and Organization*, 17(1): 1–33.

Niskanen, W. (1997). "Autocratic, democratic, and optimal government." *Economic Inquiry* 35(3): 464–479.

Olson, M. (1991). "Autocracy, democracy, and prosperity," in R. Zeckhauser (ed.) *Strategy and Choice*. Cambridge, MA: Cambridge University Press, pp. 131–157.

Schelling, Th. (1960). *The Strategy of Conflict*. Cambridge, MA: Harvard University Press.

Taylor, M. (1987). *The Possibility of Cooperation*. Cambridge: Cambridge University Press.

Tullock, G. (1987). *Autocracy*. Dordrecht: Kluwer.

Tullock, G. (1974). *The Social Dilemma. The Economics of War and Revolution*. Blacksburg: Centre for Economic Policy Research.

Voigt, S. (1999). "Breaking with the notion of social contract: constitutions as based on spontaneously arisen institutions." *Constitutional Political Economy*, 10(3): 283–300.

Voigt, S. and Salzberger, E. (2002). "Choosing not to choose: when politicians choose to delegate Powers." *Kyklos*, 55(2): 247–268.

Usher, D. (1989). "The Dynastic cycle and the stationary state." *American Economic Review*, 79: 1031–1044.

Weingast, B. (1993). "Constitutions as governance structures: the political foundations of secure markets." *Journal of Institutional and Theoretical Economics*, 149(1): 286–311.

Wintrobe, R. (1990). "The tinpot and the totalitarian: an economic theory of dictatorship." *American Political Science Review*, 84(3): 849–872.

Wintrobe, R. (1998). *The Political Economy of Dictatorship*. Cambridge: Cambridge University Press.

DIRECT DEMOCRACY

"Direct Democracy" is an umbrella term for a variety of decision processes by which ordinary citizens pass laws directly, without using representatives. The most prominent of these processes is the *initiative*, which allows citizens to place proposals on the ballot that become law if a majority of the electorate votes in favor. California's tax-cutting Proposition 13 is the best-known example. The *referendum* is a relative of the initiative that permits voters to reject proposals/laws made by their representatives but does not permit citizens to make their own proposals. European governments use referendums for issues concerning European integration, Swiss cantons and municipalities use them to approve new spending programs, American school districts require them to approve annual budgets, and many governments rely on them to amend their charters/constitutions. The *town meeting* is another form of direct democracy, albeit a dwindling one, even in its former bastions of Switzerland and New England. Although most common in the public sector, direct democracy is not a stranger to the private sector. Shareholders in many corporations vote on proposals made by management, and in some are allowed to initiate their own proposals. Referendums and town meeting type government are often employed in condominium and homeowner associations.

The choice between direct and representative democracy has interested thinkers for centuries. Madison's Federalist No. 10 contains one of the best known arguments against direct democracy, that it will lead to tyranny of the majority: "A common passion or interest will, in almost every case, be felt by a majority of the whole; a communication and concert results from the form of Government itself; and there is nothing to check the inducements to sacrifice the weaker party, or an obnoxious individual." This view was incorporated in the U.S. Constitution, and continues to feature prominently in legal scholarship.

Public choice scholarship, on the other hand, has gone down a rather different path. The study of direct and representative government from a public choice perspective began with Buchanan and Tullock (1962). As they framed the problem, the optimal form of government involves a tradeoff between "external" and "internal" costs. External costs arise when a group makes a decision unfavorable to an individual (such as when a smoker becomes subject to a cigarette tax). Internal or "decisionmaking" costs include the time and effort required to participate in a decision (e.g., costs of collecting information and time spent voting). In *The Calculus of Consent*, direct democracy was for the most part dismissed as a practical option because of the great internal costs involved in having every citizen participate (p. 213): "Direct democracy, under almost any decision-making rule, becomes too costly in other than very small political units when more than a few isolated issues must be considered. The costs of decision-making become too large relative to the possible reductions in expected external costs that collective action might produce." This argument, in some respects, is the economics principle that labor specialization is efficient, applied to political markets.

While the framework developed in *The Calculus of Consent* has stood up well over time, its conclusion about the relative costs of direct and representative democracy is less secure. For one thing, direct democracy is popular, widely used, and growing in importance across the world. For example, the best available evidence indicates that over 70 percent of American citizens currently have the initiative available to them at either the state or local level (Matsusaka, 2002). If referendums, town meetings, and county initiatives were included, the fraction of people with some access to direct democracy would be even higher. Outside the United States, Switzerland, Italy, and Australia have made use of direct democracy for decades, and virtually all countries have held national referendums at one point or another to decide important issues. The institutions of direct democracy have even spread to former Soviet Union: at least 6 of its 15 successor states have incorporated the initiative in their new constitutions. Either people are willing (and increasingly so) to live with inefficient decisionmaking procedures, or the basic theory is not capturing the benefit–cost tradeoff that is important in practice.

Much of the recent literature can be seen as fleshing out the somewhat skeletal structure of *The Calculus of Consent* to show that the calculus is not quite as unfavorable to direct democracy as it might first appear. The external costs of representative government have received the most attention, particularly the growing appreciation of agency problems. It is now well understood that elected officials sometimes fail to pursue the interests of their constituents, either because they are disproportionately influenced by "special interest" groups, corrupt, or simply ignorant (classic work includes Stigler (1971), Peltzman (1976),

Niskanen (1971), Kau and Rubin (1979), and Kalt and Zupan (1984).) When representatives "misbehave" (often defined as failing to implement the median voter policy), theory suggests that voters may be better off if they retain the right to nullify the government's laws or to propose and pass laws directly. The argument is fairly straightforward: since the median voter would never approve a policy that makes himself worse off, having the right to reject new proposals cannot hurt and possibly can help. The situation becomes somewhat more complicated when agents are asymmetrically informed, and under some conditions the initiative and referendum can make voters worse off. See Gerber (1996) for a clear development of the perfect information model, and Matsusaka and McCarty (2001) and Marino and Matsusaka (2001) for asymmetric information models of the initiative and referendum. All of these models walk in the footsteps of Romer and Rosenthal (1979). See also, the "Initiative and Referendum" entry.

The fact that elected officials have limited information gives rise to another external cost of representative government. In the original formulation of Buchanan and Tullock, external costs arise primarily from the risk that a person's wealth might be deliberately expropriated via the collective choice process. It is also possible for wealth to be expropriated inadvertently, when representatives make a bad decision based on faulty or incomplete information. In situations where the information necessary to make the "right" decision is widely dispersed in the population, centralized decisionmaking by a select group of representatives can be inefficient compared to (decentralized) direct decisionmaking by the populace as a whole. For example, representative decisionmaking is likely to be efficient for narrow technical problems, such as acceptable safety standards on a proposed dam. The necessary information can be collected from a small set of experts. However, experts cannot provide the relevant information to decide whether the power generated from the dam is worth the environmental damage from flooding upriver. This problem requires information on the preferences of the population regarding the tradeoff between power costs and environmental amenities. That information resides in each person's head and the most efficient way of tapping it may be to hold a referendum on the question. The argument, in short, is that direct democracy can be the optimal form of government for decisions in which the relevant information is widely dispersed among the population. See Matsusaka (1992) and Matsusaka and McCarty (2001) for an intuitive and formal development of these ideas, and supporting evidence.

Another line of research has begun to re-examine the assumption that the internal or decisionmaking costs of direct democracy are prohibitive. To be sure, the cost of becoming fully informed on public policy issues is substantial, and most people have better things to do with their time. Indeed, survey data confirm that voters are ignorant of even the most basic political facts. An obvious concern with direct democracy, then, is that it places decisionmaking power in the hands of the uninformed. However, a promising new line of research suggests that people may not need to be informed to vote their interests. The idea, roughly speaking, is that voters can rely on information cues (endorsements) from like-minded individuals or groups to identify if a ballot proposition in their interest. If enough cues are available, the electorate can vote as if it is fully informed without having to pay the costs of actually acquiring the information. The early evidence from laboratory experiments and actual election returns indicates that voters are quite skilled at using cues. To the extent cues are available and used, the internal costs of direct democracy may be far lower than originally suspected. The work of Arthur Lupia is central here, for example, Lupia (1994) and Lupia and McCubbins (1998). Bowler and Donovan (1998) and Kahn and Matsusaka (1997) provide additional evidence that citizens manage to vote their interests.

The building blocks for the theories just discussed enjoy empirical support — legislatures do fail to follow constituent wishes at times, agenda control does affect the nature of proposals and policy, asymmetric information is correlated with outcomes, and voters do use information cues. However, only a few attempts have been made to see if these pieces add up to a theory of institutional choice. Sass (1991) and Fahy (1998) study the choice between town meeting and representative government in samples of Connecticut and Massachusetts towns, respectively. The strongest result is that town meetings are more likely to be used in small communities, which they attribute to high decisionmaking costs from direct democracy in populous towns. But this interpretation is undercut by the fact that the initiative is much more common in large cities than small cities (Matsusaka, forthcoming.) Sass and Fahy also find a correlation between direct democracy and population homogeneity, although the relation is weaker. One interpretation is that external (deadweight) costs of rent-seeking are larger when the population is unequal, but it is not clear that this cuts disproportionately against direct democracy. The maintained assumption in these studies is that institutions adapt in the direction of efficiency. This seems like a natural starting point for inquiry, but further research is needed to assess is plausibility. Hersch and McDougall (1997) study the votes of Kansas legislators on a proposal to add the initiative to the state's constitution. They also explore the role of population heterogeneity, but are unable to find a strong relation.

A related question is what determines how often direct democracy is used, given that it is available. Banducci (1998) and Matsusaka and McCarty (2001) provide some evidence on initiative use in American states. Banducci reports that political factors are important, for example, initiatives are more likely to appear on the ballot in states with divided government (the legislature and governor's office are not controlled by a single party.) Matsusaka and McCarty (2001) find that initiatives are used more often in heterogeneous states, possibly a proxy for the difficulty of determining the (median) voter's preferences. Evidence on what issues are addressed by initiatives as opposed to legislatures appears in Matsusaka (1992). The main finding is that "divisive" issues — primarily taxes and social issues — are resolved by initiatives while more narrow issues (for example, pertaining to the administration of government or regulation) tend to be resolved by legislatures. This would be consistent with efficient decisionmaking if the so-called divisive issues are those in which information is widely dispersed.

While the empirical evidence on institutional *choice* is ambiguous, the evidence on institutional *effects* is relatively clear. One result that has emerged from study after study is that institutions matter: the process used to make decisions influences the outcomes. We are still trying to understand how and why they matter by fitting together the many empirical findings. Evidence from the United States shows that the initiative significantly changes fiscal policy of state and local governments, including the amount of spending, amount of revenue raised, centralization of spending, method of financing, and amount of borrowing (Matsusaka, 1995, 2000, 2002; Kiewiet and Szakaly, 1996). The initiative also brings about changes in social policies, the death penalty and parental abortion notification laws (Gerber, 1996, 1999). Research on Switzerland finds similar fiscal effects of the initiative and referendum at the cantonal and local level (Pommerehne, 1978; Feld and Kirchgassner, 1999; Feld and Matsusaka, 2001; Schaltegger and Feld, 2001). This is a very selective sample of recent work; see the "Initiative and Referendum" entry for more. A number of studies have also shown that cities governed by town meetings spend different amounts and on different things than cities governed entirely by representatives. See, for example, Chicoine et al. (1989), Santerre (1989), and Sass (1991).

One challenge to research on direct democracy is that its forms vary in practice. We expect town meetings to have different consequences than voter initiatives. Recent research has approached this problem by moving away from indexes of direct democracy that arbitrarily aggregate these processes. Instead, researchers are now focusing on specific procedures. This has heightened sensitivity to the role played by the mechanics of procedures, most notably the importance of agenda control (beginning with Romer and Rosenthal, 1979).

Direct democracy has received far less research attention than representative democracy, and the questions we have far exceed the answers. Yet theory suggests that the demand for direct democracy will continue to grow. The average citizen is now as educated as his representatives and with the dramatic fall in communication costs, can easily be as informed. This should push down the internal costs of direct decisionmaking, and make voters less willing to endure the agency costs of representative government. As *The Economist* (Dec. 26, 1996) recently argued, "what worked reasonably well in the 19th century will not work in the 21st century. Our children may find direct democracy more efficient, as well as more democratic, than the representative sort."

JOHN G. MATSUSAKA

REFERENCES

Banducci, S.A. (1998). "Direct legislation: when is it used and when does it pass?," in S. Bowler, T. Donovan, and C.J. Tolbert (eds.), *Citizens as Legislators*. Columbus: Ohio State University Press.

Bowler, S. and Donovan, T. (1998). *Demanding Choices: Opinion, Voting, and Direct Democracy*. Michigan: The University of Michigan Press.

Buchanan, J.M. and Tullock, G. (1962). *The Calculus of Consent: Logical Foundations of Constitutional Democracy*. Michigan: University of Michigan Press.

Chicoine, D.L., Walzer, N., and Deller, S.C. (1989). "Representative versus direct democracy and government spending in a median voter model." *Public Finance*, 44: 225–236.

Fahy, C.A. (1998). "The choice of local government structure in Massachusetts: a historical public choice perspective." *Social Science Quarterly*, 79: 433–444.

Feld, L.P. and Kirchgassner, G. (1999). "Public debt and budgetary procedures: top down or bottom up? Some evidence from Swiss municipalities," in J.M. Poterba and J. von Hagen (eds.) *Fiscal Institutions and Fiscal Performance*. Chicago, IL: The University of Chicago Press.

Feld, L.P. and Matsusaka, J.G. (2001). "Budget referendums and government spending: evidence from Swiss cantons," Working Paper, University of Southern California.

Gerber, E.R. (1996). "Legislative response to the threat of popular initiatives." *American Journal of Political Science*, 40: 99–128.

Gerber, E.R. (1999). *The Populist Paradox: Interest Group Influence and the Promise of Direct Legislation*. Princeton, New Jersey: Princeton University Press.

Hersch, P.L. and McDougall, G.S. (1997). "Direct legislation: determinants of legislator support for voter initiatives." *Public Finance Quarterly*, 25: 327–343.

Kahn, M.E. and Matsusaka, J.G. (1997). "Demand for environmental goods. Evidence from voting patterns on California initiatives." *Journal of Law and Economics*, 40: 137–173.

Kalt, J.P. and Zupan, M.A. (1984). "Capture and ideology in the economic theory of politics." *American Economic Review*, 74: 279–300.

Kau, J.B. and Rubin, P.H. (1979). "Self-interest, ideology, and logrolling in congressional voting." *Journal of Law and Economics*, 22: 365–384.

Kiewiet, D.R. and Szakaly, K. (1996). "Constitutional limitations on borrowing: an analysis of state bonded indebtedness." *Journal of Law, Economics, and Organization*, 12: 62–97.

Lupia, A. (1994). "Shortcuts versus encyclopedias: information and voting behavior in California insurance reform elections." *American Political Science Review*, 88: 63–76.

Lupia, A. and McCubbins, M.D. (1998). *The Democratic Dilemma: Can Citizens Learn What they Need to Know?* Cambridge: Cambridge University Press.

Marino, A.M. and Matsusaka, J.G. (2001). "Decision processes, agency problems, and information: an economic analysis of budget procedures," Working Paper, University of Southern California.

Matsusaka, J.G. (1992). "Economics of direct legislation." *Quarterly Journal of Economics*, 107: 541–571.

Matsusaka, J.G. (1995). "Fiscal effects of the voter initiative: evidence from the last 30 years." *Journal of Political Economy*, 103: 587–623.

Matsusaka, J.G. (2000). "Fiscal effects of the voter initiative in the first half of the twentieth century." *Journal of Law and Economics*, 43: 619–650.

Matsusaka, J.G. (2002). *For the Many or the Few: How the Initiative Process Changes American Government*. Book manuscript, University of Southern California.

Matsusaka, J.G. and McCarty, N.M. (2001). "Political resource allocation: benefits and costs of voter initiatives." *Journal of Law, Economics, and Organization*, 17: 413–448.

Matsusaka, J.G. "The initiative and referendum in American cities: basic patterns," in M.D. Waters (ed.), *The Initiative and Referendum Almanac: A Comprehensive Reference Guide to Citizen Lawmaking Around the World*. Carolina Academic Press (forthcoming) 2003.

Niskanen, W.A. (1971). *Bureaucracy and Representative Government*. Chicago: Aldine-Atherton.

Peltzman, S. (1976). "Toward a more general theory of regulation." *Journal of Law and Economics*, 19: 211–240.

Pommerehne, W.W. (1978). "Institutional approaches to public expenditure: empirical evidence from Swiss municipalities." *Journal of Public Economics*, 9: 255–280.

Romer, T. and Rosenthal, H. (1979). "Bureaucrats versus voters: on the political economy of resource allocation by direct democracy." *Quarterly Journal of Economics*, 93: 563–587.

Santerre, R.E. (1989). "Representative versus direct democracy: are there any expenditure differences?" *Public Choice*, 60: 145–154.

Sass, T.R. (1991). "The choice of municipal government structure and public expenditures." *Public Choice*, 71: 71–87.

Schaltegger, C. and Feld, L.P. (2001). "On government centralization and budget referendums: evidence from Switzerland." Working Paper, University of St. Gallen.

Stigler, G.J. (1971). "The theory of economic regulation." *Bell Journal of Economics and Management Science*, 3: 3–21.

DISCRIMINATION

Considerable misunderstanding, inefficiency and conflict that surrounds public policy on racial discrimination is partly a result of confusion and ambiguity in terminology usage by scholars, government officials and the courts. Consider the terms discrimination and prejudice. Sometimes they are used in reference to a preference or partiality in the treatment of some groups. Other times the terms refer to a judgment or opinion formed before the facts are known, what some scholars call "statistical discrimination" (Phelps, 1972). If operational definitions can be given to these terms there might be better understanding of socioeconomic forces at work.

1. Preferences

In economic theory, we postulate that each individual has a set of preferences and chooses a preferred set of objects of desire from his available alternatives. There are no objective criteria by which a third party can judge whether one set of preferences is "better" than another simply because there are no commonly accepted standards of evaluation. It is impossible to show that a preference for Bordeaux wines is superior to Burgundy or a preference for blue cars is superior to that for red cars. Preferences are generally accepted as given and the most we can objectively determine is whether, given an opportunity set, the individual is optimizing. That also applies to individual preferences for human attributes such as race, sex, nationality, religion, beauty and other attributes. From an analytical view, there is no conceptual distinction between preferences for race, nationality, sex and other preferences.

It might be rejoined that racial preferences are not comparable to other kinds of preferences in the consequences they have for society and for individuals. The indulgence of racial preferences has specific effects that the indulgence of preferences for certain wines do not have but are the preferences basically different? If so, how do they differ? The preference for Bordeaux wines "harms" Burgundy producers by reducing the value of resources that are held for Burgundy production. If the harmful consequences of preferences are generally thought to reduce the value of some resources and increase the value of others, then preferences for human physical attributes have effects similar to preferences for other objects of desire. One important difference, and by no means small, between preferences for racial features and those for wines is that the latter are not as specialized as the former. If Burgundy producers see that consumers prefer Bordeaux, they might be able to convert their resources into Bordeaux production. On the other hand, people who are black cannot become white, though this is not entirely true: one report estimated that at one time approximately 2,600 Negroes become white, "pass," each year (Eckard, 1947).

The fact that racial attributes are specialized and unchangeable, does not place them in a class by themselves. Persons with average IQs are generally preferred to those with below-average IQs, and persons who are not physically disabled are preferred to those who are, women with attractive features are preferred to comely women. In each of these cases, and many others, the less-preferred attribute is unchangeable. In each case the less-preferred person suffers a disadvantage in some competitive arena. Disadvantage and advantage are the inevitable consequences of differences in individual tastes, abilities, and traits, on the other hand, and freedom of choice in a free society on the other.

Human preferences, whether for physical attributes, such as race, or for other objects of desire such as food, child-rearing practices, alcohol consumption, addictive drugs or entertainment can have a moral dimension. There might be a moral consensus condemning preferences for forms of entertainment such as pornographic movies; there might also be a moral consensus that condemns certain race and sex preferences. The fact of a consensus on what constitutes moral or immoral preferences does not alter the fact that people do exhibit preferences and theoretically, at least, there is no commonly agreed upon standard for deciding whether one set of preferences is more righteous than another. Moreover, there is no standard or proof that one should hold neutral racial preferences with respect to any association whether it might be dating and marriage, or employment and lending.

2. Prejudice

In much of the racial literature, prejudice is usually defined as suspicion, intolerance or an irrational hatred of other races. That vision exposes analysts to the pitfalls of making ambiguous statements and advancing faulty arguments. A useful interpretation of prejudice can be found by examining its Latin root (*praejudicium*) meaning "to judge before the facts are known." Thus, economics can define prejudiced acts as decision-making on the basis of incomplete information.

Decision-making on the basis of incomplete information is necessary in a world of scarcity, uncertainty and complexity. Another common experience is erroneous interpretation of information. Furthermore, different individuals might arrive at different interpretations even if confronted with the same information. Also, different people reach different decisions on what constitutes the optimal quantity of information prior to making decisions.

Consider a simple, yet intuitively appealing, example of how decisions are made on the basis of incomplete information (and possibly erroneous interpretation of evidence). Suppose a fully-grown-tiger suddenly appeared in a room. A reliable prediction is that most individuals would endeavor to leave the area with great dispatch. Such a response to the tiger's presence is not likely to be based on detailed information about the behavioral characteristics of that *particular* tiger. The response is more likely to be based upon one's stock of information about tigers as a class. The individual pre-judges (employs stereotypes). He is not likely to seek additional information because he calculates that the expected cost of an additional unit of information is likely to exceed the expected benefit. He simply ascribes known or surmised group characteristics to the individual tiger.

In the racial discrimination literature, the words prejudice and stereotype are often used pejoratively to refer to those whose selected quantity of information, for decision-making, is deemed too small by the observer. However, what constitutes the optional quantity of information collected before decisions are made is subjectively determined by the individual's calculation of costs and benefits.

Since all of us seek to economize on information cost, we tend to substitute less costly forms of information for more costly forms. Physical attributes are cheap to observe. If a particular physical attribute is seen as being highly correlated with a more costly to observe attribute, then people may use a particular physical attribute as an estimator or proxy for the costly to observe attribute. The cheaply observed fact that an individual is short, an amputee, a black, or a woman provides what some people deem sufficient information for decision-making or predicting the presence of some other more costly to observe attribute. For example, if asked to identify individuals with doctorate degrees in physics only by observing race and sex, most of us would assign a higher probability that white males would have such degrees than black males or women. Such behavior is what decision theory expects where an unobservable attribute must be estimated from an observable one.

3. Employment Decisions

Some recruitment and hiring practices are said to reflect racial preferences, but an alternative explanation can be drawn from our discussion of prejudice. When a company seeks employees, it must discover just how productive job candidates are and whether they will be suitable for investments in training. Since gaining information about prospective candidate is costly, the company has incentive to economize. One method to economize is to select an environment where there is a high probability of success in finding suitable employees.

If a company believes there is correlation between the level of academic achievement, on the one hand, and a candidate's productivity and trainability on the other, it can reduce some recruitment costs just by knowing the job candidate's race. Recruiters know that, for example, in 1990 the average black SAT score was 737 and that for whites was 933. Recruiters might also know that only 38 percent of blacks who enter college graduate in 6 years compared to 58 percent for whites. Also, blacks who do graduate have grades that are two-thirds of a letter grade lower than whites. Given the correlation between race and academic performance, a company might assign a lower probability of finding suitable job candidates by sending recruiters to predominantly black high schools than to predominantly white high schools.

To observe a process that selects in part by skin color and to attribute its motivation to negative employer racial preferences is not only misleading but might generate unproductive public policy. For example, if it is assumed that racial preferences motivate the employer, then under the current legal structure there might be calls for anti-discrimination suits. But if the employer is seen as using race as a method to economize on information cost, a proxy for productivity, the policy might be for school administrators and students at predominantly black high schools to provide employers with reliable information about students who can meet employer productivity expectations.

Employer behavior that uses physical attributes as proxies for other attributes does not systematically differ from that of auto insurance companies that charge male drivers under twenty-five years of age higher premiums, or life insurance companies that charge women lower premiums than they charge men. In both cases, the physical attribute acts as a proxy for some other attribute. In the case of sex and driver age, in auto insurance, a higher probability of accident claims. In the case of life insurance the insured's sex indicates life expectancy. It would be misleading if we explained the auto insurance company's differential treatment of people by age and sex by suggesting they had preferences against men under 25 years of age or life insurance companies liked women better than men.

Not all men under 25 years of age are risky drivers, but auto insurance companies do not know who is and who is not a risky driver. In some cases, young men supply the insurance company with their high school or college grades or the fact that they have taken driver education classes. Auto insurance companies might have discovered a negative correlation between good grades, driver education classes and accident claim experience and charge those younger drivers a lower premium.

Merely observing the use of physical attributes such as race and sex as choice criteria permits us to say nothing unambiguous about race and sex preferences.

4. Discrimination

Discrimination may be defined simply as the act of choice. All selection necessarily and simultaneously requires non-selection; choice requires discrimination. When we preface the word "discrimination" with modifiers such as race, sex, height, education, region, and so forth, we merely state the attribute selected as the choice criteria. As such racial discrimination does not differ in any fundamental sense from any other kind of discrimination.

Our lives are largely spent discriminating for and against selected activities, objects and people. Many of us discriminate against those who have criminal records, who bathe infrequently, who use vulgar speech. Some employers discriminate against applicants who speak with a foreign accent, who have a low intelligence, cannot read or went to the "wrong" college. Most of us choose to date and marry within our own racial or ethnic group, hence discriminating against mates, save for their race and ethnicity, who might be just as suitable. There is also evidence of discrimination in politics; not many short men have been elected president of the United States. Furthermore, discrimination is not consistent. Sometimes people discriminate against theater in favor of parties, against women in favor of men; and at other times the same people do the reverse.

When a choice is made on the basis of race, that choice might or might not reflect preferences. It is impossible for an observer, simply by observing the act of choice, to say for certain whether the choice based on physical attributes reflects preference indulgence, economizing on information costs or the perception of real differences.

5. Subsidized Racial Discrimination

Government policy on race should not focus on whether people have certain racial preferences or engage in racial discrimination or employ prejudicial decision-making. Far more fruitful are efforts to insure there are no governmental acts that subsidize racial aspects of human behavior. While people can and do have racial preferences, they will not indulge those preferences at any cost. There are a number of governmental actions that lower the cost of preference indulgence thereby giving people greater inducement to indulge them.

6. Price Controls

Laws that establish minimum prices, as in the case of minimum wage legislation, and maximum prices, as in the case of rent controls, lower the cost of preference indulgence. Both tend to promote the use of non-economic attributes as criteria for resource allocation. In the case of minimum prices, there is increased resource allocation by buyer preferences and in the case of maximum prices, allocation by seller preferences. The employer who must pay a minimum wage to whomever he hires, even assuming equal productivity among employees, maximizes utility by hiring employees whose non-economic attributes are most pleasing to him. Similarly, the landlord who must charge the same rent to every tenant maximizes utility by renting to the person with attributes most pleasing to him. In both cases the cost of preference indulgence is zero.

Price controls are one of the most effective weapons in the arsenals of those holding strong racial antipathy for one group or another. During South Africa's apartheid-era, white unionists were the country's strongest supporters of minimum wage (rate for the job) laws *for blacks*. In the words of the Mine Workers' Union:

> The real point on that is that whites have been ousted by coloured labor. It is not because a man is white or coloured, but owing to the fact that the latter is cheap. It is now a question of cheap labour versus what is called "dear labour", and we consider we will have to ask the commission to use the word "colour" in the absence of a minimum wage, but when that [minimum wages] is introduced we believe that most of the difficulties in regard to the coloured question will automatically drop out (Johnstone, 1976, p. 158).

George Beetge, Secretary of the Building Workers' Union pled, "There is no job reservation left in the building industry, and in the circumstances I support the rate for the job (equal pay for equal work) as the second best way of protecting our White artisans" (Lipton, 1985, p. 209).

In 1909, the Brotherhood of Locomotive Firemen called a strike against the Georgia Railroad; one of their demands called for the complete elimination of blacks from the railroad. Instead of elimination, the arbitration board decided that black firemen, hostlers and hostlers' helpers be paid wages equal to the wages of white men doing the same job. The white unionists were delighted with the decision saying, "If this course of action is followed by the company and the incentive for employing the Negro thus removed, the strike will not have been in vain" (Spero and Harris, 1931, p. 291).

The Davis–Bacon Act of 1931 mandates that on all federally-funded or assisted construction projects prevailing wages be paid. The Labor Department, having jurisdiction, usually sets the prevailing wage at the union wage or higher and also imposes rigid union-based job classifications, restrictive apprenticeship regulations, and work jurisdiction rules. The Davis–Bacon Act produces discriminatory employment effects similar to the minimum wage.

During the legislative debate on the Davis–Bacon Act, several congressmen were explicit in their support. Georgia Congressman William Upshaw (D. GA) complained of the "superabundance or large aggregation of negro labor, which is a real problem you are confronted with in any community" (U.S. Congress, 1927). "[C]olored labor is being sought to demoralize wage rates [in Tennessee] (U.S. Senate, 1931). Alabama Congressman Clayton Allgood said, "Reference has been made to a contractor from Alabama who went to New York with bootleg labor. This is a fact. That contractor has cheap colored labor that he transports, and he puts them in cabins, and it is labor of that sort that is in competition with white labor throughout the country. ...it is very important that we enact this measure" (U.S. Congress, 1931, p. 6513).

7. Property Rights and Preference Indulgence

The structure of property rights to profits that a firm faces can influence manager decisions to whether to indulge racial preferences. There are several ways property rights to profits can be restricted. One way is an outright ban on profits as in the cases of government and other non-profit organizations, regulated profits in the case of public utilities and restricted profits through profit taxes.

If there is a tax on profits, it means the firm does not have rights to that portion of its pecuniary earnings. Restrictions on pecuniary earnings have predictable effects, namely that of a greater willingness to take earnings in non-pecuniary forms.

Consider a simple example. There is a transcribing firm whose inputs are one typist and entrepreneur. The firm can hire a black typist for $50.00 per week or hire an equally productive white typist at $75.00 per week. We might even assume that, all things being equal, the entrepreneur prefers white typists but will not indulge his racial preferences at any price.

First assume the firm is a profit-maximizer. Its balance sheet is given in Table 1.

Under the assumption of profit maximization, the firm hires the black typist. The cost (foregone profits) to indulge his racial preference would be $25, the wage differential. Assume that all else remains the same except that the government imposes a 50 percent profit tax. The new balance sheet is shown in Table 2.

The profit tax reduces the firm's property rights to profits by $50.00. One legal method to avoid part of the profit tax is to shift one's remuneration from a money form to a non-money form that is not taxable. In our example, the 50 percent profit tax gives the firm inducement to adjust its input selection where the white typist is hired as shown in Table 3.

Table 3 shows the manager indulging his racial preferences by hiring the higher cost white typist. He thereby takes more of his compensation in a non-money form because (1) to avoid a portion of the tax and (2) the tax has made preference indulgence cheaper. Prior to the imposition of the profit tax, discrimination in favor of the costlier white typist would have cost the firm $25 in foregone earnings. After the profit tax it costs the firm $12.50 in

Table 1: The balance sheet for a profit-maximizer

Total sales	Total cost
$150.00	$50.00 wages $100.00 profit
$150.00	$150.00

Table 2: The balance sheet for a profit-maximizer, including profit tax

Total sales	Total cost
$150.00	$50.00 wages $50.00 tax $50.00 after tax profits
$150.00	$150.00

Table 3: Balance sheet for a profit-maximizer including profit, after tax

Total sales	Total cost
$150.00	$75.00 $37.50 profit tax $37.50 profit after tax
$150.00	$150.00

foregone earnings to indulge his preferences. The funda-mental laws of demand apply to preference indulgence as well as other objects of desire — the lower the price, the more is taken.

Non-racial responses to attenuated rights to profit and taking compensation in non-money forms include: expense accounts for executives, ornate offices, company-paid memberships to country clubs, nepotism, hiring more pleasing and more costly employees rather than equally productive less pleasing and less costly ones (Alchian and Kessel, 1962).

The effects of restricted property rights to profit applies to organizations whose profits are regulated such as public utilities and to nonprofit organizations such as universities and to government agencies where the profit motivation is altogether absent. We can expect more discrimination of all forms will be more prevalent in regulated or in not-for-profit organizations (Becker, 1971).

Discriminated-against people have a reduced ability to modify the behavior of the owners of profit-regulated com-panies, through offering compensating differences because the rewards to efficiency cannot be fully captured by the person who acts for the company. Even more damaging to discriminated-against persons is that profit-regulated com-panies can fund the higher cost of hiring more-preferred employees by going to the regulatory commission to demand higher prices to cover the higher costs. In govern-ment, this process can be carried to the extreme because there are no profits at all and high cost employment policy can be shifted to taxpayers. Contrary to conventional wisdom, constrained profits do not serve the interest of less preferred groups (Demsetz, 1965).

8. Conclusion

As historical evidence amply demonstrates, racial prefer-ences alone are not a sufficient condition for racial prefer-ences to be effective. Preferences tell us what people would like to do; however, it is the constraints, income and prices that can tell us what they will find it in their interest to do. It took laws to facilitate racial preference indulgence and the common features of those laws is to restrict voluntary exchange and impede the operation of the market.

WALTER E. WILLIAMS

REFERENCES

Alchian, A. and Kessel, R.A. (1962). "Competition, monopoly and the pursuit of money," in *Aspects of Labor Economics*. Princeton, New Jersey: Princeton University Press, pp. 157–75.

Becker, G.S. (1971). *The Economics of Discrimination*. Chicago: The University of Chicago Press, especially Ch. 3.

Demsetz, H. (1965). "Minorities in the market place." *North Carolina Law Review*, 43(2): pp. 271–297.

Eckard, E.W. (1947). "How many negroes pass?." *American Journal of Sociology*, (May): 498–500.

Jencks, C. and Phillips, M. (eds) (1998). *The Black–white Test Score Gap*. Washington: Brookings Institution Press, p. 402.

Johnstone, F. (1976). *Class, Race and Gold: A Study of Class Discrimination in South Africa*. London: Routledge and Kegan Paul, p. 158.

Lipton, M. (1985). *Capitalism and Apartheid: South Africa 1910–84*. New Jersey: Rowman and Allanheld Publishers, p. 209.

Phelps, E.S. (1972). "The statistical theory of racism and sexism." *American Economic Review*, 62 (2; June).

Spero, S.D. and Harris, A. (1931). *The Black Worker*. New York: Kennikat Press, p. 291.

Peter Newman (ed.) (1998). *The New Palgrave Dictionary of Economics and the Law*. London: Macmillan Reference, Ltd.

U.S. Congress (1927). *Hours of Labor and Wages on Public works*. Committee on Labor, February 28: 3.

U.S. Congress (1931). *Wages of Laborers and Mechanics on Public Buildings*. Committee on Manufacturers, (March 10): 10.

U.S. Congress (1931). *Congressional Record*. p. 6513.

DYNAMIC INCONSISTENCY

The first description of dynamic inconsistency remains the most poignant:

> you must bind me hard and fast, so that I cannot stir from the spot where you will stand me … and if I beg you to release me, you must tighten and add to my bonds. — *The Odyssey*

The introduction of dynamic inconsistency into formal economic analysis came much later, in the seminal paper by Strotz (1955–1956). Strotz modeled the problem of an individual choosing a plan of consumption for a future period of time so as to maximize utility at the present moment. He posed the following question: If this individ-ual is free to reconsider his consumption plan at later dates, will she abide by it or disobey it even though her original expectations of future desires and means of consumption are verified? Strotz's model provides the same answer found in Homer's epic: the plan that is optimal at the pres-ent moment is generally one that will not be obeyed, or that the individual's future behavior will be inconsistent with the optimal plan. For example, if this inconsistency is not recognized, the individual will behave as a "spendthrift," over-consuming in the future relative to the original plan. If the inconsistency is recognized, the rational individual will do one of two things. She may "precommit" her future behavior by precluding future options to ensure that it conforms to the original plan. Or, alternatively she may modify the chosen plan to take account of future disobedience, realizing that the possibility of disobedience imposes a further constraint on the set of plans that are attainable.

Kydland and Prescott (1977) moved the application of dynamic inconsistency squarely into the arena of public policymaking. Their work had a substantial impact on the field of political economy in part because it revealed a gaping flaw in traditional analyses of public policy. Importantly, it demonstrated policy failures that have nothing to do with the underlying motivation of a policymaker, who Kydland and Prescott assume to be interested only in maximizing social welfare. As a source of policy failures, the dynamic inconsistency framework differs fundamentally from other political economy models that rest on the idea that policymakers are driven by myopia, corruption, or some other electoral incentives that cause them to deviate from socially desired goals.

The Kydland and Prescott analysis showed (most famously) that when policymakers have discretion to select the monetary policy that is best in each period, the result is excessive rates of inflation without any reduction in unemployment. The reason is that forward looking economic agents form expectations about future policy choices and, future policymakers are not likely to remain committed to choices made by the present policymakers. Suboptimal policies thus arise in the dynamic inconsistency perspective because there is no mechanism to force future policy makers to take into consideration the effect of their policy on current policymakers. Unlike the dilemma facing Odysseus, the public policy sphere offers no failsafe mechanism to bind future policy makers "hard and fast." Yet Kydland and Prescott still conclude that monetary policy should be governed by rules rather than discretion. They recommend an institutional arrangement that legislates monetary rules that become effective only after a two-year delay. In their view, such an institutional arrangement would be costly to change and thereby accommodate price stability.

Fischer (1980) illustrates the concept of dynamic inconsistency in the realm of tax policy with a useful example. Consider a government policymaker who seeks to promote long-run economic activity; this objective requires tax revenues to finance a public good. The policymaker sets taxes in two sequential fiscal cycles, period 1 and period 2, and two tax instruments are available: taxes on labor income or taxes capital income. Knowing that a tax on capital will discourage investments in productive private capital, the policy maker in period 1 levies a tax on labor income, the lesser of two evils regarding distortions in private economic activity. Firms then make irreversible investments in capital and begin to produce in period 1. In period 2, the policy maker's assessment regarding optimal tax policy changes. She now decides to tax capital income rather than labor income and thereby minimize the distortionary effects of taxation. In response to this revised policy in period 2, the labor supply increases and capital remains fixed. As this simple example illustrates, the choice of the optimal tax instrument is time-inconsistent. The best policy at one point in time is not the best policy at a future point in time, despite the fact that the government's objective remains unchanged (in this case, to maximize economic activity over the two periods).

Of course, potential capital investors might anticipate the government's future policy shift, which would temper their investments in period 1, despite the government's announced policy not to tax capital. And obviously, economic and policy decisions are made over more than two periods. Governments would not be able to make this type of policy shift more than a few times before economic agents catch on: once burned, twice shy.

This Fischer pedagogical example and the caveats again reveal that the dynamic inconsistency problem derives from two fundamental elements: (i) desired policy choices have a temporal dimension, and (ii) government policies are unenforceable contracts. In political transactions third-party enforcement is not possible simply because the parties to the agreed-upon transaction can subsequently change the rules or renege without legal sanctions. In the tax policy example, suppose the government declares that its policy to tax labor and not capital is permanent. Capital investors, one party to this agreement has no legal recourse if the government were to renege on its promise. Even if the tax policy laws were enacted, legislators (current and future) would not be bound by past agreements; they could enact new laws revoking the old.

It is important to note that the pure theory of dynamic inconsistency abstracts from potential institutional sources of durability. The very absence of legal or institutional mechanisms to maintain long-term policy commitments stands behind the suboptimal policy choice. One line of research emphasizes that political institutions and rules emerge that make currently enacted policies difficult to alter. This was the novel insight exposited by Landes and Posner (1975). In their perspective, a host of elements of the political process can be understood as durability-enhancing mechanisms (Crain and Oakley 1995).

A second approach found in a variety of theoretical models follows more closely in the mold of Kydland and Prescott. These models, sometimes labeled "strategic fiscal policy," have in common the basic theme that a current political regime might use fiscal policy variables as a means of controlling policy choices by future regimes. Once again, the inability of present period voters (or their policy making representatives in the present political regime) to make binding contracts with voters in the next period (the future regime) creates the basic dilemma. The novelty in these models, however, is that policymakers respond by making fiscal choices designed lock-in, bind, or otherwise constrain the choices available to future political decision makers. In other words, a political majority today might use fiscal policy to lock-in a current policy that a future majority would predictably oppose.

It is worth reiterating that an important wrinkle in strategic fiscal policy analysis is that inefficient government policies are driven by the representative voter and not by pressure group demands for wealth redistribution. As long as the current government can affect some policy variable that enters into its successor's decision calculus, it can influence to some degree the policy carried out by the successor government. In the process of binding future fiscal outcomes, however, the current government selects a different (and suboptimal) policy relative to what it would have preferred if it expected to remain in power. This occurs when the current and future regimes have different, or time-inconsistent, fiscal policy preferences. Three models illustrate this tradition, and surveys are provided in Perrson (1988) and Alesina (1988).

Perrson and Svensson (1989) develop a model in which a current government uses the level of the public debt as an instrument to control the level of spending by a future government. They construct a principal–agent model in which government (or the decisive voter) today is the principal and government in the next period is the agent. The intuitive example in their model posits an incumbent conservative regime that expects to be replaced in the next election by a liberal regime. The current regime will put in place a fiscal policy that features lower taxes and higher deficits than it would otherwise prefer in order to control the ability of the future liberal government to embark on large spending programs. As long as public debt enters negatively into the policy preferences of the future liberal regime, it responds to the conservative regime's legacy of deficit financing by spending less than it otherwise would prefer.

Alesina and Tabellini (1990) develop a related model, the key difference being that succeeding regimes champion different spending priorities. For example, the current regime favors large defense budgets and minimal welfare budgets, and the future regime favors the opposite policy mix. Alesina and Tabellini (1990) also assume that public debt enters negatively into the preference functions of both regimes. In the case of time-inconsistent spending preferences, the current regime moves to constrain future spending (on the welfare programs it detests) by running a larger deficit than it would if it were assured of remaining in power.

Glazer (1989) develops a strategic model in which voters have a bias toward capital-intensive projects in the absence of durability enhancing institutions. Rational voters show a consistent bias in favor of capital projects, which they would oppose were the decision theirs to make individually in a private market environment. Glazer's formal derivation is not repeated here; an intuitive understanding is straightforward and sufficient to illustrate the durability-motivated strategic fiscal choice.

Because current period voters cannot make contracts with next period's voters, one possible strategy is to limit future policy options by constructing a long-lived capital project. This maneuver eliminates from the next period the option to renew or reject the services from the capital project. An inefficiently large public capital stock is predicted under majoritarian rules, irrespective of the cost efficiency of the capital project.

Glazer's conclusion does not require any assumptions about the cost structure of the projects. Suppose that the benefits of two short-lived projects are equivalent to the benefits of one durable project, yet the costs of constructing two short-lived projects are less than the cost of building the long-lived (durable) project. Suppose further that the decisive voter in period 1 would like the services of the project in both periods. However, if the decisive voter in period 1 expects the short-term project to be rejected in period 2, he prefers the more expensive durable project in period 1. This would be the case if the benefits derived from the short-lived project over the two periods exceed the costs of the relatively more expensive durable project. In other words, the decisive voter selects a second-best outcome to prevent the worst-case outcome: no project in period 2. Glazer labels this source of capital bias a "commitment effect." Alternatively, suppose the decisive voter in period 1 has no strict preference for either the durable or the single-term project and that he expects the decisive voter in period 2 to choose the short-term project. If building the durable project is cheaper than building two successive short-term projects (i.e., there are economies of scale), the decisive voter in period 1 may select the durable project, even though the benefits are less than the cost, because it is less costly than the two short-term projects. This is what Glazer calls the "efficiency effect," which motivates a capital bias under collective choice as long as the difference in the benefits and costs of the single short-lived project exceed those of the durable project.

As this brief summary indicates, strategic fiscal models are based on the idea that choices in a given electoral period take into consideration expectations about preferences of decision-makers in succeeding periods. Fiscal variables such as spending, taxing and borrowing are used strategically as devices to control future choices if current policy makers expect the preferences of future policy makers to differ from their own. The process of binding future fiscal outcomes causes the current government to select second-best (and suboptimal) policies relative to what it would have preferred if it expected to remain in power.

Because these policy choices are second-best from the standpoint of the current regime, political conditions and the presence of institutions that enhance policy longevity should reduce the motivation to use fiscal variables strategically. Political conditions and institutions that facilitate policy durability predictably lower the incentive for strategic fiscal policy choices. In effect, strategic fiscal choices substitute for institutional sources of policy durability.

Crain and Tollison (1993) examine the tradeoff between strategic fiscal choices and institutional sources of durability using American state data. They find that such factors as term limits and the stability of the majority party controlling the state legislature reduce strategic behavior of the type described in the Perrson and Svensson (1989) and Alesina and Tabellini (1990) models. Crain and Oakley (1985) specify an empirical model to investigate implications of the Glazer model. Specifically, political conditions and institutions that facilitate policy durability predictably lower the capital intensity of government spending. Also using American state data, the findings indicate that institutions such as term limits, citizen initiative, and budgeting procedures significantly affect infrastructure spending across states. The results further indicate that political conditions such as majority party stability and voter volatility are systematically related to infrastructure differences across states. These two empirical studies indicate a fruitful common ground between models of dynamic inconsistency and the institutional models in the tradition of Landes-Posner. This ground remains largely unexplored, particularly in formal theoretical models, and represents a promising area for future research.

W. MARK CRAIN

REFERENCES

Alesina, Alberto (1988). "Macroeconomics and politics," in Stanley Fischer (ed.), *NBER Macroeconomics Annual*. pp. 13–61.

Alesina, Alberto and Guido Tabellini (1990). "A positive theory of deficits and government debt." *Review of Economic Studies*, 57: 403–414.

Crain, W. Mark, and Lisa K. Oakley (1995). "The politics of infrastructure." *Journal of Law and Economics*, 38: 1–18.

Crain, W. Mark, and Robert D. Tollison (1993). "Time inconsistency and fiscal policy: empirical analysis of US states, 1969–89." *Journal of Public Economics*, 51: 153–159.

Fischer, Stanley (1980). "Dynamic inconsistency, cooperation and the benevolent dissembling government." *Journal of Economic Dynamics and Control*, 2: 93–107.

Glazer, Amahai (1989). "Politics and the choice of durability." *American Economic Review*, 79: 1207–1213.

Kydland, Finn, E. and Edward C. Prescott (1977). "Rules rather than discretion: the inconsistency of optimal plans." *Journal of Political Economy*, 3: 473–492.

Landes, William, M. and Richard Posner A. (1975). "The independent judiciary in an interest group perspective." *Journal of Law and Economics*, 18: 875–901.

Perrson, Torsten (1988). "Credibility of macroeconomic policy: an introduction and a broad survey." *European Economic Review*, 32: 519–532.

Perrson, Torsten and Lars Svensson (1989). "Why stubborn conservatives run deficits: policy with time-inconsistent preferences." *Quarterly Journal of Economics*, 104: 325–345.

Strotz, R.H. (1955–1956). "Myopia and inconsistency in dynamic utility maximization." *The Review of Economic Studies*, 23(3): 165–180.

E

ECONOMIC FREEDOM AND ITS MEASUREMENT

Interest in the measurement of economic freedom originates from two separate lines of inquiry. The first, firmly embedded in the tradition of normative economics, focuses on freedom measurement for enlarging the narrow evaluative bases of welfare economics. The second, rooted in the libertarian tradition, tries to construct objective empirical indices of the extent of economic freedom enjoyed by countries on a world-wide basis. Despite their different origins, methodology and aims, both traditions share a common denominator that informs their theoretical underpinnings and the measures that they construct, viz., individual choice. More precisely, economic freedom measures constructed within each line of inquiry reflect different relationships between 'making choices' and 'having freedom'.

For the purposes of this review, I start with a brief illustration of the role of choice in freedom measurement. I then distinguish three perspectives on choice that are at the basis of economic freedom metrics:

1. choice as *picking up alternatives*;
2. choice as *deliberation*;
3. choice as '*undistorted*' *selection*.

I analyze the freedom metrics connected with each perspective and discuss their merits.

1. The Role of Choice in the Measurement of Freedom

Whichever line of inquiry one takes side with, the measurement of economic freedom is rooted in some relationship between economic freedom and choice. In an influential paper which originated a lively debate on the appropriate criteria for measuring freedom, Pattanaik and Xu (1990) write that,

> irrespective of which option the agent considers as the best, availability of opportunities reflects a certain degree of freedom for the decision maker which is impaired if the extent of options contracts, even if the most preferred alternative remains available. (p. 385).

Pattanaik and Xu work within the normative economics tradition. They aim at enlarging the set of intrinsically

relevant criteria that should be used in the assessment of states of affairs and — as the passage highlights — they consider freedom as 'availability of opportunities' a suitable candidate for the post. In their interpretation, access to opportunities gives to a decision maker the possibility of selecting among alternatives and, in so doing, of enjoying a certain degree of freedom. Their measure of economic freedom is based then on the idea that, as the extent of accessible opportunities increases, so does the agent's degree of liberty, unveiling therefore a direct relationship between having economic freedom and the making choices in the sense of selecting among alternatives.

Despite the different interpretation of economic freedom, a relationship with making choices can also be traced for the line of inquiry which works in the thrust of the libertarian tradition. Scholars who contributed to this line of analysis regard economic freedom as being unencumbered by unnecessary government interference in the pursuit of one's own economic activity. Necessary interference is that which guarantees protection of property rights and the smooth functioning of competitive markets. As Buchanan (1975) says,

> [u]nder regimes where individual rights to do things are well defined and recognized, the free market offers maximal scope for private, personal eccentricity, for individual freedom in its most elementary meaning. (p. 18).

But note that unnecessary government interference reduces economic freedom since it alters both the assignment of property rights and the possibility of trading at prices set by competitive markets, prices which reflect the agent's marginal valuation of resources. But, if one believes what economics has taught us, changing the value of resources at the margin affects individual choice, leading to losses of economic freedom and unveiling, once again, a relationship between enjoying economic freedom and making choices.

2. Three Perspectives on Choice

Although choice can be considered as a common denominator in the analysis and measurement of economic freedom, yet the way in which their relationship has been framed within the two lines of inquiry differs substantially. By and large, three interpretations find support in the literature. 'Choice as picking up alternatives' and 'choice as deliberation' are rooted in the normative economics tradition, whereas 'choice as undistorted selection' is pursued within the libertarian perspective.

1. Following Miller (1991), choice as picking up alternatives coincides with 'possibility to act': an agent enjoys a certain degree of economic freedom if she has alternative

opportunities or courses of action to choose from, and the larger the set of opportunities that she may access, the greater the extent of her economic freedom. Possibility to act has generated two kinds of measures. The first one, introduced by Pattanaik and Xu (1990), relies on pure cardinality: their 'Simple Cardinality-based Ordering' (SCO) compares pairs of opportunity sets on the sole basis of the number of elements that they contain. The second measure, proposed by Sen (1988, 1991, 1993), suggests that the assessment of the degree of economic freedom must depend on the preference relation of the decision maker over the available options. An opportunity set A offers greater economic freedom than B if it contains more options *and* at least weakly preferred to those in B.

Measures based on such a perspective between economic freedom and choice have become the catalyst of a number of criticisms. Some have objected to SCO's endless possibility of distinguishing opportunities, which forecloses the ground to any general classification of 'types' of opportunity (Sugden, 1998; Bavetta and Guala, 2001). Others have targeted the role of preferences in Sen and his underlying notion of economic freedom as 'doing what one wants' (cf., among the others, Hayek, 1960).

But, a further criticism applies which enjoys a stronger grip. It states that measures of economic freedom which rely either on a pure quantity assessment or on an exogeneously given preference relation do not capture an interesting interpretation of choice since they lack reference to the deliberative process. The reason is that, in order to deliberate, the decision maker must be involved in a selection effort which can neither be captured by SCO (where preferences do not enter in the assessment of economic freedom), nor by Sen's measure (where preference are exogenously given). Neither of the two measures therefore makes use of information about *how* the decision maker selects among the available alternatives and about whether she will be able to *exercise* her positive economic freedom in the decision process.

2. While a compelling challenge to the aforementioned metrics, this latter criticism is also suggestive of the way towards alternative measures. Following its thrust, some recent papers (cf. Pattanaik and Xu, 1998; Bavetta and Peragine, 2000) introduce quantitative assessments of economic freedom that capture how free is the decision maker's deliberative process. In the pursuit of such a goal, these measures endorse a different relationship between choice and economic freedom (choosing as deliberating) in which the focus is shifted from the *post* to the *pre-deliberation* stage of a choice, i.e., that stage of a decision process at which the preferences of the decision maker are not yet shaped. At that stage, the chooser is in the position for developing a will of her own (her own individuality) and the act of choosing, as

John Stuart Mill's *On Liberty* suggests, becomes the instrument for shaping it. Having options to choose from fosters individuality because certain fundamental qualities of an agent which render him autonomous, such as "perception, judgement, discriminative feeling, mental activity, and even moral preference" (Mill, 1859, p. 122) can be exercised and developed by making choices, i.e., in the deliberation process. The relationship between having economic freedom and making choices takes here a different (and more interesting) turn as choosing becomes, at the same time, *expression of* and *training for* the development of a person's autonomy. Two distinct ideas emerge: (1) choosing is an activity that is valuable in itself (autonomy as 'doing the work' of choosing, so to speak, Nozick, 1974); (2) choosing is valuable because it is functional to the development of an autonomous identity (exercising as an instrumental good). In both cases, choosing as deliberating fosters economic freedom because it develops individual autonomy.

When choice is tied to deliberation the measurement of economic freedom has to take into account the development process of individuality. Technically, this is captured by the idea of *potential preference*, i.e., all the preference relations that an agent may uphold over a set of options. Potential preferences, in turn, identify the *relevant options*, namely those options that can be chosen on the basis of a potential preference that has turned actual. An individual enjoys a wider degree of economic freedom the larger her set of relevant options. Of course, for the process of formation of individuality to be meaningful, not all potential preferences should be allowed to become actual because, in this case, we would be back to SCO. Nor we can admit shrinking the set of potential preferences to a singleton since, in this other case, we would be back to Sen (Bavetta and Peragine, 2000). A screening device is therefore necessary to select among the potential preferences. The most appropriate requires that options be *not too distant* in terms of preference from each other (Bavetta and Peragine, 2000; Bavetta and Guala, 2001).

3. The last perspective on the relationship between economic freedom and choice belongs to the libertarian tradition. It may be best illustrated by means of an example. Consider an unnecessary interference that alters the free market determination of relative prices. Just to fix ideas, let it consist of a $1 specific excise tax levied on gasoline. The tax modifies the agent's marginal valuation of resources as well as her optimal choice. Assuming a linear demand curve over the relevant range, suppose that, at the equilibrium pre-tax price of $10 an individual consumed 30 liters of gasoline per week whereas, at the equilibrium post-tax price of $11 she consumes 25 liters. The burden of the tax is $25 (which go in the government's coffers) plus $2.5 of

deadweight loss. This would be though just the 'welfare' cost of the tax which represents a measure of the distortion imposed on the free market choice but that does not capture the entire effect on economic freedom. To compute the latter we should add the consequences of the tax in terms of the mutually beneficial transactions foregone. In general, therefore, the measure of the loss in economic freedom associated with the unnecessary government intervention is given by the marginal value of the distortion multiplied by the number of transactions both undertaken and foregone.

In principle, all empirical measures of economic freedom so far constructed in the literature share these premises (cf., e.g., Gwartney et al., 2000; O'Driscoll et al., 2001). A number of complications though do arise. For example, although theoretical analysis would prescribe summing the measured distortions in each market, this is not always feasible.

In practice, to overcome these difficulties, empirical measures are contructed starting with a definition of a set of relevant economic categories where interference with individual choices may occur. These include the policy design activity of governments (trade policy, monetary and fiscal policy), as well its regulatory role (regulations on banking and finance, on the labour market, on international real and financial transactions) and its protective role (protection of property rights and control over black market activity). Once the set of variables is identified, each component is assessed. The techniques for the assessment vary with availability of data and the characteristics of the component. Finally, each component is weighed (but in some rankings all variables are equally weighed) and a grading scale is constructed which aggregates in different fashions the score assigned to each component in each country. Aggregation preserves temporal and cross-country consistency, i.e., respectively, if a country improves with time, this is reflected in its rating and the distribution of the country ratings reflects the distribution of the actual values among the countries.

The empirical measures of freedom suffer from two major limitations. The first is that appropriate microfoundations for each component are unattainable given the complexity of the information that this would require. As a consequence, for some components, the index provides us with too coarse an approximation to be reliable. A second limitation is that, though empirical measures of economic freedom are able to distinguish the free from the unfree countries, yet the indices are hardly sensitive to fine distinctions.

SEBASTIANO BAVETTA

REFERENCES

Bavetta, S. and Guala, F. (2001). "Autonomy freedom and deliberation," mimeo, CPNSS, London School of Economics.

Bavetta, S. and Peragine, V. (2000). "Measuring autonomy freedom." Economic Series Working Paper 00/27, Universidad Carlos III de Madrid.

Buchanan, J.M. (1975). *The Limits of Liberty*. Chicago: Chicago University Press.

Carter, I. (2002). "Choice, freedom and freedom of choice." *Social Choice and Welfare*, (forthcoming).

Gwartney, J., Lawson, R., and Samida, D. (2000). *Economic Freedom of the World. 2000 Annual Report*. Vancouver: The Fraser Institute.

Hayek, F. (1960). *The Constitution of Liberty*. London: Routledge.

Mill, J.S. (1859). *On Liberty*. London: John W. Parker and Son.

Miller, D. (ed.). (1991). *Liberty*. Oxford: Oxford University Press.

Nozick, R. (1974). *Anarchy, State and Utopia*. Oxford: Blackwell.

O'Driscoll, G.P., Holmes, K.R., and Kirkpatrick, M. (2001). *2001 Index of Economic Freedom*. Washington: The Heritage Foundation.

Pattanaik, P.K. and Xu, Y. (1990). "On ranking opportunity sets in terms of freedom of choice." *Réchérche Économiques de Louvain*, 56: 383–390.

Pattanaik, P.K. and Xu, Y. (1998). "On preference and freedom." *Theory and Decision*, 44: 173–198.

Sen, A.K. (1988). "Freedom of choice: concept and content." *European Economic Review*, 32: 269–294.

Sen, A.K. (1991). "Welfare, preference and freedom." *Journal of Econometrics*, 50: 15–29.

Sen, A.K. (1993). "Markets and freedoms: achievements and limitations of the market mechanism in promoting individual freedoms." *Oxford Economic Papers*, 45: 519–541.

Sugden, R. (1998). "The metric of opportunity." *Economics and Philosophy*, 14: 307–337.

ECONOMIC FREEDOM AND POLITICAL FREEDOM

> Historical evidence speaks with a single voice on the relation between political freedom and a free market. I know of no example in time or place of a society that has been marked by a large measure of political freedom that has not also used something comparable to a free market to organize the bulk of economic activity. (Friedman, 1962, p. 9)
>
> History suggests only that capitalism is a necessary condition for political freedom. Clearly it is not a sufficient condition (Friedman, 1962, p. 10)

Economic freedom refers to the quality of a free private market in which individuals voluntarily carry out exchanges in their own interests. Political freedom means freedom from coercions by arbitrary power including the power exercised by the government. Political freedom consists of two basic elements: political rights and civil liberties. Sufficient political rights allow people to choose their rulers and the way in which they are ruled. The essence of civil liberties is that people are free to make their own decisions as long as they do not violate others' identical rights. Friedman (1962) points out the historical fact that economic freedom and political freedom are inextricably connected. However, the relationships among economic freedom, civil liberties, and political rights are complex (Friedman, 1991).

In a free private market, individuals have the freedom to choose what to consume, to produce, and to give. The invisible hand leads free economic agents to pursue their own interests and voluntarily cooperate with others (Smith, 1776). Economic freedom and civil liberties are clearly related. A society whose civil liberties are incomplete is unlikely to sustain a free private market since civil liberties and economic freedom have in common the freedom from coercions by other individuals or governments. A free private market is characterized by voluntary transactions among individuals who are left alone to pursue their own ends for their economic objectives. The value of political freedom to economic freedom exactly lies in the fact that civil liberties are defined as including guarantees to limit governmental power and to protect individual autonomy. Human freedom embedded in civil liberties is the means through which economic freedom is realized.

The importance of political rights to economic freedom, however, is less clear. Friedman (1991) points out that "political freedom, once established, has a tendency to destroy economic freedom." He basically believes that the process of political competition, as determined by political rights, may generate policies that negatively affect economic freedom. Public choice scholars have long argued that competitively elected politicians and their agents in the bureaucracy are self interested and may intervene and disturb the free market to please their constituencies and sponsors. Individuals enjoying political rights use democratic forms of government to redistribute wealth from others often by interfering with the free market, by restricting competition or limiting sales through the manipulation of prices, or otherwise creating rents. The misuse of political freedom in democracies has caused an expansion of services and activities by governments far beyond the appropriate scope in which economic and human freedoms are protected and maintained. Inefficiencies of democracy fundamentally impose constraints on the workings of a free private market and hamper the full realization of economic freedom (see Buchanan and Tullock, 1962; Buchanan et al., 1980; Rowley et al., 1989; Tullock et al., 2000).

A democracy, once established, tends to limit economic freedom to some degree. More surely, an authoritarian regime is less likely to positively promote economic freedom. Suppose that a country develops a political system with a hierarchically structured bureaucratic organization that gives privileges to an elite class. In such a country, political freedom must be restricted to serve the elite minority. Even if a market exists, it must not be a true free private market. Individuals are merely agents of the state and cannot be truly competitive. Moreover, political authorities in an authoritarian regime tend to distort the market by allocating resources by coercion. The elite class controls a large part of the resources and effectively controls the entire spectrum of economic decisions. Economic freedom develops and evolves by accident, and never by design (Hayek, 1944).

Historically and logically, it is clear that economic freedom is a condition for political freedom. A core ingredient of economic freedom is private property which is fundament in supporting political freedom. Without secure private property and independent wealth, the exercise of political rights and civil liberties loses its effectiveness. Hayek (1944) maintains that "Economic control is not merely control of a sector of human life which can be separated from the rest: it is the control of the means for all our ends." People who depend on the government for their employment and livelihood have little capacity to oppose the government as they exercise their political rights. Without rights to own and utilize their properties as they want, people cannot operate a free media, practice their religions, and so forth.

In the long term, economic freedom leads to and sustains political freedom. It is no doubt that a free private market is most conducive to wealth creation (Smith, 1776). A system of economic freedom is superior to any system of planning and government management (Hayek, 1944). The market process is a spontaneous order in which resources are efficiently allocated according to individual needs voluntarily expressed by people. Without any coercions and deliberate designs, a free private market brings about economic efficiency and greater social welfare. The wealth effects of economic freedom create necessary social conditions for political freedom. Fundamentally, an authoritarian regime that represses political freedom cannot survive alongside a free private market in the long run. A free private market not only is a process for achieving the optimal allocation of resources and creating wealth, which provides material foundations for political freedom, but also provides an environment for learning and personality development that constructs behavioral foundations for political freedom. However, whether or not these conditions would lead to democracies depends on other complex factors, especially, the strategic interactions among various political groups (Przeworski, 1992).

Relations among economic freedom, civil liberties, and political rights are complex theoretically and historically. To empirically assess these relations, we face a hurdle of measuring economic and political freedom. Fortunately, several serious efforts on measuring the freedoms have recently been made. Particularly impressive are those measurements with regular upgrades. Rich panel data sets of economic and political freedoms make it possible to test various hypotheses developed in the vast theoretical literature on the two freedoms and to inspire future theoretical development based on insights derived from empirical analyses.

1. Measuring Economic Freedom

The first attempt to measure economic freedom was undertaken by Gastil and his associates at Freedom House (Gastil, 1982). Economic freedom rankings were compiled to complement Freedom House's political freedom rankings. Soon two major economic freedom indexes were published by the Heritage Foundation and the Fraser Institute (Johnson and Sheehy, 1995; Gwartney et al., 1999). The Fraser Institute and the Heritage Foundation have updated their indexes regularly. We focus on comparing the Fraser Index and the Heritage Foundation Index.

Both the Fraser Index and the Heritage Foundation Index attempt to obtain an overall economic freedom ranking for each country during a particular year based on raw scores on a variety of factors relevant to economic freedom. They follow a similar procedure that contains the following elements: defining economic freedom; selecting component variables; rating component variables; combining component ratings into the final overall rankings of economic freedom.

The Fraser Index defines core ingredients of economic freedom as personal choice, protection of private property, and freedom of exchange. In the Heritage Foundation Index, "economic freedom is defined as the absence of government coercion or constraint on the production, distribution, or consumption of goods and services beyond the extent necessary for citizens to protect and maintain liberty itself" (O'Driscoll et al., 2002). Both definitions reflect the essence of a free private market. They represent an ideal state in which a limited government focuses on protecting private property rights and safeguarding the private market for individuals to freely engage in exchanges.

Guided by their definitions of economic freedom, the two Indexes identify areas that are relevant to economic

freedom. The Fraser Index selects 21 components under seven areas: size of government; economic structure and use of markets; monetary policy and price stability; freedom to use alternative currencies; legal structure and security of private ownership; freedom to trade with foreigners; and freedom of exchange in capital markets. The Heritage Foundation Index chooses fifty variables in ten factors: trade policy; the fiscal burden of government; government intervention in the economy; monetary policy; capital flows and foreign investment; banking and finance; wages and prices; property rights; regulations; and black market activity. Apparently, the two Indexes attempt to cover essential features of economic freedom: protection of private property; reliance on the private market to allocate resources; free trade; sound money; and limited government regulations.

The two Indexes differ significantly in ways in which they rate on components of economic freedom. The Heritage Foundation Index uses a five-level grading scale to determine scores for each factor based on information collected on pertinent factor variables. However, not all factor variables are individually graded. Therefore, raw data on factor variables are combined into factor grades in a relatively subjective way. There are no explicit formulas for summarizing information on factor variables into factor grades. The Fraser Index directly assigns scores to all component variables on a 0-to-10 scale. For continuous component variables, the Fraser Index applies explicit and fixed formulas to convert original data on component variables into scores. For categorical component variables, subjective judgments are applied to obtain scores. Areas of economic freedom in the Fraser Index are rated solely on the scores of pertinent component variables. In comparison, scores on the factors in the Heritage Foundation Index seem to be obtained in a more subjective way than scores on areas in the Fraser Index. However, this practice allows the Heritage Foundation Index more liberty in using a wider range of information sources. The Heritage Foundation Index not only has more factor variables, but also covers more countries and time periods.

The two Indexes also differ in their weighting schemes for combining component ratings into their final overall rankings of economic freedom. The Heritage Foundation Index simply weights factor ratings equally. The Fraser Index uses principle component analysis to construct weights for each component variables in calculating the final scores of economic freedom. As pointed out in the Appendix of Wu and Davis (1999b), principal component analysis allows one to obtain a measure of economic freedom which is statistically objective in the sense that the final ratings of economic freedom are directly derived from the data of component variables. The method suits well for the exercise of measuring economic freedom since the final overall scores of economic freedom are derived from components that are assumed to reflect some aspects of the concept of economic freedom. The weights are based on the principal component that explains the maximum variations in the original data of component variables among all standardized linear combinations of the original data.

The Fraser Index claims to develop an objective measure of economic freedom. It is transparent and objective in scoring component variables and weighting component ratings in the final index of economic freedom. Nevertheless, these solid steps in the procedure do not change the qualitative nature of a measure of economic freedom. An economic freedom measure is not quantitative data such as national income that can be truly objectively measured. The usefulness of an economic freedom measure lies in the fact that it provides rankings of different countries over time. In other words, final scores of economic freedom are ordinal in nature. The Heritage Foundation Index applies four categories of economic freedom: Free, Mostly Free, Mostly Unfree, Repressed. The Fraser Index does not provide qualitative categories like this. Final ratings in the Fraser Index range from 0 to 10, with a higher number indicating higher degree of economic freedom. We ought not to mistake these ratings as continuous and cardinal data. The only valid and usable information in these ratings is the relative degrees of economic freedom indicated by the scores. For example, in 1997, the Fraser Index gives Hong Kong a score of 9.4, Albania 4.3, and Chile 8.2. From these numbers, we can only conclude that Hong Kong is freest economically among the three, Chile second, and Albania third. The difference between any two scores cannot be interpreted numerically. For example, we cannot say that Hong Kong is 119% freer than Albania.

The two Indexes share some similarities and some differences in their methods of measuring economic freedom. We are interested in whether the different methods would lead to differences in their final ratings of economic freedom. To statistically compare the two Indexes, we compile a data set which includes 238 country-years in 1995 and 1999. The two Indexes overlap in these two years.[1] We use data of the four categories in the Heritage Foundation Index, and accordingly collapse the inherent ten rankings (based upon the 0–10 scale) into four categories based on the final rankings in the Fraser Index.[2] Table 1 shows a cross-classification of economic freedom in the Heritage Foundation Index by that in the Fraser Index. Table 1 clearly demonstrates a pattern in which observations classified as economically freer in the Heritage Foundation Index are also classified as economically freer in the Fraser

Table 1: Cross-classification of Heritage Foundation Index by Fraser Index

Fraser Index	Heritage Foundation Index			
	Repressed	Mostly unfree	Mostly free	Free
Repressed	5	10	0	0
Mostly Unfree	8	56	14	0
Mostly Free	0	27	79	3
Free	0	0	14	22

Index.

The two Indexes classify observations similarly. Among the observations in Table 1, the total number of concordant pairs[3] is:

$$C = 5 \times (56 + 14 + 27 + 79 + 3 + 14 + 22) + 10$$
$$\times (14 + 79 + 3 + 14 + 22) + 8 \times (27 + 79 + 3 + 14$$
$$+ 22) + 56 \times (79 + 3 + 14 + 22) + 14 \times (3 + 22) + 27$$
$$\times (14 + 22) + 79 \times 22 = 13,223.$$

The number of discordant pairs of observations is:

$$D = 10 \times 8 + 14 \times 27 + 3 \times 14 = 500.$$

Of the concordant and discordant pairs, 96.36% are concordant and only 3.64% are discordant. The difference of the corresponding proportions gives a gamma $(= (C - D)/(C + D) = 92.72\%)$.

The number indicates that the Heritage Foundation Index and the Fraser Index are highly correlated. We can further explore the relationship between the two Indexes by testing the null hypothesis of independence between the two categorical variables. We simply use a Pearson chi-squared test and a likelihood-ratio chi-squared test to analyze the cross-classification as shown in Table 1. The Pearson chi-squared statistic is 218.43 which yields a P-value less than 0.0001, and the likelihood-ratio chi-squared statistic is 197.49 with a P-value less than 0.0001 (based on degree of freedom = 9). There is very strong evidence of association between these two measures even if we ignore the category orderings of the variables.[4]

2. Measuring Political Freedom

The concept of political freedom and democracy is much debated. Our task here is not to provide an exhaustive review of the debates, but to point out empirical conceptions of political freedom and democracy that cover its main features in the modern world that are relevant to statistical analyses. These narrow definitions of political freedom and democracy enable us to identify empirical cases of democracies and non-democracies. Dahl (1971) provides a useful definition of democracy by emphasizing the procedural characteristics of the political system. Democracy, as an institutional arrangement, ought to ensure the following conditions:

1. Freedom to form and join organizations;
2. Freedom of Expression;
3. Right to vote;
4. Eligibility for public office;
5. Right of political leaders to compete for support (Rights of political leaders to compete for votes);
6. Alternative sources of information;
7. Free and fair elections;
8. Institutions for making government policies depend on votes and other expressions of preferences.

When these conditions are met, the elected government is judged to be responsive to citizens' preferences, and the democracy and political freedom are established

Dahl's eight conditions describe the core of a modern democracy. For the purpose of empirically measuring political freedom, however, we need to further condense the definition and establish rules that can help categorize observations unambiguously. There exist several empirical measurements, and there is no agreement among scholars regarding the ways of actually measuring democracy (Bollen, 1980, 1993; Vanhanen, 1990; Przeworski et al., 2000; Mainwaring et al., 2001). However, Przeworski et al. (2000) point out

> ... even if regime classification has been the subject of some controversies, alternative definitions of "democracy" give rise to almost identical classifications of actual observations.

We want to compare two representative measurements.[5] One is by Freedom House and the other by Przeworski et al. (2000) (PACL, hereafter). The two measurements are both rule-based in the sense that both apply pre-determined criteria in identifying democracies. Nonetheless, Freedom House and PACL appear to represent the two "extremes" of measuring political freedom and democracy. Freedom House's political freedom rankings are based on raw scores assigned by experts, and hence, seem to be subjective. PACL's political regime classification exclusively relies on observables, and attempts to avoid subjective judgments.

Freedom House first differentiates two basic dimensions of political democracy: political rights and civil liberties. The former mainly refers to the electoral process. Elections should be fair and meaningful (choices of alternative parties and candidates, and a universal franchise). The latter implies freedom of the press, freedom of speech, freedom of religious beliefs, and the right to protest and organize. The Freedom House measure is comprehensive and related to multiple dimensions of a modern democracy. Its focus is not the form of government itself, but upon political rights and the freedom of citizens caused by the real working of the political system and other societal factors. To contrast, the PACL measure is concerned with political regimes as forms of government, and focuses on contestation as the essential feature of democracy. The authors intentionally exclude political freedom from their measurement. The narrow definition by PACL is aimed to avoid using different aspects of democracy (e.g., as defined by Dahl, 1971) that the authors believe to be of little use. The authors argue "Whereas democracy is a system of political rights — these are definitional — it is not a system that necessarily furnishes the conditions for effective exercise of these rights." (Przeworski et al. 2000) Whether or not democracy as narrowly defined by PACL is associated with political rights and other desirable aspects of democracy is a question for empirical testing.[6]

Different concepts and scopes of political freedom put forward by Freedom House and PACL underpin their rules and criteria for classifying democracies. Freedom House assigns each country the freedom status of "Free," "Partly Free," and "Not Free" based on their ratings in political rights and civil liberties. To rate political rights and civil liberties in a country, Freedom House employs two series of checklists for these two aspects of democracy. For political right ratings, Freedom House uses eight checklist questions and two discretionary questions. These questions are not only related to formal electoral procedures but also other non-electoral factors that affect the real distribution of political power in a country. Freedom House's civil liberties checklist includes four sub-categories (Freedom of Expression and Belief, Association and Organizational Rights, Rule of Law and Human Rights) and fourteen questions in total. Freedom House maintains that it does not mistake formal constitutional guarantees of civil liberties for those liberties in practice.

While the civil liberties component is broadly conceived, the political rights dimension of the Freedom House measure is more compatible with PACL's rules for regime classification.[7] These rules exclusively deal with electoral contestation and government selections. The three basic rules are labeled as "executive selection," "legislative selection," and "party." The idea is to identify democracies as regimes in which the chief executive and the legislature are elected in multi-party elections. The great majority of cases (91.8% of country-years in PACL's sample) are unambiguously classified by the three rules. PACL further introduces an additional rule ("alternation") for those ambiguous cases. The "alternation" rule is used to classify countries that have passed the three basic rules. In these countries, the same party or party coalition had won every single election from some time in the past until it was deposed by force or until now. For these cases, we face two possible errors: excluding some regimes that are in fact democracies from the set of classified democracies (type I error); including some regimes that are not in fact democratic in the set of classified democracies (type II error). PACL seeks to avoid type-II errors. Therefore, there are some regimes that meet the three basic criteria which are disqualified as democracies.

PACL rigidly and mechanically applies these four rules, but Freedom House rates countries with discretion. To be "unbiased," PACL only needs to strictly adhere to their rules while Freedom House needs to consciously maintain a culturally unbiased view of democracy and utilize the broadest range of information sources. The PACL measure is necessarily consistent because it exclusively relies on observables and objective criteria. Freedom House's checklists and ratings procedures are consistent. However, the ratings themselves could be inconsistent because of variation in information sources, raters' expertise and so on.

The distinctive spirits of the Freedom House and PACL measures are nicely reflected in their timing rules. Both measures observe countries in a period of a year. PACL codes the regime that prevails at the end of the year. Information about the real situation before the end of the year is not relevant. For example, a country that has been a democracy until the last day of a year is classified as a dictatorship in the PACL measure. For the same country, Freedom House would treat it differently and consider the political development during the whole year and assign appropriate scores. The information lost in the PACL measure is utilized in the Freedom House ratings, and the loss of information is significant for some cases, especially for many countries in political transition.

The categorization of political regimes in the PACL measure could be nominal in the sense that there is no ordering between democracy and dictatorship, or ordinal that a transition from dictatorship to democracy means some improvement. PACL's further classifications of democracy and dictatorship are nominal in nature. The difference between parliamentary, mixed, and presidential democracies is meaningful if merely qualitative and definitional. However, the difference between bureaucracy and autocracy could be quantitative. PACL classifies a dictatorship with a legislature as a bureaucracy, and not as an autocracy. Freedom House's freedom rankings are explicitly ordinal. The overall statuses of "Free," "Partly Free," and "Not Free" reflect different degrees of political freedom in countries. The base scores of political rights and civil liberties ratings are themselves ordinal. Freedom House uses a seven-point scale for the two dimensions of democracy, with 7 indicating the highest degree and 1 the lowest degree. This measurement implicitly assumes that there exists a continuum of political democracy. The two poles are the fully democratic regime (with 1 for both political rights and civil liberties) and a full autocratic regime (with 7 for both political rights and civil liberties). The underlying continuum of political regimes makes it easier to describe and analyze the rich phenomena of political transitions. Freedom House rankings make it possible to analyze the intermediate cases of semi-democracies or semi-dictatorships, and the complicated nature of democratization or reverse-democratization. Under the PACL classification, there are only two possible transition modes: from democracy to dictatorship, and from dictatorship to democracy. The simplified transition modes are less capable of capturing the transitional nature of political development.

To quantitatively compare the Freedom House and PACL measures, we use a data set that consists of 2584 country-years during the period from 1972 to 1990. This data set includes all observations that have both the PACL regime classifications and the Freedom House ratings.[8] Table 2 shows a cross-classification of political regime (PACL classifications) by freedom status (the Freedom House overall ratings).

From Table 2, we observe "Not Free" is mostly associated with "Dictatorship", and "Free" with "Democracy". For countries with a "Partly Free" ranking, more are "Dictatorship" than "Democracy". This result probably reflects the cautious stance taken by the PACL measure that tries to avoid type-II errors. Overall, these two measures are quite similar. Among the observations in Table 2, concordant pairs number at 1,361,384, and the number of discordant pairs of observations is 7,773. Thus, 99.43% are

Table 2: Cross-classification of political regime by freedom status

Political freedom	Political regime	
	Dictatorship	Democracy
Not Free	931	1
Partly Free	711	106
Free	66	769

concordant and only 0.57% are discordant. The sample gamma is 98.86%. This confirms that a low degree of political freedom occurs with non-democratic regimes and high degree of political freedom with democratic regimes. The Freedom House rankings are highly correlated with PACL political regime measures.[9]

We can further explore the relationship between the Freedom House and PACL measures by testing the null hypothesis of independence between the two categorical variables. The Pearson chi-squared statistic is 1896.62, and the likelihood-ratio chi-squared statistic is 2201.61 (based on degree of freedom = 2). Both statistics give P-values less than 0.0001. There is very strong evidence of association between these two measures even if we ignore the category orderings of the variables.

The apparent "anomalies" are cases that are reflected in up-right and bottom-left corner cells. The only one observation that is classified as "Not Free" and "Democracy" is Guatemala in 1981. The Freedom House 1981 volume's description of Guatemala (p. 352) reports: "Most opposition parties are now heavily repressed. ... Military and other security forces maintain decisive extra-constitutional power at all levels: those politicians who oppose them generally retire, go into exile, or are killed." Then the 1982 edition begins its report with the sentence (p. 296): "Until a 1982 coup Guatemala was formally a constitutional democracy on the American model." The PACL measure seems to have classified Guatemala as a democracy in 1981 while Freedom House observers clearly judged the government to be categorized by repression which was confirmed by the 1982 coup.

There are sixty-six cases that are classified as "Free" and "Dictatorship" as shown in Table 3. Among these cases, two third (66.7%) are classified according to "alternation" rules. As pointed out above, the "alternation" rules risk type-I error. So those country-years that are classified as dictatorship could actually be democracies. Using more information and discretion, Freedom House gives these observations a "Free" ranking. Botswana is a typical example. Political stability characterizes Botswana's political landscape. Botswana's Democratic Party has been ruling the country until the present. PACL "alternation" rules require Botswana during the period from 1972 to 1990 to be classified as a dictatorship. However, Freedom House rates it as "Partly Free" in 1972 and "Free" in 19 years after that, based on their information sources and survey methodology.

It is interesting to note that all those forty-four cases, in which "alternation" rules are applied, are classified as bureaucracies in PACL's more detailed regime classification. Actually, the great majority (64 out of 66) of cases

Table 3: Cases that are classified as dictatorship and free

Country	Period	Regime	Alternation rule or not
Botswana	1973–1990	Bureaucracy	Yes
Burkina Faso	1978, 1979	Bureaucracy	Yes
Djibouti	1977, 1978	Bureaucracy	No
El Salvador	1972–1975	Bureaucracy	Yes
Fiji	1972–1986	Bureaucracy	No
Gambia	1972–1980, 1989, 1990	Bureaucracy	Yes
Ghana	1981	Autocracy	No
Guyana	1972	Bureaucracy	Yes
Malaysia	1972, 1973	Bureaucracy	No
Nigeria	1983	Autocracy	No
Seychelles	1976	Bureaucracy	No
Sri Lanka	1977–1982	Bureaucracy	Yes
West Samoa	1989, 1990	Bureaucracy	Yes

rank "Free" in Freedom House surveys are classified as bureaucracies by PACL. Bureaucracies in the PACL measure are those dictatorships with legislatures, and certainly more likely to be ranked at "Free" by Freedom House than those autocracies. Among the sixty-six observations, there are only two cases in which Freedom House ranks them at "Free" and PACL classifies them as "autocracies." In the case of Nigeria, the "anomaly" is due to the timing rules used by PACL. According to Freedom House, Nigeria changed from a multiparty democracy which began in 1979 and began to change after 1982 in a series of coups, rather than a single event, which by 1984 had placed the government under the control of a military command. The judgmental nature of the Freedom House rules caused a slower reclassification.

There was a military intervention in Ghana in 1979 that led to political executions. However, the 1981 Freedom House review gives the "free" rating and begins with the sentence (p. 350): "Since Fall 1979 Ghana has been ruled by a parliament and president representing competitive parties." The 1982 report changed the rating to "not free" and noted that the country was being ruled by a military faction. It also noted that there had been some political detentions and police brutality before the 1981 coup, but "...such denials of rights have subsequently increased" (p. 295). In this instance the observers from Freedom House seem to have recognized the institution of democracy and classified the Country as "free" in 1981 but in 1982 they not only changed their rating to "not free" but also implicitly corrected their observation of the previous year.

3. Empirical Analyses on Economic Freedom and Political Freedom

With comprehensive data on economic and political freedoms becoming available, there is a surge of empirical studies on the two freedoms and the relationships between freedom and other economic and social variables.

There already existed a vast literature on the influence of political freedom on economic growth before measurements of economic freedom were published. The findings of these empirical studies are conflicting (Pourgerami, 1988; Scully, 1988; Glahe and Vorhies, 1989; Przeworski and Lomongi, 1993; Paster and Sung, 1995; Haan and Siermann, 1996). The empirical results range from positive to negative influences of political freedom on economic growth. The contradictions of the results could be attributed to contrasting model specifications and empirical measurements of political freedom. Some authors argued that the freedom which really matters in economic growth is economic freedom (Scully, 1992; Brunetti and Wedder, 1995; Knack and Keefer, 1995; Barro, 1996). This line of investigation was energized by the publication of the Heritage Foundation Index and the Fraser Index. The Cato Journal published a special issue on "Economic Freedom and the Wealth of Nations" in 1998. Positive effects of economic freedom on growth are also reported in a variety of empirical studies (Easton and Walker, 1997; Ayal and Georgios, 1998; Dawson, 1998; Haan and Siermann, 1998; Gwartney et al., 1999; Wu and Davis, 1999a, b). Economic freedom is also used to explain other aspects of economic development including income equality and human well-being (Berggren, 1999; Esposto and Zaleski, 1999).

Economic freedom as an independent variable in explaining economic growth and development is robust in numerous studies. We conclude that the arguments heard down through the centuries — a reliance upon the market place and unrestrained competition in the allocation of a society's resources is the best policy to promote economic growth — have largely been established by the experiences of the countries of the world as these have been analyzed by numerous researchers working with these new measurements. It is also the same case for economic development as a significant explanatory variable for democracy. In Lipset's classic statement, "Perhaps the most wide widespread generalized linking political system to other aspects of society is related to the state of economic development" (Lipset, 1959). Economic development, as an independent variable, has survived in a variety of rigorous empirical tests on determinants of democratic development (Diamond, 1992; Przeworski et al., 2000).

The linkages depicted in these empirical studies relate economic freedom to economic growth, and economic development to political freedom. As noted above, these two links seem to be well established. Moreover, these linkages suggest a less well established empirical the influence of economic freedom on political freedom. Such a link between economic freedom and political freedom would certainly confirm certain theoretical insights in the literature. We judge there to be a need for further studies.

Empirical analyses on the possible reverse relationship between political freedom and economic freedom are largely lacking. We will not speculate upon the reasons for the relative scarcity of studies. We simply note that it is important to learn whether the careful study of our measured history of freedoms will confirm the theoretically based arguments and observations that democracy "inherently" acts to constrain economic freedom, and whether the precise nature of such constraints can be illuminated. Further, these additional analyses are important to verify theoretical arguments about possible conflicting effects of civil liberties and political rights upon each other as well as on economic freedom. Is there a tendency for a free electoral system to work so as to limit civil rights if there is not a developed constitution and independent judiciary to prevent such an action? Do guarantees of civil rights mean that through time an electoral system will necessarily be established? Which, if not both, might be a factor in limiting economic freedom? Finally, will further empirical analyses be able to establish that there exists an endogenous relationship between economic freedom and political freedom?

There are many questions waiting to be answered and empirically established. It may be that the possible endogoniety between economic and political freedom is one of the most intriguing and perhaps the most important. If a demonstration of endogoniety can include a specification of the mechanism, if the establishment of more economic freedom really tends to lead to the development of democratic forms of government, then there are urgent reasons to hope for and expect additional studies.

WENBO-WU

OTTO A. DAVIS

NOTES

1. In the Heritage Foundation's annual report (say, in year "n") on economic freedom, authors claim that data in the current reports generally cover the last half of year "n − 2" and the first half of year "n − 1." However, it is reasonable to assume that data in the annual report of year "n" are representative of situations in year "n − 3" (Cummings, 2000).

2. To make the economic freedom ratings explicitly ordinal, it would be a good practice to assign a few broad categories of economic freedom in the Fraser Index. We construct four categories of economic freedom as follows (original final rankings in the Fraser Index are in the parentheses): Free (8–10); Mostly Free (6–7.99); Mostly Unfree (4–5.99); Repressed (0–3.99).

3. In this case, a pair is concordant if the country ranking higher in the Heritage Foundation Index also ranks higher in the Fraser Index. A pair is discordant if the country ranking higher in the Heritage Foundation Index ranks lower in the Fraser Index. For example, consider a pair of observations, one of whom is classified in the cell (Repressed, Repressed) and the other in the cell (Mostly Unfree, Mostly Unfree). This pair is concordant, since the second observation is ranked higher than the first both by the Fraser Index and by the Heritage Foundation Index. Each of the 5 observations in the cell (Repressed, Repressed) form concordant pairs when matched with each of the 56 observations in the cell (Mostly Unfree, Mostly Unfree), so there are $5 \times 56 = 280$ concordant pairs from these two cells. The 5 observations classified as Repressed by both Indexes are also part of a concordant pair when matched with each of the other $(12 + 27 + 79 + 3 + 14 + 22)$ observations ranked higher in both Indexes.

4. We can exploit the ordinality of the two measures by using the so-called uniform association model that assigns scores to the rows and columns with a coefficient that describes strength of association. The assigned scores reflect category orderings and can be modeled as equal-interval. As expected, the uniform association model predicts a greatest departure from independence of these two measures.

5. Mainwaring et al. (2001) provide a trichotomous ordinal classification of democracy for Latin American countries from 1945 to 1999. They argue that such a classification achieves greater differentiation than dichotomous classifications such as PACL regime classifications, and needs much less information that a fine-grained measure such as the Freedom House political freedom rankings would require. For our purposes, however, we need comprehensive rankings for a majority of countries in the world. That is why we focus on PACL and the Freedom House classifications. Furthermore, Mainwaring et al.'s measure is highly correlated with the PACL and Freedom House measures.

6. For the sample described below, the gamma (a statistic measuring association between two ordinal variables) for political rights and civil liberties ratings is 0.91 and the Pearson correlation is 0.92. Both statistics indicate a strong association between these two dimensions of democracy in Freedom House's surveys.

7. For the sample described below, the gamma for political rights rating and PACL regime classification is -0.98, and the Pearson correlation is -0.85. The gamma for civil liberties rating and PACL regime classification is -0.96, and the Pearson correlation is -0.80. So the associations between PACL regime classification and the two components of Freedom House's democracy ratings are very strong, and the Freedom House political rights rating is more closely related to PACL regime classification.

8. South Africa is excluded. Freedom House rated separately for "White" and "Black" in South Africa during the sample period.

9. Other measures of ordinal association further confirm the conclusion. For example, *Kendall's tau-b* is 0.742. If we ignore the ordinality of political freedom and political regime data, a high Pearson correlation (0.793) indicates a very high degree of association between these two measurements.

REFERENCES

Ayal, E.B. and Georgios, K. (1998). "Components of economic freedom and growth: an empirical study." *Journal of Developing Areas*, 32(Spring): 327–338.

Barro, R.J. (1996). "Democracy and growth." *Journal of Economic Growth*, 1(March): 1–27.

Berggren, N. (1999). "Economic freedom and equality: friends or foes?" *Public Choice*, 100(3/4): 203–223.

Bollen, K.A. (1980). "Issues in the comparative measurement of political democracy." *American Sociological Review*, 45: 370–390.

Bollen, K.A. (1993). "Liberal democracy: validity and method factors in cross-national measures." *American Journal of Political Science*, 37: 1207–1230.

Brunetti, A. and Wedder, B. (1995). "Political sources of growth: a critical note on measurement." *Public Choice*, 82: 125–134.

Buchanan, J.M. and Tullock, G. (1962). *The Calculus of Consent: Logical Foundations of a Constitutional Democracy*. Ann Arbor: University of Michigan Press.

Buchanan, J.M., Tollison, R.D., and Tullock, G. (1980). *Toward a Theory of the Rent-Seeking Society*. College Station: Texas A & M University Press.

Cummings, J. (2000). "Economic freedom indices: their use as tools for monitoring and evaluation." *SCS Working Paper* 00/01.

Dahl, R.A. (1971). *Polyarch: Participation and Opposition*. New Haven: Yale University Press.

Dawson, J.W. (1998). "Institutions, investment, and growth: new cross-country and panel data evidence." *Economic Inquiry*, 36(October): 603–619.

Diamond, L. (1992). "Economic development and democracy reconsidered." *American Behavioral Scientist*, 450–499.

Easton, S.T. and Walker, M.A. (1997). "Income, growth, and economic freedom." *American Economic Review*, 87(May): 328–332.

Esposto, A. and Zaleski, P. (1999). "Economic freedom and the quality of life." *Constitutional Political Economy*, 10: 185–197.

Friedman, M. (1962). *Capitalism and Freedom*. Chicago: University of Chicago Press.

Friedman, M. (1991). "Economic freedom, human freedom, political freedom." Speech delivered at The Smith Center for Private Enterprise Studies, California State University, Hayward.

Gastil, R.D. and followers. (1972–2002). *Freedom in the World*. New York: Freedom House.

Glahe, F. and Vorchies, F. (1989). "Religions, liberty and economic development: an empirical investigation." *Public Choice*, 62: 201–215.

Gwartney, J. and Lawson, R. (with Park, W. and Skipton, C.) (2001). *Economic Freedom of the World, 2001 Annual Report*. Vancouver: Fraser Institute.

Gwartney, J., Lawson, R., and Holcombe, R. (1999). "Economic freedom and the environment for economic growth." *Journal of Institutional and Theoretical Economics*, 155(4): 1–21.

Haan, J.De. and Siermann, C.L.J. (1996). "New evidence on the relationship between democracy and economic growth." *Public Choice*, 86: 175–198.

Haan, J.De. and Siermann, C.L.J. (1998). "Further evidence on the relationship between economic freedom and economic growth." *Public Choice*, 95: 363–380.

Hayek, F.A. (1944). *The Road to Serfdom*. Chicago: University of Chicago Press.

Johnson, B.T. and Sheehy, T.P. (1995). *The Index of Economic freedom*. Washington, DC: The Heritage Foundation.

Knack, S. and Keefer, P. (1995). "Institutions and economic performances: cross-country tests using alternative institutional measures." *Economics and Politics*, 7(November): 207–227.

Lipset, S.M. (1959). "Some social requisites of democracy: economic development and political legitimacy." *American Political Science Review*, 53: 69–105.

Mainwaring, S., Brinks, D., and Perez-Linan, A. (2001). "Classifying political regimes in Latin America, 1945–1999." *Studies in Comparative International Development*, 36(spring): 37–65.

O'Driscoll, G.P. Jr., Holmes, K.R., and O'Grady, M.A. (2002). *The 2002 Index of Economic Freedom*. Washington, DC: Heritage Foundation, and New York: The Wall Street Journal.

Paster, J. and Sung, J.H. (1995). "Private investment and democracy in the developing world." *Journal of Economic Issues*, 29: 223–243.

Przeworski, A. (1992). "The games of transitions," in *Issues in Democratic Consolidation: The New South American Democracies in Comparative Perspective*. Notre Dame: University of Notre Dame Press.

Przeworski, A., Alvarez, M.E., Cheibub, J.A., and Limongi, F. (2000). *Democracy and Development: Political Institutions and Well-being in the World, 1950–1990*. New York: Cambridge University Press.

Przeworski, A. and Limongi, F. (1993). "Political regimes and economic development." *Journal of Economic Perspectives*, 7: 51–69.

Rowley, C.K., Tollison, R.D., and Tullock, G. (1989). *The Political Economy of Rent Seeking*. Amsterdam: Kluwer Academic Publishers.

Smith, A. ([1776] 1937). *An Inquiry into the Nature and Causes of the Wealth of Nations*. New York: Random House.

Tullock, G., Seldon, A., and Brady, G.L. (2000). *Government: Whose Obedient Servant?* London: The Institute of Economic Affairs.

Vanhanen, T. (1990). *The Process of Democratization: A comparative Study of 147 States*. 1980–88. New York: Taylor and Francis.

Wu, W. and Davis, O.A. (1999a). "The two freedoms in a growth model." *Journal of Private Enterprise*, 14(2): 115–143.

Wu, W. and Davis, O.A. (1999b). "Two freedoms, economic growth and development: an empirical study." *Public Choice*, 100(1/2): 39–64.

ECONOMIC REGULATION

1. Introduction

The concept of economic regulation originally found its way into the public choice literature in Stigler's (1971) paper in the *Bell Journal of Economics*. The paper was a restatement of the time-honored capture theory of regulation, though unlike his precursors, Stigler formulated the capture theory as a testable economic model. He also showed several innovative ways to test the theory. Posner (1973) offered an assessment of how well the theory of economic regulation stacked up against competing theories.

The most important subsequent contribution to this subject is Peltzman (1976), and this is where I pick up the topic for purposes of exposition.

2. Peltzman's Generalization

In his basic paper, Stigler made the following observation: "These various political boons are not obtained by the industry in a pure profit-maximizing form" (1971, p. 6). This comment contained the seed that later led to Peltzman's (1976) generalization of Stigler's theory. Figure 1 illustrates.

Profits are measured along the vertical axis, and price along the horizontal axis. A vote-maximizing regulator/politician seeks to trade off wealth between consumers represented by the price variable and producers represented by the profit variable. Higher indifference curves for the regulator are read in a northwestern direction. Point A on the horizontal axis corresponds to a competitive industry making zero economic profits. Point B corresponds to profit-maximization by a pure monopolist or a perfect cartel. Note that the shape of the regulator's indifference curves show the nature of Stigler's conjecture. Point B is not a political equilibrium unless consumer interests are ignored totally by the regulator. (This would imply a V curve parallel to the profit axis tangent to point B.) A normal political equilibrium is given by point E, where the regulator equates his marginal rate of political substitution (of consumer for producer votes) to the slope of the transfer locus as defined by the profit hill.

Peltzman's model contains many useful implications. For example, why are certain types of industries regulated and others not? In Figure 1, it is easy to see that the improvement in regulator utility (votes) is greater when industries that are either purely competitive or pure monopolies are regulated. Movements from point such as A (pure competition) or B (pure monopoly) to point E create more

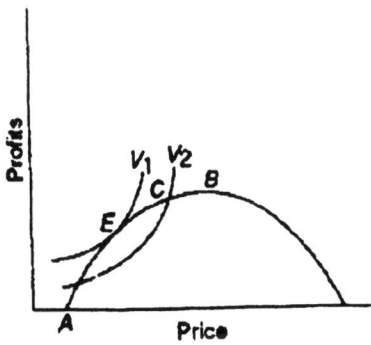

Figure 1: A regulatory equilibrium.

political wealth for the regulator than movements from intermediate positions such as C (oligopoly?). Thus, there is a vote-maximizing rationale for why one observes the extensive regulation of natural monopolies (utilities) and purely competitive industries (agriculture) and little or no regulation of the steel and automobile industries.

In a private setting, it is well known that fixed costs have no influence on short-run price and output. However, fixed costs matter to the political equilibrium level of price and profit in Figure 1. Imagine that the profit hill (which is a function of price and costs) shrank by a constant amount throughout its range, reflecting an increase in fixed costs in the industry. Obviously, the optimal political price would change. In general, the vote-maximizing regulator will make trade-offs in such a fashion that increases in industry profit are shared with consumers through a regulatory price reduction and decreases in industry profit are buffered by regulatory price increases. Hirshleifer (1976, 243) called this the principle of "share the gain and share the pain."

There are numerous other interesting applications of Peltzman's model, which is without doubt the single most important theoretical development in the post-Stigler literature on economic regulation. A few of these are summarized below.

3. The Origins of Regulation

Economists have typically taken a cross-sectional approach to the study of regulation. Given that regulation exists in some jurisdictions and not in others, differences in such variables as price and output can be compared in the two cases. Much less attention has been devoted to the question of why regulation comes into existence in the first place. In other words, what explains the timing of major regulatory events such as the passage of a new law mandating a regulatory program?

Stigler (1971) laid out a method for addressing this issue in his original paper on the subject. He attempted, with mixed results, to explain the onset (the date) of occupational regulation across U.S. states. The subsequent literature has not risen very much to Stigler's challenge on this issue, but there are some developments worth reporting.

Stigler and Friedland (1962) reported cross-sectional regression results for electricity prices across U.S. states for 1922. Their results suggested that state regulation of electricity prices had no detectable effect on the level of these prices; prices in regulated states were statistically the same as prices in unregulated states. Jarrell (1978) unraveled this conundrum by examining the timing of municipal and state regulation of electric utilities over the period prior to 1922. He found that both municipal and state regulation occurred first where the demand for regulation was the greatest, that is, where electric utility markets were the most competitive. The predicted effects of economic regulation are borne out in Jarrell's results as prices and profits rose substantially in the states that were regulated early.

Shughart and Tollison (1981) applied the timing method to explain the evolution of more liberal corporate chartering laws across U.S. states from 1837 to 1913. The older system of corporate chartering was excessively bureaucratic and cumbersome, requiring legislative enactment of a firm's charter in some cases. The new system was a great deal less costly in that obtaining a charter required going to the appropriate state office, filing the appropriate forms, and paying a fee. Shughart and Tollison sought to explain the year in which states adopted more liberal chartering laws with a model that incorporated proximate measures of the costs and benefits of such laws to local (state) manufacturing interests. Greater costs suggest later passage; greater benefits suggest earlier passage. Such a theory leads to a robust explanation of the timing of this significant episode of legal change and deregulation in U.S. history.

Explaining the timing of specific government regulations provides a challenge to economists and other students of government regulation. The progress made thus far is not really impressive, and there are many regulatory histories waiting to be written (or, one should say, rewritten).

4. Heterogeneous Firms

In the simple version of the capture theory, a unified industry captures a regulatory process at the expense of consumers. However, much economic regulation is driven by a different set of combatants. Much regulation is fueled by competitor versus competitor interests. The most obvious example of this type of regulation is where the producers of butter obtain a regulation raising the price of margarine. But this is not what is meant here; what is meant is competitor versus competitor in the same industry, that is, some butter producers against others.

Buchanan and Tullock (1975) were the first to articulate such a theory of regulation in the context of pollution controls. Since their paper, other applications of the basic concept have appeared (see, e.g., Maloney and McCormick, 1982). The basic idea is straightforward. Firms in an industry are heterogeneous with respect to costs; the industry supply curve is upward sloping to the right. This opens the door to possible regulations that impose relatively greater costs on higher-cost, marginal firms, causing some of them to leave the industry. All firms face higher costs as a result of direct regulation, but the exit of higher-cost firms raises market price in the industry. Depending upon relevant elasticities of demand and supply, the increase in price can outweigh the increase in costs for the lower-cost producers. If so, the regulation increases their wealth at the expense of both consumers and the higher-cost firms in the industry.

This approach to the explanation of regulation has been used extensively in the areas of social and environmental regulation. Fundamentally, it offers a better understanding of why direct administrative controls over production are preferred to less intrusive regulation such as environmental user fees or property rights.

In an innovative spirit, Marvel (1977) used this theory to explain the origin of the British factory acts in the 1830s. Contrary to the conventional wisdom that such laws were in the public interest because they limited the working hours of women and children, Marvel argues that the regulation of hours favored steam mill over water mill owners. The latter could only operate when the water flow was sufficient, and hence ran long hours when stream conditions were good. The hours restrictions curtailed the ability of the water-driven mills to make up for lost output when streams were low. According to Marvel's estimates, the resulting rise in textile prices transferred a significant amount of wealth to steam mill owners, who could operate on a regular basis. This is only part of the interest-group story of the factory acts, but Marvel laid out an innovative and plausible private-interest explanation of this legislation based on the idea of heterogeneous firms.

5. Social versus Economic Regulation

Stigler (1971) called his article "The Theory of Economic Regulation." This has come to be a somewhat misleading title. As the previous discussion indicated, much, if not all, of the regulation that goes under the heading of social and safety regulation has been successfully analyzed with the tools that Stigler initially deployed. In short, the best way to understand any regulatory scheme is to answer the twin questions, who wins and who loses. As Becker (1976) emphasized, it is best to think in terms of an economic theory of regulation rather than a theory of economic regulation.

Indeed, even the most innocuous sounding regulatory programs have been analyzed with the interest-group model. These include environmental, health, and safety programs (Bartel and Thomas, 1987), the British factory acts (Anderson and Tollison, 1984), various antitrust policies and practices (Mackay et al., 1987), the banning of the importation of slaves into the United States (Anderson et al., 1988), immigration restrictions (Shugart et al., 1986), apostolic decrees by the Roman Catholic Church (Ault et al., 1987), Luddism (Anderson and Tollison, 1984, 1986), population growth (Kimenyi et al., 1988), farmer opposition to futures markets (Pashigian, 1988), and still others.

6. Modern Deregulation

Deregulation is obviously an important issue for the theory of economic regulation. Not only must the theory be able to explain the onset of regulation, but it must also be able to explain the exit of regulation from the political marketplace.

Peltzman (1989) has addressed this challenge to the theory, specifically focusing on the deregulation of selected U.S. industries in the late 1970s and early 1980s. This episode of deregulation was quantitatively important, and Peltzman wanted to see if the theory of economic regulation could explain it.

He framed the issue in a general way by emphasizing that the theory of economic regulation, as presently constituted, is mostly an architecture for describing positions of political equilibrium, and it has not been expanded sufficiently to account for the process of entry into and exit from the political market for regulation. With the issue thus framed, Peltzman argued that the Chicago theory can explain episodes of deregulation, primarily as a function of regulatory-induced cost increases that increase the potential gains to the benefactors (consumers) of deregulation. In essence, he proposed a cyclical theory of regulation. Regulation (or entry) occurs and a rent-transfer process is begun; over time, the rents are eroded because the regulator cannot enforce a perfect cartel; and, finally, deregulation (or exit) becomes politically profitable. It is the present value of the regulatory transfer at the onset of regulation that drives behavior in Peltzman's dynamic model of economic regulation.

This is certainly an intriguing idea. Although it is not clear why cost increases and rent dissipation cannot be controlled by the regulator, the answer is probably traceable to Stigler's (1971, p. 6) conjecture quoted earlier. Peltzman goes on to apply this type of analysis to the various industries that have been deregulated and finds that it fits some cases but not all. Perhaps the most prominent of the latter cases is the role of rents accruing to organized labor in industries like trucking, where such rents were relatively large and the recipient group was politically powerful (apparently to no avail).

All that one can do at this stage is agree with Peltzman, who argues for further research on this issue. Peltzman, however, has pointed in a useful direction. Namely, if wealth transfers are the basis of regulation, they are surely also the basis of its decline.

7. Concluding Remarks

A lot of ground has been covered since Stigler (1971) and Posner (1974). In fact, one might say that opposing theories of regulation have been pretty thoroughly driven from the scene. Mathematical economists still spin out complex considerations of optimal regulation and so on, but the workers who toil in the empirical study of regulation and governmental behavior know better. The impact of interest groups on the economy is a fascinating problem, as scholars such as Becker (1983) and Olson (1982) have shown. A whole new type of political economy has emerged from this work which has become a dominant paradigm in political economy because it is grounded in positive economic methodology.

ROBERT D. TOLLISON

REFERENCES

Anderson, G.M., Rowley, C.K., and Tollison, R.D. (1988). "Rent seeking and the restriction of human exchange." *Journal of Legal Studies*, 17(January): 83–100.

Anderson, G.M. and Tollison, R.D. (1984). "A rent-seeking explanation of the British factory acts," in David C. Colander (ed.) *Neoclassical Political Economy*. Cambridge, Mass.: Ballinger, pp. 187–201.

Anderson, G.M. and Tollison, R.D. (1986.) "Luddism as cartel enforcement." *Journal of Institutional and Theoretical Economics*, 142(December): 727–738.

Ault, R.W., Ekelund R.B. Jr., and Tollison, R.D. (1987). "The pope and the price of meat." *Kyklos* 40(fasc. 3): 399–413.

Bartel, A.P. and Thomas, L.G. (1987). "Predation through regulation." *Journal of Law and Economics*, 30(October): 239–264.

Becker, G.S. (1976). "Comment." *Journal of Law and Economics*, 19: 245–248.

Becker, G.S. (1983). "A theory of competition among pressure groups for political influence." *Quarterly Journal of Economics*, 98(August): 371–400.

Buchanan, J.M. and Tullock, G. (1975). "Polluter's profits and political response: direct controls versus taxes." *American Economic Review*, 65(March): 39–147.

Hirshleifer, J. (1976). "Comment." *Journal of Law and Economics*, 19(August): 241–244.

Jarrell, G.A. (1978). "The demand for state regulation of the electric utility industry." *Journal of Law and Economics*, 21(October): 269–296.

Kimenyi, M.S., Shughart, W.F. II, and Tollison, R.D. (1988). "An interest-group theory of population growth." *Journal of Population Economics*, 1(October): 131–139.

Mackay, R.J., Miller, J.C. III, and Yandle, B. (eds.) (1987). *Public Choice and Regulation*. Stanford, Calif.: Hoover.

Maloney, M.T. and McCormick, R.E. (1982). "A positive theory of environmental quality regulation." *Journal of Law and Economics*, 25(April): 99–124.

Marvel, H.P. (1977). "Factory regulation: a reinterpretation of early English experience." *Journal of Law and Economics*, 20(October): 379–402.

Olson, M. (1982). *The Rise and Decline of Nations*. New Haven: Yale University Press.

Pashigian, P. (1988). "Why have some farmers opposed futures markets?" *Journal of Political Economy*, 96(April): 371–382.

Peltzman, S. (1976). "Toward a more general theory of regulation." *Journal of Law and Economics*, 19(August): 211–240.

Peltzman, S. (1989). "The economic theory of regulation after a decade of deregulation," in Martin Neal Baily and Clifford Winston (eds.) *The Brookings Papers on Economic Activity*. Washington: Brookings Institution, pp. 1–41.

Posner, R.A. (1974). "Theories of economic regulation." *Bell Journal of Economics and Management Science*, 5(Autumn): 335–358.

Shughart, W.F. II and Tollison, R.D. (1981). "Corporate chartering: an exploration in the economics of legal change." *Economic Inquiry*, 23(October): 585–599.

Shughart, W.F. II, Tollison, R.D., and Kimenyi, M.S. (1986). "The political economy of immigration restrictions." *Yale Journal on Regulation*, 4(Fall): 79–97.

Stigler, G.J. (1971). "The theory of economic regulation." *Bell Journal of Economics and Management Science*, 2(Spring): 3–21.

Stigler, G.J. and Friedland, C. (1962). "What can regulators regulate? The case of electricity." *Journal of Law and Economics*, 5(October): 1–16.

THE ECONOMIC THEORY OF CLUBS

1. Introduction

Clubs, whether one speaks of the Girl Guides, the All England Lawn Tennis and Croquet Club, a homeowners' association, or the Republican Party, are private organizations whose members collectively consume (and often produce) at least one good or service that no one person has the capacity unilaterally to finance. Clubs are thus of interest to public choice scholars because they must solve the same kinds of collective action problems government faces in the provision of public goods. Moreover, while there are exceptions to the rule (e.g., closed union shops), clubs solve these problems voluntarily rather than coercively.

This essay summarizes the theory of clubs and assesses its empirical relevance and applicability (more detailed literature reviews are contained in Sandler and Tschirhart, 1980, 1997). The second of these two tasks is not a particularly easy one because there has not been very much in the way of direct empirical testing of the theory of clubs, at least outside the literature on international alliances. However, while the effort here is not intended to be exhaustive, a sufficient number of examples will be provided so that the reader will gain a preliminary understanding of the extremely useful nature of the theory of clubs.

2. An Overview of the Economic Theory of Clubs

As developed in a seminal paper by James Buchanan (1965), the economic theory of clubs applies to goods having three key characteristics:

- Club goods are *excludable*. Individuals who do not contribute to financing the club can be prevented, at relatively low cost, from gaining access to the benefits of club membership.

- Club goods are *congestible*. Although consumption is not entirely rivalrous (there is not, as in the case of a private good, a one-to-one relationship between the amount consumed by one person and the amount available for consumption by others), each member of the club imposes a negative externality on his fellows. That negative externality materializes in the form of crowding, which degrades the quality of the benefits consumed by all.

- Club goods are *divisible*. Once a club's membership has reached its optimal size, individuals who want to join but have been excluded can form a new club to produce and consume the same good. Clubs can in principle be cloned as the demand for them warrants.

The foregoing assumptions restrict the domain of the theory of club goods to what are commonly called 'impure' public goods. A 'pure' public good, by contrast, is neither excludable nor congestible. The optimal club size in that case has no upper bound. (Exceptions exist in situations where the club can bundle the provision of a pure public good with an excludable private good, about which more below.)

With this caveat in mind, the determination of the optimal club size is, in theory at least, a straightforward exercise in equating costs and benefits at the margin. That exercise yields three conditions that must be satisfied simultaneously for optimal clubbing. These conditions are (see Mueller, 1989, pp. 150–154; Cornes and Sandler, [1986] 1996, pp. 347–56):

- A *provision condition*, which requires the optimal club size (in terms of capacity) to be determined by setting the summed marginal benefits to members from reducing congestion costs equal to the marginal cost of capacity. Holding membership constant, larger club capacity means less crowding, but supplying additional capacity is costly.

- A *utilization condition*, which ensures that this capacity is used efficiently. Club theory accordingly contemplates the charging of user fees that equate a member's marginal benefit from consumption of the club good with the marginal congestion costs the member's participation imposes on others. If the fee is set too low, the club's capacity will be overutilized; it will be underutilized if the fee is too high. Optimal capacity utilization therefore requires that the club good be priced to reflect members' tastes for crowding.

- A *membership condition*, which dictates that new members be added to the club until the net benefit from membership (in terms of lower pro-rata provision costs for existing members) is equal to the additional congestion costs associated with expanding the club's size.

These three conditions help explain the prevalence of two-part pricing of club goods. Fixed up-front membership ('initiation') fees defray the club's cost of capacity provision while per-unit charges for use of the club's facilities ensure optimal utilization. When two-part pricing is not feasible — when the club exists primarily to provide its members with a pure public good such as political lobbying, for instance — clubs may be able to price their services efficiently by bundling them with an excludable private good, furnishing what Olson (1965) calls 'selective incentives'. Member-only privileges, such as the right to subscribe to the club's magazine or journal, to buy its calendar, to have access to a group life insurance policy or to group travel packages at favorable rates, and to participate in collective wage bargaining, are examples in this regard.

But in any case, the pricing of club goods is disciplined by a 'voting-with-the-feet' mechanism as clubs compete for members (Tiebout, 1956; Hirschman, 1970). As long as clubs can be cloned freely and the members of existing clubs are free to exit, club prices will be kept in line with costs. Voting-with-the-feet also helps overcome preference revelation problems as individuals sort themselves among clubs. Those with high demands for club goods (and a corresponding willingness to pay for them) join clubs that supply high levels of output; low demanders join organizations that offer levels of output (and prices) closer to their liking.

Although the exit option helps prevent clubs from charging prices that are too high, jointness in consumption and shared responsibilities mean that free riding remains the most troublesome economic problem facing club members. Individuals have strong incentives to understate their benefits from joining so as to have their fees lowered appropriately (Laband and Beil, 1999), to 'shirk' by opportunistically reducing the effort they supply toward achieving the club's collective goals, and to otherwise take advantage of their fellow members. Apart from the three conditions for optimal clubbing stated above, the logic of collective action (Olson, 1965; Sandler, 1992) suggests that successful clubs will tend to be relatively small in size and composed of individuals having relatively homogeneous interests. Small club size raises the per-capita benefits of club membership, thereby giving individuals a greater stake in the club's success; it also lowers the costs of monitoring and controlling free riding. Hence, if the lower costs of coping with free riding in smaller groups more than offset the correspondingly higher per capita costs of club good provision, the optimal club will have fewer members than otherwise.

Small groups also have lower decision-making costs (Buchanan and Tullock, 1962), an outcome that is facilitated by homogeneity of members' interests. Group heterogeneity creates differences of opinion that make it more difficult to reach agreement on common courses of action and creates opportunities for the membership's majority to take advantage of the minority (what Buchanan and Tullock call the external costs of collective decision making). Voluntary association, voting-with-the-feet, and the ability to clone organizations as demand warrants means that diversity of tastes and preferences amongst individuals will tend to promote diversity amongst clubs rather than diversity of club membership. People will tend to associate with others who are like-minded in the sense of having similar tastes for crowding and similar demands for club good provision.

As this brief summary indicates, the theory of clubs is, in essence, the study of the private provision of congestible public goods. It differs from the study of public provision of similar goods in ways that are more matters of degree ('voluntariness' and absence of coercion) than of kind.

Clubs and government both must grapple with issues of size (capacity provision), utilization, and membership. Careful study of how actual clubs deal in practice with preference revelation, free riding, and pricing can therefore shed considerable light on the public sector's responses to similar problems. That is the subject to which the essay now turns.

3. Applications

The theory of clubs has been brought to bear in a wide variety of institutional settings. Even so, the surface has only been scratched.

3.1. International Alliances

Perhaps the most intensively investigated application of the theory of clubs is in the realm of international alliances. While the literature on alliances has been extensively and competently reviewed elsewhere (Sandler, 1993; Sandler and Hartley, 2001), it is instructive to summarize the main empirical issues briefly here, given that alliances are in a sense the paradigm for further extensions of the theory of clubs.

In the theory of alliances the observational unit shifts from the individual person to the individual country, thereby suppressing the analysis of collective action problems at the national level (see Frey, 1997). Consistent with the theory, sovereign nation-states voluntarily establish international organizations to achieve goals that are either unattainable or too costly to attain were they to act on their own. These organizations may be created for a wide variety of purposes, including mutual defense, common markets (which might be thought of as multi-product clubs), harmonious legal codes, supranational regulation of the environment, and so on.

Olson and Zeckhauser (1967) provide a cost-sharing analysis of the North Atlantic Treaty Organization (NATO) and identify the conditions under which it would be in the interest of the alliance's members to increase the size of the 'club' (also see Sandler and Forbes, 1980; Hartley and Sandler, 1999; Sandler and Murdoch, 2000). Individual members in a club arrangement bear their pro-rata shares of the costs of operating the club. In the absence of price discrimination, which allows membership prices to be scaled to individual marginal values, cost shares are computed based on the club's total costs and group size. Given the voluntary nature of club formation, each member plausibly will pay the same price, corresponding roughly to average total cost. In the case of NATO, however, Olson and Zeckhauser point out that the United States is by far the single largest contributor to alliance's coffers. Can the disparities in members' shares of NATO's total costs be viewed as reflective of each member country's valuation of the good provided by the alliance? Or do the cost shares instead represent an 'unjust' or 'unfair' distribution of the total costs?

Arguably, the benefits of NATO membership are greater to the citizens of richer nations who stand to lose more if the mutually financed defense umbrella fails to protect them. Smaller European member countries exhibit a greater willingness to participate in infrastructure expenditures, as opposed to operating expenditures, simply because the buildings will remain on their soil after the alliance dissolves (if it does). These considerations suggest that the contributions of each member country are broadly consistent with rational self-interest.

Side payments could, in theory, work to diminish the discrepancies in members' contributions. If offered by the larger countries, they would encourage the smaller countries to increase their contributions. Side payments only make sense, however, if it is in the interest of larger countries to be party to an alliance characterized by roughly equal contributions. Tollison and Willett (1979) stress the mutual interest basis of 'issue linkages'. Linking international trade relations and 'human rights' or defense assistance and foreign aid, to give two examples, provide opportunities for striking mutually advantageous bargains that move an alliance closer to the aggregate efficiency frontier.

Thus, while the United States may bear a disproportionate share of NATO's costs, other members of the alliance may contribute relatively more to foreign aid or to humanitarian relief efforts in Africa. Incorporating issue linkages into the theory of alliances promises to shed light on the overall cost-effectiveness of international cooperation. In other words, observed discrepancies in contributions may simply reflect each country's valuation of membership benefits and of the tradeoffs made on other margins. It is also worth noting, however, that, at least in the case of international trade agreements, issue linkages (between trade liberalization on the one hand and labor and environmental standards on the other) can be 'used as a pretext for protectionism' (Lawrence, 2002, p. 284).

3.2. Interest Groups

A special-interest group is the direct analog of a club. The interest group produces a pure public good for its members in the form of political lobbying and, like a club, the interest group faces the fundamental problem of controlling free riding. That is, it must be able to form and to finance its lobbying activities, and to do so, it must find means of reducing to a cost-effective minimum club members' incentive to shirk. In other words, interest groups must guard against the prospect that an individual will be able to collect his or her share of the collective benefits of group political action without supplying his or her share of the effort required to produce those benefits.

How do groups overcome free-rider problems and organize for economically efficient collective action so as to be able to gain benefits through the political process that exceed the costs of lobbying? One attempt to solve the puzzle is Olson's (1965) by-product theory of collective action. According to this theory, an association ('club') provides a private good or service to its members that cannot be purchased competitively elsewhere. By monopolistically pricing the good or service above cost, the association raises money to finance its lobbying activities.

Indeed, for whatever reason organization is undertaken, lobbying for special-interest legislation becomes a relatively low-cost by-product of being organized. This is because start-up costs have already been borne in the process forming the association for some other (non-political) purpose. A business firm is an example of an organization whose resources readily can be redeployed for political lobbying purposes, either unilaterally or in concert with other firms having similar policy interests. Workers may organize to bargain collectively with employers and then find it relatively easy to open an office in Washington to advocate higher minimum wages. Lawyers may agree collectively to a code of ethics to address such matters as attorney-client privilege and then proceed to adopt provisions in their code that, by banning advertising, for example, restrict competition among lawyers.

A handful of studies provide indirect empirical support for Olson's by-product theory. Kennelly and Murrell (1991), for instance, use observations on 75 industrial sectors in ten countries to show that variations in interest-group formation can be explained by variations in selected economic and political variables. Kimenyi (1989), Kimenyi and Shughart (1989) and Kimenyi and Mbaku (1993) model interest groups as clubs that compete for control of the political machinery of wealth redistribution. They find evidence in cross-sectional international data that governments tend to be less democratic where the competition for wealth transfers is more intense.

3.3. Religion

Iannaccone (1992, 1997, 1998) has extended the theory of clubs to religious organizations. He starts by noting that religion in modern pluralistic societies is a market phenomenon, and that competing faiths live or die according to how successful they are in convincing potential adherents that they offer a superior 'product'. This vision of near-perfect competition is seemingly marred, however, by the existence of an obvious anomaly. Although the behavioral burdens most major religious faiths impose on their adherents tend to be relatively light, as the competition for members has become more intense in recent years, the religions that appear to have been most successful, somewhat surprisingly, are the relatively small ones that make the strictest behavioral demands. Fundamentalism is everywhere on the rise.

Iannaccone maintains that the explanation for this seemingly peculiar twist in market dynamics relates to the collective nature of religious activity. He argues that a religion is a kind of club which produces an 'anticongestible' club good. By this he means that each member's participation confers benefits, not costs, on other members; in other words, there are positive returns to crowding. Iannaccone's point here has an analog in the 'superstar' phenomenon, which suggests that the benefits of consumption rise when consumers focus their attention on a small number of sports or entertainment figures.

There remains the problem of ensuring an efficient level of participation among the adherents to a particular faith. If even those who participate minimally can expect to receive full benefits (salvation), the collective good likely will be under-provided. This is the classic free-rider problem. According to Iannacocone, religious clubs may be able to minimize this problem by requiring their members to follow strict rules of behavior. Overt sacrifices (keeping kosher, shunning buttons, wearing turbans, and so on) can more readily be monitored than more subjective indicators of personal participation (i.e., intensity of belief), and this is an important advantage. Additionally, making the required sacrifice public knowledge and the individual adherent subject to the resulting social stigma raises a barrier to free riders. Only those with a high level of motivation and emotional commitment to the 'club' will participate.

Iannaccone tests his model using data on denominational characteristics. He finds that sect-like religions, which impose stricter behavioral requirements on their members, indeed seem to induce greater levels of participation. Sect members attend more religious services, contribute more money, and choose more of their closest friends from within the congregation than do otherwise comparable members of more 'mainstream' religions.

3.4. Other Applications of the Theory

Cassella and Frey (1992) analyze the problem of determining optimal currency areas. Money as a medium of exchange is a fully non-rivalrous public good, and the optimal currency area is as large as possible. But to the extent that money also serves as a source of public revenue (seigniorage) or as an economic stabilization tool, then the optimal currency area might be much smaller (consistent with the requirement that preferences over the use of money be homogeneous within the club). The recent European monetary unification promises to provide much empirical fodder for studying this issue.

Teams of productive resources, one of the defining hallmarks of the firm as an economic organization (Alchian and Demsetz, 1972), can be thought of as clubs. Leibowitz and Tollison (1980) apply this reasoning to law firms. An optimal number and mix of partners, associates and support staff members must be determined, free riding must be monitored and policed, and access to common-pool resources, such as computers, Xerox machines, and the law library, must be controlled.

Impure public goods characterized by excludability, but only partial rivalry, are at the heart of the theory of clubs. Price-fixing conspiracies, in which cartel rents represent a form of such a good to the members and in which the same basic tension exists between group size and average returns, might also be usefully modeled as clubs. The swimming pool at the country club, the student union on the college campus, condominiums, and many other similar cases (see Foldvary, 1994) suggest that the problem of determining the optimal size of the relevant club can also be related straightforwardly to the issue of federalism. For some public goods, the optimal size of the club is the entire nation; for others, it is a more delimited jurisdiction.

4. Conclusion

The theory of clubs supplies a rich framework for exploring the inner workings of collective action in private settings. Moreover, further extensions of the theory to additional examples of successful provision of impure public goods seem possible as well. This model will surely be remembered by future historians of economic thought as one of James Buchanan's key contributions.

GARY M. ANDERSON
WILLIAM F. SHUGHART II
ROBERT D. TOLLISON

REFERENCES

Alchian, A.A. and Demsetz, H. (1972). "Production, information costs, and economic organization." *American Economic Review*, 62(December): 777–795.

Buchanan, J.M. (1965). "An economic theory of clubs." *Economica*, 32(February): 1–14.

Buchanan, J.M. and Tullock, G. (1962). *The Calculus of Consent: Logical Foundations of Constitutional Democracy*. Ann Arbor: University of Michigan Press.

Cassella, A. and Frey, B.S. (1992). "Federalism and clubs: towards an economic theory of overlapping political jurisdictions." *European Economic Review*, 36(April): 639–646.

Cornes, R. and Sandler, T. ([1986] 1996). *The Theory of Externalities, Public Goods, and Club Goods*, Second Edition. New York: Cambridge University Press.

Foldvary, F. (1994). *Public Goods and Private Communities: The Market Provision of Social Services*. Aldershot, UK, and Brookfield, MA, USA: Edward Elgar.

Frey, B.S. (1997). "The public choice of international organizations," in D.C. Mueller (ed.), *Perspectives on Public Choice: A Handbook*, Cambridge: Cambridge University Press, pp. 106–123.

Hartley, K. and Sandler, T. (1999). "NATO burden-sharing: past and future." *Journal of Peace Research*, 36(November): 665–680.

Hirschman, A.O. (1970). *Exit, Voice and Loyalty*. Cambridge: Harvard University Press.

Iannaccone, L.R. (1992). "Sacrifice and stigma: reducing free-riding in cults, communes, and other collectives." *Journal of Political Economy*, 100(April): 271–291.

Iannaccone, L.R. (1997). "Toward an economic theory of 'fundamentalism'." *Journal of Institutional and Theoretical Economics*, 153(March): 110–116.

Iannaccone, L.R. (1998). "Introduction to economics of religion." *Journal of Economic Literature*, 36(September): 1465–1495.

Kennelly, B. and Murrell, P. (1991). "Industry characteristics and interest group formation: an empirical study." *Public Choice*, 70(April): 21–40.

Kimenyi, M.S. (1989). "Interest groups, transfer seeking, and democratization." *American Journal of Economics and Sociology*, 48(July): 339–349.

Kimenyi, M.S. and Mbaku, J.M. (1993). "Rent-seeking and institutional stability in developing countries." *Public Choice*, (October): 385–405.

Kimenyi, M.S. and Shughart, W.F. II (1989). "Political successions and the growth of government." *Public Choice*, 62(August): 173–179.

Laband, D.N. and Beil, R.O. (1999). "Are economists more selfish than other 'social' scientists?" *Public Choice*, 100(July): 85–101.

Lawrence, R.Z. (2002). "International trade policy in the 1990s," in J.A. Frankel and P.R. Orsag (eds.) *American Economic Policy in the 1990s*, Cambridge: MIT Press, pp. 277–327.

Leibowitz, A. and Tollison, R.D. (1980). "Free riding, shirking, and team production in legal partnerships." *Economic Inquiry*, 18(July): 380–394.

Mueller, D.C. (1989). *Public Choice II*. Cambridge: Cambridge University Press. (A revised edition of Public Choice.)

Olson, M. (1965). *The Logic of Collective Action: Public Goods and the Theory of Groups*. Cambridge: Harvard University Press.

Olson, M. and Zeckhauser, R. (1966). "An economic theory of alliances." *Review of Economics and Statistics*, 48(August): 266–279.

Sandler, T. (1992). *Collective Action: theory and Applications*. Ann Arbor: University of Michigan Press.

Sandler, T. (1993). "The economic theory of alliances: a survey." *Journal of Conflict Resolution*, 37(September): 446–483.

Sandler, T. and Forbes, J.F. (1980). "Burden sharing, strategy, and the design of NATO." *Economic Inquiry*, 18(July): 425–444.

Sandler, T. and Hartley, K. (2001). "Economics of alliances: the lessons for collective action." *Journal of Economic Literature*, 39(September): 869–896.

Sandler, T. and Murdoch, J.C. (2000). "On sharing NATO defense burdens in the 1990s and beyond." *Fiscal Studies*, 21(September): 297–327.

Sandler, T. and Tschirhart, J. (1980). "The economic theory of clubs: an evaluative survey." *Journal of Economic Literature*, 18(December): 1481–1521.

Sandler, T. and Tschirhart, J. (1997). "Club theory: thirty years later." *Public Choice*, 93(December): 335–355.

Tiebout, C.M. (1956). "A pure theory of local expenditures." *Journal of Political Economy*, 64(October): 416–424.

Tollison, R.D. and Willett, T.D. (1979). "An economic theory of mutually advantageous issue linkages in international negotiations." *International Organization*, 33(Autumn): 425–449.

ECONOMISTS VERSUS THE PUBLIC ON ECONOMIC POLICY

1. Background

Most economists know from personal experience that their perspective on the economy is unpopular. When they teach introductory students or write a basic textbook, one of their main goals is to correct students' misconceptions. What makes this task easier is that students usually share the *same* misconceptions. They resist the standard critique of price controls, doubt the benefits of free trade, and believe the economy is in secular decline. What makes this task harder, though, is that students usually resist efforts to correct their misconceptions. Even if they learn the material to pass the final exam, only a fraction are genuinely convinced. The position of the modern economic educator is, moreover, far from novel. The 19th-century experiences of Frederic Bastiat in France (1964) and Newcomb (1893) in the United States mirror those of Jeffrey Sachs (1994) in 20th-century Russia.

What often lends urgency to the economic educators' mission is their sense that the popularity of mistaken economic beliefs leads democracies to adopt foolish economic policies. The world could be much better off if only the man in the street came to understand what economists already know. Bastiat exemplifies this mentality when he explains that bad economics ...

> guides our cabinet ministers only because it prevails among our legislators; it prevails among our legislators only because they are representative of the electorate; and the electorate is imbued with it only because public opinion is saturated with it. (1964, p. 27)

Paul Samuelson put an optimistic spin on the same idea: "I don't care who writes a nation's laws — or crafts its advanced treaties — if I can write its economics textbooks." (Nasar, 1995, C1).

So there is a long tradition in economics of (a) recognizing systematic belief differences between economists and the public, and (b) blaming policy failures on these belief differences. In spite of its pedigree, however, this tradition is largely ignored in modern academic research in economics in general and public choice in particular. Most models of political failure assume that political actors — voters included — have a correct understanding of economics. Models that emphasize imperfect information still normally assume that agents' beliefs are correct *on average* (Coate and Morris, 1995). Even though this assumption runs counter to most economists' personal experience, it has received surprisingly little empirical scrutiny.

2. Evidence

Numerous surveys investigate the economic beliefs of the general public *or* economists. (Alston et al., 1992; Fuchs et al., 1998; Shiller et al., 1991; Walstad and Larsen, 1992; Walstad, 1997) These tend to confirm economists' unofficial suspicions, but only indirectly. To the best of my knowledge, there is only one study that deliberately asks professional economists and members of the general public identical questions on a wide variety of topics. That study is the *Survey of Americans and Economists on the Economy* (1996, henceforth SAEE; Blendon et al., 1997), which queried 250 Ph.D. economists and 1,510 randomly selected Americans.

The SAEE overwhelmingly confirms the existence of large systematic belief differences between economists and the public. The differences are significant at the 1% level for 34 out of 37 questions (Caplan, 2002). Moreover, the signs of the disagreements closely match common stereotypes. The public is much more pessimistic about international trade, much more concerned about downsizing and technological unemployment, much more suspicious of the market mechanism, and much less likely to believe that the economy grew over the past twenty years. Stepping back, there appear to be four main clusters of disagreement: anti-foreign bias, make-work bias, anti-market bias, and pessimistic bias.

3. Anti-foreign Bias

On any economic issue where foreigners are involved, the public tends to see exploitation rather than mutually advantageous trade. Thus, most of the public claims that "companies sending jobs overseas" is a "major reason" why the economy is not doing better; very few economists agree. The same holds for immigration: most economists see it as a non-problem, but almost no non-economists concur. Similarly, even though economists have often criticized foreign aid, few see it as a serious problem for the U.S. economy, for the simple reason that foreign aid is a miniscule fraction of the federal budget. A large majority of the public, in contrast, sees foreign aid as a heavy drain on donor economies.

4. Make-work Bias

Unlike economists, the general public almost sees employment as an end in itself, an outlook Bastiat (1964) memorably derided as "Sisyphism." They are accordingly distressed when jobs are lost for almost any reason. Economists, in contrast, see progress whenever the economy manages to produce the same output with fewer workers. Thus, economists generally view downsizing as good for the economy, an idea non-economists utterly reject. Economists do not worry about technological unemployment; the public takes this possibility fairly seriously. It is tempting to think that this gap stems from different time horizons (economists look at the long-run, non-economists at the short-run), but the data go against this interpretation. Even when asked about the effects of new technology, foreign competition, and downsizing *twenty years* in the future, a massive lay-expert gap persists.

5. Anti-market Bias

What controls market prices? Economists instinctively answer "supply and demand," but few non-economists believe so. Fully 89% of economists explain the 1996 oil price spike using standard supply and demand; only 26% of the public does the same. Non-economists tend to attribute higher prices to conspiracies rather than market forces. In a similar vein, economists see profits and executive pay as vital incentives for good performance. Most of the public, in contrast, looks upon the current level of profits and executive pay as a drag on economic performance. Overall, the public has little sense of the invisible hand, the idea that markets channel human greed in socially desirable directions.

6. Pessimistic Bias

Economists think that economic conditions have improved and will continue to do so. The public sees almost the opposite pattern: they hold that living standards declined over the past two decades, and doubt whether the next generation will be more prosperous than the current one. In addition, the public thinks the economy is beset by severe problems that most economists see as manageable: the deficit, welfare dependency, and high taxes, to take three examples.

7. Robustness

A particularly nice feature of the SAEE is that it includes an array of details about respondents' characteristics. This makes it possible to not only test for systematic belief differences, but to test various hypotheses attempting to explain them. This is particularly important because critics of the economics profession often argue that for one reason or another, the public is right and the "experts" are wrong.

Some critics point to economists' self-serving bias. (Blendon et al., 1997) Economists have large incomes and high job security. Perhaps their distinctive beliefs are the result of their personal circumstances. Do economists think that "What is good for economists is good for the country"? It turns out that there is little evidence in favor of this claim. Ceteris paribus, income level has no effect on economic beliefs at all, and job security only a minor one. High-income non-economists with tenure think like normal members of the public, not economists.

Other critics point to economists' conservative ideological bias. (Greider, 1997; Soros, 1998) The truth, though, is that the typical economist is a moderate Democrat. Controlling for party identification and ideology tends if anything to increase the size of the belief gap between economists and the public. It is true, of course, that economists endorse a variety of extremely conservative views on downsizing, profits, tax breaks, and the like. What their critics fail to appreciate, though, is that economists endorse almost as many extremely liberal views on subjects like immigration and foreign aid.

Admittedly, these empirical tests only show that economists are not deluded because of self-serving or ideological bias. It is logically possible that economists are mistaken for a presently unknown reason. Like myself, moreover, the reader probably disagrees with economists' conventional wisdom on some point or other. Still, the two leading efforts to discredit the economics profession empirically fail. At this point it is reasonable to shift the burden of proof to the critics of the expert consensus.

8. What Makes People Think like Economists?

While virtually every segment of the general population has large disagreements with economists, some segments disagree more than others. Education, being male, income *growth*, and job security consistently make people think more like economists; income *level* and ideological conservatism do not. Caplan (2001) uses the SAEE data to construct a scalar measure of the magnitude of disagreement with economists' consensus judgments. Figure 1 summarizes the results: The first bar shows that belief gap between economists and the average member of the general public; the other bars show how the belief gaps of other segments of the population compare. For example, the belief gap between economists and the most-educated non-economists is only 77% as large as the belief gap between economists and non-economists with the average level of education.

9. Policy Significance

The SAEE results suggest a simple explanation for why economists find so much fault with government policy: Most voters do not understand economics, and vote for politicians and policies in harmony with their confusion.

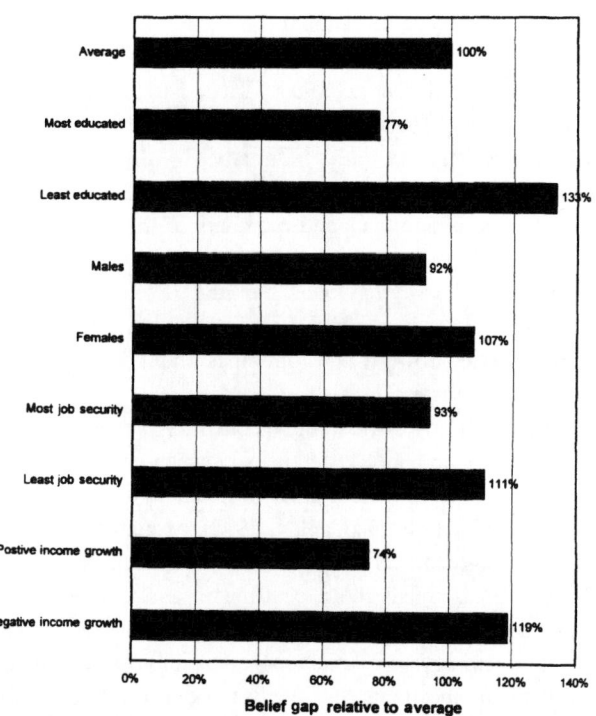

Figure 1: Size of belief gaps between economists and population sub-groups.

(Caplan forthcoming). The long history of protection and the uphill battle for free trade can be seen as an outgrowth of anti-foreign bias. Make-work bias favors labor market regulation; few non-economists recognize the potential impact on employment. The periodic imposition of price controls is unsurprising given the strength of the public's anti-market bias. Pessimistic bias is more difficult to link directly to policy, but seems like a fertile source for an array of ill-conceived policy crusades.

One question that often vexes economists is "Why isn't policy better than it is?" Popular answers include special interests, corruption, and political collusion. If you take the evidence on the economic beliefs of the public seriously, however, the real puzzle instead becomes "Why isn't policy far worse?" Part of the explanation is that the well-educated are both more likely to vote and somewhat more in agreement with the economic way of thinking. But this is far from a complete account. Figuring out the rest is one of the more interesting challenges facing the next generation of political economists.

BRYAN CAPLAN

REFERENCES

Alston, Richard, Kearl, J.R., and Michael Vaughan (1992). "Is there a consensus among economists in the 1990s?" *American Economic Review*, 82: 203–209.

Bastiat, Frederic (1964). *Economic Sophisms*. Irvington-on-Hudson, NY: Foundation for Economic Education.

Blendon, Robert, John Benson, Mollyann Brodie, Richard Morin, Drew Altman, Daniel Gitterman, Mario Brossard, and Matt James (1997). "Bridging the gap between the public's and economists' views of the economy." *Journal of Economic Perspectives*, 11: 105–188.

Caplan, Bryan (2003). "The logic of collective belief." *Rationality and Society*.

Caplan, Bryan (2002). "Systematically biased beliefs about economics: robust evidence of judgmental anomalies from the survey of Americans and economists on the economy." *Economic Journal*, 112: 1–26.

Caplan, Bryan (2001). "What makes people think like economists? evidence from the survey of americans and economists on the economy." *Journal of Law and Economics*, 44(2): 395–426.

Coate, Stephen, and Stephen Morris (1995). "On the form of transfers to special interests." *Journal of Political Economy*, 103: 1210–1235.

Fuchs, Victor, Alan Krueger, and James Poterba (1998). "Economists' views about parameters, values, and policies: survey results in labor and public economics." *Journal of Economic Literature*, 36: 1387–1425.

Greider, William (1997). *One World, Ready or Not: The Manic Logic of Global Capitalism*. NY: Simon and Schuster.

Nasar, Silvia (1995). "Hard act to follow?" *New York Times*, March 14, C1, C8.

Newcomb, Simon (1893). "The problem of economic education." *Quarterly Journal of Economics*, 7: 375–399.

Sachs, Jeffrey (1994). "Life in the economic emergency room," in Williamson, John (ed.) *The Political Economy of Policy Reform*. Washington, DC: Institute for International Economics, pp. 503–523.

Shiller, Robert, Maxim Boycko, and Vladimir Korobov (1991). "Popular attitudes toward free markets: the Soviet Union and the United States compared." *American Economic Review*, 81: 385–400.

Soros, George (1998). *The Crisis of Global Capitalism: Open Society Endangered*. NY: PublicAffairs.

Survey of Americans and Economists on the Economy (1996). The Washington Post, Kaiser Family Foundation and Harvard University, October 16, #1199. Webbed version at: http://www2.kff.org/content/archive/1199/econgen.html.

Walstad, William (1997). "The effect of economic knowledge on public opinion of economic issues." *Journal of Economic Education*, 28: 195–205.

Walstad, William and Larsen, M. (1992). *A National Survey of American Economic Literacy*. Lincoln, Nebraska: The Gallup Organization.

EDUCATION AND THE STATE

Education is typically viewed synonymously with formal schooling. Over the past century, state-provided schooling has become the norm for the industrialized world. In the United States, approximately 90 percent of children are educated in schools that are publicly financed and operated (Toma 1996). Similar statistics hold for a significant proportion of developed countries around the world (Toma, 1996). Yet public choice scholars continue to ask normative questions regarding the desirable role of the state that have been asked for at least two hundred years (Senior, 1861; Smith, 1776; Mill, 1909). Specifically, what role should the state play in providing access to schooling and does the consumption of schooling generate externalities that require a state role in provision?

Schooling fosters the development of human capital and influences the individual's lifelong choice set. Viewed from this perspective, schooling is an economic good whose consumption today influences future pecuniary and non-pecuniary wealth. In a pure market setting, parents consume schooling for their children if they choose to allocate current resources for benefits that will be reaped by their children at some point in the future. Assuming intergenerational benevolence, economists argue that parents will choose education for their children to the point where the discounted expected marginal benefits equal marginal costs.

With no interventions, a pure market outcome in schooling implies that the most disadvantaged in society would consume disproportionately small amounts of schooling because of current resource constraints. Left to the market, the poor will consume schooling in smaller amounts than the wealthy and the financial position of children at birth will influence lifelong income and wealth independent of factors such as ability or work effort.

Behind the veil of ignorance, the body politic may perceive that children who are born to families without access to financial resources should be protected and provided the same opportunities to develop human capital as those who are born to wealthier families. This conceptual notion raises a host of interesting questions that must then be decided through the political process. In its simplest form, state protection of the poor provides a guarantee of income to insure that the poor consume schooling but it does not answer the specific way in which this protection should be provided.

In a now classic work, *Education and the State* West ([1965] 1994), provides a detailed historical account of schooling developments in Great Britain and the United States. One feature of the feature of the account is the extent to which private aid was available to those who did not have resources of their own. West provides evidence that churches and other groups voluntarily contributed to the schooling of townspeople who were in economically disadvantaged straits. These contributions were occurring in a market setting prior to the development of a state system of schooling.

As the role of the state began in the late 1800s and has evolved throughout the 1900s, state protection in most of the developed world has translated into both financing of schools and provision of schooling. Implicitly, the state protection has been translated not only into a mandate that resources be redistributed so the poor can purchase schooling but it has come to mean that the poor must attend the same state-provided schools attended by others. Decisions regarding finances, curriculum to teach, the teachers to hire, the books to use, the buildings for use, and the choice of school to attend all fall under the jurisdiction of the state.

West (1965) and Lott (1990) offer public choice explanations for why the role of the state has evolved into one of provider as well as financing schools. West relied on historical data for some evidence that public provision was in part a result of political conflicts between the majority Protestants and minority Catholics. Lott portrays public provision as a means by which the state can influence the curriculum content of the schools and, thereby, indoctrinate students according to the preferences of the ruling party.

A definitive argument, either conceptually or factually, for why the state provides schooling is still outstanding. Of particular interest to public choice, however, is that the single greatest defect of public schooling that characterizes the maturation of state-provided schooling has been its failure to provide schooling for the poorest segment of society. In large metropolitan areas of the United States, for example, dropout rates commonly exceed graduation rates for the poor and minority populations. In some cities, the probability of incarceration for African American males exceeds the probability of graduation. Upper income children continue to consume the best the public system of schools has to offer (Chubb and Moe, 1990).

Observations such as these have caused scholars, even those who adhere to a state role in protecting poor children, to question whether alternative institutional arrangements might generate outcomes superior to those that have evolved under an almost complete state system of schooling. While few argue for the private donor-funded schools that preceded the state system, many examine publicly funded vouchers as an alternative mechanism to cover the cost of schooling. Under vouchers, the funding is child-centered. The funding follows the child to the school of the child's (parent's) choice. Conceptually, either public or private schools provide the schooling. This arrangement induces competition among suppliers and enhances efficiency in delivery as schools compete to attract enrollees into their school (Epple and Romano, 1998; Hoxby, 2000).

Vouchers raise several interesting public choice questions. First, once the state has assumed the role of chief provider of schooling, what conditions are necessary and sufficient to change the system toward a more market-oriented system of provision such as represented by vouchers? Scholars have examined vouchers that are targeted to a particular population group, such as the poor, versus vouchers for all children. The analyses emphasize the tax price effects of vouchers on the median voter to determine whether the public would support possible changes to the system of school finance.

Other public choice issues regarding vouchers concern the competitive effects of vouchers on student achievement. The perceived constitutional prohibitions against public funding of religious schools in the United States complicates this angle of provision. If vouchers are allowed but children are restricted in schools to which they apply, then competitive effects may be minimal. Finally, whether vouchers will lead to different configurations of housing patterns is also a public choice issue (Nechyba, 1999).

Beyond the protective, equal opportunity aspect of schooling, and its implications for funding of schooling, the other argument for a role of the state in education centers on externalities or spillovers. Arguments about spillovers have shifted over time. At heart of this question is whether the benefits to schooling are captured by the individual consumer or whether society at large captures the marginal benefits from schooling.

Historically, the externalities issue translated into a question of whether individuals (or their parents) would have the incentive to consume the optimal amount of schooling. In most of the western world, the returns to schooling are sufficiently high that few scholars seriously debate the consumption externalities issue. In developing countries, this may remain a legitimate question.

For the most part, the public choice externalities issue has shifted to another line of questioning entirely. The externalities question centers on the choice of which school to attend in the absence of state assignment of schools. In particular, the equilibrium mix of students within schools that would likely result under different financing arrangements and under alternative choice mechanisms is of interest. The mix of students expected to characterize schools if students and their families choose the school (state-provided or other) they attend is contrasted to the optimal mix of students. The mix typically refers to both the ability of students and their socioeconomic characteristics. The choice of schools and resulting mix of students is of interest because peers produce spillover consumption effects. The emerging empirical consensus is that low achieving children gain more from mixing with high achieving students than high achieving students lose by mixing with low achieving students.

Although scholars generally agree that high achieving individuals will not have an incentive to take the external peer effects into account as they choose schools under either a state or market arrangement, the question is to what extent the institutions (schools) will create mechanisms that lead to the internalization of the peer externalities. Private schools can use tuition pricing as a tool to internalize these peer externalities to some degree. Price discrimination on the part of these schools can influence enrollment patterns. High ability students can be rewarded, for example, for the positive externalities they generate via tuition discounts. To the degree that peer externalities are significant, pricing for schooling represents one tool for internalizing the spillovers. Owners of schools will have an incentive to utilize this discriminatory tool to the extent that mix of students is an attribute of schools desired by consumers.

While much of the scholarship in this area contrasts the student mix that markets yield relative to the optimal mix, public choice scholars emphasize that a relevant comparison is the market mix relative to that yielded by the state system of schooling. The benchmark for comparing alternative systems obviously has important welfare considerations.

There are other public choice considerations in education found in the literature. Many of these relate to alternative financing schemes. For example, some scholars have examined voter approval of bonds to finance school expenditures under a variety of voting rules. Fiscal federalism issues are also important in the area of education. While education historically has been financed largely from local revenues in the United States, the trend in recent years has been toward financing from state revenues. The effects of this shift on voter welfare and its implications for special interests are public choice issues.

Other issues in education are institutional in nature. State-provided schooling implies an institutional arrangement for translating voter preferences regarding education into educational output. The arrangement that has evolved in most industrialized countries is complex. At minimum, there is a bureaucratic agency charged with responsibility of the operation of schools. Issues such as selection methods and terms of office for the bureaucracy are relevant for the responsiveness of the agency to taxpayer preferences. Selection of teachers and the degree to which teachers influence educational policy also interest public choice scholars.

Today, education continues as a major public policy item not only in the industrialized world but increasingly in the developing world as well. Scholars debate whether the level of economic development results from high educational levels or whether education contributes to economic development. Many view education as the key to future development and, as such, it is not likely to decrease in importance as a topic for scholars. Public choice has much to offer in understanding the relationship between the state and education.

EUGENIA F. TOMA

REFERENCES

Chubb, John E. and Terry Moe (1990). *Politics, Markets, and American Schools*. Washington, DC: Brookings Institution.

Epple, Dennis and Richard Romano (1998). "Competition between private and public schools, vouchers, and peer-group effects." *American Economic Review*, 88(1): 33–62.

Hoxby, Caroline (2000). "Does competition among public schools benefit students and taxpayers?" *American Economic Review*, 90(3): 1209–1238.

Mill, J.S. (1909). *Principles of Political Economy*. London: Longmans.

Nechyba, Tom (1999). "School finance induced migration patterns: the impact of private school vouchers." *Journal of Public Economic Theory*, 1(1): 5–50.

Smith, Adam ([1776], 1982). *An Inquiry into the Nature and Causes of the Wealth of Nations*. Indianapolis: Liberty Fund Press.

Senior, Nassau (1861). *Suggestions on Popular Education*. London, John Murray.

Toma, E.F. (1996). "Public funding and private schooling across countries." *Journal of Law and Economics*, 39(1): 121–148.

West, E.G. ([1965] 1994). *Education and the State: A Study in Political Economy*, Third Edition. Indianapolis: Liberty Fund Press.

Zimmer, Ron and Toma, E.F. (2000). "Peer effects in private and public schools across countries." *Journal of Policy Analysis and Management*, 19(1): 75–92.

EFFICIENCY OF DEMOCRACY

In discussing the efficiency of democracy, it is helpful to consider the efficiency of market economies and dictatorships, as well. The fundamental theorems of welfare economics have been developed within the context of a market economy, while dictatorships provide a clear alternative to the democratic mode of government.

1. The First Welfare Theorem of Economics

I start with a discussion of the first welfare theorem of economics. This theorem states that if production and consumption sets are convex, there are no externalities, there is perfect competition, firms maximize their profits and consumers maximize their utility, then the Walrasian equilibrium is efficient. In a nutshell, an ideal capitalist economy is efficient.

But is a real capitalist economy efficient? One way to answer this question is to see whether the assumptions of the theorem hold.

The theorem explicitly assumes that there are no externalities. Clearly, in the real world there are many types of externalities from defense to pollution. But suppose that these externalities are dealt with elsewhere. For example, a well functioning court system that allowed for class-action suits might overcome pollution externalities that exist when there are market transaction costs. The first welfare theorem also explicitly assumes perfect competition. The degree of competition in a real economy is still subject to some debate and cannot be so easily taken off the agenda.

The theorem also contains a number of implicit assumptions, the most important being that there is no asymmetric information, thereby ruling out principal-agent problems and the costly acquisition of information. Economists tend to believe that asymmetric information is pervasive. And if asymmetric information exists, the theorem only holds under very stringent assumptions. Now there is a fallback position. Instead of unrealistically comparing the outcome to a world of perfect information, one can construct models where the outcome of competition is on average best *given* asymmetric information. So, we still have something that approximates the results of the first welfare theorem of economics. But these results rely on a whole host of assumptions and the results are not always satisfactory. For example, there may be many (possibly a continuum of) competitive equilibria, with only one being efficient. We do not have a general welfare theorem, but rather a particular model where an efficient competitive outcome may arise.

Finally, we have the core assumptions that firms maximize profits and consumers maximize utility. Only a few economists would believe that there are serious departures from these assumptions and the majority of economists have their counter-arguments. Consider for example the argument that corporations do not maximize profits because the diffuse owners of stock do not have the incentive to monitor their managers and corporate directors. Most economists would counter that the threat of a tender offer will insure that the interests of the managers are aligned with the interests of the stockholders.

As an alternative to testing the assumptions, one might measure whether a market economy is efficient. In practice this would mean a more focused study than a true test of Pareto optimality, which would require a look at the economy as whole. But even the more restricted study is rarely done. And when such a study finds inefficiency, it is easy to be skeptical. For example, suppose that a researcher claimed that a firm did not maximize profits, then others would say that some cost was not measured or that it did not make any difference because an inefficient firm would soon be eliminated from the market. Experimental economics is another venue for testing efficiency in the small. Here the cost and benefits are controlled to a greater extent by the investigator. There are many examples of money being left on the table (e.g., the ultimatum game).

How do economists react to this set of conflicting theorems and empirical studies? Certainly, some are agnostic. However, to judge by the role that the first welfare theorem plays in most graduate microeconomics texts, one would expect that a majority of the remaining economists believe that the first welfare theorem of economics is a reasonable approximation of a number of capitalist economies.

2. The First Welfare Theorem of Democratic Politics

We now turn our attention toward democracies. Democracies have a much wider scope than the Walrasian markets envisioned in the first welfare theorem. Democracies can choose whether there is a capitalist system, whether certain markets are illegal, and whether certain markets are controlled by a government granted monopoly. Democracies can also create coercive transfers: the rich can be taxed to subsidize the poor, or vice versa, and the young can be forced into military service thereby subsidizing the old.

It is relatively easy to produce a "first welfare theorem of democratic politics" — that a democratic equilibrium will be efficient. Assume that candidates want to maximize the number of votes that they receive and voters vote for the candidate that gives them the highest utility (or are more likely to vote for the preferred candidate, the greater the utility differential between the platforms). Then, if one candidate offers an inefficient platform, another candidate can offer an efficient platform that offers at least as much to every voter and strictly more to one or more of these same voters. In this way, the candidate offering the more efficient platform has a higher probability of winning the election.

Note that the assumptions of this first welfare theorem of democratic politics are less severe than the first welfare theorem of economics. One does not have to assume convex preference and production sets (e.g., no economies of scale). Nor does one have to assume away pollution externalities and the existence of public goods. As long as pollution is confined within the country, pollution is not an externality in the political process.

One should not read too much into the theorem. It does not say that government bureaucracies will produce automobiles and food or that they could produce these items as well as private industry. The theorem just says that democracies will choose that economic system which maximizes welfare. And, if the intuition of most economists is correct, that would mean a capitalist economy. Nor does the theorem tell us very much about the distribution or redistribution of income. The theorem just tells us that no pieces of the income pie will be left needlessly on the table.

It is my impression that a majority of economists would dismiss the first welfare theorem of democratic politics even if they knew it existed. With the exception of Downs (1957), most of the classical works in public choice are about government failure (see for example, Tullock, 1967; Niskanen, 1971). For the remainder of this contribution, I will argue that economists should embrace the first welfare theorem of democratic politics as readily as they embrace the first welfare theorem of economics.

3. Focusing on the Assumptions

One can attack the assumptions of the theorem. A common way to start the attack is to argue that voters are uninformed. The argument proceeds as follows: Since a person's vote is unlikely to affect the outcome of the election, it does not pay the person to be informed. We have already seen a parallel argument regarding stockholders' lack of knowledge concerning the behavior of the managers of the firm. And the counter-argument follows along somewhat similar lines, as well. In democracies, there is competition for office. This competition closely approximates a zero-sum game. What one side wants to hide, the other side wants to disclose. The cost of information gathering falls mainly on the political entrepreneurs, not the voters. If the incumbent does not do the bidding of the voters, the incumbent faces the threat of being thrown out of office.

Furthermore, the amount of knowledge necessary to vote correctly has been vastly exaggerated. Just as people consult their doctors about which pills to take rather than becoming experts in medicine, voters can ask trusted but knowledgeable friends how to vote. Political parties can also play that role for some voters.

Furthermore, being uninformed does not mean being misinformed. Voters may not know the exact amount of pork-barrel spending, but that does not mean that they on average under-estimate it rather than over-estimate it.

And perhaps most important, elections outcomes do not require that most voters are informed. Suppose for example, that there is a referendum on price controls for gasoline. If sixty percent of the voters are ignorant and just flip an honest coin (or even a dishonest coin that tells them to vote for price controls 70% of the time) and the remaining forty percent know enough economics to know that such a policy will back fire and therefore vote against the policy 90% of the time, the referendum promoting price controls will lose the election. (See Wittman, 1995, for this and other arguments.)

Other aspects of the theorem have also been attacked. But again there are counter-arguments. For example, some have argued that candidates will not keep their campaign promises. This is an example of a principal-agent problem where the voters are the principals and the agents are their elected officials. We have seen that similar arguments have been lobbed at the first welfare theorem of economics, but have been countered, ignored, or caused a retreat to a fallback position where the outcome is best on average given asymmetric information. A similar set of defensive strategies is available for the first welfare theorem of politics. Here, I will concentrate on a counter-argument (the reader can figure out the other strategies on his/her own). Political parties make commitments by their candidates more credible. Political parties support candidates for higher office if they have held their promises in lower office; and the political party often finds a role to play for their ex-office holders, thereby overcoming the last period problem (see Harrington, 1992).

Just as one can turn the first welfare theorem of economics on its head and produce contrary results (for example, production technology is not convex; therefore capitalism is inefficient), one can also generate theorems of political failure. But most of these models of government failure implicitly violate the core assumptions of economics, e.g., that uninformed voters are irrational and vote contrary to their own interests (see Grossman and Helpman, 1996, for an example).

4. Do Models of Political Failure Fit the Evidence Better?

So far I have concentrated on theoretical arguments and counter-arguments. What about the empirical evidence for the efficiency of democracy? Published cost–benefit studies are more common for government projects than for private undertakings. Many government projects have been shown to be inefficient. Furthermore, many government policies are so clearly inefficient that no cost–benefit study is necessary. Examples include rent control, protective tariffs, and many farm subsidy programs.

Does this evidence of inefficient policies undermine the efficient government hypothesis? My short answer is no unless there is a competing hypothesis that is closer to the mark. Pointing to a "failure" of the efficiency hypothesis is not sufficient grounds for rejection. Furthermore, the extent of failure is best measured by reference to the set of possible outcomes. By this second criterion, democracies are close to being welfare maximizers.

Government policies may be inefficient for a variety of reasons. I will consider two reasons for inefficiency: (1) inefficient regulation (with rent control as the example), and (2) inefficient allocation of government expenditures.

Rent control is generally believed to be inefficient. A number of cities in the United States have rent control ordinances. Nevertheless, this evidence does not undermine the hypothesis that democracies are efficient. Only a small proportion of residential housing and a negligible proportion of commercial real estate are under rent control. Therefore, it makes more sense to emphasize the rarity of rent control rather than its existence. By the measuring rod of conceivable outcomes, the outcome is close to being efficient.

Another test of the first welfare theorem of democratic politics is to compare its predictions with a model that predicts inefficiency. For illustrative purposes, I will choose the theory of rent-seeking. Rent controls are consistent with the theory of rent-seeking. In this case, the present occupants would be obtaining rents in the political sense when a rent control ordinance is enacted.

Unfortunately, the standard way of testing the rent-seeking hypothesis is misleading. To illustrate, suppose that in 30 democracies the percentage of housing under rent control varies between 12% and 15% and is on average 13%. The standard approach in the literature is to employ an asymmetric test where the efficiency hypothesis is treated as the null hypothesis. Given the above data, the efficiency hypothesis would be rejected and the rent-seeking hypothesis would be confirmed. Unfortunately, this is the wrong way to go about choosing theories.

If the rent-seeking theory merely states that there will be more rent control than the optimal amount of rent control (which is 0), then rent control merely predicts that between 0 and 100% of real estate will be under rent control. Given a uniform distribution of possibilities, this suggests that rent-seeking predicts 50% of the population will be under rent control. Since 50 is farther away from 13 than 0 is away from 13, on predictive grounds one would choose the efficiency hypothesis over the rent-seeking hypothesis. Perhaps there are refinements of the rent-seeking hypothesis that predict that 20% of the population will be under rent control, in which case the rent-seeking hypothesis would dominate the efficiency hypothesis. But this is not the way the research has been conducted. Instead, the asymmetric test of the efficiency hypothesis has been the dominant approach of the literature.

We next turn our attention toward the distribution of government goods and services.

Normative public finance predicts that governments will subsidize the production of public goods when the market is likely to fail in that endeavor. And by and large, the evidence conforms to the normative expectations. Governments subsidize vaccinations more than plastic surgeries, rather than vice versa. Governments subsidize a greater percentage of the cost of building streets than the cost of building cars, rather than vice versa. And the role of government relative to the private market is much greater in national defense than in consumption, rather than vice versa. None of these statements is very new or exciting to a public finance economist who believes in efficiency explanations for government behavior. But they are puzzling facts to those who believe in rent-seeking theory. Are those who build streets always more organized than those who build automobiles?

Again, there are plenty of exceptions to the efficiency hypothesis. But selectively choosing exceptions (one way or the other) and then "testing" them is not really good science. The sample needs to be random or at least representative. And as already shown, in choosing theories, one must compare their point predictions.

5. Are Dictatorships also Efficient?

Some of the same forces that encourage efficient outcomes in democracies also exist for dictatorships. A dictator always faces the threat of a coup and the rise of another dictator. That is, there is competition for the office. Even in the absence of competition, a dictator's desire to extort the maximum from his subjects would, other things being equal, make the dictator prefer an efficient economic system over an inefficient one. However, such forces are severely attenuated in a dictatorship. First the transaction costs of replacing a dictator can be very high; in turn, high transaction costs shield the dictator from competitive forces that eliminate inefficiency. Second, decentralizing economic control may undermine the dictator's political control; therefore, the dictator may prefer a less economically efficient but more politically malleable system. Third, the system of dictatorship makes it difficult for the truth to prevail as those below the dictator do not want to lose their positions of power (see Wintrobe, 1998). Consequently, a dictator's lunatic ideas are less likely to be challenged.

All of this brings us back to my earlier point about measuring rods. In order to judge whether democracies are efficient, we need a measuring rod. Compare West Germany to East Germany, South Korea to North Korea, and Taiwan to Mainland China. In each case the more democratic country had a much better political and economic track record than the sister Communist state. Think of Mao the next time you want to argue that democracies are inefficient.

DONALD WITTMAN

REFERENCES

Atkinson, S. and Halvorsen, R. (1986). "The relative efficiency of public and private firms in a regulated environment: the case of U.S. electric utilities." *Journal of Public Economics*, 29(April): 281–294.

Austen-Smith, D. (1991). "Rational consumers and irrational voters: a review essay on black hole tarriffs and endogenous policy theory." *Economics and Politics*, 3(March): 73–92.

Baba, S. (1997). "Democracies and inefficiency." *Economics and Politics*, 9(July): 99–114.

Becker, G. (1985). "Public policies, pressure groups, and dead weight costs." *Journal of Public Economics*, 28(December): 329–347.

Besley, T. and Coate S. (1998). "Sources of inefficiency in a representative democracy: a dynamic analysis." *American Economic Review*, 88(March): 139–156.

Breton, A. (1996). *Competitive Governments: An Economic Theory of Politics and Public Finance*. Cambridge: Cambridge University Press.

Breton, A., Galeotti, G., Salmon, P., and Wintrobe, R (eds.) (1993). *Preference and Democracy*. Dordecht: Kluwer.

Buchanan, J. and Musgrave, R. (1999). *Public Finance and Public Choice: Two Contrasting Visions of the State*. Cambridge Mass.: MIT Press.

Coughlin, P. and Nitzan, S. (1981). "Electoral outcomes and probabilistic voting and Nash social welfare maxima." *Journal of Public Economics*, 15(February): 115–121.

Coursey, D. and Roberts. R. (1991). "Competition in political and economic markets." *Public Choice*, 70(April): 83–88.

Downs, A. (1957). *An Economic Theory of Democracy*. New York: Harper and Row.

Grossman, G. and Helpman E. (1996). "Electoral Competition and Special Interest Politics." *Review of Economic Studies*, 63(April): 265–286.

Harrington, J. (1992). "The role of party reputation in the formation of policy." *Journal of Public Economics*, 49(October): 107–121.

Krueger, A. (1974). "The political economy of the rent-seeking society," *American Economic Review*, 64(June): 291–303.

Laffont, J. (2000). *Incentives and Political Economy*. Oxford: Oxford University Press.

Lindbloom, C. (1977). *Politics and Markets*. New York: Basic Books.

Rowley, C. and Vachris, M. (1994). "Why democracy does not necessarily produce efficient results." *Journal of Public Finance and Public Choice*, 12(May–December): 95–111.

Schumpeter, J. (1950). *Capitalism, Socialism and Democracy*. New York: Harper and Row.

Wintrobe, R. (1987). "The market for corporate control and the market for political control." *Journal of Law, Economics, and Organization*, 3(fall): 435–448.

Wintrobe, R. (1998). "Some lessons on the efficiency of democracy from a study of dictatorship," in S. Borner and M. Paldam (eds.) *The Political Dimension of Economic Growth: Proceedings of the IEA Conference San Jose, Costa Rica. IEA Conference Volume 119*. New York: St. Martin's Press.

Wintrobe, R. (1998). *The Political Economy of Dictatorship*. Cambridge, UK: Cambridge University Press.

Wittman, D. (1989). "Why democracies produce efficient results." *Journal of Political Economy*, 97(December): 1395–1424.

Wittman, D. (1995). "The myth of democratic failure: why political institutions are efficient." Chicago: University of Chicago Press.

Wolf, C. (1988). *Markets or Governments: Choosing Between Imperfect Alternatives*. Cambridge Mass.: MIT Press.

EFFICIENCY OF DEMOCRACY?

1. Introduction

In a sequence of publications, Donald Wittman (1989, 1995, 2003) advances the hypothesis that all democracies are efficient. Unlike George Stigler (1972, 1988) who attempted to fudge between economic and political efficiency, Wittman does not pussyfoot concerning the meaning of the term. For Wittman, efficiency means Pareto optimality (or rather, although he does not say it, Kaldor–Hicks–Scitovsky efficiency, since compensation need not be paid) honed yet more sharply into wealth maximization in order to avoid ambiguities inherent in the concept of utility (Rowley, 1997).

Wittman deploys wealth maximization aggressively. He does not argue, for example, that voters are poorly informed or that politicians shirk, but that the system is efficient because it would be too costly to have it otherwise (the transaction cost defense). Rather, he argues that voters are highly informed and that there is no shirking, that voters seek wealth maximization and that politicians broker wealth-maximizing policies under conditions of democracy.

To say that democratic political markets are economically efficient, Wittman tells us, does not imply that political markets are superior to economic markets. Rather it implies that democracies allocate to private markets those tasks in which they are most efficient and to political markets those tasks for which are best suited. That such a Panglossian perspective should have become the trade-mark of Chicago political economy following the retirement of Milton Friedman in 1976 is one of the more puzzling phenomena of the closing years of the twentieth century, a phenomenon that must cause considerable *angst* for that great author of *Capitalism and Freedom* (Friedman, 1962).

2. The Rational Choice Approach

Throughout his work in this field, Wittman deploys the rational choice postulate as the generating assumption for his theory of democratic politics. We have no quarrel with this approach. Indeed, we suggest that use of the rational choice postulate with respect to political markets is precisely what distinguishes public choice both from standard neoclassical economics and from political science. This does not imply, however, that Wittman's interpretation of the postulate conforms in all respects with that of the Virginia School. In this respect, it is important to distinguish between those aspects of rational choice that are common to both and those that are not (Green and Shapiro, 1994).

Foremost among the non-controversial assumptions is that of methodological individualism. The relevant actors in political markets are individuals, not genes, groups nations or species. From Buchanan and Tullock (1962), collective action has been viewed by public choice scholars of all kinds as nothing more than the action of individuals when they operate in groups. Second is the assumption that each individual maximizes the expected value of his own payoff, measured in terms of some utility scale relevant to that individual (Luce and Raiffa, 1957, 50).

Third is the assumption that each actor in political markets behaves in conformity with certain consistency assumptions, namely that he rank-orders all his options in terms of preference and indifference (connectedness), and that his orderings satisfy the condition of transitivity (consistency). Fourth, is the assumption that individual rationality is instrumental at least in the sense that each actor maximizes his expected utility in formally predictable ways. Together these four assumptions constitute the protected core of almost all public choice analysis.

Much more controversial, in comparing the public choice scholarship of Wittman with that of the Virginia School, is the assumption about the relevant information that political actors can normally be presumed to possess and to act on. Wittman, in common with the Chicago School of Political Economy (Becker, 1983, 1985; Stigler, 1988), assumes near perfect information and an unbounded ability of all actors to access and comprehend such information as the basis for political action. The Virginia School strongly rejects this assumption, arguing that the particular nature of political markets, notably pervading indivisibilities, lowers incentives for political actors to access and to make use of available information in political as compared with private markets. Political markets are characterized, therefore by rational ignorance and bounded rationality (Rowley and Vachris, 1993, 1995).

A second area of controversy concerns the robustness of assumptions about individual objectives, specifically whether thin or thick rationality assumptions should be deployed in public choice analysis (Green and Shapiro, 1994, 18). In thin-rational accounts agents are presumed rational in the sense that they deploy efficiently the available means to maximize expected utility, however they themselves define the latter. In thick-rational accounts, the analyst posits not only rational behavior but also some more detailed description of agent preferences and beliefs.

Wittman, of course, deploys the thick-rationality approach throughout his public choice analysis, focusing consistently on wealth maximization. There is no role for any other ideology in his analytic framework. The Virginia School, in contrast, is much more flexible. Many contributions, most notably that by Buchanan and Tullock (1962), utilize the thin-rationality approach. Although most of the empirical work of the Virginia School utilizes thick-rationality assumptions, not least because they facilitate the testing of hypotheses, wealth maximization by no means is the only focus. Virginia scholars recognize that other ideologies play significant roles in political markets, especially, for example, when expressive voting is seen to be significant, and when politicians find themselves operating under conditions of monopoly.

A third area of controversy concerns the nature and magnitude of transaction costs in political as compared with private markets. In the view of Wittman, transaction costs vary little, if at all, across these markets, a view that is not shared by scholars working within the tradition of the Virginia School (Rowley, 1997). The positive Coase theorem (Coase, 1960) sets the scene for this controversy. Wittman adheres to Stigler's incorrect interpretation of the Coase theorem, relying on the existence of zero or near-zero transaction costs in political markets. The Virginia School relies on the correct interpretation of the Coase theorem in which transaction costs are always non-zero and typically are extremely high in political markets by comparison with their private counterparts.

These distinctions in the rational choice approaches of Wittman and the Virginia School turn out to be highly significant when assessing the efficiency or otherwise of democratic politics. Let us outline the very different implications of the Virginia School's rational choice analysis for the efficiency of democracy than those advanced by Wittman in the immediately preceding *Encyclopedia* entry (Wittman, 2003).

3. The Vote Motive

In any major election, the probability that an individual voter will be decisive is vanishingly small, of the order of one in a million in U.S. presidential elections (Stigler, 1972). In such circumstances, rational individuals have no investment incentive to vote, though many do vote to manifest their support for democracy. Those who do vote have no incentive to become informed about the positions of competing candidates. Instead, they cast their votes on the basis of some past party loyalty, or on grounds of valence (for example, which candidate has more sex appeal), or they vote expressively, registering 'feel good' votes in the full knowledge that such gestures will not be decisive. Such is not the behavior of the typical individual when making private purchases in the local shopping mall. The reason for this difference of approach is the high indivisibility of the vote motive under any conceivable voting rule.

Election campaigns typically bundle several hundreds of issues into a single indivisible package, comprising complex mixes of social as well as economic policies. Even relatively sophisticated voters are obliged to choose between full-line forced packages (a practice indeed that would create antitrust problems for firms in private markets). In such circumstances, they simply cannot fine tune their political demands through a single vote opportunity. Once again, this is a distinct disadvantage of political markets by comparison with much more highly divisible private markets.

Even if well-informed voters accommodate themselves to the bundling of policies in electoral campaigns, they find themselves with very limited opportunities to signal their preferences to those who represent them. As Boudreaux (1996, 117) notes, each U.S. voter during any six year span enjoys a maximum of nine ballots to cast in four national elections. Compare this with the multitude of ballots available to the individual over such a time span in his private market activities. Yet again, this reflects high indivisibilities in political markets.

Even if all these problems are ignored, the fundamental nature of representative democracy implies that wealth maximization will not result. For the most part, democracies are based on one-man, one-vote, secret ballots. In such circumstances, vote trading is impossible. Democracies do not auction off the right to run the government to the highest bidders. Low-valued bids (from the viewpoint of wealth creation) carry equal weight with high-valued bids, at least in terms of the vote motive. If there are more low-valued active bidders than high-valued active bidders, wealth-destructive policies predictably will result under conditions of simple majority rule.

Early contributions by public choice scholars (Downs, 1957) implied that two party political systems under specified circumstances, manifest centripedal impulses that force both vote-maximizing parties (or candidates) to adopt identical positions reflecting the preferences of middle voters (Downs never used the term median voter). Let us first suppose that Downs is correct. Even in such circumstances, public good provisions are unlikely to satisfy conditions of Pareto optimality.

The public choice outcome is that rate of provision where the marginal valuation of the public good by the middle voter is equated with the middle voter's marginal tax rate. Only in exceptional circumstances will such an outcome satisy the optimality conditions defined by Paul Samuelson, namely that the vertical sum of the marginal evaluations of all individuals for that good should be equated with the marginal rate of transformation for that good (Samuelson, 1954).

In any event, the political equilibrium outlined by Downs (1957) is extremely sensitive to the assumptions on which it is predicated. If issues are evaluated in multi-space, if voters abstain as a consequence of alienation, if voter preferences are multi-peaked over policy issue space, if voters or candidates are not fully-informed, or if parties or candidates cannot move easily across issue dimension space(s), the middle voter outcome cannot be guaranteed. Indeed, the existence, uniqueness and the stability of political equilibria may be figments of the Downsian imagination (Rowley, 1984). In such circumstances, electoral outcomes are manipulable by interest group interventions.

4. Interest Groups

Prior to the seminal work of Mancur Olson (1965), both economists and political scientists took a benign view of interest groups, viewing them as infusing relevant information into political markets. Olson (1965) deployed a rational choice approach to demonstrate that individuals who sought to promote policy goals through collective action confronted a serious free-rider problem. Individuals who shirked their responsibilities to the group could not easily be denied benefits should the policy promotion prove to be successful.

In such circumstances, interest groups will differ significantly in political effectiveness. Small, homogeneous groups are the best equipped to overcome free-riding, especially if they can enforce the supply of pressure, either legally (the case of the trial lawyers) or illegally (the case of professional associations and labor unions (who break the knee-caps of those who shirk). Large, heterogeneous interest groups fare badly unless they are able to counter free-riding by the provision of private benefits at below market rates. Therefore, interest group pressures serve not only to inform political markets but to distort political outcomes from the preferred position of the median voter. In the political battle over the distribution of income and wealth, the category of interest group with which an individual associates will play a decisive role in his relative success or failure.

Just as differential transaction costs play an important role in the logic of collective action, so they exert a harmful effect on the wealth of nations. Following Tullock's seminal 1967 paper, it is now recognized that rent seeking is not a costless exercise. In a worst case scenario, efficient rent seeking outlays imply that the entire rent available to a successful interest group through political action may be wasted through dissipative rent seeking (Laband and Sophocleus, 1988; Laband and McClintock, 2001). Such waste cannot possibly be characterized as the normal cost of government since different political institutions impact significantly both on the magnitude of the rents available and on the extent to which rent seeking is dissipative of wealth (Crew and Rowley, 1988).

5. Competition in Political Markets

Wittman, like Downs (1957), relies significantly upon the assumption that democratic political markets are highly

competitive and highly contestable in deriving the middle voter equilibrium without taking into account the specific institutions through which such competitive impulses must operate. Downs, focused on the case of parliamentary democracy, composed of two competing, spatially mobile political parties, each vigorously seeking to maximize votes, recognizing that it was vulnerable to new entry should it fail to satisfy the preferences of the middle voter. This highly stylized model is not necessarily an accurate representation of real world political markets.

First, it assumes that the two competing political parties are truly independent of each other and that they will never collude. Oligopoly theory clearly advises that this is not so, as even Chicago economists such as Stigler have acknowledged in the case of private markets (Stigler, 1968). If political parties collude, in the absence of contestable markets, they enjoy discretionary power. Rational choice theory suggests that they will attempt to do so, in the absence of unresolvable differences in ideology (rejected out of hand by Wittman who believes that all individuals are imbued with a wealth maximizing ideology).

Even if the political parties fail to collude, the Cournot duopoly equilibrium will fall well short of the full competitive equilibrium, implying that the emoluments of individual politicians are significantly in excess of opportunity cost (Stigler, 1972). Given the sunk costs enjoyed by political parties with well-advertised brand images, and high incumbent re-election success rates, political markets are unlikely to be contestable, especially under 'first-past-the-post' vote rules that strongly favor two party systems.

As Stigler (1972) noted, competition in economic markets differs significantly from competition in political markets. Political products typically are exclusive in nature (for example, there is only one medicare program, only one defense program), whereas the products of private market typically are not. This is another example of pervasive indivisibility in political markets. In consequence, the outcomes even of competitive political markets are much more coercive than those of private markets, in the sense that many voters, perhaps even a majority, prefer other policies. This reality has given rise to the 'all-or-nothing' concept of political competition, which, in turn, easily metamorphoses into the concept of the state as a monopoly firm especially when one political party clearly dominates the other in a specific parliamentary election (Auster and Silver, 1979).

6. Institutions Matter

The Virginia School, from its early beginnings, has predicated its analysis on the assumption that institutions matter

(Buchanan and Tullock, 1962). The Chicago School of Political Economy has always been more ambivalent, relying more on political market competition than on the particular institutions of political markets to deliver the efficiency outcomes that it proselytizes (Becker, 1983; Stigler, 1988; Wittman, 1989, 1995).

Once again the controversy between the two Schools arises out of different interpretations of the Coase theorem. In an environment of zero transaction costs the specific nature of political institutions is unimportant. Wealth-seeking individuals will bargain around them to achieve efficient outcomes. Where transaction costs are high, however, the characteristics of political institutions become extremely important, since individuals cannot easily bargain around inefficient organizations. The Founding Fathers clearly recognized the importance of transaction costs when they wrote the United States Constitution so as to create a constitutional republic with in-built checks and balances. Even they under-estimated the resilience of the legislative and the executive branches in seeking and the weakness of the judicial branch in allowing the systematic erosion of these checks and balances since 1860.

A fundamental problem for well-functioning political institutions under conditions of democracy concerns property rights. The importance of property rights for ensuring good incentives is now widely appreciated. Untruncated property rights provide individuals with clearly defined authority to use their resources as they wish and to transfer resources to whomsoever they choose, whenever they wish, either through voluntary exchange, or as gifts and bequests. In such circumstances, resources tend to move to their highest value uses, irrespective of their initial assignment.

In political markets, however, property rights do not exist, or are so poorly defined and severely attenuated as to be devoid of efficiency incentives (Rowley and Vachris, 1993, 1995). Legislators, presidents, and bureaucrats, for the most part, cannot legally appropriate any increase in the nation's wealth resulting from political market activities; not can they be divested of their own wealth as a consequence of wealth destructive policies. They cannot easily transfer or bequest such limited property rights as they hold. They have no recourse to a system of binding commitments comparable to the law of contract in private markets.

Democratic governments, perhaps more so than dictatorships, confront fundamental obstacles to entering into binding commitments since each successive government is sovereign (Stiglitz, 1989). No parliament or Congress can bind its successor. Parliament and Congress largely determine the conditions under which individuals can sue it to recover against illegitimate appropriations of property or breach of contract. Rights to sue, predictably, are more restricted than in private markets. In such circumstances, even when transaction costs are relatively low, the Stigler version of the Coase theorem is unlikely to apply.

In the absence of a robust system of property rights, democratic political markets become feeding grounds for battles over the redistribution of wealth, battles in which middle income voters predictably extract wealth transfers from both the rich and the poor (Tullock, 1993). Such battles occur whether voters are predominantly well-informed or whether they are predominantly rationally ignorant.

In sharp contrast to the politics-as-exchange model advanced by Buchanan and Tullock (1962), much of politics concerns the struggle to gain control over public authority and the exercising of that authority (Moe, 1991, 221). When two poor individuals and one rich individual make up a polity governed by majority rule, the rich individual is in trouble. He is not in trouble because of the instability of majority rule, nor because a prisoners' dilemma prevents the three participants from realizing gains from trade. He is in trouble because the poor participants will take advantage of the public authority to invade his wealth.

In private markets, wealth redistributions occurs on a voluntary basis through charities and is utility enhancing. In political markets, wealth redistribution occurs coercively and takes the form of a negative sum game since it is costly and does not create wealth. In democratic political markets, once government expands beyond the confines of the minimal state, wealth redistribution becomes the primary focus (Rowley, 1993). In terms of wealth maximization criteria the rent-seeking society clearly fails. It is wealth-reducing, not only because of rent-seeking waste but also because many wealth transfers move opaquely and carry high excess burdens (Crew and Rowley, 1988).

7. The Economic Inefficiency of Unconstrained Democracy

The new welfare economists view private markets as failing extensively because of perceived weaknesses in property rights, pervasive externalities and public goods and widespread asymmetries in information. In contrast, they view democratic government as benevolent, omniscient and impartial in its role as the White Knight riding to rescue individuals from unavoidable private market failures (Baumol and Oates, 1988). The public choice revolution redressed this bias by analysing government as it is and not as a figment of some excessively cloistered imagination.

Buchanan and Tullock (1962) set the scene for this leveling of the playing field by demonstrating that problems posed by property right failures, externalities, publicness characteristics, and asymmetric information are greatly intensified in political markets because of pervasive indivisibilities. The rational choice approach, focusing as it does on the self-seeking motivation of all politicians, implies that politicians will behave opportunistically in this muddied market-place, rather than serving the wishes of the majority of the electorate.

Wittman is catholic in his definition of democracy, a definition that encompasses virtually any form of politics in which voting occurs (Rowley, 1997). Because of his emphasis on competition, low transaction costs and full information, he is able to downplay the role of institutions to a virtual irrelevance from the perspective of wealth maximization. Wittman views the existence or non-existence of written constitutions, the issue of universal versus limited suffrage, of direct assembly versus representative government, of unicameral versus multi-cameral legislatures, of majority versus supra-majority rule, of republican versus parliamentary democracy, of the presence or absence of the separation of powers as of minimal or even zero significance for economic efficiency. Once the unrealistic assumptions of his model are weakened, however, Wittman's case in favor of generalized democratic efficiency simply falls to the ground.

This is not to deny that government has no role to play. The minimal state, limited to ensuring law and order, the rule of law, the protection of private property rights and the defense of the realm from outside invasion clearly is superior to anarchy (Rowley, 1996). The real problem is constraining government to these limited functions. Unconstrained democracy based on universal suffrage has a sorry record. Once those with little or no property come to dominate political markets, the rational choice model advises that they will use this power to steal wealth through the political process (Tocqueville, 1848).

Let us for the moment grant Wittman his judgment that such wealth is transferred efficiently. Even then, his thesis badly fails. A large majority of economists now recognizes that a robust system of private property rights is a necessary condition for the creation of wealth. Unconstrained democracy, by Wittman's own admission, places those property rights in jeopardy. Therefore, even if democratic governments redistribute wealth efficiently, they do so by destroying the *basis* of wealth creation in society. More than two centuries ago, Adam Smith (1776) was far more sagacious than Wittman in his understanding of such matters. But then, as Smith (1782) rightly observed: "there is a great deal of ruin in a Nation."

CHARLES K. ROWLEY
MICHELLE A. VACHRIS

REFERENCES

Auster, R.D. and Silver, M. (1979). *The State as A Firm*. Boston: Martinus Nijhoff Publishing.

Baumol, W.J. and Oates, W.E. (1988). *The Theory of Environmental Policy*. Cambridge: Cambridge University Press.

Boudreaux, D. (1996). "Was your high school civics teacher right after all?" in Donald Wittman's *The myth of Democratic Failure. The Independent Review*, 1: 111–128.

Becker, G.S. (1983). "A theory of competition among pressure groups for political influence." *Quarterly Journal of Economics*, 63: 371–400.

Becker, G.S. (1985). "Public policies, pressure groups and deadweight costs." *Journal of Public Economics*, 28, 329–347.

Buchanan, J.M. and Tullock, G. (1962). *The Calculus of Consent*. Ann Arbor: University of Michigan Press.

Coase, R.H. (1960). "The problem of social cost." *Journal of Law and Economics*, 3: 1–44.

Crew, M.A. and Rowley, C.K. (1988). "Toward a public choice theory of monopoly regulation." *Public Choice*, 57: 49–68.

Downs, A. (1957). *An Economic Theory of Democracy*. New York: Harper and Row.

Friedman, M. (1963). *Capitalism and Freedom*. Chicago: University of Chicago Press.

Green, D.P. and Shapiro, I. (1994). *Pathologies of Irrational Choice Theory*. New Haven and London: Yale University Press.

Laband, D.W. and Sophocleus, J.P. (1988). "The social cost of rent-seeking: first estimates." *Public Choice*, 58: 269–275.

Laband, D.W. and McClintock, G.C. (2001). *The Transfer Society*. Washington, DC: The Cato Institute.

Luce, D.R. and Raiffa, H. (1957). *Games and Decisions*. New York: Wiley Press.

Moe, T.N. (1991). "Politics and the theory of organization." *Journal of Law, Economics and Organization*, 7: 106–129.

Olson, M. (1965). *The Logic of Collective Action*. Cambridge, USA: Harvard University Press.

Rowley, C.K. (1984). "The relevance of the median voter theorem." *Journal of Institutional and Theoretical Economics*. (March): 105–135.

Rowley, C.K. (1993). *Liberty and the State*. The Shaftesbury Papers,4. Aldershot, UK and Brookfield, USA: Edward Elgar Publishing.

Rowley, C.K. (1996). "What is living and what is dead in classical liberalism," in C.K. Rowley (ed.). *The Political Economy of the Minimal State*. Aldershot, UK and Brookfield, USA: Edward Elgar Publishing, pp. 1–23.

Rowley, C.K. (1997). "Donald Wittman's *The myth of democratic failure." Public Choice*, 92 (1–2): 15–26.

Rowley, C.K. and Vachris, M.A. (1993). "Snake oil economics versus public choice," in C.K. Rowley (ed.) *Public Choice Theory*, Volume III. Aldershot, UK and Brookfield, USA: Edward Elgar Publishing, pp. 573–584.

Rowley, C.K. and Vachris, M.A. (1995). "Why democracy does not necessarily produce efficient results." *Journal of Public Finance and Public Choice*, (December): 97–111.

Samuelson, P. (1954). "The pure theory of public expenditure." *Review of Economics and Statistics*, 36: 386–389.

Smith, A. (1776). *The Wealth of Nations*. Edinburgh: Thomas Nelson.

Smith, A. (1782). Letter to Sir John Sinclair. (14 October).

Stigler, G.J. (1968). "A theory of oligopoly." *Journal of Political Economy*, 72: 44–61.

Stigler, G.J. (1972). "Economic competition and political competition." *Public Choice*, 13: 91–106.

Stigler, G.J. (1988). *Chicago Studies in Political Economy*. Chicago: University of Chicago Press.

Stiglitz, J.E. (1989). *The Economic Role of the State*. Oxford: Basil Blackwell.

Tocqueville, A. de, (1848). *Democracy in America*. Oxford: Oxford University Press 1965.

Tullock, G. (1967). "The welfare costs of tariffs, monopolies and theft." *Western Economic Journal*, 5: 224–232.

Tullock, G. (1993). *Rent Seeking*. The Shaftesbury Papers, 2, Aldershot, UK and Brookfield, Vermont: Edward Elgar Publishing.

Wittman, D. (1989). "Why democracies produce efficient results." *Journal of Political Economy*, 97: 1395–1424.

Wittman, D. (1995). *The Myth of Democratic Failure: Why Political Institutions are Efficient?* Chicago: University of Chicago Press.

Wittman, D. (2003). "Efficiency of democracy." in C.K. Rowley and F. Schneider (eds.) *The Encyclopedia of Public Choice*. Dordrecht and Boston: Kluwer Academic Publishers.

THE EFFICIENCY OF THE COMMON LAW HYPOTHESIS

An important premise of law and economics is that the common law (i.e., judge-made law) is the result of an effort, conscious or not, to induce efficient outcomes. This is known as the efficiency of the common law hypothesis. According to this hypothesis, first intimated by Coase (1960) and later systematized and greatly extended by Posner (e.g., Ehrlich and Posner, 1974; Posner 1994), common law rules attempt to allocate resources efficiently, typically in a Pareto or Kaldor-Hicks efficient manner. Common law rules are said to enjoy a comparative advantage over legislation in fulfilling this task because of the evolutionary selection of common law rules through adjudication and the gradual accretion of precedent. Several important contributions provide the foundations for this claim. However, the scholars who have advanced theories in support of the hypothesis are often in disagreement as to their conceptual basis.

1. The Evolutionary Selection of Efficient Common Law Rules

The foundation of the efficiency of the common law thesis is the evolution of legal rules by the common law tradition of *stare decisis*. Rubin (1977), who is an important contributor in the field, maintains that the efficiency of the common law is best explained by the fact that parties will more likely litigate inefficient rules than efficient ones. The pressure for the common law to evolve to efficiency, he argues, rests on the desire of parties to create precedent because they have an interest in future similar cases. Rubin thus considers three basic situations: (1) where both parties are interested in creating precedent; (2) where only one party is interested in creating precedent; (3) and where neither party has such an interest.

Where both parties have an interest in future similar cases, and where the current legal rule is inefficient, Rubin claims that the party held liable will have an incentive to force litigation. Parties will continue to use the courts until the rule is changed. If the current rule is efficient, however, there is no incentive to change it, so it will remain in force. Where only one party has an interest in future similar cases, the incentive to litigate will depend on the allocation of liability. If liability falls on a repeat player, litigation will likely occur, whereas the other party would have no incentive to litigate. As a result, precedents will evolve in the interested party's favor, whether or not the rule is efficient. In the event that neither party is interested in precedents, the legal rule, whether efficient or not, will remain in force, and parties will settle out of court because they lack the incentive to change the current rule. Rubin thus concludes that the common law becomes efficient based on the utility maximizing decisions of litigants, rather than on judges' desires to maximize efficiency.

Economic Theories of Adjudication

Rubin's analysis was extended by Priest (1977), who articulated the idea that the common law tends to develop efficient rules independent of judicial bias in decision-making. Indeed, Priest asserts, efficient rules will develop even despite judicial hostility toward efficient outcomes. He parts with Rubin, however, on the source of the tendency toward efficiency, rejecting Rubin's conclusion that this tendency occurs only where both parties to a dispute have an interest in future similar cases and therefore have an incentive to litigate. Instead, he asserts that litigation is driven by the costs of inefficient rules, rather than the desire for precedent.

According to Priest's analysis, inefficient rules impose greater costs on the parties subject to them than do efficient rules, thereby making the stakes in a dispute greater. Where the stakes are greater, litigation is more likely than settlement. Consequently, out of the complete set of legal rules, disputes arising under inefficient rules will tend to be litigated and relitigated more often than disputes arising under efficient rules. This means that the rules not contested will tend to be efficient ones. Because efficient rules are less likely to be reviewed, especially by judges hostile to efficient outcomes, these rules tend to remain in force. Further, as inefficient rules are reviewed, the process of review provides the chance that they will be discarded in favor of more efficient variants which, in turn, are less likely to be reviewed. Thus, the selection of efficient legal rules is perpetuated in the legal system.

An important component of the theories advanced by Rubin (1977) and Priest (1977) is the criteria for the selection of disputes for litigation. In fact, only a small fraction of disputes go to trial, and even fewer are appealed. Priest and Klein (1984) develop a model of the litigation process that explores the relationship between the disputes litigated and the disputes settled. According to their one-period model of dispute resolution, the proportion of plaintiff victories in any set of cases will be influenced by the shape of the distribution of disputes, the absolute magnitude of the judgment, litigation and settlement costs, and the relative stakes of the parties. Priest and Klein show that the set of disputes selected for litigation, rather than settlement, will therefore constitute neither a random nor a representative sample of the set of all disputes. They then derive a selection hypothesis: where both parties have equal stakes in the litigation, the individual maximizing decisions of the parties will create a strong bias toward a success rate for plaintiffs at trial (or appellants on appeal) of 50 percent, regardless of the substantive law.

When the assumption that both parties have equal stakes in the dispute is relaxed (e.g., where one of the parties is a repeat player and has a stake in future similar cases), the rate of success in litigation begins to deviate from the hypothesized baseline, and the model predicts that the repeat player will prevail more frequently. Priest and Klein present a great deal of data, both derived from their own empirical investigations and from the major empirical studies of the legal system since the 1930s. While they caution against the conclusion that these data confirm the selection hypothesis, largely due to measurement problems, the data are nonetheless encouraging.

Cooter and Rubinfeld (1989) look at common law dispute resolution from an informational perspective. In their view, legal disputes are resolved at various stages of a sequential decision-making process in which parties have limited information and act in their own self-interest. An efficient resolution occurs when legal entitlements are assigned to the parties who value them the most, legal liabilities are allocated to the parties who can bear them at the lowest cost, and transaction costs are minimized. Following these premises, Cooter and Rubinfeld review economic models of legal dispute resolution, attempting to synthesize a model that provides a point of reference necessary to both an understanding of the courts, and deliberation over proposed changes in legal rules. In the first stage of a legal dispute, the underlying event, efficiency requires balancing the cost of harm against the cost of harm avoidance. Because Coasian bargaining is typically not possible, the social costs of harm are externalized. Therefore, an initial allocation of entitlements is essential to creating incentives for efficient levels of activity and precaution. During the second stage, the harmed party decides whether or not to assert a legal claim. This requires the balancing of immediate costs, such as hiring an attorney, and the expected benefits from asserting a claim. In the third stage, after a legal claim is asserted, but before trial, courts encourage parties to bargain together to reach a settlement. If the parties cannot privately settle their dispute, the court performs this function in the final stage, trial. Using their hybrid economic model of suit, settlement, and trial, Cooter and Rubinfeld come to examine the incentives parties face as they proceed through the litigation process, and make predictions based on the decisions available to the parties, with a discussion of some of the concerns that arise from the pursuit of efficiency which pervades normative economic analysis.

2. Private Choices and Public Rules: The Role of Litigants

The theories of Rubin, Priest, Klein, and to a great extent Cooter and Rubinfeld, all contain the premise that cost analysis by the litigating parties plays a role in shaping the efficiency of the common law. This premise originates from the earlier work of Landes (1971), who considered the amount of litigation in a society as a function of the way in which public court services were administered. Landes suggests that because users of the judicial system pay only nominal fees to access the public legal system, queues develop to ration the limited supply of court services. As a method of reducing backlog and court delays, Landes contemplates the requirement of larger access fees and the impact this policy choice would have on the use of courts and the demand for trials. He predicts that a money price for court access would increase the ratio of pre-trial settlements to total disputes.

In order to apply this theory to criminal cases, Landes observes that, contrary to popular belief, most criminal cases are resolved before trial, either by a guilty plea, dismissal, or other settlement arrangement between the parties. Landes then makes the assumption that both prosecutors and defendants seek to maximize their utility, subject to given constraints. Maximizing their utility, then, becomes the determining factor in deciding whether or not to settle or go to trial in a particular case. In Landes' model, the decision to settle or go to trial is influenced by factors such as the probability of conviction, severity of the offense, resources used by both the prosecutor and the defendant, costs of trial versus settlement, and degree of risk aversion. This model, in addition to the overall import of Landes' theory, provided the first empirically falsifiable hypotheses, which Landes himself tested using data from both state and federal courts.

Another more general theory of adjudication was subsequently advanced by the work of Ehrlich and Posner (1974). They outline a theory of the legal process which holds that the degree of precision in the formulation of legal commands is largely based on the desire to minimize social costs. With the knowledge that specific legal rules and general legal standards lie at opposite ends of the spectrum, Ehrlich and Posner articulate the criteria for determining the optimal degree of specificity, given cost minimization as a dominant consideration. They discuss the benefits that precision brings to the legal system, including increased predictability and the consequential reduction in litigation expenditures; increased speed of dispute resolution; and reduced information costs associated with adjudication. Yet, precision also involves costs: the costs of rule formulation, which is often substantial, given the high transaction costs of statutory decisions; allocative inefficiency arising from both the over- and under-inclusive effects of rules; and information barriers for the layman, who is more likely to understand general standards than specific rules which employ technical language.

3. Courts and Judicial Rulemaking: The Role of Judges

To understand judicial behavior, the first step is to analyze the incentives that judges have to make specific types of decisions or use particular procedures. In the federal system, law and economics has had difficulty explaining judicial behavior in economic terms in part because the federal judiciary is structured in order to remove judges from economic incentives. Posner (1994) articulates a positive economic theory of the behavior of federal appellate judges, using a model in which judicial utility is primarily a function of income, leasure and judicial voting. He argues that appellate judges are ordinary, rational people whose behavior is somewhat analogous to that of managers of nonprofit enterprises, voters, and theatrical spectators. Posner says that appellate judges are like nonprofit managers in that it is difficult to determine the quality or value of the desired output (neutral justice) from the full range of their services (rulemaking, private dispute resolution, and imposition between the government and its citizens). A rational public is reluctant to buy such services from a profit-making enterprise because a competitive market is not feasible, and they are reluctant to delegate such services to elected officials whose use of political criteria would not be easily monitored. The judiciary is called on to apply neutral justice with much discretionary power but without monetary or political compensation incentives. The judiciary's nonprofit structure enables competent people to be attracted to judging at lower wages by not forcing judges to work as hard as comparable lawyers might in private practice. However, because most judges continue their judicial activity beyond the usual retirement age of their private sector counterparts, Posner postulates that judges must derive utility in judging from something besides money and leisure. Posner believes that an appellate judge's utility function additionally contains preferences for a good reputation, popularity, prestige, and avoiding reversal. He explicitly excludes from the judicial utility function a desire to promote the public interest because he says such preference cannot be assumed across the board for all individuals. While it might explain the decisions of a few judges, it is not a good standard overall.

Posner analogizes judicial decision-making to political voting. There is pure utility in voting, as evidenced by participation in popular elections in which individuals incur a net cost in order to participate in the political process. This analogy suggests that voting on cases is one of the most important sources of judicial utility due to the deference judges' opinions receive from lawyers and the public. Judges further derive a consumption value in deciding whom or what to vote for. Judges balance this consumption against the opportunity cost of decision-making. Leisure-seeking by judges with weak preferences may result in 'going along voting': insistence that a particular decision is coerced by the law, joining opinions containing much dictum with which they disagree, or using procedural rules to avoid difficult or politically sensitive issues. Posner further suggests that this leisure-seeking explains why judges adhere to *stare decisis*, but not rigidly. With rigid adherence, they would lose the utility of discretionary power, but where there is no choice they strongly prefer to use precedent.

Posner simple formal model of the judicial utility function incorporates his articulated hypotheses to demonstrate that the behavior of ordinary federal appellate judges (and their choice to become a judge) is rational. His approach supports the theory that the conditions of judicial employment enable and induce judges to vote their values (among which Posner believes efficiency to be particularly influential), and the approach generates a number of testable economic predictions about judicial behavior which have engaged an entire generation of legal and economic scholars.

FRANCESCO PARISI

REFERENCES

Coase, R.H. (1960). "The problem of social cost." *Journal of Law and Economics*, 3: 1–44.

Cooter, R.D. and Rubinfeld, D.L. (1989). "Economic analysis of legal disputes and their resolution." *Journal of Economic Literature*, 27: 1067–1097.

Erhlich, I. and Posner, R.A. (1974). "An economic analysis of legal rulemaking." *Journal of Legal Studies*, 3: 257–286.

Landes, W.M. (1971). "An economic analysis of the courts." *Journal of Law and Economics*, 14: 61–107.

Landes, W.M. and Posner, R.A. (1975). "The independent judiciary in an interest-group perspective." *Journal of Law and Economics*, 18: 875–901.

Posner, R.A. (1994). "What do judges and justices maximize?" *Supreme Court Economic Review*, 3.

Priest, G.L. (1977). "The common law process and the selection of efficient rules." *Journal of Legal Studies*, 6: 65–82.

Priest, G.L. and Klein, B. (1984). "The selection of disputes for litigation." *Journal of Legal Studies*, 13: 1–55.

Rowley, C.K. (1989). "The common law in public choice perspective: a theoretical and institutional critique." *Hamline Law Review*, 12: 355–383.

Rubin, P.H. (1977). "Why is the common law efficient?" *Journal of Legal Studies*, 6: 51–63.

ELECTED VERSUS APPOINTED REGULATORS

A key issue in political economy concerns the accountability structures put in place to select public officials. While the principle that legislators are to be elected is now a defining feature of modern democracies, there are some offices where a plurality of selection methods survive. A key example is the case of regulators. Typically, heads of regulatory agencies are appointed by politicians, creating an insulating layer between citizens and regulators. However, a number of U.S. states have injected a degree of populism into the regulatory process by requiring that the heads of their independent regulatory commissions be directly elected. Insurance regulation has a similar structure with several states also electing their insurance commissioners.

For students of political economy this raises three key questions. First, can we develop a satisfactory theoretical understanding of the likely differences between regimes of election and appointment? Second, does the data yield robust lessons? Third, does the data square with the theory? The U.S. states provide a natural panel data laboratory for this investigation. We observe both time series and cross-sectional variation in the decision to elect or appoint.

On any first encounter with the idea of popular election of regulators, one is drawn to the proposition that consumer interests might be served more intently by elected regulators since they are more likely to have their eye on the ballot box. Indeed a number of contributions to the literature seem to begin with the observation that this is self-evident. However compelling this might seem, further thought reveals this claim to be inconsistent with the view that representative democracy yields median policy outcomes. Since those who appoint the regulators are themselves elected, then they would surely have as much interest in promoting consumer interests as directly elected regulators? Hence, we might expect either regimes with electing or appointed regulators to track the median voter's wishes on regulatory policy and authors including Baron (1995) and Laffont (1996) have modeled things this way. Any empirical differences could only be traced to differences in turnout and the composition of the electorate in different kinds of election.

A belief that election of regulators matters does require us to work with a theoretical structure outside a naive form of the Downsian model of representative democracy. Vague gestures towards support maximization a la Stigler (1971) and Peltzman (1976) are not particularly helpful either as these models rarely model the details of the institutional structure. Nonetheless, their proponents have ventured the important insight that the interplay of democracy and concentrated interests (organized or otherwise) may be important to understanding the difference between election and appointment of regulators. To use Stigler's language, the degree of *regulatory capture* by stakeholder interests may vary across regimes that elect and appoint regulators. However, sharpening insights about this does require a satisfactory theoretical account which models representative democracy and the actions of interest groups. Theoretical approaches in political economy that combine these features are still a rarity.

Besley and Coate (2000) provides the first fully developed treatment of the claim that direct election of regulators, rather than appointment by elected politicians, should lead to more consumer-oriented regulatory policies. In doing so, it makes explicit the importance of the fact that regulation is bundled with other issues when regulators are appointed. Because voters have only one vote to cast and regulatory issues are not salient for most voters, bundling provides parties with electoral incentives to respond to stakeholders in the regulated industry. Navarro (1982, pp. 126–127) has suggested an argument along these lines. The result is a sort of regulatory capture that emerges endogenously through the electoral process because of diffuse costs and concentrated benefits. If regulators are elected, their stance on regulation is the only salient issue so that the electoral incentive is to run a pro-consumer candidate. The same logic holds when producer interests are organized as an interest group capable of making campaign contributions to influence policy outcomes.

Most empirical work on the difference between electing and appointing states has concentrated on regulation of public utilities. There have been some changes in regimes over time. In 1960, fourteen states elected their utility commissioners, falling to eleven by 1997. This general trend masks the fact that six states switched their method of selecting regulators.

The large empirical literature on the effects of regulation begins with Stigler and Friedland's seminal study of electricity prices, comparing states which regulated prices with those that did not. (Stigler and Friedland, 1962; the literature as whole is expertly reviewed in Joskow and Rose, 1989). The cross-state variation between regulatory regimes in the United States has understandably been a rich testing ground for the economic effects of regulation. That institutional variation afforded by rules for appointing public utility commissioners in the U.S. provides ample scope for empirical testing. The earliest studies include Berry (1979), Boyes and McDowell (1989), Costello (1984), Crain and McCormick (1984), Harris and Navarro (1983), Navarro (1982), and Primeaux and Mann (1986), each of which looks at the evidence from a different perspective. Some of these contributions looked at rate setting, while others have looked at broader indicators of how favorable is the regulatory climate within a state. Costello's (Costello, 1984) review of the early evidence concludes that "In summary, it probably makes little difference to the average ratepayer whether a PUC is elected or appointed." (p. 104). Looking at more recently available evidence

overturns this conclusion — there is now good evidence that elected regulators are more pro-consumer in their outlook.

Formby et al. (1995) find this in their examination of electric utility bond ratings. Using data from 1979–1983 on a selection of investor-owned utilities, they find that election of public utility commissioners has a negative effect on bond ratings, consistent with a squeeze on margins due to more pro-consumer choices. Fields et al. (1997) find evidence that elected commissioners from the insurance industry are more pro-consumer. They report that the market value of life insurance companies doing business in California declined sharply following the passage of Proposition 103, which changed the method of selection of the insurance commissioner from appointment to election. Using data from 1985, Smart (1994) reports that telephone rates are lower in states that elect their public utility commissioners.

Besley and Coate (2000) look at differences in long-run (conditional) mean electricity prices for three types of tariff (residential, commercial and industrial) for a panel of 40 states that did not change their regulatory regime between 1960 and 1997. They find that residential prices are significantly lower in states that elect their regulators — their point estimates amount to around $60 per household per year at 1992 prices. The conditioning variables in the study are year fixed effects, a state specific cost index, and other demographic and economic variables. They also show that states with elected regulators are less likely to pass through cost changes into prices. Both of these are consistent with the idea that elected regulators are more pro-consumer in their outlook.

So why the difference between the older and newer work? The three studies conducted in the 1990s were looking either a different kinds of regulation (Fields et al., 1997; Smart, 1994) or at very different outcome measure (Formby et al. [1995]). Besley and Coate (2000) is more similar. However, in contrast to the previous literature, it exploits panel data and looks for long-run price differences rather than identification within a given year. This helps to alleviate the major concern within a cross-section that the decision to elect or appoint regulators is simply correlated with important unobservable differences between states. Their tests on pass through also exploit interactions between the regulatory regime and a time-varying (production costs).

A key question is who pays for lower prices in states that elect their regulators. Lower prices are likely to raise total surplus but, without lump-sum transfers there are gainers and losers. (Moreover, there are also long-run consequences to be considered to which we return below.)

In distributional terms, one (benign) possibility is that lower prices simply shift rents from shareholders to consumers. In this case, even if total surplus rises, the outcome from a welfare analysis that was sensitive to distribution would depend upon the relative weights that are placed on the payoffs of these two groups. Assuming that policy changes in the regulatory dimension are all that count, electing utility commissioners will be welfare enhancing if this rent transfer is desirable.

However, it is likely that lower prices have effects on other decisions, particularly the decision to invest. In the early years of U.S. utility regulation, the negative effects of regulator populism on incentives to invest was an abiding concern (see Troesken, 1997 for an important and persuasive discussion of this). Indeed, in part, this was behind the reason why the utilities themselves lobbied in favor of state level utility regulations to replace regulation at the local level. Once a utility had sunk its capital, it was reliant on the regulator to allow prices commensurate with earning an acceptable rate of return. Locally accountable regulators were more likely to be tempted to lower prices in order to gain popularity. In his study of gas companies, Troesken (1997) observes that "state utility commissions helped local governments credibly commit to reasonable regulatory policies. This made it easier for cities and towns to attract private capital. State regulation helped local governments commit because gas companies believed that state regulators were more sympathetic to producers than were local regulators" (p. 9). This brings into sharp relief the possible dilemma of populist regulation in a dynamic framework. These hold-up problem type of issues are recognized in the extensive theoretical literature on regulation — see, for example, the discussion in Laffont and Tirole (1993).

One important consequence of investment decisions in the United States is service reliability. This remains an important concern of regulators in the United States, the salience of which has been enhanced by the recent experience in California. Moreover, there is a feeling that there are important interactions between price regulation and service quality (see, for example Phillips, 1988, p. 507). This type of argument suggests that we might expect to see less investment in the electricity network in states that elect their regulators given our finding that prices are lower in these states. In suggestive evidence that investment may be lower, Besley and Coate (2000) use data on the number of power interruptions experienced in the States between 1984 and 1997 to show that states with elected regulators have more power interruptions.

In studies of this kind, it is important (and sometimes difficult) to be sure that being elected is not just proxying for other dimensions of regulatory rules. It is interesting to note that Navarro (1982) finds that states that elect their regulators show a more unfavorable regulatory climate according to his rankings of states gleaned from a number of commercial organizations. This is consistent with the finding that prices are lower in electing states although it is also possible that states with elected commissioners also have stronger regulatory institutions. However, looking at the measures from Norton (1985), the only states that elected commissioners in his sample were classified as weakly regulated (Norton, 1985, table 1; see also Costello, 1984, table 7.) Gormley (1981) observes that consumer movements are much more likely to be active in states where the public utility commissioner is appointed. This underlines the possibility that, over time, there can be important private responses to regulatory regimes that may affect the climate and thence become possible sources of omitted variables in empirical studies.

A key issue, which is still poorly understood, concerns the possibility that the choice of regulatory regime is endogenous. This is a tall order for empirical analysis given the relative rarity of switches in regimes. The insights from the theory and evidence suggest that this should itself be driven by the forces that shape the politics of consumer and stakeholder interests. In general, the choice of institutions remains an important, but elusive, area in empirical political economy. However, it is clearly an important agenda for the future.

The study of elected versus appointed regulators leaves little doubt that this kind of accountability structure matters in theory and practice. Moreover, the available evidence should be useful in informing debates about the design of regulatory institutions. The U.S. experiment with a more populist process does appear to yield benefits to consumers. The costs are harder to quantify. However, it is clear that election of regulators is something that merits serious consideration.

TIMOTHY BESLEY

REFERENCES

Baron, David (1995). "The economics and politics of regulation: perspectives, agenda and approaches," in Jeffrey Banks and Eric Hanushek (eds.) *Modern Political Economy*, Cambridge: Cambridge University Press.

Berry, William (1979). "Utility regulation in the states: the policy effects of professionalism and salience to the consumer." *American Journal of Political Science*, 23(2): 263–277.

Besley Timothy and Stephen Coate (2000a). "Elected versus appointed regulators: theory and evidence," NBER Working Paper 7579.

Boyes, William J. and John M. McDowell (1989). "The selection of public utility commissioners: a re-examination of the importance of institutional setting." *Public Choice*, 61: 1–13.

Costello, Kenneth W. (1984). "Electing regulators: the case of public utility commissioners." *Yale Journal on Regulation*, 2: 83–105.

Crain, W. Mark and Robert E. McCormick (1984). "Regulators as an interest group," in James M. Buchanan and Robert D. Tollison (eds.) *The Theory of Public Choice II*, Ann Arbor: University of Michigan Press.

Fields, Joseph A., Klein, Linda S., and James M. Sfiridis (1997). "A market based evaluation of the election versus appointment of regulatory commissioners." *Public Choice* 92: 337–351.

Formby, John P., Mishra, Banamber, and Paul D. Thistle (1995). "Public utility regulation and bond ratings." *Public Choice*, 84: 119–136.

Gormley, William T. (1981). "Non-electoral participation as a response to issue-specific conditions: the case of public utility regulation." *Social Science Quarterly*, 62(3): 527–539.

Harris, Malcolm C. and Peter Navarro (1983). "Does electing public utility commissioners bring lower electric rates?" *Public Utilities Fortnightly*, 112(September): 23–88.

Joskow, Paul and Roger Noll (1981). "Regulation in theory and practice: an overview," in Gary Fromm (ed.), *Studies in Public Regulation*. Cambridge, MA: MIT Press.

Joskow, Paul and Nancy Rose (1989). "The effects of economic regulation," in Richard Schmalensee and Robert Willig (eds.) *Handbook of Industrial Organization*. Amsterdam: North Holland.

Laffont, Jean-Jacques (1996). "Industrial policy and politics." *International Journal of Industrial Organization*, 14(1): 1–27.

Laffont, Jean-Jacques, and Jean Tirole (1993) *A Theory of Incentives in Procurement and Regulation*. Cambridge MA: MIT Press.

Navarro, Peter (1982). "Public utility commission regulation: performance, determinants and energy policy impacts." *The Energy Journal*, 3(2): 119–139.

Norton, Seth W. (1985). "Regulation and systematic risk: the case of electric utilities." *Journal of Law and Economics*, 28: 671–686.

Peltzman, Sam (1976). "Toward a more general theory of regulation." *Journal of Law and Economics*, 19: 211–240.

Phillips, Charles F. Jr. (1988). *The Regulation of Public Utilities*. Arlington, VA: Public Utilities Reports, Inc.

Primeaux, Walter and Patrick Mann (1986). "Regulator selection methods and electricity prices." *Land Economics*, 63(1): 1–13.

Smart, Susan R. (1994). "The consequences of appointment methods and party control for telecommunications pricing," *Journal of Economics & Management Strategy*, 3(2): 301–323.

Stigler, George (1971). "The theory of economic regulation." *The Bell Journal of Economics*, (Spring): vol 2: 3–21.

Stigler, George and C. Friedland (1962). "What the regulators regulate? The case of electricity." *Journal of Law and Economics*, 5: 1–16.

Troesken, Werner (1997). "The sources of public ownership: historical evidence from the gas industry." *Journal of Law, Economics and Organization*, 13(1): 1–25.

ELECTION MODELS

Voting is used to decide who controls power at various levels of government. Hence elected officials and individuals aspiring to hold public offices are concerned about voters' choices. Researchers have developed mathematical models of the relation *between* voters' choices *and* certain decisions that politicians make when there is an election. The material, which follows, discusses models (of this relation) developed in the public choice literature on elections. The first part of the entry sets out a general model. Then the entry discusses two important special cases, which are called "deterministic" and "probabilistic" voting models. These models are illustrated with two specific examples.

This section provides a framework which will be useful for thinking about the public choice literature on elections. This will be done by specifying a general model which is similar to ones in McKelvey (1975, pp. 817–822) and Calvert (1986: sections 2.1 and 2.4).

1. A Model (of A Two-candidate Election)

There are two candidates for a particular political office. They will be indexed by the elements in the set $C = \{1, 2\}$. Let c be a variable for the candidate index numbers. There is a set of possible strategies, X, for the candidates. The set of possible strategies is the same for both of them. A particular $x \in X$ could, for instance, specify a position on the policy issues in the election, an allocation of campaign resources, or both of these. ψ_c will be used to denote a particular strategy for c.

There is a set of individuals who can vote in the election. They will be indexed by the elements in a set, N. Let i denote an index for a voter. A particular $i \in N$ could be a number (e.g., if the voters are labeled as voters $1, \ldots, n$), a specification of various characteristics that a voter can have (such as location of residence, income, age, etc.), a vector that specifies the "ideal" positions on the various policy issues for a voter, or something else.

For each $i \in N$ and $c \in C$, there is a function

$$P_i^c: X \times X \to [0, 1]$$

that assigns to each $(\psi_1, \psi_2) \in X \times X$ a probability for: a voter randomly drawn from the individuals labeled by i - voting for c if candidate 1's strategy is ψ_1, and candidate 2's strategy is ψ_2. For each $(\psi_1, \psi_2) \in X^2$, $P_i^0(\psi_1, \psi_2) = 1 - P_i^1(\psi_1, \psi_2) - P_i^2(\psi_1, \psi_2)$ will be the probability for: the event a voter randomly drawn from the individuals labeled by i not voting (i.e., abstaining from voting), if candidate 1's strategy is ψ_1, and candidate 2's strategy is ψ_2. These can be objective probabilities or they can be subjective probabilities that are believed by both of the candidates.

F(N) will denote a σ-field of subsets of N. For example: If there is a finite set of voters, F(N) could be the collection of all subsets of N. As another example: If there is a continuum of voters and we have $N = [0, 1]$, then F(N) could be the collection of Borel sets in $[0, 1]$.

There is a probability measure, P_N, on $(N, \mathrm{F}(N))$ which assigns to each set $B \in \mathrm{F}(N)$, the probability of: a voter who is randomly drawn (from the individuals who can vote in the election) having an index $i \in B$. When P_N is a rational number (as occurs, for instance, for each B when N is finite), P_N can also be interpreted as the proportion of voters with an index in B. These probabilities can also be either objective probabilities or subjective probabilities that are believed by both of the candidates. Each candidate is concerned solely about his or her (a) expected vote, $EV^c(\psi_1, \psi_2)$, (b) expected plurality (i.e., the expected margin of victory), $Pl^c(\psi_1, \psi_2)$, or (c) probability of winning $WI^c(\psi_1, \psi_2)$.

2. Deterministic Voting Models

An important special case for the general model given above is the *deterministic voting* model. This terminology comes from analyses of models in which each candidate wants to maximize his or her expected plurality. If (for a given $i \in N$ and $(\psi_1, \psi_2) \in X^2$) we have $P_i^1(\psi_1, \psi_2) = P_i^2(\psi_1, \psi_2)$, then the expected vote from the individual(s) indexed by "i" is split evenly between the two candidates. When this occurs (since each candidate's objective is to maximize his or her expected plurality), the expected votes corresponding to the index i cancel each other out and, therefore, have no effect on $P_i^1(\psi_1, \psi_2) = P_i^2(\psi_1, \psi_2)$.

From the preceding observations it is clear that, at any given (ψ_1, ψ_2), the only voter indices that matter (to expected plurality maximizing candidates) are ones with $P_i^1(\psi_1, \psi_2) \neq P_i^2(\psi_1, \psi_2)$. When, in fact, $P_i^1(\psi_1, \psi_2) = 1$ or $P_i^2(\psi_1, \psi_2) = 1$ at a given $i \in N$ and $(\psi_1, \psi_2) \in X^2$, one of two things must be true: (a) there is one voter with the index i and the candidates believe that his or her decision will be completely determined once they choose the strategies ψ_1 and ψ_2, respectively, or (b) there is more than one voter with the index i and the decisions made by all these voters will be completely determined (and the same) once the candidates choose the strategies ψ_1 and ψ_2, respectively. Because of this, any model which satisfies the assumptions of the general voting model given above and is such that, at each $(\psi_1, \psi_2) \in X^2$ and $i \in N$ where $P_i^1(\psi_1, \psi_2) \neq P_i^2(\psi_1, \psi_2)$, either (i) $P_i^1(\psi_1, \psi_2) = 1$ or (ii) $P_i^2(\psi_1, \psi_2) = 1$, is called a "deterministic voting model."

The defining characteristic of a deterministic voting model can be restated as: For each $(\psi_1, \psi_2) \in X^2$ and $i \in N$, either the expected votes corresponding to the index i cancel each other out (and, therefore, have no effect on the candidates' expected pluralities or the decisions of the voters) corresponding to the index i will be completely determined and identical when candidate 1 chooses ψ_1, and candidate 2 chooses ψ_2. A third way of stating this characteristic is: For each $(\psi_1, \psi_2) \in X^2$ and $i \in N$, (a) $P_i^1(\psi_1, \psi_2) = 1$, (b) $P_i^2(\psi_1, \psi_2) = 1$, or (c) $P_i^1(\psi_1, \psi_2) = P_i^2(\psi_1, \psi_2) = \frac{1}{2}(1 = P_i^0(\psi_1, \psi_2))$.

The deterministic voting models that have received the most attention are ones in which

(1) each index corresponds to one voter,

(2) each voter, i, has a utility function, $U_i(x)$, and

(3a) for each voter, i, and each $(\psi_1, \psi_2) \in X^2$,

$$P_i^1(\psi_1, \psi_2) = \begin{cases} 1 & \text{if } U_i(\psi_1) > U_i(\psi_2) \\ \frac{1}{2} & \text{if } U_i(\psi_1) = U_i(\psi_2) \\ 0 & \text{if } U_i(\psi_1) < U_i(\psi_2) \end{cases}$$

$$P_i^2(\psi_1, \psi_2) = 1 - P_i^1(\psi_1, \psi_2)$$

or (3b) for each voter, i, and each $(\psi_1, \psi_2) \in X^2$

$$P_i^0(\psi_1, \psi_2) = \begin{cases} 1 & \text{if } U_i(\psi_1) = U_i(\psi_2) \\ 0 & \text{if } U_i(\psi_1) \neq U_i(\psi_2) \end{cases}$$

$$P_i^1(\psi_1, \psi_2) = \begin{cases} 1 & \text{if } U_i(\psi_1) > U_i(\psi_2) \\ 0 & \text{if } U_i(\psi_1) \leq U_i(\psi_2) \end{cases}$$

$$P_i^2(\psi_1, \psi_2) = 1 - P_i^1(\psi_1, \psi_2) - P_i^0(\psi_1, \psi_2)$$

An exception is McKelvey (1975), where it is assumed that (a) for each index, α all of the voters who are labeled by this index have the same utility function, $U_\alpha(x)$, and (b) for each index α and each $(\psi_1, \psi_2) \in X^2$,

$$(P_\alpha^0(\psi_1, \psi_2), P_\alpha^1(\psi_1, \psi_2), P_\alpha^2(\psi_1, \psi_2)) \in \{(1, 0, 0), (0, 1, 0), (0, 0, 1)\}.$$

$$[P_\alpha^1(\psi_1, \psi_2) = 1] \Rightarrow [U_\alpha(\psi_1) > U_\alpha(\psi_2)],$$

$$[P_\alpha^2(\psi_1, \psi_2) = 1] \Rightarrow [U_\alpha(\psi_1) < U_\alpha(\psi_2)].$$

This formulation provides a deterministic voting model in which abstentions can occur more frequently than just when $U_\alpha(\psi_1) = U_\alpha(\psi_2)$.

The pioneering work on deterministic voting models was done by Hotelling (1929), Downs (1957), Black (1958) and Davis and Hinich (1966, 1968). Surveys and critiques of results that have been derived in these and other analyses (using $EV^c(\psi_1, \psi_2)$, $Pl^c(\psi_1, \psi_2)$ or $WI^c(\psi_1, \psi_2)$ as the objective functions for the candidates) can be found in

Plott (1971), Kramer (1977), Mueller (1976), Rowley (1984), Ordeshook (1977) and elsewhere.

3. Probabilistic Voting Models

The other cases for the model of a two-candidate election are called *probabilistic voting* models. In other words: A model, which satisfies the assumptions of the general voting model given above, but *is not* a deterministic voting model, is called a probabilistic voting model. The terminology reflects the fact that in any such model, there is at least one pair of strategies $(\psi_1, \psi_2) \in X^2$ at which there is at least one index that matters (to expected plurality maximizing candidates) where the candidates' beliefs about the voter(s) corresponding to the index are probabilistic in a nontrivial way; in that the random variable which describes them is nondegenerate. The defining characteristic for probabilistic voting models can be restated as: There is at least one $(\psi_1, \psi_2) \in X^2$ and $i \in N$ where $P_i^1(\psi_1, \psi_2) \neq P_i^2(\psi_1, \psi_2)$ *and* $0 < P_i^1(\psi_1, \psi_2) < 1$ or $0 < P_i^2(\psi_1, \psi_2) < 1$ (or both).

One way in which a model that satisfies all the assumptions of the general voting model given above can be a probabilistic voting model is by having an index i that corresponds to two or more voters and at least one pair of possible strategies $(\psi_1, \psi_2) \in X^2$ such that the choices of the voters corresponding to index i are completely determined when candidate 1 chooses ψ_1 and candidate 2 chooses ψ_2, *but* (a) they will not all make the same choice, and (b) those who will vote are not split evenly between the candidates. The resulting model is a probabilistic voting model. This approach is the basis for the models analyzed in McKelvey (1975).

Indeed, almost any deterministic voting model can be converted into a probabilistic voting model of this sort by appropriately regrouping the indices in the deterministic voting model into indices for the probabilistic voting model.

A voting model that satisfies all the assumptions of the general voting model given above can, alternatively, be a probabilistic voting model if there is at least one voter whose choice of whether to vote and/or which candidate to vote for (if he or she votes) is probabilistic in nature. This approach is the basis for the models analyzed in Hinich and Ordeshook (1969), Davis and Hinich (1972), Hinich et al. (1972, 1973), Brams and Davis (1982), Brams (1975), Comaner (1976), Lake (1979), Coughlin and Nitzan (1981a,b), Hinich (1977) and Lindbeck and Weibull (1987). A voting model that satisfies all the assumptions given above could be a probabilistic voting model because the candidates are uncertain about the choices that voters will make and use subjective probabilities to summarize

their expectations about these choices. This is the basis for the model analyzed in Ledyard (1981, 1984). Analyses that apply to models in which any of these three interpretations can arise have been carried out in Coughlin (1983, 1984). The most closely scrutinized probabilistic voting models can be grouped into three basic categories. The first consists of models in which the description of the candidates' expectations about the voters' decisions to vote (or abstain) are probabilistic, but the description of their expectations about the choices that the voters make between the candidates are deterministic (i.e., they believe that, for each $(\psi_1, \psi_2) \in X \times X$ and $i \in N$, when candidate 1 chooses ψ_1, and candidate 2 chooses ψ_2, the voters corresponding to i who vote **will** all vote for the same candidate and the candidate who so benefits is completely determined). This category includes the models in Hinich and Ordeshook (1969), Davis and Hinich (1972), Hinich et al. (1972, 1973) and McKelvey (1975).

The second category consists of models in which there are no abstentions, but the description of the candidates' expectations about the choices that the voters will make in choosing between them is probabilistic: (a) $P_i^0(\psi_1, \psi_2) = 0$, $\forall (\psi_1, \psi_2) \in X \times X$, $\forall i \in N$ and (b) $\exists i \in N$ and $(\psi_1, \psi_2) \in X \times X$, where $P_i^1(\psi_1, \psi_2) \neq 1/2$. This category includes Brams (1975), Brams and Davis (1982), Hinich (1977), Coughlin and Nitzan (1981a,b), and Coughlin (1984).

The third category consists of models in which the description of the candidates' expectations both about voter abstentions and about the choices that the voters will make in choosing between them are probabilistic. This category includes Denzau and Kats (1977), Coughlin (1982, 1983), and Ledyard (1981, 1984).

For further discussions, see the references.

4. Examples

In the two examples stated in this section, firstly the common characteristics will be studied. Subsequently, the assumptions that differ shall be stated.

There are two candidates indexed by c = 1, 2. There are three voters, indexed by i = 1, 2, 3.

Each candidate must choose an income distribution. It will be assumed that each candidate can, in particular, choose any $\psi_c \in X = \{(x_1, x_2, x_3) \in R^3: x_1 + x_2 + x_3 = 1, x_1 \geq 0.01, x_2 \geq 0.01, x_3 \geq 0.01\}$.

Each particular voter cares only about his or her own income. More specifically, (for any given $i \in N$) for each pair x, y $\in X$: x is at least as good as y for i if and only if $x_i \geq y_i$. This implies that i prefers x to y (i.e., x is at least as good as y for i, but y is not at least as good as x for i) if and only if, $x_i > y_i$. It also implies that i is indifferent between x and y (i.e., x is at least as good as y for i and y is at least as good as x for i) if and only if $x_i = y_i$. Thus i's preferences on X can be represented by the utility function $U_i(x) = x_i$; for each pair x, y $\in$ X, $U_i(x) > U_i(y)$ if and only if x is at least as good as y for i. In addition, assume that $U_i(x)$ measures the intensity of i's preferences. More specifically, the values assigned by $U_i(x)$ have the following interpretations: $U_i(x)/U_i(y) = \frac{1}{2}$ if and only if i likes x only half as much as he or she likes y; $U_i(x)/U_i(y) = 2$ if and only if i likes x twice as much as he or she likes y; $U_i(x)/U_i(y) = 3$ if and only if i likes x three times as much as he or she likes y; and so on. This property implies that each voter's utility function is unique up to multiplication by a positive scalar. (It is, accordingly, called a *ratio-scale utility function*.)

In the examples, $P_i^c(\psi_1, \psi_2)$ will be used to denote the probability that the individual indexed by i will vote for candidate c when c = 1 chooses ψ_1, and c = 2 chooses ψ_2. Thus [at any given $(\psi_1, \psi_2) \in X^2$] the expected vote for a given $c \in C$ can be written as

$$EV^c(\psi_1, \psi_2) = \sum_{i=1}^{3} P_i^c(\psi_1, \psi_2).$$

Each candidate c is concerned solely about his or her expected plurality.

$$Pl^c(\psi_1, \psi_2) = EV^c(\psi_1, \psi_2) - EV^k(\psi_1, \psi_2)$$

(where k is the index for the other candidate), that is with his or her expected margin of victory (or, phrased differently, how much he or she expects to win or lose by). Furthermore, each candidate wants to maximize his or her expected plurality; in a candidate's view, the larger the expected margin of victory, the better. This implies that for any specification of the $P_i^c(.)$ functions, the decisions that the two candidates have to make can be appropriately modeled as a two-person, non-cooperative game, $(X, X; Pl^1, Pl^2)$, in which (1) the two players are the two candidates, (2) the strategy set for each candidate is X, and (3) the payoff functions are $Pl^1: X \times X \to R^1$ and $Pl^2: X \times X \to R^1$, respectively. By the definitions of Pl^1 and Pl^2, $Pl^1(\psi_1, \psi_2) + Pl^2(\psi_1, \psi_2) = 0$ $\forall (\psi_1, \psi_2) \in X^2$. Hence the game is zero-sum.

The next step is to consider specific assumptions about how P_i^c is related to ψ_1 and ψ_2. Example 1 in this section will be a deterministic voting model and Example 2 will be a probabilistic voting model.

Example 1. Consider the case in which, for each i $\in$ N and each pair $(\psi_1, \psi_2) \in X^2$,

$$P_i^1(\psi_1, \psi_2) = \begin{cases} 1 & \text{if } U_i(\psi_1) > U_i(\psi_2) \\ \frac{1}{2} & \text{if } U_i(\psi_1) = U_i(\psi_2) \\ 0 & \text{if } U_i(\psi_1) < U_i(\psi_2) \end{cases}$$

And

$$P_i^2(\psi_1, \psi_2) = 1 - P_i^1(\psi_1, \psi_2)$$

The resulting game, $(X, X; Pl^1, Pl^2)$, has no Nash equilibrium. Since the game is zero sum, this can also be phrased as: The game has no saddle point.

The fact that this game has no Nash equilibrium (or, equivalently, has no saddle point) can be seen quite easily. Choose any $(x, y) \in X^2$. Since the game is zero-sum, there are three possibilities:

(a) $Pl^1(x, y) = Pl^2(x, y) = 0$

(b) $Pl^1(x, y) > 0 > Pl^2(x, y)$ or

(c) $Pl^1(x, y) < 0 < Pl^2(x, y)$

Suppose that (a) or (b) holds. Identify a voter, i, who gets at least as much income at x as anyone else (i.e., for whom we have $x_i \geq x_j$, $\forall j \neq i$). Let z be the alternative in which this individual gets $z_i = 0.01$ and the others get $z_j = x_j + \frac{1}{2}(x_i - 0.01)$ (i.e., the others split the decrease in i's income). Since $x_i > 0.01$, we have $U_j(z) = z_j > x_j = U_j(x)$ for each $j \neq i$ and $U_i(z) = z_i < x_i = U_i(x)$. Therefore, $P_j^2(x, z) = 1$ and $P_j^1(x, z) = 0$ for each $j \neq i$ and; in addition, $P_i^2(x, z) = 0$ and $P_i^1(x, z) = 1$. Therefore, $Pl^2(x, z) = +1 > 0 \geq Pl^2(x, y)$. Therefore, if (a) or (b) holds, (x, y) is *not* a Nash equilibrium. Similar reasoning applies when (c) holds.

Example 1 is a game-theoretic version of the voting paradox, the fact that when majority rule is used to make collective decisions, a society can find itself in a situation where, for each social choice that could be made, there is a feasible alternative that a majority of the voters prefer (and, hence, any particular choice can be overturned by a majority vote). More specifically, this example illustrates how easy it is for the paradox of voting (and the corresponding absence of equilibrium policies) to occur when the issues that are to be resolved involve the distribution of income in the society (see Arrow, 1963; Sen, 1970).

Example 2. Consider the case in which the probabilities that describe the voters' choices satisfy the following version of Luce's axiom of "independence from irrelevant alternatives" (see Luce, 1959): For each i $\in$ N and $(\psi_1, \psi_2) \in X^2$,

$$\frac{P_i^1(\psi_1, \psi_2)}{P_i^2(\psi_1, \psi_2)} = \frac{U_i(\psi_1)}{U_i(\psi_2)} \tag{1}$$

assume also (implicit in Example 1) that each voter is going to vote; that is, for each i $\in$ N and $(\psi_1, \psi_2) \in X^2$,

$$P_i^1(\psi_1, \psi_2) + P_i^2(\psi_1, \psi_2) = 1 \tag{2}$$

Equations (1) and (2) imply that for each $i \in N$ and $(\psi_1, \psi_2) \in X^2$,

$$Pi^1(\psi_1, \psi_2) = \frac{U_i(\psi_1)}{U_i(\psi_1) + U_i(\psi_2)},$$

$$Pi^2(\psi_1, \psi_2) = \frac{U_i(\psi_2)}{U_i(\psi_1) + U_i(\psi_2)}$$

This time, the resulting game $(X, X; Pl^1, Pl^2)$ does have a Nash equilibrium. Since the game is zero sum, this can also be phrased as: The game has a saddle point.

The fact that this game has a Nash equilibrium (or equivalently, has a saddle point) can be established as follows. For each $i \in N$ and $(x, y) \in X^2$, $P_i^1(x, y) = x_i/(x_i + y_i)$. Therefore, each $P_i^1(x, y)$ is a concave function of $x = (x_1, x_2, x_3)$, and each $- P_i^1(x, y)$ is a concave function of $y = (y_1, y_2, y_3)$. This, in turn, implies that $EV^1(x, y)$ is a concave function of x and $EV^1(x, y)$ is a concave function of y. Similarly, $EV^2(x, y)$ is a concave function of y and $- EV^2(x, y)$ is a concave function of x. Therefore, candidate 1's payoff function, $Pl^1(x, y) = EV^1(x, y) - EV^2(x, y)$, is a concave function of x and candidate 2's payoff function, $Pl^2(x, y) = EV^2(x, y) - EV^1(x, y)$, is a concave function of y. By a similar argument, $Pl^1(x, y)$ and $Pl^2(x, y)$ are continuous functions of (x, y). Finally, from its definition is a compact, convex subset of R^3. Hence all of the assumptions in the premise of one of the theorems that has been labeled "Nash's Theorem" are satisfied. Therefore there is a Nash Equilibrium in this example.

Where is (or are) the Nash equilibrium (or equilibria) located? This question can be answered by solving the problem: Find the $x \in X$ that maximize(s) $U_1(x) \cdot U_2(x) \cdot U_3(x) = x_1 \cdot x_2 \cdot x_3$ over the set X. There is a unique x, which solves this problem: $x = (1/3, 1/3, 1/3)$. This implies that there is a unique Nash equilibrium in the game: $\psi_1 = \psi_2 = (1/3, 1/3, 1/3)$ (see Coughlin and Nitzan, 1981a).

PETER J. COUGHLIN

REFERENCES

Arrow, K. (1963). *Social Choice and Individual Values*. Second Edition. New Haven: Yale University Press.

Black, D. (1958). *The Theory of Committees and Elections*. Cambridge: Cambridge University Press.

Brams, S. (1975). *Game Theory and Politics*. London: MacMillan.

Brams, S. (1978). *The Presidential Election Game*. New Haven: Yale University Press.

Brams, S. and Davis, M. (1973). "Resource allocation models in presidential campaigning: implications for democratic representation." *Annals of the New York Academy of Sciences*, 219: 105–123.

Brams, S. and Davis, M. (1974). "The 3/2's rule in presidential campaigning." *American Political Review*, 68: 113–134.

Brams, S. and Davis, M. (1982). "Optimal resource allocation in presidential primaries." *Mathematical Social Sciences*, 3: 373–388.

Calvert, R. (1986). "Models of amperfect information in politics." *Fundamentals of Pure and Applied Economics*, Volume 6. Chur: Hardwood Academic Publishers.

Comaner, W. (1976). "The median voter rule and the theory of political choice." *Journal of Public Economics*, 5: 169–178.

Coughlin, P. (1982). "Pareto optimality of policy proposals with probabilistic voting." *Public Choice*, 39: 427–433.

Coughlin, P. (1983). "Social utility functions for strategic decisions in probabilistic voting models." *Mathematical Social Sciences*, 4: 275–293.

Coughlin, P. (1984). "Davis–Hinich conditions and median outcomes in probabilistic voting models." *Journal of Economic Theory*, 34: 1–12.

Coughlin, P. and Nitzan, S. (1981a). "Electoral outcomes with probabilistic voting and Nash social welfare maxima." *Journal of Public Economics*, 15: 113–121.

Coughlin, P. and Nitzan, S. (1981b). "Directional and local electoral equilibria with probabilistic voting." *Journal of Economic Theory*, 24: 226–240.

Davis, O. and Hinich, M. (1966). "A mathematical model of policy formation in a democratic society," in J. Bernd (ed.) *Mathematical Applications in Political Science*, Volume 2. Dallas: Southern Methodist University Press, pp. 175–208.

Davis, O. and Hinich, M. (1968). "On the power and importance of the mean preference in a mathematical model of democratic choice." *Public Choice*, 5: 59–72.

Davis, O. and Hinich, M. (1972). "Spatial competition under constrained choice." in R. Niemi and H. Weisberg (eds.) *Probability Models of Collective Decision Making*. Columbus: Charles E. Merrill.

Davis, O., DeGroot, M., and Hinich, M. (1972). Social preference orderings and majority rule. *Econometrica*, 40: 147–157.

Denzau, A. and Kats, A. (1977). "Expected plurality voting equilibrium and social choice functions." *Review of Economic Studies*, 44: 227–233.

Downs, A. (1957). *An Economic Theory of Democracy*. New York: Harper and Row.

Hinich, M. (1977). Equilibrium in spatial voting: the median voter result is an artifact. *Journal of Economic Theory*, 16: 208–219.

Hinich, M. (1978). "The mean versus the median in spatial voting games." in P. Ordeshook (ed.) *Game Theory and Political Science*. New York: New York University Press, pp. 357–374.

Hinich M. and Ordeshook, P. (1969). "Abstentions and equilibrium in the electoral process." *Public Choice*, 7: 81–106.

Hinich, M. Ledyard, J., and Ordeshook, P. (1972). "Nonvoting and the existence of equilibrium under majority rule." *Journal of Economic Theory*, 4: 144–153.

Hinich, M., Ledyard, J., and Ordeshook, P. (1973). "A theory of electoral equilibrium: a spatial analysis based on the theory of games." *Journal of Politics*, 35: 154–193.

Hotelling, H. (1929). "Stability in competition." *Economic Journal*, 39: 41–57.

Kramer, G. (1977). "Theories of political processes," in M. Intriligator (ed.) *Frontiers of Quantitative Economics*, Volume 3. Amsterdam: North-Holland, pp. 685–702.

Lake, M. (1979). "A new campaign resource allocation model." in S. Brams, A. Schotter, and G. Schwodiauer, (eds.) *Applied Game Theory*. Wurzburg: Physica-Verlag, pp. 118–132.

Ledyard, J. (1981). "The paradox of voting and candidate competition: a general equilibrium analysis." in G. Horwich and J. Quirk (eds.) *Essays in Contemporary Fields of Economics*. West Lafayette: Purdue University Press, pp. 54–80.

Ledyard, J. (1984). "The pure theory of large two-candidate elections." *Public Choice*, 44: 7–41.

Lindbeck, A. and Weibull, J. (1987). "Balanced-budget redistribution as the outcome of political competition." *Public Choice*, 52: 273–297.

Luce, R.D. (1959). *Individual Choice Behavior*. New York: Wiley.

McKelvey, R. (1975). "Policy related voting and electoral equilibria." *Econometrica*, 43: 815–844.

Mueller, D. (1979). *Public Choice*. Cambridge.

Mueller, D. (1976). "Public choice: a survey." *Journal of Economic Literature*, 14: 395–433.

Ordeshook, P. (1997). "The spatial analysis of elections and committees: four decades of research," in D. Mueller (ed.) *Perspectives on Public Choice*. Cambridge: Cambridge University Press, pp. 247–270.

Plott, C. (1971). "Recent results in theory of voting." in M. Intriligator (ed.) *Frontiers of Quantitative Economics*, Volume 1. Amsterdam: North-Holland, pp. 109–127.

Rowley, C.K. (1984). "The relevance of the median voter theorem". *Journal of Institutional and Theoretical Economics*, (March): 104–135.

Sen, A. (1970). *Collective Choice and Social Welfare*. San Francisco: Holden-Day.

ELECTORAL COLLEGE

The electoral college is composed of electors selected by the states of the United States to cast the votes that elect the President of the United States. According to the U.S. Constitution, as amended, in a presidential election, each state appoints a number of electors equal to the number of senators and representatives the state has in the U.S. Congress, and those electors "shall meet in their respective states" to cast votes for president. If one candidate gets votes from a majority of the electors, that person becomes the president. If no candidate gets a majority, then the House of Representatives selects the president from the three candidates with the largest number of electoral votes.

This electoral system was designed to keep the president from being directly accountable to the nation's citizens. The Founders recognized the political problems that could arise because of factions and interest groups, so deliberately wanted to insulate the president from democratic pressures. In addition to wanting to prevent a tyranny of the majority, the electoral college was designed to weight smaller states more than proportionally relative to their populations, although as discussed below, the current system actually gives the advantage to more populous states.

The U.S. Constitution has never specified how states choose their electors, and the most common way in the nation's early years was to have the state legislatures appoint the electors. In the election of 1800, ten of the sixteen states had their state legislatures choose their electors, and only one used the general ticket system that now dominates. In 1820, nine of the twenty-four states used their legislatures to select their electors, but by 1832 twenty of the twenty-four states used general ticket elections and only one — South Carolina — still had its state legislature choose their electors. South Carolinians did not vote directly for their electors until after the War Between the States. At the beginning of the twenty-first century, almost all use the general ticket method of voting, which awards all the state's electoral votes to the candidate with the most votes from the electorate. Only Maine and Nebraska divide their electoral votes, by giving the winning candidate in each congressional district one electoral vote, and awarding two electoral votes to the state's top vote-getter.

As the Founders originally envisioned it, the electoral college was to function as a search committee to identify candidates for president, and they believed that in most cases the final choice would be made by the House of Representatives (McDonald, 1994). Several features of the electoral college system were designed to keep a candidate from getting a majority unless there was widespread support for that candidate. First, the Founders thought that electors would tend to vote for candidates from their states, which naturally would spread votes to many candidates. Second, the electors were to meet in their states to cast their votes, rather than to meet together in a central location. While this is often explained by saying that transportation was slow and costly in those days, it serves the purpose of keeping electors from bargaining and logrolling to choose a president, making it more likely that the election would go to the House. Congress met in a central location, and the electors could too, if the Founders had viewed it as important.

The Constitution originally specified that electors vote for two candidates, at least one of whom had to be from a state different from the elector's. If a candidate had votes from a majority of the electors, the candidate with the highest number of votes would be president, and the candidate with the second-highest vote total would be vice president. If no candidate had votes from a majority of the electors, the House would choose the president from among the top five vote-getters, with each state (not each representative) getting one vote. After the president was selected, the candidate with the next-highest number of votes would be vice president. In 1796 John Adams was elected president under this system, and Thomas Jefferson vice president, and the disputes between them led to the Twelfth Amendment to the Constitution, ratified in 1804, which changed the system slightly. Electoral votes for president and vice president were to be cast separately, and in the event that there was no electoral majority, the House would choose among the top three vote-getters rather than the top five, still with each state getting one vote.

The Constitution never has specified how states choose their electors, and the Founders envisioned that electors would be people who would be more knowledgeable about presidential candidates, so could cast more informed votes than the general public. As already noted, the most common method in the nation's early days was to have the state's legislature choose the state's electors. Because the system was designed to prevent any but the most popular candidates from getting a majority, the Founders believed that in most cases the electoral college would present a slate of candidates to the House of Representatives, acting as a presidential search committee, and the House of Representatives would choose the best candidate from that slate. This system would insulate the president from popular opinion, allowing the president to carry out the duties specified in the Constitution without having to bow to democratic pressures.

The system rapidly evolved into a more democratic process (Holcombe, 2002: Ch. 5). In the early 1800s more states went to popular voting, and after the election of 1800, presidential elections were determined by comfortable electoral vote margins until the election of 1824, giving the impression that citizens selected the president through popular voting. In the 1824 election no candidate got an electoral majority, and the House chose John Quincy Adams over Andrew Jackson, who got the highest number of electoral votes. Citizens were outraged, called the outcome a "corrupt bargain," and complained about the elitist nature of their government (Ketcham, 1984), even though the process worked exactly as the Founders had intended. The result was the formation of the Democratic party for the specific purpose of electing Andrew Jackson as President. Jackson did win four years later, and deliberately created a more democratic government that was more directly accountable to its citizens (Schlesinger, 1945). By the 1830s the electoral college system that the Founders had intended to insulate the presidency from democratic pressures had been transformed into an electoral system in which popular voting for president, through the electoral college, selected the nation's chief executive and made the president directly accountable to voters (Holcombe, 2001).

The general ticket system that most states have used since the 1830s is designed to give each state's electoral votes the maximum possible impact. Under general ticket voting, the candidate who gets the largest number of popular votes in the state wins all of the state's electoral votes.

Many other voting systems were tried, such as tabulating votes by congressional districts, and awarding the electoral vote in each district to the candidate with the highest vote total in that district, but this type of aggregation divides a state's electoral votes, so lessens the state's impact on the outcome of the election.

As Polsby and Wildavsky (1988: 41–42) note, the electoral college system combined with general ticket voting gives a larger weighting to bigger states in presidential voting. Because each state has the same number of senators, each individual voter in a less-populous state controls a larger share of an electoral vote than each voter in a more-populous state; however, this is more than offset by the winner-take-all nature of general ticket voting that gives all of a state's electoral votes to the highest vote-getter. Winning a large state, even by a small margin, brings with it more electoral votes than winning several small states, so candidates tend to concentrate their campaigning in more populous states. This would be reversed if states awarded their electoral votes in proportion to the popular votes candidates received, rather than awarding the winner all of their electoral votes.

As the Founders intended it, the electoral college system was to be a buffer between popular opinion and the presidential selection process, but it rapidly evolved in the nation's early years to become a method for aggregating the popular vote. There is an ongoing debate about the merits of the system (Best, 1996). Compared to electing the president by popular vote, it reduces the impact of third party candidates, enhances the importance of more populous states in the election process, and reduces the incentive for people to vote in states that lean heavily toward one party. It pushes candidates to look for support beyond those states where they are the strongest, because they get no more electoral votes for increasing the size of their majority in a state, and it limits the ability to engage in fraud (it matters only in close states, and they will be closely scrutinized), and reduces the possibility of challenges and recounts. In the 2000 election, for example, attention was focused almost exclusively on Florida, the closest state, whereas with popular voting every vote in every state would have the same impact. The merits of the electoral college are sure to provoke continued debate, but it is interesting to see how the system changed so substantially prior to 1830, and that it never functioned as the Founders intended.

RANDALL G. HOLCOMBE

REFERENCES

Best, J.A. (1996). *The Choice of the People? Debating the Electoral College.* Lanham, MD: Rowman & Littlefield.

Holcombe, R.G. (2001). "The electoral college as a restraint on American Democracy: its evolution from Washington to Jackson," in J.V. Denson (ed.), *Reassessing the Presidency: The Rise of the Executive State and the Decline of Freedom.* Auburn, AL: Ludwig von Mises Institute, pp. 137–167.

Holcombe, R.G. (2002). *From Liberty to Democracy: The Transformation of American Government.* Ann Arbor: University of Michigan Press.

Ketcham, R. (1984). *Presidents Above Party: The First American Presidency.* Chapel Hill: University of North Carolina Press.

McDonald, F. (1994). *The American Presidency.* Lawrence: University Press of Kansas.

Polsby, N.W. and Aaron Wildavsky (1988). *Presidential Elections: Contemporary Strategies of American Electoral Politics*, Seventh Edition. New York: Free Press.

Schlesinger, A.M., Jr. (1945). *The Age of Jackson.* Boston: Little, Brown.

ELECTORAL COMPETITION IN MIXED SYSTEMS OF REPRESENTATION

Over the last decade electoral engineers have become increasingly cognisant of three important facts that affect worldwide electoral institutions. First, several established democracies such as Israel, Italy, Japan, New Zealand and Venezuela undertook major electoral reforms. Second, the process of democratisation in formerly communist countries brought about constitutional reforms where the design of new systems of representation is the central concern. Third, mixed-member electoral (MM) systems have been the choice of the vast majority of countries implementing electoral reform.

What are MM systems? How do they work? Bogdanor (1983, p.16) pointed out that 'although the main electoral systems are probably already known, there are undoubtedly many ingenious ways of breeding new combinations.' MM systems are one set of such ingenious combinations. These systems are hybrids using both proportional representation (PR) and plurality (PL) formulae for the election to a single representative body. Massicotte and Blais (1999) argue that such hybrids eliminate many of the weaknesses of pure PL and pure PR systems. Their aim is to provide representation to small and diffuse political groups as well as providing incentives to form stable governing majorities. In practical terms, such systems incorporate some preference-aggregating mechanisms based on PR and others based on PL. The PR mechanisms guarantee that all societal preferences, no matter how diffusely held, are represented. The PL mechanisms ensure strong incentives to form mass political formation that can prevent government instability.

MM systems are operationalized by allowing voters to cast two simultaneous votes. The first ballot for the single-member district (SMD) candidate — a Plurality (PL) ballot. The second ballot is cast for a party for the proportional allocation of seats — a Proportional Representation (PR) ballot. Shugart and Wattemberg (2000a) describe an MM system as a particular type of two-tier system. In one tier seats are allocated nominally to candidates, and in the other tier seats are allocated to party lists. In other words, in the first tier votes are cast for candidates by name and seats are allocated to individual candidates on the basis of the votes they receive. On the other hand, in the second tier votes are cast for party lists and seats are allocated on the basis of the votes received by the listed candidates.

Since each voter has two simultaneous votes available, he or she can express a double preference for a party, by voting for it in the PR ballot and for that party's candidate in the PL ballot. Alternatively, the voter can express split preferences by voting for a party in the PR ballot, but not for that party's candidate in the PL ballot. This 'split-ticket' phenomenon is a unique feature to multi-ballot elections and can significantly influence overall election strategies and results. This phenomenon has been extensively studied in the MM systems literature. Jesse (1990) and Schoen (1999) describe split-ticket voting in Germany as a product of strategic voting to support the formation of a given political coalition. Klingeman (2001), analysing elections in the same country, views the split-ticket phenomenon as a result of voters choosing candidates based on performance rather than party affiliation. According to Banducci et al. (1999), similar strategic motivations seem to guide voting behaviour in New Zealand. Navarra (1997) gives a different explanation for split-ticket voting in the Italian elections following electoral reform. Voters express split preferences in order to diversify the risk of making a wrong choice in a changing environment. Benoit et al. (2002) present a strategic model of voting behaviour in MM systems. They use Italy as a case study and estimate the relative numbers of strategic and non-strategic voters in Italian SMDs for the 1994 and 1996 elections. McAllister and White (2000) found that the individual motivations of voters are the major cause of split ticket voting in Russia principally as a consequence of weak partisanship. However, they also claim that there is evidence of voters' strategic behaviour based on their socio-economic status.

MM systems are currently used to govern about one-fifth of the world's population (Massicotte and Blais, 1999). Countries using MM systems differ in the percentages of seats allocated on the basis of the PL and PR ballots respectively (i.e., the PR/PL seat ratio). In democratic countries the PR/PL seat ratio ranges from 64/36 PR/PL split of

Georgia to 20/80 PR/PL split of the Philippines and Thailand. However, across countries it is generally true that the PL component is greater than the PR component. There are actually only four countries (Israel, Georgia, Hungary and Venezuela) with a greater PR component in the distribution of seats in the national legislature (see Shugart, 2001; Shugart and Wattenberg, 2000b for a definition and typologies of MM systems in modern democracies).

The vast majority of countries currently using MM systems adopted them as a result of recently implemented electoral reforms. Three broad results emerge in terms of electoral competition:

(1) an increase in the effective number of parties in former communist countries or in countries governed by PL systems of representation before the reform (see, for example, Boston et al., 1997, 1998 for New Zealand; Moser, 2001 for Russia; and Schieman and Benoit, 1999 for Hungary);

(2) no dramatic changes in the effective number of parties in countries previously governed by PR electoral systems (see, for example, Reed, 1999 for Japan; Mayorga, 1997 for Bolivia; Bartolini and Dalimonte, 1995 for Italy; Crisp, 2000 for Venezuela); and

(3) the formation of broad-based electoral coalitions in all countries adopting MM electoral systems (see, for example, Mudambi et al., 2001 for Italy; Hazan, 2000 for Israel; Kulisheck and Crisp, 2001 for Venezuela; Mayorga, 2001 for Bolivia).

These three general results seem to confirm that the countervailing tendencies in both the PL and PR dimensions lead to electoral competition between two opposing coalitions in a multi-party political system. Mudambi et al. (2001) and Mudambi and Navarra (2002) provide the first attempt to formulate a theory of electoral strategies in MM systems characterized by an electoral competition between two competing coalition in a multi-party context. They argue that the PR/PL seat ratio provides parties with two sets of incentives, drawn from the PL and PR components of the system. Neglecting the narrow concerns of their core supporters harms a party's performance on the PR component. Thus, narrow political formations must retain their unique identities. However, success on the PL ballot requires broad-based support. Dealing with both sets of incentives requires narrow political formations to form coalitions. Within this framework, political party strategies in SMDs are aimed at two ordered objectives. The first is the PL-driven coalition focussed objective, under which each party seeks to ensure that its coalition gains control of the government (inter-coalition competition). The second is the PR-driven party focussed objective, under which each party strives to dominate its coalition (intra-coalition competition). The power of a party within the coalition is important because it determines the importance of the party's agenda in the agenda of the coalition.

Assuming that the intra-coalition game is played non-cooperatively with Nash strategies, each coalition party is expected to exert maximum effort (and elicit maximum support from its adherents) only when the primary objective of a coalition victory is threatened. This will occur in 'marginal' SMDs where the *ex ante* belief in a coalition victory is weak. In such a constituency inter-coalition competition drives the electoral behaviour of parties. On the other hand, in 'safe' SMDs where the *ex ante* belief in a coalition victory is strong, the primary objective is not in doubt, so the secondary objective (intra-coalition competition) determines party behaviour. Here parties exert maximum effort (and elicit maximum support from their adherents) only if the candidate in the PL ballot is one of their own. If the coalition candidate is from one of their allied parties, they put virtually all their energies into fighting the PR ballot.

In order to illustrate electoral strategies in MM systems let us describe the two pathological extreme types of constituencies. Without loss of generality, suppose that the coalition candidate belongs to party i. At one extreme, the candidate receives no support from any party except for his own. Such a constituency, where coalition parties pursue their own intra-coalition objectives at the expense of coalition prospects may be termed an *internecine* constituency. In this case, the coalition vote share $V = v_i$, where V is the coalition PL vote share and v_i is the vote share of party i in the PR ballot. At the other extreme, all the parties, which adopt the approach of 'all for one and one for all', embrace the coalition candidate. Such a constituency, where the constituent parties act for all intents and purposes like one party may be termed a '*Dumas*' constituency. In this case, the coalition vote share $V = \Sigma v_k$, i.e., the sum of the shares of all the parties in the coalition.

Party behaviour in most constituencies is likely to fall between these two extremes and the actual PL vote share will also be affected by such factors as the candidate's personal popularity (or lack thereof). Thus, the coalition vote share will tend to exceed the vote share of party i, but will tend to fall short of the maximum potential vote share. But how short will it fall? This will depend on expectations of the constituent parties with regard to coalition victory in the constituency. In constituencies where coalition victory is expected, i.e., 'safe' constituencies, parties will feel free to pursue party-focused objectives at the expense of coalition-focused objectives, causing the shortfall to be large. However, parties do not have this luxury in constituencies where victory is in doubt or unlikely, and will exert themselves to obtain the best possible showing for the coalition. Thus, in such constituencies the shortfall is expected to be small.

The electoral strategies described so far can have important implications on the determination of competitive electoral equilibria. Duverger's law and Duverger's hypothesis state respectively that PL based elections with SMDs generally result in a two-party polity, while PR systems generally give rise to multi-party systems (Duverger, 1954). However, Duverger's propositions have generated controversy and have been questioned. One question has been the generality of the propositions: do we expect PL systems to result in two-party polities and PR systems to generate multi-party systems, *always* and in *all* circumstances? (see, for example, Riker, 1982; Bogdanor, 1983; Sartori, 1994). Reed (2001) analyses the 1994 and 1996 Italian national elections and demonstrates that, although there is little evidence of convergence toward a two party system, more than 80% of SMDs moved closer to bipolar competition between two candidates. Therefore, he claims that Duverger's law works as expected at the district level.

The analysis of MM system electoral strategies by Mudambi and Navarra (2002) suggests that this electoral mechanism generates incentives to create two-sided coalition-based competition with a multi-party system. They point out that MM systems have a significant PL driven component and demonstrate that this is generally sufficient to ensure that the polity can be controlled by broad-based political formations. However, the PR component ensures the persistence of many narrow focus parties, whose support can often be crucial in government formation and continuation. Thus, MM systems are multi-party systems in which the formation of coalitions leads to two-sided politics.

This analysis can also be interpreted using the spatial theory of electoral competition (Hinich and Munger, 1997). The predominant view in this literature is that candidates maximise votes or plurality and therefore see policy as a means to winning elections (Downs, 1957; Kramer, 1977). Some scholars, however, have modelled policy-oriented candidates who fight elections to achieve their own policy goals (Wittman, 1983; Calvert, 1985). Such candidates are interested not only in winning elections, but also in implementing their policy preferences. The protagonists in an MM system are the constituent parties of coalitions, rather than individual candidates. However, they face the same trade-off of balancing their individual policy positions with the coalition's overall policy position. The former affects the party's performance on the PR ballot, while the later affects its performance on the PL ballot.

Are MM systems expected to generate convergent or divergent competitive equilibria? On the basis of the discussion so far, it may be hypothesised that the answer to this question depends on the relative importance of the PR and PL ballots. If the PR ballot is much more important, intra-coalition competition is more important than inter-coalition competition. In this case parties focus on their individual policy agendas and the outcome is divergence. Conversely, if the PL ballot is more important, inter-coalition competition is more important than intra-coalition competition. This means that parties focus on creating a common coalition policy agenda to compete for the median voter and the outcome is convergence. The relative importance of the PL versus the PR ballot would typically be measured by the PL/PR ratio. For example, in Italy the PL/PR ratio is 75/25, while in Germany it is 50/50. Since Italy has a much higher ratio, the PL ballot is relatively more important, and *ceteris paribus*, we expect more convergence than in Germany (Navarra, 2002).

RAM MUDAMBI
PIETRO NAVARRA

REFERENCES

Banducci, S., Karp, J., Vowles, J. and Donovan T. (1999). "Strategic voting in the 1996 New Zealand Election: Implications for a new mixed system," Working Paper, University of Waikato.

Bartolini, S. and Dalimonte, R. (eds.) (1995). Maggioritario ma non Troppo: le Elezioni Politiche nel 1994. Bologna: Il Mulino.

Benoit, K., Giannetti, D., and Laver, M. (2002). "Strategic voting in mixed-member electoral systems: the Italian case," mimeo, University of Bologna.

Bogdanor, V. (1983). "Conclusions: electoral systems and party systems," in V. Bogdanor and D. Butler (eds.) *Democracy and Elections: Electoral Systems and Their Political Consequences.* New York and London: Cambridge University Press.

Boston, J., Levine, S., McLeay, E., and Roberts, N.S. (1997). *From Campaign to Coalition: The 1996 MMP Election.* Palmerston North, NZ: The Dunmore Press.

Boston, J., Levine, S., McLeay, E., and Roberts, N.S. (1998). "The New Zealand Parliamentarians: did electoral system reform make a difference?" *Legislative Studies*, 12: 63–75.

Calvert, R. (1985). "Robustness of the multi-dimensional voting model: candidate motivations, uncertainty and convergence." *American Journal of Political Science*, 29: 69–95.

Downs, A. (1957). *An Economic Theory of Democracy.* New York: Harper and Row.

Crisp, B.F. (2000). *Democratic Institutional Design: The Powers and Incentives of Venezuelan Politicians and Interest Groups.* Stanford, CA: Stanford University Press.

Duverger, M. (1954). *Political Parties, Their Organisation and Activity in the Modern State* (translated by B. and R. North). New York: Wiley.

Hazan, R.Y. (2000). *Parties, Elections and Cleavages: Israel in Comparative and Theoretical Perspective*. London: Frank Cass.

Hinich, M.J. and Munger, M.C. (1997). *Analytical Politics*. New York: Cambridge University Press.

Jesse, E. (1990). *Elections: The Federal Republic of Germany in Comparison*. (translated by Lindsay Batson). New York: St. Martin's.

Klingeman, H.D. and Wessels, B. (2001). "The political consequences of Germany's mixed-member system: personalization at the grass-root?" in M.S. Shugart and M.P. Wattemberg (eds.) *Mixed-Member Systems: The Best of Both Worlds?* Oxford: Oxford University Press.

Kulisheck, M.R. and Crisp, B.F. (2001). "The legislative consequences of MMP electoral rules in Venezuela," in M.S. Shugart and M.P. Wattemberg (eds.) *Mixed-Member Systems: The Best of Both Worlds?* Oxford: Oxford University Press.

Kramer, G. (1977). "On a class of equilibrium conditions for majority rule." *Econometrica*, 41: 285–297.

Mayorga, R.A. (1997). "Bolivia: electoral reform in Latin America," in *The International IDEA Handbook of Electoral System Design*. Stockholm: Institute for Democracy and Electoral Assistance.

Mayorga R.A. (2001). "The mixed-member-proportional system and its consequences in Bolivia," in M.S. Shugart and M.P. Wattemberg (eds.) *Mixed-Member Systems: The Best of Both Worlds?* Oxford: Oxford University Press.

Massicotte, L. and Blais, A. (1999). "Mixed electoral systems: a conceptual and empirical survey." *Electoral Studies*, 18: 341–366.

McAllister, I. and White, S. (2000). "Split-ticket voting in the 1995 Russian Duma elections." *Electoral Studies*, 19: 563–576.

Mudambi, R., Navarra, P., and Sobbrio, G. (2001). *Rules, Choice and Strategy: The Political Economy of Italian Electoral Reform*. Aldershot: Edward Elgar Ltd.

Mudambi, R. and Navarra, P. (2002). "Electoral strategies in mixed systems of representation." Discussion Paper, January, Research Program on Democracy, Business and Human Well-being, London School of Economics.

Navarra, P. (1997). "Voting diversification strategy: a risk-bearing model of voter behaviour in 1996 Italian National Election." *Economia delle Scelte Pubbliche, Journal of Public Finance and Public Choice*, 1: 38–53.

Navarra, P. (2002). "Spatial electoral competition in mixed-member system of representation," mimeo, University of Messina.

Reed, S.R. (1999). "Political reform in Japan: combining scientific and historical analysis." *Social Science Japan Journal*, 2: 17–193.

Reed, S.R. (2001). "Duverger's law is working in Italy." *Comparative Political Studies*, 34: 312–327.

Riker, W.H. (1982). "Two-party systems and Duverger's law." *American Political Science Review*, 76: 753–766.

Sartori, G. (1994). *Comparing Institutional Engineering: An Inquiry into Structures, Incentives and Outcomes*. New York: Columbia University Press.

Schoen, H. (1999). "Split-ticket voting in German federal elections, 1953–90: an example of sophisticated balloting." *Electoral Studies*, 18: 473–496.

Schieman, J.W. and Benoit, K. (1999). "How thick is the veil of ignorance? Uncertainty and the electoral system origins in Hungary," mimeo, Columbia University.

Shugart, M.S. (2001). "Electoral 'efficiency' and the move to mixed-member systems." *Electoral Studies*, 20: 173–193.

Shugart, M.S. and Wattemberg, M.P. (2000a). "Mixed-member electoral systems: a definition and typology," in M.S. Shugart and M.P. Wattemberg (eds.) *Mixed-Member Systems: The Best of Both Worlds?* Oxford: Oxford University Press.

Shugart, M.S. and Wattemberg, M.P. (2000b). "Are mixed-member systems the best of both worlds?" in M.S. Shugart and M.P. Wattemberg (eds.) *Mixed-Member Systems: The Best of Both Worlds?* Oxford: Oxford University Press.

Wittman, D. (1983). "Candidate motivations: a synthesis of alternatives." *American Political Science Review*, 77: 142–157.

THE ELUSIVE MEDIAN VOTER

The median voter model has been a mainstay of empirical public finance for three decades. As far back as 1943, Bowen showed how a voting model might be used to determine the level of provision of a publicly provided good (Bowen, 1943). Later refinements of the framework provided a theoretical foundation for estimating demand functions for a wide variety of public goods and services.

The typical structure assumes that individual i in community j has a utility function $U_j^i(G_j, C_j^i)$ where G_j is a collectively provided (local public) good and C_j^i is a bundle of private goods. Financing arrangements for the public good determine the tax cost $T_j(G_j, z_j^i)$ that i bears, where z_j^i is i's income or property subject to tax in j. Let p_j be a vector of private-good prices, and y_j^i be the individual's income. Then for fixed G_j, the individual chooses C_j^i to maximize U_j^i subject to the budget constraint $p_j C_j^i \leq y_j^i - T_j(G_j, z_j^i)$. This defines i's private good demand, conditional on the level of public good provision, private good prices, and i's income; call this demand function $C_j^{*i}(G_j, p_j, y_j^i, z_j^i)$. Then we can define the *induced utility function* $V_j^i(G_j, p_j, y_j^i, z_j^i) \equiv U_j^i(G_j, C_j^{*i}, (G_j, p_j, y_j^i, z_j^i))$. This induced function gives us i's preferences for different levels of the publicly provided good, taking into account the adjustments in his private good consumption as G (and therefore his disposable income) changes. Under standard assumptions about the basic utility function U and the tax-cost function T, the induced utility function V is single-peaked in G. This peak is i's ideal point G_j^{*i}. We can also think of G_j^{*i} as i's demand for the publicly provided good.

The insight of the median voter model is, of course, that — under appropriate conditions — the majority voting equilibrium choice of G_j will correspond to the median of voters' ideal points. Empirical work based on the median voter model assumes that observed levels of public services correspond to this median. The difficulty is that voters' ideal points are not observed directly; we do not know who the pivotal voter is.

If, across individuals in a given community, G_j^{*i} is monotonic in income, then the median ideal point will correspond to the demand of the person with median income. Without additional restrictions, we cannot be sure that this will be the case, even if everyone has the same basic utility function U. The direct effect of higher income may lead to an increase in demand for G. But a higher-income individual may also bear a higher tax cost if $T_j(G_j, z_j^i)$ is related to his income (this would occur, e.g., if public services are financed by an income tax. It would also happen if public services are financed by property taxes and property values are correlated with income). This second effect is like a price increase and is likely to reduce that individual's demand for the publicly provided good. The net effect of a higher income can therefore be positive for some ranges of income and negative for others. Non-monotonicity can also occur if there are underlying taste differences. Some high- and low-income residents can have similar G^*, but higher (or lower) than those with middle incomes.

One can make assumptions about the structure of preferences, the tax-cost function, and the distribution of income that guarantee that someone with median income in a community will also have median demand for the publicly provided good. Bergstrom and Goodman (1973) provide the classic development of such conditions. If these conditions hold, one can in principle use data from a cross-section of jurisdictions to estimate a "median-voter demand curve", under the maintained hypothesis that the median voter model is the correct model of public supply.

In practice, however, the conditions are not independently verified. Instead, cross-sectional studies usually just use median income and some corresponding measure of the median tax-cost directly in the empirical specifications. (Even Bergstrom and Goodman (1973), having taken pains to develop the theoretical desiderata, do not do much in the way of checking to see if the data satisfy their conditions.) While one can take this approach and even obtain sensible estimates of income and tax-price elasticities, the results are problematic. Some standard specifications, for example, imply that (if the specifications are correct) one would obtain the same empirical results if one used any fractile of the income distribution instead of the median (this is what Romer and Rosenthal (1979) call the "fractile fallacy").

There is also a measurement issue that is rarely addressed: *viz.*, which of several possible medians should one use — median household income, median family income, or some other measure — and what are the corresponding tax prices? Turnbull and Mitias (1995) find that the results are sensitive to these choices (see also Bailey and Conolly, 1998). In principle, one should also focus on the median among the politically active parts of the population, rather than the entire population. Partly for data limitations, very few studies attempt to control for this aspect of the problem (see Inman, 1978 for an exception).

One can attempt to get around the problem of inferring median demand from aggregate data by using micro data; for example, from surveys of individuals. With sufficient respondents (and subject to the usual limitations on the quality of responses), one can make inferences about demands. A careful study of this type is Bergstrom et al. (1982), using a survey in which respondents from about 100 Michigan school districts were asked whether they would like to see an increase, a decrease, or no change in the current level of public school spending in their community. With information about actual spending, together with individual-level data, this approach permits estimation of individual demand. The estimated income and price elasticities are consistent with those found in studies using aggregate data. In addition, a majority of respondents replied "no change" to the question about desired spending. This lends some support to the hypothesis that spending reflects the median preference, together with the likelihood that there is considerable clustering of residents within communities on the basis of demand for school spending. (Gramlich and Rubinfeld (1982) use a somewhat different set of questions from the same survey and get similar results.) At the same time, probably because of data limitations (surveys are expensive, relative to using aggregate data), these results are quite imprecise. The estimates of Bergstrom et al. suggest that, on average, those who said "no change" would have held this position if spending were anywhere between 67% and 150% (and, in some specifications, between 40% and 250%) of actual spending. So these results do not quite allay the concerns about the "multiple fallacy" noted, with reference to aggregate data studies, by Romer and Rosenthal (1979): *viz.*, that one cannot reject the hypothesis that observed spending corresponds not to median demand but some multiple of it.

Romer and Rosenthal (1982) and Romer et al. (1992) pointed out that aggregate voting data (the Yes–No vote split) from local public spending referenda can be used to test hypotheses about whether spending levels correspond to "median voter" outcomes. To do this, one needs to specify a model of how the proposal-maker sets spending proposals. This specification then has implications not only for what proposal we should observe, but also for the expected vote outcome. For example, one might assume that proposals come from an agenda-setter who would like to maximize the expected budget. This implies that variables relating to the reversion budget level (what happens if the proposal fails), as well as the more usual median-related variables, should be included in the "spending equation". But it also means that observed vote outcomes should be close to 50–50, and that variables that appear in the spending equation should not be significant in the "voting equation". (The agenda setter, in aiming for the highest expected budget, would take into account factors that systematically influence demand, leaving only random factors to influence the vote outcome.) By contrast, under the median-voter hypothesis, reversion variables should not affect the spending equation, but both these variables and those relating to median demand would be significant in the vote equation. (In general, there are also cross-equation restrictions implied by different specifications. These can be tested by estimating the spending and voting equations simultaneously.)

Building on these ideas, and also on Rubinfeld's (1977) analysis, Rothstein (1994) provides a useful framework for testing a variety of hypotheses about the preferences of governments and voters. The median-voter and budget-maximizing agenda-setter are two of the possible formulations concerning public supply. Using Michigan school district referendum data, Rothstein rejects both of these in favor of a model that incorporates elements of both. In particular, he finds evidence that is consistent with "budget-maximization in which the setter is poorly informed about voter preferences and voters are at least slightly uncertain about the reversion" (Rothstein, 1994, 385). His results also reinforce the point that, in order to learn anything useful about voters in a model that uses public spending data from many jurisdictions, one needs to know something about the supply side; i.e., about where the proposals are coming from. Using a quite different approach and different data, Turnbull and Chang (1998) find that the extent to which median outcomes are consistent with observations depends quite a bit on the type of jurisdictions in question and how the data are aggregated.

Assuming that we will observe median outcomes because a particular type of competitive political process determines collective choices may provide a handy and tractable analytical shorthand for some theoretical purposes. Empirical work, however, has continued to find the median voter an elusive target.

THOMAS ROMER

REFERENCES

Bailey, S.J. and Conolly, S. (1998). "The flypaper effect: identifying areas for further research." *Public Choice*, 95: 333–361.

Bergstrom, T.C. and Goodman, P. (1973). "Private demands for public goods." *American Economic Review*, 63: 280–296.

Bergstrom, T.C., Rubinfeld, D.L., and Shapiro, P. (1982). "Micro-based estimates of demand functions for local school expenditures." *Econometrica*, 50: 1183–1205.

Bowen, H. (1943). "The interpretation of voting in the allocation of economic resources." *Quarterly Journal of Economics*, 58: 27–48.

Gramlich, E.M. and Rubinfeld, D. (1982). "Micro-based estimates of public spending demand functions and tests of the Tiebout and median-voter hypotheses." *Journal of Political Economy*, 90: 536–560.

Inman, R.P. (1978). "Testing political economy's 'as if' proposition: is the median income voter really decisive?" *Public Choice*, 33(4): 45–65.

Romer, T. and Rosenthal, H. (1979). "The elusive median voter." *Journal of Public Economics*, 12: 143–170.

Romer, T. and Rosenthal, H. (1982). "An exploration in the politics and economics of local public services." *Zeitschrift für Nationalökonomie* 2(Suppl.): 105–125.

Romer, T., Rosenthal, H., and Munley, V. (1992). "Economic incentives and political institutions: spending and voting in school budget referenda." *Journal of Public Economics*, 49: 1–33.

Rothstein, P. (1994). "Learning the preferences of governments and voters from proposed spending and aggregated votes." *Journal of Public Economics*, 54: 361–389.

Rubinfeld, D. (1977). "Voting in a local school election: a micro analysis." *Review of Economics and Statistics*, 59: 30–42.

Turnbull, G.K. and Chang, C. (1998). "The median voter according to GARP." *Southern Economic Journal*, 64: 1001–1010.

Turnbull, G.K. and Mitias, P.M. (1995). "Which median voter?" *Southern Economic Journal*, 62: 183–191.

EMERGING FROM THE HOBBESIAN JUNGLE

Imagine the Hobbesian "state of nature" wherein no cooperative interaction occurs, in order to consider a positive analysis of the types of rules and institutions that simultaneously emerge, assuming (1) scarcity, (2) methodological individualism, and (3) rationality, while relying on the fundamental principles of comparative advantage and opportunity costs. These assumptions are brought to bear in the context of an uncertain world with transactions costs impeding coordination and motivation of behavior [but there is not a "veil of ignorance" a la Rawls (1971)], and both primary rules of behavior and secondary institutions of governance evolve, at least in part, to reduce such costs.

Some individuals may have or develop comparative advantages in violence, however, and therefore engage in plunder and/or extortion, as in Benson (1994, 1999). In this context, behavioral rules and governing institutions also may coordinate joint production of plunder and extortion too.

Because of scarcity, competition over the use of property is inevitable (Hume, 1751: 14–34). Thus, if rules and institutions evolve from a state of nature, they will focus on property allocation issues. Unilateral efforts to capture exclusive benefits from an asset (turn a property claim into actual ownership) requires that an individual can make a sufficiently strong threat of violence to induce others to abandon their conflicting claims and accept an obligation to recognize that individual's dominion (violence is defined as the allocation of resources to exclude other individuals from using claimed property). Since several individuals are likely to have similar incentives with regard to any particular scarce resource, however, competition through violence could consume vast amounts of resources as each invests in an effort to exclude others. Is such a "war of all against all" (Hobbes, 1651) an inevitable characterization of the state of nature? No. Anarchy can be ordered when rational individuals consider their alternatives and anticipate possible outcomes (Buchanan, 1975).

Umbeck (1981) suggests that if information was costless, each individual would recognize his relative capability for securing property, and therefore only claim the amount of property that he could defend (Umbeck, 1981: 41). This hypothetical outcome is virtually impossible, given the high cost of relevant information, but it is raised because it points to a second reason for Hobbesian conflict; scarcity means competition but uncertainty, including the uncertainty of what strategies potential rivals will adopt, turns the competition in the direction of violence. The cost of establishing property rights through violence can be considerable, however, since it includes the costs that both winners and losers have incurred. Furthermore, in a dynamic setting, winning is temporary unless the capacity for violence is maintained, and it may be temporary even then.

The Hobbesian conflict requires at least three conditions: scarcity, uncertainty, and, as stressed by Hobbes and all those who have followed him, the absence of recognized rules of what will be a multi-sided repeated game. Since conflicts over property involve more than one person, however, any subset of individuals (down to two) can reduce the costs of conflict by mutually agreeing to accept obligations to recognize some subset of each others' claims (Vanberg and Buchanan, 1990: 18), *given* that the promise each makes is credible. In an initial bargaining exchange, each individual's capacity for violence is clearly an impor-

tant determinant of bargaining strength (Buchanan, 1975: 23–25; Skaperdas, 1992: 732; Gauthier, 1986: 15), and therefore, of the initial allocation of property rights. Given the option of employing violence to secure property claims, it follows that for an individual to voluntarily adopt specified behavioral rules, "the agreement … must ration to each individual as much wealth as he could [expect to] have through the use of his own force or there will be no agreement" (Umbeck, 1981: 40). That is, individuals must expect to gain as much or more than the costs they expect to bear from voluntary constraining their behavior (Buchanan, 1990: 5). Thus, might makes rights even when the underlying rules are voluntarily agreed upon. In this way, individuals can make the private property rights to some resources more secure, perhaps without increasing their investment in violence. The substitute "investment" is giving up claims to other resources (Umbeck, 1981: 45). Clearly, both parties can be better off if they actually reduce their investments in violence (Buchanan, 1975: 23–25), but whether the individuals will reduce their investments in the tools of violence after the agreement depends on how credible the promises are, *and* on the source of the credibility.

As Hardin (1982: 2) explains, the primary theoretical developments undermining the presumption of voluntary cooperation are: (1) the one-shot prisoners' dilemma game which tends to prevent cooperation due to lack of credibility, and (2) the free rider problem which also undermines the credibility of promises even if cooperation does develop, as incentives arise to avoid the costs of cooperating while enjoying the benefits. However, Hardin (1982: 3) also stresses that widespread application of these theoretical arguments suffers from the "fallacy of static generalization." Indeed, when no one has a comparative advantage in violence, individuals may contract to recognize an equal initial distribution of private property rights to scarce resources. While Skaperdas (1992) and Rider (1993) both demonstrate that this is possible, even in a one shot game, for cooperation in the form of tacit recognition of property rights arises if conflict is sufficiently difficult for both parties, (e.g., perhaps because the marginal product of investing in conflict is very low for all parties), such cooperation is even more likely in a world of dynamic relationships. Credibility need not come exclusively from threats of violence, and non-violent institutions for mitigating free-rider incentives can also evolve.

Reductions in investments in the tools of violence under a consent contract may be modest at first, as the threat of violence remains the most important source of credibility. However, as individual begin to interact more frequently and on more dimensions, their interdependent choices become part of continuous process. As each decision becomes a link in a long-time chain of social interaction, a non-violent source of credibility arises. Repeated games do not guarantee credibility, of course, but even the repeated game situation involves weaker incentives for cooperation than those which evolve in many consensual groups (Tullock, 1985). In particular, if each individual enters into several different games with different players, then refusal to recognize widely held rules of conduct within one game can affect a person's reputation, limiting his ability to enter into other games, given that reputation travels from one game to another. When players value relationships with other reliable players more than the potential benefits associated with using violence or refusing to follow accepted conduct in any single game, the repeated-game incentives to keep promises are effectively reinforced, because anyone who chooses a non-cooperative strategy in one game will have difficulty finding a partner for any future game (Tullock, 1985: 1075–1076). Therefore, each player's dominant strategy may be to behave as expected throughout each game, whether it is a repeated or a one shot game. The credibility of threats against reputation depends on the availability of alternatives (e.g., the "exit" option, Vanberg and Congleton, 1992), so as a group expands and evolves the threat becomes more credible (Benson, 1994, 1999).

Vanberg and Buchanan (1990: 185–186) explain that once a group is formed, wherein individuals recognize various behavioral rules, the possibility for establishing other kinds of rules also develops. They define "solidarity rules" as rules targeted at all members of the group such that compliance benefits everyone in the group, as apposed to rules targeted at particular individuals in the context of interactions that benefit only those individuals. Free riding can be overcome as consensual groups evolve such solidarity rules. In particular, refusal to behave according to accepted rules of conduct can be "punished" by ostracism: exclusion from some or all future interaction with other group members (Benson, 1994, 1999). Indeed, ostracism can evolve spontaneously out of individual self-interest (as do other solidarity rules: see Benson, 1994, 1999).

If the agreement stems from an initial situation involving highly asymmetric capacities for violence, the dominant power can demand a relatively large share of property rights and wealth (e.g., property rights to some of the wealth created by other individuals). Indeed, an individual with an absolute advantage in violence will be in a position to induce another individual to accept slavery (Rider, 1993), thus concentrating all property rights (including the ownership of other persons) and wealth in the hands of one individual. But, the slave's incentives to accept the "contract" are "negative" — subjugation is expected to be better than

the alternative very high probability of losing everything through violent confrontation. Accepting slavery leaves open at least some possibility of escape in the future, after all, while death does not. Therefore, the dominant power is likely to have to maintain his relative position of dominance in order to assure credibility on the part of the weaker party (Gauthier, 1986: 195). The institutions that evolve to support the property rights arrangements will tend to rely on coercion and command. In essence, the contract is established through duress.

Between the extremes of violence-free cooperation and coercively-imposed slavery, many other possibilities exist. Some involve dispersed private property rights and high levels of cooperation, with modest payments of protection money (tribute, taxes). Indeed, it may well be that those choosing to pay the tribute could effectively produce a sufficient counter-force to over-throw the "subjugator," but if the tribute demanded is not too great, and/or if the subjugator offers something in return (e.g., protection from outside threats) thereby reducing the net cost of such extortion, the opportunity cost for highly productive individuals to invest in creating a counter-force may be too high to make it worthwhile. Thus, the subjugator is constrained in how much he can extract. In this light, a continuum of "tributes" is theoretically possible, ranging from "slavery" (Rider, 1993) when one person has an absolute advantage in violence, through situations involving a large degree of extortion and concentration of property rights to income, to modest taxes for individuals who could also produce effective violence if pressed (perhaps accompanied by some real protection services in return), to an initially equal distribution of private property rights and no coercive authority. All such systems can "naturally" evolve under different circumstances.

Since there is no unique prediction regarding the institutional arrangements that should move individuals out of the Hobbesian jungle, it becomes an empirical question, and the empirical evidence is pretty overwhelming. Essentially, all of the anthropological evidence points to the emergence of cooperation to facilitate order *within* groups rather than the emergence of coercion (Ellickson, 1993; Ridley, 1996). Hobbes' (1651) "war of all-against-all" at the individual level is rejected, even in the most primitive states of human (and pre-human) existence.. This is not surprising since significant comparative advantages in violence probably did not exist until wealth began to accumulate. However, through hard work, luck, uneven distributions of productive resources, and so on, some individuals and groups develop comparative advantages in production and expand wealth more rapidly than others. Those with a comparative disadvantage in production (i.e., a comparative advantage in violence) have incentives to engage in plunder and to develop or adapt technologies that could facilitate the taking of the wealth others are producing (Oppenheimer, 1908). The evidence is pretty overwhelming on this as well: while cooperation dominates within primitive groups (and extensive cooperation also definitely arises between some of these groups, as explained below), inter-group conflict appears to be a ubiquitous characteristic of human history (Ridley, 1996: 152–169, 189–193).

BRUCE L. BENSON

REFERENCES

Benson, B.L. (1994). "Emerging from the Hobbesian jungle: might takes and makes rights." *Constitutional Political Economy*, 5: 129–158.

Benson, B.L. (1999). "An economic theory of the evolution of governance and the emergence of the state," *Review of Austrian Economics*, 12(2): 131–160.

Buchanan, J.M. (1975). *The Limits of Liberty*. Chicago: University of Chicago Press.

Buchanan, J.M. (1990). "The domain of constitutional economics." *Constitutional Political Economy*, 1: 1–18.

Ellickson, R.C. (1993). "Property in land." *Yale Law Journal*, 102: 1315–1400.

Gauthier, D. (1986). *Morals by Agreement*. Oxford: Clarendon Press.

Hardin, R. (1982). *Collective Action*. Baltimore: Johns Hopkins University Press.

Hobbes, T. (1962 [1651]). *Leviathan*. London: Macmillan.

Hume, D. (1957 [1751]) in C.W. Hendel (ed.) *An Inquiry Concerning the Principles of Morals*. Indianapolis: Bobbs-Merrill.

Oppenheimer, F. (1914 [1908]) and Gitterman, J.M. (Tr.) *The State: Its History and Development Viewed Sociologically*. Indianapolis: Bobbs-Merrill.

Rawls, J. (1971). *A Theory of Justice*. Cambridge, MA: Harvard University Press.

Rider, R. (1993). "War pillage, and markets." *Public Choice*, 75: 149–156.

Ridley, M. (1996). *The Origins of Virtue: Human Instincts and the Evolution of Cooperation*. New York: Viking Penguin.

Skaperdas, S. (1992). "Cooperation, conflict, and power in the absence of property rights." *American Economic Review*, 82: 720–739.

Tullock, G. (1985). "Adam Smith and the prisoners' dilemma." *Quarterly Journal of Economics*, 100: 1073–1081.

Umbeck, J. (1981). "Might makes right: a theory of the foundation and initial distribution of property rights." *Economic Inquiry*, 19: 38–59.

Vanberg, V.J. and Buchanan, J.M. (1990). "Rational choice and moral order," in J.H. Nichols, Jr. and C. Wright (eds.) *From Political Economy to Economics and Back?* San Francisco: Institute for Contemporary Studies.

Vanberg, V.J. and Congleton, R.D. (1992). "Rationality, morality and exit." *American Political Science Review*, 86: 418–431.

ENDOGENOUS MORALITY

"[People] may...picture themselves as meritorious, feeling themselves guilty of no such offenses as they see others burdened with; nor do they ever inquire whether...they would not have practiced similar vices, had not...circumstances of time and place..., kept them out of the way of these vices. This dishonesty, by which we humbug ourselves and which thwarts the establishment of true moral disposition in us, extends itself outwardly also to the falsehood and deception of others." (Kant 1960: 16)

Kant's "categorical imperative" and the Golden Rule both appear to require something like unconditional cooperation (Vanberg and Congleton, 1992: 420). Indeed, from such moral perspectives, individuals should fulfill promises, respect other peoples' rights, be benevolent, practice generosity, and in general, feel "sympathy, kindness, consideration for others" (Hazlitt, 1964: 75). Even superficial observation quickly reveals that to the degree that most individuals adopt such behavior, however, they do so only under certain circumstances. Furthermore, people often feel quite "moral" (ethical, honest, honorable, meritorious, righteous) even when they violate the Golden Rule and/or behave in other ways that moral philosophers would condemn as immoral. Why? The answer proposed below is that within any institutional environment individuals "rationalize" their own selfish behavior as moral in order to reduce the costs (psychic or tangible) of achieving their objectives.

There is a growing literature that considers moral norms in the context of rational choice models (Hausman and McPherson, 1993), but Goldfarb and Griffith (1991) explain that much of this literature treats morality as part of preference functions or as constraints. (Dowell, et al. (1998) model morality as affecting both preferences and constraints). If morality is endogenous to institutions, however, the assumption that preferences are given and stable must be questioned (Cooter, 1998: 597–598). Similarly, treating morals as constraints is inadequate if different beliefs arise in different institution environments. In this context, however, Goldfarb and Griffith (1991) also explain that some models consider morality as rational strategic decision rules in certain types of games [e.g., repeated games, reputation games where cooperating is rational — for instance, see, Axelrod (1984), Ellickson (1991), Vanberg and Congleton (1992), and Ridley (1996: 53–84)]. Individuals interacting within close-knit communities rationally follow the Golden Rule, for instance, establishing and conforming to norms of honesty and generosity (e.g., benevolence, sharing rules, voluntary mutual insurance — see Benson, 2002a) because "Moral sentiments...are problem-solving devices [that evolve]...to make highly social creatures effective at using social relations [by]...settling the conflict between short-term expediency and long-term prudence in favor of the latter" (Ridley, 1996: 132).

Non-cooperative ("immoral"?) behavior can also arise in games (e.g., one period or finite repeated prisoner's dilemma games), of course, and the "moral hazard" problem has been recognized in the literature on asymmetric-information (e.g., see Hart and Holmstrom, 1987). The endogeneity of moral and immoral behavior is also recognized in the growing economics literature examining behavior within the family (e.g., Becker, 1974; Bergstrom, 1989, 1995). The literature exploring the conflicting incentives to cooperate or appropriate (e.g., Skaperdas, 1992; Rider, 1993; Anderson and McChesney, 1994; Hirshleifer, 1991; Benson, 1994b, 1999) also implicitly, and at times explicitly, suggests that moral behavior at least is endogenous. The property rights literature concludes that different types of behavior arise under different institutional arrangements [e.g., secure private property rights encourage long time horizons and voluntary cooperation such as exchange while insecure private property rights or common pools create conflict and encourage short time horizons — see Libecap (1989), Umbeck (1981), and Johnsen (1986), Benson (1984, 1994a)], and both the economics of crime literature which developed following Becker (1968) and the rent-seeking literature following Tullock (1967) also recognize that rational individuals will behave in noncooperative ways, of course, by seeking wealth produced by others, although these literatures do not explicitly address the implications of their analysis for moral beliefs. The arguments made here go beyond most of the literatures cited here, however, contending that both cooperative and noncooperative (including takings) behavior tends to be rationalized by individuals: they believe that their own behavior is morally justified (Benson, 2002a).

Microeconomics tells us that, at the margin, relative prices influence consumption choices. This may be true with moral decisions as well, given differential payoffs arising from and/or costs accruing to moral behavior in different institutional environments. If this is the case, then the question an individual faces in the context of a particular interaction is not simply, "What is the moral thing to do?" At a minimum, it also includes the follow-up: "Can I afford to behave morally in this situation?" The Golden Rule may be recognized, for instance, but rationally ignored if the expected price of morality is too high. In other words, moral behavior may be endogenous while moral beliefs themselves are exogenous. But Frank (1988) argues that it is costly for humans to pretend beliefs that are not actually adopted, so if acting as if particular beliefs are

real is desirable then it is rational to adopt them, making them part of the belief system in order to reduce the psychological costs of taking actions that otherwise would violate their conscience. Furthermore, rational individuals are not able to use conscious reason to evaluate *every* option in the array of available alternatives, because there are significant limits on abilities to reason and absorb knowledge (O'Driscoll and Rizzo, 1985: 119–122). This means that rational individuals often find it beneficial to voluntarily develop and/or conform to rules (including norms reflecting beliefs about what is moral) in order to guide their actions (Benson, 2002a) and reduce decision-making costs (Holcombe, 1992). Thus, the "Austrian School," which focuses on the knowledge problem, traces its foundations to Menger (1883) who emphasized that the origin and evolution process of many social institutions, including systems of rules, is the same as the spontaneous market process. Indeed, citing the passage of time, pervasive ignorance, and inherent uncertainty, Austrians see preferences and beliefs as continually changing as people undergo the experiences of life (Vaughn, 1994: 80). The contention that moral beliefs are endogenous does not imply that individuals simply adopt new norms to justify any behavior, however, thereby making morality irrelevant.

Norms are not likely to be as readily changeable as strategies are in game-theory models. Once beliefs are established and used to dictate behavior in an uncalculating way, they may be quite inflexible even in the face of conflicting conditions. Individuals may resist changes in institutions that would be desirable if they were fully informed, because the behavior required under the institution changes conflicts with both their established beliefs and other people's expectations of their behavior [upsetting such expectations can result in social sanctions (Benson, 2002a)]. If it becomes apparent that existing norms are in significant conflict with an individual's interests, however, so that the individual must either violate the norm or act very irrationally (e.g., repeatedly forgo obvious benefits or incur obvious costs), a moral dilemma arises and the validity of existing beliefs is questioned. Thus, while the rationalization of norms does not imply that all norms are always "rational" in the light of full information or immediate circumstances, when they evolve, the direction of evolution can be predicted assuming rationality. In this context, let us consider some of the predictions regarding moral beliefs that should arise in the process of public choice (see Benson, 2002a for more details).

Benefactors of rent seeking must openly condone the process, so they cannot acknowledge an obligation to respect other people's property rights. Thus, they not only claim but apparently believe that they have the "right" to extract rents which reduce wealth for others by restricting their property rights (Benson, 1984, 2002b). Little wonder that those who do not have the political power necessary to gain benefits from such rent-seeking transfers adopt a similar attitude toward property rights and easily turn to theft. Seeing those who gain wealth through political action as "enemies", they feel morally vindicated when they take advantage of someone in that group (e.g., steal, shirk in work) to "get back" some of what they feel is "rightly theirs". Those without political influence often believe that they are actually victims themselves so their thefts and other "crimes" are easily rationalized in their own minds as morally justified. Similarly, Nee (1998: 88) explains that "opposition norms" inevitably evolve (e.g., a "moral obligation" supporting tax evasion and avoidance). For instance, as European governments attempted to control and tax maritime trade, and granted franchises for numerous trading monopolies between 1500 and 1800, the "average merchant and seaman" responded with piracy and smuggling, and a substantial part of maritime commerce was carried out in violation of the laws of some nation-state (Rosenberg and Birdzell, 1986: 92–96). Furthermore, the middle and even the upper classes willingly wore, drank, and ate smuggled goods (Rosenberg and Birdzell, 1986: 93). Smith (1776: 898) describes the moral implications of such illegal trade, beginning with a characterization of the typical smuggler as

> a person who, though no doubt highly blameable for violating the laws of his country, is frequently incapable of violating those of natural justice, and would have been, in every respect an excellent citizen, had not the laws of his country made that a crime which nature never meant to be so…. [Furthermore, t]o pretend to have any scruple about buying smuggled goods, though a manifest encouragement to the violation of the revenue laws, and to the perjury which almost always attends it, would in most countries be regarded as one of these pedantic pieces of hypocrisy which, instead of gaining credit with any body, serves only to expose the person who affects to practice them, to the suspicion of being a greater knave than most of his neighbours. By this indulgence of the public, the smuggler is often encouraged to continue a trade which he is thus taught to consider as in some measure innocent; and when the severity of the revenue laws is ready to fall upon him, he is frequently disposed to defend with violence, what he has been accustomed to regard as just property.

Such opposition norms mean that bureaucracies are necessary for policing and punishment. Indeed, the primary purpose of most bureaucratic institutions is to facilitate the taking wealth from some and transfer it to others, but in order to do so "in good conscience", bureaucrats are likely to develop beliefs that justify their actions. Thus, for instance, in the "bureaucratic feudalism" that developed in China, Rosenberg and Birdzell (1986: 88) note that "A class of scholar-bureaucrats held classical learning in high esteem and, at the same time, cultivated a contempt for material goals or acquisition" through productive and commercial means; the authors follow that observation with the parenthetic: "Not that these values dictated an ascetic life-style to the mandarins themselves." By developing beliefs that the pursuit of "private interests" is contemptuous, bureaucrats can easily rationalize their expropriation of the wealth created by such pursuits, and their consumption of substantial benefits purchased with that wealth. They also can rationalize the activities of their bureaucracy as serving some "public good," of course, making such takings even more justifiable. As Breton and Wintrobe (1982: 152) explain, "One need not assume Machiavellian behavior, deceit, or dishonesty on the part of bureaucrats, because in all likelihood the pursuit of their own interest will be, as it is for everyone else, veiled in a self-perception of dedication and altruism."

If individuals' perceptions of morality are not endogenous, the kinds of behavior we observe in politicized societies should not exist, unless morality is simply irrelevant. However, the fact that individuals often justify their behavior in moral terms suggests that, at the very least, they believe that morality is important to those who observe their actions. If not, they are choosing to selectively violate the moral norms of cooperation because the psychological costs of such "immoral" behavior would appear to be very high when pursuing wealth through the political process.

BRUCE L. BENSON

REFERENCES

Anderson, T.L. and McChesney, F. (1994). "Raid or trade: an economic model of Indian-White relations." *Journal of Law and Economics*, 37: 39–74.

Axelrod, R. (1984). *The Evolution of Cooperation*. New York: Basic Books.

Becker, G.S. (1968). "Crime and punishment: an economic approach." *Journal of Political Economy*, 78: 167–217.

Becker, G.S. (1974). "A theory of social interaction." *Journal of Political Economy*, 84: 1063–1094.

Benson, B.L. (1984). "Rent seeking from a property rights perspective." *Southern Economic Journal*, 51: 388–400.

Benson, B.L. (1994a). "Are public goods really common pools: considerations of the evolution of policing and highways in England." *Economic Inquiry*, 32: 249–271.

Benson, B.L. (1994b). "Emerging from the Hobbesian jungle: might takes and makes rights." *Constitutional Political Economy*, 5: 129–158.

Benson, B.L. (1999). "An economic theory of the evolution of governance and the emergence of the state," *Review of Austrian Economics*, 12(2): 131–160.

Benson, B.L. (2002a). "Endogenous morality," Florida State University Working Paper presented at the American Economic Association meeting, January 1999, revised for resubmission to the *Journal of Economic Behavior and Organization*.

Benson, B.L. (2002b). "Regulatory disequilibium and inefficiency: the case of interstate trucking," *Review of Austrian Economics* 15(2–3).

Bergstrom, T.C. (1989). "A fresh look at the rotten kid theorem—and other household mysteries." *Journal of Political Economy*, 99: 1138–1159.

Bergstrom, T.C. (1995). "On the evolution of altruistic rules for siblings." *American Economic Review*, 84: 58–81.

Breton, A. and Wintrobe, R. (1982). *The Logic of Bureaucratic Control*. Cambridge, England: Cambridge University Press.

Cooter, R. (1998). "Expressive law and economics." *Journal of Legal Studies*, 28: 585–608.

Dowell, R.S., Goldfarb, R.S., and Griffith, W.B. (1998). "Economic man as a moral individual." *Economic Inquiry*, 36: 645–653.

Ellickson, R.C. (1991). *Order Without Law: How Neighbors Settle Disputes*. Cambridge, MA: Harvard University Press.

Frank, R. (1988). *Passion Within Reasons: The Strategic Control of the Emotions*. New York: W.W. Norton.

Goldfarb, R. and Griffith, W. (1991). "Amending the economist's rational egoist model to include moral values and norms. Part 2: Alternative Solutions." in K. Koford and J. Miller (eds.) *Social Norms and Economic Institutions*, Ann Arbor: University of Michigan Press.

Hart, O.D. and Holmstrom, B. (1987). "The theory of contracts." in T. Bewley (ed.) *Advances in Economic Theory*. Cambridge: Cambridge University Press.

Hausman, D. and McPherson, M. (1993). "Taking ethics seriously: economics and contemporary moral philosophy." *Journal of Economic Literature*, 31: 671–731.

Hazlitt, H. (1964). *The Foundations of Morality*. Irvington-on-Hudson, NY: Foundation for Economic Education.

Hirshleifer, J. (1991). "The paradox of power." *Economics and Politics*, 3: 177–200.

Holcombe, R.G. (1992). "The role of fiction in society," Florida State University Working Paper.

Johnsen, D.B. (1986). "The formation and protection of property rights among the southern Kwakiutl Indians." *Journal of Legal Studies*, 15: 41–68.

Kant, I. (1960), Green, T.M. and Hudson, H.H. (Trs.) *Religion Within the Limits of Reason Alone*. New York: Harper.

Libecap, G.D. (1989). *Contracting for Property Rights*. Cambridge: Cambridge University Press.

Menger, C. ([1963] 1883), Nook, F.J. (Tr.), L. Schneider (ed.) *Problems of Economics and Sociology*. Urbana, IL: University of Illinois Press.

Nee, V. (1998). "Norms and networks in economic and organizational performance." *American Economic Review Papers and Proceedings*, 88: 85–89.

O'Driscoll, G.P. and Rizzo, M.J. (1985). *The Economics of Time and Ignorance*. Oxford: Basil Blackwell.

Rider, R. (1993). "War pillage, and markets." *Public Choice*, 75: 149–156.

Ridley, M. (1996). *The Origins of Virtue: Human Instincts and the Evolution of Cooperation*. New York: Viking Penguin.

Rosenberg, N. and Birdzell, L.E. Jr. (1986). *How the West Grew Rich: The Economic Transformation of the Industrial World*. New York: Basic Books.

Skaperdas, S. (1992). "Cooperation, conflict, and power in the absence of property rights." *American Economic Review*, 82: 720–739.

Smith, A. ([1776] 1937). E. Cannan (Ed.) *An Inquiry into the Nature and Causes of the Wealth of Nations*. New York: Modern Library.

Tullock, G. (1965). *The Politics of Bureaucracy*. Washington, DC: Public Affairs.

Tullock, G. (1967). "The welfare costs of tariffs, monopolies and theft." *Western Economic Journal*, 5: 224–232.

Umbeck, J. (1981). "Might makes right: a theory of the foundation and initial distribution of property rights." *Economic Inquiry*, 19: 38–59.

Vanberg, V.J. and Congleton, R.D. (1992). "Rationality, morality and exit." *American Political Science Review*, 86: 418–431.

Vaughn, K.I. (1994). *Austrian Economics in America: The Migration of a Tradition*. New York: Cambridge University Press.

ENRON

'Enron is a big black box....' McLean (2001: 124)

'That's a good black box.' Former Enron CEO Jeffrey Skilling (US House of Representatives, Committee on Government Reform, 2001: 62)

Answers, not questions, were presumably on the minds of Enron's public relations specialists when they rolled out their 'Ask why' advertising campaign in February 2000. Only a year later, an initially maligned article in *Fortune*, entitled 'Is Enron overpriced?' (McLean, 2001), started a trickle of questions that would end up producing a flood of revelations knocking down a house of paper built on shady Special Purpose Entities, on misleading Performance Review Committee reports, on quasi-hedges of correlated risks and on a corporate culture that took pride in being impenetrable to outsiders. In one of the speediest reversals of fortune in business history, the spectacular failure of one of the world's largest and most admired companies triggered a dozen parallel congressional investigations that questioned the lack of questions by oversight authorities, such as Wall Street analysts, the Securities and Exchange Commission, Enron's Board of Directors, its legal counsel and accounting firm Arthur Andersen.

The seemingly endless parade of current and former Enron executives on the nation's TV screens was eerily reminiscent of the congressional investigations of the big tobacco companies made famous by the 1999 blockbuster movie *The Insider*. Although real life also provided a whistleblower in the person of Sherron Watkins (Watkins, 2001), it was all too apparent that members of Congress increasingly were exasperated by the drama's absence of a classic villain and the unwillingness of key players to accept any responsibility. In the words of one US representative,

> We had hoped to hear what these people thought about the loss of the jobs of thousands of employees and the savings of even more employees, shareholders, pension funds, and other investors. But most of the key players are staying silent — for what appears to be good reason. (Dingell, 2002)

Congressional frustration ultimately led to numerous calls for regulatory reform since institutional safeguards had, according to the politicians conducting the hearings, evidently failed to function.

1. Enron's Rise

Enron, headquartered in Houston, Texas, was launched in July 1985 by a merger between Houston Natural Gas and InterNorth, a Nebraska-based natural gas company. At its inception, gathering natural gas and shipping it over an approximately 37,000-mile network of inter- and intrastate pipelines comprised the core of the company's business operations. Before long, however, Order 436 (in October 1985) and, later, Order 636 (in April 1992) by the Federal Energy Regulatory Commission (FERC) required pipeline operators to provide 'open access' to other energy companies and also to separate sales from transportation services, thereby permitting other firms to ship natural gas through Enron's pipelines. FERC's regulatory orders reinforced the company's desire to broaden its business base. It did so aggressively: between 1985 and 1992, Enron won the contract to be the first company to build a new power plant after the privatization of the UK's electric industry (1988); launched GasBank, the precursor to today's wholesale energy trading business in North America and Europe (1989); established Transwestern Pipeline Company, the first transportation-only pipeline (also in 1989); and acquired Transporadora de Gas del Sur (1992), its first pipeline presence in South America (see Clayton et al., 2002, for a more detailed summary of these and other Enron transactions).

Shortly after opening the world's then-largest gas-fired power plant in the UK (1993), Enron North America set out eventually to become the foremost marketer of electricity in the US (1994) and to capture the public's imagination as one of the world's most innovative firms by utilizing the amendments to the Clean Air Act to establish itself as the leading trader of emission credits as well as one of the pioneers of the market for weather derivatives (1997). Subsequently, Enron expanded into a plethora of other businesses, both foreign (beginning construction of the Dabhol power plant in Mumbai, India, acquiring Wessex Water in the UK and obtaining power marketing licenses in Spain and Germany) and domestic (Enron Energy Services, Enron Broadband Services and EnronOnline, to name a few). This explosive growth continued almost up to its Chapter 11 bankruptcy petition filing on December 2, 2001, at which point the company reportedly had formed about 3,000 subsidiary partnerships.

2. Enron's Fall

By January 2000, Enron had been named by *Fortune* as 'The Most Innovative Company in America' for the fifth consecutive time. The magazine specifically paid tribute to the company's imaginative use of novel financial instruments. Soon, however, it would become apparent that this creativity had been extended to the firm's accounting statements, where it led to a series of premeditated obfuscations and deliberate omissions designed to draw attention to or even fabricate earnings, and to hide losses. William C. Powers, Jr., Dean of the University of Texas Law School, who chaired a special investigative committee commissioned by Enron's Board of Directors, later testified before one of the congressional committees that

> we found something more troubling than those individual instances of misconduct and failure to follow accounting rules. We found a systematic and pervasive attempt by Enron's Management to misrepresent the Company's financial condition.... [T]here's no question that virtually everyone, from the Board of Directors on down, understood that the company was seeking to offset its investment losses with its own stock. That is not the way it is supposed to work. Real earnings are supposed to be compared to real losses. (Powers, 2002)

The transactions powers referred to in his testimony are described in minute detail in Powers et al. (2002). In 1993, Enron had entered into a $500 million joint investment partnership, called by executives evidently enthralled by *Star Wars* the Joint Energy Development Investment Limited Partnership (JEDI), with the California Public Employees' Retirement System (CALPERS). Shared control allowed Enron to avoid consolidating JEDI into its financial statements. Until 1996, this device lawfully enabled Enron only to report its share of the gains and losses from the partnership and, more importantly, to keep JEDI's debt 'off the books.' However, to entice CALPERS to invest into an even larger partnership with Enron in

1996, the pension fund's share in JEDI had to be bought out. The unwillingness of Enron's management to consolidate JEDI into its financial statement necessitated finding another partner.

Being unable to identify a viable outside source of capital, Enron formed Chewco Investments, L.P. (CHEWCO) to purchase CALPERS' interest. The company's treatment of CHEWCO as a Special Purpose Entity (SPE) was permissible, though, only 'if Chewco had some independent ownership with a minimum of 3% of *equity* capital risk' (Powers et al., 2002: 7; emphasis in original). It would be determined after the bankruptcy declaration this had not been the case. But before the denouement, CHEWCO was just the first in a long line of SPEs (LJM1, LJM2 and RAPTOR I through IV) that — despite inventive attempts legally to circumvent generally accepted accounting principles — led Enron to issue financial statements from 1997 through 2001 that overstated the company's income by about $1 billion.

Moreover, Enron had hedged against losses in its merchant investments by contracting with these SPEs. Since the capitalization of these entities was overwhelmingly dependent on transfers of restricted Enron equities, Enron had in essence based its income statements on unrealized gains — and, after the decline in its share prices, unrealizable gains — in its own stock. When falling share prices made it impossible to hide the actual losses and the improperly hedged risks any longer, Enron was forced to announce, on October 16, 2001, a $544 million after-tax charge against earnings as well as a reduction in shareholder's equity of $1.2 billion related to the company's repurchase of 55 million shares of its common stock previously used to capitalize the various SEPs. The sequel was what Sherron Watkins (2000) had prophesied in her warning letter to then-Chairman Kenneth Lay, expressing fears 'that we will implode in a wave of accounting scandals.' Enron's rapid demise, an event that, at the time, represented the biggest bankruptcy in US history, wiped out the retirement savings of thousands of company employees and shattered the confidence of millions of investors in complicated — even if certified — financial statements, hastening the fall of, among others, Tyco and Global Crossing.

Reactions to Enron's implosion ranged from finding fault with 'the "transparent system" meant to protect investors...' (Hatch, 2002), to giving credit to that same system: 'Enron's fall seems to illustrate market success, rather than market failure...' (Clayton et al., 2002: 13). The latter assertion, namely that the financial market had efficiently policed itself by ferreting out the inconsistencies in Enron's accounting practices, was nevertheless a minority opinion, given the duration of the process: it took the finan-

cial experts more than three years to expose the inconsistencies. The unprecedented costs incurred by institutional and private investors alike as well as the inability of Enron employees to salvage their 401(k) savings at a time when management awarded itself hefty bonuses — shareholder lawsuits asserted that no less than 29 key executives had sold 17 million Enron shares for $1.1 billion in the three and a half years preceding the company's fall (see also Pacelle, 2001), 1.8 million shares of which supposedly were sold by Chairman Kenneth Lay for $101 million, closely followed by CEO Jeffrey Skilling (1.1 million shares for $67 million) — represented a wealth transfer of such magnitude that the impression of widespread institutional failure was inevitable. A stunned public wanted answers and politicians raced to provide them.

3. Regulatory Failure or Political Influence?

The public choice model of congressional oversight (Ekelund and Tollison, 2001, offers an inclusive overview of the relevant literature) and bureaucratic control (see Niskanen, 1971, 2001) and casts some doubt on the motives of the investigative hearings that followed Enron's collapse and the immediate announcements by the Securities and Exchange Commission (SEC) of its intent to clarify reporting rules. The interest-group theory of government posits that well-organized (and well-financed) coalitions can shape political and regulatory outcomes in their own favor by assisting politicians in their (re)election campaigns and by holding out the promise of future employment opportunities to incumbent regulators (Stigler, 1971; Peltzman, 1976; McCormick and Tollison, 1981).

There is certainly no lack of anecdotal evidence in this case that Enron had followed such a strategy. Allegations of political favorism abound. The Federal Election Commission, according to an analysis by the Center for Responsive Politics, lists $5.9 million of campaign contributions by Enron, its executives and various company-related Political Action Committees since 1989, 74% of which benefited Republicans, as well as individual donations by Kenneth Lay and his wife totaling $793,110 to Republicans and $86,470 to Democrats. Not surprisingly, this information never figured prominently in any of the many congressional hearings. There was, however, no 'smoking gun' of political influence despite the prominence of Enron advisers on Vice President Dick Cheney's task force on energy and a last-minute call by a former Clinton administration cabinet officer to the Department of the Treasury on behalf of one of Enron's chief creditors. Enron executives might have felt like they had spent 'money for nothing' (McChesney, 1997) when their calls to the White House failed to elicit expected help. Nevertheless, the political investment seemed to have paid off with regard to the SEC, which exempted Enron from several major requirements under the Investment Company Act after the company hired a close acquaintance of a leading SEC official to head its negotiation team.

The principal–agent model, as first applied by Niskanen (1971) to bureaucracy and, subsequently by others to myriad similar relations, including that between shareholders and managers, offers insight into perhaps the most revealing institutional feature of the Enron story. It describes how differences in private incentives may lead to less-than-efficient outcomes when a principal asks an agent to perform certain duties in his stead. In the Enron case, one can identify a number of such relationships interconnecting the company's Board of Directors, its management, shareholders, legal counsel and Arthur Andersen (Chang et al., 2001, review the literature addressing such multiple principal–multiple agent relations).

What is widely known as the 'revolving door' phenomenon — describing the employment of the former regulators of an industry by firms in that same industry — seemed especially prevalent in the relationships between Enron and the private organizations that were expected to provide markets with 'arms-length' evaluations of the company's financial condition. A significant number of Enron executives, among them the Chief Accounting Officer and the Chief Financial Officer, had formerly been employed by Andersen. Moreover, the Houston office of that firm over the years hired several in-house accountants from Enron, who were then assigned to work on the team in charge of auditing Enron's income statements, including Enron's Vice President of internal audit (Herrick and Barrionuevo, 2002). The same was true for Enron and its legal counsel, Vinson & Elkins (V&E):

> Enron and V&E have enjoyed one of the closest lawyer-client relationships in Corporate America. Both Enron's general counsel, James V. Derrick Jr., and his top lieutenant, deputy general counsel Robert H. Walls Jr., are former partners at the law firm. An additional 20 or so V&E attorneys have taken jobs at Enron's legal department over the past decade.... And Enron is V&E's single largest customer. In 2001, Enron accounted for more than 7% of V&E's $450 million in revenue. The law firm had several lawyers working virtually full-time on company business, including some permanently stationed in its offices. (France, 2002: 38)

Such close relationships between business entities — entities that were implicitly paid by shareholders to ensure compliance not only with the letter but also with the spirit of the applicable accounting and corporate governance laws — and Enron's executives obviously aligned the interests of the agents (Andersen and V&E) more with that of corporate management than with the interests of the principals (investors). The most compelling evidence for this incentive realignment is that both Andersen and V&E were apparently involved in advising Enron on the legality of the transactions that later led to its demise.

In addition to the perhaps criminal misconduct of some Enron executive officers, a corporate incentive structure was in place that seemed to emphasize short-term book gains over long-term profitability. The now infamous Performance Review Committees (PRCs) that rated Enron employees on a scale from 1 to 5, where the highest score often resulted in the 're-deployment' or firing of employees within six months and produced an annual turnover rate of 15% of the workforce in Skilling's division (Thomas, 2002: 42), epitomized this incentive structure, which tended to drive a wedge between the interests of senior and mid-level manager-agents and the objectives of shareholder-principals.

Unsurprisingly, in the light of this, Enron was not managed in a way that would maximize long-run value; quite the opposite. Lack of congressional oversight into new, highly complex energy trading markets, regulatory exemptions for one of the world's fastest growing firms, deficient control by the Board of Directors even as it approved controversial business structures, and conflicts of interest on the part of entities whose duty it was to ensure transparency all contributed to Enron's failure.

Relative political prices obviously have been changed by these events. Currently, stronger government regulation appears to be valued more highly by the investing public than self-regulating market forces. Lessons from public choice theory lead to the expectation that politicians will respond to this price change by supplying additional rules (McChesney, 1987, 1997). Proposals have ranged from reforming the administration of employee pension funds, most of which seem to aim for paternalistically inspired reductions in the decision rights of workers, to outlawing executives from taking stakes in any joint venture to which their company is a party, ignoring the fact that prospective partners often ask for exactly this kind of a commitment by executives ex ante. Such quick and dirty solutions dispense with another lesson of public choice theory, namely that there is no guarantee that new laws and regulations are the proper medicine, especially in the highly charged political atmosphere of an election year:

> The overall conclusion from our analysis is the negative one that politicization of market failure is unlikely to generate the ideally corrective measures which the welfare economics recommends. Only under very specific assumptions about the composition of the polity does the politically chosen solution approximate the efficient solution. (Buchanan and Vanberg, [1988] 2000: 371)

This conclusion is reinforced by the difficulties Congress faces in passing legislation creating a new independent oversight board for the accountancy profession. Overt as well as ulterior pressure applied by influential interest groups — among them the American Institute of Certified Public Accountants — to lessen the impact of the proposed legislation prompted the SEC to design an alternative set of reforms not requiring congressional approval, should the legislators decide that the political costs of added regulation outweigh the perceived political benefits (Auditors: House of correction, 2002). Claims that reputational capital and industry-wide ethics standards limit the need for additional regulation of the auditing profession were further undermined when WorldCom, an Arthur Andersen client, announced corrections to its earning statements in June 2002 that amounted to $3.055 billion for 2001 and $797 million for the first quarter of 2002.

The key question raised by the Enron scandal is whether it represents garden-variety corruption on the part of a few dishonest executives seeking personal gain coupled with serious conflicts of interest on the part of a major auditing firm hesitant to prepare accurate financial reports, thereby jeopardizing the fees paid by an important client. Or is Enron instead evidence of systemic 'market failure'? Vigorous enforcement of the criminal laws is the proper response in the first case; some serious rethinking of the hypothesis of capital-market efficiency is warranted in the second. Reinforced by the fact that it took more than three years before Enron's financial irregularities came to light, ongoing revelations of creative accounting practices elsewhere in the economy seem to undercut the conclusion that Enron is merely an isolated, albeit spectacular, violation of the trust that underpins the operation of orderly financial markets.

The broader lesson suggested by Enron is the need for careful analysis of institutional relationships, especially those involving publicly traded firms and their 'independent' auditors, prior to initiating proposed reforms. While it is not yet known whether the market failed in this case, regulatory oversight surely did. How much of this failure resulted from the 'revolving door', how much from the novelty and complexity of the markets Enron pioneered, how much from simple incompetence? One can only speculate at this point. But because, as the logic of collective action teaches, individuals and groups with concentrated interests — such as a politically well-connected company — have comparative advantages over more dispersed actors in the political process (small investors and employees), the remedy for regulatory failure is not necessarily more regulation. Public choice also teaches, however, that more, but not necessarily more effective, regulation is the predictable political response to Enron. Crisis feeds

leviathan (Higgs, 1987). It is consequently advisable for Congress to take its time in cleaning up Enron's mess. It might as well pay heed to the company's earlier 'Ask why?' advertising slogan, not forgetting to shed some light on the other 'black box' in this story, the one that describes the public sector's own interactions with Enron.

MICHAEL REKSULAK
WILLIAM F. SHUGHART II

REFERENCES

Auditors: House of correction (2002). *The Economist*, (22–28 June): 65.

Buchanan, J.M. and Vanberg, V.J. ([1988] 2000). "The politicization of market failure." *Public Choice*, 57(May): 101–113. Reprinted: J.M. Buchanan in H. Kleimt, H.G. Brennan, and R.D. Tollison (eds.) *Politics as Public Choice. The Collected Works of James M. Buchanan*, Volume 13. Indianapolis: Liberty Fund, pp. 357–371.

Chang, K.H., de Figueiredo, R.J.P. Jr., and Weingast, B.R. (2001). "Rational choice theories of bureaucratic control and performance." in W.F. Shughart II and L. Razzolini (eds.) *The Elgar Companion to Public Choice*, Cheltenham, UK and Northampton, MA, USA: Edward Elgar, pp. 271–292.

Clayton, R.J., Scroggins, W. and Westley, C. (2002). "Enron: market exploitation and correction." *Financial Decisions*, 14(Spring): 1–16.

Dingell, J.D. (2002). Statement of Congressman John D. Dingell, ranking member, Committee on Energy and Commerce: Subcommittee on Oversight and Investigations; hearing on the financial collapse of Enron. (7 February): http://www.house.gov/commerce_democrats/press/107st85.htm.

Ekelund, R.B. Jr. and Tollison, R.D. (2001). "The interest-group theory of government." in W.F. Shughart II and L. Razzolini (eds.) *The Elgar Companion to Public Choice*. Cheltenham, UK and Northampton, MA, USA: Edward Elgar, pp. 357–378.

France, M. (2002). "The Enron scandal — special report: One big client, one big hassle." *Business Week* (28 January): 38. http://www.businessweek.com/magazine/content/02_04/b3767706.htm.

Hatch, O. (2002). Statement of Senator Orrin Hatch, ranking member, Committee on the Judiciary; Accountability issues: Lessons learned from Enron's Fall. (6 February): http://www.senate.gov/~judiciary/member_statement.cfm?id=149&wit_id=51.

Herrick, T. and Barrionuevo, A. (2002). "Were auditor and client too close-knit?" *Wall Street Journal* (21 January): C1.

Higgs, R. (1987). *Crisis and Leviathan: Critical Episodes in the Growth of American Government*. New York and Oxford: Oxford University Press.

McChesney, F.S. (1987). "Rent extraction and rent creation in the economic theory of regulation." *Journal of Legal Studies*, 16(January): 101–118.

McChesney, F.S. (1997). *Money for Nothing: Politicians, Rent Extraction, and Political Extortion*. Cambridge: Harvard University Press.

McLean, B. (2001). "Is Enron overpriced?" *Fortune* (5 March): 122–126.

McCormick, R.E. and Tollison, R.D. (1981). *Politicians, Legislation, and the Economy: An Inquiry into the Interest-group Theory of Government.* Boston: Martinus Nijhoff.

Niskanen, W.A. (1971). *Bureaucracy and Representative Government.* Chicago: Aldine-Atherton.

Niskanen, W.A. (2001). "Bureaucracy." in W.F. Shughart II and L. Razzolini (eds.) *The Elgar Companion to Public Choice.* Cheltenham, UK and Northampton, MA, USA: Edward Elgar, pp. 258–270.

Pacelle, M. (2002). "Enron awards to top officials provoke outrage." *Wall Street Journal* (18 June): A2.

Peltzman, S. (1976). "Toward a more general theory of regulation." *Journal of Law and Economics*, 19(August): 211–240.

Powers, W.C. Jr. (2002). Prepared witness testimony. The Committee on Energy and Commerce: Subcommittee on Oversight and Investigation. (5 February): http://energy-commerce. house.gov/107/hearings/02052002Hearing481/ Powers781.htm.

Powers, W.C. Jr. (Chair), Raymond, S.T., and Winokur, H.S. Jr. (2002). *Report of Investigation by the Special Investigative Committee of the Board of Directors of Enron Corp.* (1 February): http://energycommerce.house.gov/107/hearings/ 02052002Hearing481/report. pdf.

Stigler, G.J. (1971). "The theory of economic regulation." *Bell Journal of Economics and Management Science*, 2(Spring): 3–21.

Thomas, C.W. (2002). "The rise and fall of the Enron empire." *Journal of Accountancy*, 193(April): 41–48.

US House of Representatives, Committee on Government Reform (2001). Enron all-employee meeting: Slide presentation and address, Kenneth Lay and Jeffrey Skilling, CEO, presenters (21 February): http://www.house.gov/reform/min/ video/pdfs/pdf_enron_ video_feb_21_trans.pdf.

Watkins, S. (2001). Letter to Enron Chairman and CEO Kenneth Lay. (August): http://energycommerce.house.gov/107/ news/layletter.pdf.

ENVIRONMENTAL POLITICS AND ECONOMIC DEVELOPMENT

1. Introduction

1.1. Environmental Problems are Political Rather than Economic

In most economic textbooks, environmental problems are considered to be economic in origin. Industrial producers of product X use the air or water system to dispose of noxious waste Z, which imposes costs on individuals who live downstream or downwind from the site at which X is produced. The lower cost of this method of disposal implies that consumers benefit from lower prices of X, while firm owners may benefit from higher profits according to market structure. In either case, neither suppliers nor consumers of X have an incentive to account for the spillover costs that the production of X imposes on persons living downstream or downwind from the site of production. Consequently, from the perspective of welfare economics, product X is overproduced and the air and water systems are overutilized as methods of waste disposal.

Of course, as Coase (1960) points out, externality problems can be solved by marketlike transactions. Those individuals affected by the spillovers could band together and pay the firm owners to use different methods of waste disposal. However, what Coase neglects is that such coordinated activities require solutions to a host of organizational problems: a method of collective decision making would have to be chosen, a method of collecting contributions would be required, and so forth. Forming such organizations are problematic, because, as Olson (1965) pointed out, such collective activities have associated public goods and political problems that few persons will have incentives to solve. Perhaps more important, the rewards of public service entrepreneurship tend to be smaller than those generated by entrepreneurship in markets, thus, fewer public goods problems tend to be solved than private goods problems.

Alternatively, rather than organizing to negotiate with producers and consumers of product X, those living downstream or downwind could lobby government to regulate or tax the production of X. That is to say, rather than form a regional organization with complete negotiation powers for the interests represented, those living downwind or downstream can form a less complex organization that attempts to persuade government to solve the problem for them. Not only does lobbying reduce the affected group's organization costs, it tends to require smaller ongoing sacrifices by individual members of the downwind group, because producers and consumers of X no longer need be fully compensated by those demanding smaller emissions. These cost advantages provide a rational choice explanation for the fact that domestic environmental policies tend to be matters decided by governments, rather than negotiated between large environmental clubs and polluters.

It bears noting that once an externality problem is brought to the attention of government, its continuation or amelioration is a result of government policy. That is to say, if no new specific or general policy is put in place, the resulting pollution level reflects incentives already present in civil law and environmental law. If new regulations are put in place, the subsequent pollution level is largely determined by the regulatory targets and the enforcement of the new environmental regulations. In this sense, it is "politics" rather than "economics" that is ultimately responsible for ongoing pollution, because it is government policies that frame the decisions of firms and consumers that generate the pollution.

This conclusion also applies to other more fundamental areas of environmental law. Resources can be privately held and managed or collectively held and managed; or private and collective management can be intermingled in a variety of ways (Ostrom, 1990). Producers may be free to use the air and water systems for waste disposal or may pay an implicit or explicit regulatory price to use these systems. In all these cases, the final use of natural resources reflects incentives latent in government policies. That is to say, all ongoing environmental problems are consequences of economic equilibria generated by ongoing political equilibria. In this sense, environmental problems are fundamentally political — outcomes of collective choice — rather than market failures.

1.2. Environmental Problems are Ancient and Fundamental

There is an unfortunate modern tendency to define "environmental policy" as that which is addressed by modern environmental agencies. This method of defining environmental policy is misleading for several reasons. The most important of these is that it focuses our attention on the subset of environmental problems that have been addressed only fairly recently, and thereby greatly understates the true dimension of environmental law and its long history. Environmental problems have long been addressed by societies, because long-term settlements or towns are only possible if a variety of water supply and waste disposal problems are solved. Either the trash has to be moved periodically out of town, or the town itself has to be moved periodically — as with nomadic villages.

Evidence of externality and environmental concerns can be found in a variety of ancient sources. For example: the Code of Hammurabi (1750 BCE) discusses the rights of property owners, and among many other rules, specifies that:

> (53) If any one be too lazy to keep his dam in proper condition, and does not so keep it; if then the dam break and all the fields be flooded, then shall he in whose dam the break occurred be sold for money, and the money shall replace the corn which he has caused to be ruined.

or

> (55) If any one open his ditches to water his crop, but is careless, and the water flood the field of his neighbor, then he shall pay his neighbor corn for his loss.

A good deal later, Aristotle (330 BCE) explicitly notes that an ideal community should take account of environmental quality:

> "I mention situation and water supply in particular because air and water, being just those things that we make most frequent and constant use of, have the greatest effect on our bodily condition. Hence, in a state which has [the] welfare [of its citizens] at heart, water for human consumption should be separated from water for all other purposes." (*The Politics*, 1969, p. 278)

Environmental prerequisites for a comfortable and healthy life have long been recognized as practical political matters essential to economic prosperity. What have varied through time have been the methods by which policies are chosen and the assessment of environmental amenities and risks. These are affected by constitutional and legal traditions, aesthetic assessments, and the technological feasibility of alternative uses of natural and human resources. Both property law and tort law are important methods for addressing externality and commons problems.

2. Contemporary Environmental Politics and Policies

2.1. The Median Voter and Environmental Policy

Within democracies, a useful first approximation of public policy is that the median voter gets what he or she wants. In most cases, voters will have a broad range of views on the ideal environmental policies. Each voter will favor the policies that maximize his or her utility given his or her understanding of the benefits and costs of environmental problems and amenities. When voters have a direct interest in environmental amenities, such as public green spaces, each voter's preferred policy will reflect both his or her marginal subjective benefit from the service and the marginal tax cost of that service. A voter's demand for such environmental services is much the same as that for roads, schools, or fire protection. Electoral demand rises as tax prices fall, median income rises, or median tastes become "greener" through time.

In other cases, the demand for environmental quality is indirect. For example, environmental regulations are often demanded as a method of reducing health risks. Here the service demanded is health or wealth rather than environmental quality, per se. In such cases, the median voter's demand for environmental quality is also affected by his or her assessment of the causal connection between particular aspects of environmental quality and health. Health is, or may be, affected by such environmental factors as household exposure to radon, lead, and arsenic; ongoing exposure to effluents transported by air and water; and indirect consequences of large- scale environmental changes as may be associated with density changes of ozone in the stratosphere or climate change. In such cases, it is clear that environmental and medical *theories* play an important role in determining the median voter's preferred environmental policy. As the median voter's perceived health risks of a given effluent increase, the median demand for environmental regulation tends to increase.

Unfortunately, the median voter cannot perfectly assess the costs or benefits of alternative environmental policies, because he or she is neither a tax expert, an environmental scientist, nor a health expert. Indeed, even experts disagree about both environmental theories and health risks. Consequently, a good deal of the median voter's demand for environmental regulation is based on secondhand knowledge of the opposing views of experts, rather than on direct personal experience — in contrast to the median demand for mass transit or public education. This is another sense in which the median voter's demand for environmental quality can be said to be indirect.

2.2. Interest Groups

A wide variety of electoral competition models yields median voter or near median voter outcomes in settings where competition is intense, voters are very well informed and vote independently, and candidates choose policy positions to maximize chances of electoral success. In other settings, the median voter model has to be modified in a variety of ways. For example, in settings where voters are imperfectly informed, organized groups may be able to persuade voters to change their minds about the relative merits of policies or be able to persuade candidates to take positions on issues that voters largely remain unaware of. Relatively few voters in the United States will know the details of the Clean Air Act, the Endangered Species Act, or of the Kyoto Protocol. In such cases, even if the general sweep of environmental policy is determined by electoral considerations (median voter interests), the details cannot be insofar as they remain largely unknown to voters. In such policy areas, elected officials may safely trade policy positions for campaign resources or adopt policies to advance their nonelectoral interests.

There is clear anecdotal and statistical evidence that interest groups have affected environmental policies, at least at the margin. For example, Coates (1995) provides statistical evidence that campaign contributions affect the voting patterns of elected legislators on environmental issues. Cropper et. al. (1992) demonstrate that EPA policies have been influenced by interest group testimony and law suits. Buchanan and Tullock's (1976) theoretical results

suggest that economic rather than environmental considerations often determine the choice of policy instruments.

The influence of interest groups is potentially greatest in areas where the demand for environmental policies is indirect, because interest groups have wider latitude to persuade voters on matters they have little or no direct experience with. In such cases, interest groups can attempt to influence the *theories* used by the median voter to assess policies in addition to his or her assessment of the direct benefits and tax costs associated with alternative policies. In the end, the policies that are chosen in democracies reflect the effects of electoral competition, which causes policies to gravitate toward median voter preferences, and the influence of politically active interest groups inside and outside government.

2.3. The Normative Valuation Problem

In some cases, the information problems confronting voters (and legislatures) can be reduced by delegating decision making to an expert bureaucracy and charging it with maximizing social net benefits. This institutional solution potentially maximizes average benefits rather than median benefits, but yields policies that advance median voter interests most of the time. To the extent that cost-benefit analysis is "honestly" applied, the resulting policies will be approximately those that the average voter would have chosen if he or she had the time and energy to be well informed on the issues being decided.

Unfortunately, in the case of environmental policy, it is often the case that benefits and costs are very difficult to estimate. This is not because environmental benefits and costs are subjective — this is always true of costs and benefits — but rather because few market proxies for costs and benefits typically exist, and, there is often significant disagreement over the effects of policy alternatives. For example, the marginal benefit of a large nature preserve in Alaska for tourists can be approximated using travel cost data, but not for nontourists who may nonetheless favor such preserves. Moreover, even for tourists it is difficult to estimate the marginal effects of small changes in the size of a nature preserve. How many fewer tourists would come if the preserve were a bit smaller? A majority of voters may favor a large preserve, but what are they willing to pay for one that is 100 square miles larger or smaller? Unfortunately, even voters rarely know this themselves. Even with completely neutral agencies interested in advancing the interests of the median voter, delegation is very difficult.

The problem of delegating environmental policy decisions becomes even more complicated when agency personnel have goals that differ significantly from those of the electoral mainstream. The EPA has failed to use cost–benefit analysis when required to do so by law. It also has used cost–benefit analysis when it was not part of its policy mandate and when cost–benefit analysis was explicitly prohibited by statute.

3. International Environmental Problems and Politics

3.1. Regulatory Externalities

One of the most interesting areas of contemporary environmental politics concerns environmental problems that span national borders. These are of special interest for political analysis because international policies address *regulatory failures* rather than conventional economic externality problems. International regulatory failures arise because individual governments have only very weak incentives to take account of the effects of their own environmental regulations on neighboring countries.

The existence of regulatory externalities often implies that unrealized gains to trade *in environmental regulations* exist. Consider the case of two neighboring democracies separated by a river into which effluents may be discharged. Each government has an incentive to regulate discharges into the boundary water insofar as its citizens (median voter) demand improved water quality — whether for recreation or health reasons. However, neither government has an electoral reason for taking account of the benefits that its policies confer upon the other country's citizens. Under the usual public choice assumptions, self-interested voters behave in the same manner as ordinary consumers and neglect the effects of their electoral demands on other citizens, both within their own countries and in neighboring countries. The combination of environmental regulations jointly determines the water quality of the boundary river by jointly determining the effluents discharged into it.

Insofar as each country's median voter values the water quality of the boundary river, each benefits from the other country's environmental regulations. Consequently, there are often mutual gains that can be realized if both countries increase the stringency of their regulations somewhat, and, moreover there are electoral reasons for attempting to realize them (Hoyle, 1991; Congleton, 1992; Fredricksson and Gaston, 2000b). Unless the two countries' environmental regulations are coordinated in some way, each tends to under-regulate its discharges into the boundary waters.

3.2. Only Coasian Solutions

National sovereignty implies that international regulatory failures can only be addressed via voluntary agreements, that is to say, via Coasian contract. A government will only sign an international agreement if it advances its own political interests, and will, subsequently, only implement policies that do so. An environmental agreement cannot implement itself, because implementation by sovereign nations requires domestic legislation. International environmental treaties, consequently, have to solve a variety of institutional problems that can be neglected in domestic environmental policy (Congleton, 1995).

The voluntary nature of international environmental agreements together with the wide range of government types and social settings implies that incentives to sign and implement international agreements vary widely (Congleton, 2001). Both the domestic environmental setting and type of government affect the ratification of environmental treaties. Murdock and Sandler (1997b) find that countries affected by upstream emissions are more likely to sign international treaties than those that are less affected by transboundary emissions. Congleton (1992) demonstrates, for example, that democracies are more inclined to sign and ratify treaties than nondemocracies. Even after a treaty is signed and ratified the overall impact of environmental treaties on domestic policies is uncertain, because, in practice, environmental treaties lack explicit enforcement provisions. The lack of international enforcement agencies implies that any Coasian contracts consummated must be self-enforcing (Barett, 1994; Schmidt, 1999). Murdock and Sandler (1997a,b) find that environmental treaties have little, if any, effect on a nation's environmental policies.

Overall, solutions to international environmental problems are clearly more difficult to resolve than those associated with equivalent domestic problems because a wider range of political considerations in several nations have to be simultaneously addressed.

4. Conclusion

4.1. Long-run Environmental Political Economy

Environmental policies, broadly interpreted, define man's relationship with the environment. They include all the rules that affect the use of natural resources — for any and all purposes. Both environmental and political considerations have long influenced the development of such rules. Political decisions largely determine "the law" insofar as political decisions standardize rules and determine which rules will be enforced by government. Significant environmental problems have often motivated collective efforts to characterize the legitimate use of property and obligations of property owners, especially those associated with various "tragedies of the commons" (Demsetz, 1967; Posner, 1972).

Polities that *properly* address environmental problems will look much different than ones that do not. Polities that fail to solve commons problems will find some resources overused and others underused, and have a citizenry that lives less comfortable and secure lives. Polities that fail to secure and protect potable water supplies will have a citizenry whose productivity is reduced by poor health and short lives. Polities that neglect land management or fail to develop institutions that address such problems may find formerly fertile farm fields reduced to wastelands. Polities that "overly protect" nature from economic uses will be less complex, less sophisticated, and poorer societies, although their natural surroundings may well be more varied and verdant.

Although the processes of economic development are complex, it is clear that the political considerations that constrain man's relationship with nature — the pattern of use rights, ownership, and regulatory restrictions — have played an important role in the course of economic development. In this respect, environmental politics is not simply a minor subarea of the economic theory of regulation, but a major engine of long- and short-term policy development with profound consequences for economic and human development. Future policies are also likely to have such effects whether new methods for addressing global environmental problems are implemented or not. Within environmental political economy, even the air that one breathes is endogenously determined!

4.2. Politics as Usual?

Nonetheless, environmental political economy is largely "politics as usual." Environmental policies are simply examples of the political equilibria analyzed by the public choice literature.

The domain of environmental policy is unusually broad, which makes the politics of environmental policies especially interesting and controversial, but not unique. Modern international environmental policy controversies address global phenomena beyond the reach of domestic governments, while raising profound normative questions about the proper response to uncertain, but possibly grave long-term risks. Modern domestic environmental policy choices are also highly contentious. Environmental regulations affect terms of trade within and between nations, and,

therefore, attract significant attention from powerful economic interest groups such as the oil, chemical, and labor lobbies. The broad implications of environmental regulations and services also attract significant interest from noneconomic interest groups whose members aim for conflicting visions of the good society. Moreover, environmental science is a relatively new field addressing issues that cut across many fields of science, and, consequently, its theories are continuously being updated. Overall, environmental politics may be ordinary, but it is "ordinary" on a grand scale.

ROGER D. CONGLETON

REFERENCES

Barett, S. (1994). "Self-enforcing international environmental agreements." *Oxford Economic Papers*, 46: 878–894.

Bevans, C.I. (1974). *Treaties and Other International Agreements of the United States of America*. Department of State Publication 8761.

Boadway, R. and Hayashi, M. (1999). "Country size and the voluntary provision of international public goods." *European Journal of Political Economy*, 15:

Buchanan, J.M. and Tullock, G. (1975). "Polluters' profits and political response, direct control versus taxes." *American Economic Review*, 65: 139–147.

Coase, R.H. (1960). "The problem of social cost." *Journal of Law and Economics*, 3: 1–44.

Congleton, R.D. (1992). "Political regimes and pollution control." *Review of Economics and Statistics*, 74: 412–421.

Congleton, R.D. (1995). "Toward a transactions cost theory of environmental treaties." *Economia della Scelte Pubbliche*, 119–139.

Congleton, R.D. (ed.) (1996). *The Political Economy of Environmental Policy*. Ann Arbor: University of Michigan Press.

Congleton, R. D. (2001). "Governing the global environmental Commons: the political economy of international environmental treaties and institutions," in G.G. Schulze and H.W. Ursprung (eds.) *Globalization and the Environment*. New York: Oxford University Press, ch. 11.

Cropper, M., Evans, W. N., Berardi, S.J., Duela-Soares, M.M., and Portney, P. (1992). *Journal of Political Economy*, 100: 175–197.

Demsetz, H. (1967). "Towards a theory of property rights." *American Economic Review*, 57: 347–360.

Feld, L.P., Pommerehne, W.W., and Hart, A. (1996). "Private provision of a public good," in R.D. Congleton (ed.) *The Political Economy of Environmental Protection*. Aldershot: Edward Elgar Publishing.

Fredriksson, P.G. and Gaston, N. (2000a). "Ratification of the 1992 Climate Change Convention: what determines legislative delay?" *Public Choice*, 104: 345–368.

Fredriksson, P.G. and Noel, G. (2000b). "Environmental governance in federal systems: the effects of capital competition and lobby groups." *Economic Inquiry*, 38: 501–514.

Fredriksson, P.G. (2001). "How pollution taxes may increase pollution and reduce net revenues." *Public Choice*, 107: 65–85.

Hoel, M. (1991). "Global environmental problems: the effects of unilateral actions taken by one country." *Journal of Environmental Economics and Management*, 21: 55–70.

Leidy, M.P. and Hoekman, B.M. (1996). "Pollution abatement, interest groups, and contingent trade policies," in R.D. Congleton (ed.) *The Political Economy of Environmental Protection*. Aldershot: Edward Elgar Publishing.

Maloney, M.T. and McCormick, R.E. (1982). "A positive theory of environmental quality regulation." *Journal of Law and Economics*, 25: 99–123.

Mueller, D.C. (1989). *Public Choice II*. Cambridge: Cambridge University Press.

Murdoch, J.C. and Sandler, T. (1997a). "The voluntary provision of a pure public good: the case of reduced CFCs emissions and the Montreal Protocol." *Journal of Public Economics*, 63: 331–349.

Murdoch, J.C., Sandler, T., and Sargent, K. (1997b). "A tale of two collectives: sulfur versus nitrogen oxides emission reduction in Europe." *Economica*, 64: 281–301.

Olson, M. (1965) *The Logic of Collective Action*. Cambridge, Mass: Harvard University Press.

Ostrom, E. (1990). *Governing the Commons: The Evolution of Institutions for Collective Action*. New York: Cambridge University Press.

Peltzman, S. (1976). "Toward a more general theory of regulation." *Journal of Law and Economics*, 19: 211–240.

Posner, R.A. (1972). *Economic Analysis of Law*. Boston: Little Brown and Co.

Sandler, T. (1996). "A game theoretic analysis of carbon emissions," in R.D. Congleton (ed.) *The Political Economy of Environmental Protection*. Aldershot: Edward Elgar Publishing.

Schmidt, C. (1999) "Incentives for international environmental cooperation: theoretic models and economic instruments," in G.G. Schulze and H.W. Ursprung (eds.) *Globalization and the Environment*. New York: Oxford University Press, ch. 10.

Schulze, G.G. and Ursprung, H.W. (eds.) (2001). *Globalization and the Environment*. New York: Oxford University Press.

Telser, L. (1980). "A theory of self-enforcing agreements." *Journal of Business*, 53: 27–44.

Tollison R.D. and Willett, T.D. (1979). "An economic theory of mutually advantageous issue linkages in international negotiations." *International Organization*, 33: 309–346.

Vaubel, R. and Willett, T.D. (eds.) (1991). *The Political Economy of International Organizations*. Boulder: Westview Press.

THE EURO

The euro is issued by the European Central Bank (ECB), an independent bureaucracy. The economic theory of bureaucracy predicts that central bank independence increases bureaucratic waste (for a test, see, Vaubel, 1997). Moreover, an international bureaucracy is farther removed from the control of voters and national politicians than a national central bank (see *International Organizations*). After-tax salaries are much higher at the ECB than at the national central banks. The staff of the ECB is still comparatively small but public theory predicts that it will ultimately be too large.

The ECB is directed by a Governing Council which consists of the Governors of the central banks of the participating states and an Executive Board of six directors who are unanimously appointed by the governments of the participating states. The Governing Council decides by simple majority. As the median member is a national central bank Governor, public choice theory predicts that the share of the Executive Board in total central bank staff will be smaller in the ECB than in national central banks (like the Federal Reserve System of the United States) where the executive board (Board of Governors) commands a majority (Fratianni and von Hagen, 1990).

The median member of the ECB Governing Council determines monetary policy and, ultimately, the inflation rate. If central bankers are appointed or proposed by the government of their home country because they share the long-run inflation preference of that government and if the governments of the member states are elected because they share the long-run inflation preference of the median voter of their country, past inflation performance or popular inflation preferences revealed in opinion polls can be used to find out which member of the ECB Governing Council has the median inflation preference. It turns out that, initially, the French members of the ECB Governing Council had the median position with respect to both inflation performance (in 1975–93) and popular inflation preferences (Vaubel, 2002).

Alternatively, the inflation rate may depend on the partisan leanings of the Council members. At the beginning, the median was a "conservative" central banker though most of the participating states had left-wing governments. Initially, one conservative government wielded effective veto power over the appointment of the Executive Board. Without the consent of the German government, which had most to lose, there would have been no European Monetary Union. In the future, however, EMU will persist even if the governments cannot agree on any appointments to the Executive Board. If the preferred long-run inflation rate was all that matters, public choice theory would predict that, in the future, newly appointed members of the Executive Board will either share the inflation preference of the median Governor or be selected two or more at a time without affecting the median. According to the same calculus, the country occupying the median position in the ECB Governing Council may veto the accession of additional member states which would deprive it of its median position. (The entry of Greece in 2001 has not deprived France of its median position.)

Since monetary policy affects the outcome of elections, the ECB may also generate political business cycles. In a monetary union, political business cycles are less likely than in a nation state because the national election dates are dispersed over time (Williamson, 1985; Fratianni, von Hagen, 1990). There is no government for the European Monetary Union, and the elections for the European Parliament are comparatively unimportant. By accident, however, there may be clusters of election dates (for example, the ten national elections between May 2002 and June 2004). The successive lowering of ECB interest rates in the fall of 2001 may be explained, inter alia, by the fact that a majority of the ECB Governing Council had been proposed by the ten incumbent governments (Vaubel, 2002).

A political business cycle is less likely when the central bank is independent. Is the European Central Bank more or less independent than the German Bundesbank, the leading European central bank prior to EMU, has been? On the one hand, the ECB is more independent because amendments of the EC Treaty require the assent of 15 parliaments (each voting by simple majority) while the Bundesbank Law may be amended by a single parliament, indeed, a single chamber of parliament (also with a simple majority). On the other hand, the individual members of the ECB Governing Council enjoy less personal independence than the members of the Bundesbank Council because the latter could always rely on being reappointed if they wished and age permitted. Moreover, the ECB would enjoy less policy autonomy than the Bundesbank, if the Council of Ministers unanimously adopted an exchange rate target for the euro. For, unlike the Bundesbank, the ECB does not have the right to abandon foreign exchange interventions which threaten price-level stability (Grüner and Hefeker, 1996).

Since the Bundesbank Law could easily be changed, the Bundesbank tried hard to maintain the support and protection of public opinion. The members of the ECB Governing Council will care less about public opinion because their policy autonomy is more secure. They will pay relatively more attention to the partisan ideology of their government and election dates at home because their personal tenure is less secure.

The revenue of the ECB is passed on to the member central banks but the shares depend on population and GDP. They differ from the countries' shares in the euro monetary base (Sinn and Feist, 1997). Hence, there are winners and losers of seigniorage. Public choice theory predicts that, other things equal, current members will prefer the accession of countries which would lose from seigniorage redistribution.

ROLAND VAUBEL

REFERENCES

Fratianni, M. and von Hagen, J. (1990). "Public choice aspects of European monetary unification." *Cato Journal*, 10: 389–411.

Grüner, H.P. and Hefeker, C. (1996). "Bank cooperation and banking policy in a monetary union: a political-economy perspective on EMU." *Open Economies Review*, 7: 183–198.

Sinn, H.-W. and Feist, H. (1997). "Eurowinners and eurolosers: the distribution of seigniorage wealth in EMU." *European Journal of Political Economy*, 13: 665–689.

Vaubel, R. (1997). "The bureaucratic and partisan behavior of independent central banks." *European Journal of Political Economy*, 13: 201–224.

Vaubel, R. (2002). "The future of the euro: a public choice perspective." in F. Capie and G. Wood (eds.) *Monetary Unions*. Basingstoke: Macmillan/Palgrave.

Williamson, J. (1985). "International agencies and the Peacock critique," in D. Greenaway and G.K. Shaw (eds.) *Public Choice, Public Finance and Public Policy. Essays in Honour of Alan Peacock*. Oxford: Blackwell, pp. 167–175.

EUROPEAN POLITICAL INTEGRATION

The dynamics of European political integration is frequently explained by the strategy of Jean Monnet: market integration in selected branches (coal, steel, manufactures, agriculture, nuclear energy etc.) and common economic policies in these areas "spill over" into more and more sectors of the economy and finally necessitate full-fledged political integration. However, there are also public choice explanations. Whenever an increase in market integration (e.g., the internal market program of 1987) is considered or new members join the club, some countries claim to be net losers and insist on new policies which would redistribute in their favor (e.g., the European Regional Policy in 1975 or the doubling of the Structural Funds in 1987–92). Moreover, market integration undermines the tax and regulatory powers of the national governments because it increases the mobility of resources. The national politicians then try to preserve their power by "harmonizing" or centralizing policies at the European level. In the absence of constitutional or natural barriers to policy collusion, market integration leads to policy cartels or monopolies (Vaubel, 1999).

Like all international organizations, the European Community/Union weakens democratic control and increases the power of organized interest groups and the bureaucracy (see *International Organizations*). In the case of the European Union, the bureaucracy is even more powerful because the Commission possesses the monopoly of legislative initiative which serves as a ratchet. It enables the eurocracy to prevent legislation that would return powers to the member states. Moreover, when the governments want to amend the Commission's proposal, the Commission decides whether a qualified majority or unanimity is required in the Council of Ministers.

The Commission, the European Parliament and the European Court of Justice all have a vested interest in the centralization of policies at the Union level. They decide by simple majority. When a simple majority of the judges interprets the Treaties in a centralizing way, the Council requires a qualified majority or unanimity to reverse the Court's decision by new legislation. The asymmetry of the quorum required in the Court and the Council generates a centralizing bias. Moreover, the Commission, sharing the centralizing inclinations of the Court, will not propose legislation reversing the Court's decision.

In many important respects, Union legislation does not require the assent of the European Parliament. Thus, the governments of the member states can evade parliamentary control by shifting legislation from the national to the European level. In 1991, for example, at least one government succeeded in raising its rate of value-added tax by means of European tax "harmonization" even though the parliament of the country was opposed to the tax increase. By setting a minimum tax rate for the European Union, the Council of Ministers can introduce taxation without representation.

The Treaties also contain a general empowering clause: the Council of Ministers may legislate even where the "Treaty has not provided the necessary powers" provided that it acts unanimously on a proposal of the Commission and such action seems "necessary to attain, in the course of the operation of the common market, one of the objectives of the Community" (Art. 308 TEC).

The parliaments of the member states do not control Union legislation but they have to ratify all amendments to the Treaties. However, all Treaty amendments have to be proposed by an Intergovernmental Conference. The governments are agenda setters. According to the Treaties, the national parliaments — unlike the state legislatures in the United States — are no longer masters of the distribution of powers.

There seems to be agreement that "the EC system is now more lobbying-oriented than any national European system" (Andersen and Eliasson, 1991: 178). There are almost 3,000 lobby organizations and 10,000 lobbyists in Brussels. The Union's favors to interest groups take three forms: protectionism, subsidies and regulation. The trade policy of the European Union is highly protectionist — especially its agricultural import levies and its "anti-dumping" measures.

As for subsidies, at least 72 percent of the Union budget is spent on favors to interest groups (Vaubel, 1994a). The bulk goes to agriculture. With regard to regulation, 78 percent of the pages of the Official Journal are devoted to special interest group legislation (Peirce, 1991: table 2). The observed interest group bias can be explained by the democratic deficit and the dominance of bureaucracy in the European Union. Bureaucrats are more accessible to interest groups and less sensitive to the wishes of voters than politicians are, for bureaucrats, unlike politicians, do not have to be reelected (Crain and McCormick, 1984).

Opinion polls and referenda in a considerable number of member countries have documented the fact that dissatisfaction with the European Community/Union is much more widespread among voters than among politicians. The European Representation Study reveals that the share of those advocating a transfer of power to the European level is much larger among the members of the European Parliament than among the national parliamentarians and the citizens (Schmitt and Thomassen, 1999: table 3.1). The citizens have considerably more confidence in their national parliament than in the European Parliament, or in the government of their home country than in the European Commission or the Council of Ministers (Eurobarometer 45, Spring 1996). The citizens believe to have much more influence on the government of their home country than on the institutions of the European Union (Eurobarometer 44.1, Nov./Dec. 1995, question 72). All this evidence indicates that the European Union suffers from a severe principal–agent-problem.

The share of respondents supporting membership in the European Union bears a significantly positive correlation with the country's EU trade integration, its net receipts from the EC budget and the duration of membership (Inglehart and Rabier, 1978; Mathew, 1980; Dalton and Eichenberg, 1993; Vaubel, 1994a).

There is a significantly negative correlation between the political rank which a Commissioner has occupied in his home country before being appointed to the Commission and the central government budget of his home country. This indicates that Popitz' Law of the attraction of the larger budget is operative in the European Union (Vaubel, 1994a).

There exists a large number of case studies applying public choice theory to particular policy areas of the European Union (for a survey, see Vaubel, 1994b; see also *The Euro*).

ROLAND VAUBEL

REFERENCES

Andersen, S.S. and K.A. Eliasson (1991). "European Community lobbying." *European Journal of Policy Research*, 20: 173–187.

Crain, W.M. and McCormick, R.E. (1984). "Regulators as an interest group," in J.M. Buchanan and G. Tullock (eds.) *The Theory of Public Choice—II*, Ann Arbor, MI: The University of Michigan Press. pp. 287–304.

Dalton, R.J. and Eichenberg, R.C. (1993). "Europeans and the European Community: dynamics of public support for European integration." *International Organization*, Summer.

Inglehart, R. and Rabier, J.-R. (1978). "Economic uncertainty and European solidarity: public opinion trends." *Annals of the American Academy of Political and Social Science*, 440: 66–87.

Mathew, D.D. (1980). *Europeanism: A Study of Public Opinion and Attitudinal Integration in the European Community*. Ottawa: Carlton University.

Peirce, W.S. (1991). "Unanimous decisions in a redistributive context: the Council of Ministers of the European Communities." in R. Vaubel and T.D. Willett (eds.) *The Political Economy of International Organizations: A Public Choice Approach*, Boulder, Co: Westview Press, pp. 267–285.

Schmidtchen, D. and Cooter, R. (eds.) (1997). *Constitutional Law and Economics of the European Union*. Cheltenham: Elgar.

Schmitt, H. and Thomassen, J. (1999). *Political Representation and Legitimacy in the European Union*. Oxford: Oxford University Press.

Vaubel, R. (1994a). "The political economy of centralization and the European Community." *Public Choice*, 81: 151–190.

Vaubel, R. (1994b). "The public choice analysis of European Integration: a survey." *European Journal of Political Economy*, 10: 227–249.

Vaubel, R. (1999). "Enforcing competition among governments: theory and application to the European Union." *Constitutional Political Economy*, 10: 327–338.

EVOLUTION OF INSTITUTIONS

1. Introduction

The powerful influence of the writings of Charles Darwin (Darwin, 1859) changed the definition of the word "evolution." Prior to Darwin, the word was a relatively unpopular synonym for the word "development." Developmental concepts had been used in numerous descriptive hypotheses from Vico (Vico, 1974) and Condorcet (Condorect, 1795) to Hegel (Hegel, 1861) and Comte (Comte, 1854). These studies were more celebrations of various "stages" of human progress through assumedly productive learning than predictive or explanatory analyses of the developmental process. A similarly non-rationalized optimism was found in Lamarck's (Lamarck, 1809) influential work on animal development through inheritable environmental adaptations. Darwin's theory burst these and related bubbles by arguing that the relatively fit have survived regardless of whether progress or retrogression has taken place. Nothing, not even divine planning, provided a better explanation of the observable characteristics of natural organisms. By the end of the 19th century, then, "evolution" came to predominantly signify a process of development in which a biological or social characteristic becomes more or less prevalent in the population depending on its ability to enhance its possessor's survival.

The following discussion accepts the newer definition and thereby concentrates on predictive discussions of the developmental process and its realized outcomes. Before proceeding, however, note that learning (or, in biology, the pre-Darwinian, Lamarck-emphasized, notion of the inheritance of environmentally acquired characteristics) is not precluded from this definition. Of course, the definition also admits natural selection: A process featuring a large number of initial varieties, a systematic inheritance of the inherited physical characteristics of one's predecessors, and a greater likelihood of survival to reproduction of those organisms whose characteristics are most suited to the environment. Darwin did not deny Lamarck's inheritance process. Nor did he discover the process of natural selection; indeed, he admits that there were several late 18th century antecedents, including the inexorable struggle for existence appearing in Malthus' First Essay on Population (Malthus, 1798).

Natural selection was first employed in a poem by Empedocles to similarly counter divine explanations of the characteristics of various animals, including humans. It was such a popular theory that Aristotle extensively reviewed it. Aristotle, the central influence on biological theory prior to Lamarck and Darwin, was critical of evolution because he did not see that natural selection could be used to explain the physical laws. Thus lacking an appropriate physical theory, he could not eliminate his prime mover as the primary cause of all observed order. Once his order-generating prime mover was admitted, Aristotle considered evolution to be superfluous. He also added, in a rather startling anticipation of 20th century anti-Darwinian thought, that our failure to observe any record of a continuum of species casts doubt on the sufficiency of natural selection as a force generating the observed variety of species in nature.

2. Roots of the Modern Economic Theory of the Evolution of Institutions

Like the modern theory of biological evolution, the modern economic theory of institutional evolution was born as a reaction against popularly held theories of rational planning. Its first articulate advocate was Edmund Burke, (Burke, 1790) who was not impressed with the "Enlightened" political theories underlying the French Revolution. Burke strenuously argued for respecting the fact that France's survival and emergence as perhaps the richest state in Europe was evidence for the efficacy of her implicit constitution. Even though it was practically impossible to rationalize this desirable outcome, Burke argued that it was not in the interest of France to overturn the pragmatic, piecemeal, trial-and-error process that had created France's institutional inheritance and political–economic dominance. Many economists endorsed this argument, which became the cornerstone of Austrian institutional conservatism through the late-19th century influence of Karl Menger (Menger, 1871) and the early 20th century works of Friedrich von Hayek (Hayek, 1973), Ludwig von Mises, (Mises, 1966) and Joseph Schumpeter (Schumpeter, 1928). All of these Austrians followed Burke in criticizing grand social reforms and praising the "spontaneous order" created by individualistic decision processes.

These Austrian institutional theories against reforming basic institutions with reason-based theories imply a conjecture that a social–evolutionary equilibrium both exists and is Pareto optimal. Remarkably, modern game theory has developed to where now, over two hundred years after Burke's original argument, we are able to establish, at least under a set of sometimes-reasonable assumptions, the veracity of this Austrian conjecture.

3. Existence and Efficiency of a Social Evolutionary Equilibrium

The problem at hand induces us to consider a set of societies, or n-person non-cooperative games, in which the individuals each experiment with a wide range of strategies. All individuals, or their replacements if they should die, adopt new strategies as a result of experience or past observations on the payoffs in dealings with other players. These strategy changes satisfy "payoff-positivity." In other words, whenever a strategy generates an-above average payoff, whether because of learning or selection, the proportion of similarly situated individuals adopting that strategy will increase.

Since we anticipate the achievement of unconstrained social optimality, the process must generally admit experimentation with all possible strategies. To achieve this, a significant-random-variation-producing process is introduced in order to generate sufficient strategic experimentation. But if excessive random variation occurs, even a most-fit organism will practically never represent a significant part of the population. The way to handle the problem is to have environmental stress increase the random variation rates and environmental success reduce these rates. Thus, following a period of social stress and experimentation, after which individuals come to unquestioningly accept a particular institution, little random variation will occur. In other words, as an organism or institution matures and establishes a successful track record, random variation rates will steadily decrease. Although some random variation is required if the organism is to be able to adopt to future shocks, as long as these external shocks approach zero, it is natural to allow random variation rates to also approach zero. The pioneering paper of Foster and Young introduce this latter assumption, albeit in a highly simplified form and under very simplifying conditions, to generate the first modern theorem demonstrating the convergence of an evolutionary equilibrium to a Nash equilibrium. Weibull has subsequently generalized this theorem to environments suitably general to fit our discussion. Although Weibull's (Weibull, 1995) convergence result requires asymmetric environments (e.g., individuals have different roles or select their strategies at different times) and individuals who are never indifferent between actions, the strategies in his model asymptotically converge (meaning that the strategies will not cycle) to Nash strategies.

Asymptotic convergence is practically important because it helps speed up the path to equilibrium. (Cycles and our variably randomized strategies could even indefinitely prolong a society's search for an equilibrium.) When dynamic paths are slow, an initial equilibrium target is very likely to have significantly shifted before the process ever even approximates it.

Of course, Nash equilibria are generally numerous and inefficient. However, our context here is an entire society, where there is an order-preserving ruling class whose members each issue committed reaction functions to inferiors in a highly asymmetric social hierarchy. These ruling-class commitments define the "institutions" that the rest of the society lives under.

Ruling out indifference between actions, which we have already done to satisfy the conditions of Weibull's convergence theorem, there is one and only one static equilibrium, and it is Pareto optimal (Thompson–Faith) (Thompson and Faith, 1981). The reason for this static efficiency is simple. Suppose that the static equilibrium (a very special Nash equilibrium) were not Pareto optimal. Then the top member of the ruling class in this hypothesized equilibrium would increase her utility by committing herself to a reaction function of the following form: "I'll substitute my part of the Pareto-superior allocation for my hypothesized equilibrium action if everyone else does; otherwise I'll do what I was doing in the hypothesized equilibrium." The others in the ruling class will similarly enhance their utilities by following with equivalent statements. The reason these utility enhancements arise is that the non-ruling class members will then rationally choose their appropriate actions and thereby move the society to the Pareto superior allocation. So the strategy of the top member of the ruling class in the hypothesized equilibrium is not a utility-maximizing strategy and the hypothesized equilibrium cannot represent a genuine equilibrium. The genuine static equilibrium must therefore be Pareto optimal.

Note that the above reasoning, originally produced under conditions of complete information about the preferences of others, obviously does not change when we replace the known utilities described above with objectively expected utilities and define Pareto optimality in terms of objectively expected rather than realized utilities.

While the Foster–Young (Foster and Young, 1990) assumptions on the nature of random variations are overly simple and the corresponding convergence theorem is not robust to some reasonable statistical generalizations (e.g., Kandori, Mailath, and Rob, (Kandori, Mailath, and Rob, 1993) and Fudenberg and Harris) (Fudenberg and Harris, 1992), it is difficult to relate the corresponding non-Nash ("risk-dominant") equilibria to either social equilibria or informationally constrained Pareto optimality. Although such an exercise will have to await future discussions, a plausible conjecture would be that the more informationally rich process would similarly convergence to a social optimum under suitably generalized definitions of social equilibrium and uncertainty-constrained social optimality.

4. Applications of the Social Evolutionary Optimality Theorem

4.1. Social Darwinism

Applying Darwinian selection to an entire society, and correspondingly arguing for the efficiency of a social–evolutionary equilibrium, has a shady past. The first application was by Herbert Spencer, a sociologist who, years before Darwin's "Origin of the Species, began pioneering a highly influential intellectual movement later called "Social Darwinism." Spencer was so impressed with the social–evolutionary equilibrium and the selection process that aided in its achievement that he regarded every attempt to help the weakest adults as an unfortunate delay in the achievement of an ideal society. If a society's least productive adults starved in the cold, it was a good thing because it hastened our move to a productive long-run equilibrium. Of course, the social–evolutionary optimality theorem has no such implication. Depending on human sympathy and the costs of social insurance, the efficient equilibrium that the society is approaching may be extremely compassionate. Moreover, even if the long-run equilibrium lacks both sympathy and social insurance, there is no apparent externality to suggest that the dynamic process leading to the long-run equilibrium is economically inefficient.

Spencer is actually the first in a long and crowded line of "cultural evolutionists," non-economists who generally lack the sophistication to deal with the normative aspects of their subject and whose economic errors are too numerous to discuss in a mere encyclopedia entry.

An economic journalist, Walter Bagehot (Bagehot, 1872), subsequently adopted a Darwinian view of international competition and thereby founded the "Struggle School" of sociology. Here, since the beginnings of society, there has been a survival of the fittest occurring in a hypothesized race in which the militarily strongest state eventually devours the others. Besides ignoring the ability to form alliances and possible diseconomies of scale, Bagehot's argument, like Spencer's, ignores the possibly excessive short-run costs of competing for the conjectured long-run gain. The argument was nevertheless popularly used to somehow rationalize British imperialism.

Finally, early in the 20th century, a Social Darwinist argument for eugenics, or "Reform Darwinism," arose. Like the other forms of Social Darwinism, this argument ruthlessly disregards the present on the basis of a hypothesis the long run will be dominated by states with a superior kind of people. Even if the conjectured long-run benefit were correct, there is no reason that a society would want to pay the costs of rushing to achieve it. Like the other forms of Social Darwinism, no dynamic failure is identified that would justify hastening the achievement of the hypothesized equilibrium. The unjustified eugenics of Hitler's Nazism was, of course, a substantial motivating factor in WWII. The fact that the Nazis lost has fortunately given eugenics, and Social Darwinism itself, such a bad name that the various postwar Social Darwinist movements have garnered but few respectable supporters.

Fortunately, professional economists have rarely adopted Social Darwinism in any form.

4.2. Applied Austrianism: A Preliminary Inspection

The most frequent application of the social–evolutionary optimality theorem by economists is, as we have indicated, extreme skepticism with respect to theory-based arguments for basic social reform. Although, logically, a novel theory might improve things, the Austrians and their optimality theorem are pointing to the high opportunity cost of theory-based reforms. Nevertheless, since almost all theory-based social reforms are reversible experiments, it is difficult to come up with an empirically persuasive Austrian policy argument.

Moreover, any Austrian policy application is necessarily a negative one: It is impossible to use the theorem to significantly reform social institutions. For all institutions are endogenous in the model and steadily evolve toward efficiency.

A more general, inefficiency-generating, evolutionary model is therefore necessary if the model is to generate positive policy applications.

4.2.1. A More General Evolutionary Model
4.2.1.1 Ideology.
Recall that objectivity was required of the learning process that enabled the ruling class to select institutions that converged to a Pareto optimum. How would members of a ruling class, whose individual utilities increase with the efficiency of the institutions they select, become non-objective in evaluating alternative institutions? The answer is that their teachers are not objective. Why would teachers be non-objective? The answer is that the teachers have formed a unified intellectual cartel that collectively biases the information that they disseminate in a direction that increases the demand for their services as teachers and government advisors.

Now the normal activities of many teachers include cultural training, which creates in students the values that make them suitable for ruling-class positions by inducing them to carry out whatever their utility-maximizing commitments happen to be. Such training requires teachers to adopt various exaggerations, which in turn require an intellectual cartel of teachers, or "school," to protect their exaggerations from the objectively justifiable skepticism of maverick teachers. Religious training is an example. But there are many others. Good business schools teach responsible business values, values that enable business leaders to attract workers, consumers, and investors. Economics and related policy subjects represent a significant exception in that ruling class evaluations of alternative institutions must be objective if efficiency is to be obtained. Whether or not a school's subjects require exaggerations in order to efficiently supply the market, as long as the various schools compete, whatever exaggerations they do teach can be counted on to generate values that maximize the utilities of the students.

However, if the schools within a field of knowledge combine into a single cartel, a professional organization with its own internal hierarchy and therefore joint-utility-maximizing organizational strategies, then the benefits of the members of the future ruling class will be traded-off against the benefits of the members of the profession. We should then expect the institutional evaluations of the students to be biased in a teacher-serving direction. When this happens, in other words, when the ruling class is captured by an "ideology," then the objective learning condition for an optimum is no longer satisfied.

While a Pareto optimum cannot be expected, it would be difficult to apply the resulting evolutionary model if ideology led to an incoherent, essentially unstable, society rather than an alternative, rapidly achieved, "ideologized" equilibrium. The existence of such an equilibrium can be established by introducing "vital institutions" into the environment. Vital institutions, such as adequate national defense expenditures, do two things. First, they greatly hasten the dynamic process by rapidly eliminating the entire set of inherently inefficient states that are incapable of generating them. Second, although ideology works by leading the ruling class to violate payoff-positivity by inducing them to reject objectively profitable institutions in favor of ideologue-benefiting institutions, no substantial bias can survive with respect to the choice of vital institutions. Hence, there are always some strategies for which payoff-positivity holds, *some* strategies such that relatively high payoffs imply increasing frequencies of the strategies. This is important because the general Weibull theorem that we have been using states that a Nash equilibrium will also be asymptotically approached if only *some* of the equilibrium strategies are payoff-positive. Hence, acknowledging the existence of vital institutions insures a rapid convergence to a static equilibrium despite its ideology-created inefficiencies.

4.2.1.2. Basic Applications.
Ideologies can be classified into two types, those that do not attack vital institutions and those that do. The former ideologies, exemplified by law and political science, are pragmatic in that the ideologues proceed by empirical observation on real world experiments with various institutional reforms. Such ideologies quickly eliminate any idea that attack a society's vital institutions because, despite the potential universal character of their ideas, it is surely not in their interest have one of their supporting societies fail. Such ideologies can therefore become "deeply rooted" in the states that adopt them. Thus, the basic forms of ancient Greek democracy and of ancient Roman law represent the founding political and legal ideologies of the modern West. Now when several ideologized nations militarily compete, those whose profession-serving ideas work to *most severely bias* the state towards military effectiveness are those that will win the competition for ultimate acceptance in the ideologized evolutionary equilibrium. Such institutions can thus be expected to be grossly inefficient.

The way to eliminate such "deeply rooted" ideologies (e.g., the militarization of youth) is to counter-educate the ruling classes, making them aware of the nature and cause of the gross legal and political inefficiencies that surround them. In the process, the society would eliminate the professional associations generating these ideas, leaving an environment in which domestic intellectuals compete by producing ideas that benefit the state rather than their professions.

Such idealistic reforms would represent great victories for insight over evolution.

Economic ideology, always noted for its abstract, theoretical, boldly reforming, character, has typically come to attack the vital institutions of its society by reforming institutions that, unbeknownst to the economists, have been vital to their societies. The result is that economics has been a perishable ideology in comparison to the more pragmatic fields of politics and law. Thus, ancient Greco-Roman economic ideology, by following the monetary theories of Plato and Aristotle, led the Ancient Roman empire to a 3rd century monetary reform that permanently eliminated the Empire's ability to issue seignorage-generating money, not understanding that the reason a government produces such money in the first place is to finance vital warfare. So, while states that retained Greco-Roman politics and legal ideologies were able to survive the dark ages, those retaining their economic ideologies did not. Similarly, soon after the rise of late Renaissance ideology, which elevated artists over merchants and thereby attacked guild entry restrictions in the name of domestic competition, began to "succeed" in eliminating guild entry restrictions, one by one, the states lost both their independence and their internal dominance by economic ideologues. Again unbeknownst to the deregulating ideologues, these entry restrictions had long been a vital source of guild military support during defensive emergencies. So early modernity witnessed a sharp shift toward Germanic pragmatism and mercantilism. The reason mercantilism was efficient solution was that it used high tariffs to appropriately internalize the externality that consumer durable imports have on a region's defense cost. These tariffs have indeed been vital to countries that face exceptionally high defense-externalities because of internal as well as external military threats. Led by the Physiocrats, the first organized school of economists in the modern period, the Enlightenment eliminated simple pragmatism, ideologizing its unfortunate victims into abandoning their mercantile protections. This leads us to the French Revolution and Mr. Burke, who laid the foundations of the ideology-ignoring Austrian argument.

Hence, rather than simply continuing or detailing the above time-line (which is done in Thompson–Hickson), we now take the opportunity to take a closer look at Austrianism in historical perspective.

4.3. A Critique of Applied Austrianism

The social–evolutionary optimality theorem, and applied Austrianism as well, fail to consider ideology. As a result, Austrians have failed to see that more general evolutionary theories, theories that recognize the perverse nature of certain evolutionary processes, may be useful in, and sometimes even necessary to, the elimination of evolutionary traps.

First consider Burke and Menger. Both had actively participated in a generation-long series of steadily expanding, free-market-ideology-based, economic reforms. Then, in the face of sudden, popularly acknowledged, evidence of the high social costs of these free-trade policies, and correspondingly sudden reforms to quickly eliminate them, they strenuously appealed to the benefits of political and economic gradualism. In retrospect, then, rather than appropriately pleading for de-ideologization, Burke and Menger worked perversely to *oppose* the appropriate operation of efficiency-generating, economically de-ideologizing, evolutionary processes.

Thus, although Burke ostensibly opposed the French Revolution because of its sudden imposition of an abstract theory on an efficient evolutionary equilibrium, the Revolution he was decrying was actually beneficial because it was *against* the theory-extolling ideologues that had, for 20 years, been capturing the French aristocracy and creating excessively laissez faire policies.

Menger's approval of the free market ideologization that had been steadily growing in France and Austria during the 1850s and early '60s led him to ignore the fact that their late '60s military failures were attributable to their extreme free market policies. So, when he saw the pragmatic German reaction to the policy failures, he reacted just as did Burke, with an appeal to gradualism that ignored the fact that the German reaction was actually a conservative movement back to an earlier, long evolved, equilibrium. As in the case of Burke, it was *appropriate* that the sudden learning of the failures of a recent ideology led to a sharp reaction against that ideology.

Hayek, Mises, and Schumpeter vociferously reacted against the egalitarian policy shocks that followed WWs I and II. Such egalitarian shocks are actually quite appropriate reflections of the domestic gratitude felt for their sacrificing masses after an expensive war fought largely by citizen soldiers, the apparent "redistributions" effecting a vital reward for successful wartime sacrifices. Because such gratitude payments — although a historical regularity in Western Europe and a result of efficiently evolved political institutions — are not part of economic ideology, these 20th century Austrian economists perversely considered them to be devastating *attacks* on the long-evolved distributional equilibrium and incorrectly predicted dire consequences.

Summarizing then, social evolutionary models ignoring the profound effects of ideology on the nature of evolutionary equilibria lead to perverse empirical beliefs. In particular, while ideology-ignoring models lead to extreme skepticism with respect to the role of theory in reforming our deeply rooted political and legal institutions, the serious inefficiencies that have predictably evolved in these long-ideologized fields can only be eliminated with a theory-based victory of insight over evolution. And while ideology-ignoring evolutionary models allow economists to freely indulge a cartel-distorted worldview that artificially increases the demand for their advice, ideology-recognizing economists admit the frequent disasters created by established economics and appreciate the ability of their highly evolved governments to solve many economic problems without the help of economists.

EARL THOMPSON

REFERENCES

Aristotle (Ca. 350 BC). *The Physics*, Books 4–8. Translated by H.P. Cooke, Cambridge, Mass, 1926.

Bagehot, Walter (1872). *Physics and Politics*. London.

Burke, Edmund (1790). *Reflections on the Revolution in France*. London.

Comte, Auguste (1854). *The Positive Philosophy*. New York.

Condorcet, Marie-Jean-Antoine (1795). *Sketch for a Historical Picture of the Human Mind*. Paris.

Darwin, Charles Robert (1859). *Origin of Species by Means of Natural Selection*. London.

Empedocles (Ca. 443 BC). *Peri Phuseos*.

Foster, D. and Young, H.P. (1990). "Stochastic evolutionary game dynamics." *Theoretical Population Biology*, 38: 219-232.

Fudenberg, D. and Harris, C. (1992). "Evolutionary dynamics with aggregate shocks." *Journal of Economic Theory*, 57(August): 420–441.

Hayek, Friedrich von (1973). *Law Legislation & Liberty, Vol. I: Rules and Order*. London & Henley.

Hegel, Georg Wilhelm Fredrick. *Philosophy of History*. Translated by J. Sibree. London, 1861.

Kandori, M., Mailath, G., and Rob, R. (1993). "Learning, mutation, and long run equilibria in games." *Econometrica*, 61: 29–56.

Lamarck, Jean-Baptiste (1809). *Philosophe Zoologique*, Paris. Translated by H. Eliot. London, 1914.

Malthus, Thomas Robert (1798). *An Essay on the Principle of Population*. London.

Menger, Carl (1871). *Principles of Economics*. Translated by Libertarian Press, 1994.

Mises, Ludwig von (1966). *Human Action*. Chicago.

Schumpeter, Joseph A. (1928). "The instability of capitalism." *Economic Journal*, 38: 361–386.

Thompson, E. and Faith, R. (1981). "A pure theory of strategic behavior and social institutions." *American Economic Review*, June: 366–381.

Thompson, E. and Hickson, C. (2001). *Ideology and the Evolution of Vital Institutions*. Boston, Dordrecht, and London.

Vico, Giambattista (1974). *Scienza Nuova*, Third Edition. Rome.

Weibull, Jorgen W. (1995). *Evolutionary Game Theory*. Cambridge MA: Harvard University Press, Ch. 5.

THE EVOLUTION OF LAW

Fuller (1964: 30) defines law as "the enterprise of subjecting human conduct to the governance of rules." Furthermore, Hume (1751) observes that the primary motivation for developing rules is so that individuals can expand wealth in the face of scarcity. Since the impetus for developing markets and law is the same, both evolve spontaneously through similar processes (Menger, 1883; Hayek, 1973; Polanyi, 1951; Benson, 2001). Importantly, however, there are two ways for an individual to expand personal wealth (Oppenheimer, 1908): (1) cooperative "economic" processes such as team production and voluntary exchange; and (2) "political" processes that take wealth produced by others through force (and/or guile). Rules and governance institutions can facilitate either of these means of seeking wealth, so a positive analysis of legal evolution requires consideration of objectives (Benson, 1998, 1999, 2001).

First, consider the evolution of rules and institutions to support Oppenheimer's economic process. Voluntarily recognized "trust rules" involve explicit or implicit agreements to adopt predictable behavioral patterns or "norms" in dealings with a limited number of identified individuals. As Vanberg and Buchanan (1990: 18) explain "Because compliance and non-compliance with trust rules are... 'targeted,' the possibility exists of forming cooperative clusters." Compliance can be made credible by threats of violent retaliation, but if individuals realize that significant benefits can arise from an ongoing relationship a rule violation can be "corrected" through "tit-for-tat" rather than through violence. As more bilateral relationships are formed and a loose knit group with intermeshing reciprocities begins to develop, competitive options for beneficial interaction arise. Thus, individuals can cooperate unconditionally with anyone known to be trustworthy, while refusing to interact with anyone known to have violated a trust rule (Vanberg and Congelton, 1992). If information spreads quickly and everyone spontaneously responds to a rule violation, the violator is excluded from all interaction in the community. Communication mechanisms can substitute for investments in capacities for violence as "solidarity rules" (obligations that are expected to be followed by all members of a group because compliance benefits everyone; Vanberg and Buchanan, 1990)-like "inform your neighbors about individuals who violate trust rules" and "ostracize untrustworthy individuals," spontaneously evolve. Related rules like "watch out for your neighbor" tend to follow and cooperation in watching to prevent theft, and in pursuit when a theft occurs is common for close-knit groups (Benson, 1992). Individuals who do not follow solidarity rules are also ostracized, undermining free-rider incentives.

Disputes inevitably arise. They can be resolved by violent "prosecution", but this can have significant negative spillover costs, particularly if opinions regarding guilt are mixed. These costs can be reduced by developing non-violent means of resolving disagreements, and by making acceptance of a judgement relatively attractive for the loser. For instance, a reputable member of the community might be chosen as a mediator or arbitrator. Since this third party must be acceptable to both disputants, "fairness" is embodied in the dispute-resolution process. An offender may also be allowed to buy his way back into the community by paying an appropriate restitution. Numerous historical and anthropological studies demonstrate that restitution and voluntary third-party dispute resolution are common institutions in close-knit groups' legal systems (Pospisil, 1971; Benson, 1991, 1992). All such institutional developments tend to be spontaneous and unplanned, but the result is a movement toward increasingly secure private property rights under "customary law" (Fuller, 1964, 1981; Benson, 1999, 2001). Indeed, "There is abundant evidence that a ... group need not make a conscious decision to establish private property rights .... People who repeatedly interact can generate institutions through communication, monitoring, and sanctioning .... without an initial conclave" (Ellickson, 1993: 1366).

Polanyi (1951: 165) stresses that the evolving spontaneous order in legal rules and institutions also may be "based on persuasion." The capacity for persuasion is likely to depend on a perception that the person is wise which in turn suggests that leadership tends to fall to productive *and* trustworthy individuals with whom others can interact in joint production or trade (Pospisil, 1971; Benson, 1999). Such "leaders" need to have no special power or authority to enforce rules. Maintenance of a network of trust is sufficient for group members to respect the leader's opinion.

Different communities may compete for the same scarce resources but they also may provide opportunities for mutually advantageous cooperation (Benson, 1995b). Even in primitive societies, extensive trade networks cross community boundaries, for instance (Benson, 1991; Ridley, 1996: 195–211), but as such arrangements evolve they also require rules and governance to function effectively. An entirely common set of rules governing all types of interaction need not be accepted, however. Individuals only have to expect each other to recognize trust rules pertaining to the types of inter-group interactions (e.g., trade) that evolve. Indeed, a "jurisdictional hierarchy" often arises wherein each group has its own norms for intra-group relationships, with a separate and possibly different set of rules applying for inter-group relations (Pospisil, 1971; Benson, 1991, 1992). Many intra-group norms will be commonly held, of course, and emulation also will occur where differences initially exist but individuals observe and perceive superior arrangements among other groups, so the evolution of common norms recognized and applied in a very extensive web of communities is clearly possible (e.g., Benson, 1989; Putnam, 1993). In other words, cooperation is one potential outcome for inter-group relations too, although the transactions costs of such cooperation are obviously relatively high, so inter-group conflict can also be expected.

Suppose that an individual has a significant comparative advantage in violence and chooses to take wealth produced by others. The result is a "negative sum" undertaking since the transfer process and any efforts to resist it consume resources that could be used to create new wealth (Tullock, 1967). Nonetheless, an individual with a comparative advantage in violence may expect to be better off by taking other's wealth than by cooperating, producing, and trading.

Given that information spreads, the individual who employs a comparative advantage in violence develops a reputation for doing so. Such a reputation can be quite valuable, as increasingly, the threat of violence alone may be sufficient to extort transfers without physically taking them. Once such a reputation develops, however, the potential for entering cooperative relationships is reduced, as anyone with whom the extortionist does not have a prior trust arrangement will not believe the extortionist's promises (Tullock, 1985). Therefore, the decision to take wealth often involves a permanent commitment to extortionist behavior, creating incentives to establish an environment that will produce a steady stream of transfers from those subjected to threats. Oppenheimer (1908) contends that the origins of the earliest states trace to precisely this situation, as nomadic hunting and/or herding communities from the relatively unfertile mountains, deserts, or sea coasts, invaded populated fertile valleys, setting up a "protection racket" (also see Carneiro, 1970; Levi, 1988: 110). Among other things, this implies that the extortionist will attempt to establish a monopoly in violence and in "law". After all, if a target for extortion can turn to another specialist in violence for help, or to a cooperative group jointly producing protection, then the extortionist's ability to extract wealth is severely limited. Thus, the extortionist must erect barriers to exit from his jurisdiction (Carneiro, 1970).

The scale of violence required to compete for and maintain power will be greater than a single individual can produce, of course, so extortionists generally establish "protection firms" for cooperative joint production. In fact, historically many examples of organized aggression involved cooperative communities with established trust relationships such as those described above, who were persuaded by an entrepreneurial "leader" (e.g., tribal war chief) that they could expand their wealth at relatively low costs through conquest.

An extortionist can also reduce the incentives for competition or resistance by transferring some wealth or a local sub-jurisdiction to potentially powerful individuals in *exchange* for an agreement to honor his jurisdictional claims. As a result, the protection racket can involve a mix of extortion of the weak and protection for the relatively powerful, and hierarchical jurisdictions that share the proceeds. In order to maintain power, extortionists also have incentives to redistribute wealth as the relative power of subgroups within his jurisdiction changes. Thus, incentives to compete for favorable treatment arise, and by focusing such competition in "advisory councils" or "representative assemblies," the cost of gathering information about the relative power of groups is reduced, as is the cost of interacting with powerful groups. An effective extortionist might also be able to simultaneously lower the cost of ruling and legitimize his claim as the monopoly source of rules by establishing adjudication backed by threats of violence, in order to divert disputes over distributional issues and to substitute for customary dispute-resolution procedures.

The potential for transfer means that all property is in a common pool open to political competition, although security of property assignments varies considerably depending on relative political power. Furthermore, large levels of extortion in the short term reduce wealth creation and the potential for transfers over the long run. Therefore, with any time horizon at all, the extortionist is likely to recognize some private property rights and allow some cooperative organizations in order to create incentives to produce wealth. His "law" must be above the norms generated by other institutions, but he is likely to claim to be the source of many laws adopted from cooperative groups, because they are low cost mechanisms for facilitating wealth creation. Thus, for instance, many early codes by kings were largely codifications of custom with modifications dictating distributional issues (Benson, 1989, 1992). However, as Hayek (1973: 51) explains, "spontaneous order arises from each element balancing all the various factors operating on it and by adjusting all its various actions to each other, a balance which will be destroyed if some of the actions are determined by another agency on the basis of different knowledge and in the service of different ends." A designed order cannot be replaced by a spontaneous order though, as

knowledge is incomplete for the rule maker (Hayek, 1973; Kirzner, 1985), and policing is imperfect (Benson, 2002). Thus, deliberate efforts to impose rules create incentives to find and exploit the uncontrolled margins in order to avoid the full consequences of the rules (Cheung, 1974; Kirzner, 1985; Benson, 2002). Rule makers are likely to respond with new institutions intended to block such maneuvers, but those subject to such legislation react again, leading to more blocking efforts, and so on. In other words, intentionally created rules also evolve, although the evolution is path dependant. As Kirzner (1985: 141–144) explains, discoveries which probably would have been made in the absence of deliberately imposed rules are not made, but a "wholly superfluous" discovery process develops in pursuit of "entirely new and not necessarily desirable opportunities for entrepreneurial discovery."

The extortionists efforts also stifle the development of trust relationships, as the honoring of any commitment tends to be perceived as arising primarily because of the deterrent effect of threatened sanctions from the sovereign. Therefore, fewer voluntary organizations are formed. Even in a society with a very strong extortionist ruler, however, some cooperative groups always remain. These groups still follow their own norms, even when doing so violates the extortionist's "law", although the customary rules that persist among close knit groups can change in light of the coercive efforts (e.g., "opposition norms" arise; Nee, 1998). Still, numerous examples of centralized coercive systems can be cited where "parallel" predominately cooperative systems of norms and institutions actually dominate many and at times even most interactions (e.g., de Soto, 1989; Acheson, 1988; Ellickson, 1991; Benson, 1989, 1995a; Bernstein, 1992). This is not surprising since the monopolized "law" serves many conflicting functions, simultaneously harassing and protecting private interests, extorting wealth and encouraging its production, maintaining the class structure and cutting across classes, integrating parts of society and disintegrating other parts. Law (in a positive sense) and justice (in a normative sense) clearly are not synonymous.

BRUCE L. BENSON

REFERENCES

Acheson, J.M. (1988). *The Lobster Gangs of Maine.* Hanover, NH: University Press of New England.

Benson, B.L. (1989). "The spontaneous evolution of commercial law." *Southern Economic Journal,* 55: 644–661.

Benson, B.L. (1991). "An evolutionary contractarian view of primitive law: the institutions and incentives arising under customary American Indian law." *Review of Austrian Economics,* 5: 65–89.

Benson, B.L. (1992). "The development of criminal law and its enforcement: public interest or political transfers." *Journal des Economistes et des Etudes Humaines*, 3: 79–108.

Benson, B.L. (1995a). "An exploration of the impact of modern arbitration statutes on the development of arbitration in the United States." *Journal of Law, Economics, and Organization*, 11: 479–501.

Benson, B.L. (1995b). "Competition among legal institutions: implications for the evolution of law," in L. Gerken (ed.) *Competition Among Institutions*, London: Macmillan, pp. 153–175.

Benson, B.L. (1998). "Economic freedom and the evolution of law." *Cato Journal*, 18(2): 209–232.

Benson, B.L. (1999). "An economic theory of the evolution of governance and the emergence of the state." *Review of Austrian Economics*, 12(2): 131–160.

Benson, B.L. (2001). "Law and economics," in W.F. Shughart II and L. Razzolini (eds.) *The Elgar Companion to Public Choice*, London: Edward Elgar, pp. 547–589.

Benson, B.L. (2002). "Regulatory disequilibrium and inefficiency: the case of interstate trucking." *Review of Austrian Economics*, 15(2–3).

Bernstein, L. (1992). "Opting out of the legal system: extralegal contractual relations in the diamond industry." *Journal of Legal Studies*, 21: 115–158.

Carneiro, R.L. (1970). "A theory of the origin of the state." *Science*, 169: 733–738.

Cheung, S.N.S. (1974). "A theory of price control." *Journal of Law and Economics*, 17: 53–72.

De Soto, H. (1989). *The Other Path: The Invisible Revolution in the Third World*. New York: Harper & Row.

Ellickson, R.C. (1993). "Property in land." *Yale Law Journal*, 102: 1315–1400.

Fuller, L. (1964). *The Morality of Law*. New Haven: Yale University Press.

Hayek, F.A. (1973). *Law, Legislation, and Liberty*, Volume 1. Chicago: University of Chicago Press.

Hume, D. (1957 [1751]) in Hendel, C.W. (ed.) *An Inquiry Concerning the Principles of Morals*. Indianapolis: Bobbs-Merrill.

Kirzner, I.M. (1985). *Discovery and the Capitalist Process*. Chicago: University of Chicago Press.

Levi, M. (1988). *Of Rule and Revenue*. Berkeley, CA: University of California Press.

Menger, C. ([1963] 1883) in F.J. Nook (Tr.), L. Schneider (ed.) *Problems of Economics and Sociology*. Urbana, IL: University of Illinois Press.

Nee, V. (1998). "Norms and networks in economic and organizational performance." *American Economic Review Papers and Proceedings*, 88: 85–89.

Oppenheimer, F. (1914 [1908]), J.M. Gitterman (Tr.) *The State: Its History and Development Viewed Sociologically*. Indianapolis: Bobbs-Merrill.

Polanyi, M. (1951). *The Logic of Liberty: Reflections and Rejoinders*. Chicago: University of Chicago Press.

Pospisil, L. (1971). *Anthropology of Law: A Comparative Theory*. New York: Harper and Row.

Putnam, R.D. (1993). *Making Democracy Work: Civil Traditions in Modern Italy*. Princeton, NJ: Princeton University Press.

Ridley, M. (1996). *The Origins of Virtue: Human Instincts and the Evolution of Cooperation*. New York: Viking Penguin.

Tullock, G. (1967). "The welfare costs of tariffs, monopolies and theft." *Western Economic Journal*, 5: 224–232.

Tullock, G. (1985). "Adam Smith and the prisoners' dilemma." *Quarterly Journal of Economics*, 100: 1073–1081.

Vanberg, V.J. and Buchanan, J.M. (1990). "Rational choice and moral order," in Nichols, J.H., Jr. and Wright, C. (eds.) *From Political Economy to Economics and Back?* San Francisco: Institute for Contemporary Studies.

Vanberg, V.J. and Congleton, R.D. (1992). "Rationality, morality and exit." *American Political Science Review*, 86: 418–431.

EXPERIMENTAL ECONOMICS AND PUBLIC CHOICE

There is a well-established tradition of using laboratory techniques to study issues in public choice, dating back to the 1970s. For example, Fiorina and Plott (1978) and Plott and Levine (1978) reported results of voting experiments, and Bohm (1972) used an experimental approach to estimate demand for public goods. This connection is reflected in the fact that the Economic Science Association (of experimental social scientists) meets jointly with the Public Choice Society each spring in the United States. This chapter provides a selective survey of experiments on public goods, common pool resources, rent seeking, and voting.

Experiments have revealed that people do free ride on others' contributions to public goods, but the problem is not as severe as economists once thought. A typical public goods experiment involves a group of people who must decide whether to contribute to a group project or account. For example, Ensminger (2001) divided a sample of East African men into groups of four. Each person was given 50 shillings and offered the opportunity to contribute some, all, or none to a "group project." The men placed their contributions in envelopes that were collected and shuffled (to preserve anonymity) and counted in front of the group. All contributions were doubled and then divided equally among the four participants. For example, a contribution of 10 shillings would be doubled to 20 and divided 4 ways, for a return of 5 shillings per person. Therefore, the individual receives a private benefit of $\frac{1}{2}$ for each shilling contributed to the group project. In the public goods literature, this private benefit is called the marginal per capita return (MPCR).

With a group of size N, the social benefit for each shilling contributed to the group project is N times the

MPCR. There is a social dilemma when the MPCR is less than 1 and greater than 1/N, which is typically the case for a public goods experiment. With a group of size 4 and an MPCR of $\frac{1}{2}$, Ensminger observed that about 60 percent of the shilling endowments were contributed to the group project. This contribution level is slightly higher than the 40 to 60 percent range that is commonly observed in the first round of a public goods experiment involving college students in the United States (Anderson, 2001; Ledyard, 1995).

Nearly 200 public goods experiments have been conducted (see the Y2K Bibliography of Experimental Economics at http://www.people.virginia.edu/~cah2k/y2k.htm). The main finding is that significant contributions are observed despite the individual incentive to free ride. Economists have designed experiments with a variety of treatments to better understand motives for contributing. Altruism provides one possible explanation, since contributions may be rational if enough utility is derived from helping others. Many studies have shown that an increase in the MPCR raises contributions, but the interpretation of this result is complicated by the fact that the MPCR affects both one's private return (the "internal return") and the benefit to others (the "external return"). It is possible to hold the internal return constant (e.g., at $\frac{1}{2}$) and increase the external return for each token contributed (e.g., $\frac{3}{4}$). Goeree et al. (2002) report that contributions are positively related to the external return, holding the internal return constant. Not surprisingly, contributions are also positively related to the internal return. Another implication of altruism is that contributions will be higher as the number of beneficiaries (i.e., group size) increases, and this is supported by a number of studies. These results are summarized in the first four rows of Table 1.

All of the experiments discussed thus far were done for a single round. In a multi-round experiment some people might reciprocate by contributing more in response to cooperative actions of others. Such reciprocity also opens up the possibility for strategic behavior, where a person might contribute more in early rounds to encourage others to do the same. This explanation is consistent with the observation that contributions decline with repetition. Contributions are also somewhat lower for people who have participated in a public goods experiment on a previous date. Despite the negative effect of repetition and experience on contribution rates, some people contribute in all rounds.

Another explanation for positive contributions is that people do not want to appear to be stingy to the researcher, who generally tracks each individual's contributions. This explanation is not supported by the work of Laury et al. (1995), who ran parallel treatments; in one case they tracked individual contributions and in the other they did not. Contributions have also been observed to depend on factors such as the ability of subjects to communicate in advance, the presence of a required level of contribution (provision point), and the ability to exclude or punish non-contributors.

Just as a contribution to a public good provides a positive externality, the use of a common pool resource provides a negative externality by reducing the value to other users. A classic example of a common pool resource is a fishery, where an increase in one person's harvest may reduce the productivity of others' fishing efforts. In a standard common pool resource experiment, each person chooses a level of effort (or usage), and the average product is a decreasing function of the sum of all efforts. Alternatively, each person can allocate effort to a private investment that has a fixed return. This is analogous to a Cournot model where individuals ignore the negative externalities associated with their own quantity decisions, and the resulting Nash equilibrium quantity is too high relative to the socially optimal level. Gardner et al. (1990) report that aggregate usage is higher than the socially optimal level and is often close to the Nash equilibrium prediction, but there is considerable variability in behavior across individuals. Many people devote all effort to the common pool resource as long as the average product exceeds the private return and otherwise switch all effort to the private investment. Over thirty papers on this topic can be found at http://www.people.virginia.edu/~cah2k/y2k.htm. Many papers examine factors that mitigate the amount of overuse, such as communication and monitoring.

Another topic that has been investigated with experimental methods is the effect of rent-seeking activities. The standard rent-seeking experiment is based on the simplest Tullock (1980) model in which the probability of obtaining a prize is equal to one's share of the total lobbying activity. Each subject chooses a level of lobbying activity, and the payoff is the prize, if it is obtained, minus the person's own

Table 1: Treatment effects in public goods experiments

Variable	Study	Effect on contribution rates
MPCR	Isaac and Walker (1988)	Positive
Internal return	Goeree et al. (2002)	Positive
External return	Goeree et al. (2002)	Positive
Group size	Isaac et al. (1994)	Positive
Repetition	Isaac et al. (1984)	Negative
Experience	Isaac et al. (1984)	Negative
Anonymity	Laury et al. (1995)	None
Communication	Isaac and Walker (1988)	Positive

lobbying cost. In a Nash equilibrium for this game, the fraction of the value of the prize that is dissipated is an increasing function of the number of competitors. Experiments show that the total cost of rent-seeking activity is significant and greater than predicted in a Nash equilibrium (Millner and Pratt, 1989, 1991; Davis and Reilly, 1998). Moreover, an increase in the number of contenders tends to raise the total cost of this rent-seeking activity (Holt, 2002, Ch. 29; Anderson and Stafford, 2002).

One area of public choice where there has been a considerable amount of disagreement is voting behavior. As a consequence, this is a fruitful area for experimental research. Early voting experiments focused on testing theoretical concepts, such as the core. Support for this notion is reported in Fiorina and Plott (1978) and Plott (1991). Subsequent studies investigated whether or not voters behave strategically in agenda-controlled committee meetings. Strategic voting requires that decisions made in the initial stages of a meeting are rational given correct expectations about what will happen in subsequent stages. Not surprisingly, subjects tend to behave more myopically in such situations (Plott and Levine, 1978). Strategic voting is more likely to arise after subjects have gained considerable experience in prior meetings (Eckel and Holt, 1989). Additionally, a considerable amount of strategic voting has been observed in single-stage voting games where backward induction is not required (Rapoport et al., 1991). Recent voting experiments have studied alternatives to majority rule. For example, Forsythe et. al. (1996) compared voting outcomes with majority rule, Borda rule and approval voting. Additionally, McKelvey and Palfrey (1998) compared outcomes with unanimity versus majority rule.

A number of excellent survey papers and collected volumes cover the topics discussed above in more depth. Ledyard (1995) is the standard reference for public goods experiments. Holt and Laury (2002) survey the more recent research on treatment effects in public goods experiments. Kinder and Palfrey (1993) is a collection of experimental papers on various topics in political science including survey-based experiments and bureaucratic agenda control. Finally, many of the experiments described above have been adapted for classroom use: Holt and Laury (1997) for public goods, Holt and Anderson (1999) for strategic voting, Goeree and Holt (1999) for rent seeking, Anderson and Stafford (2001) for tradable pollution permits, and Hewett et al. (2002) for the Tiebout hypothesis and the median voter theorem. Web-based versions of many of these experiments can be found at http://veconlab.econ.virginia.edu/admin.htm.

LISA R. ANDERSON

CHARLES A. HOLT

REFERENCES

Anderson, L. (2001). "Public choice as an experimental science," in W. Shugart and L. Razzolini (eds.) *The Elgar Companion to Public Choice*. Northampton, MA: Edward Elgar Publishing, Ch. 23.

Anderson, L. and Stafford, S. (2001). "Choosing winners and losers in a permit trading game." *Southern Economic Journal*, 67(1): 212–219.

Anderson, L. and Stafford, S. (2002). "An experimental analysis of rent seeking under varying competitive conditions." *Public Choice*, (forthcoming).

Bohm, P. (1972). "Estimating demand for public goods: an experiment." *European Economic Review*, 3(2): 111–130.

Davis, D. and Reilly, R. (1998). "Do too many cooks always spoil the stew? An experimental analysis of rent-seeking and the role of a strategic buyer." *Public Choice*, 95(1–2): 89–115.

Eckel, C. and Holt, C.A. (1989). "Strategic voting in agenda-controlled committee experiments." *American Economic Review*, 79(4): 763–773.

Ensminger, J. (2001). "Market integration and fairness: evidence from ultimatum, dictator, and public goods experiments in East Africa," Discussion Paper, California Institute of Technology.

Fiorina, M.P. and Plott, C.R. (1978). "Committee decisions under majority rule: an experimental study." *American Political Science Review*, 72(2): 575–598.

Forsythe, R., Rietz, T., Myerson, R. and Weber, R. (1996). "An experimental study of voting rules and polls in three-candidate elections." *International Journal of Game Theory*, 25(3): 355–383.

Gardner, R., Ostrom, E. and Walker, J.M. (1990). "The nature of common pool resource problems." *Rationality and Society*, 2: 335–358.

Goeree, J. and Holt, C. (1999). "Classroom games: rent seeking and the inefficiency of non-market allocations." *Journal of Economic Perspectives*, 13(3): 217–226.

Goeree, J., Holt, C., and Laury, S. (2002). "Private costs and public benefits: unraveling the effects of altruism and noisy behavior." *Journal of Public Economics*, 83(2): 257–278.

Hewitt, R., Holt, C., Kosmopoulou, G., Kymn, C., Long, C., Mousavi, S., and Sarang, S. (2002). "Voting with feet and with ballots: a classroom," experiment, Discussion Paper, University of Virginia.

Holt, C. (2002). "Webgames and strategy: recipes for interactive learning," Unpublished manuscript, University of Virginia.

Holt, C.A. and Anderson, L.R. (1999). "Agendas and strategic voting." *Southern Economic Journal*, 65(3): 622–629.

Holt, C.A. and Laury, S.K. (2002). "Theoretical explanations of treatment effects in voluntary contributions experiments," in C.R. Plott and V.L. Smith (eds.) *The Handbook of Experimental Economics Results*. Amsterdam: North-Holland, (forthcoming).

Holt, C. and Laury, S. (1997). "Classroom games: voluntary provision of a public good." *Journal of Economic Perspectives*, 11(4): 209–215.

Isaac, R.M. and Walker, J.M. (1988). "Communication and free-riding behavior: the voluntary contributions mechanism." *Economic Inquiry*, 26(4): 585–608.

Isaac, R.M., Walker, J.M., and Williams, A.W. (1994). "Group size and the voluntary provision of public goods: experimental evidence utilizing large groups." *Journal of Public Economics*, 54(1): 1–36.

Isaac, R.M., Walker, J.M., and Thomas, S.H. (1984). "Divergent evidence on free riding: an experimental examination of possible explanation." *Public Choice*, 43(2): 113–149.

Kinder, D. and Palfrey, T. (eds.) (1993). *Experimental Foundations of Political Science*. Ann Arbor: University of Michigan Press.

Laury, S.K., Walker, J.M., and Williams, A.W. (1995). "Anonymity and the voluntary provision of public goods." *Journal of Economic Behavior and Organization*, 27(3): 365–380.

Ledyard, J. (1995). "Public goods: a survey of experimental research," in J.H. Kagel and A.E. Roth (eds.) *The Handbook of Experimental Economics*. Princeton, NJ: Princeton University Press, pp. 111–194.

McKelvey, R.D. and Palfrey, T.R. (1998). "An experimental study of jury decisions." unpublished manuscript, California Institute of Technology.

Millner, E.L. and Pratt, M.D. (1989). "An experimental investigation of efficient rent seeking." *Public Choice* 62(2): 139–151.

Millner, E.L. and Pratt, M.D. (1991). "Risk aversion and rent seeking: an extension and some experimental evidence." *Public Choice*, 69(1): 91–92.

Plott, C.R. (1991). "A comparative analysis of direct democracy, two-candidate elections and three-candidate elections in an experimental environment," in T. Palfrey (ed.), *Laboratory Research in Political Economy*. Ann Arbor: University of Michigan Press, pp. 11–31.

Plott, C.R. and Levine, M.V. (1978). "A model of agenda influence on committee decisions." *American Economic Review*, 68(1): 146–160.

Rapoport, A., Felsenthal, D.S., and Maoz, Z. (1991). "Sincere versus strategic voting behavior in small groups," in T. Palfrey (ed.) *Laboratory Research in Political Economy*, Ann Arbor: University of Michigan Press, pp. 201–235.

Tullock, G. (1980). "Efficient rent seeking," in J.M. Buchanan, R.D. Tollison, and G. Tullock (eds.) *Toward a Theory of the Rent-Seeking Society*. College Station: Texas A&M University Press, 97–112.

EXPERIMENTAL PUBLIC CHOICE

Experimental public choice is concerned with the application of laboratory methodology to the study of group decision mechanisms for the provision of one or more public goods or common outcomes for each member of a collective composed of N (>1) individuals.

Every group decision mechanism has three primary components:

- a value environment
- an institution
- the behavior of the individuals

In a laboratory experiment we control the first two components and observe the third.

1. Value Environment

This defines the gains from exchange in a collective choice problem. We suppose that each individual i has a payoff, preference or utility function defined over one or more common outcomes to be chosen by the group. Thus, if there is but one public good, X, each individual, i, associates a value, $V_i(X)$, with X that is monotone increasing in units of X. X might be the size of a proposed city library, total \$ appropriations for defense in the federal budget, the outcome of an election between two candidates, with X taking on just two values, candidate A or B, the outcome of a three way senatorial race, the size of a new city opera and music center, the proceeds from a United Fund Drive, and so on. If there are two goods, X and Y, then $V_i(X,Y)$. (X,Y) might be competing alternatives: library and/or opera center, committee appropriations for education and defense. Each individual also has an endowment of a private good that can be contributed to (transformed into) creating the public good(s).

In laboratory experiments monetary rewards are most commonly used to motivate subjects. Thus $V_i(X)$ might be a table for each i associating different final outcomes with corresponding amounts of money that will be paid to i, for example, $V_i(X)$: \$10(1), \$15(2), \$19(3), \$22(4), \$24(5), \$25(6), where the amount earned is stated in dollars for various quantities, 1, 2, 3…6 units of the public good. Values may be negative indicating that the outcome is a public "bad" for some individuals. For example a proposed zoning change may increase the value of some properties, lower the value of others.

2. Institution

The institution defines the message language of the decision mechanism: vote yes or no; vote for one of the following three; choose a level for the public good and a corresponding amount you would be willing to pay if the level is achieved; contribute a sum certain to the Salvation Army. The institution also specifies the rules that define how the messages sent by individuals result in outcomes: the majority of qualified votes cast determine the winner; which of two designs are implemented for the opera center depends on the total funds contributed; an outcome is implemented if and only if the total contributions are not smaller than the cost; Roberts Rules of Order are adopted by a committee. In the literature, institutions are often referred to as "mechanisms."

In a laboratory experiment the rules are defined by the instructions for the experiment and enforced by the experimenter directly, or indirectly by the computer program, if the experiment is computerized as is now common.

3. Behavior

Individuals choose messages, given their value functions and the institution. In experiments the behavioral data are most often used to make comparisons. Does institution A yield more efficient (socially optimal) outcomes then B? Do the data correspond to the predictions of a model, e.g. does the institution exhibit free riding as predicted, or an efficient outcome as predicted? If there are two predictive behavioral models, which one is supported best by the data?

The above principles, as well as some experimental results, will be illustrated with two examples: (1) the voluntary contribution mechanism (VCM) designed to investigate the free rider problem in the provision of a public good (Marwell and Ames, 1979); (2) the "Auction Mechanism" (AM), which has been studied in various forms, but will be illustrated here as a discrete choice problem among referenda.

4. Voluntary Contribution Mechanism

Environment: Let each individual have an initial endowment representing a private good whose value to i is measured in dollars, M_i. A group of N such individuals also has available a public good whose additive value to each i is $(1/N) V(\cdot)$, where $V(\cdot)$ is a strictly increasing function of the total private good allocated to the public use by all members of the collective. If x_i is the amount of the private good retained by i, and $\Sigma_j x_j$ is the total private good spent by all j on the public good then each i associates a value with the two goods $(x_i, \Sigma_j x_j)$ equal to $M_i - x_i + (1/N)V(\Sigma_j x_j)$.

Institution: Let each individual choose a message, x_i, with $M_i \geq x_i \geq 0$, that represents the amount that i voluntarily chooses to contribute to a "group exchange" to be invested in the public good, the remainder, $M_i - x_i$, to be retained in a private exchange or account and paid in cash. Under these rules the individual return from the group exchange is given by $V(\Sigma_j x_j)$, and the total return (experiment earnings) to each individual is

$$E_i = M_i - x_i + (1/N)V(\Sigma_j x_j), \quad \text{for each i, summed over all individuals j.}$$

(Theory of) Behavior: A public goods incentive problem arises in this environment and institution if contributions to the private exchange are individually optimal, but are not optimal for the group. Since the marginal dollar earnings of the individual are given by $E_i' = -1 + (1/N)V'$, we have a public good incentive problem if $(1/N)V' < 1$; i.e., at the margin each dollar transferred from private to group use reduces the earnings of the individual. For example suppose that we have a collective of size $N = 10$ identically endowed persons, with $M_i = M$, and $V = 7.5 \Sigma_j x_j$. Then $(1/N)V' = 0.75$, and each dollar transferred to the group exchange reduces the individual's earnings by $0.25. For each individual it is therefore optimal to contribute nothing to the group exchange, yielding a payoff to i of $E_i = M$. Yet if every individual contributed M to the group exchange, each would earn $E_i = (1/10)7.5(10M) = 7.5M$.

A key parameter in understanding the experimental results in the VCM is the numerical value of $(1/N)V'$ (0.75 in the example). This is called the Marginal Per Capita Return (MPCR) for a contribution to the public good. Note, there is a free rider problem so long as we have $(1/N) < \text{MPCR} < 1$. Hence, if MPCR = 0.75 the theory implies a free rider problem for any $N > 1$.

Behavior in VCM Experiments. Hundreds of VCM experiments have reported comparisons under varying conditions: single versus repeat play, experienced versus inexperienced subjects, variations in N and MPCR, allowing communication (discussion) before each decision period, and so on. Here is a brief, much simplified, summary of the "stylized" results:

1. Free riding occurs in the sense that less than the socially optimal level of the public good is provided, but the "strong" free rider hypothesis, as predicted by the theory, is clearly rejected.

2. Sequential repetition across many periods normally increases free riding. For example in 10 period repetitions contributions in period 1 range from 40–60% of the social optimum and decline to 10–30% by period 10.

3. Using the same group of subjects in a second sequence of periods in the same session, or in a second session, tends to increase free riding.

4. Comparing a high MPCR (0.75) with a low MPCR (0.3), average contributions are greater in the former than the latter.

5. When MPCR is high, contributions actually increase with group size (comparing N = 4, 10 and 40), but the results are much more mixed when MPCR is low.

6. Communication in the form of unstructured discussion tends to increase contributions.

For a more complete summary and evaluation of the large VCM literature see Ledyard (1995).

5. Auction Mechanism

Suppose we have N individuals who must decide among P propositions which one that is to prevail. Relative to the status quo (achieved if none of the P alternatives is chosen) let V_{pi} (which may be positive, negative or zero) be the value of proposition p to individual i in dollars. A negative value for a proposition means that the individual will suffer a loss and must be compensated if she is not to be dispossessed. Let i choose a bid b_{pi} (positive, negative or zero) in dollars indicating how much she is willing to pay (or be compensated) to see p selected. A winning proposition is one for which the (algebraic) sum of the bids is nonnegative and no smaller than the sum of the bids for any other proposition. Then the net value to i of a winning proposition p is equal to

$$V_{pi} - b_{pi}, \quad \text{if } 0 < \Sigma_j b_{pj} \geq \Sigma_j b_{qi}, \quad \text{for all i and all } q \neq p,$$

$$0, \qquad \text{otherwise.}$$

If there is no winning proposition, $\Sigma_j b_{rj} < 0$ for all r, then the status quo is maintained, and relative net value is zero.

For example, consider three propositions and six individuals whose values are given by $(V_{p1}, V_{p2}, \ldots V_{p6})$:

Proposition 1 (5, −30, −30, 25, 25, 0); total = −5

Proposition 2 (60, 5, 5, −10, −10, 55); total = 105

Proposition 3 (−20, 45, 45, 0, 0, −25); total = 45

Proposition 2 clearly provides the greatest total benefit, but each person knows only his or her own private valuations and not those of others. Do groups using the auction mechanism select the best out come? Note that there is a majority rule cycle so that there is no dominant winner in pair wise voting among the alternatives: 2 beats 1, 3 beats 2, and 1 beats 3, in each case by a vote of four to two.

Six experiments have been reported using these parameters (Smith, 1977). In each experiment a maximum number of trials was specified. If on any trial there was no proposition for which the algebraic sum of the bids is positive, then the experiment proceeds to the next trial until the maximum. If on any trial the algebraic sum of the bids was positive for some proposition, the experiment was stopped and each subject was paid the difference between his value and his bid for that proposition. For example, individual 4 in one experiment bid −$35 for winning proposition 2 and collected (−$10) − (−$35) = $25. Five of the six experiments chose Proposition 2. One failed to provide a positive sum of bids on any trial.

The AM operates by unanimous consent. Indeed, in some versions this is made explicit: after each trial if one of the options provides a positive sum of bids all members are allowed to vote, and the decision is final if and only if all vote "yes." (Smith, 1980).

In an AM version of an election between two candidates each voter deposits with the election board a bid amount representing that voter's willingness-to-pay to see his or her favored candidate win. The largest sum of bids determines the winner, and the proceeds are used to compensate the losing voters: the deposit by each loser is returned plus an additional compensation equal to the deposit. Any surplus of winning bids over losing bids can be retained to help pay for the cost of the election, or prorated among the losing bidders in proportion to their amounts bid.

In addition to the experimental public goods literature there is a large literature on voting institutions such as committee choice by majority rule (Fiorina and Plott, 1978); also on agenda and committee choice (Levine and Plott, 1978).

VERNON L. SMITH

REFERENCES

Fiorina, M.P. and Plott, C.R. (1978). "Committee decisions under majority rule: An experimental study." *American Political Science Review*, 72: 575–598.

Isaac, R.M. and Walker, J.M. (1988a). "Group size effects in public goods provision: the voluntary contributions mechanism." *Quarterly Journal of Economics*, 103: 179–200.

Isaac, R.M. and Walker, J.M. (1988b). "Communication and free-riding behavior: the voluntary contributions mechanism." *Economic Inquiry*, 26: 585–608.

Isaac, R.M., Walker, J.M., and Williams, A. (1994). "Group size and the voluntary provision of public goods: experimental evidence utilizing large groups." *Journal of Public Economics*, 54: 432.

Ledyard, J. (1995). "Public goods: a survey of experimental research," in J. Kagel and A. Roth (eds.) *The Handbook of Experimental Economics*, Princeton: Princeton University Press.

Levine, M. and Plott, C.R. (1978). "A model of agenda influence on committee decisions." *American Economic Review*, 68: 146–160.

Marwell, G. and Ames, R.E. (1979). "Experiments on the provision of public goods 1: resources, interest, group size, and the free rider problem." *American Journal of Sociology*, 84: 1335–1360.

Smith, V.L. (1980). "Experiments with a decentralized Mechanism for public good decisions." *American Economic Review*, 70: 584–599.

Smith, V.L. (1997). "The principle of unanimity and voluntary consent in social choice." *Journal of Political Economy*, 85: 1125–1140.

EXPRESSIVE VOTING AND REDISTRIBUTION

Incorporating the possibility that individuals may vote partially as an act of 'expressive behavior' is one of the most promising modern extensions of the rational-voter model. The rational-voter model, founded in the work of Downs (1957), Tullock (1967), and Riker and Ordeshook (1968, 1973), assumes the voting calculus of an individual is a function of both the expected cost and benefit of voting. The cost of voting is traditionally considered to be the opportunity cost of the time, effort, and expenses required to undertake the physical act of casting a vote. As originally developed, the benefit side of the equation includes only factors relating to how much more likely the voter's most preferred outcome is to win the election if the voter chooses to cast a vote. Thus more precisely, the central factor affecting the voting decision of an individual in traditional rational-voter models is the probability that the voter will cast the 'decisive vote.'

Individuals will be more likely to vote as the probability of being the decisive voter increases because a higher probability of being the decisive voter increases the expected benefit of voting. One of the limitations of the rational-voter model is that the probability of being the decisive voter is so low in most real-world elections that the model predicts that very few people would ever turn out to vote. Actual voter turnout in elections is much greater than would be predicted by the traditional rational-voter model. The inability of the rational-voter model to explain why so many individuals vote has become known more generally as the 'paradox of voting.'

One resolution to this paradox is to extend the model in such a way as to allow the voter to receive direct utility from the act of voting itself. The theory of expressive voting, first proposed by Buchanan (1954), and further developed by Tullock (1971) and Brennan and Lomasky (1993), does precisely this. The theory of expressive voting holds that when there is a relatively low probability of casting the decisive vote, individuals will chose to vote as an act of expressive behavior, often voting along ideological or moral lines for what might be considered 'public minded' policies that are apparently against the voter's own narrow personal self interest. In essence, the notion of expressive voting extends the traditional rational-voter model by allowing voters to receive direct utility from the act of voting itself.

At first glance, the motives of a typical voter seem to run counter to the theory of expressive voting. After all, why should an individual vote in favor of a public-minded policy if it is against their own personal self interest? Tullock (1971, p. 387) explains that the answer may be found in an individual's attempt to reduce 'internal dissonance.' Tullock elaborates using an example in which an individual has the choice to give $100 to charity directly or vote on whether to be taxed the $100. According to Tullock, an individual who derives little satisfaction from charity

will not voluntarily contribute, but would be willing to vote in favor of the tax to reduce internal dissonance because the probability that he will influence the outcome is so small. Eichenberger and Oberholzer-Gee (1998) also address the more psychological factors behind expressive voting that account for why voters apparently behave more in line with social norms for fairness in their voting behavior than in market behavior.

While some economists find the assumptions underlying the theory of expressive voting to be questionable, the theory does present testable implications. In his famous 1971 article, 'The Charity of the Uncharitable,' Tullock states:

> Some further implications can be drawn from this phenomenon. As the size of the constituency in which I am voting increases, the likelihood that my vote will have any effect on the outcome decreases. Looked at from the standpoint of the voter, he can obtain the satisfaction of behaving charitably... much cheaper. (1971, pp. 388–389)

An implication of expressive voting, as noted by Tullock, is that public sector welfare spending should be directly related to the size of the voting constituency. In short, if individuals vote expressively to reduce internal dissonance, then welfare spending should be higher in larger states relative to smaller states, and at national levels of government relative to state and local levels since the probability of casting the decisive vote (or the "cost" of behaving charitably) decreases.

Empirical studies of expressive voting have been successful in explaining voter turnout (Feigenbaum et al., 1988; Kan and Yang, 2001; Copeland and Laband, 2002). In addition, using experimental methods, Carter and Guerette (1992) and Fischer (1996), provide evidence that individuals vote expressively. In these studies, individuals are given the choice to vote on earmarking funds for charity or for themselves. The authors find that individuals are indeed more likely to earmark the funds for charity as the probability of influencing the outcome declines, providing support for expressive voting.

More recently, Sobel and Wagner (2002) tested the link between expressive voting and government redistribution using biennial U.S. state-level data from 1972 to 1996. In their model, Sobel and Wagner test for evidence of expressive behavior by directly employing the probability of being the decisive voter as a regressor to explain state-level welfare spending (both measured as a percent of the budget and as a real per capita amount). They compute the probability of casting the decisive vote in each state over time using actual voter turnout data to measure the size of the voting constituency and include other traditional control variables used in previous studies explaining state-level welfare spending.

Sobel and Wagner's empirical result, which is robust to alternative specifications of the model, is that reductions in the probability of being the decisive voter are significantly correlated (at the 1 percent level) with increases in welfare spending. The magnitude of the estimated 'expressive voting effect' suggests, other factors constant, that a 10 percent reduction in the probability of casting the decisive vote would lead to a 3 to 4 percent increase in state welfare spending. Thus, Sobel and Wagner find evidence supportive of Tullock's notion that welfare spending will increase as the probability of being decisive falls because it lowers the cost of behaving charitably.

The theory of expressive voting provides an explanation for why redistributive activities should expand as the voting population expands (because it lowers the probability of casting the decisive vote and thus lowers the cost of acting ideologically or in a public minded manner). A fruitful area for future research along these lines would be to explore the role that changes in this probability played in the transition of the federal government to a large welfare state during the early 20th century. In addition, the differing involvement of national, state, and local governments in redistributive activities has the potential to be explored in more detail using this general methodology.

RUSSELL S. SOBEL
GARY A. WAGNER

REFERENCES

Buchanan, J.M. (1954). "Individual choice in voting and the market." *Journal of Political Economy*, 62(April): 334–343.

Brennan, H.G. and Lomasky, L.E. (1993). *Democracy and Decision*. Cambridge: Cambridge University Press.

Carter, J.R. and Guerette, S.D. (1992). "An experimental study of expressive voting." *Public Choice*, 73(April): 251–260.

Copeland, C. and Laband, D.N. (2002). "Expressiveness and voting." *Public Choice*, 110(March): 351–363.

Downs, A. (1957). *An Economic Theory of Democracy*. New York: Harper & Row.

Eichenberger, R. and Oberholzer-Gee, F. (1998). "Rational moralists: the role of fairness in democratic economic politics." *Public Choice*, 94(January): 191–210.

Feigenbaum, S., Karoly, L., and Levy, D. (1988). "When votes are words not deeds: some evidence from the nuclear freeze referendum." *Public Choice*, 58(September): 201–216.

Fischer, A.J. (1996). "A further experimental study of expressive voting." *Public Choice*, 88(July): 171–184.

Kan, K. and Yang, C.C. (2001). "On expressive voting: evidence from the 1988 U.S. presidential election." *Public Choice*, 108(September): 295–312.

Riker, W. and Ordeshook, P.C. (1968). "A theory of the calculus of voting." *American Political Science Review*, 62(March): 25–43.

Riker, W. and Ordeshook, P.C. (1973). *Introduction to Positive Political Theory*. Englewood Cliffs, NJ: Prentice-Hall.

Sobel, R.S. and Wagner, G.A. (2002). "Expressive voting and government redistribution: tesing Tullock's charity of the uncharitable," West Virginia University Working Paper 00-06.

Tullock, G. (1967). *Toward a Mathematics of Politics*. Ann Arbor: University of Michigan Press.

Tullock, G. (1971). "The charity of the uncharitable." *Western Economic Journal*, 9(December): 379–392.

F

FAIR DIVISION

The problem of fair division goes back at least to the Hebrew Bible. Abram (later to become Abraham) and Lot had to decide who would get Canaan and who Jordan; Solomon had to decide which of two women was the mother of a disputed baby. What was a fair solution in each case?

Before discussing criteria of fair division, consider the oldest known procedure for dividing a single divisible good like a cake between two people — "I cut, you choose," or divide-and-choose. The same procedure can be used if there are multiple items: one person divides the items into two piles, and the other person chooses one pile. If the divider has no knowledge of the chooser's preferences, he is well advised to divide the items 50–50 for himself. That way, whichever pile the chooser selects, the divider is assured of getting 50%.

The chooser, on the other hand, will get more than 50% if she thinks the two piles are unequal and selects the one she thinks is more valuable. On the other hand, if the divider knows the chooser's preferences, he can exploit this information to make one pile slightly more valuable than 50% for her — so she presumably will choose it — and keep for himself the pile he values more (assuming he values different items from her).

Is divide-and-choose fair? To make an assessment, consider the following criteria for determining what a "fair share" is:

1. *Proportionality*. Proportionality can be traced back to Aristotle, who argued in his book *Ethics* that goods should be divided in proportion to each claimant's contribution. If there are n claimants and they are all equally entitled, *proportionality* means that each thinks he or she got at least $1/n$ of the total value.

2. *Envy-Freeness*. If no party is willing to give up its portion in exchange for the portion someone else received, this party will not envy any other party. In two-party disputes, there is no difference between a proportional and an envy-free settlement. To see why this is so, assume a settlement is proportional, so you think you are getting at least 1/2 of the total value of all the items. Will you envy me? Not if you think that you have at least 1/2, because then you must think that I have at most 1/2. Symmetrically, if I think I have at least 1/2, then I will not envy you, so the settlement

is envy-free. Conversely, if the settlement is envy-free, then each of us must think that he or she is getting at least 1/2; otherwise, at least one of us will envy the other for getting more than 1/2. Thus, if there are only two parties, proportionality and envy-freeness are equivalent.

In the case of three parties, however, envy-freeness is stronger than proportionality. For example, I may think I'm getting 1/3, but if I think you're getting 1/2 (because the third party, in my eyes, is getting only 1/6), then I will envy you. On the other hand, if an allocation among three parties is envy-free, then I must think I received at least 1/3. (Otherwise, I would think the others together received more than 2/3, and I would envy the one or both who received more than 1/3.) Hence, an envy-free allocation is always proportional, even if there are more than two parties, but a proportional allocation is not necessarily envy-free.

3. *Equitability*. Equitability is an aspect of satisfaction more subtle than envy-freeness. To illustrate it in a divorce settlement, suppose you think you got 51% of the marital property but your spouse thinks she got 90% (because she had little interest in what you got). While you do not envy the portion of your spouse — in your eyes, she got only 49% — you may envy her happiness: she got more of what she wanted than you did of what you wanted.

Equitability means that both parties think they receive the same fraction of the total, as each of them values the different items. Coupled with envy-freeness, it not only means that both get more than 50% but also that both exceed 50% *by the same amount*. Thus, when both spouses think they receive 70% of the total value, they are equally pleased by their allocations.

Equitability may be a difficult property to ascertain. How does one measure whether both parties are equally happy with their allocations? In fact, it generally requires an interpersonal comparison of utilities.

4. *Efficiency*. An allocation is *efficient* if there is no other allocation that is better for some party without being worse for some other party. Efficiency by itself — that is, when not linked with properties like proportionality, envy-freeness, or equitability — is no guarantee that an allocation will be fair. For example, an allocation that gives everything to me and nothing to you is efficient: any other allocation will make me worse off when it makes you better off. It is the other properties of fairness, combined with efficiency, that ensure that the total value is distributed to everyone's satisfaction.

The modern mathematical theory of fair division has its roots in the 1940s, particularly in the work of Polish mathematicians (Brams and Taylor, 1996, 1999; Robertson and Webb, 1998). They proposed different procedures for dividing both divisible goods like a land and indivisible goods like a car, boat, or house. Procedures that involve dividing divisible goods include a plethora of cake-cutting schemes, some of which use "moving knives" that parties stop when they believe they have a fair share; others involve trimming pieces from a cake, or a set of divisible goods, to construct fair shares.

Most of these schemes are quite esoteric and, therefore, impractical to apply. Nevertheless, they include procedures that, in principle, can be used to divide a cake among any number of people so that each thinks he or she has a largest piece and, hence, does not envy anybody else.

On the more practical side, two procedures for dividing a set of items are worth describing:

1. *Strict and balanced alternation. Strict alternation* is simply taking turns: you pick an item; then I pick one; you choose again; and so on. Of course, going first can be a huge advantage; giving extra choices to compensate for going second can reduce, if not eliminate, this advantage. A specific way of balancing choices out yields a procedure called *balanced alternation*. If there are, say, eight items to be divided among persons A and B, the order of choice under balanced alternation is ABBABAAB. This procedure can be extended to more than two players.

2. *Adjusted winner.* Two players begin by independently distributing a total of 100 points across all the items to be divided, depending on the relative value they attach to each. Thus, if you consider a certain item to be worth 1/4 of the total value of everything to be divided, then you would put 25 points on it.

The term "winner" in adjusted winner comes from the next step: each party is (temporarily) given the items on which it placed more points than its opponent. Thus, if I place 24 points on the apartment, and you place 25 points on it, you will get it, at least for the moment.

Now the "adjusted" part comes in: suppose, initially, I win items totaling 55 of my points, and you win items totaling 65 of your points. Then we start transferring items from you to me, in a certain order, until the point totals are equalized (at, say, 60 points each). This order of transfer, which usually requires splitting one item, guarantees that the final allocation will satisfy envy-freeness, equitability, and efficiency if the parties are truthful.

To be sure, parties may try to manipulate a procedure to their advantage by giving false information about their preferences or making choices that do not mirror their preferences. However, most fair-division procedures provide certain guarantees, even in the face of parties that are exploitative.

In the case of divide-and-choose, as we saw, the divider can guarantee that he receives a tied-for-largest portion, whatever the chooser selects, by dividing the items 50–50 for himself. The chooser can do at least as well by selecting what she considers the larger pile, so this procedure is envy-free. However, it may be neither efficient nor equitable. Both players may do better with some other allocation, making the division inefficient. And the chooser may receive a piece she considers considerably larger than 50% when the cutter receives only 50%, making it inequitable. (Of course, the tables can be turned if the cutter has information about the chooser's preferences and uses it to get a substantially greater-than-50% portion for himself when the chooser must settle for only slightly more than 50%.)

The procedures discussed so far offer an algorithmic approach to fair division: a set of rules is specified; subject to the rules, the parties select strategies (e.g., the divider cuts the cake into two equal portions for himself) that give each certain guarantees about the resulting allocation (e.g., it will be envy-free).

Political scientists, sociologists, and applied economists have taken a more empirical tack, seeking to determine conditions under which fairness, or departures from it, occur in the world and what consequences they have for people and institutions. Psychologists, especially, have paid heed to how perceptions of fairness impinge on people's attitudes and affect their behavior.

Theoretical economists and game theorists have been more interested in finding axioms that characterize fairness (Moulin, 1995; Roemer, 1996). Their models are often nonconstructive in the sense that they establish the existence — or sometimes the nonexistence — of an allocation satisfying certain properties. (The problem of nonexistence is particularly acute in the case of indivisible goods, as illustrated by some of the paradoxes discussed in Brams et al. (2001)). But models that show existence may provide no clue as to how to construct the desired allocation.

Many analysts are interested in fairness because they desire to help people settle their differences amicably. Numerous books have been written that purport to show how to achieve "win–win" solutions. Fisher and Ury (1981) is the most popular and, undoubtedly, has helped people structure negotiations so that they are more likely to settle a dispute. One can do so, they argue, by communicating clearly, considering your opponent's interests as well as your own, and persevering in taxing situations.

Ultimately, however, you want to know on which issues you will win, on which you will lose, and on which you will have to compromise. For this purpose, fair-division procedures that can guarantee the disputants do as well as possible in realizing all the win–win potential that is available are important.

From a normative perspective, fair-division procedures can help disputants reduce the frustration, anger, and occasional violence that accompany escalating demands and endless haggling. By facilitating the disputants' bringing *their own* closure to a dispute, they help them avoid the arbitrary imposition of a settlement or continuing impasse.

STEVEN J. BRAMS

REFERENCES

Brams, Steven J. and Alan D. Taylor (1996). *Fair Division: From Cake-Cutting to Dispute Resolution*. New York: Cambridge University Press.

Brams, Steven J. and Alan D. Taylor (1999). *The Win–Win Solution: Guaranteeing Fair Shares to Everybody*. New York: W.W. Norton.

Brams, Steven J., Paul H. Edelman, and Peter C. Fishburn (2001). "Paradoxes of fair division." *Journal of Philosophy* 98(6): 300–314.

Fisher, Roger and William Ury (1981). *Getting to Yes: Negotiating Agreement without Giving In*. Boston: Houghton Mifflin (Second Edition. Penguin, 1991).

Moulin, Hervé (1995). *Cooperative Microeconomics. A Game-Theoretic Introduction*. Princeton, NJ: Princeton University Press.

Robertson, Jack and William Webb. *Cake-Cutting Algorithms: Be Fair If You Can*. Natick, MA: AK Peters.

Roemer, John E. (1996). *Theories of Distributive Justice*. Cambridge, MA: Harvard University Press.

FAME AND POLITICS

Fame-seeking was a popular topic in eighteenth century analyses of civil society and political order. David Hume (1966 [1777], p. 114) wrote of the "love of fame; which rules, with such uncontrolled authority, in all generous minds, and is often the grand object of all their designs and undertakings." American Founding Father John Adams, in his *Discourses on Davila*, staked out the extreme position that approbation-seeking is the wellspring of *all* human activity. Since that time politics and fame has been a neglected topic, but it is starting to make a comeback (Braudy 1986; Cowen and Sutter, 1997; Cowen, 2000).

Political fame has changed over the last few centuries. Since the 1920s entertainers and sports figures have displaced politicians, military leaders, and moral preachers as the most famous individuals in society, and in some cases, as the most admired. For instance, an 1898 survey asked schoolchildren which public figures they admired. Forty percent chose either George Washington or Abraham Lincoln. Seventy-eight percent of the selections came from history, both contemporaneous and past, including politicians, moral leaders, and generals. No entertainers were picked but twelve percent were characters from literature.

Another comparable poll was conducted in 1948. Only a third of the respondents chose historical figures; sports figures accounted for 23 percent, and entertainers accounted for 14 percent. Figures from comic strips received several times more selections than did Jesus Christ. When a comparable poll was held again in 1986, nine of the top ten selections were entertainers; the exception, President Ronald Reagan, also had been a movie actor (Averill, 1950; Fowles, 1992, p. 165; Cowen, 2000).

The informational distance between leaders and citizens has diminished over time. The public did not know when Grover Cleveland and Woodrow Wilson had serious health problems. Before the 1920s most Americans had never heard the voice of the President, and before the 1950s most people had never seen the President on television. In the 1930s many Americans did not know that Franklin Roosevelt used a wheelchair. Journalists knew about the sexual affairs of John F. Kennedy but did not report them. The contrast with the Clinton Presidency is obvious. Information sources have become more competitive and technologies of reproduction have become more acute, both of which mean that leaders can no longer control their public images. The modern image of a leader is not Theodore Roosevelt on horseback, charging up a hill, but rather George H. Bush vomiting in the lap of the Japanese Prime Minister. Most other developed democracies have experienced similar trends, as evidenced by the declining stature of the British monarchy.

Ideally fame incentives should serve as a magnet to induce politicians to do the right thing. Insofar as politicians look to the judgment of history, they may be able to overcome immediate electoral pressures and adopt a longer time horizon (Cowen and Sutter, 1997). Many of the great Western leaders, including the American Founding Fathers and Winston Churchill, appear to have done just that.

The evolution of mass media, however, has led many individuals to wonder whether political fame remains an active force for good. Winston Churchill asked: "Can modern communities do without great men? Can they dispense with hero-worship? Can they provide a larger wisdom, a nobler sentiment, a more vigorous action, by collective processes, than were ever got from Titans? Can nations remain healthy, can all nations draw together, in a world whose brightest stars are film stars...?" In today's world it appears that leaders court immediate approval, as do celebrities, rather than looking towards the judgment of history. They curry public favor and try to avoid public blame (Churchill, 1932/1990, p. 191; Boorstin, 1987).

The changing nature of political fame has brought mixed effects. On the negative side, society may have a weaker set of role models than in times past. This is sometimes called the "separation of fame and merit," though as we will see below this designation begs important questions. Furthermore, our incredibly intense scrutiny of Presidents and other leaders may scare off the truly honest, the truly dedicated, and attract attention-mongers in their place. Finally, as Churchill's quotation indicates, the long-run judgment of history may not exercise much sway over current political decisions.

On the brighter side, media attention helps constrain our politicians. Every move the President makes is scrutinized, photographed, reported, and analyzed on the evening news – far from the Hobbesian absolute sovereign. A celebrity politician is both a low stature politician and a constrained politician. Decreasing the stature of politicians limits political power and limits political risk-taking.

Nor need societal role models fall into complete disarray. Sometimes moral discourse operates more effectively with imperfect and blemished individuals before the public. The delinking of fame and merit allows citizens to evaluate individual's piecemeal, in terms of particular qualities, rather than imposing a uniform judgment of good or bad. More cautious forms of moral discourse may be better than the uncritical elevation of political leaders as heroes. The modern world of fame, for all its flaws, may help free notions of virtue from the cult of personality.

Nor do role models automatically induce moral (or immoral) behavior. Many individuals are already looking to act a certain way, and they seek out whichever role models validate that behavior. Citizens may interpret or reinterpret the qualities of role models accordingly, to support an agenda which is already in place. Insofar as societal role models have declined in quality, this may be an effect of basic social problems, rather than a cause of them.

Finally, the falling stature of politicians should be viewed in historical context. Fame has never been the exclusive property of the meritorious. The modern world of fame, while making it harder to become recognized for true leadership, has taken renown away from tyrants. The reallocation of fame to entertainers, for whatever crassness it has brought on, also has spelt the end of the earlier ideal of martial virtue.

Thomas Hobbes recognized that the classic "heroes" were honored for their "Rapes, Thefts, and other great, but unjust, or unclean acts," including "Adulteries... [and] Frauds." John Locke wrote: "All the Entertainment and talk of History is of nothing almost but Fighting and Killing: And the Honour and Renown, that is bestowed on Conquerours (who for the most part are but the great Butchers of Mankind) farther mislead growing Youth, who by this means come to think Slaughter the laudable Business of Mankind, and the most Heroick of Vertues." (Hobbes, 1990, Ch.10, p. 67; Locke, 1693/1989, p. 181).

TYLER COWEN

REFERENCES

Adair, Douglass (1974). "Fame and the founding fathers." in Trevor Colburn, (ed.) *Fame and the Founding Fathers*. New York: W.W. Norton and Co., pp. 3–26.

Adams, John (1851). "Discourses on Davila," in *The Works of John Adams*, Volume VI. Boston: Charles C. Little and James Brown, pp. 226–403.

Averill, Lawrence A. "The impact of a changing culture upon pubescent ideals." *School and Society*, Saturday, July 22, 1950.

Boorstin, Daniel J. (1987). *The Image: A Guide to Pseudo-Events in America*. New York: Atheneum.

Braudy, Leo. (1986). *The Frenzy of Renown. Fame and Its History*. New York: Oxford University Press.

Churchill, Winston (1990 [1932]). *Thoughts and Adventures*. New York: W.W. Norton & Company.

Cowen, Tyler and Sutter, Daniel (1997). "Politics and the pursuit of fame." *Public Choice*, 93: 19–35.

Cowen, T. (2000). What Price Fame? Cambridge, MA: Harvard University Press.

Starstruck: Celebrity Performers and the American Public (1992). Washington: Smithsonian Institution Press.

Hobbes, Thomas (1991 [1651]). in Richard Tuck (ed.) *Levianthan*. Cambridge: Cambridge University Press.

Hume, David (1985 [1777]). *Essays Moral, Political, and Literary*. Indianapolis: Liberty Classics.

Locke, John (1989 [1693]). *Some Thoughts Concerning Education*. Oxford: Clarendon Press.

FEDERAL RESERVE SYSTEM

The historical roots of the Federal Reserve System can be traced to the late 19th century debate between those defending the gold standard and those advocating the free coinage of gold and silver. Gold standard proponents painted a textbook picture of an impersonal, automatic monetary system. In practice, however, the heavy hand of the government influenced the actual operation of the standard. Contemporary observers complained about the bureaucratic inertia inherent in the Treasury's administration of currency issue. The lag between currency demand and Treasury accommodation could be weeks or months, giving rise to acute currency shortages during seasonal surges in currency demand. These shortages led to a number of reform crusades all with the goal of doing something about the "inelastic" currency.

The most famous of the crusades was the free silver movement of the 1880s and 1890s culminating in the 1896 presidential campaign between the Democratic candidate William Jennings Bryan and the Republican candidate William McKinley. Bryan's free silver movement, embodying monetary populism, was offered as an antidote to the monolithic gold standard. Currency holders would have an alternative — silver backed money — to turn to if, for whatever reason, bureaucratic supply of gold money proved sluggish. Bryan's free silver movement died with his defeat in 1896 election. But in retrospect Bryan lost the battle for currency competition but not necessarily the war. For the same fight between monetary populism and monetary monopoly was to be played out in the years leading up to the founding of the Federal Reserve.

The Panic of 1907 once again brought to the forefront the problem of the lack of seasonal currency elasticity. Reform was all but certain. And it was becoming increasingly clear that some type of central banking institution would emerge, albeit one operating within the context of a gold standard. The only question was what type of central bank? Would it be a highly centralized one as advocated by those who had defended the Treasury position as a monopoly supplier in the monolithic gold standard of the 19th century? Or would it be a decentralized system in the spirit of Bryan who had advocated 19th century currency competition?

Early victories in this central bank struggle went to the monopolists. The Republican leader Nelson Aldrich headed the National Monetary Commission charged by Congress to study the design of European central banks and offer a proposal for the United States. Aldrich presented a bill to Congress in early 1912 that followed the European model of a "monopoly" central bank. Democratic victories in the 1912 mid-term elections, however, marked a turning point. Given the new political realities no central bank bill associated with Aldrich's name could win support in Congress. Woodrow Wilson's victory in the Presidential elections of November 1912 gave added momentum to the populist movement. A central bank embodying a decentralized, competitive supply mechanism was now on the fast track.

Over the course of 1913, Wilson and the Democratic Congress hammered out the populist blueprint that would become the Federal Reserve Act and would shape the operation of the currency system during the early years (1914–1930) of the Federal Reserve. The nominal structure of the Fed was a curious mixture of private and public elements. On the private side, the Fed was to be polycentric system of 12 reserve banks, each having the power to produce a distinct currency marked by a seal indicating the district of origin, each owned by its member banks, and each required to finance itself from earnings. On the public side, the most important government element was the Federal Reserve Board, a political body that was to oversee the operation of the system.

The details of the Federal Reserve Act would determine how the private–public balance would play out. Consider first the financing arrangement. The Act forcefully rejected the typical budgetary arrangement instead of giving reserve bank management first call on earnings from discount loans, open market operations, and fees charged for providing clearinghouse services to member banks. These earnings were to be used to finance "all necessary expenses." Next, member banks were to receive a dividend payment on the paid-in capital stock. Finally, "after the aforesaid dividend claims have been fully met, all the net earnings shall be paid to the United States as a franchise tax, except that one-half of such net earnings shall be paid into a surplus fund until it shall amount to forty per centum of the paid-in capital stock of such bank." One thing the Act did not do was to authorize transfer payments from the general government to the individual reserve banks in case of a shortfall in earnings. In this sense, the reserve banks faced a bottom line somewhat akin to that faced by for-profit firms in a market setting.

With respect to ownership rights, the Federal Reserve Act nominally designated member banks as shareholders. They were required to subscribe to the capital stock of their reserve bank in an amount equal to "six per centum of the paid-up capital stock and surplus of such bank." Stock ownership, however, did not convey voting powers. Nor were there secondary markets where shares could be traded.

With respect to selection of the Fed management team, the Federal Reserve System established an interesting blend of government appointment versus "stockholder" appointment. Every member of the Federal Reserve Board was to have a government connection. In addition to five political appointees, the Board included the Secretary of Treasury and the Comptroller of Currency. Perhaps the most important power the politically appointed Board exercised was over discount policy. Discount rates set by the individual reserve banks were "subject to review and determination of the Federal Reserve Board." Thus the government, through the Board could influence, if not control, money created through the discount window.

The Federal Reserve Act contained one important loophole, however, which tended to undermine the Board's control over aggregate Fed money. According to the Act, the one margin of adjustment over which individual reserve banks unambiguously could exercise discretion was the amount of government securities to buy and sell. These open market operations were to be at the initiative of the individual reserve banks and each bank was to have first claim to the earnings generated by the government securities in its portfolio.

Whether the populist founders of the Federal Reserve were fully aware of the role the open market operation loophole might play is subject to debate. Nevertheless, the loophole emerged as the key feature of the money supply process in the 1st decade, the 1920s, of the System's peacetime operation. During slowdowns in economic activity (1924 and 1927) market rates of interest would tend to fall below administratively set discount rates. Given the relatively high discount rates, Fed money created via discount loans would tend to fall and, other things constant, the 19th century problem of seasonal shortfalls of currency would have emerged. Other things were not constant, however, as the open market operation loophole came into play. Those reserve banks having difficulty covering expenses tended to conduct open market operations. The result was that non-borrowed Fed money surged precisely when it was most needed. Over the decade of the 1920s the Federal Reserve operated as a populist, self-regulating money producing system: Competitive pressures among reserve banks fostered the adjustment of currency supplies to accommodate seasonal demands.

The Great Depression marked the end to the novel experiment in monetary populism. The Federal Reserve Board sharply raised discount rates and individual reserve banks failed to fill the void with open market operations. Numerous explanations have been offered for the restrictive depression policy. The traditional explanations have emphasized a failure in leadership, a flawed policy procedure, or rigid adherence to the gold standard. The most provocative public choice explanation has viewed the depression as a method for a self-interested Fed to kill-off non-member banks. One thing all of these explanations have in common is the presumption that these early Fed decision-makers had considerable discretionary powers that could be used to do "good or bad." According to these accounts, the Fed in the 1920s exercised this power for the "good" and in early 1930s for the "bad." There does not seem to be an appreciation of the possibility, suggested by the Federal Reserve's populist heritage, that the good monetary outcomes of the 1920s were attributable to a self-regulating system that in the 1930s was abandoned.

The Banking Acts of 1933 and 1935 rubber-stamped the change in the Federal Reserve's supply mechanism that de facto had taken place in the midst of the depression. Most importantly, the Acts once and for all closed the open market operation loophole. Open market operations now

were centralized and managed under the authority of a new agency, the Federal Open Market Committee. In addition, the Federal Reserve was no longer required to transfer excess earnings to the Treasury; all earnings from the Fed's asset portfolio could be spent exclusively on itself. The Federal Reserve, at its own initiative, changed the financing arrangement in the aftermath of WWII. In 1947, the Federal Reserve instituted a policy of transferring excess revenue to the Treasury on an annual basis. These transfers have continued up to the present time. Currently, the Federal Reserve transfers over 90 percent of revenue to the Treasury.

The 1930s change in structure from a self-regulated to a managed one would prove critical in sparking, some half century later, the interest of public choice theorists in the operation of the Federal Reserve. The organizational structure of the original Federal Reserve was worth studying in its own right. But the early supply mechanism, with the open market loophole, limited bureaucratic behavior and hence limited what a public choice theorist might add to an analysis undertaken by a neoclassical monetary economist who was cognizant of the competitive nature of the early Fed. With the reformed Fed of the 1930s came at least the potential for significant management discretion and the potential for a unique public choice perspective.

The first public choice forays, inspired by earlier work on the economics of government bureaucracies, focused on the possibility that Fed managers, particularly after WWII, might be able to set their own agenda. Federal Reserve management could use excess revenue to finance on the job amenities, but neither they nor the member bank shareholders could "take-home" profits. In this sense, the modern Federal Reserve operated as a *non-profit* monopoly firm, with expense–preference behavior as a goal. One by-product of this institutional design would be high inflation — Fed managers would be induced to increase money growth rates above optimal levels to enlarge the scope of System spending or employment.

Another strand of public choice work directed attention toward presidential and congressional pressures designed to limit the scope of bureaucratic discretion. To be sure, the Federal Reserve is neither an executive agency nor subject to a regular budgetary review. In the face of this peculiar institutional structure, the presidential control literature has posited the power of appointment as a key control mechanism. The congressional pressure literature has emphasized non-budgetary means of committee oversight.

While the public choice approach to modeling the Federal Reserve has added much to our specific knowledge of monetary policy and our general knowledge of the operation of government firms, the study of central banking may soon be the exclusive domain of public choice *historians*. This conjecture is based on the observation that as the 20th century comes to a close, technological innovation in the information sector has made competition an international phenomenon. In this New World order, monetary policy is less important in that the monopoly central banking institutions that thrived in the second half of the 20th century will have poor survival prospects in the 21st century. There will be no monetary policy, but simply monetary economics; an economics that has as its primary task the modeling of the competitive constraints within which money-producing firms must operate. Issues that in the recent past have defined the domain of monetary policy — central bank independence, the personality of the central bank chair, and discretion versus rules — are irrelevant in the face of binding competitive constraints. If this crystal ball is right, then the hey-day of the public choice approach to the Federal Reserve System may be in the review mirror. To be sure, the Federal Reserve may continue to exist into the foreseeable future just as the British monarchy continues to exist today. But as a force shaping public policy, and therefore as a subject of public choice inquiry, the days of the potent Federal Reserve may be numbered. The operation of the Fed-to-be may be studied and dissected, but primarily as lessons to be taught by history.

MARK TOMA

REFERENCES

Broz, L. (1997). *The International Origins of the Federal Reserve System*. Ithaca: Cornell University Press.

Havrilesky, T. (1995). *The Pressures on American Monetary Policy*. Boston: Kluwer Academic Publishers.

Toma, E.F. and Toma, M. (1986). *Central Bankers, Bureaucratic Incentives, and Monetary Policy*. Boston: Kluwer Academic Publishers.

Toma, M. (1997). *Competition and Monopoly in the Federal Reserve System, 1914–1951*. Cambridge: Cambridge University Press.

Woolley, J. (1984). *Monetary Politics: The Federal Reserve and the Politics of Monetary Policy*. Cambridge: Cambridge University Press.

FORECASTING PRESIDENTIAL ELECTIONS IN THE UNITED STATES

It is widely believed that U.S. presidential elections represent a referendum on the policies and achievements of the incumbent party. Pioneering studies by Kramer (1971)

and Fair (1978, 1982, 1988, 1996) found empirical support for this proposition; specifically, both concluded that more rapid growth of real output produced gains for the party of the incumbent president. Following Kramer and Fair, others have investigated empirical links between election outcomes and economic performance using a variety of techniques, specifications, and data sets. These empirical relationships are often referred to as "vote functions."

If a vote function accurately describes how changes in economic conditions determine changes in political support, one can use knowledge of prevailing conditions to predict outcomes in an upcoming election. Fair's model has frequently been cited for its use in forecasting. While it is natural to use vote functions in this manner, a useful distinction can be made between most election forecasting models and empirically estimated vote functions. The primary purpose of a vote function is to describe the behavior of voters, i.e., to test alternative theories or hypotheses about voter behavior. A good forecasting model cannot ignore knowledge of voter behavior, but its primary purpose is to use all available information to make the best possible forecast. To make the distinction clear, Fair's vote function expressly excluded pre-election polls as explanatory variables. In 1992, Fair's model predicted an easy win by incumbent George Bush, even as pre-election polls made it clear that this outcome was unlikely. Adding a poll as an explanatory variable in Fair's vote function would presumably have improved its forecast, but would not have provided any fundamental explanation for voters' dissatisfaction with the incumbent. In the remainder of this entry, attention to the behavioral issues studied by Fair and Kramer is deferred; we instead focus on the production of accurate forecasts.

One might ask why election forecasting, apart from associated behavioral issues, would be of academic interest — accurate election forecasts might be important for candidates and their campaign staff, but societal welfare gains associated with small reductions in election uncertainty are likely to be small. There are several good reasons for investing some effort in forecasting, however. First, forecasting effort is likely to produce spillover benefits related to the more fundamental issues associated with investigating voter behavior; the separation of forecasting issues from behavioral issues is somewhat illusory. For example, Gellman and King (1993) use findings about the forecasting performance of polls to draw inferences about how and when voters make their choices over candidates. Second, the specific forecasting problem presented by the institution of the Electoral College is an unusual one, so the application itself is likely to lead to innovative statistical methods. Finally, the entertainment value associated with forecasting activities cannot be dismissed, given public and media interest focused on the horse-race aspects of the campaign.

Among the simplest forecasting models are several that predict national two-party vote shares using time series data and parsimonious sets of explanatory variables. Campbell and Wink (1990) use just two predictor variables, a trial-heat poll and second quarter GDP growth in the year of the election. Lewis-Beck and Rice (1992) use a similar specification, but add variables capturing recent partisan trends. Both Campbell and Wink and Lewis-Beck and Rice report that their models produce accurate forecasts by Labor Day, roughly 60 days prior to the election. Specifically, out-of-sample forecast errors for the Campbell-Wink model had a mean absolute error of just 1.3% over the 1948–1992 period (Campbell, 1996). Other contributions in this genre include Abramowitz (1992, 1996), Lewis-Beck and Tien (1996), Holbrook (1996), and Erickson and Wlezien (1996). Notably, Hibb's two-variable "bread and peace" voting model predicts well despite its behavioral focus and the absence of any poll-based measures (Hibbs, 2000).

Although the accuracy of these models is admirable, predicting shares of the popular vote should not be the principal objective when the election winner is selected in the Electoral College. Electoral College votes are cast according to outcomes in the individual states; consequently, good forecasts of the Electoral College should be derived from vote forecasts for the states. Several models, including those developed by Rosenstone (1983), Holbrook (1991) and Campbell (1992) have taken this approach. All of these models examine election outcomes across both states and time, using a mixture of national- and state-level variables as explanatory variables. Campbell lists three limitations of the Rosenstone model: (1) values for some explanatory variables are not actually available prior to the election, (2) measurement of some explanatory variables requires subjective assessments by "experts," and (3) the model includes a very large number of explanatory variables. Holbrook's model avoids these limitations, but fails to achieve the same forecasting accuracy as Rosenstone's.

Campbell's (1992) model of state election outcomes aspires to be comparable to Holbrook in parsimony and operationality, and comparable to Rosenstone in forecasting accuracy. Following the example of his national vote-share model, Campbell includes an early-September national trial-heat poll and second quarter GDP growth as explanatory variables. The model also includes prior state deviations from national voting outcomes and other state- and region-specific indicators of partisan strength and economic performance. Although it is difficult to explain some shifting partisan alignments over time, Campbell's

model ultimately does rival that of Rosenstone's in terms of within-sample forecasting accuracy both for vote shares and Electoral College outcomes. As this is written, Campbell's model remains "state-of-the-art" in forecasting presidential elections at the state level.

Future work on econometric approaches to presidential election forecasting is likely to proceed in several directions. First, in recent years trial-heat polls for individual states have become available with increasing frequency. Since 1988, state-specific polls have been tracked and archived by the *Hotline Weekly* and its successor *National Journal*. Given that polls have demonstrated value for forecasting at short horizons before elections, it seems very likely that state-specific polls will be useful for state-specific forecasts. Holbrook and DeSart (1999) provide early evidence that this is the case. Second, it would be useful to present forecasts in terms of underlying probabilities rather than point estimates (Beck, 2000). In the literature, most assessments of accuracy are reported in terms of regression standard errors or mean absolute values of regression residuals. Given the complexity introduced by the Electoral College and the likelihood that forecast errors across states are not independent, such statistics tell us little about candidate win probabilities. A third issue concerns the timing of forecasts. Campbell's model, as many others, is designed to produce a forecast in early September, utilizing a trial-heat poll at that date. However, there is no reason forecasters should be restricted to this time horizon. Forecasts could be produced repeatedly at different pre-election horizons, using the best data available at a given time. Brown and Chappell (1999) Campbell (1996) describe methods for producing forecasts at differing pre-election time horizons.

While most scholars continue to use econometric models for forecasting elections, there is an important alternative. Researchers operating the Iowa Electronic Markets have instead used data generated by market outcomes (Forsythe et al., 1992). In the Iowa electronic markets, traders buy and sell shares prior to election day. The ultimate value of those shares is determined by the election outcome. Depending upon the type of shares being traded, market prices leading up to the election provide a measure of either a candidate's probability of winning or losing his expected vote share. If traders efficiently absorb available information about candidates' prospects, the market should give an accurate and continuously updated forecast of the election outcome. In practice, Iowa market forecasts have performed well, better than unadjusted point estimates from the major polls. Further, evidence indicates that market prices are not simply driven by the latest polls. At the very least, the Iowa market poses an interesting challenge to analysts employing econometric forecasting models: if you can produce a better forecast, why not use it to make money in Iowa?

HENRY CHAPPELL

REFERENCES

Abramowitz, A. (1992). "An improved model for predicting presidential outcomes." *PS: Political Science and Politics*, 21: 843–847.

Abramowitz, A. (1996). "Bill and Al's excellent adventure: forecasting the 1996 presidential election." *American Politics Quarterly*, 24: 434–442.

Beck, N. (2000). "Evaluating forecasts and forecasting modles of the 1996 presidential election," in J. Campbell and J. Garand (eds.) *Before the Vote: Forecasting American National Elections*. Thousand Oaks, CA: Sage Publications, pp. 161–168.

Brown, L. and Chappell, H. (1999) Forecasting presidential elections using history and polls. *International Journal of Forecasting*, 15: 127–135.

Campbell, J. (1996). "Polls and votes: the trial heat presidential election forecasting model, certainty, and political campaigns." *American Politics Quarterly*, 24: 408–433.

Campbell, J. and Wink, K. (1992) "Trial-heat forecasts of the presidential vote." *American Politics Quarterly*, 18: 251–269.

Erikson, R. and Wlezien, C. (1996). "Temporal horizons and presidential election forecasts." *American Politics Quarterly*, 24: 492–505.

Fair, R. (1978). "The effect of economic events on votes for president." *Review of Economics and Statistics*, 60: 159–173.

Fair, R. (1982). "The effect of economic events on votes for president: 1980 results." *Review of Economics and Statistics*, 64: 322–325.

Fair, R. (1988). "The effect of economic events on votes for president: 1984 update." *Political Behavior*, 10: 168–179.

Fair, R. (1996). "Econometrics and presidential elections." *The Journal of Economic Perspectives*, 3: 89–102.

Forsythe, R., Nelson, F., Neumann, G., and Wright, J. (1992). "Anatomy of an Experimental Political Stock Market." *American Economic Review*, 82:1142–1161.

Gelman, A. and King, G. (1993). "Why are American presidential election campaign polls so variable when votes are so predictable?" *British Journal of Political Science*, 23: 409–451.

Hibbs, D. (2000). "Bread and peace voting in U.S. presidential elections." *Public Choice*, 104: 149–180.

Holbrook, T. (1991). "Reading the political tea leaves: a forecasting model of contemporary presidential elections." *American Politics Quarterly*, 24: 434–442.

Kramer, G. (1971). "Short-term fluctuations in U.S. voting behavior 1896–1964." *American Political Science Review*, 65: 131–143.

Lewis-Beck, M. and Rice, T. (1992). *Forecasting Elections*. Washington, DC: Congressional Quarterly Press.

Lewis-Beck, M. and Tien, C. (1996). "The future in forecasting: prospective presidential models." *American Politics Quarterly*, 24: 468–492.

Rosenstone, S. (1983). *Forecasting Presidential Elections*. New Haven: Yale University Press.

G

GAME THEORY

Game theory is a branch of applied mathematics that provides tools for analyzing situations in which parties, called *players*, make decisions that are interdependent. This interdependence forces the players to take into account what other players might do in order to make their own best decisions, based on their goals. A solution to a game describes the "optimal" decisions of the players, who may have similar, opposed, or mixed interests, and the outcomes that may result from these decisions.

Although game theory can and has been used to analyze parlor games, its applications are much broader. In fact, game theory was originally developed by the Hungarian-born American mathematician John von Neumann, and his Princeton colleague Oskar Morgenstern, a German-born American economist, to solve problems in economics. In their book *Theory of Games and Economic Behavior* (von Neumann and Morgenstern, 1944), which was revised in 1947 and 1953, von Neumann and Morgenstern asserted that the mathematics developed for the physical sciences, which describes the workings of a disinterested nature, is a poor model for economics. They observed that economics is much like a game, wherein players anticipate each other's moves, and therefore requires a new kind of mathematics, which they called game theory. (The name may be somewhat of a misnomer, because the games of game theory do not necessarily connote the fun or frivolity that is often associated with the word "game.")

Game theory has been applied to a wide variety of situations in which the choices of players interact to affect the outcome. In stressing the *strategic* aspects of decision making, or aspects controlled by the players rather than by pure chance, the theory both supplements and goes beyond the classical theory of probability. It has been used, for example, to analyze what political coalitions or business conglomerates are likely to form, the optimal price at which to sell products or services in the face of competition, the power of a voter or bloc of voters, whom to select for a jury, the best site for a manufacturing plant, and even the behavior of certain animals and plants in their struggle for survival.

It would be surprising if any one theory could address such an enormous range of games, and, in fact, there is no single "game theory." A number of theories have been proposed, each applicable to different situations and each with its own concepts of what constitutes a solution.

Games can be classified into different categories according to certain significant features, the most obvious of which is the number of players. Thus, a game can be designated as being one-person, two-person, or *n*-person (with *n* greater than two); the games in each category have their own distinctive features. In addition, a player need not be a single person; it may be a nation, a corporation, or a team comprising many people with similar or identical interests.

In games of *perfect information*, such as chess, each player knows everything about the game at all times. Poker, on the other hand, is an example of a game of *imperfect information*, because the players do not know all the cards the other players are dealt.

The extent to which the goals of the players coincide or conflict is another basis for classifying games. *Zero-sum* (or, more generally, *constant-sum*) games are games of total conflict, which are also called games of pure competition. Poker, for example, is a constant-sum game, because the combined wealth of the players remains constant, though its distribution shifts in the course of play. In particular, if one player wins, others must lose because money is neither created nor destroyed.

Players in constant-sum games have completely opposed interests, whereas in variable-sum games they can all be winners or losers. In a labor-management dispute, for example, the two parties certainly have some conflicting interests, but both may benefit if a strike is averted. In auctions, both the seller and buyers benefit when goods are bought at what both sides consider an acceptable price.

Variable-sum games can be further distinguished as being either cooperative or noncooperative. In *cooperative games*, players can communicate and, most important, make binding agreements; in *noncooperative games*, they may communicate but cannot make binding agreements, such as sign an enforceable contract.

Sometimes games may be both cooperative and noncooperative. An automobile salesperson and a potential customer are engaged in a cooperative game if they agree on a price and sign a contract. But the dickering they do to reach this point has a noncooperative aspect if there is no certainty that they will ever reach an agreement. Similarly, when people bid independently at an auction, they are playing a noncooperative game, even though the high bidder agrees to purchase the good that he or she wins.

Finally, a game is said to be *finite* when each player has a finite number of choices to make, the number of players is finite, and the game terminates — that is, it does not go on forever. Chess, checkers, poker, and most parlor games are finite, but infinite games, which may be infinite repetitions of the same game, have been widely studied in economics and other fields.

A game can be described in one of three ways: in extensive, normal, or characteristic-function form. Sometimes these forms are combined, as in the *theory of moves* (Brams, 1994). Most parlor games, which progress step by step, one move at a time, can be modeled as *games in extensive form*. They can be represented by a *game tree*, in which each step or position is a vertex of the tree; the branches emanating from each vertex describe the players' alternative choices from each step or position (Berlekamp et al., 2001).

Games in *normal (strategic) form* are primarily used to describe two-person games. In this form, a game is represented by a *payoff matrix*, wherein each row describes the strategy of one player and each column describes the strategy of the other player. The matrix entry at the intersection of each row and column gives the outcome of row and column's strategy choices. The payoffs to each player associated with this outcome are the basis for determining whether the strategies are "in equilibrium," which determines whether or not they are stable in the sense that neither player would have an incentive to deviate.

The *characteristic-function form* of a game, which is generally used to analyze games with more than two players. It indicates the minimum value that each coalition of players — including single-player coalitions — can guarantee for themselves when playing against a coalition made up of all the other players.

Common to all areas of game theory is the assumption that players are *rational*: they have goals, can rank outcomes (or, more stringently, attach utilities, or values, to them), and choose better over worse outcomes. Complications arise from the fact that there is generally no straightforwardly best strategy for a player because of the interdependency of player choices. (Games in which there is only one player are sometimes called *games against nature* and are the subject of decision theory.)

The rules of most real-life games are equivocal; indeed, the "game" may be about the rules to be used (or abrogated). Thus, international politics is considered to be quite anarchistic, though there is certainly some constancy in the way conflicts develop and may, or may not, be resolved. Arms races, for instance are almost always nonzero-sum games in which two competitors can benefit if they reach some agreement on limiting weapons. But such agreements are often hard to verify or enforce and, consequently, may be difficult stabilize, leading to continuing conflict and even a violation of an agreement.

The story is similar is biology. When two males confront one another, whether competing for a mate or for some disputed territory, they can behave either like hawks — fighting until one is maimed, killed, or flees — or like doves — posturing a bit but leaving before any serious harm is done. (In effect, the doves cooperate while the hawks do not.) Neither type of behavior, it turns out, is ideal for survival: a species containing only hawks has a high casualty rate; a species containing only doves is vulnerable to an invasion by, or a mutation producing, hawks, because the growth rate of the competitive hawks is much higher than that of doves. In the game of survival, therefore, neither pure cooperators nor pure defectors will prevail against a mixed type, suggesting that some conflict is inevitable (Sigmund, 1993).

Applications of game theory to political science include the analysis of strategic voting in committees and elections, the formation and disintegration of parliamentary coalitions, and the distribution of power in weighted voting bodies. For example, the voting weights of members of the European Union Council of Ministers, and its decision rules for taking action (e.g., simple majority or qualified majority), have been studied with an eye to making the body both representative of individual members' interests and capable of taking collective action (Felsenthal and Machover, 1998).

Game theory can be used both to analyze existing strategic situations and to shed light on new situations that might arise were there a change in the rules, the preferences of the players, or the information available the to them. In this manner, it is well suited to providing both rigorous explanations and well-founded prescriptions if and when circumstances change.

STEVEN J. BRAMS

REFERENCES

Berlekamp, Elwyn R., Conway, John H. and Guy, Richard K. (2001). *Winning Ways for Your Mathematical Plays*, Volume 1, Second Edition. Natick, MA: A K Peters.

Brams, Steven J. (1994). *Theory of Moves*. New York: Cambridge University Press.

Felsenthal, Dan S. and Machover, Moshé (1998). *The Measurement of Voting Power: Theory and Practice, Problems and Paradoxes*. Cheltenham, UK: Edward Elgar.

Sigmund, Karl (1993). *Games of Life: Explorations in Ecology, Evolution, and Behavior*. Oxford, UK: Oxford University Press.

Von Neumann, John and Morgenstern, Oskar (1944). *Theory of Games and Economic Behavior*; Second Edition (1947); Third Edition (1953). Princeton, NJ: Princeton University Press.

GAME THEORY IN PUBLIC CHOICE

Game theory is for proving theorems, not for playing games. (Reinhard Selten, quoted in Goerre and Holt, 2001)

Game theory... has introduced a rigor in the analysis of rational behavior that was missing... [but] skepticism about the marginal value of recent theory is warranted... [because] conclusions drawn... tend to be very sensitive to the way problems are defined and to the assumptions that follow. (Sam Peltzman, 1993: 206)

Peltzman's critique, quoted above, was directed at uses of game theory in industrial organization, but could as well have been directed at uses in public choice. When compared to an earlier theoretical tradition, exemplified by Becker (1983), public choice models today tend to be more explicit about the timing of actions, and about who knows how much about what. And, as in industrial organization, this detail has come at the cost of an increased sensitivity of conclusions to assumptions, and at the cost of increased investments to become proficient in such tools.

One might also criticize public choice theory for making too *little* use of developments in game theory, however. While the theory of games has continued to advance in detail and realism over the last fifty years, the last major game theory innovation used widely in public choice theory, sequential equilibrium, was developed twenty years ago (Kreps and Wilson, 1982), and many older innovations still face widespread resistance.

One example of an older innovation still facing resistance is mixed strategies. While some public choice models allow mixed strategy equilibria (Myerson, 1993; Besley and Coate, 1997), there remains a widespread reluctance to consider such equilibria in electoral games (Ordeshook, 1986). While mixed strategy equilibria of the "divide the dollar" electoral game were described over fifty years ago (Gross and Wagner, 1950), many in public choice still consider this game to be without a satisfactory theory.

Another long-available yet little-used modeling tools in public choice is altruism. A great deal of evidence suggests that voters consider their personal benefits from policies less often than they consider benefits to their society as a whole, or to groups with which they are affiliated (Mansbridge, 1990; Caplan, 2002). Yet public choice models still typically describe selfish voters.

Public choice theory has also made little use of most of the major developments in game theory in the last twenty years. For example, signaling models in public choice (Rogoff, 1990; Lohmann, 1994) continue to favor the separating equilibria favored by the first papers on signaling, and typically justify this choice by reference to the "intuitive" equilibrium refinement (Cho and Kreps, 1987). This ignores the no less compelling "undefeated" equilibrium refinement which favors pooling equilibria (Mailath et al., 1993). Public choice theories also make little use of new generalizations of equilibrium concepts, such as rationalizable strategies,

computational approaches to agent modeling (Kollman et al., 1997), and non-expected utility models (Ghirardato and Katz, 2000; Starmer, 2000).

Game theorists have made substantial progress in the last twenty years in identifying deviations between older game theory and experimental game play, and in developing new games theories to close this gap (Goeree and Holt, 2001). Noisy game theories, such as quantal response equilibria (McKelvey and Palfrey, 1995, 1998), where players make and anticipate utility-dependent mistakes, have seen impressive empirical successes, but no public choice applications. Behavioral economics (Rabin, 1998) has been widely applied, including in law and finance (Aaron, 1999; Shleifer, 2000), but has been only rarely applied in public choice (Frey and Eichenberger, 1991).

Public choice theorists have adopted some, but far from all, of the conceptual tools developed by game theorists in the last half century. So have public choice theorists gone too far in adopting game theory tools, as many admirers of the older public choice tradition might suggest, or have public choice theorists not gone far enough in adopting game theory tools, as many game theorists might suggest?

Unfortunately, given the impoverished current state of the economics of academia, the available evidence seems roughly consistent with either conclusion. The game theory innovations that have been adopted have tended to make public choice models more complex, and the innovations that have not been adopted would have tended to make public choice models even more complex. Even if we want to evaluate the adoption of game theory in public choice only in terms of how well it promotes our understanding of public choice, ignoring other welfare effects on academics and their patrons, our main problem is that it is hard to judge the proper weight to place on model simplicity.

If we consider not just choices of basic game theories, but also the many other modeling choices made in game theory based models in public choice, we can see that modeling choices are constantly, perhaps even usually, made for reasons other than conforming to reality. Most papers with a model justify some choices by saying things like "to keep the model tractable, we assume" (Laffont and Tirole, 1991: 1092), or "the restriction to single-peaked voting is to avoid complications with equilibrium behavior under incomplete information." (Austen-Smith, 1990).

For example, unless there is a particular reason to do otherwise, models in public choice, like most economic models, tend to assume risk-neutrality, selfishness, separable or transferable utility, simultaneous actions, convexity for unique interior optima, and binary choices, cues, and signals. "Reduced form" expressions are often given as summaries of un-modeled behaviors, such as of how advertising influences voter opinion (Mueller and Stratmann, 1994). Usually, multi-period games are given identical action sets, and voters are given identical information, identical preferences, or both, as in retrospective voting models (Austen-Smith and Banks, 1989; Coate and Morris, 1995).

Given the rate at which modelers make various other assumptions for tractability, it should then not come as a surprise that game theory assumptions are made for similar reasons. So most probabilistic voting models assume convex signal distributions for no other reason than to obtain pure strategy equilibria (Coughlin, 1992), rather than the more complex mixed strategy equilibria one otherwise obtains (Hanson, 1996). Models of repeated play typically assume stationary equilibria (Austen-Smith and Banks, 1989; Baron and Ferejohn, 1989), and models with many voters typically assume voter-symmetric equilibria (Baron and Ferejohn, 1989; Feddersen and Pesendorfer, 1996). Though some have argued that such equilibria are actually more empirically plausible (Baron and Kalai, 1993), it seems clear that modelers would prefer the simplicity of such equilibria even if they were less empirically plausible.

Philosophers have long wrestled, without great progress, with the question of what level of model complexity best promotes understanding (Sober, 1975; Swinburne, 1997). On the one hand, those who favor more complex models suggest that such models tend to be closer to the truth, and suggest that excess simplicity often comes from habit and laziness. On the other hand, those who favor simpler models express concerns that more complex models hinder communication across diverse academic communities, are used to exclude those who have not mastered certain techniques, and give modelers more opportunities to select assumptions in order to obtain preferred conclusions.

In a public choice academia optimized for maximizing our understanding of public choice, modeling choices would probably weigh not only closeness to reality, but also ease of computing results, ease of summarizing the main results in simple words, comparability with other results, difficulty of biased selection of desired results, and perhaps even ability to signal the modeler's technical proficiency. Whether this would result in a faster or slower rate of adoption of game theory innovations is difficult to determine, though I suspect the reader has an opinion nonetheless.

ROBIN D. HANSON

REFERENCES

Aaron, H. (1999). *Behavioral Dimensions of Retirement Economics*. Washington, DC: Brookings Institution Press.

Austen-Smith, D. (1990). "Information transmission in debate." *American Journal of Political Science*, 34(February): 124–152.

Austen-Smith, D. and Banks, J. (1989). "Electoral accountability and incumbency," in P. Ordeshook (ed.) *Models of Strategic Choice in Politics*. Ann Arbor: University of Michigan Press.

Baron, D. and Ferejohn, J. (1989). "Bargaining in legislatures." *American Political Science Review*, 83(December): 1181–1206.

Baron, D. and Kalai, E. (1993). "The simplest equilibrium of a majority-rule division game." *Journal of Economic Theory*, 61(December): 290–301.

Becker, G. (1983). "A theory of competition among pressure groups for political influence." *Quarterly Journal of Economics*, 98(August): 371–400.

Besley, T. and Coate, S. (1997). "An economic model of representative democracy." *Quarterly Journal of Economics*, 112(February): 85–114.

Caplan, B. (2002). "Sociotropes, systematic bias, and political failure: reflections on the survey of Americans and economists on the economy." *Social Science Quarterly*, (forthcoming).

Cho, I. and Kreps, D. (1987). "Signaling games and stable equilibria." *Quarterly Journal of Economics*, 102(May): 179–222.

Coate, S. and Morris, S. (1995). "On the form of transfers to special interests." *Journal of Political Economy*, 103(December): 1210–1235.

Coughlin, P. (1992). *Probabilistic Voting Theory*. Cambridge: Cambridge University Press.

Feddersen, T. and Pesendorfer, W. (1996). "The swing voter's curse." *American Economic Review*, 86(June): 408–424.

Frey, B. and Eichenberger, R. (1991). "Anomalies in political economy." *Public Choice*, 68(January): 71–89.

Goeree, J. and Holt, C. (2001). "Ten little treasures of game theory and ten intuitive contradictions." *American Economic Review*, 91(December): 1402–1422.

Ghirardato, P. and Katz, K. (2000). "Indecision theory: explaining selective abstention in multiple elections." California Institute of Technology Social Science Working Paper 1106 (November).

Gross, O. and Wagner, R. (1950). "A continuous Colonel Blotto game." *RAND RM-408* (June). Santa Monica, California.

Hanson, R. (1996). "On voter incentives to become informed." California Institute of Technology Social Science Working Paper 968 (May).

Kollman, K., Miller, J., and Page, S. (1997). "Political Institutions and sorting in a tiebout model." *The American Economic Review*, 87(December): 977–992.

Kreps, D. and Wilson, R. (1982). "Sequential equilibrium." *Econometrica*, 50: 863–894.

Laffont, J. and Tirole, J. (1991). "The politics of government decision-making: a theory of regulatory capture." *Quarterly Journal of Economics*, 106(November): 1089–1127.

Lohmann, S. (1994). "Information aggregation through costly political action." *American Economic Review*, 84(June): 518–530.

Mailath, G., Okuno-Fujiwara, M., and Postlewaite, A. (1993). "Belief-based refinements in signalling games." *Journal of Economic Theory*, 60(August): 241–276.

Mansbridge, J. (1990). *Beyond Self-interest*. Chicago: University of Chicago Press.

McGuire, M. and Olson, M. (1996). "The economics of autocracy and majority rule: the invisible hand and the use of force." *Journal of Economic Literature*, 34: 72–96.

McKelvey, R. and Palfrey, T. (1995). "Quantal response equilibria for normal form games." *Games and Economic Behavior*, 10: 6–38.

McKelvey, R. and Palfrey, T. (1998). "Quantal response equilibria for extensive form games." *Experimental Economics*, 1: 9–41.

Mueller, D. and Stratmann, T. (1994). "Informative and persuasive campaigning." *Public Choice*, 81(October): 55–77.

Myerson, R. (1993). "Incentives to cultivate favored minorities under alternative electoral sytems." *American Political Science Review*, 87(December): 856–869.

Ordeshook, P. (1986). *Game Theory and Political Theory, An Introduction*. Cambridge: Cambridge University Press.

Sam Peltzman, S. (1991). "Review of The Handbook of Industrial Organization." *The Journal of Political Economy*, 99(February): 201–217.

Rabin, M. (1998). "Psychology and economics." *Journal of Economic Literature*, 36(March): 11–46.

Rogoff, K. (1990). "Equilibrium political budget cycles." *The American Economic Review*, 80(March): 21–36.

Shleifer, A. (2000). *Inefficient Capital Markets: An Introduction to Behavioral Finance*. Oxford: Oxford University Press.

Sober, E. (1975). *Simplicity*. Oxford: Clarendon Press.

Starmer, C. (2000). "Developments in non-expected utility theory: the hunt for a descriptive theory of choice under risk." *Journal of Economic Literature*, 38(June): 332–382.

Swinburne, R. (1997). *Simplicity as Evidence of Truth*. Milwaukee: Marquette University Press.

GENERALITY AND THE EFFICIENCY OF GOVERNMENT DECISION MAKING

1. Introduction

Most democratic governments have explicit requirements that a nation's civil and criminal law applies equally to all those who live within its boundaries. For example, the 6th and 14th amendments of the U.S. constitution assure due process and equal protection under federal law. Similar protection is assured under Article 3 of the German Basic Law, Article 1 of the French constitution, Article 14 of the Spanish constitution, and Article 14 of the Japanese constitution. Buchanan and Congleton (1998) argue that the generality principle can, and should, be applied to other areas of public law and public policy as well. For example, one can apply "equal treatment under the law" to taxation and expenditure policies, which is rarely done. Just as the

principle of equal protection under the law limits opportunities for the criminal justice system to be used to punish members of a minority, so would its application to taxation and government services limit opportunities for fiscal exploitation of minorities.

The generality principle in the context of a political constitution is the requirement that all persons within the polity be treated equally by their government. Its application can be defended on numerous grounds. For example, generality is clearly supported by democratic norms that regard all persons to be fundamentally equal as citizens — one man, one vote, by norms of procedural fairness that require all persons to play by the same rules, and by norms explicitly concerned with equality as with "equal opportunity" and "equity" norms. However, the case for adopting a constitutional generality principle can also be grounded in economic and political efficiency. That is to say, the citizens of a polity who do not broadly support democratic or egalitarian norms may nonetheless have a constitutional interest in the generality principle because it tends to increase the efficiency of democratic decision making and the policies adopted (Congleton, 1997; Buchanan and Congleton, 1998).

2. Political Efficiency and Distributional Aspects of the Funding of Pure Public Goods

The logic of the efficiency argument can be demonstrated with the classic welfare economics case for government intervention, the provision of pure public goods. A pure public good exhibits non-rivalry in consumption and is produced in a manner that precludes exclusion. Private (market) production of pure public goods tends to be suboptimal, because self-interested individuals take account of their own benefits and costs when producing or purchasing such goods and services, but neglect those realized by others. From the vantage point of a single individual, "all goods are private." In the usual characterization of equilibrium, relatively low demanders free ride on the efforts of relatively high demanders. Although low demanders are willing to contribute at the margin to secure greater service levels, transactions costs are assumed to preclude these demands from being satisfied through ordinary private markets.

Collective (government) provision can, in principle, use coercion (taxation) to fund a level of the public good or service that satisfies the Samuelsonian (1954) characterization of Pareto-efficient production, and the taxes imposed can, in principle, be apportioned so that everyone in the polity secures positive net benefits from the services produced (Lindahl, 1967; Wicksell, 1967). It is clear that government provision of a pure public good tends to be consistent with the generality principle insofar as everyone, more or less by definition, obtains the services.

However, financing the collective provision of a pure public good necessarily requires the shift of *private* (excludable) resources from the private sector to the public sector. Consequently, public finance will not automatically satisfy generality, nor the tax norms of Wicksell or Lindahl, even if the service and level funded do. Consider the following two-by-two matrix (Table 1) characterizing the net of tax benefits from a nonexcludable government service received by members of two groups in a polity of interest.

The assumed net benefits imply that the typical member of group B prefers fiscal package represented by the upper right hand cell (II) and that the typical member of group A prefers that represented by the lower left hand cell (III). Imposing the full cost of government services on the other group clearly improves the welfare of the group freed from taxes.

Suppose that majorities in the decision body of interest are slender, and consequently, the majority is alternately dominated by members of group A and group B. In this political environment, members of A and B each secure special privileges in the short run, but are bound to lose them in the long run, because all electoral winners eventually become electoral losers. In the case of an equally rotating majoritarian cycle, the members of group B and group A each determine the distribution of tax burdens approximately half of the legislative sessions. Each group benefits from democratic rule in spite of its instability, because government provision of this service is assumed to generate sizable aggregate net benefits. The average net benefit for typical members of both groups within an evenly rotating majoritarian cycle is $0.50 = 0.5(3) + 0.5(-2)$.

However, members of each group would be better off if they adopted a generality rule that restricts tax policies to ones that treat everyone equally. Note that if majoritarian decision making is constrained by a generality rule, both groups A and B will favor production with uniform taxation over non-production, $2 > 0$. The members of each group realize higher net benefits under a generality rule than under unconstrained majority rule, $2 > 0.5$. In such political settings, a generality constraint clearly increases the efficiency of majoritarian decision making.

In addition to stabilizing majoritarian politics, a generality constraint also reduces rent-seeking activities, because it reduces opportunities for preferential treatment. For example, government services such as highways, higher education, parks, medical care, and legal advice principally benefit those who use them, and are also substantially excludable. In the absence of a generality rule, relatively small groups might lobby for a new local bridge, park, or highway to be built using general tax revenues. The generality principle requires that each level of government provides its services uniformly to all within its jurisdiction or not provide them at all. This clearly reduces incentives to invest resources to secure targeted services funded by general revenues, because narrowly targeted programs and taxes are ruled out of bounds. A generality constraint reduces the scope for both majoritarian cycles and distributional conflict.

It might be argued that uniform service levels are impossible. After all, any service that is uniformly provided in some sense will be unequal in another as long as people and circumstances differ. For example, uniform service levels imply different subjective benefit levels unless all users are homogeneous. However, to the extent that benefits have measurable correlates, such as monetary net advantage or objective service levels, more generality is clearly distinguishable from less generality in a broad range of cases. The political efficiency associated with the generality principle arises because of the *predictable effects* of uniform provision of tangible services and taxes on subjective incentives for political action.

3. Generality and the Production of Government Services

Unfortunately, even if all government services are uniformly available to all taxpayers and funded by uniform proportional or lump-sum taxes, distributive conflict often remains, because government services can be produced in a variety of ways, by a variety of firms, and in a variety of locations. These distributional aspects of the production of public services are often neglected in public choice research, and can be safely neglected in cases where the

Table 1: Tax benefits from a nonexcludable government service by members of two groups

A's Obligation	B's Obligation	
	B contributes to the service	B does not contribute to the service
A contributes toward the service	I 2, 2	II −2, 3
A does not contribute to the service	III 3, −2	IV 0, 0

government is simply another consumer in a larger competitive market, as when it purchases coffee, paper goods, or personal computers for small numbers of office workers. Both local governments and small national governments often purchase goods in extensive national or world markets. In such cases, decisions that affect how and where a government purchases inputs will be relatively uncontroversial inasmuch as no profits or rents are generated by those decisions. However, in cases where government production decisions have significant effects upon the distribution of profits or rents within particular markets, this neglect is unlikely to be benign.

Beside generating political cycles, which may also cause economic cycles as government purchases are targeted and retargeted to regions favored by successive legislative majorities, the wealth effects of alternative methods of production create incentives for firms and individuals to invest significant resources in lobbying government decision makers for contracts and for high service levels. Other firms and individuals that stand to lose from higher input prices will oppose local production and favor lower service levels. To the extent that pro-service lobbies are more effective than their counterparts, service levels will exceed those which would have been sufficient to satisfy consumer demands for government services (at given tax prices).

3.1. Generality and Relative Price Neutrality in the Production of Government Services

In either case, the pecuniary interest of suppliers in securing increased demands for their services may play a significant role in determining the location and manner in which government services are produced, their output levels, and, thereby, the mix of services produced. Even in cases where government purchases take place in large well-developed competitive markets, purchases are often on such a scale as to affect relative prices and thereby the profits and wages of those producing the services provided. It is clear, for example, that a good deal of United States agricultural policy in the past half century has been predicated on such relative price effects. Similar effects are evident in cases where government services are produced by industries that are concentrated in particular regions of the polity of interest.

Generality requires that production decisions, themselves, not confer benefits or costs on specific individuals, industries, or regions of the country. That is to say, the production of government services should not itself materially alter the distribution of wealth or income.

Complete generality requires the *absence of significant relative price effects* in the production of government services and in the funding and distribution of those services. Relative price neutrality implies that no firms or factors of production stand to profit or lose from decisions regarding the allocation of production among firms or regions. In this case, neither firms nor factor owners would have a pecuniary interest in the level of government services provided. Even in cases where a program is explicitly redistributional, as might be said of welfare of social security, generality requires that the relative prices of factors used to produce those services not be materially affected.

However, aggregate price neutrality is not sufficient to reduce cycling and rent-seeking problems. Program A may drive up the demand for labor whereas program B drives up the demand for capital. In this case, labor clearly would lobby for increases in Program A, whereas capital owners would lobby for increases in Program B. Majoritarian cycles among coalitions of such groups would generate significant changes in the composition of government output and in the distribution of wealth. Aggregate relative price neutrality ameliorates these problems only in the case where the apportionment of government revenues to particular services is taken as given. In this last case, supplier incentives to lobby for (proportional) increases in the output of government services would be absent. In other cases, neutrality in the large does not necessarily improve the efficiency of majoritarian decision making. Relative price neutrality and generality are identical only if neutrality holds at the *service by service* level of analysis.

3.2. The Generality-Efficiency Tradeoff in the Production of Government Services

In a broad range of cases, there is no trade off between generality and ordinary economic efficiency in the production of government services. In such cases, distributing the production of government services more uniformly throughout a government's jurisdiction reduces relative price effects and increases the political efficiency with which services are selected without increasing the cost of government services.

On the other hand, there clearly are cases where locational economies are substantial and/or where markets for specialized inputs are too small to support more than a handful of efficiently sized producers. This might be said, for example, of the manufacture and servicing of submarines. In cases where economies of scale are significant, one can imagine settings where all voters prefer low-cost concentrated production to more costly decentralized production. Those same voters may, nonetheless, disagree about the "most advantageous" location of production insofar as specific communities gain (or lose) from securing the production site. In such cases, production should not be deliberately decentralized, but the institutions of fiscal choice should be constructed in a way that preserves the generality norm. For example, random or lottery-like selection among specific options can be used to assure *ex ante* generality at the time long-term production commitments are being contemplated. Production authority might also be delegated to a commission of "experts" whose opinions are not well known beforehand. Generality at the level of monetary net benefits may also be increased by "packaging" many production decisions into one legislative action.

4. Conclusion and Summary

The manner in which public services should be distributed and financed has long been issues at the core of welfare economics. The main stream literature that has emerged addresses a variety of questions about the optimal level of provision and methods by which such goods should be financed. Less attention has been focused on the process by which public services decisions are actually made, and on the manner by which those procedures could be improved. However, clearly, the demand and supply of government services should be analyzed in conjunction with the political institutions under which fiscal policy choices will be made.

When fiscal policies are adopted via majority rule, application of the generality principle to the production, distribution, and financing of government services reduces the range of distributional conflict that occurs and thereby increases political efficiency in several ways. Other rules for apportioning services might serve this end as well, but those distributional rules would not be as broadly acceptable as the ones implied by the generality principle, because non-general rules would only infrequently increase each person's welfare over the unconstrained case. In this sense there may not be a trade off between equity and efficiency at the constitutional level of politics.

We do observe that many public services are distributed, financed, and produced in rough accordance with the generality principle in modern democracies, as with social security programs, law enforcement, and public education. However, causal observation also suggests that political efficiency within most democratic politics could be further improved by greater deference to the generality principle. Many deviations from generality remain significant. The tax code continues to treat different kinds of income differently, and many public services are produced and

distributed in a less than uniform fashion. In many cases, the manner in which public capital projects are produced and distributed seems to reflect the effective political power of regional representative more than the generality principle. Indeed, the existence of all narrow industrial, labor, and regional lobbying groups implies that the level of generality practiced is imperfect, and that political efficiency could be improved by greater adherence to the generality principle.

ROGER D. CONGLETON

REFERENCES

Buchanan, J.M. (1976). "Taxation in fiscal exchange." *Journal of Public Economics*, 6: 17–29.

Buchanan, J.M. and Congleton, R.D. (1998). *Politics by Principle, Not Interest: Towards Nondiscriminatory Democracy.* Cambridge: Cambridge University Press.

Congleton, R.D. (1997). "Political efficiency and equal protection of the law." *Kyklos* 50(1997): 485–505.

Congleton, R.D. (1980). "Competitive process, competitive waste, and institutions," in R. Tollison and R. Congleton (eds.) *The Economic Analysis of Rent Seeking.* Brookfield Vermont: Edgar Elgar Publishing Company, pp. 101–130.

Hayek, F.A. (1960). *The Constitution of Liberty.* Chicago: University of Chicago Press.

Lindahl, E. (1967). "Just taxation — a positive solution," in R.A. Musgrave and A.T. Peacock (eds.) *Classics in the Theory of Public Finance.* New York: St. Martin's Press, pp. 168–176.

Samuelson, P.A. (1954). "The pure theory of public expenditures." *Review of Economic and Statistics*, 36: 387–389.

Weingast, B., Shepsle, K., and Johnson, C. (1981). "The political economy of benefits and costs: a neoclassical approach to distributive politics." *Journal of Political Economy*, 89: 642–664.

Wicksell, K. (1967). "A new principle of just taxation," in R.A. Musgrave and A.T. Peacock (eds.) *Classics in the Theory of Public Finance.* New York: St. Martin's Press, pp. 72–118.

GROUP ROLES IN EVOLUTION AND COGNITION

If public choice can be broadly described as the study of the mechanisms which facilitate cooperative solutions for the provision of "public goods," then the study of the evolution of cooperation should be of interest to those who study public choice. Cooperation in nature, including between modern hunter-gatherers (and presumably our Paleolithic ancestors), was made possible by the evolution of mechanisms that reduced free-riding, very often through enhanced cognitive capacity.

There are several ways that animals, including primates and our hunter-gatherer ancestors, gained from living in groups, including the gains from exchange and specialization in production, further, groups provided protection from rival groups of conspecifics and from other predators. Additionally, hunter-gatherers, who relied on hard-to-acquire large game animals for meat, reduced the variance of meat acquisition by relying on the efforts of several hunters.

Living in groups clearly allows individuals to gain from various forms of cooperation among group members, but those gains come at a cost; specifically, the individual can be harmed because self-interested individuals can also gain from exploiting the productive efforts of others by free-riding, rent-seeking, opportunistic behavior, and outright theft. The evolutionary process that eventually facilitated complex human cooperative behavior necessarily resulted in the evolution of mechanisms that suppressed free riding, thus aligning the social gains from cooperation with the private gains of the individual. The following sections are drawn, with revision, from Gifford (1999, 2000, 2002a,b).

1. Cooperation, Accounting, and Evolving Cognition

William Hamilton's (1964) development of the concept of kin selection, or inclusive fitness, and Robert Trivers' (1971) reciprocal altruism, coupled with the tit-for-tat strategy for repeated games (see, Robert Axelrod, 1984), provide models that can begin to explain why seemingly unselfish behavior can be in the interest of the individual. Hamilton shows that an individual may make sacrifices that benefit another if the following inequality holds: $B \times r > C$, where B, the expected benefit, is the expected increase in fitness to the other individual, where an increase in an individual's "fitness" increases the number of copies of its genes transmitted to the next generation relative to its competitors. The term r is the average degree of relatedness between the two individuals (the average degree to which they have inherited the same copies of their various genes), and C is the expected cost, in fitness, to the individual performing the altruistic act. So, for example, for sexually produced siblings, where $r = 0.5$, an individual will perform an altruistic act that yields a benefit to a sibling that exceeds twice the cost it bears in performing that act.

Reciprocal altruism coupled with tit-for-tat strategies, sometimes called direct reciprocity (DR), takes place in a long-term relationship between a group of non-kin where sacrifices made today by an individual that benefit another individual will be more than made up for by reciprocal sacrifices in the future. A key requirement for this strategy to work is that the players have sufficient brain power to remember the past performance of the other players and that they punish free-riding. For reciprocal altruism to evolve, an increase in the cognitive power of the individual was necessary. This increased cognitive capacity allowed the individual to maintain "mental accounts," the mental balance sheets by which it kept track of its debts to others and theirs to it, as well noting who cooperated in the past and who cheated — a process that reduced the cost to the individual caused by free riders by excluding noncooperators.

The mechanism embodied in Hamilton's rule is also an accounting system, but one maintained purely at the level of the gene, and so it tends to be inflexible, resulting in genetically preprogrammed behavior. Direct reciprocity also involves genetically motivated behavior, but that behavior is much more flexible than what is specified by kin selection. The flexibility is made possible by accounting at the cognitive level, which allows the expansion of non-simultaneous exchange to non-kin and increases the opportunities the individual has to take advantage of gains from cooperation. Two related points are important to keep in mind here: first, for DR to function it is not necessary for the individuals involved to have a conscious understanding of their social relationship, and second, their behavior is not necessarily consciously forward looking, since at this level "…foresight is not necessary for the evolution of cooperation…." Axelrod (1984: 109).

2. Complex Accounting and Complex Cognition

Richard Alexander (1987) has suggested that a much more extensive system of cooperation can be facilitated by indirect reciprocity. Indirect reciprocity (IDR) includes cooperating with those whom the individual has only observed cooperating with others in the past. "Indirect reciprocity develops because interactions are repeated, or flow among society's members, and because information about subsequent interactions can be gleaned from observing the reciprocal interactions of others." Alexander (1987: 77). Social relationships are much more complex in a system in which indirect reciprocity takes place than in relationships involving only direct reciprocity. With DR, the individual need only keep track of his obligations to each of the other individuals in the group and theirs to him. With IDR, the individual must not only keep track of these, but the behavior of all of the other group members in transactions involving the others. The complexity of the cognitive task is several orders of magnitude greater with IDR than with DR, but more importantly, the very nature of the problem is different.

Alexander (1987) also suggests that indirect nepotism (IDN) may have been an important force in the evolution of cooperation. Direct nepotism, inclusive fitness, follows from Hamilton's rule. Indirect nepotism allows the individuals involved to take advantage of the fact that, for example, among three or more siblings helping another is a non-rival good. If sibling 1 provides benefit B to sibling 3, sibling 2 receives the same expected gain as sibling 1, without having to incur the direct cost C. Recognition of the non-rivalness of altruism among individuals carrying the same genes (and between the father and mother in the case of altruism directed toward offspring) allows for a relaxation of the Hamiltonian constraint, thereby expanding the extent of possible altruistic cooperation. Of course, as with all public-goods situations, free riding is a distinct possibility, because the free rider gains a benefit without bearing a cost. Furthermore, the free-rider problem, if not solved, can result in a lower level of altruism than that predicted by Hamilton's rule. Doug Jones (2000) suggests that the free-rider problem can be solved by "conditional nepotism," where two individuals will agree to help a third using the simple rule: I will contribute "*if and only if* " you contribute. Use of this rule requires that each individual understands the other as intentional, and, unlike direct nepotism, requires conscious calculation on the part of the participants.

The modified or conditional nepotism rule for each donor brother is $2/3B > C$ (see Jones, 2000: 782). By increasing the effective coefficient of relatedness, IDN will result in an increased amount of altruistic cooperation. For indirect nepotism to work, as with IDR, the individuals involved must understand the causal nature of each other's behavior and keep mental accounts reflecting not just their own obligations to others and others to themselves, but also obligations *between* the others. Indirect reciprocity and indirect nepotism facilitate much more cooperation than either direct reciprocity or inclusive fitness, however, it is necessary that individuals be forward looking, perceive each other as intentional individuals, and be capable of creating conscious institutional constructs — in other words, be able to form intentional forward-looking social relationships, all of which represents a significant cognitive advance over what is necessary for DR to work. A major requirement for the evolution of these capabilities was the evolution of language. The next section examines cooperation among hunter-gatherers who, using IDR and IDN, maintain conscious forward looking intentional social mechanisms that facilitate complex cooperation.

3. Cooperation in Hunter-gatherer Societies

The dominant political feature of recent hunter-gatherer societies, and presumably that of Paleolithic hunter-gatherer (H-G) societies as well, was egalitarianism. Although a dominant tendency among recent H-G societies was to share large game, this egalitarianism was political, not economic. "The term *egalitarian* does not mean that all members have the same amount of goods, food, prestige, or authority.... The critical element of egalitarianism... is *individual autonomy*." Robert Kelly (1995: 296).

To maintain their egalitarianism, H-G societies form a moral community in which a significant amount of effort is expended in social control aimed at preventing or modifying antisocial behavior. It was this high enforcement cost per capita that made it difficult to extend egalitarianism to the much larger groups that came into existence with the domestication of plants and animals. The high enforcement cost was a product of the active nature of the mechanisms of control: it was necessary for each individual, in essence, to continuously consciously monitor every other individual, which required that they all more or less directly share experiences.

Decisions were made by consensus, allowing each individual to present their opinions, and consent was achieved by persuasion, not coercion (see Christopher Boehm, 1999: 60). The conscious attention required of each band member to maintain freedom meant that five to seven families was roughly the maximum number of social units that could be accommodated without a hierarchy to coordinate activities (Kelly, 1995: 211).

Language and the large brain necessary to support the H-G social contract came at an extremely high cost. "[B]ig brains are expensive organs, requiring a lot of energy to maintain — 22 times as much as an equivalent amount of muscle requires when at rest." Steven Mithen (1996: 11). For a given body size, energy production is relatively constant, and in order for more energy to be made available for a larger brain, other organs must use less. There are not significant substitution possibilities with the heart, lungs, kidneys or liver; the cheapest means of freeing up energy was the evolution of a smaller gut (see Robin Dunbar, 1996: 125). Though a smaller gut will itself use less energy, it will, other things equal, absorb less energy from ingested food. In order to maintain sufficient energy input with a smaller gut, an animal must eat foods that are higher in nutrient content or that contain nutrients that are more easily absorbed (see Dunbar, 1996: 125). Furthermore, large brains required significantly increased prenatal and postnatal nutrition levels, making increased nutrition important for pregnant women and nursing mothers (see Ann

Gibbons, 1998: 1345). A diet with an increased energy content was necessary to support the increase in brain size.

As brain size expanded, our hominid ancestors turned to meat with its high energy and nutrition content (see, Dunbar, 1996: 127; Mithen, 1996: 103). It is within this context that meat-sharing takes on its importance in human biological and cultural evolution. Meat-sharing was a form of cooperation that is much more sophisticated and complex than the simple one-on-one cooperation seen in non-human primates. And since the bands of 25 people contained from five to seven families (Kelly, 1995: 211), the meat-sharing was a form of indirect reciprocity and indirect nepotism, requiring significant forward-looking cognitive capacity.

There are significant variations in the daily returns to hunting in the hunter-gatherer environment, and where food storage is not an alternative, meat-sharing represents an efficient way of reducing the variance in access to meat facing any one family. Meat-sharing was a form of insurance that allowed hunters who were successful on a given hunt to trade lower-valued surplus meat for claims to high-valued meat in the future when their hunting was not successful. Kelly (1995) reports that a band size of 25 containing seven to eight full-time foragers and hunters was sufficient to minimize the variance associated with the uncertainty of food acquisition.

The H-G social contract required a significant amount of conscious attention and monitoring. The marginal cost of maintaining that contract increased rapidly with group size, limiting the band size to about 25 individuals. The rise of agriculture and the sedentary lifestyle that accompanied it resulted in much larger populations and in hierarchical mechanisms of governance that diminished personal freedom and autonomy. It also resulted in some unintended cultural constructs that lowered the cost of cognition. The H-G social contract was a product of biological and cultural evolution, whereas the evolutionary process of the sedentary post H-G social contract was purely cultural.

4. Culture and the Evolution of Cognition

Along with changes in the formal mechanisms of governance, the stable, sedentary, post hunter-gatherer lifestyle allowed for the development of many informal rules and norms that facilitated social interaction and lowered the cost of cognition. These informal mechanisms were, in part, social habits and routines that spontaneously evolved and operated at a non-conscious level. The stable, sedentary lifestyle allowed decision makers to off-load cognitive processes onto the environment to a much greater extent than could mobile bands. Perhaps even more importantly,

the stable environment made possible the evolution of social conventions and institutions that could not develop in mobile bands. Just as mobility made large accumulations of physical capital impractical, mobility made large accumulations of social capital impractical. Significant institution building required a stable environment within which to construct those institutions.

The symbolic mental capacity that made the H-G social contract possible allows us to create such mental constructs as promises, obligations, contracts, marriages, property, money, elections, governments, presidents, corporations, universities and football games (see John Searle, 1995: 97). Importantly, "... a system of collectively recognized rights, responsibilities, duties, obligations, and powers added onto — and in the end was able to substitute for — brute physical possession and cohabitation [that allowed for] a much more stable system of expectations ...." Searle (1995: 81). Such institutional arrangements allow for the formation of long-term expectations and constraints that lower the cognitive cost of making long-term plans. Stable cultural institutions allow for the off-loading of mental accounts onto objects in the environment, two important forms being writing and money. Though language and conscious reasoning are necessary for the construction of institutions, given the limits of reason the institutions themselves are for the most part not consciously planned.

ADAM GIFFORD JR.

REFERENCES

Alexander, R.D. (1987). *The Biology of Moral Systems*. New York: Aldine De Gruyter.

Axelrod, R. (1984). *The Evolution of Cooperation*. New York: Basic Books.

Boehm, C. (1999). *Hierarchy in the Forest: The Evolution of Egalitarian Behavior*. Cambridge, Massachusetts: Harvard University Press.

Dunbar, R. (1996). *Grooming, Gossip, and the Evolution of Language*. Cambridge, Massachusetts: Harvard University Press.

Gibbons, A. (1998). "Solving the brain's energy crisis." *Science*, 280: 1345–1347.

Gifford, A. Jr. (1999). "Being and time: on the nature and the evolution of institutions." *Journal of Bioeconomics*, 1: 127–149.

Gifford, A. Jr. (2000). "The bioeconomics of cooperation." *Journal of Bioeconomics*, 2: 153–166.

Gifford, A. Jr. (2002a). "The evolution of the social contract." *Constitutional Political Economy*, (forthcoming).

Gifford, A. Jr. (2002b). "Emotion and self-control." *Journal of Economic Behavior and Organization*, (forthcoming).

Hamilton, W.D. (1964). "The genetical evolution of social behavior." I, II. *Journal of Theoretical Biology*, 7: 1–16, 17–52.

Jones, D. (2000). "Group Nepotism and Human Kinship." *Current Anthropology*, 41: 779–809.

Kelly, R.L. (1995). *The Foraging Spectrum*. Washington, DC: Smithsonian Institution Press.

Mithen, S. (1996). *The Prehistory of the Mind*. London: Thames and Hudson.

Searle, J. R. (1995). *The Construction of Social Reality*. New York: The Free Press.

Trivers, R.L. (1971). "The evolution of reciprocal altruism." *Quarterly Review of Biology*, 46: 35–57.

GROWTH OF LOCAL GOVERNMENT IN THE UNITED STATES

The growth of government has been a topic of interest to public finance and public choice scholars for decades, but most of that interest has focused on the growth of total government, or in the U.S., the federal government, in the 20th century. This focus is understandable, because of the substantial growth in government worldwide in the 20th century. Borcherding (1977, 1985) examines government growth in the public choice tradition, focusing on 20th century federal government growth, and the influential studies of Peacock and Wiseman (1961) and Higgs (1987) incorporate political institutions into their analysis of 20th century central government growth. Campbell (1995), Holcombe (1999), Musgrave and Culbertson (1953), and Wallis (2000) are other examples of studies with this focus on 20th century federal government growth. Hughes (1977) and Holcombe (2002) have a public choice orientation, and are unusual in that they examine government growth prior to the 20th century. Local government grew in the 20th century also, but the real story of local government growth in the United States began in the 19th century.

In 1820 per capita local government expenditures were $.28 per person (all dollar figures are in constant 1914 dollars unless otherwise noted), and were 13.5 percent of total government expenditures in the United States. By 1913, the year the federal income tax was initiated, local government expenditures were $20.42 per person, and made up 64 percent of total government expenditures (Holcombe and Lacombe, 2001). Although local government expenditures continued to grow after 1913, they began shrinking as a percentage of total government expenditures up through the 1960s, because of substantial federal government growth. By the 1960s local government's share of total government expenditures stabilized and remained at slightly more than 25 percent through the end of the 20th century. The growth in local government expenditures in the 19th century was remarkable, and parallels the growth in federal expenditures in the 20th century in the sense that local government expenditures grew substantially in absolute terms and as a percentage of total government expenditures. In 1820, when local government expenditures were 13.5 percent of total government expenditures, federal government expenditures were 61 percent of the total, and by 1913, when local government expenditures had grown to 64 percent of total government expenditures, federal government expenditures were only 23.3 percent of the total.

One of the main reasons for the substantial growth of local government expenditures in the 19th century was the migration of people to cities. In 1820 only 7 percent of the U.S. population lived in urban areas, and 50 years later, in 1870, 25 percent of the population lived in urban areas. The movement of people to cities cannot explain all of the increase in local government expenditures in the 19th century, however. For one thing, expenditures per city resident were growing substantially over the period; for another, the urban population continued to grow in the 20th century, reaching 75 percent of the population by that century's end, yet federal government growth outstripped local government growth by a good margin in the 20th century.

Legler et al. (1988) analyze city government growth going back to 1850, and Holcombe and Lacombe (2001) present data going back to 1820. The data show that the growth in local government expenditures began in the 1830s. An examination of the components of local government expenditures reveals no specific expenditure component that was responsible for the overall expenditure growth. Expenditures in all categories, from police and fire protection, education, and infrastructure, grew along with the total growth in government expenditures. Thus, it is hard to conclude, for example, that the infrastructure demands of growing cities led to higher local government expenditures. One caveat is that data on 19th century local government expenditures are hard to come by, and there are few studies that examine 19th century local public finance. There is much room for further research on this issue.

There is some evidence to suggest that city government growth was more driven by the supply of revenues rather than the demand for government services. When individual city data are examined, cities appear to have spikes in their overall expenditure growth rates when they get an infusion of tax revenues, by imposing new taxes, raising rates, or more vigorously enforcing the tax laws already on the books. There is a question of causation: perhaps these revenue-enhancing activities are the result of increased demand for government services. However, increases appear to be spread among all government expenditure categories, and do not appear to be related to demand factors.

A plausible explanation for the facts is that when people move to cities, they get locational rents that governments can tax, and that this capture of locational rents by government is what produces increasing government revenue and expenditure. These conclusions are based on limited data, and this is an issue that merits more research.

In the latter part of the 19th century cities became very entrepreneurial, and issued substantial amounts of bonds to support private development (Monkkonen, 1995). The industry most often supported by public debt was railroads, because rail connections became vital to the survival of cites by the latter part of the 19th century. Towns without rail connections withered, while those with rail service thrived. But local debt was used to support other industry too. As long as borrowers repaid their loans to government, government paid off its bondholders, but it was not uncommon for governments to default on their debt when if the industry financed by the debt failed to repay government, even if the government was solvent. Bonds used to support private industry were, in effect, revenue bonds, and it was well-known that risks were greater to those holding bonds used to finance industry than, for example, bonds used to finance school construction. A more significant point is that cities were actively involved in the financing and promotion of local economic development, and local governments remained entrepreneurial up through the late 1920s, when the Great Depression crippled their financing abilities.

At the beginning of the 20th century local governments played a far more significant role in people's lives than any other level of government, in terms of the taxes they paid, in terms of services they received, and because most of their interaction with government was at the local level. But conditions were already changing as the federal government was extending its regulatory reach (Anderson and Hill, 1980; Higgs, 1989), and with the introduction of the federal income tax in 1913 and the U.S. entry into World War I a few years later, the federal government rapidly grew to eclipse local governments. Local governments became more subservient to the federal government in the 1930s, because their revenues were heavily dependent on property taxes and there was widespread default (Wallis, 1984). The federal government, with its ability to use deficit finance, stepped in and provided financial support to local governments, which substantially changed both the character of local government activity and the relationship between the federal and local governments. At the beginning of the 20th century local governments financed almost all their expenditures from own-source revenues, but by the end of the century more than a third of local expenditures were financed by transfers from federal or state government.

Federal funding of local governments has had a substantial impact on the type of activity undertaken by local governments, and perhaps also on their growth. As the traditional public finance literature has noted, federal funding affects the incentives facing local governments, so can alter the nature of their activities, and often the intent has been for federal policies to stimulate an increase in local government expenditures (Gramlich, 1968; Bradford and Oates, 1971). The incentives created by federal funding can have perverse effects, however. Tullock (1971, 1975) notes that local governments have an incentive to make themselves appear needy in order to get federal grants. Local governments may delay projects they would otherwise undertake with own-source funds in order to try to qualify for federal money. Meanwhile, local money will be allocated toward less-worthwhile projects that the federal government would be unlikely to fund. The result will be a misallocation of money toward lower-value projects, as higher-value projects are delayed while local governments engage in rent-seeking to compete for federal funding.

Tiebout (1956) shows that under certain conditions competition among local governments can result in an efficient allocation of resources toward public goods, but as McKenzie and Staaf (1978) note, federal funding of local governments tends to cartelize local governments and reduce intergovernmental competition. One reason is that with substantial local government funding coming from the federal government, there will be less variation across local governments in revenues, so there will be less intergovernmental competition over local taxes. Another is that federal grants rarely come without strings attached. Matching grants, which require local funding to receive federal funding, further act to create more homogeneity in taxation across local governments. Also, funding is often earmarked for particular programs, and because all local governments participate in the same federal programs, the output of local governments becomes more homogeneous. Federal funding reduces the ability of local governments to differentiate themselves on both the revenue and expenditure sides of their activities. The impact of federal policy toward local governments is to make local governments more homogeneous, and this reduction in differentiation reduces intergovernmental competition and sets the stage for excessively large government.

Public choice scholars have had a continuing interest in understanding the causes of government growth, but much of the focus has been on the 20th century growth of federal government. While local government growth did not keep pace with federal growth for the first two-thirds of the 20th century, it has since then, and the onset of rapid local government growth predated rapid federal government growth by nearly a century. Local government growth in the 20th century is closely tied to federal policies which have been designed to increase local government spending, and which have homogenized local governments and made them less entrepreneurial. But local government began its rapid growth long before the federal government. For those interested in understanding the origins of government growth, that naturally points toward looking at local government growth in the 19th century, but there are few studies in the area.

RANDALL G. HOLCOMBE

REFERENCES

Anderson, T.L. and Hill, P.J. (1980). *The Birth of a Transfer Society*. Stanford: Hoover Institution Press.

Borcherding, T.E. (ed.) (1977). *Budgets and Bureaucrats: The Sources of Government Growth*. Durham, NC: Duke University Press.

Borcherding, T.E. (1985). "The causes of government expenditure growth: a summary of U.S. evidence." *Journal of Public Economics*, 28(3): 359–382.

Bradford, D.F. and Oates, W.E. (1971). "The analysis of revenue sharing in a new approach to collective fiscal decisions." *Quarterly Journal of Economics*, 85: 416–439.

Campbell, B.C. (1995). *The Growth of American Government: Governance from the Cleveland Era to the Present*. Bloomington: Indiana University Press.

Gramlich, E.M. (1968). "Alternative federal policies for stimulating state and local expenditures: a comparison of their effects." *National Tax Journal*, 21: 119–129.

Higgs, R. (1987). *Crisis and Leviathan: Critical Episodes in the Growth of American Government*. New York: Oxford University Press.

Holcombe, R.G. (1999). "Veterans interests and the transition to government growth: 1870–1915." *Public Choice*, 99: 311–326.

Holcombe, R.G. (2002). *From Liberty to Democracy: The Transformation of American Government*. Ann Arbor: University of Michigan Press.

Holcombe, R.G. and Lacombe, D.J. (2001). "The growth of local government in the United States from 1820 to 1870." *Journal of Economic History*, 61: 184–189.

Hughes, J.R.T. (1977). *The Governmental Habit: Economic Controls from Colonial Times to the Present*. New York: Basic Books.

Legler, J.B., Sylla, R., and Wallis, J.J. (1988). "U.S. city finances and the growth of government." *Journal of Economic History*, 48(2): 347–356.

McKenzie, R.B. and Staaf, R.J. (1978). "Revenue sharing and monopoly government." *Public Choice*, 33(3): 93–97.

Musgrave, R. and Culbertson, J.J. (1953). "The growth of public expenditures in the U.S. 1890–1948." *National Tax Journal*, 6(2): 97–115.

Monkkonen, E.H. (1995). *The Local State: Public Money and American Cities*. Stanford: Stanford University Press.

Peacock, A.T. and Wiseman, J. (1961). *The Growth of Government Expenditures in the United Kingdom*. Princeton: Princeton University Press.

Tiebout, C.M. (1956). "A pure theory of local expenditures." *Journal of Political Economy*, 64: 416–424.

Tullock, G. (1971). "The cost of transfers." *Kyklos*, 24(4): 629–643.

Tullock, G. (1975). "Competing for aid." *Public Choice*, 21: 41–51.

Wallis, J.J. (1984). "The birth of the old federalism: financing the New Deal, 1932–1940." *Journal of Economic History*, 44(1): 139–159.

Wallis, J.J. (2000). "American government finance in the long run." *Journal of Economic Perspectives*, 14(1): 61–82.

THE GROWTH OF PUBLIC EXPENDITURE

Growth in Gross Domestic Product (GDP) per head in major industrial countries in Western Europe and North America and latterly in some Asian countries has been accompanied by a more than proportionate growth in government expenditure. This may well be regarded as the most important single influence on the evolving structure of advanced economies. It affects the structure of employment, the direction of private enterprise effort in conforming to government policies and in supplying government needs, as well as the composition of personal incomes, increasingly dependent on transfers and taxes to finance them.

1. Measuring Expenditure Growth

An important study by Tanzi and Schuknecht (2000) presents and comments on the now formidable stock of data on the growth of government spending used in the devising of policies by such international agencies as the International Monetary Fund (IMF) and the Organization of Economic Co-operation and Development (OECD).

Table 1 shows the very striking change in the growth of government expenditure over 120 years, much of it clearly concentrated in the post-WWII period. Its very generality gives rise to a number of important queries about its significance:

1. *The Definition of Government*. General Government Expenditure (GGE) includes Government Expenditure on Goods and Services (GEGS), Interest on the Public Debt, and Transfers and Subsidies and covers all layers of government. Regarded as a useful first approximation to a measure of the influence of government on the economy, narrower definitions may be used for both methodological

Table 1: Growth of General Government Expenditure (GGE) 1870–1996 (Per Cent of GDP)

Late 19th century	Pre-WWI	Post-WWI	Pre-WWII	Post-WWII			
Circa 1870	1913	1920	1937	1960	1980	1990	1996
10.8	13.1	19.6	23.8	28.0	41.9	43.0	45.0

Source: Tanzi and Schuknecht, 2000, p. 6.
Note: Average percentage for the following countries: Australia, Austria, Canada, France, Germany, Italy, Ireland, Japan, New Zealand, Norway, Sweden, Switzerland, United Kingdom and United States.

and practical reasons. GGE covers items that are not part of the GDP, notably transfers and subsidies, and exaggerates the extent of the Government's share of GDP (or strictly speaking, Gross Domestic Expenditure) that the narrower definition of GEGS conveys. Some observers prefer to exclude lower layers of government altogether on the grounds that these are only partly under the control of the central government. In short, the investigator has to check very carefully which definition is being used and why.

2. *The Scope of Government.* Wide or narrow definitions of government spending specifically exclude *public enterprises* that may obtain the bulk of their revenue from sales. This creates two problems. It may be difficult to draw the dividing line between public enterprises and government departments. More important is the question of principle. In reviewing the causes of growth in government, it may be central to the analysis to regard growing nationalisation as one of the options open in political decisions to increase the role of government[1].

3. *Time Series Problems.* The longer the period under consideration the more difficult it becomes to present a consistent and comprehensive set of data. The territorial boundaries of a country may change markedly — Germany is a prime example. This problem is partly circumvented by expressing changes in the GGE/GDP ratio in per capita terms. Political changes may dictate reallocation of functions between central government, public enterprises and lower layers of government, making it imperative for the investigator to clarify whether interest should be concentrated on the functions of government or the degree of control exercised by its different authorities. The further back in time the less reliable the data. Earlier data are largely a by-product of the administrative process rather than an integral part of economic policies that only latterly require that it is the government's function to influence macro-economic variables.

2. The Causes of Government Expenditure Growth

The growth in GGE/GDP over the long period is remarkable, it being noteworthy how much of it is concentrated in the latter half of the 20th Century, though there is a noticeable fall in its rate of increase after the 1970s. Economists and others have not been backward in coming forward with explanations. They face the inevitable difficulty that, through time, a government does not remain a constant entity. Government evolves as a succession of political decision-makers whose powers and perception of the uses to which such powers should be put evolve and change.

There is, therefore, a strong case for considering the development of ideas of government growth historically (for further elaboration, see Peacock, 1997). Wagner (1911) regarded his 'Law' as the expression of an empirical uniformity that reflected the growing role of the state as the provider of the infrastructure necessary for the industrial economy to develop. Stigler (1986) has generalised this thesis by arguing that the role of the state will fluctuate according to its perceived comparative advantage in providing goods and services.

It would be straining the concept of comparative advantage too much for it to embrace an explanation for the latter-day growth in social expenditure, notably transfer payments, or what has been termed (Peltzman, 1980) 'the demand for redistribution'. However, this immediately raises the question of the driving force in government decision-making. It is possible to envisage this demand as the anticipation by a paternalistic government of the social consequences of industrialisation, notably uncertain employment prospects and conditions of work, or even the reflection of philanthropic views of the franchised towards the unenfranchised.

A more interesting hypothesis couples the extension of the franchise in the early 20th Century onwards with the pre-tax distribution of income, thus bringing in voter support as a pre-condition for the growth of public expenditure which is consistent with the facts (see Meltzer and Richard, 1983). The degree of support would be a function of both the extension of the franchise and the degree of income inequality. Assuming a majority decision rule, the majority will benefit from redistribution the lower the median income relative to the mean but as the redistribution process continues, the post-redistribution median will approach the post-redistribution mean and gains from redistribution will gradually disappear. The neatness of this model lies in its explanation of both the expansion of GGE/GDP and its' tapering off.

The vote motive may be a necessary but hardly a sufficient condition for government expenditure growth. To assume that the public choice process is one in which the government is simply a passive reactor to a democratically elected legislature is naïve. The combination of the limited opportunities for voters to be continuously involved in the choice process and the suppression of competitors, must allow governments discretion over supply conditions. So it may be presumed that there is a built-in tendency for costs of government to rise as government increases in size.

Support for this contention has been sought in the onset of the familiar Baumol's disease (Baumol, 1993) prevalent in the services provided by government, such as law and order, education and health, because of limited opportunities to increase relative productivity in services as compared with manufacturing industries in which technological change may offset rising labour costs. Furthermore, there is a presumption that inefficiency in government services will rise as government increases in size because of growing opportunities open to budget-maximizing managers of government departments to exploit their control over information on costs and measures of performance (Niskanen, 1994).

These various hypotheses have provided a field day for econometricians, if only by revealing their methodological difficulties. Some very naïve models have been tested, such as those treating Wagner's Law as one where the sole determinant of GGE is GDP and in which the value of estimated coefficients is bound to be biased because of the exclusion of relevant variables. Competitive explanations of GGE growth cannot be regarded as mutually exclusive. However, taking account of a large number of independent variables presents formidable problems of estimation, particularly if an attempt is made to produce an integrated model, including both the perceived supply and demand influences on GE.

Furthermore, the longer the time period, the more likely that the significance of the independent variables will change and the use of fixed elasticity coefficients becomes suspect. For a full account of estimation problems, see particularly Lybeck (1986) and for methodological criticism Wiseman (1989).

3. Consequences of Government Expenditure Growth

The measurement and interpretation of GE growth has led to extensive and continuous discussion of its consequences. The particular strength of a public choice approach lies in its attempts to devise an evaluation of GGE growth that is related to the perception of citizens, rather than having to rely on some unidentifiable social welfare function or arbitrary judgment of what is good for them.

Nevertheless, considerable problems are encountered in identifying public attitudes to the growth of public expenditure. Individual citizens are clearly interested in the composition as well as the amount of expenditure. This calls for a deepening of statistical investigation to cover functional and economic classifications. GEGS is a measure of inputs and not of outputs and government outputs usually are not priced.

This problem is usually circumvented by the use of performance indicators. For example, health services may be judged in terms of the relation between growing inputs of expenditure and indicators, such as changing life expectation and changes in morbidity rates, giving rise to the difficulty of estimating changes in the quality of life. The choice of such indicators raises the question of the changing degree of participation of citizens in the political process. This itself could represent a performance indicator. Indeed, such an indicator is of particular interest to those who seek a measure of the impact of a growing public sector on personal economic freedom (Scully, 2001).

4. Concluding Remarks

The consequences of GGE growth that most exercises governments, given their financing obligations, is the growing lack of control over spending. Policy action calls for minimizing discretionary behaviour by politicians and bureaucrats suggesting a host of reforms including limits on GGE/GDP growth, development of appraisal techniques, and internal pricing systems (Domberger and Jensen, 1997). The most spectacular proposed remedy has been the privatisation of public services, but the radical change that this must produce in the culture of major services, such as health and education, whose management is largely unfamiliar with (and sometimes hostile to) market relationships has made governments wary about using it.

Public utilities, such as telecommunications, broadcasting and energy, present fewer difficulties. However, privatisation, while intended to encourage competition, is normally accompanied by extensive use of regulation of markets. Any expectation that halting the growth of government expenditure will reduce the degree of intervention in the private economy is unlikely to be fulfilled.

SIR ALAN TURNER PEACOCK

NOTES

1. The famous "Wagner Law of Increasing State Activity" specifically includes public enterprises in its formulation (Wagner, 1911), a fact that calls into question the plethora of articles

which apply econometric testing to the 'Law' but exclude public enterprises from consideration (Peacock and Scott, 2000). In the same vein, see Lybeck (1986, Ch. 3, pp. 21–49) for a useful discussion of the variation in growth in government produced by different definitions.

REFERENCES

Baumol, William, Bater, Sue Anne, and Wolff, Edward N. (1985). "Unbalanced growth revisited: asymptotic stagnancy and new evidence." *American Economic Review*, September: 806–817.

Domberger, Simon and Paul Jensen, M. (1977). "Contracting out by the public sector." *Oxford Review of Public Policy*, (4): 67–78.

Lybeck, Joham A. (1986). *The Growth of Government in Developed Economies*. Aldershot: Gower Publishing Company. Chs 3, 5.

Meltzer, Alan H. and Richard, Scott F. (1983). "Tests of a rational theory of the size of government." *Public Choice*, 41: 403–418.

Niskanen, William (1994). *Bureaucracy and Public Economics*. Brookfield: Edward Elgar.

Peacock, Alan (1997). *Public Choice Analysis in Historical Perspective*. Paperback Edition. Cambridge, England and New York: Cambridge University Press.

Peacock, Alan and Scott, Alex (2000). "The curious attraction of Wagner's law." *Public Choice*, 102: 1–17.

Peltzman, Sam (1980). "The growth of government." *Journal of Law and Economics*, October: 209–287.

Scully, Gerald W. (2001). "Government expenditure and quality of life." *Public Choice*, 108: 123–145.

Stigler, George J. (1986). *The Regularities of Regulation*. Edinburgh: The David Hume Institute, pp. 3–4.

THE GROWTH OF THE RELATIVE SIZE OF GOVERNMENT

1. How Government Grew in Wealthy Countries

Throughout the 20th century most industrialized countries experienced a remarkable growth of public expenditure, despite marked differences in their institutional and demographic structures. Up until World War I the size of public spending was relatively negligible in most industrialized countries, due perhaps to the laissez-faire outlook that prevailed during the 19th century. According to Tanzi and Schuknecht (2000), the average share of public expenditure in Gross Domestic Product (GDP) among 17 industrialized countries was a mere 12 percent in 1913, only slightly above 11 percent of 1870. After World War I, however, government spending escalated rapidly as governments took more active roles in economic and social developments,

especially so in reaction to the Great Depression. By 1937 the average size of government among Organization for Economic Co-operation and Development (OECD) countries grew to 23 percent of GDP, doubling the 1913 level.

Such a trend reached its peak between 1960 and 1980. Backed by the general optimism of government's ability to correct various market failures and perhaps by naïve perceptions of government bureaucrats' competency and public spiritedness, average public expenditure as a share of GDP rose from 28 percent to 43 percent during the period, nearly quadrupling the 1870 level. By 1980 the level of government spending in France and Germany approached nearly the half of GDP, while relatively smaller governments of Japan, UK and US kept their public expenditures well above 30 percent of GDP. Interestingly, this growth has considerably slowed down since 1980, and in some countries the share of government spending in GDP even declined, a phenomenon Tanzi and Schuknecht speculate is caused by the Reagan–Thatcher revolution which made voters and taxpayers less sanguine about state actions. From 1980 to 1990, for example, the U.K. share of public expenditure in GDP declined from 43 percent to 40 percent, and similarly so for Belgium, Ireland, New Zealand and the Netherlands. In fact, on average, government spending in all OECD countries rose by only 2.5 percentage points from 1980 to 1996 (Tanzi and Schuknecht, 2000).

Despite this recent slowdown, the growth of government's share of GDP over the past century is both impressive and unprecedented compared to the previous history of public expenditure, inviting numerous scholars to explain this extraordinary phenomenon. We believe that the literature parses the sources of government growth into two broad analytic categories- what Holsey and Borcherding (1997) term "a-institutional" and "institutional" approaches. The a-institutional approach focuses on the "mechanical" aspects of public expenditure growth, anchored in conventional neoclassical economic theory. This paradigm claims that the growth of government's relative size is a natural consequence of changing social and market conditions. On the other hand, the institutional paradigm is concerned mainly with institutional and political modelings of the public expenditure growth in the context of rent-seeking activities among voter-taxpayers, special-interest groups, and government bureaucrats.

2. A-institutional Approaches

On the whole, a-political types of modeling assume that government provision arises due to the failure of private market to provide desired levels of a given public service.

Therefore, determining whose desire is to be served by government becomes a central issue, and it is generally presumed that the median voter plays a key role in determining the level of government expenditures under majority rule. The general procedure for deriving the demand for public services is then identical to determining the median-voter's demand function, which, in turn, depends on the voters' general preferences, incomes, tax-price per unit of services, and the price of related private goods and services. For example, Borcherding and Deacon (1972) and Bergstrom and Goodman (1973) modeled nonfederal U.S. government expenditure as a function of factors that influence the median voter's demand, such as tax-price, income, and a sharing-economy element representing the degree of publicness in consumption of the services provided.

On the supply side of this a-institutional analysis, Baumol's cost disease hypothesis features most importantly. Baumol (1967) argued that because the government sector is largely labor intensive, productivity growth rates are likely lower there compared to those of private capital-intensive industries, causing the relative price of government services to rise over time. Since demands for public services are rather own-price inelastic, the increase in the relative price of government services implies an increase in the real value of government expenditures. In fact, the steady rise in the relative price of government services has been empirically supported by numerous studies, including Bradford et al. (1969); Beck (1976); Spann (1977); Peltzman (1980); Berry and Lowery (1984); Ferris and West (1996, 1999). More recently, Borcherding et al. (2002) found an 0.8 percent average growth rise of the price index of government sector output relative to the GDP deflator for private output for twenty OECD countries from 1970 to 1997. In addition, price-inelastic demands for government services are now established facts in the public choice literature. Early studies by Borcherding and Deacon (1972) and Bergstrom and Goodman (1973) indicated price-inelastic demands in the range of -0.25 to -0.50. These have been replicated by subsequent studies by Perkins (1977) and Gramlich (1985). Not surprisingly, the Baumol price effect is now generally accepted by a large majority of public choice scholars as a major source of public sector expansion (Lybeck and Henrekson, 1988; Ferris and West, 1993).

Income rise is another of the most conventional means to explain the growth of government. Over a century ago Adolph Wagner (1893) observed that as a society and its economy progress over time, the role of government in fiscal-budgetary matters expands both in absolute and relative terms in what he called "the law of expanding state expenditure." Empirically, however, most contemporary researchers are unsupportive of this idea. For "Wagner's law" to be valid income elasticities for the public expenditures must be greater than the unity. Although Pelzman (1980) claimed that the standard estimating technique resulted in downwardly biased estimates, most empirical studies have estimated income Elasticities to be much less than the unity, mostly in the range of 0.5 to 0.75, rejecting Wagner's law even after using refined estimating techniques to adjust for biases previously noted (Ram, 1987; Mueller, 1989; Gemmell, 1990; Henrekson, 1990).

Population enters into the median-voter's demand function via the offsetting effects of joint consumption economies and median voter tax-share reductions. Taking price-elasticity as zero, and given constant marginal cost of providing public goods and services, an increased level of population implies less government spending as a share of GDP, since publicly provided goods are shared amongst more people. On the other hand, this sharing aspect effectively reduces tax-price per unit of the government services to the median voter, thus increasing the quantities demanded since demands are not totally price inelastic. Borcherding (1985) demonstrated that the net effect of population change depends on both the degree of publicness of the service (not much) provided and the price elasticity of given government services (also low). He found that on the whole the two effects cancel each other out. This finding is consistent with the Peltzman's study (Peltzman, 1980) which yielded an elasticity coefficient for population on per capita government spending not significantly different from zero. A recent study by Borcherding et al. (2002) again found no significant relationship between population change and government's relative size.

3. Institutional Approaches

According to Borcherding (1985) and Borcherding et al. (2002), determinants based on traditional economic theories explain no more than fifty percent of public expenditure growth, and likely less. To complete the missing pieces of the puzzle, public choice economists have turned to neoinstitutional and political modelings of the growth of government size. Unlike the conventional method with emphasis on productive, community-service aspect of government services, this political approach typically assumes that government is a vehicle for various sorts of interest groups to promote income redistribution in their own favor, depending on their sizes and relative powers. In this neoinstitutional view of complicated processes of political competition, more powerful coalitions win redistributional gain at the expense of less politically favored groups. As the ownership structure of political influence asymmetrically alters, more redistribution takes place and the size of public expenditure increases.

Although many factors affect this aforementioned redistributional activity, the rules and procedures of the voting process that determine collective choices are crucial. Stigler's "Director's law" (1970) hypothesized that the major beneficiary of public expenditures in democracies is the middle-class, since its financing burdens the various income classes differentially. In the 19th century, Stigler notes, taxes were not tied to personal incomes, nor were benefits of public spending closely tailored to particular beneficiary groups. Instead, federal revenues came largely from tariffs and excise taxes. These severe restrictions on tax discrimination and the targeting of federal expenditures to fairly general-interest projects severely limited the redistributive role of government. Although state and local government grew slightly in relative size from 1870 until 1910, the federal share of U.S. public expenditures actually fell a bit (Borcherding, 1985). As restraints on tax discrimination and limitation on federal expenditures were relaxed in the 20th century — e.g., federal personal and corporate income taxes were introduced in the wake of the 16th amendment of 1913 — taxes and expenditures became more closely tied to income class, enabling the middle class, the putative majority coalition, to seek more redistribution through subsidies and transfer spending. Thus, a larger federal government budget materialized (Stigler, 1970). In fact, Tanzi and Schuknecht (2000) point out that changes in transfer and subsidies explain most of the growth in the U.S. public expenditures during the period of 1960 and 1990, as well as for the other wealthy OECD countries.

Building upon Director's law, Meltzer and Richard (1981, 1983) presented a rent-seeking model based on income classes in the context of the median-voter paradigm. They assume that public services serve redistributive ends and note the skew of income distribution towards the wealthy, since mean income necessarily exceeds that of the median. Given this bias, the median voter (who by hypothesis is the median income earner) sets the effective tax rates and determines the redistributive outcome. Voters with income less than the median's also favor more income redistribution, providing the necessary majority support for government expenditure growth. The key prediction of Director's law model is that the increase in indicators of income inequality (e.g., an increase in the ratio of mean to median income) leads to greater redistribution, hence greater size of government.

Two examples of such structural changes which enhance these rent-seeking fiscal effects were the extension of suffrage to lower income families in the late 19th and throughout the 20th centuries, and the effects of social security system on the number of retired persons (Meltzer and Richard, 1981). Using U.S. time-series data and econometric estimation techniques, Meltzer and Richard (1983) discovered a statistically significant positive relationship between government spending and the ratio of mean to median income. Nevertheless, subsequent studies of this phenomenon for other countries have yielded mixed results. For example, using a pooled cross-sectional time-series data for many industrialized countries, Kristov et al. (1992) show a negative correlation between government expenditures and income inequality.

Peltzman (1980) also has modeled a redistributive rent seeking of income-based coalitions, which focuses upon the vote-gathering and coalition-forming processes. While differences among groups promote redistributive rent seeking, effectiveness of these activities depends on the transaction costs and returns of forming effective coalitions and preventing the formation of blocking ones. Peltzman's model recognizes that, along with between-group inequality, within-group equality tends to increase the level of redistribution implying greater size of government. As incomes are more evenly distributed within potential beneficiary classes, the transaction costs of forming successful coalitions fall, making redistributive efforts more effective. His study concluded that the growth of government in the post-World War II period was attributed mostly to the growth of a more homogeneous middle class, which gave differential advantage to this group over the rich and poor, strengthening both the theoretical and empirical case for Director's law.

Several other scholars also appeal to competition among pressure groups to influence fiscal processes for political favor as of explanatory importance. Unlike Stigler's and Peltzman's income-class approaches to redistribution where the majority systematically manipulates the minority through the democratic process, interest group theories are driven by the assumed lower organization costs of smaller, more homogeneous groups organized on non-class bases and the ability of these to exploit larger, less-cohesive citizen groups. In general, such theories imply that (1) specialization and increased division of labor accompanied by economic development increase the numbers of powerful interest groups (Demsetz, 1982; North and Wallis, 1982, 1986), and (2) these larger numbers of interest groups tend to increase the size of government spending (Demsetz, 1982; Olson, 1982). Recently, more theoretical attention has been given to incorporating electoral politics and interest groups into fiscal choice. Becker (1983, 1985) developed a pressure group influence function, which depends on time and money spent on rent-seeking effort, as well as the degree of free riding due to increasing group size. In the

Becker model, the main determinant of the relative strength of interest-group pressure is the efficiency, or its negative complement-deadweight cost, of the tax system. He concludes that more efficient tax systems actually lower general taxpayer-voter influence relative to the pressure of the competing subsidy recipient group, thus increasing budget size. More recently, he and Mulligan (1998) have demonstrated empirically that there is a positive correlation between tax system efficiency and the size of government. The preliminary work of Dušek (2002) for the U.S. from 1940 to 1970 confirms this. Generally speaking, these findings imply that the introduction of value-added type taxes in the 1970s in all OECD countries, but the U.S., contributed importantly to the growth of public spending. Perhaps this explains why its adoption is so fiercely resisted in the U.S. (Holsey and Borcherding, 1997).

Another important strand of the budget growth literature claims that government growth may be the result of rent-seeking activities of government bureaucrats. Just as income-based coalitions in the models of Meltzer and Richard (1981) and Peltzman (1980) seek redistributional gain at the expense of others, interest groups in the Becker (1983) framework spend resources to enhance their political influences for the same purpose. Clearly, government bureaucrats and public employee unions are also motivated to transfer the wealth of general taxpaying public in their favor. Niskanen's budget-maximizing theory states that government bureaucrats are hardly benevolent promoters of the public weal, but, instead, are rational rent seekers with a desire for larger budgets. Because bureaucrats are principally motivated by "power, pay and prestige" and possess some monopoly power over the supply of public services, the budget is likely to be pushed beyond the median voter's ideal level (Niskanen, 1971). Romer and Rosenthal (1978, 1979) operationalized this theory by proposing the notion of a "budget reversion point." The budget is expanded when monopolistic bureaucrats offer an alternative budget so small that the larger, bureaucratically preferred budget is chosen. In an empirical study, Borcherding et al. (1977) also confirm the Niskanen conjecture by scrutinizing the hypothesis that the existence of civil service regulations caused higher levels of spending in state and local governments. They found that within the U.S., non-federal per capita public expenditures were positively correlated with the length of time civil service regulations were in effect.

These bureaucracy models were further developed by Brennan and Buchanan (1977) in their Leviathan theory, which added limits of various sorts on the Tiebout (1956) effects of citizen mobility and inter-jurisdictional competition to the framework of budget-maximizing bureaucrats.

The Leviathan approach reasons that greater centralization over time has increased government's monopoly power, since voters have fewer locational choices than in decades past. With less competition from other districts, government is more able to inflate its budget without seriously risking the loss of taxable income bases or other revenue sources (Brennan and Buchanan, 1977, 1978, 1980). Although empirical studies of the Leviathan theory have produced mixed results, the centralization hypothesis seems to work well as an explanation of greater nonfederal public spending in the U.S., particularly with respect to local governments where citizen mobility is otherwise less restricted (Oates, 1989).

Increased levels of fiscal illusion theory is yet another neoinstitutional force for explaining the relative growth of government. This theory basically holds that taxpayers systematically underestimate their tax burdens, while self-interested bureaucrats pursue more than the median voter's ideal level of public expenditures. Such illusions come in a variety of forms, such as "(1) complexity of tax structure, (2) renter illusion respect to property taxation, (3) income elasticity of tax structure, (4) debt illusion, and (5) the flypaper effect (Oates, 1988, 60)." While empirical studies of the fiscal illusion hypothesis generally have resulted in mixed results, renter's illusion (renters incorrectly believe that landlords pay property taxes) and flypaper effect (voters erroneously perceive lump-sum grants as lowering marginal tax price) have received wide empirical support. The fiscal illusion literature, however, does not explicitly model who manipulates and reaps the benefits of voter misperceptions (Mueller, 1989). While we suppose that Niskanean bureaucrats could be in the position of utilizing taxpayer misperceptions, neither income-based coalitions nor special interest groups can be readily overlooked as they are also, by hypothesis, able to influence the bureaucrats through electoral politics and political pressures.

Additionally, in spite of their theoretical and empirical underdevelopments, several alternative theories of government growth are also worth mentioning: (1) changing ideologies and social preferences (Lindback, 1985; North, 1985a); (2) reduced community inputs, including diminished social capital (Hamilton, 1982; Schwab and Zampelli, 1987); (3) increased household production costs (North, 1985a; Breton, 1989); and (4) rising transaction costs (North and Wallis, 1982, 1986; North, 1984, 1985a,b). These theories argue that government expenditures grew over time because citizen-consumers set higher priority on publicly provided services relative to private market services; lower levels of community resources increased the median voter's tax-price; increased geographic mobility and the participation of women in the labor force greatly increased household costs of providing the typical family services; and greater specialization and division of labor increased the transaction costs of market exchange. Interestingly, these hypotheses are concerned with changes in socioeconomic environments and their effects on demands for government services. Empirical evidence for these approaches, though hardly strong, is decidedly suggestive.

4. Concluding Thoughts

While economic theories of government growth focus upon the median voter model, institutional approaches span a wider range of frameworks, adding more social and *realpolitik* factors missing in the neoclassical analysis. Less generally recognized, however, is that the conventional budgetary measure of government size becomes a less useful indicator of the magnitude of government's influence over the economy as regulation, the alternative political instrument to fiscal activity, increases (Posner, 1971). This means that the true size of government should also incorporate an estimate of the spending equivalent necessary to obtain private sector compliance with public sector regulatory rules and directives. Without properly accounting for this "quiet side" of government activity (Leonard, 1986), public expenditures will significantly underestimate the full impact of government on the overall economy. Leonard (1986) finds several sources of budget understatement: promises of retirement benefits and social insurance, tax expenditures, subsidies in sale of public activities to favored groups, and, of course, regulatory impositions of government on the private sector. In the recent study of government growth of twenty OECD countries in the post-1970 period, Borcherding et al. (2002) used two measures of the degree of regulation to show that relatively more regulation is positively correlated with the size of public expenditures, suggesting that regulation and government spending are complements rather than substitutes for one another. They also show that although regulation adds to the relative size of U.S. government, it does not seem to increase the rate of growth in the post-1980 period, since the ratio of regulation costs to fiscal spending was roughly constant. It will be interesting to discover whether this holds generally for the other OECD countries.

Finally, our survey focused totally on the growth of spending in wealthy countries. If we were to look at the developing world, we would find that government spending shares were much smaller than for the richer countries (by 5 to 15 percentage points). We also believe that the unmeasured regulatory sector would be vastly understated. Again,

this illustrates the desirability of developing accurate measures of the regulatory side of the public sector.

THOMAS E. BORCHERDING
DONG LEE

REFERENCES

Baumol, W.J. (1967). "The microeconomics of unbalanced growth: the anatomy of urban crisis." *American Economic Review*, 57(June): 415–426.

Beck, M. (1976). "The expanding public sector: some contrary evidence." *National Tax Journal*, 29(March): 15–21.

Becker, G.S. (1983). "A theory of competition among pressure groups for political influence." *Quarterly Journal of Economics*, 98(August): 371–400.

Becker, G.S. (1985). "Public policies, pressure groups and deadweight costs." *Journal of Public Economics*, 28(December): 329–347.

Becker, G.S. and Mulligan, C.B. (1998). "Deadweight costs and the size of government." NBER Working Paper #6789.

Bergstrom, T.C. and Goodman, R. (1973). "Private demands for public goods." *American Economic Review*, 63(June): 280–296.

Berry, W.D. and Lowery, D. (1984). "The growing cost of government: a test of two explanations." *Social Science Quarterly*, 65(September): 735–749.

Borcherding, T.E. (1985). "The causes of government expenditure growth: a survey of the U.S. evidence." *Journal of Public Economics*, 28(December): 359–382.

Borcherding, T.E., Bush, W.C., and Spann, R.M. (1977). "The effects on public spending of the divisibility of public outputs in consumption, bureaucratic power, and the size of the tax-sharing group," in T.E. Borcherding (ed.) *Budgets and Bureaucrats: The Sources of Government Growth*. Durham: Duke University Press, pp. 211–228.

Borcherding, T.E. and Deacon, D. (1972). "The demand for the services of non-federal governments." *American Economic Review*, 62(December): 891–901.

Bradford, D.F., Malt, R.A., and Oates, W.E. (1969). "The rising cost of local public services: some evidence and reflections." *National Tax Journal*, 22(June): 185–202.

Brennan, G. and Buchanan, J.M. (1977). "Towards a tax constitution for Leviathan." *Journal of Public Economics*, 8(December): 255–274.

Brennan, G. and Buchanan, J.M. (1978). "Tax instruments as constraints on the disposition of public revenues." *Journal of Public Economics*, 9(June): 301–318.

Brennan, G. and Buchanan, J.M. (1980). *The power to Tax: Analytical Foundations of a Fiscal Constitution*. Cambridge: Cambridge University Press.

Breton, A. (1989). "The growth of competitive governments." *Canadian Journal of Economics*, 22(November): 717–750.

Demsetz, H. (1982). "The growth of government," in deVries Lectures, No. 4. *Economic, Legal and Political Dimensions of Competition*. Amsterdam: North-Holland.

Dušek, L. (2002). "Do governments grow when they become more efficient? Evidence from tax withholding." *Ph.D. Thesis proposal*, Department of Economics, University of Chicago (April).

Ferris, J.S. and West, E.G. (1999). "The cost disease versus Leviathan explanations of rising government cost." *Public Choice*, 98(March): 307–316.

Ferris, J.S. and West, E.G. (1996). "The cost disease and government growth: qualifications to Baumol." *Public Choice*, 89(October): 35–52.

Ferris, J.S. and West, E.G. (1993). "Changes in the real size of government: US experience 1948–1989." Carleton Economic Papers 93-01, Department of Economics, Carleton University.

Gemmell, N. (1990). "Wagner's law, relative prices and the size of the public sector." *The Manchester School*, 57(September): 361–377.

Gramlich, E.M. (1985). "Excessive government spending in the U.S.: facts and theories," in E.M. Gramlich and B.C. Ysander (eds.) *Control of Local Government*. Stockholm: Almqvist and Wiksell International, pp. 29–73.

Hamilton, B.W. (1982). "The flypaper effect and other anomalies." *Journal of Public Economics*, 22(December): 347–361.

Henrekson, M. (1990). "An economic analysis of Swedish government expenditure." *Ph.D. Thesis*, Gothenburg University.

Holsey, C.M. and Borcherding, T.E. (1997). "Why does government's share of national income grow? An assessment of the recent literature on the U.S. experience," in D.C. Mueller (ed.) *Perspectives on Public Choice: A Handbook* New York: Cambridge University Press, pp. 562–589.

Kristov, L., Lindert, P., and McClelland, R. (1992). "Pressure groups and redistribution." *Journal of Public Economics*, 48(July): 135–163.

Leonard, H.B. (1986). *Checks Unbalanced: The Quiet Side of Public Spending*. New York: Basic Books.

Lindback, A. (1985). "Redistribution policy and expansion of the public sector." *Journal of Public Economics*, 28(December): 309–328.

Lybeck, J.A. and Henrekson, M. (1988). *Explaining the Growth of Government*. Amsterdam: Elsevier Science Publishers.

Meltzer, A.H. and Richard, S.F. (1983). "Tests of a rational theory of the size of government." *Public Choice*, 41(3): 403–418.

Meltzer, A.H. and Richard, S.F. (1981). "A rational theory of the size of government." *Journal of Political Economy*, 89(October): 914–927.

Mueller, D.C. (1989). *Public Choice II*. Cambridge: Cambridge University Press.

Niskanen, W.A. (1971). *Bureaucracy and Representative Government*. Chicago: Aldine-Atherton.

North, D. (1984). "Government and cost of exchange." *Journal of Economic History*, 44(June): 255–264.

North, D. (1985a). "The growth of government in the United States: an economic historian's perspective." *Journal of Public Economics*, 28(December): 383–399.

North, D. (1985b). "Transaction cost in history." *Journal of European Economic History*, 14(September–December): 557–576.

North, D. and Wallis, J.J. (1986). "Measuring the transaction sector in the Amrerican economy, 1870–1890," in L. Engerman and R.E. Gallman (eds.) *Long-term Factors in American Economic Growth*. Chicago: University of Chicago Press.

North, D. and Wallis, J.J. (1982). "American government expenditures: a historical perspective." *American Economic Review*, 72(May): 336–345.

Oates, W.E. (1989). "Searching for Leviathan: a reply and some further reflections." *American Economic Review*, 79(June): 578–583.

Oates, W.E. (1988). "On the nature and measurement of fiscal illusion: a survey," in G. Brennan (ed.) *Taxation and Fiscal Federalism: Essays in Honor of Russell Mathews*. Sydney: Australian National University Press, p. 60.

Olson, M. Jr. (1982). *The Rise and Decline of Nations: Economic Growth, Stagflation and Social Rigidities*. New Haven: Yale University Press.

Peltzman, S. (1980). "The growth of government." *Journal of Law and Economics*, 27(October): 209–287.

Perkins, G.M. (1977). "The demand for local public goods: elasticities of demand for own price, cross price and income." *National Tax Journal*, 30(December): 411–422.

Posner, R.A. (1971). "Regulation as taxation." *The Bell Journal if Economics and Management Science*, 2(Spring): 22–50.

Ram, R. (1987). "Wagner's hypothesis in time-series and cross-section perspectives: Evidence from 'real data' for 115 countries." *Review of Economics and Statistics*, 69(May): 194–204.

Romer, T. and Rosenthal, H. (1978). "Political resource allocation, controlled agendas and the status quo." *Public Choice*, 33(Winter): 27–43.

Romer, T. and Rosenthal, H. (1979). "Bureaucrats versus voters: on the political economy of resource allocation by direct democracy." *Quarterly Journal of Economics*, 93(November): 563–587.

Schwab, R.M. and Zampelli, E.M. (1987). "Disentangling the demand function from the production function for local public services." *Journal of Public Economics*, 33(July): 245–260.

Spann, R.M. (1977). "Rates of productivity change and the growth of state and local governments," in T.E. Borcherding (ed.) *Budgets and Bureaucrats: The Sources of Government Growth*. Durham: Duke University Press, pp. 102–129.

Stigler, G.J. (1970). "Director's law of public income distribution." *Journal of Law and Economics*, 13(April): 1–10.

Tanzi, V. and Schuknecht, L. (2000). *Public Spending in the 20th Century*. Cambridge: Cambridge University Press.

Tiebout, C.M. (1956). "A pure theory of local government expenditure." *Journal of Political Economy*, 64(October): 416–424.

Wagner, A. (1893). *Grundlegung der politshen Oekonomie*. Leipzig. Third Edition.

H

HERESTHETICS AND THE EVOLUTION OF THE US CONSTITUTION

In the long run, outcomes are the consequences not only of institutions and tastes, but of the political skill and artistry of those who manipulate agendas…generate "false" issues… to exploit the disequilibrium of tastes to their own advantage. (Riker, 1980: 444)

After writing on U.S. politics and developing formal theory for nearly thirty years, William Riker came to the conclusion that "nearly anything can happen in politics" (Riker, 1980: 445). This led him to the idea of "heresthetic," the study of manipulation. The word is based on the Greek, αίρετίκοξ, "to choose," and is intended to be juxtaposed to "rhetoric" — the art of persuasion. The purpose of rhetoric may be to change the beliefs of agents, whereas that of heresthetic is to change the meaning, or understanding, of the consequence of a particular choice.

Possibly the most well-known example given by Riker of an heresthetic maneuver was the alleged 'trap' set by Abraham Lincoln for his opponent, Stephen Douglas, in the 1858 Illinois Senate race. At Freeport, in August, Lincoln asked Douglas whether it was possible for "the people of the United States Territory, in any lawful way, against the wishes of any citizen of the United States, [to] exclude slavery from its limits prior to the Formation of a State Constitution" (Fehrenbacher, 1989a: 542)

Were Douglas to answer yes, he would appeal to antislavery sentiments in Illinois, and increase his chances of winning. However, he would also anger pro-slavery southern interests, and lessen his chances of being the sole Democratic candidate in the 1860 presidential election. By answering no, it would be probable that he would lose the Senate race, and never come to represent the Democracy. Douglas did answer yes, and did indeed win the Senate race. Moreover, in 1860, the South did refuse to accept his candidacy. Riker argues that this contributed to Lincoln's victory. In fact, the logic of the situation was more complex than suggested by Riker. Lincoln's victory, I shall argue, depended very much on the profound rhetoric he utilized to persuade the North that it was threatened by the South. This threat stemmed from the Southern belief that the extension of slavery to the West was justified. In this sense, Lincoln's acts and speeches were no mere manipulation, but were

designed to change the understanding of the northern electorate about the structuring of the world. In Riker's later work, the notion of heresthetic was developed to mean something akin to rhetoric. The two are distinct, however: whereas rhetoric usually appeals to emotions, heresthetic appeals to reason and logic. I shall return to this interpretation of Lincoln's heresthetic below.

Riker's last book, published posthumously (Riker, 1996) dealt with the process of ratification of the constitution in 1787–1788. For Riker, the confederation of states that had proved successful against Britain in 1776–1783, had shown itself too weak to deal with the threat by Spain on the Mississippi. Spain had controlled Louisiana since 1783, and threatened to close the Mississippi, and New Orleans, to American shipping. This would have made it well nigh impossible for the US to expand its economy by developing the Ohio Valley. As Beard (1913) had argued much earlier, Federalists and anti-Federalists were divided over issues of debt and the Bank. The second issue of concern was the problem of factionalism: the extended republic would presumably be more exposed to factional chaos than the smaller independent states. The arguments of Jay and Hamilton in the *Federalist* (Bailyn, 1993) were designed to remind readers of the dangers of the foreign threat, while Madison's constitutional logic, as expressed in *Federalists* 10 and 51 in particular, was that the "extended republic" and the safeguards embodied in the constitution, would mitigate against factionalism.

These analyses in the *Federalist* can be seen to be an heresthetic, designed to persuade the electors of the wisdom of the choice of ratification of the Constitution.

During the administration of John Adams (1797–1800), Thomas Jefferson mounted a heresthetic campaign against Hamilton's scheme to construct a Federalist, commercially based, political economy based on a Bank and fiscal responsibility. In many ways, Hamilton's ambition was to recreate the successful regime in Britain under the Whig Supremacy and Walpole's "prime ministership" of the period 1715–1742.

Walpole's opponent in Britain was Henry St. John, Viscount Bolingbrooke, who denounced the chicanery and corruption of the Whig regime. As Pocock (1975: 447) has noted, "corruption…took the forum of credit, accompanied by the diabolic trinity of stockjobbing, faction, and standing army." Prior to the election of 1800, Jefferson made use of such rhetoric, in the same fashion as Bolingbroke, against the incipient corruption of the Federalists. In the electoral college, Jefferson and Aaron Burr both won 73 votes to 65 for John Adams and 63 for Pinckney. As a result, the vote went to the House, where eight states voted for Jefferson, and six for Burr. (Vermont and Maryland were divided.) It is believed that veiled promises by Jefferson led to the abstention of the Federalists in the two divided states. These states went Republican, giving Jefferson the presidency (Weisberger, 2000: 275). Burr had to be content with being vice-president.

What may have been a heresthetic maneuver by Jefferson led to the creation of a dominant coalitional Republican Party (later, the Democracy) that essentially remained in power until 1860.

Any close election is potentially subject to heresthetic maneuvering. The presidential election of 1824 also involved four candidates, and went to the House. In the electoral college, the results were Andrew Jackson (99), John Quincy Adams (84), William Crawford (41), and Henry Clay (37). Unlike 1800, John Calhoun won the separate vice presidential election. Clay was eliminated from the House vote, and gave his support to Adams. Cunningham (1996: 178) notes that Adams recorded in his diary that Clay and Adams "spoke of some principles of great public importance, but without any personal considerations." In the House, Adams won the six New England states, and New York (all his in the electoral college) and the three western states (Kentucky, Missouri, and Ohio) won by Clay. Jackson had won eleven states and Crawford three (Delaware, Georgia and Maryland) in the electoral college. Surprisingly, none of the three Crawford states voted for Jackson: instead, Maryland, Louisiana and Illinois switched from Jackson to Adams, giving John Quincy Adams thirteen states and the presidency. Although Clay was confirmed by the Senate as Secretary of State in March 1825, there is no evidence of collusion between Adams and Clay. In fact, Nagel (1998: 294) observed that Clay believed that joining the Adams administration was "the stupidest act of his career." However, there was a strong element of contingency (one of the underlying aspects of heresthetics). Without New York state, Adams could not have won the election, and the New York vote for Adams was the result of the choice of a single delegate, Van Rensselaer.

Clay and John Quincy Adams also feature in a complex heresthetic maneuver in 1844. In that year, the Southern delegates to the Democratic Party Convention imposed a 2/3-decision rule. This gave them blocking power, so they could stop the nomination of ex-President Martin Van Buren. After eleven ballots, a dark horse candidate, James Polk, a slaveholder from Tennessee, gained the democratic nomination and then the presidency. In the November 1844 election, Clay, the Whig candidate, gained 105 votes in the electoral college, to Polk's 170. A change of 5,000 votes in New York would have switched 35 electoral college votes from Polk to Clay, giving the the latter victory. Thomas Hart Brenton (1856) called the whole election "the most elaborate, complex and daring intrigue ever practised in an intelligent country."

One feature of the election was that it almost broke apart the intersectional (north and south) coalition of the Democracy. The story is recounted in Miller (1996), although for its origins it is necessary to start with the arrival of the schooner, *Amistad*, in August 1839, off Long Island (Jones, 1987). The schooner had been hijacked by African slaves who were alleged by the Spaniards aboard to be *ladinos* (slaves speaking Spanish, and born in Cuba). The Africans asserted they were *bozales*, captured in Africa and brought illegally to Cuba.

Legal actions, brought by the Spaniards to return the Africans to Cuba, were defeated in court in New Haven in 1839. The administration under the Democrat President, Van Buren, tried to intervene, to have the Africans shipped to Cuba. Possibly as a result of the attendant controversy, the Democratic majority in the house on January 29, 1840, passed a permanent gag rule, to "silence the abolitionist agitation," refusing to hear any petition regarding slavery. In the presidential election of November, 1840, Van Buren gained only 60 electoral college votes (mostly in the South), while the Whig, Harrison, gained 234 (123 in the North). Van Buren's commanding lead of 1836 in the North had evaporated. The Whigs also took a majority in the House in the election of that year. John Quincy Adams, ex-president and by then a House Representative, argued the case for the *Amistad* Africans in early 1841 before the Supreme Court. In November of that year, the thirty-five freed survivors sailed from New York to Sierra Leone. In January 1842 the House, under its new Whig majority, tried to censure Adams but eventually gave up the effort.

In the 1844 Democratic Party presidential nominating convention, Van Buren, and his policy opposed to annexation of Texas, gained a majority, but not the two-thirds required. Polk with a policy of "manifest destiny" (leading to the Mexican war and the attempted expansion of slavery) gained the nomination and then the presidency (Wilson 1984: 210). In December 1844, 55 Democrats, disillusioned by the double-cross of their coalition partners in the South, voted with 53 Whigs to rescind the gag rule. All Southern democrats, together with sixteen Whigs (mostly from the Western states of Ohio, Indiana, and Illinois) voted to retain the gag rule, but failed. Texas was annexed to the Union on December 29, 1845. John Quincy Adams called it the end of Civilization. He died, aged 80, in February 1848, the last Federalist.

The issue of the expansion of slavery became increasingly significant in the next decade. The *Dred Scott* decision of the Supreme Court in March 1857 appeared to deny the constitutionality of the Missouri Compromise of 1820, banning slavery from territorial land, north of 36° 31'. Indeed the decision appeared to deny the constitutional right of the Federal government to forbid slavery in any

Territory (Fehrenbacher, 1978, 2001). In speeches from June 1857, on, Lincoln argued against the validity of this decision. Moreover, his third question to Douglas at Freeport, raised the possibility that the Supreme Court could decree that *States* could not exclude slavery from their limits. Although Lincoln lost the 1858 Illinois Senate election, he was invited to New York and New Haven in February, March 1860. In his speeches there he pursued the constitutional argument against the South, arguing that the intention of the Founders was to limit slavery, while the intention of the South was to extend slavery throughout the Union (Fehrenbacher, 1989b: 115, 142).

There is no evidence that Douglas's answer at Freeport in 1858 turned the South against him. In fact, a general view in the South prior to Freeport was that while Douglas could win for the Democracy in 1860, this would bring demoralization as well as disaster to the South (Schofield, 2002). In April 1860, Southern delegates attempted a repeat of the Polk strategy of demanding a 2/3 majority.

Although Douglas gained a majority of the delegates, he was blocked from gaining 2/3, and the convention split in two. In the November election, Lincoln gained straight majorities in 15 states. The electoral college vote was split between Lincoln and Douglas in New Jersey. Only in California and Oregon would a combined Democrat slate (of Douglas and Breckinridge) have defeated Lincoln. Even in New York, where a combined "fusion" slate (Bell, Breckinridge and Douglas) was attempted, Lincoln still gained a majority. Had New York gone "Democrat" (with a 4% change), then Lincoln would have only gained 145 electoral college votes, rather than the 152 needed for a majority. In that case, as in 1824, the vote would have gone to the House, where Lincoln would probably only have won 14 states, out of 33 (Miller, 2002: 466).

After Lincoln's success in November 1860, a compromise, the Crittenden Resolutions of January 1861, was proposed which would have extended slavery to the Pacific, south of the line 36° 30'. The slave-interest backed its threat by the secession of six of the Southern states, re-affirming the Calhoun doctrine that Lincoln's election broke the logic of Union. The creation of the northern "tyrannical" majority broke this logic as expressed by Madison in *Federalist* 10. Under the compact of the Constitution, the southern states could legitimately secede. Lincoln's veto of the compromise forced another seven states to secede, often against the wishes, apparently, of a majority of their electorate.

It seems clear that the South did indeed intend to extend slavery, at least to the Pacific. Lincoln's heresthetic between 1857 and 1861 was to show this truth to the Northern electorate, and to argue that Civil War was the only way to remove this threat, while preserving the Union.

Thus, Riker's notion of heresthetic refers, in essence, to the resolution of a deep constitutional quandary by the revelation of truth through reason and logic.

NORMAN SCHOFIELD

REFERENCES

Bailyn, B. (ed.) (1993). *Debate on the Constitution.* New York: Library of America.

Beard, C. (1913). *An Economic Interpretation of the Constitution of the United States.* New York: Macmillan.

Benton, T.H. (1856). *Thirty Years in the Senate.* New York: Appleton.

Cunningham, N.E. (1996). *The Presidency of James Monroe.* Lawrence, Kansas: University Press of Kansas.

Fehrenbacher, D.E. (1978). *The Dred Scott Case: It's Significance in American Law and Politics.* New York: Oxford University Press.

Fehrenbacher, D.E. (ed.) (1989a). *Abraham Lincoln: Speeches and Writings: Volume 1, 1832–1858.* New York: Library of America.

Fehrenbacher, D.E. (ed.) (1989b). *Abraham Lincoln: Speeches and Writings: Volume 2, 1859–1865.* New York: Library of America.

Fehrenbacher, D.E. (2001). *The Slaveholding Republic.* New York: Oxford University Press.

Jones, H. (1987). *Mutiny on the Amistad.* Oxford: Oxford University Press.

Miller, W.H. (1996). *Arguing about Slavery.* New York: Knopf.

Miller, W.H. (2002). *Lincoln's Virtues: An Ethical Biography.* New York: Knopf.

Nagel, P.C. (1998). *John Quincy Adams: A Public Life, a Private Life.* New York: Knopf.

Pocock, J.G.A. (1975). *The Machiavellian Moment.* Princeton: Princeton University Press.

Riker, W.H. (1980). "Implications from the disequilibrium of majority rule for the study of institutions," *American Political Science Review,* 74(July): 432–446.

Riker, W.H. (1996). *The Strategy of Rhetoric.* New Haven: Yale University Press.

Schofield, N. (2002). "Constitutional Quandaries and Critical Elections," *Politics, Philosophy and Economics.*

Weisberger, B.A. (2000). *America Afire: The Revolutionary election of 1800.* New York: Harper Collins.

Wilson, M.L. (1984). *The Presidency of Martin Van Buren.* Lawrence, Kansas: University Press of Kansas.

HOMO ECONOMICUS

1. Introduction

The Latin term, *homo economicus,* means simply "economic man." It is also sometimes used to connote the general economic methodology which stresses maximizing behavior by individual actors. As such, this approach has proved useful, especially in its broader applications such as public choice, where the use of the economic man assumption has provided a powerful perspective from which to analyze self-interested behavior in a political setting. Nonetheless, the use of the self-interest hypothesis by economists, both in public choice and elsewhere, has proven to be and continues to be controversial and misunderstood.

2. The Economic Approach

Almost any economics textbook begins by explaining how economists approach the analysis of human behavior. Individuals are characterized as having preferences for a variety of goods. These preferences are assumed to be stable and transitive, and they can express a desire for any type of "commodity." Economic man does not have to be crass and materialistic; he can be other-regarding and loving. Economics simply does not tell us what people want.

What economics does tell us is that if we know what people want, we can predict how they will pursue their objectives; namely, economics says that people will pursue their objectives efficiently. This is what is meant by economic man, who seeks to use the resources at his disposal carefully in an effort to obtain his favored objectives in the best possible way. Thus, economic man is a maximizer, another way of saying that he does the best he can with what he has.

The economist's law of demand is an empirical proposition about such behavior. Individuals seek to minimize the effects of constraints, such as prices and income, on their behavior. The statement fact that quantity-demanded varies inversely with price, all else equal, is an expression of economic or maximizing behavior.

The fact that economists say that people maximize does not mean that they are perfect or all knowing. To the contrary, economic man is typically beset by a host of difficulties as he goes about his business, including lack of information, uncertainty, and numerous other impediments to achieving his goals efficiently. In some cases economics can deal with such issues and incorporate them into the economic man model (information costs), and in others there has been less success in this regard (uncertainty).

The important point here is that the economic man approach is a general model of human behavior. It applies not only to private behavior in markets but to behavior in general and to political behavior in particular. The genesis of the public choice revolution was the simple transference of the economic man model into the political arena. And everyone knows the story from there. Modeling political

agents as self-interested actors using economic methodology opened the door to an intellectual revolution. Political actors are not different from ordinary people. They pursue their goals (reelection) effectively, and they respond in a predictable manner. They may behave differently (bureaucrats maximize budgets; corporate executives maximize profits), but it is because the constraints they face are different and not because their fundamental behavior is different.

This is a short summary of the economic approach. As we shall see, however, the economist's model is not without its critics.

3. Is the Self-interest Axiom Relevant?

One important fact of the charges of irrelevance and lack of realism made against economic analysis is the question whether man is basically self-interested, whether maximizing behavior accurately describes the real world. Economics, it is claimed, is based on an out-dated psychological model of man. This criticism stems from a mistaken and narrow view of the economic approach. Economists recognize that humans are motivated by complex forces. However, these complex forces are not important in the examination of all questions, and it is often possible to obtain predictive results based on very simple assumptions about human motivation. It is not that the economist views the world in a simple-minded fashion, but rather that it is not necessary for him, in order to make predictive statements, to become involved in a quagmire of behavioral questions about human motivation which are outside the realm of his professional competence. This does not mean that the economist does not know that individual behavior is or can be vastly different from what his assumptions presume, or that he is denigrating the importance and origins of different types of individual behavior. It only means that in considering *some* problems he finds the effects of these differences not significant enough to warrant special attention.

Economists take maximizing behavior as a guideline, but they do not limit their consideration of maximizing behavior to economic variables alone; they also tend to look at broader trade-offs among political and other variables. The economist does not view the concept of self-interest narrowly. Individual choice is simply characterized as utility-maximizing behavior. Many human motivations, including those of love, altruism, and power, result in behavior that can be regarded as utility-maximizing. This is not to imply that economists think that man cannot change or that his preferences cannot be influenced by noneconomic forces. If we turn the economist's self-interest assumption on its head, it is possible to envisage a world of selfless people. But the critic who argues this view should try to develop consistent and predictive models of this form of behavior, and this has not been done. Moreover, where such models have been implemented (e.g., Cambodia), they have failed miserably.

The critic does play an important role in pointing out the limitations of analysis. Indeed, alternative kinds of models — an economy of love, if you will — might be quite relevant to describing some forms of human behavior, i.e., family disputes. But it should be stressed that there is competition, even in a world of saints, concerning different views of the general welfare. Consider the differences among competing religions as an example. Indeed, as Buchanan (1972) has argued, it is in part the reluctance of other social science disciplines to undertake rigorous positive examination of such behavior patterns that has led to the extension of economics into so many areas that were heretofore the realm of the other social sciences.

In general it should be stressed that economists, from their perspective that men behave in a self-interested way, recognize the importance of institutions, such as markets, that minimize the need for "good action" to solve social problems. In other words, they seek to design institutions that channel self-interest into socially desirable patterns, rather than basing social policy on appeals to the love of mankind or attempts to build character (Robertson, 1956).

Thus in considering a particular problem the economist first looks to the market for solutions. If he concludes the market is operating inadequately, he will probably propose a subsidy or tax on the grounds that the use of individual incentives is the most efficient type of intervention in markets characterized by self-interested actors. A real-life example of this can be seen in the recent clamor about the energy crisis. Where the political goal is to reduce fuel consumption, an economist will probably recommend an increase in the price of fuel, rather than suggest a campaign for voluntary energy conservation. There may be circumstances when administrative appeals to good will or voluntary action are quite appropriate, and there are clearly cases where such appeals influence behavior. But to the typical economist, if a substantial reduction in consumption is required, an increase in price is viewed as necessary.

The charge that economic theory is "cold" is largely a result of the fact that economists try to think in a calculating way about things that often have a highly emotional element. This leads those who are critical of the economic approach to the caricature of economic man. Kenneth Boulding (1969) in his presidential address to the American Economic Association argued that this attack, which comes from both the left and the right, arises from the economist's neglect of the heroic. While economic man may be a clod to some, Boulding said, heroic man is a fool, and he wondered how economic institutions had survived so long, given the fact that economic man is so unpopular. Somewhere in between the clod and the fool is the human. The important point is that economic theory does not depend on purely economic man to be valid. As Boulding (1969, p. 10) says "No one in his senses would want his daughter to marry an economic man."

Many of the criticisms leveled at economics from other disciplines stem from the tendency of economists to be primarily interested in considerations of economic efficiency. This is a natural result of their training, which teaches them to apply the concept of economic efficiency in a rigorous manner to the problems they choose to investigate. It is incorrect, however, to say that the economist is not interested in equity. On the contrary, much work in economics is devoted to the concept of equity and its application to different economic problems.

4. Relevance and Progress in the Economic Approach

The general charge that economics is irrelevant is an empty question. In fact there are two basic charges of irrelevancy. One is simply that the economic approach is the wrong kind of approach. This, of course, depends on the question being addressed. The other charge, that much of abstract economic theory has no applicability, is more related to the issue of the degree of relevance of the economic approach and also to the question of how the economic approach becomes more relevant over time.

First, the economic approach becomes more relevant as it investigates real-world problems. One way that it can do this is to broaden its utility-maximization axiom to look at non-economic factors, e.g., power, love, and so forth, and to look at motives broader than those purely economic in nature.

A second way in which economics becomes more relevant over time is by broadening the scope of investigation of economic factors. Indeed, while the methodology of modern economics has remained basically the same, there have been significant expansions to incorporate such factors as the economics of uncertainty, the cost of acquiring information, and the cost of time, to name only a few.

5. Anomalies

The modern critique of economic man models centers on the discovery of so-called anomalies in behavior, by which is meant behavior which does not comport with maximizing behavior as normally postulated by economists. Thaler (1992) has been a leader in this research. Suffice it to say here that not a lot of these anomalies refer to public choice behavior and that in general these results continue to stir up controversy. For every anomaly there is an alternative explanation based on maximizing principles. No doubt, this is a war for the soul of economists, and we shall have to wait and see how the evidence comes in.

6. Concluding Remarks

The economic man methodology has carried the Public Choice revolution a long way. It has also allowed economists to colonize other disciplines (Tullock, 1972). Properly understood, it offers a way for economics to continue to grow and expand.

ROBERT D. TOLLISON

REFERENCES

Boulding, K. (1969). "Economics as a moral science." *American Economic Review*, March: 1–25.

Buchanan, J.M. (1972). "Toward an analysis of closed behavioral systems" in J.M. Buchanan and R.D. Tollison (eds.) *Theory of Public Choice*. Ann Arbor: Michigan Press, pp. 11–23.

Robertson, D. (1956). *Economic Commentaries*. London: Staples.

Thaler, R.H. (1992). *The Winner's Curse: Paradoxes and Anomalies of Economic Life*. New York: Macmillian.

Tullock, G. (1972). "Economic imperialism." in J.M. Buchanan and R.D. Tollison (eds.) *Theory of Public Choice*. Ann Arbor: Michigan Press, pp. 317–329.

HUMAN EVOLUTION AND POLITICAL BEHAVIOR

In economic theory, tastes are taken as exogenous and outside the system. This leads to a certain looseness in theorizing; it is tempting to explain anomalous behavior by adding a particular taste to the utility function. For standard economic behavior this practice is relatively harmless, as goods are easily recognizable. However, for certain types of behavior this can seem rather arbitrary, as when Andreoni (1989) added a "warm glow" to the utility function to explain some forms of altruism. While his construct has been useful and is now relatively standard in the literature, nonetheless, it is somewhat ad hoc. Students of public choice are faced with similar problems in trying to explain particular forms of political behavior, including issues relating to the importance of ideology in political behavior and even voting.

There are an increasing number of papers in the literature explaining tastes in terms of evolution. We have those tastes that caused our ancestors to survive and reproduce, and so tastes are inherited. There are papers, for example, explaining tastes for risk (Rubin and Paul, 1979) and time preference (Rogers, 1994). For summaries, see Zak and Denzau (2001) and Robson (2001). Ridley (1997) relates evolution to economically relevant tastes. Here, I consider applications to political behavior, a less developed endeavor.

1. Positive Analysis

The analysis of evolution and political behavior is just beginning. Most evolutionary psychologists have confined their attention to individual or small group behavior, and political scientists and economists have not spent much time analyzing evolutionary theory. In what follows, I hope to show that this form of analysis has contemporary relevance and can shed light on issues that are of interest to students of public choice. Much of this discussion is based on Rubin (2002), where many additional implications can be found.

2. Evolutionary Background

Political analysis often starts with a "state of nature," a situation in which humans had no rules. But this is not a useful metaphor for studying human political behavior because such a state never existed. Humans were never humans with no rules; even chimpanzees have some political structure (de Waal, 1982, 1996). Political philosophies such as Marxism that assume complete malleability of humans are misguided and often very harmful. To understand our evolved behavior it is necessary to consider the "environment of evolutionary adaptedness" (EEA). This was a world of relatively small bands of humans or protohumans, with bands of perhaps 25–200 persons who made their living by hunting (mostly men) and gathering (mainly women.) Intelligence increased over the time of the EEA, as did pair bonding between males and females. The best discussion of this model and its implications is Barkow et al. (1992).

Humans and their closest relatives, chimpanzees, are patrilocal — groups of related males live together. This increases the possibility of male bonding and cooperation for activities such as hunting and predation against neighbors. This has been an important input into human political behavior, since patrilocalality has meant that males would have relatives with whom to form coalitions, and coalition formation is the essence of primate politics (de Waal, 1982). Moreover, a male can father more children than a female can bear. This increases the payoff to males from activities that generate access to more females. The result is that males are much more risk taking and much more political than females. Most political actors in the EEA, and even today, are males (Ludwig, 2002). Males who engaged in such activities were disproportionately likely to be our ancestors, so we have inherited tastes for these behaviors. These tastes can persist even if they are decoupled from the fitness returns that would have been common in the EEA.

Within group and between group conflict have been important factors in human behavior, and in existing primitive societies both forms of conflict are substantial. Death rates from violence are much higher than in contemporary societies. (For within group conflict, see Knauft, 1991; for between group, see Keeley, 1996). Indeed, the evolution of human intelligence requires some force with positive feedback, and the standard view is that this force has been conflict (Humphrey, 1976; Alexander, 1987; Byrne and Whiten, 1988; Whiten and Byrne, 1997). (I do not discuss the biological basis for altruism here; that is discussed elsewhere in this volume: Rubin, 2003.)

3. Group Behavior

Humans universally distinguish between in-group members and others. This distinction is made almost automatically. However, the nature of groups is very flexible. Humans can identify with almost any group, no matter how arbitrarily defined. Such group identification is based on tribal mechanisms in the EEA, where there was substantial conflict between bands or groups. This may be the basis for the ethnic conflict that we observe around the world. However, the example of the U.S. and other multi-ethnic societies indicates that such conflict is not inevitable, but rather that it can be reduced. This would be useful for those societies that are currently experiencing such conflict, particularly since ethnic conflict in today's world is not productive in any sense — either in terms of increased fitness or in terms of increased wealth. Policies in the U.S. and other advanced countries such as affirmative action that stress race are counterproductive because they can lead to race based group identity, and might well eliminate the remarkable gains the U.S. has made in reducing ethnic competition.

4. Envy

Accumulation of wealth in the EEA was probably the result of shirking and failing in a responsibility to share. Opportunities for wealth increasing activity were severely limited. As a result, humans may have developed tastes for disliking the wealthy or tastes including envy. Such tastes seem very common among humans. In today's world, most wealth accumulation is through productive activity, and so envy and tastes for envy are harmful and counterproductive.

In non-human species and in hunter-gatherer societies, hierarchies ("pecking orders") are generally used for allocation of scarce goods, including often access to females. Humans in hunter-gatherer societies resisted hierarchies, so much that Boehm (1999) referred to a "reverse dominance hierarchy," meaning that subordinates formed a coalition to limit the power of chiefs or other dominants. Humans have taken the evolved form of hierarchy and adapted it to new uses. In particular, among humans, hierarchies are used for productive as well as allocative purposes. It is likely that the widespread use of hierarchies for productive purposes came about at the time of the transition from mobile to sedentary hunter-gatherer societies, because there was probably relatively little specialization (except by gender, which is universal among humans) in earlier societies.

In the modern western world there is socially imposed monogamy and so wealthier individuals are not able to use increased wealth to engross excessive numbers of females. Moreover, individuals must be compensated if they are to take subordinate roles in hierarchies. Therefore, in modern societies, productive hierarchies are useful and beneficial for all concerned. But productive and dominance hierarchies have many features in common. In both, higher ranked individuals receive more resources, and higher ranked individuals can issue commands to lower ranked members. Therefore, humans (both normal humans and students of human behavior) often confuse the two uses. For example, the *Communist Manifesto* (Marx, 1888) with its discussion of workers as "...privates in the industrial army ... placed under the command of a perfect hierarchy of officers and sergeants." (p. 6) clearly suffered from this confusion. For both analytic and policy purposes, it is important to understand the difference.

5. Political Freedom

We are all products of natural selection. However, many of the factors involved in natural selection lead to individualism. Many processes are forms of frequency dependent games, where the optimal strategy (evolved or chosen) by an individual depends on the strategies others are playing. As a result, individual differences are an important evolved characteristic of humans.

Because of this evolved individuality, freedom has been an important characteristic of human political systems throughout most of our existence, and humans have a strong taste for freedom. On the other hand, human males and pre-human ancestors have sought political power as a way of obtaining access to females. But humans have also tried to avoid being dominated. The best evidence is that through most of human existence and the period of our evolution, when our ancestors were hunter-gatherers living in small bands, dominant individuals had relatively little power. This was not because they did not seek such power, but rather because non-dominants banded together to limit the power of the dominants. (Boehm, 1999). With the beginning of sedentary societies and of agriculture, the power of dominants increased substantially. Most of written history is the story of conflicts between various groups of dominants, or between dominants and subordinates. Until relatively recently, dominants generally won. But in most of prehistory (the time period when humans evolved to our current state) there was much more equality among males.

A necessary condition for the increase in democracy and the reduction in the power of dominants was probably socially imposed monogamy. Polygamous societies have some advantages in competition with other societies. However, they also have costs. In contemporary conditions, the advantages of monogamy seem to outweigh those of polygamy. Polygamous societies create bands of unmarried males, and control of these bands may require a coercive state. Evidence indicates that Moslem societies, which allow polygamy, are less democratic than others (La Porta et al., 1999).

6. Political Decision-making

As we have gone from living in groups of perhaps 50 individuals to our huge societies of today, we have adapted decision making mechanisms from the smaller societies. This adaptation has worked well, at least in Western societies, but not perfectly. We can see traces of earlier ways of making decisions.

A useful way to characterize human decision making is in terms of two separate mechanisms (Evans and Over, 1996). One mechanism is unconscious and makes use of all available information in an environment; the other is more formal and satisfies self conscious verbalized rules. This may explain some differences between opinions of "experts" and others on various policy issues. Humans are quite good at making decisions in many contexts using available information, and "fast and simple" heuristics can reach surprisingly good results. (Gigerenzer et al., 1999). Decisions also exhibit various forms of status quo bias, including loss aversion and endowment effects, that

probably had value in the EEA but may be less valuable now. For example, loss aversion might make it excessively difficult to terminate a government program even when it should be ended.

In many political decision problems, we pay excessive attention to identifiable individuals. In the EEA, there were only identifiable individuals, and we did not evolve to be able to make good decisions for large groups of anonymous individuals. This can lead to some errors in policy, such as insufficient use of cost–benefit analysis. Moreover, much decision making based on identifiable individuals leads to policies increasing the size and power of government, as government is enlisted to benefit indefinable persons at the cost of imposing unnoticed but real harms on the mass of society. Framing effects, which may be a result of use of the wrong decision module, can also lead to errors. For example, we tend to overemphasize intentions of actors and underestimate real effects — an error first pointed out by Adam Smith. People can deceive themselves; in politics, this self deception probably takes the form of individuals convincing themselves that policies that benefit them are socially desirable. Because we evolved in small groups where each individual has important inputs into decision making, we may have a tendency to believe that our input as an individual is more important in decision making than is in fact in our current mass societies. This may explain voting. Even though the probability of a vote being decisive is zero, humans may have evolved to believe that each person has a real impact on decisions.

7. Normative Implications

Analysis of our evolutionary background makes it possible to make strong normative statements. This is because our utility functions have evolved and evolutionary analysis can say something about these utility functions. Normative analysis then becomes objectively anchored in our evolutionary past. In particular, it becomes possible to rate societies on the basis of the extent to which they satisfy these utility functions. All political systems are not created equal. Humans do have a particular and specific set of preferences, and some systems are simply better at satisfying those preferences than are others. Edgerton (1992) and Kronk (1999) describe tribal societies with institutions that are harmful — sometimes extremely harmful, and even fatal — to their citizens. For more advanced societies with institutions that benefit powerful elites and dominants, and harm many others, we need look no farther than the Nazi or Communist regimes of the last century, which each caused tens of millions of deaths (Rummel 1995; Glover 1999.) Harmful cultures may be those that are organized to benefit dominant individuals at the expense of others, as has often been true of human societies.

The current American and Western political systems have many desirable properties. Indeed, these are the best systems that have existed, in the sense of being the most consistent with evolved human preferences and the best at satisfying these preferences. But even these systems have in the recent past had substantial problems. It was only 150 years ago that the United States had slavery, and it was only fifty years ago that many parts of the United States engaged in exceedingly unpleasant racial and ethnic policies. Although such policies are no longer legal here, some individuals still behave in racist ways. It has only been since the passage of the Nineteenth Amendment in 1920 that women were granted the right to vote in the United States, and the Civil Rights act effectively enfranchising racial minorities is even more recent. Further improvements are of course possible. Nonetheless, in almost all dimensions, modern western democracies, and particularly the United States, do a better job of satisfying evolved preferences than any other human society of the past or present. Some examples follow.

8. Individualism

As mentioned above, humans are individualistic. Political ideologies or theories that assume everyone to be the same will invariably create much human misery. We live in large anonymous societies. In these societies, there are numerous possibilities for consumption, and so we can satisfy these different tastes. Similarly, in modern capitalist societies the division of labor is extremely fine. As a result, there are many jobs and occupations individuals can fill. This again gives us possibilities to satisfy individual preferences. In earlier societies, there were more limited possibilities for consumption and for occupational differentiation, so humans had fewer opportunities to satisfy unusual or unique preferences. The contemporary United States allows widely varying life styles. The mobility created by capitalism also allows individuals to move within society in order to find a congenial life style, and geographic mobility within a given political jurisdiction is relatively easy, and is apparently becoming easier.

9. Sociality

Humans are a social species. As humans, we have always lived in groups. In the evolutionary environment, these groups would have been mainly genetic kin, but this is not the only mechanism for group identity. Group identity today is much more flexible. Humans seem to be able to easily identify with many groups, with many definitions, including even completely arbitrary identification mechanisms. This flexibility of the group identity mechanism must be counted as a desirable characteristic of humans. In today's society, it is possible to join any number of groups, with interests tailored to virtually any set of preferences, and eighty percent of individuals belong to at least one group, and many belong to several. Modern transportation and communication, products of capitalist production technologies, make finding and meeting with like minded others much easier; the Internet, an invention of modern society, is particularly useful in finding and communicating with others. There are few restrictions on forming or meeting in groups; indeed, in the United States the First Amendment to the Constitution protects the "right of the people peaceably to assemble."

10. Conflict

The negative side of our group preferences is the possibility of ethnic polarization. One group, based on ethnic, racial or religious characteristics, can engage in xenophobic predation against other ethnic groups. The United States has the advantage of not having any large majority ethnic group. Being an "American" is totally a political, not an ethnic, identification, in that many Americans are only very distantly genetically related to other Americans. This makes the risk of predation by one ethnic group against another much less likely here than in other countries. This appears to be an advantage of the United States over even Western Europe, which also includes modern liberal democracies. After all, the Nazis were in power in Germany only sixty years ago, and anti-Semitism in Europe is apparently increasing again (for example, Goodstein, 2002). Such predation has been a real risk throughout most of human existence. More generally, democracies are significantly less likely than other forms of government to engage in ethnic predatory policies (Rummel, 1994). Additionally, as incomes increase, such predatory policies also become less likely (Scully, 1997).

Although conflict is a part of modern life, for most citizens the chance of dying in a war is small. For example, in World War II only seventeen percent of the United States male population was mobilized, and only about forty percent of those served in combat units. Moreover, wars are relatively rare for major societies such as the United States — apparently on the order of about once per generation. In the twentieth century less than 1 percent of the male population, and even less of the female population, in the United States and Europe died as a result of war (All data from Keeley, 1996.) I do not want to be overly optimistic — at the beginning of the twentieth century it was commonly thought that the era of war was over and that humanity was entering an era of peace (Glover, 1999). However, for the average citizen of a western country, the risk of death in war is now quite low, and clearly much lower than in the EEA. Keeley estimates that the rate of death in tribal societies from war is twenty times larger than in the twentieth century.

11. Cooperation

We are a highly cooperative species. Cooperation in modern society works at two levels. We directly cooperate and work with others in relatively small groups where everyone knows everyone else. This is the evolutionarily old form of cooperation, and the one we intuitively understand best. But the impersonal market is a form of cooperation as well. This is a relatively new form of cooperation. It is the form of cooperation studied by economics. But it is the most powerful mechanism available for satisfying human wants, and for inducing cooperation. Indeed, in many respects almost the entire world is engaged in cooperative endeavors, coordinated through the market. Cooperation through the impersonal market is relatively new in evolutionary terms. Therefore, many do not intuitively understand it, and are excessively hostile to the market. This hostility may be based on our evolved predilection for envy, or for judging actions based on motives, rather than outcomes. But the modern west gives great scope to relatively unregulated markets, and the effects are greatly increased wealth to satisfy human desires.

12. Political Power

Our society performs well in the area of political power. Government is weaker in advanced western democracies than in other societies. The only competitor may be the band level societies of the EEA, which had reverse dominance hierarchies that limited the power of dominant individuals. But in these societies men generally had much more power than did women. For example, Edgerton (1992) points out that wife beating has been approved in "virtually every folk society." That is no longer true in western societies. Women have much more freedom and power in these societies than in any others. Indeed, it is this freedom that has allowed feminism to flourish in modern western societies. This is an important benefit, and one that should not be ignored.

In the west, we have returned to a world with relatively little power given to dominants. There are many mechanisms limiting power of dominant individuals. Governments are designed and planned explicitly to limit such power, and this is the stated purpose of the U.S. Constitution. (See also Grady and McGuire, 1999; Zywicki, 1999.) Moreover, there are many competing power centers in advanced societies, such as powerful businesses. Individuals can compete in any number of hierarchies, not merely in a governmental hierarchy. Since women now have full political equality in most of the west, it is true that today humans in the developed west have more freedom than has ever been true of the mass of humans in any society in the past. Moreover, the recent defeat of the Communist countries in the "Cold War" indicates that societies with more freedom are likely to prevail in today's world.

One important implication of the analysis is that we should be careful to restrain the power of government. Public choice scholars have always argued that government employees and politicians are no different from other humans, and that there is no strong reason to expect them to act in the "public interest" if that interest harms their private interests. But the biology strengthens this argument. Humans are strongly selected to maximize individual fitness, and if this goal conflicts with another goal, we would generally expect fitness to win out. Moreover, individuals differ from each other, and we would expect those who gain the most from using power to achieve their goals to be attracted to government service. Because humans are good at self deception, we would expect government workers to believe that they are serving the public interest, even as they are acting to maximize their own fitness. Governments have in historic times been major oppressors of humans. In the West, we have crafted a system that reduces the ability of government to engage in such oppression. But this does not mean that we can entrust government with unlimited power. Moreover, larger governments encourage more wasteful rent seeking activities, and more free riding.

It is a puzzle, however, to explain why many, including many intellectuals, want to increase the power of the government; reducing and limiting this power is one of the great human achievements. Nonetheless, although we may debate the scope of government on the margins, overall democratic western governments give less power to dominant individuals than any other form of government.

13. Economics

Modern western society is the richest society that has ever existed. Even relatively poor people in the West have access to goods and services that would have been unimaginable even to the rulers in the relatively recent past. Such goods include, for example, entertainment on TV, easy and inexpensive travel, and a wide variety of high quality foods available all year long. This level of wealth is itself a real benefit to humans. Our level of wealth and technology also makes many political activities possible. One example is the ease of communication and the consequent difficulty of government censorship. Books and videocassettes are examples; the Internet and electronic communication are others. It is also cheaper and easier to utilize the ultimate anti-government mechanism, emigration, because transportation costs are much lower than in the past. However, possibilities are limited by unwillingness of many countries to receive immigrants.

14. International Trade and Immigration

One of the most difficult tasks for economists has been to explain to others that free international trade is beneficial. We have apparently done a good job of this, and barriers to trade are lower now than at any recent time. But an analysis of the biology indicates why the task has been difficult. Humans have some innate xenophobic tendencies, and those opposed to free trade are sometimes able to invoke these tendencies in order to impose restrictions. Analysis of trade issues in military language ("trade wars") spreads this incorrect view of exchange. But reduction in trade barriers is an important task for the political system. Recent protests against "globalization" are another manifestation of tribalism and lack of understanding of the mutual benefits of exchange.

Free international trade has another important benefit. Humans desire peace, and calls for the end of war are common. One suggestion is the creation of a world government. However, even if such a government could be created, it would itself generate serious problems, as the possibility of exit as a check on government power would obviously be lacking. Increased trade between countries can increase the cost of war, and humans respond to prices and so can be expected to react to this increase in cost by reducing conflict. Moreover, increased economic interdependence can increase without bound. Thus, increased trade and economic interdependence is a more reliable engine for reducing conflict than is increasing the size and scope of government. However, as long as the possibility of conflict exists, we must realize that predation through violence is possible, and take appropriate measures for defense.

We can also gain from immigration of skilled foreigners. Such workers can increase our own welfare, as well as their own. We in the United States, which is a desirable target for immigration, could also allow more immigrants who could generate increased wealth for ourselves and for the immigrants. Increased immigration could also solve any problems with our Social Security system (Storesletten, 2000).

At various times, human xenophobic preferences have been invoked to limit immigration or confine immigration to certain ethnic groups. This is no longer an issue in US immigration policy.

PAUL H. RUBIN

REFERENCES

Andreoni, James (1989). "Giving with impure altruism: applications to charity and ricardian equivalence." *The Journal of Political Economy*, 97(6): 1447–1458.

Alexander, Richard D. (1987). *The Biology of Moral Systems*. New York: Aldine de Gruyter.

Barkow, Jerome H., Leda Cosmides, and John Tooby (eds.) (1992). *The Adapted Mind*. New York: Oxford University Press.

Boehm, Christopher, (1999). *Hierarchy in the Forest: The Evolution of Egalitarian Behavior*. Cambridge: Harvard University Press.

Byrne, Richard and Andrew Whiten (eds.) (1988). *Machiavellian Intelligence: Social Expertise and the Evolution of Intelligence in Monkeys. Apes and Humans*. Oxford: Clarendon Press.

de Waal, Frans (1982). *Chimpanzee Politics: Power and Sex Among Apes*. London: Jonathan Cape.

de Waal, Frans (1996). *Good Natured: The Origins of Right and Wrong in Humans and Other Animals*. Cambridge: Harvard University Press.

Edgerton, Robert B. (1992). *Sick Societies: Challenging the Myth of Primitive Harmony*. New York: Free Press.

Evans, Jonathan St. B.T. and David E. Over (1996). *Rationality and Reasoning*, East Sussex England: Psychology Press.

Gigerenzer, Gerd, Peter M. Todd, and the ABC (Center for Adaptive Behavior and Cognition) Research Group (1999). *Simple Heuristics That Make Us Smart*. New York: Oxford University Press.

Glover, Jonathan (2000). *Humanity: A Moral History of the Twentieth Century*. New Haven: Yale University Press.

Goodstein, Laurie (2002). "O Ye of much faith! A triple dose of trouble," *New York Times*, June 2.

Grady, Mark F. and Michael T. McGuire. (1999). "The nature of constitutions." *Journal of Bioeconomics*, 1: 227–240.

Humphrey, Nicholas (1976). "The Social Function of the Intellect," in P.P.G. Bateson and R.A. Hinde (eds.) *Growing Points in Ethology*. Cambridge UK: Cambridge University Press, pp. 303–317.

Keeley, Lawrence H. (1996). *War Before Civilization*. New York: Oxford University Press.

Knauft, Bruce (1991). "Violence and sociality in human evolution." *Current Anthropology*, 32: 391–428 (including comments and reply).

Kronk, Lee (1999). *That Complex Whole: Culture and the Evolution of Human Behavior*. Boulder. CO: Westview Press.

La Porta, Rafael, Florencio Lopez-de-Silanes, Andrei Shleifer, and Robert Vishny (1999). "The quality of government." *Journal of Law, Economics and Organization*, 15: 222–279.

Ludwig, Arnold M. (2002). *King of the Mountain: The Nature of Political Leadership*. Lexington: University of Kentucky Press.

Marx, Karl (1888). *Manifesto of the Communist Party* web edition: Project Guttenberg.

Ridley, Matt (1997). *The Origins of Virtue: Human Instincts and the Evolution of Cooperation*. New York: Viking Press.

Robson, Arthur J. (2001). "The biological basis of economic behavior." *Journal of Economic Literature*, 39: 11–33.

Rogers, Alan (1994). "Evolution of time preference by natural selection." *American Economic Review*, 84: 460–481.

Rubin, Paul H. (2002). *Darwinian Politics: The Evolutionary Origin of Freedom*. New Brunswick: Rutgers University Press.

Rubin, Paul H. (2003). "Altruism," this volume.

Rubin, Paul H. and Chris Paul (1979). "An evolutionary model of taste for risk." *Economic Inquiry*, 17: 585–596.

Rummel, R.J. (1994). *Death By Government*. New Brunswick: Transaction Publishers.

Scully, Gerald. (1997). "Democide and genocide as rent-seeking activities." *Public Choice*, 33: 71–97.

Storesletten, Kjetil (2000). "Sustaining fiscal policy through immigration." *Journal of Political Economy*, 108: 300.

Whiten, Andrew and Richard W. Byrne (eds.) (1997). *Machiavellian Intelligence II: Extensions and Evaluations*. Cambridge, UK: Cambridge University Press.

Zak, Paul and Arthur Denzau (2001). "Economics is an evolutionary science," in Albert Somit and Stephen Peterson (eds.) *Evolutionary Approaches in the Behavioral Sciences*, Volume 8. Elsevier Sciences Ltd, pp. 31–65.

Zywicki, Todd J. (1999). "The nature of the state and the state of nature: a comment on Grady & McGuire's paper," *Journal of Bioeconomics*, 1(3): 241–261.

I

IDEOLOGY

1. Introduction

Ideology is a thorn in the side of public choice. The discipline would be more powerful and more useful if it were not true that ideological factors were important in explaining political behavior. This is true for at least two reasons. First, public choice applies economic methods and theories to political behavior. But economic theory has no theory of ideology and no room for ideological factors, and so the application of public choice is weakened by the importance of factors that are outside of economics. Second, a key tenet of public choice theory is that people operate in the political realm in about the same way as in the economic realm. But in normal economic behavior, there is little room for ideological aspects of behavior. Although people may try to boycott South African products or to purchase recycled paper goods, consumption decisions of this sort are marginal and fairly unimportant. But as shown below, ideological factors are much more important in politics. Nonetheless, empirical evidence indicates that ideology is an important part of political behavior, and scholars must take the world as we find it.

Public choice scholars have examined two main issues associated with the influence of ideological factors on political behavior. First is the existence question: is there such an influence? Second is the role of the ideology of the elected representative versus the role of constituent ideology. This has been addressed as a form of "shirking": do elected representatives avoid accountability by voting their own ideological preferences instead of the interests of their constituents? We now have answers to these questions. First, ideology does matter. Second, politicians do not shirk; rather, elected representatives dependably pursue their constituents' interests. However, in the process of answering these questions, the analysis of ideology has been markedly advanced and its empirical relevance has been extensively explored. This analysis shows that ideology may be a primary building block of political conduct. I discuss each of these issues: existence, shirking, and current and new problems related to ideology.

If the question of the significance of ideology were raised today, it is unlikely that there would be much of an argument. Important political disagreements involve issues, such as abortion and homosexual rights, which are distantly removed from economic concerns as normally understood. Often the opinion of an official's "liberalism" or "conservatism" is unrelated to his or her views on economic issues, and decided entirely by the position on matters such as abortion. Moreover, positions on social and economic issues seem to be blended together: it is difficult or even impossible to find an elected official who is in favor of more economic freedom and also in favor of abortion rights, and conversely. As we shall see, both of these observations — the significance of non-economic ideological issues, and the linkage of issues so that the ideological space is one-dimensional — are consistent with what we have now come to appreciate is the nature of ideology in politics.

2. Existence

George Stigler (1971) unintentionally generated an interest in ideology. Stigler took an particularly strong stand *against* the importance of ideology, and argued that in effect all economically relevant political behaviors could be explained by economic self-interest (see also Posner, 1974; Peltzman, 1976). This idea was appealing to economists for two reasons. First, the hypothesis was sharp and was empirically testable. Second, the nature of the hypothesis was one that created sympathy among economists; economists are pleased to suppose that economic self-interest is the main motivator of human behavior. This may be because such a belief creates a stronger position for economics as a discipline, and hence is in the economic self-interest of economists (the downside of this argument is that, as Stigler 1976 indicates, economists will have little influence on policy decisions). On the other hand, it may be because economists themselves behave this way, and expect others to do so as well (see Carter and Irons, 1991). That is, economists liked this hypothesis for reasons related both to their own self-interest and to their ideology.

However, as much as we might like the hypothesis and wish it to be true, it is fair to say that the results are in, and the hypothesis has been falsified. There has been an extensive body of empirical investigation of congressional voting and it has shown that ideological factors have extensive power in explaining congressional voting; see also Mueller, 1989, for a discussion agreeing with this conclusion. The major initial contributors to the literature were James Kau and Paul Rubin (1978, 1979, 1981; Kau et al., 1982). Joseph Kalt and Mark Zupan (1984) also made a significant contribution. These scholars have found that ideology, calculated as a score on a voting scale such as one compiled by the Americans for Democratic Action (ADA) or measured by the presidential vote in the congressional district, has considerable explanatory power in predicting voting by individual congressmen. These results may be considered as confirming Schumpeter's (1950) claim that ideology is important in economic affairs (although not his claim that it would lead to the fall of capitalism, a prediction which has recently been falsified).

The basic technique has been to use voting by congressmen on issues as the dependent variable and a list of factors aimed at measuring constituent economic interests and also ideological variables as the independent variables in probit or logit regressions. The constituent characteristics generally include income, age, urbanization, race, education, unemployment, industry of employment, unionization, measures of government spending in the district, and occasionally measures of particular types of economic activity in the district. Following Kau and Rubin (1979), it is common to regress these measures on a measure of ideology such as ratings assigned by the ADA or other ideological pressure groups and then use the unexplained regression residual as the measure of "pure" ideology. Sometimes a simultaneous model is used where campaign contributions are also controlled for (e.g., Chappell, 1982; Kau et al., 1982; Kau and Rubin, 1982, 1993; also see Stratmann, 1992a for a careful analysis of this issue). Logrolling is also taken into account in some specifications (e.g., Kau and Rubin, 1979; Stratmann, 1992b.) In such analyses, the measure of ideology is invariably statistically and economically significant.

What has perhaps been just as influential in persuading many scholars that ideology is an important variable are the results of the comparatively futile attempts to challenge the hypothesis. Indeed, the original work by Kau and Rubin was projected to show that ideology did not matter, and failed in this endeavor. Peltzman (1984, 1985) later engaged in a determined effort to show that ideology was unimportant. In the 1984 paper, he controlled more carefully than others had for constituent characteristics, specifically by measuring the characteristics of those who actually voted for US Senators rather than characteristics of all voters in the electoral district (here, the state.) In this way he was able to reduce the impact of the ideological variable, but not, in general, to eliminate it. That is, Peltzman (1984) found that ideology mattered, although perhaps not as much as others had thought. Indeed, in a subsequent paper (Peltzman, 1985), he found much the same result as others: while economic factors are relevant in explaining congressional voting, and, in particular, trends in such voting, non-economic factors also are highly significant. Peltzman calls these non-economic factors

"history," but he indicates that "one could allude to regional differences in ideology as easily as to 'historical inertia' ... " (Peltzman, 1985, p. 666). In his 1985 paper, Peltzman himself relegates the results of his 1984 paper to a footnote. Thus, the existence of ideology as an important determinant of congressional voting has survived an intensive attack by a skillful econometrician (I do not offer a complete analysis of the economic literature relating ideology to passage of legislation. There are numerous papers providing such analysis. Lott and Davis (1992, footnote 1) cite 18 such papers. Kalt and Zupan (1990, footnote 2) cite 20, only partially overlapping those listed by Lott and Davis).

Further verification sustaining the importance of ideology is supplied by studies examining campaign contributions. Changes in campaign finance laws led to a large increase in the ability of a variety of groups to create Political Action Committees (PACs) and contribute to political campaigns by. Traditionally, labor unions had contributed extensively to campaigns. However, changes in the law enabled business and ideological groups to form PACs and use contributions to attempt to attain their goals (it is interesting to note that the changes in the law which generated the rise of the PACs were endorsed by labor unions, apparently because they failed to predict the effects of these changes on the ability of businesses to donate to campaigns). Both business and ideological PACs now contribute substantially to political campaigns. The structure of these contributions is analyzed more fully in Poole and Romer (1985), who show that there is an important ideological component to contributions in general.

The large volume of contributions generated by ideological PACs is itself evidence against the strong economic interest hypothesis. These contributions show that many individuals and groups are willing to spend money to attain non-economic goals. This reveals that these contributors have tastes for public goods. This observation is of course consistent with economic theory (where the elements of the utility function are unspecified) but it is not consistent with the strong claim that political action is aimed only at increasing money income. If some are willing to contribute money to change public policy for non-economic reasons, then it is not surprising that people are also willing to use their votes to achieve these same goals. It would not be surprising if citizens were willing to vote for candidates who promised to support legislation which would gratify their ideological, as opposed to economic, preferences.

This is particularly true when we remember that the act of voting is itself not understandable in terms of economic rationality, since the probability of any one vote changing the outcome of an election is infinitesimal and voting does have positive costs (Downs, 1957). However, Nelson (1994) has recently formulated a model, discussed more fully below, in which political activity, including apparently ideological activity, serves a private goal (see also Morton, 1991).

Even if we believe that the ideological PACs actually attain economic goals, economic theory still has difficulty in explaining their survival. This is because such PACs must overcome considerable free rider problems, as discussed by Olson (1965). Even for a potential contributor who believes in the goals of an organization, the optimal strategy would be to abstain from contributing and to free ride on the donations of others. Thus, when we observe individuals freely contributing to ideological PACs, we have already observed a phenomenon that contradicts the restricted view of self interested rationality. Perhaps, in addition to tastes for policies, individuals also have tastes for feeling that they themselves have influenced those policies (e.g., Andreoni, 1989). However, whatever theories may be evolved to explain these organizations, their existence and size does present a puzzle for the strong versions of the economic theory of politics.

3. Shirking

Even if it is conceded that ideology "matters" in congressional voting, an important question remains. That is the issue of whose ideology counts. Congressmen voting ideologically might simply be reflecting tastes of constituents. Alternatively, they might be indulging their own preferences (Wittman, 1977, 1983). This is essentially a principal-agent question: are legislators good agents for their constituents' (principals') ideological views, or are they shirking and representing their own views?

This question has been addressed thoroughly in the literature. There has been some confusion in many analyses, however. The initial work (Kau and Rubin, 1979) was concerned with the issue of whether non-economic factors (called ideology) influenced legislation; this work did not attempt to differentiate between the ideology of the representative and that of his constituency. For example, Kau and Rubin (1979, p. 366) stated explicitly that, "the representative (or his constituency) may be ideologically in favor of the bill ... ."

But others have conflated the question of ideological impacts on voting with the question of ideological shirking. Peltzman (1984), for example, views his analysis as testing between the impacts of constituent interest and ideology. It is possible for a representative to represent constituent ideological interest, so Peltzman's categories are not mutually exclusive.

Conceptually, issues of ideology and of shirking should be separated. It is possible to have ideologically based voting without shirking. It is also possible to have shirking without ideologically based voting. For example, a representative might vote in response to contributions received from various special interests, and thus shirk with respect to his constituents' desires, but in a way unrelated to ideology. Indeed, Kau and Rubin (1993) find exactly this form of shirking. This last possibility has not been carefully studied in the literature, which has focused on ideological shirking (see Bender and Lott 1996 for an analysis).

Kalt and Zupan (1984, 1990) argue strongly that the observed voting behavior of representatives comports well with representatives' own ideologies, and therefore represents shirking. Nelson and Silberberg (1987) test the responsiveness of their measure of shirking to changes in its relative price. However, as Bender and Lott (1996) indicate, their measure (relative strength of ADA ratings in explaining voting on general versus special-interest bills) is flawed. A better measure is the behavior of legislators in periods when reelection is not an issue; using this measure, Lott (1987) finds that legislators shirk by voting less often, but do not change their ideological positions when they do vote. Dougan and Munger (1989), following Downs (1957), argue that what appears to be ideology is actually an investment in brand-name capital — a signal of reliability and commitment providing voters with assurance that representatives will not behave opportunistically. They argue that past votes create a valuable reputational asset that makes promises of future voting behavior credible. Both Kalt and Zupan and Dougan and Munger present empirical evidence that they argue is consistent with that hypothesis. Glazer and Grofman (1989) argue that ideology is a method used by politicians to communicate with constituents, who pay limited attention to political debates.

In a recent and important paper, Lott and Davis (1992) have criticized the methodology both of Kalt and Zupan and of Dougan and Munger. More importantly, Lott and Davis (1992) and Bender and Lott (1996) have shown that voters punish shirking, to the extent that it exists, and that they are empirically quite sensitive to wandering in ideological space. One result is that senators who deviate from the interests of their constituents by as little as 1.27 percentage points are ultimately defeated. Thus, they conclude that whether or not shirking exists is unimportant since if there is shirking it is strongly punished by political markets. Kau and Rubin (1993) also find that if there is ideological shirking, it is strongly and quickly punished. The key argument is that political markets do a good job of sorting legislators. That is, a representative must be in ideological agreement with his constituency to be elected to office.

If ideological voting is based on constituent ideology, this also has created a puzzle for public choice scholars. We do not have a theory of constituent ideology. Indeed, we have no theory of political behavior in general by individuals. Revealed theory cannot explain why rational individuals vote.

Recently, however, Nelson (1994) has offered a theory that depends on ideology to motivate voting. Nelson begins with the standard Downsian observation that, because the chance of any given voter influencing the outcome of an election is trivial, there is no private motive for voting related to the expectation that any one vote will be decisive. Nelson goes on to argue, however, that there is a private motive for voting and for expressing a political (ideological) position that is distinct from "instrumental" considerations. In particular, he suggests that "political positions are...chosen not because these positions are the desired outcome for voters, but rather because one wants to associate with certain people and they have certain positions. People imitate others in choosing political positions" (Nelson, 1994, p. 92).

Nelson presents empirical evidence, relating to political behavior of ethnic groups, which is consistent with his hypothesis. For example, he shows that membership in various ethnic groups is significant in determining political affiliation (after adjusting for economic variables) and that the income of the ethnic group's members 60 years ago is significant in explaining its political orientation today. Thus, Nelson has presented a theoretical and empirical basis for constituent ideology based on private motives and normal utility maximization. This model should make the use of variables related to constituent ideology less controversial among economists.

4. Current Research and Outstanding Questions

Any future work on ideology must begin with a very important analysis that is probably the most significant public choice analysis of the US Congress. This is Poole and Rosenthal (1997), a book-length treatment of roll call voting by the House and Senate for all roll calls from the first Congress in 1789–1985. It is based on numerous articles by these authors and others; I will refer to the book rather than to the articles. Poole and Rosenthal find that what they call ideology is the basic organizing principle behind all such voting. By their definition, "voting is along ideological lines when positions are predictable along a wide set of issues" (Poole and Rosenthal, 1997, p. 4). They show that individual congressmen can be arrayed along a unidimensional continuum for most roll call votes. Almost everyone to one side of a "critical point" on this continuum

will vote one way and almost everyone to the other side will vote the other way, with errors being clustered near the critical point. The winner in any vote is then determined by the location of this critical point.

Ideology as so defined is more important than constituent economic interest in explaining voting by legislators. Moreover, it is even more important in explaining the policies that are actually selected than in explaining voting per se. Policies adopted tend to be systematically biased away from the center of the distribution of legislators and towards the ideological center of the majority party. Ideology is more important in influencing the outcome of the legislative process than in influencing voting by legislators, even though voting is what has most often been studied.

A major issue raised by Poole and Rosenthal is the nature of the voting continuum. They characterize it in several ways. It is roughly defined in terms of conflict over economic redistribution. It also generally reflects party loyalty. A key point is that the continuum reflects logrolling. That is, votes are structured so that coalitions are maintained across most issues. This explains in part why the economic interests of constituents are not significant in any one vote. The vote trading reflected in the continuum in part accounts for these interests. One theoretical treatment consistent with these arguments is Hinich and Munger (1996). However, as discussed below, the nature of this continuum is one of the most important research questions in the contemporary study of ideology.

Poole and Rosenthal also show that for most of American history, a single ideological dimension is all that is required to array votes. During two periods (the 1830s–1840s and the 1940s–1960s) a second dimension dealing with race was also useful. From the New Deal until the 1970s, they find that there was actually a three-party system in the United States (Republicans, Northern and Southern Democrats). More recently, the country has returned to a single ideological dimension and a two-party system.

This is not a logical necessity. For example, Poole and Rosenthal point out that it would be possible for two dimensions to be required, and the actual number needed is an empirical matter. They give the example of social and economic ideology, with economic liberals favoring government intervention in economic matters and social liberals opposing intervention in social or behavioral issues. It would then be possible for two dimensions to be needed to explain voting. But the fact that one dimension is sufficient is because social conservatism and economic liberalism are highly correlated, and the reverse. There are relatively few libertarians, and also relatively few individuals who favor both social and economic interventionism. This may be because individuals attracted to politics tend to be those who are interested in controlling others (Rubin, 2002).

The procedure used to estimate the continuum is called "NOMINATE." It is an iterative procedure, aimed at maximizing the probabilities assigned to the observed votes.[1] They also develop a dynamic procedure, D-NOMINATE, based on assuming that each legislator moves at most along a linear trend over his career. This assumption and resulting trend line enables Poole and Rosenthal to estimate a common issue space for all US history. (Groseclose et al., 1996 estimate a similar function.) Because of the volume of data involved (11,473 legislators, 70,234 votes and 10,428,617 total decisions), the estimation requires the use of a supercomputer. A two-dimensional model (i.e., an issue space allowing for two ideological dimensions) and a linear trend for each legislator provide as good a fit (about 85% of individual votes predicted correctly) as higher-order models (with either more dimensions or a more complex polynomial time path for legislators). Indeed, a one-dimensional model assuming that each legislator maintains a constant position predicts about 80% of the votes correctly.

Poole and Rosenthal show that the NOMINATE variable is highly correlated with more traditional measures of ideology, such as the ADA rating. This is a nice result since many researchers, including many of those discussed above, have used these scores in measuring ideology. NOMINATE is a preferred rating scale since it is more comprehensive and since traditional interest group ratings are subject to "folding" problems. That is, a legislator just a little more liberal than the ADA would get the same rating as a representative who was more conservative by the same amount. However, many of the major interest groups (e.g., the ADA and the American Conservative Union) are at or very near the (opposite) ends of the political space, so this problem is not acute.

The major theoretical issue regarding ideology is the low dimension of the ideological space, as found by Poole and Rosenthal (this is consistent with others who have examined ideology, but Poole and Rosenthal document the result much more carefully and completely). Indeed, it appears that the US political system can only handle a one-dimensional space. In those two periods when the space increased to two dimensions, catastrophe followed. The first was the Civil War. The second was the chaos of the 1960s. Thus, it appears that our institutions may have difficulty with a policy space of more than one dimension. This of course would not be surprising; many of the theoretical results following Arrow show that the only guarantee of stability is a unidimensional, unimodal issue space. But what has not been fully explored is the mechanism that constrains the US to remain in such a space.

The work of Poole and Rosenthal shows that such a mechanism must exist and that it is exceedingly important. Poole and Rosenthal have measured the issue space for congressional voting. However, the results discussed above on the absence of evidence of shirking show that the congressional issue space is congruent with the issue space of voters as well. In other words, if the ideological space for Congress is one-dimensional and unimodal, and if Congress faithfully reflects preferences of constituents, then the issue space of voters must also be one-dimensional and unimodal. This conclusion raises the question of which comes first — does the issue space facing Congress come from the underlying preferences of constituents, or does the political process somehow define the issue space for individuals?

Poole and Rosenthal provide a mechanism for using ideology in a time series analysis. Without their data, this would be difficult because each Congress faces different issues. For example: In year 1, the legislature passes a minimum wage of $2.00 per hour by a 51–49% margin. Liberal ratings services such as the Americans for Democratic Action count a vote for the minimum as a plus, so 51% of the legislature receives a positive score for this vote. In year 2, the legislature is more liberal, so it passes a $2.50 minimum wage by the same margin. The liberal rating service still counts a vote for as a plus, so again 51% of the legislature gets a positive score. Thus, even though the legislature is more liberal, conventional measures of ideology will show no change. However, by relating votes by the same legislator from year to year, Poole and Rosenthal are able to derive an intertemporally comparable index. This index can then be used in time series analyses of changes in policy. For example, Kau and Rubin (2002) show that the ideological composition of the Senate has only a small effect on the size and growth of government, and the House has no effect. Thus, it appears that ideology is important in the cross section but may be less so in the time series. This issue is clearly worth additional analysis.

Beyond this, there are fundamental questions of the nature of ideology itself. North (1990) has raised this issue and stressed its importance. He believes that the basic direction of society is determined by its ideological preferences and that we do not sufficiently understand these preferences. This means that, in addition to determining the mapping between constituent and representative preferences, the underlying structure of these preferences itself is an issue of fundamental importance.

5. Summary and Implications for Future Research

The initial interest in ideology was an effort to determine whether non-economic factors influenced economic legislation. The conclusion is that they do. The emphasis on shirking following this initial analysis has, in my view, been misguided. Constituent ideological preferences do have impacts on legislative outcomes, and the profession should devote its efforts to determining the source and nature of these beliefs. The recent work of Nelson (1994) is a good attempt at beginning this effort, and future research on ideology should focus on this issue, rather than on devising ever more scholastic tests to measure relative strength of constituent and legislator ideology. In addition, the factors that make the issue space unidimensional and unimodal are worthy of attention because these factors serve to eliminate problems of cycling and instability. Finally, the work of North (1990) tells us that the underlying structure of ideology is itself of crucial importance in ordering an economy, and we have no good theory to explain this structure.

PAUL H. RUBIN

NOTES

1. The program and data are available at Poole and Rosenthal's web site, http://voteview.gsia.cmu.edu/.

REFERENCES

Andreoni, James (1989). "Giving with impure altruism: applications to charity and Ricardian equivalence." *The Journal of Political Economy*, 97(6): 1447–1458.

Bender, Bruce and John R. Lott, Jr. (1996). "Legislator voting and shirking: a critical review of the evidence." *Public Choice*, 87: 67–100.

Carter, John R. and Michael D. Irons (1991). "Are economists different, and if so, why?" *Journal of Economic Perspectives*, 5: 171–178.

Chappell, Henry W. (1982). "Campaign contributions and congressional voting: a simultaneous probit-tobit model." *Review of Economics and Statistics*, 64: 77–83.

Dougan, William R. and Michael C. Munger (1989). "The rationality of ideology." *Journal of Law and Economics*, 32: 119–142.

Downs, Anthony (1957). *An Economic Theory of Democracy*. New York: Harper & Row.

Glazer, Amihai and Bernard Grofman (1989). "Why representatives are ideologists although voters are not." *Public Choice*, 61: 29–39.

Groseclose, Tim, Steve Levitt, and Jim Snyder (1996). "An inflation index for ADA scores," Unpublished manuscript, Ohio State University.

Hinich, Melvin J. and Michael C. Munger (1996). *Ideology and the Theory of Public Choice*. Ann Arbor: University of Michigan Press.

Kalt, Joseph P. and Mark A. Zupan (1984). "Capture and ideology in the economic theory of politics." *American Economic Review*, 74: 279–300.

Kalt, Joseph P. and Mark A. Zupan (1990). "The apparent ideological behavior of legislators: Testing for principal-agent slack in political institutions." *Journal of Law and Economics*, 33: 103–132.

Kau, James B., Donald Keenan, and Paul H. Rubin (1982). "A general equilibrium model of congressional voting." *Quarterly Journal of Economics*, 97: 271–293.

Kau, James B. and Paul H. Rubin (1978). "Voting on minimum wages: a time series analysis." *Journal of Political Economy*, 86: 337–342.

Kau, James B. and Paul H. Rubin (1979). "Self-interest, ideology and logrolling in congressional voting." *Journal of Law and Economics*, 22: 365–384.

Kau, James B. and Paul H. Rubin (1982). *Congressmen, Constituents, and Contributors*. Boston: Martinus Nijhoff.

Kau, James B. and Paul H. Rubin (1993). "Ideology, voting, and shirking." *Public Choice*, 76: 151–172.

Kau, James B. and Paul H. Rubin (2002). "The growth of government: sources and limits." *Public Choice*, 113: 389–402.

Lott, John R. Jr. (1987). "Political cheating." *Public Choice*, 52: 169–187.

Lott, John R. Jr. and Michael Davis, L. (1992). "A critical review and extension of the political shirking literature." *Public Choice*, 74: 461–484.

Morton, Rebecca (1991). "Groups in rational turnout models." *American Journal of Political Science*, 35: 758–776.

Mueller, Dennis C. (1989). *Public Choice II*. New York: Cambridge University Press.

Nelson, Douglas and Eugene Silberberg (1987). "Ideology and legislator shirking." *Economic Inquiry*, 25: 15–25.

Nelson, Philip (1994). "Voting and imitative behavior." *Economic Inquiry*, 32: 92–102.

North, Douglass C. (1990). *Institutions, Institutional Change and Economic Performance*. Cambridge: Cambridge University Press.

Olson, Mancur. (1965). *The Logic of Collective Action*. Cambridge, MA: Harvard University Press.

Peltzman, Sam (1976). "Toward a more general theory of regulation." *Journal of Law and Economics*, 19: 211–240.

Peltzman, Sam (1984). "Constituent interest and congressional voting." *Journal of Law and Economics*, 27: 181–210.

Peltzman, Sam (1985). "An economic interpretation of the history of congressional voting in the twentieth century." *American Economic Review*, 75: 656–675.

Poole, Keith T. and Howard Rosenthal (1997). *Congress: A Political-Economic History of Roll Call Voting*. New York: Oxford University Press.

Poole, Keith L. and Thomas Romer (1985). "Patterns of political action committee contributions to the 1980 campaigns for the United States House of Representatives." *Public Choice* (Carnegie Papers on Political Economy), 47: 63–113.

Posner, Richard A. (1974). "Theories of economic regulation." *Bell Journal of Economics and Management Science*, 5: 335–358.

Rubin, Paul H. (2001). "Ideology," in William E. Shughart II and Laura Razzolini (eds) *The Elgar Companion to Public Choice*. Northampton, MA: Edward E. Elgar, pp. 328–336.

Rubin, Paul H. (2002). *Darwinian Politics: The Evolutionary Origin of Freedom*, Newark: Rutgers University Press.

Schumpeter, Joseph A. (1950). *Capitalism, Socialism, and Democracy*. New York: Harper & Row.

Stigler, George J. (1971). "The theory of economic regulation." *Bell Journal of Economics and Management Science*, 2: 3–21.

Stigler, George J. (1976). "Do economists matter?" *Southern Economic Journal*, 42: 347–354.

Stratmann, Thomas (1992a). "Are contributors rational? Untangling strategies of political action committees." *Journal of Political Economy*, 100: 646–664.

Stratmann, Thomas (1992b). "The effects of logrolling on congressional voting." *American Economic Review*, 82: 1162–1176.

Wittman, Donald (1977). "Candidates with policy preferences: a dynamic model." *Journal of Economic Theory*, 14: 180–189.

Wittman, Donald (1983). "Candidate motivation: a synthesis of alternative theories." *American Political Science Review*, 77: 142–157.

THE IMPORTANCE OF THE MIDDLE IN SPATIAL POLITICS

1. Introduction

Since Hotelling (1929), almost as an after-thought in a paper on the location of economic activity, observed that there was a reason why winning Democrats and Republicans tended to favor each other, there has been a recognition of the importance of the middle in political competition. It remained for Black (1948, 1958) and Downs (1957) to develop single dimensional models of spatial politics and to observe that the median constituted a dominant strategy for a candidate or party to prevail in an election in which there are only two contenders.

Arrow (1951) turned the discussion in a different direction from that outlined by Black (1948) by proving that under reasonable conditions there was no guarantee that a social preference ordering might even exist. The fact that there might be no solution, or no dominant strategy, or no equilibrium, was a shockingly novel idea. Elections almost always produce a winner, but it was not clear just what the winner might represent. There was obviously the possibility of arbitrariness in the outcome, and that very thought was unsettling.

It would not be long, however, before the search turned to the issue of finding conditions under which there might be an equilibrium or a dominant strategy. This search is the topic that we review here. Unfortunately, since the literature is large, it is probably impossible to do full justice to all the contributions. We attempt, however, to cover the major aspects.

2. A Spatial Model

Arrow's Impossibility Theorem first inspired researchers to start to search for examples of cycles in elections (Riker, 1958). There was also the issue of interpreting the outcome of an election and, perhaps even more important, of understanding how institutions might act to resolve or diminish the importance of the possibility of encountering cycles (Riker, 1980). However, as noted above, the largest focus of attention was the search to find conditions under which there was a dominant political strategy.

Of course, it was immediately clear that if the number of dimensions (issues) is one, and if voter preferences are single-peaked, then the results of Black and Downs are applicable. A median is guaranteed to exist and it is the dominant strategy in two party elections. Since countries with serious multiple parties usually have a system in which there is a runoff election between the two parties or candidates who received the largest number of votes in the first round, this analysis is thought to be applicable so that the median still serves as the dominant strategy for a second round. Hence, the median is a powerful and attractive position for politicians who want to win and remain in office.

However, there remained a feeling, or maybe an intellectual conviction, that there had to be more than one dimension of choice. When there are two or more dimensions to the space in which issues are measured, then the Impossibility Theorem is applicable. No dominant strategy can be guaranteed. Thus, the question of finding conditions under which dominance does exist is an intellectual challenge.

Plott (1967) may have been the first to explore this issue, and he established sufficient conditions for equilibrium in multidimensional choice spaces. The most important and best known of these conditions is pairwise symmetry, which states that all nonzero utility gradients at the equilibrium must be divisible into pairs that point in opposite directions. Enelow and Hinich (1983) develop examples to demonstrate that Plott's conditions are indeed sufficient, but they are not necessary. Indeed, Plott's conditions would lead one to believe, as Shepsle (1979, p.28) states, "...unless the assumption of unidimensional or symmetrically distributed preference is satisfied, the solution to the election game posited by spatial theory does not generally exist." However, Enelow and Hinich's argument demonstrates that Plott's conditions are far stricter or constraining than need be, so equilibrium may not be so rare.

Davis and Hinich (1966, 1967) introduced a multidimensional spatial model that utilized the tools of probability theory, especially the notion of distributions. The main results of these papers, along with some extensions, is presented in Davis et al. (1970) which was aimed at reaching a wider audience. Tullock (1967) also offered a two-dimensional analysis. For the purpose of exposition, we present some elementary aspects of the Davis and Hinich model. Let x represent an n-dimensional column vector in Euclidean space and A be defined as a nxn positive definite matrix. Then if θ represents some other point in this Euclidean space, the function

$$(x - \theta)' A(x - \theta) \tag{1}$$

defines a quadratic loss function. If $\theta = x$, then the value of (1) is zero and for all $\theta \neq x$ the value of (1) is positive. Thus, x is said to be the ideal point of the individual in question. The population of voters is characterized by the density f(x). We shall see that much of the argument about conditions for dominant strategies is centered on the nature of f(x).

A voting rule is easily specified. A voter with ideal point x prefers a candidate with position θ over a candidate with position Ψ if

$$(x - \theta)' A(x - \theta) < (x - \Psi)' A(x - \Psi) \tag{2}$$

so that voting is characterized as minimization of loss. Obviously, in our Euclidean space, the voting rule (2) corresponds to distance so voters prefer the candidate whose position is nearest their own ideal point.

There is little loss of generality in defining the loss function (1) to be a quadratic. Davis and Hinich (1968) allow the components of A to be random, subject to the provision that A remains a positive definite matrix. Davis et al. (1972) observe that monotonic transformations are allowed without altering their results. Nevertheless, this formulation does provide a certain symmetry in the preference structure of the population.

3. Conditions for Dominance

As was indicated above, Plott (1967) established sufficient conditions for the existence of a dominant equilibrium strategy, but his conditions are not necessary. One can simply observe that if the distribution of voters has a point φ which is characterized by having 50% or more of the population located there, then that point φ is a dominant equilibrium strategy and it does not matter how the remainder of the distribution f(x) is distributed. There is no need for any kind of symmetry. Enelow and Hinich (1983) develop additional examples of situations in which there is dominance but Plott's condition of pairwise symmetry is not satisfied.

Davis et al. (1972) establish sufficient conditions for dominance and necessary and sufficient conditions for a transitive social preference ordering which can be obtained

by majority rule. These conditions depend, of course, upon the voting model outlined above. However, if the distribution of ideal points is given by the distribution f(x), and if this distribution has a point ϕ which is a median in all directions, which means that any hyperplane passing through ϕ divides the density f(x) into two equal parts in the sense that half of the density lies on one side or the other of the hyperplane, then ϕ is a dominant strategy. Further, this paper also established that under this condition majority rule voting defines a transitive social preference ordering over the possibilities included in the density f(x).

Davis et al. (1972) list the following as examples of distributions that are symmetric about some dominant point ϕ.

(i) A discrete distribution on a set of $2k + 1$ points in Euclidean space $\{0, x_1, -x_1, ..., x_k, -x_k\}$ such that $f(x_i) = f(-x_i)$ for all points $i = 1, ..., k$. For this distribution the dominant point $\phi = 0$. This case resembles the conditions established by Plott (1967).

(ii) A multivariate normal distribution with mean μ and non-singular covariance matrix Σ. For this distribution the dominant point $\phi = \mu$.

(iii) The probability density f defined by $f(x) = (1/2)[f_1(x) + f_2(x)]$ where f_1 is a multivariate normal density with mean μ_1 and non-singular covariance Σ and f_2 is a multivariate normal density with a different mean μ_2 but with the same covariance Σ. For this distribution the dominant point $\phi = (1/2)[\mu_1 + \mu_2]$. This example can be extended to any number of combinations of normal densities.

It should be pointed out that symmetry of this type is a sufficient condition for the existence of a dominant point, but it is not necessary. For example, if a single point carries probability $p \geq 1/2$, it is dominant regardless of how the remaining probability is distributed. For a complete social preference ordering, this symmetry is both necessary and sufficient. However, one can get "almost complete" orderings without this symmetry. In the example under consideration, if we define a very small area δ around the point with $p \geq 1/2$, then majority rule voting defines an ordering for all points outside of δ, but the ordering is not complete even though there is a dominant point.

For dominance, a major change appears to lie in the shift from finite to infinite populations. Thus for large populations of voters, where a normal or some combination of normal distributions seems satisfactory as a description of the population, then the results cited above prevail and we can expect both dominance and a social ordering. In such situations, we will have no cycles or other problems associated with the Impossibility Theorem. Thus, the importance of the middle is well established and electoral competition using majority rule should produce desirable outcomes, at least within the context of spatial analysis.

When populations are small, and especially in the committee structures of most legislative bodies, we can expect the world of McKelvey (1979) to be paramount.

4. Social Optimality

In a sense, none of the above addresses the social desirability of electoral politics as a method of public decision-making. Of course, in the value systems of most members of the free world, and especially for those who reside in developed countries, the desirability of democracy is not an issue. It is simply accepted and regarded as the best way known to organize a society.

It should also be noted that in the view of many if not most members of our society, there is a widespread belief that bureaucracies, and especially governmental bureaucracies, are inherently inefficient. Niskanen (1971) certainly argues this point in the scholarly literature. For the purpose of the following discussion, we simply accept governmental inefficiency as given.

However, accepting bureaucratic inefficiency, there remains the question of how well spatial politics does in a normative sense as an organizational principle for decision-making. Davis and Hinich (1968) address this issue. They imagine a wise and beneficient dictator who weights the individuals in his population equally, makes interpersonal comparisons, and wishes to choose a set of policies θ which minimizes the average loss of the members of the population. It is shown that the set of policies $\theta = \mu$, the mean of the distribution $f(x)$, is the unique minimum. This result does not depend upon an assumption of normality. Further, it is shown that the dictator can establish a social preference ordering based upon the idea of minimizing losses, and that this ordering amounts to the idea of choosing a given set of policies θ which is closer to the mean μ than some given alternative set of policies Ψ.

Subject to the provision about the inefficiency of the bureaucracy, it can be shown that the mean μ is a "Pareto optimal" choice. Hence, especially for normal and a mixture of normal densities, the dominant strategy is also the optimal social strategy. Spatial politics is a theory that is optimistic about the political systems of the democracies.

5. Conclusion

This essay has argued that the widespread view that the results of Arrow (1951) established the "fact" that democratic political systems are characterized by arbitrariness cycles, and ambiguity is largely an exaggeration. At least when populations are large, spatial analysis indicates that such systems are likely to be stable with a defined equilibrium strategy. Even when there are n dimensions, the observation of Hotelling (1929) that winning Democrats and Republicans tend to resemble each other remains valid.

Spatial politics is also optimistic in the sense that the dominant equilibrium strategies tend to have nice optimality properties. Of course, there is an alternative theory of electoral competition, the political theory of rent seeking (see Buchanan and Tullock (1962), Buchanan et al. (1980), Rowley et al. (1989) and Tullock et al. (2000)) which is not nearly so optimistic. Indeed, in this theory, the process of political competition breeds inefficiency beyond that noted in the above argument. Hence, even in this restricted sense, much remains to be done in the developing area of public choice.

OTTO A. DAVIS
MELVIN J. HINICH

REFERENCES

Arrow, K. (1951). *Social Choice and Individual Values*. New Haven: Yale University Press. Second Edition, 1963.

Black, D. (1948). "On the rationale of group decision-making." *Journal of Political Economy*, LVI: 23–34.

Black, D. (1958). *The Theory of Committees and Elections*. Cambridge, England: Cambridge University Press.

Buchanan, J.M. and Tullock, G. (1962). *The Calculus of Consent: Logical Foundations of a Constitutional Democracy*. Ann Arbor: University of Michigan Press.

Buchanan, J.M., Tollison, R.D., and Tullock, G. (1980). *Toward a Theory of the Rent-Seeking Society*. College Station: Texas A & M University Press.

Davis, O.A. and Hinich, M.J. (1966). "A mathematical model of policy formation in a democratic society," in *Mathematical Applications in Political Science II*. J. Bernd (ed.) Dallas, Texas: Southern Methodist University Press, pp. 175–208.

Davis, O.A. and Hinich, M.J. (1967). "Some results related to a mathematical model of policy formation in a democratic society," in *Mathematical Applications in Political Science III*, J. Bernd (ed.) Charlottesville, VA.: University of Virginia Press, pp. 14–38.

Davis, O.A. and Hinich, M.J. (1968). "On the power and importance of the mean preference in a mathematical model of democratic choice." *Public Choice*, V: 59–72.

Davis, O.A., DeGroot, M.H., and Hinich, M.J. (1972). "Social preference orderings and majority rule." *Econometrica*, 40: 147–157.

Davis, O.A., Hinich, M.J., and Ordeshook, P. (1970). "An expository development of a mathematical model of the electoral process." *American Political Science Review*, 64: 426–448.

Enlow, J. and Hinich, M.J. (1983). "On Plott's pairwise symmetry condition for majority rule equilibrium." *Public Choice*, 40: 317–321.

Hotelling, H. (1929). "Stability is Competition," *Economic Journal*, 39: 41–47.

McKelvey, R. (1979). "General conditions for global intransitivities in formal voting models." *Econometrica*, 47: 1085–1111.

Niskanen, W.A. (1971). *Bureaucracy and Representative Government*. Chicago: Aldine, Atherton.

Plott, C. (1967). "A notion of equilibrium and its possibility under majority rule." *American Economic Review*, 57: 787–806.

Riker, W. (1958). "The paradox of voting and Congressional rules for voting on amendments." *American Political Science Review*, 52: 349–366.

Riker, W. (1980). "Implications from the disequilibrium of majority rule for the study of institutions." *American Political Science Review*, 74: 432–446.

Rowley, C.K., Tollison, R.D., and Tullock, G. (1989). *The Political Economy of Rent Seeking*. Amsterdam: Kluwer Academic Publishers.

Shepsle, K. (1979). "Institutional arrangements and equilibrium in multidimensional voting models." *American Journal of Political Science*, 23: 27–59.

Tullock, G. (1967). *Toward a Mathematics of Politics*. Ann Arbor: University of Michigan Press.

Tullock, G., Seldon, A., and Brady, G. (2000). *Government: Whose Obedient Servant?* London: The Institute of Economic Affairs.

INITIATIVE AND REFERENDUM

All modern democracies rely on representatives to formulate and administer policies. Representative government takes advantage of division of labor: a small group of experts can develop expertise in policy, freeing everyone else to pursue other tasks. The downside is that elected officials may fail to pursue the interests of voters. A popular remedy for the ills of representative government is to empower the electorate at large to make policy decisions or override the decisions of their representatives. The constitutional procedures that do this are the initiative and referendum (I&R).

1. Definitions

The *initiative* process allows ordinary citizens to propose new laws by petition, that is, by collecting a predetermined number of signatures from their fellow citizens. The proposal becomes law if approved by a vote of the electorate at large. The *referendum* is a process that allows the electorate to approve or reject a proposal by the legislature. Referendums (this is the preferred plural rather than referenda according to *Oxford English Dictionary*; see Butler and Ranney (1994)) come in several flavors depending on what conditions send the measure to the voters. *Mandatory referendums* require certain proposals to be put before the voters before they go into effect. For example, most state constitutions cannot be amended without popular approval. *Legislative* or *referred referendums* are measures that the legislature chooses to put before the voters. *Petition* or *popular referendums* allow citizens to challenge measures approved by the legislature if they can collect a sufficient number of signatures. Other variants occur.

2. History

I&R as we know them first appeared as part of the 1848 Swiss constitution. Switzerland provides both processes at the federal, cantonal, and local level. Nearly 500 federal measures have come before the voters (not counting purely advisory measures). As of 1997, all 26 cantons allow the initiative and all but 1 allow mandatory or petition referendums on certain fiscal decisions. Over 80 percent of Swiss municipalities employ mandatory or petition referendums on budgetary matters. See Kobach (1994), Feld and Matsusaka (2001), and Feld and Kirchgassner (1999) for discussions of I&R in Switzerland at the federal, cantonal, and local level, respectively.

The other bastion of I&R is the United States. The initiative first appeared in 1893 in California counties. The first state to adopt was South Dakota in 1898, and the first city to adopt was San Francisco in 1899. As of 2002, 24 states and roughly half of all cities (including 15 of the 20 largest) provide the initiative, 24 states permit petition referendums, and all but 1 state require constitutional amendments to be put before the voters (Matsusaka, 2002).

Although Switzerland and the United States are the most prominent users of I&R, other countries are also active. The Italian constitution of 1947 allows petition referendums to rescind laws, no matter how long they have been on the books. Italians have decided 48 referendums, including proposals to repeal divorce laws, abortion laws, and the proportional representation system. National referendums have also been held in Europe, primarily to adopt constitutions (e.g., Denmark, France, Greece, Ireland, Poland, Turkey) and resolve questions about European integration (e.g., Denmark, France, Ireland, Italy, Norway, United Kingdom). Six of 15 successor states to the Soviet Union have initiative provisions in their new constitutions. I&R are less common outside the Western world, but not entirely absent. In Asia, referendums were used to make constitutional changes in South Korea and the Philippines, and local referendums have been held in Taiwan (on nuclear power plants) and Japan (status of U.S. base on Okinawa). South Africa ended apartheid by referendum.

And in South America, Chile began its return to democracy by rejecting a referendum on military governance. For a good overview of international I&R, see Butler and Ranney (1994).

3. Legal Forms

I&R procedures are implemented in a number of different ways. The petition process is one important source of variation. Focusing just on the United States, we see (1) differences in the number of signatures required for a measure to reach the ballot (from a low of 2 percent of the population in North Dakota to a high of 15 percent in Wyoming), (2) differences in the amount of time allowed to collect signatures (typically 90 days for referendums, often 1 year or more for initiatives), and (3) restrictions on where the signatures can be collected (such as Massachusetts, which limits the number of signatures from a single county to one-quarter of the total). There are also variations in the allowable subject matter. Some states allow initiatives to propose new statutes; others allow constitutional amendments. Some states prohibit initiatives that allocate money or raise new taxes. Many states have a single-subject rule, meaning that an initiative may address only one issue. Another source of variation is the approval process. To gain approval, some governments require a measure to be approved at two succeeding elections, allow the legislature to approve the measure before sending it to the voters, or require supermajorities. A good source for legal provisions is the Initiative and Referendum web site: www.iandrinstitute.org.

4. Theory

The internal/external cost model of Buchanan and Tullock (1962) was perhaps the first attempt in public choice to understand the tradeoffs between direct and representative democracy. They reached a fairly negative conclusion (p. 213): "Direct democracy, under almost any decision-making rule, becomes too costly in other than very small political units when more than a few isolated issues must be considered." However, their analysis compared pure forms of representative and direct democracy. I&R, which is the grafting of direct democracy devices onto representative systems, falls through the cracks.

One prominent theme of the subsequent theoretical literature is the importance of agenda control, following the path breaking work of Romer and Rosenthal (1979). Seen from this perspective, a key feature of the initiative is that it breaks the legislature's monopoly on making policy proposals. One implication with relevance for empirical work is that the initiative and referendum can have affects on policy without being used. This is because a legislature might respond to a lobbyist in order to stave off the threat of an initiative or referendum (Gerber, 1996). How I&R change policies is not entirely clear theoretically. With perfect information, both initiative and referendum drive policy closer to the median voter (compared to a government with only representatives). With asymmetric information, however, the initiative can make the median voter better or worse off (Matsusaka and McCarty, 2001) and the referendum can impede or exaggerate pro-spending biases of elected officials (Marino and Matsusaka, 2001).

Relatively little theory has been developed outside the agenda control framework. Matsusaka (1992) proposes an information economies view of I&R: representatives focus on decisions where technical expertise is important and underlying preferences are similar, while referendums are used to address issues in which the relevant information is dispersed among voters. Besley and Coate (2001) call attention to the possible role of initiatives in allowing voters to address particular issues that are usually bundled in candidates. Gerber et al. (2001) document the importance of representatives in implementing (or failing to implement) measures approved by the voters.

5. Key Research Questions

A brief (non-exhaustive) summary of some of the key issues and recent research follows.

- *For the Many or the Few?* One fundamental question is whether I&R promote majority rule or permit rich special interests to subvert the policy process. Critics have long argued that I&R increase the power of interest groups that can afford to qualify measures and fund election campaigns. Defenders argue that wealthy interests are already influential in the legislature, and that I&R allow the majority to reassert its will.

  Existing theory on this question is ambiguous. A simple agenda control model with complete information predicts that both initiative and referendum promote majority rule. Rational voters will reject proposals worse than the status quo, and adopt proposals that are better than the status quo, so they can only be made better off by having a choice (see Gerber, 1996). However, when small amounts of incomplete information are introduced, it is possible for voters to be worse off when I&R are available (see Marino and Matsusaka, 2001; Matsusaka and McCarty, 2001).

  The empirical evidence, however, generally suggests that I&R promote the interests of the many rather than the few. One example is my series of studies on state and local fiscal policy in the United States (Matsusaka, 1995, 2000, 2002). I find that since 1960, states with the initiative cut taxes, pushed spending down from state to local governments, and adopted revenue structures that were more dependent on fees and less on taxes. All three of these changes move policy in the direction preferred by a majority of voters, based on preferences expressed in polls or election returns. In contrast, the initiative drove up spending in the early twentieth century, a period where there is reason to believe that voters wanted increased government spending. Gerber (1996, 1999) provides similar evidence for social policies. She finds that initiative states were more likely than non-initiative states to adopt the capital punishment and parental abortion notification policies favored by the majority of voters.

- *Majority Tyranny?* Another fundamental question is whether the majority use the initiative to oppress numerical minorities. This possibility was an explicit motivation for the "republican" form of government adopted in the U.S. Constitution. With pure democracy, argued Madison in the celebrated Federalist No. 10, "[a] common passion or interest will, in almost every case, be felt by a majority of the whole... and there is nothing to check the inducements to sacrifice the weaker party, or an obnoxious individual." If the initiative causes policy to respond to the will of the majority, as the evidence suggests, does this endanger the rights of minorities? The answer is an empirical matter, but unfortunately the empirical work to date is unconvincing (see Matsusaka, 2002 for a review and critique). At an anecdotal level, the danger seems more theoretical than real. It is difficult to find clear instances of initiatives that trample minority rights, and the most egregious cases of majority tyranny in the last 100 years — Jim Crow in the South and internment of Japanese Americans during World War II — were instigated by representative government. Recent evidence by Hajnal et al. (2002), although indirect, points in the same direction: the majority of racial and ethnic voters are on the winning side of proposition votes 95 percent of time. Additional empirical work on this question would seem to be a high priority.

- *How do I&R Affect Policy?* A general conclusion from the empirical literature is that I&R do change policy, but without an obvious conservative or liberal bias. In the United States, the effect of the initiative on spending varies with the level of government and time period. The initiative cut combined state and local

spending during 1960–1999, but increased municipal spending in the same time period and drove up combined spending in the first decades of the twentieth century. Throughout the century, the initiative triggered decentralization of spending from state to local governments, and induced a shift in financing away from taxes and into fees for services. In Switzerland, where all evidence is post-WWII, canton initiatives reduced and decentralized spending. Cantons and cities with mandatory referendums on new spending programs also spent less. We also know that I&R change the way preferences are transformed into policies. Another pattern that seems to be robust is that mandatory referendums on debt issues reduce deficits and the amount of borrowing. See Pommerehne (1978), Romer et al. (1992), Bohn and Inman (1996), Kiewiet and Szakaly (1996), Feld and Matsusaka (2001), Schaltegger and Feld (2001), Feld and Kirchgassner (1999) and Matsusaka (2002).

- *How Do I&R Affect Economic Performance?* A number of studies touch on this question, most of them reporting that I&R improve economic performance. Pommerehne (1983) finds that Swiss municipalities with the initiative operate their refuse collection more efficiently. Feld and Savioz (1997) estimate that Swiss cantons with I&R have higher factor productivity than those without. And Blomberg et al. (2001) report that American states with the initiative grew faster during the 1969–1986 period.

- *What Role does Money Play?* This is a question that applies to political behavior in general, of course, and is the subject of a huge literature. The research on this question specific to I&R is primarily empirical. Several facts have been established. First, money certainly matters. The success of a measure depends on how much money is spent for and against it. However, the effectiveness of money is asymmetric. Virtually all studies report that spending against a measure has a big "bang for the buck," while spending in support of a measure yields an unreliable return. The most likely explanation is that raising questions about a measure is easier than convincing people of its benefits, and uncertain voters tend to vote no. Gerber (1999) is essential reading on this question, and provides links to the rest of the literature. See Broder (2000) for an illuminating view from the trenches of initiative campaigns.

- *What Explains Adoption?* I&R are usually provided as part of a government's constitution or charter. What leads some governments to adopt and not others? Unfortunately, there is virtually no theoretical or empirical work on this question. The most noteworthy study is Hersch and McDougall (1997). They provide a valuable outline of the theoretical possibilities, but have only modest success in explaining the votes of Kansas legislators on a proposal in 1994 to adopt the initiative.

- *What Explains Use?* Initiatives and referendums represent the breakdown of bargaining between the legislature and an interest group, and result in deadweight costs (to collect signatures and run campaigns). If the parties could see in advance how an initiative campaign would end, they would prefer to strike a deal above their reservation values and avoid the deadweight costs. This suggests that initiatives and referendums should be more common in environments with high levels of asymmetric information or when it is difficult for legislatures to form implicit contracts. As far as the facts go, there are important variations across time and space in initiative use. Across time, initiative use in the United States was high in the early twentieth century then gradually declined starting in the 1940s. It bottomed out in the 1960s, and then shot up in the 1980s, reaching a record high in the 1990s. Across states, initiative activity is heavily concentrated in California, Oregon, North Dakota, and Colorado. Panel regressions indicate that the number of initiatives is higher when signature requirements are low, when geographic dispersion requirements on signatures are absent, when states are heterogeneous (possibly a proxy for asymmetric information about the median voter's preferences), and when a state has divided government. See Banducci (1998) and Matsusaka and McCarty (2001).

JOHN G. MATSUSAKA

REFERENCES

Banducci, S.A. (1998). "Direct legislation: when is it used and when does it pass?" in S. Bowler, T. Donovan, and C.J. Tolbert (eds.) *Citizens as Legislators*. Columbus: Ohio State University Press.

Besley, T. and Coate, S. (2001). "Issue unbundling by citizens' initiatives." Working Paper, Cornell University.

Blomberg, S.B., Hess, G.D., and Weerapana, A. (2001). "The impact of voter initiatives on economic activity." Working Paper, Wellesley College.

Bohn, H. and Inman, R.P. (1996). "Balanced-budget rules and public deficits: evidence from the U.S. states." *Carnegie-Rochester Conference Series on Public Policy*, 45: 13–76.

Broder, D.S. (2000). *Democracy Derailed: Initiative Campaigns and the Power of Money*. Harcourt, Inc.

Buchanan, J.M. and Tullock, G. (1962). *The Calculus of Consent: Logical Foundations of Constitutional Democracy*. University of Michigan Press.

Butler, D. and Ranney, A. (eds.) (1994). *Referendums Around the World: The Growing Use of Direct Democracy*. AEI Press.

Feld, L.P. and Kirchgassner, G. (1999). "Public debt and budgetary procedures: top down or bottom up? Some evidence from Swiss municipalities." in J.M. Poterba and J. von Hagen (eds.) *Fiscal Institutions and Fiscal Performance*. The University of Chicago Press.

Feld, L.P. and Matsusaka, J.G. (2001). "Budget referendums and government spending: evidence from Swiss cantons." Working Paper, University of Southern California.

Feld, L.P. and Savioz, M.R. (1997). "Direct democracy matters for economic performance: an empirical investigation." *Kyklos*, 50: 507–538.

Gerber, E.R. (1996). "Legislative response to the threat of popular initiatives." *American Journal of Political Science*, 40: 99–128.

Gerber, E.R. (1999). *The Populist Paradox: Interest Group Influence and the Promise of Direct Legislation*. Princeton: Princeton University Press.

Gerber, E.R, Lupia, A., McCubbins, M.D., and Kiewiet, R.D. (2001). *Stealing the Initiative: How State Government Responds to Direct Democracy*. New York: Prentice-Hall.

Hajnal, Z.L., Gerber, E.R., and Louch, H. (2002). "Minorities and direct legislation: evidence from California ballot proposition elections." *Journal of Politics*, 64: 154–177.

Hersch, P.L. and McDougall, G.S. (1997). "Direct legislation: determinants of legislator support for voter initiatives." *Public Finance Quarterly*, 25: 327–343.

Kiewiet, D.R. and Szakaly, K. (1996). "Constitutional limitations on borrowing: an analysis of state bonded indebtedness." *Journal of Law, Economics, and Organization*, 12: 62–97.

Kobach, K.W. (1994). "Switzerland," in D. Butler and A. Ranney (eds.) *Referendums Around the World: The Growing Use of Direct Democracy*. AEI Press.

Marino, A.M. and Matsusaka, J.G. (2001). "Decision processes, agency problems, and information: an economic analysis of budget procedures." Working Paper, University of Southern California.

Matsusaka, J.G. (1992). "Economics of direct legislation." *Quarterly Journal of Economics*, 107: 541–571.

Matsusaka, J.G. (1995). "Fiscal effects of the voter initiative: evidence from the last 30 years." *Journal of Political Economy*, 103: 587–623.

Matsusaka, J.G. (2000). "Fiscal effects of the voter initiative in the first half of the twentieth century." *Journal of Law and Economics*, 43: 619–650.

Matsusaka, J.G. and McCarty, N.M. (2001). "Political resource allocation: benefits and costs of voter initiatives." *Journal of Law, Economics, and Organization*, 17: 413–448.

Matsusaka, J.G. (2002). *For the Many or the Few: How the Initiative Process Changes American Government*. Book manuscript, University of Southern California.

Matsusaka, J.G. "The initiative and referendum in American cities: basic patterns," in M.D. Waters (ed.) *The Initiative and Referendum Almanac: A Comprehensive Reference Guide to*

Citizen Lawmaking Around the World. Carolina Academic Press (forthcoming).

Pommerehne, W.W. (1978). "Institutional approaches to public expenditure: empirical evidence from Swiss municipalities." *Journal of Public Economics*, 9: 255–280.

Pommerehne, W.W. (1983). "Private versus oeffentliche muellabfuhr — Nochmals betrachtet." *Finanzarchiv*, 41: 466–475.

Romer, T. and Rosenthal, H. (1979). "Bureaucrats versus voters: on the political economy of resource allocation by direct democracy." *Quarterly Journal of Economics*, 93: 563–587.

Romer, T., Rosenthal, H., and Munley, V.G. (1992). "Economic incentives and political institutions: spending and voting in school budget referenda." *Journal of Public Economics*, 49: 1–33.

Schaltegger, C. and Feld, L.P. (2001). "On government centralization and budget referendums: evidence from Switzerland." Working Paper, University of St. Gallen.

INSTITUTIONS OF TRADE PROTECTION

In the United States, the primary institutions of trade protection are the congress, the president, and the bureaucracy. Within the interest group theory of politics, these institutions play the role of brokers (see Rowley et al., 1995). Voters and special interests demand protection, offering the brokers votes and campaign contributions in exchange for the wealth transfers. Consumers and others harmed by the redistributional policies supply these benefits, either unwittingly or because they cannot muster sufficient votes or contributions to resist the transfers.

Public choice theory posits that the actors in the political arena seek to maximize utility just as consumers do in the economic arena. Each group, however, has different arguments in their preference functions.

Members of Congress seek reelection. To do this they attempt to broker protectionist policies for constituents. These constituents include both workers and firms in their districts (geographic constituents) and political action committees that provide contributions (electoral constituents). Members of Congress thus tend to be responsive to narrow sectional interests. In responding to constituent demands, the fact that each representative has only one vote out of 435 and each senator only one vote out of 100 implies that legislators must engage in log-rolling trades.

The president pursues reelection if he is in his first term or a dynasty and a place in history if he is in his second term. Since his constituency is larger than that of members of Congress, he often avoids brokering protection unless electoral college calculations dictate such an action.

Bureaucrats are assumed to pursue salary, perquisites, power, patronage, and freedom from stress. Each of these benefits should increase with the bureau's budget. In the area of trade policy, more protection often leads to larger budgets for agencies, giving bureaucrats an incentive to pursue protectionism.

The policy brokers are more likely to provide protectionist benefits if they can do so behind a smokescreen. One pretext often used to broker protection is the need to ensure "fair" trade. As discussed below, policies such as antidumping and countervailing duty laws promulgated under the fair trade banner often have more to do with brokering benefits than with promoting fairness.

Because several factors attenuate the link between voters' preferences and policy outcomes (Rowley, 1984), interest groups exert a disproportionate influence on the trade policy process. Special interests pursue issues that generate large benefits to a small number of constituents while imposing small costs on a large number of constituents (Gwartney and Wagner, 1988). To obtain benefits they employ campaign contributions, blocks of votes, and persuasive advertising. They tend to be most effective when they represent small, geographically concentrated segments of society. When they represent large, diffuse interests such as those of consumers they tend to be ineffective because of free-rider problems (Olson, 1965).

There is disagreement concerning how factors form coalitions when lobbying on trade policy. Magee (1980) investigated lobbying behavior before passage of the 1973 Trade Reform Act. He found that capital and labor in an industry tended to lobby together, with both factors in export industries lobbying for free trade and both factors in import-competing industries lobbying for protectionism. More recently, Thorbecke (1997) investigated lobbying behavior before passage of the 1993 North American Free Trade Agreement (NAFTA). He found that capital and labor in an industry tended to lobby against each other, with capital favoring free trade and labor favoring protectionism.

These conflicting results reflect the broader question of how trade liberalization redistributes income. The Ricardo–Viner (R–V) theorem implies that capital and labor in export industries will gain while capital and labor in import-competing industries will lose. The Stolper–Samuelson (S–S) theorem implies that capital will gain and labor will lose. One way to reconcile Magee's and Thorbecke's findings is to note that the S–S theorem is a long run model. The legislation Magee investigated was renewed every four years, making it a short run phenomenon. NAFTA, on the other hand, represented a long run commitment to free trade. Thus the R–V theorem might provide a better guide for how factors lobby on short run issues, while the S–S theorem might provide a better guide for how factors lobby on long run issues.

Regardless of how factors lobby, their success at obtaining desired benefits depends on the institutional structure. As Milner (1997) discusses, institutions are the rules of the game within a society. The way the polity is organized affects the constraints facing actors in the political marketplace. For instance, one would expect substantially more protection if Congress is the major player than if the President is. As discussed above, members of Congress have narrower constituencies, and thus are more likely to be receptive to demands by constituents for particularist benefits.

History bears out the importance of institutional structure for trade policy outcomes. Two examples, discussed below, are the tariff reductions that occurred after the executive branch wrested tariff-setting authority away from Congress in the 1930s and the increase in administered protection after Congress began exerting more authority in the implementation of the fair trade laws in the 1970s and 1980s.

Until 1930, Congress played a major role in writing tariffs. According to the U.S. Constitution, Congress has the power to "regulate commerce with foreign nations." It used this power in the 19th and early 20th century to implement high tariffs.

The tendency of Congress to broker import protection is well illustrated by the Smoot-Hawley Tariff Act of 1930. Schattschneider (1935) reports that well-organized interest groups testified before the House seeking tariff increases, whereas many other producers were unaware of the hearings. Taussig (1931, p. 495) states that lobbyists "pretty much got what they wanted." Schattschneider also documents the extensive logrolling that Congress engaged in to secure passage of the bill. Rowley et al. (1995) discuss the opposition to the bill by women who complained that dresses would become more expensive. Speaking of them, the *New York Times* (23 May 1929, p. 28) argued that these consumers did not receive any benefits from the bill because they had no organized lobbies to testify before Congress. The final Act revised tariffs on 20,000 items, producing the highest tariff rates in U.S. history.

The Smoot-Hawley Act is a showcase for public choice theory. Well-organized special interests lobbied Congress for particularist benefits. Members of Congress brokered these transfers. To get the legislation passed they engaged in massive logrolling. More diffuse interests such as consumers were either unaware of the bill or unable to influence it.

Shortly after passage of the Smoot-Hawley Act of 1930 the U.S. experienced an economic disaster. Real U.S. net national product fell by 30 percent from 1929 to 1933. Several countries retaliated, raising tariff walls against U.S. products. U.S. exports fell from $5.2 billion to $1.7 billion and imports from $4.4 billion to $1.5 billion.

Rightly or wrongly, people attributed these economic difficulties partly to Smoot-Hawley. Newspapers throughout the country argued that high barriers to imports were a grave economic mistake. One estimate indicated that 75 percent of the people wanted lower import duties. The Republican president (Hoover) and Republican Congress, who together had produced Smoot-Hawley, were voted out of office by landslides in 1932. The experience of a depression following passage of a major tariff-raising bill strengthened the ideology, developed by Adam Smith and David Ricardo, that free trade rather than protectionism led to prosperity.

In this atmosphere President Roosevelt began seeking in 1933 to wrest tariff-setting authority away from Congress. The logrolling and tariff-raising that accompanied Smoot-Hawley convinced many that Congress could not resist narrow sectional interests. Thus the Roosevelt Administration sought, under the executive branch's treaty-negotiation authority, the right to engage in reciprocal tariff cuts with other countries. Exporters such as the auto industry lobbied in favor of the bill. The Democratic Congress, in the Reciprocal Trade Agreements Act of 1934, authorized the President to negotiate tariff cuts of up to 50 percent in exchange for similar concessions by trading partners. The executive branch has remained the major player in tariff negotiations since then, and under presidential leadership average tariffs on dutiable imports have fallen from 60 percent in 1930 to 5 percent in 1995.

Many U.S. industries were not harmed by the tariff cuts until the 1960s. Following World War II, the economies of Europe and Japan lay prostrate and U.S. industries faced little competition. It was not until the 1960s that industries such as automobiles, footwear, electrical goods, steel, and textiles faced substantial import pressure (Baldwin, 1986). These industries lobbied Congress for relief. Congress was unable to provide relief either by increasing tariffs or by using antidumping or countervailing duty laws.

This upset Sen. Russell Long, chairman of the Senate Finance Committee. Long and his colleagues were under pressure from constituents who had been damaged by imports and were unable to obtain relief. As Baldwin (1986) discusses, Long began exercising greater control over the appointment of commissioners to the International Trade Commission (ITC). His committee rejected one presidential nomination because he was too sympathetic to the executive branch. He also lectured all potential commissioners that the ITC was to be responsive to Congress, not the executive branch. His influence over the nomination process was seen by the fact that before 1967 more than half of the ITC appointees were from the executive branch and academia and less than 10 percent had Congressional backgrounds whereas after 1967 less than 10 percent were from the executive branch or academia and 50 percent had Congressional backgrounds.

As imports continued to pour into the United States in the 1970s, members of the Finance and Ways and Means Committees sought to gain greater control over antidumping (AD) and countervailing duty (CVD) rulings in order to accommodate the demands of lobbyists. In 1974, Congress gained exclusive control over the budget of the ITC. In 1979, the Ways and Means Committee complained that the antidumping and countervailing duty laws had been inadequately enforced (Destler, 1986). Congress responded by shortening the time limits in which AD and CVD rulings could be made. They also transferred authority for AD and CVD determinations to the Commerce Department, which was thought to be more responsive to the demands of business, and away from the Treasury Department, which was thought to be concerned about broader issues. As Destler (1986) has documented, these changes resulted in more AD and CVD petitions being filed, and much more relief being granted to petitioners.

However, much of this relief has been protectionist. Bhagwati (1988) has discussed that since there is no penalty for frivolous complaints, domestic rivals often file complaints to keep foreign competitors mired in expensive litigation. Finger (1991) has discussed how AD and CVD laws disenfranchise consumers and import-using firms and serve as an outlet for complaints only for import-competing firms. Further, since these laws have submerged ambiguous concepts such as dumping in technical language, they require extensive legal and accounting expertise to make rulings. In such a technical and expensive process, concentrated interests that benefit from protectionism have a greater incentive to initiate litigation than diffuse interests harmed by protectionism have to resist litigation. Thus the process greatly favors import-competing firms and harms consumers and import-using firms.

The process by which rulings are made is also illogical and anticompetitive. Unlike domestic price discrimination, dumping is determined by comparing a weighted average of the exporter's prices in his own country with each individual price charged in the U.S. As Palmeter (1989) noted, this usually leads to a finding of dumping, since an average of several numbers will be larger than some of its components. If, for example, the exporter sells the good in the U.S. and the home country for $200 one week and $100 the following week the average price will be $150. This is called the

fair value. Since this is below the price of $100 charged at one time in the U.S., this is considered dumping. Thus AD laws are very different from the Robinson-Patman Act, which governs domestic price discrimination. To quote Palmeter (1989, p. 189), "Robinson Patman requires injury to competition; the antidumping laws only require injury to competitors — which may actually enhance competition."

The institutional structure thus has important effects on trade policy outcomes. When Congress is the major player, as with tariff legislation before 1930, large amounts of trade protection are brokered. When government agencies are closely controlled by Congress, as happened with the ITC in the 1970s and 1980s, more administered protection is brokered. When the president has greater authority over trade matters, as with tariff laws since 1930, less protection is provided.

The president is not, however, immune to dispensing protection. In 2002 President Bush provided tariffs of up to 30 percent for the steel industry. The steel industry is concentrated in states such as Pennsylvania, West Virginia, and Ohio that are important for President Bush's reelection bid. Thus, even when the president is the dominant player, electoral college calculations can cause him to broker substantial amounts of trade protection.

WILLEM THORBECKE

REFERENCES

Baldwin, R.E. (1986). *The Political Economy of U.S. Import Policy*. Cambridge, Mass.: MIT Press.

Bhagwati, J. (1988). *Protectionism*. Cambridge, Mass.: MIT Press.

Destler, I.M. (1986). *American Trade Politics: System Under Stress*. Washington, DC: Institute for International Economics.

Finger, J. M. (1991). "The meaning of unfair in U.S. import policy," World Bank Policy, Research, and External Affairs Working Paper 745, The World Bank, Washington, DC.

Gwartney, J. and Wagner, R.E. (1988). *Public Choice and Constitutional Economics*. Greenwich: JAI Press.

Magee, S.P. (1980). "Three simple tests of the Stolper–Samuelson Theorem," in P. Opperheimer (ed.) *Issues in International Trade*. London: Oriel Press, pp. 138–153.

Milner, H. (1997). *Interests, Institutions, and Information*. Princeton, NJ: Princeton University Press.

Olson, M. (1965). *The Logic of Collective Action*. Cambridge, Mass.: Harvard University Press.

Palmeter, N.D. (1989). "The capture of the antidumping laws." *Yale Journal of International Law*, 14: 182–198.

Rowley, C.K. (1984). "The relevance of the median voter theorem." *Journal of Institutional and Theoretical Economics*, 140: 104–135.

Rowley, C.K., Thorbecke, W., and Wagner, R. (1995). *Trade Protection in the United States*. Brookfield, VT and Aldershot, U.K.: Edward Elgar Publishing.

Schattschneider, E.E. (1935). *Politics, Pressures, and the Tariff.* New York: Prentice-Hall.

Taussig, F.W. (1931). *The Tariff History of the United States.* New York: G.P. Putnam.

Thorbecke, W. (1997). "Explaining house voting on the North American Free Trade Agreement." *Public Choice*, 92: 231–242.

INTEREST GROUPS 1

> People of the same trade seldom meet together, even for merriment and diversion, but the conversation ends in a conspiracy against the public, or in some contrivance to raise prices. It is impossible indeed to prevent such meetings, by any law which either could be executed, or would be consistent with liberty and justice. But though the law cannot hinder people of the same trade from sometimes assembling together, it ought to do nothing to facilitate such assemblies, much less to render them necessary. (Smith [1776] 1981: 145)

> A basic principle — and conundrum — underlies the demand for legislation. The principle is that groups able to organize for less than $1 in order to obtain $1 of benefits from legislation will be the effective demanders of laws. The conundrum is that economists have little idea how successful interest groups are formed. That is, how do groups overcome free-rider problems and organize for collective action so as to be able to seek $1 for less than $1? The plain truth is that economists know very little about the dynamics of group formation and action. (Anderson et al., 2001: 343)

It is not clear why, from a theoretical perspective, the study of interest groups is a separate subfield. After all, the problem of group formation is very similar to both the problem of underprovision of public goods, and overprovision of externalities. Nonetheless, it is accurate to say that the study of interest groups constitutes a well-defined and well-established field of study (for reviews of this large and diverse literature, see Mitchell and Munger, 1991; Tollison, 1991, 1997, 2001; Austen-Smith, 1997; Ekelund and Tollison, 2001; McCormick and Tollison, 1981).

1. Interest, Particular and General

One might say that the notion of "interest" group starts with the claim by Thrasymachus, in Plato's *Republic*: "justice is nothing else than the interest of the stronger." In the dialogue that follows, Socrates and Thrasymachus debate the idea of "interest." They find interest hard to specify, because it would appear that each person may have a self-interest and a collective interest, which could

conflict. The question becomes what is interest in the first place? They argue as follows: every "art" or profession has its own interest. That interest is the "perfection" of that art. But that may cause problems. For example, should it be true that

> medicine does not consider the interest of medicine, but the interest of the body? ... no physician, in so far as he is a physician, considers his own good in what he prescribes, but the good of his patient; for the true physician is also a ruler having the human body as a subject, and is not a mere money-maker ... (Plato, *Republic*, Book I)

Jean-Jacques Rousseau and many others since have taken up the idea that the notion of "interest" should be fundamentally reconceptualized, that the conflict between the particular will and the general will should be eliminated by allowing mankind's "natural," and noncompetitive, urges to dominate social interaction.

> Man [was] perpetually employed in getting others to interest themselves in his lot, and in making them, apparently at least, if not really, find their advantage in promoting his own. Thus he must have been sly and artful in his behaviour to some, and imperious and cruel to others; being under a kind of necessity to ill-use all the persons of whom he stood in need, when he could not frighten them into compliance, and did not judge it his interest to be useful to them.... In a word, there arose rivalry and competition on the one hand, and conflicting interests on the other, together with a secret desire on both of profiting at the expense of others. (Rousseau, *Discourse on Inequality*, Part II).

Rousseau recognizes that his conception of interest, a shared conception of a general will, requires that human "nature" be remade. Whether this project is appropriate for social science is a question outside the scope of the present effort. But it is worth noting having "agreement" does not mean that interests will be reconciled. As Charles V, Holy Roman Emperor (1500–1558), said, referring to a dispute with Francis I of France: "My cousin Francis and I are in perfect accord — he wants Milan, and so do I."

2. Faction

The public choice approach takes the existence of conflicting interests as given and legitimate, rather than asserting that disagreement is a sign society is sick. It is then asked, "How do different institutional arrangements affect the clash of interests?" It may be possible to reach judgments about whether some outcomes, and therefore some institutions, are better than others, but such judgments rely on comparisons of dead-weight loss, and the likely impact on growth, rather than on more subjective conceptions of justice. In this way, public choice echoes the note sounded by James Madison in Federalist #10, and by Alexander Hamilton and Madison in Federalist #51. Consider the following claims, all starting points for the public choice theory of interest groups:

> By a faction, I understand a number of citizens, whether amounting to a majority or a minority of the whole, who are united and actuated by some common impulse of passion, or of interest, adverse to the rights of other citizens, or to the permanent and aggregate interests of the community. (Madison, *Federalist #10*)

> It is in vain to say that enlightened statesmen will be able to adjust these clashing interests, and render them all subservient to the public good. Enlightened statesmen will not always be at the helm. (Madison, *Federalist #10*)

> The latent causes of faction are thus sown in the nature of man; and we see them everywhere brought into different degrees of activity, according to the different circumstances of civil society ... The regulation of these various and interfering interests forms the principal task of modern legislation, and involves the spirit of party and faction in the necessary and ordinary operations of the government. (Madison, *Federalist #10*)

> If men were angels, no government would be necessary. If angels were to govern men, neither external nor internal controls on government would be necessary. In framing a government which is to be administered by men over men, the great difficulty lies in this: you must first enable the government to control the governed; and in the next place oblige it to control itself.... This policy of supplying, by opposite and rival interests, the defect of better motives, might be traced through the whole system of human affairs, private as well as public. (Hamilton/Madison, *Federalist #51*)

Organized interest groups, or "factions," that try to manipulate politics to their advantage, are unconcerned about other groups' welfare. Rather than relying on the forbearance of the powerful, institutions must endow the weak with the means to balance the power of factions. This is most easily done using market institutions, where the ability of the powerful to use force is circumscribed. The authors of *The Federalist* also believed that the effects of factions could be controlled by a territorially large and diverse republic, with separation of powers in governing institutions.

But what about the interest groups themselves? Are they good, or bad? How do they form?

3. Classical Interest Group Theory

The classical theorists actually had a very specific goal in mind: Describe the actual (as opposed to theoretical) process of decision-making in democracies, and evaluate its qualities compared to those claimed for abstract democratic choice. As discussed above, the framers of the American constitution had a dim view of "faction," and enlightenment thinkers generally were skeptical organized interests. In the U.S., Theodore Roosevelt and the wave of ardent "progressive" reformers that followed him tried to eliminate interests in general, and organized interests in particular, from the political process. Against this backdrop, the contribution of Arthur Bentley, in his classic work *The Process of Government*, is all the more striking.

Bentley argued that a group is simply a distinct portion of society, and recognized that any one person may be a "member" of many different groups. Further, as he famously claims in Chapter 7: "There is no group without its interest .... The group and the interest are not separate." Finally, in the same chapter, he claimed that "There is no political process that is not a balancing of quantity against quantity. There is not a law that is passed that is not the expression of force and force in tension." To simplify greatly, the advantage of groups in Bentley's view is that groups allow intensity of preference to register in policy-making, whereas "pure" democracy ignored intensity.

The difference is subtle. Imagine 25 people, choosing between two policies A and B. Imagine that 15 of these people favor policy A, and the remaining minority of 10 would prefer B. Obviously, if a vote were taken, A would win with 60% of the vote (15/25). But, in Bentley's view, it is better to think of the two groups in a kind of tug-of-war, with those who favor A pulling at a force of 60 foot-pounds (each of 15 people each pulling a rather lazy 4 f-p), and those who favor B pulling at a force of 80 foot-pounds (10 people pulling at 8 f-p each). Clearly, the "Prefer B" group will win, though they are fewer, since each member pulls twice as hard.

For Bentley, intense preferences *should* count more, because democracy doesn't get the "quantities" in policy right. He explicitly invokes Jeremy Bentham's "greatest good for the greatest number," but then claims that only group competition can calculate this quantity exactly. The general approach Bentley appears to advocating is this:

$$\sum_{i = 1 \text{ to } N_A} W_i > \text{or} < \sum_{j = 1 \text{ to } N_B} W_j$$

In our example, $N_A > N_B$, but the sum of the forces exerted by those who prefer B exceeds the force exerted by those who favor A. So, B wins.

The other "classical" interest group theorist was David Truman, (1952) whose best known work was *The Governmental Process*. Truman was sympathetic to the main normative description of Bentley, but had a much more dynamic and complex conception of interest group competition. Truman called his notion a "disturbance theory" of politics.

Suppose we start with an initial position of balance, with a stable policy. Then one group tries to increase the pressure it brings to bear, by increasing its activity and level of organization. What will happen? According to Truman, the opposition forces will likewise organize, and though the pressures on both sides may well increase markedly it is by no means clear that an attempt to organize will result in any policy change. Groups organize in "waves," as a disturbance sets off a responding surge in opposing groups, with ripples extending outward. It is not clear, in Truman's account, whether these groups then disappear once the wave of organizing is past. We turn now to the account of Mancur Olson, perhaps the most important public choice theorist of interest groups, who took up both the challenges of explaining group organization and explaining persistence of organized groups beyond their original purpose.

4. Olson and the Logic of Collective Action

The normative properties of the "classical" group theorists rested on a simple premise: if a group faced total costs of organization and action that were strictly less than the gains to the group, however distributed, the group was predicted to form and become active politically. But as Mancur Olson (1965) argued, this collective comparison of group costs and benefits is nearly irrelevant to the question of whether an effective group actually forms.

According to Olson, there are three factors that determine whether a group will form:

(1) How large is the group? Smaller groups can overcome the "collective action" problem more easily, because they can communicate and coordinate the activity.

(2) How large is the individual benefit, compared to the costs of the activity to the individual? If the individual benefits exceed the individual cost, then the activity may be thought of as private. But even if the costs exceed the benefits to the individual, the smaller the "donation" of the individual to the collective activity's success the more likely that person is to contribute.

(3) Can the nascent group provide selective incentives, or other excludable benefits connected with group membership? If such benefits (enjoyment of companionship, a magazine tied to membership dues, etc.) are valued by some people, then they will "join" the public group simply to obtain the private commodity that comes with it.

Olson's critique of the classical group theorists, and anyone else who wants to rely on group rent-seeking for benefits to society, is truly fundamental. Olson showed that there is no necessary connection between group size and the true distribution of intensity of preference profiles in the population. Most "groups" don't form. Worse, groups that do form may form around the capacity or willingness of a successful rent-seeking entrepreneur to offer selective benefits uncorrelated with the group's true goals. Consequently, politically powerful groups may simply be exploiting their own members, as well as other citizens who are not organized. The total dollar gains by the "winners" may be far less than the total dollar loss by losers.

In *The Rise and Decline of Nations*, Olson elaborated the theme of interest group competition in government by exploring some of its dynamic effects. In this portion of his theory, the links to Truman's "disturbance theory" are a bit closer. While it is true that most potential groups fail to organize, once a group has formed (for whatever reason) it is very difficult to dislodge it from its position claiming benefits and privileges in the society. Once a position of power has been obtained, any attempt to remove the benefit or disband the group disturbs those who depend on the benefit for their livelihood. Consequently, societies develop "institutional sclerosis" over time, unless some cataclysm such as war breaks the established relationships among groups and elected officials. Society devotes too much of its resources to attorneys, bureaucrats, and the writing of reports, and less to the creation of new wealth.

Olson's critique harks back to Humboldt (1993):

> We must not overlook here one particular harmful consequence, since it so closely affects human development; and this is that the administration of political affairs itself becomes in time so full of complications that it requires an incredible number of persons to devote their time to its supervision, in order that it may not fall into utter confusion. Now, by far the greater portion of these have to deal with the mere symbols and formulas of things; and thus, not only are men of first-rate capacity withdrawn from anything which gives scope for thinking, and useful hands are diverted from real work, but their intellectual powers themselves suffer from this partly empty, partly narrow employment. (pp. 29–30)

5. Chicago Interest Group Theory

There has been a long tradition of interest group theory at the University of Chicago. The earliest clear public choice result may have appeared in the late 1950s. It was named after Aaron Director, and is called "Director's Law": income redistribution, and other programs whose effect is redistribution, will focus on the middle class at the expense of the wealthy and the poor (see Stigler, 1970; Peltzman, 1980). The reason is that poor people lack the political power to be included in governing coalitions of interest groups, and the wealthy are not numerous enough to defend themselves.

The most important Chicago interest group theory, however, is the "theory of economic regulation." Stigler (1970) argued that organized interests are likely to dominate policy processes that affect their profitability. If regulation, by controlling entry into the industry and cartelizing rate structures, can increase profitability then regulation will be imposed. Stigler is skeptical of the "public interest" rationale for regulation, even if the description given by politicians is couched in public interest language. The real reason we see economic regulation, according to Stigler, is that the first-best (in terms of efficiency) solution of direct transfers from taxpayers to industries is simply too transparent. Consequently, transfers are effected through regulatory policies that have the same general effect, though with less efficiency.

Peltzman (1976) extends Stigler's model considerably, by accounting for the balancing between industry interests and consumer desires. This work brings us back a little closer to the classical interest group theorists, where the "equilibrium" among contrasting forces results in the varying levels of regulatory policy in different industries. The active agent in Peltzman's model is the politicians, since they design regulatory policies to maximize the vote that they receive. Organized voter/consumer groups can balance the power of industry very effectively, but in general the mass of consumers who pay only small individual costs are unlikely to organize, as was suggested by Olson's theory of collective action.

There have been a number of answers or criticisms of the Stigler–Peltzman model. One important work is Kau and Rubin (1982), who develop a different notion of equilibrium, or trading off of the wants of constituents, interest groups, and the members themselves. This innovative study was the first to examine the implications of ideology for the expression and control of economic "interest." The key finding is that changes in policy may not be primarily due to changes in the configuration and power of groups supporting or opposing regulation or deregulation. Instead, the explanation may be changes in ideology, or the accumulation of "errors" (from the perspective of the interest group model) in voting patterns. Another alternative is Denzau and Munger (1986), who develop institutional details within the political process that may influence the capacity of interest group to control the policy process.

Becker (1983) explicitly invokes the classical theorists in his model of group competition. The focus in this extension of the Chicago model is a subtle, but important point: from the perspective of public choice economics, transfers are not costs in any useful sense. Instead, the costs of transfers should be measured in the dead-weight losses engendered by the mechanism of the transfer itself. Becker argues that the political process will work out in such a way as to minimize the dead-weight losses, because reduced waste is a Pareto improvement.

The distribution of such gains is an indeterminate bargaining problem, and there may be transactions costs and other frictions that prevent the achievement of a zero deadweight loss solution. But, by identifying the tendency toward lower cost solutions for achieving the same transfer, Becker has brought the interest group model back toward its roots. Interest group competition is likely to force politics and policies toward efficient solutions. Those "solutions" may offend justice, since the poor are likely to lose and the middle class to win, but in terms of pure efficiency the system works smoothly, at least in the Chicago view.

6. Examples of the Public Choice Approach

A wide variety of authors have used interest group theory to understand political phenomena in the U.S. and in other countries. Consider the following examples, chosen to be diverse rather than representative:

- Ekelund et al. (1996) examine the medieval Catholic church as a rational and rent-seeking organization. This is not only a story of interest group behavior, but it is a wonderful example of the sort of questions that a carefully applied interest group model can answer. See also Ekelund and Tollison (1997), which examines the corporate form of organization and the mercantilism.

- Gray and Lowery (1996) treat interest groups from the perspective of "population ecology." The focus is on the growth and competition among groups for support, with the central premise being that the density and variety of groups will depend on the institutional environment (in this case, states). The claim by Gray and Lowery is that their findings directly contradict the Olsonian model of the "collective action" problem.

- Rowley (2000) examines the post-colonial economic performance of the nations of Sub-Saharan Africa. He argues that the failure of the economies there are primarily institutional, and gives at least the outlines of a theory of the interaction between interest group action and institutional dynamics in explaining economic performance. Along similar lines of explaining institutional and constitutional change, see Crain and Tollison

(1979), Anderson and Tollison (1985), Anderson et al. (1996), Munger and Schaller (1997).

• Holcombe (1994) argues that the traditional interest group model misrepresents the relative power of groups and legislators. It would appear that any legislator who refuses to serve groups will simply be replaced, but Holcombe points out that institutional features of modern elections render this claim suspect. Holcombe describes a variety of "barriers to entry" that leave elected officials with considerable latitude to choose among the interests they serve.

Tollison (2001) notes a series of interest group research questions that are as yet unanswered. A selection of these includes: (1) Is the interest group theory of government a theory of all government, or just off-budget, regulatory government? (2) Models of legislative voting show some, but not all, patterns in voting are explained by the constellation of interest group support and opposition. Does this mean that our models of patterns of influence are incomplete, or are there other forces at work, such as personal ideology of legislators? (3) How can the interest group model be extended to account for time-series change in patterns of regulation and policy, rather than simply cross-sectional differences? (4) How are interest group pressures perceived, and acted on, by the judiciary?

MICHAEL C. MUNGER

REFERENCES

Anderson, Gary M., Dennis Halcoussis, and Robert D. Tollison (1996). "Drafting the competition: labor unions and military conscription." *Defence and Peace Economics*, 7: 189–202.

Anderson, Gary M., William Shughart, and Robert D. Tollison (2001). "Clubs and club goods," in *Public Choice (Elgar Companion Series)*, William Shughart and Laura Razzolini (eds.) Northhampton, MA: Edward Elgar Publishing, pp. 337–356.

Anderson, Gary M. and Robert D. Tollison (1985). "Ideology, interest groups, and the repeal of the corn laws." *Zeitschrift fur die gesamte Staatswissenschaft (JITE)*, 141: 197–212.

Austen-Smith, David (1997). "Interest groups: money, information, and influence," in Dennis Mueller, (ed.) *Perspectives on Public Choice: A Handbook*. New York: Cambridge University Press, pp. 296–321.

Becker, G.S. (1983). "A theory of competition among pressure groups for political influence." Quarterly Journal of Economics, 98(August): 371–400.

Crain, William Mark, and Robert D. Tollison (1979). "Constitutional change in an interest group perspective." *Journal of Legal Studies*, 8: 165–175.

Denzau, Arthur, and Michael Munger (1986). "Legislators and interest groups: how unorganized interests get represented." *American Political Science Review*, 80: 89–106.

Ekelund, Robert B. and Robert D. Tollison (1997). *Politicized Economies: Monarchy, Monopoly, and Mercantilism*. College Station, TX: Texas A&M University Press.

Ekelund, Robert B. and Robert D. Tollison (2001). "Clubs and club goods," in *Public Choice (Elgar Companion Series)*, William Shughart and Laura Razzolini (eds.) Northhampton, MA: Edward Elgar Publishing, pp. 357–378.

Ekelund, Robert B., Robert Hebert, Robert Tollison, Gary Anderson, and Aubrey Davidson (1996). *Sacred Trust: The Medieval Church as an Economic Firm*. New York: Oxford University Press.

Gray, Virginia, and David Lowery (1996). *The Population Ecology of Interest Representation: Lobbying Communities in the American States*. Ann Arbor: University of Michigan Press.

Grier, Kevin, Michael Munger, and Brian Roberts (1994). "The determinants of industry political activity, 1978–1986." *American Political Science Review*, 88: 911–932.

Holcombe, Randall G. (1994). *The Economic Foundations of Government*. New York: New York University Press.

Humboldt, Wilhelm von (1993 [1969, original German 1854]). *The Limits of State Action*. J.W. Burrow, (ed.) Indianapolis, IN: Liberty Fund, Inc.

Kau, James B. and Paul H. Rubin (1982). *Congressmen, Constituents, and Contributors*. Boston: Martinus Nijhoff Publishing.

McCormick, Robert E. and Robert D. Tollison (1981). *Politicians, Legislation, and the Economy: An Inquiry into the Interest-group Theory of Government*. Boston: M. Nijhoff (Kluwer).

Mitchell, William and Michael Munger (1991). "Economic models of interest groups: an introductory survey." *American Journal of Political Science*, 35: 512–546.

Munger, Michael and Thomas Schaller (1997). "The prohibition amendments: a natural experiment in interest group influence." *Public Choice*, 90: 139–163.

Olson, Mancur (1965). *The Logic of Collective Action*. Cambridge, MA: Harvard University Press.

Olson, Mancur (1982). *The Rise and Decline of Nations: Economic Growth, Stagflation, and Social Rigidities*. New Haven: Yale University Press.

Peltzman, Sam (1976). "Toward a more general theory of regulation." *Journal of Law and Economics*, 19: 211–240.

Peltzman, Sam (1980). "The growth of government." *Journal of Law and Economics*, 23: 209–287.

Rowley, Charles K. (2000). "Political culture and economic performance in Sub-Saharan Africa." *European Journal of Political Economy*, 16: 133–158.

Smith, A. ([1776] 1981). *An Inquiry into the Nature and Causes of the Wealth of Nations*. Indianapolis, in Liberty Fund, Inc. (Reprint of The Glasgow Edition of the *Works and Correspondence of Adam Smith*, Volume II, R.H. Campbell and A.S. Skinner Clarendon Press, 1979.)

Stigler, George (1970). "Director's Law of Public Income Redistribution." *Journal of Law and Economics*, 13: 1–10.

Stigler, George (1971). "The theory of economic regulation." *Bell Journal of Economics and Management Science*, 2: 3–21.

Tollison, Robert D. (1991). "Regulation and interest groups," in Jack High (ed.) *Regulation*. Ann Arbor: University of Michigan Press, pp. 59–76.

Tollison, Robert D. (1997). "Rent seeking," in Dennis Mueller (ed.) *Perspectives on Public Choice: A handbook*. New York: Cambridge University Press, pp. 506–525.

Tollison, Robert D. (2001). "The interest-group theory of government: problems and prospects." *Kyklos*, 54: 465–472.

Truman, David (1952). *The Governmental Process*. New York: Knopf.

INTEREST GROUPS 2

Research on interest groups goes back at least to Cicero. He distinguished parties (partes) from factions (factio). A faction worked in its own interests whereas a party sought to discover the common good. Since then only the details of inquiry into interest groups have changed. Two thousand years on, the question of what political systems promote good interest groups still excites and maddens researchers. Thinking on this question sputtered until Montesquieu and later Madison explained how government institutions could be structured to limit the power of factions. Madison, in his #10 Federalist paper, argued that factions could be contained by dividing power between competing branches of government and by encouraging factions to be numerous so none would come to dominate government.

The greatest minds in political economy have focused on interest groups in order to understand how power flows, just as Boltzman and the atomists of the mid-19th century focused on the atom as a mental device for understanding thermodynamics. De Tocqueville, Marx, Toynbee, Orwell; the names go off like cannons. These thinkers sought to build a science of power, but their writings as those of most political sages of this century are descriptive. Their attempts at generalization are either too grand or dotted with exceptions. The leap from musings to science took place in the 1940s and 1950s with the work of Duncan Black (1958). Black drew on the writings of these earlier greats to propose the first formal model of how interest groups rise to power. His median voter model is simple but was a base from which to formulate testable hypotheses about how interest groups work.

Black's median voter model suggested that in a democracy, provided the preferences of voters over policy alternatives are ordered in a special way known as single-peaked, power will go to the median voter. The first tests of the Black model had to wait thirty years until studies such as those of Pommerehne and Frey (1976) began to see whether median income determined government spending better than mean income in both direct democracy and representative democracy. Theirs and similar studies that followed seem to vindicate the median voter view of policy-making but suffer from being joint tests of political equilibrium and the hypothesis that power flows to the median voter. If the median voter model is false, it is possible that positive results are due to a political disequilibrium.

The median voter model does not try to explain how interest groups wield power. Black was almost silent on the machinations of special interest groups and preferred to study the machinations of committees. His model rather is like the Modigliani–Miller theorem of corporate finance; a model we know to not describe reality perfectly but which frames our questions on what is missing from our understanding. Insights about the power of interest groups comes from noting "frictions" in political systems that lead politicians to deviate from the interests of the median voter. Noting what causes the deviation between median interests and politician behaviour is crucial to understanding the circumstances under which a special interest group (Cicero's *factio*) will have the whip hand over a public interest group. Can voters be consistently fooled? Are preferences single or many-peaked and so are laws subject to agenda control? Can politicians create artificial barriers to the entry of competing parties and ideas coming from public interest groups? Do special interest groups benefit from a built-in technological advantage that allows them to push their ideas ahead of others? An affirmative answer to these questions will tilt power to the side of special interests.

Knowing when power will tilt to the side of special interests has fascinated researchers because a political system that serves special interests will forgo the benefits of government projects and institutions that work in the public good. Public goods benefit everyone and are a sort of cauldron from which emerges economic growth. In *Plagues and Peoples* William H. McNeil (1976) argued that parasitism by special interests is similar to parasitism by microorganisms. Predation by the large and the small undermine cooperation and fruitful public ventures and so are forces of entropy. A society which wishes to increase its wealth must find ways either to eliminate the predators or coax them into a symbiotic union with the host of people who amass resources and so combat entropy. McNeill sees democracy as a late step in the evolution of economic predators and prey in which the parasitical overhead, or political profits that people pay for their public goods is on a downward curve greased by political competition in orderly elections.

Before we can accept McNeill's grand vision of interest group evolution we need to know the parameters that egg on interest groups. Mancur Olson (1965) used a mix of old-fashioned political economy, journalistic inquiry, and public choice insight in his investigation of collective action to argue that interest groups which have low costs of containing free riders in their ranks will have an advantage over interest groups who cannot control free riders. Political scientists took up this insight but it lay dormant in the *Public Choice* field until George Stigler reanimated it in 1971 in testable form. Stigler battened on the hypothesis that groups whose interests were concentrated would be better able to influence government than groups whose interests were diffuse. In his empirical explorations he used this hypothesis to guide him in his finding that the main beneficiaries of regulation in the consumer interest were not consumers but the regulated firms. Samuel Peltzman (1976) put Stigler's argument in maths by saying that regulators, or political brokers, maximize a value function (most often interpreted as votes gained) into which enter positively the utilities of consumers and of the predatory producers who seek through regulation to extort wealth from these consumers. Political middlemen redistribute income between the two groups to the point where the marginal loss in votes from consumers equaled the marginal gain in votes from producers.

Peltzman's article came to be one of the most cited articles in economics but its weakness was in assuming that the tradeoff between consumer and producer interests was linear. Gary Becker grafted onto Peltzman's model the insight that an interest group which preys on another is like a pickpocket. The thief damages his victim by stealing money and by forcing the victim to dash about replacing credit and identity cards. More technically the interest group harms its victim by taking money and by imposing deadweight losses. Becker's insight was to recognize that deadweight losses put an exponential break on predation. He took Harberger's insight that deadweight losses are proportional to the square of the tax, and used it to argue that a linear increase in takings by a predatory interest group will provoke a non-linear increase in the deadweight losses its victim suffers. These rapidly increasing losses will prod victims to invest equivalent sums in resisting attempts on their wealth. The advance of predators, fueled by linear incentives slows before the stiffening resistance of prey outraged by non-linear damages.

Becker's model has been seen by some as implying that politics are efficient because deadweight losses are a break to predation. This conclusion has weight if we hold constant all other forces that influence political outcomes and the conclusion fits neatly into McNeill's hypothesis (MC Neill, 1976) that virulent predators evolve into benign symbiotes, but the conclusion comes from a partial reading of Becker's model. The outcome of a contest between interest groups depends also on combatant's political savvy. Groups with the gift of intrigue, or with more guns, can laugh at deadweight losses and impose their will for generations, as the sad example of African dictatorships shows. Palda (1997) has shown that there are gaping contradictions in the fiscal policies of democracies, as in the case where governments churn their finances by transfering money to someone and taxing that money back, and Rowley and Vachris (1994) have given a thorough account of the frictions and problems inherent in evolving towards an efficient democracy. To date no one has traced the path by which political efficiency can evolve. Perhaps the best hope for such an understanding will be to carry over to public choice Thomas Ray's (1992) computer simulation (the Tierra model) of the evolution of parasites and prey by grafting some measure of the deadweight loss of government and see how this deadweight loss will evolve under different political rules.

Becker's analysis (Becker, 1983) is so general that its hull can fit around just about any sort of relation between interest groups. The model applies as well to dictatorships as it does to democracies. What is remarkable is that what some may see as a Dr. Seuss version of political modeling can make powerful testable predictions about interest groups. In a paper with Casey Mulligan (1998) Becker (Becker and Mullingen, 1998) found that governments with efficient tax systems that impose small deadweight losses per dollar raised tend to be larger than governments with inefficient tax systems. This finding is indirect confirmation of theoretical musings which have tried to weld interest groups to the median voter model.

Austen-Smith's (1987) model of interest group influence grew out of the theoretical poverty of service-induced campaign contribution models of interest groups. These earlier models were intellectual islands lying outside the Stigler–Peltzman–Becker view of politics and the Black median voter model, and saw interest groups as moustache-twirling capitalists who could buy government protection for their businesses and pet concerns with election campaign contributions. Policy played no role in the success of politicians. Empirical work by Snyder (1990) gave feeble support to this caricature.

Austen-Smith's path breaking work set out a theoretical model of policy in which interest groups can only buy influence contrary to the public interest by exploiting the public's ignorance of where politicians stand. Politicians serve two masters: voters who have preferences for a public good and special interest groups who help politicians communicate with voters for a price paid in government favours. The conclusion that comes out of Austen-Smith's model is that policy tends towards the median voter's wishes, but deviates from that tendency the greater is voter ignorance. The greater this ignorance the more can special interests sup at the public's cost. Voter ignorance in the Becker model is a function of self-interest. Special interests and their political middlemen who impose large deadweight losses on voters give voters a reason to become informed about policy and so to resist the inefficient growth of government. Becker's finding that efficient tax systems dovetail with large governments could be seen as a manifestation of political systems where efficient tax policies lull voters and allow politicians and their supporting special interests to coast like pilot fish dragging on the skins of productive citizens.

Austen-Smith (1997) believes that the modeling of interest group behaviour is in its early stages and that because we know so little about the path by which information comes to voters and resounds with them that "there is little hope of saying anything normative about whether any induced influence over policy is good or bad." This is a backhand at what is perhaps one of the most surprising and original contributions of public choice to the understanding of what drives interest groups and whether their activities are productive; the theory of rent-seeking.

Rent-seeking is a term that evokes images of landlords shaking down tenants for a few coppers. Such imagery is unfortunate because it cuts off policymakers and the public from seeing the dangers of a political system that encouragers pie-cutters above pie makers. The Holy Grail of rent-seeking research is to discover whether in the contest for government favours interest groups together spend as much or more than the prize being sought. The work of Reinganum (1982) into patent races and the huge literature in tournament theory which Lazear and Rosen (1979) spawned show that concern about whether disputes over resources destroy those resources are not restricted to the public choice field.

The rent-seeking literature takes as its basic tool a power function popularized by Tullock (1980). This "logistic power function" states that the probability a group wins government influence over other groups depends on how much it spends relative to those groups and on a parameter called political talent which translates expenditure into political success. The logistic power function is to public choice what the Cobb–Douglas function is to microeconomics: a simple, intuitive, function consistent with many different micro-formulations of power.

Rent-seeking theory says little about inner workings of interest groups. Rent-seeking theory describes the efforts interest groups will invest in forming policy given a certain reward from government, given the rules for obtaining that reward, and given how politically astute are these groups. If competing groups are of similar political skill they will each believe themselves close to the government

prize. In their striving they may dissipate all or even more than all the value of the favour government has to grant. This is both a positive and normative insight. Empirical work can proceed by looking at circumstances where politicians have the discretion to grant favours and seeing whether special interest groups are particularly active in such areas. Discretion fuels the hope of interests groups that by spending money to influence government the dice of power will roll their way. Here, for the first time in thousands of years of political research is a formal proof that political discretion carries with it a cost.

Austen-Smith's finding that voters who are informed about the public good can put a break on the activities of special interest groups gives punch to rent-seeking research. Political systems that constrain the power of politician to place artificial barriers to the flow of information such as campaign spending limits, centralized finances which discourage local governmental experiments, and a refusal to allow direct democracy, are political systems which will allow voters to become informed about the public good and will reduce the dissipative activities of special interest groups.

FILIP PALDA

REFERENCES

Austen-Smith, David (1997). "Interest groups: money, information, and influence," in *Perspectives on Public Choice*, Dennis C. Mueller (ed.) Cambridge: Cambridge University Press, pp. 296–321.

Austen-Smith, David (1987). "Interest groups, campaign contributions and probabilistic voting." *Public Choice*, 54: 123–139.

Becker, Gary S. (1983). "A theory of competition among pressure groups for political influence." *Quarterly Journal of Economics*, 98: 371–400.

Becker, Gary S. and Casey B. Mulligan (1998). "Deadweight costs and the size of government." National Bureau of Economic Research Working Paper 6789, November.

Black, Duncan (1958). *The Theory of Committees and Elections.* Cambridge: Cambridge University Press.

Lazear, Edward P. and Sherwin Rosen (1981). "Rank-order tournaments as optimum labor contracts." *Journal of Political Economy*, 89: 841–864.

McNeill, William H. (1976). *Plagues and Peoples.* Garden City, N.Y.: Anchor Press/Doubleday.

Olson, Mancur (1965). *The Logic of Collective Action.* Cambridge: Harvard University Press.

Palda, Filip (1997). "Fiscal churning and political efficiency." *Kyklos*, 50: 189–206.

Peltzman, Samuel (1976). "Towards a more general theory of regulation." *Journal of Law and Economics*, 19: 211–240.

Pommerehne, Werner W. and Bruno Frey (1976). "Two approaches to estimating public expenditures." *Public Finance Quarterly*, 4: 395–407.

Ray, T.S. (1992). "Evolution, ecology and optimization of digital organisms." Santa Fe Institute Working Paper 92-08-042.

Rowley, Charles K. and Michelle A. Vachris (1994). "Why democracy does not necessarily produce efficient results." *Journal of Public Finance and Public Choice/Economia Delle Scelte Pubbliche*, 12: 95–111.

Reinganum, Jennifer F. (1982). "A dynamic game of R and D: patent protection and competitive behavior." *Econometrica*, 50: 671–688.

Snyder, James M. Jr. (1990). "Campaign contributions as investments: the U.S. House of Representatives, 1980–1986." *Journal of Political Economy*, 98: 1195–1227.

Stigler, George J. (1971). "The theory of economic regulation." *Bell Journal of Economics and Management Science*, 2: 137–146.

Tullock, G. (1980). "Efficient Rent Seeking" in J.M. Buchanan, Robert D. Tollison, and Gordon Tullock (eds.). *Toward a theory of the rent-seeking society*. College Station: Texas A & M University Press.

INTERNATIONAL GAME OF POWER

1. Introduction

In spite of organisations like the Organization for Economic Cooperation and Development (OECD), the International Monetary Fund (IMF), the North Atlantic Treaty Organization (NATO) and the United Nations Organization (UNO), the international system is still characterised by partial anarchy. Whereas functioning nations have established a monopoly of power, and can strictly limit the use of force by their citizens to reach their ends, this is not true for the international system. Governments are still in a position to pursue international ends or to defend themselves against aggression with military force, though international legal rules and peace-furthering organisations like the UNO have been established. As long as final sovereignty rests with states, and they retain the command of armed forces instead of a world-wide organisation, this situation will prevail, wars will remain a trait of this system, and problems can only be mitigated by an evolving international body of law, international courts and organisations (Bull, 1981). For these institutions can only work to the degree their rules and decisions are accepted by states.

2. Fundamental Traits

If one of them [the crowns of France and of Spain] grows in power, the other must lose

> correspondingly. This leads between both countries ... to a kind of inherited hostility .... It can be hidden, but

never be extinguished by treaties. For the fundamentals remain ever the same, and if one country works against the other, it believes rather to preserve and to protect itself than to damage the other,...(Louis XIV, Memoirs, [1669], quoted from Schaetzel, without date: 171–172)

In contrast to the situation within nations, the governments are facing a dilemma situation in the international system (Tullock, 1974; Bernholz, 1992). Consider, for simplicity, only two countries A and B, and assume that each can win an advantage, if it alone rearms and occupies the other country. But if both rearm and perhaps go to war, they are both worse off than without rearming themselves. In a corresponding situation, sketched in Table 1, p describes the strategy of foregoing to rearm, whereas w denotes the strategy of rearming and using it either for threats or for going to war. Inside the table are given the benefits connected with the combination of the two strategies applied by the countries. The first item always refers to A and the second to B. The figures correspond to the assumptions and can be multiplied with any positive factor without affecting results. For both countries the dominant strategy is to rearm. For the rulers of A prefer strategy w, whatever strategy B might follow. If it selects p, we have a payoff of $60 > 45$ for A, and if it prefers w, $25 > 20$. The situation for B is similar. Consequently, both countries select w. But this gives the result (25, 20), which is worse than (45, 30), which they would have obtained if they both had selected strategy p. This is the so-called prisoners' dilemma applied to an international setting. A treaty not to rearm would benefit both countries. But it is better for them to break such a contract, and in contrast to the situation within states there is no authority that could punish its violation and therefore prevent it.

Not all rulers are bent on aggression. But this is no guarantee for international peace and non-aggression. For assume that the example is changed as follows (Table 2).

Table 1: A dilemma situation — 1

A	B	p	w
p		45, 30	20, 40
w		60, 15	25, 20

Table 2: A dilemma situation — 2

A	B	p	w
p		45, 30	20, 40
w		40, 15	25, 20

That is, the rulers of A would select strategy p instead of w if they knew that B were not inclined towards aggression, since now $45 > 40$. But this is not B's policy, since $40 > 30$ for this country. It follows that the rulers of A, knowing or suspecting B's intentions, have still to select w, that is to rearm, because of B's decision in favour of w, and since $25 > 20$ for A. Similar considerations apply for the case of more than two countries, though the situation becomes more complicated because of possible alliances. It follows that behaviour in the international system is strongly influenced by the aims of the most aggressive nations.

This result does not imply that international law, rules of conduct and co-operation cannot evolve. Even with only two states there are issues for which co-operation is rewarding, for which no prisoner's dilemma exists. Moreover, even in situations like those described in the examples, contracts may be kept, if the relationships are repeated, without any finite end, so that any violation of treaties can be punished by not co-operating later. That is when a repetitive game with an indefinite duration is played.

3. Characteristics of Different International Systems

Although the basic dilemma of the international system is always present except for a world-state, it may show different institutional traits resulting in different relationships among actors. Subsequently four kinds of institutional settings, namely the *Multipolar*, the *Balance of Power*, the *Bipolar System* and the *Universal Empire* will be considered (Bernholz, 1985; pp. 73–75, discusses historical cases; for an analysis of the system from a historical perspective see: Duchhardt and Knipping, 1997).

A *multipolar system* contains at least eight but usually many more countries with more or less close contacts to each other, and of which at least the eight most important ones enjoy about equal power. In such a system an aggressor or a coalition of aggressors has no motivation to preserve a defeated enemy as a necessary ally against later enemies. For there exist still enough potential allies even after an annexation of the vanquished country. Also, it follows from the geographic situation of such a system that, as Kautilya (1957: 208–209), minister of the first Maurya emperor in India, observed around 300 B.C.:

> The king who is situated anywhere immediately on the circumference of the conqueror's territory is termed the enemy. The king who is likewise situated close to the enemy, but separated from the conqueror only by the enemy, is termed the friend of the conqueror.
>
> A neighbouring foe of considerable power is styled an enemy; and when he is involved in calamities or has taken himself to evil ways, he becomes assailable; and when he has little or no help, he becomes destructible; otherwise, he deserves to be harassed or reduced ...

It follows that a tendency exists in a multi-polar system to reduce the number of countries until only seven or less essential actors remain. The term *essential actor* refers to countries whose power is strong enough not to be neglected as states striving to dominate the international system.

We conclude that multi-polar systems are unstable first, concerning their tendency of reducing the number of its members; second, as to the countries composing it. For, whereas some countries may be defeated and vanish, others may emerge if remaining countries break up because of domestic strife.

In contrast to multi-polar systems, *balance of power systems* are rather stable and lasted usually several hundred years (for the Western Balance of Power system, with a discussion of the literature by a political scientist see Sheehan, 1996; by a historian Durchardt, 1997). They mostly evolve out of multi-polar systems and comprise three to seven essential actors (Great Powers). Some small powerless countries may still be present, but they have to rely for their survival on the balance among the former or on their tolerance. Moreover, these countries are not able to upset the international balance on their own.

To understand the reason for the stability of balance of power systems, consider a situation with three essential actors (compare the game theoretical models by Wagner, 1986; Ordeshook, 1989; Selten, 1991). In time, their relative power has to change because of external or domestic reasons, so that one of them becomes stronger than each of the two others. To prevent that it gets the upper hand, the two countries have to form an alliance, to put pressure on it or even to wage a preventive war to reduce its power. But the weaker of the victorious countries has every reason to prevent the defeated state from being weakened too much or dissolved, because it needs its support as a potential ally against the stronger of the victors. Two conclusions follow: First, alliances against the strongest power and even wars are usually a necessary condition for the stability of these systems, and second, peace treaties have not to be too harsh to retain defeated countries as essential actors.

The argument presented becomes weaker if the number of essential actors increases. That it still works is confirmed by historical evidence, and may have to do with geography. Given the geographical distribution of countries it is clear that those located in the center, like Austria–Hungary and Prussia/Germany before World War I, are threatened most. But, especially if they are not the most powerful in the system, there is an interest of the nations bordering them in opposite directions to maintain them as a counterweight. This would imply five essential actors: Four in the main directions and one in the center. Still, why seven should be the upper limit as suggested by the Balance of Power System before World Wars I and II with Britain, France, Germany, Austria–Hungary (Italy instead after the WW I), Russia, the USA and Japan, is still open to question. This, though, one might argue that Austria–Hungary and Italy were not in fact essential actors at that time.

Two points are important, however: The requirement of wars to keep the system stable is not a necessary trait, if the rulers of the most powerful country restrain their foreign and military policies because of domestic reasons. Second, with more than three powers one or the other country may lose its position as an essential power, like Sweden and Spain in the 18th century, without endangering the system. The same is true if new essential actors, like Russia and Prussia in the same century, Sweden in the 17th or the USA and Japan in the 19th, enter the stage without expanding the system beyond its upper limit. But the entrance of new essential actors is difficult if not located at the rim of the system, as shown by the example of Prussia.

Though balance of power systems lasted for centuries, they all finally ended. What were the reasons? Usually the end was brought about by countries at the periphery of existing systems, for they could grow outside the system, without being hindered by any essential actor. The last balance of power system was destroyed by the Soviet Union (Russia) and the USA which had expanded over whole continents without finding substantial resistance. This was the basis of de Tocqueville's ([1835] 1945: Volume 1, 452) famous prediction *"that each of them (the USA and Russia) seems marked out by the will of heaven to sway the destinies of half the globe."* The Hellenistic balance of power system was brought down by Rome, which had grown in the West outside the system with the defeat of Carthage. The Chinese balance of power system was destroyed by Ch'in in 221 BC, which had expanded to the East of the system. And the Italian system of the Renaissance fell because of the intervention by an outside power, France. A second reason combining with this first is that politicians in power do no longer understand the workings of the system, which requires for its preservation a high standard of rational behaviour (Kaplan, 1968, states requirements for preserving the system). A harsh peace treaty like that of Versailles, St. Germain and Trianon, dissolving one of the essential actors, Austria–Hungary, and strongly weakening another, Germany, endangered the system, quite in contrast to the Vienna peace treaty restoring it after the Napoleonic wars.

The *bipolar system* is usually the result of the breakdown of a balance of power system. It contains only two essential actors, like the Soviet Union and the USA after World War II, or Rome and Carthage in the Western Mediterranean. It is unstable in the long-run, since the power of one country will outgrow that of the other. Stability can only be maintained for some time either by geographic distance or by modern nuclear arms threatening both belligerents with total destruction. Still, even with this danger present, the bipolar system of the Soviet Union and the USA broke down mainly because of the better performance of the market economy of the latter.

Universal empires are the result of the demise of balance of power or of bilateral systems, provided that rulers of the remaining "superpower" are willing and not hindered by their domestic political system to extend their country to the limit. This was done by Rome and by Ch'in which conquered the whole civilised word surrounding them (except Persia). These historical empires have only been threatened and, in the case of Rome, finally been defeated by barbarians or, like the Aztec and Inca empires, by forces from outside their civilisations.

4. Determinants of the Power and Aggressiveness of States

The military capabilities of countries, which are also, because of their threat potential, largely responsible for their political weight, are determined by several factors: The size and geographical situation of a country, the size of its population, the efficiency of its economy, the level of education and science. But military capabilities are also dependent on the political institutions, for they determine how far these factors are transformed into military power.

The importance of size and geographical situation becomes obvious by looking at two examples. England and Russia would have been conquered by Napoleon and Hitler if the former had not been an island and the latter had been of the size of France. One of the strategic advantages of the USA has been that they have been protected against other Great Powers by two oceans. Next, the size of the population determines the potential size of armed forces. But it depends itself on the size of the country and the efficiency of its economy.

The level of education and of science are also mainly determined by economic efficiency. It follows that with increasing Gross Domestic Product per capita the economic factor becomes ever more important for the relative international power. Indeed, all Great Powers in 1820 as well as in 1995 can be found by just combining two criteria: The size of GDPs and of GDPs per capita. Only the countries leading in both respects qualified as Great Powers (Bernholz, 2001).

Polititical institutions of countries are important in translating the factors mentioned into military power and into a more or less aggressive policy. It seems now that democracies wage war as often as autocracies, but that they do not fight against each other (Rummel, 1968, 1983; Chan, 1984; Weede 1984; Doyle 1986). In democracies politicians are dependent on the consent of an electorate, who are not well-informed about possible foreign dangers, but who resent the huge costs of rearmament and the danger for their lives and property in case of war. Thus leaders have a hard time and need convincing evidence, like the Japanese attack on Pearl Harbour, to convince the public that defensive efforts and even a war against the aggressive policies of autocratic regimes are necessary. It follows that democracies are usually not well-prepared against aggression, and invite attacks by autocratic regimes. Consequently they are as often involved in wars as other regimes. Moreover, it follows from the same reasoning that democracies do usually not wage war against each other. These conclusions are supported by the fact that democratic politicians try together with military leaders to develop military technology and strategy to minimise the number of victims on their own side. The wars against Iraq, against Yugoslavia (Serbia) and in Afghanistan in the last decades are examples for this policy.

Autocratic regimes enjoy, because of these domestic problems of democracies, short-term advantages in international politics. They are increased since dictators and oligarchies can usually follow a more consistent foreign policy than democratic leaders restricted by constitutions, parties, parliaments and the preferences of the electorate, which may also lead to their replacement. However, if autocracies do not succeed against democracies with market economies in the short-run, the latter will enjoy stronger economic growth, so that they develop greater potential for military power in the long-run.

4. Additional Factors Influencing the International System

The development of ever more sophisticated and less expensive weapons with the potential of mass destruction decreases the possibility for rational governments to wage war because of the risk of total destruction. Consequently, rulers will be inclined to further their aggressive or defensive aims by other means, namely guerilla warfare, terrorism and revolutions. In doing so they have to hide their involvement in such actions against other countries as much as possible. Given this development, non-government organisations can try to use the same methods and sabotage, instead of more or less peaceful demonstrations, especially if helped by the freedoms granted by liberal societies. This

danger increases if their members are adherents of an ideology demanding that they are prepared to sacrifice everything, including their own lives and that of others for its supreme values (see article on totalitarianism).

PETER BERNHOLZ

REFERENCES

Bernholz, P. (1985). *The International Game of Power*. Berlin, New York, Amsterdam: Mouton Publishers.

Bernholz, P. (1992). "The economic approach to international relations," in G. Radnitzky (ed.) *Universal Economics*. New York: Paragon House, pp. 339–400.

Bernholz, P. (2001). "Globalization and restructuring of the economy: are they new?" in Sir Hans Singer, Neelambar Hatti, and Rameshwar Tandon (eds.) *Globalization, Technology and Trade in the 21 Century*. New World Order Series 19. 3 Parts. New Delhi 2001: Vedams e-Books (P) Ltd.

Bull, H. (1981). *The Anarchical Society. A Study of Order in World Politics*. London: Macmillan.

Chan, S. (1984). "Mirror, mirror on the wall: are freer countries more Pacific?" *Journal of Conflict Resolution*, 28: 617–648.

Doyle, M.W. (1986). "Liberalism and world politics." *American Political Science Review*, 80(4): 1151–1169.

Duchhardt, H. and Knipping, F. (eds.) (1997). *Handbuch der Geschichte der Internationalen Beziehungen*, 9 Volumes. Paderborn, Muenchen, Wien: Schoeningh.

Duchhardt, H. (1997). "Balance of power und pentarchie, internationale Beziehungen 1700–1785," in H. Duchhardt and F. Knipping (eds.) *Handbuch der Geschichte der Internationalen Beziehungen*, 9 Volumes. Paderborn, Muenchen, Wien: Schoeningh.

Wagner, R.H. (1986). "The theory of games and the balance of power." *World Politics*, 38(4): 546–576.

Kaplan, M.A. (1968). "The system approach to international politics," in M.A. Kaplan (ed.) *New Approaches in International Relations*. New York: St. Martin's Press.

Kautilya ([around 300 BC] 1957). "Artha-Sastra. excerpts." in S. Radhakrishnan and Ch. A. Moore (eds.) *A Source Book in Indian Philosophy*. Princeton (N.J.): Princeton University Press.

Ordeshook, P.C. (1989). *The Balance of Power*. Cambridge: Cambridge University Press.

Rummel, R.J. (1968). "The relationship between national attributes and foreign conflict behaviour," in J.D. Singer (ed.) *Quantitative International Politics*. New York: Free Press, pp. 187–214.

Rummel, R.J. (1983). "Libertarianism and international violence." *Journal of Conflict Resolution*, 27: 27–71.

Schaetzel, W. (without date). *Der Staat*. Sammlung Dieterich 80 Second Edition. Bremen: C. Schuenemann.

Selten, R. (1991). "Balance of power in a parlour game," in R. Selten (ed.) *Game Equilibrium Models*, Volume II. Berlin, Heidelberg, New York: Springer.

Sheehan, M. (1996). *The Balance of Power. History and Theory*. London, New York: Routledge.

Tocqueville, A. de ([1835] 1945). *Democracy in America* (Translated by H. Reeve, revised by F. Bowen) Ph. Bradley (ed.) New York: Vintage Book.

Tullock, G. (1974). *The Social Dilemma. The Economics of War and Revolution.* Blacksburg (Va.): University Publications.

Weede, E. (1984). "Democracy and war involvement." *Journal of Conflict Resolution*, 28: 649–664.

INTERNATIONAL ORGANIZATION

International organizations are bureaucracies. Unlike politicians, bureaucrats do not have to be reelected. Thus, public choice theory predicts that they are less responsive to the wishes of voters and more accessible to organized interest groups (Crain and McCormick, 1984). In the public choice literature, the strong influence of interest groups has notably been documented for the European Union (see *European Political Integration*), the International Monetary Fund (in the 1980s: Fratianni and de Grauwe, 1984; Vaubel, 1991), the World Bank and the United Nations (Weck-Hannemann and Schneider, 1991).

International organizations are farther removed from the attention and comprehension of voters than national, provincial or local bureaucracies. Thus public choice theory predicts that they are less efficient and more responsive to the demands of organized interest groups than other bureaucracies. The lack of democratic control and efficiency is indicated by the fact that after-tax salaries are much higher in international organizations than in national civil services (for the OECD and, most of all, the EC see Frey, 1990; for the IMF see Vaubel, 1991). In their dealings with interest groups, international organizations can spread the burden of financing their favors over more taxpayers. As each taxpayer pays less, he has less of an incentive to inform himself about the redistribution that takes place at his expense.

A politician who is a member of a national government has less of an incentive to control an international bureaucracy than his national bureaucracy because the cost of persuasion is larger, and his share in the benefits is smaller, when he tries to increase the efficiency of an international bureaucracy (Frey, 1984: 221). Public choice theory predicts that this disincentive grows as the number of member states rises. For example, this hypothesis cannot be rejected for the International Monetary Fund and the World Bank (Vaubel, 1991, 1996).

Like all bureaucracies, international organizations fight for their survival and for more powers and resources. Thus, it is more difficult to abolish an international organization than to establish it, or to reduce its powers and resources than to increase them. International organizations prefer arrangements which increase the demand for their services, e.g., low interest rates for their lending, generous or vague eligibility requirements, etc. They dislike clear-cut rules which restrict their room of manoeuvre in negotiations with individual member governments. They prefer a case-by-case approach and the power to impose far-reaching policy conditions (Vaubel, 1991).

In sum, international organizations suffer from serious principal-agent-problems which may easily outweigh the benefits of internalizing international externalities or exploiting international economies of scale.

To the extent that an international organization is controlled by a body representing the governments of the member states, its policies depend on whether this body decides unanimously or by some sort of majority and whether the votes of the member states are weighted by their budgetary contributions and capital subscriptions or not. If the member states decide by simple or qualified majority, public choice theory predicts that the preferences of the minority tend to be ignored. This is particularly likely when the number of member states is large and the cost of logrolling is high. Expenditure will be larger than under the unanimity rule because the majority will vote for spending which benefits (primarily) the majority but is also paid for by the minority. For the same reasons, expenditure will be larger when the voting weights do not correspond to the financing weights.

Majority decisions also raise the level of regulation because they enable the majority to impose their regulations on the minority. This is the so-called "strategy of raising rivals' costs." If the regulation of the marginal (decisive) member of the majority coalition is declared to be the minimum standard for all, regulatory competition is suppressed, and the majority will further raise their regulations. These are then again extended to the minority (and so on). An iterative process of collective regulation develops.

Public choice theory has also been used to predict the division of labor between international organizations and their member states. According to the economic theory of bureaucracy, the officials in international organizations aim to maximize their power; their demand for additional powers and resources is unlimited. Thus, the division of labor is entirely supply determined. The national politicians are not likely to give away very important powers which have a decisive influence on elections ("law of inverse salience"). They will rather try to get rid of their "unpleasant" activities, their "dirty work." These are measures they consider necessary to gain or maintain the support of some interest groups on whom they depend but for which they do not want to take direct responsibility because part of the cost has to be borne by the other supporters of the ruling coalition (Vaubel, 1986). The most conspicuous examples are the European agricultural policy and the role of the IMF in propping up the large U.S. banks in the debt crisis of the 1980s.

International organizations also serve the governments of the member states to establish and enforce international cartels with respect to taxation and regulation. Such unanimous collusion has to be distinguished from the strategy of raising rivals' costs by extending taxation and regulation to others. If a single government or parliament raises taxes or regulations, taxable resources and economic activity shift abroad, and the tax base shrinks. If all member governments agree to raise their taxes and regulations, nobody can escape. Moreover, voters cannot point to the superior example of other governments ("yardstick competition"). Thus, international policy cartels weaken the corrective feedback mechanisms of "exit" and "voice." They also suppress policy innovation and policy diversification as a protection against risk.

As for case studies, the following international organizations have been analyzed from a public-choice perspective: the European Community/Union (see *European Political Integration*), the International Monetary Fund (Vaubel, 1991), the World Bank (Frey, 1986; Frey and Schneider, 1986; Weck-Hannemann and Schneider, 1991; Vaubel, 1996), the United Nations (Weck-Hannemann and Schneider, 1991; Eckert, 1991; Frederiksson and Gaston, 2000) the GATT/WTO (Moser, 1990; Finger, 1991), the OECD (Fratianni and Pattison, 1976), the International Labor Organization (Boockmann, 2001) and the International Energy Agency (Smith, 1991).

ROLAND VAUBEL

REFERENCES

Boockmann, B. (2001). "The ratification of ILO conventions: a hazard rate analysis." *Economics and Politics*, 13: 281–309.

Crain, W.M. and McCormick, R.E. (1984). "Regulators as an interest group," in J.M. Buchanan and G. Tullock (eds.) *The Theory of Public Choice — II*. Ann Arbor, MI: The University of Michigan Press, pp. 287–304.

Eckert, R.D. (1991). "U.S. policy and the Law of the Sea Conference, 1969–1982: a case study of multilateral negotiations," in R. Vaubel and T.D. Willett (eds.) *The Political Economy of International Organizations: A Public Choice Approach*. Boulder, Co: Westview Press, pp. 181–203.

Finger, J.M. (1991). "The GATT as an international discipline over trade restrictions: a public choice approach," in R. Vaubel and T.D. Willett (eds.) *The Political Economy of International Organizations: A Public Choice Approach*. Boulder, Co: Westview Press, pp. 125–141.

Fratianni, M. and de Grauwe, P. (1984). "The political economy of international lending." *Cato Journal*, (Spring/Summer): 147–170.

Fratianni, M. and Pattison, J.C. (1976). "The economics of the OECD," in K. Brunner and A.H. Meltzer (eds.) *Institutions, Policies and Economic Performance. Carnegie-Rochester Conference Series on Public Policy*. Amsterdam: North Holland, pp. 75–153.

Fratianni, M. and Pattison, J.C. (1991). "International institutions and the market for information," in R. Vaubel and T.D. Willett (eds.) *The Political Economy of International Organizations: A Public Choice Approach*. Boulder, Co: Westview Press, pp. 100–127.

Frederiksson, P.G. and Gaston, N. (2000). "Ratification of the 1992 climate change convention: what determines legislative delay?" *Public Choice*, 104: 345–368.

Frey, B.S. (1984). "The public choice view of international political economy." *International Organization*, 38: 199–223.

Frey, B.S. (1986). "The function of governments and intergovernmental organizations in the international resource transfer: the case of the World Bank," in B. Balassa and H. Giersch (eds.) *Economic Incentives*. Basingstoke: Macmillan, pp. 454–470.

Frey, B.S. (1990). *International Political Economics*, Second Edition. Oxford: Blackwells.

Frey, B.S. and Schneider, F. (1986). "Competing models of international lending activity." *Journal of Development Economics*, 20: 225–245.

Frey, B.S. and Gygi, B. (1991). "International organizations from the constitutional point of view," in R. Vaubel and T.D. Willett (eds.) *The Political Economy of International Organizations: A Public Choice Approach*. Boulder, Co: Westview Press, pp. 58–78.

Moser, P. (1990). *The Political Economy of the GATT*. Grüsch: Rüegger.

Smith, R.T. (1991). "A public choice perspective of the international energy program," in R. Vaubel and T.D. Willett (eds.) *The Political Economy of International Organizations: A Public Choice Approach*, Boulder, Co: Westview Press, pp. 142–180.

Vaubel, R. (1986). "A public choice view of international organization." *Public Choice*, 51: 39–57; revised version: R. Vaubel and T.D. Willett (eds.) (1991). *The Political Economy of International Organizations: A Public Choice Approach*. Boulder, Co: Westview Press, pp. 27–45.

Vaubel, R. (1991). "The political economy of the International Monetary Fund: a public choice analysis," in R. Vaubel and T.D. Willett (eds.) *The Political Economy of International Organizations: A Public Choice Approach*. Boulder, Co: Westview Press, pp. 204–244.

Vaubel, R. (1996). "Bureaucracy at the IMF and the World Bank: a comparison of the evidence." *The World Economy*, 19: 195–210.

Weck-Hannemann, H. and Schneider, F. (1991). "Determinants of foreign aid under alternative institutional arrangements," in R. Vaubel and T.D. Willett (eds.) *The Political Economy of International Organizations: A Public Choice Approach*. Boulder, Co: Westview Press, pp. 245–266.

INTERNET VOTING

"The Internet" is an evolving network of computer networks that enables the communication of restricted and unrestricted messages over private or public channels. Communication is based on an infrastructure of technical standards that are built into hardware and software systems.

"Internet" voting in an open communications channel started as a volunteer, non-commercial effort aimed at "democratizing" participation in all types of organizations. Initially, in the early 1980s, basic voting software tools were given away by programmers or integrated into computer-conferencing systems. A decade later, the development of World Wide Web browser interfaces and functionality made it simpler for developers to invent more advanced voting tools that made electronic voting easier and more secure. Internet browsers provided graphical online forms that made electronic ballots look more like paper ballots. Software tools were designed to use passwords to authenticate voter eligibility and to employ vote encryption to protect the integrity of the voting process. By 1995, dotcom entrepreneurs were building browser-based solutions for private Internet stockholder elections and referenda (Internet Policy Institute, 2001). While the reliability of voting in private elections is difficult to assess, Internet elections in public communications channels have not always operated smoothly. For instance, in a worldwide election conducted by ICANN (Internet Corporation for Names and Numbers) to reconstitute its leadership, system breakdowns prevented thousands of voters around the world from obtaining or submitting a ballot. However, smaller scale experiments in the US and Europe seem to have been successful (Manjoo, 2000).

Before 2000, interest in professional standards for electronic voting began to grow among companies providing online voting services, researchers and election administrators. In many US precincts, elections have been conducted for many years using local area networks (LANs). So scaling up to wide area networks (WANs) became increasingly attractive as Internet Web technology became more common. Some states experimented with Web-based registration as well as an option of participating in primary elections via the Web. In 2000, the Department of Defense conducted a pilot test of Internet voting in lieu of absentee paper ballots. And state and federal commissions studied the pros and cons of Internet voting, recommending a gradual, incremental approach (Internet Policy Institute, 2000).

Even though Internet voting may seem like the "next best" way of conducting elections, US reforms have been slowed down by declining budgets and unresolved technical and social questions about software standards.

The costs of building an Internet system are estimated to exceed ten billion dollars. Even before a declining economy and the war against terrorism changed budget priorities, election technology was a low budgetary priority. Indeed, even plans to upgrade to less error-prone computerized election equipment have encountered resistance despite the electoral problems that occurred in Florida and other states during the 2000 Presidential election.

The lack of uniform technical standards for testing election technology and certifying voting equipment have also slowed the pace of innovation in Internet voting. Voluntary standards have been coordinated by NASED (the National Association of State Election Directors) and the Federal Election Commission (FEC) (Saltman, 1988). A National Science Foundation (NSF) Workshop on Internet voting explored options for redefining technical standards to take account of emerging social needs and technological options. For instance, proposed specifications would require any system to support alternative voting methods. However NSF's report to the President did not explicitly include this user specification in its list of recommendations for further study (Internet Policy Institute, 2000).

While the US has followed a disjointed incrementalist strategy for developing Internet voting, Brazil has aggressively pursued a centralized, uniform system for conducting elections over a restricted private WAN using proprietary ATM (Automated Teller Machine) technology widely used in electronic banking. This technology, now owned by a US manufacturer of ATM solutions, has been used for several years, with approximately 300,000 voting districts using the technology in the 2000 election. Brazil's solution has been produced on the basis of a close, confidential working relationship between the government and vendor developers (Arndt et al., 2001).

Brazil's strong commitment to electronic voting in a national network was motivated by the expectation that machine processing and counting of votes would neutralize human corruption in elections. In the US, a similar faith in technology motivated interest in pre-Internet voting machines based on mechanical systems, punch cards, scanned ballots, or direct entry (e.g., touch screen) systems in local area computer networks. But experience with all of these technologies has revealed that poor management of any voting system — even paper balloting — can allow unintentional and malicious errors to undermine the integrity of an election.

The technological breakdowns of voting systems in the US 2000 presidential election have sparked an interest in building more reliable voting technology for computer networks. One goal is to build more flexible systems for determining and administering voter eligibility. These systems would allow provisional voters to cast ballots and have their eligibility verified after the polls have closed. Technologies including digital signatures, "smart" cards, and biometric authentication would enable stricter monitoring of electoral access.

Designers of computer voting solutions are also exploring new approaches to voting security. These approaches are based on new encryption techniques and computer network architectures. The effort to build impenetrable encryption techniques is evolving into a kind of arms race between computer system administrators and "crackers." Administrators can make it more difficult to break into a voting process in when votes are cast, transmitted, or counted. But crackers can become more creative in mobilizing computer resources to decipher encryption shields. This competition suggests that whenever the electoral stakes are high, malicious attacks on electronic voting processes should be anticipated (Urken, 2001).

Computer architectures, the underlying electronic structures of communications systems, are being made more modular to spur innovative approaches to building wired and wireless voting solutions. In principle, these solutions would allow plug-and-play incorporation of solutions for authentication, encryption, and new techniques for improving the reliability of computer voting. A modular computer architecture would also promote creative solutions for producing voter interfaces designed for error and for the special needs of disabled voters. Future voting systems may make use of intrusion detection and language-based security technology to make voting tools more reliable (Caltech-MIT Voting Project, 2001).

Although the evolution of Internet voting is an international phenomenon that involves tool development and experimentation around the world, the contrast between the public network approach emerging in the US and the private channel methodology being used in Brazil highlights an unresolved question: will social aspirations set the standard for designing or will voting technology be designed to maintain the status quo?

The evolution of Internet voting in the US has been driven by technological possibilities for making electronic voting in public communications channels reliable. To assure reliability, an "open" approach to developing and certifying software has been promoted. According to this approach, source code for electronic voting systems must be opened for inspection to software experts to make sure that the code does not contain hidden programs (e.g., Trojan horses). Openness can also assure that the coding is consistent with software engineering standards for building reliable software tools that will not produce "benign" errors in voting processes. These benign errors can cause

considerable administrative difficulties, but they can also be invoked to enable malicious penetration of voting systems to modify or corrupt data (Gerck, 2001).

In contrast, the private channel system in use in Brazil is based on proprietary standards. These standards are not even publicly defined, much less subject to verification of the software itself by disinterested experts. But the apparent success of WAN voting in Brazil has led ATM vendors to seek opportunities for exporting their voting systems to the US (Global/Diebold Election Systems, 2001).

While the principle of openness is important in US development of Internet voting, policymakers have not always been amenable to implementing voting tool solutions imagined by software engineers. For example, US engineers have recognized the need for integrating different voting methods into the standards for Internet voting software. Their solution would be a modular plug-and-play system that would make changing the voting method, say, from plurality voting to approval voting, as simple as filling in a checkbox on a browser form. Yet policymakers have omitted this requirement from their 2001 list of recommendations for further study submitted to the President (Internet Policy Institute, 2001). Perhaps they realized that enabling alternative voting methods could be threatening to Republicans and Democrats because changes in vote markets would introduce uncertainty into campaigning and electoral strategy. Perhaps scientists and bureaucrats considered the omission prudent to avoid jeopardizing the reception of their other recommendations.

US designers of Internet voting systems have also imposed an absolutist conception of voter privacy on the development of software voting tools. According to this absolutist principle, a vote should never be associated with the identity of a voter. Defenders of this principle contend that it is necessary for the prevention of vote trading and coercive manipulation of votes. For if a vote is to be exchanged, traders need to be able to identify the voters to trade the votes (Shamos, 1993).

This absolutist conception of privacy underlay legal action that closed down Internet voting exchanges that operated in the 2000 US presidential election. These Internet vote exchanges allowed citizens to auction their votes. And voters who wanted to help Nader achieve 5% of the popular vote made Internet deals to assure that their choices would not take away votes from Gore and thereby enable Bush to gain an electoral vote victory over Gore in the US electoral college.

An anti-vote trading policy implicitly protects the Democratic-Republican duopoly in US national politics. Moreover, the underlying privacy policy prohibits voters from being able to actively audit their vote — as they can do by verifying online that deposited monies are actually in their bank accounts or have been traded as requested.

The implementation of multiple voting methods and a more flexible voter privacy policy are issues that are being kept alive in the US by the Single Transferable Vote (STV) movement to use rank-ordering of candidates in all elections (Center for Voting and Democracy, 2002). Although this method is used in many countries, US advocates of this method contend that it would allow "instant runoffs" to be conducted in case of tied or contested electoral outcomes. These unresolved outcomes would be resolved by reprocessing citizens' rank-ordered votes until a majority winner is produced.

The social choice issues surrounding the choice of a voting method for conducting instant runoff elections have yet to be worked out. For ordinal data can be reprocessed using methods such as Condorcet scoring to resolve electoral controversies. These issues, along with the certification of voting software, voter privacy and vote trading, suggest that standards for electronic voting must take account of the complex differences found in different political cultures, even within a single state or nation-state.

As local and wide area networks become more pervasive, electronic voting tools must be flexible enough to support diverse norms while they enable the human imagination to pursue unconventional ideas. Open standards for communicating votes are not necessarily inconsistent with the development of proprietary solutions for implementing Internet protocols. As vendors from different political cultures contend for emerging markets in the US and elsewhere, they may gain competitive differentiation and sustainable strategic advantage by balancing technical requirements and social values.

ARNOLD B. URKEN

REFERENCES

Arndt, M., Engardio, P., and Goodman, J. (2001). "Diebold." *Business Week Online*, August 27 (http://www.business-week.com/magazine/content/01_35/b3746658.htm).

Caltech-MIT Voting Project (2001). "What is, what could be" (http://web.mit.edu/newsoffice/nr/2001/VTP_report_all.pdf).

Center for Voting and Democracy (2002). "Instant runoff voting" (fairvote.org. http://www.fairvote.org/irv/index.html).

Gerck, E. (ed.) (2001). "Voting system requirements." *The Bell* (safevote.com.http://www.thebell.net/papers/vote-req.pdf).

Global/Diebold Election Systems (2001). "State board of elections selects voting system vendor" December, 2001 (http://www.diebold.com/news/newsdisp.asp?id=2837).

Internet Policy Institute (2001). "Report of the National Workshop on Internet Voting: issues and research agenda." Washington, DC (http://www.internetpolicy.org).

Manjoo, Farhad (2000). "Jury still out on net elections." *WiredNews* (http://www.wired.com/news/print/0,1294,39283,00.html).

Saltman, R.G. (1988). "Accuracy, integrity, and security in computerized vote-tallying." National Bureau of Standards: Institute for Computer Sciences and Technology.

Shamos, M.I. (1993). "Electronic voting — evaluating the threat." *Computers, Freedom and Privacy*. Chicago, Illinois. (http://www.cpsr.org/conferences/cfp93/shamos.html).

Urken, A.B. (2001). "Technology alone can't fix voting problems." *Computerworld*, March 5.

IS RUSSIA A MARKET ECONOMY?

Both the European Union and the United States have recently declared that Russia now enjoys a market economy. In a further evaluation, very similar to that of EU, the U.S. Commerce Department has announced that "Russia has made tremendous econom[ic] changes…over the last decade" (Slevin, 2002). In this contribution, I question the validity of these claims and suggest that Russia remains a long way short of a fully-fledged market economy.

In one definition the term *market economy* means an economy in which most goods and services are produced and distributed through markets under the price system (Webster's 1993). Under this definition, Russia can be considered "somewhat market-oriented". In most markets there are no shortages, and forces of supply and demand determine prices; the private sector is estimated by the U.S. to control about 70% of Russia's GDP (Slevin, 2002). But the unique perversions of Russian markets call for a more rigorous analysis.

In order to make a judgment about the nature of Russia's economy, we must first investigate whether such markets coexist within an appropriate institutional environment. Superficially, Russia appears to possess private property, contract law, and a credit system; but the real question is whether these institutions function successfully, and whether the majority of Russians enjoy the benefits of these institutions.

1. The Market for Bureaucratic Decisions

In an October 2000 interview with *Le Figaro*, President Putin shrewdly remarked: "I…think that the state has a mallet, with which it only strikes one blow — to the head. So far we have not used this weapon; we have just picked it up…. However, if we are angered, we will undoubtedly use it …." While discussing the relations between tycoons and the government, Mr. Putin emphasized that the key determinant of resource allocation in Russia is the bureaucracy. The bureaucratic system possesses a mallet, and threatens to strike with that mallet in order to extort money from individuals and businesses. Bureaucrats indirectly determine who produces what, how much, and at what cost. Consumers are "sovereign" only within the framework set up by this governmental bureaucracy.

Although rent seeking exists in all economies, its scale and effects are pervasive in Russia. Federal Law #128-FZ (August 8, 2001) "On Licensing of Various Types of Business Activity" gives government officials arbitrary power to grant and revoke business licenses and to enforce compliance with any and all government standards. This power, combined with other licensing laws, gives regulators extensive oversight of just about every imaginable commercial activity. Before competing against each other for the consumer rouble, entrepreneurs first have to compete for bureaucratic favours. It is common practice for government officials to grant favours in exchange for money and non-monetary bribes — indirectly raising costs, curtailing competition, and consequently raising prices for consumers as well as limiting the variety and quality of goods in the market.

2. Property Rights

Although the rights to own, use, transform and reassign property have been increasingly vested in private citizens, the enforcement of such rights remains problematical. Since the power to enforce rights is still concentrated in the hands of the few, and is redirected to benefit a narrow circle of politicians and rising oligarchs, the most valuable resources, such as oil and gas, belong to oligarchs, while other major resources, such as urban and agricultural land, are still monopolized by the state.

Ordinary Russians possess few valuable resources, though the majority own at least one of the following: shares of stock, an apartment, a house, a suburban and/or rural land plot, a car, or a business. Shares distributed on open markets usually are poor investments and are issued by insolvent government-subsidized enterprises; shares of profitable businesses are seldom distributed in open markets. After privatization and suburban land reform, private ownership of real estate has increased, but it has caused little change — most Russians were given title to a place where they already lived or grew vegetables — and owning an apartment or a suburban land plot is no different than under Soviet rule. Semi-open markets existed in the USSR (Boettke, 1993, esp. Ch. 4; Latov, 2001; Osokina, 1998). In the Soviet Union, not only was produce grown on suburban

land widely marketed, the plots themselves were also owned and traded. Rural housing was also widely traded.

Today even if a building or land plot is privately owned, the town or regional planning committee can change without warning a property's "purpose of use" — a highly arbitrary zoning restriction. For instance, a new regulation can require turning an office building into a bakery. However, a bribe usually is enough to revert to the old purpose of use.

3. Credit System

The shortcomings of the credit system prevent money from being channelled to its highest valued uses. Private banks profit from currency speculation and from servicing state industrial enterprises and oligarchs. All government transactions, including credits to industry, pensions and unemployment insurance are done through the Central Bank, *Sberbank*.

The personal banking and credit system suffers from chronic illness. Because of lack of trust, people do not keep their money in banks. With minimal funds to lend, and little competition from other creditors, default-fearing banks offer small loans at high-interest rates and ridiculous terms. Most Russians are in fact excluded from using credit in planning their economic future. Since credit is not affordable, automobiles and real estate are purchased mostly in cash. Private banks offer a one or two year personal loan at about 20% interest (12% in foreign currency). *Sberbank* offers mortgages for a maximum of 15 years, and a car loan for up to 5 years, at over 20% (13% in foreign currency).

To obtain a loan, onerous requirements must be met. First, a valid permanent residence permit is required. (This permit states the geographical boundaries within which one is permitted to live and work legally, and functions also as an access card to state provided health care). Next one is required to submit proof of a stable source of income. On loans over $5,000 a note verifying *mental* health must be provided, on loans over $10,000 both a co-signer and some form of second collateral must be given.

These restrictions significantly reduce incentives to apply for credit. Those who already have additional collateral most likely do not need a loan, and in any case would not have income statements showing sufficient income, as tax-evasion is universal.

4. Contract Law

Contract law is still a meaningless concept in Russia. But relational contracts — contracts that combine a legal exchange of rights with a guarantee supported by the personal relationship between the parties — remain an essential part of business operations. Economic transition means increased opportunities to cheat; the law lacks clarity and enforcing power, and private systems of contract enforcement have not yet developed. How can one find a supplier for his business when the local market has not developed institutions protecting him from fraud? How can an employer effectively select employees from a pool where an overwhelming number are cheaters and shirkers?

Ignorance of "who is who" is overcome through the network of personal relationships; it is common practice to have a friend in the local government, to arrange supplies from a friend, or to employ a friend. Most job openings never reach the so-called open market. One reason is that a significant part of the economy is still underground — a "personal recommendation" ensures that employees are trustworthy and will not disclose business operations. Another reason is that many firms do not have enough staff to handle the storm of inquiries produced by an advertised job vacancy.

In Russia, where people are still learning how businesses operate, not every job has a clear description and/or requirements. Calling a recruiting agency or putting an advertisement in a newspaper is futile simply because specific knowledge of the situation is required in order to fill in the job opening with an appropriate candidate. The enormous difficulty in confirming an applicant's skills and education (certificates are falsified easily) is another reason to call a friend who can provide a reliable guarantee (Karpova, 2001).

5. Mass Media

During the last few years, the tendency has been toward less freedom of speech. All politically and economically important information is screened. Rebellious media sources are either closed down by state force or their rights are transferred to a more loyal group. Local radio channels throughout the country have been restricted recently to only a few hours of local broadcasting, and are required the rest of the time to air central broadcasting from Moscow.

Russian TV has uniform interpretations of major political and economic events, and in fact was *never* independent, except for the NTV network in the beginning of the 1st (1994) Chechen war. Otherwise, true facts about *neither* side in the Russo-Chechen conflict are revealed. Any diverse analysis in printed and broadcast media is actually oligarchs slamming the media mallet down on one another. At the same time many have access to Internet and even Western TV and radio channels. But because people have general distrust to any media reports, few (mostly intellectuals) are interested in using this as an information tool.

6. Conclusion

In the last decade Russia has certainly progressed toward more, but not necessarily freer markets. Some, like the U.S.–Russia Business Council, apparently "have no doubt that they are 'operating in Russia under market principles and market mechanisms'" (Slevin, 2002). But the principles outlined above hardly outline a free market. The state mallet is just a device used by one group of oligarchs against another.

Putin's statements in *Le Figaro* attempt to convince western investors that Russian public policy is transparent. But in reality, as one hand raises the mallet to protect a certain private business, the other renationalizes whole industries, most recently vodka production (Vladykin, 2002; Zarakhovich, 2002), and controls the investment and budgets of natural monopolies (*Monitor*, 2002).

Deals between business and government are concluded with aid of the network of personal relationships. The network has proved to be a guarantee against and a substitute for the shortcomings of market institutions in Russia; so it is and will continue for some time to be cost-effective for both Russian and Western businesses to comply rather than defend against the mallet.

Official Russian sources estimate the legal private sector as 10–12% of GDP. A recent poll indicates that at least 15–17% of the urban population is employed in the underground labour market. Counting second jobs (common for Russians) raises unregistered self-employment to 54% (Varshavskaya, 2001). Goskomstat (2002) reports that informal economic activity is especially present in agriculture, trade, industry, transportation, and investment. Correcting industrial output for illegal production increases estimates by 12.7% for 2000 and 12.4% for 2001.

Even if we believe (along with the U.S. Commerce Department), that these figures tell us of prevalence of the private sector, they are not a sufficient guarantee that private property rights for ordinary people are enforced, that there is a rule of law, and that information about markets is trustworthy. While it is true that people can buy goods of various quality and prices now with much less difficulty than before, a street booth and flee market haven is far from a free market heaven.

EKATERINA STEPYKINA

REFERENCES

Boettke, P.J. (1993). *Why Perestroika Failed?* New York: Routledge.
Goskomstat (2002) http://www.gks.ru/news/tezis/1705.doc.
Karpova, E. (2001). *Grani.ru*, January 25 (http://www.grani.ru/jobs/articles/post).

Latov Yu, V. (2001). *Ekonomika vne zakona: Ocherki po istorii i teorii tenevoi ekonomiki.* Moscow: Moskovski obschestvenni naychni fond, Ch. 6 (http://ie.boom.ru/Latov/Monograph/Chapter6.htm).

Monitor (2002). Issue 1 (April 4) (http://www.polit.ru:8081/monitor/02/0402-1/040402-1.htm).

Osokina E. (1998). *Za fasadom 'stalinskogo isobiliya'.* Moscow: ROSSPEN.

Putin, V. (2000). Interview. *Le Figaro.* As quoted by Agency WPS from *Itogi*, 51(December): 36–40.

Sberbank, http://www.sbrf.ru/ruswin/credit/crdfiz2.htm.

Slevin, P. (2002). "U.S. says Russia now 'Market Economy'." *The Washington Post*, June 7.

Varshavskaya, E. (2001). *Chelovek i trud*, No. 11 (http://www.chelt.ru/11/varshavskaja_11.html).

Vladykin, K. (2002). "Cheharda iz-za 'Stolichnoi'." *Grani.ru*, June 30 (http://grani.ru/brands/articles/stolichnaya/).

Zarakhovich, Y. (2002). "Fighting spirits." *Time Europe Magazine*, 160 (July 1).

Webster's Third New International Dictionary of the English Language (1993). Springfield, Mass.: Merriam-Webster.

IS VOTING RATIONAL?

To paraphrase William Mitchell's (2001: 5) apt analogy, if orthodox welfare economics can be thought of as a pathology of markets, public choice is a pathology of politics. Scholars working in the tradition of Pigou (1920) seem to find market failures demanding remedial government action on every street corner; scholars working in the public choice tradition seem to find the seeds of government failure in every public program and policy. As a matter of fact, 'one of the most important contributions public choice has made to our understanding of how political systems work has been to demonstrate the serious shortcomings of the simple majority rule' (Mueller, 1997: 137).

Studying collective decision making by committees and by two-party political systems, Duncan Black (1948, [1958] 1987) deduced what has since been known as the median voter theorem. Because extreme proposals lose to centrist proposals under the assumptions of that theorem, candidates and parties will move toward the middle of the political spectrum and, as a result, their policy platforms and campaign promises will tend to differ very little. Reversing US presidential hopeful Barry Goldwater's 1964 slogan, majority rule elections will present voters with an echo, not a choice. Voters do not vote under these circumstances because they are indifferent between the two candidates. Following Hotelling (1929) and Smithies

(1941), the public choice literature also teaches that, when the distribution of voter preferences is not unimodal and symmetric but multimodal or asymmetric, voters may not vote owing to alienation. That is, the position of the nearest candidate is too distant from the voter's preferred point in policy space to make voting worthwhile (Mueller, 1989: 180–182). Assuming that voters' decisions are continuous functions of candidates' positions (probabilistic voting) rather than deterministic adds generality to these results (ibid.: 199–203).

Anthony Downs (1957) added a second reason why voters might find participatory democracy to be instrumentally unrewarding under simple majority rule. Modeling the decision to vote in a rational choice context, Downs concluded that the costs of voting (registering, gathering information about candidates' positions, traveling to and from the polls, marking ballots, and so on) typically exceed the associated instrumental benefits. That is because the probability of an individual's vote being decisive (i.e., determining an election's outcome) is vanishingly small. If there are N voters and two choices (candidates) on the ballot, one person's vote will be decisive only if the votes of the other $N-1$ voters are evenly split. As N becomes large, the probability of that coincidence quickly approaches zero (Mueller, 1989: 350). Hence, if voters are narrowly rational, evaluating the act of voting purely in benefit–cost terms, they will not vote. The 'paradox of voting' to which Downs's analysis gave rise asks not why voter turnout rates are so low in democratic elections, at least in the recent American experience, but rather why millions of individuals participate voluntarily in an activity that demonstrably fails a benefit–cost test.

Low voter turnout seems to be a uniquely American (and, perhaps, Swiss) problem. More than half the eligible voting populations of these two countries routinely stay home on Election Day. Low voter turnout is of course not an issue in nations, such as Australia, Belgium and Luxembourg, where voting is compulsory and compliance is strictly enforced. However, voter participation rates elsewhere in Europe are much higher (in the range of 70–90%) even in the absence of compulsion.

As elaborated by Riker and Ordeshook (1968), an individual will vote in a two-candidate, majority-rule election only if

$$pB + D > C.$$

In this standard formulation, p is the probability that the vote will affect the election's outcome, B represents the net benefit the voter expects if his preferred candidate wins (sometimes called the 'net candidate differential', the utility difference the voter perceives between electing his first and second choices), D is the value of the non-instrumental rewards of voting (the satisfaction derived from performing one's 'civic duty', for instance), and C captures the implicit and explicit costs of casting one's ballot (also see Barzel and Silberberg, 1973; Aldrich, 1997: 377–378; Munger, 2001: 205–206).

The instrumental benefits of voting are determined according to the first term, pB. These benefits manifestly will be small if, as the median voter theorem suggests, candidates position themselves close to the same point in policy space. Even if that is not the case, however (i.e., the voter anticipates a large increase in utility if his preferred candidate wins), the instrumental benefits of voting will still be very small because p is very low. That is so independent of the expected 'closeness' of the race: the individual voter will still be one of thousands, if not millions. Which 537 of the 2,912,790 Floridians who voted Republican in the 2000 US presidential race can claim credit for George W. Bush's margin of victory? Moreover, exceptionally close elections are in fact resolved by other means — such contests are decided, not by the (disputed) vote count, but by the legislature or the courts.

Given that $pB \approx 0$ (because $p \approx 0$), voting is narrowly rational only if $D > C$, that is, the non-instrumental benefits of voting exceed the costs. Although patriotism, a feeling of being involved, and a sense of having done one's duty as a citizen by participating in the democratic process undoubtedly provide psychic rewards to some (perhaps many) individuals, preference-based explanations of human action are unsatisfying from a scientific point of view (Stigler and Becker, 1977). Performance of 'civic duty' supplies no basis for a predictive theory of voting; it serves, at best, as an ex post rationalization for observed voter turnout patterns.

Voting clearly is irrational in narrow benefit–cost terms. Yet large numbers of otherwise rational actors do indeed vote, even though their votes never 'matter'. The rational actor model of voter behavior is undermined further by the observation that turnout rates tend to be significantly lower in local elections than in national elections, despite the fact that, because the number of eligible voters is smaller in the former case, the probability of an individual's vote being decisive is higher. (The B-term might be lower in local elections, of course.) Voters do, however, seem to respond rationally to changes in at least some of the costs of voting. Turnout rates on Election Day are lower when the weather is bad (but see Knack, 1994, who finds that, contrary to conventional wisdom, rain is nonpartisan in its turnout-deterrence effects.) Similarly, fewer citizens register to vote in jurisdictions where voter registration lists are used as databases for selecting jury panels. In particular, Knack (1993) finds that aversion to jury duty depresses voter registration rates by more than seven percentage points. On the other hand, based on survey data suggesting that barely half the US population professes any knowledge of how juries are chosen, that just 42 percent of respondents think that jury panels are customarily selected from voter registration lists, and that registration rates are not disproportionately lower for self-employed individuals who face relatively high opportunity costs of jury service, Oliver and Wolfinger (1993) conclude that the avoidance of jury duty accounts for less than a one percentage point drop in voter registration rates.

Such findings point to an important distinction in the theory of rational voting. If we ask whether voter turnout rates in general can be explained in narrow benefit–cost terms, the answer seems to be no. Nevertheless, rational choice models do a reasonably good job of explaining voting behavior disaggregated by voter incomes. There are two theoretical possibilities in this regard. First, higher income voters might turn out to vote at lower rates because their opportunity costs of voting are higher. Second, higher income voters might turn out at higher rates because they have greater financial stakes in election outcomes. The weight of the empirical evidence suggests that the income effect (higher turnout) more than offsets the substitution effect (lower turnout). Voters who are older and who are more highly educated likewise exhibit greater propensities to vote than does the general voting population. The overall explanatory power of these demographic variables is quite low, though, and, indeed, models including them 'cannot predict who votes more accurately than random guessing' (Matsusaka and Palda, 1999: 431).

If instrumental benefits have little salience in decisions to vote, perhaps voters are motivated by other goals. Rejecting the expected utility model of voting, Ferejohn and Fiorina (1974, 1975) assume that voters instead follow a 'minimax regret rule' (also see Aldrich, 1997: 379–381). Given alternative courses of action, one of which must be taken before the true state of the world is revealed, individuals calculate the maximum sense of regret they anticipate, after their uncertainty has been resolved, for each action and for each end-state. They then rank-order the alternatives and select the action that yields the lowest of these maximum regrets. In the case of participatory democracy, a voter may regret deeply failing to vote if that action caused his preferred candidate to lose, but he will also regret going to the polls if that action had no impact on the electoral outcome. It turns out, under fairly general conditions, that the minimax regret rule predicts more voter turnout than is predicted by the expected utility model (ibid.: 580). Minimax regret also implies, however, that, contrary to fact, a vote for anyone other than the voter's most preferred candidate is never optimal. Similarly, rational minimax regretters do not waste their votes on candidates who have no prospect of winning (although Tullock, 1975, suggests that they should write in their own names on the ballot). Last, the model of minimax regret hinges on the voter's probability of influencing election outcomes, an assumption that subjects it to the same criticisms as the expected utility model it was intended to replace.

An alternative approach to the 'paradox of voting' models elections as affording citizens a low-cost way of expressing their policy preferences (Brennan and Buchanan, 1984; Brennan and Lomasky, 1993). Individuals engage in myriad political behaviors having no apparent instrumental consequences. They wear campaign buttons expressing support for their preferred candidates ('I Like Ike'), they affix bumper stickers to their cars ('Don't Blame Me, I Voted for [George H.W.] Bush'), and they place large signs in their front yards ('Howorth for Mayor'). In April 2001, more than 767,500 Mississippians turned out to vote in a special election called to determine whether the state flag would continue to incorporate a symbol of the Confederacy. The model of expressive voting suggests that individuals vote precisely because they know that their vote is highly unlikely to be decisive. Moreover, a rational expressive voting calculus may lead voters to make choices at the polls they would not make if their votes actually mattered.

Suppose that a voter is considering his position on a ballot measure to reduce environmental pollution (Lee and Clark, 2001: 483). Suppose further that, if the measure passes, the voter's taxes will increase by $1,100 but that he will receive only $100 worth of pollution-reduction benefits. Because the measure imposes a net cost of $1,000 on the voter, he clearly would vote against it if he thought his vote would determine the outcome. On the other hand, suppose the probability is 1/10,000 that his vote will be decisive (i.e., break what would otherwise be a tie between the measure's supporters and opponents). The expected cost of voting favorably on the measure is thus $1,000/10,000 = 10 cents. Hence, if the voter receives more than 10 cents worth of satisfaction from expressing generalized support for cleaning up the environment, he may well vote against his own economic interests.

Voting is rational in the theory of expressive voting expressly because it has little or no instrumental consequences. Thus, an individual's decision to vote cannot be divorced from the quality of the vote he casts. As Anthony Downs (1957) recognized, voters are 'rationally ignorant.'

The cost of gathering information about candidates' positions and the impact of those positions on the voter's wellbeing is high. Coupled with the negligible influence any one voter can expect to have on electoral outcomes, it simply does not pay to become well informed about the issues. Rational voter ignorance offers opportunities for decisive interest groups to engage in persuasion (Tullock, 1987), for voters to be influenced more by candidates' styles than by their substances, for voters' opinions to be swayed by the media, and for peer pressure and other random and extraneous factors to impact voters' choices (Brennan and Buchanan, 1984).

Crain et al. (1988) find indirect evidence that interest groups do in fact play decisive roles in mobilizing voters. Observing that larger electoral majorities translate into more effective interest-group influence on the legislature, they identify an incentive for the leaders of these groups to get their members to the polls. Political competition is, after all, 'more or less' not 'all or none.' Although only one party can 'win' an election, the 'losers' are not powerless to affect public policy decisions. The minority can impose costs on the majority and 'these costs will be larger, the larger the minority and the more intense its opposition' (Stigler, 1972: 100). It is therefore not proper to label 'the winning of 51 percent of legislative seats a victory and 49 percent a defeat' (ibid.: 98). Thus, for example, a president with a large vote margin (an electoral 'mandate') will be more effective in promoting his legislative agenda than one whose margin of victory is narrower. That is what Crain et al. (1988: 246) found: 'Historically, a 1 percent increase in a president's share of the popular vote leads to approximately a 1 percent increase in the amount of legislation enacted over the course of his term.' At the means of the data, 6,000 marginal voters invoke the passage of one additional bill, an investment in increased voter turnout that seems within the capacity of a well-organized interest group.

In a similar spirit, Shachar and Nalebuff (1999) combine notions of electoral 'closeness' with a 'follow-the-leader' model of political participation to develop a theory in which voters respond to the efforts of party leaders to 'get out the vote' when races are expected to be tight. Using data from the US states, they report evidence suggesting that a one percent increase in the predicted closeness of presidential elections raises voter turnout rates by 0.34 percent. Based on data from Canadian federal, provincial and municipal elections, Lapp (1999) finds weak support for the hypothesis that leader mobilization increases voter turnout. Furthermore, Radcliff (2001) adduces evidence that voter participation rates in the United States have varied directly with the organizational strength of labor unions, among the most effective mobilizers of vote blocs. Hence, taking account of the incentives of political elites and opinion leaders to internalize the benefits and costs of voting facing rank-and-file voters attaches renewed significance to George Stigler's (1972) warning against abandoning prematurely the hypothesis that voting behavior is explained by investment rather than by consumption motives.

It is nevertheless true that the act of voting, that most basic institution of democratic government, has eluded explanation on narrow self-interest grounds. The resolution of the 'paradox of voting' remains one of the most important challenges facing public choice scholars.

WILLIAM F. SHUGHART II

REFERENCES

Aldrich, J.H. (1997). "When is it rational to vote?" in D.C. Mueller (ed.) *Perspectives on Public Choice: A handbook.* Cambridge and New York: Cambridge University Press, pp. 373–390.

Barzel, Y. and Silberberg, E. (1973). "Is the act of voting rational?" *Public Choice*, 16(Fall): 51–58.

Black, D. (1948). "On the rationale of group decision making." *Journal of Political Economy*, 56(February): 23–34.

Black, D. ([1958] 1987). *The Theory of Committees and Elections.* Boston: Kluwer Academic Publishers.

Brennan, H.G. and Buchanan, J.M. (1984). "Voter choice: evaluating political alternatives." *American Behavioral Scientist*, 28(November/December): 185–201.

Brennan, H.G. and Lomasky, L. (1993). *Democracy and Decision: The Pure Theory of Electoral Preference.* Cambridge: Cambridge University Press.

Crain, W.M., Shughart, W.F. II, and Tollison, R.D. (1988). "Voters as investors: a rent-seeking resolution of the paradox of voting," in C.K. Rowley, R.D. Tollison, and G. Tullock (eds.) *The Political Economy of Rent Seeking.* Boston: Kluwer Academic Publishers, pp. 241–249.

Downs, A. (1957). *An Economic Theory of Democracy.* New York: Harper & Row.

Ferejohn, J.A. and Fiorina, M.P. (1974). "The paradox of not voting: a decision theoretic analysis." *American Political Science Review*, 68(June): 525–536.

Ferejohn, J.A. and Fiorina, M.P. (1975). "Closeness counts only in horseshoes and dancing." *American Political Science Review*, 69(September): 920–925.

Hotelling, H. (1929). "Stability in competition." *Economic Journal*, 39(March): 41–57.

Knack, S. (1993). "The voter participation effects of selecting jurors from registration lists." *Journal of Law and Economics*, 36(April): 99–114.

Knack, S. (1994). "Does rain help the Republicans? Theory and evidence on turnout and the vote." *Public Choice*, 79(April): 187–209.

Lapp, M. (1999). "Incorporating groups into rational choice explanations of turnout: an empirical test." *Public Choice*, 98(January): 171–185.

Lee, D.R. and Clark, J.R. (2001). "Is trust in government compatible with trustworthy government?" in W.F. Shughart II and L. Razzolini (eds.) *The Elgar Companion to Public Choice.* Cheltenham, UK and Northampton, MA, USA: Edward Elgar, pp. 479–493.

Matsusaka, J.G. and Palda, F. (1999). "Voter turnout: How much can we explain?" *Public Choice*, 98(March): 431–446.

Mitchell, W.C. (2001). "The old and new public choice: Chicago versus Virginia." in W.F. Shughart II and L. Razzolini (eds.) *The Elgar Companion to Public Choice*, Cheltenham, UK and Northampton, MA, USA: Edward Elgar, pp. 3–32.

Mueller, D.C. (1997). "Constitutional public choice," in D.C. Mueller (ed.) *Perspectives on Public Choice: A Handbook.* Cambridge and New York: Cambridge University Press, pp. 124–146.

Mueller, D.C. (1989). *Public Choice II: A Revised Edition of Public Choice.* Cambridge: Cambridge University Press.

Munger, M.C. (2001). "Voting." in W.F. Shughart II and L. Razzolini (eds.) *The Elgar Companion to Public Choice.* Cheltenham, UK and Northampton, MA, USA: Edward Elgar, pp. 197–239.

Oliver, J.E. and Wolfinger, R.E. (1999). "Jury aversion and voter registration." *American Political Science Review*, 93(March): 147–152.

Pigou, A.C. (1920). *The Economics of Welfare.* London: Macmillan.

Radcliff, B. (2001). "Organized labour and electoral participation in American national elections." *Journal of Labor Research*, 22(Spring): 405–414.

Riker, W.H. and Ordeshook, P.C. (1968). "A theory of the calculus of voting." *American Political Science Review*, 62(March): 25–42.

Shachar, R. and Nalebuff, B. (1999). "Follow the leader: theory and evidence on political participation." *American Economic Review*, 89(June): 525–547.

Smithies, A. (1941). "Optimal location in spatial competition." *Journal of Political Economy*, 49(June): 423–439.

Stigler, G.J. (1972). "Economic competition and political competition." *Public Choice*, 13(Fall): 91–106.

Stigler, G.J. and Becker, G.S. (1977). "De gustibus non est disputandum." *American Economic Review*, 67(March): 76–90.

Tullock, G. (1967). *Toward a Mathematics of Politics.* Ann Arbor: University of Michigan Press.

Tullock, G. (1975). "The paradox of not voting for oneself." *American Political Science Review*, 69(September): 919.

THE ITALIAN PUBLIC FINANCE CONTRIBUTION TO PUBLIC CHOICE

1. Though the influence of the Italian public finance on public choice has been recognized by such eminent representatives of public choice as Duncan Black and James Buchanan, still some aspects of the interaction between these two areas of research remain quite obscure.

Duncan Black, the first "founding father" of public choice, in his major work (Black, 1958) paid tribute to the Italian public finance, stating: "The theorizing of the book grew out of a reading of the English political philosophers and of the Italian writers on Public Finance" (Black, 1958, p. XI). In another occasion he wrote: "The Italians, in the narrower field of Public Finance, had succeeded in giving clear expression to their meaning in only the occasional passage, or in the occasional diagram, and this despite their very considerable literary abilities" (Grofman, 1981, p.19). Afterwards, in a letter addressed to me Black expressed his intention "to write a Memoir which would include an expression of obligation to some members of the 'great Italian interwar School of Public Finance'" (Black, 1983, p. 136).

James Buchanan, another "founding father" of public choice, spent a year in Italian universities during the 1950s and he has always recognized as a major influence on his work the "Italian tradition in fiscal theory," which was also the subject of an extensive essay by him (Buchanan, 1960). However, in spite of these and other authoritative expressions of admiration for the Italian studies in public finance from public choice eminent representatives, some aspects of the connections between public finance and public choice still remain unsatisfactory.

2. Though we easily recognize that classifications and definitions always keep an element of uncertainty, we feel necessary at this point to define both "public finance" and "public choice." In order to make our reasoning more sharp, we can start by a standard definition of public finance: "the complex of problems that center around the revenue-expenditure process of government" (Musgrave, 1959, p. 3).

This "complex of problems" can be studied from two different viewpoints: as a set of principles that an external entity will apply (the "benevolent despot" to which Wicksell makes reference, or Samuelson's social welfare function) or as a set of rules establishing the limits within which each individual will cooperate in order to maximize his own utility (the case of democratic institutions). In the first case the individual citizen does not take part in the public decision-making, while in the second hypothesis he is an essential part of this process.

Public finance in the first, standard meaning, has an essentially normative connotation, while in the second meaning it has a positive connotation since it becomes public choice, i.e., the "economics of politics" or (as I prefer), the "economics of non market decision-making". According to James Buchanan, "in a summary definition, public choice is the analysis of political decision-making with the tools and methods of economics" (Buchanan,

1980, p.11). Then, Buchanan continues as follows: "For specific precursors, we look to the works of the continental scholars such as Sax, Mazzola, Pantaleoni, De Viti de Marco, and most importantly to Knut Wicksell, all of whom wrote before the end of the nineteenth century. The works of these scholars differed substantially one from the other, but all shared a common objective, which was to bring the public economy within the analytical framework that had seemed so successful in explaining the working of the private economy" (Buchanan, 1980, pp. 11–12).

3. Public finance was taken into great consideration in Italy over a period of several centuries. The term "finanza" comes from the latin "finis" which applies to the settlement of a bill and apparently the Italian Guicciardini was the first writer to make use of this term.

The first attempt to apply economic methodology to public finance was that of Francesco Ferrara, whose impact was however limited by the fact that his lectures of 1850 at the Turin University remained unpublished until 1934 (Ferrara, 1934). Ferrara, a staunch supporter of liberalism (in a period when those making declarations of liberalism would be incarcerated) can be considered as an early representative of the subjectivist approach to economics. In his lectures he pointed out that in democracy the taxpayer is entitled to benefit from public expenditure (D. da Empoli and Porta, 1990).

Apart from Ferrara's anticipations, the most important contributions to public finance and public choice came from three economists: Maffeo Pantaleoni (1857–1924), Antonio De Viti de Marco (1858–1943) and Ugo Mazzola (1863–1899). It is interesting to point out that these three brilliant economists, who were also classical liberals, have been closely associated as editors of the *Giornale degli economisti* which was over a number of years the most authoritative voice against state intervention.

Pantaleoni's contribution can be considered the first application in Italy of the marginalist approach. De Viti de Marco was the author of the most complete treatment of the theory of public finance, though for some reasons we shall try to explain, Mazzola's contribution had a higher international recognition.

Apart from being the first application in Italy of the new economic theory, Maffeo Pantaleoni's essay on public expenditure, originally published in 1883 (Pantaleoni, 1883, pp. 16–27), appears to be the first contribution to the modern theory of public finance. In his work, Pantaleoni pointed out that "in the last analysis it is Parliament which decides the distribution of public expenditure" on the basis of "the opinion held by the average intelligence comprised in Parliament on the scale of marginal utilities of the various expenditures."

After a few years, two new works on the subject appeared in Austria and in Italy, by Emil Sax (1887) and by Antonio De Viti de Marco (1888), where the conditions of equilibrium were depicted as a situation where the degree of final utility of public goods for individuals equals their charge (that is, the tax they pay). Both books introduced the economic methodology in clarifying the equilibrium conditions for public goods. De Viti de Marco, whose reasoning was sharper than that of Sax (generally considered "obscure") went much further, since he presented a general framework for decision-making.

In his essay, *Il carattere teorico dell'economia finanziaria* (De Viti de Marco, 1888), De Viti de Marco initiates his discussion with the remark that government is a monopoly (a "natural monopoly"). He recognizes that public goods, because of their indivisibility, can be provided by the government only and focuses on the decision-making mechanism, pointing out how essential is to start the analysis within a relevant institutional framework (what he calls "the political constitution of the government").

Since reality provides a wide range of institutional systems, De Viti de Marco chooses to consider a typology of systems (he speaks of "types" of government), from the absolute state to the perfectly democratic ("cooperative") state. In all "types" of government, decisions are made according to an individualistic logic: comparing cost and utility and taking action only when the prospective utility exceeds the cost. In an absolute state, the ruler's aims are grounded in his own private preferences. In a democratic system, instead, government's aims are different from those of any individual, because they are the resultant (or the combination) "obtained by algebraic sum and by average" of citizens' preferences (a concept which is very close to Duncan Black's "median voter theorem").

According to De Viti de Marco, in spite of the variety of constitutions, the historical tendency is towards the democratic form of government, which "neutralizes" the monopolistic character of the government. This does not mean, quite obviously, that taxpayers in a democratic system are eager to pay taxes, because of "the intimate disposition of men, who regard as painful paying taxes and are inclined to avoid them". Another interesting ground suggested by De Viti de Marco for explaining the reluctance of the taxpayers has a psychological nature: the more efficient and satisfactory is the provision of public goods, the less intensive is their want and so the less intensive is individuals' marginal utility (quite obviously this concept coincides with Mazzola's "consolidation" theory and anticipates Puviani's theory of fiscal illusions).

This attitude by taxpayers requires government's coercion in fiscal administration, though compulsion only applies to taxpayers who are "recalcitrant" in obeying the social contract and up to the amount which represents a proper share of the burden of public goods. This share, according to De Viti de Marco, is "proper" when it equals the marginal utility of each individual. The sum of individual cost shares must equal the total cost of public goods (all the elements of the Lindahl equilibrium).

This equilibrium condition, however, is considered by De Viti de Marco essentially as a "scientific principle," since he recognizes that it "cannot be applied unlimitedly and absolutely." The reason for this preclusion is that its application would require either that the government knows the terms of each individual's "edonistic calculation" (the Wicksell's preference revelation issue) or that individuals could directly demand public goods, which is possible only for divisible goods, and not for public goods whose peculiar character is indivisibility. On the basis of these (very sensible) considerations, De Viti de Marco ends his essay by suggesting some "practical solutions," as the presumption that the utility of public goods is related to the net income, and similar suggestions which he recognizes are not "scientific" but necessary in order to approximate the "scientific equilibrium."

4. Unfortunately, De Viti de Marco's contribution to public finance, with all his public choice hints and anticipations, remained internationally ignored or at least was not widely read and understood. A great part of the tribute to the Italian public finance instead goes to Ugo Mazzola, whose essay *I dati scientifici della finanza pubblica* (1890) was the basis for Wicksell's theory of public finance.

In his work, Mazzola introduced his own theory of public goods, which was not so far distant from De Viti de Marco's theory. In Mazzola's view, the provision of public goods is a precondition for the demand of private goods (he states that public goods are "complementary" to the private goods). He fully recognizes the indivisibility of public goods and also the necessity of a public system for providing these goods. In addition, he introduces the notion of "public price" that he compares with the "private price" (while de Viti de Marco explicitly denied that taxes can be considered as "prices"). Mazzola developed the idea of "consolidation" of the satisfaction due to public goods introduced earlier by De Viti de Marco, which is the reason why this idea is normally referred to him.

Furthermore, Mazzola stated the equilibrium condition for public goods as the equilibrium between marginal utility and cost (but without pointing out, as De Viti de Marco did, that the total tax shares should sum up to the total cost). However, due to the consolidation of the satisfaction from public goods, taxpayers would try to avoid paying taxes, which would make coercion by government necessary in order to cover the cost of public goods.

5. In 1896, Knut Wicksell (Wicksell, 1896) based his theory on "A New Principle of Just Taxation" on Mazzola's views and in particular he accepted his "central thesis of equality between 'the marginal utility of public goods and their price'" [p. 80]. Wicksell appreciated the individualistic approach of Mazzola. Some expressions used by Mazzola were, however, interpreted by Wicksell as if Mazzola didn't realize that taxpayers might be reluctant to pay taxes.

In particular, Wicksell disagreed with Mazzola's conclusion that each taxpayer "... will allocate his resources ... among private and public goods ... in such a way to maximize his utility." According to Wicksell, it would be in the best interest of the taxpayer not to pay taxes. This was a misreading of Mazzola (who knew very well as all Italians know, and probably more than the Swedish, that paying taxes is painful and requires compulsion by government ....) though a very fruitful one, because in this way Wicksell made a contribution in pointing out the game theoretic approach to public choice.

Because of the quotation by Wicksell, Musgrave in all his writings on public goods, starting from his article of 1939 (Musgrave, 1939) makes reference to Mazzola's work as the basic public finance contribution of the Italian school. He quotes De Viti de Marco's work as less important, and refers to his volume of lectures which was published in English in 1936 (De Viti de Marco, 1936) and which had a mixed reception in the Anglo-Saxon world. After publishing his 1888 essay on public finance, De Viti de Marco continued his scientific activity writing on various subjects, as public debt and monetary issues. He was also a member of the Italian parliament for five terms and took part very actively in liberal battles, especially against governmental protectionist policies. His thought on the theory of public finance was expressed from year to year in his mimeographed lectures that he collected in a book almost at the end of his academic career.

That book, whose title was misleading (*First principles of public finance* appears as the title of an introductory textbook rather than of a scientific book) included very interesting developments of some of De Viti de Marco'essay original thoughts (in particular, for our purpose, may be mentioned the more conscious presentation of the parallelism of the absolute state with monopoly and of the cooperative state with perfect competition), but did not mention others and, which is worse, was not updated (e.g., neither Wicksell's nor Lindahl's works were considered). However, Musgrave and Peacock, probably because of the English edition of de Viti de Marco's lectures (and perhaps

of the wrong message sent by Wicksell), did not feel necessary to include De Viti de Marco's original essay in their volume of *Classics in the Theory of Public Finance* (Musgrave and Peacock, 1958).

6. After the contributions to public finance by Pantaleoni, De Viti de Marco and Mazzola, many other economists in Italy contributed to public finance (probably, as Buchanan said, with decreasing returns) and many of them dealt with public choice issues, but without introducing new elements relevant for public choice. The one who deserves special attention in the present context is Amilcare Puviani, whose theory of fiscal illusions was abridged in Buchanan's book, *Public Finance in Democratic Process* (Buchanan, 1967), who considered it as an important contribution to the theory of supply of public goods. As to the contribution by De Viti de Marco to the *median voter* theory, an unpublished annotation by Duncan Black [Black's Archives-Glasgow] recognizes De Viti de Marco's influence.

DOMENICO DA EMPOLI

REFERENCES

Black, D. (1958). *The Theory of Committee and Elections.* Cambridge: University Press.

Black. D. (1983). "Personal Recollections." in *Journal of Public Finance and Public Choice*, 2: 133–136.

Buchanan, J.M. (1960). "'La scienza delle finanze': The Italian Tradition in Fiscal Theory," in J.M. Buchanan (ed.) *Fiscal Theory and Political Economy.* Chapel Hill: The University of North Carolina, pp. 24–74.

Buchanan, J.M. (1967). Public Finance in Democratic Process. Durham: University of North Carolina Press.

Buchanan, J.M. (1980). "Public choice and public finance," in K.W. Roskamp (ed.) *Public Choice and Public Finance.* Paris: Cujas, pp. 11–18.

da Empoli, D. and Porta, P.L.(1990). "Soggettivismo e impostazione democratica della scienza delle finanze nel pensiero di Francesco Ferrara," in P.F. Asso, P. Barucci, and M. Ganci (eds.) *Francesco Ferrara e il suo tempo.* Roma, Bancaria Editrice, pp. 241–258.

De Viti de Marco, A. (1888). *Il carattere teorico dell'economia finanziaria.* Roma: Pasqualucci.

De Viti de Marco, A. (1936). *First Principles of Public Finance.* London: Jonathan Cape.

Ferrara, F. (1934). *Lezioni di economia politica*, Volume I. Bologna: Zanichelli.

Grofman, B. (1981). "The theory of committees and elections: the legacy of Duncan Black," in G. Tullock (ed.) *Toward a Science of Politics — Papers in Honor of D. Black.* Blacksburg, Public Choice Center, VPI, pp. 11–57.

Musgrave, R.A. (1939). "The voluntary exchange theory of public economy." *Quarterly Journal of Economics*, LIII: 213–237.

Musgrave, R.A. and Peacock, A.T. (1958). *Classics in the Theory of Public Finance*. London: MacMillan.

Musgrave, R.A. (1959). *The Theory of Public Finance*. New York: McGraw-Hill.

Pantaleoni, M. (1883). "Contributo alla teoria del riparto delle spese pubbliche." English translation in: R.A. Musgrave and A.T. Peacock (eds.) *Classics in the Theory of Public Finance*, London: Macmillan, pp. 16–27.

Sax, E. (1887). *Grundlegung der theoretischen Staatswirtschaft*. Wien: Holder.

J

THE JUDICIARY

1. Introduction

The independence of the judiciary is sometimes portrayed as necessary to ensure that this branch of government functions as an effective counterweight to the legislative and executive branches. Many scholars have defended the 'independence' of the judiciary on normative grounds, arguing that the welfare of society is thereby enhanced (cf. Buchanan, 1974). According to this view, the role of the judiciary is to protect society from unconstitutional actions by the other branches, the judges being motivated to behave in this way by their concern for the public interest. Consistent with this view, the independent judiciary might be regarded as an agent representing the interests of groups which would otherwise be unrepresented (or under-represented) in other political forums.

A large and important literature has emerged which models legislatures as firms supplying wealth transfers to competing interest groups, packaged by those political bodies in the form of legislation (McCormick and Tollison, 1981). In this model, legislatures assign property rights in wealth transfers to the highest bidder by means of contracts termed 'laws.'

What is the relationship between the operation of this market for wealth transfers and the operation of the judiciary? One interpretation would suggest that judicial rulings as well as the general behavior of judges are simply functions of the short-run interests of the pressure groups who successfully bid for political influence. Accordingly, the judiciary would not actually be 'independent' at all, but would instead tend to behave in a manner reflecting the shifting tides of interest group competition.

William Landes and Richard Posner (1975) developed an economic model in which the independent judiciary plays an important role in the operation of the political market for wealth transfers. They argue that the function of judges is to impart stability to the bargains struck between the legislature and organized interest groups. Because of its effective independence from the current legislature, the judiciary can resolve disputes involving the interpretation or constitutionality of a law or regulation in terms of the intentions of the originally enacting legislative body. Thus, legislative contracts with interest groups will not be abrogated simply because the political winds have shifted; the durability of such contracts is instead enhanced. Legislation transferring wealth becomes more valuable to interest groups than would be the case if it were vulnerable to changes in the political composition of the legislative body.

In this essay I examine this theory of the independent judiciary, explore its implications, and review the relevant empirical literature. Are the findings of these empirical investigations supportive of, or inconsistent with, the Landes–Posner model?

2. What do Judges Maximize?

Until fairly recently a view of judicial motivation held by many legal scholars and political scientists was that judges act in ways designed to preserve the integrity of the legal system, maximizing the abstract concept of 'justice' and, at the same time, the welfare of society. Economists, even while extending the model of rational self-interest beyond the domain of ordinary commercial exchange into the realm of governmental decision-making, long neglected the problem of judicial behavior and motivation.

Of course, judges might be seen as rational actors who maximize something other than their own pecuniary wealth. Adherents of this view argue that since the judiciary is insulated from monetary pressures, judges maximize along other margins, for example by basing their legal decisions on their personal ideological preferences, by seeking greater power or prestige by way of those decisions, or both. But judges are supposedly prevented from acting or deciding cases in ways that garner them greater financial benefits.

Posner (1998), for example, argues that judges are not motivated by personal economic interests which lead them to behave in ways consistent with pecuniary wealth maximization. They instead indulge their ideological preferences through their judicial decisions, acting 'to impose their policy preferences on society' (Posner, 1998, p. 583).

The question of the nature of judicial motivation has recently received quite a bit of attention from empirical economists. There is substantial evidence supporting the proposition that judges are self-interested at the margin, and that simple pecuniary wealth maximization is a dominant factor.

Cohen (1991) examined the dispositions of over 600 Sherman Act anti-trust indictments issued between 1955 and 1980. He hypothesized that self-interested judges would tend, *ceteris paribus*, to decide cases based on how they thought their rulings would affect their chances for promotion to a higher court. This is indeed what Cohen found. In cases where deciding judges saw opportunities for promotion, rulings tended to favor the prosecution (the US Department of Justice) which, of course, makes recommendations to the president on judicial appointments and court assignments. Antitrust defendants also tended to receive longer jail sentences and stiffer fines, and *nolo contendere* pleas were less likely to be accepted by the court over the government's objection, when vacancies existed on the next higher court.

In short, Cohen found that judicial rulings appear to be influenced in part by personal career ambitions. Promotion to a higher court tends to increase the present discounted value of a judge's lifetime income stream owing not only to a higher judicial salary, but also to the greater earnings prospects in private practice following (voluntary) retirement from the bench. These findings suggest that, other things being the same, judges will tend to decide cases in a manner that promotes their own self-interest, maximizing their pecuniary wealth subject to constraints.

Of course, as mentioned above, rational self-interest might conceivably express itself in the form of the pursuit of personal ideological agendas by individual judges. Kimenyi et al. (1985) subjected that proposition to empirical testing. They reasoned that if judicial decisions merely reflect personal ideological preferences, judges would tend to try more cases in jurisdictions where judicial pay is lower. Judges with ideological bents would want to try more cases because each additional decision affords them an opportunity to increase their level of personal satisfaction by imposing their ideological preferences on society. This source of utility would tend to be relatively more important to judges operating in low-pay jurisdictions than in jurisdictions where the financial returns to judgeships are higher.

For the purpose of exploring this possible relationship, Kimenyi et al. (1985) looked at the behavior of US state courts during 1980. They found that where the salaries of state supreme court judges were higher, *ceteris paribus*, the number of cases those judges decided was significantly higher, too. Therefore, lower-paid judges do not seem to compensate for lower salaries by pursuing additional opportunities to express their ideological preferences more aggressively (i.e., hearing more cases). Rather, judges appear to behave as simple wealth-maximizers, hearing cases as a positive function of their remuneration.

In sum, recent empirical studies support the hypothesis that judges are at least partly motivated in their judicial behavior by the pursuit of personal wealth, and not merely by a desire to express their ideological preferences or to maximize the welfare of society. Judges therefore seem potentially subject to influence from other branches of government exerted in the form of tangible rewards, including salary but also including other kinds of wealth-enhancement, offered with the intention of modifying the content of judicial rulings.

3. The Interest Group Theory and the Judiciary

The interest group theory of government (see Stigler, 1971; Peltzman, 1976; McCormick and Tollison, 1981 and Becker, 1983, 1985) is founded on simple economic logic. As is the case with an ordinary, private, voluntary market, the precise public policy outcome will reflect the equilibrium interaction of demand and supply. But whereas a voluntary private market will necessarily be a positive-sum game in which both demanders and suppliers mutually benefit, the public policy 'market' is a zero- (or negative-) sum game wherein the marginal benefits enjoyed by the winners are at best equal to (and frequently less than) the marginal costs suffered by the losers. Prospective recipients of the transfers are the 'demanders,' while the previous owners of the wealth being transferred are the 'suppliers.' Politicians act as brokers in this market, matching the recipients of the transfers with the sources of the wealth required to finance them, in accordance with the goal of maximizing their own political support.

A considerable body of research demonstrates the usefulness of the interest group model of government (cf. Alesina and Rodrik, 1994; and Grossman and Helpman, 1994; for a sampling of the recent literature). If government is modeled as a firm specializing in the production and distribution of wealth transfers to competing pressure groups, public policy decisions can be understood as the operational manifestation of this production process.

From this perspective, legislation is the primary mechanism by means of which government transfers are organized and distributed. The legislature functions as the broker of wealth transfers produced and marketed to pressure groups, although certain legal devices are available which permit interest groups access to wealth transfers without the intervention of that legislative body.

4. Is the 'Independent Judiciary' more than a Unicorn?

The judiciary can be described as 'independent' to the extent that the decisions rendered by courts are uninfluenced by the sorts of factors and political pressures which tend to affect legislative deliberations. Individual judges in such a setting would render decisions solely on the basis of relevant legal principles (precedent, constitutionality, and so on) and would be essentially unaffected by pressures exerted by interested parties. Those who espouse this view often go on to argue that an independent judiciary plays a key role in guaranteeing the smooth operation of a representative democracy. The functional independence of the judiciary is often merely presumed by these thinkers, who devote little or no effort towards explaining what would possibly motivate judges to act in such a public-spirited manner. Thus, it is possible to conceive of the independent judiciary as a kind of non-economic artifact, exhibiting a pattern of behavior on the part of individual judges which benefits the overall society despite the absence of a plausible motivational model explaining that behavior.

A major difficulty for this variant of the interest group story is that the existing judiciary seems to be highly independent of day-to-day partisan political pressures in actual practice. In part, this independence is built into the structure of the judiciary. Take, for example, the federal judiciary. Article III of the US Constitution imparts a substantial degree of independence to the courts by requiring federal judges to be appointed for life terms rather than being elected (partially insulating sitting federal judges from electoral politics), and prohibiting Congress from reducing their salaries while they are serving on the bench (stymieing possible efforts by the legislative branch to punish federal judges by lowering their pay).

Although a number of studies conducted by political scientists have reported finding evidence of a relationship between the political party affiliation of judges and the decisional tendencies of those jurists (Goldman, 1966; Tate, 1981), recent econometric studies cast doubt on this hypothesized relationship. For instance, consider the empirical investigation conducted by Ashenfelter et al. (1995). They analyze nearly every federal civil rights and prisoner appeals case filed in three federal court districts during FY 1981, and investigate the possibility that various characteristics of the presiding judge (including his or her political party) play a significant role in explaining judicial decisions. (Civil rights cases were included owing to the greater likelihood that these politically sensitive cases would allow judicial partisanship to affect the outcome.) They report no significant results from including the party affiliation of the ruling judge, however.

This finding, namely that there appears to be no statistically significant correlation between political party affiliations and the actual rulings issued by judges, nevertheless leaves room for ordinary 'patronage politics' in the judicial appointment process, evidence of which has been reported by a bevy of political scientists (for example, see Barrow et al., 1996). Federal judgeships are still plum appointments,

which provide the fortunate appointee with a large capital gain in connection with his or her legal career. In the context of the interest group theory of government, political party organizations represent competing wealth transfer brokerage services, and the party faithful must be rewarded for their contributions of various resources (time, effort, money, and so forth). Assuming that the political market for transfers is efficient, the behavior of suppliers should be identical regardless of party affiliation, other things held equal. Hence, while patronage politics may determine the identities of judges, it does not necessarily follow that, once they have been elevated to the bench, their decisions will be swayed by partisan political considerations. Regardless of the precise identities of the 'winners' in this patronage game, the pattern of investments by relevant interest groups will remain the same.

5. The Independent Judiciary in an Interest Group Perspective

Landes and Posner (1975) challenged the notion that the interest group theory of government implies a judiciary that automatically supports the momentary bargains struck between the legislative branch and high-bidding interest groups seeking governmentally brokered redistribution. They proposed a model in which the efficient functioning of the market for wealth transfers is significantly enhanced by a judiciary that operates in a highly independent manner.

The element of continuity and stability that is necessary for interest-group politics to operate in the context of the legislature can be provided either by the *procedural rules of the legislature* (including the committee system, parliamentary rules of order governing bill introductions, floor debates and votes, and so on), by the *independence of the judiciary*, or both (Landes and Posner, 1975, p. 878).

Landes and Posner argue that protecting the integrity of the courts will be to the advantage of the legislature because this independence will help to preserve the value of wealth transfer programs; such benefits would obviously be worth less if such programs, once enacted, were threatened by judicial interference. 'If we assume that an independent judiciary would...interpret and apply legislation in accordance with the original legislative understanding...it follows that an independent judiciary facilitates...interest-group politics' (Landes and Posner, 1975, p. 879). Consequently, they predict that a legislature will take steps to provide itself with an independent judiciary in order to protect the value of legislative contracts with interest groups.

If judicial independence is valuable to the legislature as source of durability for the wealth transfers it brokers, then the legislature presumably should reward the judiciary for providing that 'service.' In other words, the legislature should be observed to foster judicial independence. An effective device for encouraging any form of behavior is to pay for it. This suggests a possible direct test of the Landes–Posner theory: are judges who exhibit greater independence rewarded by the legislature?

There are two avenues for approaching such a test: the operating budget of the judiciary and the salaries paid to individual judges. Anderson et al. (1989) selected the latter reward mechanism for empirical testing. They investigated whether there was any statistically significant relationship between the annual salaries of state supreme court judges and the degree of independence exhibited by the judiciary in that state, after controlling for other relevant factors which might be expected to influence salaries. (The exogenous factors included measures of the opportunity cost of service on the court and of the prospective workload on that court as well as measures of statutory constraints on judges, such as lengths of judicial terms of office.)

They employed a measure of substantive due process reviews as an indicator of judicial independence. Substantive due process review is an evaluation by the court designed to determine whether a legislative act or other government regulation violates the constitutional guarantee of due process. In other words, does the legislation or regulation have the effect of violating an individual's freedom of contract, or otherwise interfere with his due process rights, without there being a vital public interest served by the law in question? [The classic substantive due process case that came before the U.S. Supreme Court was *Lochner v. New York*, 198 US 45 (1905), in which the high court ruled that a state law restricting the number of hours bakers could legally work violated the Fourteenth Amendment to the U.S. Constitution.] Although the Supreme Court refused to hear further 'substantive due process' cases beginning in early 1937, this did not foreclose state courts from continuing to undertake such reviews. All state constitutions contain due process provisions similar to that forming the basis for earlier reviews in the federal courts.

Anderson et al. (1989) argued that the willingness of state courts to overturn legislative acts on constitutional due process grounds provides a strong indicator of the effective independence of that judiciary. Courts that demonstrate a greater readiness to subject acts of the current legislature to due process review are more 'independent' of that body, better protecting the durability of all legislative contracts with interest groups. Provision of this valuable service by the judiciary should be rewarded by the legislature: other things being equal, judges who are more independent should be paid higher salaries.

Using state data, these authors found that judicial pay indeed tends to be significantly higher, *ceteris paribus*, in states where the courts have a stronger record of challenging legislative acts on substantive due process grounds. This suggests that judges receive financial rewards for behaving independently. The functional independence of the state judiciary provides a valuable service to the state legislature by enhancing the durability of past (and the expected durability of future) contracts with interest groups. Greater independence results in higher salaries for state judges, *ceteris paribus*.

Thus, the judiciary is evidently populated by rational individuals who respond in predictable ways to salary incentives offered by the legislative branch to encourage judicial independence. This implies that a degree of such independence benefits the legislature, the broker of wealth transfers to favored parties. Yet a completely independent judiciary would likely jeopardize the production of new wealth transfer contracts between the current legislature and high-bidding interest groups. We now turn to a review of this problem.

6. Partisan Politics, Judicial Independence, and Political Equilibrium

In a government driven by interest group politics, the existing degree of judicial independence represents an equilibrium outcome, and is therefore not necessarily absolute or total. There is a tension between protecting the durability of wealth transfers to interest groups brokered by past legislatures and the ability of the present legislature to enact new special interest measures. The same judicial independence that serves to protect the value of past legislative contracts tends to conflict with the ongoing operation of the legislative wealth brokering process. The rulings of a completely independent court may interfere with the ability of a legislature to enter into new contracts or to undertake the recontracting necessary to maintain political equilibrium. Efficiency requires that a balance be struck between these two competing influences.

Therefore, from the perspective of the legislature, there is an *optimal degree of judicial independence*. That optimum equates marginal cost and marginal benefit, where the costs associated with the tendency of an independent judiciary to impede the functioning of current redistributional activity just balance the benefits of enhanced durability. One implication of this equilibrium condition is that simple partisan politics may in fact exert a marginal influence on the behavior of judges. The actual equilibrium outcome may well reflect such political pressure.

Thus, the protection of judicial independence is constrained by political realities: judges may need to appease currently dominant interest group coalitions at the margin, as well as exhibiting a general 'independence' in the sense of maintaining the quality and integrity of judicial review applied to legislative contracts with interest groups.

Clearly, Article III of the US Constitution goes a considerable distance towards protecting the independence of the federal judiciary (e.g., by granting judges lifetime tenure), but that protection is imperfect. The other branches of government (the executive and the legislative) do, however, still have access to possible influence over the judiciary, for example by controlling the process of appointment and confirmation. Other margins of potential congressional influence include the size of the judiciary (which affects judicial workloads), and the fact that judicial rulings can be overturned legislatively or by (the costly and difficult) means of amending the Constitution.

However, there *is* a margin that in principle permits closer and less costly control of the courts by the current Congress, namely the annual budget of the federal judiciary. Although the US Constitution forbids the legislative branch from using actual judicial salaries as a control variable, there is no such constitutional restriction placed on the appropriation of funds for purposes of covering court operating expenses in a given year. It is possible, then, that the current Congress might employ this margin to influence federal judicial decision-making. Whether such influence is actually exerted represents an interesting empirical question.

In her provocative study of recent US Supreme Court decisions, Toma (1991) reported evidence that the Court is subject to sanctions based on the degree to which it pursues a different ideological agenda than Congress prefers. Ideological differences on the part of the Court resulted in a reduced budget allocated by the Congress.

Toma calculated the absolute value of the difference between the mean ideological ranking for a sample of Supreme Court decisions and the mean ideological ranking of the members of Congress for the period 1946 to 1977. This allowed her to address the question whether ideological differences between the Court and the Congress resulted in lower budgetary appropriations from that legislative body. If the answer were 'yes,' then this would suggest that Congress was employing budgetary appropriations to influence the ideological complexion of the Court's rulings.

That is exactly what Toma found. As the Supreme Court rulings became more consistent with the ideological preferences of members of Congress, that legislative body responded by awarding the Court with a larger budget. Given that the members of Congress were generally more conservative in their ideological rankings than justices on the Supreme Court during this time frame, this meant that the budgetary incentives rewarded the Court for deciding cases in a more conservative light. Other things held equal, as the Court's rulings became relatively more conservative, the Court's budget grew faster, but as those decisions reflected a more liberal bent, budgetary appropriations fell (or at least grew more slowly than they would have otherwise).

Congressional control is not limited to the margin of the judiciary's budget; there are a number of other means by which it can potentially exert influence on the federal judiciary. Congress can, for example, manipulate the rate at which the judiciary expands. Although the employment of particular judges is strongly insulated from political pressure (e.g., Congress cannot simply fire or otherwise replace a federal judge with whom the majority party disagrees), the creation of new judgeships *does* require joint action by the Congress and the president. The US Constitution gives the president authority to nominate and the US Senate to vote to confirm new judges; the Congress must vote in favor, and the president must sign legislation authorizing expansions of the federal judiciary.

This relationship has been studied carefully both by economists and political scientists. While caseload pressure would presumably in part explain moves by the legislative and executive branches to expand the judiciary (since more judges imply a lower caseload per judge, *ceteris paribus*), this would constitute the sole determining factor only if these political decision-makers were single-minded in their dedication to the pursuit of the 'public interest.' Assuming that a given expansion in judgeships and concomitant reduction in average caseload leads to the improvement in the quality (measured in some objective sense) of judicial decisions, then the legislation would be *institutionally efficient*. On the other hand, to the extent that political calculations figure in to the process of judicial expansion, then new judgeships would come about independently of the objective 'need' for such growth, reflecting the different pursuit of *political efficiency*.

De Figueiredo and Tiller subjected this hypothesis to econometric testing. They divided the problem into two parts, the *timing* of expansion and the *magnitude* of expansion. They employed data on judicial expansion for the Federal Appellate Court covering the period 1869 to 1991.

In one set of regressions, de Figueiredo and Tiller addressed the question of whether political factors influence the timing of bouts of judicial expansion. Their dichotomous dependent variable was defined as 1 if the federal judiciary expanded in a given year, zero otherwise. Independent variables included the average caseload per judge, the length of time since the last expansion (to control for trend effects), growth in the overall federal budget, and 'political alignment,' another dummy variable set equal to 1 if the House of Representatives, Senate, and the presidency were all controlled by the same political party, zero otherwise. Using probit analysis, they found that the only independent variable of (high) significance was 'political alignment,' which had a positive sign — indicating that successful judicial expansion was significantly more likely when the same party controlled both the legislative and executive branches.

Spiller and Gely (1992) approached the judicial independence issue from the perspective of another limited subset of court decisions, cases involving the interpretation of the National Labor Relations Act (NLRA) by the Supreme Court — a sample consisting of 249 cases decided between 1949 and 1988. They categorized each decision according to whether it was 'pro-union.' In order to measure the preferences of members of the House and the Senate, they used the relevant ideological rankings of Americans for Democratic Action (ADA). They discovered that the ADA score of the relevant House member appeared to affect the Court's probability of a pro-union decision. (Senate ADA rankings were insignificant, however.) Similarly, a pro-union decision was significantly more likely if the percentage of justices serving on the Court appointed by Democratic administrations was higher, and (sometimes) significantly correlated with the fact that the sitting president was a Democrat.

7. Conclusion

Landes and Posner offered a key extension of the interest-group theory of government by arguing that an independent judiciary performs a crucial role in protecting and preserving contracts between the legislature-suppliers and the interest group-consumers of legislated wealth transfers. Institutions that increase the level of independence of the judiciary from the political process do not place the court system outside the market for political wealth transfers but rather provide that market with the contractual infrastructure necessary to ensure its efficient operation. In sum, self-interested judges can be shown to behave in a manner consistent with the functioning of efficient markets for coercive wealth transfers for the same reasons that other rational actors participate in these markets.

GARY M. ANDERSON

REFERENCES

Alesina, Alberto and Dani Rodrik (1994). "Distributive politics and economic growth." *Quarterly Journal of Economics*, 109: 465–490.

Anderson, Gary M., William F. Shughart II, and Robert D. Tollison (1989). "On the incentives of judges to enforce legislative wealth transfers," *Journal of Law and Economics*, 32, 215–228.

Ashenfelter, Orley, Eisenberg, T., and Schwab, S.J. (1995). "Politics and the judiciary: the influence of judicial background on case outcomes." *Journal of Legal Studies*, 24: 257–281.

Barrow, Deborah J., Gary Zuk, and Gerard S. Gryski (1996). *The Federal Judiciary and Institutional Change*. Ann Arbor: University of Michigan Press.

Becker, Gary S. (1983). "A theory of competition among pressure groups for political influence." *Quarterly Journal of Economics*, 98: 371–400.

Becker, Gary S. (1985). "Public policies, pressure groups, and dead weight costs." *Journal of Public Economics*, 28: 329–347.

Buchanan, J.M. (1974). "Good Economics – Bad Law," *Virginia Law Review* 60: 483–92.

Cohen, Mark A. (1991). "Explaining judicial behavior or what's 'unconstitutional' about the Sentencing Commission?" *Journal of Law, Economics and Organization*, 7: 183–199.

Landes, William M. and Richard A. Posner (1975). "The independent judiciary in an interest-group perspective." *Journal of Law and Economics*, 18: 875–901.

Landes, William M. and Richard A. Posner (1979). "Adjudication as a private good." *Journal of Legal Studies*, 8: 235–284.

Maloney, Michael T. and Robert E. McCormick (1982), "A positive theory of environmental quality regulation." *Journal of Law and Economics*, 25: 99–124.

McCormick, Robert E. and Robert D. Tollison (1981), *Politicians, Legislation, and the Economy: An Inquiry into the Interest-Group Theory of Government*. Boston: Martinus Nijhoff.

Peltzman, Sam (1976). "Toward a more general theory of regulation." *Journal of Law and Economics*, 19: 211–240.

Peltzman, Sam (1980). "The growth of government." *Journal of Law and Economics*, 23: 209–287.

Posner, Richard A. (1974). "Theories of economic regulation." *Bell Journal of Economics and Management Science*, 5: 335–358.

Spiller, Pablo T. and Rafael Gely (1992). "Congressional control or judicial independence: the determinants of U.S. Supreme Court labor-relations decisions, 1949–1988." *RAND Journal of Economics*, 23, 463–492.

Stigler, George J. (1971). "The theory of economic regulation." *Bell Journal of Economics and Management Science*, 2, 137–146.

Tabarrok, Alexander and Eric Helland (1999). "Court politics: the political economy of tort awards." *Journal of Law and Economics*, 42: 157–188.

Tate, C. Neal (1981). "Personal attribute models of the voting behavior of U.S. Supreme Court justices: liberalism in civil liberties and economic decisions, 1946–1978." *American Political Science Review*, 75: 355–367.

Toma, Eugenia F. (1991). "Congressional influence and the Supreme Court: the budget as a signaling device." *Journal of Legal Studies*, 20: 131–146.

Toma, Eugenia F. (1996). "A contractual model of the voting behavior of the Supreme Court: the role of the chief justice." *International Review of Law and Economics*, 16: 433–447.

L

THE LAW AND ECONOMICS MOVEMENT

Law and economics is among the most successful examples of the recent surge of applied economics into areas that once were regarded as extraneous to economic analysis. Methodologically, law and economics applies the conceptual apparatus and empirical methods of economics to the study of law. Despite some resistance to the application of economics to nonmarket behavior, the important bonds between legal and economic analysis, as well as the social significance of the object of study, were in themselves a guarantee of success and fruitfulness for law and economics.

1. The Origins of Law and Economics

The origins of law and economics are traceable to Adam Smith's (1776) discussion of the economic effects of legislation regulating economic activities, and Jeremy Bentham's (1782 and 1789) theory of legislation and utilitarianism. Yet, despite such notable antecedents, it was not until the mid-twentieth century through the work of Henry Simon, Aaron Director, Henry Manne, George Stigler, Armen Alchian, Gordon Tullock, and others that the links between law and economics became an object of serious academic pursuit. The regulation of business and economic law fell within the natural interest of economists, so that the first applications of economics to law tended to focus on areas related to corporate law, tax law, and competition law.

In the 1960s, the pioneering work of Ronald Coase and Guido Calabresi brought to light the pervasive bearing of economics in all areas of the law. The methodological breakthrough occasioned by Coase and Calabresi allowed immediate extensions to the areas of tort, property and contract. The analytical power of their work was not confined to these fields, however, and subsequent law and economics contributions demonstrate the explanatory and analytical reach of its methodology in a number of other areas of the law.

A difference in approach is detectable between the law and economics contributions of the early 1960s and those that followed in the 1970s. While the earlier studies appraise the effects of legal rules on the normal functioning of the economic system (i.e., they consider the impact of legal rules on the market equilibrium), the subsequent generation of studies utilizes economic analysis to achieve a better understanding of the legal system. Indeed, in the 1970s a number of important applications of economics to law gradually exposed the economic structure of basically every aspect of a legal system: from its origin and evolution, to its substantive, procedural, and constitutional rules.

An important ingredient in the success of law and economics research has come from the establishment of specialized journals. The first such journal, the *Journal of Law and Economics*, appeared in 1958 at the University of Chicago. Its first editor, Aaron Director, should be credited for this important initiative, successfully continued by Ronald Coase. Other journals emerged in the following years: in 1972, the *Journal of Legal Studies*, also housed at the University of Chicago, was founded under the editorship of Richard Posner; in 1979, *Research in Law and Economics*, under the editorship of Richard Zerbe, Jr.; in 1981, the *International Review of Law and Economics* was established in the United Kingdom under the editorship of Charles Rowley and Anthony Ogus (later joined by Robert Cooter and Daniel Rubinfeld); in 1982, the *Supreme Court Economic Review*, under the editorship of Peter Aranson (later joined by Harold Demsetz and Ernest Gellhorn); in 1985, the *Journal of Law, Economics and Organization*, under the editorship of Jerry Mashaw and Oliver Williamson (later joined by Roberta Romano); and most recently, in 1994, the *European Journal of Law and Economics* was launched under the editorial direction of Jürgen Backhaus and Frank Stephen. These specialized journals provided, and continue to provide, an extremely valuable forum for the study of the economic structure of law.

In many respects, the impact of law and economics has exceeded its planned ambitions. One effect of the incorporation of economics into the study of law was to irreversibly transform traditional legal methodology. Legal rules began to be studied as a working system, a clear change from the Langdellian tradition, which had relied almost exclusively on the self-contained framework of case analysis and classification, viewing law as little more than a filing system. Economics provided the analytical rigor necessary for the study of the vast body of legal rules present in a modern legal system. This intellectual revolution came at an appropriate time, when legal academia was actively searching for a tool that permitted critical appraisal of the law, rather than merely strengthening the dogmatic consistencies of the system.

The marriage of law and economics has also affected the economic profession, contributing to the expansion of the original domain of microeconomic analysis, the study of individual and organizational choices in the market, to the study and understanding of other institutions and non-market phenomena.

2. The Methodology of Law and Economics

Despite the powerful analytical reach of economics, it was clear from the outset that the economist's competence in the evaluation of legal issues was limited. While the economist's perspective could prove crucial for the positive analysis of the efficiency of alternative legal rules and the study of the effects of alternative rules on the distribution of wealth and income, economists generally recognized the limits of their role in providing normative prescriptions for social change or legal reform.

Recognition of the positive nature of the economic analysis of law was not sufficient to dispel the many misunderstandings and controversies in legal academia engendered by the law and economics movement's methodological revolution. As Coase (1978) indicated, the cohesiveness of economic techniques makes it possible for economics to move successfully into another field, such as law, and dominate it intellectually. But methodological differences played an important part in the uneasy marriage between law and economics. The Popperian methodology of positive science was in many respects at odds with the existing paradigms of legal analysis. Rowley (1981) characterizes such differences, observing that positive economics follow the Popperian approach, whereby testable hypotheses (or models) are derived by means of logical deduction, then tested empirically. Anglo-American legal analysis, on the other hand, is generally inductive: lawyers use individual judgments to construct a general premise of law. Much work has been done in law and economics despite these methodological differences, with a reciprocal enrichment of the analytical tools of both disciplines.

Law and economics relies on the standard economic assumption that individuals are rational maximizers, and studies the role of law as a means for changing the relative prices attached to alternative individual actions. Under this approach, a change in the rule of law will affect human behavior by altering the relative price structure, and thus the constraint, of the optimization problem. Wealth maximization, serving as a paradigm for the analysis of law, can thus be promoted or constrained by legal rules.

The early years of law and economics were characterized by the uneasiness of some traditional legal scholars in the acceptance of the notion of wealth maximization as an ancillary paradigm of justice. Although most of the differences gradually proved to be largely verbal, and many others were dispelled by the gradual acceptance of a distinction between paradigms of utility maximization and wealth maximization, two objections continue to affect the lines of the debate. The first relates to the need for specifying an initial set of individual entitlements or rights, as a necessary prerequisite for operationalizing wealth maximization. The second springs from the theoretical difficulty of defining the proper role of efficiency as an ingredient of justice, vis-à-vis other social goals. Calabresi (1980) claims that an increase in wealth cannot constitute social improvement unless it furthers some other goal, such as utility or equality. Denying that one can trade off efficiency against justice, he argues instead that efficiency and distribution are ingredients of justice, which is a goal of a different order than either of these ingredients. Calabresi thus defends law and economics as a worthy examination of certain ingredients of justice, rather than a direct examination of justice itself.

In his well-known defense of wealth maximization as a guide for judicial action, Posner (1985) distinguishes wealth or expected utility from market prices. While market prices may not always fully reflect idiosyncratic valuations, they avoid an undertaking of interpersonal utility comparisons, with the opportunity for *ex post* rationalization of positions taken on emotional grounds. Posner's view is sympathetic to the premises of a property right approach to legal relationships, and he stresses the importance of an initial distribution of property rights prior to any calculation of wealth maximization. His paradigm of wealth maximization serves as a common denominator for both utilitarian and individualist perspectives. By combining elements of both, Posner provides a theory of wealth maximization that comes closer to a consensus political philosophy than does any other overarching political principle.

The intellectual resistance that has characterized the birth of law and economics can only be temporary. Both legal practitioners and policymakers are becoming aware of the important role of economic analysis in their discipline, and we have already mentioned notable contributions to mainstream economic theory from lawyers in the law and economics movement. Likewise, as Coase (1978) noted, economists have come to realize that the other social sciences are so intertwined with the economic system as to be part of the system itself. For this reason, law and economics can no longer be appraised as a branch of applied microeconomics; rather, it must be seen as contributing to a better understanding of the economic system itself. The study of the effects of other social sciences on the economic system will, Coase predicts, become a permanent part of the field of economics.

Coase (1978) also examines the reasons for the movement of economists into the other social sciences, and attempts to predict the future of this phenomenon. Groups of scholars are bound together by common techniques of analysis, a common theory or approach to the subject, and/or a common subject matter. In the short run, Coase maintains, one group's techniques of analysis may give it such advantages that it is able to move successfully into another field and maybe even dominate it. In the long run, however, the subject matter tends to be the dominant cohesive force. While the analytical techniques employed by economists, such as linear programming, quantitative methods, and cost–benefit analysis, may recently have aided the entry of economists into the other social sciences, Coase predicts that such a movement can only be temporary. After all, the wisdom possessed by economists, once its value is recognized, will be acquired by some of the practitioners in these other fields, as is happening in the field of law.

As the domain of law and economics continues to expand, its perspective on methodological issues has not been stagnant. While this survey emphasizes the wide range of substantive applications, some degree of controversy still surrounds several of the methodological, normative, and philosophical underpinnings of the economic approach to law. Most of the ideological differences tend to lose significance because their operational paradigms often lead to analogous results when applied to real cases. Some scholars, however, perceive that the current state of law and economics is comparable to the state of economics prior to the advent of public choice theory, insofar as an understanding of political failures was missing from the study of market failures (Buchanan, 1974; Rowley, 1989). Public choice may indeed inject a skeptical, and at times disruptive, perspective into the more elegant and simple framework of neoclassical economics, but this added element may well be necessary to better understand a complex reality. In many ways, the systematic incorporation of public choice theory into the economic approach to law has helped bridge the conflicting normative perspectives in law and economics, at least by bringing the debate onto the more solid ground of collective choice theory.

FRANCESCO PARISI

REFERENCES

Jeremy Bentham (1782). *Of Laws in General.*
Jeremy Bentham (1789). *Introduction to the Principles of Morals and Legislation.*

James Buchanan (1974). "Good economics–bad law." *Virginia Law Review*, 60: 483–492.
Guido Calabresi (1980). "About law and economics: a letter to Ronald Dworkin." *Hofstra Law Review*, 8: 553–562.
Ronald H. Coase (1978). "Economics and contiguous disciplines." *Journal of Legal Studies*, 7: 201–211.
Richard A. Posner (1985). "Wealth maximization revisited." *Notre Dame Journal of Law, Ethics, and Public Policy*, 2: 85–105.
Charles K. Rowley (1981). "Social sciences and the law: the relevance of economic theories." *Oxford Journal of Legal Studies*, 1: 391–405.
Charles K. Rowley (1989). "The common law in public choice perspective: a theoretical and institutional critique." *Hamline Law Review*, 12: 355–383.
Adam Smith (1776). *An Inquiry into the Nature and Causes of the Wealth of Nations.*

LEGAL PRECEDENTS AND JUDICIAL DISCRETION

A prominent European legal theorist, commenting on the notion of legal logic, cynically wrote: I have to confess that, as time passes, my distrust for legal logic increases (Calamandrei, 1965: 604). Calamandrei's distrust resurfaces in a number of recent legal analyses discussing the difficulties encountered in applying legal rules and judicial precedents to an ever-changing pattern of factual circumstances and underlying policy concerns. Taken as a whole, the analyses suggest that Calamandrei's distrust of legal logic can be viewed as a methodological tension with two orientations. The first orientation would limit the judiciary's role to finding the predetermined and objective meaning of legal rules. The second would expand the role of the judiciary to go beyond such a formal search for meaning, in recognition of the fact that some interpretative discretion is a necessary component of the decision-making process. This methodological tension, which some legal theorists have described as the relation between semantics and pragmatics, can be presented in many areas of application as a distinction between meaning and interpretation of legal precedents in the decision-making process.

1. *Stare Decisis* and *Jurisprudence Constante* in Early Legal Systems

The rules of precedent under common law and civil legal systems present an interesting subject matter for comparative economic investigation. Historically, the common law and civilian approach to judicial precedent share a foundation in customary law. In spite of previously held beliefs to the contrary, scholars have established that it was not until the mid-19th century that the Common law rule of precedent developed into a formal rule of *stare decisis*. As a general trend, common law jurisdictions are bound by a single court decision, whereas some civilian and mixed jurisdictions only require a continuous line of precedents before recognizing a rule of *jurisprudence constante*, which courts will follow as an authoritative secondary source of law.

There are substantial historical and conceptual differences between the doctrines of precedent in common law and civil law traditions. Both legal traditions share a common original conception of legal precedent as the presence of a sequence of consistent decisions in similar cases over time. Under Roman law, 2nd century A.D., the first conception of the authoritative force of precedent is in fact tied to the concept of a line of decisions in agreement. To a greater or lesser degree, the relevance of past decisions for the adjudication of pending cases became a universal characteristic of all early legal systems. Yet in the common law's formative stages, legal precedent, as it is known today, was not recognized as such (Hale, 1713; Postema, 1987). Under common law, the writings of Hale confirm the first notion of the evidentiary role of precedent when a series of consistent decisions over time is established (Hale, 1713: 68). The common law did not construct a system of case law through the explicit authority of cases (Sweeney, 1960). From the 12th to 17th century, judicial decisions were used to illustrate legal principles, but did not represent a binding source of law. Bracton's seminal 13th century treatise, for instance, although documenting some 500 decided cases, does not once imply the existence a doctrine of precedent (Plucknett, 1956).

2. Modern Doctrines of Legal Precedent

The principle of precedent, in its modern connotations, first emerged at the end of the 16th century when common law courts started to adhere to previous custom in matters of procedure and pleading (Berman and Reid, 1964: 446). However, it was not until the 17th and 18th centuries that a substantive rule of precedent developed, although by then it was intertwined with the tradition of customary law. The view at the time, as recorded by Blackstone, was that common law consisted of the original common custom, the effect of which the courts merely declared (Blackstone, 1764). According to the declaratory theory of precedents, legal principles exist because of their emergence and acceptance as social and legal customs, and because of their articulation in case law. Judicial decisions "find" such law

and provide a valuable written articulation of such principles, providing persuasive evidence of their content and existence. The presence of several cases recognizing the same legal principle increased the pervasiveness of such judicial articulations of common customs. In this way, the role of precedent was one of customary law, where a courts decision attained authoritative force when it was affirmed by a sequence of consistent decisions over time. In Hale's view, "a line of judicial decisions consistently applying a legal principle or legal rule to various analogous fact situations is 'evidence' of ... the existence and the validity of such a principle or rule" (Berman and Reid, 1964: 448).

At the end of the 19th century the concept of formally binding rules of precedent was established (Evans, 1987: 36–72). Under Bentham's positivist influence, the doctrine of *stare decisis* moved from practice to principle under common law, creating the notion of binding authority of precedent. The common law at that stage passed from "a time when what was said in the course of cases was evidence of law of the legal custom applying in common to all parts of the realm to a time when the law pronounced in the cases was itself the material of a substantial part of the system of law" (Evans, 1987: 36). Under the doctrine of *stare decisis*, a rule of law framed in one case under common law serves as binding authority to resolve future cases that are analogous.

Meanwhile, civilian continental systems underwent a quite different evolution driven by the greater weight recognized to the written Romanistic sources and the more codified role played by customary law in private matters. Civil law systems did not undergo such a dramatic shift from customary judge-made law to a formal theory of adjudicative legal rule-making. Instead, the notion of precedential authority remained strictly confined within the tradition of customary law. Moreover, civilian systems have, in various forms, adhered to a notion of informal precedent where it is generally held that the persuasive force of a precedent requires a sequence of analogous cases. Under French law, this doctrinal construction, also know as *arret de principe*, holds that a series of decisions, all in accord, give bearing to an established rule of law. Generally, a judge in France does not consider himself bound in any way by a single decision in a single previous instance. Rather, considerable authoritative force stems from a trend of decisions on a certain point. Indeed, as one distinguished legal writer states: "[t]he practice of the courts does not become a source of law until it is definitely fixed by the repetition of precedents which are in agreement on a single point" (Lambert, 1929: 14).

Similarly, Louisiana law provides that a precedent becomes a source of law when it has become "settled jurisprudence" (*jurisprudence constante*). As pointed out by Louisiana Supreme Court Justice James Dennis, "[w]hen a series of decisions forms a constant stream of uniform and homogeneous rulings having the same reasoning, the doctrine accords the cases considerable persuasive authority and justifies, without requiring, the court in abstaining from new inquiry because of its faith in the precedents" (Dennis, 1993). Likewise, Germany has adopted the notion that a long line of decisions on a certain subject may be taken to create a sort of judicial custom. A line of precedent that has been standing for some time is referred to as "permanent adjudication" (*standige Rechtsprechung*) (Dainow, 1974). These examples are representative of a general trend within civilian jurisdictions of according a continuous line of jurisprudence the authority of customary law.

Of course, both the common law and civilian approaches to precedent reflect fundamentally different views as to the nature and source of law-making. Whereas, under civil law, legislation and custom are considered the primary sources of law, the common law emphasizes court decision-making as a principal source of law. These historically different roles of the judiciary in the civil and common law traditions are related to the different ideological emphasis placed on certainty, equity, and discretion in court decisions in those legal traditions.

The argument is sometimes made that both systems have converged. Civilian systems increasingly recognize the binding force of vertical precedents formally when originating from the highest national court, while at the same time the influence of precedent has been gradually weakened in the U.S. Both approaches resemble — more in theory, less in practice — different answers to the questions of when a court decision creates a binding rule of law.

3. Economic Theories of *Stare Decisis* and Legal Precedents

Judge Posner's famous claim that the common law is efficient, whereas statute law is more concerned with redistribution toward special interest, rests largely on an intuitive theory of judicial behavior. Since judges are isolated from market pressure and they lack the tools for distributive policy-making, the remaining benchmark is the efficiency criterion (Posner, 1992). Despite their intuitive appeal, subsequent attempts to measure judicial utility functions in terms of economically relevant and observable variables have not been very successful (Higgins and Rubin, 1980).

Apart from normative claims of judicial preference for utility maximization, subsequent evolutionary models have focused upon the conflicting and procedural nature of common law litigation, of which the rule of precedent is a major component. Broadly, there are two ways in which a precedent-based process may affect the overall efficiency of the common law. From an evolutionary perspective, the rule of precedent might drive the legal system to outcomes that are, in economic terms, efficient. Otherwise, the process of precedent may provide a cost-effective mechanism for judges to allocate the legal system's scare resources in adjudication, a type of internal or allocative efficiency.

A pioneering strand of literature claims that the common law tends towards a natural selection of efficient law. This is done regardless of any bias or competence on behalf of judges, yet it is done as a result of utility maximizing decision-making by litigants. Under these litigant-driven models of evolutionary change, inefficient precedents are more likely to be subject to repeated litigation because they impose deadweight losses on the losing parties (Rubin, 1979), create larger stakes on which to litigate (Priest, 1977), and lead those that stand to benefit from an efficient rule to increased investment in litigation expenses (Goodman, 1979). The main contribution of these studies is the shift of focus from tentative theories of judicial behavior to the wealth maximizing behavior of litigants. Over the years, the litigant-driven models of evolutionary change have been challenged on several fronts. In particular, the incorporation of a true system of precedent into the analysis of evolutionary models of the common law grants significant weight to aged decisions. Since current decisions have small and symmetric effects on the state of the law or balance of precedents, the decisions will be taken into account by parties when deciding to litigate. Most importantly, rather than facing a binary, all-or-nothing outcome, a litigant seeking to reverse a precedent will need to take into account the possibility that precedent may also be strengthened rather than simply reversed or maintained (Landes and Posner, 1979: 260). Given the high probability of obtaining an analogous decision to the precedent, it can be expected that efficient, rather than inefficient, decisions will be relitigated, leading them to be strengthened (affirmed), instead of weakened (reversed) (Landes and Posner, 1979: 261). The effect of a precedent-based system and the symmetric nature of relitigation decisions thus cuts against the evolutionary drive towards efficiency. Furthermore, litigant driven evolutionary change — without judicial insight — might improve the law relative to what it would be in its absence, but there is no systematic propensity towards a maximum economic efficiency or continuous improvement thereof (Cooter and Kornhauser, 1980). Also, as Roe (1996) points out, the predictive value of the evolutionary model is constrained by such factors as accidental conditions, path dependence and evolutionary accidents.

However, public choice arguments may in fact tilt the balance in the opposite direction. Independent of efficiency, the law can be expected to favor whichever party could most easily organize and mobilize resources to reverse unfavorable precedents (Gallenter, 1974). In this sense, common law and statutory law may not be so different after all (Tullock, 1980). Similarly, where attorneys have a financial interest in the outcome of litigation, their interest in precedent may decide the build of the law, especially in areas of law where there are no other organized parties with strong interests in precedent, such as tort law, divorce, and criminal law (Rubin and Bailey, 1994: 825–828). In a recent paper dealing with the public choice aspects of tort law, Zywicki (2001) maintains that the doctrine of *stare decisis* creates high-priced opportunities for special interest groups. Because *stare decisis* generates long-term, stable precedents that secure returns over extended time, it increases the stakes of litigants and induces rent-seeking expenses. Depoorter and Parisi (2001) present a comparative economic investigation of the rule of precedent under both common law and civilian legal systems. Their economic model suggests that the Court should follow precedent when the savings in litigation costs and adjustment costs expected to flow from such a move outweigh the expected error costs associated with the precedent. In other words, the Court generally recognizes exceptions to the rule of *stare decisis* only when the expected error costs associated with keeping a precedent outweigh the litigation and adjustment costs expected to result from overruling that precedent. The optimal timing for the consolidation of binding precedents depends on environmental parameters such as the technical difficulty of the decision, the likelihood of judicial errors, the political stability, and honesty of the judiciary. Longer time requirements for the consolidation of precedents reduce the capture ability of rent-seekers trying to manipulate the course of the law through leading cases.

On a different level, the internal or allocative economic efficiency of a precedent controlled system of adjudication is straightforward. The procedural rules of the common law, with their communication and information-enhancing aspects, provide key components to the effectiveness of common law's alleged efficiency. *Stare decisis* thus serves the purpose of preserving the integrity of information within the judiciary. Conform with standard solutions in communication theory that prescribe the usage of redundancy in settings of noise problems a non-hierarchical, resource limited judiciary uses a redundancy-based transmission system in the form of *stare decisis*. The theory of precedent thus resembles a "redundancy" communication tactic — the introduction of repetition or pattern into messages — whereby the value of precedents is not informative as much as communicative (Macey, 1989). The U.S. system of the rule of precedent can be understood by regarding the judiciary as a resource-constrained team that seeks to minimize the expected number of correct decisions within its fixed limitations. Thus, strict vertical precedent at the trial level and strict horizontal precedent at the appellate level are in line with the organizational aim of maximizing the expected number of correct decisions, while minimizing judicial resources per case (Kornhauser, 1995).

More generally, uncertainty in the system prevents legal actors from responding optimally to all information that might be used in the judicial process. The limitations faced by rational actors in handling complex and non-local information used in legal decisions created the need for courts to reason by analogy with past decisions, such as is the case under *stare decisis* (Heiner, 1986). Finally, *stare decisis* has also been explained as result of judges' preference for the doctrine. A game theoretic model demonstrates how *stare decisis* offers a superior mechanism for judges to impose their normative views, beliefs and mores, while preventing destructive competition among them (O'Hara, 1993).

BEN DEOORTER
FRANCESCO PARISI

REFERENCES

Bentham, Jeremy (1989). *Of Laws in General*. London: University of London, Athlone Press.

Berman, Harold J. and Reid, Charles J. Jr. (1996). "The transformation of English legal science: from Hale to Blackstone." *Emory Law Journal*, 45: 437.

Blackstone (1764). *Commentaries*. Chicago: University of Chicago Press, 1979.

Calamandrei, Pietro (1965). "La funzione della giurisprudenza, nel tempo presente." *Opere giuridiche*, I: 602–604.

Cooter, Robert D. (1983). "The objectives of private and public judges." *Public Choice*, 41: 107–132.

Cooter, Robert D. and Kornhauser, Lewis A. (1980). "Can litigation improve the law without the help of judges?" *Journal of Legal Studies*, 9: 139–163.

Crew, Michael A. and Twight, Charlotte (1990). "On the efficiency of law: a public choice perspective." *Public Choice*, 66: 15–136.

Cutler, A. and Nye, D. (1983). *Justice and Predictability*. London: Macmillan.

Dainow, Joseph (1974). *The Role of Judicial Decisions and Doctrine in Civil Law and Mixed Jurisdictions*. Baton Rouge: LSU Press, pp. 133–164.

Dennis, James L. (1993). "The John Tucker, Jr. lecture in civil law: interpretation and application of the civil code and the evaluation of judicial precedent." *La. Law Review*, 54(1): 15.

Depoorter, Ben W.F. and Parisi, Francesco (2001). "Stare decisis, Jurisprudence Constante and the optimal timing of legal precedents." Unpublished manuscript.

Evans, Jim (1987). "Change in the doctrine of precedent during the nineteenth century," in L. Goldstein, Laurence (ed.) *Precedent in Law*. Oxford: Clarendon Press, pp. 35–72.

Gallanter, Marc (1974). "Why the haves come out ahead: speculation on the limits of legal change." *Law and Society Review*, 9(Fall): 95.

Goodman, John C. (1979). "An economic theory of the evolution of the common law." *Journal of Legal Studies*, 7: 235.

Hale, Matthew (1713). *The History of the Common Law of England*. Chicago: University of Chicago Press (1971).

Heiner, Ronald A. (1986). "Imperfect decisions and the law: on the evolution of legal precedent and rules." *Journal of Legal Studies*, 15: 227–261.

Higgins, Richard S. and Rubin, Paul H. (1980). "Judicial discretion." *Journal of Legal Studies*, 9: 129–138.

Kornhauser, Lewis A. (1995). "Adjudication by a resource-constrained team: hierarchy and precedent in a judicial system." *Southern California Law Review*, 68: 1605.

Lambert (1929). "Case method in Canada." *Yale Law Journal*, 39: 1.

Landes, William M. and Posner, Richard A. (1976). "Legal precedent: a theoretical and empirical analysis." *Journal of Law and Economics*, 19: 249–307.

Landes, William and Posner, Richard (1980). "Legal change, judicial behavior, and the diversity jurisdiction." *Journal of Legal Studies*, 9: 367–386.

Macey, Jonathan R. (1989). "The internal and external costs and benefits of stare decisis." *Chicago-Kent Law Review*, 65: 93–113.

Macey, Jonathan R. (1994). "Judicial preferences, public choice, and the rules of procedure." *Journal of Legal Studies*, 23: 627–646.

Moreno, Richard D. (1995). "Scott v. Cokern: of precedent, jurisprudence constante, and the relationship between Louisiana commercial laws and Louisiana pledge jurisprudence." *Tulane European and Civil Law Forum*, 10: 31.

O'Hara, Erin (1993). "Social constraint or implicit collusion? Toward a game theoretic analysis of stare decisis." *Seton Hall Law Review*, 24: 736–778.

Plucknett, Theodore F.T. (1956). *A Concise History of the Common Law*. London: Butterworth.

Posner, Richard A. (1992). *Economic Analysis of Law*, (Fourth Edition). Boston: Little, Brown.

Postema, Gerald J. (1987). "Some roots of the notion of precedent," in L. Goldstein (ed.), *Precedent in Law*, 9. Oxford: Clarendon Press.

Priest, George L. (1977). "The common law process and the selection of efficient rules." *Journal of Legal Studies*, 6: 65–82.

Roe, Mark J. (1996). "Chaos and evolution in law and economics." *Harvard Law Review*, 109: 641–668.

Rubin, Paul H. (1977). "Why is the common law efficient?" *Journal of Legal Studies*, 6: 51.

Rubin, Paul H. (1982). "Common law and statute law." *Journal of Legal Studies*, 11: 205–223.

Rubin, Paul H. and Bailey, Martin J. (1994). "The role of lawyers in changing the law." *Journal of Legal Studies*, 23: 807.

Schwartz, Edward P. (1992). "Policy, precedent, and power: a positive theory of Supreme Court decision making." *Journal of Law, Economics, and Organization*, 8: 219–252.

Shapiro, Martin M. (1972). "Toward a theory of stare decisis." *Journal of Legal Studies*, 1: 125–134.

Stewart, Richard B. (1979). "The resource allocating role of reviewing courts: common law functions in a regulatory era," in Clifford S. Russell (ed.) *Collective Decision Making*. Baltimore: Johns Hopkins University Press, p. 205.

Tullock, Gordon (1980). *Trails on Trail: The Pure Theory of Legal Procedure*. New York: Columbia University Press.

Von Wangenheim, Georg (1993). "The evolution of judge made law." *International Review of Law and Economics*, 13: 381–411.

Zywicki, Todd (2001). "A supply analysis of efficiency in the common law." Unpublished manuscript.

LEGAL RULES AND STANDARDS

1. Costs of Rules and Standards

Rules are those legal commands which differentiate legal from illegal behavior in a simple and clear way. Standards, however, are general legal criteria which are unclear and fuzzy and require complicated judiciary decision making (Diver, 1983; Kaplow, 1992). A speed limit whose violation leads to a fine of 100 $ is a rule, whereas a norm for car drivers to "drive carefully" whose violation leads to damage compensation is a standard. In the latter case the legal norm leaves open what exactly the level of due care is and how the damage compensation is to be calculated (Ulen, 1999).

The principal choice between rules and standards has to do with the relative size of the various costs associated with the formulation and enforcement of legal norms. There are systematic factors which affect the relative cost of rules and standards. One of the first and most important contributions to the matter of rules versus standards is the work by Judge Posner, who has identified the central efficiency implications (Posner, 1998). His main contention is that standards may have lower initial specification costs, but they have higher enforcement and compliance costs than rules. There are thus three different costs associated with a legal norm, (1) the costs of norm specification, (2) the costs of rule adjudication, and (3) the costs of compliance with a legal norm, especially the costs resulting from legal uncertainty. For instance, promulgating the standard "to take reasonable care in all matters" is extremely easy and does not generate any specification cost at all. However, applying this standard in practice would generate significant costs for both judges, who have to determine whether the defendants have complied with the standard (costs of adjudication), and for the defendants, who had to determine what level of precaution was necessary in their view in order to escape liability. In the case of precise rules, the relative size of costs is exactly vice versa. Judge Posner concludes that the desire to minimize total costs should be the dominant consideration in the choice between precision and generality, that is between rules and standards.

An important insight brought up by Kaplow may substantially help decide when to use rules and when to use standards and has to do with the extent to which the law should be given content before individuals act (rules) rather than waiting until afterwards (standards) (Kaplow, 1992, 1999). Since the cost of specifying a rule is initially greater than for a standard, but results in savings for judges and individuals later on. Individuals must must take costly decisions not knowing how the law applies to behavior and judges must apply the law to past behavior. It follows that the relative advantage of rules lies in situations in which there will be frequent application of the rule and the incidence of adjudication may also be frequent. As a result, the central factor influencing the desirability of rules and standards is, to a great extent, the frequency with which a law will govern conduct. If a specific mode of conduct will be frequent, the additional costs of designing rules — which have to be borne only once — are likely to be exceeded by the savings of judges and individuals. Examples are situations that occur frequently in the lives of many people such as traffic laws. In contrast, standards are more efficient when the the law is related to more heterogeneous areas. Determining the appropriate content of the law for all such contingencies would be very expensive and, in many cases, simply a waste. It can therefore be concluded that in those areas of the law in which economic and social conditions change frequently and with them the optimal set of legal decisions standards are more efficient than rules.

2. Rules versus Standards and the Division of Labour between the Legislator and the Judiciary

Another important aspect is that the degree of preciseness in legal statutes defines to a large extent the division of labor between parliaments on the one hand and the judiciary as well as the bureaucracy on the other. A law consisting of rules leaves little or no discretionary power to those

who administer it. And a law consisting of imprecise standards delegates the refinement of the standard to the judiciary or the bureaucracy. If parliaments have little knowledge about what a reasonable standard of care is, they are well advised to delegate these decisions to courts. Courts, or better the system of courts, can then learn in a decentralized way. Gradually, by way of many different court decisions which become unified by supreme court rulings, the imprecise standard is gradually transformed into more precise rules. This also gradually reduces costs of uncertainty for the citizens, who have to comply with legal norms. This mechanism, however, requires a civil service and a judiciary which is well trained to cope with unstructured decision situations and has the skill and the information to arrive at precise and efficient decisions on the basis of unclear rules.

3. Rules can Reduce the Costs of Monitoring

The use of imprecise standards which give ample space for discretionary decisions creates additional possibilities for corrupt behavior in countries where corruption of government officials and the judiciary is a problem. If for instance the use of all toxic substances is forbidden there is more ample space for corruption of officials without a complete list containing all these substances, because this leaves the decision to sort out what is toxic to the official (Kaplow, 1999). If an official turns a blind eye to the use of a substance which is on a list, his corrupt behavior can be easier monitored in case of a rule than in case of a standard which leaves the definition of toxicity to the official himself. This holds for many other administrative legal norms, such as import and export restrictions, safety regulation, food and drug control, regulation of banks and capital markets. The same holds for the rules of property, contract and tort law. A corrupt judge who adjudicates rules is therefore subject to easier monitoring and critique than in a system which requires subtle arguments for adjudication. For the same reason per se rules which apply without the possibility of a defense by the defendant might be preferable. Any defense, for instance an efficiency defense in antitrust cases, might lead to decisions which are obscured for an outside observer and therefore might widen the scope for willful decisions of administrators and courts.

For similar reasons it has been argued that precise rules which leave little descretion to administrative agencies can better protect civil liberties and political rights than standards, as the violation of the law can easily be observed (Sunstein, 1995). The "void for vagueness" doctrine is based in part on this observation.

The contention that rules always lead to better information and easier monitoring is however not unchallenged. Rules may be enacted so as to give the impression of taking some action. In reality the rule may be a poor one inaccurate and not enforced (Baldwin, 1995). Or rules may be contradictory thus increasing rather than reducing discretion of agencies. Or they may be overcomplex with exceptions and exceptions from the exceptions.

4. Rules Allow for the Concentration of Human Capital

The use of imprecise standards in legal texts and their superiority over rules is often defended on the grounds that the central authority lacks the information to set a good rule and that the administration of the legal norm should be left to the decentralized system of court decisions. Thus the legal norms, which might be very fuzzy in the beginning, become more and more precise by way of precedents set by the higher courts. And the fuzzy legal command to act carefully is then transformed into a long list of precise prescriptions related to various categories of damages. This decentralized learning and with it the gradual transformation of imprecise standards into precise rules is regarded as one of the major advantages of the court system in which judges have ample space for decisions.

But this system might not work very well, if the decision makers have little information or little expertise or if they are not well trained for taking complex decisions. This might be the case in poor countries, where information is more difficult to obtain and the stock of human capital is lower than in developed countries. The learning process of a judiciary might then be too slow, legal uncertainty prevails over too long periods and the result is not a gradual shift from standards to judge made rules but a long-lasting and costly uncertainty for those who are obliged to obey legal norms. A legal system, which allows judges to take routine decisions which require little information processing might be a more appealing system for developing countries.

5. Parliament Rules and Standards from an Interest Group Perspective

Advocating more precise rules by parliaments disregards the findings of the positive theory of regulation. Regulatory laws are often not in the public interest because influential interest groups can induce parliaments to enact statutes in their favor. Legislation might be influenced by corruption, capture and by the interests of the state bureaucracy. The court system as a whole, however, cannot easily be influenced by interest groups. Even if parts of the judiciary are corrupt, the eventual outcome of the decentralized learning process of the judiciary is more difficult to push into a certain direction than decisions of parliament.

The development of judge made law based on vague standards might therefore lead to superior solutions as compared to parliamentary law, independent of all considerations regarding the division of labor between parliament and the judiciary and the different knowledge and expertise of judges and members of parliament. Shifting rule making more to parliaments might aggravate the problems of interest group influence — an adverse effect which has to be traded off against the gains of more precise parliamentary rules.

6. From Rules to Standards, some Evidence from History

A historical tendency of a development from rules to standards is observable since the age of mercantilism, i.e. the period from the late 16th century. In Europe this period is marked by two outstanding legal developments, the rise of regulatory law and a state bureaucracy on the one hand, and the codification of other legal materials especially civil law on the other.

Politeia law (in German Polizeyrecht) evolved in Europe since the early 16th century. It regulated many areas of life hitherto either unregulated or regulated by local custom or law. In the 16th and 17th century many countries such as Sweden, Denmark, German states, the Netherlands, Spain and Italian states issued statutes regulating in detail personal and economic behavior (Stolleis, 1996). Also in England comparable statutes were introduced

The codifications of the 18th and 19th century provide another example of rule based law, which was aimed at leaving little discretionary power to judges in general and to judges of lower instances in particular. It was even at times forbidden to write commentaries to the law, because every decision should be deducted from the legal text by way of pure syllogistic deduction. In the state of Pruzzia the "Preussisches Allgemeines Landrecht", enacted 1794 after decades of drafting, had more than 19,000 articles, four times more than the modern civil code and the criminal code of Germany taken together. In the early codes any standards were regarded with the utmost distrust by the lawmakers. If a judge had doubts about the interpretation, he had to ask a royal commission for an authoritative interpretation. The authors of these codifications were aware that not all cases could be solved by way of deduction from the legal text, but they tried to make the law as crystal clear as possible and to have the solution of all future cases contained in it as far as possible. Also in France the prevailing view was that of a judge taking syllogistic decisions. "Le juge est le bouche de la lois".

A predominant view among legal historians is that the high level of preciseness in the codes was driven by the strive for power of the absolute Monarchs, who made and enacted the laws by decree and did not wish to share power with the administration and judiciary. But an alternative explanation might be that this concentration of decision power at the central level of the legal system was a substitute for human capital at lower levels.

Legal centralization faded away during the 20th century. For example in Germany it seems to be little disputed that in the 20th Century legislators in Germany more often than before resorted to standards, and that the supreme courts increasingly used vague standards for the interpretation of the law. It is a well established fact that between 1890 and 1930 the German civil courts changed substantially their jurisdiction and based it on standards and not — as before- on rules. Hedemann (1933) refers to the vague standard of the "*exceptio doli generalis*" in contract law. This exception from the rule based formality of the civil law was seldom used in practice until the end of the19th century according to Hedemann. It was never used by the Reichsgericht (Supreme court) during the first 17 years of its existence after 1879, and only ten times during the first 30 years. But after the year 1900 jurisdiction became "overflooded" with its use (Hedemann, 1933). This development can be shown for other standards in the German civil code as well, whose importance was originally very limited but later became predominant in many fields of Civil Law. Large fields of the law, in which the legislator remained inactive, were newly developed by judges, such as labor law, antitrust law, housing law, copyright law and corporation law by resorting to the interpretation of vague standards. Bona fides, originally a norm to deal with some exceptional cases, became an important legal principle of German contract law.

Thus there is some conclusive evidence that at least in some European states the law of modern times was rule based at the beginning and later on developed to a more standard based system, in which far reaching decisions are made by the administration and the courts. This supports the view that economic development causes the legal system to shift towards standards with the resulting effect of a decentralisation of competences.

HANS-BERND SCHAEFER

REFERENCES

Baird, D.G. and Weisberg, R. (1982). "Rules, standards, and the battle of the forms: a reassessment of §2-207." *Virginia Law Review*, 1217–1262.

Baldwin, R. (1995). *Rules and Government*. Oxford, Clarendon Press

Diver, C.S. (1983). "The optimal precision of administrative rules" *Yale Law Journal*, 93: 65–109.

Ehrlich, I. and Posner, R.A. (1974). "An economic analysis of legal rulemaking." *Journal of Legal Studies*, 3: 257–286.

Ebel, W. (1956). *Geschichte der Gesetzgebung in Deutschland*. Hannover.

Hedemann, J.W. (1933). *Die Flucht in die Generalklauseln, Eine Gefahr für Recht und Staat*. Verlag Mohr: Tübingen.

Kaplow, L. (1992). "Rules versus standards, an economic analysis." *Duke Law Journal*, 557–629.

Kaplow, L. (1999). "General characteristics of rules," in Boudewijn Bouckaert and Gerrit Dem Geest (eds) *Encyclopedia of Law and Economics, Volume. V, The Economics of Crime and Litigation, No. (9000)*. Cheltenham: Edward Elgar, pp. 502–528.

Kennedy, D. (1976). "Form and Substance in private law adjudication," *Harvard Law Review*, 1685–1778.

Nonet, P. and Selznick, P. (1978). *Law and Society in Transition: Toward Responsive Law*. New York.

Posner, R.A. (1998a). Economic Analysis of Law (Fifth Edition). New York: Aspen Law and Business.

Posner, R.A. (1998b). "Creating a legal framework for economic development." *World Bank Research Observer*, 13: 1.

Rose, C.M. (1988). "Crystals and mud in property law." *Stanford Law Review*, 577–610.

Stolleis, M. (1996). (Hrsg.) *Polizey im Europa der frühen Neuzeit*. Frankfurt/Main.

Sunstein, C.R. (1995). "Problems with rules." *Cal. Law. Rev.* 83: 953–1023.

Ulen, Thomas S. (1999). "Standards und direktiven im lichte begrenzter rationalität," in Ott and Schäfer (eds.) *Die Präventivwirkung zivil- und strafrechtlicher Sanktionen*. Tübingen, pp. 346–380.

LEGISLATIVE POLITICS

> In framing a government which is to be administered by men over men, the great difficulty lies in this: you must first enable the government to control the governed; and in the next place oblige it to control itself. (James Madison, *Federalist* No. 51)

'All politics is local', according to the late Massachusetts Democrat and House Speaker Thomas P. ('Tip') O'Neill. Nowhere is that adage truer than in geographically based representative democracies.

Direct democracy, whereby political decisions are taken by the enfranchised polity as a whole, is certainly not unknown. That method of collective decision-making is utilized in many townships in the United States and some municipalities in Switzerland. Voter referenda and citizen initiatives for such purposes as approving bond issues and amending constitutions are common features of US state and local governmental processes (Sass, 2001: 157); referenda are likewise used extensively in the EU for important constitutional issues. Moreover, the institution of direct democracy is likely to be exploited more frequently in future as changes in information technology continue to lower its costs. It is nevertheless true that, because the cost of group decision-making rises sharply with group size (Buchanan and Tullock, 1962; Olson, 1965), in most democratic societies ordinary citizens delegate decision-making authority to politicians they elect to represent them in a legislature or parliament.

The legislative assemblies that, through the enactment of laws, conduct the ordinary political business of representative democracies exhibit astonishing diversity around the globe. Buchanan and Tullock (1962: 223–224) identify four key constitutional variables that shape the form and functioning of these democratic institutions. First are the rules for electing the members of the legislature. Are legislative representatives elected by a plurality, by a simple majority, or by a qualified (say, two-thirds) majority of the enfranchised citizenry? Second are the rules that define the basis of legislative representation. Do legislators represent functional interests (e.g., labor, agriculture, property), do they have geographical constituencies, or is representation in the legislature instead based on legislators' political party affiliations and proportional to party strength in legislative vote totals? Are legislators elected at large, or is the basis of representation apportioned amongst single-member constituencies? Third are the rules that determine the degree of representation (i.e., the number of voters per representative) and, hence, the size of the legislative assembly. Fourth are the rules that govern action by the legislature itself. Can a simple majority of the members enact laws, or is a more inclusive majority required?

The constitutionally specified number of legislative chambers also belongs on this list. Is the legislature unicameral, consisting of a single body, or is it bicameral, comprising two chambers, an upper house (e.g., a Senate, a House of Lords, or a Bundesrat) and a lower house (e.g., a House of Representatives, a House of Commons, or a Bundestag)? In any case, these four (or five) variables interact to determine the constellation of interests that get represented effectively in the legislature. They do so, chiefly, by affecting two types of costs the members of the legislative assembly face. The first of these is *decision-making costs*, the direct and indirect (opportunity) costs of gathering information, negotiating vote trades, and achieving the level of agreement required for taking legislative action. Other things being the same, decision-making costs tend to rise as the size of the legislature increases, as the interests of the

constituencies represented become more heterogeneous, and as legislative voting rules become more inclusive. The second category of costs is *external costs*, the reduction in utility the members of any random minority can expect to have imposed on them because of actions taken by any random majority. Increases in the degree of representation, greater homogeneity of constituents' interests, and voting rules that are more inclusive tend to lessen these costs.

To illustrate, consider a unicameral legislature and a bicameral legislature yielding equal degrees of representation (i.e., having the same number of constituents per representative). If legislative action can be taken by simple majority votes in both cases, it follows that, in the absence of a vote cycle, similar legislative outcomes will emerge under unicameral and bicameral structures unless the members of the latter's two chambers have different bases of representation (i.e., serve different constituencies). With the same total size and the same basis of representation, the cost of obtaining a legislative majority is the same; the fact that one legislature has two houses is purely cosmetic. Now suppose that the basis of representation of the bicameral legislature's upper house differs from that of its lower house, and that legislative action requires a simple majority vote in both chambers. Given that a majority of the representatives of two constituencies, dissimilar in their respective interests, must vote favorably before the legislature acts, the cost of obtaining a legislative majority is plainly higher than it would be in a unicameral legislature of the same total size, the members of which have the same basis of representation. By increasing the cost of legislative agreement, bicameralism serves as a brake on an activist legislature.

The costs of enacting legislation in a bicameral legislature also rise with greater disparities in chamber sizes. If chamber sizes are unequal and the legislature's decision-making costs increase at an increasing rate, the cost of buying one more vote in the larger chamber will exceed the savings from buying one less vote in the smaller chamber. Assuming independence between the two chambers, it follows that the total cost of securing a bill's passage will be greater the more unequal are the sizes of a bicameral legislature's upper and lower houses (McCormick and Tollison, 1981: 44–45). These observations also suggest that legislative structures trade off in predictable ways with legislative voting rules: other things being the same, outcomes in unicameral legislatures will approximate those of bicameral legislatures only if unicameral legislatures operate by voting rules that are more inclusive than simple majority.

Total legislature size, by itself, has an ambiguous effect on the cost of legislating. On the one hand, by reducing the average number of constituents per member of the legislative assembly, larger legislatures tend to lower voters' costs of monitoring their elected representatives. On the other hand, because each member of a large legislature will have less influence on the legislative process, such monitoring will pay fewer dividends. By diluting the value of each legislator's vote, large legislatures also lower the price at which interest groups can buy influence. The effect of legislature size on the price of influence is offset to some extent by the logic of collective action (Olson, 1965), which suggests that it will be more difficult in large legislatures for a majority of the members to reach the agreement necessary to enact legislation. Votes are cheaper in large legislatures, but to assemble a majority coalition more of them must be bought.

Citizens delegate decision-making authority to their elected representatives in order to reduce their own decision-making costs. Insofar as these representatives are utility-maximizing human actors, that delegation creates a principal–agent problem for voters: legislators will pursue their own self-interests to the extent allowed by given political constraints. The seeking of personal wealth, the consuming of the perquisites of legislative office, and the angling for post-legislative-career job opportunities supply incentives for legislators to 'shirk', either by voting against their constituents' interests (Bender and Lott, 1996), or by indulging their own ideological preferences (Kau and Rubin, 1979, 1993; Rubin, 2001).

Perhaps the most salient personal goal of an elected representative is to win reelection. Because the mass of voters is rationally ignorant of the impact most of the business of the legislature has on their private wellbeing (Downs, 1957) and, moreover, because voters face serious free-rider problems in monitoring the behavior of their elected representatives and in removing them from office, the members of the legislative assembly have little motivation to advance the interests of their constituents as a whole. Bolstered by the well-known advantages of incumbency, legislators will instead cater to the demands of special-interest groups that are well organized and willing to deliver political support (i.e., campaign contributions and vote blocs) in return for promises of favorable legislative treatment.

'Pork barrel' politics is the predictable outcome of legislators' tendencies to advance the parochial interests of relevant electoral coalitions, 'however unimportant the interests may be from a national standpoint' (Posner, 1969: 83). Particularly in a geographically based representative democracy, the members of the legislative assembly will have strong incentives to support programs and policies whose benefits are concentrated on the individuals and groups important to them politically, but whose costs are distributed diffusely over the polity as a whole. While the representatives of the constituencies who will bear the tax burden of financing projects from which they derive little or no benefit would otherwise vote against the proposal, they have pet projects of their own designed to benefit their political supporters at the taxpaying public's expense. Although no one pork barrel project would pass if voted on in isolation — because its costs summed over all voters exceed the value of its narrowly focused benefits — there are obvious gains to be had from legislative vote trades. These gains can be exploited through bilateral or multilateral agreements in which a majority of the legislators each promise to vote for the others' projects ('logrolling'), or by packaging the proposals together in an omnibus spending bill that each member of the majority is obliged to support in order to secure approval for his own project. Explicit or implicit vote trades facilitate the playing of a legislative negative-sum, prisoner's dilemma game from which no one member can withdraw and hope to retain his seat.

The necessity of monitoring compliance with logrolling bargains helps explain why most legislative voting takes place near the end of the legislative session (Crain et al., 1986). (Ex-post settlements are another means of enforcing legislative vote trades.) The ordinary business of the legislature, which consists primarily of brokering wealth transfers among various identifiable groups within the polity, is facilitated by a legislative committee system that assigns responsibility for overseeing defined policy areas (agriculture, defense, commerce, and so on) to subsets of the legislature's membership. Legislative committees, who members have immediate political interests in the policies they oversee, help control the legislative agenda (Leibowitz and Tollison, 1980), thereby averting vote cycles, monitor the executive branch agencies that implement legislative policies (Weingast and Moran, 1983), and serve as proving grounds of party loyalty (Crain, 1990). Public choice analysis has been applied fruitfully to these and other institutional features of legislatures (Tollison, 1988).

When the Founding Fathers of the US constitutional republic designed the national legislature, they were well aware that its members would be subject to the influence of politically powerful special-interest groups, or 'factions'. Although James Madison strongly opposed the Constitutional Convention's 'Great Compromise', which granted the states equal representation in the Senate, he later wrote eloquently in defense of the separation of powers embodied in a bicameral Congress. Composed of a lower house, its members having relatively short terms (two years) and its seats apportioned on the basis of population, paired with an upper house, its members having relatively long terms (six years) and its seats apportioned equally among the states, 'no law or resolution can now be passed without the concurrence, first, of the people, and then, of a majority of the States' (*Federalist* No. 62). Recognizing the value of impediments 'against improper acts of legislation', Madison clearly understood that what might be called the industrial organization of the legislature (Weingast and Marshall, 1988) — its structure and operating rules — has an important influence on legislative outcomes.

WILLIAM F. SHUGHART II

REFERENCES

Bender, B. and Lott, J.R. Jr. (1996). "Legislator voting and shirking: a critical review of the literature." *Public Choice*, 87(April): 67–100.

Buchanan, J.M. and Tullock, G. (1962). *The calculus of Consent: Logical Foundations of Constitutional Democracy*. Ann Arbor: University of Michigan Press.

Crain, W.M. (1990). "Legislative committees: a filtering theory," In W.M. Crain and R.D. Tollison (eds.) *Predicting Politics: Essays in Empirical Public Choice*. Ann Arbor: University of Michigan Press, pp. 149–66.

Crain, W.M., Leavens, D.R., and Tollison, R.D. (1986). "Final voting in legislatures." *American Economic Review*, 76(September): 833–841.

Downs, A. (1957). *An Economic Theory of Democracy*. New York: Harper & Row.

Kau, J.B. and Rubin, P.H. (1979). "Self-interest, ideology, and logrolling in congressional voting." *Journal of Law and Economics*, 22(October): 365–384.

Kau, J.B. and Rubin, P.H. (1993). "Ideology, voting, and shirking." *Public Choice*, 76(June): 151–172.

Leibowitz, A. and Tollison, R.D. (1980). "A theory of legislative organization: making the most of your majority." *Quarterly Journal of Economics*, 94(March): 261–277.

McCormick, R.E. and Tollison, R.D. (1981). *Politicians, Legislation, and the Economy: An Inquiry into the Interest-group Theory of Government*. Boston: Martinus Nijhoff.

Olson, M. (1965). *The Logic of Collective Action: Public Goods and the Theory of Groups*. Cambridge and London: Harvard University Press.

Posner, R.A. (1969). "The Federal Trade Commission." *University of Chicago Law Review*, 37(Autumn): 47–89.

Rubin, P.H. (2001). "Ideology," in W.F. Shughart II and L. Razzolini (eds.) *The Elgar Companion to Public Choice*. Cheltenham, UK and Northampton, MA, USA: Edward Elgar, pp. 328–336.

Sass, T.R. (2001). "The anatomy of political representation: direct democracy, parliamentary democracy, and representative democracy," in W.F. Shughart II and L. Razzolini (eds.) *The Elgar Companion to Public Choice*. Cheltenham, UK and Northampton, MA, USA: Edward Elgar, pp. 157–179.

Tollison, R.D. (1988). "Public choice and legislation." *Virginia Law Review*, 74(March): 339–371.

Weingast, B.R. and Marshall, W.J. (1988). "The industrial organization of Congress; or why legislatures, like firms, are not organized as markets." *Journal of Political Economy*, 96(February): 132–163.

Weingast, B.R. and Moran, M.J. (1983). "Bureaucratic discretion or congressional control? Regulatory policymaking by the Federal Trade Commission." *Journal of Political Economy*, 91(October): 765–800.

LEGISLATORS

1. Introduction

One way to think about legislators is in terms of the interest-group theory of government and the demand and "supply" of legislation (McCormick and Tollison, 1981). Keep in mind that the use of "interest-group" as a modifier in this context is not meant to be pejorative. Individual citizens can want or demand laws for any reason — e.g., the law makes the world a better place, the law promotes the production of a public good, and so forth — but they will generally act in some group context to obtain the passage of a desired law or the defeat of an undesired law. A basic principle underlies the demand for legislation. The principle is that groups who can organize for less than one dollar in order to obtain one dollar of benefits from legislation will be effective demanders of legislative output.

In the interest-group theory, the supply of legislation is an inverse demand curve. Those who "supply" wealth transfers are individuals who do not find it cost effective to resist having their wealth taken away. In other words, it costs them more than one dollar to resist having one dollar taken away. This concept of a supply curve of legislation or regulation suggests that the costs of political activity to some individuals exceed the potential gains (or avoided losses). The supply of legislation is, therefore, grounded in the unorganized or relatively less-organized members of society. It should be kept in mind that "supply" in this discussion differs from standard usage in economics; it implies coercion and not willingness.

Who runs this supply–demand process? The individuals who monitor the supply–demand process are legislators, bureaucrats, and other political actors. These individuals may be conceived of as brokers of legislation, and they essentially act like brokers in a private context — they pair demanders and suppliers of legislation. That is, they seek to pair those who want a law or a transfer the most with those who object the least. In the usual logic of the interest-group theory, brokers will concentrate on legal arrangements that benefit well-organized and concentrated groups for whom the pro rata benefits are high at the expense of diffuse interests, each of which is taxed a little bit to fund the transfer or legislation. By efficiently pairing demanders and suppliers of legislation, the political brokers establish an equilibrium in the market for legislation. In return, these brokers extract an economic return for their services in the form of votes, campaign contributions, and future job offers.

Legislators are at the heart of the study of legislation and legislative processes, and the remainder of this entry focuses on certain aspects of their behavior. Also, depending on the particular structure of the legislature (total size, number of committees, voting rules, and so on), the brokerage process will operate at different levels of "costs." (Crain, 1979). Stricter voting rules, for example, raise the cost to legislators of finding diffuse minorities to "supply" taxes and transfers. In effect, a legislative production function will impact on the rate of passage of legislation. This production function undergirds the process by which legislation is supplied and is itself an integral part of the study of legislators.

2. Broker Preferences

The public choice literature contains a great deal of discussion about the degree to which ideology affects the voting behavior of elected representatives. In simple terms, does the politician exercise his or her personal value judgments in voting, as opposed to voting strictly in terms of constituents' interests? The answer is obviously yes to some degree, and the debate in the literature is over the degree.

The general form of the debate goes as follows. A model of representative voting behavior is specified, including constituent interest and ideological measures (such as the Americans for Democratic Action voting ratings). If the ideological measures prove to have a statistically significant impact in the test, ideology is held to influence the behavior of politicians at the margin (Kau and Rubin, 1979). Sam Peltzman (1985) challenged this conclusion with the argument that the inclusion of better measures of the "economic" variables affecting voting behavior in the models that are being tested would reduce the statistical significance of the ideological variables.

The whole issue is mired in difficulties. A simple example suffices to illustrate. Representative A is from an oil district and yet votes "no" on an oil import fee bill. Did the representative express his ideological preferences in this case? Because his voting "no" in exchange for votes on other issues is entirely probable, it is not at all clear that he voted "no" on ideological grounds. Vote trading or logrolling obscures the role of ideological voting on *single* issues. Many post offices and dams are built on such principles, and, in some cases, the post office or the dam generates more local political benefits for the representative than the oil import fee.

On the broader scale of voting across all issues, it seems reasonable to predict that ideology plays an economically rational role in such behavior. Nelson and Silberberg (1987) put the matter nicely. Narrowly focused bills where the final destination and distribution of funds are well known make ideological voting more costly; hence, less is observed. More general bills where effects are unknown or unpredictable make ideological voting less costly; hence, more such behavior is observed. Ideological voting obeys the law of demand — more is observed where engaging in such behavior is cheaper. Nelson and Silberberg (1987) presented evidence from voting on defense appropriations bills to suggest that this approach to ideology and voting is a useful one.

The issue, then, is not whether ideology matters at all to political behavior, but how much and under what conditions.

3. Seniority

Legislators are not homogeneous, which means that their influence is not homogeneous either. They will differ in their natural abilities as politicians, and they will differ in terms of their institutional status in the legislature. A measurable way in which representatives are different is in their length of service or tenure in the legislature. Seniority leads to heterogeneous political influence. Seniority assumes this role because rank and influence in the legislature (e.g., committee assignments) increase with legislator tenure. For example, agenda control opportunities will be provided by seniority (through committee chairmanships) where cycles exist.

The reasons for this conclusion are mostly a priori at present, but nonetheless convincing (Stigler, 1976). The legislature is organized, in many dimensions, like a prototype labor union with a strong form of monopoly power. The increase of legislator influence over political outcomes as a function of seniority is just one part of the union analogy, but it suffices to illustrate the basic point. To predict policy outcomes such as the economic impact of government programs across representative districts, one must control for seniority and related differences of legislators; all representatives are not created equal.

4. Committees

Economists have produced a significant amount of work on legislative committees. One body of literature, pioneered by Kenneth Shepsle (1978), focuses on the role of committees in determining "structure-induced equilibria." In other words, rather than cycling about endlessly as predicted by Arrow (1951), legislatures actually reach decisions and produce laws. In Shepsle's approach, outcomes are induced, indeed predicted and controlled, by the structural characteristics of the legislature, including committees, committee assignments, and so forth.

A second major issue in the literature is the control by the legislative committee over its relevant bureaucratic dominion. William Niskanen's (1971) theory of bureaucracy set the stage for this debate. Niskanen argued that because of its superior information, a bureau had greater bargaining power with regard to its budget than did the bureau's oversight committee. Subsequent work on the economic theory of bureaucracy has been largely in this tradition. However, Barry Weingast and Mark Moran (1983) offered an alternative principal–agent theory, which predicts that the oversight committee (the principal) has most of the relevant bargaining power, including the ability to remove or to hamper the career of the bureau head (the agent). They tested this theory with data concerning the Federal Trade Commission (FTC), and found supporting evidence.

The issue raised in this debate is an important one. Are government bureaus out of control or are they merely docile agents following the commands of voters as expressed through their elected representatives on the relevant committees? The Weingast approach suggests that political incentives should be compatible as between the legislature and the bureaucrat. The legislator observes a particular political trade off in the election. Imposing that trade off on his bureaucratic agent is in the legislator's interest. In this approach bureaucracy is not out of control but is closely monitored and controlled by Congress.

Committees have other functions and roles than those discussed here. But in the economic theory of legislation, their role is seen as promoting the passage of legislation. They are engines for finding out what laws people want and who will pay for them, conducting preliminary votes, screening and controlling bureaucratic appointments, and so on.

5. The Compensation of Legislators

McCormick and Tollison (1978) examine the issue of legislator pay. With regard to the legal pay of legislators, they analyzed the legislature as analogous to a union or wage cartel. In some states legislator pay is set by the state constitution; in others it is set by the legislature. The latter case amounts to a very strong form of wage-setting power because few, if any, substitutes for legislator services exist in a given state. McCormick and Tollison found that legislator wages in the "union" states (wages set by the legislatures) are much higher (100–200%) than in the "non-union" states (wages set by the state constitutions), all else the same.

Not all legislator pay is above the table. Outside-the-legislature pay comes in a variety of legal, quasi-legal, and illegal forms. McCormick and Tollison (1981) developed a theory of outside legislator pay that is based upon the occupational composition of a legislature. Imagine the following scenario: an auctioneer starts to call out legislator wages to elicit a labor supply curve for legislators. The first group to volunteer to run for and to serve in the legislature is composed of lawyers. They are the most effective at combining service in the legislature with making outside income. The lawyer who is also a legislator has a particular appeal for certain potential clients: in effect, the derived demand for the services of a lawyer *qua* legislator is more inelastic than the derived demand for plain old lawyers. Thus, low pay results in a greater number of lawyers in the legislature. As legislator pay rises, businesspeople will sign up next for legislative service. They sign up for the same reason as lawyers, only they are not as proficient as lawyers at earning outside income. Finally, at high levels of legislator pay, people are drawn to run for office who are attracted by the high level of pay per se because they are not adept at combining legislative service with procuring outside income (farmers).

McCormick and Tollison tested this theory using data on the occupational composition of state legislatures and found its implications strongly supported. Lawyers and business-types dominate low-pay legislatures; farmers dominate high pay legislatures.

6. Legislators as Rent-extractors

Fred McChesney (1997) recently expanded the concept of the politician's role in the interest-group theory of government in a sensible and significant way. He stressed that in the traditional interest-group theory, the role of the politician is to create rents and returns that interest groups in turn compete to capture. In this case the politician is a passive broker. McChesney went on to argue that the politician cannot only create rents, he can also extract them. Individuals and firms in the economy develop specific and expropriable capital in certain lines of endeavor. Politicians can force side payments from these individuals by threatening them with taxes and/or regulation designed to expropriate their specific capital.

Building on this insight, McChesney developed a very interesting theory of rent extraction by politicians: legislators introduce a bill that threatens an industry's return on capital unless the industry contributes to their legislative campaigns. His theory provides insights into a range of government gestures in the direction of industry: for example, committee investigations and hearings, political speeches mapping out new legislative proposals, and governmental commissions to study "problems."

7. Campaign Spending

The literature on campaign spending can be easily summarized — campaign spending is a means of entry into politics. A challenger's advertising expenditures perform the important function of introducing the unknown candidate to the electorate; the incumbent's cannot do much more than remind his constituency of his virtues. The empirical literature that examines the impact of campaign spending shows that the advertising elasticity of challenger spending with respect to votes is larger than that for incumbent spending (Grier, 1987). The moral of this body of work is simple — campaign spending laws are incumbent protection laws. As such, campaign finance legislative can be seen as an effort by legislators to impose entry barriers into politics.

Of course, not all incumbents support campaign finance limits. If they did so, surely such limits would be in place. Powerful, senior members of the Congress, including almost all committee chairmen, are opposed to campaign finance reform, whatever their public stances on this issue, because such reforms would weaken the protection that they receive from high levels of committee-based campaign funding.

Ironically, and fortunately, their self-serving opposition to campaign finance reform, in the long term, serves to enhance the competitive nature of the democratic political process and to weaken the very monopoly privileges that they seek to reinforce.

8. Concluding Remarks

An approach based on an economic theory of legislation none offers rich scientific and empirical opportunities to study legislatures. This is by no means the only approach to study legislatures, but it is provocative to think of the legislature as an institution guided by mostly private interests. After all, no man is safe when the legislature is in session.

ROBERT D. TOLLISON

REFERENCES

Arrow, K.J. (1951). *Social Choice and Individual Values*. New York: Wiley.

Crain, W.M. (1979). "Cost and output in the legislative firm." *Journal of Legal Studies*, 8(1979): 607–621.

Grier, K.B. (1989). "Campaign spending and senate elections, 1978–1984." *Public Choice*, 60(December): 201–219.

Kau, J.B. and Rubin, P.H. (1979). "Self-interest, ideology, and logrolling in congressional voting." *Journal of Law and Economics*, 22(October): 365–384.

McChesney, F.S. (1997). *Money for Nothing*. Cambridge: Harvard

McCormick, R.E. and Tollison, R.D. (1978). "Legislatures as unions." *Journal of Political Economy*, 8(February): 63–78.

McCormick, R.E. and Tollison, R.D. (1981). *Politicians, Legislation, and the Economy*. Boston: Kluwer.

Nelson, D. and Silberberg, E. (1987). "Ideology and legislator shrinking." *Economic Inquiry*, 25: 15–25.

Peltzman, S. (1985). "An economic interpretation of the history of congressional voting in the twentieth century." *American Economic Review*, 75(September): 656–675.

Shepsle, K.A. (1978). *The Giant Jigsaw Puzzle*. Chicago: University of Chicago Press.

Stigler, G.J. (1976). "The sizes of legislatures." *Journal of Legal Studies*, 5(January): 17–34.

Weingast, B.R. and Moran, M.J. (1983). "Bureaucratic discretion on congressional control? Regulatory policymaking by the Federal Trade Commission." *Journal of Political Economy*, 91(5): 765–800.

LEVIATHAN MODELS OF GOVERNMENT

Geoffrey Brennan and James Buchanan first developed the Leviathan model of government, in their 1980 book *The Power to Tax*. In this early formulation government is *assumed* to act as a monopolist that maximizes tax revenues. Such representation is driven by the other fundamental assumption that the authors make, namely, that rational ignorance, fiscal illusion and outright collusion among elected officials deprive taxpayers-voters of any control they may have over government. Hence the reference to Hobbes' Leviathan. In *The Power to Tax*, Brennan and Buchanan develop the fiscal consequences of the revenue maximizing government and point out the constitutional provisions that may hinder the Leviathan in its drive to appropriate taxpayers' resources.

The sheer originality and the intuitive plausibility of the Leviathan model can be appreciated by contrasting its predictions to those of the traditional Musgravian public finance. To begin with, the fundamental problem of taxation is quite different in the two conceptualisations of the state. In the traditional vision, the government is a benevolent public good provider, which seeks to raise a given amount of revenues subject to certain efficiency and equity constraints.

With a revenue-maximising Leviathan, instead, citizens must impose constraints on the government that limit its ability to raise revenues to a given amount. Also the standard analysis of excess burden is turned on its head. With the amount of revenues to be raised by taxation fixed, the optimal tax base is the one that induces the minimum amount of distortion of taxpayers' choices, namely, the most inelastic sources of revenues. With the amount of revenues to be raised the maximand, the citizens seek to limit the government to the more elastic tax bases, so to shelter parts of their income and wealth from the Leviathan. The Leviathan model provides a justification of the normative public finance principle of horizontal equity, but for quite different reasons than the standard one, to treat equals equally. A citizen writing a tax constitution to constrain the Leviathan would require that the government impose uniform tax schedules across persons to limit the government's capacity to engage in tax discrimination as a means of expanding revenues. A similar logic leads to a preference for progressive over regressive taxes, since fewer revenues can typically be raised by tax schedules imposing high marginal tax rates than by schedules imposing low ones. Moreover, the Leviathan model provides an additional justification for Wicksell's (1896) prescription that expenditure proposals be tied to the taxes that would finance them. Wicksell puts forth this argument as a means to ensure informed choices by citizens as to the benefits and costs of public projects. With a revenue-maximising Leviathan around, the proposal is motivated by the need to ensure a balanced budget and to force the government to provide some public benefits in exchange of the revenues raised. Also debt and money creation are for the Leviathan additional, shrouded means to raise revenues. Puviani (1903) provides a classical treatment of this point. Balanced-budget provisions as well as limitations on the government capacity to print money — to the possible extent of a complete denial of such power (Brennan and Buchanan, 1980, p. 130) — are the best constitutional response. Finally, Brennan and Buchanan argue that, as long as some individuals and firms are mobile, fiscal decentralization forces governments to engage in tax competition, thereby destroying Leviathan's monopoly on taxation and bringing government spending closer to the preferences of citizens. Hence the empirical restriction that "total government intrusion into the economy should be smaller, *ceteris paribus*, the greater the extent to which taxes and expenditures are decentralized" (Brennan and Buchanan, 1980, p. 15).

The empirical testing of the Leviathan model has begun in the 1980s and is still an active line of research. The results that can be evaluated as "mixed" at best. Early studies concentrate on data sets drawn from American and Canadian states. Nelson (1986) finds those states that tax personal income have significantly larger government sectors as implied by the Leviathan model; however, a Granger causality test on the estimates suggests that causality may run other way. Nelson also found that the relative size of the government sector varies inversely with the number of local government units. If one assumes that having more local government units signifies a stronger federalist structure and more intensive constraints on government through intergovernmental competition, then this result also supports the Leviathan model. Marlow (1988) and Zax (1989) find that total government size varies inversely with the relative importance of a local government, another result consistent with the Leviathan hypothesis.

At the cross-national level, several studies have also found that federalist structures inhibit government growth (Cameron, 1978; Schneider, 1986). However, Oates (1985) and Forbes and Zampelli (1989) conclude that having a federalist constitutional structure has a negative, but statistically insignificant effect, on the growth rates of public sectors in developed countries. Oates also found that the degree of centralization of tax revenue, a source of fiscal power emphasized by Brennan and Buchanan (1980, p. 185), is either not statistically significantly related to government growth or inversely related at both cross-national and cross-state levels of growth. More recently, Stein (1999) demonstrates that fiscal decentralization is actually associated with *larger* government in Latin America. Joulfaian and Marlow (1990) find similar results for a cross section of OECD countries, but rationalize them in a way consistent with the Leviathan model. They suggest that greater decentralization enhances citizens' trust in government, which then allows them to demand more public goods. In reviewing all these contrasting results Oates (1989) resolves most discrepancies among the empirical studies and concludes that, at the local level where citizens are assumed to have the greatest mobility, the evidence is supportive of the Leviathan hypothesis; in all other situations, the Leviathan is a "mythical beast" (Oates, 1989).

Oates (1989) review essay is certainly not the end of the story. In a recent paper Rodden (2002) persuasively argues that existing cross-national studies are insufficient to dispel the myth of Leviathan for two reasons. First, they employ cross-section averages or single year snapshots. They thus shed little light on the dynamic nature of decentralization and the growth of government, both of which are processes that unfold over time. In particular, governance in many countries around the world is undergoing a major transformation since the 1980s. Cross-national empirical analyses (such as Panizza, 1999) demonstrate that a pronounced trend towards fiscal decentralisation is strongly linked with transitions to democracy, especially in large, formerly centralised countries. For these countries, average state and local expenditure as a share of the total government sector have almost doubled from the 1980s till now. Thus it may be inappropriate to conduct empirical analysis as if all countries have reached a long-term equilibrium. Second, until very recently, insufficient attention has been given to the precise institutional incentives created by different forms of decentralisation. If decentralisation is to have a constraining effect on the growth of government, it must occur on both the expenditure and revenue sides. In the vast majority of countries, however, increased state and local expenditures are funded increasingly by grants, shared revenues, or other revenue sources that are controlled and regulated by the central government. Expenditure decentralisation without corresponding local tax powers will not engender the tax competition that drives the Leviathan model, nor will it strengthen the agency relationship between local citizens and their representatives. On the contrary, decentralisation funded by "common pool" resources like grants and revenue sharing might have the opposite effect. By breaking the link between taxes and benefits, mere expenditure decentralisation might turn the public sector's resources into a common pool that competing local governments will attempt to over-fish, with the result to intensify the growth of government. Once these effects are controlled for, Rodden (2002) finds results that are in line with the Leviathan hypothesis in a pooled sample of 70 countries.

Other critiques to the Leviathan hypothesis are moved at a theoretical level. In their public choice approach to taxation, Hettich and Winer (1999), among others, question the Leviathan model as it *assumes*, but does not explain the source and the stability of the dictatorial power of the Leviathan. However, political economics models of political accountability, such as Persson et al. (1997), provide an explanation of why and to what extent *rational* taxpayers-voters allow the government to secure rents for itself at the expense of taxpayers-voters welfare. These models can be considered as a theoretical development of the early Leviathan model. The Brennan and Buchanan (1980) formulation can be reinterpreted in the logic of the political accountability models, as a government that is not accountable at all. Moreover, models of political accountability provide and explanation of the source and stability of a government behaviour in Western-type democracies that is characterized by a significant degree of Leviathan-style rent appropriation. As such, they provide the reply to the Hettich and Winer (1999) critique.

Interestingly, these models are biased against providing Leviathan-style results, because they suppose rational, rather than fiscally illuded, voters and see the constitutional rules as a weak, rather than the only, device to constrain the behaviour of elected officials. Constitutions are incomplete contracts, which do not offer to elected politicians an explicit incentive scheme that associates well-defined payoffs with actions in all states of the world. This makes it hard to tie specific rewards or punishments to the decisions a politician takes. Basically, constitutions reward elected politicians simply by allowing them to remain in office and sanction them simply by throwing them out of office. The mechanism that distributes such rewards and sanctions is the electoral process. Thus, unlike Brennan and Buchanan (1980), the models of political accountability study whether ordinary politics, as opposed to constitutional politics, is able to tame the Leviathan. The base of the argument is that the electoral process must carry out an adverse selection process of searching for potential candidates that are less likely to behave discretionally and divert rents from the public budget at the expense of the welfare of taxpayers-voters. Two are the sources of this discretional power: (1) an *asymmetry in action*. When citizens elect their representatives, they temporarily delegate the exclusive decision making authority over policy making to the holders of public office. This creates room for abuse of power between elections. (2) An *asymmetry in information*. In many cases, politicians have access to much better information on the relative merits and precise consequences of alternatives policies than the population at large. This also creates room for potential abuse by the holders of public offices.

Clearly, any abuse of power reduces the electoral accountability of the system and the utility of voters. To minimize the welfare loss, voters coordinate on a *voting strategy* that makes the elected officials as accountable as possible, given the incomplete nature of the contract embedded in the constitution. The strategy is based on an intertemporal trade off: if the elected official diverts too many resources today, he is not elected again, i.e., he is removed from office and will not be able to appropriate resources tomorrow. The amount of diversion depends on the severeness of the asymmetries in action and information of above and on the institutional framework.

The simplest possible case is when voters share the same information as politicians and the institutional setting is a "pure" presidential democracy, i.e., one where political decisions are taken by a single branch, which for convenience we call the executive, elected by the voters. The elected officials derive utility at the expense of voters only because of the asymmetry in action, created by time interval between two elections. For simplicity all elected officials are the same, so the results are driven from the institutional framework, rather than by the competence of officials. The executive decides over the budget, i.e., it supplies a certain amount of public good, from which voters derive utility, using tax revenues. The executive can also appropriate these revenues, entirely or in part. To the extent that the executive diverts revenues from the production of the public good, the executive's utility increases and that of the voters decreases. Since voters know the "technology" available to the executive for transforming revenues into the public good, they can also infer the amount of resources the executive has appropriated for personal use. Based on this information, they decide whether to reelect the executive or not.

Persson et al. (1997) show that the immediate conclusion that voters decide not to reelect the executive if it has appropriated any nonzero amount of revenues is not in voters' best interest. If voters adopt such a voting strategy, the executive anticipates that it will be thrown out of office at the end of its mandate, and appropriates as many resources as possible. Such strategy is clearly inefficient for voters. The efficient strategy is to allow the executive to appropriate the amount of resources that makes it just indifferent between being reelected for an iteration of future terms, or appropriate everything now and not be reelected. Essentially, democracy, because of the incompleteness of the contract that the constitution establishes between voters and their delegates, has a cost in terms of resources that citizens must transfer to elected officials to motivate them to hold office. This is an endogenous Leviathan equilibrium.

Voters' welfare further decreases when there is not only an asymmetry in action, but also an asymmetry in information. Suppose that the technology with which the executive transforms revenues into public good changes randomly, possibly because of the dynamics of the economy; suppose also that voters cannot observe the technology currently available, while the executive can. In this case voters cannot tell whether the, say, small amount of public good they receive is due to the executive having appropriated a large amount of resources for personal use or to a poor realization of the technology. In this case they coordinate on a voting strategy centered on a minimum amount of public good consumption. If they get that amount or more, they reelect the executive; if they get less, they throw it out of office. Faced with this voting strategy the executive seeks reappointment only if the available technology is sufficiently favorable; in this case it gives the voters the minimum amount of public goods they want. Otherwise the executive knows that, even if it diverts no resources from those it is to administer, it will not be reappointed. Hence, it has a clear incentive to appropriate as many revenues as possible. Persson et al. (1997) show that voters are hurt by incomplete information, while the executive captures some of the informational rents. In this setting, the executive diverts more

resources than under fully informed voters and does so relatively more when the economic conditions are so poor as to make reelection unlikely.

Persson et al. (1997) explore the robustness of these results under different institutional regimes (parliamentary or congressional systems, different budget approbation procedures and the like) and find that in all these forms of democracies it is always rational for voters to allow holders of office to appropriate a nonzero amount of rents. Modern democratic governments are neither a monopolistic Leviathan as in Brennan and Buchanan (1980) nor the political counterpart of the perfect competition model (Becker, 1958), but something in between. Padovano (1995) argues that, to place the equilibrium government behaviour as far away from the Leviathan endpoint as possible, one must shorten and fix the length of the legislatures, adopt majoritarian electoral systems and expand the number of political positions assigned through direct electoral processes rather than through indirect designation. Furthermore, Padovano et al. (2002) find that an independent judiciary may reduce the amount of discretion of the Leviathan.

In conclusion, the Leviathan model of government has started as a logical and fearsome possibility, has gone through the rogue waters of empirical tests and theoretical questioning of the plausibility of the underlying hypothesis, only to be reformulated in what seems to be a less extreme, but more general and solid vision of modern democracies.

FABIO PADOVANO

REFERENCES

Becker, G.S. (1958). "Competition and democracy." *Journal of Law and Economics*, 1: 105–109.

Brennan, G. and Buchanan, J.M. (1977). "Towards a tax constitution for Leviathan." *Journal of Public Economics*, 8: 255–273.

Brennan, G. and Buchanan, J.M. (1977). *The Power to Tax. Analytical Foundations of a Fiscal Constitution.* Cambridge: Cambridge University Press.

Cameron, D.R. (1978). "The expansion of the public economy: a comparative analysis." *American Political Science Review*, 72: 1243–1261.

Forbes, K.F. and Zampelli, E.M. (1989). "Is Leviathan a mythical beast?." *American Economic Review*, 79: 568–577.

Hettich, R. and Winer, S. (1999). *Democratic Choice and Taxation.* Cambridge: Cambridge University Press.

Joulfaian, D. and Marlow, M.L. (1990). "Government size and decentralization: evidence from disaggregated data." *Southern Economic Journal*, 56: 1094–1102.

Marlow, M.L. (1988). "Fiscal decentralization and government size." *Public Choice*, 56: 259–269.

Nelson, M.A. (1986). "An empirical analysis of state and local tax structure in the context of the Leviathan model of government." *Public Choice*, 49: 283–294.

Oates, W. (1985). "Searching for Leviathan: an empirical study." *American Economic Review*, 75: 748–757.

Oates, W. (1989). "Searching for Leviathan: a reply and some further reflections." *American Economic Review*, 79: 578–583.

Padovano, F. (1995). "A Theory of Political Collusion and Government Growth." Ph. D. Thesis, George Mason University.

Padovano, F., Fiorino, N., and Sgarra, G. (2002). "Judicial branch, checks and balances and political accountability." *Constitutional Political Economy*, (forthcoming).

Panizza, U. (1999). "On the determinants of fiscal centralization: theory and evidence." *Journal of Public Economics*, 74: 97–139.

Persson, T., Roland G., and Tabellini, G. (1997). "Separation of powers and political accountability," *Quarterly Journal of Economics*, 112: 1163–1202.

Puviani, A. (1903). *Teoria dell'Illusione Finanziaria*. Palermo.

Rodden, J. (2002). "Reviving Leviathan: fiscal federalism and the growth of government." Working Paper, Department of Political Science, MIT.

Schneider, M. (1986). "Fragmentation and the growth of local government." *Public Choice*, 48: 255–263.

Stein, E. (1999). "Fiscal decentralization and government size in Latin America." *Journal of Applied Economics*, 11: 357–391.

Wicksell, K. (1896). *Finanztheorische Untersuchungen*. Jena.

Zax, J.S. (1989). "Is there a Leviathan in your neighborhood?" *American Economic Review*, 79: 560–567.

LOGIC OF COLLECTIVE ACTION

> What are the common wages of labor depends every where upon the contract usually made between those two parties, whose interests are by no means the same. The workmen desire to get as much, the masters to give as little as possible. The former are disposed to combine in order to raise, the latter in order to lower the wages of labor.
>
> It is not, however, difficult to foresee which of the two parties must, upon all ordinary occasions, have the advantage in the dispute, and force the other into a compliance with their terms. The masters, being fewer in number, can combine much more easily.... (Smith [1776] 1976: 83–84)

One of public choice's key insights is that outcomes in political markets differ from those in ordinary markets, not because the behavioral motivations of individuals are different in the two settings, but because of fundamental differences in the institutional frameworks within which rational actors pursue their self-interests. One implication of this line of reasoning is that group action differs markedly from individual action. Shared goals and joint responsibilities create indivisibilities that, we shall see, represent the most distinctive feature — and the most important barrier — to the mobilization of political influence in the interest-group society.

Private choices take place within the context of a system of well-defined, well-enforced and transferable property rights that generate price and profit signals to which individuals have powerful incentives to respond; public choices take place within the context of ill-defined, contractually unenforceable and non-tradable property rights that force decision makers to act without the benefit of explicit market indicators. Private choices are unilateral; public choices are multilateral. Private choices entail consequences that are for the most part borne by the decision maker himself; the benefits and costs of public choices must be shared with others. Individuals participate in private transactions voluntarily; in politics, decisive factions access the coercive powers of the state to compel the obedience of indecisive factions. Private exchanges are positive-sum; exchanges mediated by the public sector may be zero-sum or, more frequently, negative-sum. Competitive markets supply buyers and sellers with alternatives to which they readily can turn; monopoly in the public sector provides limited options among which the costs of switching tend to be high.

In the private sector, decision makers make choices without first obtaining the approval of others. Under open market conditions, sellers decide independently of their rivals what products to offer, which features to include, and what prices to charge. Buyers likewise act on their own accounts in deciding what products to purchase, which sellers to patronize, and what prices to pay. Each seller strives to maximize his profits by reference to firm-specific revenue and cost functions, and each buyer strives to maximize his utility by consulting his income-constrained personal preference orderings. Outcomes in ordinary markets, in short, emerge from the interactions of autonomous economic agents seeking only their own private gains.

While decisions in the private sector are the result of individual action, decisions in the public sector demand collective action. Depending on the voting rules in place, a democratic society cannot act without the concurrence of a plurality, a majority, or a supermajority of the citizenry. Collective action problems arise most frequently in the provision of pure and impure public goods — national defense, highways, clean air, parks, and so on — which provide benefits to a group of individuals, but which no one of them has the independent capacity to finance (Azfar, 2001: 59). Nevertheless, in modern western democracies the realm of collective action has expanded far beyond the provision of public goods to include pensions, health care, education, the dole, and the many other ornaments of the *dirigiste* welfare state. Global environmental treaties and military alliances elevate collection action to the level of the nation-state.

The logic of collective action helps to identify the groups that will tend to be successful politically. Prior to 1965, it was widely assumed that 'groups of individuals with common interests … act on behalf of their common interests much as single individuals are often expected to act on behalf of their personal interests' (Olson, 1965: 1). That monolithic view of group action, which ignored the diversity of the interests of group members, was exploded by Mancur Olson's seminal contribution to the public choice literature. Olson recognized that, unlike individual action, group action requires the agreement of others. Because each member of a group is a rational actor, his personal interests will not coincide perfectly with those of his fellows. The insight that not every group member will necessarily gain the same benefits from — nor bear the same costs of — collective action made possible a richer analysis of the behavior of groups seeking to exploit political processes for their own ends.

Olson's logic suggests that the most effective collective actors will be groups that are relatively small and composed of individuals with relatively homogeneous interests. Small group size raises the expected per capita return to group membership, thereby giving its members greater personal stakes in the group's success. Suppose that collective action promises a total benefit of $1,000,000 and that the members of the group will share the benefit equally. It should be obvious that the incentives to participate in collective action will be stronger when 100 members will divide the benefits than it would be in a group having 1,000,000 members. In the first case, each member can anticipate a gain of $10,000 if the group is successful; the expected per capita gain in the second case is only $1. Since no member of a group rationally will invest more of his own resources in collective action than he expects to gain, small groups will have comparative advantages as collective actors. Their members will supply more effort on the group's behalf, contributing more time and money to achieving the group's goals than otherwise. Small groups also face lower costs of monitoring and controlling free riding. Each group member has incentive to collect his share of the group's gains while avoiding his pro rata costs of supporting the activities necessary to attain the group's objectives. Such free-riding behavior is easier to detect, and sanctions against it (including expulsion from the group) are easier to impose, when the group is small than when it is large.

Small groups also have lower decision-making costs, an advantage reinforced by homogeneity of members' interests. Group heterogeneity creates differences of opinion that make it more difficult to reach agreement on common courses of action, and creates opportunities for the membership's majority to take advantage of the minority (what Buchanan and Tullock, 1962, call the external costs of collective decision making). Voluntary association, voting-with-the feet (Tiebout, 1956; Hirschman, 1970), and the ability to clone groups as demand warrants means that diversity of tastes and preferences amongst individuals will tend to promote diversity amongst groups rather than diversity of group membership. People will tend to associate with others who are like-minded in the sense of assigning similar values to the benefits they anticipate from collective action. There is thus much common ground between Olson's logic and the economic theory of clubs (Buchanan, 1965; Cornes and Sandler, [1986] 1996; Anderson et al., 2001).

Groups engaged in political action frequently were organized initially for some other purpose. Recognizing that many of the costs of group formation are start-up costs, Olson proposed a 'byproduct theory' of collective action. Once a group has been organized for any reason — individuals with common interests on some issue have been identified and contacted, a membership list has been compiled, dues have been paid, the association's officers have been elected, and office space has been leased — the cost of redirecting the group's efforts to the political arena is relatively low. Political action becomes a byproduct of the organization because start-up costs have already been borne in the process forming the association for some other (non-political) purpose. Indeed, for whatever reason organization is undertaken, lobbying for special-interest legislation becomes a relatively low-cost byproduct of being organized. Workers, for example, may organize to bargain collectively with employers and then find it relatively easy to open an office in the national capital to advocate higher minimum wages. (As a matter of fact, Olson devoted an entire chapter to the collective action problems of labor unions; see Sandler, 1992: 113–114, for a succinct summary.) A business firm is another example of an organization whose resources can be redeployed at low cost for political lobbying purposes, such as seeking the enactment of protectionist trade policies or 'right-to-work' laws. Lawyers may agree collectively to a code of ethics to address such matters as attorney-client privilege and then proceed to adopt provisions in their organization's code that, by banning advertising, for example, restrict competition among lawyers and raise their fees. The National Collegiate Athletic Association (NCAA) organizes to control violence and reduce player injuries in college sports, and then lobbies for exemption from the antitrust laws in order to capture rents from student-athletes. Industry trade associations, agricultural cooperatives, private charitable trusts, groups of individuals afflicted by the same disease, and organizations of retired people are a few of the many groups that, once formed, are well-positioned to act politically.

A key point of contention in the literature is whether individuals can be motivated to join such organizations in the absence of coercion (e.g., laws mandating 'closed shops') and, moreover, to supply the funds necessary to finance the group's political activities. Lobbying is, after all, itself a public good and free riding consequently will plague its provision. It is Olson's attentiveness to the 'publicness' of shared political goals and, hence, the formidable barriers effective factions must overcome, that distinguishes his logic of collective action from the efficiency theories of pressure-group politics put forward by Becker (1983, 1985) and Wittman (1989, 1995).

Olson advanced a theory of 'selective incentives' to address the free-riding problem that disadvantages collective action relative to individual action. According to that theory, an association provides a private good or service to its members that cannot be purchased competitively elsewhere. By tying this good or service to membership and monopolistically pricing it above cost, the association can raise money to underwrite its lobbying activities. The Sierra Club, among the most venerable organizations of American 'greens', sells calendars to its members, for instance. Membership in the American Association of Retired Persons (AARP) provides access to a group life-insurance policy and to discounts on prescription drugs and travel packages. The members of BUND, the German affiliate of Friends of the Earth International, get to purchase automobile insurance at favorable rates because, as the organization's publicity materials state, 'we know that you … will drive especially responsibly and environmentally friendly'. The NCAA supplies member schools with a schedule of regular-season games and post-season tournaments.

Olson's byproduct theory was originally dismissed by George Stigler (1974), who argued that there is no good reason for assuming that interest groups will have monopoly power over the provision of particular private goods to their members. How, then, could they generate monopoly rents to finance their lobbying activities? One answer overlooked by Stigler is that many interest groups creatively use their tax-exempt status under section 501(c)(3) of the Internal Revenue Code to reallocate monies raised for legitimate organizational activities to support their political agendas (Bennett and DiLorenzo, 1998). The basic point, however, is that Olson's hypothesis about the use of selective incentives is testable; it simply cannot be dismissed as a theoretical curiosity. It is entirely plausible, for example, to argue that the demand for Sierra Club calendars is downward sloping and that the Sierra Club therefore has sufficient monopoly power in the calendar market to finance many of its lobbying activities with the associated rents. Moreover, the point goes well beyond the trivial example of calendars to such selective benefits as group insurance policies, a variety of member discounts, and, in some cases, such as the American Medical Association, the right to practice one's profession.

Mulvey (1994) investigated the use of selective incentives by the AARP, and found that they are directly related to association membership, which is a proxy for interest-group clout. She also found support for the fungibility of organizational funding as between tax-exempt activities and (non-exempt) political lobbying. This limited evidence suggests that Olson's byproduct theory of interest-group formation may be more empirically relevant than commonly assumed, but additional research along these lines is nevertheless needed.

Public choice economists know very little about the dynamics of interest-group formation (but see Wagner, 1966, who suggests that political entrepreneurs play creative roles in this regard). No matter their origins, the logic of collective action nevertheless suggests that small, cohesive factions will tend to dominate the democratic political process. Because such groups are in position to supply votes, campaign contributions, and other forms of support to politicians and policy makers, these officials will respond favorably to their demands. The mass of voter-taxpayers is everywhere at a disadvantage in the competition for wealth transfers that characterizes interest-group politics. Just as it is not worth spending more than $1 to gain $1, it is not worth spending more than $1 to avoid having $1 expropriated for transfer to a politically more effective group. Owing to their large numbers, their lack of organization, and their inability to articulate a coherent political agenda, the polity as a whole predictably will be vulnerable to a 'tyranny of the minority'. It is thanks to Mancur Olson that we now understand why this plain fact of democratic politics seems so obvious.

WILLIAM F. SHUGHART II

REFERENCES

Anderson, G.M., Shughart, W.F. II, and Tollison, R.D. (2001). "Clubs and club goods," in W.F. Shughart II and L. Razzolini (eds.) *The Elgar Companion to Public Choice*. Cheltenham, UK and Northampton, MA, USA: Edward Elgar, pp. 337–353.

Azfar, O. (2001). "The logic of collective action," in W.F. Shughart II and L. Razzolini (eds.) *The Elgar Companion to Public Choice*. Cheltenham, UK and Northampton, MA, USA: Edward Elgar, pp. 59–82.

Becker, G.S. (1983). "A theory of competition among pressure groups for political influence." *Quarterly Journal of Economics*, 98(August): 371–400.

Becker, G.S. (1985). "Public policies, pressure groups, and dead-weight costs." *Journal of Public Economics*, 28(December): 330–347.

Bennett, J.T. and DiLorenzo, T.J. (1998). *Cancerscam: Diversion of Federal Cancer Funds to Politics*. New Brunswick, NJ: Transaction Publishers.

Buchanan, J.M. (1965). "An economic theory of clubs." *Economica*, 32(February): 1–14.

Buchanan, J.M. and Tullock, G. (1962). *The Calculus of Consent: Logical Foundations of Constitutional Democracy*. Ann Arbor: University of Michigan Press.

Cornes, R. and Sandler, T. ([1986] 1996). *The Theory of Externalities, Public Goods and Club Goods*, Second Edition. Cambridge and New York: Cambridge University Press.

Hirschman, A.O. (1970). *Exit, Voice and Loyalty*. Cambridge: Harvard University Press.

Mulvey, J. (1994). "Paying physicians under medicare: an empirical application of the interest-group theory of government." Unpublished doctoral dissertation. George Mason University, Fairfax, VA.

Olson, M. (1965). *The Logic of Collective Action: Public Goods and the Theory of Groups*. Cambridge and London: Harvard University Press.

Sandler, T. (1992). *Collective Action: Theory and Applications*. Ann Arbor: University of Michigan Press.

Smith, A. ([1776] 1976). *An Inquiry into the Nature and Causes of the Wealth of Nations. The Glasgow Edition of the Works and Correspondence of Adam Smith*, Volume I, R.H. Campbell, A.S. Skinner, and W.B. Todd (eds.) Oxford: Oxford University Press.

Stigler, G.J. (1974). "Free riders and collective action: an appendix to theories of economic regulation." *Bell Journal of Economics and Management Science*, 5(Autumn): 359–365.

Tiebout, C.M. (1956). "A pure theory of local expenditures." *Journal of Political Economy* 64(October): 416–424.

Wagner, R.E. (1966). "Pressure groups and political entrepreneurs: a review article," in G. Tullock (ed.) *Papers on Non-market Decision Making*. Charlottesville, VA: Thomas Jefferson Center for Political Economy, University of Virginia, pp. 161–70.

Wittman, D.A. (1989). "Why democracies produce efficient results." *Journal of Political Economy*, 97(December): 1395–1424.

Wittman, D.A. (1995). *The Myth of Democratic Failure: Why Political Institutions are Efficient*. Chicago: University of Chicago Press.

THE LOGIC OF LIBERTY

1. Introduction

In 1970, Amartya Sen launched an extensive debate on the relationship between individual liberty and the Pareto principle in his famous article on the "Impossibility of a Paretian Liberal" (Sen, 1970). In this article, Sen claimed to prove that a principle reflecting liberal values even in a very mild form cannot be combined with the weak Pareto principle, given an unrestricted domain. "If we do believe in these other conditions, then the society cannot permit even minimal liberalism" (Sen, 1970, 157); and "While the Pareto criterion has been thought to be an expression of individual liberty, it appears that in choices involving more than two alternatives it can have consequences that are, in fact, deeply illiberal" (ibid.).

For the most part, scholars who have engaged Sen unsuccessfully in this debate have done so in terms of Sen's own definitions of liberalism and of the Pareto principle (see, however, Peacock and Rowley, 1972 and Rowley and Peacock, 1975, for exceptions). In this paper, we return to the debate to place the key concepts under close scrutiny and to suggest that the Sen paradox does not exist once the concepts are more carefully defined and more thoroughly evaluated.

2. The Nature of the Sen Paradox

Sen (1970) sets out the following conditions for social choice (the following are direct quotes):

CONDITION U (Unrestricted Domain): Every logically possible set of individual orderings is included in the domain of the collective choice rule.

CONDITION P (Weak Pareto): If every individual prefers any alternative x to another alternative y, then society must prefer x to y.

CONDITION L (Liberalism): For each individual i there is at least once pair of alternatives, say (x, y), such that if this individual prefers x to y, then society should prefer x to y, and if this individual prefers y to x, then society should prefer y to x.

Sen's intention is to permit each individual the freedom to determine at least one *social choice*, "having his own walls pink rather than white, other things remaining the same for him and the rest of society" (Sen, 1970, 153).

On the basis of these three conditions, Sen (1970) argues that the following impossibility theorem holds:

Theorem I: There is no social decision function that can simultaneously satisfy Conditions U, P, and L.

Sen (1970) then weakens the condition of liberalism to allow the condition of liberalism only to a proper subset of individuals:

CONDITION L* (Minimal Liberalism): There are at least two individuals such that for each of them there is at least one pair of alternatives over which he is decisive, that is, there is a pair of x, y, such that if he prefers x (respectively y) to y (respectively x), then society should prefer y (respectively y) to y (respectively x).

Sen (1970), on this basis, subsumes Theorem I with Theorem II:

Theorem II: There is no social decision function that can simultaneously satisfy Conditions U, P, and L*.

SEN's Proof takes the following form:

Let the two individuals referred to in Condition L* be 1 and 2, respectively, and let the two pairs of alternatives referred to be (x, y) and (z, w) respectively. If (x, y) and (z, w) are the same pair of alternatives, then there is a contradiction. They have, therefore, at most one alternative in common, say x = z. Assume now that person 1 prefers x to y, and person 2 prefers w to z (= x), and let everyone in the community including 1 and 2 prefer y to w. There is no inconsistency for anyone, not even for 1 and 2, and their respective orderings are: 1 prefers x to y and y to w, while 2 prefers y to w and w to x. By Condition U this should be in the domain of the social decision mechanism. But by Condition L*, x must be preferred to y, and w must be preferred to x (= z), while by the Pareto principle, y must be preferred to w. Thus, there is no best element in the set (x = z, y, w) in terms of social preference, and every alternative is worse than some other. A choice function for the society does not therefore exist.

Next, let x, y, z, and w all be distinct. Let 1 prefer x to y, let 2 prefer z to w and let everyone in the community including 1 and 2 prefer w to x and y to z. There is no contradiction for 1 or 2, for 1 simply prefers w to x, x to y, and y to z, while 2 prefers y to z, z to w, and w to x. By condition U this configuration of individual preferences must yield a social choice function. But by Condition L* society should prefer x to y and z to w, while by the Pareto principle society must prefer w to x, and y to z. This means that there is no best alternative for this set, and a choice function does not exist for any set that includes these four alternatives. Thus, there is no social decision function satisfying Conditions, U, P, and L*, and the proof is complete (Sen, 1970, 154).

Sen illustrates the type of impossibility that is involved by taking a special case of two individuals and three alternatives. There is one copy of a somewhat salacious book, say *Lady Chatterley's Lover*, which is viewed differently by Mr. Prude and by Mr. Lascivious). The three alternatives are: that Mr Prude reads the book (x), that Mr. Lascivious reads it (y) and that no one reads it (z). Mr. Prude's preference ordering is z, x, y, whereas the preference ordering of Mr. Lascivious is x, y, z. The explanation of these preference orderings is that both individuals are meddlesome with respect to each other.

According to Sen (1970), if the choice is between x and z, then Condition L* requires that society should prefer z to x. Mr. Prude should not read the book. Similarly, if the

choice is between y and z, then Condition L* requires that society should prefer y to z, with Mr. Lascivious reading the book. However, the solution in which the book is handed over to Mr. Lascivious is Pareto inferior since both individuals prefer that Mr. Prude should read the book. By reference to conditions U, P, and L* there is a cycle reflective of an inconsistency of choice.

3. Condition U (Unrestricted Domain)

In his 1970 essay, Sen simply argues that Arrow's (1950) condition of collective rationality can be seen to be "merely a requirement that the domain of the collective choice rule should not be arbitrarily restricted" (Sen, 1970, 153).

There is a set of possible social states, each of which is a complete description of society, including every individual's place in it. Each individual i (i = 1, 2,..., m) has a preference ordering R_i over S; An ordering by definition is complete, reflexive and transitive. A collective choice rule C is a function determining, for each M-tuple $(R_1, R_2, ..., R_m)$ of orderings on S, a social preference relation R on S. Condition U requires that the domain of C includes every logically possible M-tuple $(R_1, R_2, ..., R_m)$ of orderings on S.

One possible way out of Sen's impossibility dilemma is the weakening of Condition U (Fine, 1975; Blau, 1975). What does this imply? "If a particular configuration of individual preferences is 'outside the domain' of a social decision procedure, then nothing can be deduced from that procedure if such a configuration were to arise" (Sen, 1976, 233). Suppose that such a configuration does occur? According to Sen (1976, 233) to say that it is outside the domain of a procedure is merely an admission of defeat as far as that procedure is concerned. For this reason he comes down against all attempts to rely on this means of resolving the dilemma. Peacock and Rowley (1972) sharply disagree with this judgment, arguing that a bounded domain for collective choice is essential for the preservation of liberty in society. We shall return to this important issue later in this essay following clarification of the other conditions.

4. Condition P (the Weak Pareto Principle)

Sen's (1970) Condition P is a very weak version of the Pareto principle. Under condition P, if someone prefers x to y and everyone else regards x to be at least as good as y then x is need not be socially superior to y. Condition P requires only that if everyone in society prefers x to y then x is socially superior to y. Sen is reluctant to identify the Pareto principle with the unanimity rule (Sen, 1976, 219), since the unanimity in question is not of the whole preference but only over the pair. This latter pair-wise unanimity rule (UR) will yield the Pareto principle only where social preference over any pair depends only on individual preferences over that pair. This last condition, following Arrow (1951), is the independence of irrelevant alternatives. The Pareto principle has this independence quality and this takes us beyond the unanimity rule (UR).

Sen derives from the independence property of the Pareto principle a result that he calls the "Paretian epidemic". He defines a person as being "decisive" both ways over a pair x and y if and only if x is judged to be socially better than y whenever he prefers x to y, and vice versa. A weaker form of decisiveness is "semi-decisiveness" which requires that society judge x to be at least as good as y whenever a person prefers x to y, no matter how others rank x against y. Sen (1976) purports to prove that if social-preference cycles are to be avoided, irrespective of the nature of individual preferences, then a person who is decisive both ways over any pair of social states must be semi-decisive both ways for all pairs of social states. If correct, this suggests that under the rule of the Pareto principle no one "can be given an inch without being given an ell" (Sen, 1976, 220).

The impossibility of the Paretian liberal, evidently, is an immediate corollary of the Paretian epidemic. If one person is made decisive over one pair, representing a tiny protected sphere of personal choice, Sen argues that by virtue of the Paretian epidemic he is potentially semi-decisive over *every* pair of social states. The limited element of independence implicit in the Pareto principle, combined with the inter-pair consistency of always avoiding preference cycles is sufficient to spread decisiveness of a person from one pair to every pair, albeit in the weakened form of semi-decisiveness.

It is by no means clear that Sen's interpretation of Condition P withstands close scrutiny. He sidesteps two important limitations in both his 1970 and his 1976 contributions. The first limitation is the concentration of his discussion on *pair-wise* comparisons between x and y, whether Mr. Prude or Mr. Lascivious should read *Lady Chatterley's Lover*. The third choice, z, namely that *no-one* should read the book, is simply ignored. Yet, we know that Mr. Prude favors z over either of the two alternatives. Given this preference, the Pareto principle is incapable of providing a social choice over the three alternatives under consideration and the issue of a Paretian epidemic simply does not arise.

Sen's error, so far unrecognized in the literature, is to focus on *pair-wise* rather than on *overall* comparisons. Of course, Sen may do so if he so wishes, but he cannot then label Condition P as the Pareto condition. Mr. Prude and Mr. Lascivious disagree as to whether the book should or should not be read, and that silences the Pareto principle properly defined.

The second limitation relates to the nature of the value judgments that justify the use of the Pareto principle. Here, Sen (1976) acknowledges an important area of contention but evades its full implications. Unambiguously, the Pareto principle rests on the value judgment that social welfare should be defined in individualistic terms, with concern extending to all individuals in society.

More controversially, one could refine Pareto optimality by requiring each individual to be considered the best judge of his own welfare (Rowley and Peacock, 1975). If this value is maintained, then no individual may impose his own preferences on any other individual, no matter how well founded those preferences may appear to be in terms of prevailing ethical standards. Preferences that are meddlesome simply would not register in any social welfare function defined by reference to the Pareto criterion thus defined.

The economics profession is divided concerning the acceptability of this latter value judgment. The large literature on merit goods and paternalism suggests the existence of an influential *dirigiste* cohort of economists who are willing to impose their preferences on others if the political process provides such opportunities.

Suppose that meddlesome preferences are denied social relevance in terms of Condition P. Then the Sen impossibility theorem is significantly weakened. There may be no inconsistency between Conditions P and L*. For example, in Sen (1970), the meddlesome preferences of Mr. Prude and Mr. Lascivious would simply be suppressed by the social decision-maker in resolving the apparent conflict between Condition P and Condition L*.

Sen (1976) confronts such a possibility in his responses to insights provided by Blau (1975) and by Farrell (1976). Blau (1975) introduced the concept of ordinal intensity of preferences into the discussion, defining ordinal intensity as follows: If a person prefers x to a, a to b, and b to y, then his preference for x over y I stronger than his preference for a over b. A person is meddlesome according to Blau if and only if his preference over the two alternatives in his own assigned pair is weaker than his opposition to someone else's preference over that person's assigned pair.

Blau defends Condition P over Condition L* and proposes a modified liberalism that makes libertarian rights conditional upon preferences being non-meddlesome in the sense that he has defined. Sen (1976) questions this judgment: "Since libertarian values come into their own in defending personal liberty against meddling, one can argue that the presence of meddling makes libertarian values more (not *less*) important. If everyone meddles in the sense of Blau, surely libertarian values should demand that the meddling part of each person's preferences be ignored but the non-meddling parts dealing with one's own affairs be defended against other people's meddling" (Sen, 1976, 221). For reasons that we shall make clear, we agree with Sen's (1976) judgment on this issue.

Farrell (1976) also explores the avenue of amending an individual's preferences so that he is deemed indifferent between any pair of states for which some other individual is to be decisive. He outlines a method of moving from true preferences $\{R_i\}$ of the individuals to amended preferences $\{R_i'\}$ without running into social preference cycles. Farrell rejects such a procedure on the grounds that it falsifies preferences. Sen nevertheless concludes that "Farrell's approach seems to have much merit in it" (Sen, 1976, 232).

Ultimately, however, Sen comes down reluctantly against the solution of preference amendment, arguing that 'the set of individual orderings in general provides too little information for deciding what to do' (Sen, 1976, 237). The same set of individual orderings under one interpretation of the motivations underlying the preferences might suggest the dropping of condition P, while under another interpretation of the motivations it might point the finger at Condition L*. Once again, we agree with Sen's (1976) judgment.

In our view, it would be a dangerous error to resort to a process of preference amendment to resolve the Sen paradox. Such a process would place discretionary power in the hands of social decision-makers who would inevitably abuse it, with serious implications for the preservation of individual liberty. Economists rightly have shown themselves to be reluctant to speculate on the reasons behind preferences, given the subjective nature of such speculations.

5. Condition L* (Minimal Liberalism)

The condition of minimal liberalism, as outlined by Sen (1970, 1976), asserts that some choices between alternative social states may involve differences that are personal to some individual. For example, with everything else the same, Jack sleeps on his back (x) or on his belly (y). Such choices may be taken to be the concern only of the relevant person and to lie in that person's 'protected sphere' (Hayek, 1960).

Let us examine the nature of the conflict a little more closely in terms of two examples introduced into the discussion by Allan Gibbard (1974).

First, suppose that I have a right to choose the color of my bedroom walls. If I prefer white bedroom walls to yellow, then no matter who wants my walls to be yellow, it is preferable for them to be white. Condition L* (unlike Condition L) claims that everyone has rights in this sense, or in the modest version put forward by Sen (1970) that

everyone has at least one such right. Suppose now that I am a perverse non-conformist in that I want my bedroom walls to be a different color from Mrs. Grundy's. Mrs. Grundy, however, is a conformist. She wants her bedroom walls to be the same color as mine.

There are four social states available in this situation, namely a_{ww}, a_{wy}, a_{yw}, and a_{yy}. These social states differ only in the color of our respective bedroom walls. The first index gives the color of my walls and the second that of Mrs. Grundy's. Denoting P_1 for my preferences and P_2 for Mrs. Grundy's preferences, it follows respectively from $a_{yw}P_1a_{ww}$, $a_{ww}P_2a_{wy}$, $a_{wy}P_1a_{yy}$, and $a_{yy}P_2a_{yw}$ that $a_{yw}Pa_{ww}$, $a_{ww}Pa_{wy}$, $a_{wy}Pa_{yy}$, and $a_{yy}Pa_{yw}$. According to Condition L* each of the available alternatives ought not to be chosen. This is an interesting result because it demonstrates that a liberal paradox may arise without reference to the Pareto condition.

Second, suppose that Angelina wants to marry Edwin but will settle for marrying the judge, who wants whatever she wants. Edwin wants to remain single, but would rather marry Angelina than see her marry the judge. There are then three alternative social states:

W_E: Edwin weds Angelina;
W_J: the judge weds Angelina and Edwin remains single;
W_O: both Edwin and Angelina remain single.

Angelina prefers them in the order W_E W_J W_O; Edwin prefers them in the order W_O W_E W_J. Here Sen's notion of rights and the Pareto principle combine to yield a cycle. First, Angelina has a right to marry the willing judge instead of remaining single, and she prefers W_J to W_O. Hence W_JPW_O. Second, Edwin has the right to remain single rather than to wed Angelina, and he prefers W_O to W_E, where the only difference between the two is whether or not he weds her. Hence W_OPW_E. Finally, since all three prefer W_E to W_J, by Condition P we have W_EPW_J. The cycle is complete: W_JPW_O, W_OPW_E, and W_EPW_J. This outcome is known as *Gibbard's Paradox*.

In 1970, Sen was inclined to infer from the impossibility result that Condition P should be questioned in the context of social choice questions in which there are personal issues for which Condition L* makes sense. While recognizing that unanimity is a powerful reason for a policy to be pursued, Sen warned that it is important "not merely... to know who prefers what, but also *why* he has this preference" (Sen, 1970b, 83).

6. The Perspective of Game Theory

A number of critics of Sen's paradox utilize the social choice framework adopted by Sen (1970) while rejecting

	Lascivious	
	Reads LCL	Does Not Read LCL
Prude Reads LCL	a, c	b, c'
Does Not Read LCL	a', d	b', d'

Figure 1:

the particular notion of rights deployed in his analysis (Bernolz, 1974; Sugden, 1985; Buchanan, 1996). In the view of Bernholz (1974) and Buchanan (1996), rights are not to be interpreted to allow individuals to choose among social states. Rather, individuals are assigned rights "to control defined elements which, when combined with the exercise of mutually-compatible rights of others, will generate a social state as an outcome of an interaction process, not of a 'choice' as such, by either one or many persons" (Buchanan, 1996, 124). Nevertheless, rights are assigned through the political process, essentially as part of a constitutional contract. Sugden's (1985) view, which is much closer to our own, will be discussed later in this section.

Let us first focus on the view of Buchanan (1996), using the example of *Lady Chatterley's Lover*. Let us define four states of society as follows:

I. Prude reads LCL; Lascivious reads LCL.

II. Prude does not read LCL; Lascivious reads LCL.

III. Prude reads LCL; Lascivious does not read LCL.

IV. Prude does not read LCL; Lascivious does not read LCL.

In this depiction, unlike that of Sen (1970) the social state depicted by I is deemed to be possible. Its inclusion does not violate the spirit of his example. Figure 1 sets out these alternatives in matrix form.

According to Sen (1970), the payoffs for Prude are arrayed as follows: $b' > b > a' > a$. For Lascivious, the payoffs are arrayed as follows: $c > c' > d > d'$. In each case, these are payoffs over the full set of completed states. Sen's explicit ranking of social states guarantees that the independent adjustment outcome in Cell II is non-optimal in the sense that it is Pareto-dominated by the outcome in Cell III. Since Sen's purpose is limited to that of deriving an ordering over complete social states, there is no issue of assigning or partitioning rights among separate individuals.

However, if individuals are to be allowed to interact, one with another, as Buchanan (1996) suggests, their separate assignments in the interaction process must first be specified. At this stage, the rule of libertarianism comes into play. This rule assigns to each person a protected domain or sphere of private action that he can enforce, if he so desires,

as a part of any social outcome. In the post-constitutional situation, once such rights have been assigned, the Pareto criterion offers a means of evaluating potential transfers of rights among individuals. "In the end, the 'meddlesome preferences' may prevail, but only if those who hold them are willing to pay for their exercise" (Buchanan, 1996, 124).

Sugden (1985) strips the starting point right out of the social choice mechanism. He views the notion of the personal sphere — the area of individual action that is protected against social encroachment — as a central idea in the tradition of classical liberal thought. On this he quotes John Stuart Mill (1848):

> Whatever theory we adopt respecting the foundation of the social union, and under whatever political institutions we live, there is a circle around every individual human being which no government, be it that of one, of a few, or of the many, ought to be permitted to overstep. ..... That there is, or ought to be, some space in human existence thus entrenched around, and sacred from authoritative intrusion, no one who professes the smallest regard to freedom or dignity will call in question. (1848, Book 5, Ch. 11, Sec. 2).

Sugden (1985) utilizes this insight to offer a radically different interpretation of Gibbard's paradox to that accepted by Sen. Sugden illustrates this difference with an example more central to classical liberal doctrine than the color of walls. Let x be a social state in which one individual Liz writes a private diary expressing controversial political views. Let y be another social state identical to x in all respects accept that the sentiments Liz records in her diary are nonpolitical. According to Sen (1970) the pair of social states {x,y} should be assigned to Liz's personal sphere. If Liz prefers x to y, this implies that she would not choose x if y were available to her. The tie between social preferences and choice is hypothetical.

Suppose now that there is a second person, Ken, who also keeps a personal diary and who also might or might not wish to record controversial political opinions. Then we may distinguish four social states: Let v be the state in which Liz and Ken both keep political diaries; let w be the state in which Liz's diary is nonpolitical and Ken's is political; let x be the state in which Liz's diary is political and Ken's is not; and let y be the state in which both diaries are nonpolitical.

According to Sen the pairs {v,x} and {w,y} should be assigned both to Liz and to Ken. The paradox is that if the two individuals' preferences happen to take certain forms, this assignment of pairs of social states to personal spheres generates a logical contradiction. Specifically, if Liz's preference ordering, in strict descending order, is x, w, v, y and if Ken's is v, y, w, x, then the assignment of pairs of social states to personal spheres generates a cycle of

	Ken's Strategy	
Liz's strategy	Political	NonPolitical
Political	v	x
Nonpolitical	w	y

Figure 2:

social preference: x is socially preferred to y, y to w, w to v, and v to x.

In reality, however, in even remotely free societies, each individual chooses the content of his own diary. This is not a choice between social states. The content of any one person's diary is a characteristic of a social state and not a social state itself. According to Sugden (1985), the best way to describe this kind of procedure is as a game form (Figure 2).

It is not clear how Liz and Ken would play this game given the preferences outlined above. What strategy is best for Liz depends on what Ken is going to do, and vice versa. If they each choose according to maximin/minimax, then the outcome will be v. Both Liz and Ken will have political diaries. According to Sen, this outcome fails to respect Liz's personal sphere. The pair {w,v} belongs to Liz's sphere and she prefers w to v. Therefore, society ought not to choose v if w is available. Her hypothetical choice is not being respected.

Yet, if liberty is understood in terms of noninterference, it is surely Liz's actual choice — to keep a political diary — that has the first claim on society's respect. An uncompromising classical liberal would assert that each individual has a right to write whatever he chooses in a private diary, and that the whole purpose of the personal sphere is to protect that individual from other individuals' desires to meddle. This is so, argues Sugden (1985), even if "such a claim cannot be formulated in the language of conventional social choice theory" (Sugden, 1985, 229). In this judgement, Sugden comes close to our own view, though he still appears to allow personal spheres to be determined through the mechanism of social choice itself and he does not distinguish, as we shall, between rights and liberties.

7. The Perspective of Classical Liberal Political Economy

In his book, *On Liberty* (1859), John Stuart Mill set out to identify the nature and limits of the power that can be legitimately exercised by society over the individual. Under conditions of autocracy, the aim of patriots was to set limits to the power which the ruler should be suffered to exercise over the community; and this limitation was what was meant by liberty. As autocracy gave way to representative government, and as the holders of power were made regularly accountable to the community, Mill recognized that the limitation of the power of government over individuals loses none of its importance. The 'tyranny of the majority

now must be included among the evils against which society requires to be on its guard (Mill, 1859, 8).

> Society can and does execute its own mandates: and if it issues wrong mandates instead of right, or any mandates at all in things with which it ought not to meddle, it practices a social tyranny more formidable than many kinds of political expression, since though not usually upheld by such extreme penalties, it leaves fewer means of escape, penetrating much more deeply into the details of life, and enslaving the soul itself.

and

> There is a limit to the legitimate interference of collective opinion with individual independence: and to find that limit, and maintain it against encroachment, is as indispensable to a good condition of human affairs, as protection against political despotism.

In *On Liberty*, Mill asserts one simple principle to govern the dealings of society with the individual in the way of compulsion and control: "the sole end for which mankind are warranted, individually or collectively, in interfering with the liberty or action of any of their number, is self-protection. ... [t]he only purpose for which power can be rightfully exercised over any member of a civilized community, against his will, is to prevent harm to others. His own good, physical or moral, is not a sufficient warrant... Over himself, over his own body and mind, the individual is sovereign" (ibid., 13).

For Mill (1859) the freedom of an individual to act upon his own opinions at his own risk and peril, so long as such actions do not harm others, is essential to his development as a human being:

> He who lets the world, or his own portion of it, choose his plan of life for him, has no need of any other faculty than the ape-like one of imitation. He who chooses his plan for himself, employs all his faculties. He must use observation t to see, reasoning and judgment to foresee, activity to gather materials for decision, discrimination to decide, and when he has decided, firmness and self-control to hold to a deliberate decision. And these qualities he requires and exercises exactly in proportion as the part of his conduct which he determines according to his own judgment and feelings is a large one. It is possible that he might be guided in some good path, and kept out of harm's way without any of these things. But what will be his comparative worth as a human being? It really is of importance, not only what men do, but also the manner of men they are that do it. (ibid., 59).

Mill was especially energized to protect individuality from societal pressures to conform to so-called public opinion, recognizing that once such conformity has been established it is very difficult to jettison:

> The demand that all other people shall resemble ourselves, grows by what it feeds on. If resistance waits till life is reduced *nearly* to one uniform type, all deviations

from that type will come to be considered impious, immoral, even monstrous and contrary to nature. Mankind speedily become unable to conceive diversity, when they have been for some time unaccustomed to see it. (ibid., 74).

As many subsequent scholars have emphasized Mill's harm principle provides at best only necessary and not sufficient conditions for the restriction of liberty. It tells us that individual liberty may be limited only to prevent harm to others; it does not indicate which circumstances constitute harms of sufficient magnitude and it does not identify how great an imposition on liberty is justified in order to preclude such harms.

In *Before Resorting to Politics* (1996), Jasay addresses these *lacunae*. He argues that the Kaldor-Hicks potential compensation test, central to modern welfare economics, provides an unsound guide to political action because it cannot resolve the fundamental problem posed by Pareto of making interpersonal comparisons of utility. Where no balance can be struck between the good and the bad consequences of political action, Jasay suggests that the Hippocratic precept applies: *"first, avoid doing harm"* (Jasay, 1996, 5–9).

Making sure to avoid doing harm before trying to do good sets a strong presumption against balancing offsetting interests and determining which should carry a greater weight. Such a precept ensures that the individual should be free to do whatever is not expressly forbidden rather than that he should be allowed to do only what has been expressly approved by the state (Jasay, 1997).

This presumption against using the coercive powers of the state mandates some bounding of the domain of politics and the removal of at least some alternatives from the reach of social choice. From the particular perspective of the paradoxes raised in the Sen literature, the basic rule derived from Jasay's (1996, 1997) analytical framework is that an individual is free to do what is feasible for him to do subject to two compatibility conditions (Jasay, 1996, 5–23).

One condition relates an individual' actions to his own obligations, which in turn, are the rights of other individuals. The other condition relates his actions to harm to other individuals. If neither of these constraints binds, the individual confronts no burden of proof concerning the admissibility of feasible actions. The burden of proof rests with those who would challenge his liberty to undertake them.

Let us define as 'liberties' those feasible actions that an individual is free to execute. Some actions are inadmissible because they would infringe the rights of others. Such rights may be the natural rights of the individual to his life, liberty and property (Locke, 1690). Other rights may arise as a consequence of contractual relationships between individuals. Some actions may also be inadmissible because

they would infringe the like liberties of others (Mill, 1859). All other feasible actions by an individual are permissible. In combination, these liberties and rights define the private space of an individual, the domain of his negative freedom that may not be coercively invaded by any other individual or by any government.

8. The Logic of Liberty

In this perspective, an admissible action is the exercise either of a right or of a liberty. Let us henceforth refer to this as Condition L** and use this concept to resolve the various paradoxes that have been posed in the literature induced by the 1970 essay of Amartya Sen.

8.1. Purely Private Choices

Let us first consider the implications of Condition L** for entirely private choices such as: John sleeps on his back or John sleeps on his belly. John may sleep on his back or his belly, irrespective of the preferences of all others. This kind of choice is neither social nor inter-personal in nature. To distinguish this claim from other libertarian claims let us call it the "decisive libertarian claim".

To keep track of these elements of choice a "decisive private sphere set", (DPS_i) is designated for each individual. For entirely private choices the decisive libertarian claim is:

Condition L**: $(\forall(i \in N))(\exists(x,y \in DPS_i \subset X, |DPS_i| \geq 2)$
$(x,y \in DPS_i \rightarrow ((xP_iy \rightarrow xPy) \,\&\, (yP_ix \rightarrow yPx))))$.

Condition L** sends elements of X to the decisive private sphere of each individual in a manner that conforms with the *maximum principle*, the objective of which is to maximize the liberty of any one individual consistent with the like liberty of all other individuals. In the case of private choices, this rule takes the form:

Condition L**
for $j,k \in N$, $j \neq k$, $x \in X$:
$(\forall j)(f_L: X \rightarrow DPS_j \,|(\forall j,k)(x \in DPS_j \Rightarrow x \notin DPS_k))$

For each individual, the rule sends elements of X to each individual's decisive private sphere. This is done under the qualification that if an element is in the decisive private sphere of individual j, it is not in the decisive private sphere of individual j. Thus, it is entirely appropriate under this rule for John to decide whether he will sleep on his back or on his belly. It is equally appropriate for Karl to decide whether he will sleep on his back or on his belly.

It is entirely inappropriate for John to decide whether Karl will sleep on his back or on his belly or for Karl likewise to make such decisions for John. Neither is socially decisive over the other person's choice. Condition L* as designated by Sen (1970) fails to make this characterization. Condition L** clearly resolves the Sen paradox in the specific case of private choices. The outcomes are mutually compatible across individuals and conform to the like liberty of all others. They are resolved appropriately at the private and not the social level.

8.2. *Multiple Purely Private Choices*

This result generalizes to the many private choices available to many individuals. The same general rule sends each element of choice to the private sphere of each individual. No individual has the right to dictate the choice of any other individual with respect to any matter of private choice. These mutually exclusive outcomes are compatible across individuals, conform to the like liberty of all others, and are resolved appropriately at the individual level. John, Karl, James and Keith may each sleep as he pleases, each may choose where to live as he pleases, etc., without placing any restrictions on the like liberties of each other. There can be no Paretian epidemic from this libertarian perspective.

This category of choices we designate as *decisive libertarian claims (DLC)*.

8.3. *The Indecisive Libertarian Claim*

The *decisive libertarian claim* (DLC) applies to a multitude of entirely private choices. Individuals may choose freely without the consent of any other individual. However, the logic of liberty extends far beyond this domain. Interpersonal dependences are pervasive features of any society. We shall argue in this section that many such interdependencies can be handled by the logic of liberty without recourse to social choice in the sense required by Sen (1970). We shall show that the set of interpersonal choices requires mutual consent between individuals defined by reference to prior rights. Let us call this the "indecisive libertarian claim". Such choices are personal, not social choices; yet, they are not entirely private.

Let us now recall the Lady Chatterley's Lover example as outlined by Sen (1970). Mr. Prude (P) and Mr. Lascivious (L), are each endowed with meddlesome preferences. Sen (1970) presents us with the following three subset social states, of U:

x = Prude reads LCL; y = Lascivious reads LCL; and z = no one reads LCL.

Mr. Prude prefers z from {x,z} and {x,y,z} but prefers x from {x,y}. Mr. Lascivious prefers y from {y,z} but prefers x from {x,y,z} and {x,y}. By Condition L*, $zP_px \rightarrow zPx$ and $yP_lz \rightarrow yPz$; but by Condition P, xPy. Hence there is an apparent cycle. Under our formalization, no elements of choice are shared between Mr. Prude and Mr. Lascivious from the perspective of social choice. Sen (1970) has them sharing element z. The choice that no one should read the book is viewed as being in each of their choice domains and yet is ignored by Condition P.

Contrast our fuller characterization of liberty with that implicit in Sen (1970) statement. There is no decisive solution, in terms of the logic of liberty over any of these pairs. The choice is no longer entirely private. When moving from the private realm to the interpersonal realm it is necessary to change the decision-rules. In interpersonal, not private, matters mutual consent is required perhaps constrained by the prior rights of any individual. Of all the commentators on this debate perhaps only Peacock and Rowley (1972), together with Nozick (1974) have recognized the importance of this logic.

Let us now revisit this example from the perspective provided by the logic of liberty. According to Sen (1970) there is only one copy of *Lady Chatterley's Lover* available either to Mr. Prude or to Mr. Lascivious. It is feasible for either Mr. Prude or for Mr. Lascivious to read or not to read the book. Everything now depends on which of the two individuals owns the book.

If Mr. Prude owns the book, he has a liberty to read or not to read it. By a similar line of reasoning, if Mr. Lascivious owns the book he has a liberty to read or not to read the book. Ownership provides either party with a prior right that trumps the liberty of the other party. If the individual who does not possess the right of ownership wants to meddle in the affairs of the person who owns the right he can do so only by contracting with that person. If Mr. Prude owns the book he will not read it and he will not allow Mr. Lascivious to read it unless a contract determines such a transfer of rights. If Mr. Lascivious owns the book, he has a liberty to read the book. He will do so unless Mr. Prude intervenes, via contract, to exchange the right to read the book. All of this falls within the logic of liberty. If there is no prior right, then the logic of liberty implies that he who has access to the book has the liberty to decide.

Suppose now that the choice situation becomes more complex in the sense that individual preferences are even more complex. Even in the "perverse non-conformist case", the logic of liberty also resolves Sen's (1976) dilemma. Let us illustrate with respect to the Mrs. Grundy example, which exemplifies "Gibbard's paradox".

8.4. Gibbard's Paradox

Suppose that I am a perverse non-conformist. It is feasible for me to paint my bedroom walls any color that I choose. My choice is not constrained by any prior contract. Therefore, I have a liberty to choose my color scheme. Mrs. Grundy, likewise, has a liberty to make her own choice. Suppose that I have the right to choose the color scheme; then Mrs. Grundy has no liberty to intervene.

Suppose, alternatively, that Mrs. Grundy holds this right. To realize my preference for non-conformity, I now must contract with Mrs. Grundy, paying her to enter into an obligation not to match my color scheme. If I fail to achieve such a contract, Mrs. Grundy is free to choose the color scheme that maximizes her preferences. The logic of liberty clearly resolves this dispute.

In the "perverse non-conformist case", the logic of liberty resolves the apparent Sen (1970) dilemma. It is feasible for me to paint my bedroom walls any color that I choose as long as my choice does not imply any obligation to Mrs. Grundy. Therefore, I have a liberty to choose my color scheme. Mrs. Grundy, likewise, has a liberty to make her own choice. To realize my preference for non-conformity, I must contract with Mrs. Grundy, paying her to enter into an obligation not to match my color scheme.

From the same perspective, let us now evaluate the case of marital preferences. It is clear that Angelina, Edwin and the judge each has a liberty to remain single. None of the three has a right to marry any of the other participants. If Edwin's preferences are as listed by Sen (1970), he will successfully contract with Angelina to marry him. He has a liberty so to do, but no right. If Angelina declines his offer, then Angelina has a liberty to interact with the judge who has no right to marry her without consent.

9. Conclusions

The logic of liberty and its associated rules enables us to deal with purely private choices, multiple private choices and choices involving interpersonal utilities always assuming that tortious liability is not involved. John may live in New York, read *Lady Chatterley's Lover*, sleep on his back, worship God through Christ, etc. All the while, Karl may live in Massachusetts, read *Das Capital*, and deny the existence of God through Christ. These choices are mutually compatible and respect the like liberty of all others.

This outcome is not compatible, of course, with the *one best choice* viewed as some aggregation of utilities, whether utilitarian or Paretian, refracted upon society by a benevolent social decision-maker. For those who would allow meddlesome preferences to interfere with strictly private choices, it might appear that society would be better off as a whole if John were constrained to live in Massachusetts, to read *Das Kapital*, and to deny the existence of God through Christ, etc., even though his strictly private preferences are opposed to such a choice.

Sen (1970) would put all this into the melting pot of social choice. Let us not pretend, however, that such a judgment has anything to do with the logic of liberty.

EMORY PETERS
CHARLES K. ROWLEY

REFERENCES

Arrow, K. (1963). *Social Choice and Individual Values*, 2nd edn. New York: John Wiley.

Barry, B. (1986). "Lady Chatterley's Lover and Doctor Fischer's Bomb Party," in J. Elster and A. Hylland (eds.) *Foundations of Social Choice Theory*. Cambridge: Cambridge University Press.

Basu, K. (1984). "The right to give up rights." *Economica*, 51(204): 413–422.

Bernholz, P. (1974). "Is a Paretian liberal really impossible?" Public choice, XX, Winter, 99–107.

Blau, J. (1975). "Liberal values and independence." *Review of Economic Studies*, XLII: 395–401.

Buchanan, J.M. (1996). "An ambiguity in Sen's alleged proof of the impossibility of a Pareto Libertarian." *Analyse & Kritik*, 18: 118–125.

Farrell, M. (1976). "Liberalism in the theory of social choice." *Review of Economic Studies*, XLIII: 3–10.

Fine, B.J. (1975). "Individual liberalism in a Paretian society." *Journal of Political Economy*, 83: 1277–1282.

Gaertner, W., Pattanaik, P.K., and Suzumura, K. (1992). "Individual rights revisited." *Economica*, 59: 161–177.

Gibbard, A. (1974). "A Pareto-consistent libertarian claim." *Journal of Economic Theory*, 7: 388–410.

Hayek, F. (1960). *The Constitution of Liberty*. Chicago, Illinois: University of Chicago Press.

Hillinger, C. and Lapham, V. (1971). "The impossibility of a Paretian liberal: comment by two who are unreconstructed." *Journal of Political Economy*, 79: 1403–1405.

Jasay, A. de (1996). *Before Resorting to Politics*, Brookfield, Vermont: Edward Elgar.

Jasay, A. de (1997). *Against Politics*, London: Routledge.

Mill, J.S. (1848). *Principles of Political Economy*. London.

Mill, J.S. (1859). *On Liberty*. London. S. Collini (ed.) 1989. Cambridge: Cambridge University Press.

Nozick, R. (1974). *Anarchy, State and Utopia*. Oxford: Blackwell.

Nozick, R. (1976). "Distributive Justice." *Philosophy and Public Affairs*, 3: 45–126.

Peacock, A.T. and Rowley, C. (1972). "Pareto Optimality and the Political Economy of Liberalism." *Journal of Political Economy*, May/June: 476–490.

Rowley, C.K. and Peacock, A.T. (1975) *Welfare Economics: A Liberal Restatement*. Oxford: Martin Robertson.

Sen, A. (1970). "The possibility of a Paretian liberal." *Journal of Political Economy*, 78: 152–157.

Sen, A. (1976). "Liberty, unanimity and rights." *Economica*, 43(171): 217–245.

Sen, A. (1992). "Minimal liberty." *Economica*, 59(234): 139–159.

Sugden, R. (1985). "Social Choice and Individual Liberties." *Economics and Philosophy*, 1: 213–229.

LOGROLLING 1

Vote trading between legislators or committee members is a common phenomenon. The economics and political science literature defines logrolling or vote-trading as follows:

Let (x,y) and (z,w) be pairs of mutually exclusive issues and let voter preferences with respect to each pair be separable. A logrolling situation exists if

xPy and zPw, but ywPxz

where P stands for social preference as defined by the voting rule employed (Bernholz 1974, p. 53). For many logroll theorems it suffices if the first two social relationships are characterized by R (e.g., x and z do not lose to y and w, respectively).

Logrolling is illustrated in Figure 1. Voters 1, 2, and 3 vote on issues A and B using simple majority rule. The payoffs for these three voters on issue A are 5, -1, and -1, and the payoffs for the voters on issue B are -1, 5, and -1. If everyone votes sincerely, issue A and issue B both fail to obtain a majority of votes; neither issue is passed. However, voters 1 and 2 have an incentive to form a vote trade agreement: voter 1 agrees to vote for B and in exchange the second voter agrees to vote for A. Without vote trading no issue passes. In the presence of the vote trade agreement — which implies sophisticated voting and therefore a misrepresentation of preferences — both issues pass. In this example, total utility is increased by 3 units for

	ISSUES	
VOTER	A	B
1	5	-1
2	-1	5
3	-1	-1

Figure 1:

each issue and society is better off overall. The trade is welfare enhancing in this case, and logrolling resulted in a positive sum game. However, if the -1's in the table shown in Figure 1 are replaced by $-3'$ a negative sum game will be the result. Voters 1 and 2 still have an incentive to trade votes and while these two voters benefit individually for their vote trade, society is worse off overall, by -1 for each issue.

The normative discussion of logrolling evolves around the issue of logrolling being a positive or negative sum game. It has been argued that vote trading coupled with unanimity rule will result in a positive sum game (Wicksell, 1896). Legislators may deal with public goods issues that could potentially make society better off. In this case logrolling may produce a collective choice that brings society closer to the provision of a socially optimal level of public goods by allowing for an expression of different intensities of preferences through vote trading (Buchanan and Tullock, 1962). Logrolling may result in a negative sum game is if the electoral system does not define jurisdictions according to the spillover of public goods (Tullock, 1959). In Tullock's road example, voters have to decide on the maintenance of access roads to a main highway, with a few farmers served by each access road. Here, each access road is a local public good. The problem here is that voters other than the voters affected by the public good decide on the production of the good. The entire community decides which roads to maintain via simple majority rule. Tullock shows that members of the coalition repair the roads beyond optimal levels because they do not have to bear the full costs of the repair if costs are shared equally among all farmers. Some of the costs are borne by farmers not in the winning coalition. In this case majority rule with trading can lead to too much government spending.

Regardless as to whether logrolling is a positive or negative sum game, vote trading outcomes may not be stable, implying a lack of equilibrium in the vote exchange market (Mueller, 1967; Park, 1967). If trade agreements are broken, instability may arise, and shifting coalitions may lead to a decrease in welfare. The close relationship between vote trading and cyclical majorities can be illustrated by using Figure 1. From this table, four combinations of issue pairs arise: (A,B), (~A,B), (A,~B), and (~A,~B). It is possible to show that a cycle exists over these issue pairs. After voters 1 and 2 have agreed to form a logroll coalition for the passage of both issues (A,B), voter 3 has an incentive to approach voter 2 for the passage of the (A,~B) pair. This combination makes voter 2 better off by 3 units and voter 3 better off by 2 units of utility. Next, voter 1 has an incentive to approach voter 3 with the proposal to pass none of the issues (~A,~B). 3 will abandon the coalition with 2 to enter a more favorable coalition with 1. From this point, the cycle can start all over again with the combination (A,B). Bernholz (1973) shows formally that preferences that allow for a logroll imply the existence of a voting cycle.

The centralized vote trading model stands in stark contrast to the previous model in its optimism about the vote trading process (Haefele, 1971; Koford, 1982). In the central vote exchange model reneging is not possible as vote trades are organized centrally by party leaders. Votes are prices paid for the passage of legislation. Costs of passing the bill are costs incurred by legislators who are opposed to the legislation but vote for it. These costs are minimized: leaders have incentives to select those legislators to help pass a bill for whom it is cheapest to do so. Further, legislators pass only bills for which benefits exceed costs. Thus vote trades exist within the confines of a positive sum game. Koford (1990) argues that transactions costs, i.e., the costs of informing citizens how their representative voted on a bill, lead to logroll coalitions which are organized along party lines.

One expects the vote trading coalition to be a minimum winning coalition (Riker, 1962). Every unnecessary member included in the winning coalition implies that the net payoff is smaller for the members than needed to secure victory. The largest share for each member is secured when the coalition has the minimum number of members to ensure passage of the bill. However, minimum winning coalitions are potentially unstable (Tullock, 1981). Losers always have an incentive to reformulate the platform, so they are included in the winning coalition. Tullock suggests that stability can be induced by forming a majority that includes nearly every voter in a legislature. Recent work makes this argument using formal models (Groseclose and Snyder, 1996).

Logrolling models give little guidance on how to proceed with identifying vote trades empirically, or how to test implications that are associated with vote-trading models. However, we know that votes that are potentially subject to logrolling are votes where a minority of legislators are intensely in favor (opposed), while the majority of legislators are mildly opposed (in favor) or indifferent. Logrolling gives a specific prediction: xPy and zPw but $ywPxz$. Vote trades are predicted on issues that would not pass if every legislator votes his or her honest preferences but that are passed if logroll coalitions are formed. Likely candidates are votes where the minority interest has won. Among this set of votes, applying Riker's (1962) size principle, likely candidates are votes in which the outcome has been reasonably close. Using this reasoning and the statistical method outlined above, Stratmann (1992) identifies logrolling statistically among agricultural interests on amendments to the 1985 farm bill. The findings indicate that representatives from tobacco districts traded votes with legislators representing other agricultural commodity interests, specifically sugar and peanut farmers. Fairly equal size on the peanut vote coefficient in the sugar regression and the sugar vote coefficient in the peanut regression provided evidence for reciprocity and coalition formation.

Stratmann's evidence suggests that those legislators who are the cheapest to buy for membership are most likely to be members of the vote trade coalition. For example, on an amendment on peanut subsidies, it was found that 120 legislators switched their vote due to a vote trade agreement. These legislators made up a disproportionate share of those who had a probability between 0.3 and 0.4 and 0.4 and 0.5 of voting for peanut subsidies: 90 percent of legislators who were in the 0.3 and 0.4 range switched and 65 of 134 (48.5 percent) legislators who were in the 0.4–0.5 range switched. This is consistent with the hypothesis that party leaders arrange low cost trades which in turn enhances stability. Recent work by Irwin and Kroszner (1996) shows that final, party-line voting masks a rich vote trading dynamic. They examine logrolling coalitions and show that vote-trading between oil and lumber interests was one of the factors that determined the outcome of tariff-legislation in the 1930s.

If instability were widespread in Congress, evidence for reciprocity in vote trades should be virtually non existent, supporting the view that trading is anarchic. The notion that trading involves instability and shifting coalitions is not supported by Stratmann (1992, 1996). He finds reciprocity among members from agricultural districts voting for their colleague's commodity price supports, quota restrictions, etc. To date, empirical findings appear to point to stable coalitions. For example, the ongoing vote trading coalitions between farm, city, labor and western interests has been documented for over a period spanning from 1947 to 1962 (Mayhew, 1966; Stratmann, 1995). Further, the evidence for reciprocity in vote trades suggests no wide-spread reneging on vote trade agreements.

So far, the evidence on vote trading appears to be consistent with the hypothesis that leaders efficiently organize vote trades: many of the legislators who voted for a bill because of a logroll agreement were legislators marginally opposed to the passage of the bill. Thus, representatives for whom it was cheapest to vote against constituency interests were solicited as members of the logroll coalition. These results suggest that these coalitions are not formed as suggested by the cycling theorems. At one step in a cycle, high demanders form a winning coalition with very low demanders, opposing those with moderate intensity. For example, at some point in the cycle wheat farm representatives are expected trade and form a winning coalition with legislators strongly opposed to peanut subsidies. This implies that legislators with a low probability of voting for peanut subsidies vote for these subsidies due to the vote trade agreement. The evidence is not consistent with this prediction as many of the traders are legislators marginally opposed to subsidies (Stratmann, 1992). More empirical studies are needed to test for logrolling, how coalitions are formed, and whether vote-trading is, on net, a positive or negative sum game.

THOMAS STRATMANN

REFERENCES

Bentley, A.F. (1907). *The Process of Government.* Chicago: University of Chicago Press.

Bernholz, P. (1973). "Logrolling, Arrow paradox and cyclical majorities." *Public Choice,* 15: 87–95.

Bernholz, P. (1974a). "Communication." *American Political Science Review,* 68: 961–2.

Bernholz, P. (1974b). "Logrolling, Arrow paradox and decision rules — a generalization." *Kyklos,* 27: 49–61.

Bernholz, P. (1975). "Logrolling and the paradox of voting: are they logically equivalent?" *American Political Science Review,* 69: 961–962.

Bernholz, P. (1978). "On the stability of logrolling outcomes in stochastic games." *Public Choice,* 33(3): 65–82.

Black, J.D. (1928). "The McNary-Haugen Movement." *American Economic Review,* 18: 426ff.

Buchanan, J.M. and Tullock, G. (1962). *The Calculus of Consent.* Ann Arbor: University of Michigan Press.

Caplin, A. and Nalebuff, B. (1988). *On 64%-Majority Rule. Econometrica,* 56: 787–814.

Coleman, J.S. (1966). "The possibility of a social welfare function." *American Economic Review,* 56: 1105–1022.

Coleman, J.S. (1967). "The possibility of a social welfare function: reply." *American Economic Review,* 57: 1311–1317.

Coleman, J.S. (1983). "Recontracting, Trustworthiness, and the Stability of Vote Exchanges." *Public Choice,* 40: 89–94.

Downs, A. (1957). *An Economic Theory of Democracy.* New York: Harper and Row.

Downs, A. (1961). "In defense of majority voting." *Journal of Political Economy,* 69: 192–199.

Farquharson, R. (1969). *Theory of Voting.* New Haven: Yale University Press.

Fenno, R.F. (1973). *Congressmen in Committees.* Boston: Little Brown.

Ferejohn, J.A. (1974). *Pork Barrel Politics: Rivers and Harbors Legislation 1947–1968.* Stanford: Stanford University Press.

Fiorina, M.P. and Plott, C.R. (1978). "Committee decisions under majority rule: An experimental study." *American Political Science Review,* 72: 575–598.

Froman, L.A. (1967). *The Congressional Process: Strategies, Rules and Procedures.* Boston: Little, Brown and Company.

Gibbard, A. (1973). "Manipulation of voting schemes: A general result." *Econometrica,* 41: 587–602.

Groseclose Tim and James M. Snyder (1996). "Buying supermajorities." *American Political Science Review,* June, 90(2): 303–315.

Haefele, E.T. (1971). "A utility theory of representative government." *American Economic Review,* 61: 350–367.

Hylland, A. and Zeckhauser, R. (1979). "A mechanism for selecting public goods when preferences must be elicited." KSG Discussion Paper 70D, Harvard University.

Irwin, Douglas A. and Kroszner, Randall S. (1996). "Log-Rolling and Economic Interests in the Passage of the Smoot-Hawley Tariff," Carnegie-Rochester Conference Series on Public Policy, December, 173–200.

Jackson, John E. (1974). *Constituencies and Leaders in Congress.* Cambridge: Harvard University Press.

Kadane, J. B. (1972). "On division of the question." *Public Choice,* 13: 47–54.

Kau, J.B. and Rubin, P.H. (1979). "Self-interest, ideology, and logrolling in congressional voting." *Journal of Law and Economics,* 22: 365–384.

Koehler, D.H. (1975). "Vote trading and the voting paradox: A proof of logical equivalence." *American Political Science Review,* 69: 954–960.

Koford, K.J. (1982). "Centralized vote-trading." *Public Choice,* 39(2): 245–268.

Koford, K.J. (1987). "Scale economies and rent-seeking in legislative parties." *Public Choice,* 52: 35–55.

Koford, K.J. (1990). "Dimensions, transaction costs and coalitions in legislative voting." *Economics and Politics,* 2: 59–82.

Mayhew, D.R. (1966). *Party Loyalty Among Congressmen: The Difference Between Democrats and Republicans.* Cambridge: Harvard University Press.

McKelvey, R.D. (1976). "Intransitivities in multidimensional voting models and some implications for agenda control." *Journal of Economic Theory,* 12: 472–482.

McKelvey, R.D. and Ordeshook, P.C. (1980). "Vote trading: An experimental study." *Public Choice,* 35(2): 151–184.

Mueller, D.C. (1967). "The possibility of a social welfare function: Comment." *American Economic Review,* 57: 1304–1311.

Mueller, D.C. (1973). "Constitutional democracy and social welfare." *Quarterly Journal of Economics,* 87: 60–80.

Mueller, D.C. (1989). *Public Choice II.* Cambridge: Cambridge University Press.

Mueller, D.C., Philpotts, G.C., and Vanek, J. (1972). "The social gains from exchanging votes: A simulation approach." *Public Choice,* 13: 55–79.

Musgrave, R.A. (1959). *The Theory of Public Finance.* New York: McGraw-Hill.

Niemi, R.G. (1983). "Why so much stability?: Another opinion." *Public Choice,* 41(2): 261–270.

von Neumann, J. and Morgenstern, O. (1953). *The Theory of Games and Economic Behavior,* 3rd edition. Princeton: Princeton University Press.

Oppenheimer, J.A. (1975). "Some political implications of vote trading and voting paradox: A proof of logical equivalence: A comment." *American Political Science Review,* 69: 963–966.

Ordeshook, P.C. (1986). *Game Theory and Political Theory.* Cambridge: Cambridge University Press.

Park, R.E. (1967). "The possibility of a social welfare function: Comment." *American Economic Review*, 57: 1300–1304.

Philpotts, G. (1972). "Vote trading, welfare, and uncertainty." *Canadian Journal of Economics*, 3: 358–372.

Riker, W.H. (1962). *The Theory of Political Coalitions.* New Haven and London: Yale University Press.

Riker, W.H. (1974). Communication. *American Political Science Review*, 68: 1692.

Riker, W.H. and Brams, S.J. (1973). "The paradox of vote trading." *American Political Science Review*, 67: 1235–1247.

Satterthwaite, M.A. (1975). "Strategy-proofness and Arrow's conditions: Existence and correspondence theorems for voting procedures and social welfare functions." *Journal of Economic Theory*, 10: 187–217.

Schwartz, T. (1975). "Vote trading and Pareto efficiency." *Public Choice*, 24: 101–109.

Schwartz, T. (1981). "The universal-instability theorem." *Public Choice*, 37(3): 487–501.

Schofield, N. (1987). "Coalitions in West European Democracies: 1945–1986." St. Louis: Washington University, 1987, mimeo.

Shepsle, K.A. (1979). "Institutional arrangements and equilibrium in multidimensional voting models." *American Journal of Political Science*, 23: 27–59.

Shepsle, K.A. and Weingast, B.R. (1981). "Structure-induced equilibrium and legislative choice." *Public Choice*, 37(3): 503–19.

Stratmann, T. (1992). "The effects of logrolling on congressional voting." *The American Economic Review*, (82)5: 1162–76.

Stratmann, T. (1996). "Instability in collective decisions? Testing for cyclical majorities." *Public Choice*, 88: 15–28.

Stratmann, T. (1995). "Logrolling in the U.S. Congress." July, *Economic Inquiry*, 23: 441–456.

Smith, V. (1977). "The Principle of Unanimity and Voluntary Consent in Social Choices." *Journal of Political Economy*, 85: 1125–1139.

Tullock, G. (1959). "Some problems of majority voting." *Journal of Political Economy*, 67, 571–579, reprinted in Arrow and Scitovsky (1969, pp. 169–178).

Tullock, G. (1974). Communication. *American Political Science Review*, 68: 1687–8.

Tullock, G. (1981) "Why so much stability?" *Public Choice*, 37(2): 189–202.

Wicksell, K. (1896). "A new principle of just taxation." *Finanztheoretische Untersuchungen.* Reprinted in Musgrave and Peacock (1967, 72–118).

LOGROLLING 2

Logrolling refers to a political practice of forming majority coalitions to support a potpourri of minority positions. Hence it involves each politician giving up some things to gain some other things of greater value. Typically, it refers to legislative vote trading, but it certainly has broader connotations than that. Indeed, Olson's (1982) argument regarding the decline of empires was predicated on the more general notion that minority interests can logroll successfully to stop efficient growth. As Stein and Bickers (1994) have pointed out even in legislatures its meaning is a bit ambiguous. Some have argued that 'pork-barrel' type legislation (in which a large number of specific projects, each with a very narrow constituency are pulled together to create a majority) is a consummate example of logrolling. Others have pointed to the passage of a number of disparate bills being passed by a narrow legislative committee structure. Still others have claimed that the initial political push for a program may be quite narrow, but to maintain a long-term base of support, the benefits have to broaden, and so a sort of logroll occurs to broaden the impact of the programs.

There have been a number of separate lines of inquiry regarding the subject of logrolling and vote trading. For purposes of this essay I divide them up as: logrolling and the social choice problem; universalism, efficiency, and distributive concerns; empirical studies. I deal with them each in turn.

1. Logrolling and the Social Choice Problem

Binary trades, the mainstays of markets, has long appeared to be the sure ticket to Pareto improvements. In the last decades some of the luster associated with trades has worn off. First came the observation that at the base of all trades seemed to be a less soluble prisoner's dilemma game (each side would like to move second: take the money and run, so to speak). Only the existence of property rights underlying market transactions seem to stabilize the outcomes (see Schwartz, 1981).

This casual observation did not prevent some political observers from conjecturing an amelioratory relationship between social choice paradoxes and the practice of vote trading. The brashest of these claims was by James Coleman (1966) who erroneously argued that vote-trading and other forms of political bargaining implicit in logrolling required a cardinality of the social decision space which would obviate the Arrovian problems of social choice. This, in spite of the early warning by Anthony Downs (1957) that the formation of a "winning coalition" from a coalition of minorities could lead to problems of cyclic outcomes.

The general relationship between creating a victory, when there is no Condorcet Winner and vote cycles was first stipulated by Kadane (1972) and then continued and extended in a number of papers and articles on the trading of votes and general problems of cycles in the 1970's (Bernholz, 1974; Miller, 1975; Oppenheimer, 1975, 1979; Schofield, 1980). Eventually this literature was pulled together into one simple and elegant proof by Thomas Schwartz (1981). Schwartz showed that regardless of the type of institution, any time a trade *had* to take place for an outcome to be reached (i.e., it could not be reached by the mere aggregating of purely individualistic maximizing behavior), there was an implicit cycle going on. This analysis pulled together a number of problems including that of the "Liberal Paradox" (Sen, 1970) which had been shown to be related to cycles (Bernholz, 1976) and the prisoner dilemma (Miller, 1977b).

2. Universalism, Efficiency, and Distributive Concerns

The fact that log-rolling involves cycles doesn't deal with its values and functions. Gordon Tullock (1967) argued that it was an engine for the pernicious growth of majoritarian governmental budgets. In a similar voice, Olson (1982) argued but with a more general voice, that the narrow minorities would form stable blocking coalitions. Of course, this notion flies in the face of the above generalizations, which pointed out that there was no stability in such coalitional structures. Of course, other aspects of the political environment could generate stability to coalitions of minorities, much as Arrow's instabilities can be blocked by violating one or more of his "desiderata" (such as non-dictatorship).

Weingast began to consider one of the fundamental bases for logrolls: that a typical logroll includes many a project where each project's benefits are divisible and concentrated in just a few legislative districts. The funds come from universal taxation. Note that any set of projects would define a winning and a losing set of districts. The concern is why do these sorts of "pork-barrel" projects pass so regularly and easily. The first successful search for an explanation for the creation of stable minorities coalitions came from Weingast (1979). He argued that super-inclusive universal coalitions could form so long as the politicians are left uncertain as to which coalitions might form, and hence fear being left out of the winning coalitions. Indeed, under those conditions, universal coalitions form as the "core" of the cooperative legislative game so as to secure maximum ex ante expected value for the each of the members in a legislature when their inclusion in the winning coalition is at risk.

Weingast et al. (1981) went on to conjecture that strong parties, which could secure membership in winning logrolls for its members, could lead to more efficient, smaller coalitions. This has led to a new argument, that universalism would hold only within majority parties, not across parties whenever the parties are strong enough to keep disciplined coalitions winning (Cox and McCubbins, 1993).

3. Empirical Studies and Conclusions

Recently, the theoretical conjectures outlined above supporting universal log rolling coalitions have been subject to testing (Collie, 1988 presents an overview; Stein and Bickers, 1994 presents interesting and careful tests). In all cases, the results have proven the theoretical conjectures very vulnerable. The results showed that most programs with divisible benefits are passed in bills that benefit very few districts: far fewer than had been conjectured, either by the early universalist conjectures, or by the later party-centric arguments. Indeed, the number of programs and bundles of programs that reward more than a small segment of districts is small. This doesn't mean that there is no vote — swapping and logrolling. But it does mean that the dynamics must be somewhat different than has been conjectured to date. Rather, what is implied is that the premises in the arguments ought to be reassessed.

Some of the premises which are suspect include (1) that the voters track the benefits going to the district; (2) that the legislator can influence benefits by getting a project for her own district; (3) that voters reward legislators for the flow of benefits to their districts. Stein and Bickers note that universalization of benefits was argued for as a strategy to increase reelection chances. There are other strategies which may be more attractive.

But it appears that as long as humans have been around, there has been 'trading' and trading by politicians across programs, often in the currency of votes, is just one form of the activity. It is likely to play a role in the securing of all political outcomes, and perhaps is the reason for the popular notion: "politics makes strange bedfellows."

JOE OPPENHEIMER

REFERENCES

Arnold, R. Douglas (1981). "Legislators, Bureaucrats, and Location Decisions." *Public Choice*, 37: 107–132.

Bernholz, P. (1976). "Liberalism, logrolling and cyclical group preferences." *Kyklos*, 29: 26–37.

Bernholz, P. (1974). "Logrolling, arrow paradox and decision rules: A Generalization." *Kyklos*, 27: 49–61.

Bickers, Kenneth N. and Stein, Robert M. (1994). "Response to Barry Weingast's Reflections." *Political Research Quarterly* 47(June): 329–333.

Buchanan, James and Tullock, Gordon (1962). *The Calculus of Consent.* Ann Arbor: University of Michigan Press.

Coleman, James (1966). "The possibility of a social welfare function." *American Economic Review*, 56: 1105–1122.

Collie, Melissa P. (1988). "The legislature and distributive policy making in formal perspective." *Legislative Studies Quarterly*, 13(November): 427–458.

Cox, Gary and McCubbins, Mathew (1993). *Legislative Leviathan.* Berkeley: University of California Press.

Downs, A. (1957). *An Economic Theory of Discovery.* New York: Harper and Row.

Kadane, Joseph (1972). "On division of the question." *Public Choice,* 13(Fall): 47–54.

McKelvey, Richard D. and Ordeshook, Peter C. (1981). "Experiments on the Core." *Journal of Conflict Resolution,* 25(4): 709–724.

Miller, Gary J. and Oppenheimer, Joe A. (1982). "Universalism in Experimental Committees." *American Political Science Review,* 76 (2, June): 561–574.

Miller, N.R. (1983). "Pluralism and Social Choice." *American Political Science Review,* 77: 734–747.

Miller, N.R. (1975). "Logrolling and the arrow paradox: A note." *Public Choice,* 21: 107–110.

Miller, N.R. (1977a). "Logrolling, vote trading and the paradox of voting: A game theoretic overview." *Public Choice,* 30(Summer): 51–70.

Miller, N.R. (1977b). "Social preference and game theory: A comment on the dilemmas of a paretian liberal." *Public Choice,* 30: 23–28.

Niou, Emerson and Peter Ordeshhok (1985). "Universalism in Congress." *American Journal of Political Science,* 29(May): 246–258.

Olson, Mancur (1982). *The Rise and Decline of Nations: Economic Growth, Stagflation, & Social Rigidities.* New Haven: Yale Univeristy Press.

Oppenheimer, Joe (1975). "Some political implications of 'vote trading and the voting paradox: a proof of logical equivalence': a Comment." *American Political Science Review,* 69(3): 963–969.

Oppenheimer, Joe A. (1979). "Outcomes of logrolling in the bargaining set and democratic theory: some conjectures." *Public Choice,* 34: 419–434.

Schofield, Norman (1980). "The bargaining set in voting games." *Behavioral Science,* 25: 120–129.

Schwartz, T. (1981) "The Universal Instability Theorem." *Public Choice,* 37(3): 487–502.

Sen, A.K. (1970). "The Impossibility of a Paretian Liberal." *Journal of Political Economy,* 78(Jan/Feb): 152–157.

Shepsle K. and Weingast, Barry (1981). "Structure induced equilibrium and legislative choice." *Public Choice,* 37(3): 503–520.

Shepsle K. (1979). "Institutional arrangements and equilibrium in multidimensional voting models." *American Journal of Political Science,* 23(1): 27–59.

Stein, Robert M. and Bickers, Kenneth N. (1994). "Universalism and the electoral connection: A test and some doubts." *Political Research Quarterly,* 47(June): 295–317.

Tullock, Gordon. (1967). *Toward A Mathematics of Politics.* Ann Arbor: University of Michigan Press.

Weingast, Barry R. (1979). "A rational choice perspective on congressional norms." *American Journal of Political Science,* 23(May): 245–262.

Weingast, Barry R., Shepsle, Kenneth A., and Johnsen, Christopher (1981). "The Political Economy of Benefits and costs: A neoclassical approach to distributive politics." *Journal of Political Economy,* 89(August): 642–664.

Weingast, Barry R. (1994). "Reflections on distributive politics and universalism." *Political Research Quarterly,* 47(June): 319–327.

M

MEDDLESOME PREFERENCES AND RENT EXTRACTION: THE TOBACCO SHAKEDOWN

Tobacco has become an arena of civil warfare throughout the Western world over the past half-century or so. This war has been fueled by an ideological rhetoric that speaks of the costs that smokers place on nonsmokers (Office of Technology Assessment, 1985, 1993). The state claims to wage the war to protect innocent nonsmokers from predatory attacks by smokers. This claim has now been thoroughly refuted, starting with Tollison and Wagner (1988), as extended in Tollison and Wagner (1992). Whereas Tollison and Wagner argue that those costs are borne wholly by smokers, such authors as Manning et al. (1989), Gravelle and Zimmerman (1994), and Viscusi (1997) argue that there are some modest costs shifted onto nonsmokers, but that those costs are significantly less than the excise taxes that are currently imposed on cigarettes. As a result, smokers do not impose costs on nonsmokers but rather subsidize nonsmokers. Yet the war on tobacco continues, and in a big way. What the continuation of the war perhaps illustrates is the interaction between meddlesome preferences and rent extraction.

A social democracy with the large government it entails carries within itself tendencies to transform tolerant preferences into meddlesome preferences (Buchanan, 1986). A market economy supports tolerance across different preferences within a society, a collective economy does not. If health care is organized through private property within a market economy, people are responsible for the costs of their health care. People who engage in risky occupations, dangerous leisure time activities, or unhealthy lifestyles would bear the medical costs associated with those personal choices. If people who ride motorcycles incur higher medical costs on average than people who do not, they will bear the higher costs. If people who smoke incur higher medical costs, they will bear those costs. The provision of medical care within the framework offered by the principles of property and contract does nothing to undermine support for the liberal principle of mutual toleration over preferences.

As health care comes increasingly to be financed collectively, however, tolerance over personal choices can give way to intolerance, due to the shifts in political and personal incentives that collectivization creates. The actuarial evidence shows that people who smoke have lower average life expectancies than nonsmokers, though there are many smokers who lead long lives and nonsmokers who die early. Insurance within a market economy charges different prices to people in different risk categories that reflect the different costs of providing service (McCormick et al., 1997).

It is different with collective provision and its replacement of market pricing with tax financing or state-regulated pricing. People who make relatively low use of a service form a natural interest group, whose members have interests that are opposed to those who might make relatively high use. What was a matter of a simple toleration of different choices of lifestyles under market arrangements becomes a matter of political interest and activity. In the presence of collective provision, the costs of activities that entail above-average costs will be shifted partially onto those whose activities entail below-average costs. The transfer of medical care from a market-based to a collective-based mode of organization generates pressures for a similar transfer of control regarding a variety of other personal choices. Activities that have expected costs of health care that are higher than average become of concern to people who dislike those activities, because they now are paying for some of the costs associated with those activities. Toleration recedes as collective provision replaces market provision, as tolerant preferences are transformed into meddlesome preferences.

The state necessarily becomes a battleground for the adjudication of disputes over personal lifestyles. When economic activity is organized according to the principles of property and contract, a society can tolerate peacefully a variety of such lifestyles because those who conduct more costly patterns of life pay for them. But once the market principle of personal responsibility is abridged for some principle of collective responsibility, interest groups are automatically established that will bring personal lifestyles onto the political agenda, which in turn generates opportunities for rent extraction.

A huge literature on rent seeking has been inspired by Gordon Tullock's (1967) seminal articulation. Fred McChesney (1997) advances rent extraction as a closely related cousin to rent seeking. Rent seeking and rent extraction are to politics what bribery and extortion are to ordinary people. For ordinary people, these kinds of activity are wrong. But in politics they are business as usual. Rent seeking describes what people have in mind by lobbying. It refers to the payments people make to secure political favors. A sports magnate would like special tax treatment for a stadium he is building. He lobbies to get this enacted.

Or, more likely, hires someone to do this for him. In this regard, it is noteworthy that few defeated or retired legislators return to their home districts. Most of them stay in Washington, where their value as lobbyists is high.

But rent seeking is only part of the story of money and politics, and perhaps only the smaller part. Rent extraction may be even more significant. It refers to the payments people make to avoid being victimized by politically harmful measures. If rent seeking would be called bribery if it occurred between private persons, rent extraction would be called extortion. McChensey (p. 2) uses Citicorp as an example of how corporations react to political rent extraction. "The nation's largest banking company employs eight registered lobbyists in its Washington office. In addition, six law firms represent Citicorp's interests on Capitol Hill. No one should judge this strike force ineffective by how little banking legislation gets through: The lobbyists spend most of their time blocking and blunting changes that could hurt Citicorp's extensive credit-card operations, student-loan business or ever-broadening financial-service offerings."

McChesney notes that rent extraction by politicians is similar to the practice of "mud farming" that William Faulkner described in *The Reivers*. Late at night, farmers would plough up portions of the dirt roads in front of their houses, and then soak the roads. The cars that passed by during the day would get stuck in the mud. The drivers faced a choice. They could abandon their cars. Or they could pay the farmers to hitch up their mules and pull out the stuck cars — for a price, of course.

There is one vital difference between rent seeking and rent extraction that should not be ignored, and which may explain why the former has received more attention than the latter. With rent seeking, politicians are portrayed as relatively passive victims. They are deluged by lobbyists, and on occasion capitulate to them. The politician is caught in a squeeze between the intensity of special interests and the quietude of the public interest.

With rent extraction, however, politicians are in the forefront of the action. They are the active initiators who continually look for targets. Those targets, like the drivers who came across the mud farmers, have a choice. They can ignore the politicians and lose a lot of their wealth. Or they can participate politically, thereby softening their losses.

Not all rent extraction must be produced politically. Rent extraction can be farmed out, much as with the tax farming of old. A practice called tax farming has been traced back at least 4000 years to ancient Mesopotamia (Webber and Wildavsky, 1986). Real farmers raise food from their land. Tax farmers raised revenue from the people who inhabited the lands of some ruler. It is only natural that a practice that has been employed in so many places over 4000 years would show many differences in the particular details by which it operated.

The central idea of tax farming, however, was the same everywhere. A ruler wanted to extract revenue from his subjects, and hired someone to do the extraction. Typically a tax farmer would be awarded a monopoly to harvest taxes from a particular area. In many cases a ruler would assign a revenue quota to the tax farmer. A tax farmer who failed to deliver his quota of revenue would be liable for the shortage.

Tax farmers were generally wealthy men who became even wealthier through tax farming. The ruler's chief concern was to get his desired revenue. If the tax farmer failed to extract sufficient revenue from the people, the ruler could collect the shortage from the tax farmer himself. A ruler would not want to hire a tax farmer who was poor because only a wealthy tax farmer could assure satisfaction of the ruler's appetite for revenue.

While tax farmers were liable for shortages, tax farming was generally a profitable business. Whatever wealth a tax farmer started with, he could generally add to it nicely through tax farming. Tax farmers who extracted revenues beyond their quotas could keep the difference. Such a tax farmer would not invoke a ruler's wrath so long as he raised sufficient revenue for the ruler. From time to time rulers would use such devices as soliciting bids for the right to be a tax farmer, in an effort to increase their share of the tax farmer's harvest.

Tax farming has been widely regarded as a practice of autocracy and not of democracy, for in democracy taxation is the province of the legislature. Despite this common presumption, it would seem as though a form of tax farming has erupted recently in the United States. It takes the form of lawyers filing class action suits, where the results of those suits replace what otherwise would have required legislation to accomplish. The tobacco settlement is a recent case in point (Wagner, 1999). The major tobacco companies settled a suit with all state governments throughout the land for $246 billion. The revenues are already accruing to the states, and are being used for a wide variety of purposes from A to Z.

The lawyers in this case are modern-day tax farmers. They have used the tobacco companies as a vehicle for collecting taxes on smokers. Instead of state legislatures roughly doubling their tobacco taxes, the lawyers collected the taxes themselves through the tobacco settlement. What makes the analogy with tax farming complete is that the lawyer-tax farmers were able to keep many billions of dollars for themselves. The majority of the revenue collected by the tax farmers of old went to the rulers. It is the same for our new form of tax farming.

The tobacco settlement is not the first case of modern tax farming and other cases are now in process. Before tobacco, there was asbestos. Since tobacco, there is gun manufacturing (Levy, in press). What exists in these cases is a form of tax farming, only the farmers wear suits and work mostly in offices. They find people from whom to extract revenue, and typically focus on the easiest and most lucrative targets, which are those targets whose pockets are thought to be the deepest. The new tax farmers keep a good chunk of the revenue they collect for themselves. The remainder goes to politically favored purposes in one form or another. The tobacco litigation involved the state attorneys general in hiring private law firms, and with many of those firms making contributions to political campaigns on behalf of their sponsors.

The recent settlement between the major tobacco companies and the American states illustrates modern tax farming at work. The states could have legislated tax increases on cigarettes, as they have often done. Perhaps influenced by a political calculus that forecast strong opposition to tax increases, they supported suits instead. They farmed out tax collection to law firms rather than resorting to legislation. Meddlesome preferences that were generated in a context of rational ignorance and Paretian non-logical conduct (Pareto, 1935), made this shakedown appear to most people to be not a disguised form of tax but rather justice at work. Most legislators are lawyers, and the growth of democratic tax farming may well strengthen the commingling of law and politics.

RICHARD E. WAGNER

REFERENCES

Buchanan, J.M. (1986). "Politics and Meddlesome Preferences," in R.D. Tollison (ed.) *Smoking and Society: Toward a More Balanced Assessment*. Lexington, MA: Lexington Books, pp. 335–342.

Gravelle, J.G. and Zimmerman, D. (1994). *Cigarette Taxes to Fund Health Care Reform: An Economic Analysis*. Washington, D.C.: Congressional Research Service.

Levy, R. (2003). "Taxation through Litigation," in D. Racheter and R.E. Wagner (eds.) *Politics, Taxation, and the Rule of Law*. Boston: Kluwer Academic Publishers.

Manning, W.G. et al. (1989). "The Taxes of Sin: Do Smokers and Drinkers Pay Their Way?" *Journal of the American Medical Association*, 261: 1604–1609.

McChesney, F. (1997). *Money for Nothing: Politicians, Rent Extraction, and Political Extortion*. Cambridge: Harvard University Press.

McCormick, R.E., Tollison, R.D., and Wagner, R.E. (1997). "Smoking, Insurance, and Social Cost." *Regulation*, 20: 33–37.

Office of Technology Assessment (1985). *Smoking Related Deaths and Financial Costs*. Washington, D.C.: Office of Technology Assessment.

Office of Technology Assessment (1993). *Smoking-Related Deaths and Financial Costs: Office of Technology Assessment Estimates for 1990*. Washington, D.C.: Office of Technology Assessment.

Pareto, V. (1935). *The Mind and Society: A Treatise on General Sociology*. New York: Harcourt Brace.

Tollison, R.D. and Wagner, R.E. (1988). *Smoking and the State*. Lexington, MA: D.C. Heath.

Tollison, R.D. and Wagner, R.E. (1992). *The Economics of Smoking*. Boston: Kluwer Academic Publishers.

Tullock, G. (1967). "The Welfare Cost of Tariffs, Monopolies, and Theft." *Economic Inquiry*, 5: 224–232.

Viscusi, W.K. (1992). *Smoking: Making the Risky Decision*. New York: Oxford University Press.

Wagner, R.E. (1999). "Understanding the Tobacco Settlement: The State as a Partisan Plaintiff." *Regulation*, 22 (4): 38–41.

Webber, C. and Wildavsky, A. (1986). *A History of Taxation and Expenditure in the Western World*. New York: Simon and Schuster.

THE MEDIAN IN POLITICS

The controversies surrounding democratic institutions can be simplified and brought into clearer focus by considering the properties of the median of a probability density on the line (the "population median") or the median of a sample drawn from that density. Two short contributions by Francis Galton to *Nature* of 1907, in which he demonstrated that one could move from the properties of estimation to the properties of voting, ought to have made it clear to later workers that the median is an appropriate mathematical model of a one-dimensional majoritarian decision-making process, Galton (1907a, b). Any position other than the median, as Galton pointed out, would lose in competition with the median.

Galton's demonstration seems to have been too far advanced for non-statisticians to appreciate, David Levy and Sandra Peart (2002). Most importantly, Duncan Black (1958) from who no predecessor is hidden, described Galton's contribution as an minor forerunner of his own work in which the population of those voting is fixed. Thus Black missed how Galton moves in the context of randomly selected jury from *estimation* to voting. Once one appreciates that voting and estimation can be represented by the same mathematical structure, the way is clear for the entire apparatus of mathematical statistics to be focused upon the issues of political presentation, Gilbert Bassett and Joseph Persky (1999). Indeed, thinking in terms of political representation as an estimation procedure makes it obvious that democracy procedures are wider than simple voting, encompassing such historically intriguing institutions as the

Athenian practice of election by lot in which representatives are selected at random, Levy (1989).

These two ways of thinking about the median in politics help make clear that democratic institutions can be viewed apart from the subjectivist interpretation of voting which rather naturally follows from the neo-classical economic approach to politics adopted by the founders of public choice, by Black (1958), Kenneth J. Arrow (1963), James Buchanan and Gordon Tullock (1962) and those later scholars whose contributions are surveyed by Dennis Mueller (1989). Voting as estimation approach allows an objectivist interpretation of politics. When Galton considered the members of a jury giving numerical votes damages to be awarded he not unnaturally assumed that there was some sense to the proposition that there was in fact some underlying damage to be redressed and so he tested his formalized intuition by studying how the median guess recovered the true weight of a dressed ox!

Using the two-fold interpretation of the median in politics, we consider three contentious issues of political theory: the intensity-blindness of majority rule politics, the possibility of multiple equilibrium in democracy and the problem of lack of influence in an election.

Intensity. The world seems divided between those for whom "one person one vote" resonates and those for whom "one dollar one vote" appeals. This question of intensity occurs at the center of the interpretation we put upon median voter theory because once multiple dimensions are introduced in politics then the possibility of vote trading — "log-rolling" in the American idiom — opens (Buchanan and Tullock, 1962) and there is no reason to believe, save in the symmetrical Plott conditions (Charles Plott, 1967), that the median will prevail issue by issue (Richard McKelvey, 1979).

Violations of median voter desires via log rolling, vote trading, agenda control are positive issues. What interpretation do we put on such results? Those for whom intensity matters will likely approve such institutions as representative democracy where such a political market can be effected. Those for whom interest group politics are distasteful might well prefer such institutions as single-issue direct democracy, as exemplified in citizen initiatives, where the majority's judgment is more likely to be decisive.

Weighting votes by dollars raises throny questions of income distribution. Fortunate that the complication which intensity of preference raises in politics can be considered in the abstract definitions of mean and median. The first property worthy of remark of the population median is that its existence is no more or less problematic than that of probability itself. For whenever there is a probability

density, a function f such $f(x) \geq 0, \int_{-\infty}^{\infty} f(x)dx = 1$ we can construct the median as that v for which $\int_{-\infty}^{v} f(x)dx = 1/2$. On the contrary the existence of the first moment of the random variable X (the "population mean") $\mu = E(x) = \int_{-\infty}^{\infty} xf(x)dx$ depends upon the delicate question of absolute convergence. Intuitively, if values of X far from center occur with sufficient frequency, the first moment is not defined.

Existence can be guaranteed by making the distribution finite. We may express the sample mean (median) rather neatly as the mean (median) of empirical probability distribution $\hat{F}$ which puts mass $1/n$ at each point $x_1, x_2 \ldots x_n$. This evades rather than solves the problem although the fragility of the sample mean, *the* textbook estimator, even when there is a symmetric unimodal F underlying the $\hat{F}$, was perhaps not fully appreciated until the work of the Princeton robustness study (Tukey et al., 1972). Outside the case of a normal distribution in which context it is ideal — which in linear regression form is equivalent to the supposition that the modeler's specification is incapable of improvement! (Levy, 1999/2000) — the mean's performance relative to the median's ranges from mediocre to ghastly. The robustness of the median, and thus the plausibility of issue by issue majority rule, was totally clear to Galton when he pointed out of in a jury setting, the use of the *average* estimate of damage would be hostage to the vote of a single "crank" and that in proportion to his "crankiness." Bassett and Persky (1999) by formulating voting and estimation as equivalents are able to transfer robustness considerations from statistical theory to public choice.

Stability. One aspect of Plato's criticism of democracy in *Republic*, its theoretical instability, has been verified when Arrow and Black demonstrated the phenomenon of cyclical majorities even when the issue is constrained to a single dimension. Constraint to a single dimension is enormously helpful because it tells us that the problem of instability cannot be one of intensities where a vote on one issue is traded for a vote on another. Black's evocative diagnosis of the problem is that the "single peaked" conditions failed; that is to say, some voter in the population has preferences which look like Figure 1 where X is an issue and F(X) is the preference over that issue. Of course, Black takes the population as given and so inquire into the properties of the population median.

Suppose instead of the preferences of an individual voter, Figure 1 represents the population of factionalized voters. There is a smaller faction at A and a larger one at C and nothing much between then. If a small number of votes change (Downs, 1957) the median can be moved rather dramatically. This can be expressed by the fact that in the

F(x)

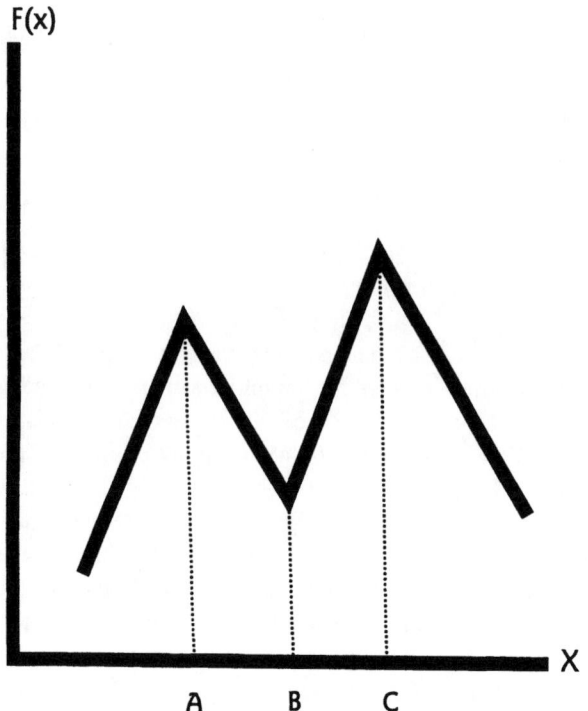

Figure 1: A problem for a median.

context of a bimodal distribution, the influence curve of sample median can be unbounded (Frederick Mosteller and J.W. Tukey, 1977). It is perhaps in this context that worries of factional violence in democracy, as expressed by Plato, make sense. Kill a Cs and the election moves close to A. In this same context, the justification for election by lot becomes clear (Levy, 1989); killing a Cs will only change the probability of the election results slightly.

The advantage of drawing Figure 1 explicitly is that is becomes obvious that, under either interpretation, we are in the presence of a non-convexity. Extremes are preferred to averages; tails are more massive than the center. From standard considerations with non-convexity discontinuous behavior and multiple equilibria can be expected.

Votes without influence. The doctrine of rational ignorance developed at length by Downs (but found in rather earlier in Robert Filmer) supposes that since an individual in a large-number election has no influence to speak out, it is not rational for him to acquire much in the way of information. But this assumes that the voter thinks that being influential is an unmixed blessing. The problem of majority-rule voting in a bimodal distribution suggest that perhaps a rational individual would just as soon not be of much influence. If an individual vote by itself has an important influence then the absence of that vote would also have an influence.

DAVID M. LEVY

REFERENCES

Andrews, D.F., Bickel, P.J., Hampel, F.R., Huber, P.J., Rogers, W.H., and Tukey, J.W. (1972). *Robust Estimates of Location.* Princeton: Princeton University Press.

Arrow, Kenneth J. (1963). *Social Choice and Individual Values.* 2nd edition. New Haven: Yale University Press.

Bassett, Gilbert, Jr. and Robert Persky. (1999). "Robust voting." *Public Choice,* 99: 299–310.

Black, Duncan (1958). *Theory of Committees and Elections.* Cambridge: At the University Press.

Buchanan, James M., and Gordon Tullock (1962). *Calculus of Consent.* Ann Arbor: University of Michigan Press.

Downs, Anthony (1957). *Economic Theory of Democracy.* New York: Harper & Row.

Filmer, Robert (1949). *Patriarcha.* Peter Laslett, (ed.) Oxford: Basil Blackwell's.

Galton, Francis (1907a). "One vote, one value." Letter to the Editor of *Nature,* 75: 1949: 414.

Galton, Francis (1907b). "Vox Populi." *Nature,* 75: 1949: 450–451.

Levy, David M. (1989). "The statistical basis of Athenian–American constitutional theory." *Journal of Legal Studies,* 18: 79–103.

Levy, David M. (1999/2000). "Non-normality and exploratory data analysis: problem and solution." *Econometric Theory,* 15: 427–428; 16: 296–297.

Levy, David M. and Sandra J. Peart. (2002a). "Francis Galton's Two Papers on Voting as Robust Estimation." *Public Choice,* 113: 357–365.

McKelvey, Richard D. (1979). "Global conditions for global intransitivities in formal voting models." *Econometrica,* 47: 1085–1113.

Mosteller, Frederick, and Tukey, J.W. (1977). *Data Analysis and Regression.* Reading, MA: Addison-Welsey.

Mueller, Dennis C. (1989). *Public Choice II.* Cambridge: Cambridge University Press.

Plato. (1980). *Republic.* Translated by Paul Shorey. Loeb Library.

Plott, Charles (1967). "A notion of equilibrium and its possibility under majority rule." *American Economic Review,* 57: 787–806.

THE MEDIAN VOTER MODEL

1. Introduction

Most analytical work in public choice is based upon relatively simple models of majority decision making. These models are widely used even though the researchers know that real political settings are more complex than the models seem to imply. The use of such simple models can be defended for a variety of reasons: First, simple models allow knowledge to be transmitted more economically from one person to another than possible with more complex models. Second, simple models provide us with engines of analysis that allow a variety of hypotheses about more complex phenomena to be developed, many of which would be impossible (or uninteresting) without the frame of reference provided by models. Third, it is possible that simple models are all that is necessary to understand the main features of the world. The world may be less complex that it appears; in which case simple models that extract the essential from the observed will serve us well.

All of these defenses of simple models apply to the median voter model, which is, perhaps, the simplest possible model of majoritarian decision making. There is no more transparent nor easily communicated explanation of political outcomes in a democracy than that all political outcomes reflect median voter preferences. Moreover, testable implications of the median voter model abound. If the median voter gets more or less what he or she wants, then anything that affects the median voter's assessment of the relative merits of alternative policies or candidates will also affect political outcomes. For example, the median voter's age, sex, income, information, ideology and expectations should all systematically affect public policy. Moreover, to the extent that these predictions are largely borne out by empirical research, the median voter model can be regarded not only as a convenient method of discussing majoritarian politics and a fruitful engine of analysis, but also *a fundamental property of democracy*.

2. Origins of the Median Voter Theory

For all of its simplicity, the median voter model is by no means obvious. Although majoritarian voting is clearly a very ancient method of group decision making, which doubtless has been used in tribal councils since before the dawn of recorded history, there is no clear statement of the median voter theorem until approximately 1950. For example, there is no mention of the concept of a pivotal or decisive voter in Aristotle's analysis of political decision making written in 330 B. C.. Condorcet, an eminent French mathematician and philosopher, discovered the idea of a pivotal voter and also noted how the accuracy of decisions can be improved by majority decisions in juries, but includes no clear statement of the median voter theorem. Political pundits have noted (and lamented) tendencies for candidate positions to converge in democratic elections, as did the occasional economic theorist, Hotelling (1929), but the median voter theorem awaited Duncan Black's work on majority voting (1948), and Anthony Downs' extension to representative democracy (1957).

That such a simple idea took so many centuries to emerge may seem surprising given the clarity of the result, but both the rational choice framework and statistical basis of median analysis also emerged at surprisingly late dates. In the case of political analysis, analysis of the properties of simple majority rule may have been delayed for historical as well as methodological reasons. The use of national elections to select governments or government policies is a fairly recent innovation for *national* political systems. Even in the United States where elections have used to select representatives to various state and local governmental bodies for many centuries, the members of the U. S. Senate were appointed rather than elected prior to the passage of the 17th amendment in 1913.

3. An Illustration: Direct Democracy and the Median Voter

To appreciate the logic of the median voter model, consider a setting where three individuals: Al, Bob and Charlie are to choose a restaurant to eat lunch at. Al prefers a restaurant where lunch can be had for $5.00, Bob favors a bit better fare at a restaurant serving $10.00 lunches, and Charlie wants a gourmet restaurant where lunch will cost around $20.00. Bob can be said to be the *median voter* because exactly the same number of individuals prefer a more expensive restaurant than Bob as prefer a less expensive restaurant than Bob, here one each. For convenience assume that, given any two options, each member of the lunch group prefers restaurants with prices closer to their preferred restaurant to ones that are farther from it. Now consider some majority decisions over alternative restaurants:

Options	Pattern of votes			Result
$10 vs. $20	A: 10	B: 10	C: 20	10
$5 vs. $20	A: 5	B: 5	C: 20	5
$5 vs. $16	A: 5	B: 5	C: 16	5
$10 vs. $5	A: 5	B: 10	C: 10	10

The *weak form of the median voter theorem* says the median voter always casts his or her vote for the policy that is adopted. *Note that Bob always votes in favor of the outcome that wins the election.* Note also Bob's preferred $10 restaurant will defeat any other. If there is a median voter, his (or her) preferred policy will beat any other alternative in a pairwise vote. (The median voter's ideal point is always a Condorcet winner.) Consequently, once the median voter's preferred outcome is reached, it can not be defeated by another in a pairwise majoritarian election. The *strong form of the median voter theorem* says the median voter always gets her most preferred policy.

4. Illustration: Electoral Competition and the Median Voter

Similar results are associated with representative democracy where voters select policy makers rather than policies. The case of most relevance for the median voter model is that in which there are two major candidates or parties, one of which will be given the power make public policies until the next election. If voters cast their vote for the party or candidate closest to their most preferred feasible policy, it turns out that the candidate who is closest to the median voter always wins the election. This follows because the candidate closest to the median voter is also closest to the ideal points of more than half of the electorate. (This "distance-based" model of voter preferences is sometimes called the spatial voting model.) Consequently, the winning candidate always receives the vote of the median voter, and the *weak form of the median voter theorem holds*.

If candidates can freely choose policy positions to maximize their share of the votes, both candidates will attempt to adopt policy platforms that are closer to the ideal policies of the median voter than the other. Consequently, major party candidates will both tend to select platforms that are relatively close to the median voter's preferred policies. Moreover, as each candidate competes for the favor of the median voter, the positions of both candidates converge toward the policy positions that maximize the median voter's welfare. In the limit, both candidates adopt the same platforms, and both candidates receive essentially the same number of votes. However, it doesn't matter which candidate wins the election in this limiting case. In either case, the *strong form of the median voter theorem* will hold for national public policies. The median voter gets exactly what he or she wants–to the extent that the elected candidate delivers on his or her campaign promises.

This line of reasoning can be generalized within limits. In electoral contests between two policy alternatives, candidates or parties, if a median voter exists government policy will maximize the welfare of the median voter in equilibrium. Median preferences determine a very wide range of policies if this conclusion can be applied to the broad range of decisions made by majority rule in modern democratic societies.

5. Illustration: The Median Voter's Demand for Public Policy

The strong form of the median voter model allows government policy to modeled as a straightforward application of the rational choice model developed in microeconomics.

For example, consider the following model of the median voter's preferred level of environmental regulation. Suppose that environmental quality is a function of regulatory stringency R and national income, $E = e(R, Y)$. Suppose also that the median voter gets a constant fraction "a" of national income, $Y^m = aY$, which is decreasing in regulatory stringency, $Y = y(R)$. Suppose further that voters care about their own income and environmental quality. The constraints and definitions can be substituted into the median voter's utility function: $U = (ay(R), e(R, y(R)))$, which can be differentiated with respect to R to characterize the median voter's ideal stringency of environmental regulation R^*. R^* will satisfy $U_Y aY_R + U_E (E_R + E_Y Y_R) = 0$. The first term is the median voter's marginal cost of environmental regulation and the last is his marginal benefit from more stringent environmental regulation.

The median voter will select policies that equate her marginal benefits with her marginal costs ($U_Y aY_R = U_E (E_R + E_Y Y_R)$). As these marginal costs and benefits change, so will the median voter's preferred environmental regulation. The implicit function theorem can be used to determine the comparative statics of environmental regulation with respect to parameters of the median voter's optimization problem.

6. Policy Implications of the Median Voter Model

Models have been developed for the median voter's demand for other forms of regulation, for public goods and services, for transfers to the poor and elderly, and for national and domestic defense by changing the constraints to fit the policy of interest. This is part of the versatility of the median voter model. It can easily be used to analyze a wide range of public policies. Given the strong form of the median voter theorem, such characterizations ,of the median voter's preferred policies provide (qualitative) forecasts of public policy in a well functioning democracy.

However, even without a specific characterization of the median voter's preferred policy, the median voter model has a number of clear implications. One implication is that public policies will tend to be moderate middle-of-the-road policies, e.g., drawn from the exact middle of the political spectrum. Such policies can be regarded as "moderate" essentially by definition. Another implication is that many, perhaps most, people will be at least partly displeased with the policies chosen. Voters tend to have different ideal point insofar as their tastes, age, income, tastes, ideology, or information differ. (However, although most people are dissatisfied with government policy, they may still prefer majoritarian decision rules to all the other methods of collective choice that they are aware of).

A third implication is that increases in the dispersion of the distribution of voter preferences (increased radicalism) will have little, if any, effect on public policies unless increased dispersion also affects the median of the distribution of voter ideal points. *This implies that median voter policies tend to be relatively more stable than would have been the case if average rather than median voter opinions determined policy.* The properties of median implies that public policies will be relatively stable (robust) through time as voters are subject to life's vicissitudes, technological progress, and political shocks.

To go beyond these general properties of medians, the strong form of the median voter theorem is usually invoked. Given the strong form of the median voter model, any change in circumstance that changes the constraints of the median voter or the identity of the median voter is predicted to have systematic effects on the size and composition of government programs. For example, the median voter's demand for government services tends to increase through time as median income increases and as government services become relatively cheaper than private alternatives. However, as in ordinary microeconomic analysis, not every median voter model yields unambiguous predictions about the effects of changes in the median voter's choice problem on the electoral demand for government services. For example, the median voters demand for government services depends in part on the tax system used to finance them. Government services are generally normal goods in the sense used by economists, however when financed by an income tax the tax price of those services increases as voter income increases. This tax-price effect may partly or totally offsets the normal-goods effect of increases in median voter income.

7. The Normative Properties of Median Voter Policies

The normative properties of median voter outcomes are clearly of considerable interest for political theorists. Insofar as median voter outcomes tend to emerge in open democracies, evaluation of median policy preferences allows the merits of unconstrained democracy to be assessed.

Although the median voter model implies that the median voter gets what "she wants," it does not imply that public policies will be efficient in the usual Paretian sense of welfare economics. There are many reasons for this. First, the median voter model implies that minority interests do not directly affect policies, essentially by definition, and thus every majoritarian policy is likely to impose externalities on the minority. Second, even within the majority, votes rather than the intensity of desire or willingness to pay determine policy in electoral settings. Some voters

who feel intensely about an issue may be willing and able to compensate others to adopt policies that differ from those otherwise favored by the median voter. Unrealized gains to trade may exist at the median voter's ideal policy.

A third source of normative difficulty for the median voter model is that the policy information available to the median voter is often fairly limited. It is clear that the task of assessing the relative merits of alternative policies can be a very time consuming and information intense task. Many policy analysts spend a lifetime to master the details of a single policy area such as tax or energy policy. In such areas, voters clearly can not be fully informed about the choices that they confront. In the case where the median voter's expectations are none-the-less unbiased, the median voter will still receive, *on average*, the package of government services and policies that he or she wants, although mistakes will be made. In cases where informational problems lead to biased expectations about the consequences of policies, the median voter will not get what *truly* advances his or her interests, but rather what is misperceived as advancing those interests.

Fourth, voter ignorance opens the door to the strategic games of interest groups and the bureaucrats who may manipulate voters by appropriately subsidizing various kinds of information and act counter to median voter interests (agency costs, bribery) in policy areas where the median voter is unlikely to be well informed. (It can be argued that essentially the whole special interest group/rent-seeking literature is predicated on informational problems of these kinds in open democratic societies).

8. A Theoretical Problem for the Median Voter Model

There also is a well-known theoretical problem with majority rule that appears to reduce the applicability of the median voter model. A *median voter does not always exist.* For example, suppose there are three voters, Al, Bob and Cathy who must choose among three policy alternatives, I, II, and III. Suppose that Al prefers option III to II to I, while Bob prefers I to III to II and Cathy prefers II to I to III. Note that the pattern of votes will be, III > II and II > I, but I > III! Majority rule can lead to inconsistent rankings of policy alternatives, and to unstable policy choices. Duncan Black (1948) pointed out that *single peaked* preferences are sufficient to guarantee the existence of a median voter in one dimensional issue spaces. However, in 2-dimensional cases, a median voter exists *only* in cases where voter tastes are very symmetrically distributed. In other cases, intransitive cycles are endemic even if voter preferences are single peaked! In such cases, no median voter exists, and every policy has a non-empty *win set*.

(The win set of policy vector z is the set of policy vectors which is preferred to z by a majority of the electorate). The absence of a median voter equilibrium may also arise in models where candidates can manipulate information and voter turnout. Chaos and indecision are predicted features of majority voting in such models.

9. Empirical Support for the Median Voter Model

Although theoretical arguments suggest that the applicability of the median voter model may be very limited, the empirical evidence suggests otherwise. There is a large body of evidence that suggests median voter preferences over policies are (largely) of the sort which can be mapped into a single issue space while retaining "single peakedness" Poole and Daniels (1985) find that 80–90% of all the recorded votes in the US Congress can be explained with a one dimensional policy space. Stratmann (1996) finds little evidence of cycling across Congressional votes over district specific grants.

Moreover, the median voter model has a very good empirical track record in public finance as a model of fiscal policy across states and through time. Recent studies show that the median voter model can explain federal, state, and local spending, as well as international tariff policies. Congleton and Shughart (1990) Congleton and Bennett (1995) suggest that the median voter model provides a better explanation of large scale public programs than comparable interest group models. This is not to suggest that the median voter always exercises the same degree of control over public policy irrespective of political institutions. Holcombe (1980) and Frey (1994) report significant policy difference between representative and direct forms of democracy that would not exist unless significant agency problems exist within representative government. Moreover, statistical tests can never prove that a particular model is correct, only that it is more likely to be correct than false. However, in general, the median voter model appears to be quite robust as a model of public policy formation in areas where the median voter can credibly be thought to understand and care about public policy.

The empirical evidence suggests that the median voter model can serve as a very useful first approximation of governance within democratic polities. As a consequence, the median voter model continues to function as an analytical point of departure for more elaborate models of policy formation within democracies in much the same way that the competitive model serves the micro economics literature.

ROGER D. CONGLETON

REFERENCES

Alberto Alesina, John Londregan, and Howard Rosenthal (1993). "A model of the political economy of the United States," *The American Political Science Review*, 87: 12–33.

Arrow, K.J. (1963). *Social Choice and Individual Values*, 2nd edition, New Haven: Yale University Press.

Besley, Timothy and Coate, Stephen Source (1997). "An economic model of representative democracy," *Quarterly Journal of Economics*, 112: 85–114.

Black, Duncan (1948). "On the Rationale of Group Decision-making," *Journal of Political Economy*, 56: 23–34.

Black, Duncan (1987). *The Theory of Committees and Elections*. Dordrecht: Kluwer Academic Publishers.

Boylan, R.T. and McKelvey, R.D. (1995). "Voting over economic plans," *American Economic Review*, 85: 860–871.

Buchanan, J.M. and Tullock, G. (1962). *The Calculus of Consent*. Ann Arbor: University of Michigan Press.

Congleton, R.D. (2001). "Rational ignorance, rational voter expectations, and public policy: a discrete informational foundation for fiscal illusion," *Public Choice*, 107: 35–64.

Congleton, Roger D. and Bennett, Randall W. (1995). "On the political economy of state highway expenditures: some evidence of the relative performance of alternative public choice models." *Public Choice*, 84: 1–24.

Congleton, R.D. and Shughart, W.F., II (1990). "The growth of social security: electoral push or political pull?," *Economic Inquiry*, 28: 109–132.

Downs, A. (1957) *An Economic Theory of Democracy*. New York: Harper Collins.

Feld, Lars P. and Savioz, Marcel R. (1997). "Direct democracy matters for economic performance: an empirical investigation," *Kyklos*, 50: 507–538.

Frey, B. (1994). "The role of democracy in securing just and prosperous societies direct democracy: politico-economic lessons from Swiss experience," *American Economic Review*, 84: 38–342.

Holcombe, R. (1980). "An empirical test of the median voter model," *Economic Inquiry*, 18: 260–274.

Hotelling, H. (1929). "Stability in competition," *Economic Journal*, 39: 41–57.

Kramer, G. (1971). "Short term fluctuations in US voting behavior, 1896–1964," *American Political Science Review*, 65: 131–143.

Lott, J. and Kenny, L. (1999). "Did Women's Suffrage Change the Size and Scope of Government?" *Journal of Political Economy*, 107: 1163–1198.

McGuire, M.C. and Olson, Mancur, Jr. (1996). "The economics of autocracy and majority rule: the invisible hand and the use of force," *Journal of Economic Literature*, 34: 72–96.

Meltzer, A.H. and Richard, S.F. (1981). "A rational theory of the size of government," *Journal of Political Economy*, 89: 914–927.

Mueller, Dennis C. (1989). *Public Choice II*. New York: Cambridge University Press.

Noam, E.M. (1980). "The Efficiency of Direct Democracy." *Journal of Political Economy*, 88: 803–810.

Piketty, Thomas (1995). "Social mobility and redistributive politics," *Quarterly Journal of Economics*, 110: 551–584.

Romer, T. and Rosenthal, H. (1979). "The elusive median voter," *Journal of Public Economics* 12: 143–170.

Stratmann, T. (1996). "Instability of collective decisions? testing for cyclic majorities," *Public Choice*, 88: 15–28.

Turnbull, G.K. and Chang, C. (1998). "The median voter according to GARP," *Southern Economic Journal*, 64: 1001–1010.

Turnbull, G.K. and Djoundourian, S.S. (1994). "The median voter hypothesis: evidence from general purpose local governments," *Public Choice*, 81: 223–240.

Wittman, Donald (1989). "Why democracies produce efficient results," *Journal of Political Economy*, 97: 1395–1424.

MEDIEVAL CHURCH

The medieval Roman Catholic Church was an economic entity while at the same time undeniably pursuing social and spiritual goals. Large and powerful enough by the eleventh or twelfth centuries for Europe to be called "Christendom," the Church took on the character of a sophisticated modern corporation. A primary task of the social sciences has been to delineate the role that institutions and technology played in the development of western civilization. Over the past 20 years, the economic role in that development has come to the fore (Ekelund et al., 1996) as part of the overall economics of religion.

Economists are latecomers in the analysis of a number of implicit markets, including that of religion. However the fundamental premise undergirding these new approaches is that economic elements come to play in all markets, implicit as well as explicit. Thus, while it may be the case that economic motives do not necessarily dominate every decision, the "science of choice" may be applied to problems that have heretofore been labeled psychological, sociological, anthropological, political, legal or religious. Increasingly, therefore, the tools of modern microeconomics, public choice (especially as interest group analysis) and property rights are being applied to issues thought to be the exclusive matter of other social sciences. The medieval Roman Catholic Church is one of these issues.

The facts of the medieval church may be stylized and put into the context of an economic model. After the twelfth century, Roman Catholicism (with only insignificant fringe competition from Jews and Moors) came to dominate large parts of Western Europe. The legal system of the Church, canon law, was beginning to supplant and eventually dominate civil law in (then) loosely organized "states" and other political entities. Ecclesiastical officials enacted laws respecting all aspects of the "supply" decision of such goods as "assurances of eternal salvation," political support from the papacy and clergy and social services of all kinds. Marriage, trade and all manner of behavior were regulated in conjunction with the supply of these services. Kings, princes and aristocrats of all kinds owed much of their power to the approbation of the Roman catholic authorities who, with full complements of upstream and downstream agents, helped negotiate trade deals, wage wars and maintain armies. The Roman Church, moreover, was immensely wealthy and was a huge landholder during the medieval period. The retail side of the church offering religious, medical and social services of all kinds was also a primary source of revenues in addition to payments (taxes and other forms of rents) from monarchs, politicians and the local religious establishments (monasteries, parish churches, etc.).

The organization of the church was that of an M-form corporation with the pope as CEO, a financial division called the Papal Camera, upstream directors (the Curia and Cardinals), and a geographically dispersed downstream retail division. The primary role of the upstream church was to provide doctrine and dogma relating to the essential principles of membership (e.g., interpretations of the Holy texts) and to collect downstream rents. It established, with authority centralized in the Pope after the Council of Trent (1545–1563) but formalized only later in the nineteenth century, the often-labyrinthine conditions for eternal salvation and the penalties for violating any of those conditions.

Downstream were the geographically dispersed purveyors of local Roman Catholicism. These included the regional mendicant and contemplative religious orders, monasteries, some of which were as much production units of agricultural and other goods as sellers of religious services, and parish priests and other local clergy. While rents were collected at all levels, primary revenues came from these retail ends of the downstream church. Enforcement policies and assigned agents of the centralized Roman authorities were necessary to prevent opportunistic behavior in distant locales of the church.

Entry control was obviously necessary to maintain the strength of demand for the Roman monopoly. Malfeasors, when caught, were subject to severe punishments. Interdict, whereby the "sinner" could not have contact or truck with other Christians, was one form of punishment. Most severe was excommunication of the wrongdoer — a total separation from the body Catholic and a sentence of eternal damnation if repentance was not made. Heretics of all kinds (those who did not adhere to the main body of Catholic dogma and interpretations) were of course excommunicants, but many were also subject to violent death through the various "holy wars" or crusades of the middle ages. Later, even more virulent punishments were meted out to Protestants and other "heretics" through Inquisitions in Spain, Rome and elsewhere. These punishments may be seen as attempts to maintain monopoly.

Doctrinal manipulations were also used by the Roman Catholic Church to make its demand curve more inelastic and/or to shift it rightward. The conditions attached to the Church's chief product — assurances of eternal salvation — were manipulated throughout the middle ages in order to increase revenues and the number of demanders. Marriage markets, largely of secular and civil concern prior to the Church monopoly, were taken over by the Church with conditions attached to the simple contract respecting endogamy, presence of a priest, posting of bans, and so on. Regulations respecting "divorce" or marriage dissolution were intricate and varied with income and circumstances of petitioners. Such price discrimination manifestly increased the Church's rents over the medieval period. Another doctrine that was almost manipulated out of recognition was that respecting usury and "just price." When the church was a debtor, it seems, usury prohibitions were enforced, but not when it was a creditor. The same manipulations attended church rules respecting monastery thithes and taxes, the granting of indulgences, jubilee attendance, and benefices granted to bishops and cardinals. Such methods and practices of rent collection reached something of a limit in the sixteenth century precipitating the Protestant Reformation (Ekelund et al., 2002).

The economic view of the medieval church featuring the principles of public choice, industrial organization and microanalytic behavior, while still under construction, offers new insights into the development of western institutions. The old Weber-Tawney view of the church, as least as popularized, was that the Roman church and its policies had a negative impact on economic growth and development, a view that contrasts with that of Sombart and Schumpeter. The new microeconomic perspective eschews, to a large extent, these important macroeconomic issues. Rather, a theory of rational behavior permits an understanding of the church as an economic entity — one that benefited from increasing secularization of European society but one that recognized that science, technology and humanism would ultimately weaken the kind and form of "magic" the church was selling. If "belief in Christ and Christian principles" were the main issue, it would be difficult to explain how Roman Christians issued crusades against other "Catholics," the eastern orthodox Christian church or (later) Protestant Christians of all stripes. Moreover, the emergence of fierce censorship of all kinds in the sixteenth and earlier centuries is also difficult to understand (Galileo was a devout Catholic) except in an economic context, that is, the context of monopoly rent seeking by interest groups in the Church. Economists objectively viewing these policies and doctrines

see them as examples of monopoly behavior and all that the model entails. If religious organizations, in this case the Roman church, were acting solely in the public interest, they would behave as a "good government" — one that provides information, spiritual goods and social goods to the faithful at competitive, i.e., marginal cost, rates. An "economic" examination of the behavior of the medieval church does not provide overwhelming support for this view.

ROBERT B. EKELUND, JR.

REFERENCES

Ekelund, Robert B. Jr., Robert F. Hebert, Robert D. Tollison, Gary M. Anderson and Audrey B. Davidson (1996). *Sacred Trust: The Medieval Church as an Economic Firm*. New York: Oxford University Press.

Ekelund, Robert B. Jr., Robert F. Hebert and Robert D. Tollison. (2002). "An economic analysis of the rise of protestantism." *Journal of Political Economy*, 110, 646–671.

MERCANTILISM

Mercantilism, as stylized in standard parlance, is that system of state building and state controls that existed chiefly in European nation states between 1500 and 1776 (sometimes dated 1500–1650 or 1500–1650). Dating at 1776 is apt since the term "mercantilism" was coined by Adam Smith in his *Wealth of Nations* to describe a loose system of controls epitomized in dispersed writings by an equally dispersed group of pamphleteers of many nationalities (British, French Spanish, Flemish and Scandinavian among others). These writers shared a number of common concerns but no common analytical tools and, as such, the term mercantilism is ambiguous if it refers to some "system" of ideas or theories. There are fundamentally two methods of dealing with mercantilism in the literature of economics. First, mercantilism is characterized as a collection of ideas with a corollary as the history of and ideas leading to controls and state power. A second and newer approach considers mercantilism as a process featuring the declension of economic controls wherein rent-seeking individuals and groups alter constraints establishing a political economy leading to freer trade and the modern world.

There are ideational rationales aplenty for mercantilism and many are of significant historical value. As commentaries on international trade and domestic policies, mercantile writers such as Thomas Mun, Gerard de Malynes, Bernard de Mandeville and many others offered invaluable commentary on the economic history of their time.

Mandeville and others in fact espoused variants of what came to be known as "laissez faire" (Chalk, 1951, 1966). Gold or specie acquisition, foreign trade regulation, colonization, or suppression of the poor is served up as objectives in much of this literature and such goals have become the *sine qua non* of ideational mercantilism. But the most famous ideational-historical argument for mercantile controls over trade (e.g. tariffs, quotas, prohibitions, etc.) is that they were the objects of "state power." The origins of this argument are found in the late nineteenth century (Schmoller, 1897) and continue in the magisterial study of Heckscher (1934 [1931]). The modern literature on mercantilism is awash with filigree on these themes but it is far more confused and contradictory than the earlier work of Heckscher (1934) and Viner (1937).

Nowhere does this historical literature consider let alone answer the questions "who is the State" or "why are these policies followed or advocated in place of others?" Only an approach that features rational behavior *as an informant of history* is able to provide satisfactory answers to these questions. That approach combines modern microeconomic theory and the insights of public choice in order to explain how rational economic actors under extant constraints altered (or were unable to alter) political and economic institutions that created (or did not create) the Industrial Revolution. *In Mercantilism as a Rent-Seeking Society* (1981) and later in *Politicized Economies* (1997) Ekelund and Tollison described how public choice and contemporary neoclassical economic theory explain the declension of mercantilism in England and its stubborn persistence in France and Spain.

In England there was a fundamental shift in authority from the monarchy to the British Parliament — that is, rent-seeking interest groups altered the source of property rights in the economy. This was accomplished in several ways. First, jurisdictional disputes of the two court systems (royal and common law) shifted the authority to alter property rights from the monarch to nascent democratic institutions. The common law courts often settled these disputes, many over the locus of controls over business and the granting of monopoly, (with Justice Coke often presiding) in favor of Parliament rather than the monarch. Secondly, the decline of internal controls took place due chiefly to the opportunistic behavior of Crown agents and to the self-interested activities of businesses. A prime example of this sort of behavior was the attempted enforcement of the Statute of Artificers (1563). Local guilds after having received monarchical privileges in London and elsewhere to set up regional monopolies were thwarted in their aims by *unpaid enforcers* of the regulations. Sheriffs, and other unpaid enforcers, were predictably self-interested and made deals that undermined the Statute. The ability of illegal competitors to

escape to the countryside (where any enforcement was more costly) also helped make the regulations ineffective. Thus, the "process view" of mercantilism emphasizes that public choice — wherein manipulations by rent-seeking self-interested groups create property rights changes — is at the center of the explanation of how mercantilism was undermined and freer competition emerged. Naturally, these developments were at first fragile. Commitments to tripartite democratic institutions during the seventeenth century (during the Restoration) had ultimately to be credible (North and Weingast, 1989) and this period of instability carried over into the eighteenth century (Wells and Wills, 1998).

While England had long enjoyed some nature of checks on the authority of the monarchy, especially checks on taxation, France and Spain did not. Colbertism — the name given to mercantilism in France — reigned supreme as monarchical authority established domestic and trading monopolies of many different kinds. As rent-seeking agent for the French Crown, Jean-Baptiste Colbert established a tobacco monopoly in 1681 regulating all aspects of tobacco production, importation, manufacture and sale. This state monopoly, and others like it such as in textiles, generated enormous rents for the Crown with tobacco regulations alone bringing in 500,000 *livres* in 1681 and 30 *million* in 1789. In other matters such as the state purchase of inputs, the state acted as a monpsonist. Cartelization or franchising monopoly through competitive bidding also followed a pattern with finished goods the object of rational rent-seeking by the French Crown. Such policies included the retardation of invention, innovation, the arts and academics. French *intendents* located in the provinces and accountable directly to Crown ministers were the enforcers of all this regulation. Malfeasors and cheating of any kind was dispensed with harshly.

In Spain, mercantilism and centralized control of areas of the economy proceeded with at least as much vigor as in France. Crown and "aristocratic" monopolies were imposed over virtually all domestic and international commerce. Combined with theocratic elements of the Roman Catholic reconquest (persecution of Moors, Jews and Protestants through the Inquisition), Spanish mercantile patterns were more virulent if somewhat less effective due to traditional Spanish "separatism" than in France. These policies often had disastrous effects. The monopolization of sheep farming, for example, into an organization called the Mesta reduced the amount of farming to levels that created periodic famine. Regulatory rents and ever-increasing taxes went to finance the glory of the monarchy and the waging of costly wars. These factors plus strong class differentiation, enormously skewed income distributions, religious persecutions, huge bureaucracy at regional and, later at national levels, and a rent-seeking regulatory death grip on trade all contributed to the later "tragedy" of Spain's lack of economic development.

Mercantilism touched all nations over the period, including colonies. Colonization was indeed the object of European nation states, but rent flows guided the path of colonization. American colonists were asked to conform to trade regulations, production prohibitions and price controls set up by the English monarch and the Parliament. Although they did so imperfectly due to opportunistic behavior on the part of British governors and American agents, customs officials were given extraordinary powers under the Navigation Acts passed between 1660 and 1696. Decrees and Parliamentary legislation of the time, e.g., the Hat Act of 1732, cannot be attributed to "state power" however. Rather it is demonstrably the result of rent-seeking self-interested behavior on the part of individuals and groups within the polity of England. All such moves towards control of European colonies may be viewed in this light.

Mercantilism then is most fruitfully conceived as a problem in constitutions, interest groups and rational behavior. This view offers, unlike the ideational-historical perspective, a means of analyzing institutions that cause and those that hinder economic growth and development. The tools of public choice and neoclassical economics are essential to that critical undertaking.

ROBERT B. EKELUND, JR.

REFERENCES

Chalk, Alfred (1951). "Natural law and the rise of economic individualism in England," *Journal of Political Economy*, 59: 330–347.

Chalk, Alfred (1966). "Mandeville's fable of the bees: a reappraisal," *Southern Economic Journal*, 33: 1–16.

Ekelund, Robert B. and R.D. Tollison (1981). *Mercantilism as a Rent-Seeking Society: Economic Regulation in Historical Perspective*. College Station: Texas A&M University Press.

Ekelund, Robert B. and Tollison, R.D. (1997). *Politicized Economies: Monarchy, Monopoly, and Mercantilism*. College Station: Texas A&M University Press.

Heckscher, E.F. (1934 [1931]). *Mercantilism*. Trans. M. Shapiro, 2 vols. London: George Allen and Unwin.

North, D.C. and Weingast, B.R. (1989). "Constitutions and commitment: the evolution of institutions governing public choice in seventeenth-century England." *Journal of Economic History*, 49: 803–832.

Schmoller, G. (1897). *The Mercantile System and its Historical Significance*. New York: Macmillan.

Viner, Jacob (1937). *Studies in the Theory of International Trade*. New York: A.M. Kelley.

Wells, John and Douglas Wills (2000). "Revolution, restortion,and debt repudiation: the jacobite threat to England's institutions and economic growth," *Journal of Economic History*, 60: 418–441.

MONETARY POLITICS

In many countries monetary policy institutions have been designed to minimize "political" influences on decision-making, but given the motivations of politicians, these protections will always be imperfect. This entry describes the most important political influences on monetary policy. We first consider monetary policy cycles related to the timing of elections, then those involving partisan change. Next considered are political models of inflationary biases, including applications of the time inconsistency problem and models of bureaucratic behavior. Finally, monetary policy choices are briefly described in the context of public choice models of committee decision-making.

1. Electorally Motivated Political Monetary Cycles

In Nordhaus's (1975) model of the political business cycle, vote-seeking politicians opportunistically manipulate the economy to gain the support of myopic voters who are concerned with current macroeconomic conditions. Incumbent politicians engineer pre-elections booms to gain votes; these booms are then followed by post-election contractions. Political business cycles could be produced with either fiscal or monetary policies, but monetary policy changes can be implemented quickly and without special enabling legislation.

The Nordhaus model was probably inspired by the 1972 U.S. presidential election. In that year, incumbent Richard Nixon was the beneficiary of a healthy pre-election boom, a boom that many suspected was engineered with the cooperation of Chairman Arthur Burns at the Federal Reserve (Fed). Woolley (1984) carefully reviewed Fed decision-making in that year, and concluded that the Fed's Federal Open Market Committee (FOMC) was not directly motivated by a desire to insure Nixon's reelection. However, price controls imposed by the Nixon administration transferred intense political pressure to the Fed — any move by he Federal Reserve to raise interest rates in a regime of controlled price and wages would surely have drawn ire from politicians and the public. Thus, while the Fed's accommodative stance probably reflected bureaucratic self-protection, the effect nevertheless advanced the reelection prospects of the incumbent.

Systematic quantitative evidence of political monetary cycles also exists. Grier (1987) estimated a monetary policy reaction function for the U.S. that was augmented with dummy variables to account for electoral timing. He found that the electoral dummies were statistically significant, supporting the hypothesis of cycles. These results were questioned by Beck (1987), who suggested that the electoral pattern primarily reflected accommodation of fiscal policy pressures, but Grier (1989), using more flexible empirical specifications, later found evidence of electoral cycles even when the stance of fiscal policy was accounted for. Subsequent evidence has been mixed, but the hypothesis of a monetary political business cycle clearly cannot be dismissed.

2. Partisan Political Business Cycles

In a pioneering cross-country study, Hibbs (1977) found that unemployment rates were lower under left-leaning than right-leaning political regimes, reflecting the underlying concerns of the parties' core constituencies. Supporting this theme in the monetary policy arena, Beck (1984) concluded that U.S. monetary policy is easier under Democratic presidents than Republicans; Cowart (1978) and Minford and Peel (1982) provided similar evidence for left- and right-leaning governments in Europe and the U.K. Grier (1991, 1996) provided striking evidence that the partisan composition of Congressional oversight committees affects the stance of monetary policy in the U.S.

With the advent of the rational expectations revolution, political business cycle models of both partisan and electoral varieties were questioned, and ultimately reformulated. A rational model of electoral cycles was presented by Rogoff and Sibert (1988) and rational partisan models were formulated by Alesina (1987), Alesina and Sachs (1988), and Chappell and Keech (1986, 1988). In the rational partisan models, election uncertainty causes partisan-related policy surprises and fluctuations in real economic outcomes. Chappell and Keech (1988) empirically linked election-related surprises in monetary policy to changes in unemployment in the U.S., finding modestly-sized partisan impacts. Alesina, et al. (1997) found broad supportive evidence for rational partisan cycles and related patterns in monetary policy across a panel of 18 OECD countries.

3. Channels of Influence

Partisan and political business cycle models require that politicians control, or at least influence, fiscal or monetary policies. How do they do so? Building on the arguments of Kane (1980), Havrilesky (1995) suggests that, in the U.S., presidential influence over monetary policy derives in part from the Fed's need to deflect Congressional threats to its independence — i.e., the Fed accommodates presidential wishes; in return, it is understood that the president will protect the Fed from threatening legislative

intrusions. The Congress implicitly gains from this stand-off as well: it can publicly "bash" the Fed for its bad performance, while escaping direct responsibility for economic outcomes. Havrilesky's (1988, 1995) statistical evidence showed that the Fed was responsive to direct executive branch "signals" of monetary policy preferences reported in the press.

Politicians also influence monetary policy through the power of appointment. Havrilesky and Gildea (1992) have argued that economists are particularly reliable ideologues and that presidents, recognizing this, choose economists for their early-term appointments. Waller (1992) also investigates the appointments process, developing a model of bargaining between an appointing executive and a confirming legislature. Both Waller (1989) and Keech and Morris (1997) have noted that if influence over policy comes primarily through the power of appointment, policy shifts associated with regime changes in the executive branch may be gradual and delayed; it takes time for a president to "pack the Board" with loyal supporters. Chappell et al. (1993) have used dissent voting data to infer that U.S. presidents' partisan influences over monetary policy come primarily via the power appointment rather than direct pressure. This poses a particular challenge for rational partisan models described earlier: rational partisan models require that elections produce policy surprises, but election-related surprises will be minimal if policy change must await a packed Board.

4. The Political Origins of Inflation

In most economies the price level rises over time. In the absence of a strong case for the desirability of inflation, one is led to suspect a political bias toward inflationary policies. The time inconsistency problem, described by Kydland and Prescott (1977) and applied to monetary policy by Barro and Gordon (1983), provides a possible explanation for such a bias. According to this theory, policymakers value both low inflation and output in excess of its natural rate. If the public expected zero inflation, policymakers would have an incentive to increase output with a positive money supply surprise. But if the public had rational expectations, this incentive would be anticipated, rendering a zero inflation equilibrium untenable. Rather, inflation will be positive in equilibrium, and will persist at a level where the marginal costs of inflation and the associated marginal (short-run) gains in output are balanced. Although it is not widely appreciated, a similar result was described by Nordhaus (1975) in a setting where expectations were adaptive rather than rational.

To avoid a suboptimal inflationary equilibrium, some have proposed that politicians might wish to appoint "conservative" central bankers (i.e., those who are less concerned with output gains than their political principals) and grant them independence in day-to-day policymaking (Rogoff, 1985). Such a solution is problematic: it is not clear how conservatives are to be identified and selected, nor is it clear how their independence is to be protected given the incentives of political principals (Toma, 1997). These issues aside, a substantial empirical literature has developed on the relationship between central bank independence and inflationary performance across countries. After exhaustive study, Cukierman (1992) concluded that the preponderance of the evidence supports the view that independence and low inflation are connected, but that evidence is not overwhelming.

Inflation may also arise from the desire of governments to directly extract revenue via money creation — it is widely recognized that hyperinflations have political origins in the need to raise revenue without levying explicit taxes. Using a model that employs the logic of the time inconsistency problem, Cukierman (1992) has shown that the revenue motive can produce an inflation rate exceeding the steady-state seigniorage-maximizing rate. He also provides some empirical support for the seigniorage motive from cross country evidence — seigniorage is a more important source of revenue when tax institutions are less efficient and political systems less stable. For the U.S., Toma (1997) has described how institutional changes affecting the Federal Reserve's revenue generating capacities have mirrored changes in the government's need for seigniorage revenue.

Although most theories focus on the political "demand" for inflation, the political "supply" is also an important public choice issue. In the U.S., the operating budget of the Federal Reserve bureaucracy is funded by interest earnings on government bonds that it holds. When the Fed exchanges money for bonds, it trades an asset that bears no interest for one that does, providing a bureaucratic incentive for monetary expansion (Toma, 1982). Tollison and Shughart (1983) have provided empirical support for Toma's model by demonstrating that expansions in Federal Reserve employment have been related to expansions of the monetary base.

5. Committee Decisions

Monetary policy decisions are usually made by committees, and committee decision-making is a topic of intrinsic interest in public choice. In the U.S., monetary policymaking provides an excellent opportunity to study committee decisions because the FOMC meets repeatedly to consider a single issue (the degree of ease or tightness in the policy stance) and because there are extensive records describing both the preferences of individual members and FOMC decisions. Formally, monetary policy directives require majority approval by the FOMC. Members must cast assenting or dissenting votes; these votes are recorded and later made available to the public.

Investigations of dissent voting patterns have shown that there are systematic differences in policy preferences across members. For example, district Reserve bank presidents tend to favor tighter policy than Federal Reserve Board governors (Belden, 1989), and Democratic appointees favor ease relative to Republicans (Havrilesky and Gildea, 1991). Policy preferences of FOMC members are also related to educational background, profession, and other career characteristics (Havrilesky and Schweitzer, 1990; Chappell et al., 1995). Econometric analysis of FOMC voting patterns also reveals that the Fed Chairman has disproportionate weight in committee decisions, undermining the simple median voter hypothesis (Chappell et al., 1993).

The availability of information on policy preferences of individual committee members suggests a fruitful direction for research on politics and monetary policy. Political influences, whatever their source, must operate through the decisions of individual policymakers. This in turn suggests that political influences may be more clearly detectable when individuals provide the unit of analysis, rather than a governmental entity that has already aggregated those preferences. A nice illustration of this is provided by McGregor's (1996) investigation of political monetary cycles using data describing individual FOMC members' votes. McGregor found that FOMC members who were appointed by the party of the incumbent president tend to favor pre-election ease, while members appointed by the opposition favored pre-election tightness. At the individual level political influences were abundantly clear; at the level of committee outcomes these influences were obscured.

HENRY CHAPPELL

REFERENCES

Alesina, A. (1987). "Macroeconomic Policy in a Two-Party System as a Repeated Game." *Quarterly Journal of Economics* 102: 651–678.

Alesina, A., Roubini, N., and Cohen, G. (1997). *Political Cycles and the Macroeconomy*. Cambridge: MIT Press.

Alesina, A. and Sachs, J. (1988). "Political parties and the business cycle in the United States." *Journal of Money, Credit and Banking*, 20: 63–82.

Barro, R. and Gordon, D. (1983). "A positive theory of monetary policy in a natural rate model." *The Journal of Political Economy*, 91: 589–610.

Beck, N. (1984). "Domestic political sources of American monetary policy": 1955–1982. *Journal of Politics*, 46: 786–817.

Beck, N. (1987). "Elections and the Fed: is there a political monetary cycle?" *American Journal of Political Science*, 31: 194–216.

Belden, S. (1989). "Policy preferences of fomc members as revealed by dissenting votes." *Journal of Money, Credit and Banking*, 21: 432–441.

Chappell, H., Havrilesky, T., and McGregor, R. (1993). "Partisan monetary policies: presidential influence through the power of appointment." *Quarterly Journal of Economics* 108: 185–218.

Chappell, H., Havrilesky, T., and McGregor, R. (1995). "Policymakers, institutions, and central bank decisions." *Journal of Economics and Business*, 47: 113–136.

Chappell, H. and Keech, W. (1986). "Party differences in macroeconomic policies and outcomes." *American Economic Review*, 76: 71–74.

Chappell, H. and Keech, W. (1988) "The unemployment rate consequences of partisan monetary policies." *Southern Economic Journal* 55: 107–122.

Cowart, A. (1978) "The economic policies of European governments, part I: monetary policy." *British Journal of Political Science* 8: 285–311.

Cukierman, A. (1992). *Central Bank Strategy, Credibility, and Independence*. Cambridge: MIT Press.

Grier, K. (1991). Congressional oversight committee influence on U.S. monetary policy. *Journal of Monetary Economics*, 28: 201–220.

Grier, K. (1996). "Congressional oversight committee influence on U.S. monetary policy revisited." *Journal of Monetary Economics*, 38: 571–579.

Grier, K. (1989). "On the existence of a political monetary cycle." *American Journal of Political Science*, 33: 376–389.

Grier, K. (1987). "Presidential politics and federal reserve independence: an empirical test." *Southern Economic Journal*, 54: 475–486.

Havrilesky, T. (1988). "Monetary policy signaling from the administration to the Federal Reserve." *Journal of Money, Credit and Banking*, 20: 83–101.

Havrislesky, T. and Gildea, J. (1991). "The policy preferences of fomc members as revealed by dissenting votes: comment." *Journal of Money, Credit and Banking*, 23: 130–138.

Havrilesky, T. (1995) *The Pressures on American Monetary Policy*. Boston: Kluwer Academic Publishers.

Havrislesky, T. and Gildea, J. (1992). "Reliable and unreliable partisan appointments to the Board of Governors." *Public Choice*, 73: 397–417.

Havrilesky, T. and Schweitzer, R. (1990). "A theory of FOMC dissent voting with evidence from the time series." in T. Mayer, (ed.) *The Political Economy of American Monetary Policy*. New York: Cambridge University Press.

Hibbs, D. (1977). "Political parties and macroeconomic policy." *American Political Science Review*, 71: 1467–1487.

Kane, E. (1980). "Politics and fed policymaking: the more things change, the more they remain the same." *Journal of Monetary Economics*, 6: 199–211.

Keech, W. and Morris, I. (1997). "Appointments, presidential power, and the Federal Reserve." *Journal of Macroeconomics*, 19: 253–267.

Kydland, F. and Prescott, E. (1977). "Rules rather than discretion: the inconsistency of optimal plans." *Journal of Political Economy*, 85: 473–492.

McGregor, R. (1996). "FOMC voting behavior and electoral cycles: partisan ideology and partisan loyalty." *Economics and Politics*, 8: 17–32.

Minford, P. and Peel, D. (1982). "The political theory of the business cycle." *European Economic Review*, 17: 253–270.

Nordhaus, W. (1975). "The political business cycle." *Review of Economic Studies*, 42: 169–190.

Rogoff, K. (1985). "The optimal degree of commitment to an intermediate monetary target." *Quarterly Journal of Economics*, 100: 1169–1189.

Rogoff, K. and Sibert, A. (1988). "Elections and macroeconomic policy cycles." *The Review of Economic Studies*, 55: 1–16.

Tollison, R. and Schughart, W. (1983). "Preliminary evidence on the use of inputs by the Federal Reserve System." *American Economic Review*, 73: 291–304.

Toma, M. (1982). "Inflationary bias of the Federal Reserve system: a bureaucratic perspective." *Journal of Monetary Economics*, 10: 163–190.

Toma, M. (1997). *Competition and Monopoly in the Federal Reserve System 1914–1951*. Cambridge, UK: Cambridge University Press.

Waller, C. (1992). "A bargaining model of partisan appointments to the central bank." *Journal of Monetary Economics*, 29: 411–428.

Waller, C. (1989). "Macroeconomic policy games and central bank politics." *Journal of Money, Credit, and Banking*, 21: 422–431.

Woolley, J. (1984). *Monetary Politics: The Federal Reserve and the Politics of Monetary Policy*. New York: Cambridge University Press.

N

THE NEW DEAL

> I pledge you, I pledge myself, to a new deal for the American people. (Franklin Delano Roosevelt)
>   The Great Depression is to economics what the Big Bang is to physics. (Margo, 1993)

Whatever else might be said about the New Deal — and scholars and polemicists alike have said much — the fact of the matter is that it did not work. Despite unprecedented federal government spending over the period 1933 to 1939, recovery from history's worst depression, in the United States at least, ultimately awaited Pearl Harbor: GNP in 1958 prices remained below that of 1929 for more than a decade (Couch and Shughart, 1998: 26). By contrast, 'recovery occurred in 1932 for New Zealand; 1933 for Japan, Greece, and Romania; 1934 for Chile, Denmark, Finland, and Sweden; 1935 for Estonia, Hungary, Norway, and the United Kingdom; 1936 for Germany; and 1937 for Canada, Austria, and Italy' (Romer, 1993: 23–24).

There are a number of reasons why the policies and programs set in motion by FDR failed to achieve at least the first two of his stated goals of 'relief, recovery and reform'. One is the First New Deal's (1933–35) wrong-headed strategy of responding to a colossal decline in real output by implementing programs that had the effect of reducing production even further (Higgs, 1987: 174). Confusing effect with cause, the operation of salutary market forces was shortcircuited by the administration's efforts to prop up farm prices by drastically reducing the number of acres under cultivation and by actually destroying crops and livestock; to prop up wages by fostering unionization and by enacting minimum wage and 'prevailing wage' laws; and to prop up industrial prices by exempting from the antitrust laws codes of 'fair competition' negotiated under the National Industrial Recovery Act. Another reason for failure is a series of disastrous monetary policy initiatives, beginning with a sharp contraction in the money supply at the depression's onset, and ending with a doubling of the banking system's required reserve ratios at a time (1936–37) when recovery seemed finally to be underway (Friedman and Schwartz, 1963: 299–545). Yet another reason is the uncertainty created by the administration's

anti-capitalist rhetoric, which turned especially virulent during the Second New Deal (1935–39). FDR's notorious plan to 'pack' the Supreme Court and his nomination of ultraliberal Senator Hugo Black to that suddenly complaisant body combined with the administration's attacks on business to chill investment incentives by outwardly threatening the separation of powers and constitutional protections for private property (Higgs, 1997).

When FDR began his first term of office on March 4, 1933, the US economy was in shambles: 'net national product in current prices fell by more than one-half from 1929 to 1933 and net national product in constant prices by more than one-third' (Friedman and Schwartz, 1963: 299). Real incomes dropped by 11 percent between 1929 and 1930, 9 percent between 1930 and 1931, 18 percent between 1931 and 1932, and 3 percent the next year. 'These are extraordinary declines for individual years, let alone for four years in succession. All told, money income fell 53 percent and real income 36 percent' (ibid.: 301). American workers were losing their jobs in unprecedented numbers. Beginning in the last half of 1929, unemployment rates rose steadily until fully 25 percent of the US labor force had been idled (Stein, 1984: 30). Indeed, the annual rate of unemployment has reached double-digit levels in the United States in only 17 of the last 100 years for which data are available. Ten of these milestones occurred during the Great Depression (Vedder and Gallaway, 1993: 75).

Facing 'an emergency more serious than war' (Higgs, 1987: 159), the Roosevelt administration's response was both swift and massive. FDR's legendary First One Hundred Days were legislatively the most active of any US chief executive before or since. Many of the alphabet agencies of the New Deal, addressing 'virtually all basic economic activity of the nation, such as banking, employment, unemployment, housing, agriculture, transportation, salaries and wages, credit, insurance, and regional economic development' (Hosen, 1992: 8), were hastily put in place. As Arthur Schlesinger describes it,

> on adjournment on June 15, 1933, the President and the exhausted 73rd Congress left the following record: March 9 — the Emergency Banking Act, March 20 — the Economy Act, March 31 — the establishment of the Civilian Conservation Corps, April 19 — abandonment of the gold standard, May 12 — the Federal Emergency Relief Act, setting up a national relief system, May 12 — the Agricultural Adjustment Act, establishing a national agricultural policy, with the Thomas amendment conferring on the President powers of monetary expansion, May 12 — the Emergency Farm Mortgage Act, providing for the refinancing of farm mortgages, May 18 — the Tennessee Valley Authority Act, providing for the unified development of the Tennessee Valley, May 27 — the Truth-in-Securities Act, requiring full disclosure

in the issue of new securities, June 5 — the abrogation of the gold clause in public and private contracts, June 13 — the Home Owners' Loan Act, providing for the refinancing of home mortgages, June 16 — the National Industrial Recovery Act, providing both for a system of industrial self-government under federal supervision and for a $3.3 billion public works program, June 16 — the Glass-Steagall Banking Act, divorcing commercial and investment banking and guaranteeing bank deposits, June 16 — the Farm Credit Act, providing for the reorganization of agricultural credit activities, and June 16 — the Railroad Coordination Act, setting up a federal Coordinator of Transportation. (Schlesinger, 1958: 20–21)

That was only the beginning, however. Over the next six years, the New Dealers spent prodigally in an attempt to jump-start the economy. The most famous of the New Deal agencies, the Works Progress Administration (WPA), was launched in early April 1935 with an appropriation of $5 billion, at the time the single largest budget request in American history (Conkin, 1975: 56). Headed by Harry Hopkins, the WPA financed tens of thousands of public works projects, including paving and repairing 240,000 miles of roads, constructing 153 air fields and laying 280 miles of runway, erecting 4,383 new school buildings and repairing 30,000 others, and building or refurbishing more than 2,000 sports stadiums (Couch and Shughart, 1998: 113–14). Ostensibly believing that the work provided should match the skills of the jobless as closely as possible, Hopkins financed thousands of projects that employed out-of-work painters, sculptors, actors, and other artists (ibid.: 114). The common perception that the WPA is synonymous with the New Deal has some basis in fact: it and other public works programs accounted for 34 percent of total federal emergency spending during the depression years (Couch and Shughart, 2000: 108).

Charges of fraud and waste were quite common and, in fact, the WPA, dubbed 'We Piddle Around' by its many critics, is credited with adding the word 'boondoggle' to the English language. The conventional wisdom about the WPA in particular and the New Deal in general, however, is that it saved American capitalism from its own excesses. Were it not for the federal government's active intervention at a time when markets seemed incapable of self-correction, the demands of a beaten people would have forced far more drastic policy changes, perhaps propelling the nation into the waiting arms of the socialists. As one contemporary admirer put it,

> federal policy providing work for the jobless ... has been of inestimable value to millions of workers who otherwise would have been idle and, in many instances, without means of subsistence. Furthermore, the demonstration that a democracy could assure to a substantial

fraction of its jobless workers an opportunity to work as well as the actual work that was accomplished represented priceless gains to the American people as a whole. (Howard, 1943: 841)

With billions of dollars available for distribution in the form of direct relief, work relief, subsidized loans and insurance, it should come as no surprise that the competition for federal dollars was intense, or that complaints by some state and local politicians of constituents being shortchanged frequently were strident. Congressional delegations from the South, a region that FDR often referred to as the 'nation's number one economic problem', were especially vocal in charging that the New Dealers responsible for allocating funds had their eyes on more than simple economic need. It was not until much later, however, that serious empirical study of the New Deal's spending priorities became possible.

The modern literature on the New Deal was launched by Leonard Arrington's (1969) announcement of his discovery of a set of documents prepared by the Roosevelt administration in 1939 to showcase its economic policy accomplishments, and by his own descriptive statistical analyses of the data showing wide disparities in the cross-state distribution of funds (also see Arrington, 1970). Don Reading (1973) was the first economist to exploit Arrington's dataset econometrically. He found modest support for a 'relief' hypothesis of New Deal spending. In particular, states experiencing the most severe declines in per capita incomes between 1929 and 1933 received more federal aid per person (summed over the entire 1933–39 period) than did less hard-hit states. Nevertheless, most of the cross-state variation in the distribution of New Deal funds was explained, not by other indicators of economic distress (the level of income per capita in 1933, the unemployment rate in 1937, and the percentages of the population that were either black or engaged in tenant farming in 1930), but by variables controlling for the presence of national assets in a state (the fraction of state lands owned by the federal government and the number of highway miles per capita).

Reading's most enduring contribution to the literature, however, was to speculate that his failure to find empirical support for the New Deal's stated goals of promoting economic recovery and fostering institutional reform left room for political explanations of the administration's spending priorities. Perhaps, Reading (1973: 803) suggested, states were rewarded or punished according to the roles they played in electing FDR in 1932. A variant of that hypothesis was subsequently tested by Gavin Wright (1974), who found that a measure of 'closeness' of presidential vote shares in a state, along with the standard deviation of that variable, explained nearly 59 percent of the variation in the interstate distribution of New Deal funds. Other things being the same, states where presidential races historically were tight and party vote shares were more volatile received more New Deal largesse. FDR would have anticipated higher political returns per dollar spent in such states, compared with others where the Democratic Party's vote share traditionally had been both either very large or very small and stable (reflecting entrenched voter positioning).

Wright's presidential vote-buying model of New Deal spending thus supplies a public choice explanation for why the solidly Democratic South received proportionately less federal aid than other regions of the country. Importantly, variables controlling for economic need (the decline in income per capita between 1929 and 1932, the fraction of the population on relief in 1935, and the unemployment rate in 1937) were not statistically significant when Wright estimated a more general model of the determinants of the cross-state distribution of New Deal funds. Other than the two political variables, only the percentage of state land owned by the federal government and the fraction of the population living on farms (which Wright included as a proxy for the political effectiveness of the farm lobby) contributed significant explanatory power. Similar findings emerged when Wright investigated the allocation of WPA jobs across states.

In sum, Wright's empirical evidence pointed to presidential politics as the chief determinant of New Deal spending. These results were later confirmed and extended by Anderson and Tollison (1991), who also found evidence of congressional influence on New Deal priorities, and by Couch and Shughart (1998), who exploited annual state employment indices developed by Wallis (1987) for the depression period to disaggregate the data by year and by expenditure category.

In a series of papers, John Joseph Wallis (1984, 1987, 1989, 1991) offered an alternative explanation for the failure of prior studies to find a significant relationship between New Deal spending and economic conditions in the states. In particular, Wallis argued that implicit and explicit matching requirements, whereby the states were required to share the cost of financing many of the New Deal's programs, are decisive in explaining the cross-state distribution of federal funds. Indeed, when a two-equation model designed to capture the interrelationships between federal spending and state spending during the New Deal was estimated (Wallis, 1984) or, alternatively, lagged federal grants were included in a single-equation model of federal spending across states (Wallis, 1987), economic conditions in the states became statistically significant. Moreover, the estimated signs on these variables were consistent with the hypothesis that the New Dealers responded to economic need, thereby helping

'restore a measure of credibility to the traditional view of the New Deal' (ibid.: 519). One interpretation of Wallis's matching hypothesis is that ideological opposition to the New Deal on the part of the region's political elites explains the South's comparative relative neglect: southerners simply balked at contributing the money necessary to attract significant federal aid.

Exploiting data on the matching requirements actually used by the Works Progress Administration, Couch and Shughart (2000) find, however, that the funding formula was itself perverse. They report a negative relationship between state matching contributions and state income. States hit harder by the Great Depression, in other words, were required to bear larger shares of the cost of financing WPA projects. They also find that, holding income per capita and other variables constant, states making smaller matching contributions tended to receive larger federal grants. (Consistent with regional differences in the marginal vote-buying power of New Deal spending, significantly less WPA money was allocated to the southern states than predicted by their cost shares.) With respect to the WPA at least, it does not appear to be the case that states with healthier economies benefited disproportionately from the New Deal merely because they had more resources available for matching purposes. (If that were true, why would such a formula have been adopted for distributing emergency relief funds in the first place?) What does appear to be the case is that Harry Hopkins rewarded his agency's supporters: funding for work relief projects was more generous in states represented by US Senators who voted to pass the Emergency Relief Appropriation Act of 1935, the legislation authorizing the creation of the WPA.

Public choice interpretations of the New Deal have yielded significant insights into the political forces that shaped the US government's responses to the unprecedented economic events of the 1930s. Many questions remain unanswered, of course, but we can now be reasonably confident that a vote motive belongs on the list of reasons why the New Deal failed to achieve its stated goals. Although he denied saying it, the New Dealers were for the most part motivated, not by public spirit, but by Harry Hopkins's celebrated call to political arms: 'we shall tax and tax, and spend and spend, and elect and elect'.

WILLIAM F. SHUGHART II

REFERENCES

Anderson, G.M. and Tollison, R.D. (1991). "Congressional influence and patterns of New Deal spending." *Journal of Law and Economics*, 34: 161–175.

Arrington, L.J. (1969). "The New Deal in the West: A preliminary statistical inquiry." *Pacific Historical Review*, 38: 311–316.

Arrington, L.J. (1970). "Western agriculture and the New Deal." *Agricultural History*, 44: 337–353.

Conkin, P.K. (1975). *The New Deal*. New York: Thomas Y. Crowell Co.

Couch, J.F. and Shughart, W.F. II (1998). *The Political Economy of the New Deal*. Cheltenham, UK and Northampton, MA, USA: Edward Elgar.

Couch, J.F. and Shughart, W.F. II (2000). "New Deal spending and the states: the politics of public works," in J.C. Heckelman, J.C. Moorhouse and R.M. Whaples (eds.) *Public Choice Interpretations of American Economic History*. Boston: Kluwer Academic Publishers, pp. 105–122.

Friedman, M. and Schwartz, A.J. (1963). *A Monetary History of the United States, 1867–1960*. Princeton: Princeton University Press.

Higgs, R. (1987). *Crisis and Leviathan: Critical Episodes in the Growth of American Government*. New York and Oxford: Oxford University Press.

Higgs, R. (1997). "Regime uncertainty: why the Great Depression lasted so long and why prosperity resumed after the war." *Independent Review*, 1: 561–590.

Hosen, F.E. (1992). *The Great Depression and the New Deal*. Jefferson, NC: McFarland and Co.

Howard, D.S. (1943). *The WPA and Federal Relief Policy*. New York: Russell Sage.

Margo, R.A. (1993). "Employment and unemployment in the 1930s." *Journal of Economic Perspectives*, 7: 41–59.

Reading, D.C. (1973). "New Deal activity and the states, 1933–1939." *Journal of Economic History*, 33: 792–810.

Romer, C.D. (1993). "The nation in depression." *Journal of Economic Perspectives*, 7: 19–39.

Schlesinger, A.M. (1958). *The Coming of the New Deal*. Boston: Houghton Mifflin.

Stein, H. (1984). *Presidential Economics: The Making of Economic Policy from Roosevelt to Reagan and Beyond*. New York: Simon and Schuster.

Vedder, R.K. and Gallaway, L.E. (1993). *Out of Work: Unemployment and Government in Twentieth-Century America*. New York: Holmes and Meier.

Wallis, J.J. (1984). "The birth of old federalism: financing the New Deal." *Journal of Economic History*, 44: 139–159.

Wallis, J.J. (1987). "Employment, politics, and economic recovery during the Great Depression." *Review of Economics and Statistics*, 49: 516–520.

Wallis, J.J. (1989). "Employment in the Great Depression: new data and hypothesis." *Explorations in Economic History*, 26: 45–72.

Wallis, J.J. (1991). "The political economy of New Deal federalism." *Economic Inquiry*, 29: 510–524.

Wright, G. (1974). "The political economy of New Deal spending: an econometric analysis." *Review of Economics and Statistics*, 56: 30–38.

NONPROFIT ORGANIZATIONS

Although public choice theorists and other researchers typically dichotomize the economy into the private and public sectors, a large and growing segment of the U.S. economy does not appropriately belong in either category: nonprofit entities. The terms "third sector" and "independent sector" are used to refer collectively to nonprofit organizations and to emphasize how they differ from for-profits firms and governmental bodies.

Nonprofits are artificial creations of the federal tax code under section 501(c) and can be further divided into not-for-profits and charities. Not-for-profits operate exclusively to serve a specific membership or client group, e.g., the American Automobile Association which aids member motorists. Charities or nonprofits, at least in theory, benefit society as a whole and are far more important in the size and scope of their activities than not-for-profits. Thus, my discussion is limited to charitable organizations which are classified by the Internal Revenue Service (IRS) as having 501(c)(3) or 501(c)(4) status and religious organizations. Such entities engage in a myriad activities including, but not limited to, health (hospitals, clinics, nursing homes, and physical fitness facilities), museums, education (college, university, and other institutions), disease research, public policy, and addressing society's ills — disaster relief, illness, homelessness, unemployment, abuse of humans and animals, and hunger, for example.

Conventional wisdom holds that most charities help the unfortunate in society who cannot help themselves, "but only about 10 percent of charities do that. Many organizations, declared to be charities by the IRS, serve the wealthy and middle class. ..." (Johnston, 1987). A survey by the Urban Institute "of 3,400 human service organizations revealed that the poor comprised the majority of the clients of only about 30 percent of the agencies, and that for half of the agencies, the poor constituted less than 10 percent of the clientele" (Salamon, 1985, p. 44).

Some nonprofits are national in scope, collect and spend hundreds of millions of dollars each year, and employ thousands of staff members, e.g., the American Red Cross, while others may serve only a small local constituency through volunteer effort with a small budget, e.g., a local soup kitchen aiding the hungry or a shelter for the homeless. There is no "typical" nonprofit in terms of size of staff, scope of activities, budget, functions, or any other operating dimension.

The term "nonprofit" is rather misleading in that most of these entities do, indeed, earn profits, in the sense that their revenues exceed costs. There are two primary characteristics of every charity: (1) there are no residual claimants, i.e., the "profits" — the excess of revenues over costs — cannot be distributed to any person or group and (2) society as a whole must, at least in theory, benefit from the organization's operations.

Nonprofit entities have "been a feature of Anglo-American law for nearly a millenium," (Hansmann, 1980, p. 884), and in his classic work, *Democracy in America*, Alexis de Toqueville (p. 198) praised the extensive voluntary activity that he observed and asserted that "Nothing ... is more deserving of our attention than this sector." Charitable activity is a significant and growing fraction of economic activity in the United States. As shown in the Table 1, there were 1.23 million charitable organizations in 1998 (including social welfare and religious congregations) with 10.9 million full-time and part-time employees who account for approximately 7.1 percent of total employment. These entities received $664.8 billion in revenues in 1997 from private contributions, dues, fees, and charges, and government grants and other sources. Moreover, the nonprofit sector is growing rapidly: Between 1982 and 1998, the number of nonprofits rose by 437,000 (55.1 percent); their revenues soared by $453 billion (213.7 percent); paid staff increased by 4.4 million; and the number of volunteers in full-time equivalents climbed by 1.2 million (26.7 percent).

Nonprofits are unique from all other organizations in society in that only they can call forth the energies of volunteers and donations of money and goods from private households. Independent Sector, a trade association for nonprofits, estimates that in 1998, 55.5 percent of Americans volunteered, some 109.4 million persons, who contributed 19.9 million hours of their time which was valued at $225.9 billion. Some 70.1 percent of households on average contributed $1,075 to charitable activities in 1998. (Independent Sector, 2001)

Table 1: Size and scope of the nonprofit, tax-exempt sector[a] in the U.S., selected years, 1982–1998

Attribute	1998	1992	1987	1982
Number of organizations (millions)	1.23	1.03	.907	.793
Total revenues ($ billion)	665[b]	509	317	212
Paid staff (full- and part-time) (millions)	10.9	9.1	7.4	6.5
Full-time equivalent volunteers (millions)	5.7	5.5	5.1	4.5

Notes
[a] Includes 501(c)(3), 501(c)(4), and religious organizations.
[b] This figure is for 1997.
Source: Independent Sector (2001).

Although the rationale for nonprofit status has never been explicitly stated by Congress, three economic justifications have been offered: "thin markets," "market failure," and "public goods." A university press, for instance, publishes books that most commercial publishers would disdain because the market for the books is so limited that their production would not be profitable, but society is better off with the book, despite its small readership. "Market failure" is used to justify nonprofit hospitals; e.g., the market failure occurs because consumers are supposedly incapable of judging the quality of their medical care. Removing the profit motive by having nonprofit provision in theory helps overcome the principal-agent problem in such cases, a rather questionable notion given that both for-profit and nonprofit hospitals and other medical facilities exist. The public goods argument applies to museums; volunteer labor and private contributions efficiently produce a cultural and artistic heritage that is highly desirable to society at little cost to the state.

To encourage charitable activity, nonprofits are heavily subsidized to reduce their operating costs. Nonprofits are exempt from local, state, and federal income, sales, and property taxes; they receive special treatment from the federal government regarding unemployment insurance, minimum wages, securities regulation, bankruptcy, antitrust restrictions, and copyright; charities enjoy a host of exemptions from onerous state and local laws and regulations regarding franchises, inspections, bonds, and so forth. Employees of nonprofits are even treated differently under the law; an employee of a charity can contribute more to a retirement fund than can an employee of a for-profit. Nonprofit postage is subsidized, and these organizations can mail literature and catalogs at much lower costs than their for-profit counterparts. Finally, contributors to a charity with 501(c)(3) status obtain a deduction from federal, state, and local income taxes. (Bennett and DiLorenzo, 1989, pp. 9–11.)

From an economic perspective, the most critical characteristic of charities is that they are virtually insulated from both marketplace competition that disciplines managers of private firms and electoral constraints faced by politicians in the public sector. Nonprofits are run by self-perpetuating boards of directors, so there is never an election contest to oust incumbents, and there are no shareholders demanding accountability — after all, the *sine qua non* of the nonprofit form is that profits may not be distributed. The directors are volunteers who serve part time, so professional, full-time staffs have wide discretion in controlling the organization and its agenda and are able to divert resources to perquisites that benefit the staff. Research has shown that although charities describe themselves as "volunteer" organizations, a large portion (half or more) of the budget typically goes for staff salaries, benefits, and perquisities; substantial wealth is held in reserve at the same time that fund raising is relentless. Indeed, fund raising and organizational survival and growth become the primary objectives of long-established charities after professional staffs gain control (Bennett and DiLorenzo, 1994). X-inefficiency is a characteristic of nonprofit institutions (Duizendstraal and Nentjes, 1994). In large, bureaucratic nonprofits directed by professionals, charitable activity is undertaken primarily as an adjunct to the fund raising function. Many programs are not intended to benefit the public but rather to give publicity to the organization to aid fund raising (Bennett and DiLorenzo, 1999). Small, local charitable organizations serving a specific clientele and operated mainly by volunteers and religious institutions tend to be more charitable in the traditional sense.

Three trends are emerging which have major implications for nonprofits in the long run. First, spurred on by the success of AIDS activists in obtaining ten millions of dollars from local, state, and federal governments, many charities are increasingly seeking funding from the public sector to support their programs (Smith and Lipsky, 1993). The taxpayer is viewed as a much more reliable source of funding than contributions from corporations or individuals. Although this approach may increase revenues in the short run, the inherent problems is that with government funds come bureaucratic restrictions about how nonprofits must operate, who must be served, and so forth. Second, and relatedly, nonprofits are becoming much more active in the political arena as advocates of various public policies, some of which stray far from the realm of traditional charity. (Bennett and DiLorenzo, 1998, 2000). Taken together, these two trends imply that nonprofits are diminishing their separate identities as "independent" organizations and inevitably becoming more like adjuncts of government.

The third trend involves ties between nonprofits and for-profits, i.e., the commercialization of the nonprofit sector through endorsements and "seals of approval" on products of commercial firms and through nonprofits' own commercial activities (Bennett and DiLorenzo, 1989, 2001). Weisbrod (1998, pp. 287–288) has observed that "Nonprofit organizations' are bringing revolutionary changes in traditional behavior, and in the process they are blurring the distinction between nonprofits and private firms." The issue with commercialization of charity is that charity, in a sense, is the antithesis of commercialism. In the world of commerce, consumers expect goods and services in return for payments to producers. In the world of charity, donors expect nothing in return for their contributions, and

society benefits from the benevolence of the giver. As commercialism of charities becomes more widespread — again driven by the search for revenue — different individuals assume importance in the organization. Marketing and production experts gain power at the expense of those dispensing charity. Goal displacement is inevitable in the long run.

Taken together, three trends imply that nonprofits are becoming more closely tied to government and more like commercial enterprises. Thus, their unique role and functions in society are being steadily diminished. If donors perceive that nonprofits are adjuncts of government or commercial in nature, private contributions and other support may wane for these institutions that have important roles to play in contemporary society.

JAMES T. BENNETT

REFERENCES

Bennett, J.T. and DiLorenzo, T.J. (1989). *Unfair Competition: The Profits of Nonprofits*. Lanham, MD: Hamilton Press.

Bennett, J.T. and DiLorenzo, T.J. (1994). *Unhealthy Charities: Hazardous to Your Health and Wealth*. New York: Basic Books.

Bennett, J.T. and DiLorenzo, T.J. (1998). *CancerScam: The Diversion of Federal Cancer Funds to Politics*. New Brunswick, NJ: Transaction Publishers.

Bennett, J.T. and DiLorenzo, T.J. (1999). *The Food and Drink Police: America's Nannies, Busybodies, and Petty Tyrants*. New Brunswick, NJ: Transaction Publishers.

Bennett, J.T. and DiLorenzo, T.J. (2000). *From Pathology to Politics: Public Health in America*. New Brunswick, NJ: Transaction Publishers.

Bennett, J.T. and DiLorenzo, T.J. (2001). *Public Health Profiteering*. New Brunswick, NJ: Transaction Publishers.

de Toqueville, A. (1956). "*Democracy in America*," in R.D. Heffner (ed.) New York: Mentor Books.

Duizendstraal, A. and Nentjes, A. (1994). "Organizational slack in subsidized nonprofit institutions." *Public Choice*, 81: 297–321.

Hansmann, H. (1980). "The role of nonprofit enterprise." *Yale Law Journal*, 89 (April): 835–906.

Independent Sector (2001). The nonprofit almanac in brief: facts and figures on the independent sector 2001. http:\\www.independentsector.org/nonprofitinformation center/information_center. html.

Johnston, D. (1987). "IRS seeks to impose curbs on lobbying by charities." *Los Angeles Times*, January 1.

Salamon, L.M. (1985). *Partners in Public Service: Toward a Theory of Government-Nonprofit Relations*. Washington, DC: Urban Institute.

Smith, S.R. and Lipsky, M. (1993). *Nonprofits for Hire: The Welfare State in the Age of Contracting*. Cambridge, MA: Harvard University Press.

O

THE ORIGINS OF SOCIAL CHOICE THEORY

The term "social choice" originated with Arrow's (1951) theoretical analysis of the problem of aggregating the transitive preferences of individuals into a transitive collective preference outcome. The concept of social choice is also associated with "collective choice" analysis rooted in an economic analysis of the logic of democratic consent found in the work of Buchanan and Tullock (1962).

Both of these analytical approaches are related to earlier, relatively unknown studies of the properties of voting methods. From the Roman Republic until today, voting analysts have identified methodological properties and dilemmas. But it was not until late in the 18th century that this knowledge began to be developed cumulatively within a common theoretical framework. Instead, the insights of one analyst in defining and approaching a problem were often lost. So later analysts had to start from scratch, often with very different analytical tools, concepts, and objectives.

The history of voting ideas has an ambivalent status in social choice and collective choice theory. On the one hand, pursuing the goal of a deductive science of voting seems to reduce historical developments to purely antiquarian significance. For in principle, the generality of theories makes it unnecessary to know historical background in order to learn how to apply modern concepts. Consequently traditional or historical definitions of problems are often redefined within the frameworks of contemporary mathematical models. On the other hand, the history of voting provides a rich source of theories, experiences, and problems that challenge us to rethink our interpretation of voting processes. These challenges are not purely analytic; they direct our attention to applications outside the traditional sphere of elections. In addition, by examining voting arguments from the past, we can learn about the underlying metaphysics of contemporary normative debates such as the choice of the "best" voting system.

Voting theory and its contemporary social and collective choice derivatives can be seen as pathways in the development of a deductive, experimental science of voting. In Kuhnian terms, there still is no "normal" paradigm for voting science. Theoretical ideas about voting lack a common framework of concepts, models, and predictions that are essential for defining the science as paradigmatic. Instead there are divergent arguments about the goals of voting as well as the interpretation of standards for measuring consensus. Some see this diversity as an obstacle to intellectual progress; others see divergent intellectual directions as a creative force that enriches problem solving.

Pliny the Younger (1995), who confronted a dilemma associated with casting a vote when the agenda consists of more than two choices, did the earliest known analysis of a social choice phenomenon. Before Pliny, voters in traditional cultures typically faced binary choices, so these dilemmas did not occur.

The institutional context for Pliny's analysis was a Senate tribunal rendering a verdict in a murder trial of former slaves of a Roman consul, who had been found dead. Instead of conducting separate votes for each verdict alternative — banishment, death, and acquittal, Pliny arranged an agenda of binary choices among the three verdict alternatives and attempted to manipulate the collective outcome by controlling the agenda of binary choices. Writing retrospectively to a colleague in A.D. 105, Pliny describes his attempted manipulation and asks if what he did was a mistake.

Pliny's discomfort about strategic manipulation of the agenda highlights the complexity of voting analysis. This complexity can make it difficult for others to answer and discuss questions such as Pliny's. We do not know if Pliny received a response from his correspondent, but subsequent voting theorists also struggled with developing a dialogue about empirical and normative issues. In fact, an underlying current in early voting analyses is the tension between two criteria for evaluating collective outcomes: preference aggregation and making the "right" choice.

This tension became institutionalized in the social contexts of theorists from Pliny until the 18th century. Whether the norms were secular or religious, the tension was a characteristic of pre-modern legislatures, which not only voted to produce new laws, but also served as juries to render verdicts in criminal and civil cases. These dual functions sustained a concern with producing the right choice, a concern that continues in contemporary political decision making.

Between Pliny and the 18th century, Ramon Lull and Nicolas Cusanus explored social choice ideas in religious institutions. Lull's (1914) novel, *Blanquerna*, written in 1285, addresses voting procedures as part of a story about a hermit who becomes a monk, abbot, bishop, and the pop. Lull outlines a voting system based on pairwise comparisons of ranked choices. His didactic exposition makes it clear that not following the "art" can produce dire consequences. For when electors choose *Blanquerna* as bishop without following the "art," they generate an indecisive outcome and the decision must be appealed to the Pope to produce a winner.

Lull's more scholarly work such as *De Arte Eleccionis (1937)*, written in 1299, outlines a pairwise election method that clearly resembles a Condorcet procedure. Lull's use of matrix notation and his recommendation that the number of voters be odd (to prevent ties) distinguish him as an imaginative precursor of ideas that did not emerge until for nearly 500 years. But Lull never found an audience in which his analytical ideas could grow.

Nicolas Cusanus developed in an intellectual environment in which Lull's works were part of the curriculum even though Lull was reputed to be a dangerous thinker. Although Lull and Cusanus were both intellectuals in a Catholic culture, Cusanus (Häegele and Pukelsheim, 2000) was more focused on the problem of ending a long schism in the papacy by designing a voting procedure for the election of a Holy Roman Emperor — rather than a Pope. Approximately 130 years after Lull had outlined an "honest" method of elections for the Church, Cusanus proposes a Borda system and criticizes attempts to control the collective outcome by manipulating electors. Cusanus also applies the Borda method to votes on propositions with more than two possibilities, contrasting it with the binary procedure in use in Venice for propositions and elections. The Venetian method, similar to approval voting (Lines, 1986), simplified the process of selecting 41 electors from an initial assembly of 1500 members.

In the Church, unanimous collective outcomes were valued as a sign of divine inspiration. But when voting outcomes were not unanimous, the custom of distinguishing between the *sanior et major pars* (sounder — as in "more correct" — and greater part) was adopted (Moulin, 1958). In some cases, the authority of an individual or subset of voters was used to overrule a plurality coalition. Gradually, however, divisiveness caused by defining the *sanior* voters led to reliance on the *greater* part as a criterion for defining a consensus.

The tension between selecting the right choice and the most popular choice continued in the analyses of voting in the 18th century French Academy of Sciences (FAS). Members of the FAS were generalists, scientists who shared a concern with managing problems associated with electing and promoting members of the Academy. LaPlace, Poisson, and Lavoisier all developed mathematical models to support their arguments about how to elect or promote the "right" or most meritorious candidates (Rapaport, 1967). But it was Borda who first raised the issue in a 1770 FAS paper, "On Elections by Ballot," (Borda, 1784) in which he showed that the conventional plurality method would not select what is now known as the Condorcet winner. To remedy this problem, Borda recommended a method in which each candidate would receive points according to his ranking in voter preference orderings. Although FAS papers were normally published within three years, Borda's paper did not appear until 1784, when it was published with an introductory note by Condorcet, the Secretary of the FAS. Condorcet was responsible for setting the publication schedule and may have delayed publication for political reasons.

One year after the publication of Borda's paper, Condorcet (1785) presented his analysis of voting, 13 "hypotheses" about the effects of voting procedures on the group probability of making a correct collective choice. The 1785 Essai includes the first statement of the inconsistency between individual and collective transitivity in voting. Condorcet viewed this inconsistency as an "effect" — not a "paradox" — that was significant because it effected the performance of the group in selecting a correct choice.

There is no evidence that Condorcet and Borda — or surrogates — actually debated voting methods. To some extent, the issue of voting methods was overshadowed by political animosity between Condorcet — who wanted to modernize the French state by introducing popular representation — and Borda — an ardent supporter of absolute monarchy. And although Condorcet explored the properties of different voting methods, he seemed to recognize that plurality voting was easier to manipulate than Borda voting. For Condorcet's election as FAS secretary was a manipulation that was facilitated by plurality voting (Urken, 1991).

After the 1789 Revolution, Condorcet supported the Republican cause and wrote a constitutional plan that included a practical voting method that had nothing to do with his 1785 Essai. However when the design of a jury for the trial of King Louis XVI was debated, Condorcet proposed a jury size and voting method based on a mathematical argument extracted from his 1785 Essai (Urken, 1991).

Condorcet's 1785 Essai and practical proposal were read by Lhuilier, 1794), who showed that the practical method could not select the Condorcet winner. Later theorists like Nanson (1882) were influenced by Condorcet's analysis. But there is no evidence that Jefferson, Madison, or Carroll ever read the 1785 Essai (Urken, 1991; McLean and Urken, 1992).

After the Revolution, when the FAS was reconstituted into the Institute of France (IOF), internal political conflicts once again prevented French scientists from clarifying their ideas and developing their arguments experimentally (McLean and Urken, 1996). Napoleon, an IOF leader before ascending to political power, appointed a special commission to study voting methods for the IOF. The commission included Borda and Daunou, an expert in literature who had worked on voting problems with Condorcet before the Revolution. The IOF adopted a Borda method. Daunou wrote a scathing critique of IOF problems created by strategic manipulation of Borda voting. But when Napoleon, as political leader, unilaterally changed the method back to plurality voting, there is no evidence that he was influenced by Daunou's analysis. It seems that Napoleon, like Condorcet, appreciated the ease of manipulating collective outcomes under plurality voting.

None of these pre- or post-Revolutionary French works on social choice were studied at all in France for approximately 65 years, when a French economist rediscovered, but did not revive, the classical tradition. Duncan Black's (1958) path-breaking FAS archival work and economic analysis resuscitated awareness of the classical tradition in the middle of the 20th century. However his interpretation of the dualism in social choice theory was to relegate Condorcet's analysis of the probability of making a correct choice in voting processes to jury decision making. And the name that Black coined, the "jury theorem," has become a conventional reference for Condorcet's 1785 Essai even though Condorcet's primary objective was to design social choice procedures to maximize the group probability of making a correct choice in all collective choices, which in his view, did not theoretically or practically differentiate between legislative, electoral, or jury environments.

Condorcet viewed his 1785 Essai as a starting point for developing experimental knowledge about voting processes. But preference aggregation is still the dominant framework in social choice theory following Arrow's "impossibility" results and "paradox of voting." In some respects, we have not advanced much in balancing the analyses of preferences aggregation and making the right choice. For example, the current—sometimes metaphysical—debate between advocates of Borda and Approval voting about the "best" voting method are reminiscent of the adversarial debates that occurred in the 18th century FAS (Mackenzie, 2000). However contemporary appreciation of the "jury theorem" has extended Condorcet's analysis of competence in social choice and begun a tradition of rigorous experimental analysis of social choice problems in juries (Guarnaschelli et al., 2000) that takes account of aggregating preferences and making a correct choice.

ARNOLD B. URKEN

REFERENCES

Arrow, K. (1951). *Social Choice and Individual Values*. New York: Wiley.

Black, D. (1958). *The Theory of Committees and Elections*. Cambridge: Cambridge University Press.

Borda, J.-C. de (1784). "On elections by ballot," in I. McLean and A.B. Urken (eds.) *Classics of Social Choice*. Ann Arbor: University of Michigan Press.

Buchanan, J.M. and Tullock, G. (1962). *The Calculus of Consent*. Ann Arbor: University of Michigan Press.

Condorcet, M.J.A.N., marquis de [1785] (1972). *Essai Sur L'application De L'analyse À La Probabilité Des Décisions Rendues À La Pluralité Des Voix*. New York: Chelsea Publishing Co. Facsimile reprint of original published in Paris by the Imprimerie Royale.

Guarnaschelli, S., McKelvey, R., and Palfrey, T. (2000). "An experimental study of Jury decision rules," *American Political Science, Review*, June 2000.

Häegele, G. and Pukelsheim, F. (2000). *Lulls Schriften zu Wahlverfahren*. Universität Augsburg. Institut für Mathematik. Report No. 434.

Lhuilier, S. (1794). Examination of the election method proposed to the National Convention of France in February 1793, and Adopted in Geneva, in I. McLean and A.B. Urken (eds.) *Classics of Social Choice*. Ann Arbor: University of Michigan Press.

Lines, M. (1986). "Approval voting and strategy analysis: a venetian example." *Theory and Decision*, 20: 155–172.

Lull, R. [ca. 1285] (1914). *"Blanquerna,"* in A.M. Alcover (ed.) *Obres Originals del Illuminat Doctor Mestre Ramon Lull*, Volume 9. Palma: Commissió Editora Lulliana.

Mackenzie, D. (2000). "May the Best Man Lose," *Discover*. Volume 21(11).

McLean, I. and Urken, A.B. (1992). "Did Jefferson or Madison understand Condorcet's social choice theory?," *Public Choice*. 73: 445–458.

McLean, I. and Urken, A.B. (1996). "La Réception des Oeuvres de Condorcet sur le Choix Social: 1794–1803: Lhuillier, Morales, et Daunou," in P. Crépel (ed.) *Nouvelles Recherches sur Condorcet*. Paris: Minerve.

Moulin, M.L. (1958). "Sanoir et major pars: note sur l'Évolution des techniques Électorales dans les Ordres religieux du Vie au XIIIe siécle," *Revue historique du droit français et étranger*.

Nanson, E.J. (1882). "Methods of Election." Paper read to the Royal Society of Victoria on 12 October 1882, in I. McLean and A.B. Urken (eds.) *Classics of Social Choice*. Ann Arbor: University of Michigan Press.

Pliny the Younger (1995). "Letter to Titius Aristo, A.D. 105," in I. McLean and A.B. Urken (eds.) *Classics of Social Choice*. Ann Arbor: University of Michigan Press.

Rapaport, R. (1967). "Elections in the French Academy of Sciences," *Essays in Honor of Henri Guerlac*. Ithaca: University of Cornell Press.

Urken, A.B. (1991). "The Condorcet-Jefferson connection and the origins of social Choice theory," *Public Choice*, 72, 213–236.

P

THE PARADOX OF REBELLION

In the mythology of revolution, the people rising to
throw off a tyrannical ruler is the dominant theme ...
Most of the mythology concerns a people driven
beyond endurance by the vicious oppression of their
masters rising up and establishing a noble and just
republic. I regret to say that this myth is mainly myth.
Gordon Tullock, *Autocracy* (Tullock, 1987: 53)

Rebellious activities are illegal activities directed at a
change in the policies or leadership of a political regime or
in the nature of the regime itself. They are usually, but not
always, instances of collective action, i.e. they require
the participation of two or more individuals and — if
successful — produce an outcome that may be enjoyed by
everyone sympathizing with the rebellion, irrespective of
participation. But in that respect rebellion is, even when
bad, a collective good and hence open to the problems of
free-riding so familiar to economists. The problem has
perhaps been most eloquently summarized by the late
philosopher, Gregory Kavka:

Imagine a country in which a small elite rules over and
exploits the vast majority of the citizens. All the members
of the exploited group know that if they acted together,
they could easily overthrow the present regime and set up
a new and just government that would better serve their
interests. Furthermore, the elite regime has not rendered
the exploited so fearful that they fail to communicate
their dissatisfaction to one another. Initially, it seems
obvious that, if the members of the exploited group are
rational, they will pursue their common interests by
revolting against the regime, toppling it, and establishing
a new government in its place. But now consider the
question of participation in the revolution from the point
of view of an individual member of the exploited group.
It would appear that, for him, the substantial costs of participation — the risk of being punished by the regime for
participating or of dying in the fighting — will greatly
exceed the expected benefits. For, in the first place, it is
highly unlikely that his participation would significantly
increase the chances of the revolution succeeding. And,
in the second place, the benefits of better government
that would follow a revolution are essentially public
goods, i.e. the average individual would receive them
even without being an active participant in the revolution.
Hence, if he maximizes expected utility, our potential
revolutionary will not join in the revolt. Nor, for like reasons, will his fellows; and as a result, there would not be
a revolution. (Kavka, 1982: 455)

The basic reasoning has been known at least since the
writings of the English 17th century 'Leveller' political
activist John Lilburne, and Vladimir I. Lenin may be seen to
have drawn attention to the neglect of the problem in the
thought of Karl Marx. However, the first to explicitly identify the collective good nature of rebellious activities and
submit it to public choice analysis were Mancur Olson
(Olson [1965] 1971: 105–109, 161–162) and Thomas
Ireland (Ireland, 1967), and it was Gordon Tullock who first
devoted considerable attention to the problem and who
coined the phrase 'the paradox of revolution' (Tullock, 1971,
1974, 1987). The problem identified is, however, much more
general than revolution alone and may logically be extended
to rebellion in general, so it is no doubt more fitting to speak
of a 'paradox of rebellion' (Kurrild-Klitgaard 1997) and a
resulting 'rebel's dilemma' (Lichbach, 1995), and this line of
analysis has influenced the treatment of rebellious activities
in a long list of publications (e.g., Silver, 1974; Salert, 1976;
Buchanan, 1979; Kirk, 1983; Finney, 1987; Taylor, 1988;
Coleman, 1990; Sandler, 1992).

The basic logic of the paradox may be expressed by a
modified version of Olson's logic of collective action,
i.e. by an inequality which must be satisfied if it is to be
rational for a potential rebel to contribute to collective
rebellious action:

$$V_i \Delta R_i + B - C > 0,$$

where V_i is the potential rebel's 'share' of the collective
good produced by a successful rebellious act, ΔR_i is the
change in the probability of success of the rebellious act
given the individual's contribution, B are the benefits he
may derive from the process itself, while C represents all
the costs he may incur from participating. Tullock's point is
that rebellious activities usually are large-scale phenomena
where the typical individual's contribution is insignificant,
and where the expected value of the collective good
accordingly goes to zero. The individual's problem then is
that if we for the moment disregard the private benefits,
then all that is left are the costs. In other words, in the
absence of private, participation-related benefits, it will
never be rational for an individual to participate; he will
rather choose to free-ride on the risks taken by his fellow
comrades. But if they all are similarly rational, the potential rebels will find themselves in a situation resembling a
n-person Prisoners' Dilemma, and there will never be any
collective rebellious action at all.

To many such conclusions seems completely at odds with
a reality, where after all there are many examples of revolutions, rebellions, riots, not to mention coups and instances of
terrorism. On the other hand, the analysis highlights an
important, but neglected fact, namely that the occurrence of

large-scale collective rebellious action may be a highly over-estimated phenomenon: While some rebellious activities, e.g., coups, occur frequently in some societies, empirical examples of large-scale collective activities is in fact quite rare, and when they do occur, it is rare to find more than five percent of the relevant sympathizers participating (Lichbach, 1995: 11f, 17f; Kurrild-Klitgaard, 1997: 124ff).

Unless one adopts the view that real-world rebels are irrational or completely rejects public choice analysis as such, the reasoning indirectly gives rise to two central and related questions: (1) Given the public goods problem, why do some collective rebellious action occur at all? (2) Why do some rebellious activities end up as large-scale revolutions, while others become rebellions, riots, or simply just coups or terrorism?

The answer given by Tullock to the question of why rebellious activities occur at all is basically a by-product explanation that may be called the Tullock Model: Events such as a revolutions do not occur because of the collective good that is officially sought or that is sometimes produced, but rather, first and foremost, because of the private benefits to be reaped by the participants, or they may occur in those rare situations, where there are no costs associated with the rebellious actions. As such Tullock himself has found the model useful for explaining the student rebellions of the late 1960s and the frequently occurring coups in societies with large rents to be reaped by a political class as well as the general absence of large-scale rebellions (Tullock, 1971, 1974, 1987).

Tullock's analysis has been submitted to fierce criticism from a number of sides. Observers have often felt that it was simply absurd to think that, e.g., ideology and the policies of a regime should be unimportant for the level of rebellious activities. Even among rational choice theorists the view has often been that the analysis is too simplistic (DeNardo, 1985), less than fruitful (Buchanan, 1987: 14; Mueller, 1989: 175), or partly misapplied (Kurrild-Klitgaard, 1997). Against this it must, however, be kept in mind that Tullock's claim is not that no individuals ever act altruistically; it is only the more modest (if only slightly less cynical) that most of the time people do not act predominantly altruistically, and that when personal costs are high and the expected utility of contributing to the collective good is small, large-scale collective action is unlikely. And whereas the critics usually point out that some forms of rebellious action, obviously do occur, the Tullockian answer would probably be: Yes, but very rarely, and usually only when some Olsonian selective benefits are applied.

Other analysts working within the rational choice paradigm have put the emphasis elsewhere, and there is by now a very wide range of types of 'solutions' that have been proposed to the paradox of rebellion (cf. Lichbach, 1994; Lichbach, 1995; Kurrild-Klitgaard, 1997). In particular, many studies have focused on the possibility of including some 'softer' values in the calculations of individual rebels, thereby changing the payoff so as to be positive. Many such suggestions have focused on, e.g., Kantian moral reasoning, notions of group solidarity, class consciousness, etc. (Muller and Opp, 1986, 1987; Elster, 1988; Finkel et al., 1989; Opp, 1989; Motyl, 1990; Opp, 1994). But what is less obvious is how that alone necessarily will do the trick; it seems that either such a type of reasoning simply represents an increase in the collective good value, or it is a question of acting in the interest of the group, but where the individual action still remains insignificant for the outcome. Either way this alone seems logically insufficient to solve the collective action problem (Buchanan, 1979; Kurrild-Klitgaard, 1998). If anything, it must be the case that the values included in the calculus refer to benefits connected directly with the process itself, e.g., a sense of doing one's duty, a 'moral satisfaction', etc.

A different line of research has been to focus on the importance of the size of the relevant group of rebels. If relatively few individuals are required in order to achieve the desired outcome, the efficacy of the typical individual rebel may be much bigger than in settings requiring thousands of participants, just as the transaction costs associated with coordinating plans and utilizing common resources effectively are smaller for small groups. Together these aspects are seen as playing a part in the explanation of the frequency of coups relative to grand revolutions (e.g., Kurrild-Klitgaard, 2000). They also suggest an explanation of the relative success of terrorist acts and guerilla warfare (cf. Tullock, 1975; Sandler and Scott, 1987; Popkin, 1988; Tong, 1988). On the other hand, there is a certain safety in numbers, i.e. the risks of being caught or injured are often relatively smaller in the case of thousands of rioters than in the case of small groups of conspirators or individual demonstrations of civil disobedience (DeNardo, 1985).

Yet another line of research has focused on the dynamics of rebellious action and the role of expectations (Gunning, 1972; Chalmers and Shelton, 1975; Roeder, 1982; Mason, 1984; DeNardo, 1985; Oberschall, 1993, 1994; Kuran, 1989, 1991, 1995; Kurrild-Klitgaard, 1997, 1998). The point of such studies have often been that it may be misleading to portray the decision of a potential rebel as either joining or not joining an already ongoing collective act; the decision will rather be influenced by certain expectations as to how many others will be participating, how many will be needed, how much the individual can contribute, etc. Incorporating such elements into the calculus of the potential rebel makes it much more likely that the situation will resemble a coordination game than a Prisoners' Dilemma.

Finally, the analysis of the Tullock Model may be too stylized to be descriptive of real world situations, where there may often be considerable differences in the talents and the intensity of the preferences of the potential rebels, and where organizations exist. What rebellious movements need in order to be successful at overthrowing a regime is, first and foremost, political entrepreneurship (cf. Wagner, 1966; Frohlich et al., 1971; Frohlich and Oppenheimer, 1974). This has been argued both theoretically and in connection with a number of case studies, where it has been shown how the presence of radicals acting as political entrepreneurs may help rebels overcome the initial collective action problems and thereby change the dynamics of the situation (Popkin, 1979; Popkin, 1988; Taylor, 1988; Kurrild-Klitgaard, 1997; Parikh and Cameron, 2000).

What seems to be lacking in the public choice analysis of rebellious activities are two things. First, at the theoretical level there is a lack of explanations for why collective rebellious action sometimes become 'big' (revolutions and rebellions), other times 'small' (riots), and sometimes do not get off the ground at all. Second, there is a lack of detailed public choice based analyses of specific events, e.g., in the form of analytical narratives. What could seem to be a fruitful line of research would be studies trying to incorporate public choice analysis into grander historical case studies (cf. Goldstone, 1994).

PETER KURRILD-KLITGAARD

REFERENCES

Buchanan, A. (1979). "Revolutionary motivation and rationality." *Philosophy and Public Affairs*, 9(Fall): 59–82.

Buchanan, J.M. (1987). "The qualities of a natural economist," in C.K. Rowley (ed.) *Democracy and Public Choice: Essays in Honor of Gordon Tullock*. Oxford: Basil Blackwell, pp. 9–19.

Chalmers, J.A. and Shelton, R. (1975). "An economic analysis of riot participation." *Economic Inquiry*, 13: 322–336.

Coleman, J.S. (1990). *Foundations of Social Theory*. Cambridge: Belknap Press.

DeNardo, J. (1985). *Powers in Numbers: The Political Strategy of Protest and Rebellion*. Princeton: Princeton University Press.

Elster, J. (1988). "Marx, revolution and rational choice," in M. Taylor (ed.) *Rationality and Revolution*. Cambridge: Cambridge University Press, pp. 206–228.

Finkel, S.E., Muller, E.N., and Opp, K.-D. (1989). "Personal influence, collective rationality and mass political action." *American Political Science Review*, 83(3): 885–903.

Finney, L. (1987). A rational choice theory of revolution and political violence. College Park: University of Maryland, Unpublished dissertation.

Frohlich, N. and Oppenheimer, J.A. (1974). "The carrot and the stick: optimal program mixes for entrepreneurial political leaders." *Public Choice*, 19(Fall): 43–61.

Frohlich, N., Oppenheimer, J.A., and Young, O.R. (1971). *Political Leadership and Collective Goods*. Princeton: Princeton University Press.

Goldstone, J.A. (1994). "Is revolution individually rational? Groups and individuals in revolutionary collective action." *Rationality and Society*, 6(1): 139–166.

Gunning, J.P. (1972). "An economic approach to riot analysis." *Public Choice*, 8(Fall): 31–46.

Ireland, T. (1967). "The rationale of revolt." *Papers on Non-Market Decision Making*, 3(Fall): 49–66.

Kavka, G.S. (1982). "Two solutions to the paradox of revolution." *Midwest Studies in Philosophy: Social and Political Philosophy*, 7: 455–472.

Kirk, R. (1983). "Political terrorism and the size of government: a positive institutional analysis of violent political activity." *Public Choice*, 40(1): 41–52.

Kuran, T. (1989). "Sparks and prairie fires: a theory of unanticipated political revolution." *Public Choice*, 61(1): 41–74.

Kuran, T. (1991). "The East European revolution of 1989: is it surprising that we were surprised?" *American Economic Review*, 81(Papers and Procedings)(2): 121–125.

Kuran, T. (1995). *Private Truths, Public Lies: The Social Consequences of Preference Falsification*. Cambridge: Harvard University Press.

Kurrild-Klitgaard, P. (1997). *Rational Choice, Collective Action and the Paradox of Rebellion*. Copenhagen: Institute of Political Science, University of Copenhagen & Copenhagen Political Studies Press.

Kurrild-Klitgaard, P. (1998). Politik, rationalitet og det Moralske Dilemma. *Politica*, 30(4): 423–439.

Kurrild-Klitgaard, P. (2000). "The constitutional economics of autocratic succession." *Public Choice*, 103(1–2): 63–84.

Lichbach, M.I. (1994). "Rethinking rationality and rebellion: theories of collective action and problems of collective dissent." *Rationality and Society*, 6(1): 8–39.

Lichbach, M.I. (1995). *The Rebel's Dilemma*. Ann Arbor: University of Michigan Press.

Mason, T.D. (1984). "Individual participation in collective racial violence: a rational choice synthesis." *American Political Science Review*, 78: 1040–1056.

Motyl, A.J. (1990). *Sovietology, Rationality, Nationality: Coming to Grips with Nationalism in the USSR*. New York: Colombia University Press.

Mueller, D.C. (1989). *Public Choice II*. Cambridge: Cambridge University Press.

Muller, E.N. and Opp, K.-D. (1986). "Rational choice and rebellious collective action." *American Political Science Review*, 80(2): 471–488.

Muller, E.N. and Opp, K.-D. (1987). "Rebellious collective action revisited." *American Political Science Review*, 81(2): 561–564.

Oberschall, A.R. (1993). *Social Movements: Ideologies, Interests, and Identities*. New Brunswick: Transaction Publishers.

Oberschall, A.R. (1994). "Rational choice in collective protests." *Rationality and Society* 6(1): 79–100.

Olson, M. (1971 [1965]). *The Logic of Collective Action: Public Goods and the Theory of Groups*, Second Edition. Cambridge: Harvard University Press.

Opp, K.-D. (1989). *The Rationality of Political Protest: A Comparative Analysis of Rational Choice Theory.* Boulder: Westview Press.

Opp, K.-D. (1994). "Repression and revolutionary action." *Rationality and Society*, 6(1): 101–138.

Parikh, S. and Cameron, C.M. (2000). "Riot games: A theory of riots and mass political violence," Paper presented at 7th Wallis Institute Conference on Political Economy, University of Rochester, 19–20 October.

Popkin, S.L. (1979). *The Rational Peasant: The Politcal Economy of Rural Society in Vietnam.* Berkeley: University of California.

Popkin, S.L. (1988). "Political entrepreneurs and peasant movements in Vietnam," in M. Taylor (ed.) *Revolution and Rationality.* Cambridge: Cambridge University Press, pp. 9–62.

Roeder, P.G. (1982). "Rational revolution: Extensions of the 'by-product' model of revolutionary involvement." *Western Political Quarterly*, 35: 5–23.

Salert, B. (1976). *Revolutions and Revolutionaries: Four Theories.* New York: Elsevier.

Sandler, T. (1992). *Collective Action: Theory and Applications.* Ann Arbor: University of Michigan Press.

Sandler, T. and Scott, J.L. (1987). "Terrorist success in hostage-taking incidents." *Journal of Conflict Resolution*, 31(1): 35–53.

Silver, M. (1974). "Political revolution and repression: An economic approach." *Public Choice*, 17: 63–71.

Taylor, M. (1988). "Rationality and revolutionary collective action," in M. Taylor (ed.) *Revolution and Rationality.* Cambridge: Cambridge University Press, pp. 63–97.

Tong, J. (1988). "Rational outlaws: rebels and bandits in the Ming dynasty," pp. 1368–1644, in M. Taylor (ed.) *Revolution and Rationality.* Cambridge: Cambridge University Press, pp. 98–128.

Tullock, G. (1971). "The paradox of revolution." *Public Choice*, 11: 89–100.

Tullock, G. (1974). *The Social Dilemma: The Economics of War and Revolution.* Blacksburg: Center for Study of Public Choice.

Tullock, G. (1975). "Column war," in G. Tullock (ed.) *Frontiers of Economics.* Blacksburg: Center for Study of Public Choice, pp. 79–98.

Tullock, G. (1987). *Autocracy.* Dordrecht: Kluwer.

Wagner, R.E. (1966). "Pressure groups and political entrepreneurs: a review article," *Papers on Non-Market Decision Making*, 1: 161–170.

PARCHMENT VERSUS GUNS

It is widely thought that just as a market economy is an expression of economic freedom, so is a democratic polity an expression of political freedom. A market economy and a political democracy would thus seem to combine to form a constitution of liberty for a free society. In this respect, the renowned constitutional scholar Charles McIlwain once noted that "constitutional government is by definition limited government" (McIlwain, 1947, p. 21). Without some explanation as to how it is possible truly to limit government, however, this common formulation is perhaps more sentimental than realistic. The task of giving that sentiment some grounding in reality is a difficult one that raises some knotty issues regarding the institutional framework of a free society.

The very idea of limited government implies that government is not the source of personal rights, for government itself is limited by the prior and superior rights of the people who form it. People form government, government doesn't form people, a theme that is developed crisply in an economic context in James Buchanan and Gordon Tullock (1962). One use that people make of their rights is to create governments to preserve and protect those rights. Without government, people would be subject to predatory attack, both from each other and from outsiders. Rights are of little value if they cannot be preserved and protected. For government to pursue this protective task, it must be sufficiently powerful to subdue potential predators, both domestic and foreign. Government thus must be the locus of predominant force within a society, for otherwise it could not fulfill its protective role.

The eternal question that won't go away is how, or whether, it is possible to design a government that will use its power to preserve and protect without using that same power as an instrument of predation (Scott Gordon (1999) presents several historical episodes where different societies have taken different approaches to limiting government). It is easy to illustrate the problem of limiting government. If two people acting privately cannot rightfully take the property of a third person, neither should they be able to do so simply because they comprise a political majority. Suppose Primo, Secundo, and Terzo comprise a town. Primo's property contains some marshland which he plans to drain and fill to create a shopping center. Secundo and Terzo each prefer to see the land remain as marshland, even if it means they must go elsewhere to do their shopping.

The institutional framework of the market economy provides an easy way for Secundo and Terzo to secure their desired marshland. All they have to do is to get Primo's permission to keep the land as a marshland rather than turn it into a shopping center. There are many particular ways they could accomplish this. A simple way would be for them to buy the relevant portion of Primo's land. Alternatively, Secundo and Terzo could lease the land from Primo, say for 99 years. They could act on their own behalf in doing this, or they could act in the name of a conservation trust which they established. In any case, the basic principles of property and contract that provide the legal framework for a market economy provide a set of simple rules within which market participants can create quite complex patterns of governance to carry out their desired transactions (Epstein, 1995). Regardless of the particular form that a transaction might take, the market framework provides a consensual method for resolving this divergence of opinion among Primo, Secundo, and Terzo. If Secundo and Terzo place a higher value on using the land as a bird sanctuary than Primo places on building a shopping center, Secundo and Terzo will be able to convince Primo to give up on the shopping center and let the marshland serve as a bird sanctuary instead.

For Secundo and Terzo, the problem with this method of resolving this difference of opinion is that they have to pay full price to get their way. Yet they comprise a majority in the town. So long as political decisions can be made by majority vote and do not require unanimity, Secundo and Terzo can do better for themselves by adopting a motion to treat the construction of a bird sanctuary on Primo's land as a town project. The cost of securing the land would now come from town funds. Public financing of the bird sanctuary thus allows the winning majority to transfer some of the cost onto the losing minority. The extent to which such a transfer occurs depends on the type of tax system the town uses. A very simple tax system would be one that imposes equal cost sharing across residents. In this case, Secundo and Terzo would each pay but one-third of the cost, whereas under the market-based method of creating the bird sanctuary they would each pay one-half the cost.

To be sure, Primo would not voluntarily sell the land to the town under these circumstances because refusing to sell the land would prevent the tax from being imposed. Secundo and Terzo would have to use the name of the town to invoke eminent domain to get the land. Doing this allows the majority to take Primo's land against his will, and to force him to accept only two-thirds of the compensation the town offers, because his taxes also cover one-third of that compensation.

The Fifth Amendment to the American constitution allows governments to take private property through eminent domain, but also places tight restrictions on the use of this power. One such restriction is that any such taking must be to advance some legitimate public (as distinct from private) purpose. Another restriction is that the owners of property be justly compensated for any such taking. As Richard Epstein (1985) explains, the history of eminent domain over the past century or so has increasingly run in the direction of governments taking property for what are private uses and paying only partial or token compensation in the process.

Despite its clear wording about public use and just compensation, the Fifth Amendment does not seem to be a strong bar against governments taking private property for private use while failing to pay just compensation. The Fifth Amendment, along with any constitutional document, is just a piece of parchment. While parchment paper is stronger than ordinary writing paper, apparently it is not sufficiently strong to deter rapacious governments and interest groups from using government as an instrument of predation.

In Federalist No. 48, James Madison noted that legislatures in Virginia and Pennsylvania had repeatedly violated their state constitutions, acting thereby as an instrument of predation on behalf of some people at the expense of others, in sharp contrast to acting as an instrument of protection and preservation. Madison concluded his examination by noting "that a mere demarcation on parchment is not a sufficient guard against those encroachments which lead to a tyrannical concentration of all the powers of government in the same hands." The articulation on parchment of a declaration of limited government to protect and preserve is not by itself sufficient to generate protection and preservation as the core activity of government.

There is a tenuous balance between liberalism or capitalism on the one hand and democracy on the other, as the American Founders recognized. A system of economic organization based on private property will require some measure of government activity, if to do nothing else than protect people's rights of person and property. Liberalism is grounded in individual freedom and private property. In this scheme, government itself is simply a reflection of people's use of their rights of person and property, and is not a source of those rights. Governmental authority is limited to securing individual rights.

Even though there may be general agreement about the proper principles of governmental activity, that agreement often dissolves in the specifics of particular practice. Primo, Secundo, and Terzo might all affirm the principle of limited government, and yet Secundo and Terzo will participate willingly and even eagerly in taking Primo's property when doing so allows them to promote a favored project at lower cost to themselves. To be sure, Secundo and Terzo may have some moral qualms about their use of politics to circumvent the market in building their bird sanctuary. To subdue such qualms, they might invoke such doctrines as strategic holdouts and free riders as a kind of therapy to ease their minds. This would allow Secundo and Terzo to deceive themselves into believing that Primo really valued the bird sanctuary, only refused to say so because he was holding out to get a higher price.

As Vincent Ostrom (1984) explains with particular cogency, government involves a Faustian bargain: instruments of evil — power over other people — are to be employed because of the good they might do, recognizing that evil will also result. This raises the issue of the terms of that bargain. There are two principle approaches to securing more favorable terms. One approach looks primarily to education and related processes for cultivating virtue and wisdom within a population (Walker, 1990). The claim here is that the wiser people are about the dangers of the Faustian bargain, the less eagerly they will embrace it. Parchment will serve as a stronger barrier to predatory uses of government as people become wiser in their understanding about such predatory uses of government.

The other approach looks primarily to a kind of opposition of interests to limit government predation. Metaphorically speaking, this alternative approach looks to guns more than to parchment (Wagner, 1987, 1993). The basic principle behind this approach is for governmental action to require some concurrence among different participants with opposed interests. Such concurrence, it should be noted is exactly what market exchange promotes. Within the frameworks of property and contract, Primo, Secundo, and Terzo will all concur in the market-generated outcome concerning the use of Primo's marshland. If that land becomes a bird sanctuary, this will be because Primo concurs with Secundo's and Terzo's desire to exercise dominion over the marshland. The testimony about Primo's concurrence lies in his willingness to cede control over the land to Secundo and Terzo. If that land becomes a shopping center, this will be because Secundo and Terzo concur with Primo's desire to build a shopping center. The testimony about Secundo's and Terzo's concurrence lies in their unwillingness to make an offer that would be sufficient to convince Primo to cede control over the land.

Both approaches reflect a presumption that self-interest is predominant in all human activity, in government as well as in commerce. The justification for government resides in the need to control the darker side of self-interest. With self-interest being ineradicable, the problem of constitutional control becomes one of how to control the operation of self-interest within government while allowing government the ability to perform those governing tasks that its justification requires. Ultimately, the task would seem to require both parchment and guns, that is, both knowledge pertinent to the task and rightly aligned incentives to act consistently with that knowledge. Knowledge and incentive, moreover, do not act in separable fashion, for knowledge is generated through practice and practice is shaped by incentive, as Richard Wagner (2002) explains. For instance, Charles Warren (1932) describes how the general welfare clause of the American constitution underwent a transformation from a strong limit on the ability of

Congress to appropriate money to a situation where Congress could appropriate for whatever it chooses, so long as it pronounces that it has some good civic reason for doing so. The process Warren describes is clearly one of a continuing spiral involving both belief or knowledge and incentive or interest. One of the central themes of the classical approach to moral education was that morality was simply good conduct that was reduced to habit through practice. The ability successfully to take property through politics instead of relying upon market transactions is to engage in a contrary form of practice. This alternative form of practice, where legislative takings replace market transactions, may, if repeated sufficiently, become sufficiently habitual to promote alternative beliefs as to what comprises just conduct. Knowledge and incentive, parchment and guns, would seem to be nonseparable ingredients of constitutional order in the final analysis. This interaction between knowledge and incentive was clearly recognized in the Germanic branch of constitutional economics that is known as ordnungstheorie, a founding statement of which is Eucken (1950), whose subsequent literature is represented nicely in Stützel, Watrin, Wilgerodt, and Hohmann (1981), and which is given a nice textual presentation in English in Kaspar and Streit (1998).

RICHARD E. WAGNER

REFERENCES

Buchanan, J.M. and Tullock, G. (1962). *The Calculus of Consent.* Ann Arbor: University of Michigan Press.

Epstein, R.A. (1985). *Takings: Private Property and the Power of Eminent Domain.* Cambridge, MA: Harvard University Press.

Epstein, R.A. (1995). *Simple Rules for a Complex World.* Cambridge: Harvard University Press.

Eucken, W. (1952). *Grundsätze der Wirtschaftspolitik.* Tübingen: Mohr Siebeck.

Gordon, S. (1999). *Controlling Government.* Cambridge: Harvard University Press.

Kaspar, W. and Streit, M.E. (1998). *Institutional Economics: Social Order and Public Policy.* Cheltenham, UK: Edward Elgar.

McIlwain, C.H. (1947). *Constitutionalism: Ancient and Modern.* Revised Edition Ithaca, NY: Cornell University Press.

Ostrom, V. (1984). "Why governments fail: an inquiry into the use of instruments of evil to do good," in J.M. Buchanan and R.D. Tollison (eds.) *Theory of Public Choice II.* Ann Arbor: University of Michigan Press, pp. 422–435.

Stützel, W., Watrin, C., Wilgerodt, H., and Hohmann, K. (eds.) (1981). *Gurndtexte der Sozialen Marktwirtschaft.* Stuttart: Fischer.

Wagner, R.E. (1987). "Parchment, Guns, and the Maintenance of Constitutional Contract," in C.K. Rowley (ed.) *Democracy and Public Choice: Essays in Honor of Gordon Tullock.* Oxford: Basil Blackwell, pp. 105–121.

Wagner, R.E. (1993). "Parchment, Guns, and Constitutional Order," in C.K. Rowley (ed.) *Property Rights and the Limits of Democracy.* Cheltenham, UK: Edward Elgar.

Wagner, R.E. (2000). "Complexity, governance, and constitutional craftsmanship."*American Journal of Economics and Sociology*, 61: 101–117.

Walker, G. (1990). *Moral Foundations of Constitutional Thought.* Princeton, NJ: Princeton University Press.

Warren C. (1932). *Congress as Santa Claus.* Charlottesville, VA: Michie.

POLITICAL AND CULTURAL NATIONALISM

Nationalism is an emotional identification with fellow subjects of a state on the basis of shared language, customs, values, religion or culture. Nationalism is not a sense of loyalty to international organizations such as the United Nations, or to non-governmental bodies such as Amnesty International. There is no such thing as "Prozac Nation," even if that term is an arresting metaphor. However, it would be a mistake to insist too strongly upon a bond to a *de jure* state. It was meaningful to speak of nineteenth-century German nationalism before the unification of that country, even as it is meaningful to speak of Quebec nationalism today. On the other hand, one may distinguish between nationalism and a purely local attachment to one's city or region. There is no such thing as Virginia nationalism today, although it might have been different in 1861 when Robert E. Lee followed his "country" into secession.

The definition of nationalism also excludes a bond to a diverse state whose subjects cannot be said to share core set of values or a common culture. Before World War I, there was no such thing as Austro-Hungarian nationalism. In such cases, one should distinguish between nationalism and patriotism, for the first but not the second term seems to require a common set of values.

Nationalism is also a normative political theory under which a geographically compact distinct people has a right to self-determination (Ignatieff, 1993: 145). Since an "ought" cannot be derived from an "is," one might admit the existence of a Serbian nation prior to World War I, while denying that the break-up of the Austro-Hungarian Empire was benign.

The opposite of normative nationalism is a normative universalism, which asserts that (1) norms must be universalizable if they are to count as norms; and (2) purely national norms which cannot be universalized are necessarily suspect. Modern political theory is almost always universalist, and based upon an abstract deliberation of the rights and duties common to all men without regard to their nationality. The universalist may point to such extreme cases as Serbia as an object lesson of the vices to which nationalism might be prey (Gomberg, 1990; Nussbaum, 1996).

Nationalism is often identified with a conservative perspective, particularly when employed to justify barriers to immigration, or (in the case of English conservatives) opposition to European integration. However, anti-globalists who reject free trade also appeal to a sense of nationalism.

1. A Curious Omission

Marxism was faulted for lacking a theory of nationalism, and the same charge may fairly be leveled at public choice theory and political theory scholarship. Recently Robert Goodin and Philip Pettit excluded a section on nationalism in their recent book of essays because it "hardly counts as a principled way of thinking about things" (Goodin and Pettit, 1993: 3). But since nationalism is one of the most potent sentiments in the political arena, this argues for more, not less, scholarly attention.

Forty years ago it was easier to imagine that nationalism had been all but dissolved in the acid baths of rationalism and modernism. In its place, scholars on the left proposed an internationalism based on more encompassing structures such as the United Nations or broader ideologies such as socialism; meanwhile, scholars on the right, who saw political choice through the prism of narrow economic calculation, or who espoused libertarian principles, typically regarded nationalism as an atavistic sentiment that had lost its appeal. Moreover, those on the right who supported less encompassing structures, such as the states rights movement in the United States, usually asserted that the strongest attachments were local and never national. The nationalism of Charles de Gaulle was thought faintly ridiculous, and the few academics who responded to such appeals believed themselves on the losing side of history. When George Grant (1978) wrote his account of Canadian Prime Minister John Diefenbaker's 1963 defeat at the hands of a continentalist Liberal party, he called it *Lament for a Nation: The Defeat of Canadian Nationalism.*

It is no longer possible to dismiss the appeal of national sentiment. Communism did not bury nationalism; instead, communism lies buried, to an important extent by the nationalism it had dismissed. In the first world, the rise of nationalist movements in Quebec, Scotland and Corsica have led to a devolution of powers from central governments. In the United States, the terrorist attack of September 11, 2001 awoke powerful nationalist sentiments. Finally, the darker varieties of nationalism that emerged in the Balkans remind us that the progressive defense of universalism cannot entirely be dismissed.

2. Theories of Nationalism

Nationalism's continuing importance invites one to consider its benefits and costs. The simplest explanation for nationalism's appeal is that it is one of the particularistic emotions, like love of family and friends, that bind us to others, and that constitute the sense of *solidarity* or community that is one of the most basic human goods (Weil, 1955). Ignoring such bonds drains the life and ideals out of the particular content that alone gives it substance.

The second benefit of nationalism is related to the first. Nationalism fosters a homogenous culture, high and low, and what a common culture may offer, to those who were formerly Bretons or Lorrainois, is the ability to deal with each other across increased distances with lower *transaction costs*. Dialects disappear and a single language emerges, with all of the gestures and facial clues that are the common currency of exchange in a conversation. "To 'do business with each other'," notes Charles Taylor, or to "operate a system of courts, run a bureaucratic state apparatus and the like, we need millions who can communicate without difficulty in a context-free fashion" (Taylor, 1998: 192).

Such theories have been thought to explain the rise of European nationalism in the nineteenth century. Prior to then, the impulse to solidarity found its expression through membership in more encompassing religions, such as Christendom prior to the Reformation, or through more local attachments. For Ernest Gellner (1997), nationalism was a response to the anomie of modernity that followed on the shift from an agricultural to an industrial economy. Nationalism united an alienated society, with "*Gessellschaft* using the idiom of *Gemeinschaft*." The deserted village was reinvented in the nation-state, and a "mobile anonymous society simulate[d] a closed cosy community" (Gellner, 1997: 74; see also Berlin, 1999).

Purely local bonds, to town or region rather than state, were also stronger prior to the expansion of transportation that followed the Industrial Revolution. As commerce became national, so too did the need for national sentiments as a means of reducing the transaction costs across a country. Extrapolating further, one might predict the decline of national sentiments in an era of transnational free trade agreements such as the North American Free Trade Agreement and intergovernmental structures such as the European Union.

German history might seem broadly consistent with this view of nationalism. There was relatively little national sentiment prior to the nineteenth century, but the flow of people and commerce across the Germanic states that followed the customs union contributed to the sense of nationalism. A similar story may be told of nineteenth century Italian nationalism. In addition, the decline in international trade during the 1930s might plausibly be linked to the subsequent rise of perverse nationalistic political parties during that decade.

The difficulty with such explanations is that, resting on a naive Whig view of history, they make nationalism seem over-determined. Religious sentiments did not weaken during the nineteenth century. If anything, they were strengthened during the Victorian period, even among the elites. And while the decline in free trade produced pathological brands of nationalism in some European states, in others they produced wholly marginal figures such as Sir Oswald Mosely. Indeed, one should not underestimate the extent to which fascism was an international anti-democratic movement, linking national parties in states such as Spain, Italy and Germany.

The third benefit of nationalism is that, by bonding us more closely to our fellows, nationalism increases altruistic impulses and reduces *free riding*. We are more willing to perform acts for the general good — serving in the military, contributing to charity — when we feel a kinship to others. This promotes the trust that is the cement of our society.

In this way, nationalism might actually reduce the possibility of war. While some wars are fought on nationalist grounds, patriotism plausibly decreases the likelihood of conflict by increasing the costs of aggressive war. The patriot can be readily enlisted to defend his homeland, but persuading him to invade another country may be a harder sell. Non-patriots might fight for private ends, for glory or material gain, but not so effectively as the patriot who defends his country. So viewed, patriotism increases the costs of imperialist or aggressive wars by reducing the probability of success. When the war requires mass armies (or mass support through taxation), securing patriotic backing is critical in the war effort, and the bias towards defensive wars will reduce the overall likelihood of war. The success of the Russian forces in the "Great Patriotic War" is consistent with this thesis, and so too is English resistance to Hitler. "What has kept England on its feet during the past year?," asked George Orwell in 1941. It was not the desiccated liberalism of an H.G. Wells or George Bernard Shaw. Rather, it was "the atavistic emotion of patriotism, the ingrained feeling of English-speaking peoples that they are superior to foreigners" (Orwell, 1984: 196).

A fourth explanation of the emergence of nationalism sees it as shaped by elite opinion-makers who *rent seek*.

For example, Jean-Luc Migué (1979) attributes the remarkable degree of support for separatism among francophone intellectuals in Québec to the political plums that would be available in a sovereign Quebec. In particular cases, such theories might have much to commend them; but as a general explanation of nationalism they resemble the reductionist accounts of religion associated with vulgar Marxism.

3. Varieties of Nationalism

The intensity of nationalist sentiment varies among nations. In addition, nationalist sentiments may be distinguished on the basis of their membership rules. A very thick criterion of inclusion might have its members share a common language, religion, culture, and even ancestry. At the other extreme, liberal nationalism emphasizes core political values while downplaying other aspects of national identity. While the United States remains relatively unilingual, cultural and religious bonds are weak. What increasingly takes the place of a cultural heritage is a common adherence to liberal legal traditions, as seen by the prominent role played by the Bill of Rights in American society. If *gessellschaft* used the idiom of *gemeinschaft* in Gellner's (1997) analysis of nineteenth-century nationalism, with the state emerging from shared cultural norms, the cultural norms must arise from the state in liberal nationalism and gemeinschaft builds upon gessellschaft.

Early forms of English nationalism were intertwined with the philosophical emphasis on individual rights and the humanitarian enthusiasm for liberty, and this was inherited in America. Even during the American Revolution, those of the Patriot side appealed to the "common rights of Englishmen." The absence of ethnic uniformity, even in colonial times, shifted the nexus of nationalism from culture to the libertarian ideals of the Founders.

French nationalism also has an important ideological component that dates from the Revolution. However, these ideals were univeralized so as to provide a justification for Napoleonic wars of "liberation." After the fall of the First Empire, nationalism became closely identified with the anti-Dreyfusard right, including antiliberals such as Charles Maurras.

German writers and intellectuals were quite critical of the universalistic ambitions of French nationalism. Instead, German nationalism was based on the cultural identity of the German people and their traditions. The German historic school stressed the priority of customary acceptance of rules and institutions over reason. According to this school, there is no absolute notion of just social and legal order. To the contrary, the different historical heritage of the various nations may justify differences between their national aspirations. The German premises were thus more respectful of the historical differences among the various national traditions and skeptical of any attempt at formulating universal principles that could govern the process of unification of the German people.

FRANK BUCKLEY
FRANCESCO PARISI

REFERENCES

Anderson, Benedict (1991). *Imagined Communities: Reflections on the Origin and Spread of Nationalism*. London: Verso.

Berlin, Isaiah (1999). "*The Roots of Romanticism*," in Hendry Hardy (ed.) Princeton: Princeton University Press.

Buckley, F.H. (2000). "Liberal Nationalism," *UCLA Law Review*, 48: 221–264

Gellner, Ernest (1997). *Nationalism*. New York: New York University Press.

Goodin, Robert and Pettit, Philip (1993). *A Companion to Contemporary Political Philosophy*. Cambridge, MA: Blackwell.

Gomberg, Paul (1990). *Patriotism is like Racism*, 101 ETHICS 144.

Grant, George (1978). *Lament for a Nation: The Defeat of Canadian Nationalism*. Ottawa: Carleton University Press.

Ignatieff, Michael (1993). *Blood and Belonging: Journeys into the New Nationalism*. New York: Farrar, Straus, and Giroux, 1994.

Migué, Jean-Luc (1979). *Nationalistic Policies in Canada*. Montreal: The C.D. Howe Institute.

Nussbaum, Martha C. (1996). "Patriotism and cosmopolitanism," in Joshua Cohen (ed.) *For Love of Country: Debating the Limits of Patriotism*, Volume 2. Boston: Beacon Press.

Orwell, George (1984). "Wells, Hitler, and the World State," in *The Penguin Essays of George Orwell*.

Taylor, Charles (1998). "Nationalism and Modernity," in John A. Hall (ed.) *The State of the Nation: Ernest Gellner and the Theory of Nationalism*. New York: Cambridge University Press.

Weil, Simone (1955). *The Need for Roots: Prelude to a Declaration of Duties of Mankind*. London: Routledge.

POLITICAL BUSINESS CYCLES

Few concepts in political economy are more widely known than the political business cycle (PBC). Nor have many given rise to such heated debate among scholars. The extent of debate reflects the highly mixed empirical evidence that has been found, but the heat of the debate has come largely from the challenge to the economists' favorite assumption — rationality — posed by traditional formulations of the political business cycle theory. This in turn follows from the roles of macroeconomists and political scientists in the early contributions to political business cycle analysis. (For discussions of these see Drazen, 2000; Keech, 1995; Paldam, 1997.)

The expositions that focused widespread attention on the topic were by Keynesian oriented economists (William Nordhaus, 1975; Duncan MacRae, 1977) and a political scientist (Edward Tufte, 1978). The basic idea rested on the political assumption that favorable economic conditions before elections help incumbent office seekers and the then common macroeconomic assumption that inflation — unemployment tradeoffs are much flatter in the short run than in the long run. As a result a well-timed expansion before an election could result primarily in an expansion of output and decline in unemployment before election day with most of the concomitant increase in inflation being delayed until safely after the election. This opportunistic or office-seeking motivated version of political business cycle theory, sometimes referred to as 'election cycles,' implied similar behavior by governments of both the left and the right before elections and quickly became an important challenger to the more traditional "partisan" view in political science of the politics of macroeconomic policy. Here cycles were generated by the different priorities of left and right wing governments as each came to power (see Hibbs, 1987). There are other examples of how government action can generate fluctuations based on a radical economics view (Kalecki, 1943; Feiwel, 1974; Boddy and Crotty, 1975; Sherman, 1979) or on the monetarist view of long and variable outside lags in monetary policy (Friedman, 1970). We will not focus on these here.

The opportunistic version assumed candidates were only interested in reelection. Although the original formulation by Nordhaus assumed that incumbents would always manipulate the economy to win elections and hence produce regular macroeconomic cycles, systematic policies of this type cannot be expected to occur at every election in part because of the rational expectations critique (see below). Not surprisingly, the empirical evidence clearly rejects such systematic cycles for the industrial countries in economic target aggregates such as unemployment and output. Moreover, Nordhaus's model was developed using a voting function approach. If instead governments observe approval ("popularity") ratings to monitor their likelihood of reelection, then incumbents with partisan objectives would only be expected to manipulate the economy to win elections when a significant 'popularity deficit' exists. During other times they would pursue policies based on ideologies and the interest of their support groups ('partisan view'). Hence both considerations are likely to be of relevance and were neatly combined in the 'contingent partisanship' formulation of Frey and Schneider (1978).

Along with the emerging literature on the politics of monetary policy (which entry see) and mounting evidence of government policy actions that tended to destabilize economies and generate high inflation, such contributions dealt a powerful blow to the traditional assumption of Keynesian economists that macro economic policies were set on public interest criteria free of political pressures (see Buchanan and Wagner, 1977). This helped stimulate growing interest in institutional arrangements to lessen political influences on monetary and fiscal polices (see Willett, 1988).

The basic proposition that good economic conditions enhance the popularity of incumbents enjoys massive empirical support. There is a large body of literature on voting and approval functions (see Lewis-Beck, 1998; Nannestad and Paldam, 1994). Fair regularly updates his specifications before U.S. elections (see, e.g., Fair, 1996, 2000). The specific trade offs among economic variables, the relative influence of levels versus rates of change, and the extent of retrospective versus prospective voting based on consumer-voter expectations (MacKuen et al., 1992; Norpoth, 1996) are nod clearly understood and some of these relations clearly vary over time. For example, during the 1990s electorates in Europe were tolerant of much higher average levels of unemployment than in the 1970s, and even in the U.S., incumbents could not have received relatively high approval ratings in the face of very high inflation and unemployment levels in the '70s and early '80s. There is also evidence that voters give as much or more weight to aggregate economic conditions as to their own circumstances. (On such sociotropic voting see Lewis-Beck, 1988.) Thus while precise relationships are still the subject of dispute, the general proposition that economic conditions have a strong influence on vote and popularity functions is a safe one.

More controversial is the idea of inflation — unemployment trade offs — the Phillips curve. The 1970s saw the rise to prominence of new classical macroeconomics with its twin emphases on rational expectations and flexible wages and prices. Along with the earlier contributions by monetarists such as Milton Friedman (1968). this approach stressed the distinction between anticipated and unanticipated policies. It was only unanticipated changes in macroeconomic policies that would face fairly flat short run inflation unemployment trade offs. But if the opportunistic political business cycle game were played before every election, then regular pre election expansions could hardly be a surprise so continued electoral success would seem to require irrationality on the part of voter expectations. While Nordhaus (1989) indicated his comfort with the assumption of irrational expectations formation, to many economists this was quite unappealing. Thus more than a few economists felt an obligation to discredit opportunist PBC theory; and in some cases, to undertake reformulations consistent with rational expectations (Minford and Peel, 1982; Alesina, 1988). The Alesina version has been labeled a rational partisan cycle and results not from opportunistic pre-election behavior by governments but from the responses of private sector behavior to the outcomes of uncertain elections. This "surprise" element should be greater, the higher the level of uncertainty pre-election about the outcome. The effect would give rise to post election shocks rather than cycles per se, but the literature has loosely interpreted the term political business cycle to include almost any type of political influence on the economy or economic policy variables. The concern with rational expectations has led to the development of ingenious models with imperfect information under which the surprise elements of election outcomes generate rational partisan cycles after elections (Alesina, 1988) or signal an incumbent's competence (Rogoff and Siebert, 1988) and even PBC elements in a real business cycle model (Blomberg and Hess, 2002). There has been extensive empirical testing only of the rational partisan model where the results are mixed with Alesina and his coauthors generally interpreting their studies as being supportive (e.g., Alesina et al., 1997) and most other authors being less impressed (see Drazen, 1990).

Had the initial disputants been more familiar with public choice theory, these early debates could have been more productive. In its early stage of development macroeconomic rational expectations analysis tended to assume that actors had high levels of information. These have proved to be overly optimistic for many economic actors with strong interest at stake and are even more so for many voters who have little direct incentive to be informed about macroeconomic policies. The public choice concept of rational ignorance in the face of information costs is tremendously important in this context (see Willett, 1988).

Of course if played regularly information on PBCs would spread and limit their effectiveness, but in political markets informed voters do not cancel out uninformed voters the way they tend to in financial markets (see Willett, 1988) so the spread of disincentives for PBCs could be slow, especially when the PBC is not played at every election. And the evidence is clear that it is not. It is widely conceded that President Richard Nixon did practice the Nordhaus-Tufte model, in part because President Eisenhower was unwilling to do so when then Vice President Nixon first ran for the presidency (and in his view lost as a result). And Jimmy Carter played the opportunistic-PBC backwards, following expansionary policies when he first came in office (on the frequency of this type of partisan PBC behavior see the discussion and references in Paldam, 1997). President Carter was forced by accelerating

inflation to tighten before the next election. While this episode conflicts with the opportunistic PBC, Carter's subsequent loss of his re election bid could be interpreted as support for the belief that incentives to play the PBC game still exist — in part because it has not been played at every election. One way to make sense of the mass of often contradictory or inclusive findings of empirical studies on PBCs is that no one version is played with consistent regularity, but that both opportunistic and partisan versions have some explanatory power. For the OECD countries partisan patterns tend to show up more regularly in the data (see the discussion and references in Drazen, 2000), but we cannot safely conclude that well-informed rational voters have eliminated all incentives for opportunistic PBC behavior. And anecdotal evidence suggests the possibility that opportunistic PBC behavior is much more common in the so far seldom studied developing countries than in the industrial world. Shi and Svensson (2000), in a study of 123 industrial and developing countries, find that on average budget deficits are larger in pre-election years by an average of one percent of GDP, but that for the developing countries the average was two percent. Remmer (1993) also finds considerable evidence of electoral patterns in Latin American economics, but these do not conform to the traditional PBC. They suggest that this reflects both greater incentives for politicians to stay in office due to corruption, and a less informed electorate as a result of lower press freedom.

For the OECD countries the evidence of election cycles is much stronger for policy instruments (monetary and fiscal policy) than for real outcomes (output and unemployment). One possible interpretation would be that voters are better informed than policy makers so that continued efforts by politicians are offset by the public à la the rational expectations critique. Also consistent with this interpretation is the tendency to find some evidence of cycles in inflation rates. While such a scenario could be plausible with respect to a set of key private sector decision makers, it doesn't seem plausible for the public at large.

A more likely explanation in our judgment starts with focus on the incentives for micro oriented PBCs that have macro consequences. It is hardly a surprise that politicians tend to give out favors prior to elections to improve the likelihood of success at the polls. One of the strongest regularities in the OECD data is that fiscal transfers tend to rise before elections, while tax cuts are much more likely then tax increases. These actions of course result in a cycle in the fiscal deficit, but this needn't have had any connection with desires to exploit the inflation-output trade offs emphasized in the traditional opportunistic PBC models. Pissarides (1980) is the only study we are aware of, where a policy instrument, tax rates in this case, enters a popularity function directly. Perhaps because the literature on PBCs has been dominated so heavily by macroeconomists, the micro incentives for political cycles have received insufficient attention. (Important exceptions include Drazen, 2000; Rogoff and Siebert, 1988; Shughart and Tollison, 1985; Tufte, 1978.)

Such cycles in fiscal policy can also explain non-opportunistically motivated cycles in monetary policy. This also helps explain another apparent anomaly. Nordhaus's model focuses on monetary policy as the government's policy instrument. However, in the United States and an increasing number of other countries the government does not directly set monetary policy. This is done by central banks with some degree of political independence. Why would independent central banks generate political business cycles? Laney and Willett (1983) suggest that even nonpartisan independent central banks may be political in the sense that they are concerned with criticisms of high interest rates and are especially sensitive to this in pre-election periods. (For evidence on the latter for the US see Willett, 1990). Where the central bank has a desire to avoid interest rate fluctuations then a cycle in the fiscal deficit would generate a corresponding cycle in the monetary aggregates. (For discussion and references to further literature on such "passive" monetary cycles see Drazen, 2000; pp. 236–237, 242–243; interesting examples for recent episodes of political pressure on monetary policy in the U.S. can be found in Woodward, 2000.)

Note also that such micro motivated cycles in policy instruments would likely occur much closer to elections than would macro oriented ones since the micro benefits would come immediately with the expenditure increases and tax cuts while the macro effects would occur only with (possibly substantial) lags. Indeed the post election lagged macro effects of pre election micro oriented pre election polices could be part of the explanation for why the standard opportunistic PBC model appears to explain only a quite limited amount of the OECD data.

Of course micro focused PBC analysis would lead us to look for cycles in non-budgetary items such as trade protectionism (which see). Also under explored are the international dimensions of PBC behavior. While the effects of alternative exchange rate regimes on the incentives for opportunistic PBCs was addressed relatively early on (see Willett and Mullen, 1982), there has been relatively little empirical research, but many anecdotes about political cycles in payments deficits and exchange rates — especially in the developing countries. For example, Rudiger Dornbusch (2001: 241) points out that for Mexico "with surprising regularity, the currency collapsed every

six years, shortly after each new president took office." (For recent evidence on the effects of elections on exchange rate policies in Latin America see Blomberg et al., 2002; Frieden and Stein, 2001 and on industrial countries see Bachman, 1992; Bernhard and Leblang, 2002; Blomberg and Hess, 1997; Lobo and Tufte, 1998.)

There has of course also been interest in the effects of the incentives for PBCs generated by alternative political institutions such as parliamentary versus presidential systems and fixed versus variable election dates (see Drazen, 2000) for institutional mechanisms such as balanced budget requirements, independent central banks, and fixed exchange rates to limit PBC behavior. One interesting theoretical conclusion is that while a regime of high capital mobility and fixed exchange rates would effectively limit the ability of a government to manipulate mandatory policy directly to generate an opportunistic PBC, under these conditions an increase in the fiscal deficit would force a PBC in the money supply even if there were an independent central bank (see Willett, 2001). This illustrates the need to carefully examine the full range of possibilities when proposing institutional solutions.

THOMAS D. WILLETT
MANFRED W. KEIL

REFERENCES

Alesina, A. (1988). "Macroeconomics and politics," in O. Blanchard and S. Fischer (eds.) *NBER Macroeconomics Annual*. Cambridge, MA: MIT Press.

Alesina, A., Roubini, N., and Cohen, G. (1997). *Political Cycles and the Macroeconomy*. Cambridge, MA: MIT Press.

Bachman, D. (1992). "The effect of political risk on the forward exchange bias: the case of elections." *Journal of International Money and Finance*, 11: 208–219.

Bernhard, W. and Leblang, D. (2002). "Democratic processes and political risk: evidence from foreign exchange markets." *American Journal of Political Science*, 46: 316–333.

Blomberg, S. and Hess, G. (1997). "Politics and exchange rate forecasts." *The Journal of International Economics*, August: pp. 189–205.

Blomberg, S. and Hess, G. (2002). "Is the political business cycle for real?" *Journal of Public Economics*, forthcoming.

Blomberg, S., Frieden, J., and Stein, E. (2002). "Sustaining fixed rates: the political economy of currency pegs in Latin America," Working Paper.

Boddy, R. and Crotty, J. (1975). "Class conflict and Macro-policy: the political business cycle." *Review of Radical Political Economy*, 1–19.

Buchanan, J. and Wagner, R. (1977). *Democracy in Deficit: The Political Legacy of Lord Keynes*. New York: Academic Press.

Dornbusch, R. (2001). "Fewer monies, better monies." *American Economic Review*, May: 238–247.

Drazen, A. (2000). *Political Economy in Macroeconomics*. Princeton: Princeton University Press.

Fair, R. (1978). "The effect of economic events on votes for President." *Review of Economics and Statistics*, 159–173.

Fair, R. (1996). "Econometrics and presidential elections." *Journal of Economic Perspectives*, 89–102.

Fair, R. (2000). "Actual outcome — November 2000," *Mimeo*, Yale University.

Feiwel, G. (1974). "Reflections on Kalecki's theory of political business cycle." *Kyklos*, 21–47.

Frieden, J. and Stein, E. (eds.) (2001). *The Currency Game: Exchange Rate Politics in Latin America*. Washington, D.C.: Inter-American Development Bank.

Frey, B. and Schneider, F. (1978). "An empirical study of politico-economic interaction in the U.S." *Review of Economics and Statistics*, 174–183.

Friedman, M. (1968). "The role of monetary policy." *American Economic Review*, 1–17.

Friedman, M. (1970). *The Optimum Quantity Theory of Money and Other Essays*. Chicago: Chicago University Press.

Hibbs, D. (1987). *The American Political Economy: Macroeconomics and Electoral Politics in the United States*. Cambridge, MA: Harvard University Press.

Kalecki, M. (1943). "Political aspects of full employment." *Political Quarterly*, 322–331.

Keech, W. (1995). *Economic Politics: The Costs of Democracy*. Cambridge: Cambridge University Press.

Laney, L. and Willett, T. (1983). "Presidential Politics, Budget Deficits, and Monetary Policy in the United States: 1960–1976." *Public Choice*, 53–69.

Lewis-Beck, M. (1988). *Economics and Elections*. Ann Arbor: University of Michigan Press.

Lobo, B. and Tufte, D. (1998). "Exchange rate volatility: does politics matter?" *Journal of Macroeconomics*, 20: 351–365.

MacKuen, M., Erikson, R., and Simson, J. (1992). "Peasants or Bankers? The American Electorate and the U.S. Economy." *American Political Science Review*. 597–611.

MacRae, D. (1977). "A political model of the business cycle." *Journal of political economy*, 239–263.

Nannestad, P. and Paldam, M. (1994). "The VP-function. A survey of the literature on vote and popularity functions." *Public Choice*, 213–245.

Minford, P. and Peel, D. (1982). "The political theory of the business cycle." *European Economic Review*, 253–270.

Nordhaus, W. (1975). "The political business cycle." *Review of Economic Studies*, 169–190.

Nordhaus, W. (1989). "Alternative approaches to the political business cycle." *Brookings Papers on Economic Activity*, 2: 1–68.

Norpoth, H. (1996). "Presidents and the prospective voter." *Journal of Politics*, 776–792.

Paldam, M. (1997). "Political business cycles," in Dennis Mueller (ed.) *Perspectives on Public Choice*. Cambridge: Cambridge University Press.

Persson, T. and Tabellini, G. (2000). *Political Economics: Explaining Economic Policy*. Cambridge, MA: The MIT Press.

Pissarides, C. (1980). "British Government popularity and economic performance." *Economic Journal*, 569–581.

Remmer, K. (1993). "The political economy of elections in Latin America, 1980–1991." *American Political Science Review*, 87(2)(June): 393–407.

Rogoff, K., and Sibert, A. (1988). "Elections and macroeconomic policy cycles." *Review of Economic Studies*, 1–16.

Sherman, H. (1979). "A Marxist theory of the business cycle." *Review of Radical Political Economy*, 1–23.

Shi, M. and Svensson, J. (2000). "Conditional Political Business Cycles." Harvard University and Institute for International Economic Studies, Stockholm University, processed.

Shugart, W. and Tollison, J. (1985). "Legislation and political business cycles." *Kyklos*, 43–59.

Tufte, E. (1978). *Political Control of the Economy*. Princeton: Princeton University Press.

Willett, T. (ed.) (1988). *Political Business Cycles: The Political Economy of Money, Inflation, and Unemployment*. Durham, N.C.: Duke University Press for the Pacific Research Institute.

Willett, T. (1990). "Studying the fed: towards a broader Public choice perspective," in Thomas Mayer (ed.) *The Political Economy of American Monetary Policy*. Cambridge: Cambridge University Press.

Willet, T. (2001). "The political economy of external discipline: constraint versus incentive effects of capital mobility and exchange rate pegs," prepared for delivery at the 2001 Annual Meeting of the American Political Science Association, San Francisco, August 30–September 2, 2001.

Willett, T. and Mullen, J. (1982). "The Effects of Alternative International Monetary Systems on Inflationary Biases and Macroeconomic Discipline," in Raymond E. Lombra and Willard E. Witte (eds.) *Political Economy of International and Domestic Monetary Relations*. Ames, Iowa: Iowa State University Press, pp. 143–155.

Woodward, B. (2000). *Maestro*. New York: Simon and Schuster.

POLITICAL ECONOMICS AND PUBLIC CHOICE

Political economics is a strand of literature that emerged in the mid-1980s and mostly deals with the same topics as public choice. A quick look at the indexes of two of the most widely read reviews of the literature (Persson and Tabellini, 2001; Drazen, 2000) gives a sufficient idea of how much the interests of political economics overlap with those of public choice. We read "economic models for political analysis," "electoral competition," "median voter equilibria," "laws, institutions and delegated authority," "rent seeking and predation," "lobbying" "legislative bargains," "electoral cycles"... and the list could be longer.

This overlap in topics is in striking contrast with the limited interaction between the two research communities. Very few political economics scholars participate to meetings of the public choice societies publish in journals such as *Public Choice* and quite seldom refer to contributions of the public choice school (short of the *Calculus of Consent* and with the exception of the two above mentioned literature reviews).

If we take the textbooks as an indicator of the attitude of one discipline towards the other, we keep the impression that the dialogue does not flow exactly seamlessly. On the one hand, public choice handbooks like Mueller (1997) and Shughart and Razzolini (2001), do not consider political economics as a separate discipline. They do cite and examine single contributions, like the theory of the strategic use of the debt (Tabellini and Alesina, 1990) or the innovations to the theory of the political business cycle (Alesina, 1987; Rogoff, 1990). The same applies to the forthcoming *Public Choice III*. On the other hand, political economists look at the relation between their discipline and public choice in two different and contradictory ways. Persson and Tabellini (2001) basically state that political economics analyses the same subject matter as public choice but with superior theoretical rigor. In their words "... Researchers in [public choice] tradition were reluctant, however, to use formal game-theoretic tools or to impose strong notions of individual rationality. As a result, the initial work sometimes relied on weaker theoretical or microeconomic foundations" (Persson and Tabellini, 2001, p. 3, italics added). Political economics, instead, borrows the methodology of the new classical macroeconomics and of the rational choice theory. It can thus be defined as a discipline that "... adopts the equilibrium approach of macroeconomic theory of policy and exploits the tools of rational choice in analysing some of the classic problems in public choice" (Persson and Tabellini, 2001, p. 4).

Drazen (2000) acknowledges that the differences between public choice and political economics are blurred. "Many treatments of the new political economy would not make a distinction between the fields, arguing that public choice is an integral part of the new political economy" (Drazen, 2000, p. 9). Drazen, however, argues that a distinction can be made in terms of topics: in his view public choice is interested in politics *per se*, while political economy focuses on the effect of politics on economic outcomes. Never he points out to a difference in methodology or analytical rigour, as Persson and Tabellini do.

In this entry we try to represent the Venn diagram of these two sets, public choice and political economics. We will focus, however, exclusively on the areas where they do not intersect and therefore may learn from each other. In science, however, two disciplines may dialogue and corroborate each other provided that they share the paradigm. We must therefore assess first whether the two disciplines are methodologically incompatible, as Persson and Tabellini state, or not.

Public choice theory is founded on the axiom that human behaviour, as described by the rational choice paradigm, is invariant with respect to the environments where the individual makes its choices; the outcome depends on the constraints that characterize these environments, be they monetary, legal, institutional, or related to the information available, but the process remains the same. Indeed, public choice owes its success to the first application of the paradigm of rational choice to the political process. This application was, from the beginning, so rigorous as to interpret the lack of participation of most individuals in politics as a form of *rational ignorance* (Downs, 1957), i.e., as the result of a rational calculus that evaluates the individual's opportunity cost of being informed about political matters higher than the expected rates of return. These rigorous behavioural postulates forced political scientists to a paradigm shift that yielded the rational political science of the Rochester school and economists to abandon the Keynesian presupposition that political economy was chosen by a benevolent despot aiming to maximize a social welfare functional.

In particular, the public choice critique of Keynesian political economy represents the first crossroads between public choice and political economics. Political economics develops from the New Classical Macroeconomics and especially Kydland and Prescott's (1977) conclusion that not all policies are equally plausible; only those that the policymaker has no incentive to abandon become credible or "time consistent." A technology is needed to make it impossible for policymakers to use their discretionary power and thus make time consistent choices; rules, the constitution, the institutional framework in which and by which policies are decided supply that technology. By that, around the early 1980s political economics arrives to the long-standing public choice tenet that "institutions matter."

It seems thus fair to conclude that both disciplines adopt a positive approach where economic policies and outcomes are the result of rational agents that maximize their private interests subject to institutional constraints. The two literature strands are based on the same paradigmatic plank. The critique of insufficient rigour that Persson and Tabellini move to public choice seems therefore misplaced. It is true that a few public choice models deflect from rational choice paradigm: for instance, the explanation of high public deficit in terms of fiscal illusion (Buchanan and Wagner, 1977), as a critique to the Ricardian equivalence theorem; the theory of expressive voting (Brennan and Buchanan, 1984); and, obviously, the philosophical explorations of the foundations of society (Buchanan,

1975; Brennan and Buchanan, 1985). But besides these offshoots, it seems unjustified to accuse the Chicago school and the Rochester school of public choice of adopting "weaker theoretical and microeconomic foundations," not to mention the Virginia school whose theoretical restrictions receive strong empirical support both from econometric and experimental analyses.

A difference between the two strands of literature may appear not in terms of methodologies, but of analytical devices used in the models. Political economics seems to have exploited to a greater extent than the Virginia and the Chicago schools of public choice the non-cooperative game theory, as Persson and Tabellini also affirm. These models are apt to represent the interrelations between agents within a specific institutional set-up. The rules (extensive forms) of the games may represent the institutional frameworks under scrutiny, the sequence of the moves the relative agenda setting power of the players, and the solution to the game is the economic and/or political outcome. This analytical approach has allowed political economics to produce significant processes in the analysis of comparative economic systems and of general equilibrium models of government. A case in point is the analysis of electoral accountability and the separation of powers among the different branches of government (Persson et al., 1997). Public choice scholars had already dealt with the issue, which is central to the analysis of modern democracies (Breton, 1996). Yet only within the precise specification of the institutional set-up allowed by the extensive form of the game is it possible to derive under what conditions the government system (parliamentary, congressional or presidential) will converge towards a competitive equilibrium, with fully functioning systems of checks and balances, or towards a collusive, oligarchic equilibrium. Furthermore, the insistence on non-cooperative game theory has moved the interests of political economics from policies to political process; witness the proliferation of research on electoral accountability and on budget processes. The distinction proposed by Drazen, that tends to confine public choice to political processes and political economics to policy outcomes, seems thus less and less appropriate, if it has ever been so.

On the other hand, the analytical device that public choice theory has exploited most often is the principal-agent model, both because of its original interest in government failures and for its focus on the behaviour of agents within a single institution: the legislative, the bureaucracy, or regulatory agencies. By isolating one relationship between, say, voters and legislators, public choice models cast the other influences on the behaviour of legislators under a *ceteris paribus* conditions. Hence, another

distinction that can be traced between public choice and political economics is in their perspectives. Public choice tends to adopt a Marshallian, partial equilibrium approach, whereas political economics models are more often (but not always) couched in a Walrasian, general equilibrium perspective.

This difference in perspectives creates excellent opportunities for gains from trade between the two disciplines. While a Walrasian perspective is certainly broader and more complete than a Marshallian one, the partial equilibrium approach adopted in public choice allows a greater precision in the description of the institutional details where political and economic decisions are taken. In a more and more integrated world for what it concerns economic processes, political differences are increasingly the most important source of variation among countries and of asymmetries in economic performances: the lesson of the literature on budget rules as the determinant of cross country difference in fiscal performance is clear in this respect. This literature, among others, confirms that one must pay attention to the details in order to understand how different institutional frameworks yield different economic outcomes. In this field, a Marshallian perspective is often the sole possible approach.

Furthermore, this approach is generally more amenable for empirical testing. The level of abstraction needed to keep a general equilibrium political model tractable often opens a wide gap between the theory's predictions and empirical reality. This distance is not only due to lack of institutional detail, but also to the need to choose variables in the econometric models that are loose and often disconnected proxies of their theoretical counterparts. Many political economics models, even relatively simple ones, are often quite problematic to test: for instance the war of attrition explanations of fiscal outcomes tend to confound notions of institutional ex post stability with political, ex ante stability, which is a relevant problem in cross section tests (Padovano and Venturi, 2001). The risk to produce mixed results is *ceteris paribus* lower from a partial equilibrium, public choice perspective, than from a general equilibrium approach. These tests, however, provide firmer grounds for further theoretical developments. Hence the existence of gains from trade.

Finally, there are topics that the two disciplines have so far left completely one to the other. For instance, political economics has developed an interesting theory of the optimal size and number of countries (Alesina and Spolaore, 1997; Bolton and Roland, 1997). These theories explain the forces, such as income redistribution, preferences over policies, risk sharing with respect to exogenous shocks, which lead to a breakdown and formation of countries and political unions. New insights can thus be drawn on the causes of the breakdowns of countries, like many that formerly belonged to the socialist bloc, as well as on the dynamics of political unions, such as the process of European integration. On the other hand, public choice is expanding its analysis of political system from democracies to autocracies or dictatorships. To witness the importance of this development, one must bear in mind that most countries of today's world (not to mention historical times) are ruled by dictatorships. Moreover, the most delicate issues in international affairs revolve around the relationship between democratic systems and dictatorial countries.

In conclusion, one can be assured that political economics and public choice share the same rational choice paradigm and areas of interest. The main difference, and not a great one, is a prevalence of partial equilibrium models in one strand of literature and of general equilibrium ones in the other. But once these differences are presuppositions for scientific progress, trying separate the two research fields or to assess the superiority of one over the other is a futile enterprise.

FABIO PADOVANO

REFERENCES

Alesina, A. (1987). "Macroeconomic policy in a two party system as a repeated game." *Quarterly Journal of Economics*, 102: 651–678.

Alesina, A. and Spolaore, E. (1997). "On the number and size of nations." *Quarterly Journal of Economics*, 112: 1027–1056.

Bolton, P. and Roland, G. (1997). "The breakup of nations: a political economy analysis." *Quarterly Journal of Economics*, 112: 1057–1090.

Brennan, G. and Buchanan, J.M. (1984). "Voter choice: evaluating political alternatives." *American Behavioral Scientist*, 28: 185–201.

Brennan, G. and Buchanan, J.M. (1985). *The Reasons of Rules. Constitutional Political Economy*. Cambridge: Cambridge University Press.

Breton, A. (1996). *Competitive Governments: An Economic Theory of Politics and Public Finance*. Cambridge: Cambridge University Press.

Buchanan, J.M. (1975). *The Limits of Liberty. Between Anarchy and Leviathan*. Chicago: University of Chicago Press.

Buchanan, J.M. and Wagner, R.E. (1977). *Democracy in Deficit. The Political Legacy of Lord Keynes*. New York: Academic Press.

Downs, A. (1957). *An Economic Theory of Democracy*. New York: Harper and Row.

Drazen, A. (2000). *Political Economy in Macroeconomics*. Princeton: Princeton University Press.

Kuhn, T. (1962). *The Structure of Scientific Revolutions*. Chicago: University of Chicago Press.

Kydland, F. and Prescott, E. (1977). "Rules rather than discretion: the inconsistency of optimal plans." *Journal of Political Economy*, 85: 473–491.

Mueller, D.C. (ed.) (1997). *Perspectives on Public Choice: A Handbook*. Cambridge: Cambridge University Press.

Padovano, F. and Venturi, L. (2001). "Wars of attrition in Italian government coalitions and fiscal performance, 1948–1994." *Public Choice*, 109: 15–54.

Persson, T., Roland, G., and Tabellini, G. (1997). "Separation of powers and political accountability." *Quarterly Journal of Economics*, 112: 1163–1202.

Persson, T. and Tabellini, G. (2001). *Political Economics*. Cambridge: MIT Press.

Rogoff, K. (1990). "Political budget cycles." *American Economic Review*, 80: 1–16.

Shugart, W.F. and Razzolini, L. (eds.) (2001). *The Elgar Companion to Public Choice*. Chelthenam: Edward Elgar.

Tabellini and Alesina (1990). "Voting on the budget deficit." *American Economic Review*, 80: 37–49.

THE POLITICAL ECONOMY OF FEMA DISASTER PAYMENTS

A central contribution of public choice theory to the analysis of government activity is in viewing the activities of government, not as determined by some single altruistic dictator, but rather as the result of a process involving individual political agents who react to the incentives they face. Federal disaster relief, administered by the Federal Emergency Management Agency (FEMA), is one activity that is ripe for political influence due to the process of disaster declaration and relief. After a disaster strikes a particular state, the governor makes a request to the president for disaster assistance. Following a governor's request, the president then decides whether to declare the state or region a disaster area. Only after a disaster has been declared by the president can disaster relief be given. FEMA is in charge of determining the level of relief funding for the area, but additional appropriations are determined by congress in cases requiring large amounts of funding beyond FEMA's allocated budget. The Act which governs the rules of federal disaster declaration and expenditures gives the president the authority to declare a disaster without the approval of congress. Furthermore, the Act prohibits the use of any arithmetic formula to determine levels of disaster relief to any area. The potential thus exists for political influence to affect the disaster relief process at two distinct stages; whether or not a disaster is declared by the president, and how much money is allocated through

FEMA and congress for disaster relief after a disaster has been declared by the president.

FEMA was created by an executive order of President Carter in 1979 that essentially merged many separate disaster relief agencies that had already been in existence. The vast majority of FEMA operations and expenditures are undertaken under the rules and processes established by the Robert T. Stafford Disaster Relief and Emergency Assistance Act (Public Law 93-288), hereafter called the Stafford Act. This act establishes the process for requesting a presidential disaster declaration, defines the types of relief that are available for relief expenditures, and the conditions for obtaining assistance. From a budgetary standpoint, expenditures under the Stafford Act come from the portion of FEMA's budget known as the President's Disaster Relief Fund. Besides FEMA's activities under the Stafford Act, there are several additional, smaller programs undertaken outside the Stafford Act such as the flood insurance program and the U.S. Fire Administration. The activities of FEMA are subject to congressional oversight by several committees. In the House of Representatives, for example, there are four committees partially responsible for the oversight of FEMA. Two of these committees oversee the activities of FEMA under the Stafford Act, while the other two oversee the smaller, non-Stafford Act activities. A similar process is present on the Senate side of congressional oversight of FEMA.

The process for FEMA disaster relief suggests there are two potential sources by which political influence may enter into the FEMA disaster relief process. The first avenue of political influence is the process of disaster declaration. Because this is a decision left entirely up to the president, and because there is such a wide range of possible weather phenomenon (such as thunderstorms and snowstorms) for which disasters may be declared, it is possible that he may be more likely to declare a disaster in a state that is politically important. Also, because the Stafford Act allows the president to unilaterally declare a disaster without the approval of congress, it is possible that the president may use this power to punish or reward legislators who support or oppose his policies, or just simply tarnish the image of opposing party legislators in hopes of reducing their probability of reelection.

The second avenue through which political influence may affect FEMA expenditures is through congressional oversight. It is important for the agency to be in good standing with the oversight committees, as these committees can have considerable influence over the agency. In public choice theory, this relationship between congress and a bureau such as FEMA is traditionally examined within a framework known as the congressional dominance model, which postulates that bureaus are very responsive to the wishes of congress and the president [see Moe (1987, 1997); Weingast and Moran (1983); Weingast (1984); Anderson and Tollison (1991); Couch and Shughart (1997); Young et al. (2001)]. Specifically, the model suggests that congressional committees having both budget and oversight responsibilities see that bureaucrats carry out the policy preferences of the legislators. In 1992, for example, the House Appropriations Committee found evidence of excessive and wasteful spending by several senior executives at FEMA, such as chauffeur-driven cars. The Appropriations Committee readily cut several executive positions and reduced the budgets of others. Given the power of oversight committees, it is thus possible that states who are represented on these committees overseeing FEMA receive a disproportionally larger amount of money for disaster relief to remain in the good graces of the oversight committees. This possibility is augmented by the fact that the Stafford Act explicitly prohibits the use of any formula to determine levels of disaster payments.

Using FEMA disaster expenditure and disaster declaration data for all 50 states over the period 1991 to 1999, Garrett and Sobel (2001) measure the impact presidential and congressional influences have on disaster relief. To assess the impact of presidential influence, they hypothesize that the decision of presidential disaster declaration in a state is a function of several state socioeconomic characteristics, the electoral importance of a state [Willet (1989) and Tabellini and Alesina (1990)], whether or not the state governor is of the same political party as the president, and the percent of congressional representation from the state that is of the same political party as the president. Given that a disaster has been declared in a state, Garrett and Sobel hypothesize that the level of FEMA disaster relief to a state in a given year depends upon the size of the natural disaster (which they proxy with private insurance disaster payments and Red Cross disaster assistance), and the number of legislators from the state that are on one each the FEMA disaster payment oversight committees. In addition, they test for differences in disaster declaration and expenditures during election years versus non-election years.

Their results support the predictions of the public choice model. They find that political incentives facing the president do significantly affect the decision of disaster declaration. Those state having greater electoral importance have a higher rate of presidential disaster declaration. They also find evidence that the mean rate of presidential disaster declaration is higher during election years compared to a non-election year, and for all years in the sample the mean rate of disaster declaration was highest in the year of Bill Clinton's reelection campaign in 1996.

Garrett and Sobel also find strong evidence that political incentives in congressional oversight are significant determinants of FEMA disaster relief payments. They find that those states having greater representation on FEMA oversight subcommittees received higher FEMA disaster relief payments. On average, each additional member on a FEMA oversight committee results in $20 million in additional FEMA disaster payments to the committee member's state. Focusing on differences in Senate and House representation, they find that House representation on either a Stafford Act or non-Stafford Act committee significantly impacts the level of disaster relief (roughly $30 million in additional FEMA disaster payments, on average), but Senate representation does not. This is possibly because House members have a higher percentage of their constituency impacted by a disaster than a corresponding Senator. This finding also supports Goff and Grier (1993) who suggest that Senators will be less politically effective and less likely to apply influence relative to House members.

Garrett and Sobel use their empirical estimates to determine how much of FEMA disaster relief is due to political influence. They find that, on average, 44.5 percent of total FEMA disaster payments over the sample period were a result of congressional representation on FEMA oversight committees. Thus, their calculations reveal that nearly half of all FEMA disaster relief is explained by political influence rather than actual need based on disaster severity and frequency.

Although FEMA is often promoted as a savior for individuals and communities hit by a disaster, Garrett and Sobel find evidence that disaster declaration and the level of FEMA disaster expenditures are both politically motivated. Their results lend further support to the congressional dominance model, and the public choice model of government more generally. Their findings cast doubt on FEMA's altruistic goal of financial assistance to those most in need, and questions the role of government versus private agencies in providing disaster relief.

THOMAS A. GARRETT

RUSSELL S. SOBEL

REFERENCES

Anderson, G. and Tollison, R. (1991). "Congressional influence and patterns of new deal spending, 1933–1939." *Journal of Law and Economics*, 34: 161–175.

Couch, J. and Shughart II, W. (1997). *The Political Economy of the New Deal*. Cheltenham, UK and Northampton, MA: Edward Elgar.

Garrett, T. and Sobel, R. (2001). "The political economy of FEMA disaster payments." West Virginia University Working Paper 01-06.

Goff, B. and Grier, K. (1993). "On the (mis)measurement of legislator ideology and shirking." *Public Choice*, 76: 5–20.

Moe, T. (1987). "An assessment of the positive theory of congressional dominance." *Legislative Studies Quarterly*, 12: 472–520.

Moe, T. (1997). "The positive theory of public bureaucracy," in Dennis C. Mueller (ed.) *Perspectives on Public Choice: A Handbook*. New York: Cambridge University Press, pp. 455–480.

Tabellini, G. and Alesina, A. (1990). "Voting on the budget deficit." *American Economic Review*, 80: 37–49.

Weingast, B. (1984). "The congressional-bureaucratic system: a principal agent perspective (with applications to the SEC)." *Public Choice*, 44: 147–191.

Weingast, B. and Moran, M. (1983). "Bureaucratic discretion or congressional control? Regulatory policy-making by the federal trade commission." *Journal of Political Economy*, 91: 132–163.

Willet, T. (1989). *Political Business Cycles: The Political Economy of Money, Unemployment and Inflation*. Durham, NC: Duke University Press.

Young, M., Reksulak, M., and Shughart II, W. (2001). "The political economy of the IRS." *Economics and Politics*, 13: 201–220.

THE POLITICAL ECONOMY OF ITALIAN ELECTORAL REFORM

1. Introduction

In the public choice tradition, politics is seen as a market activity in which individual preferences are revealed and translated into public policies through a 'production' process. In this framework, a sequence of elections may be considered as a repeated game in which the preferences of society are expressed and find representation (Ordeshook, 1997). The expression and implementation of societal preferences and the production of implied policies are guaranteed by the repeated nature of the game. The market where this game is played is the electoral market.

To apply this perspective to the understanding of elections we require a model of a typical market whose basic elements are the demand side, i.e., the behavior of buyers, the supply side, i.e., the behavior of sellers, and a set of rules that constrain buyers' and sellers' market activities (Navarra and Mudambi, 2001). The supply side of the electoral market is composed of political parties that mainly produce policies. The demand side is made up of voters who select their preferred policies through the electoral process — the expression and representation of societal preferences. The set of rules governing the way elections are implemented is the electoral system that represents the mechanism through which electoral choices are translated into implemented policies through the selection of elected representatives. In this framework, electoral systems are the rules that regulate the electoral game in which democracy is practiced (Grofman and Reynolds, 2001).

The actions of political agents in the electoral game are linked with one another by a complex system of incentives. Since this system of incentives is affected by the election rules, any alteration of the rules alters the incentives of the different agents in the game (Myerson, 1999). Thus, we are obliged to consider changes in rules as well as particular choice options available within the set of rules that exist.

In this essay we review the literature on the change of the electoral rules in Italy during the 1990s. The extant proportional representation system was changed to a system with strong elements of plurality at both the national and local level. Following Mudambi et al. (2001a,b), we strive to unify constitutional political economy with public choice analyzing both choices between rules and choices subject to rules (Rowley, 1997). When we deal with choices subject to rules we are concerned with the behavior of political agents under a given electoral system, whereas when we consider choices between rules we focus on behavior when the electoral system itself is in the process of being changed. The change of the electoral system in Italy was a process of choice between different electoral rules that, once taken, affected decision-making on both the demand- and the supply-side of the electoral market.

2. Choices between Rules

Alternative electoral rules have several consequences for a political system. Mudambi et al. (1996, 1997, 1999) compare the two systems of representation regulating Italian local elections before and after the implementation of the electoral reform. The electoral systems whose peculiarities they investigate are proportional representation (PR) and a system incorporating many elements of plurality (PL). They compare empirically the two systems of representation with respect to the following variables: the information engendered to voters, their commitment in participating in the electoral process, the dilution of the power of elected representatives and the degree of proportionality in translating votes into seats.

As argued by Stigler (1971) indirect democracy naturally results in elected representatives with considerable latitude in interpreting the wishes of their constituents. This suggests two important measuring rods that may be used to compare electoral systems. The first is the amount of information that the system engenders amongst the voters. The second is the level of interest that they elicit from the voters. Mudambi et al. (1996, 1997) use Olson's (1965) theory of groups as the basis upon which to construct a *proxy* for the information level and electoral turnout as the *proxy* for voter commitment. Comparing local elections in Italy before and after the electoral reforms, Mudambi et al. (1996) find strong evidence for higher levels of information and voter commitment under the old PR system than under the new system incorporating significant elements of plurality.

In a different paper Mudambi et al. (1999) compare the effects of two variables on the power wielded by elected representatives electoral systems before and after the reform: the information level engendered amongst the eligible voters and the effectiveness of the electoral process in translating votes into seats (i.e., the degree of proportionality). Again the proxy for the information level is based on Olson's theory of groups. The measure of power dilution is constructed using the index of control developed by Cubbin and Leech (1983). Finally, the effectiveness of the electoral system in translating votes into seats is measured an index proposed by Mudambi (1997). They find that both information level and the degree of proportionality had a negative effect on power dilution in the 1985 and 1990 PR elections. However, these two effects disappear in the results of an identical model run for the 1994 PL elections.

3. Choices Subject to Rules

Once the electoral properties of alternative electoral systems have been compared and the choice amongst them has been made, the selected rules constrain political behavior on both the demand and the supply side of the electoral market. Most of the literature analyzing the effects of the new Italian electoral rules on the choices of voters and political parties has focused on their impact on representation at national level. In particular, researchers have analyzed the election of representatives to the Chamber of Deputies (CD), i.e., the Lower House of the Italian Parliament. The new system of representation adopted at for the elections to the CD is a mixed-member (MM) system. These systems incorporate elements from both PR and PL electoral rules. The Italian case is characterized by a 75%/25% PL/PR split, i.e., 75% of the members of the CD are elected in single-member constituencies (SMCs) using a PL system, while 25% are elected on the basis of a list PR system from multi-member constituencies.

3.1. The Supply-side of the Electoral Market

Countries that have adopted MM systems have generally witnessed the generation of political competition between two broad political coalitions. This is one of the most important features of MM systems. Italy is no exception. Electoral competition under the new Italian rules is characterized by two sets of incentives created by the PL and PR components of the MM system. Competing in small single-member PL constituencies requires the creation of broad coalitions capable of winning majorities in geographically cohesive but politically diverse districts. However, political parties must maintain their unique identities in order to maintain their appeal to their core supporters in the large multi-member PR districts (i.e., plurality maximization vs. vote maximization; Navarra and Lignana, 1997).

Mudambi and Navarra (2002) analyze party electoral strategies that emerge from the incentive structure generated by the Italian MM system. Parties craft their strategies on the basis of two-ordered objectives. The primary objective is a coalition-focused objective of achieving a coalition victory in each SMC. The secondary objective is a party-focused objective aimed at minimizing the margin of victory of candidates from other coalition parties, while attempting to maximize the margin of victory of the party's own candidates. They show how party strategies in a given electoral coalition are sensitive to the nature of the coalition as well as the nature of the individual SMC electoral contest in which the parties are engaged. Finally, they estimate the impact of intra-coalition behavior on the probability of victory in SMC races.

The analysis of electoral competition by Mudambi and Navarra (2002) has two main implications, both of which derive directly from the game theoretic nature of the contest. First, parties in coalitions face two sets of rivals — parties in other coalitions and parties within their own coalition. In the pursuit of their electoral objectives, there are circumstances in which intra-coalition rivals are considered more serious threats than extra-coalition rivals. Second, coalitions are often composed of heterogeneous parties that have joined for purely electoral purposes with significant differences in their political platforms. Such purely electoral coalitions are likely to be extremely unstable (Mudambi et al., 2001a,b).

The distinction between electoral and political coalitions is fundamental to understanding the dynamics of the formation and collapse of Italian governments in the years following electoral reform. Giannetti and Laver (2001), drawing from Laver and Kato (2001), suggest that the inherent features of the new system of representation produce two interacting party systems: one for the 'electoral politics' and the other for the 'legislative politics'. The *electoral* party system is viewed as responding to the centripetal logic of PL races in SMCs producing the formation of large electoral coalitions. On the other hand, in the parliamentary party system, the PR component that supports the centrifugal logic of parties to maintaining their separate identities by breaking away from electoral coalitions and bargaining as smaller units over government formation. The interaction between electoral and legislative party systems creates forces that have destabilizing effects on the incumbent government.

Italian Government instability in the post-reform period has been also analyzed by Mudambi et al. (2002). In this paper, as in Giannetti and Laver (2001), the decisive structure of the legislature is an endogenous and dynamic product of the government formation process (Laver and Shepsle, 1996). The formation of government with heterogeneous parties is modeled as a two-stage game. In the first stage, parties form electoral coalitions to fight the elections. In the second stage the parties in the winning coalition bargain over the division of net benefits from office. Extreme elements in each of the coalitions have the least in common with each other, but also have the least to gain from the continuation of the government in office. Therefore they have a shared interest in undermining the stability of the government. Finally, they show the conditions under which rational parties play the two-stage game as a dynamic game in which electoral victory is subsidiary to government stability in the formation of the electoral coalitions.

The most important objective of the Italian reformers was the generation of a bipolar party system (Duverger, 1954) that in turn would lead to effective governance and alternation in power. The introduction of an MM system with a significant PL component was seen as the means to achieve this goal. Katz (1996) suggests that Italian electoral reform did not produce the two-party politics it was supposed to provide according to Duverger's predictions. However, Reed (2001) demonstrates that Duverger's law not only works in Italy, but it does so rapidly and powerfully. Following Wildasky (1959) and Riker (1986), he points out that the electoral system effects operate at the district level and it is by agglomerating these district level effects that politics at the national level affected. He uses three indicators of party competition and shows that the MM system not only reduced the number of candidates per district but also produced a movement towards two-candidate competition. In Reed's view, bipolar candidate competition at the district level should be understood as the first stage of a process that is likely to be lead to two-party competition at the national level.

3.2. *The Demand-side of the Electoral Market*

MM systems are operationalized allowing each voter to cast two ballots. The first ballot is a PL ballot cast for the selection of a candidate in the SMC; the second vote is a PR ballot for the most preferred political party list in a larger multi-member district. This mechanism implies that voters may vote for a candidate of one party (or coalition) in the SMC and for the list of a different party at the PR level. As argued by Cox (1997), different voting systems confront voters with different problems of strategic electoral choice. The introduction of a significant PL component in the electoral formula for transforming votes into seats (75% of the total seats in the Lower House) implies that casting a vote for the most preferred candidate, i.e., voting 'sincerely', is not always the best way to have an impact on the outcome of the election. Did the Italians vote strategically in the elections governed by the new rules?

Benoit et al. (2002) estimate the level of strategic voting in the 1994 and 1996 Italian national elections. They group Italian voters into three categories. The first category comprises 'loyalist' voters. These voters vote for their most preferred party in the PR ballot, find a candidate from that party in the PL ballot and vote for him. The second and third categories comprise 'strategic' and 'non-strategic' voters. They vote for their most preferred party in the PR ballot, but find a candidate from a different party in the PL ballot. Strategic and non-strategic voters differ in their behavior in SMC races. The former vote for a candidate from a party within the same coalition as their most preferred party, whereas the latter vote for a candidate of a party that is *not* in the same coalition of their most preferred party. Benoit et al. (2002) apply King's (1997) technique of 'ecological inference', to estimate the relative number of strategic and non-strategic voters in each SMC. They find that a higher proportion of supporters of the Center-left coalition (*Ulivo*) are strategic as compared to supporters of the Center-right (*Polo*). Center-left voters, therefore, voted more strategically since they did not split their PR and PL votes between the two competing coalitions to extent that Center-right supporters did. Analyzing a risk-bearing model to capture the extent of strategic voting emerging from the implementation of the MM system in the 1994 Italian national elections, Navarra (1997) reaches similar conclusions.

Majoritarian electoral formulae provide strong incentives for abstention due to the 'wasted votes' phenomenon (Cox, 1997). Given the strong elements of PL in the Italian MM system, one would have expected high abstention rates. However, the change in the electoral rules had no effect on the abstention rate, which continued to grow following to a long-established trend. The abstention level maintained its classic geographical and social pattern and further, there was no significant difference between the rate for PL and PR races. In sum, in the PL ballot, where voters have a direct influence on the outcome in terms of candidates and majority voting, turnout (a) was no higher than before; (b) was no higher than in the PR races, and (c) was not affected by the degree of uncertainty in the particular electoral contest.

RAM MUDAMBI
PIETRO NAVARRA
GIUSEPPE SOBBRIO

REFERENCES

Benoit, K., Giannetti, D., and Laver, M. (2002). "Strategic voting in mixed-member electoral systems: the Italian case," paper presented at the 2000 Annual Conference of the American Political Science Association.

Cox, G.W. (1997). *Making Votes Count*. New York: Cambridge University Press.

Cubbin, J. and Leech, D. (1983). "The effect of shareholding dispersion on the degree of control in British companies: theory and measurement." *Economic Journal*, 93: 351–369.

Duverger, M. (1954). *Political Parties: Their Organization and Activity in the Modern State*. New York: Wiley.

Giannetti, D. and Laver, M. (2001). "Party system dynamics and the making and breaking of Italian governments." *Electoral Studies*, 20: 529–553.

Grofman and Reynolds (2001). "Electoral systems and the art of constitutional engineering: an inventory of the main findings," in R. Mudambi, P. Navarra, and G. Sobbrio (eds.) *Rules and Reason: Perspectives on Constitutional Political Economy*. New York: Cambridge University Press.

Katz, R.S. (1996). "Electoral reform and the transformation of party politics in Italy." *Party Politics*, 2: 31–53.

King (1997). *A Solution to the Ecological Inference Problem*. Princeton: Princeton University Press.

Laver, M. and Giannetti, D. (2001). "Party system dynamics and the making and breaking of Italian governments." *Electoral Studies*, 529–553.

Laver, M. and Kato, J. (2001). "Dynamic approaches to government formation and the generic instability of decisive structures in Japan." *Electoral Studies*, 20: 509–527.

Laver, M. and Shepsle, K.A. (1996). *Making and Breaking Governments: Cabinets and Legislatures in Parliamentary Democracies*. New York: Cambridge University Press.

Lijphart, A. (1984). *Democracies: Patterns of Majoritarian and Consensus Government in Twenty-One Democracies*. New Haven: Yale University Press.

Mudambi, R. (1997). "A complete information index for measuring the proportionality of electoral systems." *Applied Economics Letters*, 4: 101–104.

Mudambi, R. and Navarra, P. (2002). "Electoral strategies in mixed-member electoral systems," London School of Economics Working Paper, Research Program in Democracy, Business and Human Well-Being, January.

Mudambi, R., Navarra, P., and Nicosia, C. (1996). "Plurality versus proportional representation: an analysis of Sicilian elections." *Public Choice*, 86: 341–357.

Mudambi, R., Navarra, P., and Patty, J. (2002). "A complete model of strategic alliances in the context of electoral reform." SDS Discussion Paper, Carnegie Mellon University.

Mudambi, R., Navarra, P., and Sobbrio, G. (1997). "Voter information and power dilution: evidence from Sicilian provincial elections." *Public Choice*, 92: 169–180.

Mudambi, R., Navarra, P., and Sobbrio, G. (1999). "Changing the rules: political competition under proportionality and plurality." *European Journal of Political Economy*, 15: 547–567.

Mudambi, R., Navarra, P., and Sobbrio, G. (2001a). "The electoral cost imposed on coalitions by constituent parties: the case of Italian national elections," in R. Mudambi, P. Navarra, and G. Sobbrio (eds.) *Rules and Reason: Perspectives on Constitutional Political Economy*. New York: Cambridge University Press.

Mudambi, R., Navarra, P., and Sobbrio, G. (2001b). *Party Strategies and Voting Behaviour: the Political Economy of Italian Electoral Reform*. Aldershot: Edward Elgar.

Myerson, R. (1999). "Theoretical comparisons of electoral systems." *European Economic Review*, 43: 671–697.

Navarra, P. (1997). "Voting diversification strategy: a risk-bearing model of voter behavior in 1996 Italian national election." *Economia delle Scelte Pubbliche, Journal of Public Finance and Public Choice*, 1: 38–53.

Navarra, P. and Lignana, D. (1997). "The strategic behaviour of the Italian left in a risk-sharing framework." *Public Choice*, 93: 131–148.

Ordeshook, P.C. (1997). The spatial analysis of elections and committees: Four cases of research. In D.C. Mueller (ed.) *Perspectives on Public Choice*. New York: Cambridge University Press.

Reed, S.R. (2001). "Duverger's law is working in Italy." *Comparative Political Studies*, 34: 312–327.

Riker, W.H. (1986). "Duverger's law revisited," in B. Grofman and A. Lijphart (eds.) *Electoral Systems and their Political Consequences*. New York: Agathon Press.

Rowley, C.K. (1997). "The relevance of public choice for constitutional political economy." *Public Choice*, 90: 1–10.

Stigler, G.J. (1971). "The theory of economic regulation." *Bell Journal of Economics*, 2(Spring): 3–21.

Wildasky, A. (1959). "A methodological critique of Duverger's political parties." *Journal of Politics*, 21:303–318.

POLITICAL TRANSACTION-COST MANIPULATION

"Political transaction-cost manipulation" is a general theory of the growth of government that integrates diverse analyses in the public choice literature. Its core idea is that federal officials have both the incentive and the opportunity to manipulate private citizens' (and other government officials') transaction costs of taking political action on measures that alter the national government's authority. The theory provides an explanation of how government often grows even when the public does not want it to grow, and why government usually doesn't shrink even if the public would prefer it to shrink.

Political transaction costs by definition here denote costs of reaching and enforcing agreements regarding the role and scope of government. If federal officials are able to raise the transaction costs of opposing government-expanding measures, they can block public resistance and thereby enable the national government's authority to grow (and remain) beyond the level that otherwise would be tolerated (Twight, 1983, 1988, 1992). Treating political transaction costs as endogenous, this model analyzes in detail government officials' incentives to engage in transaction-cost manipulation, the specific forms the behavior takes, and its implications for the growth of government. Political transaction-cost manipulation thus provides a unifying framework that integrates and extends important aspects of prior scholarly work on fiscal illusion, cost concealment, strategic use of information, government autonomy-enhancing strategies, agenda control, credit claiming, blame avoidance, and related forms of congressional and bureaucratic behavior (Twight, 1994).

1. Natural versus Contrived Political Transaction Costs

Political transaction-cost manipulation theory distinguishes "natural" from "contrived" transaction costs, focussing primarily on the latter. Natural transaction costs are those that would exist even if all political actors tried to minimize transaction-cost impediments to political exchange. They are what most people think of when they consider the transaction costs of political action. For example, in the absence of other incentives, the high transaction costs of organizing large groups whose members naturally have small individual stakes in the outcome may preclude their formation into viable interest groups (Olson, 1965). Such political transaction costs inhere in the nature of reality: they are not created by federal officials.

"Contrived" political transaction costs, on the other hand, are created by federal officials, a product of their self-interested use of the mechanisms of government. The key insight is that political transaction costs often are increased intentionally: political actors manipulate them strategically to achieve personal political objectives. Such contrived political transaction costs alter either people's perceptions of the costs and benefits of government authority in a given sphere, or the costs of taking political action based upon those perceptions. For example, politicians long have understood that by disguising the outcome of governmental policies or by purposely concentrating a policy's benefits and dispersing its costs, public resistance can be curtailed. In these and myriad other ways, government officials thus often manipulate the costs of collective action encountered by the public or by others in government (Twight, 2002).

2. Rent-seeking through Political Transaction-cost Manipulation

Clearly, political transaction-cost manipulation is a form of rent-seeking. Consistent with Tullock's (1967) rent-seeking insight, the creation of contrived political transaction costs enables lawmakers, bureaucrats, executive branch officials, and others in government to obtain more of what they — and any interest groups they serve — personally value, at the expense of the general public.

3. Determinants of Political Transaction-cost Manipulation

The question is, what circumstances make support for a transaction-cost-increasing measure more feasible and attractive to a government official? The theory of political transaction-cost manipulation identifies variables that shape a federal official's decision to support or oppose such a measure. Variables that encourage support for a transaction-cost-increasing measure include: an appealing rationale; complexity (which reduces the likelihood that the measure will be understood, while allowing informed sponsors later to feign mistake); executive support for the measure; political job security and perquisites associated with it; third-party payoffs; party support; and high perceived importance of the measure to the official's constituents. Ideology is another key determinant: the theory predicts that government officeholders will favor laws, regulations, and policies that increase transaction costs associated with disapproval of programs that they personally favor on ideological grounds. Media attention to the transaction-cost-increasing features of a measure is predicted to negatively influence support for the measure. Time plays a more ambiguous role: it may increase support for a transaction-cost-increasing measure by facilitating

formation of interest groups likely to benefit from it, yet it may decrease support for the measure by providing greater opportunity for those harmed to discover the measure's likely effects (Twight, 1988, 2002).

4. Transaction-cost Manipulation in the Private Sector

Of course, transaction-cost-increasing behavior also occurs in the private sector. Although firms in perfectly competitive markets have no leeway to increase transaction costs, most businesses operate in imperfectly competitive markets that allow possible benefits to firms that engage in such behavior. Fraud is one example of these market strategies (Darby and Karni, 1973); firms' attempts to raise their rivals' costs provide another (Salop and Scheffman, 1983). Nonetheless, although transaction-cost augmentation by private firms sometimes does occur in the short run, associated direct costs as well as long-run competition and potential legal prosecution reduce its viability and appeal.

Constraints on transaction-cost manipulation are weaker in the public sector. In the private sector, consumers' desire not to be misled operates as a significant constraint on private actors' ability to effect contrived transaction costs. In political markets, the incentive of private individuals to acquire and act upon information relating to governmental officeholders' performance is minuscule by contrast. Higher natural transaction costs create greater slack in the political process, which in turn allows greater scope for transaction-cost manipulation. Reduced private incentives to acquire information also dampen incentives of potential "competitors" in political, bureaucratic, and judicial markets to reach citizens with information regarding changes in political transaction costs. Moreover, government officials who raise transaction costs to voters by lying about the nature of a government program or by mislabeling a statute face no legal penalty for their behavior that is comparable to punishment for private sector fraud.

Costs generated by adopting measures that increase relevant transaction costs thus do not impinge upon government decision makers as direct costs to the same extent that they do upon private decision makers engaged in analogous behavior. As a result, the government sector provides more fertile ground for such activity (Twight, 1988, pp. 140–145).

5. Intra-governmental Manipulation of Political Transaction Costs

In addition to changing private citizens' transaction costs, government officials also have incentives and ability to manipulate each other's transaction costs. Just as changes in political transaction costs facing the public may result from legislative, executive, judicial, or administrative action, so too the transaction costs facing government functionaries in each branch may be altered by actions of their government counterparts both within and outside their particular branch of government. For example, those serving on key congressional committees are in prime positions to manipulate information flowing to the rest of Congress. Bureaucratic cost concealment directed at other government officials supplies another well-documented example (Niskanen, 1971, 1975). Spiller and Tiller (1997) have described other examples that illustrate transaction-cost manipulation between Congress and government agencies and between Congress and the courts. The result of all such behavior is intragovernmental alteration of targeted government officeholders' transaction costs of perceiving and reacting to the costs and benefits of actual or proposed government authority in a given sphere. Intragovernmental manipulation of political transaction costs is expected to be responsive to the variables discussed above, though the relative importance of specific variables will vary with the particular governmental context.

6. Types of Political Transaction-cost Manipulation

The actions that fall under the rubric of political transaction-cost manipulation are varied, united by their common ability to alter the transaction costs of resistance to government authority-expanding measures. The main forms of political transaction-cost manipulation are those involving "information costs" on the one hand and "agreement and enforcement costs" on the other. Alternatively, these two categories might be termed "perception costs" and "action costs." However diverse the practices involved, they are cut from the same cloth.

The common ground shared by the superficially dissimilar forms of behavior identified below has not been widely understood. It has not been intuitively obvious that behavior as diverse as, for example, labeling statutes euphemistically, dispersing programmatic costs, unilaterally reinterpreting statutory law, and inserting parochial riders in politically safe omnibus bills might be reflections of the same impetus to manipulate political transaction costs. The transaction-cost-manipulation approach strives to systematically identify these linkages, developing a taxonomy of the different forms of this behavior.

On the information-cost manipulation side, the behavior includes such things as semantic efforts to alter public perception of the costs and benefits of government activities;

distortion of information, or restriction of access to information, about the nature and consequences of government activities; forms of taxation that change people's perception of the tax burden imposed on them; forms of subsidy that alter public perception of the benefits and costs implied; forms of regulation that obscure its cost to the individual; off-budget techniques; and incrementalism in expanding government authority. Prohibiting legitimate private contracts so as to increase the information costs of evaluating private alternatives to government control also falls under this heading.

On the agreement- and enforcement-cost side, the behavior encompasses all transaction-cost manipulation strategies that restructure costs of political *action* rather than costs of political information. One such category is "unilaterally changing the locus or scope of government decision-making authority in ways that shift the transaction-cost burden entailed in effectuating or forestalling change in the role of government" (Twight, 2002, p. 54). An example here is changing the meaning of the Constitution by means of the U.S. Supreme Court rather than through the formal amendment process established by Article V. When the Supreme Court expanded the meaning of the Constitution's interstate commerce clause, for instance, it turned the formal amendment process upside down. Instead of requiring those who wanted to expand the government's role to amend the Constitution as specified by Article V — a process designed to protect the original Constitution by making it costly to change the document — the Supreme Court made the change by judicial fiat. As a result, any subsequent effort to restore the Constitution's prior meaning required defenders of the original Constitution to incur the high transaction costs of amendment that had been intended for those who wanted to alter the original document, a complete reversal of the transaction-cost burdens of constitutional change. Whenever the Supreme Court has reinterpreted various provisions of the Constitution so as to expand the reach of federal authority, the court has shifted transaction cost burdens in this way.

Other subcategories of agreement- and enforcement-cost manipulation include: deliberately concentrating the benefits and dispersing the harm born of government action; changing the cost to private individuals of effecting administrative or judicial challenge to the government's interpretation of its existing powers; directly changing the cost to private citizens of achieving political agreement to revise the scope of government authority; interaction between government agencies that alters the cost to individuals of revising the scope of government authority;

and adopting procedural strategies that alter costs to congressmen of implementing their decision-making authority (e.g., tying different legislative proposals together into a single bill to make it a package deal). These and other subcategories are identified, with examples of each, as part of the model's taxonomy of transaction-cost manipulating strategies (Twight, 1994, p. 203).

Empirical Evidence

Evidence consistent with this theory is now abundant. Research has shown that political transaction-cost manipulation was pivotal in developing and implementing key federal programs and policies that touch the lives of all Americans. Creation and expansion of Social Security, income tax withholding, federal education controls, Medicare and related health care regulation, and federal database mandates and surveillance measures, for instance, all entailed such manipulation.

The Social Security Act was passed in 1935 through a variety of transaction-cost manipulating techniques. People at the time did not want compulsory old-age insurance for everyone; rather, they wanted means-tested public assistance for the aged poor. As Carolyn Weaver (1983) has shown, Franklin Roosevelt secured Social Security's passage only by tying it to other more popular measures, controlling information flowing to Congress and the public, dominating the agenda with the FDR-backed bill, and refusing to sign individual sections of the bill if separated from the other sections. All of these strategies increased the political transaction costs of opposing the Social Security Act.

Today, because of deliberate increases in political transaction costs, resisting this program is virtually impossible. Employers are required by law to extract payroll taxes from wages without employees' consent, making the cost of the tax less apparent than it would be if wage-earners had to write a check for the same amount. Government officials continue to tell Americans that they have a contractual right to Social Security benefits, despite the U.S. Supreme Court's 1960 ruling that people who have paid Social Security taxes for their entire working lives have no contractual right to anything as a result. The payroll tax itself is said to be "split" between employers and employees, with the employer shouldering half of the 12.4% Social Security tax.

In truth, economists and government officials have known for decades that employees bear almost the entire 12.4% tax — both halves — the "employee's" half through payroll tax deductions noted on their pay stubs, and the "employer's" half in the form of reduced contractual wages. As Edgar Browning (1975, p. 381) stated, "the dual nature of the levy does not influence the incidence of the tax," so that "its only impact" is on "voter awareness of the costs." Nonetheless, government officials continue to misrepresent the extent of the tax burden borne by employees, deliberately raising the transaction costs to voters of perceiving the full impact of the Social Security tax — and thus reducing public resistance to it.

Similarly, federal income tax withholding was mandated in 1943 by means of a variety of transaction-cost-manipulating techniques. For example, legislators told the public that withholding was for the benefit of taxpayers and would lower their tax burdens. Yet in congressional hearings at the time they discussed the revenue that needed to be "fried out" of taxpayers, how they could not "get those fellows" without withholding, and how withholding would increase future federal tax revenues (Twight, 2002). From 1943 to the present, mandatory withholding has dramatically increased the political transaction costs of resisting federal income taxes and thus the expanded power of government.

Laws establishing federal controls over education likewise were passed and implemented by means of transaction-cost manipulation. For example, legislators secured passage of a 1958 law by calling it the "National Defense Education Act," although they acknowledged among themselves that the tie to national defense was a "gimmick," a "sales argument," a way of providing federal revenues even to students studying "social welfare work, automobile driving or ... flower arranging" (Twight, 2002, pp. 147, 153). Similar techniques were used to pass the 1965 Elementary and Secondary Education Act. For example, although the bill was said to be part of President Lyndon Johnson's "war on poverty," congressional hearings show that the Act's antipoverty rationale was a sham, with the bill's benefits in fact designed to disproportionately benefit the affluent, not the poor. Legislators also claimed that these laws would not result in federal "control" over education, yet deliberately established such control by requiring states and localities to comply with federal educational goals in order to obtain federal funding.

Passage of the 1965 Medicare law as well as more recent federal health care controls hinged on similar strategies. Incrementalism, lying, and tying were used repeatedly. After decades of failed political efforts to mandate compulsory health insurance for all Americans, advocates deliberately narrowed the proposal to compulsory national health insurance for the aged. This incremental strategy proved crucial to passage of the 1965 Medicare law. In addition, the Medicare bill was made part of the Social Security Amendments of 1965, which contained a 7% increase in cash benefits for Social Security recipients. Tying these measures together meant that a legislator could not vote against Medicare without voting against the Social Security benefit increase, thus increasing the political transaction costs to legislators and to private citizens of opposing the Medicare bill. In addition government officials deliberately misrepresented Medicare, claiming that it provided coverage for catastrophic illness when they knew it contained no such provision. Moreover, once in place it was implemented with the familiar transaction-cost-increasing strategies of withholding and ostensible "splitting" the Medicare tax. Today, government officials tell us that if we decline Medicare hospital insurance benefits, having paid Medicare and Social Security taxes our entire working lives, we will forfeit all Social Security benefits. It would be difficult to devise a more powerful strategy for forcing people not to resist Medicare.

Similar strategies were used in passage and implementation of the 1996 Health Insurance Portability and Accountability Act (HIPAA). Though legislators represented the bill as a benign measure aimed at assuring that workers could retain health insurance upon changing jobs, the bill also contained privacy-endangering features of the previously rejected Clinton Health Security Act of 1993. A provision labeled "Administrative Simplification" contained requirements for "unique health identifiers" for all Americans, uniform electronic databases of personal medical information, and standardized data formats nationwide. By obscuring these provisions and tying them to more appealing measures, government officials increased the political transaction costs of resisting HIPAA and facilitated its passage. Misrepresentation continued at the implementation stage when government officials assured Americans that the new electronic databases would not be harmful because of HIPAA-mandated privacy regulations adopted by the Clinton and Bush administrations. Again, it was a transaction-cost-manipulating untruth: the so-called "privacy" regulations in fact dramatically reduced Americans' medical privacy.

Detailed empirical studies of these and other policy measures document the ubiquity and deliberateness of political transaction-cost manipulation, showing the linkage between the variables discussed above and federal officials' decisions to use transaction-cost-increasing strategies. Evidence consistent with the model's predictions is found in congressional hearings, the *Congressional Record*, and other official federal documents.

Impact on the Growth of Government

Manipulating costs of political decision making in order to achieve results initially inconsistent with actual public preferences has been a recurrent strategy in capturing and maintaining increased government authority over U.S. citizens. In contrast to some economists' visions of a transaction-cost-minimizing state, this model and associated empirical work have documented government officials' characteristic willingness and ability to increase the political transaction costs facing others on issues that influence the scope of government authority. The result has been steady expansion of the role and scope of government, buttressed by resistance-blocking mechanisms deliberately embedded in our institutional structure. Political transaction-cost manipulation thus has allowed government to grow beyond the level that otherwise would be tolerated, making a vastly expanded central government now largely self-perpetuating.

CHARLOTTE A.L. TWIGHT

REFERENCES

Browning, E.K. (1975). "Why the social insurance budget is too large in a democracy." *Economic Inquiry*, 13: 373–387.

Darby, M.R. and Karni, E. (1973). "Free competition and the optimal amount of fraud." *Journal of Law and Economics*, 16(1): 67–88.

Niskanen, W. (1971). *Bureaucracy and Representative Government*. New York: Aldine-Atherton.

Niskanen, W. (1975). "Bureaucrats and politicians." *Journal of Law and Economics*, 18: 617–643.

Olson, M. (1965). *The Logic of Collective Action: Public Goods and the Theory of Groups*. Cambridge: Harvard University Press.

Salop, S.C. and Scheffman, D.T. (1983). "Raising rivals' costs." *American Economic Review*, 73: 267–271.

Spiller, P.T. and Tiller, E.H. (1997). "Decision costs and the strategic design of administrative process and judicial review." *Journal of Legal Studies*, 26(2), part 1: 347–370.

Tullock, G. (1967). "The welfare costs of tariffs, monopolies, and theft." *Western Economic Journal*, 5(June): 224–232.

Twight, C. (1983). "Government Manipulation of Constitutional-Level Transaction Costs: An Economic Theory and Its Application to Off-Budget Expenditure Through the Federal Financing Bank," Ph.D. Dissertation, Seattle: University of Washington.

Twight, C. (1988). "Government manipulation of constitutional-level transaction costs: a general theory of transaction-cost augmentation and the growth of government." *Public Choice*, 56(2): 131–152.

Twight, C. (1992). "Constitutional renegotiation: impediments to consensual revision." *Constitutional Political Economy*, 3(1): 89–112.

Twight, C. (1994). "Political transaction-cost manipulation: an integrating theory." *Journal of Theoretical Politics*, 6(2): 189–216.

Twight, C.A. (2002). *Dependent on D.C.: The Rise of Federal Control Over the Lives of Ordinary Americans*. New York: Palgrave/St. Martin's Press.

U.S. Supreme Court (1960). *Flemming v. Nestor*. 363 U.S. 603.

Weaver, C.L. (1983). "The economics and politics of the emergence of social security: some implications for reform." *Cato Journal*, 3: 361–379.

PRESSURE GROUPS AND UNINFORMED VOTERS

During the last quarter of the twentieth century, economic and political science journals were filled with models of interest group politics. Their details differed, but, with certain exceptions (most of which are noted below), the message was the same: politicians tradeoff good policy in return for campaign contributions from special interests. The appeal of these models was the plausibility of their assumptions and the apparent realism of their conclusions. Since voters are often persuaded by political advertising, it makes sense that candidates would move their policies away from the median voter in order to gain the pressure group contributions that pay for such advertising. In this essay, I take a closer look at how uninformed, but rational voters, respond to such advertising. In the process, I show that pressure groups play a much more beneficial role in elections then generally believed.

1. The Standard Model and its Critics

Uri Ben Zion and Eytan (1974) and Welch (1974) published the first formal models showing the relationship between campaign funding by pressure groups and the behavior of the uninformed voters. In these models, a candidate maximizes vote share, which is a positive function of the candidate's position and campaign expenditures on advertising. An interest group donates money to the candidate in turn for the politician choosing a policy closer to the pressure group's preferred policy. The politician will agree to this quid pro quo if the politician gains more votes from advertising than are lost from choosing an inferior policy position. For want of a better term, I will refer to this and similar models as the standard model.

A large body of research incorporated the basic insights of this argument [see Mitchell and Munger (1991) and Morton and Cameron (1992) for surveys of the early literature]. This argument was also an important justification behind a whole host of articles even when the articles did not explicitly deal with voters. Consider Becker (1983,

1985) who assumes an interest group influence function — other things being equal, the greater the expenditure by the group, the more that the group will get its way in the political sector. How this money is turned into political pressure is not specified — it may be used for bribes or for informing legislators. But certainly an important motivating force for acceptance of Becker's model is that the money could be used for campaign advertising.

In the late 1980s and early 1990s several authors attacked the standard modeling of pressure group influence. Wittman (1989, 1995) argued that these models suffer from a meta-theoretical inconsistency — if voters believe that the standard model is correct, then voters would not act in the way posited. In particular, if the median voter knew that advertising comes at the cost of the candidate moving away from the median, then the median voter would vote for the candidate doing less advertising. Thus the standard model makes no sense when the voters understand the model. In the words of Lohmann (1998), the standard model requires "voter illusion."

Now in the standard model, the behavior of the voters is treated as a functional form — the more advertising, the more votes for the candidate. But as Austen-Smith (1991), in his critical review of *Black-Hole Tariffs and Endogenous Policy Theory* pointed out, voters should be modeled as utility maximizers rather than as mere automatons. While Austen-Smith did not provide any model in his review, he did list the requirements for a rational model of voter behavior — that voters will include in their calculations the knowledge that parties seek to win office and lobbies seek to influence policy.

For the most part, these arguments seemed to fall on deaf ears during the 1990s. Prominent examples include Baron (1994) and Grossman and Helpman (1997). In their models, a pressure group again provides money for advertising in exchange for a policy move by the candidate. They divided voters into two groups — informed voters who vote purely on policy grounds and uninformed voters whose vote for a candidate depends only on the candidates' advertising expenditures. So the uninformed voters are again just automatons. And once again, a candidate moves away from the median voter toward the preferred position of the pressure group whenever the candidate gains more votes from the uninformed through advertising than the candidate loses from the informed by taking a less desirable position.

If the uninformed voters had an ounce of wisdom in their heads, they would abstain and let the informed make the decision for them (see Fedderson and Pesendorfer (1998) for the argument); and, as already noted, if the median uninformed voter had two ounces of wisdom in his head, he would realize that the candidate doing more advertising is farther away from the median and, consequently, would vote for the candidate doing less advertising.

The question for the most of the remainder of this essay is: under what circumstances would uninformed but rational utility maximizing voters be more likely to vote for a candidate when the candidate spends more money on advertising.

The short answer is rational voters only respond positively to more advertising if the voters are on average better off by doing so. But how can the voter be better off? There are two ways this question has been answered. (1) There is some benefit that the rational uninformed voter gains in return for the candidate choosing an inferior position. And (2) advertising moves the outcome toward the preferred position of the median uninformed voter. We start with the first answer.

2. Uniformed Voters Gain some Benefit in Exchange for an Inferior Policy

Maybe voters gain enjoyment from political advertising and rationally vote for the candidate doing more advertising. Frankly, I am skeptical that the entertainment value of political advertising is very high.

A more convincing approach is that voters may tradeoff reduced risk for an inferior policy. Congleton (1986) argued that advertising increases information about the candidate's policies, thereby reducing policy risk. Austen-Smith (1987) developed this insight about risk-reduction into a model of political campaigns. In his model, the median voter is willing to vote for a candidate whose expected policy is worse than the other candidate's expected policy if the risk (variance) is lower for the first candidate. At the same time, the pressure group is willing to provide money for advertising if the candidate moves away from the median voter toward the pressure group's most preferred position. So the median voter rationally votes for the candidate doing more advertising whenever the reduction in risk compensates for the loss in expected policy position. Extensions of the Austen-Smith model were made by Ingberman (1992) and Gersbach (1999). Ingberman assumed that more is known about the incumbent, while Gersbach considered the case where candidates have policy preferences.

Several authors have assumed that the pressure group has inside information regarding the relative quality (e.g., honesty or leadership skills) of the candidates. Voters know the positions of the candidates, but not their quality (or, in some models, voters have only a weak signal of quality). All of the voters prefer higher quality to lower quality. The pressure group provides information about the quality of the high-quality candidate in return for the high-quality candidate moving toward the position of the pressure group and away from the median. Voters are willing to tradeoff the inferior policy for a higher-quality candidate.

Prat (1999, 2000) and Gerber (2001) model the process as one of costly signaling. In these signaling models, there is no content to the advertising; rather voters infer quality from the amount of advertising. The models are similar. I concentrate on Gerber's model, which is somewhat easier to understand but employs stronger assumptions. In his basic model, the candidates' positions are given. The voters, but not the pressure group, value quality per se. The pressure group and challenger observe a signal (high or low) regarding the quality of the challenger. The pressure group then enters into a contract with the challenger to exchange money for favors (since voters dislike favors, this can be interpreted as policy along a different dimension). During the campaign, the voters get their own signal of quality and are also able to observe the amount of campaign expenditures, thereby inferring the pressure group's signal, as well. High campaign expenditures indicate a high-quality challenger. Under plausible assumptions this means that the median voter is better off voting for the candidate that is doing more advertising even though he has sold more favors. Like most signaling models, this one has many equilibria.

Wittman (2001a) employs a model of cheap talk endorsements where content is important. Again, voters know the positions of the candidates, but not their relative quality. Here, the pressure group also values quality. In his model, both candidates' positions are endogenous. Although the pressure group can lie and endorse the low-quality candidate as the high-quality candidate, in equilibrium the pressure group tells the truth. Therefore, the uninformed voters become fully informed after observing the endorsement. Although competition for endorsement by the pressure group means that the high-quality candidate moves away from the median voter, the median voter gains more by having the high-quality candidate elected than she loses in policy. If there are pressure groups on both sides of the median, the equilibrium outcome is that all of the pressure groups endorse the high-quality candidate who is at the median voter's most preferred position.

3. Advertising Provides Information about Position to the Uninformed

The second approach assumes that some of the voters are uninformed about the true position of the candidates. Political advertising and/or endorsements provide the requisite information. As a result, the candidates move away from the median informed voter toward the median of the uninformed voters, making the median uninformed voter better off. Clearly, the pressure group provides such information only in the case where it is made better off by such a move.

Seminal work by McKelvey and Ordeshook (1984, 1985) showed how uninformed voters could make use of poll data and endorsements to make rational inferences about the positions of the candidates. In their model, uninformed voters do not know the position of the pressure group. An endorsement by the pressure group tells the uninformed voter which candidate is to the left and which is to the right. The uninformed voter also knows where he stands on the distribution of voters (informed and uninformed), all of whom have linear symmetric loss functions. Suppose that the particular uninformed voter is considerably to the left. If the poll data says that more than 50% of the voters prefer the left candidate, then that indicates that this particular uninformed voter should prefer the left candidate, as well. In a sequence of polls, the uninformed voters become more informed, and they have a greater say in the election.

Wittman (2001b) also assumes that that there are two types of voters, informed and uninformed, and that candidates are only interested in winning. In contrast to McKelvey and Ordeshook, the uninformed do not have access to poll data. Uninformed voters may have preferences that differ from the informed voters. If the median uninformed voter is closer to the pressure group than the median informed voter is to the pressure group, then it may pay the pressure group to contribute to a candidate's advertising campaign. In a series of models, Wittman shows how the uninformed, combining their understanding of the political process with bits of information derived from advertising and/or endorsements, can become fully informed. The outcome is at the median of all voters. In the absence of advertising, the outcome would be at the median of the informed voters. So pressure group contributions move the outcome toward the median voter, overall.

Schultz (2001) and Wittman (2000) consider the case where truthful advertising about the relative positions of both candidates can be directed to a subset of voters. In both papers, those who do not receive advertising can make intelligent inferences. For example, not receiving information from a candidate informs the voter that she is not being favored by that candidate. Schultz assumes that there are two candidates with policy preferences and a certain amount of money to be given to n groups. He shows that information and subsidies will go to those who are marginally uninformed and unbiased toward either candidate. Wittman considers office-motivated candidates within the

context of a single-dimensional policy framework. In equilibrium, all voters are informed and the winning candidate is at the median voter's most preferred position.

Coate (2002) assumes that political parties represent perfectly opposing ideological preferences. Each party's candidate is either ideological or office oriented, the latter taking a less extreme position vis a vis the median voter. The positions of the ideological and office oriented candidates are exogenous in the model. Ordinary voters cannot distinguish between the ideological and office motivated candidate, but the pressure group can. Other things being equal, the members of the political party prefer the ideological candidate. In contrast, the pressure group is more interested in getting its policy implemented. Here advertising is always truthful. Only moderate candidates will be supported by pressure groups since only moderate ideologies will gain voters. The net result from pressure group contributions is that parties tend to choose candidates closer to the median.

To sum up the micro-foundations literature: rational voters vote for the candidate doing more advertising only if the voters are on average better off by voting for that candidate than the other. Stated in this way, this is not a surprising result. It just contradicts a very large literature.

4. Do Pressure Group Contributions Aid or Hinder the Political Process?

A more subtle question is whether pressure group contributions aid the political process, and if so, by how much. Generally, the results depend on the degree of competition, on who makes the offers, the distribution of preferences, the response function of the voters, the nature of the information provided, and, in the signaling models, on equilibrium selection and whether there is a pooling equilibrium. If there is more than one pressure group, then competition is likely to shift the surplus from the pressure group to the candidates, which ultimately means the median voter (when the candidates maximize votes). If the pressure group makes an all or nothing offer, this gives more power to the pressure group; if it is the candidates who make offers to the pressure group, then the superior candidate captures some of the surplus. Again this surplus will accrue to the median voter if the candidates are maximizing votes. The effect of the distribution of preferences on the equilibrium outcome is more complicated (see Wittman (2001a) for a discussion). Generally, when uninformed voters are rational, pressure group contributions for advertising are more likely to aid the political process than do it harm. That is, the median voter's welfare is likely to be improved in comparison to the situation where there are no pressure groups and no advertising. But with sufficient ingenuity, one can still construct models where the competition for endorsements makes the voters worse off.

5. Future Research

The question of how uninformed but rational voters make use of information that comes from sources who have their own agenda is an extremely interesting one. The answers provided here are only the beginning. Undoubtedly, this question will inspire a large body of research in the coming years.

DONALD WITTMAN

REFERENCES

Austen-Smith, David (1987). "Interest groups, campaign contributions, and probabilistic voting." *Public Choice*, 54: 123–139.

Austen-Smith, David (1991). "Rational consumers and irrational voters: A review essay on *Black hole tariffs and endogenous policy theory by Stephen Magee, William Brock, and Leslie Young* (Cambridge University Press 1989)." *Economics and Politics*, 3: 73–92.

Austen-Smith, David (1997). "Interest groups: money, information and influence," in Dennis Mueller (ed.) *Perspectives on Public Choice*. Cambridge: Cambridge University Press.

Baron, David P. (1994). "Electoral competition with informed and uninformed voters." *American Political Science Review*, 88: 33–47.

Becker, Gary (1983). "A theory of competition among pressure groups for political influence." *Quarterly Journal of Economics*, 96: 371–400.

Becker, Gary (1985). "Public policies, pressure groups and deadweight costs." *Journal of Public Economics*, 28: 330–347.

Ben-Zion, Uri and Eytan, Zeev (1973). "On money, votes and policy in a democratic society." *Public Choice*, 17: 1–10.

Cameron, Charles and Enelow, James (1993). "Asymmetric policy effects, campaign contributions and the spatial theory of elections." *Mathematical and Computer Modeling*, 16: 117–132.

Coate, Stephen (2002). "Political contributions with campaign contributions and informative advertising," NBER Working Paper 8693.

Congleton, Roger (1986). "Rent-seeking aspects of political advertising." *Public Choice*, 49: 249–263.

Congleton, Roger (1989). "Campaign finances and political platforms." *Public Choice*, 62: 101–118.

Dixit, Avinash and Londregan, John (1998). "The determinants of success of special interests in redistributive politics." *The Journal of Politics*, 58: 1132–1135.

Fedderson, Timothy and Pesendorfer, Wolfgang (1998). "Abstentions in elections with asymmetric information and diverse preferences." *American Political Science Review*, 93: 381–398.

Gerber, Alan (1999). "Rational voters, candidate spending and incomplete information," Yale University Working Paper.

Gersbach, Hans (1999). "Elections and campaign contributions, divided support and regulation." Alfred-Weber Institut Working Paper.

Grofman, Bernard and Norrander, Barbara (1990). "Efficient use of reference group cues in a single dimension." *Public Choice*, 64: 213–227.

Grossman, Gene M. and Helpman, Elhanan (1996). "Electoral competition and special interest politics." *Review of Economic Studies*, 63: 265–286.

Grossman, Gene M. and Helpman, Elhanan (1999). "Competing for endorsements." *American Economic Review*, 89: 501–524.

Hinich, Melvin and Munger, Michael (1989). "Political investment, voter perceptions, and candidate strategy: an equilibrium spatial analysis," in Peter Ordeshook (ed.) *Models of Strategic Choice in Politics*.

Ingberman, Daniel (1992). "Incumbent reputations and ideological campaign contributions in spatial competition." *Mathematical and Computer Modeling*, 16: 147–170.

Lohmann, Susanne (1998). "An information rationale for the power of special interests." *American Political Science Review*, 92: 809–828.

Magee, Stephen P., Brock, William A., and Young, Leslie (1989). *Black Hole Tariffs and Endogenous Policy theory*. Cambridge: Cambridge University Press.

McKelvey, Richard and Ordeshook, Peter (1984). "Rational expectations in elections: some experimental results based on a multidimensional model." *Public Choice*, 44: 61–102.

McKelvey, Richard and Ordeshook, Peter (1985). "Elections with limited information: a fulfilled expectations model using contemporaneous poll and endorsement data as information sources." *Journal of Economic Theory*, 36: 55–85.

McKelvey, Richard and Ordeshook, Peter (1986). "Sequential elections with limited information: a formal analysis." *Social Choice and Welfare*, 3: 199–211.

Mitchell, William and Munger, Michael (1991). "Economic models of interest groups: an introductory survey." *American Journal of Political Science*, 35: 512–546.

Morton, Rebecca and Cameron, Charles (1991). "Elections and the theory of campaign contributions: a survey and critical analysis." *Economics and Politics*, 4: 79–108.

Mueller, Dennis and Stratmann, Thomas (1994). "Informative and persuasive campaigning." *Public Choice*, 81: 55–77.

Pelzman, Sam (1976). "Toward a more general theory of regulation." *Journal of Law and Economics*, 19: 211–240.

Potters, Jan, Sloof, Randolf, and Winden, FransVon (1997). "Campaign expenditures, contributions, and direct endorsements: The strategic use of endorsements and money to influence voter behavior." *European Journal of Political Economy*, 13: 1–31.

Prat, Andrea (Forthcoming). "Campaign spending with office-seeking politicians, rational voters, and multiple lobbies." *Journal of Economic Theory*.

Schultz, Christian (2001). "Strategic campaigns and special interest politics," University of Copenhagen Working Paper.

Puy, M. Socorro (2000). "Lobby groups and the financial support of election campaigns." *Journal of Public Economic Theory*, 2: 319–348.

Sloof, Randolph (1998). *Game Theoretic Models of the Political Influence of Interest Groups*. Kluwer.

Snyder, James M. (1989). "Election goals and the allocation of campaign resources." *Econometrica*, 57: 637–660.

Welch, William (1974). "The economics of campaign funds." *Public Choice*, 20: 83–97.

Welch, William (1980). "The allocation of political monies: economic interest groups." *Public Choice*, 35: 97–120.

Wittman, Donald (1989). "Why democracies are efficient." *Journal of Political Economy*, 97: 1395–1424.

Wittman, Donald (1995). *The Myth of Democratic Failure: Why Political Institutions are Efficient*. Chicago: University of Chicago Press.

Wittman, Donald (2000). "Targeted Information and Uninformed Voters," University of California Santa Cruz Working Paper.

Wittman, Donald (2001a). "Candidate quality, pressure group endorsements, and uninformed voters," University of California Santa Cruz Working Paper.

Wittman, Donald (2001b). "Rational voters and political advertising," University of California Santa Cruz Working Paper.

PRINCIPAL–AGENT RELATIONSHIPS IN THE THEORY OF BUREAUCRACY

The theory of the firm has many applications to political markets, and principal-agent theory in particular has been used to describe the relationship between Congress and the bureaucracy. The principal-agent model of the bureaucracy addresses the importance of property rights and contracts in political markets. In this regard, the development of this model parallels the evolution of the theory of the firm that has stressed the significance of transactions costs associated with using the price mechanism. Coase (1937) describes how firms emerge within a market to minimize transactions costs, and Alchian and Demsetz (1972) describe how institutions emerge within a firm to minimize transaction costs. Similar developments have occurred in the theory of bureaucracy and representative government.

The application of principal-agent theory to bureaucratic outcomes finds its roots in the theory of regulation developed by Stigler (1971), who maintained that, as a rule, regulation is acquired by an industry and designed and operated primarily for its benefit. The basic resource of the state, the power to coerce, is a commodity freely traded in the political market place and moved to its most efficient margins by competing pressures. Stigler's theory was extended and formalized by Peltzman (1976). Like Stigler, Peltzman assumed that transfers of wealth were at stake in the regulatory process, not usually in cash form, but rather indirectly in the form of regulated prices, entry restrictions and the like. The legislator is viewed as vote maximizing by allocating transfers in response to the competing bids of political coalitions. Generally, the legislator (as broker) has incentives to provide welfare transfers as long as the gain in political support from the winners outweighs the loss of support from the losers. From this generating assumption, Peltzman formulated a theory of the optimum size of effective political coalitions within a framework of a general model of the political process. Becker (1983) presented a theory of competition among pressure groups for political influence that built on Peltzman's analysis. Political equilibrium was shown to depend on the efficiency of each group in producing pressure, the effect of additional pressure on the influence of the group, the number of persons in different groups, and the deadweight cost of taxes and subsidies.

Building upon this concept of political equilibrium, Weingast and Marshall (1988) used the theory of the firm to show how the institution of the committee system developed in the legislature to minimize the transactions costs of delivering services to constituents once the political equilibrium was reached. Following Williamson (1985), three conditions determine a contractual breakdown; (1) bounded rationality, (2) opportunism, and (3) asset specificity. Each of these conditions are present in the legislative market for votes. The legislators operate under the constraints of bounded rationality because the nature and benefits of all future bills cannot be known at the time of the vote trade. The problems of noncontemporaneous benefit flows and nonsimultaneous exchange in vote trading result in opportunistic behavior, and legislators invest their time and staff resources into issues that are specific to their constituency. Weingast and Marshall argue that reputational effects of repeat play alone cannot overcome these contractual failure conditions; therefore the congressional committee system emerged and gained power in order to facilitate efficient trading and enforcement between legislators. Legislators, acting alone, cannot ensure the provision of services to their districts; therefore, gains from trade exist in the legislature. Instead of trading explicitly in votes to capture the gains from exchange, legislators sacrifice the property right of agenda power over some policy areas in exchange for a committee assignment in which they have near monopoly rights over a subset of policy areas.

Congressional committees, then, reflect the specialization of legislators in order to provide their constituents with services. While the committee system helps legislators to serve their constituents, the committee cannot directly provide all of the appropriate services. Instead, the legislators delegate the provision of some of these services to bureaus that trade a total budget for a total output of these services. As in the team production case of Alchian and Demsetz (1972), marginal productivity is costly to observe; so bureau shirking may occur. Weingast (1984) argues that the delegation will only occur if bureau production (complete with shirking) provides greater net benefits than any other method of providing the service.

In summary, the simple principal-agent model of the relationship between Congress and the bureaucracy described above incorporates many facets of the theory of the firm. The congressional committee system is seen as a governance structure that emerged to solve contractual problems in the market for votes so legislators could capture gains from trade. Legislators sacrifice control over some policy areas in exchange for near monopoly rights over policies that benefit their constituencies. The committees delegate the provision of some services to bureaus; hence, a principal-agent relationship develops. The principal-agent problems can be alleviated if the committees develop efficient incentive structures to discipline the bureaus.

This simple principal-agent theory is appropriate for analyzing a two-tiered organization. Recent work in the theory of the firm has recognized the need to explore more complex hierarchical structures. Specifically, the principal-agent model has been extended to incorporate a third tier, that of an intermediate supervisor who monitors the agent for the principal. Tirole's (1986) formal presentation of the three-tier principal-supervisor-agent (P-S-A) model illustrated how this lengthening of the hierarchy introduces the possibility of collusion between the supervisor and the agent, which could decrease the efficiency of the organization. Further work by Laffont (1990), Tirole (1992), and McAfee and McMillan (1995) show that adding a supervisor increases the extent of the principal-agent costs of operating the hierarchy, and thus, decreases the efficiency of the organization.

In this respect, the P-S-A model finds its roots in von Hayek (1945) who argued that organizational costs develop because knowledge is dispersed among individuals within the hierarchy who have incentives to exploit their informational advantage. This loss of information control was formally modeled by Williamson (1967) who showed that there exist diminishing returns to scale which serve to limit the optimal firm size. In the McAfee and McMillan (1995) version of the P-S-A model, each layer added to the hierarchy is predicted to double amount of rent. As the source of the information (the agent) becomes further removed from the decision-making unit (the principal), this distortion of information increases exponentially, resulting in organizational diseconomies of scale.

Much of the literature that applies principal-agent theory to bureaucratic oversight focuses on the relationship between one congressional oversight committee and one bureau; however, the pattern of congressional oversight in practice is much more complicated, indicating that use of the principal-supervisor-agent model may be more appropriate.

At the supervisory level of the hierarchy there are, in fact, many supervisors of the bureaucracy agents. First, there is legislative oversight. There exist jurisdictional overlaps in the legislature, that is, the legislative committee jurisdictions are not always aligned with the jurisdictions of the bureaucracy, and most bureaus are actually overseen by two or more standing legislative committees.

Even if one of the oversight committees can be shown to dominate, the multiplicity introduced by bicameralism cannot be ignored. Oversight activities occur through both House and Senate committees. If both chambers pass measures in different forms and if these differences cannot be resolved via amendments, a compromise bill must be forged in a conference committee before the bill can be sent forth for Presidential review.

Another legislative supervisor of the bureaucracy is revealed by the budgetary process. In addition to responding to multiple oversight committees, each bureau's budget must be approved by a subcommittee of the Appropriations committee of the relevant chamber. Appropriations committee proposals can then be amended by the full chamber before being passed. Often there can be a conflict of goals between the appropriations and oversight committees.

The jurisdictional overlaps in the legislative oversight system, then, offer a challenge to one of the major assumptions in the simple principal-agent model: that the near monopoly power of committees solves the contractual problems of vote trading in the legislature. The simple principal-agent theory concludes that for a policy change to occur, there must be a substantial change on the oversight committee. The weakening of the agenda power of committees through jurisdictional overlaps within and between chambers means that entities other than oversight committee members have an influence on bureau policy. Any change in policy, in all likelihood, may not be traced back to one particular committee.

In addition to legislative oversight, the President is another supervisor within the hierarchy. The power struggle that may occur between the President and the legislature would seem to have a great influence on bureau policy, whether the agency is independent or part of the President's cabinet. Budgets of bureaus are submitted to the Office of Management and Budget (OMB) for approval who then prepares a total federal budget for Presidential review. It is the President, then, who presents the total budget to Congress, a budget that reflects his goals for the nation.

Finally, another supervisor with influence over federal policy is the judiciary that interprets legislation. Supreme Court decisions often lead to reforms in the body of legislation, and the precedents set in the courts have an impact on federal policy.

The existence of multiple supervisors overseeing the bureaucracy may result in a greater role for bureaucratic preferences in the political market. If the interaction among supervisors leaves room for the bureaucracy to assert power, the model must be amended to include incentives for the bureaus to monitor themselves. Indeed, these incentives were incorporated into the theory of the firm in the literature on the separation of ownership and control (Jensen and Meckling, 1976; Fama, 1980). In this literature, monitoring of agents is accomplished by the presence of efficient capital markets and the outside managerial labor market. These devices, however, are not available to cure the monitoring problems inherent in the bureaucratic model.

In the political market, there does not exist a tool like the capital market to signal the performance of a bureau. Indeed, the outputs of most bureaus are extremely difficult to measure. Unlike stockholders, legislators cannot shift costlessly among investments, because the rank (and thus, power) of a legislator on a committee depends on his seniority on that committee; a move to another committee would entail a loss of such seniority. A committee assignment is seen as a long-term investment by the legislator rather than as a portfolio diversification (Rowley and Elgin, 1988).

The monitoring of bureaucrats also does not seem to come from the outside managerial labor market. Public sector managers do not have incentives to monitor themselves in order to improve their promotion chances within or outside the bureau because salaries and promotions are strongly linked to seniority. The difficulty of measuring bureau performance extends to the evaluation of managers. The performance qualification that can be measured and is most likely to be rewarded is that of obtaining budget increases for one's bureau rather than that of operating more efficiently.

Thus, it seems that the property rights that are available in the private sector to mitigate principal-agent problems, are severely attenuated in the bureaucratic version of the model. Rowley and Vachris (1993) explain how nonexistent or poorly defined property rights cause inefficiencies in political markets. Unlike economic markets, which are proprietary in nature and in which individuals bear the full consequences of their choices, political markets are largely non-proprietary, and individuals do not necessarily bear the full consequences of their choices. Moe (1990) discusses how the uncertainty of property rights in political markets distorts the choices made by political actors. Delegation of authority to federal bureaus is not the result of legislators putting their property to the most efficient use. Rather, those in power today are most concerned with setting up a governance scheme for the bureaucracy that cannot in turn be amended or reversed by those who may be in power tomorrow. To ensure that opponents do not control the bureaucracy in the future, then, the legislature purposely gives up control over it in the present. The same can be true of the industry special interest groups that demand the services provided by the bureau in the first place. Bureaus are given great discretion in order to insulate policy outcomes from future changes in the balance of political power. The bureaus, themselves, also favor insulation from political uncertainty; and once agencies are set up, bureaucrats predictably take steps to increase their autonomy. They can accomplish this independence partly by gaining expertise, or asset specificity, in their field.

The ultimate principal in the political market is the "demander" of the bureaucratic services. Just as there are multiple agents and supervisors in this hierarchy, it can be argued that there are also multiple principals or demanders. Voters are one source of demand. As a principal in the hierarchy, voters could exert control over supervisors (that is, legislators and Presidents) who did not provide appropriate levels of service. According to the median voter theorem, legislators and Presidents cater to the median voter's demands instead of attempting to appease the preferences of all voters in the country because median voter preferences determine a political market equilibrium (Downs, 1957). Rowley (1984) has shown that the outcome predicted by the median voter theorem is dependent upon a set of very stringent and unrealistic assumptions about the election process. If, for example, more than two political parties contest an election, or if voters refrain from voting, then the median voter theorem does not hold. Therefore, we cannot generally assume that the median voter's preferences dominate in the political market.

Without the equilibrium solution of the median voter, the extent of control that voters have over legislators and Presidents is necessarily diminished. Rowley and Vachris (1995) discuss other reasons why the vote motive cannot serve as an efficient control mechanism in political markets. First, unlike private markets, voting processes do not guarantee that the highest bidder wins the right to office; instead, the distribution of bids from politicians to voters also matters (McCormick and Tollison, 1981). Second, voters cannot transfer their property rights predictably and cannot abandon them without high transactions costs such as emigration or revolution. Third, political choices are bundled, so voters lose control over specific issues. Finally, the problems of voter memory decay and rational ignorance prevent voters from effectively punishing politicians for deviating from voter preferences.

If voters are incapable of effective oversight over the supervisors in the political hierarchy, special interest groups may be able to capitalize upon this market failure and exert control over policy outcomes. Stigler's (1971) capture theory of regulation points to industry special interest groups as demanders or principals in this sense. The interactions of these special interest groups play a role in determining the policy outcome. Yes, politicians predictably will cater to successful interest groups, but such an outcome can hardly be described as politically efficient. Rowley and Vachris (1995) argue that special interest groups achieve their redistributive goals through wealth dissipating rent-seeking. These groups exacerbate the informational asymmetries in political markets because opaque policies are more likely to be enacted than transparent ones; therefore, they achieve their goals with a high degree of technical inefficiency.

In summary, then, the institutional description provided above of the many agents, supervisors and principals involved in the oversight of the bureaucracy indicates that the simple principal-agent model is not a reflection of institutional reality. In the case of federal antitrust enforcement, at the bottom of the hierarchy, the Antitrust Division and the Federal Trade Commission serve as multiple agents. The separation of powers and the jurisdictional overlaps in the legislature serve to widen the hierarchy at the supervisory level in that the President, the judiciary, and several legislative committees influence antitrust policy. At the top of the hierarchy, multiplicity of principals result from the failure of the median voter theorem and the logic of collective action. Voters and various special interest groups all demand antitrust services and thus influence the pattern of enforcement. In reality, then the hierarchy is widened at all three levels, making an efficient outcome difficult to obtain.

MICHELLE A. VACHRIS

REFERENCES

Alchian, A. and Demsetz, H. (1972). "Production, information costs and economic organization." *American Economic Review*, 68: 777–795.

Becker, G.S. (1983). "A theory of competition among pressure groups for political influence." *Quarterly Journal of Economics*, 63: 371–400.

Coase, R.H. (1937). "The nature of the firm." *Economica*, 4: 386–405.

Downs, A. (1957). *An Economic Theory of Democracy*. New York: Harper and Row.

Fama, E. (1980). "Agency problems and the theory of the firm." *Journal of Political Economy*, 88: 288–307.

Jensen, M.C. and Meckling, W.H. (1976). "Theory of the firm: managerial behavior, agency costs, and ownership structures." *Journal of Financial Economics*, 3: 305–360.

Laffont, J. (1990). "Analysis of hidden gaming in a three-level hierarchy." *Journal of Law, Economics and Organization*, 6(2): 301–324.

McAfee, R.P. and McMillan, J. (1995). "Organizational diseconomies of scale." *Journal of Economics and Management Strategy*, 4(3): 399–426.

McCormick, R.F. and Tollison, R.D. (1981). *Politicians, Legislation and the Economy: An Inquiry into the Interest-Group Theory of Government*. Boston: Martinus Nijhoff.

Moe, T.M. (1990). "The politics of structural choice: toward a theory of public bureaucracy," in O. Williamson (ed.) *Organization Theory*. New York: Oxford University Press, pp. 116–153.

Peltzman, S. (1976). "Towards a more general theory of regulation." *Journal of Law and Economics*, 19: 211–240.

Rowley, C.K. (1984). "The relevance of the median voter theorem." *Journal of Institutional and Theoretical Economics*, (March): 104–135.

Rowley, C.K. and Elgin, R.S. (1988). "Government and its bureaucracy: a bilateral bargaining versus a principal-agent approach," in C.K. Rowley, R.D. Tollison, and G. Tullock (eds.) *The Political Economy of Rent Seeking*. Kluwer Academic Publishers.

Rowley, C.K and Vachris, M.A. (1993). "Snake oil economics versus public choice," *Public Choice Theory*, Vol. III. Aldershot: Edward Elgar Publishing, pp. 573–584.

Rowley, C.K. and Vachris, M.A. (1995). "Why democracy in the United States does not necessarily produce efficient results." *Journal of Public Finance and Public Choice*, (December): 97–111.

Stigler, George J. (1971). "The theory of economic regulation." *Bell Journal of Economics and Management Science*, 2 (Spring): 3–21.

Tirole, J. (1986). "Hierarchies and bureaucracies: on the role of collusion in organizations." *Journal of Law, Economics and Organization*, 2 (Fall): 181–214.

Tirole, J. (1992). "Collusion and the theory of organizations," in J. Laffont (ed.) *Advances in Economic Theory: Proceedings from the Sixth World Congress of the Econometric Society*, Vol. 2. Cambridge, England: Cambridge University Press, pp. 151–206.

von Hayek, F.A. (1945). "The use of knowledge in society." *American Economic Review*, 35: 519–530.

Weingast, Barry R. (1984). "The congressional bureaucratic system: a principal agent perspective." *Public Choice*, 44: 147–191.

Weingast, Barry R. and Marshall, William J. (1988). "The industrial organization of congress; of why legislature, like firms, are not organized as markets." *Journal of Political Economy*, 96: 132–163.

Williamson, O.E. (1967). "Hierarchical control and optimal firm size." *Journal of Political Economy*, 75(2): 123–138.

Williamson, O.E. (1985). *The Economic Institutions of Capitalism*. New York: Free Press.

PROHIBITION

The policy of prohibition is an extreme measure directed at the production, distribution, and consumption of a good or service. Whereas policies such as regulation, taxation, price controls and licensing seek to control and limit a market, prohibition is intended to completely eliminate the market. Historically, prohibition has been applied to markets that have been deemed to be morally repugnant to society and in conflict with state religion or ideology. Therefore we find that prohibition has been applied to such activities as usury, prostitution, insider trading of corporate securities, and nudity and to goods such as alcohol, tobacco, narcotic drugs, marijuana, firearms and freon. Because prohibition has generally been limited to highly dangerous products and activities of a questionable moral character they can be viewed as serving the public interest. Additionally, the production and consumption of these goods and services are typically associated with self-destructive behavior, harm to the social and civic order, increases in crime, accidents, and the spread of disease and the degradation of the environment.

The primary problem with the public interest view of prohibition is that the policy cannot in fact achieve the result of prohibiting the targeted good or service. A strictly enforced prohibition will eliminate the legal market, but will also result in the establishment of a black market. As market suppliers leave the market, price of the product rises in the black market; tighter enforcement increases cost, especially risk of capture, increase price further and result in a smaller quantity demanded. Becker and Stigler (1974) argue that the trouble with prohibition is that suppliers enter the black market in response to higher prices, so that increased enforcement only serves to increase potential earnings. However, the more vexing problem of prohibition is that it changes the entire nature of the market. For example, Paul and Wilhite (1994) note that prohibition removes government from the role of enforcing property rights and that the alternative regime of violence and coercion not only sets up opportunities for the collection of monopoly profits, but also results in the production of significant negative externalities.

In total, the economics of prohibition shows that the policy cannot in fact remove the good from society, that prohibited products are more dangerous and are consumed under conditions of greater risk and ignorance, and that black markets increase the amount of violence and crime in society (Thornton, 1991a). As applied to the market for illegal drugs and alcohol, prohibition results in products of a higher level and variability of potency. This effect combines with increased ignorance concerning product quality and adulterates and results in a product that is much more dangerous than its counterpart in the legal marketplace (Thornton, 1998a). Prohibition-related crime includes the production, distribution, and consumption of the illegal product, all the acts of violence committed to enforce contracts and sales territories, acts of violence inflicted on innocent bystanders, corruption of politicians, public officials, and law enforcement officers, and the criminal acts committed by consumers in order to pay black market prices. Prohibition can even increase crime by reducing the number of legal market job opportunities available in the workforce (Beil and Thornton, 2000). The full economic cost of prohibition also includes the direct enforcement costs, civil liberties and privacy rights lost in the attempt to improve the effectiveness of enforcement and all the expenditures by the public to insulate itself from the ravages of prohibition.

Although economists generally supported prohibitions such as alcohol prohibition based on the 18th Amendment to the U.S. Constitution, long periods of experience and evidence with these prohibitions have made economists increasingly skeptical of prohibition and increasingly supportive of alternative policy regimes (Thornton, 1991b; Miron and Zwiebel, 1995). Public choice economists have recently turned their attention to prohibitions such as the "Noble Experiment" with alcohol prohibition (1920–1933) and the prohibition of narcotics (1917–present) and marijuana (1938–present) known as the "War on Drugs." These investigations have provided great insight into the public choice nature of these policy regimes, additional evidence on the public choice nature of governmental institutions, and provided useful insights into the workings of black markets.

In retrospect, alcohol prohibition in the United States during the 1920s was a highly unusual policy that would seem to lend support to Arrow's impossibility theorem; imposed as it was by Constitutional Amendment and ended with the only repeal of an Amendment in history. Thornton (1991, 1996, 1997) however shows that this policy was proceeded by a long history of government intervention into alcohol markets including colonial prohibitions, heavy taxes, licensing, local option, state prohibitions and that these policies were ineffective and tended to cycle as a result. These interventions, in turn created criminal and social externalities and helped turn temperance organizations into the first public interest groups such as the Anti-Saloon League and the Prohibition Party. With the demand-side bolstered by rent-seeking commercial interests and the 17th Amendment that gave women the right to vote and the supply-side weakened by conditions created by World War I, national prohibition became a reality.

Boudreaux and Pritchard (1994) adopted an explicit public choice perspective to analyze the 18th and 21st Amendments. They argue that representatives ignored their constituents' desire for alcohol prohibition because the Federal government received approximately 1/3 of its total revenue from taxes on alcohol. The passage of the 16th Amendment, which permitted the Federal government to tax income, created a new and significant source of revenue. The Income Tax quickly dwarfed alcohol as a source of revenue and therefore greatly lowered the cost of voting for prohibition and thus nicely explains both the adoption and timing of prohibition. They go on to show that the Great Depression resulted in falling income tax revenues in 1931 and that this reduced the cost of Congress voting for the 21st Amendment repeal prohibition in 1933 and restarting the flow of alcohol tax revenue.

Goff and Anderson (1994) also examined the votes in the U.S. Senate for the Prohibition and Repeal amendments from a public choice perspective. They modeled support or opposition to the amendments as a function of constituent preferences, interest group activity, political party activity, and legislator ideology and they found support for the idea that economic interests played in an important role in the passage of both Amendments. Munger and Schaller (1997) examined the Amendments using a cross-section of state-level voting. They also found that the preferences of citizens and economic interests played important roles in both votes. In addition, they found that that economic interests in the alcohol industry were insignificant in opposing the passage of prohibition while Goff and Anderson measure of the alcohol industry was significant. Thornton and Weise (2001) add that tax revolts against local governments during the early years of the Great Depression were an important component in the political push for Repeal and the returning flow of alcohol tax revenues.

The public choice approach has been extremely useful in dissecting the modern war on drugs. One important conclusion in the public choice literature on prohibition runs counter to the argument that increased enforcement leads to decreased crime (Benson et al., 1994). This literature (Benson and Rasmussen, 1991; Benson et al., 1992; Rasmussen et al., 1993; Sollars et al., 1994; Benson et al., 1995; Bumgarner and Sjoquist, 1998) stresses that the incentives and strategies to increase drug law enforcement actually result in more violence and criminal activity and bigger budgets for law enforcement. Of course, prohibitions are also a major cause of corruption (Benson, 1981; Benson, 1984; Benson and Baden, 1985; Thornton, 1991a).

Rasmussen and Benson (1994) provide a book-length examination of the war on drugs from a public choice and property rights perspective that explains why drug policies have produced results that are far different than policy makers and citizens expect. For example they show that increased drug law enforcement encourages crime by reducing the probability of arrest and that increased enforcement efforts knock drug dealers out of spatial equilibrium resulting in large increases in violence on the part of drug dealers in order to restore equilibrium. They also demonstrate that laws permitting the confiscation of drug dealer property create incentives for law enforcement that reduces the probability of apprehension for non-drug crimes and increases crime rates. In conclusion, they argue that the criminal justice system is a common property resource and drug laws only encourage the exploitation of this resource, resulting in a tragedy of the commons.

The public choice literature indicates that prohibition, once established is generally stable, or that it cycles between prohibition and "sin taxes" because prohibition is supported strongly by ideology, special interests, and bureaucracy. However, the public choice literature on the war on drugs has greatly supplemented the economic literature and further depicts prohibition as an unworkable, self-defeating, or ineffective policy and this knowledge could contribute to a counter-ideology to prohibitionism, which along with a victims-of-prohibition interest groups, might serve to undermine that stability (Thornton, 1995, 1998a).

MARK THORNTON

REFERENCES

Beil, R.O. and Thornton, M. (1998). "The economics of prohibition-related crime: contests with externalities." *Advances in Applied Microeconomics*, 7: 179–201.

Beil, R.O. and Thornton, M. (2000). "An economic theory of prohibition-related crime." *Perspectiva Econômica*, 35: 45–50.

Benson, B.L. (1981). "A note on corruption by public officials: the black market for property rights." *Journal of Libertarian Studies*, 5 (Summer): 305–311.

Benson, B.L. (1984). "Rent seeking from a property rights perspective." *Southern Economic Journal*, 51: 388–400.

Benson, B.L. and Baden, J. (1985). "The political economy of government corruption: the logic of underground government." *Journal of Legal Studies*, 14: 391–410.

Benson, B.L., Kim I., and Rasmussen, D.M. (1994). "Estimating deterrence effects: a public choice perspective on the economics of crime literature." *Southern Economic Journal*, 61: 161–166.

Benson, B.L., Kim I., Rasmussen, D.W., and Zuehlke, T.W. (1992). "Is property crime caused by drug use or drug enforcement policy?" *Applied Economics*, 24: 679–692.

Benson, B.L. and Rasmussen, D.W. (1991). "The relationship between illicit drug enforcement policy and property crimes." *Contemporary Policy Issues*, 9: 106–115.

Benson, B.L., Rasmussen, D.W., and Sollars, D.L. (1995). "Police bureaucracies, their incentives, and the war on drugs." *Public Choice*, 83: 21–45.

Boudreaux, D.J. and Pritchard, A.C. (1994). "The price of prohibition." *Arizona Law Review*, 36: 1–10.

Bumgarner, M. and Sjoquist, D.L. (1998). "The impact of crack enforcement on police budgets." *Journal of Drug Issues*, 28: 681–699.

Goff, B. and Anderson, G. (1994). "The political economy of prohibition in the United States, 1919–1933." *Social Science Quarterly*, 75: 270–283.

Miron, J.A. and Zwiebel, J. (1995). "The economics case against drug prohibition." *Journal of Economic Perspectives*, 9 (Fall): 175–192.

Munger, M. and Schaller, T. (1997). "The prohibition-repeal amendments: A natural experiment in interest group influence." *Public Choice*, 90 (1–4): 139–163.

Paul, C. and Wilhite, A. (1994). "Illegal markets and the social costs of rent-seeking." *Public Choice*, 79 (1–2): 105–115.

Rasmussen, D.W. and Benson, B.L. (1994). *The Economic Anatomy of a Drug War: Criminal Justice in the Commons*. Lanham, MD: Rowman and Littlefield.

Rasmussen, D.W., Benson, B.L., and Sollars, D.L. (1993). "Spatial competition in illicit drug markets: The consequences of increased drug enforcement." *Review of Regional Studies*, 23 (Winter): 219–236.

Sollars, D.L., Benson, B.L., and Rasmussen, D.W. (1994). "Drug enforcement and deterrence of property crime among local jurisdictions." *Public Finance Quarterly*, 22: 22–45.

Thornton, M. (1991a). *The Economics of Prohibition*. Salt Lake City, UT: University of Utah Press.

Thornton, M. (1991b). "Economists on illegal drugs." *Atlantic Economic Journal*, 19: 73.

Thornton, M. (1995). "The repeal of prohibitionism," in T.R. Machan and D.B. Rasmussen (eds.) *Liberty for the Twenty-First Century: Contemporary Libertarian Thought*. Lanham, MD: Rowman & Littlefield, pp. 187–204.

Thornton, M. (1996). "The fall and rise of puritanical policy in America." *Journal of Libertarian Studies*, 12 (Spring): 143–160.

Thornton, M. (1997). "Prohibition: the ultimate sin tax," in W.F. Shughart (ed.) *Taxing Choice: The Predatory Politics of Fiscal Discrimination*. New Brunswick, NJ: Transaction Publishers, pp. 171–198.

Thornton, M. (1998a). "The potency of illegal drugs." *Journal of Drug Issues*, 28 (Summer): 725–740.

Thornton, M. (1998b). "Perfect drug legalization," in J. Fish (ed.) *How to Legalize Drugs: Public Health, Social Science, and Civil Liberties Perspectives*. Northvale, NJ: Jason Aronson, Inc, pp. 638–660.

Thornton, M. and Weise, C.D. (2001). "The great depression tax revolts revisited." *Journal of Libertarian Studies*, 15 (Summer): 95–105.

Weise, C.D. (1998). "The Political Economy of Prohibition and Repeal: Ideology, Political Self-Interest, and Information Control." Masters Thesis. Auburn, AL: Auburn University.

PUBLIC CHOICE AND SOCIALISM

The idea of constructing a rational economic order through state control dominated 20th century public policy. The theory of socialism swept the intellectual world by grabbing the higher moral ground, and in the policy realm, socialism exerted its influence by creating political revolutions in Russia, China, and throughout the underdeveloped world. Less obvious, but no less important, was socialism's influence on the policies of non-socialist countries. The great "liberal" democracies all moved in the socialist direction in terms of public policy throughout the 20th century. The rise of the democratic welfare state in the UK and US and the explosion of the government's regulatory role in these economies are all manifestations of the socialist victory in the world of ideas.

The socialist experiment proved to be a failure. It proved not only an isolated failure, but also a global one — every political and economic system influenced by socialism suffered from a severe crisis in the last decades of the 20th century. The soft socialism of the democratic welfare states suffered from fiscal crises in the 1970s and 1980s and led to dramatic policy transformations in the UK (Thatcher), and US (Reagan). Other highly regulated and egalitarian societies followed the Thatcher/Reagan path in the 1980s and 1990s — New Zealand, Ireland, and even the Scandinavian welfare states had to adjust their fiscal houses. Of course, perhaps the most dramatic political-economic event of the 20th century was the collapse of real-existing socialist states throughout East and Central Europe in 1989 and the dissolution of the former Soviet Union in 1991 (the only other contender for most dramatic event this century is the Great Depression of the 1930s). A century that began with increasing demands for the regulation of business and economic planning by government to achieve more efficient production and a more egalitarian distribution of income, ended with a worldwide privatization revolution and a generalized recognition of the innovative benefits that accrue from entrepreneurship. The intellectual demand for state control of economic life was replaced by a "gains from trade" understanding of how the world works. Public choice theory played no small role in this dramatic shift in the intellectual climate of opinion. More pertinent for our purposes here, public choice theory provided the intellectual apparatus needed to pierce the Romantic veil of socialist ideology and lay bear the ugly reality of the political economy of socialism.

1. The Austrian Contribution

Before detailing the public choice contribution to our understanding of real-existing socialist economies, we will discuss the economic debate over socialism that took place in the 1930s and 1940s that set the stage for the development of public choice theory in the 1950s and 1960s. The Austrian economist Ludwig von Mises (1920, 1922, 1949) challenged advocates of socialism to provide an answer to the problem of rational economic calculation in the socialist society. Mises, building on the earlier work of Barone, Pareto and Wieser, pointed out that if socialism was to operate efficiently and rationalize the process of production as was claimed, it would have to replicate the marginalist principles that had been detailed in the neoclassical analysis of the market economy. In other words, there was a formal similarity in the efficiency propositions of capitalism and socialism. The crucial difference was that socialism promised to achieve efficiency through an alternative institutional regime. Mises asked the advocates of socialism to detail exactly how the institutions of collective ownership and centralized economic planning would replicate the functional roles played by private property, free pricing and profit and loss accounting within the coordination of economic activities (also see Hayek, 1948). Mises pointed out that no such argument could in fact be made. Without private ownership in the means of production, there would not be a market for the means of production. Without a market in the means of production, there would not be any exchange ratios established for the means of production. Without exchange ratios reflecting relative scarcities of the means of production, economic planners would not be able to rationally calculate alternative uses of scarce capital resources in production. This constituted Mises' famous argument that rational economic calculation under socialism is impossible.

It is important for our purposes, however, to point out that Mises' analysis of socialism raised at least four objections to the economic practicality of socialism: (1) private property rights and economic incentives; (2) prices as economizers of information within a complex system of exchange and production; (3) profit and loss accounting and the problem of economic calculation; and (4) politics and the problem of the abuse of power and tyranny (see Boettke, 2000a, 2001). Mises (and later Hayek, 1948) tended to emphasize the problems of economic calculation and knowledge precisely because during the debate over socialism questions of incentives and complexity were eliminated by hypothesis by their opponents. Lange, for example, argued that questions of incentives lie outside the bounds of economic discourse (Lange, 1936–37a and 1936–37b: 127). Such questions are best left to sociology, and to introduce them would violate the maxims of value-free economic analysis, at least that is what Lange and other pro-socialist

economists contended. Moreover, Lange also maintained that developments in computational technology would solve the complexity problems associated with the coordination of economic activities (Lange, 1969). So it makes sense that Mises and Hayek would emphasize the issues of calculation and dispersed knowledge in the debate with the market socialists. The calculation argument was the decisive intellectual argument because it could not be answered by assumption in the way that incentives and computational complexity could. The reason for this inability to assume away the problem was that the calculation argument was grounded in an *institutional context*. Outside of the institutional context of private property economic calculation was not just difficult; it could not take place. Of course, in the examination of real existing socialist economies, the problems of incentives and computational complexity were damaging enough from the point of view of successful economic coordination. Socialist economies were characterized by inefficient production, and pervasive shortages of poor quality consumer goods (see Boettke, 1993: 12–45).

A useful way to view the Austrian "calculation" argument is that it serves the same function within the analysis of socialism that Ronald Coase's argument that in a zero transaction cost world firms would not exist serves within the development of the theory of the firm. The Austrian argument served to establish what real-existing socialism could not be, and thus enabled scholars to look inside the "black-box" of Soviet-type economy (see Boettke, 1998). Unfortunately, much of the 1950s–1960s literature in comparative economic systems was diverted into two unproductive research paths — mathematical models of optimal planning, and macroeconomic econometric examinations of comparative economic growth rates. Both of these research programs, at best, added little to our understanding of Soviet-type economies, and at worst, significantly distorted that understanding (e.g., see Besancon, 1980). This distortion was most evident in the claims made by leading economists, such as Paul Samuelson, that Soviet planning techniques rationalized production, and that the Soviet economy would catch-up and outperform the market-oriented economies of the west in the near future.

On the other hand, the Austrian "impossibility" theorem, interpreted as we have suggested, sets the stage for a microeconomic analysis of how economic life within the politicized environment of the Soviet-type system actually operated. It strips the 'Romance' from socialist ideology and instead demands "realism" in political-economic analyses of socialism. As we have suggested by analogy to Coase's work on the firm, the Austrian argument opened the "black box" of real-existing socialism. And once opened, a public choice analysis allowed us to look inside and understand the incentive structures in operation internal to real-existing socialist economies.

2. From Romance to Realism in the Economic Analysis of Socialism

The Soviet system could not operate as the socialists of the late 19th and early 20th century had promised it would. It is important to remember the outlandish promises made on behalf of socialism. The socialists claimed that their system would out-perform capitalism by abolishing private property and rationalizing production. In substituting production for direct use for production for exchange by way of a settled economic plan, the socialist system would achieve unprecedented levels of material progress and do so in a manner that ensured harmonious social relations. The exploitation of man by other men would be abolished, and our state of alienation would be transcended. Mankind would move from the Kingdom of Necessity to the Kingdom of Freedom (see, Roberts, 1971; Boettke, 1990). Even the more informed arguments by economists, such as Lange, retained aspects of this earlier utopianism. Lange argued that while in theory socialism merely performed as well as capitalism, in reality it would outstrip capitalism's productive capacity and ensure an egalitarian distribution of income (Lange, 1936–37b: 127).

Such socialist promises for enhanced economic performance and greater social justice proved chimerical on all levels. First, socialism in practice could not abolish private property rights completely because real collective property is conceptually incoherent — someone must retain control rights (Barzel, 1989). The Soviet system had an attenuated private property rights system in which decision makers retained control rights, but not cash-flow rights (see Boyko, Shleifer, and Vishny, 1995: 33–38).

The Soviet industrial sector was characterized by the literal monopolization of production. However, these monopoly firms were inefficient and required continuous subsidization from the central government. This created the problem that economic enterprises confronted a "soft-budget" constraint (Kornai, 1986).

Furthermore, bureaucratization of economic production was pervasive. The original advocates of planning did not believe this would be a problem (e.g., Bukharin and Preobrazhensky, 1919). According to socialism's advocates, in abolishing private property socialism would overcome the division of labor. This being the case, individuals would be constantly shifting in and out of the different bureaus. The organizational reality of socialism, however, revealed just the opposite. In order to operate in a non-chaotic manner, a standing bureaucracy had to be formed. Thus, behavior in the Soviet bureaucracy, just as in its counter-part in the Western democracies, could be rendered intelligible through an economic analysis of bureaucratic incentives (Tullock, 1965).

Finally, the glue that held the Soviet economic system together was the "rents" to be had both internal and external to the plan. The Soviet economy was one of pervasive shortages where administrative prices were not allowed to adjust upwards to clear the market. The shortage situation created costs to buyers, (e.g., queuing), that were not simultaneously benefits to sellers. In such a situation, sellers have a strong incentive to transform these costs to buyers into benefits for themselves — either in monetary rewards or non-monetary compensation (e.g., the exercising of a preference). Building on Tullock's (1967) basic model, several scholars have attempted to depict the Soviet system as a rent-seeking society. David Levy (1990), for example, argued that the bias in Soviet pricing was to set prices below market clearing levels because this generated "rents" to those in control of the distribution of goods. Shleifer and Vishny (1992) developed a similar model to explain the pervasive shortages under socialism. Anderson and Boettke (1997) apply the "rent-seeking" model further to explain the entire mature Soviet industrial structure, and through an argument by analogy relate the Soviet system to earlier mercantilist domestic arrangements for fiscal issues. In the absence of a well-ordered tax system, both the monopolistic industrial structure and the elaborate mechanisms in place to ensure that structure are designed to raise state revenue via the means of monopoly privilege and venality.

3. Public Choice and Transition Strategy

James Buchanan has stressed that work in political economy, if we desire to retain some level of realism and relevance, must begin with the "here and now" and not just postulate whatever start-state of analysis might be desired to make the model tractable (see, e.g., Buchanan 1975: 78). Unfortunately, most models of socialist transition that have been developed fail to appreciate the *de facto* organizing principles that governed life in the Soviet-type system. Concentration has instead been focused on the *de jure* statements of what constituted the system.

The Soviet system was made up of a series of interlocking "contracts" and "vested interests," and any attempt to change the system must begin with this institutional inheritance. *If* the Soviet system was actually a land without any ownership claims, then post-communist reforms would be immeasurably simpler than they are — even given the cultural conditioning often invoked to explain the resistance to reform. But the social fact is that many limited — though tacitly legitimated — ownership claims had been established throughout the economic system. The implication of this fact for the transition is that what is required is the divesture of some interests, the legitimation of others, and the creation of conditions so that others can be determined in the new social arena of politics and law. As Boycko, Shleifer and Vishny (1995: 36) put it: "The structure of ownership under Soviet socialism was thus both different from the textbook model and highly inefficient. The politicians had almost all the control rights, and no cash flow rights either. The managers had some of the control rights, but no cash flow rights either. The objectives of the politicians who possessed the control rights were very far removed from the public interest. The virtually complete political control without countervailing cash flow rights to moderate political temptations did not constitute an inefficient ownership structure." Given the reality of this ownership structure, the reformer's primary goal is to depolitize economic life. Thus, Boycko, Shleifer and Vishny argue that "controlling managers is not nearly as important as controlling politicians, since managers' interests are generally much closer to economic efficiency than those of the politicians. Once depoliticization is accomplished, the secondary goal of establishing effective corporate governance can be addressed" (1995: 65).

The socialist regime did not abolish the market anymore than the prohibition on alcohol in the 1920s stamped out the buying and selling of liquor. We know from historical examination of the War Communism period (1918–1921) that even during the height of the campaign against all forms of capitalist relationships (and the threat of death) some individuals still found it advantageous to enter the "black market." Of course, in both the attempt to eliminate commodity production in the Soviet Union and the attempt at prohibition in the United States, the nature of the market was transformed by the *de jure* structure. But if we want to understand how the market actually operated, the *de facto* rules must be the focus of our attention (see, Hewett, 1988; Boettke, 1993).

At the time of the introduction of radical market reforms in Russia (January, 1992) there existed an array of ownership claims. The right of ownership constitutes a claim to (1) the right to use the asset, (2) the right to appropriate the returns from the asset, and (3) the right to change the asset's form and substance (see Furubotn and Pejovich, 1974). Institutions are the formal and informal rules governing the social intercourse under discussion. In this regard, when discussing the institution of ownership we are attempting to specify those formal and informal rules that govern the use, transfer and capitalization of an asset. In a world where formal rules are absent or defined in an incoherent manner, informal rules emerge to provide a governance structure within which economic decisions will be made. How effective or ineffective this system of governance will be is an empirical matter. Both formal and informal rules can imperfectly define rights and lead to social conflict. In pre-Yeltsin Russia, private property was not abolished despite the formal rules that said this was so. As Yoram Barzel put it: "The claim that private property has been abolished in communist states and that all property there belongs to the state seems to me to be an attempt to divert attention from who the true owners of the property are. It seems that these owners also own the rights to terminology" (1989: 104, fn. 8).

Markets are embedded within (and operate on the basis of) a governance structure, the formal component of which has in contemporary history been the domain of the Nation-State. But the Nation-State is itself embedded within a set of underlying cultural beliefs. Governance is required for the market to operate in a manner conducive to modern industrialization, but governance is also a function of market forces. Rules of the game engender patterns of exchange and production, and the emerging pattern of exchange and production aid in the selection between different regime rules. The political center is rarely, if ever, truly uninhibited — even in a totalitarian system. Pockets of civil society (perhaps *sub rosa*) emerge to challenge the legitimacy and power of the center. The center is inhibited, not only by formal rules of limited government, but also by the legitimating authority of civil society. Successful political and economic transformation, however, requires the development of transparent formal rules to subordinate the center to the rule of law. The key issue for this transformation is how to work through the indigenous institutions of informal inhibition to legitimate formal rules of subordination. The contrast is not really between the state and the market. It is between the state and civil society, within which market activity and non-market voluntary association co-exist. In an ironic twist, the public space required by civil society for political voice might only be possible when the private space of market competition is guaranteed. Looking at the issue this way leads to widely different implications for the manner in which privatization (and transition policy in general) should be pursued. Constraints on actions come not only from formal rules of governance, but from the informal rules rooted in "culture" as well. Hayek (and others) has stressed the tacit presumption that undergirds the formal adoption of law

(1973). In this sense, law is seen as a codification of rules of the social game that already attained a level of legitimacy through *de facto* observance, rather than as the creation of new rules. Attempts to impose rules unconnected to pre-existing social practices then are severely limited (see Boettke, 1996).

The path from "here to there" in former socialist countries then requires not only an idea of the "there" intended, but also the "here" from which one is starting, *before* an appropriate strategy for the path can be determined. With regard to the question under examination (i.e., the transfer of ownership) the steps required for the divesture of property from some owners, the legitimization of property held by others, and the establishment of conditions for the attainment, use, transformation, capitalization, and transfer of assets for new owners should be the focus of our attention. The appropriate policy path is necessarily multidimensional and grounded in the previous historical pattern of ownership. As David Stark (1996) has pointed out, postcommunist developments are following a path-dependent trajectory. Therefore, it is more appropriate to view post-communism as a process of transforming existing institutions, than it is to view post-communism as a transition to a new economic order lying outside of history.

4. Conclusion

Building upon the Austrian argument against the possibility of a rational socialist economy, public choice economics offers crucial insight into the actual workings of real-existing socialist societies. Demonstration of the perverted incentive structure necessarily confronted under central planning, and the disastrous effects such an incentive structure generates under real-existing socialism is a great credit to the theory of public choice. Furthermore, in bringing to bear much-needed emphasis on the true nature of real-existing socialist societies as societies characterized by *de facto* property rights operating against the distorting backdrop of *de jure* property prohibition, public choice offers an invaluable insight into the way successful post-communist reform in Eastern and Central Europe must be undertaken. Public choice sheds light on the fact that a realistic reform strategy must be predicated on a realistic model of political economy that recognizes that the transition from real-existing socialism to the market cannot be achieved costlessly. Entrenched bureaucrats in the central planning system face strong incentives to resist reform, and however illegitimately, these bureaucrats must be viewed as 'property holders' who need to be dealt with accordingly if real reform is to take place at all. Without the crucial analysis offered by public choice theory, both our understanding

of the true nature of real-existing socialism, the functioning of this system and appropriate method of dealing with the transition process would be seriously compromised.

PETER J. BOETTKE
PETER T. LEESON

REFERENCES

Anderson, Gary and Boettke, Peter (1997). "Soviet venality." *Public Choice*; reprinted in Boettke (2001), pp. 140–153.

Barzel, Yoram (1989). *Economic Analysis of Property Rights*. New York: Cambridge University Press.

Boettke, Peter (1990). *The Political Economy of Soviet Socialism: The Formative Years, 1918–1928*. Boston: Kluwer Academic Publishers.

Boettke, Peter (1993). *Why Perestroika Failed: The Politics and Economics of Socialist Transformation*. London: Routledge.

Boettke, Peter (1996). "Why culture matters." reprinted in Boettke (2001), pp. 248–265.

Boettke, Peter (1998). "Coase, communism and inside the "Black Box" of the soviet economy." Reprinted in Boettke (2001), pp. 66–76.

Boettke, Peter (ed.) (2000a). *Toward a History of the Theory of Socialist Planning*, Volume 1.

Boettke, Peter (ed.) (2000b). *Socialism and the Market: The Socialist Calculation Debate Revisited*. 9 volumes. London: Routledge.

Boettke, Peter (2001). *Calculation and Coordination: Essays on Socialism and Transitional Political Economy*. London: Routledge.

Boycko, Maxim, Shleifer, Andrei, and Vishny, Robert (1995). *Privatizing Russia*. Cambridge, MA: MIT Press.

Buchanan, James (1975). *The Limits of Liberty*. Chicago: University of Chicago Press.

Buchanan, James (1996). *Post-Socialist Political Economy*. Aldershot, UK: Edward Elgar Publishing.

Bukharin, N. and Preobrazhensky, E. (1919). *The ABC of Communism*. Ann Arbor, MI: University of Michigan Press, 1966.

Furubotn, E. and Pejovich, S. (1974). *The Economics of Property Rights*. Lexington, MA: Ballenger Publishing.

Gregory, P. (1990). *Restructuring the Soviet Economic Bureaucracy*. New York: Cambridge University Press.

Hayek, F.A. (ed.) (1935). *Collectivist Economic Planning*. London: Routledge.

Hayek, F.A. (1948). *Individualism and Economic Order*. Chicago: University of Chicago Press.

Hayek, F.A. (1973). *Law, Legislation and Liberty*, Volume 1. Chicago: University of Chicago Press.

Hewett, Ed (1988). *Reforming the Soviet Economy: Equality versus Efficiency*. Washington, DC: Brookings Institution.

Kornai, J. (1986). "The soft budget constraint." *Kyklos*, 39; reprinted in Boettke (ed.) (2000), Volume V, pp. 193–220.

Lange, O. (1936–37a). "On the economic theory of socialism: part one." *Review of Economic Studies*, 4; reprinted in Boettke (ed.) (2000), Volume IV.

Lange, O. (1936–37b). "On the economic theory of socialism: part two." *Review of Economic Studies*, 4; reprinted in Boettke (ed.) (2000), Volume IV.

Lange, O. (1969). "The computer and the market," reprinted in Boettke (ed.) (2000), Volume VIII.

Levy, D. (1990). "The bias in centrally planned prices," *Public Choice*; reprinted in Boettke (ed.) (2000), Volume IX, pp. 53–66.

Mises, L. (1922). *Socialism: An Economic and Sociological Analysis*. Indianapolis: Liberty Fund, 1981.

Mises, L. (1949). *Human Action: A Treatise on Economics*. New Haven, CT: Yale University Press.

Roberts, Paul Craig (1971). *Alienation and the Soviet Economy*. Albuquerque, NM: University of New Mexico Press.

Shleifer, A. and Vishny, Robert (1992). "Pervasive shortage under socialism." *Rand Journal of Economics* (Summer); reprinted in Boettke (ed.) (2000), Volume IX, pp. 67–76.

Stark, David (1996). "Recombinant property in East European capitalism." *American Journal of Sociology*, 101.

Tullock, G. (1965). *The Politics of Bureaucracy*. Washington, DC: Public Affairs Press.

Tullock, G. (1967). "The welfare costs of tariffs, monopolies and theft." *Western Economic Journal*, 5(June).

PUBLIC CHOICE AND THE CHICAGO SCHOOL OF ANTITRUST

Be true to your school. (The Beach Boys, 1963)

1. Economists and Antitrust: Background

Antitrust — meaning statutory prohibition of contracts and practices deemed anticompetitive — is essentially an American invention. English common law included jurisprudence concerning restraints of trade, and the civil law sometimes outlawed certain commercial practices. But until Congress passed the Sherman Act of 1890, there was no general legislation against contracts "in restraint of trade" or practices in pursuit of "monopolization," to use the language of the statute's operative sections. (Some American states had previously enacted their own antitrust laws.)

The statute did not define these terms, leaving courts to pour content into them. Leaving controversial and (as discussed below) politicized issues for judges to decide did not produce felicitous outcomes. Vertical contracts explicable only in terms of greater efficiency, mergers involving two firms in industries with thousands of competitors, or single-firm actions that explicitly increased output, nonetheless were condemned because the results (such as increased price competition) reduced the number or significance of rival firms. Especially once the second important antitrust statute (the Clayton Act of 1914) established private rights of action

for alleged antitrust violations, courts found it hard to separate firms' actions that anticompetitively reduce social welfare from socially-beneficial competition that just harms competitor-plaintiffs, who can use antitrust to raise rivals' costs in court. Economists studying antitrust's important cases have concluded that a majority were decided wrongly as a matter of welfare-maximizing economics (Rubin, 1995).

Many of the practices subject to antitrust scrutiny after 1890 were ones that economists had analyzed very little. Things like mergers (horizontal and vertical), tying, information sharing, and resale price maintenance were not matters of general familiarity, nor were their welfare implications well understood. As antitrust cases stimulated economists' interest in such contracts and practices, however, economists typically condemned practices they could not explain using models of perfect competition. All of that began to change with the rise of the Chicago school.

2. Chicago's Welfare Analysis of Antitrust

The fame of the Chicago school approach to antitrust rests on its normative, social-welfare analysis of practices theretofore subject to judges' and economists' condemnation. Chicago influence dates from the 1950s, the seminal work beginning with Aaron Director and the Antitrust Project at the University of Chicago Law School (Kitch, 1983). Chicagoans perceived the logical fallacy of condemning practices just because they are absent in the perfect competition model, which assumes away transaction costs, information costs, contractual opportunism and free-rider problems. In the real world, businessmen cannot assume away such things. The Chicago school explained how many practices condemned under antitrust actually are welfare-enhancing.

The contributions made along these lines by pioneers like Robert Bork, Yale Brozen, John McGee and Lester Telser have been summarized elsewhere (e.g., McChesney, 1993; Kitch, 1983). The impact of the Chicago school revolution in antitrust has been remarkable, both in the courts and in the academy. By the 1980s, it had become the dominant mode of antitrust analysis, acknowledged as the reigning paradigm even outside Chicago (e.g., Joskow, 1991).

3. Positive Analysis of Antitrust

Increasing realization that much of antitrust had been wrong-headed from the start, treating as competitively malign things that in fact are quite benign, prompts questions of a positive rather than normative sort. Why does antitrust exist at all? How does it function? Has it increased social welfare? Such questions were downplayed during the more normative debates over Chicago-school welfare analysis. But with the normative issues for the most part resolved in Chicago's favor, economists' focus has increasingly shifted to the positive issues.

Several points are useful in addressing the positive issues. First, antitrust is a political creature. In the United States, Congress created and sustains it, and political appointees enforce it. Second, antitrust is a form of economic regulation, punishing certain types of economic behavior while allowing others. Antitrust lends itself, therefore, to positive analysis under the general economic theory of regulation.

Under the economic theory of regulation, the stated goals of the particular regulatory regime are of little help in deciding whether that regime is economically beneficial. One must look at actual performance — the demonstrated costs and benefits of the regulation — to reach a defensible positive conclusion. But, finally, an analyst must be mindful that much regulation exists for political, not social-welfare, reasons.

So, a positive analysis of antitrust must begin with appraisal of its benefits and costs. In considering the benefits, however, one should realize that cartels and monopolies, the twin evils identified in antitrust law, are usually transient phenomena. Cartels set up a prisoner's dilemma wherein the dominant strategy for all participants is to defect, thus ending the collusion. (Courts themselves early recognized that price fixers soon start chiseling on price.) Monopoly, on the other hand, can only be sustained if there are barriers to entry into markets, and even potential entry restrains the prices a firm with market power can charge.

The benefits of laws against cartels and monopolies thus depend on the relative costs of legal intervention relative to natural dissolution of cartels and natural erosion of monopoly by new entry. Whether antitrust has benefits is an empirical question. There has been no systematic showing of any antitrust benefits. Quite the contrary. All existing evidence, notably the sophisticated statistical analyses performed by George Bittlingmayer, indicates that antitrust has imposed net costs on American economic performance. Antitrust enforcement (including the uncertainty caused by constantly shifting amounts and patterns of enforcement) decreases output (Bittlingmayer, 1996) and business investment (Bittlingmayer, 2001). With the suspension of antitrust enforcement under the National Industrial Recovery Act (NIRA) in the 1930s came increases in output (Bittlingmayer, 1995). These results, noteworthy in their own right, help explain Sproul's (1993) finding that in markets undergoing antitrust prosecution prices actually *rise* when cases are filed. The results are also corroborated by other work: antitrust case activity leads to increases in unemployment, for example (Shughart and Tollison, 1991).

The effects of antitrust enforcement on stock returns parallel antitrust's negative effects on real activity (output, investment and employment). Antitrust case filings are associated with large and significant declines in overall stock prices (Bittlingmayer, 1992; see also Bittlingmayer and Hazlett (2000) concerning the stock-return effects of the *Microsoft* case). Not surprisingly, then, with the suspension of antitrust altogether under the NIRA came an increase in stock prices as well as a jump in industry output (Bittlingmayer, 1995).

In short, no economic case has been made that antitrust has any net benefits. At the same time, antitrust clearly is costly. More important than the sheer administrative costs of operating many (two federal plus 50 state antitrust regimes), wrongfully decided cases deter efficient business practices. Questions necessarily arise: why were antitrust laws passed and, since they are on net more costly than beneficial, why do they survive?

4. Antitrust: The Public Choice Perspective

Deleterious economic regulation ordinarily owes its origin and survival to politics. Antitrust, researchers find, is no different. DiLorenzo (1990) shows empirically that there was no economic rationale for the Sherman Act. The trusts against which the Sherman Act supposedly was directed were expanding output many times faster than overall production was increasing nationally; their prices were falling faster than overall prices nationally. But the Sherman Act was a politically useful smokescreen, allowing the Republican Congress in an election year to pose as anti-business populists while passing the legislation of true political value to them, new tariffs. Several subsequent analyses provide additional evidence that trace the origins of antitrust to interest-group pressures (e.g., Libecap, 1992; see also McChesney, 1995: 331).

The origins of antitrust legislation other than the Sherman Act have likewise been traced to politics. The Clayton Act in 1914 was passed after a presidential campaign in which the perceived need for stronger antitrust laws was a principal plank of the Republican, Democratic and Bullmoose parties. Not surprisingly, then, the Act itself is explained by the politics of wealth transfers, including transfers to small firms engaged solely in intrastate commerce and so immune from the Clayton Act (Ekelund et al., 1995). State antitrust laws that preceded passage of the Sherman Act also passed for political, not economic reasons. Midwestern farm interests in particular found antitrust useful in combating more efficient, centralized meat processing firms in cities like Chicago (Boudreaux et al., 1995).

Subsequent enforcement of antitrust laws has likewise been a function of politicians' self-interest, including response to political pressure. Bittlingmayer (2001: 297) notes that, historically, "its [antitrust's] enforcement has often had a substantial political component," starting with Teddy Roosevelt's celebrated trust-busting. Elsewhere, he notes several more recent examples, including the Microsoft case (Bittlingmayer, 1996: 372–73; see also Bittlingmayer and Hazlett, 2000).

Statistical analyses of particular enforcement areas find that politics rather than economics explain antitrust activity. In theory, antitrust is a useful form of political rent extraction; and in fact, political influence helps explain why the government brings but then dismisses cases (Faith et al., 1982). Merger enforcement policy cannot be explained in efficiency terms; the statistical evidence indicates that efficient mergers are the ones challenged (Eckbo and Wier, 1985). But a model of political pressure to stop mergers can explain patterns of merger enforcement (Coate et al., 1990).

The foregoing leaves much of the public choice literature concerning antitrust unmentioned. The point, however, is to indicate that public choice scholars have produced a body of theoretically based and empirically validated work on antitrust which finds that politics explain the origins and survival of a regulatory system that overall has proven costly to social welfare.

5. Chicago Positive Opinions on Antitrust

If antitrust is just economic regulation, a political system with no discernible net benefits, one would think that Chicago — one of the earliest hubs of economists working within the economic theory of regulation — would view antitrust with at least suspicion. Instead, Chicagoans have viewed antitrust with respect, even enthusiasm. The first notable "Chicago school" scholar of antitrust, Henry Simons, in the 1930s saw monopoly as the source of the Depression, which he feared would destroy American democracy. Vigorous antitrust enforcement was the solution, Simons wrote. "The Federal Trade Commission must become perhaps the most powerful of our government agencies" (1948 reprint: 58).

Subsequent Chicago analysts of antitrust, while perhaps not as exuberant as Simons, still have had nothing but praise for it. George Stigler, the best known Chicago scholar of industrial organization during his time, was a member of the National Committee to Study the Antitrust Laws, which in 1955 issued a report advocating aggressive enforcement of the law. Earlier, he had called for "dissolution of a few score of our giant companies." Thirty

years later, he still believed that antitrust was "a sort of public-interest law" (Hazlett, 1984: 46).

One could add any number of other Chicagoans to the list of antitrust fans. Ignoring any costs of antitrust, Posner writes (2001a: 2) that the value of efficiency "establishes a prima facie case of having an antitrust policy." Robert Bork, part of the original Antitrust Project at Chicago, likewise claims that efficiency explains the Sherman Act (1978). That claims rests on his reading of the statute's legislative history, that is, what politicians said as they legislated.

It is difficult to imagine a mode of analysis further from public choice than evaluating government policy in terms of putative benefits (without costs), or in terms of what politicians say about those claimed benefits. Indeed, that perspective would be anathema in Chicago itself, were the subject not antitrust. Stigler himself (1975: 140) wrote, "The announced goals of a policy are sometimes unrelated or perversely related to its actual effects, and the *truly intended effects should be deduced from the actual effects.*"

Antitrust causes Chicagoans to transgress their general mode of positive economic analysis (summarized, e.g., in Reder (1982)) in other ways. For instance, there is the general Chicago stance (Reder, 1982: 31) that "objectives that cannot be achieved except through the state are to be scrutinized carefully and sceptically. ... [Chicago takes] a generally adverse view of government intervention. Any reformer must either refute it or minimize its importance." The burden therefore is on those who think a particular government regulation or policy works to demonstrate that fact.

But not when it comes to antitrust. How to deal with all the evidence (some of it mentioned above) concerning antitrust's net costs? Posner (2001a: 2) dismisses the bad case law as dated, though little of it has been overruled, and ignores the statistical showings of antitrust's other costs. How, next, to deal with the public-choice explanations for antitrust's birth and growth — much of it appearing in journals published by the University of Chicago? Posner (2001b: 942, citations omitted) again dismisses the evidence without explanation: "There is a history of efforts to explain antitrust enforcement as just another example of interest-group politics, an approach that has worked for a number of government agencies and programs. But the efforts have not been successful." How then does Posner explain antitrust? "Looking over the entire history of U.S. antitrust law, I conclude that the most powerful explanatory variable is simply the state of economic opinion" (Id.). Antitrust regulation is due to some economic *Zeitgeist*, not the ordinary political reasons that explain most other forms of economic regulation.

One exception to the general approval of antitrust in Chicago should be noted. Coase (1988) complained that antitrust, nominally a subset of industrial organization, had in fact swallowed up the entire subject. Economists' fascination with 'the monopoly problem,' as he called it, had distracted their attention from the true object of industrial organization, the behavior of firms. In addition, Coase continued, economists too quickly ascribe unfamiliar business practices to monopoly power. Coase may well be right in both respects, but his points have nothing to do with public choice, an area about which he has shown only scepticism (Coase, 1994: 42–46). The questions noted above remain: why was antitrust created and why has it survived?

One other Chicagoan belatedly reached the same stage in evaluating antitrust. Shortly before his death, Stigler (1993: 401) recanted his previous approbation of antitrust: "at the risk of being called fickle, many economists (I among them) have lost ... our enthusiasm for antitrust ... The declining support for antitrust policy has been due to the often objectionable uses to which that policy has been put." Like Coase, though, Stigler suggested no reasons to explain antitrust's century of "objectionable uses," nor any for its survival (indeed, robust growth) during that time. His disavowal therefore stopped well short of embracing the alternative public-interest model of antitrust.

In Hyde Park, Stigler's recantation is perhaps viewed as apostasy. No other Chicagoan has come forward to join the growing group of economists noted by Stigler who have lost their antitrust enthusiasm, much less to join the growing public-choice group that has begun to answer the questions that Chicago does not ask.

FRED S. McCHESNEY

REFERENCES

Bittlingmayer, George (1992). "Stock returns, real activity and the trust question." *Journal of Finance*, 47(December): 1701–1730.

Bittlingmayer, George (1995). "Output and stock prices when antitrust is suspended: the effects of the NIRA," in Fred S. McChesney and William F. Shughart II (eds.) *The Causes and Consequences of Antitrust: The Public Choice Perspective*. Chicago: University of Chicago Press, pp. 287–318.

Bittlingmayer, George (1996). "Antitrust and business activity: the first quarter century." *Business History Review*, 70(Autumn): 363–401.

Bittlingmayer, George (2001). "Regulatory uncertainty and investment: evidence from antitrust enforcement." *Cato Journal*, 20(Winter): 295–325.

Bittlingmayer, George and Thomas W. Hazlett (2000). "DOS Kapital: has antitrust action against Microsoft created value in the computer industry?" *Journal of Financial Economics*, 55: 329–359.

Bork, Robert (1978). *The Antitrust Paradox*. Boston: Little Brown.

Boudreaux, D.J., DiLorenzo, T.J., and Parker, S. (1995). "Antitrust before the Sherman Act," in Fred S. McChesney and William F. Shughart II (eds.) *The Causes and Consequences of Antitrust: The Public Choice Perspective*. Chicago: University of Chicago Press, pp. 255–270.

Coase, R.H. (1988). "Industrial organization: a proposal for research," in Victor R. Fuchs (ed.) *Policy Issues and Research Opportunities in Industrial Organization*, Vol. 3 of *Economic Research: Retrospective and Prospect*, Cambridge: National Bureau of Economic Research, pp. 59–73 (originally published in 1972).

Coase, R.H. (1994). "Economics and contiguous disciplines," in R.H. Coase (ed.) *Essays on Economics and Economists*. Chicago: University of Chicago Press.

Coate, Malcolm B., Higgins, Richard S., and McChesney, Fred S. (1990). "Bureaucracy and politics in FTC merger challenges." *Journal of Law and Economics*, 33(October): 463–482.

DiLorenzo, T.J. (1990). "The origins of antitrust." *Regulation*, 13: 26–34.

Eckbo, B. Espen and Wier, Peggy (1985). "Antimerger policy under the Hart-Scott-Rodino Act: a reexamination of the market-power hypothesis." *Journal of Law and Economics*, 28(April): 119–149.

Ekelund, Robert B., McDonald, Michael J., and Tollison, Robert D. (1995). "Business restraints and the Clayton Act of 1914: public- or private-interest legislation?" in Fred S. McChesney and William F. Shughart II (eds.) *The Causes and Consequences of Antitrust: The Public Choice Perspective*. Chicago: University of Chicago Press, pp. 271–286.

Faith, Roger L., Leavens, Donald R., and Tollison, Robert D. (1982). "Antitrust pork barrel." *Journal of Law and Economics*, 25(October): 329–342.

Hazlett, Thomas W. (1984). "Interview with George Stigler." *Reason* (January): 44–48.

Joskow, P.L. (1991). "The role of transaction cost economics in antitrust and public utility regulatory policies." *Journal of Law, Economics and Organization*, 7: 53–83.

Kitch, E.W. (ed.) (1983). "The fire of truth: a remembrance of law and economics at Chicago, 1932–1970." *Journal of Law and Economics*, 26(April): 163–234.

Libecap, Gary D. (1992). "The rise of the Chicago packers and the origins of meat inspection and antitrust." *Economic Inquiry*, 30: 242–262.

McChesney, F.S. (1993). "Antitrust," in David R. Henderson (ed.) *The Fortune Encyclopedia of Economics*. New York: Warner Books, pp. 385–390.

McChesney, F.S. (1995). "Be true to your school: Chicago's contradictory views of antitrust and regulation," in Fred S. McChesney and William F. Shughart II (eds.) *The Causes and Consequences of Antitrust: The Public Choice Perspective*. Chicago: University of Chicago Press.

Posner, Richard A. (2001a). *Antitrust Law*, Second Edition. Chicago: University of Chicago Press.

Posner, Richard A. (2001b). "Antitrust in the new economy." *Antitrust Law Journal*, 68: 925–943.

Reder, Melvin W. (1982). "Chicago economics: permanence and change." *Journal of Economic Literature*, 20: 1–38.

Rubin, P.H. (1995). "What do economists think about antitrust? A random walk down Pennsylvania Avenue," in Fred S. McChesney and William F. Shughart II (eds.) *The Causes and Consequences of Antitrust: The Public Choice Perspective.* Chicago: University of Chicago Press, pp. 33–62.

Shughart, William F. II and Tollison, Robert D. (1991). "The employment consequences of the Sherman and Clayton Acts." *Journal of Institutional and Theoretical Economics*, 147(March): 38–52.

Simons, Henry C. (1948). "A positive program for laissez faire: some proposals for a liberal economic policy." Reprinted in *Economic Policy for a Free Society.* Chicago: University of Chicago Press.

Sproul, Michael F. (1993). "Antitrust and prices." *Journal of Political Economy*, 101: 741–754.

Stigler, George J. (1975). "Supplementary note on economic theories of regulation," in G.J. Stigler (ed.), *The Citizen and the State.* Chicago: University of Chicago Press.

Stigler, George J. (1993). "Monopoly." in David R. Henderson (ed.), *The Fortune Encyclopedia of Economics.* New York: Warner Books, pp. 399–403.

PUBLIC CHOICE IN ITALY

Italian scholars are at the forefront of research in public choice if we accept the view that the strand of literature generally termed "political economics" (Persson and Tabellini, 2001) is germane in methodology and subject matters to traditional public choice. Outstanding researchers in this fields are Italians, Guido Tabellini, Alberto Alesina, Roberto Perotti to name a few, publish regularly in first class journals, such as AER JPE, QJE, *Econometrica* and are enrolled in Economics departments of top American Universities.

But even if we prefer to keep political economics and public choice as two separate strands of literature, there are more Italian researchers active in this field and, consequently, the country's contribution to the progress of public choice is more significant today than at the times when Buchanan won the Nobel prize. A few facts support such claim. During the entire decade of the 1980s, only two articles by an Italian scholar was published in the journal *Public Choice* (Fratianni and Spinelli, 1982; Forte, 1987); during only the year 2001 no less than 8 Italians published in the same journal and 3 in *Constitutional Political Economy*. Between 1990 and 2002 three meetings of the European Public Choice Society have been organized by Italian Universities (Torino, Siena and Piemonte Orientale) while only one in the 1980s (Reggio Calabria, 1986). Quantity wise, since 1995 Italian scholars are steadily the more numerous national group within the EPCS; quality wise, in 2002 an Italian won (*ex aequo*) the Wicksell Prize for the best paper by a scholar under 30 years of age presented to the EPCS meeting.

However, similar remarks might have been stated about public choice in other countries. What makes Italy special for public choice?

The answer requires a bit of history of public choice ideas. Italian scholars of public finance of the XIXth century, such as De Viti de Marco, Mazzola, Puviani, Pantaleoni, have been precursors and a source of inspiration for the development of the public choice paradigm (da Empoli, 1993; Buchanan, 1960). In 1861, Italy was created as a state from the unification of several smaller states, most of them with a long history of bad government (Mack Smith, 1996). Some of the unwelcome legacies of the pre-unitary states for the new kingdom were a very high public debt, budget unbalances and unequal levels of development across regions. The link between types of government and fiscal and economic outcomes was clear under the eyes of the Italian public finance scholars and became an underlying theme of their research. By and large they published in Italian, and knowledge of their contributions was mostly confined to Italians and to scholars such as Buchanan who learned the language of Dante. Da Empoli (1993) points out that many of Buchanan's contributions to public choice and public finance have been inspired by the Italian school. If Buchanan derived from Wicksell the emphasis on decision-making rules, he absorbed from the Italians the ideas of contractarianism and of government failure.

However, this school did not last long as the cultural background of the Italian economic profession. The onset of the Keynesian revolution, the influence within the country of economists such as Franco Modigliani and Paolo Sylos Labini in favor of state manipulation of the economy, the economic prosperity of the postwar years persuaded the Italian economists of the desirability of an increasingly active role of the state into the economy. From the 1960s to the early 1980s the Italian climate was not favorable for public choice. Few scholars, like Domenico da Empoli, Emilio Giardina and Francesco Forte, were pursuing a public choice research agenda then.

Until the late 1970s, these scholars, as well as some others affiliated to them, tried to diffuse the new paradigm into the country's economic culture mainly by translating works of Buchanan, Tullock and Olson[1] and by trying to re-tie the knot between modern public choice and the Italian school of public finance. The goal was twofold. First, pointing out the relevance of these theories to explain structural problems of the Italian economy, the rising public debt to name one, and institutional setup. Second to show that public choice had deep roots into our cultural heritage. These efforts were, however, insufficient to displace the country's prevailing the-state-should-intervene attitude. What lacked was a robust and wide-ranging research program that applied public choice theories to Italian cases.

In the early 1980, four events created the preconditions for such a program to emerge. First, in 1983 Da Empoli published the journal *Economia delle Scelte Pubbliche — Journal of Public Choice and Public Finance*. The journal aimed to establish a connection between researches in public choice conducted on the American and European side of the Atlantic (as well as on the Italian shores of the Mediterranean). To this end the journal was published increasingly in English; most of all, in several issues, articles by very well known economists (Buchanan, Tullock, Stigler, Duncan Black, Lejonhufvud, Allais among others) were side by side with articles by (much) lesser known scholars (such as myself). The Editor's strategy was to attract Italian scholars to the field of public choice, as well as trying to raise new researchers. Secondly, in 1986 Giorgio Brosio published *Economia e Finanza Pubblica*, the first Italian textbook of public finance that paid considerable attention to public choice. The innovation of the book was not to treat public choice theories as a topic *per se*, but as perspective from which to explain public finance topics. The (still) wide circulation of this textbook within Italian universities contributed to the diffusion of public choice ideas among undergraduate students. Third, in the 1980s some Italian professors began to send their graduate students to American Universities specialized in public choice. George Mason University, the University of Maryland as well as other larger though less specialized Departments received a string of Italian students. This is also the period when people like Tabellini, Alesina, and Perotti studied in American Universities that subsequently hired them. A new generation of Italian scholars was created that not only received a systematic training in the field, but also learned to do research from people who regularly published in high level scientific journals.

To an extent all these events were endogenous results of the deterioration of Italy's economic and political situation in the 1970s to the 1980s. The worsening situation of the public finances, the spreading of corruption within the political elite and the public sector, ultimately due to the lack of alternation in government, pointed out, within the economic profession, that Keynesian macroeconomics lacked explanations and solutions that public choice instead could offer. Although, as Keynes himself pointed out, ideas change with generations, and still the majority of

Italian economists (and people) tend to see the government as the solution, rather than the problem, from the early 1990s on the Italian climate became more pleasant for the public choice paradigm.

Today, several academic groups pursue a public choice research agenda, often publish in international journals, develop theories inspired by Italian experiences and apply public choice models to Italian cases. A first group (in a strict geographical order from North to South) holds its intellectual center in Turin; among the various topics, this group is active in the study of political business cycle, fiscal federalism and comparative economic systems. Rome has three research groups. One, centered around Political Sciences at La Sapienza (da Empoli) and the Center for Economics of Institutions at Roma Tre, studies the relation between political institutions and economic performance in terms of output growth, budget outcomes and tax structure at the national and local level; the public choice of international organizations; and, as a new research agenda, how the internal structure of government affects legislative production. The branch of this group at La Sapienza publishes the *Journal of Public Choice and Public Finance*. A second research group is located at the Law School of La Sapienza, studies checks and balances and law and economics. Within this group Gianluigi Galeotti is, with Albert Breton and Pierre Salmon, one of the founders of the *Villa Colombella Group*, which promotes a series of international research seminaries. The Department of Economics of La Sapienza is the base of the newly founded *European Center for the Study of Public Choice*, which invites international scholars and pursues a research agenda chiefly interested in constitutional political economy. Other members of the Department work on government coalitions and bureaucracy. Sicily has no less than three groups: the University of Messina focuses on electoral rules and outcomes, both at the local and at the national levels; the University of Palermo is active in social choice; the University of Catania studies rent seeking, devolution of government powers and public expenditures in support of the arts.

Two further research groups deserve attention. A first is in Milan, between the IGIER (at the Bocconi University) and the Cattolica University. Led by Guido Tabellini, this group is one of the most important and active springs of research in political economics. Several of their working papers, after having been published in top journals and widely circulated collected works, are cited very often. Another, more recent group is composed by young Italian scholars who work abroad and share the London School of Economics as their *Alma Mater*. This group is composed by political economists, political scientists, public choice scholars and cover fields such as interest groups, economics of corruption, media, information and politics, as well as others.

Italy's economic and political situation tends to mold the research culture in favor of applied work over basic theorizing. Hence the evolution of public choice research within the country and the attention to such ideas appears related to the economic and political situation of the country. The worse the economic situation, especially in the area of the public finances, and the more significant the evolution of the institutional framework, the greater was the interest in public choice. It is no accident that the peaks were in the XIXth century, after the unification of the state, and today, after the crisis of the so-called First Republic, the federalist reorganization of the state and the acceleration of the process of European integration. With respect to the scholars of the XIXth century, however, the diffusion of contemporaneous Italian works in public choice is no longer limited by the language; the future of public choice research in Italy will be more closely correlated with the paradigm's fortune worldwide. Similarly, public choice research in general, which so far has suffered of excessive Americanism, will take advantage of the contribution of a country that has proved to be inspiring as well as, unfortunately, a particularly interesting case study.

FABIO PADOVANO

NOTES

1. Da Empoli translated *The Limits of Liberty, Liberty Market and State, Democracy and Deficit*; Martelli translated the *Calculus of Consent*; Eusepi translated *Cost and Choice*; Villani the *Reason of Rules*; the Italian version of *The Logic of Collective Action* was published in 1982. Carrubba and Da Empoli (1975) and Forte and Mossetto (1973) published translations of selected articles by well-known public choice scholars.

REFERENCES

Buchanan, J.M. (1960). "'La scienza delle finanze': the Italian tradition in fiscal theory," in J.M. Buchanan (ed.), *Fiscal Theory & Political Economy: Selected Essays*. Chapel Hill: The University of North Carolina Press, pp. 24–74.

Carruba, S. and Da Empoli, D. (eds.) (1975). *Scelte Pubbliche*. Firenze: Le Monnier.

Da Empoli, D. (1993). "Public Choice in Italy." *Public Choice*, 77(1): 75–84.

Forte, F. (1987). "The Laffer Curve and the theory of fiscal bureaucracy." *Public Choice*, 52: 101–124.

Forte, F. and Mossetto, G. (eds.) (1973). *Economia del Benessere e Democrazia*. Milano: Franco Angeli.

Fratianni, M. and Spinelli, F. (1982). "The growth of government in Italy: evidence from 1861 to 1979." *Public Choice*, 39: 221–243.

Mack Smith, D. (2000). *Storia d'Italia dal 1861 al 1997*. Bari: Laterza.

Persson, T. and Tabellini, G. (2001). *Political Economics*. Cambridge: MIT Press.

PUBLIC ENTERPRISE

A public or political enterprise is a government-owned business firm. To understand the nature of these firms, it is useful to examine why they exist and how they behave.

Hypotheses why *private* firms exist hinge on transaction costs, the firm being a nexus of contracts formed to solve the shirking-information problem of joint production (Coase, 1937, 1988; Alchian and Demsetz, 1972; Williamson, 1975, 2000; Grossman and Hart, 1986; Furubotn and Richter, 1997; Holmstrom, 1999; Demsetz, 2002). Hypotheses why *public* firms exist span a broader spectrum, including a taste for government ownership, patronage, failure to understand how markets work, and limitations of the market system, whether inherent or imposed (Pashigian, 1976; De Alessi 1982, 2001; Eggertsson, 1990; Levy and Spiller, 1994; Troesken, 1997). These hypotheses, which are not mutually exclusive, are examined next.

Public enterprises may arise if individuals have a taste for them, that is, are willing to give up other commodities in order to have more of them. Individuals, however, presumably choose one kind of firm over another because they believe that the consequences benefit them. The evidence bears this out; taste is not a significant explanatory variable (Pashigian, 1976).

Public enterprises may arise to facilitate patronage. Individuals with a comparative advantage in the exercise of political power have incentive to use the state to benefit themselves and groups they favor; concurrently, politicians have incentive to provide such benefits to gain political support (McChesney, 1997). Accordingly, public enterprise may be established to mask or ease wealth transfers. For example, exempting state enterprises from property and other taxes lowers their production outlays, encouraging their existence and benefiting their clients at the expense of taxpayers. A related hypothesis is behavior modification. Thus, individuals can be encouraged to behave in certain ways by having public enterprises produce and sell appropriate commodities at subsidized prices.

Public enterprises may arise because individuals misunderstand how markets work. For example, a sharp increase in price caused by a sharp increase in demand or decrease in supply provides information and incentive for producers to increase output or consumers to reduce consumption. Such events, however, offer special interest groups an opportunity to argue that the market has failed and seek patronage through production by public firms.

Public enterprises may arise from limitations of the market, whether inherent or imposed. If the costs of establishing, enforcing, and exchanging private property rights are too high or the market is too small, private firms may not arise, thereby offering scope for public firms. Such conditions may exist in an open market or may result from government actions that make private property rights insecure and otherwise increase transaction costs.

Public enterprises, like private enterprises, may also arise to solve the shirking-information problem of team production. The higher are the costs of monitoring whether a commodity meets the specifications provided in a procurement contract, the greater is the opportunity for all parties to shirk, reducing the gains from specialization (contracting out) and encouraging vertical integration. This incentive is particularly acute in government when terms such as "for the public good" and "in the public interest" appear. These terms are not specific enough to define the rights and duties of the parties involved, expanding the opportunity to shirk.

Other explanations, such as the desire to provide a check on the performance of private enterprises, are variants of the hypotheses already discussed or mere rhetorical noise. The actual or fancied reasons for the existence of public enterprises, however, affect behavior only to the degree that they are reflected in binding constraints on the enterprises' decision makers. To predict a firm's behavior, it is necessary to focus on the cost-reward structures embedded in its organizational form and examine their economic consequences.

A distinguishing characteristic of public enterprises is that ownership shares in their specialized assets are not transferable. Taxpayers who wish to change their portfolio of shares in public enterprises must change the political jurisdictions in which they work and live or the way in which the political enterprises operate. This lack of transferability implies that individuals cannot specialize in the ownership of public enterprises and risk bearing and that the future consequences of managers' decisions are not reflected (capitalized) in the shares' current transfer prices. The results include a loss of information on economic performance and a reduced incentive by owners to monitor managers.

Thus, managers of political enterprises may be expected to have weaker constraints on their choices than managers of comparable private enterprises. The latter are subject to the discipline of the market and must respond to market signals if their firms are to survive. Managers of public firms, on the other hand, are less constrained by market considerations, finding it easier to obtain subsidies and mask discretionary behavior under the guise of fulfilling various social goals. Public enterprises, especially those with politically influential clients, can survive for long periods, and their managers prosper, in the presence of persistent losses and mismanagement.

Managers of political enterprises have greater opportunity for discretionary behavior than managers of comparable private firms. In particular, they have more opportunity to increase the resources (e.g., staff and assets) under their supervision and to allocate these resources in ways designed to enhance their own welfare. Their salaries and other contractual pecuniary rewards, however, often are subject to ceilings, whereas those paid to managers of private enterprises are not. This difference implies that managers of public firms have greater incentive to allocate resources to enhance their job security, thereby increasing the present value of all future job-related benefits. Such benefits, however, cannot be capitalized and human life is finite. Moreover, it is costlier for owners to monitor the acquisition of non pecuniary than pecuniary benefits. Thus, the cost of non pecuniary benefits is lower and managers of political enterprises acquire more of them.

The analysis implies that managers of public enterprises are more likely to adopt policies that enhance their position, ease their work load, and generally make their jobs more rewarding as they see it. For example, they are more likely to choose pricing policies that are easier to administer. This strategy includes changing output prices less frequently, tailoring them less closely to existing demand and supply conditions, favoring influential special interest groups, and giving subordinates across-the-board wage increases. Similarly, they are more likely to hire subordinates with characteristics they prefer, discriminating on the basis of race, sex, education, and congeniality, and giving such subordinates benefits designed to reduce friction. They also have incentive to reduce risk and enhance their survival by engaging in anti competitive behavior, including predatory activities. In general, public enterprises may be expected to be less responsive to consumer wants, less efficient by market standards, and more aggressive in inhibiting competition.

These implications are supported by the evidence (De Alessi, 1982; Borcherding et al., 1982; Millward and

Parker, 1983; Boardman and Vining, 1989), including evidence from the current world-wide privatization movement (Villalonga, 2000). Compared to regulated private firms, for example, municipal electric utilities generally charge lower prices, apply fewer peak-related tariffs, favor business relative to residential users and voters to non voters, change prices less frequently and in response to larger changes in economic determinants, relate prices less closely to the costs of serving particular user groups, sell wholesale electric power at lower prices and buy it at higher prices, spend more on plant construction, have greater capacity and higher operating costs, adopt cost-reducing innovations less readily, offer a smaller variety of output, maintain managers in office longer, and exhibit greater variation in rates of return.

Evidence from other industries provides additional support for these and other implications. Relative to regulated private enterprises, municipal water utilities have lower tariffs with fewer service categories and fewer blocks within each category, have rate structures that favor more politically active groups, use more capital-intensive production techniques, and are less efficient by market standards. Relative to both regulated and unregulated private enterprises, public enterprises are less successful in satisfying consumer wants for urban transit, are less efficient by market standards in providing bank and airline service, and incur higher costs in providing fire prevention and refuse collection services. Evidence from the U.S. hospital industry suggests that public enterprises have more binding and explicit internal monitoring rules, make less use of market information, are more likely to give across-the-board rather than selective wage increases, are less likely to use cost-minimizing input combinations, are more likely to respond to an increase in occupancy by increasing the proportion of administrative personnel at the expense of medical and other services, are less efficient by market standards, and emphasize the production of those services more easily monitored by trustees and legislators.

Managers of public enterprises are also more likely than managers of comparable private firms to engage in anti competitive behavior (Lott, 1999; Sappington and Sidak, 1999). That is, they are more likely to seek to raise competitors' costs, block entry of prospective competitors, evade regulations intended to encourage competition, and sell below cost to drive competitors out of business.

In summary, theory and evidence indicate that, relative to private enterprises, public enterprises are less responsive to consumer wants, less efficient by market standards, and more likely to engage in discretionary and anti competitive behavior.

LOUIS DE ALESSI

REFERENCES

Alchian, A.A. and Demsetz, H. (1972). "Production, information costs, and economic organization." *American Economic Review*, 62(5): 777–795.

Boardman, A.E. and Vining, A.R. (1989). "Ownership and performance in competitive environments: A comparison of the performance of private, mixed, and state-owned enterprises." *Journal of Law and Economics*, 32(1): 1–34.

Borcherding, T., Pommerehne, W.W., and Schneider, F. (1982). "Comparing the efficiency of private and public production: The evidence from five countries." *Zeitschrift fur Nationalokonomie*, Suppl. 2: 127–156.

Coase, R. (1937). "The nature of the firm." *Economica*, 4(6): 386–405.

Coase, R. (1988). *The Firm, the Market, and the Law*. Chicago: University of Chicago Press.

De Alessi, L. (1982). "On the nature and consequences of private and public enterprise." *Minnesota Law Review*, 67(1): 191–209.

De Alessi, L. (2001). "Property rights: private and political institutions," in W.F. Shughart II and L. Razzolini (eds.) *The Elgar Companion to Public Choice*. Cheltenham: Edward Elgar, pp. 33–58.

Demsetz, H. (2002). "Property rights and the firm," in T.L. Anderson and F.S. McChesney (eds.) *Property Rights: Contract, Conflict, and Law*. Princeton: Princeton University Press.

Eggertsson, T. (1990). *Economic Behavior and Institutions*. Cambridge: Cambridge University Press.

Furubotn, E.G. and Richter, R. (1997). *Institutions and Economic Theory: The Contribution of the New Institutional Economics*. Ann Arbor: University of Michigan Press.

Grossman, S.J. and Hart, O.D. (1986). "The costs and benefits of ownership: A theory of lateral and vertical integration." *Journal of Political Economy*, 94(4): 691–719.

Holmstrom, B. (1999). "The firm as a subeconomy." *Journal of Law, Economics, and Organization*, 15(1): 74–102.

Levy, B. and Spiller, T. (1994). "The institutional foundations of regulatory commitment: A comparative analysis of telecommunications regulation." *Journal of Law, Economics, and Organization*, 10(2): 201–246.

Lott, J.R. Jr. (1999). *Are Predatory Commitments Credible? Who Should the Courts Believe?* Chicago: University of Chicago Press.

McChesney, F.S. (1997). *Money for Nothing: Politicians, Rent Extraction, and Political Extortion*. Cambridge: Harvard University Press.

Millward, R. and Parker, D.M. (1983). "Public and private enterprise: comparative behaviour and relative efficiency," in R. Millward, D.M. Parker, L. Rosenthal, M.T. Summer, and N. Topman (eds.) *Public Sector Economics*. New York: Longman, pp. 199–274.

Pashigian, B.P. (1976). "Consequences and causes of public ownership of urban transit facilities." *Journal of Political Economy*, 84(6): 1239–1259.

Sappington, E.M and Sidak, J.G. (1999). "Incentives for anticompetitive behavior by public enterprises," Working Paper 99-11. Washington, DC: AEI-Brookings Joint Center for Regulatory Studies.

Troesken, W. (1997). "The source of public ownership: historical evidence from the gas industry." *Journal of Law, Economics, and Organization*, 13(1): 1–25.

Villalonga, B. (2000). "Privatization and efficiency: Differentiating ownership effects from political, organizational, and dynamic effects." *Journal of Economic Behavior and Organization*, 42(1): 43–74.

Williamson, O.E. (1975). "*Markets and Hierarchies: Analysis and Antitrust Implications*." New York: Free Press.

Williamson, O.E. (2000). "The new institutional economics: Taking stock, looking ahead." *Journal of Economic Literature*, 38(3): 595–613.

PUBLIC FINANCE AND THE MEDIAN VOTER MODEL

The median voter model is a model of demand aggregation under majority rule. Economists find the market demand for private goods by horizontally summing the demand curves of all individuals in that market; similarly, when individual demands are aggregated through majority rule voting, the demand of the entire group is the demand of the median voter. The idea can be traced back at least to Hotelling (1929), who suggested it in an article on spatial competition. Black (1948a, 1948b, 1948c) developed the median voter model in detail, discussed the cyclical majority problem, and used the median voter model to lay the foundation for the development of modern public choice theory.

The median voter model is really not a single model, but a conclusion that is generated through a family of similar models. The median voter conclusion is that when collective decisions are made by majority rule, the demand of the median voter is the demand of the group. Bowen (1943) demonstrates this in a model of referendum voting, and Black (1948a, 1958) analyzes democratic decision-making in a committee setting in detail, and arrives at the same conclusion. Black also explains the cyclical majority and discusses conditions under which the median voter result will not hold. Downs (1957) extends the formulation of Hotelling (1929), and presents the median voter result in a model of representative democracy. Downs goes well beyond discussing voting to give an insightful analysis of many aspects of representative democracy, and both Downs (1957) and Black (1958) are among the classic works in public choice that enabled it to emerge as a separate sub-discipline. Taking formulations of Bowen (1943), Black (1958), and Downs (1957) together, the median voter model suggests that in many different institutional settings — referenda, committee decision-making, or representative democracy — when decisions are made by majority rule, the median voter's demand is the group's demand.

By the early 1970s the median voter model was being used as a description of both the supply and demand sides of public sector resource allocation. Articles in prominent journals, such as Barlow (1970), Borcherding and Deacon (1972), and Bergstrom and Goodman (1973) developed empirical results based on the assumption that the output produced by the public sector is the output most preferred by the median voter. At this point, the median voter model was generally accepted not just as a model of demand aggregation, but as a more general model of public sector resource allocation. The median voter model was one of the most substantial and long-standing models in the young discipline of public choice, and by the early 1970s was often depicted as concluding that the public sector produces what the median voter wants.

The median voter model fell out of favor during the 1970s, as Holcombe (1989) describes. Niskanen's (1971) model of bureaucratic resource allocation argued that public sector output is much larger than the median voter would prefer, immediately calling into question the model's broad interpretation. Still, Niskanen used the median voter model for the demand side of his model, and his innovation was the modeling of the supply side of the public sector, which up to that time had mostly been neglected. A more substantial blow to the median voter model came from a theoretical literature, led by McKelvey (1976), which argued that in general, majority rule voting would not produce a unique and stable outcome, and the median voter result would hold only in the most narrow of special cases. The possibility of cyclical majorities had been well-known by public choice scholars. Black (1948a) illustrated the possibility clearly, and Arrow (1951) began his book with a discussion of cyclical majorities. Black (1948a, 1958) showed that they would arise only if individual preferences were not single-peaked, and for decades public choice scholars assumed that preferences were likely to be single-peaked, so cyclical majorities would be rare occurrences. McKelvey (1976) argued that once a framework like Black's is extended from one to many dimensions, cycles would be expected even when all preferences are single-peaked. This created quite a debate in the literature.

Some, such as Riker (1980), argued that this inherent tendency for cycles meant that political markets were fundamentally different from economic markets, and that there could be no political equilibrium as such. Others, such as Tullock (1982) argued that political outcomes were, in fact, more stable than market outcomes, and challenged public choice scholars to explain why. One outcome of this debate was a closer integration of voting models with political institutions, log-rolling, and interest group politics (Weingast, Shepsle, and Johnsen, 1981; Holcombe, 1986). This emphasis on institutions pushed pure voting models like the median voter model into the background and brought aspects of the political bargaining process into more prominence.

In addition to being used as a theoretical foundation for public choice models, the median voter model has also been subject to direct empirical tests, almost always using cross-sectional data on local governments in the United States. Barr and Davis (1966) showed that public sector expenditures were correlated with median incomes across jurisdictions, and McEachern (1978) looked at local debt levels across states and found results consistent with the median voter model. Holcombe (1980) calculated the median voter's preferences from school finance referendum data, and found that referenda tended to produce the outcome most preferred by the median voter. Inman (1978) examined whether the median income voter explained local expenditure levels better than average income or other variables, and his results supported the median voter model. While most empirical tests of the median voter model tend to support it, Romer and Rosenthal (1979, 1982) find inconclusive results that do not support the median voter model. The median voter model does seem to hold up well to empirical testing, but it is worth noting that it has been tested almost exclusively with state and local government data because cross-sectional data are readily available, and because of institutional differences, the results may not extrapolate to national data.

While theorists as far back as Downs (1957) have tried to incorporate factors affecting voter turnout into the median voter model, it has never been done in a convincing way, and the model does not account for the impact of political campaigning and interest groups on voter preferences. Rather, the model assumes that voter preferences are fixed and that candidates and parties adjust to them. Furthermore, the model assumes that voters always vote their true interests, which has been insightfully questioned by Brennan and Lomasky (1993). These omissions could be viewed as shortcomings of the model, or as simplifying assumptions. As simple and unrealistic as the model is in some regards, it still goes a long way toward explaining how voter demands are aggregated through democratic decision-making.

The median voter model is best viewed as a model of demand aggregation which concludes that under majority rule, the aggregate demand of a group of voters will be the demand of the median voter. Interpreted in this way, the model offers substantial insights into the democratic decision-making process, and empirical evidence suggests that it is descriptive of actual collective decision-making outcomes.

RANDALL G. HOLCOMBE

REFERENCES

Arrow, K.J. (1951). *Social Choice and Individual Values*. New Haven: Yale University Press.

Barlow, R. (1970). "Efficiency aspects of local school finance." *Journal of Political Economy*, 78(Sept./Oct.): 1028–1040.

Barr, J.L. and Davis, O.A. (1966). "An elementary political and economic theory of the expenditures of state and local governments." *Southern Economic Journal*, 33(October): 149–165.

Bergstrom, T. and Goodman, R. (1973). "Private demand for public goods." *American Economic Review*, 81(June): 280–296.

Black, D. (1948a). "On the rationale of Group decision-making." *Journal of Political Economy*, 56(February): 23–34.

Black, D. (1948b). "The decisions of a committee using a special majority." *Econometrica*, 16(July): 245–261.

Black, D. (1948c). "The elasticity of committee decisions with an altering size of majority." *Econometrica*, 16: 262–270.

Black, D. (1958). *The Theory of Committees and Elections*. Cambridge: Cambridge University Press.

Borcherding, T.E. and Deacon, R.T. (1972). "The demand for services of non-federal governments." *American Economic Review*, 62(December): 891–901.

Bowen, H.R. (1943). "The interpretation of voting in the allocation of economic resources." *Quarterly Journal of Economics*, 58(November) 27–48.

Brennan, G. and Lomasky, L. (1993). *Democracy and Decision: The Pure Theory of Electoral Preference*. Cambridge: Cambridge University Press.

Downs, A. (1957). *An Economic Theory of Democracy*. New York: Harper & Row.

Holcombe, R.G. (1980). "An empirical test of the median voter model." *Economic Inquiry*, 18(April): 260–274.

Holcombe, R.G. (1986). *An Economic Analysis of Democracy*. Carbondale: Southern Illinois University Press.

Holcombe, R.G. (1989). "The median voter model in public choice theory." *Public Choice*, 61: 115–125.

Hotelling, H. (1929). "Stability in competition." *Economic Journal*, 29(March): 41–57.

Inman, R. (1978). "Testing political economy's 'as if' assumption: Is the median income voter really decisive?" *Public Choice*, 33: 45–65.

McEachern, W.A. (1978). "Collective decision rules and local debt choice: A test of the median voter hypothesis." *National Tax Journal*, 31: 129–136.

McKelvey, R.D. (1976). "Intrasitivities in multi dimensional voting models and some implications for agenda control." *Journal of Economic Theory*, 12(June): 472–482.

Niskanen, W.N. (1971). *Bureaucracy and Representative Government*. Chicago: Aldine-Atherton.

Riker, W.H. (1980). "Implications from the disequilibrium of majority rule for the study of institutions." *American Political Science Review*, 74(June): 432–446.

Romer, T. and Rosenthal, H. (1979). "The elusive median voter." *Journal of Public Economics*, 12: 143–170.

Romer, T. and Rosenthal, H. (1982). "Median voters or budget maximizers: evidence from school expenditure referenda." *Economic Inquiry*, 26: 556–578.

Tullock, G. (1982). "Why so much stability?" *Public Choice*, 37: 189–202.

Weingast, B.R., Shepsle, K.A. and Johnsen, C. (1981). "The political economy of benefits and costs: A neoclassical approach to distributive politics." *Journal of Political Economy*, 89(August): 642–664.

PUBLIC FINANCE IN DEMOCRATIC PROCESS

The origins of public finance, as a field of study though most certainly not as an object of practice, can be traced to the emergence of the cameralists after 1500 in central Europe (Backhaus and Wagner, 1987). The focal point of cameralist concern was on survival of the regime, which in turn, required a military capacity and economic development. This concern about development took place within absolutist regimes that existed in a highly competitive, Tiebout-style (1956) environment. The Peace of Westphalia in 1648, for instance, recognized more than 300 independent units of governance within the cameralist lands. Joseph Schumpeter (1954: 143–208) described the cameralists well when he referred to them as "Consultant Administrators." They were both consultants and administrators. They were consultants to the various kings, princes, and other royal personages who ruled throughout those lands. The cameralists were not, however, anything like contemporary academic consultants. They were real-world administrators as well. They were engaged in such activities as managing mines or glass works. Many of the cameralists also held academic posts (as noted in Albion Small's (1909) thorough but more descriptive than analytical examination).

If one were to construct a model of the cameralist vision of the state, it would look like a model of a business firm. The state's lands were potential sources of revenue. Forests could be harvested, game could be caught, and mines could be worked. The ruler would also sponsor an assortment of commercial enterprises, as in operating a glassworks or a brewery. Taxes occupied a secondary position as a source of revenue. They were a last resort option for public finance, and not the first source of revenue.

The cameralist absolutisms have long given way to democracies throughout the Western world. In many respects, however, public finance has not kept pace with this change in political regime. Cameralistic public finance was a choice-theoretic approach to public finance. The phenomena of public finance, state revenues and expenditures, arose out of some ruler's optimizing choices. It is quite different in modern democratic regimes. The phenomena of public finance do not arise from someone's optimizing choice, but rather arise through interaction among the many participants within the fiscal process. This interactive or catallactic approach to public finance leads often to quite different implications for public finance than does the choice-theoretic approach (Wagner, 1997). A good deal of contemporary public finance has maintained the choice-theoretic orientation toward public finance, as if fiscal phenomena are still generated through the same processes that were in place in mercantilistic and cameralistic times. This astonishing situation was noted in 1896 by Knut Wicksell (1958: 82), when he observed that the theory of public finance "seems to have retained the assumptions of its infancy, in the seventeenth and eighteenth centuries, when absolute power ruled almost all Europe."

The distinction between a choice-theoretic and a catallactic orientation toward fiscal phenomena is a central fault line that runs throughout contemporary public finance. The seminal articulation of the choice-theoretic orientation can be attributed to the British economist Francis Edgeworth (1897). The seminal articulation of the catallactic orientation can be attributed to the Swedish economist Knut Wicksell (1896). While both of these authors are now more than a century behind us, their central orientations toward public finance are readily visible in contemporary fiscal scholarship.

The Edgeworthian, choice-theoretic orientation treats public finance as the study of government intervention into the economy, typically expressed as maximizing some form of social welfare function. In particular, Edgeworth raised the question of how a government would impose taxes within a nation if it wanted to raise those taxes with a minimum amount of sacrifice to taxpayers. For a given amount of revenue to be raised, Edgeworth's ideal state would be one that imposed the least amount of sacrifice upon taxpayers in raising its revenue. This Edgeworthian, choice-theoretic approach to public finance treats the phenomena of public finance as arising from the maximizing choices of a benevolent entity, the state. The state stands outside the market economy and its participants. The people who participate in the market economy may write the first draft, so to speak, but it is the state that revises and perfects the manuscript.

The Wicksellian, catallactic orientation treats public finance as the study of how people participate through government to achieve their various ends (Wagner, 1988). This orientation, with its emphasis on fiscal institutions in place of the Edgeworthian emphasis on resource allocations, is illustrated with striking lucidity in James Buchanan (1967). The state does not stand above the market economy and its participants. The same people who participate in the market economy participate in state governance as well. Fiscal phenomena are not the product of some ruler's maximizing choices, but rather emerge through interaction among people. This interaction might be beneficial for everyone or nearly everyone, or it might be beneficial for only a few, and costly for many others. The state is treated as a nexus of contractual and exploitive relationships. The extent to which those relationships are contractual or exploitive depends on the constitutive structure of governance that is in place.

As a matter of general principle, political relationships are both contractual and exploitive. It is fine to say that taxes are the prices we pay for civilization, to recall the inscription attributed to Oliver Wendell Holmes that is chiseled above the main entrance to the headquarters of the Internal Revenue Service in Washington, D.C. This doesn't mean, however, that the relationship between citizens and state is the same as the relationship between customers and the retail outlets they frequent. A customer can refuse to buy and, moreover, generally can return merchandise that turns out to be defective or otherwise unsatisfactory. There is no option to do this in politics. To say that civilization is being priced too highly and to withhold payment will only land the protester in prison. And there is certainly no point in asking for a refund by claiming that the state's offerings weren't as good as its advertisements claimed them to be.

To speak of a catallactical approach to public finance is not to claim that the phenomena of public finance arise through voluntary interaction among people. It is only to say that those phenomena arise through interaction among people, the very same people as who interact with one another within the market economy. Much of the phenomena of public finance surely arise through duress and not through genuine agreement. This aspect of duress was given particular stress in a good deal of the Italian scholarship on public finance, and which is surveyed in James Buchanan (1960).

Within the Wicksellian, catallactical tradition, primacy of analytical attention is placed upon the institutions of governance, both market governance and, especially, political governance. This contrasts sharply with the Edgeworthian, choice-theoretic tradition where the primary analytical attention is placed upon prices and resource allocations. The state is not treated as some exogenous force that perfects and corrects the outcomes of the market economy. The actual fiscal conduct of the state emerges through complex interactions among fiscal and political participants, and the precise character of those interactions is constrained and shaped by a governing institutional and constitutional framework.

A choice-theoretic approach to public finance was suitable in cameralist and mercantilist times. A cameralist ruler could reasonably be described as seeking to use his fiscal means to promote his dynastic ends. For the cameralists it was historically accurate to ascribe the phenomena of public finance to the choices of the rulers. The state's revenues depended on the ruler's choices about how to operate his mines and how to farm his lands. The extent to which state expenditures were directed to projects that might increase future productivity were likewise objects of choice for the ruler. Suppose two kingdoms were observed to undertake different expenditure programs. In Primo's kingdom, expenditures were heavily oriented toward such investments as draining swamps and building roads that would be likely to increase future production. The budget in Secundo's kingdom, however, did little about swamps and roads, and instead spent lavishly on amusements for Secundo and his court. It would be reasonable in this case to compare the budgetary choice of the two kingdoms, and to say that Primo had a lower time preference, or was otherwise more far-sighted than Secundo. To the extent it is possible to make inferences about preferences from the observation of choices with respect to private choices, it would be possible to do the same thing with respect to state choices within the cameralist setting. To be sure, the conduct of cameralist rulers was relatively civilized, and nothing like the experience with dictators in the 20th century. The conceptual construction of a benevolent despot perhaps finds historical validation in the cameralist period. That does not, however, validate the use of constructions based on benevolent despots in public finance today.

Whether budgets are tilted toward amusements or capital projects would not be directly a source of information about some ruler's preferences in a democratic regime. Budgets emerge out of interactions among participants, and those interactions are governed and shaped by a variety of procedural and constitutive rules. The people who participate in a market make their various choices, but it makes no sense to speak of the market itself as making choices. The market simply registers and reflects the choices and interactions among the participants. It is the same with budgetary outcomes within a democracy. Furthermore, the same set of people can generate quite different budgetary outcomes, depending on the institutional framework within which the budgetary process proceeds. In this respect, there are an indefinitely large number of particular budgetary processes that can be imagined, and it is conceivable that a wide variety of budgetary outcomes could be generated, if the experiment were performed of having the same people engage in successive interactions across differing institutional frameworks. This consideration suggests immediately that a post-cameralist public finance would place particular importance and significance on the institutional framework within which fiscal outcomes emerge.

Taxation is most surely a Faustian bargain, as Vincent Ostrom (1984) explains. Excess burden is one of the primary tools that is employed in public finance. The claim on behalf of excess burden is that taxes have burdens beyond the burden associated with the revenues that taxes collect, due to the changes in market choices that people make in response to taxation. Despite the widespread use that is made of excess burden analytics, the concept suffers from some deep institutional problematics within a democratic political system, as Richard Wagner (forthcoming) explains. In a pure Wicksellian framework, public projects are approved to the extent that political participants value the resulting public programs more highly than they value the private alternative they had to sacrifice. It simply makes no sense to speak of excess burden in a Wicksellian-like institututional setting. In non-Wicksellian settings, the democratic fiscal process involves significant elements of domination and subordination. Those who are subordinated may well bear costs beyond the gains that are attained by the dominating classes, but this is simply to say that any process by which some people are taxed for the benefit of others will involve costs beyond the directly observed budgetary magnitudes. There is nothing surprising about this. Taxation transforms private property governance into common property governance (Wagner, 1992), and the balanced budget multiplier that results from this transformation is generally negative. Taxation does truly represent a Faustian bargain, particularly outside the framework of Wicksellian or consensual governance.

RICHARD E. WAGNER

REFERENCES

Backhaus, J.G. and Wagner, R.E. (1987). "The cameralists: a public choice perspective." *Public Choice*, 53: 3–20.

Buchanan, J.M. (ed.) (1960). "The Italian tradition in fiscal theory," in *Fiscal Theory and Political Economy*. Chapel Hill: University of North Carolina Press, pp. 24–74.

Buchanan, J.M. (1967). *Public Finance in Democratic Process*. Chapel Hill: University of North Carolina Press.

Edgeworth, F.Y. (1897). "The pure theory of taxation," in R.A. Musgrave and A.T. Peacock (eds.) *Classics in the Theory of Public Finance*. London: Macmillan, 1958, pp. 119–136.

Ostrom, V. (1984). "Why governments fail: an inquiry into the use of instruments of evil to do good," in J.M. Buchanan and R.D. Tollison (eds.) *Theory of Public Choice II*. Ann Arbor: University of Michigan Press, pp. 422–435.

Schumpeter, J.A. (1954). *History of Economic Analysis*. New York: Oxford University Press.

Small, A. (1909). *The Cameralists: The Pioneers of German Social Polity*. New York: Burt Franklin.

Tiebout, C.M. (1956). "A pure theory of local expenditures." *Journal of Political Economy*, 64: 416–424.

Wagner, R.E. (1988). "The calculus of consent: a Wicksellian retrospective." *Public Choice*, 56: 153–166.

Wagner, R.E. (1992). "Grazing the budgetary commons: the rational politics of budgetary irresponsibility." *Journal of Law and Politics*, 9: 105–119.

Wagner, R.E. (1997). "Choice, exchange, and public finance." *American Economic Review*, Proceedings, 87(May): 160–163.

Wagner, R.E. (forthcoming). "Some Institutional Problematics of Excess Burden Analytics." *Public Finance Review*.

Wicksell, K. (1896). "A new principle of just taxation," in R.A. Musgrave and A.T. Peacock (eds.) *Classics in the Theory of Public Finance*. London: Macmillan, 1958, pp. 72–118.

PUBLIC GOODS

Public goods are goods with benefits that extend to a group of individuals. The interest in public goods can be traced back to classical economics. David Hume and Adam Smith agreed that government intervention is needed to supply goods and services characterized by collective benefits. If left to the spontaneous action of individuals or organizations, these goods would not be adequately provided.

A theory of public goods was first developed with the publication in 1954 of Paul Samuelson's seminal paper "The Pure Theory of Public Expenditure." Since then, research interest in the topic has grown rapidly. Economists have studied systematically pure public goods and distinguished them from the opposite case of pure private goods. Pure private goods do not involve collective benefits, are rival in consumption and can be efficiently allocated by the private market. On the other hand, pure public goods are characterized by non-rivalry of benefits and non-excludability. For these reasons, collective provision is considered a necessity for these goods.

1. Characteristics of Public Goods

Two characteristics mostly distinguish public goods from private goods. Pure public goods are non-rival in consumption and non-excludable. Consumption of a good is *non-rival* if a person can increase her consumption without reducing the quantity of the good available for anyone else's consumption — the principle as stated by Samuelson in 1954 "one man's consumption does not reduce some other man's consumption." This contrasts with pure private goods, in that consumption by a person reduces availability to others. A fireworks display or a television broadcast are examples of non-rival goods, as long as the view is unobstructed or one has access to a TV set; and so are vaccination programs and national defense. A public good may also create disutility or negative benefits. Consider air pollution: the disutility suffered by one person does not reduce the disutility suffered by anybody else in the community.

Non-rivalry in consumption means that public goods can be consumed by more than one person at a time, and the marginal cost of extending the service to an additional individual user is zero. In this sense, non-rivalry creates market inefficiencies regarding the allocation of these goods.

The second characteristic is non-exclusion. Public goods are *non-excludable* whenever the benefits from the good are available to all once the good is provided and nobody can be excluded from consumption. Fireworks displays, street lighting and national defense are non-excludable public goods, since it is impossible or very costly to exclude individuals from consumption once they have been provided. Once a good is excludable, private property rights can be created and a price can be charged in order to access consumption. Non-exclusion creates additional market inefficiencies.

2. Public Goods and Market Inefficiencies

The main problem caused by non-rivalry is that consumers are not motivated to reveal their preferences. Once the good is provided, there is no incentive for individuals to disclose their willingness to pay for the good, since everybody can consume it without decreasing the amount available to others. Individuals become "free riders" and thus enjoying the benefit from a good that others are providing, without having to pay for their consumption. Furthermore, since everyone can free ride, no one has an incentive to produce the public good. Everyone tends to wait for others to produce it. As a result, the public good will be underproduced, if produced at all. Experimental evidence suggests, however, that this outcome is not as prevalent as the theory indicates and individuals tend to contribute to the provision of public goods even if not at the efficient level.

Non-rivalry also implies that the marginal cost of adding any additional consumer is zero. For this, society's welfare would be maximized when the good is available for consumption at no cost to everyone who places a positive value on it: that is, no individual should be excluded from consumption. However, even if it is inefficient to exclude individuals from consumption, the market does not have a good way of allocating the public good to all individuals who place a positive value on it. In fact, a private firm would be able to provide these goods and sustain the production costs only if it could raise a revenue by charging

user fees to consumers. Such charges would obviously cause some potential user to forego consumption, thus causing a loss in efficiency.

The main obstacle to charging user fees resides in the non-excludability property of public goods. If potential users cannot be excluded from consumption, then private sellers are unable to use prices to finance production. The only alternative available is to rely on voluntary contributions by users, and this will be unlikely to provide the efficient amount of public goods. Free riding, in fact, will always be an option: to enjoy the good no matter whether or not a person contributed to it.

3. Efficient Provision of Public Goods

With private goods consumers decide what quantity to buy for any given market price. Individual demand curves show the willingness to pay for any quantity of the good and the market demand is found by horizontally adding the individual demand curves, determining for each price level the total quantity requested by the market.

With public goods, on the other hand, there is only one level of output and consumers are willing to pay different prices for each level. Therefore, the market demand for a public good is found by vertically adding all the individual demand curves. For each potential level of public good output, the market demand reveals the total amount that consumers are willing to pay. An efficient allocation would then require producing the public good as long as society's total willingness to pay for it is greater than the marginal cost of producing the good. This is the so-called Samuelsonian condition, stating that an allocation will be efficient if the sum of marginal benefits from the public good equals the marginal cost of providing it. The intuition behind this condition is straightforward: since the benefits from a public good are not exclusive to any individual, the marginal benefit is obtained by summing each person's willingness to pay, or marginal valuation, over all individuals.

4. Lindahl Prices

The Lindahl pricing system (after the Swedish economist who first proposed it) suggests a pricing system according to which "prices" for a public good are set so that each individual pays a price equal to the marginal benefit he/she derives from the public good. Lindahl "prices" are personalized prices. Even though consumers are all consuming the same quantity of a public good, they all enjoy the good differently and are willing to pay different amounts. With private goods, individuals all face the same price for the good, and choose the quantity they wish to consume, and these quantities differ among individuals. With a pure public good the opposite situation arises: everyone consumes the same quantity of the public good, but individuals' "prices" are different. While the price of a private good is the price that people actually face in the market, Lindahl prices are hypothetical prices and this explains the quotation marks. They are the prices that individuals would be willing to pay for an additional unit of the public good. The main advantage of Lindahl prices is that when they are charged, every individual prefers and demands the same level of output for the public good, and such a level of output is the efficient one.

The Lindahl pricing system, however, has a number of drawbacks. The main one is the lack of relevant information to actually calculate the prices. To implement Lindahl prices, in fact, one must know the individual's demand curves for the public good. As we have argued above, individuals in general lack the proper incentives to reveal their preferences toward public goods, and this makes the calculation of Lindahl prices a difficult undertaking.

5. Government Provision of Public Goods

All societies face the problem of providing public goods. Individuals are better off if all participate in to the provision of public goods rather than if all choose not to do so, but each individual at the same time is better off if she alone does not pay for the public good. For these reasons, public goods are of particular interest to public policy makers because they tend to be inefficiently provided by the market or by private arrangements.

Government production of a public good has a main advantage, because a government can impose taxes and fees to pay for the public good. Still, the main problem of deciding the optimal level of public good production remains. To determine it, the government would need to know its citizens' preferences. However, as we have previously argued, since exclusion is not possible, nothing forces citizens to reveal their true preferences. Furthermore, citizens are not willing to reveal their willingness to pay for the public good if the actual payment they will be assessed depends in some way on their reported willingness to pay. Mechanisms have been designed to induce true preference revelation under specified conditions and to attain an efficient provision of public goods. For instance, the Clarke (1971) demand revealing mechanism is one of such mechanisms. It has been defined by Tideman and Tullock as "a new and superior process for making collective choices" (Tideman and Tullock, 1976). These mechanisms, however, are subject to the same criticisms as the Lindahl prices, particularly concerning their practicality.

Societies have dealt with government provision of public goods in different ways: a dictator may choose for the people, a representative political body may represent people's preference, or citizens may vote directly. Voting is a common way to decide the allocation problem, whether people vote directly on local public goods issues or vote to elect representatives who will in turn decide about the public goods. Most voting contests are decided according to majority rule voting. Under majority rule, the level of spending chosen will be the one preferred by the median voter, though not necessarily the efficient level.

Often, when economists think about the market failure caused by public goods they concentrate on the fairness issue of some individuals having to pay for the consumption of others. The far more serious issue regarding public goods, however, is not that few individuals have to pay for somebody else's consumption, but that not enough individuals pay and the public goods are not provided at all, even though it would be socially beneficial to do so. Hence, societies often must rely on governments to provide public goods, if not by producing them, then at least by paying for their production with tax revenues.

LAURA RAZZOLINI

REFERENCES

Clarke, Edward (1971). "Multipart pricing of public goods." *Public Choice*, 11: 17–33.

Hume, David (1739). *Treatise of Human Nature*. Oxford: Oxford University Press, 1941.

Mueller, Dennis C. (1989). *Public Choice II*. Cambridge: Cambridge University Press.

Samuelson, Paul (1954). "The pure theory of public expenditures," *Review of Economics and Statistics*, 36: 387–389.

Tideman, T.N. and Tullock, G. (1976). "A new and superior process for making social choices." *Journal of Political Economy*, 84: 1145–1160.

PUBLIC SCHOOLS

State and local governments spend more on the primary and secondary public school system than on any other government function. Its critical role in the development of skills is noted in numerous state supreme court rulings on the constitutionality of public school finance systems. Public school systems also have provided an important laboratory for testing various theories that have been developed in public choice.

One of the first major contributions of public choice was the recognition of the key role played by the median voter. Pioneering empirical studies of the demand for government services replaced the mean income measure used in earlier public finance studies with median income. Subsequently others have realized that the median voter need not have the jurisdiction's median income. To take an important example, the distribution of preferred spending levels for public schools depends on how many families send their children to private school. Some of the community's richest families utilize a private school to obtain the school quality they prefer, which is higher than the school quality chosen by the median voter. Having chosen private school, these parents are best off minimizing their tax burden, and consequently voting for low public school spending. A coalition of poor parents and private school parents thus favor low spending, implying that the median voter has an income that is less than median income. Romer and Rosenthal (1982) searched over the income distribution to see which decile best explained school spending. They got the best fits using the fourth decile income and the fifth decile income (i.e., median income), with the fourth decile income providing a slightly better fit than the median income. This suggests that the median voter has an income that is a little lower than median income, perhaps due to private school parents aligning themselves with poorer families.

We have concluded that relatively rich parents turn to private schools when public schools do not provide the quality these parents desire. Thus the demand for private school is expected to be greater when the typical school district has a larger fraction of families making much more than median voter. This hypothesis receives empirical support in studies by Hamilton and Macauley (1991), and by Schmidt (1992). To provide a more equitable education, some state governments have made it harder for rich school districts to provide the quality of schooling their voters demand. As expected, Husted and Kenny (2002) find that private school enrollment has risen in the relatively affluent metropolitan areas in states that have limited the variation in school spending across school districts.

The price facing the median voter depends on the distribution of income in the community. Lovell (1975, 1978) showed that if taxes are proportional to income then the price facing the median voter is proportional to the ratio of the median voter's income to mean income in the jurisdiction. In a Tiebout (1956) world, where households sort into communities providing their preferred spending levels, communities are homogeneous and thus the ratio of median to mean income equals one. In a more typical setting with imperfect sorting and the distribution of income skewed toward the

rich, the ratio of median to mean income is less than one. This ratio is smaller in communities with more *relatively* rich households to tax to help pay for the median voter's government services. That is, the price of government services facing the median voter is lower if there is a greater subsidy resulting from the higher taxes levied on richer households. Lovell (1978) explains spending in Connecticut school districts. He finds support for the prediction that a fall in the price of schooling, measured by ratio of median income to mean income, leads to higher spending.

The median voter theory implies that the pivotal median voter's preferences will be reflected in spending decisions. But there has been concern that the institutional structure of spending referenda may allow budget maximizing bureaucrats to induce the median voter to spend more than that voter would prefer. Romer and Rosenthal (1978, 1979, 1982) hypothesize that these bureaucrats take advantage of a low reversion budget to obtain approval for a budget that is slightly more preferred than the reversion budget and is higher than the median voter's preferred budget. Utilizing the larger K-12 school districts in Oregon that approved a school budget in 1971–72, Romer and Rosenthal (1982) find that minimum-spending reversion levels result in higher spending levels, which is consistent with their theory. On the other hand, increases in the reversion level above this minimum level are associated with higher spending, contrary to their prediction. Holcombe (1980) utilized school referenda results from Michigan to compare the level of school expenditures chosen in school spending elections with that preferred by the median voter. Utilizing a referendum's proposed and reversion spending levels, the fraction of voters supporting the proposed spending level, and estimates of the dispersion of preferred spending levels, he is able to estimate the median preferred spending level under the assumption that the distribution is normal. On average, actual spending is 2.4 percent *less* than that preferred by the median voter. Munley (1984) gets very similar results using school spending referenda in New York. This research suggests that the median voter is getting the budget that he prefers and is not being induced to approve a higher level of spending, which would appeal to budget maximizing school bureaucrats.

On the other hand, there is some evidence that school boards often select a date for a school spending referendum that favors higher spending. In general elections, federal and state races are being decided. Turnout is much lower in special school elections, in which little else is decided. Special school elections tend to be dominated by parents and teachers, who have more at stake in the outcome. Not surprisingly, Pecquet et al. (1996) find that there is more support for higher spending in special elections. School boards appear to recognize the benefit from getting a favorable mix of voters. Dunne et al. (1997) report that only 5 percent of school spending referenda in Oklahoma are scheduled for the same date as the general election, and only 3 percent take place in the summer, when it is harder to reach parents. Dunne et al. also examine the selection of school bond election dates in twenty states in which school boards can set the election date. The timing of school board elections plays a crucial role in this decision. School boards elected in general elections tend to set school bond elections for general elections, and school boards elected in special elections tend to choose special elections for bond elections. In each case, the school board is picking an electoral setting that would be preferred by the voters who selected the school board. Thus scheduling school board elections as special elections results in excessive school spending.

The incentives that voters have to vote and to gather information about elected officials and the performance of government agencies are quite limited. But this monitoring of elected officials and of government agencies is crucial to the development of strong incentives for elected officials to do what voters wish and for government agencies to be efficient. A number of state supreme courts have ruled that the state system of education finance was unconstitutional because it was inequitable. The *Serrano* ruling in California, for example, permitted very little variation in spending across school districts. Furthermore, some state legislatures, perhaps anticipating an adverse ruling from the court, restructured the education finance system to reduce the inequality in school spending across school districts. These changes give school districts less latitude in determining educational spending. As a result, voters have less at stake in school board elections and in school spending referenda and are expected to devote less effort to monitoring school district performance, resulting in less efficient schools. Consistent with this reasoning, Husted and Kenny (2000) find that a representative drop in spending inequality caused average SAT scores to fall by 4 to 21 points, holding various school and parental inputs constant. Reducing voter autonomy in school decisions thus appears to make schools less efficient.

Comparison across jurisdictions helps voters monitor governmental performance, and competition among jurisdictions may force governments to be more efficient. Zanzig (1997) found that public school efficiency increased as the number of school districts per county rose from 1 to approximately 4. Further increases in the number of school districts had no effect on school efficiency, implying that only 4 districts are needed to reap the full benefits of competition among school districts. A lack of competition raises the cost of education, which should lead to higher spending.

Kenny and Schmidt (1994) conclude that spending is 12 percent higher, other things equal, in states with little competition among school districts. The effects of reduced efficiency and excessive spending are especially pronounced in Hawaii, with a state-wide school district, and in states with countywide school districts (Florida, Louisiana, Maryland, Nevada, Virginia, West Virginia).

These studies of public schools have provided valuable evidence on public choice theories. Families with slightly less than median income appear to be decisive voters in the determination of school spending, perhaps because private school parents are joining with poor families in voting for lower spending levels. Rich parents choose private schooling when the public schooling districts are not sufficiently homogeneous or when rich districts are constrained in raising school quality. Public school spending is higher when the median voter can tax richer families to help pay for better schools. Although the evidence suggests that the median voter is getting his preferred school spending, school boards sometimes manipulate the identity of the median voter; utilizing special school elections instead of general elections results in a median voter who views higher school spending more favorably. Schools become more efficient when school districts have more autonomy, giving families a greater benefit from political participation, and when there is competition between school districts, which facilitates comparison of district performance.

LAWRENCE W. KENNY

REFERENCES

Dunne, S., Reed, W.R., and Wilbanks, J. (1997). "Endogenizing the median voter: public choice goes to school." *Public Choice*, 93(October): 99–118.

Hamilton, B.W. and Macauley, M.K. (1991). "Determinants and consequences of the private-public school choice." *Journal of Urban Economics*, 29(May): 282–294.

Holcombe, R.G. (1980). "An empirical test of the median voter model." *Economic Inquiry*, 18(April): 260–274.

Husted, T.A. and Kenny, L.W. (2000). "Evidence on the impact of state government on primary and secondary education and the equity-efficiency trade-off." *Journal of Law and Economics*, 43(April): 285–308.

Husted, T.A. and Kenny, L.W. (2002). "The legacy of *Serrano*: the impact of mandated equal spending on private school enrollment." *Southern Economic Journal*, 68(January): 566–583.

Kenny, L.W. and Schmidt, A.B. (1994). "The decline in the number of school districts in the U.S.: 1950–1980." *Public Choice*, 79(April): 1–18.

Lovell, M.C. (1975). "The collective allocation of commodities in a democratic society." *Public Choice*, 24 (Winter): 71–92.

Lovell, M.C. (1978). "Spending for education: the exercise of public choice." *Review of Economics and Statistics*, 60(November): 487–495.

Munley, V.G. (1984). "Has the median voter found a ballot box that he can control?" *Economic Inquiry*, 22(July): 323–336.

Pecquet, G.M., Coats, R.M., and Yen, S.T. (1996). "Special versus general elections and the composition of the voters: evidence from Louisiana school tax elections." *Public Finance Quarterly*, 24(April): 131–147.

Romer, T. and Rosenthal, H. (1978). "Political resource allocation, controlled agendas, and the status quo." *Public Choice*, 33(4): 27–43.

Romer, T. and Rosenthal, H. (1979). "Bureaucrats versus voters: on the political economy of resource allocation by direct democracy." *Quarterly Journal of Economics*, 93(November): 563–587.

Romer, T. and Rosenthal, H. (1982). "Median voters or budget maximizers: evidence from school expenditure referenda." *Economic Inquiry*, 20(October): 556–578.

Schmidt, A.B. (1992). "Private school enrollment in metropolitan areas." *Public Finance Quarterly*, 20(July): 298–320.

Tiebout. C.M. (1956). "A pure theory of local expenditures." *Journal of Political Economy*, 64(October): 416–424.

Zanzig, B. (1997). "Measuring the impact of competition in local government education markets on the cognitive achievement of students." *Economics of Education Review*, 16(October): 431–441.

PUBLIC UTILITY REGULATION

Public utility regulation originates from the problem of natural monopoly. Where there are overwhelming scale economies as in the case of public utilities, traditionally, electric, gas, water and telephone, the cost to society is arguably minimized by having one supplier. The problem with one supplier is that it allows for monopoly exploitation with the resulting efficiency losses from monopoly. The Marshallian Triangle ABC in Figure 1 is the efficiency loss and the rectangle EAB"F is the monopoly exploitation. The latter is also the monopoly profits and constitutes a transfer from consumers to the monopolist. As such it is not an efficiency loss. However, following Tullock's (1967) insight on rent seeking, this rectangle is much more important to the process of natural monopoly regulation. It consists of the rents from monopoly and, indeed, will normally be much larger than the triangle. Indeed, it becomes the principal bone of contention in the regulatory process and the quest for these monopoly rents is the main driver of the process and is critical to understanding the process.

The first problem of regulation is an old one involving second-best issues. If regulation set price at C where the allocative efficiency losses ABC were totally eliminated

the firm would not cover its fixed costs and would either have to go out of business or recover them by some form of lump-sum subsidy. Here is the source of the rent-seeking dilemma. Regulation has to find a way of covering the firm's costs. It would traditionally do this by moving to the second best optimum of C', which provides an efficiency gain of AB'C' and the monopoly rents are all taken by consumers. This second-best optimum effectively recognizes that the maximum gain of ABC is not attainable.

For many years this simple view of the regulation of natural monopoly was rather generally accepted with few exceptions (Averch and Johnson, 1961; Posner, 1969, 1974). This is evidenced by the fact that prior to the 1980s there were two dominant forms of natural monopoly regulation, viz. public enterprise (PE), and cost-of-service or rate-of-return regulation (ROR). PE was the predominant form of regulation in most of Europe and ROR predominated in North America. During the 1970s and 80s a change took place in the views of economists with the result that increasingly these regulatory institutions were the subject of greater criticism and in the 80s a new form of regulation, incentive regulation or price-cap regulation (PCR) became increasingly important. This was spawned by political changes in United Kingdom with the election of Margaret Thatcher in 1979 and her program of privatization of public enterprise. Along with privatization, changes in regulation were required. Stephen Littlechild (1983), a long time critic of ROR, proposed PCR for British Telecom, the former Post Office Telephones and PCR spread to other public utilities in the United Kingdom Meanwhile, theorists — most notable being Jean-Jacques

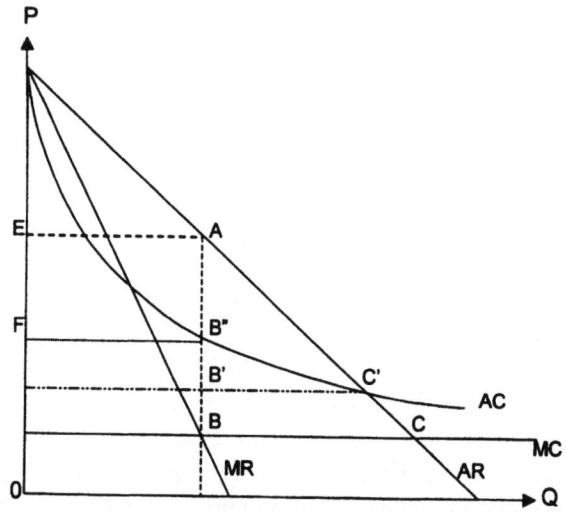

Figure 1: The welfare cost of monopoly.

Laffont and Jean Tirole (1993) — developed elegant mechanism design theories of incentive regulation. In the 80s incentive regulation came alive. However, by the mid 90s the façade of incentive regulation started to crack and hybrid systems known as performance-based regulation (PBR) appeared on the scene. What was it that Littlechild and most economists found so problematical about ROR and why did regulatory practice partially turn against PCR?

The feature of ROR that most offended economists was that it coupled revenue and cost together. The firm earned revenue by demonstrating that its costs were at a particular level and its regulators then allowed revenues based on the proof of these costs. Thus, revenue directly depended on costs. The greater its costs the greater the revenue allowed. Given the asymmetry of information about the firm's costs it was very difficult for a regulator to determine whether the firm's costs were minimized. The firm was able to take some of the monopoly rents in the form of higher costs entirely consistent with the much earlier notion of J.R. Hicks (1935) that the "quiet life" was the "best of all monopoly profits." It was this internal inefficiency or X-inefficiency that was at the root of most economists' distaste for ROR and PCR was an attempt to overcome these inefficiencies.

PCR, by setting price, broke the link with costs and provided incentives for internal efficiency absent under ROR. In terms of the Figure 1 it created a discontinuity in the firm's marginal revenue curve. Unfortunately, PCR offered no free lunch as readily became apparent in theory and practice. Laffont and Tirole's exploration of information asymmetries provides a very clear basis for understanding why PCR might be extremely problematical in practice. This can be seen from examining their assumptions and realizing that they are extremely unlikely to be met in practice. They assumed that the firm's costs were known accurately only to the firm but that both the firm and the regulator had common knowledge of the probability distribution of costs, i.e., of the likelihood that the regulated firm's actual costs were at various levels. Under these circumstances they were able to show that the firm would operate in a least-cost manner provided it was able to appropriate the rents attributable to its information advantage and (emphasis added) *provided the regulator allowed it to continue to retain these rents*. They showed that if a regulator later changed his mind and attempted to appropriate these information rents that the firm would lose its incentives to operate at least cost. They dubbed this a failure of commitment. But, as history has demonstrated, regulators simply cannot promise to leave rents on the table, whether or not this might be theoretically justified. Thus, in practice, under PCR, regulatory commitment and

reneging was a significant problem. When the firm made significant profits, regulators adjusted PCR parameters to appropriate them. When the firm showed signs of approach financial distress, regulators relaxed the PCR regime. The required theoretical commitment of the regulator to a stable regime was not in evidence in practice, with the end result that PCR has been difficult to implement in practice. Thus, Laffont and Tirole's contribution has been to indicate the importance of information rents in regulation and their framework has turned out to provide effectively an impossibility theorem for the direct application of PCR, since real regulators are not able to comply with the commitment requirements theoretically required for PCR to work.

In the United States PCR was rarely embraced so enthusiastically as it was in Europe. Could it be that years of regulatory practice had bred a concern about the regulator's congenital inability to commit? Put more gently, there was a long established practice in regulation of pragmatism or "working things" out as you go along. Goldberg (1976) argued that regulation should be seen as a complicated form of contract for which all eventualities could not be specified and saw the regulator as the intermediary between consumers and the firm to address problems as unforeseen eventualities arose. An alternative argument developed from Tullock (1967) would see the regulator as a broker distributing the rents dependent on changes in the political equilibrium, as developed in Crew and Rowley (1988). Either interpretation is consistent with the way practice developed in the United States PBR is a hybrid of PCR and ROR. The firm's ability to make profits is attenuated by a sharing rule, whereby above or below an upper and lower limit respectively the firm shares profits or losses respectively. This provides a process for attenuating the regulator's ability to take away what are perceived as excess profits by agreeing up front on a process for limiting the scope for excess profits on the upside and limiting the exposure faced by the firm for losses on the downside. Clearly, incentives for X-efficiency are weakened in the process but this may be the best that it is achievable now given the state of technology in regulatory economics today.

This brief sketch notes the two predominant forms of regulation in the past: rule-based and regulator-based. Rule-based regulation, like pure PCR, is intended to bind the hands of the regulatory agency to a formula, on which the regulated firm can rely in its future planning. Regulator-based regulation may have some overriding principles, typically set in place by authorizing statutes, but it is intended to leave considerable judgment to the regulator(s) in determining policies and outcomes going forward. Where is the future of regulation of network industries, the traditional public utilities, likely to lie? The steady progress of new technologies may erode economies of scale and scope sufficiently so that regulation will just fade away, the Posnerian vision. A major hurdle to this, of course, are rent-seeking strategies of incumbents and their supporters. At present, it seems likely that regulated utilities will be with us for at least a few more years. Given the rents at stake, the most likely form of regulation will likely continue to be regulator-based, building on some forum, like state and federal commissions, that provides a semi-opaque process for dividing these rents, while providing a modicum of protection for small consumers with no other options against monopoly exploitation. This sort of regulation may seem a lame approach to the problem, and the regulator in this approach may be subject to capture by one or another of the contending protagonists to the regulation game, as in Stigler (1971) and Peltzman (1976). However, it does at least provide for a managed resolution of the continuing contingencies that arise when society attempts to control or influence economic organizations through regulation. Notwithstanding a number of promising experiments over the past century, and some progress in understanding the incentives engendered by regulation, such regulator-based governance structures seem likely to remain the vehicle of choice for "public utility" regulation.

MICHAEL A. CREW

PAUL R. KLEINDORFER

REFERENCES

Averch, Harvey and Johnson, Leland L. (1962). "Behavior of the firm under regulatory constraint." *American Economic Review*, 52(December): 1052–1069.

Crew, Michael A. and Kleindorfer, Paul R. (2001). "A critique of the theory of incentive regulation," in M.A. Crew and P.R. Kleindorfer (eds.) *Future Directions in Postal Reform*. Boston: Kluwer Academic Publishers.

Crew, Michael A. and Rowley, Charles K. (1988). "Toward a public choice theory of monopoly regulation." *Public Choice*, 57(1)(March): 49–67.

Goldberg, Victor P. (1976). "Regulation and administered contracts." *The Bell Journal of Economics*, 7-2(Autumn): 426–448.

Hicks, J.R. (1935). "Annual survey of economic theory." *Econometrica*, 3: 1–20.

Laffont, Jean Jacques and Tirole, Jean (1993). *A Theory of Incentives in Regulation and Procurement*. Cambridge: MIT Press.

Littlechild, Stephen C. (1983). *Regulation of British Telecommunications' Profitability*. London: Department of Trade and Industry.

Peltzman, S. (1976). "Toward a more general theory of regulation." *Journal of Law and Economics*, 19(August): 211–240.

Posner, Richard A. (1969). "Natural monopoly and its regulation." *Stanford Law Review*, 21(February): 548–643.

Posner, Richard A. (1974). "Theories of economic regulation." *Bell Journal of Economics*, 5(Autumn): 335–358.

Stigler, George J. (1971). "The theory of economic regulation," *The Bell Journal of Economics and Management Science*, 2(1)(Spring): 3–21.

Tullock, Gordon (1967). "The welfare costs of tariffs, monopolies and theft." *Western Economic Journal*, 5(June): 224–232.

R

RATIONAL CHOICE APPROACHES TO ECONOMIC AND POLITICAL HISTORY

Douglass North, Mancur Olson and William Riker have each, in their various ways, attempted to develop "rational choice" approaches to the evolution of society.

North's approach is perhaps the most wide-ranging. Work with Thomas (North and Thomas, 1973, 1977) attempted an economic explanation of the transition from hunter/gatherer societies to agriculture. Later, he proposed a "neoclassical theory of the state", wherein "Leviathan" contracts to set up a system of property rights and taxes (North, 1981). His later work has focused on institutions, and how they change as a result of incentives, knowledge and beliefs (North, 1990, 1994). One of his most persuasive pieces is his work with Weingast (North and Weingast, 1989) on the Glorious Revolution in 1688 in Britain, and how this transformed Britain's ability to manage debt, fight wars (particularly with France), and develop an empire.

Riker's earliest work was on American Federalism, particularly the logic underlying the need for Union in 1787 (Riker, 1953, 1964) and the stability of parties as coalitions (Riker, 1962). After working for a number of years on rational choice theory (Riker and Ordeshook, 1973), Riker returned to American political history, to interpret key events in terms of heresthetics (see "Heresthetics and the Evolution of the U.S. Constitution": this Encyclopedia).

Much of Olson's work has attempted to grapple with understanding how some societies are successful and others much less so. In his early book, Olson (1965) used the idea of the prisoner's dilemma to suggest that cooperation may fail, as individuals pursue their selfish ends (by strikes, revolutions, etc.) and indirectly constrain economic growth. Later, Olson (1982) used this argument to provide a "declinist" explanation of why stable democracies such as Britain and the U.S. appeared less vital (in the 1980s) than the newer democracies of the post World War II era (such as France, Germany, Japan, etc.). Olson's argument at that time had some similarities with an historical one put forward by Paul Kennedy (1987). Based on the evidence from the "decline" of Spain after 1600, of France after 1815, and of Britain after 1945, Kennedy suggested that empires tended to engage in military adventures, at great cost, eventually

weakening their own economic structure. The U.S., in 1987, appeared, to Kennedy, to be just such a declining military power. In fact, in 1990, U.S. military expenditure accounted for about 5% of GNP and 20% of government expenditure, while the parallel shares for the Soviet Union were 10% and 43% respectively. Olson's last book published posthumously (Olson, 2000) attempted an account of how the predatory state apparatus of the Soviet Union could induce relatively rapid industrial growth in its initial phase, and then collapse as abruptly as it did in the 1990s.

One way to attempt an integration of these various analyses of economic history is to use the idea of factor coalitions. Rogowski (1989) has used the notion, from economic theory, that there can be assumed to be three factors of production: land, labor and capital. External and internal features may grant advantages to particular coalitions of these factor "interests." For example, the U.S. in the late 1700s could be characterized as abundant in land, with both labor and capital relatively scarce. Principal imports were manufacturers, intensive in capital and skilled labor. Thus protection in the form of tariffs would necessarily benefit capital and "industrial labor." In contrast, since land was abundant, this economic interest, together with agricultural labor, would benefit from free trade. Consequentially, the political conflict between the commercial Federalist Party and the agrarian Jeffersonian Republicans, at the election of 1800, can be interpreted in factor terms. However, some of the elements of this controversy can only be understood with respect to earlier factor conflicts in Britain, from 1688 on.

North and Weingast (1989) had argued that the creation of the Bank of England in 1693 provided a method of imposing credible commitment on Parliament. The dilemma facing any government of that time was that war had become more expensive than government revenue could cover. Consequently, governments, or monarchs, became increasingly indebted. Risk-preferring, or war-loving, monarchs, such as Philip II of Spain or Louis XIV of France, were obliged to borrow. As their debt increased, they were forced into repudiation, thus making it more difficult in the future to borrow. Since the Bank of England "managed" the debt in Britain after 1693, there was an incentive for Parliament to accept the necessary taxation, and also to avoid repudiation. However, it was clear in 1688 that William would pursue the war with France with great vigor and cost. Contrary to the argument of North and Weingast, this escalating debt could, in fact, force Parliament to repudiation. Until 1720, it was not obvious how Parliament could be forced to commit to fiscal responsibility. How this was done was through the brilliant strategy of Robert Walpole, first "prime" minister.

The fundamental problem was that the majority of members of both Commons and Lords were of the landed interest. The obvious method of funding government debt (which had risen to 36 million pounds sterling by 1713) was by a land tax. Indeed the land tax raised approximately 50% of revenue. War weariness had brought in a Tory government in 1710, and the obvious disinclination of the Tory landed gentry to pay increasing land taxes forced up the interest rate on long term government debt from 6% to 10% (Stasavage, 2002). In some desperation the government created the South Sea Company in 1711. After Queen Anne died in 1714, and the Hanoverian, George I, became sovereign, increasing speculation in South Sea Company stock and then the collapse of the "bubble" in September 1720, almost bankrupted the government. Walpole stabilized confidence in the Company by a swap arrangement with the Bank of England. In April 1721, Walpole, now Chancellor of the Exchequer and First Lord of the Treasury, began his scheme to stabilize government debt by instituting a complex system of customs and excise. By restricting imports, mostly foodstuffs and land intensive commodities, this system had the effect of supporting the price of the scarce commodity, land. From 1721 to 1740, these excise taxes and customs raised an increasing share of government revenue. As Brewer (1988) has described, the system required a sophisticated and skilled bureaucracy. The Walpole device had many effects. Firstly, it ushered in a long period of Whig dominance (at least until the 1800s). Protection of land remained in place until the Repeal of the Corn Laws in May 1846. As McLean (2001) has described, the Repeal was effected by Robert Peel, leader of the Tories (or conservatives), together with Wellington in the Lords, against the interests of the majority of their party. Famine in Ireland made it obvious to Peel and Wellington that unless food prices were lowered then social unrest could lead to civil strife. The Walpole "bargain" of 1721 essentially created a compact between the "commercial" Whig interests and both Whig and Tory "landed" interests. By supporting land prices, the bargain led to increased investment in agriculture, and (possibly counter-intuitively) the decline of the agricultural labor force. Increased food prices may have reduced the real wage of industrial labor (Floud and McClosky, 1994).

Although agricultural output increased in Britain, the population grew even more rapidly, and Britain became increasingly defendant on food imports, particularly from the U.S.

Jefferson was well aware of the implications of the Walpole bargain. His reading of the works of Henry St. John, Viscount Bolingbroke, led him to believe that the land–capital bargain led to corruption, and the filling of Parliament by placemen. In fact, Bolingbroke's arguments against Walpole were, to some degree, invalid, since the compact did make it possible for Britain to manage its debt, fight its wars, and create an empire. Bolinbroke's logic was, however, valid for the U.S. Hamilton's attempt in 1793 to recreate a Walpole system would have necessitated both a land tax and a tariff system. Since U.S. imports were primarily manufactures, a tariff would protect the scarce factor, capital, associated with these imports. In Jefferson's view, this would have disadvantaged the landed interest. By creating an agrarian coalition, essentially of the southern slave-owning landed interest, and western free farmers, Jefferson created a long-lasting compact under which the U.S. became the food supplier for Britain. Just as the Walpole compact persisted until 1846, so did Jefferson's agrarian coalition survive until 1860. At that point, the southern demand for expansion to the Pacific destroyed the Jeffersonian–Jacksonian Democracy.

The aftermath of the Civil War created a new coalition, of commercial interests and industrial labor, as represented by the presidential victory of the Republican, McKinley, over the populist Democrat, William Jennings Bryan in 1896.

From this perspective, U.S. politics in the period 1896–1956 can be interpreted in terms of a single factor dimension, capital, since we can regard the interest of land to be generally, in opposition to capital. Thus in the 1930s, the inclination of Republicans for the preservation of a hard money or gold standard rule was in opposition to the need for available credit in the agricultural sector.

In the 1960s, agitation for greater civil rights brought the labor axis into prominence. L.B. Johnson's positioning on this axis contributed to his great electoral victory in 1964, but also opened the way for the Republican Party to adopt an increasingly conservative social position and gain political control in the southern states (Miller and Schofield, 2002).

In Britain, since 1846, all these factors have played a role at various times. For example, McLean (2002) has observed that the success of the Reform Bill, under the Conservative, Disraeli, in 1867, depended on beliefs about Empire. For industrial labor, "Empire" meant the opportunities for emigration and a better life in the Dominions of America, Canada and South Africa. By using the rhetoric of "Empire", the conservatives could hope to appeal to working class voters. In fact, such rhetoric was an important aspect of Thatcher's electoral success in the 1980s. Indeed, recent empirical analysis of electoral beliefs in Britain (Martin et al., 2002) make it clear that in addition to the usual economic (or "capital") axis, it is necessary to employ a second "social" axis. This axis incorporates "civil rights," but is also characterized by attitudes to European Union.

Conservative MPs' responses to a questionairre on this topic suggests that they are strongly opposed to the incorporation of Britain within the European Union. In other words, political beliefs, that were founded on an economic rationale dating back over a hundred years, are still relevant, in a somewhat different form, today.

This narrative suggests that preferences, or interests, on economic factors or dimensions, play an important role in political decisions. However, the manner in which these interests are transformed into beliefs is, to a considerable degree, still a matter of conjecture. Indeed, how these beliefs take political expression seemingly depends on the perception and strategies of political leaders such as Walpole, Peele, Disraeli, Jefferson, Lincoln or Johnson.

It has been a long standing controversy in rational choice theory whether political economy is best described by the concepts of "equilibrium" or "chaos" (Austen-Smith and Banks, 1998). In his later work, after 1980, Riker opted for chaos, and focused on key "contingent" events like the Ratification of the U.S. Constitution in 1788, or the onset of the Civil War in 1860–61.

The brief description of British and U.S. political history offered here suggests that there can be long periods during which political economic equilibrium is quite stable. However, equilibria can be destroyed and dramatically transformed at key historical periods, as described above. Denzau and North (1994) have adopted ideas from evolutionary theory in biology (Eldredge and Gould, 1972) and from the notion of "informational cascades" (Birhchandani et al., 1992) and proposed the concept of "punctuated social equilibrium." As they suggest, this idea is an analogue in the social realm of Kuhn's notion of scientific revolution (Kuhn, 1962). At least intuitively, the notion of "punctuated social equilibrium" would seem entirely relevant to the puzzle of the collapse of the Soviet Union that so intrigued Olson. Indeed, it is entirely possible that the apparent relative decline of the U.S. and Britain (which seemed so obvious to Olson in 1982 and Kennedy in 1987) has been reversed, as the underlying political economic equilibrium has been transformed in these two countries since 1980. Constructing a historically based theory of social, political and economic evolution to explain these phenomena is the task facing the next generation of scholars.

NORMAN SCHOFIELD

REFERENCES

Austen-Smith, D. and Banks, J. (1998). "Social choice theory, game theory, and positive political theory." *Annual Review of Political Science*, 1: 259–287.

Birhchandani, S., Hirschleifer, D., and Welsh, I. (1992). "A theory of fads, fashion, custom and cultural change as information cascades." *Journal of Political Economy*, 100: 992–1026.

Brewer, J. (1988). *The Sinews of Power*. Cambridge, MA: Harvard University Press.

Denzau, A.T. and North, D. C. (1994). "Shared mental models: ideologies and institutions." *Kyklos*, 47: 3–31; reprinted in A. Lupia, M.D. McCubbins and S. Popkin (eds.) *Elements of Reason*. New York: Cambridge University Press, pp. 23–46.

Eldredge, N. and Gould, S. (1972). "Punctuated equilibria: an alternative to phyletic gradualism," in T. Schopf (ed.) *Models in Pealeobiology*. San Francisco, Freeman, pp. 82–115.

Floud, R. and McCloskey, D. (eds.) (1994). *The Economic History of Britain Since 1700*, Volume 1: 1700–1960. New York: Cambridge University Press.

Kennedy, P. (1987). *The Rise and Fall of the Great Powers*. New York: Random House.

Kuhn, T. (1962). *The Structure of Scientific Revolutions*. Chicago: University of Chicago Press.

Martin, A., Miller, G., and Schofield, N. (2002). "Economic factors, and political ideologies: elections in Britain and the U.S.," Typescript, Washington University in St. Louis.

McLean, I. (2001). "Irish potatoes, Indian corn and British politics: interests, ideology, heresthetic and the repeal of the Corn Laws," in F. McGillivvay, I. McLean, R. Pahre, and C. Schonhardt-Bailey (eds.) *International Trade and Political Institutions*. Cheltenham, UK: Edward Elgar, pp. 99–145.

McLean, I. (2002). *Rational Choice and British Politics*. Oxford: Oxford University Press.

Miller, G. and Schofield, N. (2002). "Activist coalition formation, partisan realignment and majority rule instability in the U.S.," Typescript, Washington University in St. Louis.

North, D.C. (1981). *Structure and Change in Economic History*. New York: Norton.

North, D.C. (1990). *Institutions, Institutional Change and Economic Performance*. New York: Cambridge University Press.

North, D.C. (1994). "Economic performance through time." *American Economic Review*, 84: 359–368.

North, D.C. and Thomas, R.P. (1973). *The Rise of the Western World: A New Economic History*. New York: Cambridge University Press.

North, D.C. and Thomas, R.P. (1977). "The first economic revolution." *Economic History Review*, 30: 229–241.

North, D.C. and Weingast, B. (1989). "Constitutions and commitment: the evolution of institutions governing public choice in 17th century England." *Journal of Economic History*, 49: 803–832.

Olson, M. (1965). *"The Logic of Collective Action."* Cambridge, MA: Harvard University Press.

Olson, M. (1982). *The Rise and Decline of Nations*. New Haven: Yale University Press.

Olson, M. (2000). *Power and Prosperity: Outgrowing Communist and Capitalist Dictatorships*. New York: Basic.

Riker, W.H. (1953). *Democracy in America*. New York: Macmillan.

Riker, W.H. (1962). *The Theory of Political Coalitions*. New Haven: Yale University Press.

Riker, W.H. (1964). *Federalism: Origin, Operation, Maintenance.* Boston, MA: Little Brown.

Riker, W.H. and Ordeshook, P.C. (1973). *An Introduction to Positive Political Theory.* Englewood Cliffs, NJ: Prentice Hall.

Rogowski, R. (1989). *Commerce and Coalitions.* Princeton: Princeton University Press.

Stasavage, D. (2002). *Public Debt and Political Representation.* New York: Cambridge University Press.

RATIONAL IGNORANCE

1. Theory

Information is a good like any other. The primary benefit of information is that it reduces the probability of acting on false beliefs; the primary cost is that acquiring information requires time. Basic microeconomics predicts that (ignoring risk-aversion) individuals acquire information up to the point where the expected marginal benefits equal the expected marginal costs (Stigler, 1961). Beyond that point, acquiring information becomes selfishly counter-productive; while you will avoid more mistakes, it is on balance cheaper to commit them.

A corollary is that if the marginal benefits of information are always zero, the rational economic decision is to be ignorant. If the market pays nothing for knowledge of ancient Egypt, there is no reason to spend time learning about it. In general terms, then, "rational ignorance" refers to any situation where individuals know little or nothing because the expected benefits of knowledge are negligible.

However, it has long been recognized that rational ignorance has far more empirical relevance in public choice than in other branches of economics. Why? Suppose that spending one more hour learning about politicians' voting records allows you to shift your vote to a candidate whose policies, if adopted, would be $100 better for you. The *expected* marginal benefit of an hour of study is emphatically not $100, but $100 multiplied by the probability that you cast the decisive vote, tipping an otherwise deadlocked outcome. In virtually any real-world election, that probability will be essentially zero, implying an expected marginal benefit of zero as well (Olson, 1965; Downs, 1957).

The upshot is that imperfect information matters far more in politics than in markets. Consumers are not omniscient, but they have clear incentives to roughly figure out whether a piece of merchandise is worth the asking price. They are ignorant of details of the marketplace, not its basics. In contrast, voters' have no more incentive to study the *basics* of politics than they have to study the minutiae! Even if a person voted in a completely random manner,

he could still enjoy personal comfort and security. A person who consumed in a completely random manner could not.

2. Evidence

At any rate, this is what the economics of information tells us. But do these predictions hold up empirically? Obviously they are not literally true. Everyone knows something about politics. Nevertheless, the empirical evidence on political knowledge reveals that citizens are ignorant to a shocking degree. Consider the following table showing the percentage of adult Americans aware of various elementary political facts.

Item	%
Know President's term is 4 years	94
Can name governor of home state	89
Can name vice president	78
Know which party has U.S. House majority	69
Know there are two U.S. senators per state	52
Can name their Congress member	46
Aware Bill of Rights is first ten amendments to U.S. Constitution	41
Can name both of their U.S. senators	39
Can name current U.S. secretary of state	34
Know term of U.S. House members is 2 years	30
Can name one of their state senators	28

Source: Dye and Zeigler, *The Irony of Democracy* (1996, p.132).

More comprehensive works (e.g. Delli Carpini and Keeter, 1996) are quite consistent with this outline; in fact, they show that knowledge of foreign affairs is even more limited. It is particularly striking that such a small percentage knows unchanging characteristics of the U.S. Constitutional structure like the number of senators each state has or the length of House members' terms. Without this knowledge, it is hard to see how voters could hold the politicians who represent them accountable for anything. Politicians' low level of name recognition is less surprising, but similarly disheartening: if voters are unable even to *name* their representatives, it is wishful thinking to imagine that they keep track of their voting records and reward or punish them accordingly in the next election. Politicians' party affiliations obviously simplifies this problem to some degree, but voter knowledge of the party to which second-tier politicians belong is also quite limited.

3. Consequences

One of the main themes of public choice is that democracy is paradoxically run for the benefit of "rent-seeking" special interests rather than the general public. Rational ignorance is at the root of most efforts to model this outcome. If voters have no idea what politicians are doing, then politicians can safely cater to the special interests who make it their business to closely follow whatever aspects of policy they depend on. This pattern often goes by the name of "concentrated benefits, diffuse costs." Each piece of special interest legislation takes only a few cents from the average voter, but provides millions for the special interests who back it. No voter, therefore, will bother to even learn of the existence of the legislation, but its beneficiaries may well employ a full-time staff of lobbyists to protect their livelihood (Olson, 1965; Weingast et al., 1981; Rowley et al., 1988; Magee et al., 1989).

A more complex account of the connection between rational ignorance and the predominance of special interests focuses on campaign contributions. Special interests can use their money to buy politicians' support. These politicians then use donations to pay for misleading political advertising. Precisely because voters are so uninformed, this misleading advertising is generally an effective way to get votes. In equilibrium, of course, politicians have to strike a balance between special interests and voter interests, but the less informed the voters are, the less their interests count (Grossman and Helpman, 1994).

4. Responses

The empirical evidence on voter ignorance is widely, though not universally, accepted. A minority of scholars maintain that "political IQ" tests understate the true competence of the individual voter (Popkin, 1991; Lupia and McCubbins, 1998). The most effective critiques of the standard analysis, however, concede voters' severe ignorance, but maintain that even so, democracy works remarkably well.

The leading version of this argument is sometimes called "the miracle of aggregation" (Page and Shapiro, 1992; Wittman, 1995; Hoffman, 1998). Suppose that only 10% of voters are well-informed; they vote for the candidate who puts more weight on voter welfare. The remaining 90% are completely uninformed and vote by flipping a coin. Common sense says that this situation is hopeless. Basic statistics, however, implies that as the size of the electorate increases, the randomness of individual voters matters less and less. In percentage terms, errors tend to cancel each other out. In fact, for a reasonably large electorate, we can practically guarantee that in a two-party race, each candidate gets half of the uninformed vote. No matter what a candidate does, he gets at least 45% of the votes. To win, though, a candidate needs more; and the only way to get more is to court the informed voters. What

fraction of the well-informed does a politician need to win? 51%. In other words, whichever candidate *the majority of well-informed voters prefers* wins the election, even though by assumption the well-informed are out-numbered 9:1.

A parallel argument holds for ignorance about policy. Suppose that most voters are ignorant about international economics. As long as this ignorance leads equal fractions of voters to over- or under-estimate the benefits of free trade, the equilibrium policy remains the same. Voter ignorance by itself therefore does not imply that protectionism prevails. As long as errors are random rather than systematic, and the electorate is large, an ignorant electorate acts "as if" it were fully informed.

This sort of reasoning is especially persuasive to economists because it is an obvious extension of the familiar rational expectations assumption. Most formal economic models routinely represent imperfect information as measurement error; they assume that individuals observe the "true value plus noise." In Akerlof's (1970) famous article on asymmetric information, for example, ignorant car buyers know the *average* value of used cars, but nothing about any particular car. From a rational expectations standpoint, systematic errors are by definition "irrational," a condition that most economists are unwilling to invoke.

Aside from the miracle of aggregation, another source of optimism in the face of voter ignorance emerges from the economics of crime (Becker, 1968). This literature suggests that politicians can be kept in check even if voter ignorance occasionally rises up to 100%. All that is necessary is that politicians have a strictly positive *probability* of being caught if they abuse the public trust. If so, voters have a simple way to deter abuses: over-punish whoever they catch. If a politician has a 1% chance of being caught taking a $1 bribe, bribery has to be punished with far more than a $1 fine. Voters could penalize wayward politicians for even minor infractions by throwing them out of office, demonizing them, or putting them in jail. This is not idle theorizing, either; a number of politicians have ruined their careers by saying the wrong word at the wrong time, or by misusing a trivial amount of official resources.

The "concentrated benefits, diffuse costs" story has also been specifically challenged. Perhaps if there were only a single program in the federal budget that fit this description, that program would survive indefinitely. But most economists concerned about programs with concentrated benefits and diffuse costs believe that they number in the thousands. If so, there is a simple way to get rid of them: set up some sort of omnibus repeal bill (Wittman, 1995). Bundle thousands of tiny affronts against the average taxpayer into one bill that pulls the plug on all of them. In this way, politicians could overcome the dilemma that no one program is big enough to attract voters' attention. Interestingly, after economists raised this theoretical possibility, U.S. politics provided a clear empirical illustration with the post-Cold War base closings bill.

Finally, even if one believes that voter ignorance remains a serious problem for democracy, it is important to carefully work through the direction of the effect. Rational ignorance has generally been thought to make government inefficiently large. But standard asymmetric information models actually predict the opposite (Breton and Wintrobe, 1982). In the Akerlof lemons model, to take the canonical example, informed sellers and uninformed buyers leads the used car market to shrink. The reason is that buyers realize that they are unable to judge product quality, and therefore become more reluctant to buy. In a parallel manner, if political insiders know more about program quality than voters, voters' rational response is, in effect, to say "When in doubt, vote no." In equilibrium, then, asymmetric political information tends to make government smaller, not bigger.

BRYAN CAPLAN

REFERENCES

Becker, Gary (1968). "Crime and punishment: an economic approach." *Journal of Political Economy*, 76: 169–217.

Breton, Albert, and Wintrobe, Ronald (1982). *The Logic of Bureaucratic Conduct: An Economic Analysis of Competition, Exchange, and Efficiency in Private and Public Organizations*. New York: Cambridge University Press.

Delli Carpini, Michael, and Keeter, Scott (1996). *What Americans Know About Politics and Why it Matters*. New Haven: Yale University Press.

Downs, Anthony (1957). *An Economic Theory of Democracy*. New York: Harper.

Dye, Thomas and Zeigler, Harmon (1996). *The Irony of Democracy: An Uncommon Introduction to American Politics*. Belmont: Wadsworth Pub.

Grossman, Gene and Helpman, Elhanan (1994). "Protection for sale." *American Economic Review*, 84: 833–850.

Hoffman, Tom (1998). "Rationality reconceived: the mass electorate and democratic theory." *Critical Review*, 12: 459–480.

Lupia, Arthur and McCubbins, Mathew (1998). *The Democratic Dilemma: Can Citizens Learn What They Need to Know?* Cambridge: Cambridge University Press.

Magee, Stephen, Brock, William, and Young, Leslie (1989). *Black Hole Tariffs and Endogenous Policy Theory: Political Economy in General Equilibrium*. Cambridge: Cambridge University Press.

Olson, Mancur (1965). *The Logic of Collective Action: Public Goods and the Theory of Groups*. Cambridge: Harvard University Press.

Page, Benjamin and Shapiro, Robert (1992). *The Rational Public: Fifty Years of Trends in Americans' Policy Preferences*. Chicago: University of Chicago Press.

Popkin, Samuel (1991). *The Reasoning Voter: Communication and Persuasion in Presidential Campaigns*. Chicago: University of Chicago Press.

Rowley, Charles, Tollison, Robert and Tullock, Gordon (eds.) (1988). *The Political Economy of Rent-Seeking*. Boston: Kluwer Academic Publishers.

Stigler, George (1961). "The economics of information." *Journal of Political Economy*, 69: 213–225.

Weingast, Barry, Shepsle, Kenneth and Johnsen, Christopher (1981). "The political economy of benefits and costs: a neoclassical approach to distributive politics." *Journal of Political Economy*, 89: 642–664.

Wittman, Donald (1995). *The Myth of Democratic Failure: Why Political Institutions are Efficient*. Chicago: University of Chicago Press.

RATIONAL IRRATIONALITY

1. Puzzles for Rational Ignorance

Economists have long been aware of voters' rational ignorance. But the beliefs of many voters seem anomalous even taking their severe ignorance into account. Voters frequently have *systematic biases* rather than random errors. They underestimate the economic benefits of free trade, overestimate the percentage of the budget spent on welfare, and misinterpret low economic growth as absolute economic decline (Caplan, 2002; National Survey of Public Knowledge of Welfare Reform and the Federal Budget, 1995; Survey of Americans and Economists on the Economy, 1996). From a rational expectations standpoint, such systematic errors are by definition a sign of "irrationality" rather than ignorance. Even on less restrictive cognitive assumptions, the further beliefs diverge from the truth, the harder it becomes to interpret them as honest mistakes.

Another puzzle is that people are often *emotionally committed* to their political beliefs (Hoffer, 1951). They look at new evidence and empirical tests more as a threat than an opportunity to learn. The modern history of socialism provides a standard example: as evidence of its failures mounted, a large fraction of socialists refused to acknowledge not only its inadequacies, but true disasters such as the collectivization famines under Lenin, Stalin, Mao, and others. Similar mindsets are easy to find across the political spectrum. A new study finding that the Laffer curve peaks at a marginal rate of 90% would probably antagonize or even enrage conservative proponents of tax cuts, but is unlikely to make many conservatives rethink their views.

A related oddity about voters' beliefs is the extreme certainty with which many voters hold them. The basic economics of information predicts that the poorly informed will be open-minded. The less you know, the more you must recognize how many possible ways you could have gone wrong. In politics, though, extreme ignorance often co-exists with dogmatism. Passionate protectionists are rarely able to correctly explain the principle of comparative advantage, few fierce opponents of government spending are aware of the composition of the budget, and so on. As the saying goes, "Don't confuse me with the facts."

2. A Simple Model of Rational Irrationality

These are some of the reasons that led Caplan (2000, 2001c) to introduce the concept of *rational irrationality* as a rival to the better-known concept of rational ignorance. The standard analysis of rational ignorance indicates that when there are weak incentives to reach correct answers, individuals realize this fact and accordingly choose to gather little information. Caplan proposes that agents optimize along a second margin as well: their *degree of rationality* itself (Akerlof and Dickens, 1982). When there are weak incentives to reach correct answers, an otherwise intelligent person may opt to turn off his critical faculties and believe whatever makes him feel best.

If comforting beliefs are false, there is a obviously trade-off between your beliefs' psychological benefits and your material well-being. The key assumption of rational irrationality is that agents on some level have rational expectations about this trade-off. Suppose for convenience that the trade-off is linear. Then like any other product, we can draw a demand curve showing the "quantity" of irrationality a consumer selects at any given "price" (Figure 1).

For example, a doctor may want to believe that he can perform surgery while drunk without additional risk, but this belief would have high expected material costs from law suits and loss of business. The same doctor could however vote on the basis of lame economic sophisms without fear of negative consequences. Since his vote is almost certain to have no effect on the outcome anyway, he could safely indulge irrational political beliefs at the ballot box even though he refrains from such cognitive excesses on the operating table.

In terms of Figure 1, the standard neoclassical assumption is that demand for irrationality is vertical at $q = 0$; that is, that individuals are fully rational regardless of the practical relevance of the question. Voters are as rational as consumers. But if we relax this polar assumption, there is a strong reason to expect people to become markedly *less* rational when they turn to political questions. If a consumer acts on the basis of irrational beliefs, he bears the full costs of the errors. If a citizen votes on the basis of irrational beliefs, in contrast, he bears only an infinitesimal fraction of the costs. In markets, rational expectations is a private good; in politics, it is a public good.

Like rational ignorance, rational irrationality is relevant to matters other than public choice. Caplan (2001c) suggests, in particular, that religious beliefs often fit the same basic pattern. Most religious adherents are highly certain of their religious beliefs, in spite of their unfamiliarity with rival doctrines. But in most cases, religions focus on questions with little practical relevance. Unless one wishes to be a professional biologist, for example, how you would hurt your career prospects by embracing creationism over evolution? Here again, then, people might retain irrational beliefs indefinitely because the material costs of error are minimal. In a sense, rational irrationality provides an economic account of the parallels between political ideology and religious faith emphasized so eloquently by Eric Hoffer in *The True Believer* (1951).

Rethinking political failure. Caplan (2001c) emphasizes that rational irrationality allows for a great many political failures that rational ignorance cannot sustain (Wittman, 1995). Rational irrationality can take many public choice intuitions about political failure and put them on a stable theoretical foundation.

Consider, for instance, the common argument that voter ignorance of international economics leads to protectionist policies. This story has been shot down on the grounds that purely random errors resulting from lack of information should cancel out. If voters are ignorant about international trade, leading some to overestimate the benefits of protectionism and others to underestimate them, there is no reason to expect the equilibrium platform to be biased in a protectionist direction. In contrast, if voters are rationally irrational, they could systematically tend to overestimate

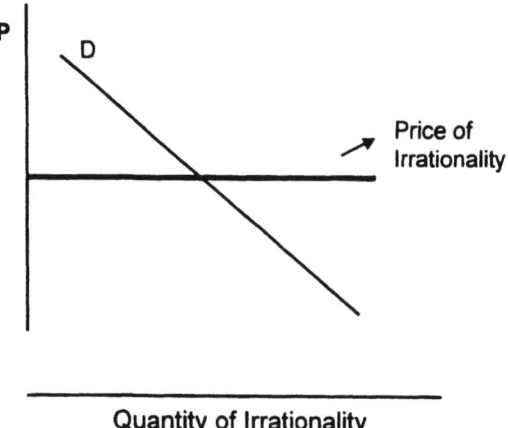

P

D

Price of Irrationality

Quantity of Irrationality

Figure 1: The demand for irrationality.

the benefits of protectionism, driven perhaps by xenophobia. Their systematic overestimate would in turn push the political system to adopt the protectionist policies that voters believe to be beneficial.

Indeed, such policies could in principle win *unanimous* support (Caplan, 2003). Suppose, following Becker (1958), that all voters have identical preferences and endowments. If protectionist policies prevail, each voter is $1000 worse off than under free trade. But each voter gets $10 of surplus from believing in the economic benefits of protectionism. Then a voter is better off holding this irrational view as long as -$1000*$p$ + $10 > 0$, where p is the probability of voter decisiveness (Brennan and Lomasky, 1993). As long as $p < 1\%$, each and every voter will put his faith in protection and vote accordingly, leading to a per capita loss of $990.

Critics of rational ignorance arguments point out, in addition, that voters have a variety of simple strategies for coping with their own ignorance. The most obvious is "When in doubt, vote no." When voters learn that a politician advocates programs of unknown quality, they could automatically count such advocacy against them. Admittedly, this argument sounds strange and forced. But why? A natural explanation is that voters' problem is irrationality rather than ignorance. In a sense, they want to be fooled. If they were buying a used car, they would apply extra caution to compensate for their own ignorance. When they vote, however, they rarely bother. They want to *believe* that new programs will make the world a better place. Questioning that assumption would disturb their worldview without significantly raising the probability that better programs prevail.

In many brands of public choice, special interests are presumed to be the driving force behind inefficient policy. What makes this approach problematic is that inefficient policies are frequently *popular* (Caplan, 2002, 2001a). The public pays little attention to the details of trade policy; but when they do hear about protectionist measures, they are usually supportive. The same goes for many of the policies economists question, from price controls to drug regulation. Rational irrationality provides a simple alternative account of political failure: The main cause is not special interests, but voters themselves. This hardly implies, however, that counter-productive policies are somehow efficient. Democracy creates a pervasive voter-on-voter externality. The fact that most individuals choose to pollute does not imply that laissez-faire delivers the socially optimal level of pollution. Similarly, the fact that most individuals vote in favor of a policy does not mean that democracy delivers socially optimal policy.

BRYAN CAPLAN

REFERENCES

Akerlof, George and Dickens, William (1982). "The economic consequences of cognitive dissonance." *American Economic Review*, 72: 307–319.

Becker, Gary (1958). "Competition and democracy." *Journal of Law and Economics*, 1: 105–109.

Brennan, Geoffrey and Lomasky, Lòren (1993). *Democracy and Decision: The Pure Theory of Electoral Preference*. Cambridge: Cambridge University Press.

Caplan, Bryan (2000). "Rational irrationality: a framework for the neoclassical-behavioral debate." *Eastern Economic Journal*, 26: 191–211.

Caplan, Bryan (2001a). "What makes people think like economists? Evidence from the survey of Americans and economists on the economy." *Journal of Law and Economics*, 44: 395–426.

Caplan, Bryan (2001b). "Rational irrationality and the microfoundations of political failure." *Public Choice*, 107: 311–331.

Caplan, Bryan (2001c). "Rational ignorance versus rational irrationality." *Kyklos*, 54: 3–26.

Caplan, Bryan (2002). "Systematically biased beliefs about economics: robust evidence of judgmental anomalies from the survey of Americans and economists on the economy." *Economic Journal*, 112: 1–26.

Caplan, Bryan (2003). "The logic of collective belief." *Rationality and Society*.

Hoffer, Eric (1951). *The True Believer: Thoughts on the Nature of Mass Movements*. New York: Harper and Row.

National Survey of Public Knowledge of Welfare Reform and the Federal Budget (1995). Kaiser Family Foundation and Harvard University, January 12, #1001. URL, http://www.kff.org/content/archive/1001/welftbl.html.

Survey of Americans and Economists on the Economy (1996). The Washington Post, Kaiser Family Foundation and Harvard University, October 16, #1199. URL, http://www2.kff.org/content/archive/1199/econgen.html.

Wittman, Donald (1995). *The Myth of Democratic Failure: Why Political Institutions are Efficient*. Chicago: University of Chicago Press.

RECIPROCITY

The concept of reciprocity assumes peculiar importance in a world where there is no external authority to enforce agreements, that is, in a Hobbesian state of nature. In many game-theoretic situations, reciprocity permits the emergence and stability of cooperative outcomes, even in a lawless world when agreements between the players are not enforceable. Not surprisingly, the principles of reciprocity gain particular practical and historical importance in the field of international law, given the absence of an overarching legal authority with compulsory jurisdiction to enforce agreements. Reciprocity has effectively become a meta-rule for the law of nations, an essential principle for the practice of sovereign nations. Many structural similarities exist, in fact, between the emergence of legal rules in a lawless environment and the formative process of international law, including the lack of a supreme legislative body. The rules governing international relations are left to the spontaneous interaction of states (custom) or to contracts expressly entered into (treaties).

1. Reciprocity Constraints and the Rules of Social Interaction

Game theory is a useful tool for the study of the behavior of sovereign states, since it focuses on interactions where parties can determine only their own strategies and thus have no direct control of the outcome.

According to the theory of norms, there are two formative elements of spontaneous social rules: (1) the practice should emerge out of the spontaneous and uncoerced behavior of various members of a group, and (2) the parties involved must subjectively believe in the obligatory or necessary nature of the emerging practice (*opinio iuris*). The first element is essentially a rather standard assumption of rational choice, while the second element may be viewed as a belief of social obligation, emerging in response to game inefficiencies, in support of rules of behavior that avoid aggregate losses from strategic behavior.

While these elements represent two necessary conditions for the emergence of customary rules, they do not provide much information on the remaining conditions for the emergence of efficient custom. Some additional structural conditions for the emergence of spontaneous social rules are necessary, whenever the strategic conditions of the game are such that socially optimal outcomes are not achievable through Nash strategies.

The stylized settings considered below shed light on the more problematic cases of conflicting incentives with inconsistent individual preferences over alternative outcomes. In conditions of stochastic or induced symmetry, spontaneous processes of law formation may be successful even in the presence of originally misaligned individual interests of the Prisoners' Dilemma type and of the asymmetric Battle of the Sexes type.

1.1. The Ideal Setting: Structural Reciprocity (Perfect Incentive Alignment)

Perfect incentive alignment occurs when the parties' rankings of preferences converge toward a mutually desirable outcome. This condition implies that neither party has an incentive to defect unilaterally, nor has a reason to fear defection by the other party. Structurally symmetrical situations are relatively easily characterized by stable relationships of mutual cooperation. Because strategies that maximize individual expected payoffs also maximize group welfare, no one has any reason to challenge the emerging equilibrium.

The perfect alignment of interests can be induced either (i) endogenously or (ii) exogenously. The former case implies that the players naturally find themselves in such a heavenly relationship. The latter case implies that the parties have been able to overcome a conflict of interests through exogenous devices. Such is the case of an exchange supported by a perfect contract enforcement mechanism. Paradoxically, therefore, there is no need for law or norms in an environment already characterized by perfect incentive alignment, as contracts and social arrangements are self-enforcing.

The perfect alignment of individual interests, however, rarely occurs in real life situations. In the absence of proper enforcement mechanisms, even a Pareto improving exchange opportunity creates a temptation for shirking and *ex post* opportunism. When shirking and post-contractual opportunism becomes a dominant strategy for one or both players, the exploitation of opportunities for mutual exchange becomes difficult or unobtainable (Kronman, 1985). The absence or inadequacy of contract enforcement mechanisms leads to the search and eventual emergence of alternative safeguards.

The following discussion focuses on conditions of reciprocity and role-reversibility as alternatives to the above described structural harmony.

1.2. The Golden Rule: Induced Reciprocity (Symmetry Constraint)

Golden rules of reciprocity can be thought as the result of a successful binding of each player's strategy to that of his opponent. Automatic reciprocity of the golden-type creates a symmetry constraint on the players' strategies, producing an important change in the traditional results.

Unlike the atomistic world of non-strategic economics, suboptimal equilibria may emerge in a game theoretic setting because players are only allowed to choose strategies, and cannot single-handedly determine outcomes. Because of the potential accessibility of off-diagonal, non-cooperative outcomes, players are tempted to defect from optimal strategies, generating outcomes that are Pareto inferior for all (Buchanan, 1975).

By eliminating the accessibility of the asymmetric outcomes of the game, golden rules of reciprocity induce the parties to choose strategies after taking into account the effect of a reciprocal choice of the other player. In other words, golden-type reciprocity renders the reward for unilateral defection unobtainable. As a result, no rational player will employ defection strategies in the hope of obtaining higher payoffs from unilateral defection, nor will rational players be induced to select defection strategies as a merely defensive tactic. Automatic reciprocity mechanisms thus guarantee the destabilization of mutual defection strategies and the shift toward optimizing cooperation. Two figures will illustrate this point.

Figure 1 depicts the equilibrium obtained in the absence of a reciprocity constraint. Two players are faced with a cooperation problem. Strategies I, II, and III represent three levels of cooperation (with strategy I being the highest level and strategy III being the lowest). Even though mutual cooperation at level I generates the highest aggregate payoff, strategy III dominates in equilibrium, as it is shown by the Nash arrows for the two players. For a similar argument relying on tit-for-tat strategies in iterated games, see Axelrod (1981, 1984).

This equilibrium should be contrasted with the outcome induced by a reciprocity constraint as illustrated in Figure 2.

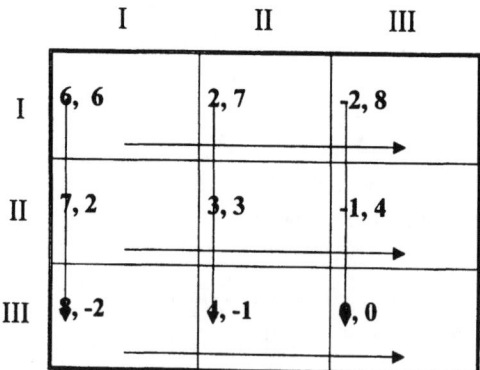

Figure 1: A cooperation problem without constraint.

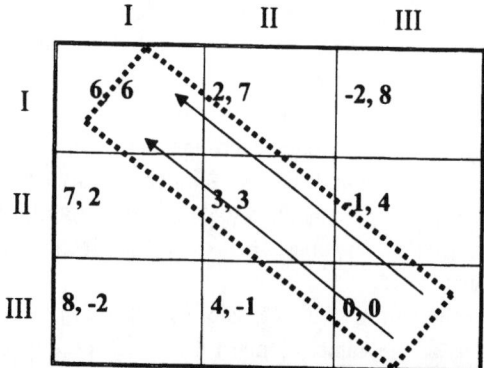

Figure 2: A cooperation problem with a reciprocity constraint.

Figure 2 shows the effect of a reciprocity constraint on the equilibrium obtained in Figure 1. By eliminating the accessibility of asymmetric outcomes, golden-type reciprocity compels the parties to take into account the effect of the opponent's reciprocal choice when selecting their optimal strategy. In this way, the dominance of strategy III obtained in Figure 1 is transformed in a dominance of strategy I, with optimal levels of cooperation for the two players.

Interestingly, where custom is recognized as a primary source of law, mechanisms of automatic reciprocity are generally regarded as meta-rules of the system. The so-called law of nations (the system that governs the relationship between states) serves as an example. The process of voluntary recognition of rules by sovereign states implies that, absent a commonly accepted standard of conduct, lawless freedom applies. Lawless environments are characterized by structural reciprocity. In its original form, custom emerges in the absence of an established legal system or commonly recognized rule of law.

Rules of reciprocity are among the oldest principles of customary law. In the absence of law, reciprocity implies that parties can do back to others what has been done to them, subject to the limits of their reciprocal strengths. Ancient customs of retaliation, based on conceptions of symmetry and punitive balance, provide an intriguing illustration of the principle of reciprocity at work. While practices of literal retaliation are formally discouraged, the principle of reciprocity is recognized as a crucial pillar for the process of international law formation.

Often, situations of post-contractual behavior capable of modifying states' obligations arise in the law and practice of international relations. The international law process provides states with numerous occasions for opportunistic behavior, including hold-out strategies and free-riding. Left unconstrained, states' unilateral defection strategies would dominate in equilibrium (Figure 1). For example, having signed a treaty, states may introduce unilateral reservations at the time of ratification. Standards of compliance in treaty implementation also rely heavily on the subsequent practice of states. The post-contractual behavior of states can shape and modify the content of an already finalized agreement, or even abrogate a treaty.

To cope with this reality, basic norms of reciprocity have emerged as international customary law. Art. 21(1)b of the 1969 Vienna Convention articulates an established custom of reciprocity, creating a mirror-image mechanism in the case of unilateral reservations: "Legal Effects of Reservations and of Objections to Reservations: A reservation established with regard to another party ... modifies those provisions to the same extent for that other party in its relations with the reserving state." The effects of this automatic reciprocity mechanism are similar to a tit-for-tat strategy without the need for active retaliation by states: whenever a treaty is modified unilaterally in favor of one state, the result will be as if all the other states had introduced an identical reservation against the reserving state. By imposing a symmetry constraint on the parties' choices, this rule offers a possible solution to Prisoners' Dilemma problems.

As an additional illustration, one can think of a voluntary contribution game between several people for the realization of a common project. If the benefits from the realized project are non-excludable, the various players are faced with a usual public good problem, with dominant free-riding strategies. As an application of a golden-type reciprocity constraint, imagine that the parties agree (and credibly commit) to a "lower denominator" matching grant solution. Every player agrees to contribute to the common cause an amount equal to the least of the other players' contributions. The players are now faced with a choice of strategy subject to a credible reciprocity constraint. By unilaterally defecting (i.e., offering a contribution of zero), each player can precipitate the failure of the joint enterprise. No player can obtain the unilateral defection (temptation) payoff, because by withholding or reducing the amount of his contribution, each player causes a mirror-image revocation or reduction of the other players' contributions. Thus, although no player can unilaterally determine the success of the joint enterprise (because unanimous participation is necessary), each individual player can determine its failure. Under most circumstances, this arrangement is capable of preventing unilateral defection and free-riding strategies from dominating in equilibrium. The ability of each player to lower the minimum denominator in the group adds robustness to the cooperative solution in spite of the apparent fragility occasioned by the unilateral veto effect of the reciprocity rule.

As an important consideration, one should note that, while the principle of reciprocity solves conflict situations characterized by a Prisoners' Dilemma structure (in both symmetric and asymmetric cases), golden-type reciprocity is on its own incapable of correcting other strategic problems. When a conflict occurs along the diagonal possibilities of the game (such that the obtainable equilibria are already characterized by symmetric strategies), a reciprocity constraint will not alter the dynamic of the game. Reciprocity constraints are effective only where incentives for unilateral defection are present. This reciprocity will be ineffective for Battle of the Sexes games and unnecessary in the Inessential Game and Perfect Incentive Alignment cases.

1.3. The Silver Rule: Stochastic Reciprocity (Role Reversibility)

Silver-type reciprocity requires a stochastic symmetry in the relationship between two or more players. This stochastic symmetry could result from a random distribution of asymmetric payoffs in an iterated game or, more commonly, it could result from an alternation of roles among the various players.

Unlike golden-type reciprocity, silver-type reciprocity further necessitates a pre-commitment of each player to a meta-strategy for the entire duration of the play. That is to say, a player cannot adopt different strategies at different nodes of an iterated game, but must choose a strategy (be it pure or mixed) that he will unconditionally follow for entire duration of the supergame. Under such conditions, the optimal meta-strategy will be that which maximizes the present value of the expected flow of payoffs from the supergame. In situations of silver-type reciprocity with a relatively high probability of future interaction and a relatively low time preference, cooperative strategies will be more likely to dominate in equilibrium.

An important consideration in most analyses of spontaneous cooperation is the discount factor, which serves two purposes. First, it acts as a function of the players' time preference. Faced with very high time preference, players in a repeat game become less likely to give up part of their present payoff for an expected increase in the payoffs from future interactions. As time preference increases, the present discounted value of future payoffs decreases. Where time preference is infinite, payoffs from future interactions have zero value. Second, the discount factor is a function of the probability of future interactions. When the probability of future interactions is low, players are less likely to give up part of their present payoff for an expected increase in the payoffs from future iterations. As the probability of future interactions increases, so does the present expected value of cooperation.

One should further note that, unlike golden reciprocity, silver reciprocity does not in itself correct repeated Prisoners' Dilemma problems. Indeed, even if the players found themselves in such an iterated game, silver-type reciprocity would not alter the usual results obtained in the Chainstore paradox (Selten, 1978: 127–159) and the Folk theorem (Fudenberg and Maskin, 1986: 533–554). Conversely, silver-type reciprocity is capable of correcting other strategic problems that the golden-type rule cannot effectively address, such as the asymmetric Battle of the Sexes game.

The history of customary law provides illustrations of silver-type reciprocity at work. During the formative period of the medieval mercantile law, traveling merchants acted in the dual capacity of buyers and sellers in order to exploit price differentials between various medieval markets. In their commercial dealings they committed themselves to following a set of rules and customs that would govern all their future business transactions. This privately created body of law, known as the law merchant (*lex mercatoria*), applied indiscriminately to commercial contracts entered into by professional merchants, without possibility of a dual standard. If those rules were biased in their favor of merchants in their role as sellers, they would have the opposite effect when the same merchants acted as buyers, and vice-versa. In this setting, Fuller (1969) observed that frequent role changes fostered the emergence of mutually recognized and accepted duties in a society of economic traders: "By definition the members of such a society enter direct and voluntary relationships of exchange. ... Finally economic traders frequently exchange roles, now selling now buying. The duties that arise out of their exchanges are therefore reversible, not only in theory but in practice" (Fuller, 1969: 24).

In this mercantile context, role reversibility changed an otherwise structurally asymmetrical situation (i.e., buyer v. seller) into one that was stochastically symmetrical, eliminating the temptation to articulate one-sided rules. The law merchant therefore illustrates a successful system of spontaneous and decentralized law.

The emergence of cooperative strategies for the supergame requires, as indicated above, an effective precommitment of the players to a single strategy (pure or mixed) to be followed for the entire duration of the game. This will ensure that the *ex ante* choice of a given rule will not be followed by an *ex post* breach of the rule, once the roles are reversed.

In real life, where relational rules are violated following role reversal, norms of social reprobation play a collateral yet crucial role in sanctioning case-by-case opportunism. Likewise, a merchant who invokes a particular rule when buying yet refuses to abide by the same rule when selling would be regarded as violating a basic norm of business conduct, and would suffer reputational costs within the business community. The group's ability to impose a sanction depends on the recordation of an individual's past behavior. Reputation serves as a source of collective knowledge regarding past actions (Benson, 1992: 5–7; Greif, 1989). Conditions of role reversibility, coupled with norms that generate disincentives for the adoption of opportunistic double standards, are therefore likely to generate optimal rules via spontaneous processes.

2. Conclusion: The Nature of Reciprocity

Reciprocity constraints of the golden type serve an important function when applied to simultaneous or sequential Prisoners' Dilemma games. At the origin of the problematic results of the Prisoners' Dilemma lies the fact that players cannot choose outcomes, but rather only select strategies. Outcomes are beyond the control of any individual player, generated instead by the combination of selected strategies.

Reciprocity constraints of the golden type eliminate this problematic feature of the game by preventing asymmetric combinations of strategies. Under a golden rule of reciprocity, players know that by selecting a strategy, they are actually determining the outcome of the game. The incentives for unilateral defection are eliminated because the reciprocity constraint would transform a situation of unilateral defection into one of mutual defection with reciprocal losses for both players.

Regarding the silver rule of reciprocity, one should think that, following the same optimization logic they employ for all economic choices, individuals choose among alternative rules of behavior. They are unlikely to reveal strategic preferences when individual interests are not aligned. Traditionally, such strategies are viewed as hindrances to the spontaneous emergence of cooperation. Strategic preference revelation has no effect in situations of role reversibility or stochastic symmetry (Parisi, 1996). Because the expected costs and benefits of alternative rules are the same for all members of the group, each member has the incentive to agree to a set of rules that benefits the entire group, thus maximizing his expected share of the wealth.

In long-term human interactions, reciprocity and close-knittedness provide individuals with an optimal set of incentives for choosing optimizing strategies. Recent analyses indicate that individual incentives are more likely to be aligned where the horizons of individual maximization are extended to include the payoffs from future interactions and there is a concern for the well-being of close members within the group. The presence of reciprocity constraints allows for a far more optimistic prediction of spontaneous order. This insight is consistent with the prediction of evolutionary models of social interaction, where low discount rates for future payoffs and the close-knittedness of the group are found to be positively correlated with the emergence of optimal social norms. These conclusions are qualitatively similar to those discussed above for the case of role reversibility. Repeat game situations with role reversibility, reciprocity constraints, and structural integration facilitate the emergence and recognition of rules of custom. In consideration of reciprocal constraints undertaken by the other members of the community, individuals who frequently exchange roles in their social interactions have incentives to constrain their behavior to conform to socially optimal norms of conduct. An even stronger logic explains the emergence of cooperation in situations of induced reciprocity. In both cases, the non-idealistic and self-interested behavior of human actors is yet capable of generating optimal norms.

FRANCESCO PARISI

REFERENCES

Axelrod, R.M. (1981). "The emergence of cooperation among egoists." *American Political Science Review*, 75: 306.

Axelrod, R.M. (1984). *The Evolution of Cooperation*. New York: Basic Books.

Benson, B.L. (1992). "Customary law as a social contract: international commercial law." *Constitutional Political Economy*, 3: 1.

Buchanan, J.M. (1975). *The Limits of Liberty: Between Anarchy and Leviathan*. Chicago: University of Chicago Press.

Ellickson, R.C. (1991). *Order Without Law: How Neighbors Settle Disputes*. Cambridge, MA: Harvard University Press.

Fuller, L.L. (1969). *The Morality of Law*. New Haven, CN: Yale University Press.

Fudenberg, D. and Maskin, E. (1986). "The folk theorem in repeated games with discounting or with incomplete information." *Econometrica*, 54: 533–554.

Greif, A. (1989). "Reputation and coalitions in medieval trade: evidence on the maghribi traders." *Journal of Economic History*, 49: 857.

Kronman, A. (1985). "Contract law and the state of nature." *Journal of Law, Economics and Organization*, 1: 5.

Parisi, F. (1995). "Toward a theory of spontaneous law." *Constitutional Political Economy*, 6: 211–231.

Parisi, F. (1996). "Law as a voluntary enterprise," in S. Ratnapala and G. Moens (eds.) *The Jurisprudence of Liberty*. Sidney: Butterworth Publishers.

Parisi, F. (2000). "The cost of the game: a taxonomy of social interactions." *European Journal of Law and Economics*, 9: 99–114.

Scott, K.E. (1994). "Bounded rationality and social norms." *Journal of Institutional and Theoretical Economics*, 150: 315–319.

Selten, R. (1978). "The chain-store paradox." *Theory and Decision*, 9: 127–159.

Tucker, A.W. (1950). "A two-person dilemma," Unpublished manuscript; reprinted in P. Straffin (1980), "The prisoner's dilemma." *UMAP Journal*, 1: 101.

REDISTRIBUTIVE POLITICS 1

Most governments redistribute funds. Indeed it seems likely that a particular type of redistribution accounts for the original foundation of the institution of government. We have no direct records of government of the founding days, but it seems likely that an individual with a special talent for the use of violence decided that he would tax his neighbors instead of simply working for his income. Once the chief had established himself he would find it useful to create a certain number of public goods. He would object to competition whether from other tribesmen who want the property of others or from neighboring tribes. Thus establishing a police and court system to prevent competition from within the tribe, and military forces to prevent outside competition seems reasonable. Something in the way of a very simple road system would also pay from the standpoint of the tribal ruler.

Although this involves wealth going from one person to another without voluntary agreement on both sides, it is not what we normally mean by redistribution. Usually "redistribution" is nominally intended to help the worst off members of society. In fact, however, the government frequently uses its powers to increase the well-being of people or institutions already well-off. In this contribution, I use the word "redistribution" in a more general sense in which there is government movement of wealth from one person or group to another regardless of their initial wealth. If we examine political redistribution throughout history we find many cases in which the redistribution actually is from people who are poor to people who are much better off. The current American farm program is an example, and the tax support which the medieval church received is another. Of course there are some poor farmers and there were some poor monasteries. But most of the transfers until very recently went to people who were reasonably well off.

There is a further case in which redistribution does not seem to be aimed at supporting the poorest individuals. Citizens of most of the Western countries and the more prosperous of the Eastern countries like Japan and Singapore have much higher incomes than the citizens of countries like India and Bangladesh. The transfer of wealth from people who are perceived as wealthy in the United States to those perceived, as being poor in United States is a shift of wealth around among the top 20 percent of the world's population. Only a little wealth is redistributed from the citizens of the United States or Switzerland to the citizens of Uganda or Ethiopia. There does not seem to be any explanation for the actual patterns except simple nationalistic self-interest.

Until recently, I was a professor at the University of Arizona in Tucson. I knew many people mainly in the political science department who were very strongly in favor of taxing the wealthy in order to help the poor. In conversation I would point out that 100 miles south of Tucson there was an international border with Mexican incomes being very much lower than the incomes of people in United States who received such transfers. I never was given a rationalization for this pattern by these aggressive believers in income redistribution. In general they refused to discuss the matter. Since we are a country where speech and, in this case, silence are unregulated, there was nothing I could do to straighten the matter out. To repeat, vigorous self-interested nationalism is the only reasonable explanation.

The more wealthy nations do in fact transfer some money to citizens of the poor nations, but this is a small fraction of the money that they transfer to their own citizens they regard as poor by the standards of their own country. It is also true that the wealthier members of the population are taxed heavily, to the extent that they fail to avoid taxes. People, who are poor by American standards, even if wealthy by the standards of poor countries, receive some transfers which can be considered as payments from the rich. Lebergott's calculation of such transfers go back to 1830 and they show that the poor, unemployed or sufferers from other misfortunes did about as well from government relief in terms of share of national income as they do today.

The really big transfers in the modern welfare state, leaving aside such things as the farm programs, come by way of Prince Bismarck's invention, the Social Security programs. These are essentially compulsory insurance programs with a redistributive component. The average U.S. citizen pays approximately 15 percent of his income throughout his working career into the so-called social security trust fund. Prince Bismarck and Frankin Roosevelt were both brilliant politicians, albeit without many scruples. They believed correctly that they could fool the workers by collecting half of this directly from the workers and the other half by a tax on their employers. Of course the employers reduce the wages enough to pay the tax. Politically, however, the program worked very well. The workers are fooled so they vote for a program that they think costs them half as much as it does.

To clarify the matter for the United States, let us assume that instead of the tax and payment by the federal government, Congress had simply required that each citizen pay six percent of his income to a private insurance company of his choice for the purchase of an annuity for his old age. Further let us say that your employer is also required to pay six percent of the worker's wage to the same insurance company which will be added to the payments for his annuity. Note that I am ignoring the special provision for medical insurance for older people and some impoverished people. This is simply to make the example easy to follow.

Since the insurance company would invest the premiums in interest-bearing securities and would actuarially compute the number of its policyholders who would die, the return would be apparently considerably more than the return on the current Social Security payments. This of course is simply an example of another way of permitting the person paying in to get an investment return on his payments. In

practice, however, over time average incomes rise as a result of technical progress. Congress has from time to time increased the tax payments and the pension to keep up. As a result, the average retired person gets a pension that is not too much below what he would get if his payments had been invested and the interest added to his pension.

This however is the average person. The pension was originally adjusted to the payments which had been made in, so that upper-income people received more money when they retired. This arrangement has been adjusted so as to provide for a limited transfer from upper-income people to lower income people. Still, it is not radically different from an arrangement under which individuals are required to purchase annuities. Thus this procedure is more a transfer for the individual from his youthful and middle age income to his retirement than from the rich to the poor.

There are however significant transfers and redistributions which are not in essence a redistribution of income over the life span of individuals. The farm program has already been mentioned and people who are unemployed or ill may receive significant payments. There are other cases of transfers. People in the military for example are underpaid while on active service and then receive generous pensions when they leave. They also have medical service provided free. Here again it is a transfer along the lifetime income stream without necessarily changing the total income over the life.

Why the transfer, however? Normally it is discussed as a sort of charity with the poor and elderly the beneficiaries. There is no doubt that this is part of the explanation. Most governments have transferred money to the poor almost regardless of the form of government. There are bio-economic reasons why this may be true. Further, of course, religious considerations may be important and we may simply indoctrinate children with this preference. Statistics show voluntaty gifts to charity of 2 or 3%. But the fact remains that many of the transfers go to people who are not poor. I have mentioned the agricultural program, which is much worse in Europe and Japan than in United States. There are however many other programs which benefit particular enterprises or persons who are not poor.

It seems certain then that charitable motives are by no means the only reason for redistributive programs. In general there are three possible reasons for voting for transfers in a democracy. The first of these is charity and desire to help those who are not as well-off as the median voter. The second is simply the consequence of successful rent seeking. The third is a feeling that too much inequality is politically dangerous. In practice, although direct transfers to people who use their votes to get them are important, they are much smaller than the Bismarckian transfers which are normally referred to as the welfare state. The rapid growth of government expenditures in most democratic countries in the 20th century is mainly the result of these Bismarckian expenditures. Even here, it is likely that much of the political drive for these expenditures comes from the beneficiaries. As pointed out above the method of taxes used to support them is deliberately deceptive. In United States the so-called gray tigers are active in getting support and the program is referred to as the "third rail of American politics." A politician who touches it dies.

It is easy to argue in favor of charitable distributions to the worst off part of society. It is also easy to argue for transfers from the upper-income groups to fund them. Indeed the members of the upper income part of society may be in favor of such transfers, and indeed make many voluntary transfers. If the forceful transfers were repealed it is possible that the voluntary transfers from the wealthy would approximately make up for that. Most people do not want to try the experiment.

Looked at ex-ante the Bismarckian system for helping the old by transferring money through the Social Security system would not seem to the very sensible. People now drawing the pensions, did not however buy the type of insurance mentioned above in their younger days. Thus the younger people would have to continue supporting the existing older people so the burden on them would be high. It would only be in the next generation that there would be no net transfer between generations. There is also the fact that the age distribution of the population is changing, so that the number of young people per aged person is shrinking. The tax on the younger people per capita will have to be the sharply raised.

Still discontinuing the system would be painful. Apparently everybody over the age of 50 would lose if the program was simply abolished and those under that age would gain. Of course many of the people under 50 have parents who are drawing pensions and would find it desirable to supplement their parents income out of their own pockets if the pensions were repealed. Altogether the system we have although lacking any real justification, as an effort to help the poor or injure the wealthy appears to be politically invulnerable (Tullock, 1970, 1983, 1986, 1988).

GORDON TULLOCK

REFERENCES

Tullock, G. (1970). *Private Wants, Public Means: An Economic Analysis of the Desirable Scope of Government.* New York: Basic Books.

Tullock, G. (1983). *Economics of Income Distribution.* Hingham, MA: Kluwer Academic Publishers.

Tullock, G. (1986). *The Economics of Wealth and Poverty.* London: Wheatsheaf Press.

Tullock, G. (1988). *Wealth, Poverty & Politics.* Oxford: Basil Blackwell.

REDISTRIBUTIVE POLITICS 2

All policies have distributive consequences, and redistributive motives drive a good deal of politics. There are many pathways for redistributive policy. Some of these work through labor markets (as in the wage setting institutions of some corporatist regimes), or regulation of products and prices, or provision of public services. This essay focuses, instead, on a type of explicit redistribution in democratic polities, *viz.*, policies that directly redistribute income among people through a system of taxes and transfers.

Much of the work on the positive theory of this kind of redistribution has relied on a "workhorse model" in which the parameters of a linear income tax function are chosen by majority rule (Romer, 1975; Roberts, 1977; Meltzer and Richard, 1981). People differ in their endowments or income-earning capacities. Taxes are levied in proportion to before-tax income, and are redistributed in the form of a lump-sum transfer ("demogrant") to everyone. Even though this appears to be a rather special kind of redistributive scheme, it is a good place to start, for several reasons. (1) It is the simplest framework that allows for progressivity, in the sense that average tax rates are increasing in income. The higher is the demogrant, the greater the progressivity and higher the degree to which income is redistributed. (2) Considerations such as incentive effects of taxes and transfers can readily be incorporated in the analysis. (3) The political problem can be reduced to one of choosing a single tax parameter: either the tax rate or, equivalently, the size of the demogrant. This makes the analytical problem of establishing voting equilibrium much easier than in settings with more policy dimensions.

In models of this type, the usual prediction is that the political equilibrium under majority rule will be the tax policy (or degree of redistribution) most preferred by the citizen with median before-tax income. For an interesting range of special cases, this result can be sharpened further to the following: For actual income distributions, the median is typically below the mean. This means that, for the pivotal voter, the "tax price" of a dollar of transfers is less than a dollar. The further away the median is from the mean, the lower is this tax price. The equilibrium level of redistribution will be decreasing in median before-tax income (for a given average before-tax income) and increasing in average before-tax income (for a given median). In other words, as the median before-tax income gets further from the average, the amount of politically-enacted redistribution will increase. The ratio of median to mean income is one measure of income inequality: the lower this ratio, the greater the inequality. So the result can be interpreted to mean that, at least in democracies, we should expect to observe more redistribution where, *ceteris paribus*, there is greater inequality in before-tax incomes. (This does not mean, of course, that the after-tax distribution will be more equal when there is more before-tax inequality.)

An important point in connection with the above results is that they concern a majority-voting equilibrium. The segment of the population that does not vote — perhaps because they do not have the right to vote or because, for other reasons, their political importance is systematically very low — will not affect the collective choice. So the relevant distribution of income in the interpretation of the results is the distribution of income among the politically effective population. Increased political participation by low-income groups — due, for example, to extension of the franchise together with political mobilization — will lower the median before-tax income relative to the mean. This will increase the equilibrium level of redistribution. (Of course, there may be a considerable lag between the time of enfranchisement and the mobilization required to have an effect on policy.) On the other hand, holding the effective median before-tax income constant, a fall in the income of those below the median will lead to less redistribution.

Cross-country comparisons are fraught with difficulties, but recent work by Milanovic (2000) sheds some light on these hypotheses. He looked at data on factor incomes (before taxes and transfers) in 24 democracies over the period 1974–1997. He compared these with disposable incomes (after taxes and transfers). Unremarkably, the distribution of disposable income is generally more equal than that of factor income — evidence of the pervasiveness of redistribution in democracies. But, in addition, this *reduction* in inequality is greater in countries with higher before-tax inequality. This is consistent with the hypotheses of the basic model. At the same time, Milanovic's data also suggest that people in the middle of the factor-income distribution gain very little from redistribution. This implies that, overall, the pure majoritarian framework assumed by the median-voter setup may not be quite the right model of the political process.

The standard model has been elaborated in many ways. Here I will note only a few main issues that have attracted attention recently: multiple jurisdictions, uncertainty, and endogenous formation of beliefs about the incentive effects of redistribution.

One can consider redistributive politics when there are many jurisdictions, each of which can redistribute within its own borders. Bolton and Roland (1997) use the linear-tax framework to examine how redistributive politics can affect the stability of federal arrangements. A majority of a region's residents may prefer to stay (or become) politically independent, rather than be subject to the transfers that would occur under the redistributive policy chosen by a unified government. Political support for secession in a region is more likely when there are significant inter-regional differences in income distribution and the efficiency gains from unification are relatively small. Such secession threats can sometimes be forestalled by adjustments in the redistributive policy of the central government. This may mean increasing redistribution to gain the support of lower-income regions; in other situations it may mean reducing redistribution in response to the political pressures of relatively high-income regions.

When people can move across jurisdictional boundaries, the incentive effects of taxes and transfers include locational decisions. Redistributive politics can induce sorting of households among jurisdictions. In a metropolitan area with many communities, this can be one of the sources of income stratification (i.e., clustering by income groups), even when people do not have a direct preference to live among others of similar incomes (Westhoff, 1977; Epple and Romer, 1991; Epple et al., 2001). This sorting, in turn, limits the extent of redistribution that can occur when taxing authority is decentralized.

Returning to the single-jurisdiction framework, incorporating uncertainty into the analysis can change some of the predictions of the standard model. (For a consideration of redistribution and uncertainty in a multi-jurisdiction framework, see Persson and Tabellini (1996).) When income streams are uncertain, redistribution acquires a "social insurance" motive. This kind of insurance typically pays benefits in the event of a "negative shock" such as unemployment. Suppose that insurance is a normal good. Then increasing inequality (holding mean income constant) lowers the median voter's demand for social insurance. At the same time, it increases the demand for direct redistribution, as in the standard model with no uncertainty. The net effect on redistributive policy is ambiguous, and will depend on details such as the degree of risk aversion. Moene and Wallerstein (2001) present a model in which one obtains a U-shaped relationship between redistribution and inequality. When inequality is low, the insurance aspect predominates and increasing inequality leads to less redistribution. At higher levels of inequality, the direct redistribution motive is stronger and increases as inequality grows. Bénabou (2000), in a different model in which the insurance motive plays an important role, also derives such a U-shaped relationship. Moene and Wallerstein provide empirical evidence that supports this relationship, using data on social expenditures in 18 countries.

Uncertainty can also play a more subtle role in shaping people's attitudes toward redistribution. Suppose that individual before-tax incomes are the result not only of costly individual effort but also of inherited factors (or "opportunities") and luck. For a given level of effort, someone with better luck or more affluent social background will, on average, generate more income. From an individual's point of view, the link between effort and income is uncertain. Piketty (1995) analyzes a linear-tax model of this type, where people rationally use observations about the income dynamics of their own families to form beliefs about the incentive effects of taxation. Since someone with poor parents is more likely to have low income than someone with rich parents (holding effort constant), people with different histories will form different beliefs. Those who come to believe that effort is important will be less willing to support redistribution than those who think predetermined factors or luck are more important. In this framework, people with the same income (and same underlying preferences) can therefore have different attitudes (or, more precisely, induced preferences) toward redistribution, and these differences can persist in a dynamic equilibrium. The equilibrium choice of redistributive policy will still correspond to the median of preferred tax rates, but the pivotal voter need no longer be someone with median before-tax income. Two countries with similar current income distributions but different histories can therefore have different current redistributive policies.

The median-voter framework of the standard model applies most cleanly to direct democracy, or to systems with first-past-the-post elections contested by two vote-maximizing political parties. With proportional representation and more than two parties, the analytical task of deriving politico-economic equilibrium is more complicated. Policy depends on legislative bargaining among parties. Relative bargaining strengths of the parties depend on electoral outcomes. The economic choices and voting decisions of the population depend, in turn, on forecasts of legislative bargains. In general, the pivotal voter in such a setting will be endogenously determined, and the results one obtains are likely to be quite sensitive to how the model is specified. Austen-Smith (2000) develops a linear-tax model in which three parties compete under PR. Each party represents an economic interest group or occupational category. (Parties are assumed to be "ideological" and do not change their interest-group allegiances.) Redistributive policy affects choices of occupations, which in turn affect the relative electoral strengths of the parties. For a plausible range of cases, Austen-Smith shows that the PR policy equilibrium leads to more redistribution than would occur in a two-party majoritarian setting. This seems to be consistent with the stylized facts from the U.S. and Western Europe.

Another departure from the standard model is to move away from the essentially one-dimensional policy space of that framework. In one such formulation, voters care about a non-economic issue (such as race relations or religion) as well as about their own economic well-being. Two parties compete by taking positions on both issues, so that a platform consists of a redistributive policy as captured by a proposed tax rate in the linear-tax framework, together with a stance with respect to the non-economic dimension. Suppose that parties are again ideological, in the sense that they maximize the expected post-election well-being of particular groups of voters. So, as in Roemer's (1998) analysis, a "Left" party might represent the anti-clerical poor while a "Right" party stands for the pro-clerical rich. If there are enough pro-clerical poor voters, it may be optimal for the Left party to moderate its stance on redistributive policy — i.e., make it economically more conservative. Because the two policy dimensions cannot be unbundled, redistributive platforms — and the resulting policy equilibrium — in the two-dimensional setting end up being different from what they would be in the absence of the non-economic dimension. An increase in the salience of the non-economic issue can cause a party to deviate further from its ideal point on the redistributive dimension. Which party is affected more in this way depends on the distribution of voter preferences over the two dimensions. Roemer (1998) suggests that in the U.S. there was an increase in the salience of non-economic ("values") issues from the mid-1970s to the mid-1990s, together with a move by the Democratic party toward a less-redistributive platform.

Even restricting the focus to explicit redistribution, a broad range of issues remain to be analyzed. For example, the dynamic interactions among political participation, redistributive politics, and economic performance are only beginning to be understood. (See Bénabou (2000) for a start in this direction). On this and other fronts, there is great scope for further theoretical exploration together with detailed empirical work that draws on the implications of theory.

THOMAS ROMER

REFERENCES

Austen-Smith, D. (2000). "Redistributing income under proportional representation." *Journal of Political Economy*, 108: 1235–1269.

Bénabou, R. (2000). "Unequal societies: Income distribution and the social contract." *American Economic Review*, 90: 96–129.

Bolton, P. and Roland, G. (1997). "The breakup of nations: A political economy analysis." *Quarterly Journal of Economics*, 112: 1057–1090.

Epple, D. and Romer, T. (1991). "Mobility and redistribution." *Journal of Political Economy*, 99: 828–858.

Epple, D., Romer, T., and Sieg, H. (2001). "Interjurisdictional sorting and majority rule: an empirical investigation." *Econometrica*, 69: 1437–1465.

Meltzer, A.H. and Richard, S.F. (1981). "A rational theory of the size of government." *Journal of Political Economy*, 89: 914–927.

Milanovic, B. (2000). "The median-voter hypothesis, income inequality, and income redistribution: an empirical test with the required data." *European Journal of Political Economy*, 16: 367–410.

Moene, K.O. and Wallerstein, M. (2001). "Inequality, social insurance, and redistribution." *American Political Science Review*, 95: 859–874.

Persson, T. and Tabellini, G. (1996). "Federal fiscal constitutions, part II: risk sharing and redistribution." *Journal of Political Economy*, 104: 979–1009.

Piketty, T. (1995). "Social mobility and redistributive politics." *Quarterly Journal of Economics*, 110: 551–584.

Roberts, K.W.S. (1977). "Voting over income tax schedules." *Journal of Public Economics*, 8: 329–340.

Roemer, J.E. (1998). "Why the poor do not expropriate the rich in democracies: an old argument in new garb." *Journal of Public Economics*, 70: 399–424.

Romer, T. (1975). "Individual welfare, majority voting, and the properties of a linear income tax." *Journal of Public Economics*, 4: 163–185.

Westhoff, F. (1977). "Existence of equilibria in economies with a local public good." *Journal of Economic Theory*, 14: 84–112.

REGULATING GOVERNMENT

The common perception is that one of the primary functions of government is to assure the proper functioning of market economies by regulating a wide range of private economic activity. This perception is quite the opposite of the type of regulation that is needed. Regulation is needed for market economies to function properly, but it is regulation *of* government, not regulation *by* government that is crucial.

We are not arguing that private economic activity requires no regulation. It is obvious to anyone who understands the degree of coordination required among literally hundreds of millions, indeed billions, of individuals to create even a modicum of wealth (much less the amount that those of us lucky enough to live in capitalist countries enjoy routinely) that a great deal of economic regulation is required. But the most effective economic regulation is

provided by the information and motivation contained in market prices. The communication that takes place through market prices motivates people from all over the globe to pursue their own interests in ways that do the most to promote the interests of others.

Yet, a strong case can be made that government is necessary for a market economy to function properly. Without collective action backed up by the threat of government coercion, the coordination and cooperation that is the hallmark of properly-functioning markets can be undermined by a number of prisoners' dilemmas — situations in which it is in the interest of each to make choices that are destructive to the interests of all. A market economy, it is argued, requires the protection of private property against domestic predators; the enforcement of contracts; the provision of critical public goods such as national defense (protection of private property against foreign aggressors); the internalization of major externalities such as those associated with serious pollution problem; and possibly the financing of certain types of infrastructure where the costs of charging each user an amount corresponding to his use would be exorbitant (e.g., city streets).

For the purposes of our argument, we accept the case that without government forcing people to contribute to some collective goods, the prisoners' dilemma temptations would result in less than the efficient amounts of them being provided, although we readily acknowledge that strong opposing arguments can be made. For example, see, Friedman (1989: Chs 28–31) and Benson (1990) for arguments that private property can be protected and contracts enforced by strictly voluntary arrangements, or Coase (1974) who pointed out that lighthouses, a widely used example of a public good that requires government provision, were widely provided privately in eighteenth-century England. But even if you accept that government coercion is necessary to overcome the prisoners' dilemma that would otherwise prevent the optimal provision of the above goods, the case favoring that coercion is subject to far more qualifications than commonly realized — qualifications that explain the necessity of regulating government if markets are to work properly.

While it is theoretically possible for government to use its coercive powers to resolve the prisoners' dilemmas that prevent the optimal provision of certain collective goods, the exercise of that coercion creates other prisoners' dilemmas that can be, and often are, more destructive than the ones supposedly eliminated. Consider some examples.

If government is to produce the services that people value most, but which supposedly won't be provided through the private market, consumer/taxpayers must be able to accurately communicate their preferences to political authorities. Voting is surely the best way for the general public to transmit information on which government services they believe are worth more than the cost. While voting may be the best way to keep politicians informed on the wide-ranging preferences of the public at large, it suffers from a serious problem by putting each voter (or potential voter) in a number of prisoners' dilemmas.

For example, citizens would be better off collectively if they all became well informed on the positions of political candidates vying for their votes, and on the issues the winning candidate will decide upon, and then cast their vote accordingly. Suppliers provide better service when their customers are well informed, and this is true whether the suppliers are politicians or used-car dealers. But there are costs to becoming politically informed and each voter knows that, as opposed to becoming informed on a private purchase, his political choices will have no effect on the government services he receives or how much he pays for them, no matter how informed his votes. This is true no matter what he thinks other voters will do, unless he foolishly expects the highly unlikely possibility that other voters will split their votes evenly, in which case his vote will be decisive. So the rational choice for each citizen is to avoid the cost of becoming politically informed (which is reflected in polls showing that most people are woefully uninformed about candidates and issues) even though the resulting widespread "rational ignorance" leads to the worst outcome for citizens in general. Uninformed citizens are left vulnerable to the political exploitation of special-interests, as will be discussed momentarily.

Even if information were freely acquired and citizens were fully informed politically, they would still be in a voting prisoners' dilemma. There are private costs incurred by those who take the time to register and vote. These costs are not large, but they are far larger than any private benefits realized from shifting political decisions in the direction the voter prefers, a benefit that is effectively zero given the miniscule probability that any one vote will be decisive in an election. So even though it would be collectively rational for all informed voters to go to the trouble to vote, since this would keep politicians more responsive to the general concerns of the public, voting is irrational (a least for the purpose of affecting the outcome) from the perspective of each voter. This prisoners' dilemma is commonly referred to as "rational apathy."

A natural response is that rational apathy cannot be a serious prisoners' dilemma since many people do vote, which means that they must realize personal benefits from voting that aren't captured by the effect their votes have on election outcomes. This argument has merit, but it tells us

that those voters who avoid the prisoners' dilemma of ration apathy do so by becoming entangled in another one. Some people realize an expressive benefit from voting that has nothing to do with the election's outcome. They simply feel good about expressing themselves in favor of, or in opposition to, particular policies and candidates. And because no individual vote is likely to affect the outcome, the cost of achieving expressive satisfaction through voting is effectively zero for each voter. So if it makes a person feel good about himself to support "helping the poor" or "protecting the environment," he will likely vote for government programs that purport to accomplish these noble goals (or for candidates that support them) no matter how much these programs will cost him in higher taxes *if they pass*. The tax cost has little influence on his voting decision since that decision has no affect on whether a proposal passes. Of course, if a majority of the voters yield to the temptation of "expressive voting" then all taxpayers end up paying much higher tax bills than any of them would vote for with a decisive vote. But, because of the prisoners' dilemma that expressive voting creates, each voter judges himself better off getting his "expressive voting" benefit no matter how he thinks others will vote. See Brennan and Lomasky (1993) for a more complete discussion of expressive voting.

Once voters empower government to take more of their money for noble purposes, they find themselves in another prisoners' dilemma. Making sure that their tax money is spent to actually accomplish the advertised objectives requires that taxpayers follow up on their votes by monitoring how politicians and bureaucrats spend that money. Although taxpayers would be collectively better off if all contributed to the cost of monitoring, each taxpayer is better off not contributing, no matter what she thinks others will do.

The resulting lack of taxpayer oversight means that once a government program has been approved, always in the name of accomplishing some noble purpose, organized interest groups working behind the scenes will make sure the program is implemented so that it does more to benefit them than to accomplish the noble purpose. Because these groups are relatively small and have a dominant interest, they are able to overcome the prisoners' dilemma that prevents the general taxpayer from organizing for effective political action. Of course, members of organized interest-groups could, like voters, use their political influence with noble social goals in mind. But, because an interest group's political actions are far more decisive than a vote, using its influence to promote social goals is extremely costly in terms of sacrificed private benefits.

But interest groups also find themselves in a destructive prisoners' dilemma because of their ability to gain private benefits at public expense through political influence. Piracy is profitable when the victims are many and the pirates are few. But everyone is worse off when almost everyone becomes a pirate and few are left shipping the goods. And today almost everyone is a member of some interest group that is benefiting from some government program that harms the general public. But even though everyone would be better off if all such groups reduced their claims on others, no group is motivated to do so. Who wants to lower their Jolly Roger and go back to shipping the goods when he is surrounded by pirates?

A government regulated only by the right of everyone to vote is an unregulated government — a government that soon destroys the market economy and the freedom and productivity that are impossible without the socially benevolent regulation of private property and market prices. Unless government is regulated by constitutional limits that prevent most political activity that would win majority support, voting becomes little more than the means by which voters choose who represents them in the mutually destructive attempt of each to live at the expense of each other. These constitutional limits take the form of substantive restrictions that prevent government from doing particular things (such as taking private property without just compensation, and then only for genuinely public purposes), and restrictions that put procedural roadblocks in the path of government action (such as the executive veto, judicial review, and supra majority votes).

Unfortunately, political democracy has been elevated in the public mind as the primary means of protecting human rights (Bethell, 1998: 335), with preventing government from doing anything a majority votes for (or would vote for) being seen as undemocratic. This represents a dramatic shift in public opinion from the healthy skepticism toward political actions that prevailed during the founding of the American republic and which continued to prevail in large measure until the end of the nineteenth century. This shift in public opinion is a serious threat to constitutional regulation of government. As Henry Simon (1951: 20) observed: "Constitutional provisions are no stronger than the consensus that they articulate. At best, they can only check abuses of power until moral pressure is mobilized; and their check must become ineffective if often overtly used."

J.R. CLARK
DWIGHT R. LEE

REFERENCES

Benson, B. (1990). *The Enterprise of Law: Justice Without the State*. San Francisco: Pacific Research Institute for Public Policy.

Bethell, T. (1998). *The Noblest Triumph: Property and Prosperity Through the Ages*. New York: St. Martins Press.

Brennan, G. and Lomasky, L. (1993). *Democracy and Decision: The Pure Theory of Electoral Preference*. Cambridge: Cambridge University Press.

Coase, R. (1974). "The lighthouse in economics." *Journal of Law and Economics*, October: 357–376.

Friedman, D. (1989). *The Machinery of Freedom: Guide to a Radical Capitalism*. La Salle, Ill.: Open Court.

Simon, H. (1951). *Economic Policy for a Free Society*. Chicago: University of Chicago Press.

REGULATORY TAKINGS

[N] or shall private property be taken for public use, without just compensation. (U.S. Const. Amend. V)

[W]hile property may be regulated to a certain extent, if regulation goes too far it will be recognized as a taking. (Pennsylvania Coal v. Mahon, 260 U.S. 393, 415 (1922). Justice Holmes)

The Takings Clause of the Fifth Amendment of the United States Constitution is the basis for regulatory and non-regulatory takings claims. The Clause allows government — federal, state, or local — to take private property only if government uses it for a legitimate state interest and justly compensates citizens for what it takes.

Governments may take property by physically appropriating (condemning) it or by taking title to it. Such outright takings are an old prerogative of the sovereign, and are referred to as the "eminent domain" power. When a government entity physically appropriates, or invades, property (e.g., when land is flooded in order to build a dam) a *per se* taking exists.

In an eminent domain case, a court considers whether or not an appropriation of private property, by physical invasion or by title transfer, occurred; whether the property was taken for a public use; and if so, whether the government paid the owner just compensation (Eagle, 2001). If all of these conditions exist, the appropriation is constitutional.

In cases involving a regulatory taking, property is not appropriated physically. Rather, by regulation, a government reduces the range of permissible uses to which the citizen may put his property. Such restrictions oftentimes reduce the value of the property substantially. A regulatory taking exists, for example, when a state government enacts legislation forbidding all building, or other use or development, of property that previously could be developed (Lucas v. South Carolina Coastal Council, 1992).

Not all government actions that prevent property owners from using their property as they wish are regulatory takings. When a government enforces property-use restrictions that existed when the owner acquired the property, there is no taking and the government need not compensate the property owner.

In a regulatory-takings case, a court will follow a balancing approach introduced by Justice Holmes in Pennsylvania Coal and reiterated in the 1978 Penn Central case. Courts will make an *ad hoc*, factual determination of the unique circumstances of the case, paying close attention to the following three concerns: the nature of the government action; the severity of the economic impact of that action; and, the degree to which the action interferes with the property owner's reasonable, investment-backed expectations (Pennsylvania Central Transportation Co. v. New York City at 124).

Richard Epstein notes that takings jurisprudence is both complex and paradoxical (Epstein, 1998). Over time, takings jurisprudence developed in ways that provide citizens with strong protection against physical intrusion, or the taking of title by government entities. At the same time it affords relatively little protection to persons whose properties are subjected to strict limits on uses (Lawrence, 1990). Thus, some sticks in the bundle of rights that make up common-law property rights, such as the right to be free from unwanted physical invasion, receive much greater protection than do the "use" and "development" sticks.

Both regulatory and non-regulatory takings place the rights of private citizens to use their property as they wish in conflict with the desire of government officials to use this property differently. In particular, specific private-property rights typically compete with the state's police powers. Over the past century, as the scope of these powers has expanded the conflicts between government actions and private-property rights have multiplied.

From a public-choice perspective, government's increasing size and scope raises the specter of special-interest groups lobbying for the use of police powers to gain access to property rights that they would otherwise have to purchase (Fischel, 1988). If the costs associated with the lobbying activity are less than the expected benefits to the interest group of acquiring property on the market, then groups will use the political process to seek rents via property regulation (Levmore, 1990).

Uncompensated takings present a variety of problems including, as Epstein notes: decreased investment activity, unfair distribution of "gains" from the coerced transfer, and decreased overall economic efficiency as properties are redistributed to a lower-value use from owners who place higher values on them (Epstein, 1998). These various drawbacks lead Epstein to note that the compensation requirement, "force[s] the state to internalize the cost of its

initiatives. Just compensation just operates as a pricing mechanism in a world of compulsory purchase" (Epstein, 1998: 564).

However, special-interest groups continue to resort to the political process to acquire private property. This very real problem is illustrated by the case of Casino Reinvestment Dev. Auth. v. Banin, 320 N.J. Super 342 (1998), involving an attempt by developer Donald Trump to use the state's eminent domain power to acquire land he wished to use for a parking lot at one of his casinos. Interest group lobbying may also help explain the popularity of wetlands' regulations in the United States. These regulations, particularly section 404 of the Clean Water Act, limit the ability of homeowners and developers to use their property, in order to protect a resources — wetlands — that environmentalists value. The regulation shifts the costs of wetlands' protection from environmentalists and others who place some value on wetlands protection to property owners, who may place very different values on these resources (Ceplo, 1995).

The problem that lies at the heart of efficiency concerns as they relate to regulatory takings is that of differential valuation. Using the wetlands example, if special-interest groups lobby government to restrict the use of private wetlands it is clear that they place some value on the control of private-property rights. We can infer that special-interest groups value the protection of wetlands, or the restriction of property rights, up to the amount they are willing to spend in lobbying efforts. But it is not clear that these special-interest groups value the property rights as highly as do the rights' holders. After all, the property owners paid for their land and would, presumably, be willing to sell the land, or certain rights to use the land, at some price.

If government regulates and restricts the use of private wetlands transfers value from property owners, and gives it to individuals who are unwilling to pay market prices for the resource. Relying on the regulatory process to accomplish their ends, interest groups limit their transaction costs to those associated with lobbying. If they succeed, interest groups who rely upon regulatory action to accomplish their ends avoid the costs associated with purchasing rights from myriad owners. Importantly, such non-market transactions restrict the flow of information concerning alternative uses of resources that market prices convey.

Developing a strict rule that private-property owners must be compensated when government takes property rights goes some way toward addressing the efficiency concern outlined above because the requirement forces government, through the taxpayers, to bear the costs of restricting or altering property use. If government must pay for the property rights it takes, then government officials must calculate which rights are worth the price of compensation. The compensation requirement will not eliminate the problem posed by interest group lobbying; interest groups will still seek, and politician still provide, regulation. But because government revenue has alternate uses, a compensation requirement will more tightly constrain the urge of officials to regulate property uses.

A compensation requirement does not, however, impose the costs of regulation directly on the interest groups that lobby for them. So, in the case of wetlands regulation, if government were required to compensate owners of private wetlands for the loss of value caused by regulation, taxpayers as a whole would bear the cost of protecting the resource; private owners would not be forced to bear this cost alone. Environmentalists would still accomplish their goal of restricting the use of property that they do not own at a cost to them that is less than the full cost to the general fisc. Thus, while compensation for regulatory takings would improve matters, it would not eliminate interest group politics.

Differential valuation is also an issue when courts examine the "reasonable, investment-backed expectations" of private property owners whose property is regulated. Beginning with the Pennsylvania Coal decision and followed by the Penn Central, Lucas, and Palazzolo, takings jurisprudence developed in such a way that courts will find no compensation requirement for owners whose property is regulated if, after the regulatory action, the property retains some value.

The questions of who defines "reasonable," and which types of investments will be considered relevant, are clearly important, but have not yet been directly addressed by the courts, although the Supreme Court has noted that reasonableness will be determined in light of state property law (Lucas v. South Carolina Coastal Council, 1992, footnote 7). As Steven Eagle notes: "Regulatory schemes … are subject to an upward spiral. The more regulation there is, the more regulation the public may expect, and the more regulation is permitted in accordance with the public's expectation" (Eagle, 2001: 914) And as Eagle points out, this "upward spiral" of regulation leads to a "downward spiral" of diminishing expectations concerning the protection of private-property rights.

Another issue that presents some difficulties is the "parcel as a whole" doctrine. This doctrine requires courts faced with regulatory takings claims to consider the value of affected property in its entirety. If the entire parcel retains some value, the taking is not compensable. For example, if a 50-acre parcel contains a 20-acre area of wetlands, and if the property owner is unable, due to a regulatory scheme, to develop the 20 acres of wetlands, a court will consider the value remaining in the other 30 acres of land before making a compensation decision. If the 30 non-wetlands acres retain value, the owner will receive no compensation for the loss of value associated with the regulation of the 20 wetlands acres.

Until relatively recently, the Supreme Court was reluctant to find that a compensable taking occurred when government did not take either physical possession of or title to private property (Eagle, 2001). Regulations that reduced a property's value were typically not found to be compensable takings. So, for example, in the 1887 case of Mugler v. Kansas, the Supreme Court found that a state statute forbidding the manufacture of alcohol was not a compensable taking of a formerly lawful private brewery. In a 1915 case, the court reviewed a Los Angeles statute that outlawed brickyards and brick kilns in certain parts of the city. The case involved a brick maker named Hadacheck who was arrested and imprisoned for continuing to make bricks on his property. Arguing that his actions did not constitute a public nuisance, Hadacheck claimed the government action took approximately 90% of his property's value. Despite this fact, the court refused to find a taking and held that the City did not have to compensate Mr. Hadacheck (Hadacheck v. Los Angeles, 1915).

Not until 1922 did Justice Holmes make his now-famous comment that government regulation might go "too far" and effect a taking. Despite the comment, the Supreme Court did little to enforce the takings clause against the growing use government police powers. Four years after Holmes' statement, the Court allowed a broad zoning ordinance to stand in Village of Euclid v. Ambler Realty Co., despite the fact that the new regulation reduced the value of the property by 75%, and substantially altered the owner's rights to use their property. Six years later, the Court decided that a Virginia law requiring all red cedar trees located within two miles of any apple orchard be cut down, if the cedars had cedar rust, did not "take" property from a man who was forced to cut down a large number of cedar trees on his property (Miller v. Shoene, 1928).

Because of this reluctance to limit governments' use of police powers, actions such as zoning ordinances, rent-control laws, a host of environmental laws, civil forfeiture laws, historic preservation laws, and others were found to be valid under the U.S. Constitution, so long as the state could articulate a "rational basis" for such regulation. Charles Rowley sees this development as a "process of constitutional disregard … [by which the Supreme Court] justices enabled the legislature to suborn the U.S. economy from capitalism to socialism as that legislature pursued its own ambitions to become the presidium of a rent-seeking, transfer society" (Rowley, 1992: 103).

This position of exceptional deference to the government's extension of its police powers culminated in the 1978 case of Pennsylvania Central Transportation Co. v. City of New York. The case involved New York City's Historic Preservation Law, which required owners of historic buildings to maintain the exteriors of these buildings, and which forbade their alteration without prior approval by the Historic Preservation Commission (O'Hara, 1995). The plaintiff, Penn Central, owned Grand Central Station in New York, a designated historic landmark. The company entered into a lease with another company, UGP Properties, to rent air space over the terminal so that a fifty-story office building could be built. The lease was entered into after passage of the Historic Preservation Law and the court upheld the City's denial of approval for building over the space.

Applying the *ad hoc*, factual analysis to the case, the Court found the plaintiffs could not establish a "taking" simply by showing that they had been denied the ability to exploit a property interest that they believed was available for development. The Court found that the Landmarks Law did not interfere with the terminal's established uses or with the plaintiffs' key expectation concerning its use of the parcel. Further, the development restrictions were substantially related to the promotion of the general welfare. These restrictions not only permitted reasonable beneficial use of the landmark, i.e., reasonable return on investment, but also provided the plaintiffs with other opportunities to improve the terminal site and other properties it owned (as Epstein says in his landmark work, Takings, "'reasonable return' on investment is simply a euphemism for the confiscation of private property, bit by bit and year by year." Epstein, 1985: 188).

Rowley notes that the decision not only "demonstrated an appalling ignorance of the nature of property rights and of the meaning of the eminent domain clause, but a shrewd understanding of the dominant political agenda of the legislature and its special interests at that time" (Rowley, 1992: 115). It was not until the 1980s that the court began to limit ever-expanding use of police powers to regulate a wide variety of activities.

In a case from 1980, Agins v. City of Tiburon, the Supreme Court articulated a two-prong test for deciding if a regulatory action had unconstitutionally taken property. The first prong asks if the regulation advances a legitimate state interest. Next, a court must ask if the regulation denies the property owner economically viable use of his land. In the case, the plaintiffs owned very valuable property overlooking San Francisco. The city rezoned the land for single-family residence or open space only, rather than condemning it, because it believed condemnation would be too expensive. The property owner alleged that the zoning amounted to a taking. The Court disagreed. The Agins test is often applied in cases of facial changes to a statute or regulation, where a plaintiff claims that "on its face" the regulation fails to advance a legitimate state interest or takes all economic value from an owner. If a statute or regulation meets the Agins facial challenge, it might still be challenged under the Penn Central balancing test "as applied" to a particular plaintiff.

1987 was a watershed year for takings jurisprudence, with the Supreme Court deciding four cases involving regulatory takings. Three of these decisions finally breathed life into Justice Holmes' statement that government regulation could go "too far." One case continued the tradition of strong deference to government use of police powers to restrict property use.

In First English Evangelical Lutheran Church of Glendale v. County of Los Angeles, the Court found that a temporary taking of property had occurred and that the plaintiff should be compensated for its loss. This decision resolved the question of whether or not just compensation is a remedy for a regulatory taking as opposed to a simple invalidation of the offending statute or ordinance (Lawrence, 1990). It is also seen as an elevation, by the Supreme Court, of substantive as well as procedural protection for private-property rights (Siegan, 1997: 124).

The facts of the case are these: in 1979 the County of Los Angeles passed an ordinance prohibiting the building or reconstruction of any structure in a particular flood-prone area, pending further study. In 1981 the interim ordinance was replaced by a permanent ordinance that allowed limited construction or reconstruction in the floodzone. The plaintiff church had run a campground in the area since 1957 (in 1978, during a severe flood, all the buildings at the campground were destroyed). The church subsequently filed suit, alleging that the ordinance took all use of their property.

The Court assumed, for purposes of reaching a decision, that the ordinance took all use of the church's property. It was held that invalidation of the ordinance alone would be insufficient to compensate the plaintiff for its loss, and so compensation was due despite the fact that the county government did not invoke its eminent domain powers and despite the fact that the taking was temporary, not permanent.

Also in 1987, in Nollan v. California Coastal Commission, the Court invalidated an attempt by the California Coastal Commission to tie the granting of approval for shorefront development to a requirement that property owners dedicate a public easement across their private beaches.

The Nollans leased, then purchased, beachfront property, one-quarter mile from a county park and public beach. A run-down cottage was located on this property. The Nollans wanted to tear the cottage down and build a two-story home. They applied for a permit to build, and the Coastal Commission approved the permit on condition that the Nollans allow the public to walk across their property. This condition was imposed in recognition of a California statute that required public access in case of new development or certain instances of reconstruction.

The plaintiffs argued that the regulation worked a *per se* physical taking, because the public-access requirement might lead to constant public presence on their property. Further, they argued that the regulation imposed upon them the costs associated with creating a public benefit. Justice Scalia, writing for the majority, found that the regulation did create a *per se* taking and so the Court did not need to balance interests in making a compensation determination. The court also discussed the issue of whether or not the Nollans were being asked to bear the costs of creating a public benefit. Applying the Agins test, the Court found that there was no "essential nexus" between the regulation's means (an easement over private property) and its ends (public access to the ocean). Thus, the regulation did not advance a legitimate state interest; therefore, it was an unconstitutional taking.

Nollan introduced the idea that there must be a nexus between government means and ends when it regulates property use. It also established the idea that a regulation that negatively affects property use must substantially advance a legitimate state interest. This requirement significantly less deferential to the use of government's police powers is the older, rational-basis requirement. By raising the bar on what was acceptable government regulatory behavior, the Court gave property owners increased abilities to challenge government actions limiting property uses.

In Hodel v. Irving, the Court determined that part of a federal statute, the Indian Land Consolidation Act of 1983, which restricted the ability of Native Americans to devise small interests in land to their heirs violated the Takings Clause. The court noted that the legislation might, in fact, serve a legitimate government interest in resolving the problem of very small landholdings among Native Americans. The court also noted that, given that most of the land was leased, there were few investment-backed concerns that might be affected. Despite this, the Court found that taking a traditional stick from the bundle of property rights — the right to pass property to one's heirs — was such an extreme measure that it was a taking, for which just compensation must be paid, despite the fact that the value of property affected was small. In a concurring opinion,

Justice Stevens stated: "[t]he Fifth Amendment makes no distinction between grand larceny and petty larceny" (Hodel v. Irving, 1987: 2089).

Finally, in Keystone Bituminous Coal Association v. DeBenedictis (1987), the Court determined that a Pennsylvania law prohibiting coal mining in certain cases where ground subsidence might occur is not an unconstitutional taking of property. Mine operators and individual coal companies who were, as a result of the law, forced to leave substantial amounts of unmined coal in the ground, brought the suit (Siegan, 1997). The Court found that the State of Pennsylvania asserted genuine public interests in preserving land and a variety of public and non-commercial buildings, including dwellings. Thus the statute advanced a legitimate state interest. Additionally, because it did not prohibit all mining of coal, the plaintiffs were left with some economically viable use of their land. Moreover, the Court analogized mining in cases where there was a threat of subsidence to a public nuisance, and noted that the government could legitimately act to prohibit such nuisances. As the nuisance exception to takings jurisprudence was well established, the Court determined that no compensable taking had occurred.

In Keystone, the Court found no taking and so the case did not provide as much protection of property rights as the mine owners would have liked. However, the Court's acceptance of the principles surrounding the judicial review of takings claims first elaborated Agins v. City of Tiburon represents "an approach generally more protective of property rights than had long existed in that hallowed tribunal" (Siegan, 1997: 114). The approach was borne out in the later 1987 decisions of First English, Nollan, and Hodel and in the subsequent, much-publicized cases of Lucas v. South Carolina Coastal Council and Dolan v. City of Tigard.

In Lucas, a 1988 state statute was found to take all economic value of a piece of property, triggering the just compensation requirement of the Fifth Amendment. The statute prohibited the building of any permanent habitable structure on certain ocean-front property in South Carolina. The plaintiff spent close to $1 million to purchase two ocean-front lots in 1986 before the statute was enacted. The purpose of the law was to create a natural buffer against high-tides, storm surges, and hurricanes, thus protecting natural habitat, promoting tourism, and preserving the South Carolina beach and dune system (Siegan, 1997).

The plaintiff argued that the statute rendered his property valueless and that therefore, his property was taken. The state claimed that development of the property would create a serious public harm and that compensation is not due to owners when government acts to prevent such harm. In the majority opinion, Justice Scalia wrote that when regulation deprives an owner of all economically viable use of land, a *per se* taking occurs and the government must compensate the owner unless the regulation deals with a nuisance, or the regulation is a part of the state's background principles of real property law (Callies, 1996).

Lucas is a landmark decision in which the Court placed some (highly specific) limits on the government's ability to take property through regulatory action. The case was hailed by property-rights advocates as a major victory. Coupled with the 1987 pro-property rights cases, the Court seemed poised to roll back decades of restriction on the liberty of citizens to use their property. This impression received further support in the 1994 case of Dolan v. City of Tigard.

In Dolan, the plaintiff, who owned an electric and plumbing supply store wanted to demolish one building and replace it with a larger one and a parking lot. The property was located in a business district zone so that the city could restrict development to take transportation and other public needs into account. The city's zoning requirements obligated property owners to meet a 15% open-space requirement. Dolan's permit was approved by the city planning commission on condition that she dedicate a 15-foot easement to be used for a storm-drainage system, and also that she dedicate an eight-foot easement for a pedestrian and bicycle path. The commission found that the easements were reasonably related to the increased use that the property would generate.

Mrs. Dolan sued, arguing that the easements took her property. She also argued that, after Nollan, partial takings are constitutional only if an essential nexus exists between the restriction and the proposed action. Here, she contended, there was no such nexus.

The Supreme Court reversed the ruling of the Oregon court. It found that the city did not show a reasonable relationship between the easements and Mrs. Dolan's proposed construction. This "reasonable relationship" requirement amended the first-prong of the Agins test that an essential nexus exist between the regulation and legitimate state interests. The Dolan decision requires courts to ask not only if the regulation advances a legitimate state interest, but also if the means and ends of the regulation are reasonably connected. The Court said that there must be a "rough proportionality" between these means and ends, a proportionality that was not evident in the Dolan case.

With the Dolan decision the Supreme Court might have reached the limits of its willingness to revive protection of private-property rights. In two subsequent takings decisions, Palazzolo v. State and Tahoe-Sierra, the Court further clarified when regulatory action will require compensation, and when such action will be constitutionally sound.

In Palazzolo, the Court considered the following: if regulation was in place before an owner purchased property, was the owner barred from bringing a regulatory takings claim?

The Court also considered the issue of economic viability. How much value need remain after regulation for property to have economic viability? At issue in Palazzolo were 18 acres of coastal wetlands. The owner, Mr. Palazzolo, filed a variety of building/development permit requests for this land over the course of more than 20 years. From 1960 to 1978, Mr. Palazzolo was sole shareholder of Shore Gardens, Inc., which held title to the property. From 1978 on, he owned the property outright.

In 1960, the Town of Westerly approved a plat for the property, subdividing it into 80 lots. Some of the lots were sold, but these parcels were located on "uplands" that could easily be developed. No parcels in the wetlands area were sold. In 1962, Mr. Palazzolo submitted a request to dredge a pond on the property. This application was returned because it was incomplete. In 1963, Mr. Palazzolo submitted another request to build a bulkhead, dredge the pond, and fill the wetlands. When this application was filed, there was no requirement that the state approve the filling of a wetland, however, there was a requirement that a person wishing to dredge a pond obtain approval from the Division of Harbors and Rivers. For reasons that remain unclear, Mr. Palazzolo did not fill the wetlands at this time.

In 1965, Rhode Island passed a wetlands protection act that required that the Department of Natural Resources approve all requests to fill coastal wetlands. In 1966, Mr. Palazzolo once again applied with DNR to dredge the pond, fill the wetlands, and build a beach facility. This request was approved in 1971, but then the approval was revoked. Mr. Palazzolo did not appeal the revocation. In 1971, the Coastal Resources Management Council was created. In 1977 this agency forbade the filling of coastal wetlands unless it approved the project.

In 1983, Palazzolo submitted a proposal with the CRMC to dredge the pond and fill his wetlands. This proposal was rejected and the rejection was not appealed. Tenacious, if nothing else, Mr. Palazzolo submitted another request to build a beach facility in 1985. This request was denied, appealed by Mr. Palazzolo, and the appeal denied.

Mr. Palazzolo filed his takings claim in 1986. The Supreme Court of Rhode Island determined that his claim was not ripe, because of faults found with his previous applications. Because Mr. Palazzolo's applications were not complete, the Rhode Island court determined that he had not yet received a final decision concerning the application of the wetlands-protection regulations to his property. Further, the state court found that "a regulatory takings claim may not be maintained where the regulation predates the acquisition of the property" (Palazzolo v. Rhode Island, at 715). In other words, the court said that because of changes in the regulatory regime in the 1960s, Mr. Palazzolo had notice, when he became the property's owner in 1978, that his title was limited by wetlands development restrictions. The court also held that Mr. Palazzolo retained some economic viability in the property because he could build on the uplands parcels and because he could make an open-space gift of the wetlands portion, worth about $150,000.

Mr. Palazzolo appealed to the Supreme Court. The Court held that, in fact, Mr. Palazzolo's claim was ripe, because the CRMC reached a final determination when it denied his 1983 and 1985 applications. The Court further held that Mr. Palazzolo's acquisition of title after the wetlands protection regulations took effect did not bar his takings claim. The Court rejected the Rhode Island court's rule, suggesting that to adopt it would be to absolve the state of the need to defend against excessive and capricious land-use regulations in all cases of post-regulatory transfer.

Finally though, the Court found that Mr. Palazzolo did retain significant economic value in his land because he could build on the upland portion. Applying the Lucas rule, Mr. Palazzolo was not deprived of *all* economic viability of the property, and so the Court remanded the case for further consideration which, as of this writing, has not been finalized. The Court did point out, though, that in cases where owners are not able to show a categorical (i.e., 100%) taking, "[t]he economic impact of the regulation on the claimant and ... the extent to which the regulation has interfered with distinct investment-backed expectations' are keenly relevant to takings analysis generally" (Eagle, 2001. Cumulative Supplement, 43).

Most recently, in Tahoe-Sierra Preservation Council, Inc. v. Tahoe Regional Planning Agency (2002), the Supreme Court again addressed the issue of regulatory takings. In a decision viewed as a set-back for property owners, the Court held that a temporary moratorium on building is not a taking.

The case involved a challenge to restrictions placed on construction at Lake Tahoe. The plaintiffs were hundreds of individuals who purchased undeveloped lots around the lake, with the expectation that they would be able to build. The Tahoe Regional Planning Authority imposed two moratoria, lasting 32 months, on building in the Lake Tahoe Basin while it studied the impact of development in the area and crafted a land-use plan (August, 1981–August, 1983 and August, 1983–April, 1984). Property owners brought suit, alleging the moratorium took their property, and that under the Lucas rule they should be compensated. At trial, the court found that there was no partial taking under the Penn Central test, but that under Lucas there was a categorical, if temporary, regulatory taking.

On appeal, the Ninth Circuit distinguished Tahoe from Lucas, noting that in Lucas the regulations at issue prohibited all development in perpetuity, while in this case, the moratorium, although lengthy, was temporary. Therefore, no categorical taking had occurred. Instead, a "temporal slice of the [plaintiffs'] fee interest" had been impacted. Further distinguishing Tahoe from First Evangelical Lutheran Church the court noted that the issue in the latter case was a remedial one: the proper way to calculate compensation for a taking, not the determination of whether such a taking had, in fact, occurred.

The Supreme Court affirmed the Ninth Circuit's decision. It held that the mere enactment of the regulations implementing the moratoria did not constitute a *per se* taking of the landowners' property. The Court determined that the issue of whether a taking occurred depended upon consideration of the landowners' investment-backed expectations, the actual impact of the regulation on the landowners, the importance of the public interest involved, and the reasons for imposing the temporary restriction. Thus, the Court relied upon the *ad hoc* balancing test of the Penn Central. (But, in Tahoe, the Court found that the owners did not challenge the trial court's finding that there was no partial taking, so the Court did not revisit this issue.)

Additionally, the Court suggested that adopting a categorical rule that any deprivation of all economic use, no matter how brief, constituted a compensable taking would impose unreasonable financial obligations upon governments for the normal delays involved in processing land-use applications and would improperly encourage hasty decision making. This was unacceptable to the majority and so a categorical rule based on the Lucas reasoning was rejected.

Tahoe, along with Palazzolo, signals at least a modification of the movement towards increased protection of private property rights by the highest court. Nothing in the plain language of the Fifth Amendment, or in economics, justifies government refusals to compensate property owners for the value losses caused by such regulation. The market value of such losses can be determined. And when a deprivation is less than complete, a diminution in value may also readily be determined. The Tahoe and Palazzolo cases, therefore, leave in unjustified scope for government regulation, permitting government to regulate and take property in violation of the Constitution.

In conclusion, current takings doctrine most vigorously protects owners against physical invasions, while regulatory takings that result in less than complete economic deprivation are permitted. Partial takings, after Dolan, are permissible, but only if an essential nexus exists between the government restriction and the state interest being pursued . And finally, regulatory takings that take all value, but that are temporary, are not unconstitutional.

Thus, despite the 1987 decisions and the subsequent cases in the 1990s, in most cases governments will not be required to compensate property owners if a regulation impairs the owner's right to use his land. The result is that property owners with regulatory takings claims still face a substantial burden to overcome the presumption that government police powers are being exercised constitutionally. Property rights remain at odds with government police powers.

KAROL BOUDREAUX

REFERENCES

American Jurisprudence 2nd Ed. (2000). 26 Eminent Domain, Section 12.

Callies, David L. (1996). "After Lucas and Dolan: an introductory essay," in D. Callies (ed.) *Takings: Land-Development Conditions and Regulatory Takings after Dolan and Lucas*. Chicago, IL: American Bar Association.

Ceplo, Karol (1995). "Land-rights conflicts in the regulation of wetlands," in B. Yandle (ed.) *Land Rights*. Lanham, Maryland: Rowman & Littlefield.

Clegg, R. (ed.) (1994). *Regulatory Takings: Restoring Private Property Rights*. Washington, DC: National Legal Center for the Public Interest.

Eagle, Steven ([1996] 2001). *Regulatory Takings*. New York: Lexis Publishing.

Epstein, Richard (1985). *Takings: Private Property and the Power of Eminent Domain*. Cambridge, MA: Harvard University Press.

Epstein, Richard (1998). "Takings," in Peter Newman (ed.) *The New Palgrave Dictionary of Economics and the Law*. London: Macmillian, Reference, Ltd.

Fischel, W. (1988). "Introduction: utilitarian balancing and formalism in takings." *Columbia Law Review*, 88: 1581–1599.

Lawrence, Nathaniel (1990). "Regulatory takings: beyond the balancing test," in *Regulatory Takings: The Limits of Land Use Controls 191–245*. Chicago, IL: American Bar Association.

Levmore, Saul (1990). "Just compensation and just politics." *Connecticut Law Review*, 22: 285.

O'Hara, Erin (1995). "Regulatory takings: an oxymoron?" in B. Yandle (ed.) *Land Rights*. Lanham, Maryland: Rowman & Littlefield, pp. 31–65.

Rowley, Charles (1992). "The Supreme Court and takings judgments: constitutional political economy versus public choice," in N. Mercuro (ed.) *Taking Property and Just Compensation*. Boston: Kluwer, pp. 79–124.

Siegan, Bernard (1997). *Property and Freedom*. New Brunswick, NJ: Transaction Publishers.

CASES

Agins v. City of Tiburon, 447 U.S. 255 (1980).

Dolan v. City of Tigard, 114 S. Ct. 2309 (1994).

First English Evangelical Lutheran Church of Glendale v. County of Los Angeles, 107 S. Ct. 2378 (1987).

Hadacheck v. Los Angeles, 239 U.S. 394 (1915).

Hodel v. Irving, 107 S. Ct. 2076 (1987).

Keystone Bituminous Coal Association v. DeBenedictis, 107 S. Ct. 3141 (1987)

Lucas v. South Carolina Coastal Council, 505 U.S. 1003 (1992).

Miller v. Shoene, 276 U.S. 272 (1928).

Mugler v. Kansas, 123 U.S. 623 (1887).

Nollan v. California Coastal Commission, 107 S. Ct. 3141 (1987).

Palazzolo v. Rhode Island, 746 A.2d 707 (R.I. 2000).

Palazzolo v. Rhode Island, 533 U.S. 606 (2001).

Pennsylvania Central Transportation Co. v. City of New York, 438 U.S. 104 (1978).

Tahoe-Sierra Preservation Council, Inc. v. Tahoe Regional Planning Agency 122 S.Ct. 1465 (2002).

Village of Euclid v. Ambler Realty Co., 272 U.S. 365 (1926).

RENT DISSIPATION

The "rent" whose dissipation is the subject of this item is the rent derived by rent seeking, not the rent on buildings or farms, etc. This is a relatively recent category in economics, because the discovery of the whole phenomenon of rent seeking is recent (Tullock, 1967). Modern states devote a great deal in the way of resources to activities or expenditures that benefit only narrow groups. It is probable that although each of these activities benefits only a small and distinct group, there are so many of them and they are so widely distributed that almost everyone benefits from at least one, and pays for many others well in excess of any benefits received.

The farm program is an excellent example of rent seeking in action. The farmers and associated industries lobby government heavily for farm protection policies. The government responds munificently. Very large amounts of money are transferred to farmers by the rest of population, partly in the guise of direct government subsidies and partly in the form of price floors. Government outlays, in response to rent seeking on the part of interest groups, accounts probably for more than 50 per cent of total government expenditures. This total must be augmented by the cost of inefficient regulations imposed in response to rent-seeking outlays. These latter restrictions, designed to benefit special groups, do not appear in the budget, but they are significant.

Most economists are agreed that these benefits are not distributed solely as the result of the goodwill of benificent politicians. They are mainly the result of active lobbying or something worse by the potential beneficiaries. The problem of rent dissipation is to discover how these things are paid for. This is not to imply that they are necessarily responses to bribery or other forms of massive corruption.

Anyone visiting the capital of any major country, Washington for example, must be aware of the wide range of expensive entertainments and restaurants. Lobbyists provide major support for these services by entertaining and dining politicians and their staffers in the expectation that their generosity will be repaid through the legislative and/or the regulatory process. But large though that industry is, it clearly could not absorb even a small part of, let us say, the farmers gains from government action. Further, although the politicians are paid off partly through votes, it is clear that a representative of a metropolitan area does not gain votes directly from the farm program. Nevertheless many such representatives vote for programs that do not benefit their own constituents..

The explanation is simple although not widely known. It is the phenomenon of logrolling. In essence congressman from one district pay for things for their district by voting for things for other districts. The author of this note lives in Washington DC. Many in this area feel that we need another bridge across the Potomac and do not want it to be a toll bridge. Some of them are naive enough so that they think it can and should be provided free by the federal government or the state of Virginia if there are no tolls. In fact, of course, the residents of Washington will be taxed to pay for many bridges among them there may be one over the Potomac. The logrolling bargain is made negotiated by congressmen through their committees and their caucuses.

Although almost everybody knows about logrolling it is seldom dealt with carefully in traditional political science texts. Further congressmen normally only mention the things they get for their district when addressing their constituents. On occasion they will say that they had to vote for something in other districts in order to get something for their own. But mainly the individual voters are not told directly how they have paid for the project. Getting them however is vital to the congressmen. Congressman Watts, an important black member of the Republican hierarchy in the House has decided to withdraw. Apparently one of the reasons for this is that a large self propelled gun which was to be manufactured in his district has been canceled. Thus some of his constituents will lose jobs. His response, if that is what it is, surprises no one.

The rents then are in fact provided in the currency of other rents. I seek for, and perhaps receive, a bridge across the Potomac. Directly this is a free benefit for me, but I may be paying for dikes along the Mississippi or in the modern environmental age, the removal of such dikes. Whether I make a net gain or a net loss reflects largely the skill of my congressman and various random events in the negotiating process. On matters like roads it is probable that I do not do too badly in the overall compromise. But the allocation of government funds is very far from wealth maximizing for society or evenly distributed across the population.

Roads and many other things provided by the government are positively beneficial even if provided in a less than optimal way. There are other things the government does that are clearly harmful even if they happen to be evenly distributed. I mention the farm program one aspect of which is raising the price of milk. This could be regarded as an anti-baby action although clearly that is not its motive. Similarly the rest of the farm program does not directly match injury to the food eating population.

Protective tariffs are a clear-cut case of a government policy that, with minor exceptions, impose net costs on society. They are returns to rent seeking by usually small minorities paid for by various types of logrolling. It is a clear-cut example of the government production of "illth" (a word invented by John Stuart Mill as the opposite of "wealth").

This note deals with rent dissipation in a democratic and specifically American context. It will be found however in almost all kinds of political process. The dictator after all must keep the officials happy, and simply paying them is expensive. If he allocates road funds in such a way that the road leading to the hacienda of a prominent general is improved, this may be a cheaper way of getting his support than direct payment. The distribution of road funds in a dictatorship may not differ very much from that which would be found in a democracy. Trading of favors is important in all governments, and is not obviously avoidable. We must accept governments as we find them and internal trading among their officials is normal. We can hope to develop mechanisms for reducing the amount of rent dissipation, but we should not pretend that governments and lobbyists who stand to lose money and votes from their introduction are likely to respond positively to reforms that are designed to increase the overall wealth of society (Tullock, 1967, 1993).

GORDON TULLOCK

REFERENCES

Tullock, G. (1967). "The welfare costs of tariffs, monopolies and theft." *Western Economic Journal*, 5: 224–232.

Tullock, G. (1993). "Rent seeking," The Shaftesbury Papers, No. 2. Aldershot: Edward Elgar Publishing.

RENT EXTRACTION

> You had better hold on
> Hold on to what you got. (Joe Tex, 1965)

Formal economic analysis of rent extraction is a relatively recent development in public choice theory (McChesney, 1987, 1998). The basic model of rent extraction has been found useful in related fields where price theory is applied to analyze regulation. For example, it has been called "one of the most influential [developments] in law and economics of the last decade" (Sidak, 1998: 657).

As part of the Virginia School approach to political economy, the concept of rent extraction traces its intellectual roots to the seminal work on rent seeking by Tullock (1967). Whereas rent seeking is based on the idea of private individuals benefiting themselves through the political process, rent extraction points out that politicians are themselves players in the regulatory auction. Further, politicians have more than one strategy to benefit themselves. They gain not only when compensated by successful rent seekers, but also by threatening private individuals or groups with losses and then allowing themselves to be bought off rather than make good on the threats. Private wealth is extracted in the process.

1. Overview

William Mitchell (1988: 107) identifies the particular contribution of Virginia School public choice as its "theory of the failure of political processes." Given the costs and rewards facing politicians and bureaucrats, "inequity, inefficiency, and coercion are the most general results of democratic policy formation."

Part of the "inequity and inefficiency" to which Mitchell refers stems from rent seeking by favored groups. The idea that politicians can create rents for some groups (e.g., via tariffs for steel producers) at the expense of others (steel purchasers) is now well explored. (See entries by Tollison and by Tullock, this volume.) In the simplest rent-seeking models, gains from legislation go to the highest private bidders. Losses accrue to those who do not bid enough to stave off the legislation.

Complementing the fundamental rent-seeking model, rent extraction focuses on the political "coercion" mentioned by Mitchell. Recognition of the rent extraction strategy starts with the realization that (a) as rational maximizers, politicians are interested in transferring wealth to others only to the extent that it generates benefits for themselves; (b) if politicians can transfer wealth to others, they can transfer it to themselves; and (c) that there are

various ways to transfer wealth to government actors. Therefore, politicians must be seen as more than mere passive auctioneers of rents (McCormick and Tollison, 1981). They actively seek wealth-increasing opportunities, like everyone else. A fully-specified model of political behavior takes into account the many ways a politician's property rights allow him to improve his situation, net of the costs of doing so.

Outside politics, *homines economici* improve their lots in two fundamental ways. First, they can contract or otherwise cooperate voluntarily, leaving both sides better off (Axelrod, 1984). But much human interaction is non-cooperative (Schelling, 1960). One can improve his situation at the expense of another by just taking the latter's wealth, for example.

So it goes in politics. A person can contract with politicians for special favors — that is the essence of rent seeking. But a politician with the power to bestow those special favors often has the power to take wealth for himself while leaving the other side worse off. In fact, he can take for himself merely by threatening private parties' wealth, then allowing himself to be bought off.

Consider a tax increase. Politicians have the constitutional ability to levy taxes, and taxes on income already earned or other wealth already in place offers an attractive taxation target. But an ability to tax necessarily entails the discretion *not* to tax, that is, to propose taxation but then not levy the tax threatened. Proposing onerous legislation and then — for a price — agreeing not to push or even to withdraw the legislation proposed is the essence of rent extraction. Rent-extracting games are observed routinely as part of tax legislation proposals: private individuals pay, not for special favors, but to avoid disfavor (Doernberg and McChesney, 1987).

Likewise, consider threats of price controls, such as those that the Clinton administration proposed for the medical, pharmaceutical and insurance industries in 1993–94. Had these measures been imposed, the costs to the affected industries would have been enormous. In each industry, there are large stocks of specific capital, including human capital, which generate income flows over time. Quasi-rents are earned as compensation on prior investments (education, product research and development). But just as wealth previously earned can be confiscated by taxation, expected future returns can be imperiled by price controls such as those jeopardized by the Clinton's. Rather than submit to the price controls threatened, the industries that would have suffered paid millions over to politicians to avoid them (McChesney 1997: Ch. 4).

Politicians have figured out any number of other ways to extract private wealth (Beck et al., 1992). Yandle (2001: 600), for example, notes the "not-in-my-back-yard" response to proposed pollution-control measures. "[T]he politician can indicate that electric utilities are being targeted for dramatic reductions in sulfur dioxide emissions. Then, instead of the industry organizing to seek favors or rents conferred by regulation, the industry organizes and lobbies to deflect or soften the proposed rules."

Regardless of the tactics chosen, the strategy of rent extraction is essentially the same. Proposed government action (e.g., a legislative bill to be voted on) that imposes costs on a person or group presents the putative victims with a choice: pay up for relief of the threat or endure the consequences. If the expected cost of the threatened act exceeds the value of what the parties threatened must surrender to avoid legislative action, they rationally will hand over the payment demanded of them.

Thus, in a public-choice approach to government, rent seeking is to rent extraction as bribery is to extortion. In a rent-extraction/bribery game, potential beneficiaries from political action compensate politicians for their gains. In a rent-extraction/extortion game, potential victims pay politicians not to impose losses. The implications for the payers are completely different — a gain versus a loss — but the politician gains in either sort of game.

2. Politician Rent Extraction vs. Private Rent Seeking

Distinguishing rent extraction from rent seeking is not always easy, as both involve payments to politicians. "Bribery and extortion substantially overlap. ...The same envelope filled with cash can be both a payment extorted under a threat of unfairly negative treatment and a bribe obtained under a promise of unfairly positive treatment" (Lindgren, 1993: 1700). But politically the two are quite distinct strategies for raising money, as politicians themselves recognize. They label their rent-extracting proposals (i.e., bills submitted just to elicit money *not* to enact the bills) with names like "juice bills" ' or "milker bills." Ralph Nader has referred to some such proposed legislation as a "cash cow" for politicians.

The necessary conditions for rent extraction are the same as those for rent seeking. There must exist potential gains to some person (or group) from using political power to transfer wealth to himself (or itself). Second, the benefits of the transfers must outweigh the costs of achieving them. In principle, both the benefits and costs of political wealth transfers are a function of anterior constitutional rules concerning political transfers. Rules that protect private citizens from transfers reduce the benefits and increase the costs of both rent seeking and rent extraction. Such constitutional

protections have weakened considerably in most developed nations (e.g., Anderson and Hill, 1980), increasing the extent of both rent seeking and rent extraction.

However, rent extraction differs from rent seeking in three ways. First, the principal beneficiary from a successful rent-extraction strategy is not a private person or group, but politicians themselves. Private payments *not* to legislate tax increases or price caps go directly to politicians. That is, rent extraction is a two party game between politicians and would-be private victims, compared to rent-seeking, which involves three parties: potential winners, potential losers and the politicians who decide the winners and losers.

Second, rent extraction is typically more difficult to detect than rent seeking. Rent seeking ordinarily requires specific legislation or regulation to shift one group's wealth to another. Rent extraction, to the contrary, requires only a threat of action to induce payment from would-be victims. Successful rent extraction is measured by what does *not* result in legislation or regulation. Thus, more rent extraction will take place than can be observed.

The difference in observed amounts of rent seeking relative to rent extraction is all the greater, given the different process costs attached to the two strategies. Enacting rent creating proposals typically requires satisfaction *ex ante* of high-cost procedures (hearings, votes) and will be subject to predictable *ex post* obstacles (court challenges, bureaucratic amendment). The American steel industry's success in winning tariff protection in 2002, for example, was the result of a sustained campaign of lobbying, political contributions and the like before the fact. After Congressional enactment and presidential signature, however, it still faced court tests and bureaucratic interpretation of its complicated definitions and procedures.

From a politician's standpoint, the beauty of rent extraction is precisely that it is primarily covert, and procedurally low-cost. It is virtually costless to submit a bill that threatens tax increases, price caps or other private wealth, current or future. It costs little, either, to withdraw the bill (or let it die for lack of support), once the requisite payments are made to forestall the bigger loss that actual passage of the legislation would entail.

3. The Social Costs of Rent Extraction

The money surrendered by those who otherwise would suffer by the political actions threatened is only a transfer. But rent extraction has real economic costs, measured along several margins. The very process of mounting the threat and then negotiating over its removal entails deadweight losses. Even when threats are ultimately bought off, then, the threatened firm is left worse off (Beck et al., 1992).

Perhaps most important costs of rent extraction are its longer-term effects. The private wealth (current or expected) that politicians can credibly imperil derives from productive private investments. Potential rent extraction represents an expected future levy reducing the net benefit of the investment today. At the margin, therefore, the specter of rent extraction reduces the amount of investment made, just as any tax reduces the amount of the activity taxed. Potential rent extraction is also costly in altering the types of investments made. At the margin, the specter of future threats increases the relative returns of investments that are less visible to would-be extracting politicians.

Thus, rent extraction in more advanced economies is analytically no different from outright nationalization in less prosperous countries. In the former setting, politicians demand (and get) a fraction of an individual's or firm's wealth. In the latter situation, politicians take a larger fraction, perhaps the entire investment. Regardless of setting and amount taken, however, politicians have the effective ability to take some or all of the wealth over which they preside. Any stock of relatively immobile private capital offers potential gain from regulatory threats. The short-term costs in negotiating over just how much will be taken, and the long-term effects on investment incentives, are straightforward.

Once the political opportunities and social costs of rent extraction are appreciated, other aspects of basic public choice theory are seen in a different light. A group's ability to organize, for example, is seen as unambiguously good in the rent seeking model. But the extent of organization, while useful for seeking rents, also offers politicians lower-cost opportunities to extract the group's existing wealth (McChesney, 1991). In a world where both rent seeking and rent extraction strategies are part of a politician's total portfolio of wealth-maximizing choices, group organization is not unambiguously desirable.

FRED S. McCHESNEY

REFERENCES

Anderson, T.L. and Hill, P.J. (1980). *The Birth of a Transfer Society*. Stanford: Hoover Institution Press.

Axelrod, R. (1984). *The Evolution of Cooperation*. New York: Basic Books.

Beck, R., Hoskins, C., and Connolly, J.M. (1992). "Rent extraction through political extortion: an empirical examination." *Journal of Legal Studies*, 21: 217–224.

Doernberg, R.L. and McChesney, F.S. (1987). "On the accelerating rate and decreasing durability of tax reform." *Minnesota Law Review*, 71: 913–962.

Lindgren, J. (1993). "Theory, history, and practice of the bribery-extortion distinction." *University of Pennsylvania Law Review*, 141: 1695–1740.

McChesney, F.S. (1987). "Rent extraction and rent creation in the economic theory of regulation." *Journal of Legal Studies*, 16: 101–118.

McChesney, F.S. (1991). "Rent extraction and interest-group organization in a Coasean model of regulation." *Journal of Legal Studies*, 20: 73–90.

McChesney, F.S. (1997). *Money for Nothing: Politicians, Rent Extraction and Political Extortion*. Cambridge, MA: Harvard University Press.

McChesney, F.S. (1998). "Rent from regulation," in P. Newman (ed.) *The New Palgrave Dictionary of Economics and the Law*, Vol. 3. London: Macmillan, pp. 310–315.

McCormick, R.E. and Tollison, R.D. (1981). *Politicians, Legislation, and the Economy: An Inquiry into the Interest-Group Theory of Government*. Boston: Martinus Nijhoff.

Mitchell, W.C. (1988). "Virginia, Rochester and Bloomington: twenty-five years of public choice and political Science." *Public Choice*, 56: 101–119.

Schelling, T. (1960). *The Strategy of Conflict*. Cambridge, MA: Harvard University Press.

Sidak, J.G. (1998). "The petty larceny of the police power." *California Law Review*, 86: 655–670.

Tullock, G. (1967). "The welfare costs of tariffs, monopolies and theft." *Western Economic Journal*, 5: 224–232.

Yandle, B. (2001). "Public choice and the environment," in W.F. Shughart II and L. Razzolini (eds.) *The Elgar Companion to Public Choice*. Cheltenham, UK: Edward Elgar, pp. 590–610.

RENT SEEKING

1. Introduction

Rent seeking is the socially costly pursuit of wealth transfers. The concept of rent seeking was introduced to the economics profession by Tullock (1967). In his original presentation the basic idea that transfer seeking could lead to social costs was so simple that it has been automatically assumed that the idea had to have clear precursors in the literature. Nonetheless, even though one can find vague resemblances to the idea in many earlier writings, no one has uncovered a forerunner to Tullock's idea. His 1967 paper represents an original and important development in economic theory.

The early doctrinal development of the theory of rent seeking proceeded as follows. Krueger (1974) gave the field a name in her paper "The Political Economy of the Rent-Seeking Society." Although she presented some empirical estimates of the costs of rent seeking, Krueger's paper was primarily theoretical in nature, showing how rent seeking can lead to social costs in the adoption of policies to restrict international trade. Krueger was unaware of Tullock's paper. Posner (1975), who was aware of Tullock's paper, wrote the first empirical paper about rent seeking. His estimates suggested that the social costs of rent seeking in the regulated sector of the U.S. economy could be substantial. Finally, in an effort to solidify the earlier contributions and to stimulate work in the field, Buchanan (1980) and Rowley et al. (1988) published collections of papers on rent seeking that have been both widely cited and influential in the subsequent development of the field.

The remainder of this essay will detail the various aspects of the theory of rent seeking as it has evolved since Tullock's seminal paper.

2. Definitions and Semantics

Tullock originally framed his theory of rent seeking in contrast to the prevailing wisdom in the late 1950s and early 1960s, which held that the deadweight costs of monopoly and tariffs were empirically quite small. Harberger's (1954) famous calculations on the extent of monopoly power in the United States is a good example of this type of thinking. Monopoly as a source of market failure evidently was on the verge of being trivialized. Tullock advanced an argument that rectangles as well as triangles matter in the calculation of the social costs of such policies as tariffs and monopolies; that is, Tullock introduced the concept of a trapezoidal society.

Tullock's point was simple though full of potential pitfalls. He argued that expenditures made to capture a transfer were a form of social cost. The social cost arises because the resources used for transfer seeking have a positive opportunity cost somewhere else in the economy with respect to engaging in positive-sum activities. Transfer seeking is at best a zero-sum activity in that it simply shuffles dollars among people and groups and is probably negative-sum if traditional deadweight costs result as a by-product of such activities. Social costs clearly arise in the process by which resources are shifted from positive-to-zero- and negative-sum activities. Rent seeking thus embodies a social cost in terms of the foregone product of the resources employed in rent seeking.

Several points should be kept in mind. The theory of rent seeking does not condemn all types of profit seeking. As Buchanan (1980) articulated clearly, traditional competitive profit seeking or entrepreneurship in the competitive model (seeking quasi-rents) does not qualify as rent seeking. Such profit seeking is productive; it creates value such as new products. Rent seeking is unproductive; it destroys value by wasting valuable resources.

Normally, the concept of rent seeking is applied to cases where governmental intervention in the economy leads to the creation of artificial or contrived rents. Seeking such

returns leads to social costs because output is fixed by definition in, for example, a government regulation. Entrepreneurship in this setting can only be said to be negative; it will simply dissipate rents and lead to no increase in output. Nonetheless, it is possible to conceive of rent seeking as taking place in a nongovernmental setting. Buchanan (1983), for example, argued that the rivalry of siblings for an inheritance can lead to rent-seeking activities within families, although Anderson and Brown (1985) offer a critique of this approach based on the idea that parties in this case are simply maximizing their utility.

Another point to keep in mind is that to the degree that the process of rent seeking involves the provision of utility or real income to participants in the process, these benefits should be netted out against the cost of rent seeking. As Congleton (1988) has argued, if the rent seeker takes the regulator out to dinner, the value that the regulator places on the dinner must be subtracted from the social costs of rent seeking. In-kind provisions, of course, come with excess burdens attached.

Once artificial rents have been created, it is hard to avoid the implication that rent seeking will occur along some margin. If a tax deduction is offered, tax shelters will be created and used. If civil servants are paid a wage in excess of their marginal revenue products, queues will develop for government jobs. All of these processes involve the use of scarce resources to seek transfers; the process is relentless.

3. Theory

Posner (1975) stated the first version of a rent-seeking game, describing a constant-cost game in which the probability of winning is proportional to investment and the available rents are exactly dissipated. He posited risk-neutral bidders, a fixed prize, and a given number of bidders. Where, for example, the pool of rents equals $100,000 and there are ten rent seekers, each bidder will offer or expend resources of $10,000 to capture the rents. In Posner's model rent seeking is analogous to buying a lottery ticket with a one in ten chance of being successful. Under such conditions rents are exactly dissipated; $100,000 is spent to capture $100,000.

Posner's exact dissipation hypothesis is popular in the literature because it makes empirical work easier. A rectangle is a definite area whose value can be reasonably estimated. Moreover, Posner's model is robust with respect to the free entry and exit of bidders (Higgins et al., 1985). That is, it naturally generalizes to a concept of a long-run equilibrium of bids and bidders. Rents are perfectly competed away with an endogenous number of bidders, and the prize to the winning rent seeker represents only a normal rate of return on his rent-seeking investment.

This does not mean, however, that all or even most rent-seeking contests are perfectly competitive in nature. Tullock (1980) presented classes of models where rent seeking is imperfectly competitive in the sense that the competitive process for rents leads to over- or under-dissipation of the available rents. That is, more or less than the value of the rents is expended to capture them. Rent seeking in these models does not take place under constant-cost conditions. These cases are interesting, and they are generated by assumptions about risk aversion, limitations on the number of bidders, imperfect information, and so on.

As between Tullock's analysis of over- and under-dissipation possibilities, the overdissipation possibility does not seem to be very plausible, at least in the setting of repeat play games. In this case, rent seekers are somehow led to bid more than the value of the prize. That is, they would be better off by not playing the game in the first place.

Underbidding, where rent seekers in the aggregate spend less than the value of the prize, is another matter. There are several plausible bases for underbidding equilibria, including risk aversion (Hillman and Katz, 1984), comparative advantage among monopolizing inputs (Rogerson, 1982), and game-theoretic considerations (Tullock, 1980).

4. Measurement of Rent-Seeking Costs

There are numerous empirical results on the social costs of rent seeking, depending on the methodology, coverage, and economy analyzed by the author. Krueger (1974) suggested that 7 percent of Indian GNP was wasted in rent seeking and 15 percent of Turkish GNP was lost due to rent seeking for import licenses. Posner (1975) estimated that as much as 3 percent of U.S. GNP was lost due to the social costs of monopolization through regulation. These are obviously substantial sums of money in any economy. Cowling and Mueller (1978) derived an estimate that the rent-seeking and deadweight costs of private monopoly in the United States were 13 percent of gross corporate product.

Subsequent empirical work in this area has proceeded along several lines. A reasonable amount of work has followed the lead of Krueger in seeking to examine the rent-seeking costs of trade intervention in various economies. In general, these works come up with higher numbers than Krueger. Magee et al. (1989: Ch. 15) provide a survey of this research.

Other work has attempted to estimate the costs of rent seeking for economies as a whole. This analysis has taken two general forms. First, there are the lawyer regressions. Various authors (see, for example, Murphy et al., 1991) have added lawyers in various regression formats set up to explain GNP or rates of growth in GNP, both in the United States and across countries. The robust conclusion of this work is more lawyers, lower growth, lower GNP. Some of these admittedly simplistic regression estimates suggest that lawyers reduce aggregate income by as much as 45 percent. Nontheless, lawyers are a key input in the rent-seeking process across societies.

Eschewing a regression-based approach, Laband and Sophocleus (1988) attempted an aggregate, sector-by-sector accounting of rent-seeking costs in the U.S. economy. They counted expenditures on such items as locks, insurance, police, and the military as being driven by rent-seeking or rent-protecting incentives. On this basis they estimated that almost one-half of the U.S. GNP in 1985 was consumed by such costs. Their approach will surely be controversial. A small sample of the categories that they treated as rent-seeking costs include crime prevention (FBI), police (corrections), restraint of trade (FTC), residential investments (locks), commercial investments (guards), educational investments (library theft), property-rights disputes (tort litigation), and government (defense, lobbyists, PACS). Following an accounting-like procedure, these authors go sector-by-sector to obtain their estimates of rent-seeking costs.

As with all empirical work, these various approaches are only as good as the theories and models upon which they are based. Buying a lock, for example, is a response to the security of property rights in a society. This security can be produced in a variety of ways (including moral exhortation), but in the face of the relevant probabilities, buying a lock can hardly be seen as an unproductive investment. Given the prevailing ethos, a lock protects property rights, and the protection of property rights enhances the productivity of resources over what they could produce without the lock. To argue that one can be wealthier without locks and lawyers implies that there are feasible reforms in behavior that will reduce such costs. This is certainly believable, but this is exactly the burden that estimators of the costs of rent seeking face. The lock and the lawyer are only wasteful to the extent that these resources can be feasibly reallocated to more productive uses. Alternatively, contributions to churches should be regarded as substitutes for locks.

In principle, the cost of rent seeking is simply the increase in GNP that would result if a feasible way to reallocate resources from locks and lawyers to more productive uses could be found by a political entrepreneur. This figure could be high or low, but it is probably low given the ability of rent-seeking inputs to resist such reallocations. And the mere resistance of the inputs is yet another reason not to waste resources attempting such a reallocation (Tollison and Wagner, 1991).

A related concept is Tullock's (1975) transitional gains trap. In this case regulatory-created rents are dissipated by cost-increasing competition (e.g., more airline flights at a given time of day), so that consumers and producers are "trapped" in a situation from which no Pareto-like improvement is possible. Producers make normal returns on their investments after rent dissipation, and consumers pay higher than competitive prices. The capital losses facing producers in this case preclude a Paretian argument for deregulation.

5. Rent Protection

Not only do individuals use real resources to seek transfers, but they also sometimes use real resources to protect their rents from encroachment by other rent seekers. In contrast to rent seeking, this behavior is called rent protection. The basis for such behavior is clear. Not all "suppliers" of wealth transfers find it economically rational to allow their wealth to be taken away (why spend a dollar to save a dime?). Some will find it worthwhile to fight back (spend a dollar to save two dollars).

Virtually all welfare analyses of monopoly and regulation ignore rent-protecting activities of organized opponents of such governmental programs. A more general welfare analytics will include traditional dead-weight costs, rent-seeking costs, and rent-protecting costs. An important contribution to this literature in recent years has been McChesney's (1997) concept of rent extraction. He has generated results on rent seeking in which regulation or legislation is threatened and then withdrawn as a way to stimulate the formation of interest groups from which politicians can exact tribute. In other words, politicians are passive actors in the theory of rent seeking, whereas they are pro-active in the formation of interest groups in the theory of rent extraction.

6. Rent Seeking and the Distribution of Income

There will not be an equal distribution of rent-seeking ability in a society. Thus, the mechanism by which rents are assigned is likely to affect the distribution of wealth to the extent that Ricardian rents are earned in rent seeking. Consider a regulatory-hearing mechanism for assigning rents and suppose that some lawyers or economists earn inframarginal rents in rent seeking. On average, these individuals will be wealthier than their marginal competitors and wealthier than they would be without a rent-seeking

mechanism of the particular type that rewards their skills. The choice of such a transfer mechanism increases the demand for lawyers (and possibly economists) above that which would hold with (say) an auction mechanism for assigning monopoly rents. So, first of all, the mechanism will alter the distribution of wealth by occupation. Moreover, if the requisite talents of the favored occupation cannot be reproduced at constant costs, the inequality of wealth in society may be further affected. For example, suppose the qualities of a good businessman/speculator are more fungible among the population than the qualities of a good lawyer; then inframarginal rents will accrue to the best of the legal profession in regulatory hearing cases. With an auction no Ricardian rents would be earned. The distribution of wealth would differ between these two societies as a consequence.

7. Conclusion

Tullock's theory of rent seeking is a novel and important development in economic theory. Time will tell, but it is possible to say now that rent-seeking theory offers a way for economists to understand better the positive and normative effects of government in an economy. For a long time this analysis was only about triangles. Tullock lifted our vision to rectangles and trapezoids (Tollison, 1982).

ROBERT D. TOLLISON

REFERENCES

Anderson, G.M. and Brown, P.J. (1985). "Heir pollution: A rate on Buchanan's 'laws of succession' and Tullock's 'blind spot.'" *International Review of Law and Economics*, 5: 15–24.

Buchanan, J.M. (1980). "Rent seeking and profit seeking," in J.M. Buchanan, R.D. Tollison, and G. Tullock (eds.) *Toward a Theory of the Rent-seeking Society*. College Station: Texas A&M University Press, pp. 3–15.

Buchanan, J.M. (1983). "Rent-seeking, noncompensated transfers, and laws of succession." *Journal of Law and Economics*, 26: 71–86.

Congleton, R.D. (1988). "Evaluating rent-seeking losses: do the welfare gains of lobbyists count?" *Public Choice*, 56: 181–184.

Cowling, K. and Mueller, D.C. (1978). "The social costs of monopoly power." *Economic Journal*, 88: 727–748.

Harberger, A.C. (1954). "Monopoly and resource allocation." *American Economic Review*, 44: 77–87.

Higgins, R., Shughart, W.F., and Tollison, R.D. (1985). "Free entry and efficient rent-seeking." *Public Choice*, 46: 247–258.

Hillman, A.L. and Katz, E. (1984). "Risk-averse rent-seekers and the social cost of monopoly power." *Economic Journal*, 94: 104–110.

Krueger, A.O. (1974). "The political economy of the rent-seeking society." *American Economic Review*, 64: 291–303.

Laband, D.N. and Sophocleus, J.P. (1988). "The social cost of rent seeking: first estimates." *Quarterly Journal of Economics*, 107: 959–984.

Magee, S.P., Brock, W.A., and Young, L. (1989). *Black Hole Tariffs and Endogeneous Policy Theory*. Cambridge: Cambridge University Press.

McChesney, F. (1997). *Money for Nothing: Politicians, Rent Extraction, and Political Extortion*. Cambridge: Harvard University Press.

Murphy, K.M., Schleifer, A., and Vishny, R.W. (1991). "The allocation of talent: implications for growth." *Quarterly Journal of Economics*, 106: 503–531.

Posner, R.A. (1975). "The social costs of monopoly and regulation." *Journal of Political Economy*, 83: 807–827.

Rogerson, W.P. (1982). "The social costs of monopoly and regulation: a game-theoretic analysis." *Bell Journal of Economics*, 13 (Autumn): 391–401.

Rowley, C.K., Tollison, R.D., and Tullock G. (1988). *The Political Economy of Rent Seeking*. Boston: Kluwer.

Tollison, R.D. (1982). "Rent seeking: a survey." *Kyklos* 35(face. 4): 575–602.

Tollison, R.D. and Wagner, R.E. (1991). "Romance, reality, and economic reform." *Kyklos*, 44: 57–70.

Tullock, G. (1967). "The welfare costs of tariffs, monopolies, and theft." *Western Economic Journal*, 5: 224–232.

Tullock, G. (1975). "The transitional gains trap." *Bell Journal of Economics and Management Science*, 6: 671–678.

Tullock, G. (1980). "Efficient rent seeking," in J.M. Buchanan, R.D. Tollison, and G. Tullock (eds.) *Toward a Theory of the Rent-Seeing Society*. College Station: Texas A&M Press, pp. 97–112.

RENT SEEKING AND POLITICAL INSTITUTIONS

1. Introduction

Gordon Tullock's (1967) analysis of "The Welfare Costs of Monopolies, Tariffs, and Theft" revealed that these outcomes are more inefficient than implied by traditional welfare economics, because individuals use scarce resources to secure these undesirable outcomes. To secure tariffs, resources are devoted by domestic firms who may profit from trade protection, and to avoid them, by those who expect to be harmed by import duties. Obtaining monopoly power often requires similar investments to secure and avoid government-enforced entry barriers. In the case of crime, the aim of rent seekers and rent avoiders is not to influence government policy, but involves a similar sort of conflict. Criminals invest resources to redistribute resources from owners to themselves and owners invest

resources in locks and guns to foil the efforts of potential criminals. Tullock points out that the total output of valuable goods and services is necessarily smaller than would have been the case if those resources had been used to produce new consumer goods rather than wasted in games leading to inefficient outcomes. Static welfare economics had *under measured* the losses generated by tariffs, monopoly, and theft by focusing attention on final outcome and neglecting the processes by which those outcomes were generated (Posner, 1975).

The private advantage of rent seeking is largely determined by the "rules" of the rent-seeking contest. These "rules" determine both the acceptable range of rent-seeking methods and the payoffs of private investments in rent-seeking contests. To the extent that existing formal and informal rules can be modified or new formal rules introduced rent-seeking losses can clearly be reduced (or increased) through institutional design. The "rules of the game" are simply another name for the array of formal and informal institutions under which the rent-seeking contest takes place (Congleton, 1980, 1984). Institutions can both induce and curtail rent-seeking activities.

2. Institutions and the Rent-seeking Society

To see how institutional design affects the magnitude of rent-seeking efforts and losses, consider the following characterization of a rent-seeking society. Suppose that the expected payoffs from contest j are of the form: $R_{ij} = s_j(f_j(x_{ij}), g_j(x_{oj})) P_j - c_j(x_{ij})$, where x_{ij} is the investment by the i-th rent seeking in contest j and x_{oj} is the investment of all other rent seekers. P_j is the prize or profit at stake, f_j and g_j are influence production functions, c_j is a cost function reflecting the value of resources in other non-rent-seeking activities such as farming and leisure. Function s_j is a sharing rule or probability function for contest j. It is normally assumed that model rent-seeking contests are such that *relative influence* rather than absolute influence determines shares of the prize, or the probability of winning the entire prize. If all players simultaneously double their influence, each player's share of the "prize" is unaffected.

Nonetheless, investing in rent-seeking contests can be entirely rational in the sense that self-interest leads individuals and groups to play such socially unproductive games as a means of securing private advantage. The typical rent seeker will invest in rent-seeking contests up to the point where: $c_{j\,xi} = P_{j\,sj} F f_{j\,xi}$ across all games. That is to say, rent seekers devote resources to a rent-seeking contest up to the point where the expected marginal advantage in pursing the prize equals its marginal opportunity cost, which implies that marginal returns are equalized across rent-seeking contests. The level of investment in each game is affected by the magnitude of the prize, the sharing rule, and the production of influence functions, which partly determine $s_j F$ and f_{jxi}.

Note that both the production of influence and the effect of influence on a player's share of the prize, f_{jxi} and $s_j F$, are partly determined by the efforts of other contestants and *partly by the institutions* that determine how influence can be produced and how the prize will be divided (for example, winner take all or proportional shares). Both the institutional setting and the magnitude of P are usually assumed to be exogenous.

The assumed structure of the sharing rule and influence production functions implies that a grand prisoner's dilemma exists. All players would be better off if every rent seeker's investment was reduced by the same proportion, because this pattern of reduction would not affect individual shares in the prize(s), but would free resource for other more valuable uses. In such contests, *essentially all the resources invested in these contests are wasted*, insofar as they are consumed by the influence-production processes without increasing the quantity or variety of available goods and services. However, no individual has an interest in reducing his own investment in a rent-seeking contest unless the others do the same.

Informally solving this form of the prisoner's dilemma is not an easy task, because as the players reduce their efforts, the advantage of rent-seeking investments tends to *increase at the margin for each individual player*. "Cheating" on whatever informal rules come to be adopted becomes an increasingly attractive option as effort levels decline.

The ability of affected groups to devise and implement formal rules to curtail investments in these unproductive games remains in the interest of all those in the game, insofar as costs can be reduced for all (including the winners). For example, institutions that eliminate the possibility of influence, by setting $f_{jxi} = 0$, or that eliminate the effect of "influence" on individual shares of the pie, by setting $s_j F = 0$, eliminate all interest in rent-seeking contests by eliminating the gains from rent seeking. The institutional design question is whether such institutions can be adopted, and whether they necessarily reduce rent-seeking expenditures or simply redirect conflict into other channels. Unfortunately, the same incentives tempt individuals to cheat in the ordinary play also exist at the level of institutional reform. Each participant at a constitutional convention naturally prefers rules that increase their own influence relative to potential rivals (Wagner and Tollison, 1991). Moreover, efforts to curtail one form of rent seeking may simply divert efforts to other equally wasteful contests

as marginal returns in other "unregulated" games are re-equated.

3. Institutional Remedies for the Rent-seeking Dilemma

The rent-seeking literature has demonstrated that a number of institutions can affect the extent of rent-seeking expenditures. For example, if the prize in a particular contest decreases, all rent seekers will realize smaller marginal benefits from their rent-seeking activities in that game. A smaller prize induces each rent seeker to invest less in the game of interest, which also diminishes the total investment in rent seeking in the most commonly analyzed games. Consequently, political arrangements that reduce the fraction of national resources distributed in response to rent-seeking efforts tend to attract smaller individual investments in rent seeking from all rent seekers. Here we may note that private property rights, civil and political liberties, and a takings clause all bound the domain of government policies and tend to reduce the level of rent-seeking loss relative to governments where the domain of public policy is larger (Buchanan, 1980; Rowley et al., 1988).

The size of the prize sought by rent seekers is also affected by laws that protect rents once obtained. For example, monopoly contracts may be enforced by a nation's judicial system or not. If cartel agreements are not enforced, increased uncertainty about the value and durability of a monopoly privilege tends to reduce the expected value of the prize and, thereby, the level of effort invested to organized monopolistic organizations, or to create entry barriers.

In addition to political and legal institutions that affect the size of the prizes potentially available to rent seekers, rent-seeking contests are also characterized by *institutions* that determine how individual and aggregate rent-seeking efforts produce influence and how influence affects the distribution of the prize or the probability of winning the prize. The manner in which influence is produced by the efforts of individuals, $f_j(x_{ij})$, and groups is partly determined by *procedural rules* that determine legitimate methods of producing influence. For example, access to policy makers may be unrestricted, determined by familial ties, political activism, reputation, or lottery, and so forth. Regulatory deliberations may invite only a few people or groups to comment on proposed regulation or many. Campaign contributions may be explicitly linked to votes on pending legislation or only implicitly linked. Bribery may be legal or illegal, and, if illegal, enforcement may be more or less intense. In all these cases, the ability of any interest group to influence the policy outcomes is partly determined by its own efforts, partly those of other groups, and partly by the institutional setting. The institutional setting determines the general productivity of some forms of influence relative to others, and may favor some groups relative to others. For example, entry barriers in rent-seeking contests often reduce rent-seeking losses for those in the game, but imply that some groups cannot win the prize, (Corcoran, 1984).

In addition to the institutions that determine the productivity of alternative methods of producing influence, there are others that determine how the influence produced can affect the assignment of the prize in the contest of interest. In contest environment sketched out above, function s_j specifies how influence affects the distribution of the prize among rent seekers. This may be based upon the relative production of influence, or describe a probability function for winning the entire prize is affected by their relative efforts, $S_j = s_j(f(x_{ij}), g(x_{oj}))$.[1] The process that determines the allocation of the prize may be made by a generality rule, a true lottery, a single policy czar, or a committee. Such a committee may choose the winner(s) of the contest using unanimous agreement or majority rule. The prize may be awarded all to one player, distributed only among all those who participate, or distributed within an industry or to all citizens. If the prize is shared, the amounts given out may be equal or unequal, and the shares may be affected by rent-seeking efforts or not.

In all these cases, it is clear that both the decision and allocative rules have effects on both the kind and extent of the rent-seeking investments made by each individual rent seeker, and, consequently, on the aggregate rent-seeking losses. For example, majority rule tends to attract smaller investments in rent seeking than one-man rule, and winner take all apportionment rules tend to attract greater efforts than proportional share games or lotteries (Congleton, 1983).

Other institutional characteristics of the setting in which the rent-seeking contest is played also affects the size and scope of rent-seeking activities. For example, federalism tends to reduce the size of the prize contested and reduce the number of rent seekers who participate in a particular game (insofar as players must reside within the jurisdictions of interest). Both these effects tend to reduce rent-seeking expenditures (Warneryd, 1998). Participation in rent-seeking contests may be sequential as when eligibility for a final prize is determined from a sequence of games (Baik and Lee, 2000).

All these analyses demonstrate that the modification of formal institutions is one method by which rent-seeking losses can be controlled, even if rent-seeking losses cannot be avoided altogether. Moreover, several models of the emergence of civilization from anarchy argue that political and legal institutions are adopted in order to escape from the Hobbesian jungle, which is an unmitigated rent-seeking society. In these analyses, political and legal institutions are invented "whole cloth" as a means of reducing the waste of resources in rent-seeking games (Tullock, 1972; Skogh and Stuart, 1982; Skaperdas, 1992; Hirschliefer, 2001).

Rationality implies that efforts to devise institutions to address the problems will tend to reflect the potential net advantage of solving particular rent-seeking problems. If losses are large, great efforts are worth undertaking. If the costs of solving a problem are low, less effort is necessary to solve the problem. It seems clear that rent-seeking games that generate large losses that can be easily avoided will be revised through institutional reform or ordinary legislation. Laws may be adopted which restrict transfer of real property to nonviolent and voluntary means. Murder, theft, dueling and street racing may be declared illegal and punished. Bribery may be outlawed and violators exiled or jailed. Other productive forms of conflict may be promoted by enforcing contracts and devising transferable packages of use rights.[2]

If the cost of adopting loss reducing institutions is also large, wasteful rent-seeking contests may remain unsolved. For example, violent conflict between nations over boundaries often involves large scale losses, but history suggests that those losses are very difficult to eliminate completely. Moreover, conflict over policies within a nation are inevitable as long as governments are able to adopt policies that have distributional consequences. Insofar as nearly all policies have distributional consequences, it is unlikely that domestic rent-seeking loses can be completely eliminated, although they can be reduced by intelligent institutional design. There are problems for which institutional solutions to rent-seeking losses are unlikely to be adopted, and others for which the solutions adopted are unlikely to work in the long run.

4. Institutions and Rent-seeking Costs

If the welfare economists prior to 1967 under counted the cost of tariffs, monopoly, and theft, it is possible that Tullock and others exploring the normative implications of rent-seeking have overstated them. Given human nature, both rent-seeking and *cost-avoiding* efforts by *all available means* are to be expected. If the costs of rent-seeking can be reduced, it is clearly in the interest of those involved in rent-seeking contests to reduce them in some way. If these costs cannot be reduced, they would not be costs in the sense that economists use the term but rather technological facts of life analogous to ordinary production or transactions costs (Buchanan, 1969). Both lines of argument imply that the true cost of rent-seeking tends to be smaller than suggested by the literature on rent-seeking contests.

The second of these possibilities, what might be called the "transactions cost" argument, is clearly false. Rent-seeking losses can be controlled in a variety of ways as noted above. Formal and informal institutions can reduce rent-seeking losses by changing the rules and rewards of rent-seeking contests. Such rules affect the relative returns of rent-seeking activities within a particular contest and also across the wide range of contests that might be played. In this sense, rent seeking is clearly a costly activity.

Whether policy-relevant rent-seeking costs exist or not depends on whether existing formal and informal institutional arrangements have already reduced rent-seeking losses as much as is humanly possible. Analysis of rent-seeking contests can direct our attention to reforms that could make us all better off in settings where new institutions can be devised that reduce the losses associated with rent-seeking games. On the other hand, if rent-seeking losses have already been minimized, analysis of rent-seeking advances the conservative policy agenda of defending existing institutions that curtail those losses. *In either case, a thorough understanding of rent-seeking contests is clearly central to our efforts to devise more effective institutions and to understand the institutions that we already have* (Tollison and Congleton, 1995).

ROGER D. CONGLETON

NOTES

1. The most common specification of this relationship resembles a lottery where one's probability of winning the prize or one's share of the prize depends on the number of lottery tickets purchased, x_i, relative to total ticket sales, $S = x_i / (\Sigma_j x_j)$.
2. Note that the efforts of firms who compete in well-functioning markets resembles rent-seeking as far as firms are concerned. However, competition in markets tends to increase the size of the prize to be distributed, and distribute much of that prize to individuals not directly involved in the contest, namely to consumers.

REFERENCES

Baik, K.H. and Lee, S. (2000). "Two-stage rent seeking contests with carryovers." *Public Choice*, 103: 285–296.

Baik, K.H. and Lee, S. (2001). "Strategic groups and rent dissipation." *Economic Inquiry*, 39: 672–684.

Buchanan, J.M. (1969). *Cost and Choice*. Chicago: Markham Publishing Co.

Buchanan, J.M. (1980). "Rent seeking and profit seeking," in J.M. Buchanan, R.D. Tollison, and Gordon Tullock (eds.) *Toward a Theory of the Rent-Seeking Society*. College Park: Texas A&M Press.

Buchanan, J.M., R.D. Tollison, and G. Tullock (eds.) (1980). *Toward a Theory of the Rent-Seeking Society*. College Park: Texas A&M Press.

Congleton, R.D. (1980). "Competitive process, competitive waste, and institutions," in J.M. Buchanan, R.D. Tollison, and Gordon Tullock (eds.) *Toward a Theory of the Rent-Seeking Society*. College Park: Texas A&M Press.

Congleton, R.D. (1984). "Committees and rent-seeking effort." *Journal of Public Economics*, 41: 441–448.

Corcoran, W.J. (1984). "Long-run equilibrium and total expenditures in rent seeking." *Public Choice*, 43: 89–94.

Hirshliefer, J. (2001). *The Dark Side of the Force: Economic Foundations of Conflict Theory*. New York: Cambridge University Press.

Posner, R.A. (1975). "The social costs of monopoly and regulation." *Journal of Political Economy*, 83: 807–827.

Rowley, C.K., Tollison, R.D., and Tullock, G. (1988). *The Political Economy of Rent Seeking*. Boston: Kluwer Academic Publishers.

Skaperdas, S. (1992). "Cooperation, conflict and power in the absence of property rights." *American Economic Review*, 82: 720–739.

Skogh, G. and Stuart, C. (1982). "A contractarian theory of property rights and crime." *Scandinavian Journal of Economics*, 84: 27–40.

Tollison, R.D. and Congleton, R.D. (1995). *The Economic Analysis of Rent Seeking*. Aldershot: Edgar Elgar Publishing.

Tullock, G. (1967). "The welfare costs of monopolies, tariffs and theft." *Western Economic Journal*, 5: 224–232.

Tullock, T. (1972). *Explorations in the Theory of Anarchy*. Blacksburg: Center for Study of Public Choice.

Warneryd, K. (1998). "Distributional conflict and jurisdictional organization." *Journal of Public Economics*, 69: 435–450.

RENT-SEEKING GAMES

Models of rent seeking consider players who engage in a contest, with each expending costly effort to increase his chances of winning a given prize. The effort can take many forms, such as campaign contributions, bribery, and advertising. The prize can also take many forms: passage of a favored policy, the grant of a profitable defense contract, or the reduction of a tax. Rent-seeking models can thus be applied to many issues which involve firms and individuals competing to transfer wealth.

The theoretical literature focuses on how much effort each player exerts, on how aggregate effort compares to the value of the prize (that is, the degree of rent dissipation), on how aggregate effort varies with the number of participants, and on how different rules for allocating the prize affect effort.

The theory of rent seeking relates to the theory of auctions. But the emphases and some of the assumptions differ. Rent seeking supposes that the effort represents a social cost rather than a transfer (see Tullock, 1967; Krueger, 1974; Posner, 1975; Bhagwati, 1982; Tollison, 1982). And whereas much of the work on auctions looks for rules which would maximize the seller's expected revenue, in rent seeking the design of a game is usually taken as fixed. Lastly, most analyses of auctions suppose that a bidder is uncertain about the values other bidders place on the object, whereas models of rent seeking usually supposes that these valuations are common knowledge.

In the following we will consider three types of contests.

1. Tullock Contest

Consider n firms competing for a prize. For simplicity, suppose they value the prize identically, at 1. For the Tullock contest (Tullock, 1967) let firm i's effort on rent-seeking be y_i. Each of the other firms spends y. A firm's probability of winning the prize equals the ratio of its spending on rent seeking to total spending by all firms on rent seeking. Thus, firm i's expected profits are $y_i/\sum_j^n y_j - y_i$.

This formulation is analytically tractable, but does not maximize social welfare or the benefits to the agency awarding the prize. Skaperdas (1996) offers an axiomatic justification of a more general contest success function:

$$\frac{y_i^{\alpha_i}}{\sum_j^n y_j^{\alpha_j}}. \tag{1}$$

The Tullock form supposes that $\alpha_i = 1$ for all i.

In a Nash equilibrium for the Tullock contest, firm i chooses y_i to maximize its expected profits, so that y_i must satisfy the first-order condition

$$\frac{\sum_{j \neq i} Y_j}{(\sum_j^n y_j)^2} = 1. \tag{2}$$

In equilibrium, all firms spend the same amount, so that y satisfies

$$y = \frac{n-1}{n^2}. \tag{3}$$

Total spending on rent seeking is thus $(n-1)/n$, and rent dissipation is incomplete — though for large n it approaches unity, for $n = 2$ it is 1/2.

The basic Tullock model has been extended in many directions, with emphasis on rent dissipation. Risk aversion

can either decrease or increase rent seeking effort (see Konrad and Schlessinger, 1997). The ambiguity is the consequence of two effects of increased spending on rent-seeking. First, an increase in effort reduces wealth in all states of the world (whether the player wins the prize or not). Second, increased effort also increases the likelihood of the favorable outcome of winning the rent-seeking prize, and so provides a form of self-insurance. More risk averse persons will seek more insurance by spending more on rent seeking to increase the likelihood of success, but they will also be inclined to spend less on rent seeking because of its inherent riskiness.

When there are only two identical players, the ability of one player to commit to his effort before the other does makes no difference to the outcomes, but if the two players place different values on the prize, the outcome of the sequential game differs from the simultaneous game (Dixit, 1987).

2. All-Pay Auction

The literature offers a different model, which predicts full rent dissipation even with only two players — the all-pay auction. Such an auction resembles conventional auctions in supposing that the highest bidder wins the prize. But it differs from most auctions in supposing that both the winner and the losers must pay their bids. A reasonable interpretation is that firms make contributions to politicians, with the firm which spends the most winning the prize. (See Hirshleifer and Riley, 1992; Hillman and Riley, 1989; Baye, Kovenock, and de Vries 1993, 1996.) This is the contest form that appears when $alpha = \infty$ in the contest success function (1).

We can readily see that no equilibrium in pure-strategies exists in such a contest: for if firm 1 spent y, then firm 2 could win for sure by spending $y + \varepsilon$, with ε arbitrarily small. Instead in a Nash equilibrium contenders choose their rent-seeking outlays as a mixed strategy: that is, the Nash equilibrium is a probability distribution from which contenders draw their efforts at random. For any number of identical participants exceeding one, expected aggregate spending on rent seeking equals the value of the prize: rent dissipation is complete.

3. Menu Auction

The menu auction model of governmental decisions was introduced by Grossman and Helpman (1994). In this model each firm confronts the government with a contribution schedule, which maps every policy vector government may choose into a payment from the firm to the government (or politician).

One element of an equilibrium is a set of contribution schedules such that each firm's schedule maximizes its expected profits, taking as given the schedules of the other firms. Suppose a politician adopts that policy which maximizes his utility, which for our purposes means that he maximizes the payments he will receive.

In such a game, the contribution schedules will be locally truthful: each firm sets its contribution schedule so that the marginal change in the contribution for a marginal change in the probability that it wins the prize equals the firm's benefit from the change in this probability. It can also be shown that the contribution schedule is linear, with an intercept of 0. That is, each firm offers to pay x for getting a share x of the prize (or, equivalently, for the probability x of winning the prize). This means that, as in the all-pay auction, rent dissipation is complete.

4. Asymmetric Valuations of Prize

By the envelope theorem, if different players place different values on the prize, then the player with a higher valuation must have a higher expected utility. Say this player values the prize at V_H. Since his utility cannot be negative, his effort cannot exceed the probability of winning the prize. But this means that the efforts of other players must be less than V_H, and rent dissipation cannot be complete.

Notice that when firms are identical, both all-pay auctions and menu auctions extract the full surplus of firms. Thus, no auction mechanism can give the agency a higher return. And the same holds if the firms differ. In any mechanism which extracts the maximum possible surplus, the marginal firm earns zero economic profits. An inframarginal firm will earn profits equal to the difference between its valuation of the prize and the valuation to the marginal firm. Both mechanisms yield that result; both therefore also predict the same value of expected payments. Empirically distinguishing between the two auction models of rent seeking is thus difficult.

AMIHAI GLAZER

REFERENCES

Baye, Michael, Kovenock, Dan, and De Vries, Casper (1993). "Rigging the lobbying process: An application of the all-pay auction." *American Economic Review*, 83: 289–294.

Baye, Michael, Dan Kovenock, and Casper De Vries (1996). "The all-pay auction with complete information." *Economic Theory*, 8: 291–305.

Douglas, Bernheim B. and Whinston, Michael D. (1986). "Menu auctions, resource allocation and economic influence." *Quarterly Journal of Economics*, 101(1): 1–31.

Bhagwati, Jagdish N. (1982). "Directly unproductive, profit-seeking (DUP) activities." *Journal of Political Economy*, 90: 988–1002.

Dixit, Avinash (1987). "Strategic behavior in contests." *American Economic Review*, 77: 891–898.

Grossman, Gene M. and Helpman, Elhanan (1994). "Protection for sale." *American Economic Review*, September: 833–850.

Hillman, Arye and Riley, John (1989). "Politically contestable rents and transfers." *Economics and Politics*, 1: 17–39.

Hirshleifer, Jack and Riley, John G. (1992). *The Analytics of Uncertainty and Information.* Cambridge: Cambridge University Press.

Konrad, Kai and Schlesinger, Harris (1997). "Risk aversion in rent-seeking and rent-augmenting games." *Economic Journal*, 107: 1671–1683.

Krueger, Anne O. (1974). "The political economy of the rent-seeking society." *American Economic Review*, 64: 291–303.

Milgrom, Paul (1988). "Employment contracts, influence activities, and efficient organization design." *Journal of Political Economy*, 96: 42–60.

Posner, Richard (1975). "The social costs of monopoly and regulation." *Journal of Political Economy*, 83: 807–827.

Skaperdas, Stergios (1996). "Contest success functions." *Economic Theory*, 7: 283–290.

Tollison, R. (1982). "Rent-seeking, a survey." *Kyklos*, 35: 575–602.

Tullock, Gordon (1967). "The welfare cost of tariffs, monopolies, and theft." *Western Economic Journal*, 5: 224–232.

RENT SEEKING IN DEVELOPMENT

The term rent seeking was coined by Anne Krueger (1974), and her discussion of the issue placed it squarely in a development context. In particular, she modeled rent seeking as a competition for import licenses when quotas are used to restrict international trade. This type of trade restriction has been widely used in developing countries. Further, as discussed below, rent seeking may arise in response to a wide array of other policies which have also been frequently used by developing countries. Thus, it was quickly realized that the phenomenon identified by Krueger was of major importance to developing economies.

The precise definition of rent seeking has proved to be elusive, as the term has been applied to a very wide range of activities. For the purpose of the discussion here, I will consider rent seeking to be a subset of what Bhagwati (1982) has dubbed Directly-unproductive profit-seeking (DUP) activities, where the government policy (e.g., the level of the import quota) is taken as given, and rent seeking arises in response to this fixed policy. This working definition corresponds well with the rent-seeking game developed by Tullock (1980) and may also include monopoly seeking which was first discussed by Tullock (1967).

It does not include tariff seeking as first described by Tullock (1967) and later developed by many authors.

Krueger's insight appears to have a clear policy implication: if the level of protection of a domestic industry is taken as given, a tariff is preferable to a quota, since a quota gives rise to rent seeking. Bhagwati and Srinivasan (1980) introduce the concept of revenue seeking under which individuals spend real resources in an attempt to obtain the revenue raised by a tariff. While there may be a general sense that rent seeking for import licenses is likely to be more costly than revenue seeking, ultimately this is an empirical question.

Price controls have been widely used in developing countries and are another policy which may have high rent-seeking costs attached. When binding price controls cause a shortage, black markets tend to develop. In addition, the gap between the official price and the black market price implies that there is a rent associated with being able to purchase a good at the official price. One way rent-seeking can be manifested in this case is a rationing of the good by the expenditure of time, i.e., waiting in line. (See, among others, Deacon and Sonstelie [1989].)

Krueger provided first estimates of the cost of rent seeking in developing countries. She estimated that the costs of rent seeking associated with the trade regime were 15% of GNP in Turkey in 1968 and 7.3% of national income in India in 1964. Mohammad and Whalley (1984) take a broader look at rent seeking, by including investment licensing, price controls and labor market controls in addition to quota restrictions in the trade regime when they estimate the costs of rent seeking. They estimate that the costs of rent seeking range between 30 to 45% of Indian GDP in 1980/81. Krueger and Mohammad and Whalley assume that rents are fully dissipated, while the actual extent of rent dissipation is an unresolved question which has been debated in the literature following Tullock's (1980) contribution.

Rent seeking can raise the economic costs of distortions imposed on the economy by the government. However, it also has the potential to reduce welfare when it occurs in response to policies which would otherwise be welfare enhancing. The International Coffee Agreement (ICA) is a vehicle by which rich consuming nations provide disguised foreign aid to poor producing nations by agreeing to pay higher prices for coffee. The signatories agree to buy their coffee only from ICA members who restrict sales in order to raise prices. This is an arrangement which should benefit the exporting members of the ICA which are poor to middle income developing nations. The restriction in the sale of coffee within the ICA is achieved through the use of export quotas. Bohman et al. (1996) suggest, at least for the case of Indonesia, that costs associated with rent seeking for the export quotas may outweigh the benefits of higher coffee prices.

After Krueger's work, it was recognized that rent seeking could cause large reductions in the level of income in developing countries, but in the context of Solow type growth models, rent seeking would not affect an economy's long run rate of growth. Since the mid 1980s, when the work of Paul Romer (1986, 1990) revived the field of growth theory, the search has been on for explanations of the widely varying growth experience found in the developing world. Several authors have since incorporated rent seeking into endogenous growth models.

In a research and development based model of growth, Grossman and Helpman (1991) find that quota induced rent seeking always reduces the growth rate by causing the removal of resources from the productive sector of the economy. As a result, less research and development takes place and growth is slower. In Sturzenegger and Tommasi (1994), entrepreneurs may devote effort to innovation or to a rent-seeking contest in which they may obtain a subsidy from the government. When political access is distributed unequally across the sectors of the economy, the authors find that less effort is devoted to the rent-seeking contest and that the growth rate is higher as a result.

Murphy et al. (1991) develop a model in which growth results from knowledge spillovers. In particular, productivity growth is determined by the most talented individual located in a sector in the previous period. In this model, rent seeking always reduces the level of output, and may reduce the growth rate of the economy. This depends on the technology of rent seeking and on whether it induces the most talented individual in the economy to become a rent seeker. The authors provide a crude test of their model by regressing cross-country per capita growth on college enrollments in law and engineering, where the law enrollments are taken as a proxy for talent allocated to rent seeking. They find that per capita growth is negatively related to law enrollments and positively related to engineering enrollments.

Pecorino (1992) develops a model of growth driven by the accumulation of human capital. There are two rent-seeking technologies in this model. Under the first, agents seek rents from within the productive sector of the economy. These agents do not specialize in rent seeking. Under the second technology, agents specialize in the rent seeking activity and acquire (socially) unproductive human capital which enhances their ability to seek rents. Rent seeking undertaken by specialists reduces the level, but not the growth rate of output. Rent seeking undertaken by individuals otherwise engaged in productive activity does reduce the economy's growth rate. Productive human capital is effectively unemployed during the time these agents spend seeking rents. As a result, the rate of return on investment in human capital and the growth rate of output are both reduced. As with the result of Murphy et al. (1991), the specifics of the of rent seeking technology determine whether or not rent seeking has long-run growth effects.

Recently, the topic of corruption has attracted a great deal of attention in the development literature. Rent seeking and corruption are closely related for two reasons. First, as discussed by Krueger (1974), competition for government positions in which bribes may be obtained can be considered a form of rent seeking. As a result, there may be resource costs associated with bribes that might otherwise be considered a pure transfer. Second, policies which give bureaucratic discretion in the award of economic rents (e.g., import licenses) will tend to encourage corruption. Shleifer and Vishny (1993) relate the costs of corruption to the industrial organization of bribe taking. Competition among bribe takers selling government inputs which are perfect substitutes can drive bribe taking to zero, but decentralized monopolists selling complementary inputs will lead to very high costs associated with bribe taking. Shleifer and Vishny argue that the need to keep corruption secret is one of the reasons that it is damaging to growth. Mauro (1995) presents empirical evidence showing that there is a negative relationship between corruption and growth which is manifested through the investment channel. For an in depth discussion of corruption and development, see Bardhan (1997).

Agents engaged in rent seeking may acquire human capital which is specific to this and other DUP activities such as tariff seeking, but which may not be easily transferable to activities in the productive sector of the economy. (See, e.g., Krueger, 1990: 210–213.) If this is true, it may have important implications for economic reform, and may help explain why reforms are difficult and prone to failure. Conlon and Pecorino (1998) develop a model in which there is both rent seeking and lobbying for import protection through the use of an import quota. The use of an import quota leads to rent seeking. Sector specific skills cause the labor market for rent seekers and lobbyists to be segmented from the market for labor in productive sector of the economy. A reform which reduces available rents leads to a negative feedback effect through an increase in the lobbying activity. As a result, the distortion in the trade regime is worsened and the initial fall in rents may be partially offset. By contrast, a reform which targets the lobbying activity will reduce the trade policy distortion and may reduce the levels of rents. A positive feedback effect (the reduction in available rents) is possible, but not guaranteed

under a reform which targets lobbying, while a negative feedback effect (increased lobbying activity) is guaranteed under a reform which targets the rent-seeking activity.

Rent seeking is an important development issue because policies which can give rise to rent seeking have been very widely used in the developing world. Rent-seeking activity reduces the level of productive economic activity in the economy and may reduce the growth rate as well. The same policies which lead to rent seeking are likely to foster corruption. This is an additional avenue through which these policies may retard growth.

PAUL PECORINO

REFERENCES

Bardhan, P. (1997). "Corruption and development: A review of the issues." *Journal of Economic Literature*, 35: 1320–1346.

Bhagwati, J.N. (1982). "Directly-unproductive, profit-seeking (DUP) activities." *Journal of Political Economy*, 90: 988–1002.

Bhagwati, J.N. and Srinivasan, T.N. (1980). "Revenue seeking: A generalization of the theory of tariffs." *Journal of Political Economy*, 88: 1069–1087.

Bohman, M., Jarvis, L., and Barichello, R. (1996). "Rent seeking and international commodity agreements: the case of coffee." *Economic Development and Cultural Change*, 45: 379–404.

Conlon, J. and Pecorino, P. (1998). "Primary and secondary reform." *Economic Inquiry*, 36: 590–602.

Deacon, R.T. and Sonstelie, J. (1989). "Price controls and rent-seeking behavior in developing countries." *World Development*, 17: 1945–1954.

Grossman, G.M. and Helpman, E. (1991). "Growth and welfare in a small open economy," in E. Helpman and A. Razin (eds.) *International Trade and Trade Policy*. Cambridge, MA: MIT Press, 141–163.

Krueger, A.O. (1974). "The political economy of the rent-seeking society." *American Economic Review*, 69: 291–303.

Krueger, A.O. (1990). "The political economy of controls: American sugar," in M. Scott and D. Lal (eds.) *Public Policy and Economic Development*. Oxford: Clarendon Press.

Mauro, P. (1995). "Corruption and growth." *Quarterly Journal of Economics*, 110: 682–712.

Mohammad, S. and Whalley, J. (1984). "Rent-seeking in India: its cost and policy significance." *Kyklos*, 37: 387–413.

Murphy, K.M., Shleifer, A., and Vishny, R.W. (1991). "The allocation of talent: implications for growth." *Quarterly Journal of Economics*, 106: 503–530.

Pecorino, P. (1992). "Rent seeking and growth: the case of growth through human capital accumulation." *Canadian Journal of Economics*, 25: 944–956.

Romer, P.M. (1986). "Increasing returns and long run growth." *Journal of Political Economy*, 94: 1002–1037.

Romer, P.M. (1990). "Endogenous technological change." *Journal of Political Economy*, 98: S71–102.

Shleifer, A. and Vishny, R.W. (1993). "Corruption." *Quarterly Journal of Economics*, 108: 599–617.

Sturzenegger, F. and Tommasi, M. (1994). "The distribution of political power, the costs of rent-seeking and economic growth." *Economic Inquiry*, 32: 236–248.

Tullock, G. (1967). "The welfare costs of tariffs, monopolies and theft." *Western Economic Journal*, 5: 224–232.

Tullock, G. (1980). "Efficient rent seeking," in J.M. Buchanan, R.D. Tollison, and G. Tullock (eds.) *Toward a Theory of the Rent-Seeking Society*. College Station, Texas: Texas A&M University Press.

THE RULE OF LAW

> The great Question which in all Ages has disturbed Mankind, and brought on them the greatest part of thos Mischiefs which have ruin'd Cities, depopulated Countries and disordered the Peace of the World, has been, Not whether there be Power in the World, nor whence it came, but who should have it.
>
> — John Locke

Western political thought has been dominated, since the beginning, with an interest in the procedures by which political power is applied. Theorists as early in the history of the field as Aristotle were primarily concerned not with what a state does, but how a state once entrusted with power will make decisions. In other words, according to what rules will political power be exercised. Perhaps even more dominant than political theory has been the example of the semitic tradition of submission of magesterial authority and citizens alike to *ex ante*, written law. One of the critical products of this ferment, applied with varying degrees of consistency, over the past 2500 years of Western history has been the political and legal doctrine that has come to be known as *the rule of law*.

There are two ways that political and legal power can be applied. One way is for coercive power to be exercised by rulers according to their discretion and in reaction to events as they arise. This has been called the application of "discretionary power" or "the rule of man." The alternative norm — the rule of law — demands that the actions of political and legal bodies be bound by a body of *ex ante* laws. Thus the "rule of law" literally means "rule by the law," as opposed to "rule by those in power." The rule of law, as a principle, is ultimately meant to constitute a seal between the application of coercive power and the justification for its use. In some sense, public choice theory can be viewed as an analysis of the effects of breaches in this seal.

But this is only the broadest way of understanding a term generally used with a much more nuanced meaning. There are implications of the norm as described above that are considered more important than others and are generally more descriptive of the benefits attributed to the norm. This more descriptive criteria for the rule of law says that the use of political and legal power must be applied, ahistorically, impersonally, and generally. It is these three features — impersonality, a historicity, and generality — that make up the norm as it is conventionally used.

The rule of law first of all implies that law is applied impersonally. That is, the law is not created in order to satisfy the preferences of any individuals. The impersonal nature of the rule of law creates a seal between the application of political and legal power (which is necessarily in the hands of persons in positions of leadership) and the justification of the use of that power (which is assigned to the law itself). This is perhaps the most important aspect of the rule of law as it effectively bars the arbitrary use of power. The scope of the use of power is bound and delimited by a fixed source that has neither personality nor preference. Therefore the application of power cannot be used as a means for attaining individual ends. The implications of this aspect of the rule of law should be clear for public choice theorists. If the rule of law is perfectly applied, it is not possible for political action to be a result of personal preferences. Because public choice fundamentally studies political leaders as fulfillers of personal preferences, public choice is fundamentally the study of breaches in the seal constituted by the rule of law.

This depersonalization is accomplished via the law's fundamental *a historicity* and *ex ante* character. The rule of law is said to be in place only in circumstances where applications of power are bound by rules set forth *prior* to any of that power's applications. The *ex ante* nature of law under the rule of law can be read in one of two ways. The law can fulfill the norm by having been developed prior to its applications in historical time. Alternatively, and more broadly, this *a historicity* can be read as a demand that law be independent of events in the world. That is, the rule of law is said to fulfill its *ex ante* character only if law is created without reference to or motivation from particular circumstances or individuals. In either case, under the doctrine, the law must have a certain independence from the particularities of history.

The flip side of the depersonalization of the law implied by the rule of law is the general nature of the law. This third feature of the rule of law has been called the generality norm. Because law must be developed without regard to particular events in the world, and applied without regard to the preferences of its appliers, it cannot apply discriminately. The rule justifying an exercise of power can never be unique to a particular individual or even a particular grouping of people. It must apply generally. This, too, implies a fundamental seal constituted by the rule of law — under the generality norm, all persons are safe from the arbitrary use of power against them especially on the basis of particular characteristics.

It must be kept in mind, however, that these characteristics of the rule do not imply that the law cannot make distinctions among groups. In fact it is certainly possible for the *ex ante* body of law to single out groups on the basis of gender, race or even ideology and still conform to the rule of law. The salient feature of the rule is only that these laws must not waver on the basis of particular individuals or individual groups in historical time. They must be blind to particular individuals, and not necessarily to groups defined *ex ante* to the law's applications. It is also important to note that the rule of law does not necessarily do away with the need for a legislature or judiciary. Political and legal leaders ultimately must still interpret and apply the law under the norm and the publication of new laws are possible within the framework. But the scope of law, the social and economic spheres it may affect, and the reasoning behind any future legislation are set up and controlled by a body of law that is defined prior to any such applications. The actions of the political and legal authority are ultimately bound, shaped and justified by an impersonal, non-historical and general body of law.

There are several results of the application of the rule of law that make it a desirable norm. One of these is that the law is made to be ultimately predictable. Because the law does not change as quickly as the preferences of leaders, it is relatively consistent over time. If the law is given in a written form this is especially true. However, even the common law has a consistency to it because it changes only very slowly over time — or at any rate, more slowly than discretionary law. The upshot of this predictability is that individuals under a regime of rule of law can make social and economic plans under the assumption that the basic rules of social interaction are not subject to change. This stability allows individuals to, especially, make long term plans, whereas under discretionary law, long term planning is a risky and uncertain thing. It is this aspect of the rule of law that lead Hayek to refer to it as an "instrument of production" (1945, 1973).

The rule of law also implies that no individuals have coercive power over others. That is, as Hayek argues, individuals have some degree of liberty from the will of other persons. Because all coercive power is held by the state, and the state is governed by *ex ante* law (which has no personality and therefore no personal conflicts), coercive power can never be used to bend the will of one person to the will of another. Conflicts of interest under the rule of law must be resolved using some set of fixed procedural rule and cannot boil down to coercive conflict. Within the bounds of the fixed law, individuals must settle conflicts peacefully and mutually. Thus the rule of law alone accomplishes much of the liberal program. Individuals have fundamental freedom, at least from the will of other individuals. This freedom, with open recourse to political conflict barred, allows for the development of a contractual rather than coercive system of relationships between individuals. And, importantly to economists, this is the *sine non qua* of markets. As Hayek puts it: "The classical argument for freedom in economic affairs rests on the tacit postulate that the rule of law should govern policy in this as in all other spheres" (1960, 220).

Neither the liberal program nor Pareto improvement is necessarily accomplished by the rule of law, however. A body of *ex ante* law can, after all, still demand the enforcement of illiberal policies. Laws, for instance, enforcing segregation, punishing consensual sexual acts, or banning criticism of the state are all perfectly consistent with the concept of the rule of law. Neither does the rule of law ensure any degree of Pareto efficiency. Government can still legitimately block Pareto improvements and even cause Pareto regresses under the norm. Thus while the rule of law implies freedom from the will of other persons, it does not imply freedom from coercion by the state (see, e.g., Hasnas, 1995).

Finally, the rule of law is generally taken to imply public knowledge of the law by all individuals subject to the law. This feature of the rule of law is less clearly derived from the doctrine itself. However, it is difficult to imagine an implementation of the doctrine without a public understanding of the law. Because, by the generality norm, no individuals have a privileged relationship to the law, all individuals must be capable of holding others accountable to the law. Although the *ex ante* law in principle dictates the process by which enforcement of the law happens, it also must apply to those enforcers. The solution to this problem — who will enforce the law on the enforcers of the law — is a motivating subject of Constitutional theory and political economy (see Buchanan and Tullock, 1962 and Buchanan, 1975). Knowledge of the law allows the possibility of electoral or literal revolutions against those leaders who do not themselves obey law. Constitutional theory — like public choice theory — can be viewed as a study of the mechanisms that hold the rule of law in place. Mechanisms in constitutional theory such as the division of power allow for an alternative to revolution by creating game-strategic balances between branches of enforcers of the law. These mechanisms, too, generally rely on an informed population since they are predicated on the idea that political and legal leaders will leverage the public's knowledge of the law as an implicit threat against power seeking political rivals.

The classical defenses of the rule of law have usually been connected to the strands of liberalism, egalitarianism and rationalism inherent in political philosophy over the course of the field in the West. The traditional desire for a *rational* political order demanded that law not be governed by the passions (read: preferences) of leaders, for reason and the passions were believed to be opposed to one another. Thus rational law had to be set up *ex ante* and based on philosophy in order to avoid taking on an arbitrary character in the hands of political leaders. Plato's ideal republic was a construction of reason and one of the major concerns of the Republic was the development of leadership that would not corrupt and would remain subservient to its rational law. Egalitarian concerns motivated the construction of the rule of law through the generality norm in Aristotle, for example, who was concerned, in great measure, with the balancing of power among the classes in the polis in order to generate temperate law. Finally, as has been mentioned, the rule of law is a necessary but not sufficient condition for most forms of liberalism that have dominated political thought since the enlightenment. Thus the provision of liberty from the coercive will of other persons has also been a classical defense for the rule of law. Exemplary here are the arguments and intuitions behind the liberality of the body of common law that formed the English constitution. All of these pieces of the classical defense are rooted in the West's fundamental suspicion of those in power.

It is this suspicion, too, that lies at the root of the two major justifications for the rule of law offered by political economists in the twentieth century. The first of these is that the rule of law, interpreted strictly, does away with the possibility of political economic problems such as rent seeking. As has been mentioned, the rule of law, by depersonalizing the law, creates a seal between personal preferences and political power. Political leaders are incapable of applying coercive power discriminately. But without the ability to apply some sort of discriminatory political power, political leaders have nothing to sell to rent seekers. Other political problems like vote buying are likewise barred by the doctrine. Once again, candidates have no political currency with which to purchase support; the growth of government is controlled by the *ex ante* law and not the appliers of the law. The political economic problems of interest to public choice theory only arise when the generality norm is violated because the rule of law has been weakened in some way (see Buchanan and Congleton, 1998).

The second of the contemporary political economic justifications of the rule of law, offered by Hayek (who was also concerned with a defense of liberalism generally) favors the rule of law as a precondition for the blessings of the extended order of the market economy. In Hayek's thought, the rule of law creates an atmosphere of predictability that allows long term economic plans to develop. Capital formation, trading conventions and extensive price systems are impossible without a stable institutional environment to grow in. Further, as has been mentioned, without the rule of law, confiscation and arbitrary punishment, fueled by rent seeking, become viable (and often less risky) alternatives to production and contracting. But this alternative is ultimately a zero sum game, offering none of the growth and innovation offered by markets.

Indeed, there has been some evidence presented in the modern growth literature that the rule of law is strongly connected to growth and thus concludes that Hayek's conjecture about the rule of law as an instrument of production may indeed be right (see Barro, 1997 and Mahoney, 2001). This modern literature fits with historical explanations that place the emergence and adoption of a rule of law — which provided secure and predictable backdrop for economic actors instead of the uncertain and arbitrary backdrop that characterized unbound political rulers — as a primary cause for the economic growth experienced in West from the middle-ages onward (see Birdzell and Rosenberg, 1986). The difficulties of the transition from socialism in East and Central Europe and the former Soviet Union throughout the 1990s, and the failure of development in Africa and other less developed regions has led to a renewed appreciation of the underlying institutional regime required for economic growth. It is now not uncommon for economists to conclude that without private property and freedom of contract, encrusted in a rule of law, and economic actors will be thwarted in their attempts to realize the mutual gains from exchange and economic growth will be stalled as the economic and financial institutions required for advanced material progress will fail to emerge (La Porta et al., 1998). The question that now has moved to center stage of political economy scholarship is how does one successfully grow a rule of law in these reforming economies (see Rubin, 1997).

PETER J. BOETTKE
RYAN OPREA

REFERENCES

Barro, Robert (1997). *Determinants of Economic Growth: A Cross-Country Empirical Study*. Cambridge: MIT Press.

Birdzell, L.E. and Rosenberg, N. (1986). *How the West Grew Rich*. New York: Basic Books.

Buchanan, J.M. (1975). *The Limits of Liberty*. Chicago: University of Chicago Press.

Buchanan, J.M. and Congleton, R.D. (1998). *Politics by Principle, Not Interest*. New York: Cambridge University Press.

Buchanan, J.M. and Tullock, G. (1962). *The Calculus of Consent*. Ann Arbor: University of Michigan Press.

Hasnas, John. (1995). "The myth of the rule of law." *Wisconsin Law Review*, 199.

Hayek, F.A. (1945). *The Road to Serfdom*. Chicago: University of Chicago Press.

Hayek, F.A. (1960). *The Constitution of Liberty*. Chicago: University of Chicago Press.

Hayek, F.A. (1973–1979). *Law, Legislation and Liberty*, 3 volumes. Chicago: University of Chicago Press.

La Porta, R., Lopez-de-Silanes, F., Shliefer, A., and Vishny, R. (1998). "Law and finance." *Journal of Political Economy*, 106(6): 1113–1155.

Mahoney, P. (2001). "The common law and economic growth: hayek might be right." *Journal of Legal Studies*, 30(2): 503–525.

Rubin, P. (1997). "Promises, promises," in C.K. Rowley (ed.) *Classical Liberalism and Civil Society*. Cheltenham, UK: Edward Elgar Publishing, 1997.

RULES VERSUS STANDARDS

In crafting laws, lawmakers cannot effectively foresee all the particular circumstances to which their laws could apply. This renders legislation general in nature and incomplete as a matter of practical necessity, leaving an unavoidable margin of discretion to judges when interpreting laws and applying general principles to the specific situation at bar (Posner, 1989). To guide judges through the margins of discretion, lawmakers may opt to incorporate rules or standards into the laws they write. The functionality of these rules or standards, the consequences of their incorporation into laws, and their significance from an economic perspective, are all the subject of the present study.

A "standard" is the legal or social criterion that adjudicators use to judge actions under particular circumstances. In that sense, standards are circumstantial; they are open-ended, allowing the adjudicator to make a fact-specific determination such as whether a driver used "reasonable care" in given situation. Standards such as reasonableness are largely intuitive, which makes them easy to understand for the general public. A "rule," conversely, withdraws from the adjudicator's consideration the circumstances that would be relevant to decision-making according to a standard. Rules are more specific than standards; they create bright line tests such as whether a driver exceeded the speed limit of 55 miles per hour. Greater specificity decreases the flexibility of a rule, often at the expense of an optimal fit between the coverage of a rule and the regulated conduct.

When legislators choose between rules and standards, they must consider when, and at what cost, the rules and standards should be applied to specific situations. For instance, rules require advance determination of the law's content because of the high degree of specificity involved in their formulation. Lawmakers must perform research in advance to determine the appropriate rule to create, *ex ante*. Therefore, rules are more costly for legislators to promulgate than general standards, which require less specificity. Standards, however, are more costly for legal advisors to predict or adjudicators to apply because they require determinations of the law's content *ex post*. Hence, in the event of a car accident where the driver was traveling more than 55 miles per hour, liability would be automatic under a 55 miles per hour rule. However, under a standard such as "reasonableness," the judge or jury would have to determine the facts and circumstances at the time of the accident, and decide whether to impose liability. The application of a standard is more fact specific, but naturally less consistent in the long run. Thus, from an *ex ante* perspective, rules are typically optimal, and from an *ex post* perspective, standards are typically optimal.

1. The Problem of Judicial Interpretation

The optimal degree of specificity of laws has been a frequent subject of debate for centuries. Legal theorists have long attempted to formulate principles that should guide judges when interpreting incomplete legal precepts. In ancient Greece, Aristotle (350 B.C.) realized the unavoidable necessity of incomplete laws. He advocated the doctrine of original intent in legislative interpretation, suggesting that, given the unavoidable incompleteness of legal rules, techniques of legislative interpretation should be developed to give guidance to judges and interpreters when applying such general laws to specific circumstances. In the process of legislative interpretation, judges should fill the void of the letter of the law with the finding of how the original lawmakers would have specified the rule in light of the specific facts, if they had foreseen the problem and dealt with it explicitly.

Incompleteness of legal rules is not only a matter of unavoidable necessity. At times, incomplete legal precepts can be purposefully enacted as a way to delay the decision-making process, transferring to the judiciary some of the tasks that would otherwise have to be carried out *ex ante* by the legislature. In this setting, Jeremy Bentham (1776) addressed the question of optimal specificity of laws, providing fertile ground for the modern debate on rules versus standards. Bentham's idea of a two-tiered system, where the public learns of the general rules while the judges hear individual cases with some freedom to depart from the *ex ante* rule, provides a good example of the possible role of purposeful incompleteness of legal rules. In Bentham's world, judicial discretion would not necessarily depend upon the lack of specificity of the *ex ante* rule, but could well coexist with detailed and fully specified *ex ante* rules, since judges would have some adjudicatory flexibility when applying the *ex ante* rule to the case (see, e.g., Dan-Cohen, 1984; and Parisi, 1992).

Going beyond Bentham, it is true that the use of standards would allow the judiciary to adhere to more flexible decision rules, with the option to deviate from conduct rules in specific circumstances. This approach would avoid running into the limits of the two-tiered analysis, given the fact that if too many decisions are issued against the original meaning of the rule, the *ex ante* value of the rule may be corroded with an emerging public distrust in the legislative and judicial functions of government. With rational expectations, the general public would anticipate the likely *ex post* interpretation of the rule, with a further corrosion of the *ex ante* function of the legislative enactment.

The recognition of the unavoidability of incomplete laws is an important stepping-stone towards the discovery of optimal specificity of laws. Within the margins of reasonable foresight, lawmakers have some choice on the degree of specificity of legal rules. Laws that are not fully specified upfront impose greater implementation and decision-making costs by judicial and administrative bodies at a later stage. The optimal degree of specificity of law thus critically depends on the relative costs and political advantages of lawmaking by different branches of government. The evaluation of comparative advantages in lawmaking necessarily rests on the full understanding of the public choice implications of alternative allocations of lawmaking power. Erlich and Posner (1973) conjecture that when the rule is statutory and the conduct to be regulated is politically controversial, the cost of promulgating a rule is highest. The formulation of a statutory rule requires negotiation among the legislators. The analysis of transaction costs in other contexts suggests that the costs of legislative negotiation are likely to be substantial due to the number of legislators whose agreement must be secured. The costs of negotiation will be even higher when the proposed rule is controversial. Transaction costs increase with the number of parties whose agreement is necessary for the transaction to occur. The presence of so many parameters that affect the choice of optimal degree of detail of legal rules has led Diver (1983: 76) to conclude that, while some laws may better serve their purpose as rules and others as standards,

"[g]eneralizations about optimal rule precision are inherently suspect."

1.1. Under-Inclusion and Over-Inclusion Problems

From an efficiency perspective, there are both under- and over-inclusive effects that occur when deciding to implement a rule to specific circumstances that were not specifically envisioned by the lawmaker. Ehrlich and Posner note that coupling a rule with a standard can solve the problem of under-inclusion. For example, it can thus be made unlawful to drive more than 70 miles per hour *or* to drive at any speed that is unreasonably fast given the particular circumstances of the case. While under-inclusion can be remedied by backing the rule with a standard, the result of adding a standard can diminish the benefits of legislating with rules, namely the low cost for adjudicators in determining when an individual has violated the rule.

When implementing a rule or a standard, there are also over-inclusive effects. The problem of over-inclusion is frequently dealt with by allowing enforcement officials to waive *ex post* the application of the rule or standard (e.g., speeding violations can be excused in case of emergency, etc.). As a matter of theory, a rule could be formulated with sufficient level of detail to contemplate all the possible exceptions, excuses and justifications. In practice, however, it may be less possible to envision *ex ante* all possible contingencies, or too costly to allow case-by-case exceptions to be made at the enforcement level.

The problems of over-inclusion and under-inclusion are more serious the greater the heterogeneity of the regulated conduct, and the faster the rate of change of the regulated environment. Kaplow (1992) suggests that even an activity that may appear homogeneous and objectively ascertainable such as speeding contains overriding elements of heterogeneity. The reasonableness of speeding depends on the particular circumstances of the case. A single speed limit, or even a number of speed limits contingently set in consideration of particular circumstances, would by necessity lead to occasional under-inclusiveness or over-inclusiveness. The lack of a perfect fit between the *ex ante* legal rule and the circumstances of the case occasions potential social losses. Over-inclusion and under-inclusion impose social costs that vary according to the relative size of the value of the regulated activity and the gravity of the negative externalities of the activity, absent legal constraints. In this context, Ehrlich and Posner suggest that minimizing the social loss function with respect to potential under-inclusion and over-inclusion costs maximizes efficiency and predict that rules will be more common in areas of homogenous conduct.

2. Rules, Standards, and the Social Cost of Lawmaking and Adjudication

Law and economics scholars have often considered the criteria for determining the optimal degree of specificity of legal rules. Scholars who have entered the debate have utilized instruments from optimal decision theory, public choice theory, and constitutional political economy, with differing and often antithetical results. Much attention has been paid to the difference between standards and rules in the law and economics literature. Generally, scholars have postulated that laws articulated as "standards" leave a greater margin of discretion to judges and administrative agencies in the implementation of the legal norms. To the contrary, "rules" are laws that are specified upfront with a greater level of detail and thus leave a lesser margin of discretion in the implementation of such norms.

There are, of course, costs and benefits to governing with rules or with standards, and such costs should be taken into account in choosing the optimal specificity of a law. Such variables that bear on the choice of optimal degree of specificity of legal rules include the law's intended objective, the frequency of the application of the legal rule, and the total cost of lawmaking, net social welfare, and the cost of legal advice.

The law's intended objective is important because if the law's purpose is deterrence of specific conduct, criminal or otherwise, rules are typically preferable (Diver, 1983: 77). This is because laws written with deterrence in mind send strong, clear signals to the population at large that certain conduct will yield certain consequences, regardless of extraneous or mitigating factors. Where deterrence is not the primary goal, standards are often more appropriate (Diver, 1983: 77). When crimes have already been committed, for example, lawmakers may prefer to equip adjudicators and enforcers with specific standards that permit the consideration of extraneous or mitigating factors. Rules and standards may come together in this way so that rules efficiently govern conduct and standards govern punishment (see Dan-Cohen, 1984).

The frequency of a law's application is important to consider in determining optimal specificity so that lawmakers can strike the right balance between promulgation and enforcement costs. If a law is frequently applied, enforcement costs will tend to be higher than promulgation costs. This necessarily means that rules will be more efficient than standards when the law is frequently applied. Since legislators must absorb promulgation costs only once, standards have the potential to cost significantly more because adjudicators accrue enforcement costs each time there is a violation (Kaplow, 1992: 577). Rules are also more efficient because individuals are more easily able to learn about them, thus improving their chances of complying with the rules instead of violating them.

The total cost of lawmaking is another factor that economists weigh heavily in determining the optimal specificity of legal rules. Ehrlich and Posner have advanced the notion that total cost (i.e., promulgation cost, enforcement cost, and all other costs) should ultimately control a legislature's determination. As stated before, rules require a high degree of specificity and therefore have higher promulgation costs which may include detailed research (Kaplow, 1992: 570). Standards, on the other hand, will be costlier to enforce for adjudicators, draining more resources from the judicial system (Kaplow, 1992: 577). Adjudicators must give content to standards, which is a key factor in high enforcement costs (Kaplow, 1992: 570).

Economists concerned about net social welfare tend to favor rules because they guarantee greater certainty, consistency, and predictability to private parties (Sullivan, 1992). Sullivan argues that rules promote judicial economies by minimizing the need for a detailed consideration of facts and circumstances each time a law is applied (Sullivan, 1992: 63).

The cost of legal advice is a final factor in determining the optimal specificity of legal rules. For standards, this cost — meaning the cost of consulting with an attorney to determine whether certain conduct violates the law — is higher than it would be for rules (Kaplow, 1992: 571). Attorneys will convey a more concrete understanding of the consequences of an actor's conduct where rules are concerned, because they are easier to apply *ex ante*. Given the cheaper cost factor, more individuals are likely to become informed in a regime dominated by rules (Kaplow, 1992: 574).

2.1. Rule, Standards and Information Costs

Economists note that there is an information cost associated with promulgating and enforcing rules and standards, particularly with regard to compliance with rules and standards. Under rules, informed individuals can fully identify the content of the law since legal provisions are fully articulated up-front and, as a result, individuals may more easily conform their behavior to the law. Rules are precise and it is easier to conform conduct to a precise rule. Under a standard such as reasonableness, what is "reasonable" under the circumstances can vary widely. Applying standards may require some guesswork by less experienced legal actors. As a result, standards tend to be more costly for individuals to interpret when deciding how to act. When individuals can determine the application of rules to their potential acts more clearly, their conduct is more likely to reflect the previously promulgated rules. This is because standards will be given content and substance only after individuals act. Under rules, individuals are more likely to be informed, and under standards, individuals are likely to be relatively uninformed. Kaplow suggests that uninformed individuals act based on their best guess about how the law will apply to their contemplated conduct. Informed individuals, on the other hand, act based on actual knowledge of the law.

2.2. Lawmaking as a Production Function: The Optimal Scale Problem

The law making process is, in a sense, a production function with both fixed and variable costs. In this way, the creation of the law can be thought as the fixed cost investment in the production of legal order. Lawmakers choose the level of specificity of legal rules by allocating fixed capital in the production process (Parisi and Ghei, 2001). A greater level of specificity of the law generally increases the cost of creation of the law, but requires lower implementation costs by courts and administrative agencies. Thus the greater the fixed investment (i.e., the more specified the law is), the lower the variable costs for its implementation will be.

Further, Parisi and Ghei note that lawmakers choose the timing of legal intervention and revision of legal rules. In this production analogue, the lawmakers' choice corresponds to the investment decision in the fixed production capital and the choice of timing of replacement of obsolete capital. The degree of specificity and the timing of legal intervention are critical control variables for the social planner's attempt to maximize the net present value of legislation. Parisi and Ghei illustrate how the optimal balance of timing and specificity is affected by exogenous parameters such as (a) the expected frequency of application of the legal rule; (b) the degree of uncertainty in the regulated environment; (c) the extent to which lawmaking costs are irreversible (i.e., sunk); and (d) the time preference rate of the social planner.

The choice of a well specified rule is likely to require a larger up-front investment, but has lower operating costs later. Enacting a rule requires a large outlay in the initial acquisition of information, but because the rule is simple to understand and apply, the operating costs are low. A standard requires a smaller investment initially, as it requires less information and legislative detail to enact. However, it requires larger outlays in its enforcement, in that it is more costly for individuals to acquire information about

a standard and it requires greater implementation and interpretation efforts by the courts.

In this context, Kaplow suggests that regulation is sometimes served better with a rule, and other times better served with a standard, depending on frequency of application of the relevant law. For legal issues that arise frequently in settings with common characteristics, a rule would tend to be desirable. Because learning about a rule is cheaper, individuals may spend less in learning about the law and may be better guided by a rule since the law's content can be readily ascertained. Conversely, where legal issues rarely arise and the circumstances are varied, designing a rule that accounts for every relevant contingency would be wasteful, as most of such hypothetical circumstances would never arise in actual cases. Since rules have a higher fixed cost than standards, whereas standards generally have a higher variable cost, Kaplow shows that when frequency is low, a general standard is preferable.

The solution to this lawmaking problem generates several implications concerning the patterns of lawmaking under different legal, social and economic conditions. This leads to the hypothesis that legal systems respond to exogenous changes in the external environment by adopting varying patterns of lawmaking, thus maximizing the value of a legal intervention. This hypothesis provides the basis for further consideration of the likely departures from such optimal lawmaking pattern due to specific public choice failures.

2.3. The Obsolescence Problem

It is important to consider that circumstances change with time. Thus, an important cost of legal regulation by means of rules is the cost of altering rules to keep pace with social, economic or technological change. For example, the development of the air bags and anti-lock brakes on vehicles altered the relative costs of accident avoidance. Such changes and advancements can even render rules obsolete. Posner and Ehrlich suggest that the more detailed a rule is, the more often it will have to be changed. For detailed rules, the cost of change is high.

Obsolescence, however, is not as much of a problem with governance by standards as it is with rules. Standards are relatively unaffected by changes over time since a standard indicates only the types of circumstances that are relevant, and not particular, specific circumstances. The reasonableness standard directs the decision maker to determine, *ex post*, what behavior by the parties would have minimized the sum of the expected accident costs and the accident avoidance costs. This concept can be followed despite that the optimal course of conduct changes immensely with time. The optimal rule maker, then, would use more specific rules when there is a stable environment, and general standards when there is a fast rate of change.

Enacted legal rules are subject to obsolescence given the changes in the external environment. Detailed rules are more sensitive to exogenous, unforeseen changes in the regulated environment and thus are more prone to obsolescence. Ehrlich and Posner note that detailed judge made rules of liability, derived from standards and characteristic of the nineteenth, century have given way in this century to detailed traffic and other safety codes that, through the doctrine of negligence *per se*, operate as rules of tort liability as well as standards. The rise in the rate of economic and technological change over time has increased the cost of the judicial process. While the judicial process is not well suited to the rapid alteration of rules, a general standard can accommodate more change. However, the first adjudication under a standard constitutes a precedent for future enforcement proceedings and nearly transforms the standard into a rule.

2.4. Lawmaking under Uncertainty

An important dimension of the optimal specificity problem concerns the conditions of uncertainty that exist in the enactment of any law. The fundamental premise of recent law and economics research is that lawmaking can be analogized to an investment, where the process of lawmaking imposes a present cost in the expectation of future benefits (Dixit and Pindyck, 1994). In the presence of uncertainty, legal systems can thus be viewed as making investment decisions that create present lawmaking costs and which generate uncertain future benefits. With this in mind, the creation of legal rules often imposes initial lawmaking costs that are at least partially sunk.

The assumption that initial lawmaking costs are at least partially sunk is based on the simple observation that lawmaking costs cannot be recovered if the enacted rule proves to be ineffective or undesirable at a later time. In general, there are a variety of sunk costs in lawmaking. First, there are the obvious costs of legal intervention, which include the direct legislative and political costs, publication, and notice costs. Second, there are the learning costs for courts, enforcement agencies, lawyers and general public. These costs may be substantial and are for the most part irreversible, given the limited value of having learned a law, once the law is repealed. Third, there may be sunk costs of legal innovation whenever there is a change in the existing set of legal entitlements, given the disequilibrium that is likely to take place as a result of legal changes. Finally, there may be institutional costs involved in the change in

the legal rule. For example, there may be sunk costs associated with the discontinued operation of an existing rule, given the lost value in the specialization of legal operators and other sunk investments by law enforcement agencies.

The irreversibility of lawmaking costs has important implications for our understanding of optimal lawmaking behavior. It makes lawmaking especially sensitive to various forms of uncertainty over the future costs and benefits derived from the enforcement of the new rule and the rate of change of the regulated environment that may induce obsolescence in the enacted rule.

Quite notably, any model of optimal lawmaking that fails to consider the option value of delaying innovation is necessarily assuming — explicitly or implicitly — that the legal system can avoid all the above sunk costs, and can abrogate and enact laws without sunk expenditures. For most real life applications, however, there are likely to be substantial sunk costs involved in regulatory or legal innovation, which necessitate a revision of the net present value rule in the context of lawmaking. Like in any investment decision, there is the choice on the timing of the investment. Lawmakers need to choose the timing for legal intervention. Given uncertainty about future returns, investment can be postponed to acquire more information. Likewise, legal intervention or revision of current rules can be postponed. But delays in such investment decisions often come at a cost, given the forgone benefits of the investment in the immediate future.

As the emerging investment theory literature has amply shown (see e.g., Pindyck, 1991), the ability of an investor to delay an irreversible investment profoundly changes the logic to be followed in reaching a decision on whether to invest. Traditionally, investment theory under uncertainty suggested that given such tradeoff of costs and benefits, an investment should be carried out whenever it generated a net increase in present value. These conclusions have been revisited in light of option pricing theory (McDonald and Siegel, 1985; Pindyck, 1991) which have revealed that the optimal choice of an investment under uncertainty is not the one generated by net present value calculations, but the one generated taking into account the full value of the option to invest. The results of the investment literature have important implications for the choice of optimal timing in lawmaking.

Given the different sunk investment of a rule as opposed to a standard, the option value of delaying legal intervention varies in the two cases. Thus, in the presence of uncertainty and sunk investment costs, the lawmaker is faced with a wedge between the economies of scale obtainable with the implementation of a specified rule and the increased value of the foregone option to postpone the lawmaking decision.

The dual optimization problem facing the lawmaker, then, is that of determining the optimal level of specificity and timing of intervention in consideration of the above factors. The understanding of the optimal timing problem presented in Parisi and Ghei, in conjunction with the optimal specificity problem presented in the previous law and economics literature (Erlich and Posner, 1973; Schwartz and Scott, 1995; and Kaplow, 1992), would serve as building blocks for a more complex model of lawmaking where timing and degree of specificity are allowed to vary simultaneously. The two optimization problems can then be set up to tackle the interesting problem of the simultaneous choice of optimal timing and specificity of legal rules. Indeed, at any point in time, lawmakers decide their legislative action controlling both the timing and the degree of detail of legal rules, with a likely awareness of the important interrelationship between the two variables.

2.5. Optimal Timing and Specificity of Legal Rules: Bridging the Gap

Parisi and Ghei have also tackled the issue of optimal timing of lawmaking using the insights of option pricing theory. Parisi and Ghei observe that the choice of optimal-timing in lawmaking should be derived considering the option-like characteristics of lawmaking decisions. The authors show that the net present value methodology is inappropriate for dealing with lawmaking decisions under uncertainty. They reach their conclusion by illustrating the different results obtained considering the option value of deferring legal intervention, showing how the resulting lawmaking rules depend on various parameters of the regulated environment.

Building upon the contributions in the existing literature, the problem of optimal specificity can be reconsidered in a dynamic fashion, examining a world where there is a single supreme lawmaker whose business it is to create law. Differently from the existing models in the literature, the lawmaker has two major control variables: first, the option to innovate (or delay intervention); second, the choice of either fully specifying the rule *ex ante* (i.e., choosing a "rule" in Erlich and Posner's terminology) or to state the law in general terms, which requires an *ex post* interpretation of the law (i.e., choose a "standard" in Erlich and Posner's terminology).

3. Conclusion: Policy Implications

As discussed extensively above, the use of rules versus standards has broad implications on judicial interpretation

and the cost and benefits of lawmaking. But choosing the optimal specificity of legal rules also has an impact on public policy that is useful to consider. Legislatures enact general laws that affect large classes of individuals, whereas litigation in the judicial system has a more focused and limited impact. Legal decisions made in the legislatures lack precedential value and therefore affect only interested parties. From a public choice perspective, lobbying before legislatures presents a collective action problem that would be avoided in the case of judicial decision-making.

As a policy matter, Schäfer (2001) suggests that the use of rules over standards has the advantage of reducing corruption, concentrating human capital, and cutting down on court delays caused by complex decisions. Schäfer's conclusions are based primarily on the idea that rules-based systems are preferable in developing countries. Using China as an example, Schäfer declares that efforts there to find the optimal degree of specificity of laws are unsuccessful because the judiciary is composed of largely untrained or unqualified personnel. Adjudicators apply the standards haphazardly and so frequently that no clear signals are sent to the public.

Schäfer's argument depends critically on the debatable premise that legislatures are inherently less corrupt and better informed than the judiciary. Additionally, the regulated environment in developing countries may be more volatile than those of industrialized countries. Volatility of the external environment creates an increased opportunity for obsolescence of legal rules. This in turn would render standards preferable to specific rules, prevent the legislature from constantly having to incur the cost of legislative amendment to modify previous legal enactments after each new development in the external environment.

FRANCESCO PARISI

REFERENCES

Aristotle (350 B.C.). "Nicomachean ethics, bk. V. §10," in Roger Crisp (ed. and Trans.), *Nicomachean Ethics*. New York: Cambridge University Press, 2000.

Bentham, J. (1776). "A fragment on government," in J.H. Burns and H.L.A. Hart (eds.) *A Comment on the Commentaries and a Fragment on Government*. London: University of London Althone Press, 1977.

Dan-Cohen, M. (1984). "Decision rules and conduct rules: on acoustic separation in criminal law." *Harvard Law Review*, 97: 625.

Diver, C.S. (1983). "The optimal precision of administrative rules." *Yale Law Journal*, 93: 65.

Dixit, A.K. and Pindyck, R.S. (1994). *Investment Under Uncertainty*. Princeton: Princeton University Press.

Kaplow, L. (1992). "Rules versus standards: an economic analysis." *Duke Law Journal*, 42: 557.

McDonald, R. and Siegel D.R. (1985). "Investment and valuation of firms when there is an option to shut down." *International Law Review*, 26(2): 331.

Parisi, F. (1992). "*Liability for Negligence and Judicial Discretion*." 2nd edition. Berkeley: California University Press (IAS Series).

Parisi, F. and Ghei, N. (2001). The value of waiting in lawmaking. George Mason University School of Law working paper No. 01-16. Social Science Electronic Publishing.

Pindyck, R.S. (1991). "Irreversibility, uncertainty and investment." *Journal of Economic Literature*, 29: 1110.

Posner, R.A. (1989). "Legislation and its interpretation: a primer." *Nebraska Law Review*, 68: 432.

Ehrlich, I. and Posner, R.A. (1973). "An economic analysis of legal rulemaking." *Journal of Legal Studies*, 11(January): 257.

Schwartz, A. and Scott, R.E. (1995). "The political economy of private legislatures." *University of Pennsylvania Law Review*, 143: 595.

Schäfer, H. (2001). Rules versus standards in developing countries, should poor countries have a more rule based legal system? Unpublished manuscript from University of California at Berkeley.

Sullivan, K.M. (1992). "The justices of rules and standards." *Harvard Law Review*, 106: 22.

S

SELF-INTEREST

"It is not from the benevolence of the butcher, the brewer, or the baker, that we expect our dinner, but from their regard to their own interest." (Adam Smith, The Wealth of Nations, p. 14.)

1. Introduction

The self-interest assumption has an impressive pedigree in economics. From Adam Smith to Gary Becker it has been the lynchpin of many models of human behavior. Put simply, "self-interest" postulates that individuals, in making economic choices, take into account only their own well-being and ignore the welfare of others. The proviso that individuals act in this way simplifies and clarifies arguments wonderfully.

However, it is important, at the outset, to clear up a common misunderstanding of the term. In the Public Choice tradition, choice is assumed to be governed by preferences. Sometimes, self-interested behavior is interpreted as any choice driven merely by one's preferences. This must be contrasted with the meaning, in the current literature (Cox et al., 2001; Rabin, 1993; Sen, 1977; Hoffman et al., 1994). In the literature, self interest reflects an (empirical) assumption restricting preferences to those which rule out direct concern for the welfare of others. Of course, any such self-interested actor needs to take into account how the changed welfare of others leads to objective circumstances affecting her own welfare. Such consequential interactions are *not* ruled out by the self-interest assumption. Indeed, acting to obtain such benefits is usually referred to as 'enlightened self-interest.'

By cutting out consideration of others' welfare from the economic agent's calculus, the self-interest assumption allows the theorist to focus solely on the effects of choice on the chooser. It allows for a theory of choice in which each individual's preferences are separable from those of others: the interactions of individuals' preferences need not be considered.

This simplification has allowed economic theory to model the logic of market choices by considering the direct valuation to the traders of the goods and services exchanged. Models of choice need not take into account the particulars of: from whom a particular person is buying, to whom that person is selling, or what the effect of the transaction is on another party. This modeling has fostered the development of a clear distinction between the positive analysis of economic behavior and the normative concerns of welfare economics. For example, by assuming self-interest, in any given situation, one can identify both the likely market outcome, and any associated externalities. Externalities are parsed out of the actors' decisions and can be separated for purposes of public policy analysis.

2. The Complexity of the Alternatives to Self-Interest

Relaxing the self-interest assumption allows others' well being to enter directly into one's decisions. This shift forces the theorist to specify precisely how others' welfare enter into the decisions. Many possibilities arise. Increasing the welfare of some others might be positively valued, some of the time, and negatively some of the time. In either case, exactly how much value is to be placed on the others' welfare would have to be specified. And of course, the relationship could be different for each pair of actors. To complicate matters further, individuals may also be concerned about the distributional properties of a given exchange: say about some notion of 'not being bested,' or of fairness of distribution. The list of factors that might appear once the theorist peeked into the other-regarding box could be very long indeed.

So it is not surprising that for a very long time models of economic decision making held firmly to the self-interest assumption. And the fruits of adhering to this spare model have been plentiful. General equilibrium theory (Arrow and Hahn, 1977), Samuelson's models of public goods (Samuelson, 1954), and, indeed, most major results in the field have flowed from the simple behavioral assumptions of rationality *and* self-interest. Becker, 1981, has even modeled family behavior on the basis of self-interest.

3. The Empirical Problem of Self-interest

But there has always been a problem: self-interest is never more than an approximation of observed behavior. Taken literally, *in extremis*, the self-interest assumption involves essentially socio-pathic behavior: it implies that one would take any payoff, no matter how small, even if it caused horrendous harm to others but was free of direct consequences to one's-self. In most contexts the implications of self-interested behavior are not damaging, and *can* be observed, regularly. But everyday observation and common sense also reveal countless acts of seemingly unselfish behavior among friends, family, and even casual strangers. And alas, acts of enmity and revenge can also be found. Other-regarding behavior, both benevolent and malevolent, is easy to find if one only looks for it. A few theorists who, as early as the 1950's (Valavanis, 1958 and Preston, 1961 were among the earliest), began producing preliminary models of other-regarding behavior recognized this stubborn fact.

Casual observation also contradicted the predictions of some early models in the Public Choice field. Olson (1965) argued that voluntary contributions to public goods would not occur in large groups without selective incentives, but charitable donations violating that prediction were easy to observe. A similar anomaly was found in voting. Despite the predictions of some models to the contrary, voters, even in very large electorates, vote (Downs, 1957; Barry, 1970 gives some early comments concerning the difficulties). Extensions of the self-interest model to moral philosophy (consider the movement toward ethical egoism in the late 50's as captured by Feldman, 1978; Kalin, 1970; and Medlin, 1957) and political philosophy, sped the development of criticism. Self-interest was seen as too impoverished an assumption to capture the moral side of behavior, and hence was deemed to be an inadequate model of human psychology (Frankena, 1963). A few theorists proposed models of other regarding preferences to deal with the anomalies (Frohlich, 1974; Sen, 1977; Margolis, 1982) but little empirical work existed at that time to test their constructs.

4. Experimental Empiricism and Current Responses

But it wasn't until the applications of the rational choice model to non-market problems caught on in other disciplines that economists and other users of preference models of behavior seriously questioned self-interest. The testing of theories of collective action, or public goods problems, often modeled as a Prisoners' Dilemma Games, led to a body of controlled observations that appeared to contradict the self-interest assumption. Individuals were found, consistently, to contribute to attempts at providing public goods in unorganized groups. The scope of the anomalous behavior varied by context, but rarely was it less than 15% (1995; Dawes, 1980).

The growth of experimental economics and the desire to test the results in game theory provided the motivation and the mechanism for direct formal tests of the self-interest assumption. Miller and Oppenheimer (1982) argued that experimental data regarding committee behavior required a reformulation of the independent preferences hypothesis. Frohlich et al. (1984) demonstrated that, in a simple money allocation experiment, individuals exhibited a variety of other-regarding behaviors, ranging from altruism, through malevolence. Meanwhile results from ultimatum games (see Dawes, and Richard, 1988 and Roth, 1995 for a relatively comprehensive review) turned up anomalous results in which subjects rejected offers of cash, seemingly, on the basis of an unfavorable comparison of their proposed payoff to that of the allocator. The persistence of these anomalies sparked the hypothesis that the anomalous behavior in ultimatum games was an artifact of the implicit bargaining strategic structure inherent in the ultimatum games. To deal with this, economists developed a genre of experiment called dictator experiments. These removed all strategic elements from the interactions. But the ensuing series of experiments revealed persistent other-regarding behavior. Experimentalists began to identify aspects of the choice environment which affected the form of other-regarding behavior (Hoffman et al., 1996; Eckel and Grossman, 1996; Frohlich et al., 2001; here again, see Roth, 1995, for a comprehensive overview of the earlier literature).

The next step was a series of attempts to account for the observed data manifesting other-regarding behavior. (Rabin, 1993, Fehr and Schmidt, 1999; Cox et al., 2001 among others.) Each was posited on a multi-functional utility function, but none has achieved predominance. At this writing, the status of the self-interest assumption is under attack. While it may continue to enjoy prominence in certain theoretical areas where it appears to be a reasonable approximation to reality, (such as in large market interactions, etc.) theorists are attempting to identify how to model behavior in situations in which its failure generates unacceptably inaccurate predictions.

NORMAN FROHLICH

JOE OPPENHEIMER

REFERENCES

Arrow, K.J. and Hahn, F.H. (1977). *General Competitive Analysis*. Amsterdam: North Holland Publishing Company.

Barry, Brian M. (1970). *Sociologists, Economists, and Democracy*. London: Collier-McMillan Ltd.

Becker, Gary S. (1981). *A Treatise on the Family*. Cambridge, MA: Harvard University Press.

Cox, James C., Sadiraj, Klarita and Sadiraj, Vjollca (2001). "A theory of competition and fairness without equity aversion," Paper presented at the International meetings of the Economics Society of America, Barcelona, Spain, June.

Dawes, Robyn M. (1980). "Social dilemmas." *Annual Review of Psychology*, 31: 169–193.

Dawes, Robyn M. and Thaler, H. Richard (1988). "Anomalies: cooperation." *Journal of Economic Perspectives*, 2(#3, summer): 187–197.

Downs, Anthony (1957). *An Economic Theory Of Democracy*. New York: Harper and Row.

Eckel, Catherine C. and Grossman, Philip J. (1996). "Altruism in anonymous dictator games." *Games and Economic Behavior*, 16: 181–191.

Fehr, Ernst and Schmidt, Klaus M. (1999). A theory of fairness, competition, and cooperation. *Quarterly Journal of Economics*, 817–868.

Feldman, Fred (1978). "Egoism," in *Introductory Ethics*. Englewood Cliffs, NJ: Prentice Hall, pp. 80–96.

Frankena, William K. (1963). *Ethics*. Englewood Cliffs, NJ: Prentice Hall.

Frohlich, Norman (1974). "Self-interest or altruism: what difference?" *Journal of Conflict Resolution*, 18, 55–73.

Frohlich, Norman Joe Oppenheimer, w Pat Bond, and Irvin Boschman (1984). "Beyond economic man." *Journal of Conflict Resolution*, 28(1): 3–24.

Frohlich, Norman, Oppenheimer, Joe and Moore, Bernard (2001). "Some doubts about measuring self-interest using dictator experiments: the costs of anonymity." *Journal of Economic Behavior and Organization*, 46(3): 271–290.

Hoffman, Elizabeth, McCabe, Kevin, Shachat, Keith, and Vernon, Smith (1994). Preferences, property rights and anonymity in bargaining games. *Games and Economic Behavior*, 7(3): 346–380.

Hoffman, Elizabeth, Kevin McCabe and Vernon L. Smith (1996). "Social distance and other-regarding behavior in dictator games." *American Economic Review*, 86(3): 653–660.

Kalin, Jesse (1970). "In defense of egoism," in David P. Gauthier, (ed.) *Morality and Rational Self-interest*. Englewood Cliffs, NJ: Prentice Hall, Inc 64–87.

Ledyard, John O. (1995). "Public goods: a survey of experimental research," in *The Handbook of Experimental Economics*, John H. Kagel and Alvin E. Roth (eds.) Princeton: Princeton University Press, pp. 111–194.

Margolis, Howard (1982). *Selfishness, Altruism, and Rationality*. Cambridge: Cambridge.

Medlin, Brian (1957). "Ultimate principles and ethical egoism." *Australasian Journal of Philosophy*, XXXV: 111–118.

Miller, Gary J. and Oppenheimer, Joe A. (1982). "Universalism in experimental committees." *American Political Science Review*, 76: 561–574.

Olson, Mancur (1965). *The Logic of Collective Action*. Cambridge: Harvard University Press.

Preston, Lee E. (1961). "Utility interactions in a two-person world." *Journal of Conflict Resolution*, 5(4): 354–365.

Rabin, Matthew (1993). Incorporating fairness into game theory and economics. *American Economic Review*, 83(5). 1281–1302.

Roth, Alvin E. (1995). "Bargaining experiments," in John H. Kagel and Alvin E. Roth (eds.) *The Handbook of Experimental Economics*. Princeton: Princeton University Press pp. 253–342.

Samuelson, Paul (1954). "The pure theory of public expenditure." *Review of Economics and Statistics*, 36: 387–389.

Sen, A.K. (1977). "Rational fools: a critique of the behavioral foundations of economic theory," *Philosophy and Public Affairs* 6(4): 317–344.

Smith, Adam (1937). *The Wealth of Nations*. New York: Modern Library Editions.

Valavanis, Stefan (1958). "The resolution of conflict when utilities interact," *The Journal of Conflict Resolution*, 2: 156–169.

SELFISH GENE

The "selfish gene" is a biological term that has considerable application in the human sciences. Paradoxically, the selfish gene may lead people to engage in apparently charitable behavior. Before dealing with the details of this however it is important to note that human behavior is only controlled by genetic inheritance in the most general way. Human beings walk on their feet, not their hands, wear clothing in cold weather because they have no fur, and in many other ways their genes control their behavior. Genes exert control over the behavior of human beings, however, to a lesser degree than nature controls the physical design of human beings. Nevertheless, some degree of control occurs.

Genes are transmitted from generation to generation and they will only be translated if the individual controlled in part by them acts in such a way as to stay alive and reproduce. Thus the gene, to speak as if it thought things through, wants more genes duplicating itself in the next generation. In fact of course it has no preferences at all, but if it does increase the number of the duplicates in the next generation then it will thrive. Thus to refer to the gene as selfish is showing some poetic license, but does not actually mislead biologists. Economists and public choice scholars should accept this notion on the same terms.

The intriguing feature of this kind of "selfishness" is that it leads to behavior that appears to be unselfish, even generous. To take a famous example Mr. Smith has a certain gene and there is a 50 percent chance and that his sibling also has it. Thus if the genes of Mr Smith cause him to sacrifice his life to save three siblings, the number of genes providing for such a sacrifice would be larger in the next generation. Action on the part of the gene to save copies of itself, albeit at the sacrifice of itself, is what is referred to as selfish behavior in a gene. Naturally this example is an extreme one. Still parents sacrificing for their children are less extreme examples of the same phenomenon. In general any action that reduces one's expectancy of producing viable genes in the next generation while suitably increasing the likelihood of such genes being produced by someone else, implies that those genes will be more frequent in the next generation and hence will multiply over time.

All of this is good biological theory. Since human beings are a biological species it should apply to them.

Most biologists think that it does, and I see no reason to doubt that. Nevertheless except in close family relations I do not conclude that it has a great deal of influence on human behavior. This is unfortunate because a greater degree of generosity and kindness would make the world a pleasanter place. But there is no reason to believe that evolution selects traits in terms of their pleasantness. If an individual is too generous he willl have fewer descendents than if he displays just the right amount of generosity. The right amount is not zero, in most cases, but outside the family it comes close to that.

GORDON TULLOCK

SEPTEMBER 11, 2001

> War is a mere continuation of policy by other means. (Carl von Clausewitz, [1832] 1976: 87)
> Except at harvest-time, when self-preservation enjoins a temporary truce, the Pathan tribes are always engaged in private or public war. Every man is a warrior, a politician and a theologian.... Every village has its defence. Every family cultivates its vendetta; every clan, its feud. The numerous tribes and combinations of tribes all have their accounts to settle with one another. Nothing is ever forgotten, and very few debts are left unpaid. (Winston S. Churchill, [1930] 1996: 134)

Afghanistan has almost always been on the verge of disintegration. Straddling the mountain passes that link the plains of India with Central Asia and beyond, it was a frequently moved pawn in the Great Game played out in the late nineteenth century between the British and Russian empires, each seeking a buffer zone against the other's expansionist aims. Before that, Afghanistan sat astride the path of vital East-West trade convoys moving over the famous Silk Route. More recently, control of the Afghani mountain passes has been sharply contested by local warlords and Mafia-like criminal organizations trafficking in drugs and contraband. Foreign powers, great and small, have long sought 'spheres of influence' in this 'strategic frontier' (Pigou, [1921] 1941: 27), sometimes intervening directly, but more often by courting tribal warlords with money and guns.

The proximate cause of Afghanistan's descent into chaos at the close of the twentieth century was American neglect in the wake of the withdrawal of Soviet troops in 1989, bloodied in a decade-long conflict with the mujaheddin, and the subsequent overthrow, following the USSR's collapse in 1991, of its puppet regime in Kabul (Rashid, 2000: 21). Fighting one of the Cold War's eleventh-hour battles by proxy, the United States had supported the mujaheddin generously with some $4 to $5 billion worth of modern weaponry (ibid.: 18), including 900 Stinger missiles (ibid.: 44), which it funneled covertly to them through the Pakistani government's Interservices Intelligence (ISI) agency. Victory won, 'the Americans... washed their hands of Afghanistan...' (Elliot, 1999: 24), leaving a country 'divided into warlord fiefdoms' over which 'all the warlords... fought, switched sides and fought again in a bewildering array of alliances, betrayals and bloodshed' (Rashid, 2000: 21), and 'ordinary Afghans with a widespread feeling of having been betrayed' (Elliot, 1999: 24).

Into this power vacuum stepped the Taliban. A series of military successes over tribal factions contending for local or regional supremacy, crowned by the capture of Kabul in September 1996, triggered hopes that peace and stability would finally be restored, at least to Afghanistan's southern provinces. To Pakistan, 'desperately keen to open up direct land routes for trade with the Central Asian Republics...' (Rashid, 2000: 26), and to the United States, interested both in a strategically located partner to its anti-Iran policy and in a regime that would help ensure the success of a joint American-Saudi-financed, trans-Afghanistan natural gas pipeline long delayed by civil war (ibid.: 46), the Taliban seemed to be a godsend. Neither country was much off-put by the Taliban's virulent anti-modernism and subjugation of women implemented under a strict interpretation of the Sharia law. Not until feminist pressure was brought to bear on the Clinton administration in late 1997 did US policy begin turning around, a reversal soon solidified by the Taliban's refusal to endorse the pipeline project (ibid.: 176).

Despite its need for continued American aid, Pakistan remained faithful to the Taliban because, under Mullah Omar, the regime kept its promise of restoring 'peace', albeit the peace of authoritarian repression. By eliminating the petty warlords who had disrupted the lucrative smuggling trade over the southern mountain passes, the Taliban overcame a tragedy of 'anticommons', arising from multiple rights to exclude (Buchanan and Yoon, 2000). Roving bandits were displaced by a stationary bandit (McGuire and Olson, 1996). In 1993, travelers on the 130-mile-long route from Quetta to Kandahar 'were stopped by at least 20 different groups, who had put chains across the road and demanded a toll...' (Rashid, 2000: 22). Soon after entering the fray in late 1994, 'the Taliban cleared the chains from the roads, set up a one-toll system for trucks entering Afghanistan at Spin Baldak and patrolled the highway from Pakistan. The transport mafia was ecstatic...' (ibid.: 29). Tolls fell to 'an average of 6,000 rupees (US$150) for a truck traveling from Peshawar to Kabul, compared to

30,000–50,000 rupees, which truckers paid before' (ibid.: 191). Although the Pakistani economy was heavily damaged by the widespread evasion of customs' duties the Taliban facilitated, the 'enormous nexus of corruption' that emerged in Afghanistan's neighbor ensured governmental complaisance (ibid.).

The roots of September 11, 2001, go much deeper than the Soviet Union's collapse, however. A fundamental problem is cartography. Afghanistan, like many of the nation-states fashioned from the carcass of the Ottoman Empire in the aftermath of the First World War (Fromkin, 1989), is an artificial construct. Its southern border was drawn in the late nineteenth century by Sir Mortimer Durand, the colonial government of India's foreign secretary, expressly to divide the Pashtun (or Pathan) tribe's homeland in half, thereby establishing a buffer state on India's northwest frontier. When the Pashtunis who found themselves on the Indian side of the Durand line failed to integrate themselves quietly under the Raj, the North-West Frontier Province (NWFP) was sliced off from the Punjab to establish a second, inner buffer. These two 'tribal belts' were formally incorporated within the boundaries of Pakistan when that nation separated from a newly independent India under the Partition Plan effective 14 August 1947; the Durand line stood (Hilton, 2001).

Afghanistan's northern border was drawn by Josef Stalin. Formalized in the 'Settlement of 1922', a series of treaties between the Soviet Union and its southern neighbors (Fromkin, 1989: 559), the new boundary lines carved up a region, 'comprising modern day Tajikistan, southern Uzbekistan and northern Afghanistan', that had been 'one contiguous territory for centuries' (Rashid, 2000: 146). Like Sir Mortimer Durand, Stalin was apparently keen to create his own buffer zone against the Pashtuns (and the Raj) by stranding sizeable Tajik and Uzbek populations in what thenceforth was northern Afghanistan.

What emerged was the map of a wholly synthetic nation-state comprising at least 20 distinct ethnic groups. Heading the list are the Pashtuns, concentrated in the south and accounting for between 30 and 40 percent of the total Afghani population. Then there are the Turkmen, Tajiks and Uzbeks of northern Afghanistan, a region less populous than the southern Pashtun provinces, but containing '60 percent of Afghanistan's agricultural resources and 80 percent of its former industry' (ibid.: 55). Nuristanis, claiming descent from the armies of Alexander the Great, dominate the western provinces, while remote, mountainous central Afghanistan is the homeland of the Hazaras, 'distant offspring of the armies of Chingiz Khan' (Elliot, 1999: 52–53).

The map's failure to respect customary tribal territorial claims and to accommodate existing regional trade patterns

and social networks has had disastrous consequences for Afghanistan, as it also has had in much of sub-Saharan Africa (e.g., Rowley, 1999). In both cases, members of some close-knit ethnic groups find themselves on opposite sides of new, unwanted national borders; others are compelled to share ground with their enemies of old. Ethnic violence is the predictable outcome as each group seeks control of local, regional and national levers of political power. Strongmen rise and fall as their supporters gain the upper hand. Political authority is exercised, not by sharing power with rivals, but by repressing them.

A factional disease demands a republican cure. Short of redrawing the map of Central Asia, as has been proposed for sub-Saharan Africa (Kimenyi, 1999), the cycle of ethnic conflict can only be stopped by constitutional means. A federal system of government that shifts most political decision-making authority away from the center toward regions having a high degree of autonomy, combined with a representative legislature empowered to resolve tightly defined questions of national policy, offers a time-tested way of accommodating the diverse insular interests of an ethnically heterogeneous polity (Frey and Eichenberger, 1999). The history of the Middle East in general (Friedman, [1989] 1995; Lewis, 1995), and of Afghanistan in particular (Lewis, 2001), suggests, however, that even republican forms of government may be unworkable. Indeed, the UN-sponsored transitional government already has drawn fire from Uzbeks angered at the appointment of Tajiks by interim Prime Minister Hamid Karzai, a Pashtuni, to head the high-profile defense, foreign affairs and interior ministries (Schaeffer, 2001). Starting with existing national borders, new constitutions that provide for orderly means of secession and self-determination may be the only trouble-free path to regional political stability.

The 'spongy no-go area between Pakistan and Afghanistan, a land of fierce and complicated tribal loyalties and equally ferocious tribal feuds, of gunrunning, drug dealing, and smuggling…' (Hilton, 2001: 60), provided a natural refuge for Osama bin Laden, the architect of September 11, 2001. Awash with money and weapons, some of which had been supplied to bin Laden directly by the United States to help equip the camps he built to train mujaheddin units during the Soviet invasion (and to establish theological colleges — madrassas — to inoculate them with Islamist zeal), the region evolved into a terrorist nursery. After the Soviets withdrew, bin Laden redeployed his military infrastructure in support of the Taliban's drive to restore Pashtunis to their self-claimed place as the rightful rulers of Afghanistan.

His reasons for doing so are bound up in the constellation of theological, cultural and political crosscurrents that have plagued the Middle East for millennia. One of the most important of these is Wahhabism, a movement launched in the eighteenth century by Muhammad ibn Abd al-Wahhab (1703–1787), an Arabian cleric who fathered 'a campaign of purification and renewal. His purpose was to return the Muslim world to the pure and authentic Islam of the Prophet, removing and, where necessary, destroying all later accretions' (Lewis, 2001: 59). Wahhabi doctrine was embraced by the House of Saud, the rulers set over Arabia by Britain in the interwar period. The Taliban's rejection of modernity, a central tenant of that doctrine, attracted covert support from at least some members of Saudi Arabia's royal family, to whom bin Laden had developed close ties (and amassed a personal fortune) through his father's construction business (Rashid, 2000: 131–132). Bin Laden's involvement with the Taliban was also animated by the centuries-old sectarian division between Shia and Sunni Muslims, grounded in a doctrinal dispute over the proper line of succession (hereditary versus elective) to the Prophet Muhammad. The Talibans are fiercely Sunni. Seeing a threat to its own security in the collapse of the Afghan state, neighboring Iran, the only nation where Shias constitute a majority of the population, backed the opposition forces (ibid.: 196–206).

At the end of the day, bin Laden became the Taliban's single most important financial backer, supplying an estimated $100 billion in cash and military assistance to the Afghan regime over the past five years. These monies came not from his own bank account, but 'from three primary sources: legal and illegal businesses or front companies bin Laden operates directly or indirectly; tribute payments he receives from several Persian Gulf states, companies or individuals that give him funds so he and his al Qaeda supporters will stay out of or minimize activities in their countries; and entities that are masked as charities' (Woodward, 2001). The Taliban leadership's economic dependency on bin Laden helps explain why they continued to protect and shelter him after September 11 rather than save their own necks (ibid.).

The withdrawal of US support for the Taliban in the late 1990s added to bin Laden's list of grievances against the 'Great Satan', a list that includes the American victory over Iraq in the Gulf War, the continued presence of US troops in Saudi Arabia after Kuwait's liberation, America's *rapprochement* with post-Khomeini Iran and, not least, its long-standing support of Israel (ibid.: 133). Bin Laden became a household name in August 1998, following the bombings of the US embassies in Kenya and Tanzania, which claimed 220 lives. He may also have had a hand in earlier attacks against American interests. Bin Laden has been blamed for the 18 US soldiers killed in Mogadishu,

Somalia, in 1993; for a 1995 bombing in Riyadh, which caused the deaths of five American servicemen; and for another 19 Americans killed in Dhahran in 1996. His involvement is suspected in bombings in Aden in 1992 and at the World Trade Center in 1993, in a plot to kill President Clinton during his 1994 state visit to the Philippines, and in a plan to destroy 12 US civilian aircraft in 1995 (ibid.: 134–135).

September 11, 2001, was the unforgettable pinnacle of Osama bin Laden's campaign of terror. A preliminary effort to assess the economic impact of that day's events suggests that the attacks on the World Trade Center and the Pentagon imposed immediate costs exceeding $100 billion, in the forms of property damage and values of lives lost, and of up to $2 trillion in lower future corporate profits (Navarro and Spencer, 2001).

A reasonably alert US intelligence service would have been better prepared. Bin Laden had already demonstrated American vulnerability to a terrorist strike on its homeland. Nonetheless, an administration weakened by the Monica Lewinsky affair and lacking basic foreign policy expertise (according to Elliot, 1999: 76, Secretary of State Madeline Albright was so uninformed about Afghanistan that, during her first trip to the country, she had to be told the names of the different Afghan parties) failed to avert tragedy.

Neither did the airline industry heed the alarm bells that had been ringing 'since 1988, when a bomb in a suitcase destroyed Pan Am Flight 103 over Lockerbie, Scotland…' (Yeoman and Hogan, 2002: 43). As a matter of fact, the industry's lobbyists — a cadre counting, among others, ten former members of Congress, two former transportation secretaries, three former officials of the Federal Aviation Administration and the wife of Senate Majority Leader Tom Daschle — have worked hard to water down or defeat every subsequent proposal to beef up airport security, 'including the recommendations of two high-profile presidential commissions' (ibid.: 42). For example, apparently worried about the costs of implementing new security procedures and of annoying the flying public, the airlines fought a plan floated in the midst of the 1996 presidential election campaign by Vice President Al Gore, chair of the White House Commission on Aviation and Security, to require the affirmative matching of all passengers with their baggage. In the weeks following the Vice President's decision to reverse course and accept the industry's weaker alternative proposal, calling only for monitoring the baggage of 'suspicious passengers', the airlines contributed some $500,000 to the Democratic Party (ibid.: 45).

Interest-group politics thus stalks explanations for why and how commercial aircraft were so easily turned into weapons of terror on September 11. Even now, the airlines warn that unprecedented focus on security threatens to delay the implementation of promising accident-prevention technologies, such as air-turbulence detection devices, and they have apparently convinced the Bush administration not to require prospective employees of the new federal airport security service to have high-school diplomas (Pasztor, 2001).

While terrorism is probably as old as mankind, its modern use as a strategy for influencing public opinion and public policy by groups lacking the means to wage war on a national scale can be traced to 1967, when Israel captured the West Bank and Gaza Strip, thereby angering supporters of Palestinian statehood. The end of the Cold War and the breakup of the Soviet Union added fuel to the terrorist fire as ethnic factions maneuvered for regional autonomy (Enders and Sandler, 1995: 215). Terrorism is likely to continue for the foreseeable future in the Middle East and Central Asia as diverse groups forced for a century or more to live on a map drawn by foreign powers, their ancient conflicts suppressed temporarily, first, by Ottoman and Persian, and, later, by British, French and Soviet hegemony, 'regroup to create new political identities for themselves'. After all, 'it was only at the end of the nineteenth century, with the creation of Germany and Italy, that an accepted map of western Europe emerged, some 1,500 years after the old Roman map started to become obsolete' (Fromkin, 1989: 565).

Pakistan threatens to become the next powder keg. Allowing itself to become the key staging area for the Taliban's incursions into Afghanistan, Pakistan was also complicit in that group's assistance to the Kashmiri separatist movement in next-door India (Rashid, 2000: 186). What goes around comes around. Demands for independence or autonomy on the part of the Kurds, 'a scattered, tribal people who inhabit the plateaus and mountains where Iraq, Iran, Russian Armenia, and Turkey now overlap' (Fromkin, 1989: 503), 'which had been on the agenda in 1921', but 'somehow disappeared from [it] in 1922' (ibid.: 560), remain unfulfilled. Ethnic grudges are not in short supply.

The tools of economics can be applied fruitfully in analyzing terrorist behavior and in assessing alternative antiterrorism policies. Terrorists are rational actors who select their targets and modes of attack cost-effectively, and respond predictably to changes in the expected benefits or costs of terrorist action (Enders and Sandler, 1995). The design and implementation of public policies toward terrorism accordingly merits careful thought, lest terrorists be given incentive to husband their limited resources by committing fewer, but even more dramatic acts than that which riveted the world's attention on September, 11, 2001. While priority clearly must be assigned to protecting innocent lives and property by suppressing al Qaeda and similar terrorist networks, as well as their sponsors in, among others, Egypt, Iraq, Libya, Pakistan, Saudi Arabia and Somalia, the public choice lesson of September 11 is that new national boundaries and new constitutions promise the only lasting solutions to the terrorism of the twenty-first century.

WILLIAM F. SHUGHART II

REFERENCES

Buchanan, J.M. and Yoon, Y.J. (2000). Symmetric tragedies: commons and anticommons. *Journal of Law and Economics*, 43: 1–13.

Churchill, W.S. ([1930] 1996). *My Early Life: 1874–1904*. New York: Touchstone.

Clausewitz, C. von ([1832] 1976). *On War*. (ed.) and trans. by M. Howard and P. Paret. Princeton: Princeton University Press.

Elliot, J. (1999). *An Unexpected Light: Travels in Afghanistan*. New York: Picador USA.

Enders, W. and Sandler, T. (1995). "Terrorism: theory and applications," in K. Hartley and T. Sandler (eds.) *Handbook of Defense Economics*, vol. I, 213–249. Also in K.J. Arrow and M.D. Intriligator (eds.) *Handbooks in Economics*, vol. 12. Amsterdam: Elsevier.

Frey, B.S. and Eichenberger, R. (1999). "A new proposal for federalism and democracy in developing countries," in M.S. Kimenyi and J.M. Mbaku (eds.) *Institutions and Collective Choice in Developing Countries*, pp. 315–326. Also in J.M. Mbaku and M.S. Kimenyi (eds.) *Public Choice and Developing Societies*. Aldershot: Ashgate.

Friedman, T.L. ([1989] 1995). *From Beirut to Jerusalem*. New York: Anchor Books.

Fromkin, D. (1989). *A Peace to End all Peace: The Fall of the Ottoman Empire and the Creation of the Modern Middle East*. New York: Henry Holt.

Hilton, I. (2001). The Pashtun Code. *New Yorker*: 58–71.

Kimenyi, M.S. (1999). "Spatial competition, ethnicity, and the optimal size and composition of units of collective choice," in M.S. Kimenyi and J.M. Mbaku (eds.), *Institutions and Collective Choice in Developing countries*, pp. 355–380. Also in J.M. Mbaku and M.S. Kimenyi. (eds.) *Public Choice and Developing Societies* Aldershot: Ashgate.

Lewis, B. (1995). *The Middle East: A brief history of the last 2,000 years*. New York: Touchstone.

Lewis, B. (2001). "The revolt of Islam." *The New Yorker*, November 19, 50–63.

McGuire, M.C. and Olson, M. (1996). the economics of autocracy and majority rule: the invisible hand and the use of force. *Journal of Economic Literature*, 34: 72–96.

Navarro, P. and Spencer, A. (2001). "September 11, 2001: assessing the costs of terrorism." *Milken Institute Review*, 2(4): 16–31.

Pasztor, A. (2001). "Focus on security may delay progress in airlines' accident-prevention efforts." *Wall Street Journal*, A3 & A10.

Pigou, A.C. ([1921] 1941). *The Political Economy of War*, new and revised. edition. New York: Macmillan.

Rashid, A. (2000). *Taliban: Militant Islam, Oil and Fundamentalism in Central Asia*. New Haven and London: Yale Nota Bene.

Rowley, C.K. (1999). "Rent seeking and rent extraction from the perspective of Africa," in M.S. Kimenyi and J.M. Mbaku (eds.) *Institutions and Collective Choice in Developing Countries*, pp. 223–254. Also in J.M. Mbaku and M.S. Kimenyi (eds.) *Public Choice and Developing Societies* Aldershot: Ashgate.

Schaeffer, J. (2001). *Taliban Still Pose Threat to Afghans*. Associated Press (December 28).

Woodward, B. (2001). "Bin Laden said to 'own' the Taliban." *Washington Post*, A1.

Yeoman, B. and Hogan, B. (2002). "Airline insecurity." *Mother Jones*, 40–46.

SINGLE-PEAKED PREFERENCES AND MEDIAN VOTER THEOREMS

Many important choices are made by majority rule. However, as is widely known, Condorcet (1785) discovered an important problem with majority rule: For a given set of alternatives, it may be the case that, for each alternative, there is some other alternative which is preferred by a majority of the eligible voters. For a simple example where each alternative can be beaten under majority rule, see (for instance) Kelly (1988: 16).

The problem discovered by Condorcet has led researchers to identify assumptions about voter preferences which imply that there is an unbeaten alternative. The best known assumptions (about voter preferences with unbeaten alternatives) are ones where the voters have what are known as "single-peaked" preferences.

The distinguishing feature of single-peaked preferences was described in Black (1948: 24), where this special term was first introduced. His description was specifically for a "committee considering different possible sizes of a numerical quantity and choosing one size in preference to the others." The following description was for any particular member of the committee:

> Once he had arrived at his view of the optimum size, the farther any proposal departed from it on the one side or the other, the less he would favor it. The valuations carried out by the member would then take the form of points on a single-peaked or 1-shaped curve.

Significantly, Black (1948) established that (when the members of a committee have single-peaked preferences) if a committee member's most preferred alternative is (in a certain specific sense) a median for the corresponding distribution of the members' most preferred alternatives, then that alternative is unbeaten under majority rule.

Black's reasoning can also be used in certain other settings where public choices are made (for instance, Black noted that his reasoning has similar implications for an analogous model of multicandidate elections). Drawing on research that has built on Black's work, this entry will *both* discuss some of the key assumptions and results in Black's original research *and* state assumptions and results for a more general model (which applies to various settings where public choices are made).

1. Alternatives, Individuals and Preferences

Black (1958) stated: "By a *committee* we will mean any group of people who arrive at a decision by means of voting" (p. 1). He also stated: "A *motion* we define as any proposal before a committee which it may adopt or reject by a method of voting" (p. 1). Black also assumed that the committee has a finite number of members and that each member has preferences on the set of motions.

The more general model for this entry will use the following notation and assumptions.

X will denote a set of alternatives. $N = \{1, \ldots, n\}$ will be an index set for a finite set of individuals who get to vote on the alternatives. For each $i \in N$, R_i will be a binary preference relation on X, where xR_iy means "x is at least as good as y, for i". xP_iy will mean "x is preferred to y, for i" (i.e., xR_iy holds, but yR_ix does not). It will also be assumed that R_i is an ordering on X — that is, R_i is

(i) complete (For all distinct $x, y \in X$: xR_iy or yR_ix),

(ii) reflexive (For all $x \in X$: xR_ix),

(iii) transitive (For all $x, y, z \in X$: $[xR_iy$ and $yR_iz] / [xR_iz]$).

[Note: The terms that have been used for assumptions about preferences vary from one reference to another (see, for instance, the discussion about terms in Sen (1970: 8–9)); the specific terms listed above are the ones adopted by Sen (1970: 8–9)].

1.1. Examples

Two simple examples will be used to illustrate various aspects of the material in this entry. In the next paragraph, they will be used to illustrate the assumptions stated above. Later on, additional features will be added to the examples — so that they can be used to illustrate other things. In order to keep the discussion as clear as possible, the examples have been tailored to illustrate the basic concepts and theorems that are covered.

Both of the examples will have the following common features: A committee is considering the budget of a particular government agency. The set of alternatives available to the committee is $\{r, s, t\}$, where r denotes retrenchment (with large budget cuts), s denotes the same budget as at present, and t denotes a tremendous increase in the agency's budget.

Example 1. There are three individuals, $i = 1, 2, 3$, on the committee. Their preferences are rP_1sP_1t, sP_2tP_2r, and tP_3sP_3r respectively (where xP_iyP_iz means: xP_iy, yP_iz, and xP_iz).

Example 2. There are four individuals, $i = 1, 2, 3, 4$, on the committee. $i = 1, 2, 3$ have the same preferences as in Example 1 and $i = 4$ has rP_4sP_4t.

2. Utility Functions and Linear Orders

The preferences of the four individuals used in the two examples can be represented by the following utility functions:

$u_1(r) = 3,$	$u_1(s) = 2,$	$u_1(t) = 1,$
$u_2(s) = 3,$	$u_2(t) = 2,$	$u_2(r) = 1,$
$u_3(t) = 3,$	$u_3(s) = 2,$	$u_3(r) = 1,$
$u_4(r) = 3,$	$u_4(s) = 2,$	$u_4(t) = 1,$

(where the subscript denotes the individual whose preferences are being represented).

For graphing a voter's utility function in a Cartesian plane, it will be helpful to have a way of "lining up" the elements in X (so that we will know what order they should be put in when we locate them on an axis). For instance, if the elements are the real numbers, they could be potentially "lined up" by using a weak inequality (or) or by a strict inequality ($<$ or $>$). More generally: As in Rubin (1967) and Denzau and Parks (1975), the way in which the elements in X will be "lined up" can be made precise by specifying a binary relation, $_o$, on the set X which is

(i) complete (For all distinct $x, \tilde{y} X$: $x_o y$ or $y_o x$),

(ii) transitive (For all $x, y, \tilde{z} X$: $x_o y$ and $y_o z$] / [$x_o z$]), and

(iii) anti-symmetric (For all $x, \tilde{y} X$, [$x_o y$ and $y_o x$] / [x and y are not distinct]).

As in Rubin (1967) and Denzau and Parks (1975), this relation will be called a "linear order."

Some references (for instance, Mas-Colell et al. (1995: 801)) assume that the relation used to "line up" the alternatives has properties (i)–(iii) *and* is reflexive (For all $\tilde{x} X$: $x_o x$) — as with the weak inequalities for a set of real numbers. Some references (alternatively) assume that the

relation has properties (i) and (ii) *and* is irreflexive (For all $\tilde{x} X$, it is not the case that $x_o x$) — as with the strict inequalities for a set of real numbers. References where this second approach is used include Arrow (1963: 77), Fishburn (1970: 487; 1972: 94–95; 1973: 75, 102), Kelly (1988: 29), and Moulin (1988: 225, 263–264).

The first approach explicitly assumes that the relation has properties (i), (ii) and (iii) *and* adds an assumption. The second approach explicitly assumes that the relation has properties (i) and (ii) *and* assumes that the relation is is irreflexive. Since the second approach uses a relation that is transitive and irreflexive, the relation is also anti-symmetric (see, for instance, Fishburn (1973: 72–73)). Hence, when either of these approaches is used, the relation has properties (i), (ii) and (iii). So these two approaches are special cases for the definition of a linear order used by Rubin (1967) and Denzau and Parks (1975).

In a linear order, some (or all) of the comparisons can be "strict" comparisons. A strict comparison in a linear order will be denoted by the symbol $<_o$. More specifically, for a given linear order $_o$ (on the set X) and any pair $x, \tilde{y} X$, we will be using $x <_o y$ to mean: $x_o y$ holds, but $y_o x$ does not hold.

In the examples, the interpretation of $x_o y$ will be "x is either to the left of y or in the same place as y." In the examples, the interpretation of $x <_o y$ will be "x is to the left of y." So, in the examples, the linear order $_o$ will give us a way of lining up the alternatives from left to right when graphing a voter's utility function. For the examples, it will be assumed that the linear order is: r is to the left of s, s is to the left of t, and (hence) r is to the left of t (i.e., $r <_o s$, $s <_o t$, and $r <_o t$).

3. Graphing the Voters' Utility Functions

In the examples, the utility function for any given individual $i \{1, 2, 3, 4\}$ can be graphed as follows. First, place r, s, and t on the horizontal axis with r to the left of s and s to the left of t (corresponding to the linear order being used for the examples). Second, letting the vertical axis be measured in utility units, place dots at the three points with the following Cartesian coordinates $(r, u_i(r))$, $(s, u_i(s))$, and $(t, u_i(t))$. Third, draw lines connecting $(r, u_i(r))$ with $(s, u_i(s))$ and connecting $(s, u_i(s))$ with $(t, u_i(t))$.

When the graphs are drawn, it becomes clear that, for each individual, the three dots "take the form of isolated points on single-peaked curves" Black (1948: 24).

In the examples, if you start at the leftmost alternative (r) and move to the right, you can see that:

(i) for $i = 1$ and $i = 4$, the curve that you have drawn consistently goes down [from $(r, u_i(r)) = (r, 3)$ to $(s, u_i(s)) = (s, 2)$ and then to $(t, u_i(t)) = (t, 1)$];

(ii) for $i = 3$, the curve that you have drawn consistently goes up [from $(r, u_3(r)) = (r,1)$ to $(s, u_3(s)) = (s, 2)$ and then to $(t, u_3(t)) = (t, 3)$];

(iii) for $i = 2$, the curve that you have drawn first goes up [from $(r, u_2(r)) = (r, 2)$ to $(s, u_2(s)) = (s, 3)$] and then goes down [to $(t, u_2(t)) = (t,1)$].

Thus each curve is "one which changes its direction at most once, from up to down" Black (1958: 7).

When each voter has a most-preferred alternative, this statement implies that each voter has a single "peak" for his preference ordering. In the examples, this property can be seen by looking at the graphs for the voters' utility functions.

4. Single-Peaked Preferences

Black (1948: 24–25) used the following terminology (in the context of his committee model):

"We shall refer to the motion corresponding to the peak of any curve — the most-preferred motion for the member concerned — as his optimum." Black's concept of an "optimum" can be extended (so that it applies to any individual's preference relation R_i) by using the following more general definition: $\tilde{x}_i X$ is an optimum for $\tilde{i} N$ if and only if $x_i P_i y$, for all $\tilde{y} X — \{x_i\}$.

As in Black (1948, 1958), in what follows it will be assumed that each individual in N has an optimum. In the examples, the committee members' optima are $x_1 = x_4 = r$, $x_2 = s$, and $x_3 = t$.

In the preceding paragraphs, the preferences of the four individuals in the examples have been used to illustrate the idea behind the concept of single-peaked preferences. Assuming that each voter i has an optimum x_i, the concept itself can be stated precisely as follows (following Denzau and Parks (1975), for instance): R_i is "single-peaked with respect to $_o$" if and only if, for each pair $y, \tilde{z} X$,

$[y <_o z \ \& \ z <_o x_i]/[zP_i y]$

and

$[x_i <_o y \ \& \ y <_o z]/[yP_i z]$.

5. Comparisons Based on Majority Rule

We will consider certain pairwise comparisons (of alternatives) that are based on majority rule. More specifically, we will consider comparisons where a majority of the non-indifferent voters prefer one particular alternative to another. The statement that $\tilde{x} X$ "gets a majority over" $\tilde{y} X$ will mean $|\{\tilde{i} N : xP_i y\}| > |\{\tilde{i} N : yP_i x\}|$, where $|A|$ denotes the number of elements in (or "cardinality of") the finite set A.

In Example 1: s gets a majority over both r and t. In Example 2: no alternative gets a majority over every other alternative — but, at the same time, there is also no alternative that gets a majority over either r or s.

6. The Population of Voter Optima

Since each voter has an optimum, the voter optima constitute a population (as that term is used in Statistics). This population can be summarized with a probability distribution as follows: The distribution of voter optima is the discrete probability distribution P(■) on X that satisfies

$P(x) = |\{\tilde{i} N : x_i = x\}| / n$, for $\tilde{x} X$.

In this distribution: For any $\tilde{x} X$, $P(x)$ is simply the proportion of voters for whom x is the best alternative. In Example 1, the distribution of voter optima is: $P(r) = P(s) = P(t) = 1/3$. In Example 2, it is: $P(r) = \frac{1}{2}$ $P(s) = P(t) = \frac{1}{4}$.

When thinking about a distribution it is sometimes helpful to measure its center by using the concept of a median. In this context, a median will be defined in the following way: $\tilde{m} X$ is a median for the distribution of voter optima with respect to $._o$ if and only if

$P(\{\tilde{x} X : \tilde{x}_o m \}).\frac{1}{2}$

and

$P(\{\tilde{x} X : m_o x\}). \frac{1}{2}$.

Other references that have applied the same statistical notion of a median to distributions of voter optima include Black (1948, 1958), Fishburn (1973), Denzau and Parks (1975), Enelow and Hinich (1984) and Mueller (1989). In general: *If* the underlying statistical notion of a median is applied in a setting where (as in the context being studied here) (1) discrete probability distributions are used to summarize populations and (2) a population can potentially have an *even* number of things in it, *then* there is the possibility of having more than one median (see, for instance, Johnson et al. (1992: 51)). Because of this possibility, some statistical references use an alternative notion of a "median" for a discrete distribution which will assure that there is a unique median (see, for instance, Johnson et al. (1992: 42) — although that approach will not be adopted here.

Recall that, for the examples, the linear order is: r is to the left of s, s is to the left of t, and (hence) r is to the left of t (i.e., $r <_o s$, $s <_o t$, and $r <_o t$). In Example 1, there is a unique median $m = s$ (the unique alternative that beats every other alternative). In Example 2, there are two medians $m' = s$ and $m'' = r$ (the two unbeaten alternatives).

A voter whose optimum is a median for the distribution of voter optima (with respect to a linear order) is, accordingly, called a "median voter" (with respect to the given linear order). In Example 1, $i = 2$ is the unique median voter. In Example 2, every individual except $i = 3$ is a median voter.

7. Median Voter Theorems

The following two "median voter theorems" are generalizations of results that were established by Black (1948: 27, 28, respectively) in the context of his committee model. Proofs of these theorems are provided in Denzau and Parks (1975).

Theorem 1. Suppose that X is finite, each voter has an optimum, each voter's preference ordering is single-peaked with respect to $._o$, and n *is odd*. Then the voter optimum x_i gets a majority over every other alternative in X if and only if x_i is a median for the distribution of voter optima (with respect to $._o$).

Corollary 1. Suppose that X is finite, each voter has an optimum, each voter's preference ordering is single-peaked with respect to $._o$, and n *is odd*. Then the voter optimum x_i gets a majority over every other alternative in X if and only if i is a median voter (with respect to $._o$)

When the premise for Theorem 1 is satisfied, the discrete distribution of voter optima necessarily has a unique median. Therefore Theorem 1 implies that, when its premise is satisfied, there exists a unique voter optimum which gets a majority over every other alternative. Theorem 1 and this implication are both illustrated by Example 1 (where n is the odd number 3 and $x_2 = s$ gets a majority over both r and t).

In Example 1, $i = 2$ is a unique median voter. However, while Theorem 1 implies that (under its premise) there is a unique voter *optimum* that beats every other alternative, Corollary 1 implies that (under the same premise) there are cases where there is more than one *median voter*. For instance, suppose $N = \{1, 2, 3\}$ and $rP_i \, sP_i \, t$, for each $\tilde{i} \, N$. Then r is a unique voter *optimum* that beats every other alternative *and* each voter is a *median voter*. When the premise for Theorem 1 is satisfied and there is more than one median voter, it follows from Theorem 1 that each median voter has to have the same optimum.

Theorem 2. Suppose that X is finite, each voter has an optimum and each voter's preference ordering is single-peaked with respect to $._o$, and n *is even*. Then there is no alternative in X that gets a majority over the voter optimum x_i if and only if x_i is a median for the distribution of voter optima (with respect to $._o$).

Corollary 2. Suppose that X is finite, each voter has an optimum, each voter's preference ordering is single-peaked with respect to $._o$, and n *is even*. Then there is no alternative in X that gets a majority over the voter optimum x_i if and only if i is a median voter (with respect to $._o$).

When the premise for Theorem 2 is satisfied, the discrete distribution of voter optima has at least one voter optimum that is a median and no more than two distinct voter optima that are medians. Therefore Theorem 2 implies that (when its premise is satisfied) there is at least one voter optimum that is unbeaten and no more than two distinct voter optima that are unbeaten. Corollary 2 implies that (under the same premise) there may be more than two median voters. These observations are illustrated by Example 2 (where n is the even number 4, voters 1, 2, and 4 are the median voters and the optima that are unbeaten under majority rule are $x_2 = s$ and $x_1 = x_4 = r$).

In some settings where voting is used, there is an individual (such as a committee chairman) who can break ties. If the premise of Theorem 2 is satisfied, there are two distinct optima that are unbeaten *and* we add the assumption that there is an individual in N who can break ties, then the unbeaten optimum that is closer to that individual's optimum will be the final decision.

It should be noted that Arrow (1963), Fishburn (1970, 1972, 1973), Sen (1970), Denzau and Parks (1975) and others have proven some closely related theorems (which have premises that are variations on the ones used above).

It should also be noted that Black (1948) predicted that his theorems would "provide the basis for a theory of the equilibrium distribution of taxation or of public expenditure" (23). Significantly, his theorems (and extensions of them) have been widely applied in studies of the public sector — see, for instance, Atkinson and Stiglitz (1980: ch. 10)) the plus the references that they cite.

PETER J. COUGHLIN

REFERENCES

Arrow, K. (1963). *Social Choice and Individual Values*, Second Editon. New Haven: Yale University Press.

Atkinson, A. and Stiglitz, J. (1980). *Lectures on Public Economics*. New York: McGraw-Hill.

Black, D. (1948). "On the rationale of group decision making." *Journal of Political Economy*, 56: 23–34.

Black, D. (1958). *The Theory of Committees and Elections*. Cambridge, England: Cambridge University Press.

Condorcet, M. (1785) *Essai sur l'application de l'analyse a la probabilite des decisions rendues a la pluralite de voix*. Paris. (For an English translation of the relevant parts of Condorcet's essay, see: McLean, I. and Hewitt, F. (1994) *Condorcet*. Aldershot, England: Edward Elgar Publishing.)

Denzau, A. and Parks, R. (1975). "The continuity of majority rule equilibrium." *Econometrica*, 43: 853–866.

Enelow, J. and Hinich, M. (1984). *The Spatial Theory of Voting*. Cambridge, England: Cambridge University Press.

Fishburn, P. (1970). "Intransitive individual indifference and transitive majorities." *Econometrica*, 38: 482–489.

Fishburn, P. (1972). "A location theorem for single-peaked preferences." *Journal of Economic Theory*, 4: 94–97.

Fishburn, P. (1973). *The Theory of Social Choice*. Princeton: Princeton University Press.

Kelly, J. (1988). *Social Choice Theory*. Berlin: Springer-Verlag.

Johnson, N., Kotz, S., and Kemp A. (1963). *Univariate Discrete Distributions*, Second Editon. New York: Wiley.

Mas-Colell, A., Whinston, M., and Green, J. (1995). *Microeconomic Theory*. Oxford, England: Oxford University Press.

Moulin, H. (1988). *Axioms for Cooperative Decision Making*. Cambridge, England: Cambridge University Press.

Mueller, D. (1989). *Public Choice II*. Cambridge, England: Cambridge University Press.

Rubin, J. (1967). *Set Theory for the Mathematician*. San Francisco: Holden-Day

Sen, A. (1970). *Collective Choice and Social Welfare*. San Francisco: Holden-Day.

THE SOCIAL COST OF RENT SEEKING

Consider two entrepreneurs: Smith and Jones. Each has $10 million to invest. Smith invests his money in a shoe factory. Gross sales of shoes each year come to $3 million; operating expenses are $2 million annually. Thus, Smith makes a nominal profit of $1 million per year. However, Smith could have invested his capital in a restaurant, earning a net return of $500,000 per year so relative to the next-best alternative use of his capital, Smith is earning a 5 percent rate of return on his investment. That is, consumers value his production of shoes more, $500,000 per year more, than they value the dining services provided by the restaurant. Smith becomes a wealthy man by making the right decision about what consumers value. Smith's wealth, then, is a reflection of the value he creates for society.

Jones invests her money in bribing ... er .... successfully explaining to Alabama politicians why they should give her a tax break worth $1 million per year. (It doesn't take much money to 'explain' things to Alabama politicians). Jones also has an opportunity cost of $500,000 per year, as she could invest her $10 million capital in the same restaurant that Smith could invest in. Relative to her opportunity cost, Jones is, like Smith, earning a 5 percent rate of return on her investment. Thus, from the perspective of the two individuals, their behavior is identical — each 'invests' available capital in the highest-return employment.

However, in terms of social welfare, the two entrepreneurs are completely different. Whereas Smith's profits

result from his creation of previously unrealized value for society, Jones' profits do not reflect value created for society. Critically, they are derived only from redistribution of existing wealth, not from creation of new wealth (Baumol, 1990; Bhagwati, 1982; Hirshleifer, 1994). Even though Jones put only her own capital at risk, in lobbying for the tax break, this action is socially harmful. How so? Because her capital could have been employed in producing restaurant services that society valued, on net, at $500,000 per year. Employment of Jones' capital in an activity that society valued at zero, 'costs' society $500,000 worth of value that otherwise might have been realized. This unrealized potential value is the social cost of rent seeking (Tullock, 1967).

We know that rent seeking takes place, so there is a cost borne by society. The question is, how significant is the social cost of rent seeking? There have been three general approaches taken to answering this question. One approach is indirect: if we can specify the relationship between rent seeking activity and the size of the rents to be had, then identification of the aggregate amount of governmentally-arranged wealth transfers permits conclusions to be drawn about the magnitude of the implied social cost. This approach easily has drawn the most attention of Public Choice scholars (Tullock, 1971; Browning, 1974; Krueger, 1974; Posner, 1975; Paul and Wilhite, 1991; Dougan and Snyder, 1993). In theory, fully-informed and rational individuals would, collectively, spend 100 percent of the value of the expected transfer, less an ordinary rate of return, in efforts to achieve/block the transfer. That is, there would be complete dissipation of the expected rent(s). However, even slight deviations from the assumption of full information can lead, in theory, to over or under-dissipation.

Theory notwithstanding, our everyday experience seemingly suggests that successful rent seekers do not pay much for the wealth transfers that politicians arrange for them (Tullock, 1988, 1989, 1997). The most obvious example of this is the disparity between the amounts of money special interest groups donate to politicians and the value of legislative protection provided. The latter typically is many multiples of the former. However, the fact that the observed 'price' of special favors seemingly is low does not mean that the social cost of rent seeking is low or that rents are not substantially dissipated away in efforts to capture them.

Unobserved investments in the rent seeking process may loom large in the final reckoning of social cost. Such investments not only may take non-cash forms, they also may not even flow to politicians in control of the political apparatus that determines the supply of rents. Labor unions and other special interest groups commonly provide labor and votes for politicians. They also provide commercial advertisements in support of a politician and/or against his opponent(s). They invite (and pay) politicians to speak to their organizations. They invite politicians to lunch, sporting and entertainment events, and the like (Laband et al., 1994). They provide well-paid jobs for the politician's family members and friends. But these investments that target specific politicians only are made after identifying the imperative to do so in the first place. Such imperative derives either from identifying an opportunity to gain rents or perceiving a threat that some other special interest group is lobbying for political action that would be harmful to your group. Timely identification of both opportunities and threats requires constant investment in information about current events and activities in the world generally, and especially in all branches and levels of government, not just by active rent seeking entities, but also by everyone who wishes to avoid being victimized by the rent seeking efforts of others. It simply must be the case that such investments by all potentially affected parties, even though they may be small on the margin, are enormous in the aggregate (Laband and McClintock, 2001).

Even if the relationship between the size of the rents and the degree of dissipation was well understood, which it is not, imputation of the social cost of rent-seeking from determination of the size of the rents understates the social cost. This is because resources also are expended by individuals who seek to become suppliers of the rents themselves (this has, of course, been a major cause of wars throughout history) and thus the beneficiaries of subsequent rent-seeking activity (Buchanan, 1980). The next two approaches avoid this mis-measurement problem.

A second approach to gauging the social cost of rent-seeking is direct measurement of rent-seeking expenditures. For example, one could identify the expenditures in a given year for all federal and state licensed political lobbyists, expenditures by individuals seeking public office, donations by special interest groups to political campaigns, and so forth. This accounting approach yields estimated expenditures on wealth redistribution activity in the U.S. in the hundreds of billions of dollars annually in recent years (Laband and Sophocleus, 1992; Laband and McClintock, 2001). Remember, these are expenditures that could have been, but are not, put to use in producing positively-valued goods and services.

A third approach to assessing the social cost of rent-seeking is historical or comparative analysis of the effects of rent-seeking on a country's economic performance. The theory is straightforward: as more of a nation's resources are devoted to rent-seeking rather than productive activity, less real economic growth is forthcoming (Olson, 1965; Murphy et al., 1991; Rauch, 1994). Although researchers do not measure rent-seeking activity directly, they use the presence of institutional structures that facilitate or inhibit rent-seeking activity as a proxy for the activity itself. The strong and consistent finding by researchers is that the economic performance of countries with strong protectionist regimes is markedly lower than the economic performance of countries in which competitive forces are not stifled (Olson, 1965; Ekelund and Tollison, 1981, 1997).

DAVID N. LABAND

REFERENCES

Baumol, W.J. (1990). "Entrepreneurship: Productive, unproductive, and destructive." *Journal of Political Economy*, 98: 893–921.

Bhagwati, J.N. (1982). "Directly unproductive profit-seeking activities." *Journal of Political Economy*, 90: 988–1002.

Browning, E.K. (1974). "On the Welfare Cost of Transfers." *Kyklos*, 27: 374–377.

Buchanan, J.M. (1980). "Rent Seeking and Profit Seeking," in J.M. Buchanan, R.D. Tollison, and G. Tullock (eds.) *Toward a Theory of the Rent-Seeking Society*. College Station: Texas A&M University Press, pp. 3–15.

Dougan, W.R. and Snyder, J.M. (1993). "Are Rents Fully Dissipated?" *Public Choice*, 77: 793–814.

Ekelund, R.B. and Tollison, R.D. (1981). *Mercantilism as a Rent-Seeking Society*. College Station: Texas A&M University Press.

Ekelund, R.B. and Tollison, R.D. (1997). *Politicized Economies: Monarchy, Monopoly, and Mercantilism*. College Station: Texas A&M University Press.

Hirshleifer, J. (1994). "The dark side of the force." *Economic Inquiry*, 32: 1–10.

Krueger, A.O. (1974). "The political economy of the rent-seeking society." *American Economic Review*, 64: 291–303.

Laband, D.N. and Sophocleus, J.P. (1992). "An estimate of resource expenditures on transfer activity in the United States." *Quarterly Journal of Economics*, 107: 959–983.

Laband, D.N., Mixon, F., and Ekelund, R.B., Jr. (1994). "Rent seeking and hidden resource distortion: Some empirical evidence." *Public Choice*, 78: 171–185.

Laband, D.N. and McClintock, G.P. (2001). *The Transfer Society: Economic Expenditures on Transfer Activity*. Washington: The Cato Institute.

Murphy, K.M., Shleifer, A., and Vishny, R. (1991). "The allocation of talent: Implications for growth." *Quarterly Journal of Economics*, 106: 503–531.

Olson, M. (1965). *The Rise and Decline of Nations*. New Haven: Yale University Press.

Paul, C. and Wilhite, A. (1991). "Rent-seeking, rent-defending, and rent dissipation." *Public Choice*, 71: 61–70.

Posner, R. (1975). The social cost of monopoly and regulation. *Journal of Political Economy*, 83: 807–827.

Rauch, J. (1994). *Demosclerosis*. New York: Times Books.

Tullock, G. (1967). "The welfare cost of tariffs, monopolies, and theft." *Western Economic Journal*, 5: 224–232.

Tullock, G. (1971). "The cost of transfers." *Kyklos*, 24: 629–643.

Tullock, G. (1988). "The costs of rent seeking: A metaphysical problem." *Public Choice*, 57: 15–24.

Tullock, G. (1989). *The Economics of Special Privilege and Rent Seeking*. Boston: Kluwer.

Tullock, G. (1997). "Where is the Rectangle?" *Public Choice*, 91: 149–159.

SORTITION

[T]he appointment of magistrates by lot is thought to be democratical, and the election of them oligarchical …
(Aristotle, *Politics*: 1294b, 5–10)

Sortition is decision by a random process, such as the drawing of lots. It was widely used by the ancient Greeks. In Athens, in the fifth and fourth centuries B.C., virtually all administrative positions (excluding a few requiring specialized abilities, such as military leaders) were filled by lot. It was also used in renaissance Venice and Florence. Those governments employing sortition were administered more regularly, honestly and successfully than contemporaneous states utilizing other methods, and, in fact, compare favorably to modern states (Headlam, 1933: 173; Finlay, 1980: 29; Queller, 1986: 4, 8). Any comparison between ancient and modern states is, of course, impeded by the dramatically more expansive role of modern states.

As Aristotle noted, the Athenians considered selection by lot as essential to democracy. They believed other known methods of election were inherently susceptible to manipulation by organized interest, and would prevent rule by the demos (Headlam, 1933: 12–32, 177). Greek critics of the lot (including Socrates) were also critics of democracy, generally, and criticized the lot *because* it was democratic (Headlam, 1933: 13–14).) In renaissance Italy, Florence employed sortition more broadly than Venice and, as a result, was regarded as more democratic (Gilbert, 1968: 473). Election by lot, there, was considered coincident with liberty and equality. One of the purposes of the lot was to diminish the powers of the magistrates, thus retaining governance by the people, rather than a ruling political class (Hansen, 1992: 236).

The Greeks recognized decision by lot as a defense against faction (Aristotle, *Rhetoric to Alexander*: 1424a, 13–16; *Politics*: 1303a, 15–20; Headlam, 1933: 38), as did the Venetians and Florentines (Finlay, 1980: 31, 38; Queller, 1986: 6). The random element in the selection process reduces the return to political rather than productive enterprises. Sortition may also reduce political violence relative to voting, by removing the benefit of eliminating a few key voters in close elections (Levy, 1991: 146–147).

The role of chance in sortition is sometimes interpreted as revealing divine intent (Plato, *Laws*: Book III, 690c; Book VI, 759c; Homer, *The Iliad of Homer*: 3:316, 7:161; Proverbs 16:33; Hansen, 1990: 58; Headlam, 1933: 4–8).

There are a variety of ways in which an element of randomness can be incorporated into a collective decision making procedure. One familiar manner is the use of a random method, such as a coin toss, to select an alternative where a voting procedure fails because of a tie. Other methods of incorporating some degree of randomness include voting where some of the alternatives considered are lotteries across single-valued alternatives, as well as the single-valued alternatives themselves (Zeckhauser, 1969; Fishburn, 1972; Machina, 1985). A more sophisticated decision technology, sometimes called the average rule, is discussed in Coleman (1973), Intriligator (1973, 1982) and Freixas (1984). Individuals are permitted to express their preferences as vectors. These vectors can represent the probabilities with which an individual believes they would be most satisfied with the alternatives covered, or may represent a weighted ranking which reflects they strengths of their preferences. For instance, each voter might be given 100 votes which they may allocate however ever they choose across the set of alternative (they may choose to give their most favored alternative 50 votes, their second choice 30, etc.). Taking the average of the weighting for each alternative yields a probability distribution that can be applied to create a social ordering or select among the alternatives. A simpler method is to permit electors to mark their preferences on ballots, but rather than counting them, draw one at random, which becomes the social choice. This is sometimes referred to as a proportional lottery (Fishburn and Gehrlein, 1977; Gehrlein, 1991; Gehrlein and Berg, 1992) or proportional majority voting (Mueller, 1989).

In the Social Choice literature, spawned by Arrow's seminal impossibility theorem (Arrow, 1950, 1963), various criteria have emerged by which to evaluate the desirability of collective decision-making technologies. Procedures incorporating a degree of randomness often perform well under these criteria. Arrow's theorem states that any social welfare function that is complete, transitive, defined for all individual orderings, exhibits a positive association between individual preferences and the social preference, and is independent of irrelevant alternatives, must either be imposed or dictatorial. In fact, Arrow himself noted that probabilistic decision methods are not necessarily subject to his famous proof (Arrow, 1963: 20–21). Nandeibam (2000) shows that it is possible to construct probabilistic criteria corresponding to Arrow's deterministic ones, such that a class of decision mechanisms satisfies the criteria (i.e., is neither dictatorial nor imposed).

With reference to Arrow's criteria, sortition is not decisive, in that there is not a unique outcome for any given set of votes. From the same set of expressed preferences, the procedure may select alternative A one time, and alternative B the next. Sortition is complete, in that for any given set of alternatives, one of which is to be randomly selected, a selection can be made. This is in contrast to voting, which fails to select among alternatives in those instances resulting in a tie.

Sortition, unlike voting systems, can be independent of irrelevant alternatives. Susceptibility to irrelevant alternatives is observed when third party candidates, with no chance of winning, siphon votes away from a major candidate, such that the winning candidate is not the first choice of a plurality of the voters. Under sortition, any alternative that is included could potentially be drawn, regardless of the low probability of such an event. Therefore there are no irrelevant alternatives to be independent of.

Collective decision mechanisms that are not independent of irrelevant alternatives are susceptible to manipulation through preference falsification. Participants may be able to improve the outcome of the election by misrepresenting their preferences. This weakness is common to all voting systems deciding among three or more alternatives, except those incorporating a significant element of chance (Gibbard, 1973; Satterthwaite, 1975; Barberà and Peleg, 1990). Some forms of sortition, including the proportional lottery, however, are strategy-proof (Kelly, 1977; Barberà, 1978, 1979). Decision technologies that are susceptible to misrepresentation of preferences will be biased towards voters who have less regard for honesty as a normative standard. The accurate revelation of preferences has value beyond determining the outcome of a particular election, as in guiding the development of future policy proposals. Decision technologies that are less vulnerable to manipulation would seem preferable, *ceteris paribus*.

Forms of sortition, including the average rule and proportional lottery, are unanimous. If all lots are marked with the same alternative, it is selected with certainty. These forms of sortition are also strongly monotonic. That is, an increase in the relative standing of an alternative in the individual rankings of one or more electors increases the probability of that alternative being selected. This is in contrast with decisive voting procedures where, although an increase in the relative standing of an alternative in individual rankings cannot reduce the probability of an alternative being selected, it only increases the probability of selection when that alternative was within one vote of

being tied. This strong monotonicity in these forms of sortition means that there is a benefit in seeking as near a unanimous consensus as possible in the selection or development of any proposed alternative. This is unlike plurality voting mechanisms, where consensus beyond a plurality of voters has no effect on the probability of success.

Sortition is typically anonymous and neutral. All voters are treated identically, as are all alternatives. Sortition is not transitive. If alternative A is selected over alternative B, and B over C, it is not certain that A would be selected over C. In fact, because of the random element, if A is selected over B, it is not certain that in an additional drawing from the same lots that A will be selected over B again.

Stochastic decision methods are currently accepted in some applications, and not in others. A more or less random selection of jurors is generally regarded as acceptable. During the Vietnam conflict a lottery was used to determine who would be conscripted. A coin toss before the kickoff of football games is accepted as an appropriate device to determine who will receive the ball. Fishburn (1978) offers a list of characteristics relating to the acceptability of lotteries as decision mechanisms. He cites (1) a set of two or more qualifying agents that have met some criteria, (2) a prize (or duty) to be awarded to one of the candidates, (3) more or less homogeneous attitudes towards accepting the prize or duty, (4) general acknowledgement of an equal right to receive the prize (or evade the duty), and (5) the lack of a competition to persuade others that one candidate is more deserving of selection than the other. Fishburn notes that he knows of no circumstance that does not meet these five criteria in which decisions are currently made stochastically.

Political contests clearly do not meet Fishburn's fourth and fifth characteristics. It is interesting to note, however, that renaissance Venice, which did employ selection by lot, did attempt to have their collective political decision-making meet those criteria. Politicking was forbidden in Venice. It was illegal for Venetians to suggest that they themselves, or anyone else should be nominated to the pool of candidates or electors, from which selection would be made by lottery. So great was concern regarding political intrigue advancing the interests of one clan or faction over another, that virtually all social gatherings where political alliances might be advanced were regulated or prohibited, including large dinners, weddings and baptisms (Queller, 1986: 77–78).

Sortition has the potential to protect against the tyranny of the majority — that is, the threat that a dominant majority will suppress the interests of a persistent minority. Although majorities may shift over time under the plurality-voting rule, it may well be that a few dominant factions rotate power amongst themselves, while the most vulnerable minorities are permanently suppressed. The inherent susceptibility of plurality voting to manipulation makes this unfortunate outcome more likely. The very real possibility that a minority coalition will eventually become dominant can be expected to temper the temptation for any currently dominant faction to exploit its position too aggressively. Under the average rule and proportional lottery a position that is held by 20% of the populace will win out, on average, 20% of the time. On the other hand, the fact that a viewpoint is only held by a minority may be interpreted as an *a priori* indication that it is, in fact, desirable for that viewpoint to be suppressed. Some viewpoints remain in the minority because they are abhorrent to a majority of the populace. One strength of sortition in the balancing the interests of minorities and majorities is that it can be implemented such that the probability of an alternative being selected is proportional to the strength of support it has. It is also possible for sortition to be implemented such that an alternative must receive some minimum level of support to be included in the lottery.

Stochastic decision mechanisms severely impair the effectiveness of efforts to affect the outcome of collective decisions. For this reason, the returns to rent-seeking efforts are significantly lower where sortition is employed. Therefore, the proportion of resources directed to rent-seeking, as opposed to productive efforts, should be markedly lower in societies that employ probabilistic decision mechanisms. The inverse relationship between the degree of randomness in collective decision making, and the amount of resources directed to capturing transfers (as opposed to creating wealth) is a theme that runs through Tullock's *Efficient Rent-seeking* article, and the literature that surrounds it (Tullock, 1980; Lockard and Tullock, 2000).

Sortition served well those states that used it as a collective decision making technology, where it was regarded it as the very essence of democracy. It restrains the growth of an independent political class, impedes manipulation of the political apparatus, impairs factional discord, restrains state power, protects vulnerable minorities and reduces rent-seeking. Decision methodologies incorporating some degree of randomness hold promise for addressing instances of governmental failure revealed through the public choice analysis of political institutions.

ALAN A. LOCKARD

REFERENCES

Aristotle, *Politics*, [ca. 330 BC], 1298a, 20–25, 1294b, 5–10, 1300b, 1–5, 1303a, 15–20.

Aristotle (attribution believed spurious), *Rhetoric to Alexander*, [ca. 330 BC], 1424a, 13–19.

Aristotle, *Constitution of Athens*, [ca. 330 BC], 8.1, 22.5, 43. 1, 55.1, 62.1.

Arrow, K.J. (1950). "A Difficulty in the Concept of Social Welfare." *The Journal of Political Economy*, 58(4): 328–346.

Arrow, K.J. (1963). *Social Choice and Individual Values*. New York: John Wiley & Sons.

Bandyopadhyay, T., Deb, R., and Pattanaik, P.K. (1982). "The structure of coalitional power under probabilistic group decision rules." *Journal of Economic Theory*, 27, 366–375.

Barberà, S. (1978). "Nice Decision Schemes," in H.W. Gottinger (ed.) *Decision Theory and Social Ethics: Issues in Social Choice* Dordrecht, Holland: D. Reidel Publishing Co. pp. 101–117.

Barberà, S. (1979). "A note on group strategy-proof decision schemes." *Econometrica*, 47(3): 637–640.

Barberà, S. and Peleg, B. (1990). "Strategy-proof voting schemes with continuous preferences." *Social Choice and Welfare*, 7: 31–38.

Coleman, J. (1973). *The Mathematics of Collective Action*. Chicago: Aldine Publishing Co.

Finlay, R. (1980). *Politics in Renaissance Venice*. New Brunswick, NJ: Rutgers University Press.

Fishburn, P.C. (1972). "Lotteries and Social Choices." *Journal of Economic Theory*, 5: 189–207.

Fishburn, P.C. (1978). "Acceptable Social Choice Lotteries," in H.W. Gottinger (ed.) *Decision Theory and Social Ethics: Issues in Social Choice*. Dordrecht, Holland: D. Reidel Publishing Co. pp. 133–152.

Fishburn, P.C. and Gehrlein, W. (1977). "Towards a theory of Elections with Probabilistic Preferences." *Econometrica*, 45(8): 1907–1924.

Freixas, X. (1984). "A cardinal approach to straightforward probabilistic mechanisms." *Journal of Economic Theory*, 227–251.

Gehrlein, W.V. (1991). "Coincidence probabilities for simple majority and proportional lottery rules." *Economics Letters*, 35: 349–353.

Gehrlein, W.V. and Berg, S. (1992). "The effect of social homogeneity on coincidence probabilities for pairwise proportional lottery and simple majority rules." *Social Choice and Welfare*, 9: 361–372.

Gibbard, A. (1973). "Manipulation of schemes: A general result." *Econometrica*, 41(4): 587–601.

Gibbard, A. (1977). "Manipulation of schemes that mix voting with chance." *Econometrica*, 45(3): 665–681.

Gilbert, F. (1968). "The venetian constitution in Florentine political thought," in N. Rubinstein (ed.) *Florentine Studies: Politics and Society in Renaissance Florence*. London: Faber and Faber.

Gradstein, M. and K.A. Konrad. (1999) "Orchestrating rent seeking contests." *The Economic Journal*, 109(458): 536–545.

Hansen, M.H. (1992). *Athenian Democracy in the Age of Demosthenes*. Cambridge, MA: Blackwell.

Headlam, J.W. (1933). *Election by Lot in Athens*. London: Cambridge University Press.

Intriligator, M.D. (1973). "A probabilistic model of social choice." *Review of Economic Studies*, 40(4): 553–560.

Intriligator, M.D. (1982). "Probabilistic Models of Choice." *Mathematical Social Sciences*, 2: 157–166.

Kelly, J.S. (1977). "Strategy-proofness and social choice functions without singlevaluedness." *Econometrica*, 45(2): 439–446.

Kooreman, P. and Schoonbeck, L. (1997). "The specification of the probability functions in Tullock's rent-seeking contest." *Economics Letters*, 56: 59–61.

Levy, David. (1991) *The Economic Ideas of Ordinary People.* New York: Routledge.

Lockard, Alan and Gordon Tullock (eds.) (2000). *Efficient Rent Seeking: Chronicle of an Intellectual Quagmire.* Boston: Kluwer.

Machina, M.J. (1985). "Stochastic choice functions generated from deterministic preferences over lotteries." *Economic Journal*, 95(379): 575–594.

Mueller, D.C. (1989). "Probabilistic majority rule." *Kyklos*, 42(2): 151–170.

Nandeibam, S. (2000). "Distribution of coalitional power under probabilistic voting procedures." *Mathematical Social Sciences*, 40: 63–84.

Nurmi, H. (2001). "Resolving group choice paradoxes using probabilistic and fuzzy concepts." *Group Decision and Negotiation*, 10: 177–198.

Pattanaik, P.K. and Peleg, B. (1986). "Distribution of power under stochastic social choice rules." *Econometrica*, 54(4): 909–921.

Plato, *Laws* Book III, 690c, Book VI, 759c.

Plato, *Republic*, Book V, 460 A, 461 E, Book VIII, 557 A.

Queller, D.E. (1986). *The Venetian Patriciate: Reality versus Myth.* Chicago: University of Illinois Press.

Satterthwaite, M.A. (1975). "Strategy-Proofness and Arrow's Conditions: Existence and Correspondence Theorems for Voting Procedures and Social Welfare Functions." *Journal of Economic Theory*, 10: 187–217.

Tullock, G. (1980). "Efficient Rent Seeking," in J.M. Buchanan, R.D. Tollison, and G. Tullock (eds.) *Toward a Theory of the Rent-Seeking Society.* College Station: Texas A&M University Press, pp. 97–112.

Zeckhauser, R. (1969). "Majority Rule with Lotteries on Alternatives." *Quarterly Review of Economics*, 83(4): 696–703.

STANDARD OIL AND MICROSOFT: ANTITRUST LESSONS

Until the mid-1970s, American antitrust regulators and courts too-often confused "competition" with "competitors." Today this confusion occurs much less frequently. The reason is twofold: first, sensible economics is more likely to guide antitrust's application, and second, consumer welfare (rather than producer welfare, or "democratic values," or some other goal unrelated to competition) is now the near-exclusive standard by which antitrust regulation is judged.

But improved as it is, in this writer's view antitrust's benefits still fall short of its costs. The need for government to ensure that competition prevails is not at all obvious, while the actual record of antitrust regulation being used to stymie competition is long and clear.

Support for these two claims is found in two of the most famous antitrust cases — the first coming early in antitrust's history (*United States v. Standard Oil, Inc.*, 1911), the second occurring very recently (*United States v. Microsoft Corp.*, 1999). Despite being separated by nearly ninety years, these two cases share important similarities. Both cases involved highly visible companies in new industries on technology's frontier, and both companies were founded and led by outspoken, aggressive entrepreneurs, each famous for the unprecedented fortune he amassed in business. Also, each firm was accused of using unfair and ruthless means of garnering the large market shares that each enjoyed. Chief among these allegedly illegal means of exclusion is predatory price-cutting.

Indeed, Microsoft's Bill Gates is often compared with Standard Oil's John D. Rockefeller (Murray, 1998). Unfortunately, the comparison is with the mythical rather than the real Rockefeller.

1. Standard Oil

John D. Rockefeller founded Standard Oil in 1870. That year, Standard sold 4% of all kerosene sold in the United States and the price of kerosene was 26¢ per gallon. By 1885, Standard's market share approached 85% and each gallon of kerosene sold for 8¢. Kerosene's price continued to fall — to just under 7.5¢ in 1890 and to 5.91¢ in 1897. Also, Standard's market share continued to rise. This share was about 90% for much of the 1890s.

The steadily falling price of kerosene (Standard's chief product during its formative and its controversial years) reflected Standard's steadily increasing production efficiency. Standard's average cost of refining a gallon of kerosene in 1870 was 3¢. Fifteen years later, at 0.452¢, this cost was less than one-sixth of its 1870 level.

Not surprisingly, the petroleum-industry's output rose during this time. In 1880, output was 840 million gallons of kerosene; by 1897 output had more than tripled to 2.6 billion gallons (Boudreaux and Folsom, 1999: 557–560).

Standard's dramatic cost cutting resulted largely from the obsession of Rockefeller and his lieutenants for efficiency. Many of the practices that critics highlighted as evidence of Rockefeller's ruthless quest for monopoly are, when considered dispassionately, better seen as benign cost-cutting measures that harm only those rivals who were unable or unwilling to match Standard's intrepid drive for efficiency. For example, by exercising extraordinary quality control over the production of its refineries, Standard saved money by self-insuring. And because of the large volume that it shipped, Standard was able to self-insure its products against being damaged in transit. Also, Standard integrated backward into barrel production (including buying large tracks of timber), which cut its marginal cost of acquiring barrels by nearly 62% (Armentano, 1982: 58).

Did Standard augment its undoubted commercial and industrial acumen with monopolizing tactics? No. For a half-century following Standard's forced break-up in 1911, unchallenged opinion held that much of Standard's success was achieved through predatory pricing — that is, pricing below cost with the intention of ruining rivals in order to gain monopoly power in the future. A now-classic study by John McGee, however, found no evidence of predatory pricing by Standard (McGee, 1958). Subsequent research (both empirical and theoretical) supports McGee's finding (Easterbrook, 1981; Elzinga and Mills, 1989).

But none of Standard's successes — not its pioneering organization of the petroleum-refining market; not its creation of several products that never before existed (e.g., petroleum jelly); not its immense size; not its significant market share; not even its obsessive drive for continuing efficiency improvements — carved out for it a market free of competition. Standard's share of the market for refined-petroleum products began to fall in the late 1890s. By 1907 (the year President Theodore Roosevelt's administration inaugurated its antitrust case against Standard Oil), its market share had fallen from about 90 percent (in the late 1890s) to 68 percent. By the year (1911) that the United States Supreme Court upheld the break-up of Standard, its market share had fallen further, to 64 percent (Boudreaux and Folsom, 1999: 560).

The judgment of *Wall Street Journal* writer Alan Murray (1998) that "[o]nly after the government busted the Standard Oil trust did anything like free-market competition return" is clearly mistaken. Historians Ralph and Muriel Hidy (1955: 477) more accurately noted that "even before the breakup of the combination, the process of whittling Standard Oil down to reasonable size within the industry was already far advanced."

In summary, two features of Standard's success are noteworthy. First, it was the result of unusual acumen, creativity, and entrepreneurial and administrative drive, rather than the result of tactics that can fairly be described as monopolizing; second (and supporting the first) never did this success yield monopoly power for Standard, if "monopoly power" is understood to be the ability to harm consumers.

This second claim might strike many readers as preposterous, for how is it that a firm with such overwhelming

market share — in excess of 90% for several years in the late 19th century — can be said *not* to possess monopoly power?

This question and its answer are vital to a proper understanding of competition, and, hence, to a better understanding of the *Microsoft* case.

2. The Market Process

Markets exist in time. A snapshot of a firm's market share no more reveals the realities of a market than does a snapshot of a jet reveal the realities of flight. Some facts are revealed, but the essentials of the phenomena remain unexposed. A large market share might be evidence of unusual ability to please consumers — that is, a special skill at behaving competitively — or it might be evidence of discordant special privileges. The closest we can come to telling if a large market share is evidence of consumers being well served or of consumers being harmed is to look at the firm's actual treatment of consumers.

Only if the firm raises its (real) prices and cuts its output is it reasonable to conclude that it possesses monopoly power. But if the firm cuts its prices and *increases* its output, the most plausible conclusion is that the firm has no monopoly power. Neither of these conclusions is ever correct beyond question; reality is too complex for such strong statements. But each of these conclusions is the *best* that non-omniscient observers can offer. Any other conclusions are more likely to be mistaken.

Because Standard Oil consistently (and considerably) cut its real prices and expanded its output, we have no reliable evidence that it possessed monopoly power. A monopolist likely would not have acted in this way. The available evidence of what matters most — Standard's pricing and output practices — screams "competition."

It will not do to assert that Standard *could* have raised its prices and cut its output. Of course it *could* have done so. But what would have happened if, contrary to actual fact, it had acted like a monopolist?

We do not know for sure. Perhaps price hikes and output restrictions would have raised Standard's profits even higher without significantly increasing the speed at which rivals threatened its market share. But no one has ever been in a better position to make this assessment than were Rockefeller and his fellow executives at Standard back in the late 19th century. Presumably, they wanted to maximize their firm's net present value; I assume (reasonably) that they were genuine profit-maximizers. So the fact that Standard did not behave as a monopolist points to the conclusion that Standard was in fact no monopolist — or, at least, that Rockefeller and other executives at Standard did not believe Standard to be a monopolist.

Almost any firm can increase its immediate profits by restricting output and raising price. The local Holiday Inn probably *could* inform the guest who requests an extra-night stay that the price of this extra night is five percent higher than is the price he paid for each of the previous few nights. After all, the guest probably won't want to go to the trouble of packing his bags and finding another motel just to avoid paying a five-percent premium. But while such a price hike would raise Holiday Inn's immediate profits, it is likely to diminish its profits in the long-run because rival motels will become relatively more attractive to consumers. Firms are forever sacrificing immediate opportunities for higher profits in exchange for a longer stream of expected higher profits.

The mere ability to raise price and increase profits in the short-run is not sufficient evidence of monopoly power.

No one today can say for sure what reasons motivated the decisions of Standard Oil's executives. Perhaps they were simply too daft to recognize the enormous monopoly power that their large market share bestowed upon them. Perhaps they feared government retaliation if they took advantage of their monopoly power. Or perhaps — and this reason strikes me as the most sensible — they understood that if they ever acted like a monopolist, the dynamic forces of competition would quickly enough destroy their large market share and reduce their firm's net present value.

The historical record shows that even without behaving like a monopolist, Standard's market share was eventually cut by rivals. So there is sound reason to believe that Standard's executives understood that their market "dominance" was never as indomitable as many people simply assumed it to be. For them to act like a monopolist likely would have revealed that Standard was indeed not a monopolist — and that acting like one without really being one causes profits more quickly to fall rather than to rise.

3. Microsoft

The history of Microsoft is remarkably similar to that of Standard Oil. In just a few years of its incorporation, Microsoft become one of America's most famous companies and a massive presence in a new industry regarded as essential to the country's economic and military vitality. And its founder, Bill Gates, like J.D. Rockefeller, became well-known by the public and detested by his rivals.

Two other similarities are critical. First, the prices of products sold by Microsoft, like those sold by Standard Oil, fell steadily since Microsoft's founding. Second, Microsoft's business practices, like those of Standard Oil, were denounced by its rivals and by the government as predatory and otherwise aimed at choking off market opportunities for other producers.

The price (in constant 1999 dollars) of Microsoft's operating-system software (MS-DOS, then Windows) fell steadily and significantly during the 1990s — from $225 in 1990 to $106 in 1998 (McKenzie, 2001: 40). At the same time, the quality and number of tasks performed by this software steadily increased.

Significant drops in real prices and improvements in quality occurred for nearly all of the products Microsoft offered. Especially telling is the fact that prices in those markets in which Microsoft offered software products fell faster than in those markets in which Microsoft did not offer such products (Liebowitz, 1998; Liebowitz and Margolis, 1999: 153–157).

As for charges of predation, they ring hollow. Space does not permit a detailed review of the many reasons advanced by critics for believing that Microsoft's pricing policies were out of line with the interests of consumers. Certainly, software prices over the years have radically fallen. But to assess current claims of predation requires peering into the future, because while it is occurring predatory pricing in practice is indistinguishable from competitive pricing.

The most compelling evidence on this matter is supplied by George Bittlingmayer and Thomas Hazlett (2000), who examined how the share prices of software firms (excluding Microsoft) moved with each change in Microsoft's fortunes on the antitrust front. Examining current share prices (which are set by the expectations of millions of investors) is perhaps the closest we can come to peering into the future.

Bittlingmayer and Hazlett found that the market valuation of firms complementary to Microsoft — both hardware and software producers — fall whenever Microsoft's fortunes on the antitrust front grow dimmer and rise whenever they brighten. This evidence suggests that investors do not generally believe that Microsoft's actions threaten to monopolize those markets in which it competes. The reason is that monopolization by Microsoft would raise consumers' full cost of computing and, therefore, reduce the demand for products supplied by hardware and software producers. Firms complementary to Microsoft would suffer. The fact that investors in these firms respond negatively to antitrust actions against Microsoft is powerful evidence that Microsoft's actions are competitive rather than predatory.

And if Microsoft's actions are competitive, this fact, in turn, casts doubt on the prevailing wisdom that Microsoft enjoys monopoly power. Like Standard Oil, Microsoft does serve a substantial share of a market, but unlike a genuine monopolist, it does not raise prices or restrict output.

The soundest conclusion, therefore, is that Microsoft is no monopolist.

Much of antitrust's intellectual support comes from mistaken history. Standard Oil was clearly no monopolist, if by monopolist we mean a firm that raises prices, restricts output, and reduces consumer welfare. And nor is Microsoft a monopolist. The time has come for economists to devote more time to looking at actual market performance of real-world firms and less time spinning out esoteric scenarios of possible harm that can emerge from vigorous competition.

DONALD J. BOUDREAUX

REFERENCES

Armentano, D.T. (1982). *Antitrust and Monopoly*. New York: John Wiley Interscience.

Bittlingmayer, G. and Hazlett, T.W. (2000). "DOS Kapital: Has antitrust action against microsoft created value in the computer industry." *Journal of Financial Economics*, 55(March): 329–359.

Boudreaux, D.J. and Folsom, B.W. (1999). "Microsoft and standard oil: radical lessons for antitrust reform." *Antitrust Bulletin*, 44(Fall): 555–576.

Elzinga, K.G. and Mills, D.E. (1989). "Testing for predation: Is recoupment possible?" *Antitrust Bulletin*, 34(Fall): 869–893.

Easterbrook, F.H. (1981). "Predatory strategies and counterstrategies." *University of Chicago Law Review*, 48(Spring): 263–377.

Hidy, R. and Hidy, M. (1955). *Pioneering in Big Business: 1882–1911*. New York: Harper and Row.

Liebowitz, S.J. (1998). "Bill Gates's secret? build better products." *Wall Street Journal* (October 20): A22.

Liebowitz, S.J. and Margolis, S.E. (1999). *Winners, Losers, and Microsoft*. Oakland, CA: The Independent Institute.

McGee, J. (1958). "Predatory price cutting: The Standard Oil (N.J.) Case." *Journal of Law and Economics*, 1(October): 137–169.

McKenzie, R.B. (2001). *Trust on Trial*, revised Edition. Cambridge, MA: Perseus Publishing.

Murray, A. (1998). "Reading Rockefeller and Busting up trusts." *Wall Street Journal* (May 18): A1.

STATE-SPONSORED MURDER AS A RENT-SEEKING ACTIVITY

State-sponsored murder is quite common. In the 20th century, some 170 to 360 million innocents were murdered by their governments, and the 21st century is not starting off well. These killings are more than four times those of war. The Soviets, Communist Chinese, and the Nazis killed on an appalling scale. The rogues' prize goes to the Khmer Rouge, who liquidated a third of the population of Cambodia. But, no continent is free of killing. When the state murders the general population, the term is democide; when it murders minorities, it is genocide.

1. The Demand for Democide

There is a rough inverse relationship between per capita income (GDP) and the amount of state-killing. Where per capita income is low, life is viewed as cheap. Where income is high, states are constrained, since killing the population is dear. This suggests that price (measured by a unit of real gross domestic product destroyed) constrains the amount of state-sponsored murder.

Democide mainly occurs in authoritarian regimes. Terror is a signal that the price of opposition is high. The benefit of democide is continued rule; the cost is destroyed output. A cold calculus suggests that a rational dictator will murder the population to the point where the marginal benefit equals the marginal cost. Marginal benefit in this context is continued rule and a share in the rents that dictators generate through centralized political and economic control plus any pleasure obtained from inflicting terror. Marginal cost is the incremental national output lost from the killing. Civilized people view government-sponsored murder as demented, the acts of barbarians and sociopaths. But, many aspects of life that we judge as bads, nevertheless, obey the law of demand.

Does democide obey the law of demand? Yes, it does. For my sample of 31 nations that killed 10,000 or more of their citizens, I find that a one percent increase in price (the logarithm of RGDP) is associated with a 1.4 percent decline in the number of citizens murdered. The regression coefficient is highly significant, and about half of the variation in democide is associated with the logarithm of per capita RGDP. (Scully, 1997)

So, there is some evidence that rising per capita income constrains murder by the state. This fact may help us understand the slowdown in the pace of killing in the Soviet Union and China. Under Stalin, about 43 million were murdered; after him, about 8 million. Under Chairman Mao, 35 million died; since then, less than a million. While economic performance was poor under socialism, there was some growth and economic advance. Comrades were getting more expensive to liquidate.

And, there is some crude historical evidence, as well. In the 13th century, 32 of 360 million people were murdered — about 9 percent of the population. And, this was a time before gunpowder. In the 17th century, the killing rate had fallen by half. In the 19th century, about 44 million were killed (3.7 percent of the world's population).

Alas, the fascists and communists reversed the trend in the 20th century, when 7.3 percent of the world's population were killed. Absent the 75 million killed by Hitler, Stalin, and Mao, about 2.5 percent of the world's population perished at the hands of their governments.

2. Democide and Genocide as Rent-seeking Activities

Humans prefer to dominate, and they dominate those they distrust and dislike. Antipathy may be official policy or it may arise spontaneously and be tolerated by government. The extreme form of antipathy is murder; less pernicious is discrimination. Enmity has economic implications. Discrimination transfers income from the minority to the majority, and is a form of rent-seeking.

Among authoritarian states, restrictions on minorities are fairly common. Such domination and rent-seeking arises through restrictions on occupational choice, denial of education, licensing, confiscation of land, nationalization of business, and so on. The dominant group earn rents from sanctioned restrictions, and has a vested interest in maintaining them. The rulers benefit from maintaining domination (bribery and corruption are endemic throughout the authoritarian world). Thus, part of the motivation for maintaining rule is to protect the rent-seeking capacity of the dominant group. Politicians extract a fee for providing the use of the coercive power of the state for that service.

Murder is the extreme form of enmity. Terror has been usefully employed to enforce ideology (the Inquisition, the Cultural Revolution, Muslim fundamentalism, etc.) or policy (e.g., the Soviet collectivization scheme). It is employed by authoritarian states to maintain power. Terror has an obvious chilling effect on enemies.

While it is impossible to know the value (not necessarily, pecuniary) of democide to the officials who have practiced it, it is possible to crudely calculate the lost national output arising from it. Democide makes life and property insecure. Such insecurity lowers savings. Reduced capital formation lowers the rate of economic growth. I hypothesize that the path of per capita income in nations that practice democide is below the path of income in nations that do not engage in it. By making comparisons of the paths of per capita income it is possible to estimate the order of magnitude of this form of rent-seeking activity.

3. Evidence

In principle, the rent-seeking loss associated with democide can be calculated by comparing the evolution of the economy before and after the democide with its path during the killing. But, that comparison would be dubious. Political murder often is not infrequent. We would not know whether the path of per capita income prior to demo-cide is free of political uncertainty or whether people fully recovered from it after. A better comparison would be with the growth path of countries that are broadly similar in political and economic development, but that have not committed democide.

To eliminate differences in income among countries, per capita real gross domestic product data were converted to indices, with 1960 as the base year. To compare growth paths, a comparison sample of non-democidal nations with a more or less similar stage of economic and political development is required. My comparison sample contained 23 countries (e.g., Egypt, Ivory Coast, Morocco, Dominican Republic, Jordan). A composite index was obtained by weighing each RGDP by its population share and summing. There are 33 democide nations in the sample (e.g., Algeria, Ethiopia, Rwanda, Guatemala, Iran, Pakistan). These nations were converted to an index of a representative democidal nation by weighing as described previously. Dividing the index of the democidal nations by the index of the non-democidal nations yielded an average value of 0.81. Thus, democidal rent-seeking is estimated to cost 19.2 percent of GDP.

To insure that the result is not a figment of the mix of comparison nations, I constructed a sample of eleven other mostly freer, less-developed, non-democidal nations (e.g., Botswana, Barbados, Jamaica, Fiji). The path of the index of this sample of nations lies above that of the index of the 23 autocratic, non-democidal nations. This is not surprising, since it is known that nations with freer institutions grow more rapidly than nations with less freedom.

It may be that the effect of democide on the path of real per capita income is not uniform across countries or continents. The scale of the killing may differ, people's attitude toward it may vary, and some may be better informed about what is going on. On this basis, Africa has suffered the most. Democidal rent-seeking is estimated to reduce per capita income by 25 percent. There is not much difference between Asia and Latin America (18.6 and 18 percent, respectively). Of the countries that were examined separately, the range was 18.2 percent (Philippines) to 61.6 percent (Angola).

4. Conclusion

Democide and genocide seemingly are activities of majority group domination and authoritarian rule. State-sponsored murder on a large scale has a long history. Despite crude weaponry, the Chinese emperors from the

Chin dynasty (221 BC) to the Ching (1911), exclusive of the Mongols, murdered 34 million. The Mongols did in 30 million in a tenth of the time. (Rummel, 1992, 1993)

But, exclusive of communist democide, there has been a historical decline in the rate of state-sponsored murder. I believe that this is due to rising per capita incomes, which make the cost in terms of lost national output too high, rather than to more humanity among dictators. Comparison of the growth path of the representative democidal nation with that of the representative non-democidal nation indicates that state-sponsored murder reduces national wealth by about 20 percent.

GERALD W. SCULLY

REFERENCES

Rummel, R.J. (1992). *Pre-20th Century Government Killing.* University of Hawaii at Manoa, Honolulu, Hawaii.

Rummel, R.J. (1993). Appendices: Centi-kilo murderers, 1900–1987. Haiku Institute of Peace Research.

Scully, G.W. (1997). "Democide and genocide as rent-seeking activities." *Public Choice*, 93(1–2): 77–97.

STRUCTURE-INDUCED EQUILIBRIUM

Why so much stability? (Tullock, 1981)

The Marquis de Condorcet (1785), who ultimately lost his head to Dr Guillotin's infamous invention, was the first known scholar to recognize that political outcomes under simple majority rule are inherently unstable (Rowley, 1987). Consider the problem of dividing a gift of $100 among three persons (Mueller, 1989: 63–64). Suppose that two of them reach an agreement to split the $100 between themselves, with $60 going to one and $40 to the other. The third person, who receives nothing, has an incentive to strike a bargain with the second, offering a split of, say $50–$50, which makes both of them better off than they would be under the initial proposal. Faced with desertion, the first person can destabilize the new coalition by offering to accept $45 for himself, leaving $55 for one of the others. And so on. While it can easily be shown that the Nash equilibrium to this zero-sum, pure redistribution game is an equal division of the $100 between two of the three players, the identities of the members of the winning coalition are indeterminable a priori. The game has three possible (and equally likely) outcomes, namely (V_1, V_2), (V_1, V_3), and (V_2, V_3), where the Vs denote the voter-players, and it is impossible to predict ahead of time which of these outcomes, if any, will emerge.

The theoretical possibility that simple majority rule can lead to an endless series of changing winning coalitions — a phenomenon known as 'cycling' — was revisited by Charles Dodgson ('Lewis Carroll') ([1876] 1987) a century after Condorcet first recognized it. Lost once again, the message from the eighteenth century French academicians ultimately was retrieved by Duncan Black (1948). Kenneth Arrow (1951) and other modern public choice scholars have since studied cycling at length (see Enelow, 1997, for a summary of the literature). Despite the theoretical possibilities, however, majority rule outcomes seem to be remarkably stable in practice. Committees, legislatures, and voters actually make decisions by simple majority rule and these decisions are not usually plagued by endless cycling. Why so much stability (Tullock, 1981)?

One answer to Tullock's question is that institutions exist which help prevent majority rule decisions from being subject to renegotiation or which facilitate the formation of stable winning coalitions. Equilibrium is induced by structure (Shepsle, 1978; Shepsle and Weingast, 1981). There are several possibilities in this regard. The most obvious of these involves the designation of an agenda-setter, someone with the authority to determine the order in which issues are brought to a vote. Supplemented by a set of mutually agreed-to constraints on the collective decision-making process, such as those provided by *Robert's Rules of Order*, which limit the possibility of defeated proposals resurfacing, the agenda-setter can block embryonic cycles. Of course, the agenda-setter may also use his authority to manipulate the order of votes in ways that produce outcomes more consistent with his own preferences than with those of the majority (McKelvey, 1976; Munger, 2001: 229–236). The agenda setter's position may confer fewer advantages in parliamentary systems, however, owing to the existence of multiple equilibria within the governing coalition (Helpman and Persson, 1998).

Stability in majority rule decision-making is also promoted by the common practice of adopting 'reversion points', or fallback positions that serve as baseline alternatives to the proposal being considered (for a general discussion, see the papers collected in Shepsle and Weingast, 1995). Spending reverts to its current level if a proposal to increase an agency's budget is defeated, for instance. The accepted interpretation of the law stands (*stare decisis*) unless the court votes affirmatively to overturn it. Baseline budgeting, deference to legal precedent, and similar such decision rules help avert cycling by reducing the dimensionality of the decision space. Only certain options compete against one another at a given time. In the limit, each vote is one-dimensional, namely a choice between the status quo and a well-specified alternative to it. Only two outcomes are then possible. Either the alternative fails to attract the support of a majority, in which case the status quo prevails, or the alternative dominates the existing equilibrium and the majority votes to displace it. If in the latter case the victorious alternative is adopted as the reversion point for subsequent decisions, the chances of cycling back to the status quo ante become remote.

This begs an important question: how is the dimension-reducing decision rule selected in the first place? If voters are sophisticated, they will foresee that restrictions on the range of options they are permitted to choose among also limit the range of possible outcomes, perhaps eliminating some of their most preferred alternatives from contention. As such, the adoption of a reversion point is itself a collective decision-making problem that transforms a superficially one-dimensional vote into a two-stage game (see Ordeshook, 1986).

By limiting the range of options voters may select among and, hence, making it less likely that the existing majority coalition will unravel, reversion points tend to sustain equilibrium outcomes. Logrolling, or vote trading, provides another source of stability in majority rule decisions (Stratmann, 1997). Individuals exchange their votes on collective decisions in which they have few pressing interests so as to form winning coalitions in support of issues in which they have greater personal stakes. Tullock's (1959) example is instructive. Three farmers face the problem of repairing the roads giving them individual access to the main highway. If maintenance proposals are voted on separately, none of the roads will be repaired because all of the benefits of collective action accrue to a single voter. Farmers A and B will vote against a proposal that requires them to contribute toward the repair of farmer C's access road, A and C will vote against repairing B's road, and so on. However, at least two of the roads will be repaired if the beneficiaries agree to support each other's spending proposals. Farmer B might agree to vote to repair farmer A's road in return for A's pledge to vote in favor of repairing B's, for instance.

Logrolling can facilitate the formation of stable winning coalitions, provided that voters' preferences differ in intensity (farmer A is willing to pay more for B's vote than C is, for example); cycling cannot be ruled out otherwise. (Bernholz, 1973, in fact argues that a cycle in votes will produce a cycle in vote trades.) Additionally, when the benefits of collective action exceed the costs, vote trading can be welfare enhancing in the sense that it enables proposals to be approved that would be bypassed in its absence. On the other hand, when the costs of financing collective benefits are shared equally, logrolling can lead to excessive spending owing to the fact that the members of the majority coalition do not bear the full costs of their own actions, some of which are shifted to the minority. Downs (1961) and Mueller (1989: 333–334) challenge this conclusion, however.

The observation that agenda-setters, reversion points, and logrolling are all part and parcel of the rules of the game that govern the normal workings of committees, legislatures, and other institutions of collective choice suggests that no one of them is sufficient by itself to ensure stability in majority rule decision-making. Indeed, there are a number of other institutional constraints that impose structure on collective decisions which, along with those discussed previously, evidently play complementary roles in promoting and maintaining majority-rule equilibria. Among these other institutional constraints are the assignment of proposals to subcommittees composed of individuals with strong interests in particular issues who control the items placed on the full committee's agenda, the appointment of independent commissions to work out the details of proposals that the majority has approved in principle, and the use of conference committees to resolve differences between the alternative versions of bills passed by the two chambers of a bicameral legislature (Basuchoudhary et al., 1999). Stability in majority-rule decision-making is also enhanced by the power of the executive veto (Crain and Tollison, 1979b; Carter and Schap, 1987), the brand-name capital of the legislature's majority party (Crain et al., 1988), the independent judiciary (Landes and Posner, 1975; Anderson et al., 1989; Shughart and Tollison, 1998), and the constitution itself (Crain and Tollison, 1979a; Anderson et al., 1990). The 'checks and balances' built into the Swiss political system, the division of responsibilities between the European Parliament and the EU Commission, and the delegation of monetary policymaking to independent central banks seem to have similar purposes and effects (Moser, 2000). In short, many of the institutions of democratic government learned by every schoolchild who studies European and American constitutional systems comprise the structure that induces equilibrium in majority rule decisions.

WILLIAM F. SHUGHART II

REFERENCES

Anderson, G.M., Martin, D.T., Shughart, W.F. II, and Tollison, R.D. (1990). "Behind the veil: The political economy of constitutional change." In W.M. Crain and R.D. Tollison (eds.), *Predicting politics: Essays in empirical public choice*, pp. 89–100. Ann Arbor: University of Michigan Press.

Anderson, G.M., Shughart, W.F. II, and Tollison, R.D. (1989). "On the incentives of judges to enforce legislative wealth transfers." *Journal of Law and Economics*, 32(April): 215–228.

Arrow, K.J. (1951). *Social Choice and Individual Values*. New York: Wiley.

Basuchoudhary, A., Pecorino, P., and Shughart, W.F. II (1999). "Reversal of fortune: The politics and economics of the super-conducting supercollider." *Public Choice*, 100(September): 185–201.

Bernholz, P. (1973). "Logrolling, Arrow paradox and cyclical majorities." *Public Choice*, 15(Summer): 87–95.

Black, D. (1948). "The decisions of a committee using a special majority." *Econometrica*, 16(July): 245–261.

Carter, J.R. and Schap, D. (1987). "Executive veto, legislative override, and structure-induced equilibrium." *Public Choice*, 52(3): 227–244.

Condorcet, Marquis de (1785). *Essai sur l'application de l'analyse à la probabilitié des décisions rendues à la pluraliste des voix*. Paris: De l'imprimerie royale.

Crain, W.M., Shughart, W.F. II, and Tollison, R.D. (1988). "Legislative majorities as nonsalvageable assets." *Southern Economic Journal*, 55(February): 303–315.

Crain, W.M. and Tollison, R.D. (1979a). "Constitutional change in an interest-group perspective." *Journal of Legal Studies*, 8(January): 165–175.

Crain, W.M. and Tollison, R.D. (1979b). "The executive branch in the interest-group theory of government." *Journal of Legal Studies*, 8(June): 55–89.

Dodgson, C.L. ([1876] 1987). "A method of taking votes on more than two issues," in D. Black (eds.) *The Theory of Committees and Elections*, Boston: Kluwer Academic Publishers. pp. 224–234.

Downs, A. (1961). "In defense of majority voting." *Journal of Political Economy*, 69(April): 192–199.

Enelow, J.M. (1997). "Cycling and majority rule," in D.C. Mueller (ed.) *Perspectives on Public Choice: A Handbook*, pp. 149–162. Cambridge: Cambridge University Press.

Helpman, E. and Persson, T. (June, 1998). "Lobbying and legislative bargaining." NBER Working Paper 6589.

McKelvey, R.D. (1976). "Intransitivities in multidimensional voting models and some implications for agenda control." *Journal of Economic Theory*, 12(June): 472–482.

Moser, P. (2000). *The Political Economy of Democratic Institutions*. Cheltenham, UK and Northampton, MA, USA: Edward Elgar.

Mueller, D.C. (1989). *Public Choice II: A Revised Edition of Public Choice*. Cambridge: Cambridge University Press.

Munger, M.C. "Voting," in W.F. Shughart II and L. Razzolini (eds.) *The Elgar Companion to Public Choice*. Cheltenham, UK and Northampton, MA, USA: Edward Elgar, 197–239.

Ordeshook, P.C. (1986). *Game Theory and Political Theory: An Introduction*. Cambridge: Cambridge University Press.

Rowley, C.K. (1987). "Borda, Jean-Charles de," in J. Eatwell, M. Milgate, and P. Newman (eds.) *The New Palgrave: A Dictionary of Economics*, vol. 1. London: Macmillan. pp. 262–263.

Shepsle, K.A. (1978). *The Giant Jigsaw Puzzle: Democratic Committee Assignments in the Modern House*. Chicago: University of Chicago Press.

Shepsle, K.A. and Weingast, B.R. (1981). "Structure-induced equilibrium and legislative choice." *Public Choice*, 37(3): 503–519.

Shepsle, K.A. and Weingast, B.R. (1995). *Positive Theories of Congressional Institutions*. Ann Arbor: University of Michigan Press.

Shughart, W.F. II and Tollison, R.D. (1998). "Interest groups and the courts." *George Mason Law Review*, 6(Summer): 953–969.

Stratmann, T. (1997). "Logrolling," in D.C. Mueller (ed.), *Perspectives on Public Choice: A Handbook*. Cambridge: Cambridge University Press, pp. 322–341.

Tullock, G. (1959). "Some problems of majority voting." *Journal of Political Economy*, 67(December): 571–579.

Tullock, G. (1981). "Why so much stability?" *Public Choice*, 37(2): 189–202.

SUPPLY OF PUBLIC GOODS

According to the theory of public finance built under the "social welfare function" maximisation principle (Atkinson and Stiglitz, 1980), governments must fiscally supply "public goods," i.e., the goods that have a complete or very important indivisibility: so that rivalry in consumption and exclusion of those who do not pay cannot be applicable (Samuelson, 1954, 1955) A general equilibrium system of equations may then be constructed in which, in addition to functions relating to market economy goods offered at their equilibrium prices, functions relating to pure and impure public goods also appear paid by tax prices or other public measures modelled on the nature and size of the relevant market failures. The reasoning goes on arguing that because the benefits of these goods may be enjoyed independently from their tax prices, citizens try to under-assess their preferences so that public goods are under supplied. The same conclusion is reached with a game theory approach in an institutional vacuum, assuming that each individual or group acting independently produces public goods that automatically provide benefit to others affecting their choice: the outcome is a Nash equilibrium characterised by under-production. (Cornes and Sandler, 1986). And the task of politicians committed to the public interest should therefore be that of re-addressing the balance in the allocation of resources between private and public goods. This set of theories, that so many academicians consider so obvious, is greatly misleading.

First of all, the aggregate social welfare function is a myth (Rowley and Peacock, 1975). In democracy, governments represent only the preferences of a majority of the electors, mostly the median voters. Furthermore, politicians are loose agents of them and operate by bureaucracies with their opportunistic behaviour. Parliaments do not vote on comprehensive social welfare functions but on budgets. And because of the intrinsic looseness of the principal-agent paradigm in representative democracy, what citizens may convey to their political representatives are, at best, sets of preferences. Arrow's theorem of impossibility of consistent choices applies to majority decisions (Arrow, 1951). And the prevailing majority may tax the minorities to finance goods benefiting majority (Wicksell, 1896; Peacock [on Toqueville], 1992; Buchanan and Tullock, 1962). It has been shown that this is also likely to happen under qualified majority, in normal parliamentary decisions, because this voting rule creates a quasi monopolistic situation making the political market non contestable (Forte, 1985). An excess of public expenditures on their benefits is likely to emerge since those who decide and get particular benefits (politicians, bureaucrats, pressure groups) do not pay the costs financed by taxes and debts. The assertion that Governments under-supply public goods because of the intrinsic imperfection of the fiscal nexus in the connection between taxes and public services rests on a wrong assumption. Precisely because public goods are paid by the fiscal nexus, i.e., through a "non market" transaction, disconnecting public goods from their "tax prices" government and bureaucracies are not constrained by the free market demand and financing. And therefore, as William Niskanen (1971) has argued, bureaucracies in search of power, may rationally expand the gross product to the point where the entire consumer surplus is destroyed. Or as I have argued (Forte, 2000), behaving as managers not considering the value for the stockholder, but the gross revenue under constraint of a minimum profit, bureaucrats may expand gross product to a point where citizens-taxpayers are left only with a minimum surplus, just enough to avoid their revolt. X inefficiency and leisure on the job (Peacock, 1983) are also likely to emerge in public bureaucracies. With a prisoner dilemma trap, one can show that the natural rational tendency of individual action, as for public goods, is not to under-supply but to over-supply. Indeed, each individual or group tries to get public supplies to their benefits paid by the general community. At the end everybody gets less benefits than the individual costs. If there is no institutional constraint to this tendency, taxpayers, who do not try to get expenses for their benefits with costs thrown on the community, act irrationally from the individual point of view. As for the prices functions, markets failures derive from *imperfections* of the signals whereas governments failures derive from the *absence* of price constraints.

At minimum, public supplies, if undertaken by public entities, should be provided by entrepreneurial organisations imitating, as far as possible, market economy firms and should be monitored with similar product and productivity parameters (Forte, 1983). A likely replay shall be that appropriate parameters here are intrinsically different. Actually public bureaucracies do not like to be organised and controlled with private firms techniques and resist, with their inherent power, to them.

A constitutional choices level must be set forth, with rules that constrain fiscal choices done at the ordinary level. (Buchanan and Tullock, 1962) Competition among governments operating at different jurisdictional levels and at the same level in different territorial areas may improve the chances of electors-taxpayers of having their preferences satisfied, if they have the choice of entering and leaving given governments as a clubs (Tiebout, 1956; Buchanan, 1965). But limits to mobility and imperfect information reduce the possibility of the citizens of considering governments as competing entities. For some public goods the effects spill-over from the area of the supplying "club" to the clubs with jurisdiction in different areas. And systems of taxation cannot be easily forged to connect the supply of goods of each government with tax prices on the members of their club (Oates, 1972; Oates and Schwab, 1988). Public institutions may be improved to develop a broader and bigger application of the club principle, particularly by single good provision (as for instance elementary schools). Nevertheless one must recognise that while, as for the market system, market failures appear as imperfections and limits, as for governments, supplies failures are intrinsic to the possibilities of collective action through democratic choices and the related principal-agents paradigms (Moe, 1984), from citizens to politicians and from politicians to bureaucracies. Thus one cannot argue that whenever there is an element of public good, there is a case for a public supply.

Nozick (1974) has shown that for so called pure public goods, as defence, justice and public order, the exclusion of those who do not want (or can) pay for them is technically possible. But, as he has argued, the supply of these goods by private market firms may lead to a monopoly, with a dangerous power of exploitation. Why one may assume that Governments could not exploit an unconstrained monopoly power given to them? Simply because welfare economists impose a nice social welfare function that enlightened politicians are supposed to maximise? In a public choice approach, federalism and clubs, with a multiplicity of competing government units, appear necessary, for the reduction of conflicts of preferences and of the dangers of exploitation (Pauly, 1970). However, it must be recognised that in addition to the monopoly argument a main reason why Government are charged of providing services of law and order in modern states is the interdependence of utilities of the members of a wide community as for these goods (or bads). Thus, some of them must be supplied uniformly to every one in the given wide community, independently from the specific willingness to pay. And the upper level of Government on the broadest available jurisdiction may appear as the most appropriate one, for some of these goods (Forte, 1977). Interdependence and conflict, not non excludability and non rivalry dominate this issue with a difficult equilibrium (Fedeli and Forte, 2001). On the other hand, since these goods are intrinsically divisible, some of them, may be appropriately left to the private associations: for instance private associations of professionals as the certified accountants, as it may be the case for the "correct accounting rules" for the corporations and groups of companies accounts. In the area of justice, arbitration may replace much of the official courts activities in civil cases and labour controversies, leaving the production of the rules on which to decide to the laws of the parliaments and to the customs.

For such goods as a lighthouse or many roads and tunnels or bridges and public transportation services the theoretical welfare economics argument for public supply are non rivalry, lack of (easy) excludability and external economies. Fixed costs often prevail and therefore pricing at average costs or close to it would imply a great wastage of consumer surplus (Dupuit, 1933; Hotelling, 1938). And even price at marginal cost might be wrong because of externalities as reduction of pollution and traffic congestion by public transportation services. All this is fine in a partial equilibrium analysis. But one must consider that the free provision or the supply in deficit must be paid by taxes or public debt. These too create distortions between marginal costs and prices plus additional welfare losses through transaction costs (Coase, 1946, 1947, 1988). And without the market economy budgetary constraint, X-inefficiency and excessive output may arise. Public economy failure must be compared with the private economy failures to which they are supposed to remedy. As for external economies the case for public intervention by subsidies and tax expenditures is limited by the fact that these have costs and are subject to failures, as stated by Buchanan (1962) in his criticism of the Pigouvian margins as allocation principle. Furthermore contracts among the interested persons, on the basis of improved property legal rules, may internalise externalities (Coase, 1960). The requisite of non excludability may change by a re consideration of the transaction costs involved. Lighthouses, a classic example of non excludable public goods, in the past have actually been financed by a toll on the ships that were approaching the ports (Coase, 1974; Peacock, 1979) and

this policy is even more feasible now with electronic means for all the ships that are aided in their navigation. Highways may be financed by tolls and the traffic may be eased by credit cards and telepass. Scientific research and cultural production may have components of public goods: but a reinforcement of legal institutions as patents and copy-right may increase the scope for scientific research and cultural activities with pecuniary remuneration (Forte, 1983, p. 150). Young may not be able to pay for their higher education and their parents may be unwilling or unable to cover these expenses. And one may argue that here there is a market failure, because banks could provide loans to the students to be repaid after graduation when employed if they had adequate information on their future gains and assurance that they would not cheat. But to remedy to this failure student loans scheme may be devised with public guarantee, that have a minimum cost for the government or no cost at all because of the possibility of taxing the incomes of the former students (Friedman, 1955; Peacock and Wiseman, 1964; Barr, 1991; Creedy, 1993). On the other hand, one may argue on public goods arguments, that higher education of merit students, being particularly beneficial to the cultural and scientific capital of the society, should be supported by community. But in fact several private institutions provide fellowships to students with good qualifications, precisely on the basis of these public good arguments, some times for their own interest, some times for prestige reasons and some times for altruism. Paretian redistribution does exist on private rational basis (Hochman and Rogers, 1969). One cannot argue that whenever there is a collective good argument there is a need for a public supply. Individual action by consumers of important shares of collective goods and collective action by non profit institutions may some time do the job.

But are all public goods those with the intrinsic "public nature" of non rivalry and non excludability? One can easily observe that most of the goods *actually supplied by governments* are not of this kind. Education, health, welfare intrinsically are rival and excludable supplies. Externalities may play some role in justifying their public supply, but hardly one may say that the "welfare state imperial construction" rests on external economies foundations. Welfare and education public supplies cannot be justified by non rivalry and non excludability. Their foundation is twofold: the equality of opportunity principle, i.e., a redistribution in favour of those who are unable to pay for these services; and limited rationality as "acrasia" or weakness of will and lack of adequate information for those who can pay for these merit goods. In ordinary choices they tend to under assess their future wellbeing while at as higher level of rationality they understand that this lack of telescopic sight is against their interest, so that they self constrain their action (Musgrave, 1959; Elster, 1979; Forte, 2000). Paradoxically to remedy the "acrasia" that induces people to overlook the future, grandiose public pension schemes mostly based on a pay as you go system and pervasive public health services funded by the tax system have been created that reduce the propensity of individuals to save for the future. The justification of spoiling the individuals of any responsibility for their health and old age rests only on a conception of the state as a Leviathan. In a different approach, with responsible actors more conducive to economic growth and distributive justice (Buchanan, 1986) a broader room must be left for individual choice about health and retirement providence. In this optic there is no reason to give a more favorable tax regime to the social security contribution and benefits than to the complementary contributions to private analogous insurance and pension funds. But if the foundation of the public supplies are redistribution and self constraint on irrational choices, why a monopolistic government supply should be preferred to other ways of supply with broader room for individual choice?

The main question is then why public goods of the various kinds so far considered should be supplied by public entities (Forte, 1967) rather that by private firms or non profit institutions. The reasons why one should prefer a supply of public goods by public institutions over a supply of them by private entities, given the above considered intrinsic failures of the public production, must be analysed case by case (Peacock, 1984; Blanckart, 1985; Byatt, 1985; Marchese, 1985), without a priori case in favour of the public supply as it is often implicitly done, confusing the case for a collective action by "public goods" with a case for a "public supply" of these public goods.

For the public goods that are grounded by supply side arguments, as the risks of private monopolies, the case for a public supply may be stronger than for those that are justified on the demand side by imperfect rationality and/or by distributive considerations. Admittedly services as those of external defence imply a political power that cannot be given to private armies. But procurement by outsourcing may be extensively practised, following the Coase-Williamson theory of the firm (Coase, 1937; Williamson, 1975, 1979). In the area of public museums, the service to the public may be assigned by a bid to private firms that shall finance themselves by tickets and other revenues from the visitors, revenues of collateral services and copy rights. Government officials may merely control this activity. As for the conservation of the museums items the Government in charge may rent the service of custody from private organisation and outsource to private professionals the task of cataloguing the items. Prisons too might be run by private firms under public control paid for their services (Forte, 1967). Historical and artistic buildings as heritage of the past as public good to be preserved for the present and future generation, do not need to be a public property, which often means nobody's property. Private owners, compensated by fiscal benefits on investment and maintenance expenditures, for the public constraints of proper preservation, may do a far better job, with a much lower cost for the Government, because more interested in their properties. Big bridges like that planned to connect Sicily to the continent that certainly shall provide a wide range of positive externalities may be built by project financing based primarily on revenues from tolls with the public subsidy becoming a minor factor. One cannot argue that the tolls shall leave some capacity unutilised, it is likely that they shall avoid the external economies of congestion. And one cannot argue that the government should provide subsidies in an amount equivalent of these externalities and for ever since these externalities shall be enduring. Beside the fact that they are hardly measurable, this is clearly an "all or nothing choice," so that much of the externalities are inframarginal (Buchanan and Stubblebine, 1969). Generally for public works projects with deferred profitability and important externalities private supply by project financing mostly financed by the market may conform to correct allocation principles and may do a better job with a much lower public cost than a public supply. Even for local streets and public lighting where to charge a toll is impossible, private initiative may be called for by project financing: instead of getting prices from the users, the private firms engaged in these activities, may get, by some kind of incentive contract, payments from the government proportioned to the units of services rendered. There is not much difference between a public subsidy to a municipal transportation service and a current transfer paid to private firms that undertake the above described supply of public highways and streets. Truly one might distinguish between "search (public) goods" where the effectiveness of the supply may be observed when it is made, by considering its objective qualities and quantities and "trust (public) goods" where the effectiveness of the supply can be assessed in the individual situations only with prohibitive cost and/or ex post, after a period o time (Tirole, 1988). This last may be the case of the pure scientific research. One may claim that for these trust good would be inefficient to rely on contract with private firms because it is difficult to currently control the effectiveness of the theoretical work done, as the pecuniary remuneration may be an insufficient motivation in pure science. Thus one may argue that this is a typical case of public goods where a supply by government entities is appropriate. But pure scientific research need not be done by governmental entities only. There are other institutions that, by their reputation, may be "trusted," among the non profit and quasi private as many Universities.

Let us now consider the public goods whose foundation lie on the failures of the market mechanism on demand side, as those in the area of education, arts, health, social security and aid to the "least favoured," where the state, as a paternalistic entity that "knows better," as mostly developed. As for the "welfare" goods that become public because of distributive reasons and imperfect rationality of individuals, *prima facie* vouchers (Peacock, 1983) and compulsory insurance (and a combination of the two) should be suggested to allow the individuals to be free to choose among the different suppliers. Vouchers appear well suited to health and education expenditures, but as it has been written for the British experience "the voucher was a challenge to the formidable fortress of paternalism, professional corporatism, monopoly and political authority that had long ruled British education. That the ramparts did not fall to the first intellectual assault was almost predictable" (Seldon, 1986, section VI). Compulsory private insurance, with freedom of choice of the insurers, is already applied for automobile accidents. It may be applied for accidents on work. It may be extended to the pensions area for retired workers to replace the pay as you go approach. One may argue that if all European countries that apply the pay as you go system for the retirement pensions schemes where shifting to the private insurance systems with funding schemes, there would not be enough supply of financial products on the market to satisfy this demand. In addition one may argue that a shift to funding schemes while paying the pensions via the pay as you go system is extremely difficult. But retirement compulsory private insurance with funding schemes need not to be alternative to the public system. They may be complementary to them. But it is extremely difficult to make these changes because here too there is a formidable fortress of paternalism, corporatism, monopoly and political authority. As for health one may argue that to replace the public health service with compulsory insurance would cause a perverse selection against the older and those with a bad health conditions. But compulsory insurance with private institutions may be suggested for some professions that have peculiar health risks. Granting that there is case for a *basic* free public health service, does not follow that this service should be provided by public institutions or that these should behave as monopolies in the territory in which are located. The case for a public supply of hospital services needs to be demonstrated by specific arguments as economies of scale (if any), better accountability of public institutions as for these delicate trust goods supplies because of the political responsibility and competition (Tirole, 1988). And central government gigantic public monopolies as those theorised and realised in the welfare state policies, hardly shall pass this scrutiny. Here again the voucher system for the free choice of the services may enhance efficiency and effectiveness of the supply.

At best the economic theories of public goods *per se* provide grounds to (not unlimited) public transfers and regulations, not to public supplies and public monopolies by governments and by their enterprises. Why the supply of public goods should be public in the various components of its supply and in its global financing needs to be demonstrated case by case, with the case for a public monopoly as a true exception.

FRANCESCO FORTE

REFERENCES

Arrow, K. (1951). *Social Choice and Individual Values*. New York: John Wiley and Sons. (Revised Edition 1963.)

Atkinson, A.B. and Stiglitz, J. (1980). *Lectures on Public Economics*. New York: McGraw-Hill.

Barr, N. (1991). "Income-contingent student loans: an idea whose time has come," in G.K. Shaw (ed.) *Economics, Culture and Education*. Brookfield: Elgar.

Buchanan, J.M. (1962). "Politics, policies and pigouvian margins," *Economica*.

Buchanan, J.M. (1965). "An economic theory of clubs." *Economica*, 32: 1–14.

Buchanan, J.M. (1986). *Liberty, Market and The State, Part Three: An Exploration in The Theory of Justice.* London: Harvester Press.

Buchanan, J.M. and Stubblebine, C. (1969). "Externality," in K.J. Arrow and T. Scitovsky (eds.) *Readings in Welfare Economics*. London: American Economic Association.

Buchanan, J.M. and Tullock, G. (1962). *The Calculus of Consent. Logical Fundations of Constitutional Democracy*. Ann Arbor: University of Michigan Press.

Coase, R. (1937). "The nature of the firm." *Economica*, 4.

Coase, R. (1946). "The marginal cost controversy." *Economica*, 13.

Coase, R. (1947). "The marginal cost controversy: some further comments." *Economica*, 14.

Coase, R. (1960). "The problem of social cost." *Journal of Law and Economics*, 3.

Coase, R. (1974). "The lighthouse in economics." *Journal of Law and Economics*, 17: 357–376.

Coase, R. (1988). *The Firm, The Market and The Law*. Chicago: University of Chicago Press.

Cornes, R. and Sandler, T. (1986). *The Theory of Externalities, Public Goods and Club Theory*. Cambridge: Cambridge University Press.

Creedy, J. (1993). *The Economics of Higher Education*. Broockfield, Vermont: E. Elgar.

Dupuit (1933). "De L'utilité Et De Sa Mesure," in M. De Bernardi (ed.) *Scritti Scelti*. La Riforma Sociale: Torino.

Elster, J. (1979). *Ulysses and The Sirens*. Cambridge: Cambridge University Press.

Fedeli, S. and Forte, F. (2001). "Minimising frustrations versus median voter's equilibria. A reasonable choice procedure." *Jahrbuch Für Neue Politische Ökonomie*. Tübingen: Mhr-Siebeck.

Forte, F. (1967). Why public goods should be public? Papers In Non-Market Decision Making.

Forte, F. (1977). "Principles for the assignment of public conomic functions in a setting of multi layer government," in *Studies on The Perspectives for The Public Finance Functions of The Community*, in *Report of The Study Group (Mc Dougall) on The Role of Public Finance In European Integration*, vol. II, *Individual Contribution and Working Papers, Commission of Te European Communities*, Vol. II, Bruxelles.

Forte, F. (1983). "Monitoring the productivity of bureaucratic behaviour," in H. Hanusch (ed.) *Anatomy of Government Deficiencies. Proceedings of a Conference Held at Diessen, July 22–25, 1980*. Berlin: Spinger-Verlag.

Forte, F. (1985). "Control of public-spending growth and majority rule," in A Cura, Di F. Forte and A Peacock (eds.) *Public Expenditure and Government Growth*. Oxford and New York: Blackwell, pp. 132–142.

Forte, F. (2000). *Principi Di Economia Pubblica*, Fourth Edition. Milano: Giuffré.

Friedman, M. (1955). "The role of ghovernment in education," in R.A. Solo (ed.) *Economics and Public Interest*. New Brunswik: Ritgers University Press.

Hochman, H.M. and Rogers, R. (1969). "Pareto optimal redistribution." *American Economic Review*, 542–557.

Hotelling, H. (1938). "The general welfare in relation to problems of taxation and of railways and utility rates." *Econometrica*, 242–269.

Marchese, C. (1985). "Market and non- market alternatives in the supply of public goods: Some empirical evidence," in F. Forte and A. Peacock (eds.) *Public Expenditure and Government Growth*. Oxford and New York: Blackwell.

Moe, T.M. (1984). "The new economics of organization." *American Journal of Political Science*, 28.

Musgrave, R.A. (1959). *The Theory of Public Finance*. Mc Graw Hill.

Niskanen, W.A. (1971). *Bureaucracy and Representative Government*. Chicago: Aldine.

Nozick, R. (1974). *Anarchy, The State and Utopia*. New York: Basic Books.

Oates, W.E. (1972). *Fiscal Federalism*. New York: Harcourt, Brace and Jovanovich.

Oates, W.E. and Schwab, R. (1988). "Economic competition among jurisdiction: efficiency enhancing or distortion inducing?" *Journal of Public Economics*, 35: 333–354.

Pauly, M.V. (1970). "Optimality, 'public goods', and local government: A general theoretical analysis." *Journal of Political Economy*, 78: 572–585.

Peacock, A.T. (1979). "The limitations of public goods Theory. The Lighthouse Revisited," in A.T. Peacock (ed.) *The Economic Analisys of Government and Related Schemes*. Oxford: Robertson.

Peacock, A.T. (1983). "Education Voucher Schemes — Strong Or Weak?" *Economic Affairs*, 3, 2.

Peacock, A.T. (1983). "Public inefffeciency: informational and institutional constraints," in H. Hanusch (ed.) *Anatomy of Government Deficiencies. Proceedings of A Conference Held At Diessen, July 22–25, 1980*. Berlin: Spinger-Verlag.

Peacock, A.T. (1984). "Privatisation in Perspective." *The Three Banks Review*.

Peacock, A.T. (1992). *Public Choice Analysis in Historical Perspective*. Cambridge: Cambridge University Press.

Peacock, A.T. and Wiseman, J. (1964). *Education for Democrats*, Institute of Economic Affairs, London.

Rowley, C.K. and Peacock, A.T. (1975). *Welfare Economics a Liberal Restatement*. Oxford: Martin Robertson.

Samuelson, P. (1954). "The pure theory of public expenditure," *Review of Economic and Statistics*, 36: 387–389.

Samuelson, P. (1955). Diagrammatic exposition of A pure theory of public expenditure, *Review of Economic and Statistics*, 37: 350–356.

Seldon, A. Ed. (1986). *The Riddle of The Voucher. An Inquiry Into The Obstacles To Introducing Choice and Competition In State Schools*. London: Institute of Economic Affairs.

Tiebout, C.M. (1956). "A pure theory of local expenditures." *Journal of Political Economy*, 64: 416–424

Tirole, J. (1988). *The Theory of Industrial Organisation*, Cambridge, Mass: The Mit Press.

Wicksell, K. (1896). "A New Principle of Just Taxation," in R.A. Musgrave and A.T. Peakock (eds.) *Classics in the Theory of Public Finance*. London: McMillan (1958).

Williamson, O. (1975). *Markets and Hierarchies*. New York: Free Press.

Williamson, O. (1979). Transaction costs economics: The governance of contractual relations. *Journal of Law and Economics*, 22: 233–262.

THE SUPREME COURT

For many decades, the attention devoted to the U.S. Supreme Court by positive political analysis lagged behind study of the executive and legislative institutions much like public and media attention. Historians, biographers, and legal theorists provided most of the articles and books regarding the Court. Even among the constitutional framers, the discussions concerning the Court's structure paled in comparison with the other branches. The main debate turned on the method of judicial selection that the framers thought would best insulate judges from external influences. These debates are related in many sources such as James Madison's notes (Scott, 1893) as well as anti-federalist collections.

In spite of the framers stated intention to insulate justices from political incentives by appointing them for a "term of good behavior," social scientists in economics, political science, and law have increasingly searched for incentive effects on judicial behavior in general and Supreme Court behavior in particular. Baum (1997), Epstein and Knight (1998), and Clayton and Gillman (1998) provide comprehensive discussions of positive explanations of judicial decision making. In the broadest terms, these explanations can be divided along two lines: (i) those stressing incentives internal to the Court, and (ii) those stressing incentives external to the Court.

Among the studies that investigate incentives internal to the Court, "attitudinal" models rely on the personal ideologies of the justices along with the roots those ideologies in the background and experiences of justices. Segal and Spaeth (1993), and Epstein et al. (1998) are examples of this kind of approach that lies on the border between psychology and public choice. A second strand of the internal incentive explanations emphasizes Court rules and traditions. For example, Segal and Spaeth (1996) examine the importance of the doctrine of *stare decisis* on justice behavior. On a third front developing in more recent years, several authors have directed their attention to bargaining and influence games arising among justices in their search for majority coalitions. Baird et al. (1995) extensively reviews these kinds of game theoretic situations in legal settings. Ferejohn and Weingast (1992a,b) and Wahlbeck et al. (1998) provide empirical analysis of bargaining incentives for judges and Supreme Court justices.

Landes and Posner's (1975) landmark contribution paved the way for the other line of research emphasizing incentives external to the Court. While the contributions cited above can all be viewed as positive political models, this second category initiated by Landes and Posner is more indicative of traditional public choice models in its focus upon the influence of interest groups, legislators, and voters. The Landes and Posner article postulates that the judiciary maximizes the present value of legislation from the perspective of the enacting legislature. In spite of the Court's ability to overturn legislation, Landes and Posner develop the idea that the independent judiciary functions to make bargains struck between voters and legislative more durable. In this way, Landes and Posner turn the stated intentions of the constitutional framers on their head.

Rather than limiting interest group politics, the independent judiciary structure promotes and facilitates it. Their empirical support for their model is not extensive. In an appendix they estimate preliminary results for Court reversals, looking at factors such as tenure of justices and the number of bills passed by Congress

Subsequent contributions have more fully developed theoretical and empirical models of external influences on the Court. Some look specifically at the Supreme Court while others examine the federal judiciary at large. The constraints considered include the power of Congress to remove justices, alter the number of justices, and determine judicial branch funding. For example, Toma (1991) finds Congress can signal justices its desires and influence outcomes through the budgeting process. Using data from both the Supreme Court and lower federal courts, De Figueiredo and Tiller (1996) find that Court expansion is linked to political alignment in Congress. In addition to congressional influence, other studies have considered the effects of public opinion on the Court. McCubbins et al. (1995) find evidence that changes in the size of the federal judiciary have had an effect upon legal theories. Gely and Spiller (1992) find that while Roosevelt's court packing threat had little influence on voting behavior of justices, their decisions were closely linked to electoral outcomes. Spiller and Spitzer (1992) explain legal doctrines in terms of the current political environment.

Most contributions analyzing Court behavior have examined majority opinions of the Court or shifts in those majority opinions. A much smaller set of studies examines variations in consensus among justices. Descriptive data compiled by Epstein et al. (1996) documents the abrupt breakdown in consensus after the 1930s as measured by the proportion of cases decided by a one-vote margin, with concurring opinions, and with a dissenting opinion, and others. Posner (1996: 357) identifies the increased caseload facing the Court and the accompanying decline in the percent of cases reviewed as the "standard explanation" for the decline in consensus. As the caseload increases and the percent reviewed declines, the cases selected for review grow more difficult and contentious. However, this explanation is little more than speculative to date in that little or no evidence has been presented supporting the claim. The other common explanation is that statutory change, such as the Judges Bill of 1925, altered jurisdiction over cases and led to greater dissension. Haynie (1992) reviews the evidence.

Beyond these external influences, factors internal to the courts have been used to explain the fluctuation in consensus. For instance, Walker et al. (1988) highlight the role of the Chief Justice in maintaining "consensual norms." Calderia and Zorn (1998) develop an error correction model of dissenting and concurring opinions stretching from 1800 to 1991 and find evidence that the breakdown in consensus can be attributed, in part, to leadership of the court.

In evaluating the explanations of either majority opinions or variations in consensus, surprisingly few contributions have stressed the *ex ante* screening of Supreme Court justices as a means by which interest groups influence subsequent voting behavior and disagreements between justices. Landes and Posner do include tenure of justices in their model of Court reversals, but it only indirectly measures similarities and differences among justices based on characteristics of the screen. As is well known, the selection screen for the U.S. Supreme Court consists of two primary components — the presidential nomination and the confirmation hearings and vote by the Senate. The influence of this power is seen in the fact that nearly all justices are appointed from the same party as the President. The power of the confirming Senate resides in its effective veto power over nominees. Other than debates about which of these screens influences Court composition most heavily, the importance of these screens for Court outcomes are still largely unexamined.

Another seldom-studied aspect of the Supreme Court is its influence on socioeconomic outcomes. Almost all the attention has focused on effects on the Court rather than effects of the Court. What efforts have been made primarily examine the impact of individual Court decisions or policy shifts on specific issues. Becker and Feeley (1973) is an example. Johnson (1979) broadened the scope somewhat by looking at the effect of the Supreme Court on lower court decision making. The study taking the widest view to date is probably Bussiere (1998), who looks at the impact of the Court on the growth of the welfare state. Rosenberg (1991) considers the potential for broader social impact of the Court.

Beyond the effects of majority outcomes, the variations in Court consensus may also have important, but as yet, unstudied effects. Posner (1996) suggests that greater dissension within the Supreme Court reduces its ability to perform its tasks as efficiently and reduces the consistency and long-run stability of decisions. The importance of stability in basic institutions of political economy for economic development has long been emphasized and more recently confirmed using cross-country studies such as Barro (1997). Where there is broad agreement between justices on a given Court or across Courts over time, the basic rules-of-the game for society remain relatively stable. Divisive decision making within or across Courts amounts to the decision for millions of people resting in the hands of one swing vote on the Court and lack durability. Rather than relying on a relatively stable set of basic rules based on Court consensus, individual and organizational decision makers face greater uncertainty when Court divisiveness increases.

BRIAN GOFF

REFERENCES

Baird, D.G., Gerner, R., and Picker, R.C. (1995). *Game Theory and the Law*. Cambridge: Harvard University Press.

Barro, R.J. (1997). *Determinants of Economic Growth: A Cross-Country Empirical Study*. Cambridge, MA: MIT Press.

Baum, L. (1997). *The Puzzle of Judicial Behavior*. Ann Arbor: University of Michigan Press.

Becker, T.L. and Feeley, M.M. (eds.) (1973). *The Impact of Supreme Court Decisions*. New York: Oxford University Press.

Bussiere, E. (1998). "The Supreme Court and the development of the welfare state: judicial liberalism and the problem of welfare rights," in C. Clayton and H. Gillman (eds.) *Supreme Court Decision-Making: New Institutional Approaches*. Chicago: University of Chicago Press.

Caldiera, G. and Zorn, C.J.W. (1998). "Of time and consensual norms in the Supreme Court." *American Journal of Political Science*, 42(July): 874–902.

Clayton, C. and Gillman, H. (eds.) (1998). *Supreme Court Decision Making: New Institutionalist Approaches*. Chicago: University of Chicago Press.

De Figueiredo, J.M. and Tiller, E.H. (1996). "Congressional control of the courts." *Journal of Law and Economics*, 39(October): 435–462.

Epstein, L. and Knight, J. (1998). *Choices Judges Make*. Washington, DC: Congressional Quarterly Press.

Epstein, L., Hoekstra, V., Segal, J.A., and Spaeth, H.J. (1998). "Do political preferences change? A longitudinal study of U.S. Supreme Court justices." *Journal of Politics*, 60(August): 801–818.

Epstein, L., Segal, J.A., Spaeth, H.J., and Walker, T.G. (1996). *The Supreme Court Compendium: Data, Decisions, and Developments*. Washington, DC: Congressional Quarterly Press.

Ferejohn, J.A. and Weingast, B.R. (1992a). "Limitation of statutes: strategic statutory interpretation." *Georgetown Law Journal*, 80(February): 565–582.

Ferejohn, J.A. and Weingast, B.R. (1992b). "A positive theory of statutory interpretation." *International Review of Law and Economics*, 12(2): 263–279.

Gely, R. and Spiller, P.T. (1992). "The political economy of Supreme Court constitutional decisions: The case of Roosevelt's Court-packing plan." *International Review of Law and Economics*, 12(1): 45–67.

Haynie, S.L. (1992). "Leadership and consensus on the U.S. Supreme Court." *Journal of Politics*, 54(November): 1158–1169.

Johnson, C.A. (1979). "Lower court reactions to Supreme Court decisions: a quantitative examination." *American Journal of Political Science*, 23(November): 792–804.

Landes, W.M. and Posner, R.A. (1975). "The independent judiciary in an interest group perspective." *Journal of Law and Economics*, 18(December): 875–091.

McCubbins, M., Noll, R.G., and Weingast, B.R. (1995). "Politics and the courts: a positive theory of judicial doctrine and the rule of law." *Southern California Law Review*, 68(September): 1631–1683.

Posner, R.A. (1996). *The Federal Courts: Challenge and Reform.* Cambridge, MA: Harvard University Press.

Rosenberg, G.N. (1991). *The Hollow Hope: Can Courts bring about Social Change.* Chicago: University of Chicago Press.

Scott, E.H. (ed.) (1893). *Journal of the Constitutional Convention, kept by James Madison.* Chicago: Scott, Foresman, and Company.

Segal, J.A. and Spaeth, H.J. (1996). "The influence of *stare decisis* on the votes of U.S. Supreme Court justices." *American Journal of Political Science*, 40(November): 971–1003.

Segal, J.A. and Spaeth, H.J. (1993). *The Supreme Court and the Attitudinal Model.* New York: Cambridge University Press.

Spiller, P.T. and Spitzer, M. (1992). "Judicial choice of legal doctrines." *Journal of Law, Economics, and Organization*, 8(March): 8–46.

Toma, E. (1991). "Congressional influence and the Supreme Court: the budget as a signaling device." *Journal of Legal Studies*, 20(January): 131–146.

Wahlbeck, P., Spriggs, J. and Maltzman, F. (1998). "Marshalling the Court: bargaining and accommodation on the U.S. Supreme Court." *American Journal of Political Science*, 42(January): 294–315.

Walker, T., Epstein, L., and Dixon, W.J. (1988). "On the mysterious demise of consensual norms in the United States Supreme Court." *Journal of Politics*, 50(May): 361–389.

T

TAKINGS AND PUBLIC CHOICE: THE PERSUASION OF PRICE

The Fifth Amendment of the United States Constitution concludes, "nor shall private property be taken for public use without just compensation." What is known as the "just compensation" or "eminent domain" or "takings" clause is also present (or judicially construed to be present) in every state constitution and in the officially-proclaimed practice of most governments around the world. Yet the takings issue remains controversial, as is suggested by the many treatments of it by scholars who reflect the public-choice tradition (Ellickson, 1977; Epstein, 1985; Farber, 1992; Fischel, 1995; Levmore, 1991; Miceli and Segerson, 1996; Siegan, 1980; Wyeth, 1996). This essay will illustrate how a public choice approach can illuminate some of the important issues. The plan is to explain how the present distinction between physical takings and regulatory takings causes governments to choose too much regulation.

The idea that owners of property should be compensated is relatively uncontroversial when applied to actions in which the government takes physical possession of the property in question, as when it seeks to build a road, a dam, or a public building on private land. Compensable "physical invasion" includes instances in which the government itself takes title (even if it does not occupy the property), entitles private parties to trespass without taking title, or causes a detrimental physical occupation by water or foreign material. In most physical invasion cases, the government attempts first to buy the land (or an easement) on the open market. Unlike most other market participants, however, the government's right of eminent domain entitles it to force reluctant landowners to give up title in return for a court's determination of just compensation. Just how much compensation is "just" is often a matter of controversy (Goldberg et al., 1987; Kanner, 1973), but that something is owed by the government is usually not disputed in these instances.

The more controversial aspects of takings arise when the government establishes or changes a regulation that causes some properties to decline in value. Examples include rezoning formerly residential (but undeveloped) land for open space, restricting economic activity in certain areas because of the presence of wetlands or endangered species, and requiring that underground mining be curtailed to protect surface owners. In these instances, the government usually declines to offer just compensation even though the loss to the owner may be almost as great as if the government had taken the property for a roadway. This dichotomy in compensation practice — almost always pay for physical invasion, almost never pay for regulation — is the focus of this essay.

In the public choice view, government is not a neutral, third-party referee in matters concerning regulations and eminent domain. The scope and content of regulations will depend crucially on how the costs are distributed. This is in contrast to the black-letter law on the subject, which does little to inquire about the political process and usually takes the government's justifications for its actions at face value. The epitome of this deference is the U.S. Supreme Court's view of the "public use" clause, which many commentators regard as prohibiting the government from taking private property (with compensation) and giving it to another party for his private use (Epstein, 1985; Merrill, 1986; Paul, 1987). The Court agrees that takings must be for public use, but it accepts without inquiry almost any legislative declaration that, say, a private shopping center or an automobile assembly plant is a "public use." The possibility that private parties may be operating through the legislative process to further their private interests is largely disregarded.

The public choice approach regards the government as responding to the economic interests of those involved in the process. The obligation to pay will shape the behavior of the government's actions; they are not "exogenous" to the model. In this respect, a government agency's behavior is analogous to that of a private firm. The agency possesses a budget constraint, and officials have to decide whether purchase of certain inputs exceeds the priority of other items in its budget, or whether it is worth requesting the legislature to raise taxes to obtain additional funds to purchase them. In weighing these considerations, the government undertakes the same sort of benefit-cost analysis that private individuals must do when making a purchase: Would the money spent on purchasing the land possibly be better spent on some other project or left in the hands of taxpayers?

In introductory microeconomics, a private firm's decisions about how to produce something depends not just on technology and resources, but the relative prices of those resources. Farmers can produce raw food and fiber, for example, with inputs of land, labor, and capital. If labor is inexpensive, farm owners will hire many workers to plant, cultivate, and harvest their crops. They will substitute towards labor and away from expensive machinery and other forms of capital. If labor becomes relatively costly, however, farm owners will find it worth their while to purchase and employ sophisticated machinery to plant, cultivate, and harvest. The relative prices of inputs will also affect what crops they raise. Those that require intensive husbanding by hand will be planted where labor is less costly, while those that can be tended largely by machinery will be planted where labor is expensive.

The "inputs" for the government must be characterized differently than they would for a private firm. The government often has a choice between accomplishing its goals by acquiring title to land or by regulating it while leaving it in the hands of the private owners. The alternative inputs, in other words, are not labor and capital, but regulation and acquisition.

To provide a concrete example of a trade off, consider government efforts to protect an urban area along a major river from flooding. The government could build flood-control dams upstream in order to prevent the floods from occurring. This would obviously involve acquisition of land for the dam and for the area subject to periodic inundation. (As one can see, what the dam does is shift the flood damage upstream to presumably cheaper land in rural areas.) Another way to reduce flood damage in urban areas, though, is to regulate development in flood-prone areas downstream (White, 1986). Such regulation is not entirely paternalistic, in the sense that property owners are prevented from accepting risks of flooding to themselves. In major floods, buildings that become unmoored by the torrent become additional agents of destruction as they hit other buildings and bridges downstream, and personal liability for such damage is nearly impossible to establish after the fact.

As the reader can easily surmise, cost-minimizing flood control programs would most likely involve a combination of regulation of downstream land and acquisition of upstream land to build dams and levies. The difficulty arises from the fact that one input to flood control, regulation, can seem much cheaper than the other, acquisition, if regulation does not require compensation. For example, an optimal amount of flood control might involve a dam that costs $50 million and regulations that reduce downstream floodplain owner's property value by $30 million (net of the gain to property value from less flood damage). To be scrupulous in this comparison, it should be noted that the $50 million for the dam must include, besides the opportunity cost of the resources taken, the costs of condemnation and the excess burden of additional taxes needed to finance the compensation.

Assume now that the same degree of flood control could be had by building no dam at all but adopting more widespread and stringent land-use regulations that impose a net

cost of $100 million. Clearly the former method (dam and moderate regulation) is less costly by $20 million. But if the government agency charged with flood control does not have to compensate landowners for regulation, it may be tempted to undertake the latter strategy (regulation only), even though it is more costly to society. Moreover, it may be tempted to use its regulatory powers to extend flood "protection" to areas where the costs of such protection exceed the benefits to those protected.

In general, underpricing regulatory activity relative to acquisition in most circumstances induces overregulation and excessive expansion of government activities. The agency responds rationally to the price schedule it faces, just as a firm would expand its labor-intensive activities if it did not have to pay for labor. One exception arises when those burdened by the regulation are politically influential and thus can constrain the agency's choices. Indeed, some historical accounts of the development of just compensation for landowners in England points to the political influence of land-owning barons (Stoebuck, 1972). But the political defense often fails for regulation, since those victimized by the regulation may be a small minority who are not even resident in the jurisdiction, which is commonly the case for suburban landowners (Ellickson, 1977). Moreover, the government agency may be captured by interest groups who receive the benefits of its regulatory activities but do not bear its costs. Such agencies may be sufficiently independent — indeed, may have been deliberately made independent — that they can resist political pressure from those who bear the costs.

The objection voiced by many scholars who are not influenced by public choice is that the government simply does not make such calculations. Defenders of the status-quo (no compensation for regulation) argue that the government is different from a private actor. Government agencies are supposed to promote the public welfare, not make a profit for shareholders. Because the agency is charged with maximizing well-being, it actually does take account of the value of economic opportunities that are foregone as a result of regulation.

There is a situation in which a regulator might actually behave this way. Private developers sometimes acquire large amounts of contiguous land on which to build houses. Prior to selling the houses (or the prepared lots), the developer often imposes covenants that bind the purchasers to observe a list of regulations. These regulations look much like those of a typical government-imposed zoning ordinance, except that the private regulations are often much more detailed and intrusive. They go beyond saying where the houses must be placed and what they can be used for. These private regulations often dictate what kinds of vehicles may be placed in driveways, what color the homes may be painted, and what sort of furniture may be put on the front porch.

Yet the private developer does not pay anyone to accept these regulations. To the contrary, he expects buyers of homes to pay a premium for their existence. He does not have to price his regulations explicitly because he feels the full opportunity cost of them. If he adopts regulations that repel most buyers, it will lower the value of his assets. If he adopts too lenient a set of regulations, buyers will likewise be shy of living in a densely-developed community in which their neighbors may be able to do things that lower their property's value.

It is arguable that sometimes governments behave the same way as private developers do. A small municipality consisting entirely of homeowners and whose land is used only for housing is apt to be governed by members of their own group. If they propose a general regulation that prohibits renting homes to students from a nearby university, they are apt to feel both the benefit and cost of such a decision. The benefit would be a more peaceable neighborhood and hence higher home values, while the cost would be the foregone revenue that each owner might have gotten had she decided to rent her property to students. In this situation, a decision to adopt such a regulation is not much different from that which a private developer would do.

The situation changes greatly, however, when the government agency can subject to regulation the property of people who are not members of the governing faction. Here a more explicit cost in the form of just compensation can be helpful to prevent the excessive use of regulation. I will describe a famous example that came to light in Lucas v. South Carolina Coastal Council, 505 U.S. 1003 (1992).

The South Carolina Coastal Council had in 1988 altered the land-use regulations pertaining to building on private property along the oceanfront beaches of the state. Seaward of a Council-drawn line in the sand, no development of any kind was permitted. The Council was complying with a recently passed state legislation. The legislature cast its rationale for the prohibition on development as a matter of preventing public harms such as beach erosion, storm damage to homes, and destruction of wildlife habitat. In order to insulate the Council's land use decisions from political influence, the legislature decreed that the decisions of the Council were not subject to landowner requests for variances or other exceptions.

David Lucas owned two beachfront lots, each about one-third acre in area, that were within the new zone on which no permanent structures could be built. He had purchased the two parcels prior to the adoption of the new regulations for about one million dollars. The effect of the new regulations was to leave his investment nearly worthless. Having no means of appealing his classification, Mr. Lucas sought in court to compel the state to pay him for the denial of economic use of his land.

The trial judge held the Council's new regulation to be a taking, given that no economic use for Lucas's land remained. The state supreme court reversed. Accepting the state legislature's determination that building along the beach was a "harmful" activity, the state court held that no compensation was due despite the complete wipeout of economic use. Faced with Lucas's Fifth Amendment claim that this amounted to a regulatory taking, the South Caroline Supreme Court declared that regulations meant to prevent "harms," as declared by the legislature, were not compensable.

The U.S. Supreme Court reversed the South Carolina Supreme Court. Justice Scalia's opinion expressed a public-choice insight. He worried that if the Court always deferred to regulatory legislation that prevented "harms," the legislature would go about recasting the language of its regulations to avoid the obligation to compensate. A highway, to use an example not used by Justice Scalia, could be built much more cheaply if existing homes and businesses in a projected right of way could be said to be "harmful" to the public.

And from the road-builder's point of view, such buildings are harmful to his mission. It is not difficult to see how people who specialize in a single activity can persuade themselves that activities inconsistent with their enterprise can be so perverse as to be labeled "harmful." Environmental and planning agencies would seem no different from highway departments in this respect.

Yet if government agencies were given this license, they could obtain property rights of great value that the government would otherwise be unwilling to pay for. Wildlife preserves, scenic views, and open space could be established without the need to compensate owners whose activities were curtailed. They could even leverage regulation into acquisition at low cost by downzoning (under the harm-prevention rubric) the desired land and then purchasing it at the now-diminished price. To forestall this opportunism in cases of complete economic wipeout, Scalia's opinion held that such regulations were compensable under the takings clause unless grounded in "background principles" of state law. While the provenance of such principles remains unclear, the thrust of Scalia's idea is that they should sufficiently remote in time as to be removed from verbal manipulation by the present legislature.

The Lucas decision is subject to the criticism that its holding can be invoked only against regulations that are so extreme as to leave owners with no viable economic use whatsoever. Few regulators are so dull as to be unable to meet this criterion by, say, allowing a few tents on land best suited for homes, thereby keeping it from being developed. The property owner who can get some economic use by pitching tents but not houses on her land gets nothing under the *Lucas* criterion.

Lucas is not invoked here to explicate Constitutional principles, though. It is to show how perceptions of cost affect government behavior. The eventual outcome in *Lucas* exquisitely illustrates how government agencies respond to changes in relative prices. The evidence emerged not in the court opinion but in the subsequent settlement of the case. After the U.S. Supreme Court's decision, the state of South Carolina decided to settle the case by purchasing Mr. Lucas's two lots. What did it do with the lots whose development it had argued was irreparably harmful to the environment? Well, it had just paid almost a million dollars for them. It decided to recoup its money by selling them to a developer to build houses upon (Fischel, 1995, ch. 1; Lucas, 1995). The state even declined the offer by an inland neighbor who sought to purchase one of the lots (for about eighty percent of the asking price) and keep it undeveloped in order to preserve his seaward view. When I revisited the site with Mr. Lucas and his attorney, Jerry Finkel, in March of 2000, there was a large house on one of the lots, and the other was still on the market.

Some see this story as an example of government hypocrisy — professing one thing but doing another. Public choice tends to make one less judgmental, even of this remarkable about-face. The *Lucas* outcome is an example of how the price one has to pay affects behavior. Prior to the *Lucas* decision, South Carolina perceived the price of Lucas's lot (and others like it) as being low, since it did not expect to have to pay for them. At that price — zero dollars and zero cents — even the least environmentally-sensitive legislator would have to concede that environmental values surely should prevail. No highways or hospitals or airports — that is, alternative uses for the state's money — needed to be given up to preserve the coast. The legislature did not have to risk the wrath of voters by raising taxes to pay for the lots. All it had to do was pass a regulation, whose burden fell upon a small number of landowners.

Once the state came into possession of the land, however, it had reason to pay attention to its market price relative to its environmental value. Agents of the new owner (the state) now surely noticed that the properties in question were among the few lots along several hundred yards of this beach that did not already have large homes upon them. They are packed side-by-side, so that Lucas's vacant lots look like two missing pickets in a long fence. The state's agents then surely noticed that developers were willing to pay nearly half a million dollars for each of the lots, and the state's agents did what rational and faithful public servants should do: They sold the lots to developers.

The state had not changed its intrinsic values. It valued the environment no less after the case than before. The state simply responded to the higher price of preserving this tiny (less than one acre) stretch of the beach and did the sensible thing. It is no more hypocritical for them to have done so than it would be for an owner of a farm to switch from human pickers to mechanical pickers once the wages of farm laborers went up.

The just compensation clause can viewed as a device that keeps government officials from excessive enthusiasm. Having to pay money out of scarce budgetary resources makes officials calculate whether it is worthwhile to undertake a particular project. By applying methods of analyzing individual choice to the public sector, public choice offers insights into an important constitutional question that other approaches might not.

WILLIAM A. FISCHEL

REFERENCES

Ellickson, Robert C. (1977). "Suburban growth controls: An economic and legal analysis." *Yale Law Journal*, 86 (January): 385–511.

Epstein, Richard A. (1985). *Takings: Private Property and the Power of Eminent Domain.* Cambridge, Mass.: Harvard University Press.

Farber, Daniel A. (1992). "Economic analysis and just compensation: An anti-discrimination theory of takings." *International Review of Law and Economics*, 12: 125–138.

Fischel, William A. (1995). *Regulatory Takings: Law, Economics, and Politics.* Cambridge, MA: Harvard University Press.

Goldberg, Victor P., Thomas W. Merrill, and Daniel Unumb (1987). "Bargaining in the Shadow of Eminent Domain: Valuing and Apportioning Condemnation Awards between Landlord and Tenant." *UCLA Law Review*, 34 (April): 1083–1137.

Kanner, Gideon (1973). "Condemnation Blight: Just How Just Is Just Compensation?" *Notre Dame Lawyer*, 48 (April): 765–810.

Levmore, Saul (1991). "Takings, Torts, and Special Interests." *Virginia Law Review*, 77 (October): 1333–1368.

Lucas, David (1995). *Lucas vs. the Green Machine: Landmark Supreme Court Property Rights Decision by the Man Who Won It Against the Odds.* Charleston, SC: Alexander Books.

Merrill, Thomas W. (1986). "The Economics of Public Use." *Cornell Law Review*, 72 (November): 61–116.

Miceli, Thomas J. and Kathleen Segerson (1996). *Compensation for Regulatory Takings: An Economic Analysis with Applications.* Greenwich, CT: JAI Press.

Paul, Ellen Frankel (1987). *Property Rights and Eminent Domain.* New Brunswick: Transaction Press.

Siegan, Bernard H (1980). *Economic Liberties and the Constitution*. Chicago: University of Chicago Press.

Stoebuck, William B (1972). "A General Theory of Eminent Domain." *Washington Law Review*, 47 (August): 553–608.

White, Gilbert F (1986). "Human Adjustment to Floods," in Robert W. Kates and Ian Burton (eds.) *Geography, Resources, and Environment*, vol. 1. Chicago: University of Chicago Press.

Wyeth, George (1996). "Regulatory Competition and the Takings Clause." *Northwestern University Law Review*, 91 (Fall): 87–143.

TERM LIMITS 1

Term limitation is an institutional option in representative democracy that, if taken, sets some maximum amount of time that an individual can serve in some public office. In contemporary America, for example, the president, most state governors, nearly half the states' legislators, and some 3,000 officials at the local level are term limited. Why these laws exist and what effects these laws have are questions that have spawned a large literature in economics and political science. I survey this literature elsewhere (López, 2002a). Here I will focus on two aspects of term limitation that both describe its essence and also provoke unresolved issues.

1. The Tenure-Turnover Trade off and Welfare Effects of Term Limits

Consider a president who is popular enough to win his re-election bid. Voters benefit from the job experience that the president gains from being in office a long time. But the president would benefit from being able to dissuade effective challengers, and this is a skill that may be acquired, along with job experience, from being in office a long time. If the president then uses this electoral security to his own benefit rather than to better representation of his constituents, voters would be harmed.

Now consider a Member of Congress who is popular among his district constituents. Voters benefit from him accumulating job experience with greater tenure. But his tenure relative to the tenure of other members is also valuable if it means he can bring higher net benefits to the district (perhaps in the form of an increase in net transfers). But the member would benefit, like the president, from erecting some barriers to effective challengers. If the member then uses this electoral security to his own benefits, and fails to represent constituents' preferences along the way, voters are again harmed.

These hypothetical examples illustrate the tenure-turnover tradeoff that voters face and that term limitation addresses. Rapid replacement of politicians is costly to voters because inexperienced people run the government. In legislatures, it is costly for voters to replace their representative too frequently because their representatives do not stay in office long enough to acquire important powers to direct net transfers toward the district. These are turnover costs. In contrast, it is costly to leave officials in office for too long because they may erect entry-barriers to effective challengers and pursue their own ends. They may also impose excessive deadweight loss on the economy in directing rents to themselves and their electoral constituents. These are tenure costs.

Term limitation is a mechanism for keeping tenure costs low and therefore a benefit to voters. However, term limitation also increases turnover costs. Theoretically, the optimal term limit would be set at the length of tenure at which the marginal tenure cost just equals the marginal turnover cost (cf. Adams and Kenny, 1986). Thus, the welfare effects of adopting term limits are conceptually straightforward. However, complications arise in estimating the tenure and turnover costs. More serious complications arise when the tenure and turnover costs of one political entity (such as a state or congressional district) depend systematically on the tenure and turnover costs in other entities. This is the case with legislative and congressional term limits.

The welfare effects of congressional term limits depend firstly on whether legislators from all districts are term limited. In state legislatures with term limits, every legislator is term limited. A strong case can be made that a reduction in average tenure with a preserved distribution of relative tenure is welfare enhancing; at least it would explain why voters might support term limits (Dick and Lott, 1993). But the welfare effect would still depend on the concavity of voter utility over turnover and tenure costs (e.g., Lee, 2002). In the case of Congress, however, 23 states unilaterally passed term limits during a wave of state-level reform in the early 1990s. (The Supreme Court later struck down these laws.) This almost certainly would have harmed voters in the term-limited districts to the benefit of voters in the non-limited districts. So why did voters in these states pass term limits? This is an issue that is not well understood (López, 2003). And it runs parallel to related and equally puzzling question.

2. Supporting Incumbents and Term Limits

The Congressional incumbent reelection rate exceeded 90% for all elections in the 1990's. Yet opinion polls in the mid-1990s routinely indicated supermajority support for term limits among voters. And voters revealed strong preferences for term limits at the voting booth: term limits on state legislators and Congress passed 22 of the 23 times they appeared on state referenda.

Why might voters support incumbents and also support legislative term limits? Here again the tenure-turnover tradeoff comes into play. Because districts compete for net transfers vis-à-vis one another, and more tenured legislators are typically more productive in acquiring net transfers, it is primarily relative tenure that is valuable to voters in a given district. Now suppose that increased tenure enables legislators to capture rents instead of passing them on to constituents. That is, legislators become electorally secure and begin to shirk as they acquire more tenure. Voters in all districts would capture welfare gains from a general reduction in tenure. But the importance of relative tenure creates a free-rider problem: if all districts agreed to replace their incumbent through electoral defeat, each would then have the incentive to cheat. Term limitation is the mechanism to enforce such an agreement (Dick and Lott, 1993). Hence, voters are not behaving inconsistently when supporting incumbents and universal term limitation.

Unilateral term limitation is a separate case, and the more puzzling as well. Is it rational for voters to support their own incumbents while voting to limit the terms of their own Congressional delegation? The free-rider argument only explains universal term limits, and further research on this topic has been inconclusive (see López, 2003 for discussion). It is possible, then, that this conundrum presents the opportunity to uncover more advanced strategic motivations behind voter support for institutional change. Consider that five of the 23 states that passed term limits did so conditional on a majority of the other states also doing so. Sophisticated behavior was also evidenced when Congress considered term limits. Prior to the Supreme Court decision that struck down the unilateral state laws, a representative's vote on term limits was systematically related to whether he or she was from a state that had unilaterally self-imposed. But when Congress considered the same bill two years later, the vote was unaffected by whether the state had self-imposed (López, 2002). In general, a district's support for term limits has exhibited a clear awareness of whether other districts have supported them or will support them. A promising direction for theoretical research would be to model multiple districts in a sequential game with payoffs related to tenure-turnover costs in each district, whether the district had passed term limits, and whether other districts had. Such a game could generate hypotheses relating states' support for term limits to population, income, net transfers, homogeneity of constituents, and other seemingly important variables.

3. Empirical Work

Most empirical work involving term limitation seeks to estimate the effects of term limits on dependent political variables (such as tenure, party balance, shirking, and the value of holding office), policy variables (such as constitutional features and fiscal stability), and economic variables (such as growth). Close to no empirical work has sought to explain the origins of term limits, for example by estimating the likelihood of a state passing term limits. Why did certain states pass term limits while others did not? Of theoretical significance to this would be, among other variables, the state's net transfer profile and the tenure of its delegation. Since term limits laws were passed via referendum/initiative, a variable that indicates whether the state constitution allows for referendum/initiative would also be of theoretical significance. This estimation is prevented by the fact that every state that allows for referendum/initiative also passed term limits. As such, we are left with the uninteresting result that states passed term limits because their constitution featured a direct democracy institution. However, if term limits and direct democracy are determined by different political-economic processes, then this result is also wrong. If they are determined differently, the likelihood of term limits should be estimable using instrumental variables. This depends on whether exclusion restrictions can be convincingly argued and reliably measured for the estimation of the instrument. Future empirical work could take up this question, as well as the efficiency effects of term limits, toward valuable contributions to our understanding of the origins and effects of term limits.

EDWARD J. LÓPEZ

REFERENCES

Adams, J.D. and Kenny, L.W. (1986). "Optimal tenure of elected public officials." *Journal of Law and Economics*, 109: 303–328.

Dick, A.R. and Lott, J.R. Jr. (1993). "Reconciling voters' behavior with legislative term limits." *Journal of Public Economics*, 50: 1–14.

Lee, K. (2002). "An analysis of welfare effects of legislative term limits." *Public Choice*, 110(3/4): 245–260.

López, E.J. (2002). "Congressional voting on term limits." *Public Choice*, 112: 405–431.

López, E.J. (2003). "Term limits: Causes and consequences." *Public Choice*, 114: 1–56.

TERM LIMITS 2

A term limit is a statutory or constitutional restriction on the number of terms that an individual is allowed to hold a particular elected office. The term limit may or may not be grandfathered. Full grandfathering allows officeholders at the time that term limits are enacted to be exempt from term limits, whereas limited grandfathering allows such officeholders to be treated as if they have previously served no terms. Some term limits allow an individual who is forced out of office by term limits to hold the same office again after a specified period of time has elapsed while many do not. In recent years there has been heated debate over the desirability of term limits.

1. Historical Background

The concept of a term limit goes back at least to Aristotle, who praised the merits of a legislature of citizens with each holding office for a short time. This frequent succession of citizens in an office is referred to as rotation in office. Term limits were not uncommon in colonial America and, although not included in the United States Constitution, were debated at length during the Constitutional Convention. Indeed, George Washington was widely praised for retiring from the presidency after two terms. While voluntary rotation in office was commonplace in the U.S. Congress until the late nineteenth century, Polsby (1968) documents the rise of the career congressman and the institutionalization of the Congress that took place thereafter. Not only did the average number of terms served by congressmen steadily increase over time, but the Congress itself developed an increasingly complex committee system accompanied by growth in congressional staff and the rise of the seniority system.

Although today the prevalence of professional politicians indicates at best a modicum of enthusiasm on their part for rotation in office, term limits do exist for many state and municipal elected offices. Most states have term limits for governor. Term limits also have been imposed in a large number of states and municipalities, many in the 1990s, on the offices of state representative, mayor, and city councilman. At the federal level the twenty-second amendment to the U.S. Constitution limits a president to two elected terms.

The two elected federal offices that are notably free of term limits are U.S. senator and U.S. representative, and it is the question of the imposition of term limits for these offices that has generated the most controversy in recent years. In the early 1990s twenty-three states passed voter referenda or laws limiting the number of terms that their congressmen could serve. These referenda and laws subsequently were overturned by the U.S. Supreme Court in 1995 in *U.S. Term Limits, Inc. v. Thornton*. Although there is little question that public support for term limits exists, it is not obvious that this support is an explicit cry for term limits or an expression of frustration with the way that government has been operating.

2. Issues Surrounding Term Limits

The focus of debate in recent years has been on the likely effects of term limits imposed on congressmen. Some important issues raised include the impacts of term limits on the composition of the Congress, the type of legislator who will serve, the degree to which legislators will faithfully represent their constituents' interests, and the level of federal government expenditures or the size of government. The issues are not necessarily independent of each other. Analysis is difficult because the absence of term limits on congressmen throughout the history of the Congress means that there are no data on the behavior of congressmen under term limits. Consequently, analyses are normative, theoretical, or indirect when empirical.

2.1. Composition of the Congress

Legislative tenure almost certainly will be reduced if term limits are imposed. Reed and Schansberg (1994) estimate that a six-term limit for congressmen will reduce the expected number of terms served by a congressman from 8.9 to 3.2 with the maximum being 6.0. Furthermore, there initially will be large influxes of freshman congressmen every twelve years (six terms), but the magnitudes of these influxes will dampen over time. There will be times after the imposition of term limits when the Congress will have historically high percentages of inexperienced congressmen.

It should be noted that these estimates of the effect of term limits on expected tenure are based on historical continuation rates (for the period 1985 through 1991) for congressman and do not take into account how the term limits themselves can alter behavior and therefore continuation rates. Grofman and Sutherland (1996) argue that strong challengers may postpone running for office until term limits force an open-seat election, while Francis and Kenny (1997) argue that term limits in a higher office (e.g., the U.S. Senate) may encourage more holders of lower office (e.g., the U.S. House) to run for higher office by generating more open-seat elections for higher office. More generally, the probability of reelection depends on the degree to which congressmen serve their constituents' interests, and term limits may alter congressmen's incentives to serve those interests.

A related implication of term limits is the likely demise of the seniority system, under which committee chairmanships are assigned on the basis of length of tenure in office, because the number of congressmen with the maximum possible seniority may well exceed the number of committee chairmanships. It is not clear what would replace the seniority system.

Finally, there are partisan implications of term limits. Gilmour and Rothstein (1994) conclude that term limits will impact the partisan composition of the Congress by favoring Republicans. This is because in recent years Democratic incumbents have had lower retirement rates and higher reelection rates than Republican incumbents and Republican challengers have been more likely to win open-seat elections than Democratic challengers following the retirement of incumbents from their respective parties. The relative magnitudes of the parties' retirement rates, reelection rates, and open-seat election rates taken together favor Republicans under the forced-retirement regime of term limits.

2.2. Type of Congressman

Term limits will impose the rotation in office that had once been voluntary. It has been argued (Petracca, 1996) that rotation in office guards against concentration of political power in the hands of career legislators and professional politicians and is consistent with the belief that in a democracy governance should be carried out by amateurs who shortly return to their lives as private citizens. Presumably such citizen-legislators, understanding that they are free from the task of continually seeking reelection and that they shortly will return to the private sector to live under the rules contained in their own legislation, would be more inclined to represent the true interests of their constituents and to not pursue their private interests and would be less susceptible to influence from special interest groups and their promises of campaign contributions.

The logic of this argument is not convincing. Why should a mandated limited time in office, effectively the constraint that it is not possible to make a career of that office, cause these citizen-legislators to better represent their constituents interests and to not pursue private gain? This is a particularly relevant question because the threat of not being reelected constrains legislators to take the interests of unorganized constituents into account (Denzau and Munger, 1986). In order to make the claim that term limits will produce a legislature of citizen-legislators more

inclined to represent constituent interests it would be necessary to make a convincing argument that term limits will influence the self-selection of citizen-candidates in this manner. No such argument has yet been made. Indeed, it has been argued that the interruption of a private sector career in order to serve a brief time in office under term limits may attract a higher proportion of independently wealthy individuals and opportunists than does the current system without term limits (Polsby, 1991).

It also is not clear that term limits actually will lead to a legislature of amateurs, let alone amateurs who efficiently and faithfully represent their constituents. It is more likely that term limits will not discourage politically ambitious people from running for office but will instead channel their ambitions in different directions. In lieu of the prospect of a potentially long career in Congress, the congressman will consider how to optimally manage a career that may include a succession of different political offices or periodic stints working in the private sector, perhaps as a lobbyist for firms with interests before the Congress (Garrett, 1996). While the congressman's decision-making calculus will give weight to the interests of his constituents, it necessarily will give weight to the interests of his potential future constituents or private-sector employers as well. Furthermore, the limited time horizon in office under term limits implies that the congressman has both less time to learn and less incentive to invest time in learning the substance of the issues being considered by the Congress because a shorter time horizon means a shorter time to collect the returns from such an investment.

2.3. Representation of Constituents' Interests

There has been considerable debate on whether and to what extent term limits will alter the level of shirking by congressman. "Shirking" refers to a congressman's failing to fully represent the interests of his constituents. A congressman whose interests do not coincide with his constituents' interests has an incentive to shirk. The threat of not being reelected by the voters because of this shirking acts to reduce shirking. However, a "last-period problem" arises when a congressman, knowing that he is in his last term in office and therefore does not have to face reelection, can costlessly shirk as much as he likes and will do so if his interests do not coincide with his constituents' interests. A last-period problem does not arise for a congressman who is defeated for reelection because this congressman is not aware that he has served his last term in office until after defeat, whereas a potential last-period problem does arise for every congressman who retires from office. If voters can detect shirking earlier in a congressman's career, then it is likely that the last-period problem will not be important because congressmen who are inclined to shirk will be defeated for reelection before their voluntarily leaving office. Studies by Lott (1987, 1990) and Van Beek (1991) indicate little difference between congressmen's voting on legislative bills in their last term before retirement and their voting on legislative bills in their previous terms served, thereby suggesting that voters do tend to remove shirking congressmen from office prior to voluntary retirement.

Term limits, which would force many congressmen to leave office prior to electoral defeat, guarantee that the last-period problem will arise more frequently. The relatively short three-term and six-term limits that have been suggested for congressmen likely will cause the degree of shirking associated with the last-period problem to increase nontrivially by not giving voters enough time to remove shirking congressmen prior to their last terms before forced retirement under term limits. These term limits also will prematurely remove from office those congressmen who are inclined to shirk little and whom the voters would like to retain in office.

Focusing only on the last period is, however, an oversimplification. Although shirking by a congressman will be greatest in the last period because the reelection constraint is no longer binding, shirking likely will occur throughout a congressman's career.

Dick and Lott (1993) argue that tenure itself can be a source of shirking. A congressman with longer tenure has greater seniority on committees and likely has developed greater ability to utilize the rules of the Congress and greater skill at logrolling. These factors will increase the ability of the congressman to transfer wealth to his district from the rest of the country relative to a congressman with shorter tenure. Voters are therefore reluctant to remove from office a congressman with relatively long tenure. This allows the congressman to shirk with respect to other interests of the voters without unduly risking electoral defeat. The longer a congressman's tenure, the greater is the potential amount of shirking by a congressman without endangering reelection. By forcing all congressmen to leave office after a specified number of terms, term limits make it less costly for voters to discipline their congressmen at the polls. Dick and Lott believe that the resulting reduction in shirking will more than offset the increase in shirking generated by the last-period problem occurring more frequently under term limits.

While Dick and Lott make valid points that shirking can increase with tenure because the ability to transfer wealth increases with tenure and that term limits can reduce shirking from this source, their contention that any increase in shirking induced by term limits will be only in the form of more last-period shirking reflects too narrow a focus. Bender et al. (2001) argue that given a finite time horizon in office a congressman will optimally shirk throughout his congressional career (i.e., there is a time path of optimal shirking). In this dynamic context optimal shirking means that in each term the congressman's degree of shirking reflects a tradeoff between the benefit of additional utility from additional shirking in the current term and the cost of the reduction in expected present value of the utility received in future terms from the reduction in probability of reelection at the end of the current term induced by additional shirking in the current term. The less time remaining in the horizon, the smaller is the cost of electoral defeat and therefore the larger is the optimal amount of shirking. Term limits reduce the time horizon of the congressman and therefore raise his optimal amounts of shirking in each of his terms in office. The threat of electoral defeat becomes less effective in controlling shirking when term limits are present because the return to not shirking is diminished by the reduced time horizon under term limits. This impact on shirking is magnified to the extent that the reduced return to lower shirking causes the pool of potential candidates to consist of candidates who are on average more inclined to shirk. Term limits not only increase shirking by existing congressmen but also encourage potential shirkers to run for office.

2.4. Size of Government

Over the years both the average tenure of congressmen and the level of government expenditures, a proxy for the size of government, have been increasing. Some proponents of term limits argue that they will reduce the size of government based on a presumed positive and causal relationship between tenure and spending. It has been hypothesized that the longer that congressmen are in office the more likely they are to be drawn into a culture of spending or shirk more by supporting legislation for more spending than their constituents desire or develop more expertise at logrolling. However, Reed et al. (1998) test these hypotheses and find at best weak evidence that a relationship between congressional tenure and support of government spending exists and consequently little empirical support for the proposition that term limits will reduce the size of government.

3. Conclusions

The list of issues above is not exhaustive. Certainly the impact of term limits on the influence of lobbyists and on the relative power of the executive and legislative branches of government could be added to the list. The unavailability of data on the behavior of congressmen under a term-limits regime precludes direct empirical testing of all of the issues. This inability to test directly the hypotheses about the impacts of term limits may continue to leave the desirability of term limits an open question.

BRUCE BENDER

REFERENCES

Bender, B., Haas, T.C., and Kim, S. (2001). "Sorting, shirking, and term limits. Mimeo," paper presented at the Public Choice Society Meetings, San Antonio, March.

Denzau, A.T. and Munger, M.C. (1986). "Legislators and interest groups: how unorganized interests get represented." *American Political Science Review*, 18 (March): 89–106.

Dick, A.R. and Lott, J.R. Jr. (1993). "Reconciling voters' behavior with legislative term limits." *Journal of Public Economics*, 50 (January): 1–14.

Francis, W.L. and Kenny, L.W. (1997). "Equilibrium projections of the consequences of term limits upon expected tenure, institutional turnover, and membership experience." *Journal of Politics*, 59 (February): 240–252.

Garrett, E. (1996). "Term limitations and the myth of the citizen-legislator," *Cornell Law Review*, 81: 623–697.

Gilmour, J.B. and Rothstein, P. (1994). "Term limitation in a dynamic model of partisan balance." *American Journal of Political Science*, 38 (August): 770–796.

Grofman, B. and Sutherland, N. (1996). "The effects of term limits when competition is endogenized: a preliminary model," in B. Grofman (ed.) *Legislative Term Limits: Public Choice Perspectives*. Boston: Kluwer Academic Publishers, pp. 175–182.

Lott, J.R. Jr. (1987). "Political cheating." *Public Choice*, 52 (March): 169–187.

Lott, J.R. Jr. (1990). "Attendance rates, political shirking, and the effect of post-office employment." *Economic Inquiry*, 28 (January): 133–150.

Petracca, M.P. (1996). "A history of rotation in office," in B. Grofman (ed.) *Legislative Term Limits: Public Choice Perspectives*. Boston: Kluwer Academic Publishers. pp. 247–277.

Polsby, N. (1968). "The institutionalization of the U.S. House of Representatives," *American Political Science Review*, 62 (March): 144–168.

Polsby, N. (1991). "Constitutional mischief: what's wrong with term limits." *The American Prospect* (Summer): 40–43.

Reed, W.R. and Schansberg, D.E. (1994). "An analysis of the impact of congressional term limits." *Economic Inquiry*, 32 (January): 79–91.

Reed, W.R., Schansberg, D.E., Wilbanks, J., and Zhu, Z. (1998). "The relationship between congressional spending and tenure with an application to term limits." *Public Choice*, 94 (January): 85–104.

Van Beek, J.R. (1991). "Does the decision to retire increase the amount of political shirking?" *Public Finance Quarterly*, 19 (October): 444–456.

TERRORISM

Terrorism is defined as 'the systematic employment of violence and intimidation to coerce a government or community into acceding to specific political demands' (The New Shorter Oxford English Dictionary, 1993). Whether or not such an act is viewed as good or evil depends on particular circumstances and involves a normative judgment.

For example, during the early stages of the French Revolution, adherents or supporters of the *Jacobins* advocated and practiced methods of partisan repression and bloodshed in the propagation of principles of democracy. Many French citizens viewed such terrorist acts favorably, at least until the Revolution of 1789 descended into the Terror of 1793–94 under the Directorate dominated by Danton, Robespierre and Marat (Hugo, 1874, 1998). Yet these same terrorist acts were viewed throughout as evil by most members of the French Aristocracy and by many others loyal to the Crown and fundamentally opposed to French republicanism.

Similarly many Irish American Catholics revere and fund acts of terror perpetrated against the United Kingdom by the *Irish Republican Army*, whereas the large majority of United Kingdom citizens view these same acts as evil applications of atheistic, Marxist-Leninist dogma.

Most recently, the governments of several countries in Africa and the Middle East, notably Afghanistan, Somalia, Iraq, the Yemen, Sudan, Libya, Syria, Pakistan, Iran, and Saudi-Arabia, have nurtured and financially supported the training of terrorists broadly defined as members of *al Qaeda* to enable them to launch a sequence of successful terrorist attacks on the United States and to threaten similar attacks on other advanced Western nations. Yet, the vast majority of citizens of all civilized, advanced nations despise *al Qaeda* as the epitome of evil, indeed as the Godless perpetrators of torture, pillage, enslavement of women and mass murder and mutilation.

1. The Heterogeneous Nature of Terrorist Groups

Terrorist groups manifest themselves in a wide variety of shapes and sizes. Some groups, like the *Irish Republican Army, La Cosa Nostra Fatah, Hamas and Hezbollah, Baader-Meinhof* and *The Shining Path*, are geographically concentrated and culturally and politically homogeneous.

Other groups, like *al Qaeda* are geographically dispersed and culturally and politically diverse. More rarely, terrorists take the form of lone individuals, like the *Unabomber*, who respond violently, perhaps to mental illness, perhaps to perceived personal failure to perform satisfactorily in civilized society.

Small homogeneous groups organize their activities rather like the special interest groups depicted in Mancur Olson's (1965) logic of collective action. They overcome the free-rider problem that confronts all organizations pursuing goals that are public goods or bads, in part by privatizing the benefits from collective action and in part by enforcing supply either through physical intimidation or by moral suasion. Because they operate illegally and cannot enforce contracts through the legal system, they must rely heavily on networks of trust, based either on religious fanaticism or on excessive greed for wealth, but always reinforced by violence against individuals and the families of individuals who seek to defect from or to betray the group. In such circumstances, individuals who join a tightly knit terrorist group confront the equivalent of a serious transitional gains trap that strongly deters exit (Tullock, 1975).

Large, heterogeneous terrorist groups confront more serious difficulties in building membership and in deterring defections and betrayals. Mancur Olson (1965) predicted that large groups pursuing goals with pronounced publicness characteristics tend to be less successful than smaller, more homogeneous groups unless they are organized for some other purpose that provides private benefits to their members. In essence, such terrorist groups by-product terrorism by providing selective benefits.

For example, the *al Qaida* leadership preys on illiterate, simple-minded male drop-outs drawn primarily from a range of Middle Eastern countries (but also from Europe, North America Africa, Australasia and Asia) by indoctrinating them in fanatical Islam, by focusing hostility towards such 'Western values' as capitalism and individualism and by promising each terrorist such Heavenly pleasures as rivers of sweet honey and holy wine, 72 virgin brides and free passes to Paradise for 70 of his friends and relatives should he die in an attack on the Infidels. Of course, not all terrorists are sufficiently stupid as to believe in such nonsense. Many are coerced into engaging in suicide attacks by threats of torture or by death threats to their families should they refuse to serve coupled with promises of long-term financial support for their dependents should they successfully complete their mission.

Senior members who actively plan or execute terrorist attacks are provided with affluent lifestyles and international travel that are unattainable through ordinary market transactions. The *Fatah* motivates its membership into launching suicidal attacks on Israel by promising the establishment of a socialist State of Palestine and the removal of the Jewish occupation. *Hamas* and *Hezbollah* motivate membership by promising the elimination of Israel from the map of the Middle East.

Large terrorist groups that are not grounded in one nation state clearly confront serious problems of free riding that cannot be overcome solely by reliance on selective benefits. To effect supply, the larger umbrella organizations, such as *al Qaida*, encourage the emergence of a network of much smaller cells motivated and trained through a wide range of geographically dispersed training camps. The network externalities provided by the umbrella group allows such a terrorist group to obviate the impact of changing national borders that otherwise would tend to weaken the internal cohesion of the group (Olson, 1982). The small nature of each cell also allows cell leaders to foster an atmosphere of trust and a fear of exit conducive to high risk-taking among the membership. Because the cells operate independently of each other, the identification of any one cell by the victims of an act of terrorism does not automatically or easily expose other cells or the umbrella organization to effective retributive action.

Furthermore, pan-Islam disposes adherents of that faith to view themselves as Muslims first, and as citizens of particular countries second. Clearly, this doctrine helps *al Qaeda* and other multi-national terrorist groups to overcome the logic of collective action.

2. Linkages with Nation States

Terrorist groups often enjoy the geographical protection and financial support of countries that share common terrorist objectives but that desire to avoid the international sanctions that would be invoked by overt action. Such has been the case of successive governments of the Irish Republic that until recently provided covert support for the *IRA*. It continues to be the case in Palestine, with respect not only to *Fatah* but also to *Hamas* and *Hezbollah*. It is clearly the case of Iraq, the Yemen, Syria, Pakistan, and Saudi-Arabia with respect to *al Qaeda*.

The relationship between terrorist groups and nation states, however, is more complex than a simple sharing of hatreds. The insecure governments of certain nation states pay off terrorists within their borders to avoid destabilizing military attacks and/or to secure their support in attacking border enemies. Such is the case with Egypt, Saudi-Arabia, Pakistan, and the Yemen with respect to *al Qaeda* and of Palestine with respect to *Hamas* and *Hezbollah*.

The temporary controlling authorities in such failed states as Somalia, the Yemen, Sudan and, most spectacularly,

Afghanistan go yet further, allowing themselves to be purchased by such well-funded terrorist groups as *al Qaeda*, placing themselves on the payroll of the terrorists and effectively becoming handmaidens to their designs. The public choice analysis of such hijacked states does not yet exist. Inevitably, a relevant literature will emerge in the wake of September 11, 2001 (Shughart, 2003).

3. The Goals of Terrorists

By the nature of its terrain, terrorism undoubtedly attracts the services of a number of mentally unstable individuals, whose behavior cannot be subjected systematically to economic analysis. For the most part, however, such individuals are the exception rather than the rule, and, typically, do not achieve significant leadership roles in substantive terrorist groups. They do not do so because terrorist groups pursue rational goals that would be subverted or nullified by unpredictable behavior. Those who are mentally disturbed are used by the rational leaders of terrorist groups, as are the ignorant, religiously indoctrinated fanatics who seek an early entry into Paradise, and or who seek large financial side payments to their families, as compensation for engaging in acts of self-destruction.

The leaders of all successful terrorist groups are rational actors motivated by the maximization of some combination of expected wealth, power, fame and patronage, much in the way of other members of society. They differ markedly from most other individuals with respect to their attitudes towards risk, typically manifesting risk preference in relatively extreme forms such as a relatively low regard for human life and a relatively low level of genuine attachment to associates and colleagues. Because these latter preferences differ so markedly from those of other individuals, their behavior appears to be irrational. Fundamentally, however, this is not the case.

Individuals with similar preferences and attitudes towards risk occupy many legitimate areas of activity. Examples include William Jefferson Clinton in politics, Michael Milken in stock trading and Jimmy Bakker in the populist religion market. Such individuals respond to perceived rewards and penalties, albeit while skirting the edges of potential personal disaster.

Terrorist leaders likewise respond rationally to expected costs and benefits. They can be deterred or diverted by actions that manifestly lower the net expected benefits of terrorist attempts (Shughart, 2003). Their rational goals imply that they seek to impose the maximum possible terrorist cost for any given outlay of resources (Enders and Sandler, 1995). Because they operate in environments unregulated by any rule of law, their behavior is less constrained as it edges towards extremism than typically is the case of those with similar pathological symptoms who remain more or less within the civilized sectors of society.

4. The Relevance of Religion

Many of the Middle Eastern terrorist groups, notably *al Qaeda, the Palestinian Islamic Jihad, Hamas and Hezbollah* organize themselves around the rhetoric of a radical interpretation of Islam and seek to impose this religion on Middle Eastern countries that are deemed to have betrayed the Muslim faith. It is doubtful whether the affluent leaders of these groups, for example Osama bin Laden in the case of *al Qaeda*, or Dr. Rathi Abd al-Aziz and Sheikh 'As' ad Bayyud al-Tamimi in the case of the *Palestinian Islamic Jihad*, have any serious use for the Muslim faith other than as a device for attracting followers. Certainly their respective life-styles do not conform to the stringent standards required by that faith. Such, however, is not the case for the large majority of their footsoldiers.

Although it is currently politically correct to refer to Islam as a peaceful religion, this is a less than accurate interpretation even with respect to its less radical versions. Contemporary Muslim faith, rather like medieval Christianity, is very rule oriented, in the sense that it sets out precise requirements for prayer, fasting, alms and economic exchange.

This type of rule-oriented doctrine leads to dogmatic and precise rule-following behavior on the part of ignorant and ill-educated Muslims and provides a fertile breeding ground for terrorism when manipulated by charismatic leaders. Such strict adherence to doctrine also fosters conflict between Islamic sects on the basis of relatively minor differences of interpretation. For example, Shias consider Sunnis to be apostates and vice versa.

Unlike Christianity, the Muslim faith has experienced no modernization to accommodate the requirements of a developing world. Indeed, contemporary Islamic thought is impoverished as a consequence of the suffocation of Muslim intellectual activity since the tenth century (Kuran, 1995, p. 176). As Kuran notes (ibid.) the Islamic scholar Mohammed Arkoun makes two distinctions in characterizing public discourse in the Islamic world. One is between the *thinkable* and the *unthinkable*, the other between the *thought* and the *unthought*.

Noting that past generations of Muslims treated key tenets of the European Enlightenment as unthinkable, Arkoun argues that present generations of Muslims cannot even conceive of applying the methods of historical criticism to sacred texts and cherished traditions (ibid.). In consequence, the 'resurgence of Islam is taking place on the basis of an immense unthought accumulated over centuries.'

If Arkoun is correct, he provides an explanation of the process through which educated leaders of terrorist groups secure such a powerful grip over the minds of their followers. By transferring beliefs from the realm of the thinkable to that of the unthinkable, social pressures within the group induce the withdrawal of those beliefs from public discourse. Members of the group become progressively less conscious of the disadvantages of what is now publicly favored and increasingly more conscious of the advantages. As a result, private opinion moves against the publicly disfavored alternatives. This offers an explanation of why groups go to extremes.

5. The Relevance of Geography

With the singular and important exception of *al Qaeda*, modern terrorist groups typically emerge within specific countries to eliminate governments that are perceived to be inimical, on religious, political or other grounds, to the goals of their leadership. The evidence strongly suggests that the large majority of countries that attract such terrorist groups are relatively small countries, surrounded geographically by other countries.

Hosts that manifest dictatorial oppression, religious conflict, periodic wars and periodically changing borders are especially attractive to such parasites. Countries that have access to sea routes and, therefore, that benefit from the comparative advantage of international trade, appear to be relatively less attractive as potential hosts. Presumably, the perceived economic advantages of trade outweigh the trade-destructive rhetoric of fighting for Islam typically utilized by terrorist leaders to motivate the local population into violence.

Many of the host countries are vulnerable to terrorism because they are the victims of artificial geographical boundaries imposed by former colonial Empires without regard to ethnic composition. Such is the case within much of the Middle East and much of sub-Saharan Africa (Rowley, 2000). Such synthetic nation-states, especially when they do not federalize in order to reflect customary tribal preferences, predictably result in ethnic violence and become breeding grounds for terrorist parasites (Shughart, 2003). The single party systems and outright dictatorships that dominate much of the Middle East and sub-Saharan Africa are highly attractive to pathological terrorist leaders not least because such politically vulnerable regimes tend to pay off rather than to confront terrorists by offering them safe harbor and subsidized access to economic resources.

6. The Asymmetric Nature of Terrorist War

In the early twenty-first century, the United States is the world's only superpower, comparable in terms of military dominance to the ancient Roman Empire during the first two hundred years, A.D., and to the British Empire at its peak in the mid-nineteenth century. In principle, it should be invulnerable to its enemies, credibly capable of annihilating them should they dare to challenge its private space. Yet, the United States is peculiarly vulnerable to terrorist attack ironically because its human and physical capital is so valuable.

The term 'asymmetric warfare' was coined first in the USSR during its unsuccessful attempt to defend its imperial seizure of Afghanistan against the 'Holy Warriors' of the *Mujahedeen*. The term entered into the US military lexicon only in 1995 defined with elegant simplicity as 'not fighting fair' (Bray, 2002, p. 25). Asymmetric warfare implies that singularly weaker forces are capable of imposing devastating costs on a massively stronger enemy without necessarily fearing the ultimate penalty of a nuclear or a nuclear-equivalent response. September 11, 2001 was the first manifestation of this phenomenon. This may prove to be the foretaste of yet more spectacular devastations should the terrorist presence not be substantially eradicated by forceful American action.

In order to understand the varying degrees to which terrorists engage in violence and the varying levels of devastation that they are prepared to impose it is important to distinguish between two types of terrorist groups, namely those that are stationary and those that are non-stationary (McGuire and Olson, 1996).

Stationary terrorists, such as the *IRA, Fatah, Hamas* and *Hezbollah*, that operate from well-defined territories and seek to advance the interests of members within the same or closely adjacent locations, predictably will engage in strictly localized and limited terrorist attacks. To engage in nuclear, biological or chemical attacks of any magnitude would be to run significant risks of harming their own members as well as of inducing equally devastating retaliations from those harmed. In a sense, rational stationary terrorists that have an *encompassing interest* (Olson, 1993) in the territory within which they operate are constrained from acts of widespread destruction.

Of course, if terrorists establish themselves as parasites on a host that believes that victims of terrorism will not retaliate by annihilating the host population — as was the case with *al Qaeda* in Afghanistan prior to September 11, 2001 — these constraints will not apply. For such terrorists have no encompassing interest in the host country from which they operate.

Non-stationary or roving terrorists operating through networks of inter-active cells located secretly in many countries are the most dangerous of all, since such cells have no encompassing interest whatsoever in the countries from which they operate and confront minimal risks of major retaliation even if their location is discovered following a terrorist attack. This is the reason the American victory in Afghanistan over Taliban and *al Qaeda* forces in the months following September 11, 2001 is only a first step in the war against terrorism. The non-stationary cells of *al Qaeda* located, it is estimated, in some forty to sixty countries world wide are significantly more dangerous than were those located in Afghanistan under the leadership of Osama bin Laden and Mohammed Omar.

Because rogue states like Iraq and Pakistan may be willing suppliers of weapons of mass destruction both to stationary and to non-stationary terrorist groups, the war on terrorism cannot be deemed to be successful until their autocratic leaders have been removed and their political systems have adjusted to secure individual liberties, private property rights, limited government and the rule of law.

7. The Cost of Terrorism

Because of the nature of an asymmetric war, terrorists are able to impose very high costs on their enemies at seemingly trivial costs to themselves. September 11, 2001 is the most extreme example to date of this asymmetry. It has been estimated that the successful attacks launched on that day against the United States may have cost the terrorists no more than $200,000. (The terrorist lives lost were at most costless since the perpetrators were expediting their journey to Paradise).

The present value of the economic damage to the United States economy, however, has been estimated to be perhaps as much as two trillion dollars (Navarro and Spencer, 2001). Immediate costs, counting the value of lives lost, property damage and lost production are well in excess of $100 billion. The annual cost of airport and airline anti-terrorist measures is estimated to be in excess of $40 billion. Although the initial stock market estimates of the collapse of market capitalization undoubtedly were excessive at $2 trillion, nevertheless, the loss of investor confidence (animal spirits) together with the drag on economic incentives likely to ensue from greater government involvement in the economy and from larger budget deficits predictably will extract a savage toll on the rate of growth of the US economy over the following several years.

Since September 11, 2001 involved only a very limited strike at localized US assets, and since credibly *al Qaeda* agents have access to weapons of widespread destruction,

the expected cost of terrorism to the United States and to its other seriously committed allies is dramatically higher than the two trillion dollar estimate by Navarro and Spencer, at least in the absence of a successful war on the terrorist network. Yet, in an environment in which weapons of mass destruction become ever cheaper and easier to hide, the very notion of a successful war against roving networks of terrorists is at best likely to prove ambiguous.

Fundamentally, moreover, the economic costs of terrorism against the United States pale into insignificance by comparison with the loss of liberties and the erosion of the rule of law that the war on terrorism inevitably imposes. The American criminal laws, already badly crippled by complex rules of discovery, by excessively lax bail facilities, by televised trial circuses and by a decrepit jury system (Tullock, 1997) are clearly incapable of dealing effectively with accused terrorists. Inevitably, the administration has resorted to a *de facto* suspension of *habeas corpus* and to reliance on military tribunals in order to skirt the manifest limitations of the American trial courts.

Equally serious are the adverse implications of the war on terrorism for the freedom of movement and protection against search of innocent American citizens. Such freedoms, hard won in the eighteenth century by the Founding Fathers, almost squandered in the mid-nineteenth century during the War of Northern Aggression, and only slowly re-established thereafter, are in process of being shredded once again.

The most significant costs imposed on Americans by the successful terrorist attacks of September 11, 2001 undoubtedly are those arising from the erosion of individual freedoms, private property rights, limited government and the rule of law.

ANNE RATHBONE
CHARLES K. ROWLEY

REFERENCES

Bray, C. (2002). "How the press gets the military wrong — and why it matters." *Reason/2.02*, 33(9): 22–31.

Enders, W. and Sandler, T. (1995). "Terrorism: Theory and applications," in K. Hartley and T. Sandler (eds.) *Handbook of Defense Economics*, vol.12. Amsterdam: Elsevier.

Hugo, V. (1874, 1998). *Ninety Three*. New York: Carroll & Graf Publishers.

Kuran, T. (1995). *Private Truths, Public Lies: The Social Consequences of Preference Falsification*. Cambridge: Harvard University Press.

McGuire, M.C. and Olson, M. (1996). "The economics of autocracy and majority rule: The invisible hand and the use of force." *Journal of Economic Literature*, 34 (March): 72–96.

Olson, Mancur (1965). *The Logic of Collective Action.* Cambridge: Harvard University Press.

Olson, Mancur (1982). *The Rise and Decline of Nations: Economic Growth, Stagflation, and Social Rigidities.* New Haven: Yale University Press.

Olson, M. (1993). "Dictatorship, Democracy and Development" *American Political Science Review*, 87(3), (September): 567–576.

Navarro, P. and Spencer, A. (2001). "September 11, 2001: Assessing the costs of terrorism." *Milken Institute Review*, 2(4): 16–31.

Rowley, C.K. (2000). "Political culture and economic performance in sub-Saharan Africa." *European Journal of Political Economy*, 16 (March): 133–158.

Shughart, W.F. II (2003 forthcoming). "September 11, 2001," in C.K. Rowley and F. Schneider (eds.) *The Encyclopedia of Public Choice.* Dordrecht: Kluwer Academic Publishers, 520–524.

Tullock, G. (1974). *The Social Dilemma: The Economics of War and Revolution.* Blacksburg: Center for Study of Public Choice.

Tullock, G. (1975). "The Transitional Gains Trap." *Bell Journal of Economics and Management Science*, 6(2): 671–678.

Tullock, G. (1997). *The Case Against the Common Law.* The Blackstone commentaries, Vol.1. Fairfax: The Locke Institute.

THE THEORY AND MEASUREMENT OF ECONOMIC FREEDOM

Social scientists recognize three broad categories of freedom: political, civil or legal, and economic. A matter of great philosophical dispute is whether freedom or liberty is natural (negative) or human (positive). For example, does one have the right to choose how one labors (a natural right occupational freedom) or does one have a right to a minimum living standard for that labor (a human or positive right that requires government to redistribute economic outcomes on the basis of some notion of distributional justice)? We will not engage in that debate here. I will take freedom to be a procedural concept rather than a notion about positive outcomes. Thus, political freedom is about the right of the polity to choose who governs them, not who governs. Civil liberty is about the right to be ruled by law rather than by man. Rule of law is about fair procedures, and not about fair outcomes or justice. Economic freedom is about the right to organize one's pecuniary affairs with minimal interference by the state, and not about just economic outcomes. While the measurement of political and civil liberty has been with us for four decades or so, the measurement of economic freedom is more recent.

To my knowledge, Freedom House (1987) made the first attempt to measure economic freedom (it did so once,

and then abandoned the project). The organization has had a long involvement in measuring political and civil liberty, with those measures going back to 1973 for virtually all nations. As with previous attempts at measurement, their measures of political and civil liberty are not without controversy. A number of human or positive freedoms and subjective criteria are included among the variables used to construct their ratings. Freedom House's thinking about economic freedom is even more woolly. Broadly, they based their measure of economic freedom on sub-indices of the right to private property, freedom of association, freedom of travel, and the right to information. But, freedom of property contains measures of land reform, which is frequently confiscation without compensation, the extent of social services, and income distribution. Freedom of association includes the right to collude to redistribute income. Freedom of travel includes the degree of discrimination and socioeconomic mobility in society. The right to information includes such attributes as price controls, subsidies, and minimum wage.

A quantitative measure of economic freedom should be more comprehensive and more precise in definition of the attributes that aggregate to an overall measure of economic liberty than is found in the attempt at measurement by Freedom House. Thus one would want to include, among others, such items as the right to private property, freedom of contract, the rule of law, the size of government and its command over resources, the extent of the fiscal state, the degree of government economic regulation of business, labor, and markets, the monetary framework and monetary policy, commercial policy (free trade versus protectionism), and so on.

Along with a colleague, in 1991, (Scully and Slottje, 1991) I published the first set of measures of economic freedom based on a more comprehensive set of attributes, and ones selected on natural or negative criteria rather than on human or positive criteria. In all some 15 attributes went into the construction of the index. The economic freedom index was calculated for 1985, and for 144 nations. The results made sense, in that countries that one would have thought had a high (low) level of economic freedom indeed had a high (low) ranking based on the measure. But, while the index is based on objective criteria, those country rankings in between high and low are a matter of dispute. Nevertheless, the measure of economic freedom that I constructed was significantly related to the rate of economic growth across these countries. That is a reassuring finding, but it is not necessarily definitive about how accurately economic freedom is measured.

Let me give some criticism of my index of economic freedom, which also holds to a lesser degree for the economic liberty indexes that have followed my effort. In my rankings (the average of the ranks of the 15 attributes), the United States has a rank of 1.0, but so does Ireland, Liechtenstein, and Luxembourg. New Zealand has a rank of 5.73 and Hong Kong has a rank of 11.93, which is not too much better than the rank for Sweden (13.93). Now, most scholars knowledgeable of these countries would rank Hong Kong first in the world and New Zealand fairly low, at least for 1985. Hong Kong, despite being relinquished by Britain to China, remains the freest economy on earth. New Zealand, in 1984, was the most heavily regulated economy outside the socialist block. True enough, market-based reforms were undertaken in the post-1984 period but this would not have showed up in my measures, in 1985. Ireland was still heavily regulated and taxed in 1985. Liechtenstein and Luxembourg have fairly large public sectors, and certainly would rank below the United States.

In general, the problem with these measures of economic liberty, no matter how objective, is that they can distinguish the free from the unfree, but they are based on attributes that are not sufficiently fine to distinguish degrees of economic freedom among countries that are generally free or not free. This means that more research needs to be undertaken on this topic, and, perhaps, a much wider array of attributes needs to be considered.

The Fraser Institute took over the project on measuring economic freedom. James Gwartney and his associates (Gwartney and Lawson, 2001) have recently published the fifth edition of *Economic Freedom of the World: Annual Report 2001*. Their measure of economic freedom is the best that is available. For 2001, it is for 123 countries and is based on 21 components. The 7 broad categories of objective measures that go into the construction of the index are: the size of government, the structure of the economy and use of markets, monetary policy and price stability, freedom to use alternative currencies, legal structure and property rights, freedom to trade with foreigners, and freedom of exchange in capital and financial markets. Based on their components, Hong Kong ranks highest (9.4 on a scale to 10.0), followed by Singapore, New Zealand, United Kingdom, United States, Australia, Ireland, Switzerland, Luxembourg, and the Netherlands (8.4). But, Finland, Austria, Germany, and Iceland are not far behind, and clearly there is heavy intervention by the state in these economies. And, Bahrain and Oman rank higher than Spain in economic freedom. Thus, while the Fraser Institute's measure of economic freedom is objective and is much improved over previous measures, it still suffers from a lack of fineness in the components used to construct it. (Rabushka, 1991, Gwartney, Lawson and Block, 1996).

Part of the problem in the construction of economic freedom index is that a trade-off between inclusiveness of variables and comprehensiveness of coverage is encountered. That is, if you want to include countries such as Madagascar, Myanmar, and so on, not a great deal of objective data is available. Recognizing this problem, the authors have constructed a more comprehensive index of economic freedom for 58 countries. This index is based on 45 components. The main source of expansion of the attributes is the addition of information on the extent of regulation of capital, financial, and labor markets. With the incorporation of these data, some changes in the rankings do occur, and some of these changes make a good deal of sense. For example, Taiwan's rank dramatically improves, while that of France and Italy fall considerably. But, now Italy is not much freer than Egypt or Haiti, and is less free than Argentina and Bolivia. Unfortunately, when one correlates these two measures of economic freedom (the economic freedom index and the comprehensive index), one finds a correlation coefficient between the index ratings of .95 and between the rankings of .94.

Most indices of freedom weigh each attribute equally. Such an egalitarian standard implies, for example, that people have a social welfare function that equally weighs whether property is private or collective or whether the garbage is picked up privately or by the state. Clearly, they do not. So, part of the problem in constructing an aggregate measure of economic freedom may arise from the method of weighing the attributes.

Ideally, one would be able to specify a social welfare function in which rights are ranked lexicographically. Weights based on the relative rankings of the attributes would be employed to construct an overall measure of economic freedom. But, that approach is not possible. Alternatively, the researcher might impose his/her own weights or survey knowledgeable people for their opinions, but this is too ad hoc. There are two objective methods of weighing that attributes that have some theoretical justification and intuitive appeal. Since many of these attributes are correlated with each other, why not take advantage of that fact, and weigh by variances? This is the method of principal components. Each factor (an agglomeration of some of the attributes) is not correlated with any subsequent factors. Alternatively, one can weigh by regression coefficients using instrumental or hedonic estimation. Thus, per capita GDP might be the instrumental variable, and the coefficients of the attribute of economic liberty on per capita income would give a measure of how that attribute is valued. There are some other techniques for finding weights, but they are not suitable in this context.

In the creation of my measures of economic freedom, I constructed measures based on equal, principle component, and hedonic weights. When these indices are correlated with one another, one finds massive inter-correlation. Thus, choice of the weighing technique had little impact on the rank of economic freedom.

The finding that how one weighs the attributes in constructing an overall measure of economic liberty does not matter particularly may tell less about the problem of weighing than it tells us about the problems of the objective attributes. That is, the objective attributes may be insufficiently fine to reveal much difference within the set of generally free or generally not free nations. Or, they are so inter-correlated with one another that weights are irrelevant. A way of thinking about this issue is that, for the objective criteria that we have, countries that get institutions and policies right get them all right, and countries that get institutions and policies wrong get them all wrong.

GERALD W. SCULLY

REFERENCES

Gwartney, J. and Lawson, R. (2001). *Economic Freedom of the World: Annual Report 2001*. Vancouver: Fraser Institute.

Gwartney, J., Lawson, R., and Block, W. (1996). *Economic Freedom of the World: 1975–1995*. Vancouver: Fraser Institute.

Rabushka, A. (1991). "Preliminary definition of economic freedom," in W. Block (ed.) *Economic Freedom: Toward a Theory of Measurement*. Vancouver: Fraser Institute.

Scully, G.W. and Slottje, D.J. (1991). "Ranking economic liberty across countries," *Public Choice*, 69: 121–152.

TOTALITARIANISM

1. Introduction

Totalitarianism has been defined differently since the 1920s (Schlangen, 1970; Linz, 2000) when the scientific analysis of a presumably new phenomenon began with the takeover of power by Communists in Russia, Fascists in Italy and later by National Socialists in Germany. Four definitions will be mentioned. The first takes the sphere of life subordinated to the dictate of the state as its characteristic. Mussolini's definition in the *Enciclopedia Italiana* (1929: 847 f.) is an example:

> for the Fascist everything is within the state and there exists nothing human or spiritual ... outside the state. In this sense Fascism is totalitarian and the Fascist state interprets, develops and multiplies the whole life of the people as a synthesis and unit of each value.

This definition has been accepted by scientists like the sociologist Andreski (1965), but has obvious disadvantages.

First, it can include all possible regimes, even democracies. For in a *Total Democracy* there would be no sphere free from government regulation determined by majority voting. Second, a *Theocracy* in which about all aspects of life were regulated by religious prescriptions would also be a totalitarian regime. But in the first case at least a majority has to agree to this all-encompassing state activity, and in the second case nearly the whole population believing in the religion may agree to these regulations.

A second definition (Friedrich and Brzezinski, 1956) employs five characteristics:

1. A dominant totalitarian ideology;
2. A monopoly party;
3. A secret police applying terror;
4. A monopoly of information and
5. A planned economy.

This definition has also several weaknesses. First, why should a monopoly party and a planned economy be necessary for a totalitarian regime? What happens, if instead a priesthood and an economy restricted by the values of an ideology are present? Second, can terror not be applied by other organizations than a secret police? Third, is an overwhelming influence of the ideology on information not sufficient? Moreover, theories of this kind are too static to account for the rise, the development and the breakdown of totalitarian regimes.

Another definition has scarcely been influenced by those mentioned, but has relationships to the old theory of autocracy (Tullock [1974], 1987). This approach taken by the theory of Public Choice has applied the methods of economics to create formal models, and assumed that a dictator employs government power to maximize his utility under certain restrictions. The utility depends only on the wealth, income or consumption of the dictator, whereas the restrictions refer, e.g., to the means to maintain his power, or make a distinction between whether the dictator is a roving or a stationary bandit (Olson, 1993; McGuire and Olson, 1998). This assumption implies that the latter is more interested in long-term exploitation than the former, so that he exploits his subjects less in the present to be able to use their resources also in the future.

The most advanced of these models has been developed by Wintrobe (1998). He enriches the theory by introducing power besides consumption into the utility function of the dictator and, by using a richer set of restrictions, tries not only to explain ordinary dictatorships, but also totalitarian regimes. The latter are the outcome of great weight given in the dictator's utility function to power as compared to consumption, and of a production function efficiently producing loyalty with the help of a well organized party and a strong ideology. In spite of its merits, Wintrobe's model suffers from the assumption that the dictator is mainly interested in power, and that ideology is only a means to maximize it. But ideologies define the very aims of totalitarian regimes. To mention one example: Why should Hitler devote scarce transportation facilities and armed forces to transport people to Auschwitz, when they were badly needed to support the struggling German armies? If power had been his predominant aim, he would never have done so. But his behavior is understandable if ideology entered his utility function.

Subsequently the following definition is preferred (Bernholz, 1997, 2001; Piekalkiewicz and Penn, 1995):

> A totalitarian regime is an ideocracy which has not yet reached the aims implied by its supreme values, and which tries to pursue them with the spiritual and secular power available after it has gained domination of a state.

In this definition two concepts, *ideocracy* and *supreme values*, have to be explained. Supreme values are postulated by an ideology to be lexicographically preferred to everything else, even to the life of those believing in them and to the lives of others. An ideocracy is a political system in which all aims in society are subordinated with the help of spiritual and secular power to the rules implied by the supreme values. Besides totalitarian regimes there exist thus other ideocracies, called *mature ideocracies*, in which about the whole population believes in the rules postulated by the supreme values, so that no secular power has to be applied to enforce them, except in rare cases of transgression. For instance, a theocracy is a mature ideocracy in which the supreme values are defined by a religion.

The above definition makes only sense as a building block of a theory. Its usefulness becomes clear by sketching this theory.

2. Origins of Totalitarianism

No totalitarian regime has ever come into being without a powerful *ideology*, a *Weltanschauung*, claiming to be a more or less comprehensive and ultimate explanation of reality (Maier and Schaefer, 1997). Such an ideology contains *supreme values* which it insists have to be preferred lexicographically by all believers, so that no efforts and no sacrifice, even of one's own life or of the lives of others have to be spared to reach the ends postulated. All people able to become believers have to be converted, be they for instance Aryans in the case of national socialist, or proletarians in the communist, or the whole of humanity in Christian or Muslim ideologies.[1] According to certain ideologies some people, however, cannot be converted, like Jews according to Nazi and capitalists and bourgeois according to Communist ideology. Such groups are enemies of the true creed, and have consequently either to work as subjects of the believers for reaching the ends of the ideology, to be forced into emigration or to be eliminated.

An ideology is usually invented or revived by individuals who win a following by their charismatic personality. Their creed is often contained in holy scriptures whose absolute truth cannot be doubted, but interpreted by a selected leadership.

An ideology is a *necessary* but not a *sufficient* condition for the evolution of a totalitarian regime. For this to arise, *spiritual* and *secular* power have to be combined, that is, the government of at least one country has to be taken over by believers. To reach this end an organisation with a leadership or a leader having the monopoly right to interpret the ideology have to be created. It is needed to win votes in a democracy or to infiltrate armed forces and bureaucracy in authoritarian regimes to grasp power. This aim would be endangered if many believers were allowed to interpret the creed, since this would weaken the *movement* by splitting it up into different sects.

Finally, to be able to grasp power, a severe *crisis* has to occur. For to convert non-believers, they must doubt their present believes and way of life in view of the promises to solve the crisis contained in the ideology.

Even then, a *mature ideocracy* instead of a *totalitarian regime* may develop, if the groups of believers can emigrate to a thinly settled country and create a political system like the Puritans in Massachusetts or the "state" established by the Jesuits in Paraguay. For in this case nearly only believers are present so that no wide-spread force or terror characteristic of totalitarian regimes have to be applied. Consequently, a peaceful regime is established, if the supreme values do not ask for further expansion. It follows that mature ideocracies and totalitarian regimes are both ideocracies, but that the latter in contrast to the former has not yet reached the aims postulated by the respective ideology.

3. Domestic Policies after Gaining Secular Power

If secular and spiritual power have been combined, the supreme values can be enforced, as required by their absolute truth. Opponents have to be converted. If they resist, they as well as non-convertible people (like Jews under the Nazis or Bourgeois and Landlords under Communism) have to be made subservient and used for the ends of the regime, to be driven into exile or to be eliminated. If necessary, brutal force and terror have to be applied.

True believers should do this with good conscience since they work (or pretend to do so) for the realization of the supreme values, and not for their own benefit or because they are evil sadists. In fact, they are themselves prepared to sacrifice their lives.

This policy implies the subjugation of all organs of the state, the dissolution or *Gleichschaltung* of all organizations which may hinder or oppose the regime. The legal system has to be adapted to the requirements of the ideology and the judiciary to be made subservient. A different constitution containing the rules prescribed by the creed has to be implemented, which is not a constitution of liberty. In this process the existing organization(s) of believers like a party or a priesthood may play a prominent role. The leaders continue their dominant role, since they have the sole right to interpret the constitution and the meaning of law according to the ideology.

4. The Flourishing and Demise of Totalitarian Regimes

When the totalitarian movement has consolidated its power, converted all potential believers and removed or put to work all inconvertibles for its purposes, it may turn into a mature ideocracy, if its ideological aims do not call for further expansion. For instance, if its ideology is religious, it may turn into a theocracy, like the Israel of antiquity,[2] Tibet, or Iran since Ayatollah Khomeini.

Things are different if the ideology asks either for a conversion of all people on earth, or for the subjugation of them by a selected group, or for more limited aims, like the unification under one government of all people speaking the same language. Whereas this aim has a chance to be reached after some time by political pressure on and war with other nations, if it is not too ambitious, it is nearly impossible to complete the task of dominating the globe. Consequently, a totalitarian regime with such an aim will either be defeated in war, or has to reinterpret its ideology. This will be easier if a second or third generation of leaders does no longer believe, but only pretends to do so to use ideology to maintain power. A defeat in war is probable, especially since ideology encourages an unrealistic view of power relationships. The defeat of Germany under Hitler is a telling example. The communist regime under Stalin, by contrast, postponed the World Revolution and limited itself to *Communism in One Country* for the time being. Finally, Deng and Gorbachev began with fully-fledged and, for their regimes, dangerous reinterpretations of the ideology. As a consequence the regime changes its nature and moves towards an ordinary authoritarian or finally perhaps even into a pluralistic or democratic regime. As can be seen

for the Soviet Union, the state may even fall apart in the process. It is, however, also possible that the reinterpretation only removes the expansionary traits of the ideology. In this case a mature ideocracy may evolve.

5. Totalitarian Regimes in History

In Table 1 a list is presented of the regimes in history that have been totalitarian according to the definition given above together with sources. Moreover, the table contains estimates of the numbers of people killed by them. There may be some cases of totalitarianism which are missing. This is especially true for border cases. The Mahdi rebellion in the Sudan in the 19th century was certainly a totalitarian movement which turned into a theocracy. But it was soon after the early death of its founder defeated by the British Empire under the leadership of Lord Kitchener. When Iran was turned into a theocracy (the Islamic Republic) between 10,000 and 20,000 opponents were killed. This means that there existed a short totalitarian period before a mature ideocracy was firmly established. Similar developments happened with the Taliban's effort to establish a theocracy in Afghanistan.

The Christian crusades to Palestine were totalitarian movements, since they were motivated by ideology and led under the banner of the Cross. They led in scarcely two centuries to the death of between 800,000 and 900,000 Arabians. The Crusaders killed between 50,000 and 60,000 Jews and Arabians (Heinsohn, 1998) when they conquered Jerusalem in 1096. But they were not the army of a totalitarian state, except that they founded the kingdom of Jerusalem. The same is true for other crusades.

There is broad agreement among scholars who analysed the question as to which regimes were totalitarian during the 20th century. No such agreement exists concerning the first seven regimes which have been included in Table 1. So justification has to be given, why they fit our definition. Consider first the Mongols. According to Voegelin (1941; see also de Rachewiltz, 1973):

> The thesis [in the documents] that Genghis Khan is the only and supreme Lord of the Earth may be considered as part of a dogmatic system explaining the true nature of government in the cosmos ... But since ... at least the earthly part of it, is a world in the making, the formula proves to be a claim to rulership for Genghis Khan and to submission by all other earthly powers ... It is brimming with dynamic energy and pregnant with the fanatical acts born of the desire to transform the world of man into a likeness of God's rule in Heaven (405).

> In such cases of a regrettable lack of understanding for the perfectly peaceful and law abiding intentions of the Mongol Imperial Government who did nothing but

carry out an Order of God, punitive expeditions had to be undertaken — like that of 1241, carried into Eastern and Central Europe, which had been the proximate cause for the Papal mission of 1245 (406).

We turn to the Aztecs and quote Conrad and Demarest (1988: 38):

> imperial cosmology held that the Mexica must relentlessly take captives in warfare and sacrifice them; the spiritual strength of the sacrificed enemy warriors would strengthen the sun and stave off its inevitable destruction by the forces of darkness. Thus, it was specifically the Mexica's sacred duty to pursue a course of endless warfare, conquest, and sacrifice to preserve the universe from daily threat of annihilation. The new vision of the cosmos accelerated the pace and scale of human sacrifices beyond all previous measure, associating these ancient rites specifically with the Mexica state and the expansion of the Triple Alliance.

The Taiping rebellion in China originated with the creation of a half-Christian movement, the Association of God Worshipper, by Hung Xiuquan, who believed to be the son of god, and his organizer Feng Yun Shan. Hung Xiuquan founded the Heavenly Kingdom of Great Peace and became Heavenly King in 1851. The supreme values of the ideology included a Christian-inspired communism and equality of the sexes. The kingdom's armies conquered Hunan, Wuhan and Nanking, and moved as far as Tientsin before they were finally defeated in 1864 (Michael and Chung-Li, 1966–71).

A description of Geneva, the Muenster Anabaptists and the Inca Empire as totalitarian regimes is presented in Bernholz (1997:185–290), together with the sources.

It remains to discuss the figures in Table 1. Since totalitarian regimes have a strong tendency to suppress and eliminate people who are not convertible according to their ideologies, or who resist the supreme values contained in them, the number of victims killed by these regimes directly or indirectly, that is for instance by forced labour and starvation, is huge. A comparison of the numbers of victims caused by democratic, authoritarian and totalitarian regimes in the 20th century, 2, 26.7 and 138 million

Table 1: List of totalitarian regimes

Country	Period	Number of victims (Thousand)	Historical source
Mongols	13–15th Ctr.	29927	Morgan (1986)
Incas	Till 16th Ctr.	n.a.	Conrad and Demarest (1988)
Aztecs	Till 16th Ctr.	1000	"
Calvin's Geneva	1542–46	0.058	Choisy (1902), Zweig ([1936], 1983)
Anabaptist's Muenster	16th Ctr.	n.a.	van Dühlmen (1974)
French Revolution (Jacobin Terror)	1794–94	263	Greer (1935), Ladouce (1988)
Taiping Revolution	1851–64	20–34000	Shih (1972), Chesneaux (1973)
Soviet Union	1917–87	61911	Rummel (1990), Courtois et al. (1997)
Nazi Germany	1933–45	20946	Rummel (1992)
Communist regimes:			
China	1949–87	35236	Rummel (1991)
Vietnam	1954–87	1678	Rummel (1996)
Cambodia (Khmer Rouge)	1975–79	2035	Kiernan (1996)
North Korea	1948–87	1663	Rummel (1998)
Poland	1946–48	400	Checinski (1983)
Eastern Europe	1917–89	1000	Courtois et al. (1997)
Cuba	1959–96	15–17	Courtois et al. (1997)
Ethiopia	1974–91	2 000	Human Rights Watch (1990)

Sources for numbers: Elliott (1972), Dobkowski and Walliman (1992: 167), Rummel (1996: 12), completed and corrected by Heinsohn (1998).
For Calvin's Geneva: Meyers Konversationslexikon (1903).
Note: Figures by other authors diverge widely in some cases, for instance for the Soviet Union even by a factor of 0.5. Still, all estimates agree on general magnitudes.

(of which 110.3 million by communist regimes) (Rummel, 1996:15), demonstrates the deadly nature of totalitarian regimes. In these estimates the victims of the wars are excluded, whose number has been estimated as amounting to 34 million (Rummel 1996: 15).

But not only absolute figures matter. Of the different groups persecuted as non-convertibles, the group of proprietors (capitalists, bourgeois, kulaks) suffered the greatest number of deaths, between 40 and 50 million by communist regimes. But if we look at relative figures of victims, for instance as a percentage of the total population or of the persecuted groups, a different picture emerges. The total number of people killed in Geneva because they did not adhere to the right protestant creed is small, but so was the population of Geneva. And the percentage of the total population killed in Cambodia, about 21% (Kiernan, 1996: 458), seems to be the highest among all totalitarian regimes of the 20th century. If one looks, on the other hand, at the proportion of people killed of groups of victims, the number of Jews, 67% of Jews in Nazi Europe (Rummel, 1996: 120), of Ukrainians (mainly Kulaks), 41% (Conquest, 1986: 306), or Tibetans in Communist China, 33.3% (Rummel, 1996: 120), then these numbers overshadow everything else.

PETER BERNHOLZ

NOTES

1. Religions are considered to be ideologies for the purpose of explaining totalitarian regimes. This does not imply that their metaphysical truth concerning last human values is denied.
2. This concept was first coined by Flavius Josephus (Contra Apionem 2: 165) around 94 A.D. to contrast the organization of Jewish society with the political systems conceptualized by classical Greek theory. Compare Taubes (1987).

REFERENCES

Andreski, S. (1965). *The Uses of Comparative Sociology.* Berkeley and Los Angeles: University of California Press.

Bernholz, P. (1997). "Ideology, Sects, State and Totalitarianism: A General Theory," in: H. Maier and M. Schaefer (eds.) *Totalitarismus und politische Religionen. Konzepte des Diktaturvergleichs*, vol. II. Paderborn, Muenchen, Wien, Zuerich: Ferdinand Schoeningh, 271–298.

Bernholz, P. (2001). "Ideocracy and Totalitarianism: A Formal Analysis Incorporating Ideology." *Public Choice*, 108: 33–75.

Checinski, M. (1983). "Terror and Politics in Communist Poland." *Research Paper* 13 (October). Jerusalem: The Soviet and East European Research Center, Hebrew University.

Chesneaux, J. (1973). *Peasant Revolts in China, 1840–49.* New York: W.W. Norton.

Choisy (1902). *L'Etat chrétien calviniste à Genève.* Paris.

Conrad, G.W. and Demarest, A.A. (1988). *Religion and Empire.* Cambridge and New York: Cambridge University Press.

Courtois et al. (eds.) (1997). *Le livre noir du communisme: Crimes, terreur, répréssion.* Paris: Robert Laffont.

Dobkowski, M.N. and Wallimann, L. (eds.) (1992). *Genocide in Our Time: An Annotated Biography with Analytical Introductions.* Ann Arbor (Mich.): Pierian Press.

Elliott, G. (1972). *Twentieth Century Book of the Dead.* London: Allan Lane, The Penguin Press.

Friedrich, C. and Brzezinski, Z. (1965). *Totalitarian Dictatorship and Autocracy.* Cambridge: Harvard University Press.

Heinsohn, G. (1998). *Lexikon der Völkermorde.* Reinbeck bei Hamburg: Rowohlt Taschenbuch, rororo.

Greer, D. (1935). *The Incidence of Terror during the French Revolution: A Statistical Interpretation.* Cambridge, MA: Harvard University Press.

Human Rights Watch (1991). *Evil Days: Thirty Years of War and Famine in Ethiopia.* New York: Human Rights Watch.

Kiernan, B. (1996). *The Pol Pot Regime. Race, Power and Genocide in Cambodia under the Khmer Rouge, 1975–79.* New Haven and London: Yale University Press.

Ladouse, I. (1988). Was France the Fatherland of Genocide? *The World and I.* January: 683–690.

Linz, J. (2000). *Totalitarian and Authoritarian Regimes.* Boulder, Colorado: Lynne Rienner.

Maier, H. and Schaefer, M. (eds.) (1997). *Totalitarismus und politische Religionen. Konzepte des Diktaturvergleichs*, vol. II. Paderborn, Muenchen, Wien, Zuerich: Ferdinand Schoeningh, 271–298.

Meyers Grosses Konversationslexikon (1903). *Calvin*, Sixth Edition, Second vol. Leipzig and Wien: Bibliographisches Institut, pp. 108–109.

Michael, F.H. and Chung-Li, C. (1966–71). *The Taiping Rebellion. History and Documents*, Three vols. Seattle: University of Washington Press.

Olson, M. (1993). "Dictatorship, Democracy and Development." *The American Political Science Review*, 87: 567–575.

Olson, M, and McGuire, M. (1998). "The Economics of Autocracy and Majority Rule: A Study of Dictatorship," in S. Borner and M. Paldam (eds.) *The Political Dimension of Economic Growth.* Houndmills, Basinkstoke, London and New York: Macmillan, 38–73.

Morgan, D. (1986). *The Mongols.* Oxford: Blackwell.

Piekalkiewicz, J. and Penn, A.W. (1995). *Politics of Ideocracy.* State University of New York Press: Albany.

Rachewiltz, Igor de (1973). Some Remarks on the Ideological Foundations of Chingis Khan's Empire. *Papers on Far Eastern History*, vol. 7: 21–36.

Rummel, R.J. (1990). *Lethal Politics: Soviet Genocide and Mass Murder since 1917.* New Brunswick, NJ: Transaction Publishers.

Rummel, R.J. (1991). *China's Bloody Century: Genocide and Mass Murder since 1900.* New Brunswick NJ: Transaction Publishers.

Rummel, R.J. (1992). *Democide: Nazi Democide and Mass Murder.* New Brunswick NJ: Transaction Publishers.

Rummel, R.J. (1996). "Death by Government," in I.L. Horowitz (ed.). New Brunswick NJ: Transaction Publishers.

Schlangen, W. (1970). "Der Totalitarismus Begriff," in *Aus Politik und Zeitgeschichte. Beilage zur Wochenzeitung Das Parlament* 44: 3–46.

Shih, V.Y.C. (1972). *The Taiping Ideology: Its Sources, Interpretations and Influences*. Seattle: University of Washington Press.

Taubes, J. (ed.) (1987). *Religionstheorie und Politische Theologie*. Muenchen and Paderborn: Wilhelm Fink und Ferdinand Schoeningh.

Tullock, G. ([1974], 1987). *Autocracy*. Dordrecht, Boston and Lancaster: Kluwer.

van Dühlmen, R. (1974). *Das Täuferreich zu Münster 1534–1535*. Reports and Documents. München: Deutscher Taschenbuch Verlag.

Voegelin, Eric (1941). The Mongol Orders of Submission to European Powers, 1245–1255. *Byzantion*, XV: 378–413.

Wintrobe, R. (1998). *The Political Economy of Dictatorship*. Cambridge University Press: Cambridge.

Zweig, S. ([1936], 1983). *Castellio gegen Calvin oder Ein Gewissen gegen die Gewalt*. Frankfurt/Main: Fischer.

TRADE PROTECTIONISM

> If we had a situation where these [steel workers] were our constituents and someone was breaking in their house and raping and robbing and pillaging them, we would want to send in a policeman to do something. In this instance, they [importers of foreign steel] are just coming in and taking their future, they are taking their jobs, they are taking all of their dreams away ... We must stand up for the people of this nation. We must stand up with a force of steel and with a backbone of steel. (Mr. Klink, Pennsylvania, *Congressional Record*, 1999)

> ... the [steel import quota] bill before the Senate is a job killer, a trade war starter, and it is a bill that will destroy 40 jobs in steel-using industries for every one job it saves in steel producing. (Mr. Gramm, Texas, *Congressional Record*, 1999)

1. If Free Trade is Efficient why isn't it Universal?

Explaining trade protectionism has been one of the most fruitful areas for the application of public choice analysis. Economists have long faced a conundrum. If our theory is correct that seldom do deviations from free trade improve economic efficiency, why is it that in the real world free trade is the exception rather than the rule? Public choice analysis provides the answer. In common practice, economists ascribe the property of aggregate economic efficiency to any policy moves that create sufficient gains so that the winner could compensate the losers with something left over, i.e., to any policy which expands the utility possibility frontier beyond the initial equilibrium. In practice, however,

such compensation is seldom paid; a policy that expands the utility possibility frontier often makes some worse off. From the standpoint of political economy, policies that potentially raise everybody's utility have much less appeal than policies that actually make everybody better off. Despite the frequency with which international trade theory is mischaracterized, it does not prove that everyone gains from free trade, even when there are no domestic market failures. It proves only that in money terms the gains from free trade in total are greater than the losses, in the sense that there is some set of transfers from winners to losers that could make everybody better off (Willett, 1995). If we assume that most individuals and groups are more interested in their own costs and benefits than in those for their country or the world, then it is perfectly consistent with rational behavior for some individuals and groups to favor trade protection for their industries.

2. Why isn't Protectionism more Prevalent?

Before public choice analysis became widely known, some economists predicted that free trade eventually would reign. These predictions were based on the public interest assumptions that so often dominated discussion of economic policy or else on naïve political science models that predicted that any selective protection measures would be defeated, since a substantial majority would lose from such protectionism. The rent-seeking model of public choice makes quite different predictions. This model stresses costly information and the incentives for free riding that imply many voters will be rationally ignorant or not vote. Concentrated efforts by well-organized producer groups give them incentives to be highly active politically and generally result in more producer than consumer influence on the political process. The prevalence of protectionist tariffs, quotas, and voluntary export restraints (VERs) are a direct result of this process. Thus public choice analysis yields powerful insight into the formation of trade policy.

Despite the importance of its insights, there is a serious problem with such applications of simple rent seeking theory to trade policy. It explains too much!

Having shown how rent seeking theory can explain protection, the current challenge for public choice analysis is to explain why protectionism is not much more prevalent. While the United States does have many formal and informal trade barriers today, they are relatively minor compared with the high levels of protection provided by the Smoot-Hawley tariffs of the 1930s. The story is the same for many other countries as well.

The search for answers to this question has led public choice analysts and political scientists to focus on a wider range of considerations such as the roles of ideas and institutions, the objectives of the executive branch, and the emergence of anti-protection interest groups. It is important to recognize that this richer menu of considerations offers complements to, not substitutes for, rent seeking theory.

3. The National Interest, Interest Groups and Protectionism

Most of the early analysis of trade policy took the country as the basic unit of analysis and focused on calculations of the so-called optimal tariff whereby a country with market power could use trade barriers to improve its terms of trade. Optimality came from balancing these gains against the portion of the standard efficiency costs of protectionism borne by the home country. Retaliation reduces the scope for gains but sometimes they remain positive. Such optimum tariff models were used to provide a rationale for international agreements like GATT to dampen countries' incentives to play such games. However, with the exception of cases of economic warfare, such optimal tariff modeling provides fairly little insight into the actual formulation of trade policies or the best design for institutions to limit protectionism.

Considerably more explanatory power seems to flow from both the standard rent seeking models and modern mercantilist models in which national leaders believe trade surpluses are good for the national economy and/or national power and security. Naturally, for the latter to be an argument for tariffs one must ignore the truth that under a flexible exchange rate or in the long run under the specie-flow mechanism, protectionism is unlikely to improve the trade balance, because import tariffs depreciate the currency, expanding net exports. Of course, rent seeking, mercantilism and bad economics are all tied together, for rational interest groups will attempt to take advantage of mercantilist ideologies and bad economics (Ekelund and Tollison, 1981).

Unified rational actor or billiard ball views of nation states also characterize what has traditionally been the dominant school of thought in the literature on international political economy written by international relations scholars. Dubbed realist or modern mercantilist, this approach focuses on the countries' search for power and security and the role of international power structures in shaping outcomes in the international system. It is widely accepted that such views have considerable explanatory power for France, Japan, and a number of the newly industrializing countries. Foreign policy and national security objectives do not always militate for trade protectionism, however. In the United States during the postwar period the idea that liberal trade policies helped promote U.S. foreign policy and national security considerations was a powerful force behind efforts by both Democratic and Republican administrations to promote trade liberalization and fight protectionism (Finger, 1991).

Such foreign policy concerns and learning from the disaster of the Great Depression combined to foster institutional reforms designed to treat trade policy as an aspect of foreign policy, not just domestic policy, and to strengthen the hand of the executive branch relative to Congress in setting trade policy. These are the major explanations for the progressive lowering of US trade barriers during the first several decades of the postwar period. [see Goldstein (1993); Ikenberry et al. (1988); Rowley et al. (1995)].

Willett (1995) argues that the slowing of the U.S. movement toward trade liberalization can be explained by the weakening of both national security concerns and the clout of the executive branch relative to Congress combined with the growth of interest group pressure. Thus while the standard realist interpretation sees the increase in U.S. protectionism as resulting from a strong government, Willett's interpretation sees this process as a result of a weakening of the power of the state relative to domestic societal (rent seeking) pressures.

4. The Public Choice Approach to Protectionism: Some Theory

4.1. Rent Seeking

An important early contribution to the public choice approach to protection is Tullock (1967), which argues that the resources absorbed in lobbying for protection may outweigh the cost of protection itself. Krueger (1974) develops a similar theme. She models the resources sacrificed in the competition for import licenses. But, she stresses the important idea that in many economies government restrictions upon economic activity are pervasive facts of life, giving rise to rents, and people often compete for the rents, a process called rent seeking and one that uses up resources. Bhagwati (1982) notes that in a distorted economy profit-seeking activities, including lobbying for protection, smuggling and competing for import licences, while not directly productive, may be indirectly welfare enhancing, by using up resources that are doing damage elsewhere. Krueger also emphasizes that rewarding rent seekers undermines the faith of the public in the fairness of markets, which leads to more government intervention and hence a vicious circle of ever increasing rent seeking.

4.2. The Median Voter

Markussen et al. (1995, ch. 19) offer an accessible review of the literature and we draw on their discussion. Much of public choice modeling is based on the idea that public officials enact policies to maximize the probability of their being reelected. Suppose that the voters in an electorate are arranged on a line, in order of the level of protectionism that they support. If the level of protectionism is to be decided by referendum, the bill with the most support will be that which appeals to the median voter. If voting is by a legislature, legislators who support the level of protection supported by the median voter will tend to be elected.

In most economies, voters own disparate amounts of capital, so there are a few who own much capital and many who own none, but all voters own similar amounts of the factor labor. Consequently, the median voter is likely to vote according to the interests of labor. The Stolper-Samuelson theorem states that when both labor and capital are mobile between sectors and certain other conditions are satisfied, labor will benefit or suffer from protection depending on whether labor is the country's scarce or plentiful factor. The empirical implication of this is that labor-scarce countries are likely to have higher tariff rates on average than labor-abundant countries, even though for all countries, if they are too small to influence world prices, protection is harmful, in the sense that the gainers from free trade could compensate the losers and still be better off. Similar results occur in the overlapping generations model of Gokcekus and Tower (1989). They find that when a labor-scarce country liberalizes, even if all citizens have an identical pattern of asset accumulation over their lifetimes, those who have already accumulated assets are capitalists who will gain from liberalization, while the young, who are workers now but will be capitalists later in life, may either win or lose. If most of the population is young, free trade may be resisted in a labor-scarce economy, even though it benefits the whole economy.

Even though free trade alone may be politically unpopular, by combining a trade bill with an income redistribution bill, the bill with the most appeal should include free trade for a country that faces fixed world prices. Moreover, even if world prices are not fixed, the cooperative arrangement with other countries that should meet with the widest approval is free trade combined with an appropriate transfer between nations (Copeland et al., 1989). These mechanisms should limit protectionism.

4.3. The Status Quo Bias

Uncertainty associated with trade liberalization also helps explain why tariffs remain. Those who would be hurt by liberalization are easy to identify. Those who will gain better jobs through expanding opportunities in non-traded and export sectors are harder to identify. Thomas Shelling (1984) points out that voters tend to empathize with the easily identifiable. Consequently, governments may spend large sums of money to rescue one identifiable individual, even though that money could have been better used to save the lives of many unidentified individuals through medical research. Similarly, to the extent that voters empathize with obvious losers from freer trade, there may be little political pressure for trade liberalization, though the opportunity cost of each job protected may be vast. There is also some evidence from experimental economics (Knetsch, 1989) that people tend to value more highly what they own than prospective possessions. Both of these ideas suggest what has been referred to as *status quo bias* against liberalizing trade policy. This bias is reinforced by Corden's (1974) *conservative social welfare function*, which implies that society will support policies that prevent falls in real income for any significant group. As Rodrik (1993) points out, this uncertainty may explain "why reforms that are instituted by an authoritarian regime against prevailing political sentiment survive the return of democracy (think of Pinochet's trade reforms in Chile)."

A further implication is that liberalization will be more likely in boom times, when incomes are rising, than in recessions. However, for the counter argument see Rodrik (1985, p. 1487) who argues that "a deep economic crisis relegates distributional considerations to second place behind economy-wide concerns and therefore allows an agenda-setting government to seek trade policy reforms alongside macroeconomic reforms.

4.4. Picking the Form of Protection

Public choice also informs the choice between production subsidies, import tariffs and import quotas as ways to protect import competing industry. The welfare loss per unit of protection to the protected industry from quotas generally exceeds that from tariffs which exceeds that from subsidies. Thus consumers should rank the three policies in the indicated order. Home producers, *protection seekers*, are aware that quotas are less visible than subsidies or tariffs, and consequently are likely to rank quotas above the other two. Those who benefit from government spending, *revenue seekers*, are likely to prefer the revenue raising tariff to the neutral quota, and both are preferred to the revenue absorbing subsidy.

Yet another option is import quotas with the quota rights accruing to foreigners. Some of these are called VERs, or "voluntary" export restrictions, because the foreigners "voluntarily" restrict exports to avoid other forms of protection by the U.S. If set at the appropriate level, VERs turn competitive foreign firms into monopolists. These foreigners' ideal form of protection is a VER set at their ideal level. These quotas, by restricting sales to the U.S. market and jacking prices up, enable foreigners to act as a cartel and buy off foreign resistance to U.S. protectionism (Kaempfer and Willett, 1989). Finally, Krueger (1983) has argued that all forms of import-substituting protection are inferior to export subsidies as ways of encouraging particular sectors, because the former have no budgetary cost, and are therefore more likely to be used excessively.

Becker (1983) provides an elegant solution to the question of why we end up at neither free trade nor autarky. He argues that the level of protection of the import competing sector at the expense of the rest of the economy is a function of the expenditure by lobbies for the two sectors. Each sector will expend time, energy and money on political pressure up to the point of balance between the expected incremental costs and benefits of further lobbying.

From Becker's logic it follows that as the level of protection rises, further incremental increases in protection will yield smaller benefits to the favored sector relative to the costs to the harmed sector. This shrinks the level of lobbying by the former relative to the level of lobbying by the latter, resulting in an equilibrium level of protection. In essence, Becker argues if lobbying is balanced that the political system will tend to generate efficient outcomes.

Consequently, the political process will tend to choose efficiently between tariffs, the various forms of quotas, and subsidies. However, Cassing and Hillman (1985) and Kaempfer and Willett (1989) emphasize that the political process is most likely to coalesce support around the forms of protection that generate the best tradeoff between the goals of those groups who are best able to mobilize rent seeking resources.

Dixit et al. (1997) emphasize the deadweight cost of lobbying. They suggest that the polity may have an incentive to pass a constitutional amendment to prevent the government from using efficient policies (like lump sum taxes and subsidies) to redistribute income, because restricting the choice to inefficient policies may shrink rent-seeking expenditures. Thus, their model suggests a new way by which distorting policies might emerge as a political equilibrium (also, see Rodrik, 1985). A related issue is explored by Panagariya and Rodrik (1993). They build rigorous models to demonstrate that under certain circumstances welfare may be enhanced by forcing the government to protect only through a uniform tariff. Uniformity creates a free-rider problem, which reduces the incentives for tariff lobbying. Second, if there are imported inputs used in import-competing sectors, uniformity again reduces lobbying by those sectors. Finally uniformity may force future governments to limit their attempts to use tariffs to redistribute income.

Irwin (2002, in progress) notes that in the early 1800s, the industrialized North-Eastern U.S. wanted tariffs to protect manufacturers, the developing West wanted tariffs for the revenues they generated, and the agricultural exporting South wanted free trade. But the revenue seekers were able to gang up with the protection seekers to muster enough political power to defeat the free traders. But the protection seekers do not always gang up with the revenue seekers, because as Pincus (1980) notes in the early years of the U.S., protectionists wanted the tariff above the maximum revenue level, while revenue seekers wanted it below.

4.5. Antidumping and Administered Protectionism

In recent years the use of antidumping statutes has become increasingly important. In the U.S. for an antidumping duty to be activated, the U.S. International Trade Commission (formerly the U.S. Tariff Commission) must find that imports have injured the domestic industry and the U.S. Department of Commerce must find that imports are priced unfairly.

"Foreign firms who charge not only higher prices abroad than they do at home, but also higher prices than their domestic competitors, are still saddled with dumping margins of 50 percent and higher. AD no longer has anything to do with predatory pricing. Even more to the point, all but AD's staunchest supporters agree that AD has nothing to do with keeping trade 'fair.' AD has nothing to do with moral right or wrong, it is simply another tool to improve the competitive position of the complainant against other companies." "The ongoing tinkering with the AD statutes has weakened the law sufficiently that little real evidence of injurious dumping is required before duties are levied" (Blonigen and Prusa, 2002).

They argue with precision and passion that U.S. AntiDumping statutes create perverse incentives. "A foreign industry can almost guarantee it will not be subject to AD duties if it charges sufficiently high prices in its export markets. On the other hand, a domestic industry might resist lowering its prices … [and] might lay-off more workers than expected" as high import penetration and low domestic industry employment are used by the U.S. International Trade Commission to infer injury, which is a critical prerequisite for winning an AD case.

Political pressure matters in how the U.S. International Trade Commission handles antidumping complaints. As

Blonigen and Prusa note, two oversight House and Senate subcommittees control the USITC's budget and three studies all find that industries located in the districts of oversight committee members receive better treatment from the commission. Hansen and Prusa (1996, 1997) find that an additional oversight representative increases the probability of a finding of injury by about 8 percent. Moreover, they obtain an even more sinister result: "PAC contributions to the oversight members also improve an industry's chances, which suggests that political pressure is generated not just by employment concerns, but also by re-election financing concerns."

Antidumping opens up yet another channel for the distribution of rents. Hartigan and Rogers (forthcoming) find a pattern of insider buying in the two months preceding the filing of antidumping complaints, even though the Securities and Exchange Commission prohibits insider buying on the basis of material information that is not yet in the public domain.

5. Protectionism: Empirical Results

Gawande and Krishna (forthcoming) survey empirical approaches to the political economy of trade policy. Baldwin (1985) finds that, for the U.S., sectors with low wages and a high ratio of labor to output tend to be highly protected. This implies that protection is used to help low-income groups. He also finds that protection levels are positively related to industry employment levels, supporting the *adding machine model* which implies that trade protection for an industry is related to its voting strength. Finally, he finds that protection is inversely related to the number of firms in the industry. This suggests that oligopolistic industries find it easier than competitive industries to overcome the free rider problem to muster protectionist legislation [confirming a result found by Pincus (1977) for the tariff act of 1824].

Dutt and Mitra (2001) empirically explore the Stolper-Samuelson argument discussed above. They find that all countries protect, but an increase in the gap by which the capital-labor ratio of the median family falls short of the average for the country raises protectionist barriers in capital-abundant countries and lowers them in labor-abundant countries, providing tentative support for the median voter theory. Magee and Baldwin (2000) provide further support for the theory, with their finding that a high proportion of less educated workers in an electorate, i.e., a lower endowment of human capital per worker, makes a U.S. Representative more likely to vote for protectionist legislation. Similarly, Kaempfer and Marks (1993) find that votes for fast-track authority (for the

Bush administration to negotiate the Uruguay Round and NAFTA) were positively related to the average wage (human capital) and negatively related to labor PAC contributions.

A number of studies have examined the role of campaign contributions to legislators as a determinant of congressional voting on protectionism, e.g., Baldwin (1985), Tosini and Tower (1987), and Fisher et al. (2002). All these studies find that campaign contributions are an important determinant of congressional voting on protection. FGT found that protection can be bought cheaply. One thousand dollars from steel PACs paid to a Republican who is initially receiving no contributions raises the probability that he votes in favor of steel import quotas by 7 percentage points. Similarly, Gawande and Krishna (forthcoming, p. 20) remark how small political contributions are compared to the efficiency losses that trade distortions cause.

Gibbs et al. (2002) explore yet another channel of political influence buying. They find that congressional campaign contributions by the steel industry purchased commentary in the Congressional Record in favor of the steel import quota bill of 1999, with the price of an additional word being quite low: less than $100.

Tosini and Tower (1987) also finds that a protectionist vote is more likely from a U.S. Senator who faces an election in the near future or a congressman whose electorate suffers from lots of unemployment or whose electorate exports relatively little of its output. Similarly, McArthur and Marks (1998) find that lame duck legislators are less protectionist, concluding that legislators tend to favor the general welfare if it doesn't cost them too much.

Takacs (1981) finds that, for the U.S., unemployment tends to foster higher tariffs while inflation tends to lower them. Irwin (1998) suggests this effect is due to the widespread use of specific tariffs, or tariffs that are fixed per unit of good not per unit of value (ad valorem tariffs). However, since the type of tariff used is itself a choice of the policy makers, this counter-cyclical trend in tariff levels is probably intentional on more than one level. That is, not only *are ad valorem* rates raised and lowered in recessions and booms, but protection instruments are used that react in the same way to the economy without needing legislative or bureaucratic adjusting.

Consistent with this research, Magee et al. (1989) find that Republican administrations generate more protection than Democratic administrations do. Their mechanism is Republicans tend to be more ardent inflation fighters, which brings on recession and pressure for protectionism.

The level of protection also depends on who is enfranchised. Hall et al. (1998) find that after women got the vote in U.S. national elections in 1920, tariffs fell. Their explanation is that women purchased the families' consumption goods and blamed tariffs for raising prices, whereas men attributed to the tariff favorable impacts on factor rewards.

Finally, Gardner and Kimbrough (1992a,b) document that, in the U.S., as revenue demands increased, first excise taxes then the income tax were enacted, and both times tariff levels were cut. Once the fixed costs of these two new taxes had been paid, it made sense to rely less on the use of tariffs.

6. Conclusion: The Dracula Effect

Self-serving special interests will always fight to protect themselves. What can economists and political scientists do to limit protectionism? Bhagwati (1988, p. 85) in a marvelous rhetorical flourish articulates what he calls the Dracula effect. Just as Dracula shrivels into nothingness when the morning sunlight hits him, "exposing evil to sunlight helps to destroy it." Similarly, economists for a long time have been illuminating fallacies in protectionist reasoning and documenting the costs and unintended consequences of protectionism. It is only more recently that political economists have shed light on the role of the political process in generating protectionism. All of this analysis combines to convincingly demonstrate that protection is the costly product of a negative sum political game, rather than the product of a government benignly maximizing a social welfare function designed to put us somewhere on the maximal tradeoff between equity and efficiency.

F.Y. Edgeworth (1908), Keynes' predecessor as editor of the *Economic Journal*, anticipated much of the public choice response to various models that justify protection when he wrote in response to Bickerdike's exploration of the idea that the national advantage could be served by the optimum tariff:

> Thus the direct use of the theory is likely to be small. But it is to be feared that its abuse will be considerable. It affords to unscrupulous advocates of vulgar Protection a particularly specious pretext for introducing the thin edge of the fiscal wedge. Mr. Bickerdike may be compared to a scientist who, by a new analysis, has discovered that strychnine may be administered in small doses with prospect of advantage in one or two more cases than was previously known; the result of this discovery may be to render the drug more easily procurable by those whose intention, or at least whose practice is not medicinal ... Let us admire the skill of the analyst, but label the subject of his investigation POISON.

WILLIAM H. KAEMPFER
EDWARD TOWER
THOMAS D. WILLETT

REFERENCES

Baldwin, R.E. (1985). *Political Economy of U.S. Import Policy*. Cambridge: MIT Press.

Baldwin, R. and Magee, C. (2000). "Is trade policy for sale? congressional voting on recent trade bills," *Public Choice*, 105: 79–101.

Becker, G.S. (1983). "A theory of competition among pressure groups for political influence." *The Quarterly Journal of Economics*, 98 (August): 371–400.

Bhagwati, J.N. (1980). "Lobbying and welfare." *Journal of Public Economics*, 14 (December): 355–363.

Bhagwati, J.N. (1982). "Directly unproductive, profit-seeking (DUP) activities." *Journal of Political Economy*, 90 (October): 988–1002.

Bhagwati, J.N. (1988). *Protectionism*, Cambridge: MIT Press.

Blonigen, Bruce A. and Prusa, T.J. (2002). "Antidumping," in K. Choi and J. Harrigan (eds.).

Cassing, J.H. and Hillman, A.E. (1985). "Political influence motives and the choice between tariffs and quotas." *Journal of International Economics*, 19 (November): 279–290.

Choi, K. and Harrigan, J. (eds.) (2002). *Handbook of International Economics*. Oxford: Basil Blackwell.

Copeland, B., Tower, E. and Webb, M. (1989). "Quota wars and tariff wars." *Oxford Economic Papers* 82 (October): 774–788.

Dixit, A., Grossman, G.M. and Helpman, E. (1997). "Common agency and coordination: General theory and application to government policy making." *Journal of Political Economy*, 105 (August): 752–769; reprinted as chapter 1 of Grossman and Helpman (2002).

Dutt, P. and Mitra, D. (2001). Endogenous Trade Policy Through Majority Voting: An Empirical Investigation. Manuscript.

Edgeworth, F.Y. (1908). "Appreciations of mathematical theories." *Economic Journal*, 18 (December): 541–556.

Ekelund, R. and Tollison (1981). *Mercantilism as a Rent Seeking Society*. College Station: Texas A&M University Press.

Finger, J.M. (1991). "The GATT as an international discipline over trade restrictions: A public choice approach," in R. Vaubel and T.D. Willett (eds.) *The Political Economy of International Organizations: A Public Choice Perspective, 125–141.* Boulder: Westview Press.

Fisher, R., Gokcekus, O., and Tower, E. (2002). "Steeling house votes at low prices for the Steel Import Quota Bill of 1999." Duke University Working Paper, http://www.econ.duke.edu.

Gardner, G.W. and Kimbrough, K. (1992a). "Tax smoothing and tariff behavior in the United States." *Journal of Macroeconomics*, 14 (Fall): 711–729.

Gardner, G.W. and Kimbrough, K. (1992b). "Tax regimes, tariff revenues, and government spending." *Economica*, 59: 75–92.

Gawande, K. and Krishna, P. (forthcoming). "The political economy of trade policy: Empirical approaches," in Choi and Harrigan (eds.) (2002).

Gibbs, R., Gokcekus, O., and Tower, E. (2002). "Is talk cheap? Buying congressional testimony with campaign contributions." Duke University Working Paper, http://www.econ.duke.edu.

Gokcekus, O. and Tower, E. (1989). "Does trade liberalization benefit old and young alike?" *Review of International Economics*, 6 (February): 50–58.

Goldstein, J. (1993). *Ideas, Interests and American Trade Policy.* Ithaca: Cornell University Press.

Grossman, G.M. and Helpman, E. (2002). *Interest Groups and Trade Policy.* Princeton: Princeton University Press.

Hall, H.K., Kao, C., and Nelson, D. (1998). "Women and tariffs: Testing the gender gap hypothesis in a Downs-Mayer political-economy model." *Economic Inquiry*, 36(2): 320–332.

Hansen, W.L. and Prusa, T.J. (1996). "Cumulation and ITC decision making: The sum of the parts is greater than the whole." *Economic Inquiry*, 34: 746–769.

Hansen, W.L. and Prusa, T.J. (1997). "The economics and politics of trade policy: An empirical analysis of ITC Decision Making." *Review of International Economics*, 5 (May): 230–245.

Hartigan, J.C. and Rogers, C. (forthcoming). "Equity purchases by insiders and the filing of antidumping petitions." *Review of International Economics.*

Ikenberry, G.J., Lake, D., and Mastanduno, M. (eds.) (1988). *The State and American Foreign Economic Policy.* Ithaca: Cornell University Press.

Irwin, D.A. (1998). "Changes in U.S. tariffs: The role of import prices and commercial policies." *American Economic Review*, 88 (September): 1015–1026.

Irwin, D.A. (2002). "Internal improvements and antibellum tariff politics." Dartmouth College Working Paper in Progress.

Kaempfer, W.H. and Marks, S.V. (1993). "The expected effects of trade liberalization: Evidence from U.S. congressional action on fast-track authority." *World Economy*, 16 (November): 725–740.

Kaempfer, W.H. and Willett, T.D. (1989). "Combining rent seeking and public choice theory in the analysis of tariffs versus quotas." *Public Choice*, 56 (October): 77–86.

Kaempfer, W.H., Tower, E., and Willett, T.D. (1989). "Performance-contingent protection." *Economics and Politics*, 1 (November): 261–275.

Knetsch, Jack L. (1989). "The endowment effect and evidence of nonreversable indifference curves." *American Economic Review*, 79 (December): 1277–1284.

Krueger, A.O. (1974). "The political economy of the rent seeking society." *American Economic Review*, 64 (June): 291–303.

Krueger, A.O. (1983). *Trade and Employment in Developing Countries: Volume 3 Synthesis and Conclusions.* Chicago: University of Chicago Press.

Magee, S.P., Brock, W.A., and Young, L. (1989). *Black Hole Tariffs and Endogenous Policy Theory: Political Economy in General Equilibrium.* Cambridge: Cambridge University Press.

Markusen, J.R., Melvin, J.R., Kaempfer, W.H., and Maskus, K.E. (1995). *International Trade: Theory and Evidence.* Boston: McGraw-Hill.

McArthur, J. and Marks, S.V. (1998). "Constituent interest versus legislator ideology: The role of political opportunity cost." *Economic Inquiry*, 26 (July): 461–470.

Panagariya, A. and Rodrik, D. (1993). "Political economy arguments for a uniform tariff." *International Economic Review*, 34 (August): 685–704.

Pincus, Jonathan J. (1977). *Pressure Groups and Politics in Antebellum Tariffs.* New York: Columbia University Press.

Pincus, Jonathan J. (1980) "Tariffs," *Encyclopedia of American Economic History, vol. 1.* New York: Scribner's 439–450.

Rodrik, D. (1985). "Political economy of trade policy," in G.M. Grossman and K. Rogoff (eds.), *Handbook of International Economics, vol. III.* Amsterdam: North Holland.

Rodrik, D. (1993). "The positive economics of policy reform." *The American Economic Review, Papers and Proceedings* 83 (May): 356–361.

Rowley, C., Thorbecke, W., and Wagner, R. (1995). *Trade protection in the United States.* Cheltenham: Edward Elgar.

Shelling, T.C. (1984). *Choice and Consequence: Perspectives of an Errant Economist.* Cambridge: Harvard University Press.

Takacs, W.E. (1981). "Pressures for protectionism: An empirical analysis." *Economic Inquiry*, 19(4): 687–693.

Tosini, S.C. and Tower, E. (1987). "The textile bill of 1985: The determinants of congressional voting patterns." *Public Choice*, 54 (May): 19–25.

Tullock, G. (1967). "The welfare cost of tariffs, monopoly and theft." *Western Economic Journal*, 3 (June): 224–232.

Willett, T.D. (1995). *The Public Choice Approach to International Economic Relations*, Fairfax: Center for Study of Public Choice.

TRANSITIONAL ECONOMIES

Theories of economic transition were revolutionized by the dramatic events of 1989, when several East European states openly broke with the Soviet Union and expressed desires for more democratic rights and free markets. As Soviet domination of Eastern Europe dissolved, there was not only understandable jubilation in Europe, but also expressions of shock throughout capitals of the world. Radio Free Europe in Berlin exclaimed, "Our jaws cannot drop any lower." By 1991, communism also collapsed in the Soviet Union, and fifteen more states emerged with similar hopes for democracy and markets. With twenty-seven states in Europe and Eurasia interested in establishing free markets and democracy in the early 1990s, policies on transition were rapidly needed to help guide economic reforms.

Initial policy ideas to transform dysfunctional socialist economies in Eastern Europe were derived from basic textbook economics representing the so-called *Washington consensus* (Williamson, 1990). Policy makers who advocated the Washington consensus argued that to initiate a transition to market, governments needed to liberalize prices, stabilize the macroeconomy through tight monetary policy and implement the privatization of state run firms (Blanchard et al., 1991). Ten years of evidence show these policy ideas to be deficient. Price liberalization lead to an unexpected and precipitous fall in output throughout the region that was much longer than anyone anticipated (Kornai, 1993). Stabilization has been very difficult to achieve in many counties due to soft budget constraints associated with state run enterprises and the inability of governments to withdraw generous subsidies and welfare entitlements to citizens. Mass privatization in many countries was frequently stalled or blemished by extensive asset stripping.

We know with the benefit of hindsight, that many deficiencies in policy prescriptions were related to limited understandings of economic change and misunderstandings about the role of economic and political institutions for fostering economic growth. Much has changed since the beginning of the 1990s. Transitional economics now has well-developed dynamic theories of economic reforms that draw heavily on standard arguments in public choice theory (Roland, 2000). This article explores the major contributions of public choice theory to theories of transitional economies by focusing on the dynamics of economic reform programs in East European countries.

1. Transition Types

Prior to 1989, economists had limited experience in the rapid transformation of economies to free market systems and no experience with the type of transformations occurring in Eastern Europe. Although countries such as Chile, Argentina and South Korea attempted significant market reforms in the 1970s and 1980s, they did so under conditions of authoritarian rule. Other communist countries, such as China and Vietnam, introduced incremental economic reforms in existing socialist systems. In each of these cases, when market reforms were introduced, the political institutions of each country remained essentially unchanged. However states in Eastern Europe and the former Soviet Union instituted so called dual transitions, where political and economic systems were changed simultaneously. This meant the scope and degree of change was much wider in East European transitions than almost all previous transitions to market, involving unprecedented changes in institutions of governance and market development (Balcerowicz, 1994; Voorhees, 1995).

The road to free market democracy promised to be long and hard in Eastern Europe. Former communist societies had no private property rights, large and inefficient state run industries, centralized planning of all facets of the economy, misallocation of labor, production and resources. Considerable restructuring efforts would be needed to achieve even limited market functioning. These societies also had no established judicial or regulatory bodies, poorly developed civil societies, and little or no prior experience with liberal democracy (Szacki, 1994). Instituting free elections might take weeks, but overhauling these political institutions would take years

with no exact blueprint for what would happen as reforms progressed.

As policy-makers developed new blueprints for the dual transitions occurring in Eastern Europe, it quickly became evident that these states would encounter very new problems during reforms. For example, policy measures designed to help develop markets and eliminate the legacies of socialist planning might conflict with measures introduced to develop democracy. Early research on dual transitions therefore focused on the dynamics of instituting political and economic reforms simultaneously and the problems associated with these dynamics. We begin with the initial constraints facing policy-makers.

2. Constraints on the Transition to Market: Rational Actors

To understand the problems facing new East European governments, first consider the issue of enacting economic reform programs within democratic political arrangements. Using the perspective of a rational voter, we can ask how they might react to economic reform packages. Even if it is assumed that a majority of voters are certain they will benefit from an economic reform program, rational voters, who place sufficiently high discount rates on future gains from reform, will not prefer a reform program to the *status quo*. The actual constraints on reform minded governments, however, are more severe. Market reforms would result in contractions in existing socialist economies. In addition, there was considerably uncertainty among citizens about the effects of different reform programs on these economies. When these facts are coupled with either risk attitudes among citizens or actual uncertainty with respect to the potential distributive effects on an individual, it is easy to see why rational voters might attempt to resist market reforms. Since their expect utility from reform programs is likely to be small, they will prefer the *status quo* to new reform programs.

Governments in transitional economies can expect opposition *ex ante* to economic reform programs from rational citizens. If these governments are democratically elected, as all governments in East European transitions, then a natural question concerns how potentially costly reform programs can be initiated within democratic regimes. Transitional economics, borrowing heavily from theories of public choice, provide two general answers to this problem. The first answer focused on compensation or side-payments to citizens in transforming economies (Przeworski, 1991). By providing redistributive transfers (or a commitment to make transfers), governments could compensate losers to change their preferences on reform programs. This idea has been explored extensively in different versions of public choice theory including cooperative games, collective action and social choice theory (Ordeshook, 1986; Sen, 1970). However since this strategy was potentially costly, it could also undermine budgetary reforms in transitioning economies. For this reason it was not seriously pursued by most mainstream economists or policy-makers.

The second answer focused on the role of agenda-setters in democratic institutions. Since it is unlikely that a majority of rational voters would prefer reforms to the *status quo*, policy experts suggested making heavy use of the agenda setting powers of the executive to both craft economic reform packages as well as usher these reform packages through newly established legislatures (Sachs, 1993). By making reform packages take it or leave it offers with few or no amendments, governments avoided the problem of transaction costs associated with democratic bargaining (Black, 1958; Buchanan and Tullock, 1962) as well as problems of cycling in democratic legislatures (Riker, 1982). This strategy would not only facilitate the passing of reform programs in democracies, but would also help obviate the inevitable preference for the *status quo* shared by most citizens. Governments throughout Eastern Europe used this strategy extensively to initiate reform programs.

Once governments enacted economic reform programs, post-socialist systems would face sustained contractions in the economy. Although the duration and severity of economic contractions was uncertain, policy makers feared that a protracted recession would cause politicians to reverse market reforms when faced with mass political pressure. Transitional economists therefore believed governments would face opposition to reform programs *ex post*, besides *ex ante* constraints to the introduction of reforms. Given the possibility of such opposition, policy-makers attempted to evaluate the optimality of various strategies designed to move from socialist to market economies (Aslund, 1995; Hellman, 1998; Przeworski, 1991). To evaluate these strategies, policy-makers focused on the speed of reform programs, the potential for reversing reform programs and the probability of political backlash.

3. Transitions Strategies and Transition Dynamics

Policy-makers advocated two major types of reform strategies to deal with potential problems associated with economic reforms in Eastern Europe and Eurasia. One reform strategy, known as 'shock therapy' or the 'big bang' approach to economic transitions, suggested that governments should promote a fast and comprehensive transition from socialism to capitalism (Balcerowicz, 1995; Sachs, 1993). According to this reform strategy, governments should institute a radical process of change that introduced liberalization, stabilization and restructuring measures in an economy simultaneously, and implement these measures as quickly as possible (Lipton and Sachs, 1990; Aslund, 1995). This would lead to spontaneous adjustments to market reforms throughout society and quickly move elements of the economy to a free market system. The main justifications for this plan was to take full advantage of the political opening created by the new political climate after the fall of communism and to use this political capital to help weather the inevitable economic downturn caused by the introduction of market reforms (Balceorwicz, 1995).

In contrast to shock therapy approaches, other transitional economists advocated a more gradual process of transition from socialism to capitalism (Dewatripont and Roland, 1992; McMillan and Naughton, 1992; Murrell, 1992). Under a gradualist strategy, reforms would be carefully sequenced in terms of both the priority and feasibility of implementing reforms. Although both strategies would implement liberalization, stabilization and privatization policies, the speeds of implementation would be different. Gradualist reforms strategies insisted, moreover, on extensive institutional restructuring of economic organizations, early in transition process, whereas shock therapy assumed institutional restructuring should occur later.

There are several potential advantages to gradual reform strategies over 'shock therapy' approaches. First, by instituting gradual reforms, it would be easier to identify those who are worse off in the transition and compensate 'losers' from reform through social programs. This could help prevent a political backlash to reform. Second, by carefully sequencing economic reforms, governments could demonstrate clear policy successes when these policies yielded social benefits. This would make it easier to build political coalitions for future reforms in the economy and help sustain political momentum for economic reforms. Third, if transition policies resulted in mistaken economic outcomes, gradualist strategies could arrest these reforms because reversal costs were lower than 'shock therapy' approaches (Dewatripont and Roland, 1995). Gradualism therefore lowers the cost of experimenting with reform programs and may make the move away from the *status quo* more acceptable to a majority of citizens over time.

An important point of contention between these different economic reform strategies concerned their respective assumptions on the cost of halting or reversing reforms. Some policy-makers preferred rapid transitions because it was believed that the costs associated with reversing these policies would be very high. Consequently, rapid transitional policies would most likely result in a long-term commitment to a market economy or structural reforms in the economy that could not be reversed by new governments. Other policy-makers preferred gradualist strategies because reversal costs were lower. Gradualist policies could avoid reforms that led to inefficient market outcomes that could not be undone because of high reversal costs. Consequently, correcting or learning from policy mistakes would be much easier for governments committed to gradual reforms in the economy.

4. Public Choice Theories of Reform Reversals

The concepts used to explain why East European democracies might slow, halt or even reverse economic reforms programs, are directly linked to public choice theories of collective action and rent-seeking. One viewpoint suggests that policy reversal would most likely emerge from a coalition of dissatisfied voters and anti-reform politicians (Przeworski, 1991). To understand this viewpoint, recall that as economic reforms progress, they will likely generate higher social costs. Citizens or groups hurt most by reforms, such employees of state run enterprises, unemployed workers or pensioners, will naturally seek special exemptions or special protection from the government.

Unfortunately politicians normally face elections before the benefits of economic reforms materialize; therefore many will be tempted to provide special benefits to favored constituencies to gain electoral support. This could weaken the long-term beneficial effects of reform policies on the economy. Social interests seeking protection from economic reforms therefore pose serious risks to economic restructuring *ex post*. A similar mechanism can be used to explain political backlash against reformers. As the cost of reform materializes throughout the society and uncertainty about distributional costs decreases, opposition to transitional reforms increase. As elections approach, citizens react to the cost of reforms by voting out reform parties and replacing them with anti-reform politicians to halt restructuring policies.

These explanations for policy reversals view the reform of socialist economies as a public good that can be eroded by special interests seeking protections from emerging market forces. An alternative viewpoint suggests that elites will halt economic transitions because they stand to benefit from partial or incomplete reforms of an economy (Hellman, 1998). To understand this argument, we need to

remember that post-socialist economies were full of *nomenklatura* bureaucrats who remained extremely strong after the initiation of transitional reform programs (Aslund, 1995). These officials frequently remained in government, continued to run old state enterprises or direct newly privatized firms, banks and industries.

Many of these bureaucrats also enjoyed windfall profits from early and incomplete economic reforms. For example, weak property rights allowed managers to strip their firms' assets. Bankers benefited from profitable arbitrage in distorted financial markets, while local party officials prevented new firms from entering local markets. If a government enforces property rights, legislates additional regulation of financial sectors and strengthens banking laws and enterprise regulations, any additional reforms would reduce or eliminate rents arising from partial reforms. *Nomenklatura* insiders clearly have powerful incentive to prevent such additional reforms to maintain their privilege rents in transitional states.

Besides their economic and political power, the privileged position of *nomenklatura* insiders derives from collective action advantages associated with size. These groups have relatively few members with similar interests, while civil society groups in Eastern Europe are much larger, weaker and more heterogeneous (Howard, 2002). Because the benefits of their rents are concentrated and private while the costs are diffused over the entire society, *nomenklatura* members have stronger incentives to block reforms than civil society groups have to maintain reforms. In contrast to other threats to reform, this rent-seeking insight interprets the problem of economic reform reversals coming from *nomenklatura* insiders who arrest market reforms so they can continue to enjoy monopoly benefits from partial economic reforms.

5. Public Choice and Transitional Economics

Transitional economics focuses on how states can transform their existing economy into a free market system. A decade ago it was commonplace for economists outside public choice theory to discuss market reforms in isolation from the existing rules and institutions that regulated market behaviors. However, the dynamics of transition in Eastern Europe provides a host of examples to illustrate the importance of institutions for the development of markets and the interaction of market development with politics. Public choice has traditionally rejected the idea that markets can be understood independently of politics. After some early policy setbacks, economists have incorporated this principle into their theories of transition.

When considering the dynamics of reform processes, *ex ante* and *ex post* constraints on democratic government are powerful influences on the outcome of reform strategies. *Ex ante* constraints can be mitigated either through compensation packages or various types of agenda control. *Ex post* constraints can be mitigated either by increasing or lessening reversal costs, depending on whether democratic threats to reform are expected to come from popular interest groups or elite rent-seekers. Strategies to reform the economy are selected to deal optimally with these constraints. Whatever strategy is pursued, public choice theories suggest that governments can expect to face different types of collective action problems when implementing reform programs.

MICHAEL J.G. CAIN

REFERENCES

Aslund, A. (1995). *How Russia Became a Market Economy.* Washington: The Brookings Institution.

Balcerowicz, L. (1994). "Understanding post communist transitions." *Journal of Democracy,* 5(4): 75–89.

Balcerowicz, L. (1995). *Socialism, Capitalism, Transformation.* Budapest: Central European University Press.

Black, D. (1958). *The Theory of Committees and Elections.* Cambridge: Cambridge University Press.

Blanchard, O., Dornsbusch, R., Krugman, P., Layard, R., and Summers, L. (1991). *Reform in Eastern Europe.* Cambridge: MIT Press.

Buchanan, J.M and Tullock, G. (1962). *The Calculus of Consent.* Ann Arbor: University of Michigan Press.

Dewatripont, M. and Roland, G. (1992). "Economic reforms and dynamic political constraints." *Review of Economic Studies,* 59(4) October: 703–730.

Dewatripont, M. and Roland, G. (1995). "The design of reform packages under uncertainty." *American Economic Review,* 85(5) December: 1207–1223.

Fish, S.M. (1998). "The Determinates of Reform in the Post-Communist World." *East European Politics and Societies,* 12(1): 31–78.

Hellman, J. (1998). "Winner take all: The politics of partial reform in postcommunist transitions." *World Politics,* 50(2): 203–234.

Howard, M.M. (2002). "The weakness of post-communist civil society." *Journal of Democracy,* 13(2): 157–169.

Kornai, J. (1993). "Tranformational Recession: A General Phenomenom Examined through the Example of Hungary's Development." *Economie Appliquée,* 46(2): 181–227.

Lipton, D. and Sachs, J. (1990). "Creating a market economy in Eastern Europe: The case of poland." *Brookings Papers on Economic Activity,* (1): 75–133.

McKelvey, R.D. (1976). "Intransitives in multidimensional voting models and some implications for agenda control." *Journal of Economic Theory,* 12: 472–482.

McMillan, J. and Naughton, B. (1992). "How to reform a planned economy: Lessons from China." *Oxford Review of Economic Policy.* 12(3) Spring: 130–143.

Murrell, P. (1992). "Conservative Political Philosophy and the Strategy of Economic Transition." *East European Politics and Societies,* 6(1): 3–16.

Ordeshook, P. (1986). *Game Theory and Political Theory.* Cambridge: Cambridge University Press.

Przeworski, A. (1991). *Democracy and the Market.* Cambridge: Cambridge University Press.

Riker, W. (1982). *Liberalism Against Populism.* Prospect Heights, IL: Waveland Press.

Roland, G. (2000). *Transition and Economics: Politics, Markets, and Firms.* Cambridge: MIT Press.

Roland, G. (2002). "The Political Economy of Transition." *Journal of Economic Perspectives,* 16(1): 29–50.

Sachs, J.D. (1993). *Poland's jump to the market economy.* Cambridge: MIT Press.

Sen, A.K. (1970). *Collective Choice and Social Welfare.* New York: North-Holland Press.

Szacki, J. (1994). *Liberalizm po Komunizmie.* Warsaw: Społeczny Instytut Wydawniczy Znak, Fundacja Im. Stefana Batorego.

Williamson, J. (1990). "What Washington Means by Policy Reform," in John Williamson (ed.), *Latin American Adjustment: How Much Has Happened.* Washington DC: Institute for International Economics.

Voorhees, J. (1995). "The transition to market economies and political pluralism. *East-Central European Economies in Transition* in J.P. Hardt and R.F. Kaufman (eds.), New York: M.E. Sharpe.

TRANSITIONS FROM AUTOCRACY TO DEMOCRACY

1. Introduction

Most countries have been dominated by kings, dictators or oligarchies during most of written human history. Moreover, in many cases such *autocracies* were based on ideologies prescribing supreme values to be followed by all believers, so that they were at the same time mature ideocracies like for instance *theocracies* (Flavius Josephus, 1994–1996: 2, 165) or *totalitarian regimes* (see article on totalitarianism). By contrast, democracy as a political regime has been invented rather late in classical Greece, vanished in the following centuries, and was widely successful only during the last centuries.

This is not surprising, since larger political entities, states, with some exceptions like the Swiss Confederation or the United States of America, were mostly formed by force (Ruestow, 1950), often by "roving" or "stationary" bandits applying force to exploit a subjugated productive population (Olson, 1993; Olson and McGuire, 1998). And why then should rulers give up their privileges for a broader participation in political decisions? Why should they agree even to be bound by their own laws instead of remaining above the law?

2. Economic Development as Rulers' Motivation to Limit their Discretionary Powers

> It is certain that despotism ruins individuals by preventing them from producing wealth much more than by depriving them of what they have already produced: it dries up the sources of riches, while it usually respects acquired property. Freedom, on the other hand produces far more goods than it destroys (de Tocqueville [1835] 1945: 220 f.)

A dictator or an oligarchy afraid of soon losing its power (Olson's roving dictator) has not much interest in saving the subjugated population from extreme exploitation. It is motivated to get as many spoils as possible and to transfer them to safe places for the time after its fall. Things are different if rulers feel certain that they, and perhaps even their descendants, will remain in power for a long, perhaps an indefinite period (Olson's stationary bandits). For if they allow people to retain most of the goods they acquire and convince them that there is no danger of irregular interventions into their business affairs, then individuals will be prepared to save, to invest and to innovate, provided that they believe that this policy will be maintained in the future. As a consequence, the amount of goods produced increases, and with it the value of the share reserved by the rulers (see Roll and Talbott, 2001, and Weede, 1986, for the influence of free institutions on wealth). It follows that rulers are motivated, given these conditions, to set up and to be bound by a system of legal rules.

Moreover, because of these relationships, and of their wish not to be endangered by coups d'etat or violent overthrows dictators have reason to increase the probability of staying in office. This can be done by buying the support of the leaders of the armed forces and of important individuals, by trying to create a hereditary kingdom with a hereditary class of supporters (nobles) or by supporting the regime by an ideology legitimising its permanent existence. The more rulers succeed in this endeavour, the more they will be motivated to take the long-term perspective concerning the development of resources.

But as historical experience shows, such a development towards greater security of rulers to be able to maintain their

power in the future, and as a consequence the introduction of some rule of law is not a necessary outcome. If no ideology can be created, that is believed also by the immediate supporters of a dictator, his rule is always threatened by the very leaders of the armed forces, by important noblemen, by influential ministers or even by members of his own family, on whose support the ruler depends. As a consequence, more coup d'etats can be observed in history, which have led to a replacement of one autocratic ruler by another, than changes to other, more pluralistic political regimes. On the other hand, if an ideology is present or can be created, which is believed by the members of the supporting elite, this danger is diminished. But at the same time, the supreme values contained in the ideology may be such that they prevent favourable economic developments (Bernholz, 1995).

3. The Importance of Competition among Several Political Units

> Now the states are already in the present day involved in such close relations with each other that none of them can pause or slacken in its internal civilisation without losing power and influence in relation to the rest; and hence the maintenance, if not the progress, of this end of nature is, …, secure even by the ambitious designs of the states themselves. Further, civil liberty cannot now be easily assailed without inflicting such damage which will be felt in all trades and industries, and especially in commerce: and this would entail a diminution of the powers of the state in external relations…Hence the restrictions on personal liberty of action are always more and more removed, …And thus it is that…the spirit of enlightenment gradually arises as a great good which the human race must derive even from the selfish purposes of aggrandisement on the part of its rulers, if they understand what is for their own advantage (Kant [1784] 1959: 31)

It follows from the conclusions drawn that additional factors must be at work to increase the probability that rulers are prepared to limit their discretionary powers in favor of their subjects. So let us ask again: Why should the ruling elite in an autocracy agree to strong and secure property rights, to minimal state intervention, to limitation of taxes, and thus of its own powers to command and to take away goods at their own discretion? But this time we ask the question by taking into account international relations. Given these conditions, sociologist Baechler (1995) and the so-called 'New Economic Historians' have tried to provide an answer (North and Thomas, 1973; North, 1981; Jones, 1981; Bernholz et al., 1998). They stress that 'European disunity has been our good luck.' In Europe, feudalism with its many power centers developed during the Middle Ages and a split opened up between religious and temporal powers. Rivalry arose among the many rulers to preserve and to extend their powers by foreign policy and military endeavours. This forced them to become interested in the loyalty of their subjects and in economic development to secure a greater tax base and thus stronger armies. However, economic development itself depended on establishing adequate property rights, a reliable legal system, free markets and limited taxes. Consequently, those states were successful in this fierce foreign policy and military competition in the long run who, by chance or by design, made the greatest progress in introducing such institutions. Thus, competition among states forced on unwilling rulers a limitation of domestic powers. The development of competing legal systems, of the rule of law and of safe property rights was helped not only by interstate competition but also by the increasing separation of church and state, by preventing a theocracy (Berman, 1984). These latter events made it impossible, too, that supreme values embodied in earlier religious thinking, like usury laws or the suppression of developments in the sciences and in technology, put obstacles in the path of economic growth. Because of these developments limited government and a pluralistic society arose in Europe as a pre-democratic achievement. First capitalism and later democracy were their progeny.

From Europe these developments spread to other parts of the world, because other countries tried to imitate the successes reached in Europe and in former European colonies like the USA, Canada, Australia and New Zealand. For international competition among states has remained a driving force for the introduction of free institutions until today, motivating rulers like in Japan in the Meiji Era, or Gorbatchew and Deng in the Soviet Union and China since 1979, respectively, to limit their domestic powers to strengthen their economies as a base of international power. Whether the institutional reforms taken were adequate and thus successful is, of course, another question.

4. From Economic Freedom to Democracy

Until now it has only been shown that it is in the interest of autocratic rulers, especially when fierce international political and military competition is present, to allow free markets, safe property rights and a reliable contract law, and not to burden their subjects too much with taxes and regulations obstructing the free play of markets. This implies a wide extension of economic freedom to subjects and a self-limitation of discretionary powers on the part of rulers. But it does not mean that pluralistic or even democratic rights of participation in political decisions are bestowed on the population. Why then should there be a chance that democratic regimes may emerge out of this long process favouring economic freedoms?

It seems that several factors are working in this direction. First, the further developed an economic system, the more complex it becomes. Consequently, an always better education and greater freedom to take decisions have to be granted to individuals, to allow the process of economic growth to proceed. Second, given this situation, more and more people may ask themselves, whether the ruler and the elite surrounding him have the competence to decide the increasingly complicated questions of economic and social policy. As a consequence, and accustomed to the growing sphere of economic freedom they enjoy, they may ask themselves why they should not be allowed to participate in the decisions of political issues. Fourth, because of the complexity of problems to be solved, the ruler himself is dependent on a growing number of experts. All these factors work together with international military and political competition, to incline rulers or to put them under pressure to grant more and more political rights to a growing number of citizens.

The developments sketched seem to have played an important role in many historical cases. Favourable economic developments have preceded regularly the rise of pluralism and democracy, and the surge in the number of democratic regimes during the last two centuries followed in the wake of the growth of capitalistic economic systems. It should also provide food for thought that in modern complex societies democracies seem to have existed and still to exist only in market economies with extended private property, whereas the opposite is not true.

Still, the chain of events described is not a necessary sequence. Dictators may prefer to maintain absolute domestic power at the cost of unfavourable economic developments and the danger of being threatened by foreign powers, or to be unable to extend their power internationally. For the wealth they want or need personally and for their supporters may be available even if the dominated country remains relatively poor. And the small size of a country they dominate may hinder them anyhow to move to parity with superior foreign countries, however favourably their own economy might develop. Finally, if autocracy takes the form of an ideocracy its supreme values may forbid the move to safe private property rights and towards a decentralized market economy. As a consequence a change to an efficient and innovative economic system may be prevented permanently or for decades even in view of international military and political competition (see article on Totalitarianism). A telling example is provided by the persistence of a Communist totalitarian regime in the Soviet Union for about 70 years, though even this system could not withstand reality in the very long run.

5. Other Factors Influencing the Transition from Autocracy to Democracy

One factor preventing or delaying the transition from autocracy to democracy has just been mentioned: Supreme values of an ideology contradicting the requirements of an efficient and innovative economic regime. The resulting economic and, therefore, fiscal and military weakness may even be compensated for an extended period because of some advantages an autocracy experiences compared to democracies. First, it can make up for its economic inefficiency by enforcing a lower level of consumption in favour of higher investments and a higher share of gross national product devoted to military expenditures. Second, in its foreign policy it can follow a more consistent and, if wanted, more expansionary position than democracies, which are in their policies dependent on and limited by parliaments, political parties, interest groups and the consent of their citizens. Consequently, autocracies may be able to defeat or even subjugate democracies of a similar size in the short run. And if this happens they are able to turn them, too, into autocracies, and later to prevent their transition to democracy. This is especially the case if an adequate ideology is available, which helps to overcome resistance and to maintain dominance.

On the other hand, if autocracies and totalitarian regimes do not succeed in time with such policies, democratic market economies will develop more strongly. This means that they will enjoy greater fiscal and military capabilities in the long run, even though their share of government in gross domestic product is sizeably lower than in these regimes. For the higher investment rate can after some time no longer compensate for the greater efficiency and especially innovative potential (for a comparison of the innovative breakthroughs reached in free market vs. communist so-called planned economies see Kornai, 1971: 271–280).

By contrast, the transition of authoritarian to pluralistic and democratic regimes may be furthered by three other factors. First, they may be defeated in war and democracy may be introduced by the victors (as in West Germany and Japan after World War II). Second, after power has been shared with a wider circle of privileged people in a complex society with a market economy, that is when a kind of oligarchy has been reached, infighting may occur between different groups within this political elite. But then it may happen, that the fighting factions seek the support of other segments of the population by promising them political participation. Third, the rulers may be unable to solve a severe economic or other crisis and helplessly step down in favour of a democratic regime. This has happened several times to military regimes in Latin America during the last decades.

Apart from these three, several institutional factors seem to play a role in determining whether efforts are undertaken to transform autocracies into democracies and whether these efforts are successful (Linz, 1990; Linz and Stepan, 1996). Among them it appears to be important whether the country has had a democracy before, whether co-operation between parts of the old regime and the opposition is possible during the transition process and which form of democratic system is envisaged. The transformation process becomes especially difficult if economic institutions have to be changed at the same time together with the political institutions. For since the beneficial consequences of even well-designed economic reforms materialize only after some time, the costs are felt by a great part of the population very soon. Consequently the reformers lose credit and it is necessary that a functioning opposition exists (mostly related to those members of the old regime who have been prepared to abolish autocracy) who can take over the government, and who are willing to adhere to the tenets of establishing the rule of law and democracy and to the fundamentals of economic reforms.

In totalitarian regimes one of the reasons for changes may also be a weakening of the ideology. This is especially probable if the rulers of the second or third generation after its foundation or rejuvenation do no longer believe in it, but only pretend to do so to maintain their dominance. In this case they may be willing to move towards a free market economy by reinterpreting the ideology because of fierce international political and military competition. And in this case the forces discussed above begin to work. Whether, however, the reforms introduced by the rulers are successful depends on their knowledge of the underlying relationships and on the resistance they meet. There remains, therefore, still the possibility that a totalitarian or ideocratic regime ends up not as a democratic but as a simple autocratic regime.

PETER BERNHOLZ

REFERENCES

Baechler, J. (1995): *Le capitalisme, I. Les Origines*. Paris: Gallimard.

Berman, H.J. (1983). *Law and Revolution*. Cambridge, MA/London: Harvard University Press.

Bernholz, P. (1995). "Supreme Values, Tolerance and the Constitution of Liberty," in: Gerard Radnitzky and Hardy Bouillon (eds.) *Values and the Social Order*, vol.1. Aldershot: Avebury Ashgate, pp. 235–250.

Bernholz, P., Streit, M., and Vaubel, R. (eds.) (1998). *Political Competition, Innovation and Growth. A Historical Analysis*. Berlin, Heidelberg and New York: Springer.

Flavius Josephus (1994–1996). *Contra Apionem.*

Kornai, J. (1971). *Anti-Equilibrium. On Economic Systems Theory and the Tasks of Research.* Amsterdam and London: North Holland.

Jones, E.L. (1981). *The European Miracle.* Cambridge: Cambridge University Press.

Kant, I. ([1784] 1959). "Idea of a Universal History from a Cosmopolitan Point of View." Translated by W. Hastie, in: P. Gardiner (ed.) *Theories of History.* New York: The Free Press.

Linz, J.J. (1990). Transitions to Democracy. *The Washington Quarterly,* 13: 143–164.

Linz, J.J. and Stepan, A. (1996). *Problems of Democratic Consolidation: Southern Europe, South America, and Postcommunist Europe.* Baltimore: Johns Hopkins University Press.

North, D.C. and Thomas, R.P. (1973). *The Rise of the Western World: A New Economic History.* Cambridge: Cambridge University Press.

North, D.C. (1981). *Structure and Change in Economic History.* New York: W.W. Norton & Co.

Olson, M. (1993). "Dictatorship, Democracy and Development." *The American Political Science Review,* 87: 567–575.

Olson, M, and McGuire, M. (1998). "The Economics of Autocracy and Majority Rule: A Study of Dictatorship," in: S. Borner and M. Paldam (eds.) *The Political Dimension of Economic Growth.* Houndmills, Basinkstoke, London and New York: Macmillan, pp. 38–73.

Roll, R. and Talbott, J. (2001): *Why Many Developing Countries Just Aren't.* Internet: http://www.worlddevelopmentnoc.com/id21.htm.

Ruestow, A. (1950). *Ortsbestimmung der Gegenwart.* 3 vols. Zuerich.

Tocqueville, A. de ([1835] 1945). *Democracy in America,* vol. 1. New York: Vintage Books.

Weede, E. (1986). "Catch-up, distributional coalitions and governments as determinants of economic growth or decline in industrialized societies," *British Journal of Sociology,* 37: 194–220.

TRIANGULATION

> Things fall apart; the center cannot hold. … (W.B. Yeats, *The Second Coming*)

When the members of the 104th US Congress took their seats in January 1995, President Bill Clinton faced Republican majorities in both legislative chambers. Forty years of Democratic Party hegemony in the House of Representatives had come to an abrupt end, signifying a political realignment that had eluded even Ronald Reagan's grasp. The Republican congressional victory, usually attributed to the failed health care reform initiative spearheaded by First Lady Hillary Clinton and to the political popularity of the 'Contract with America,' the brainchild of

Speaker of the House to be Newt Gingrich (R-GA), was the nadir of Mr. Clinton's first term of office.

Like 'Jason' of the *Halloween* series of horror movies, Bill Clinton returned from near political death, miraculously reviving his standing in the polls as he had done during his maiden presidential campaign and was to do many times over before leaving the White House in January 2001, by adopting a strategy of 'triangulation.' In ordinary usage, that term refers to the trigonometric method whereby navigators, surveyors and spycatchers determine the position of an unknown point given a known baseline and two Cartesian coordinates. Political consultant Dick Morris is credited for using it to describe the supposedly novel scheme by means of which the president cobbled together a governing coalition from a modern American electorate divided roughly evenly between Democrats, Republicans, and so-called independent voters. However defined (and the term seems to have at least three possible interpretations), triangulation was intended to co-opt the middle of the political spectrum. It is, in essence, a restatement of the median voter theorem, a central principle of public choice deduced by Duncan Black (1948, [1958] 1987).

The median voter theorem can be stated as follows (see Munger, 2001, for a more formal treatment). If voters' preferred outcomes can be arrayed along a single dimension (e.g., left-right), voters' preference orderings are 'single-peaked' (have unique maxima), and collective decisions are taken by simple majority rule, then the preferences of the voter located at the median of the preference array will be decisive. Any proposal (or candidate) to the left or the right of the median will be defeated in a majority rule election by one positioned closer to the median voter's preferred outcome. Because extreme proposals lose to centrist proposals under the assumptions of the median voter theorem, candidates and political parties rationally will move toward the middle of the political spectrum in order to gain or retain political power.

Subsequent extensions of the theorem showed that the decisive voter need not be located exactly at the center of the distribution of the preferences of the eligible voting population (see, e.g., Hinich and Munger, 1997). Not everyone who can vote does vote. Some voters may be alienated from the process because the positions of the candidates are too distant from the policies they prefer. Other voters may abstain because they perceive no important differences between the candidates' positions. These richer statements of the median voter theorem suggest that candidates will move about in policy space (without the aid, sadly, of a political theodolite), trading expected vote gains against expected vote losses, until their electoral support is at a maximum.

In political context, one meaning of triangulation is illustrated by a (possibly apocryphal) aphorism of President Richard Nixon, 'run to the right and govern to the middle'. The two-stage electoral gauntlet run by aspiring US presidents demands that candidates first secure nomination by the delegates to their parties' quadrennial political conventions. Since these delegates tend to come from the ranks of the parties' most active and most ideologically committed members, successful candidates must position themselves accordingly. Republican presidential candidates will 'run right' during the primary election season in order to appeal to the nominating convention's median delegate, whose political preferences will in general be more conservative than those of the general voting population. Candidates for the Democratic Party's nomination will for similar reasons 'run left.' Once the parties' presidential nominees have been selected, however, both candidates will move toward the center, since victory in the general election demands catering to the median of the preference distribution of all likely voters, which includes Democrats, Republicans, and independents. 'Triangulation' under this interpretation implies that presidential candidates will first shore up their partisan bases and then reposition themselves for the general election campaign. It also implies that, once elected, a sitting president will 'govern to the middle' in order to maximize his reelection prospects.

A second meaning of triangulation suggests that, far from shoring up their political bases, candidates can safely ignore the preferences of the party faithful. Voters located at the extremes of the left–right preference array are unlikely to switch their allegiances to the other party's candidate, no matter how persuasive or charismatic he may be. Hence, candidates for presidential office can triangulate the electorate, increasing their chances of election or reelection, by selectively taking positions that appeal to the median voter, but offend their staunchest supporters. Trading on liberal political credentials secured by stances on core issues, such as abortion and affirmative action, a Democrat such as Bill Clinton can proclaim that 'the era of big government is over' and promise to 'end welfare as we know it,' thereby picking up support from moderate voters without risking the loss of his left-wing nucleus. Knowing that right-wing voters are unlikely to support a liberal Democratic candidate, a Republican such as George W. Bush can likewise safely scold his conservative political base, complaining that, 'too often, on social issues, my party has painted an image of America slouching toward Gomorrah,' and accusing them of wanting to 'balance the budget on the backs of the poor.'

A third interpretation of triangulation comes from Dick Morris himself. In the transcript of an interview with Australian reporter Kerry O'Brien, Morris defined the strategy as an attempt 'to take the best of each party and combine them' (O'Brien, 2000). For example,

> The liberals in the US, the left, said, 'We need to have gun control and we need to let people out of prison early.'
> The Republicans said, 'We should not control guns and we should keep them in jail.'
> The public said, 'I want the gun control from the left and the long prison sentences from the right.'
> And Clinton said, 'OK, I'm going to give that to you. I'm going to advocate those two steps. And I'm going to forget about the left wanting parole and I'm going to forget about the right wanting no restrictions on guns.' (ibid.)

Whether or not Mr. Morris had accurately gauged public opinion in this particular case, his idea of triangulation seems to be one of identifying policy issues on which voters are sharply divided, and then combining them in ways that appeal to a larger political constituency than could be marshaled in support of either one separately. An alternative construal of Morris's strategy is that of opportunistically appropriating selected policy positions of one's political opponents, yielding ground on issues where the expected political gain is less than expected cost. So, if liberals care more about gun control than they care about prison populations, and if conservatives are willing to back 'reasonable' restrictions on gun ownership in return for stiff sentences for convicted felons, then packaging support for gun control with opposition to tolerant parole policies would defeat consistently hard-left or hard-right positions on both issues.

Bill Clinton's perspective on modern American politics was undoubtedly colored by his experiences during the 1992 presidential election, when Reform Party candidate Ross Perot garnered 19% of the popular vote, perhaps denying George H.W. Bush a second term and propelling a Democrat into the White House for the first time since Jimmy Carter occupied it 12 years previously. Mr. Clinton's election by a less-than-50% plurality of the votes cast may have been reason enough to think that a 'third way' — not Democrat nor Republican — must be found for building a ruling coalition that included a significant fraction of the 'undecided,' 'independent' voters in the middle of the political spectrum. But 'triangulation' is nothing new. Successful politicians have always been required to operate in multidimensional issue space, seeking the location of the median of the distribution of voters' preferences over policy alternatives. The tradeoffs that inevitably must be made in constructing a set of support-maximizing policy proposals are an essential feature of a collective choice process in which the preferences of the median voter hold a privileged position.

WILLIAM F. SHUGHART II

REFERENCES

Black, D. (1948). "The decisions of a committee using a special majority." *Econometrica*, 16 (July): 245–261.

Black, D. ([1958] 1987). *The Theory of Committees and Elections*. Boston: Kluwer Academic Publishers.

Hinich, M.J. and Munger, M.C. (1997). *Analytical Politics*. Cambridge: Cambridge University Press.

Munger, M.C. (2001). "Voting," in W.F. Shughart II and L. Razzolini (eds.) *The Elgar Companion to Public Choice*, 197–239. Cheltenham, UK and Northampton, MA, USA: Edward Elgar.

O'Brien, K. (2000). Transcript: Dick Morris on Bill Clinton. *7.30 Report* (May 17): http://www.abc.net.au/7.30/stories/s127980.htm.

U

UNDERGROUND GOVERNMENT: THE OFF-BUDGET PUBLIC SECTOR

Politicians and bureaucrats have a great disaffinity for constraints placed on their discretionary behavior, particularly with regard to their ability to spend and to borrow. Government spending permits politicians to direct benefits to their constituents in general and especially to their political supporters. Debt is favored because repayment occurs in the future (perhaps while others are in office) while the benefits of the expenditures are reaped in the present period. In the United States, both statutory and constitutional restraints on government spending and indebtedness greatly limit the abilities of politicians and bureaucrats at the state and local levels of government to spend and to incur debt. These restrictions historically arose because of the egregious fiscal excesses during the nineteenth century when canals and railroads were under construction. In the heady days of the "robber barons," bonds were issued by state and local governments to attract the railroads, and defaults were not uncommon. To restore fiscal integrity — and the faith of investors, many of whom were foreign — statutory and constitutional restraints were imposed on the fiscal actions of governments. For example, at the state level of government, forty-five states now have either a constitutional or statutory requirement that the governor must submit a balanced budget; forty require the legislature to enact a balanced budget; and thirty-seven states mandate that the budget signed by the governor must be balanced (Council of State Governments, 2001, p. 260, table 6.3). Thus, the ability of politicians and bureaucrats to spend and borrow are markedly constrained.

In response to fiscal constraints on their behavior, public officials have devised a means to move government activities "off the books" or "underground" by creating "off-budget enterprises" (OBEs) which permit them to evade statutory and constitutional constraints on borrowing. An OBE is a corporation established by a charter from the federal or a state or local government that has significant ties to the governmental entity that charters it. Typically, the members of the board of directors of the OBE are appointed by elected officials in the jurisdiction that established the OBE, so politicians ultimately control the OBE. Because the OBE is an entity separate from the governmental unit that established it, its financial operations are not subject to the statutory or constitutional restraints imposed on government itself. OBEs spend, borrow, hire and fire, contract for services, and engage in all sorts of activities free from the limitations imposed on governments.

As Bennett and DiLorenzo (1983, p. 35) discuss, the first attempt at off-budget activity occurred in the city of Waterville, Maine at the close of the nineteenth century when the city fathers wanted to build a new city hall, but taxpayers rejected the bond inititative required to finance it. Undeterred, the politicians established the Waterville New City Hall Commission, a corporate entity, donated a building lot to the Commission, and hired a contractor who was to be paid from the proceeds of a bond offering made by the Commission. Debt service on the bonds was to be provided from rent paid by the city to the Commission for use of the building. But, because the source of the rent was taxes, "the Commission was held unconstitutional in 1898, because the court ruled that the arrangement was a disguised mortgage that violated the debt limitation imposed on the city by the Maine constitution." Waterville politicians then regrouped to evade the constitutional debt limits that limited their actions. The next year, 1899, the Kennebec Water District was established as a separate corporation — the nation's first OBE — that would issue its own bonds to purchase the private water companies operating in the area. Revenues from providing water services to residents would pay the interest, retire the debt, and finance the corporation's operations. The Supreme Judicial Court of Maine held that this debt was not the obligation of the city or the taxpayers, so the constitutional restriction on borrowing did not apply, and the scheme passed judicial scrutiny (Morris, 1958).

From this modest beginning, OBEs have proliferated in both numbers and activities. The most comprehensive census of these entities is reported in the *Census of Governments* (U.S. Census Bureau, 1997, p. vii) where OBEs are called "special district governments" (excluding school districts) "that exist as separate entities with substantial administrative and fiscal independence from general purpose local governments ... [These] entities must possess three attributes: existence as an organized entity, governmental character, and substantial autonomy." According to the *Census of Governments* (pp. vii–viii), the number of OBEs has increased dramatically: "As a group, special district governements are by far the most rapidly growing type of government, rising to a total of 34,683 [in 1997], an increase of about 3,128, or 9.9 percent, since the 1992 Census of Governments. ... [T]he number of special district governments reported in 1997 is almost three times the number ... reported in 1952."

Of significance is the Census Bureau's admission that the reason for the dramatic growth of OBEs is motivated by financial constraints on government: "The increasing number of special districts often reflects financial considerations. As new programs are initiated, or new services required, the establishment of special districts may reduce the need to increase the burden on general purpose governments which may be unable to meet the fiscal requirements necessary to implement these new programs. *Debt and tax limitations are further stimulants for creating special districts* for raising both capital construction and operating expenditure funds." (Ibid., emphasis added.)

OBEs engage in a wide range of activities, including (but not limited to) operating airports, fire protection, cemeteries, hospitals, industrial development, mortgage credit and housing, parking facilities, recreation and parks, electricity generation and distribution, gas and water supply, sewerage, mass transit, and the construction and maintenance of highways. They are generally designated as authorities, commissions, or districts by the governmental body that creates them. OBEs tend to be concentrated in the most populous states: in 1997, 11 states had more than 1,000 OBEs, with California (3,010), Illinois (3,068), Texas (2,182), and Pennsylvania (1,919) having the most. Four states (Alaska, 14; Hawaii, 15; Louisiana, 39; and Rhode Island, 76) and the District of Columbia (1) had fewer than one hundred OBEs (U.S. Census Bureau, p. 13 table 9). A small number of OBEs have been chartered by the federal government, because their operations involve more than one state; most notable is the Port of New York Authority which operates transportation facilities for metropolitan New York City, an area that includes New Jersey.

Another indicator of the economic significance of OBEs is their debt. For state and local governments, two types of debt exist: full-faith-and-credit debt which is approved by the taxpayers in a bond referendum and "nonguaranteed" debt incurred by OBEs. The term full faith and credit indicates that taxpayers have agreed to tax increases if needed to guarantee payment of principal and interest. For OBEs, revenues from operations are pledged in the bond indenture to cover principal and interest payments; the taxpayer does not guarantee repayment, and taxpayer approval is not sought when OBEs issue bonds. Interest payments on both full-faith-and-credit and nonguaranteed debt are exempt from federal taxation.

As shown in Table 1, at the state level of government, nonguaranteed debt issued by OBEs outstanding was a small fraction of voter-approved debt in 1942, the earliest date for which information is available. In 1942, $5.80 in full-faith-and-credit debt existed for each $1 of nonguaranteed debt at the state level. By 1970, however, the amounts

of the two types of debt outstanding were roughly equal. Since 1980, nonguaranteed debt outstanding has risen by roughly a factor of five while full-faith-and-credit debt outstanding has only increased by a factor of about 2.4. At the local level of government, a similar pattern emerges. The amount of nonguaranteed debt issued by OBEs was nearly equal in 1980 to the amount of voter-approved debt outstanding, approximately $100 billion. Since that time, however, nonguaranteed debt has risen by a factor of 4.5 while full-faith-and-credit debt outstanding went up only by a factor of three. These trends since 1980 reflect that "Since 1978 … activists have proposed and passed initiatives limiting taxing and spending by state governments in the United States" (New, 2001, p. 1). Off-budget activities conducted by OBEs, that is underground government, was the natural response of politicians and bureaucrats to these tax and expenditure limitations (Bennett and DiLorenzo, 1982).

A number of disquieting public policy issues arise in the context of off-budget enterprises. First, if the activities of OBEs are truly in the public interest, why does the public not vote on the bonds issued by these entities? Indeed, full-faith-and-credit debt always carries a lower interest rate than does nonguaranteed debt, for lenders demand compensation for the higher risk of default of nonguaranteed bonds. Thus, capital cost considerations favor the elimination of OBEs and the movement of their activities on-budget. Of course, the sticking point is the constitutional and statutory limitations on government debt which lead to the creation of OBEs in the first place. But those restraints raise an important issue: If these contraints are no longer relevant, shouldn't they be repealed? And, if the constraints are still relevant, should OBEs be used to evade them?

Second, politicians assert that OBEs provide superior service to the public because they are far less bureaucratic and offer much greater flexibility than traditional government agencies that are supposedly hamstrung by red tape, civil service regulations, and bidding requirements. Rather than being an argument in favor of OBEs, however, such claims are a clarion call for the reform of bureaucratic red tape and regulations. If regulations and red tape hamper government operations without compensating benefits, reform is essential. Much closer to the truth is that OBEs offer politicians greater opportunities for nepotism and favoritism in rewarding their supporters than does on-budget government agencies where freedom-of-information legislation typically mandates an openness and transparency from which OBEs are exempted as "private" corporations.

Third, a persuasive argument can be made that OBEs should be disbanded and their actitivities turned over to

Table 1: State and local government debt by type, selected years, 1942–1997 ($ millions)

	State debt		Local government debt		Total	
Year	Full faith and credit	Nonguaranteed	Full faith and credit	Nonguaranteed	Full faith and credit	Nonguaranteed
1942[a]	$2,641	$455	__[b]	__[b]	__[b]	__[b]
1952	$4,926	$1,714	$17,510	$4,571	$22,436	$6,285
1960	$8,912	$9,216	$32,738	$15,938	$41,650	$25,154
1970	$17,736	$21,167	$57,601	$34,911	$75,337	$56,078
1980	$49,364	$70,457	$100,439	$102,196	$149,803	$172,653
1990	$74,972	$240,518	$170,147	$355,641	$245,119	$596,159
1995	$116,195	$304,994	$261,080	$406,112	$337,275	$711,106
1997	$119,514	$335,002	$296,152	$454,275	$415,666	$789,277

Notes: [a] First year for which data are available. [b] Not available.
Source: J. Scott Moody, ed. 2001. *Facts and figures on government finance*, 35th edition, Washington DC: Tax Foundation, table E14 (p. 207) and table F12 (p. 284).

private firms. OBEs obtain revenues from providing goods or services, so the eclusivity criterion so crucial to the concept of public goods is not applicable. In short, those who do not pay for the electric service or the highway tolls, for example, can easily be denied such services. Thus, virtually all of the activities of OBEs could be conducted by private firms, even if government subsidies were required (as might be the case for mass transit). A large and growing literature on *privatization of public services* shows unequivocally that private provision is typically far more efficient than government provision, so taxpayers would benefit from higher quality services at less cost.

Finally, scholars and researchers should be aware that the public sector, particularly at the state and local level of government in the United States, is much larger in terms of revenues, expenditures, and employment than is generally reported — OBEs are extensions of government. In terms of both numbers and outstanding debt, OBEs are clearly important components of the public enterprise broadly conceived. Off-budget enterprises are not unique to the United States by any means, but exist in Britain and other countries where they are called "quangos," an acronym for quasi-autonomous nongovernmental organizations. Underground government and off-the-books operations are prominent features of the political landscape that benefit politicians more than their constituents.

JAMES T. BENNETT

REFERENCES

Bennett, J.T. and DiLorenzo, T.J. (1982). "Off-budget activities of local governments: the bane of the tax revolt". *Public Choice*, 39(3): 333–334.

Bennett, J.T. and DiLorenzo, T.J. (1983). *Underground Government: The Off-Buget Public Sector*. Washington, DC: Cato Institute.

Morris, C.R. (1958). "Evading debt limitations with public building authorities: the costly subversion of state constitutions". *Yale Law Journal*, 68(December): 34–45.

New, M.J. (2001). "Limiting Government Through Direct Democracy: The Case of State Tax and Expenditure Limitations: Policy Analysis 420", Washington, DC: Cato Institute.

U.S. Census Bureau. (1999). *1997 Census of Governments, Vol. 1, Government Organization*. Washington, DC: U.S. Government Printing Office.

V

THE VALUE OF VOTING RIGHTS

In almost all democratic national elections an individual vote matters only in highly unlikely situations. It can be said that it is more likely to win the jack pot of a national state lottery than to become once the decisive voter in a lifetime, or to be hit in a thunderstorm than to change the voting results. Thus, it can be said that individual voters generally cannot alter such an election result regardless of whether they vote or not and how they vote. The fact that nevertheless many individuals voluntarily participate in such elections suggests that people care about democracy as such.

In public choice theory it is assumed that individuals as voters act rationally, i.e., by their voting behavior they try to maximise their own benefits. The rational voter theory was first developed by Downs (1957), Tullock (1967), Riker and Ordeshook (1968), and it is summarized e.g., by Mueller (1989, Chap. 18), Struthers and Young (1989), and Schram (1991). Given the fact that voting means to invest some effort (gathering and evaluating information, going to the polling booth or asking for the ballot-papers for postal vote), the extremely low probability for one's own vote being decisive makes voting apparently irrational. Because of this conclusion it is often asked why people vote, and many scholars have tried to give reasons in order to explain the discrepancy between the theoretical prediction and empirical observations refered to as "vote participation paradox."

According to public choice theory, voters' decision to participate in a vote is driven by individual costs and benefits involved. The typical reason given by public choice theorists why benefits should be close to zero is the extremely low probability that the own vote is decisive (Mueller, 1989; Struthers and Young, 1989). Besides the low probability justification for not voting ("my vote won't matter"), the costs of voting offer another justification. These costs include the necessary preparations (one needs the voting card or, as in the United States, is not even registered automatically by the authorities but has to take the initiative oneself) as well as the costs of information, i.e., in the case at hand the costs of making up one's mind which party one should vote for. A clear-cut position about the support for one party or another is usually the result of

gathering information and reevaluating, reinterpreting or even neglecting facts. By deciding not to vote, all these mental efforts can be avoided. Furthermore, important costs of voting are, of course, the opportunity costs in terms of lost working or leisure time.

The rational voter theory as applied in the literature on political support functions (for a survey see Nannestad and Paldam, 1994) somehow neglects the low probability argument for not voting and claims that people decide in public elections as in economic situations. In other words: a voter chooses that party or coalition whose program or expected policy is best for him or herself personally. According to such a view, parties are nothing more than competing firms trying to satisfy the voters' demands (given a perfect competitive political system).

To justify such an approach one has to argue why the low probability-argument does not apply. One way would be that most voters' subjective probabilities for being decisive are rather unrelated to the objective probabilities (for a discussion see Struthers and Young, 1989; a related argument referring to self-deception and diagnostic voting is given by Quattrone and Tversky, 1985). In the minimax-regret model of Ferejohn and Fiorina (1974) voting is interpreted as a decision under uncertainty, i.e., voters are unable to estimate the probabilities of the alternative outcomes and, consequently, neglect them by concentrating on the outcomes themselves.

The theory of low-cost decisions, on the other hand, is serious about the low-probability argument. Voting decisions are identified as situations where the individual decision is irrelevant for the individuals themselves and for all other individuals, though the collective decision is relevant for all individuals (Kirchgässner, 1992). The decision takes place behind a "veil of insignificance" (Kliemt, 1986) resulting in "wrong" decisions being without significant consequences for the decision-makers. One important aspect in this context is whether voters decide rationally between the alternatives, once they have decided to participate in the vote (Brennan and Buchanan, 1994 or Kliemt, 1986). The other dimension is to decide whether or not to vote. The theory of low-cost decisions suggests that because hard (economic) incentives are missing, soft incentives like those created by moral rules or psychic costs can exert a strong impact for such decisions. Consequently, the main difference between economic and voting decisions is that costs of following social (moral) rules are usually high in economic decisions but rather low in voting decisions.

As already Riker and Ordeshook (1968) argued, citizens may receive some utility from their act of voting independent of the outcome. Citizens may enjoy the act of voting because participating in democratic elections awakens political interests and thereby all the fun and inspirations induced by more or less active participation in political debates. Voters may also be concerned to maintain democracy (Downs, 1957) or derive some sort of satisfaction from complying with the ethic of voting or with "civic duty." According to this view, the rewards of voting are considered to be twofold: voting is not exclusively instrumental to determine the winning party or coalition, but also is a private consumption act from which benefits accrue independent of the outcome of the election. The distinction made is between the investment and consumption value of voting (e.g., Stigler, 1972 or Guttman et al., 1994) or between instrumental and expressive voting (Fiorina, 1976).

In empirical studies there is quite a lot of evidence that changes in the relevant variables, as e.g., in expected closeness, cause changes in the turnout rate (e.g., Kirchgässner and Schimmelpfennig, 1992). For an explanantion of the high turnout level, however, other variables turn out to be relevant like the sense of duty, inter- and intragroup relations or respondent's level of political interest (see, for instance, Blais et al., 2000 for an empirical study conducted during the 1993 Canadian federal election campaign, or Schram and Sonnemans (1996) for evidence from a participation game experiment).

In an experiment Güth and Weck-Hannemann (1997) investigate the value of democratic voting rights by providing the participants the chance to sell them. More specifically, an incentive compatible mechanism was used to elicit the (willingness-to-accept) value of the voting right in the election of the German Bundestag in October, 1994. Moreover, a postexperimental questionnaire made it possible to assess the relative importance of answers to the question "why do people vote?"

The results are striking though consistent with observed turnout levels: Most of the participants did not want to sell their voting right even at the top price offered; only a small minority of participants would have sold their voting right for any positive price, i.e., only very few people view their individual voting power as inessential as suggested by the "why do people vote?" paradoxon; and another intermediate group was willing to sell their voting right for substantial prices, but refused to do so at very low prices.

The bids which, from a normative point of view, should reveal the true values for one's voting right thus show a strong non-willingness to sell one's voting right. Furthermore, the group of voters who hardly assign any positive value to their voting right is close to being negligible. Among the reasons why to vote most subjects viewed voting as a civic duty or as a possibility to state one's opinion as the most important for their own decision.

In total, one may conclude (following Blais, 2000 as well as Kirchgässner and Pommerehne, 1993) that the rational choice model of voter participation is useful, but only in explaining behavior at the margins of social norms and other-regarding behavior, and that the importance and impact of low-cost decisions have to be fully recognized and more carefully studied in the future in public choice analysis.

HANNELORE WECK-HANNEMANN

REFERENCES

Blais, André, Young, Robert, and Lapp, Miriam (2000). "The calculus of voting: An empirical test." *European Journal of Political Research*, 37, 181–201.

Brennan, Geoffrey and Buchanan, James M. (1984). "Voter choice: evaluating political alternatives." *American Behavioral Scientist*, 28(2): 185–201.

Downs, Anthony (1957): *An Economic Theory of Democracy*. Harper & Row: New York.

Ferejohn, John A. and Fiorina, Morris P. (1974). "The paradox of not voting: A decision-theoretic analysis." *American Political Science Review*, 68: 525–536.

Fiorina, Morrism P. (1976): "The voting decision: instrumental and espressive voting." *Journal of Politics*, 38: 390–413.

Güth, Werner and Weck-Hannemann, Hannelore (1997): "Do people care about democracy? An experiment exploring the value of voting rights." *Public Choice*, 91: 27–47.

Guttman, Joel M., Hilger, Naftali, and Shachmurove, Yochanan (1994). "Voting as investment vs. voting as consumption New Evidence." *Kyklos*, 47(2): 197–207.

Kirchgässner, Gebhard (1992). "Towards a theory of low-cost decisions." *European Journal of Political Economy*, 8: 305–320.

Kirchgässner, Gebhard and Pommerehne, Werner W. (1993): "Low-cost decisions as a challenge to public choice." *Public Choice*, 77: 107–115.

Kirchgässner, Gebhard and Schimmelpfennig, Jörg (1992). "Closeness counts if it matters for electoral victory: some empirical results for the United Kingdom and the Federal Republic of Germany." *Public Choice*, 73, 283–299.

Kliemt, Hartmut (1986). "The veil of insignificance." *European Journal of Political Economy*, 2/3, 333–344.

Mueller, Dennis C. (1989): *Public Choice II*, Second Edition. Cambridge, MA: Cambridge University Press.

Nannestad, Peter and Paldam, Martin (1994). "The VP-function: A survey of the literature on vote and popularity functions after 25 years." *Public Choice*, 79(3)–4, 213–245.

Quattrone, George A. and Tversky, Amos (1985). "Self-deception and the voter's illusion," in Jon Elster (ed.) *The Multiple Self*. Cambridge: *Cambridge University Press*, MA pp. 35–58.

Riker, William H. and Ordeshook, Peter C. (1968). "A Theory of the Calculus of Voting." *American Political Science Review*, 62: 25–42.

Schram, Arthur (1991). *Voter Behavior in Economic Perspective*. Berlin: Springer.

Schram, Arthur and Sonnemans, Joep (1996). "Why people vote: experimental evidence." *Journal of Economic Psychology*, 17: 417–442.

Stigler, George (1972). "Economic competition and political competition." *Public Choice*, 13(Fall), 91–106.

Struthers, John and Young, Alistair (1989). "Economics of voting: theories and evidence." *Journal of Economic Studies*, 16(5): 1–42.

Tullock, Gordon (1967). *Toward Mathematics of Politics*. Ann Arbor: University of Michigan Press.

VOTES FOR WOMEN

In the United States, Wyoming and Utah were the first states to grant women the right to vote, in 1869 and 1870, respectively. They were followed over two decades later by Colorado in 1893 and Idaho in 1896. The list of states approving female suffrage then grew steadily from 1910 to 1920, when the 19th Amendment to the U.S. Constitution expanding the voting franchise to women was ratified.

It took many more years for female suffrage to spread around the world. Finland granted women the right to vote in 1906 and was followed over the next quarter century by many European countries. It was not until 1929 that the first Latin American and Asian countries — Ecuador and India — allowed women to vote. Expansion of women's suffrage continued across these continents through the late 1950s. Moslem countries were among the last to grant women the right to vote, many doing so between 1949 and 1963. In 1971, Switzerland became the last major developed country to allow women to vote.

There are several interesting questions involving women's suffrage that have been addressed in public choice research. What factors played a role in determining support for women's suffrage and its early adoption? How long did it take for women to fully respond to their new voting privilege? What impact did the resulting shift in the composition of voters have on government policies?

There has been very little research on the sources of political support for women's suffrage. Jones (1991) explains voting behavior in the U.S. House and Senate on a constitutional amendment giving women the right to vote, and Kenny (2002) studies the timing of U.S. states approving women's suffrage provisions. Not surprisingly, Jones finds that legislators from states that had granted women the right to vote supported amending the U.S. Constitution to expand the voting franchise to women across the country.

More fundamentally, support for women's suffrage depended on the ratio of women to men and on the fraction of women who were married. Granting women the right to vote was less costly to men in states where there were fewer women and thus a smaller change in the equilibrium due to suffrage. The scarcity of women in frontier states should have given women a greater share of marital income (Becker, 1981), and thus more privileges. Furthermore, having women's suffrage may have helped states with few women attract more women, which would be valued by single males in these states. Consistent with this reasoning, legislators from states with relatively few women were more likely to support the 19th Amendment (Jones, 1991), and states with few women granted women the right to vote earlier (Kenny, 2002). Similarly, granting women the right to vote should have had a smaller impact on political outcomes in states in which more women were married, and thus internalizing in their marriage the gains from marital specialization and from efficient statistical discrimination in the labor market (Hunt and Rubin, 1980). As predicted, Kenny finds that states with a larger fraction of women married adopted women's suffrage sooner.

The greater difficulty that women in rural states faced in organizing a successful grass roots movement hampered their success in obtaining the right to vote. Kenny's finding that the adoption of women's suffrage occurred later in more rural states is consistent with Stigler's (1971) evidence that occupations obtained licensure later in less urbanized states.

How long did it take for women to fully utilize their newly obtained voting privilege? For many individuals, the various benefits from voting appear to barely cover the cost of voting. But some political capital is needed to be able to select the candidate or policy that is best for a citizen. Lott and Kenny (1999) argue that the acquisition of this political capital, and the voter participation that it facilitates, is unlikely to be profitable for an older person who has just been given the right to vote but should be beneficial for a newly enfranchised 25 year old. As time passes, older cohorts of women who did not take advantage of their new right to vote are replaced by young cohorts of women who, with a lifetime of voting ahead of them, find it worthwhile to vote. This process of cohort replacement thus results in higher voter turnout. There is, however, very little evidence on how long it takes for voter turnout to fully respond to a major change in the voting franchise.

Lott and Kenny estimate the impact of giving women the right to vote on voter turnout in gubernatorial races in 1870–1940. Approximately half the ultimate increase in turnout occurs immediately. As time passes since women obtained the voting franchise, turnout continues to rise but at a decreasing rate. Under a spline specification, after nine years have passed the rate of increase in turnout as time passes falls to one third the initial rate of increase. Under a quadratic specification, turnout is estimated to increase until 54 years have passed since women were granted the right to vote. Both results suggest that it takes a very long time for the full effects of granting women the right to vote to be observed.

Other evidence is consistent with it taking a generation before turnout fully responds to a sharp rise in the incentive to vote, due to the repeal of a poll tax. Filer et al. (1991) find that the poll tax, which was repealed in 1964 by the 24th Amendment, was still depressing turnout 16 years later. Lott and Kenny (1999) estimate that it took at least 20 years for voter turnout to fully recover after the poll tax was removed.

Adding women to the ranks of voters is hypothesized to have resulted in higher government spending. Divorced women often have been unable to obtain full compensation for their family-specific investments through alimony. And programs that favor the poor are more valued by women, who tend to have lower incomes than men. Thus women who are single or concerned about becoming single may prefer government programs that transfer resources to the poor over uncertain alimony payments. Lott and Kenny (1999) use the estimated growth in turnout due to granting women the right to vote, which was described above, to measure the growing importance of women in the ranks of those who vote. Allowing women to vote is estimated to have raised state spending by 14 percent immediately, by 21 percent after 25 years, and by 28 percent after 45 years. The growth in spending that is attributed to women's suffrage accounts for approximately 16 percent of the 88 percent growth in real per capita state spending between 1913 and 1922. Lott and Kenny's other finding that state congressional delegations became more liberal after women were allowed to vote also is consistent with suffrage leading to greater government spending.

Women in Switzerland obtained the right to vote in 1971, at least 25 years after women in neighboring France, Germany, and Italy had started to vote. Abrams and Settle (1999) take advantage of this natural experiment to estimate the impact on government spending of women participating in elections. Enfranchising women is hypothesised to result in a new decisive voter who is poorer. According to Meltzer and Richard's (1981) model, this should lead to a rise in pure redistributive government spending. Abrams and Settle provide support for this prediction. They find that social welfare spending rose 28 percent. Husted and Kenny (1997) show that spending on government services falls if the income effect associated with the new decisive voter being poorer is greater than the substitution effect due to this voter facing a lower price for government services. Abrams and Settle find that government spending on final goods and services fell by 6 percent as a result of women being granted the right to vote, which is consistent with the empirical generalisation that the income elasticity for government services typically exceeds the price elasticity (Husted and Kenny, 1997, p. 55).

There also is some evidence that the legal and regulatory structure became more favorable to women after they were given the right to vote. Lott and Kenny (1999) report that states that had approved women's suffrage laws were more likely to pass legislation that restricted alimony to women and allowed alimony to be granted permanently. Women played a dominant role in the temperance movement. Lott and Kenny find that states were more likely to pass state laws banning the consumption of alcohol once women started voting. Similarly, the 18th Amendment to the U.S. Constitution establishing Prohibition received more support in state houses and senates in states that had given women the right to vote (Munger and Schaller, 1997).

To summarize, states with relatively few women and in which most women were married were among the first to grant women the right to vote. It took several decades for turnout to fully respond to this expansion of the voting franchise. As women began to vote and then turned out in greater numbers, state congressional delegations became more liberal, state spending increased, and state divorce laws became more favorable to women. State legislatures also responded to the influence of female voters by outlawing the consumption of alcohol in the state and supporting a constitutional ban on alcohol for the nation.

LAWRENCE W. KENNY

REFERENCES

Abrams, B.A. and Settle, R.F. (1999). "Women's suffrage and the growth of the welfare state." *Public Choice*, 100(September): 289–300.

Becker, G.S. (1981). *A Treatise on the Family*. Cambridge: Harvard University Press.

Filer, J.E., Kenny, L.W., and Morton, R.B. (1991). "Voting laws, educational policies, and minority turnout." *Journal of Law and Economics*, 34(October, part 1): 371–393.

Hunt, J.C. and Rubin, P.H. (1980). "The economics of the women's movement." *Public Choice*, 35(3): 287–295.

Husted, T.A. and Kenny, L.W. (1997). "The effect of the expansion of the voting franchise on the size of government." *Journal of Political Economy*, 105(February): 54–82.

Jones, E.B. (1991). "The economics of woman suffrage." *Journal of Legal Studies*, 20(June): 423–437.

Kenny, L.W. (2002). "Explaining the puzzle of why men gave women the right to vote." University of Florida working paper.

Lott, J.R. Jr. and Kenny, L.W. (1999). "Did women's suffrage change the size and scope of government?" *Journal of Political Economy*, 107(December): 1163–1198.

Meltzer, A.H. and Richards, S.F. (1981). "A rational theory of the size of government." *Journal of Political Economy*, 89(October): 914–927.

Munger, M. and Schaller, T. (1997). "The prohibition-repeal amendments: a natural experiment in interest group influence." *Public Choice*, 90(March): 139–163.

Stigler, G.J. (1971). "The theory of economic regulation." *Bell Journal of Economics and Management Science*, 2(Spring): 1–21.

VOTING EQUIPMENT, MINORITIES AND THE POOR

"...the old and cheap, outdated machinery is usually found in areas with populations that are of lower income people, minorities, and seniors on fixed incomes." (Al Gore, November 28, 2000)

"...everybody knows that the worst voting machinery is concentrated in poor areas." (*The Economist*, June 9, 2001)

In the aftermath of the 2000 Presidential election and the disputed vote in Florida, controversy arose over the previously obscure issue of differences in voting equipment across jurisdictions. The American public became acquainted with the potential for punch card voting mechanisms to produce large numbers of invalidated ballots. A widespread perception emerged among politicians and in the news media that the use of punch cards, and of antiquated voting machinery more generally, was more common in counties with a greater percentage of minorities and poor people. A series of editorials and op-ed articles in the Washington Post claimed that "it is mainly affluent counties that have switched" from punch cards to more modern equipment while "poor and minority voters tend to be stuck with less accurate machines," that African Americans "were far more likely to be stuck with the lousy machines than were affluent whites," and that "the most error-prone machines tend to be in the poorest counties."

This conventional wisdom that emerged so rapidly in late 2000 was superficially plausible for two reasons. First, the proportion of ballots for which no valid presidential choice was registered was much higher in areas heavily populated by minorities and the poor than elsewhere. Second, income and ethnicity are often strongly related to the quality of other public services, such as education. It seems reasonable to assume that where incomes and local tax revenues are low, election administration would be less well funded, and inferior voting technology — namely, punch card equipment — would still be in use.

There are several flaws in this logic, however. First, although there were several previous local elections in which incompletely punched-out chad produced controversial recounts, there was no universal consensus among election administrators that they produced the highest rates of voter error. The drawbacks of punch cards are now well known: voters often punch the holes in the wrong places, or apply insufficient force so that incompletely-removed chad results in undervotes; because no candidate information is printed directly on the cards, it is difficult for voters to discern mistakes by examining their cards. However, technical studies of voting equipment (e.g., Saltman (1988), have also documented problems with lever machines, optical scan systems, and direct electronic recording (DRE) systems (which use touch screens, push buttons or keyboards). In fact, empirical analyses find virtually no difference overall in the rates of invalidated ballots produced by DRE and punch card systems (Caltech/MIT, 2001; Knack and Kropf, 2002a).

Second, minimizing invalidated ballots is only one of several criteria by which election administrators have typically assessed the performance of voting technology. Although the media now revile any technology that appears to produce voter error, until after the 2000 election the media's interest was only in producing quick vote totals on election night — and by that criterion, punch card systems performed far better than optical scan systems, particularly for large jurisdictions such as Los Angeles County.

Third, election administration, and voting equipment more specifically, represents only a tiny fraction of any county's budget, regardless of the type of voting equipment it uses. (In most states, elections are administered by county governments.) Moreover, it had never been a salient issue, or a visible item in county budgets. In counties with high income levels, with strong tastes for education, public parks and other services, election administration may receive as little public attention and as little funding as in a poorer county. For example, the only county in Maryland still using punch cards in 2000 (Montgomery) has the wealthiest, best-educated population in the state, and spends more per capita on education, parks and other services than almost any county in the nation.

Historical and idiosyncratic factors appear to be influential determinants of voting equipment in use. In the early 1960s, hand-counted paper ballots were used in most small counties, while lever machines were used in large counties. As many of the smaller counties have grown, they purchased optical scanning equipment, which use ballots very similar to the hand-counted ballots. Many lever machine counties switched to punch cards beginning in 1964; others retained lever machines until DREs became available more recently, while others still use the lever machines.

Because so few people within county government know much about voting equipment, election administrators often have a high level of discretion in choosing equipment type, and their choices are likely to reflect their own experiences, and those of their colleagues in other counties. Some election administrators are likely to be highly risk averse, and unwilling to adopt a system not already in wide use elsewhere. Some of them may have budgets allowing them to attend conferences and learn what has worked well and what has failed in other counties.

To the extent that cost does matter, income per capita may not predict quality as well as county size. Volume discounts from vendors, and economies of scale in setting up new systems, favor larger counties. As noted in FEC (1982: 11):

> New voting systems are, typically, first adopted by large metropolitan jurisdictions where the complexity of the ballots and the volume of voters create pressures for improved vote recording and tabulating techniques. Such jurisdictions are also blessed with the fiscal, technical, and managerial resources equal to the challenge. Only when new devices are tested and debugged in this way are they normally then adopted by intermediate-sized jurisdictions.

Minorities tend to live in larger counties, so may benefit from more modern voting equipment, to the degree that cost matters. Tennessee is an illustrative case. In 1998, fewer than one fifth of all the state's counties had electronic voting systems. However, these included the three largest counties of Shelby (Memphis), Davidson (Nashville), and Knox, which account for a disproportionate share of the state's poor, minorities, and Democratic voters. Shelby County alone is home to nearly one half of the state's African Americans, but just over one tenth of its whites.

Statistical analyses reported in Knack and Kropf (2002b) overwhelmingly reject the conventional wisdom that minorities and the poor disproportionately reside in areas using punch card and other inferior voting equipment. They combined county-level data on voting equipment in use in 1998 with U.S. Census data on minority and poor populations, county size, income levels, and property tax revenues per capita. For the U.S. overall, black-white differences in punch card use were negligible: 31.9% for whites and 31.4% of African Americans live in counties using this voting technology. Hispanics were much more likely to live in punch card counties than either whites or blacks. However, this difference was entirely attributable to Los Angeles County, where nearly one in seven Hispanics in the country reside. (About 1 in 10 voters using punch card equipment in 1998 lived in L.A. County.) Whites (27.7%) were more likely than blacks (21.8%) to live in optical scanning counties, but blacks (37.8%) were much more likely than whites (26%) to live in counties using either of the technologies for which "overvoting" is impossible if machines are programmed correctly: DRE and lever machines.

In Florida, African Americans were only slightly more likely than whites to live in punch card counties. The notable difference again was for Hispanics, 84% of whom live in punch card counties, compared to just over 60% for whites and African Americans. This difference is entirely attributable to the use of punch card voting in Miami-Dade County, home of more than one half of Florida's Hispanics, but fewer than one in seven whites and fewer than one in five African Americans.

Findings are similar when looking at voting equipment used by the poor (persons living below the poverty level) and non-poor. The poor are slightly more likely (33.4% compared to 31.8%) to live in punch card counties than the non-poor nationwide, but they are also slightly more likely (9.8% to 8.6%) to use the most modern technology (DRE).

These comparisons were also conducted on a state-by-state basis, for the 29 states in which some but not all counties used punch card technology. In 18 of the 29 states, whites were more likely than African Americans to live in punch card counties. Whites were more likely than Hispanics to live in punch card counties in 21 of the 29 states. In 21 states, the non-poor are more likely than the poor to reside in counties using punch card voting equipment.

Other results in Knack and Kropf (2002b) provide little evidence for the importance of "affordability," as measured by county size, per capita income, or property tax revenues per capita. Punch card counties in Florida are much larger, wealthier, and more revenue-rich than counties using any other type of voting equipment. Similarly, for the U.S. as a whole, punch card counties are larger and wealthier on average than those using any other voting system. Counties using electronic voting constitute the group with the lowest incomes on average, and — by a wide margin — the lowest property tax revenues per capita.

Similar findings are produced by state-by-state comparisons across counties for the 28 states in which some counties use punch cards while others use modern (optical scanning or electronic voting) equipment. In 17 of the 28 states, punch card counties tend to be larger than counties with modern equipment. In 17 (but not the same 17 as in the case of county size) of the 28 states, punch card counties tend to have higher average incomes. Similarly, in 17 of the 28 states, punch card counties on average had higher property tax revenues per capita. Florida fits these general patterns. Population, income and tax revenues were all significantly higher in its 15 counties using punch cards in 1998 than in its 24 optical scan counties (electronic voting had not yet been approved for use in Florida).

Higher rates of invalidated ballots in heavily-minority areas cannot, therefore, be attributed to a greater likelihood that minorities must vote using punch card equipment. Controlling for the type of voting equipment in use, invalidated ballots remain higher in counties with more African Americans, Hispanics, and poor persons (Knack and Kropf, 2002b). However, although voting equipment is distributed in a race-neutral way, it may have effects that are not race-neutral. Several studies have found, using both precinct-level and county-level data, that the association between invalidated ballots and African American population is particularly strong where punch cards are used, but disappears where voting technology is used that can be programmed to prevent overvoting (Herron and Sekhon, 2001; Kimball et al., 2001; Tomz and Van Houweling, 2001; Knack and Kropf, 2002a).

The explanation for this pattern is not obvious. Survey data indicate that differences in deliberate undervoting between whites and blacks are fairly small, and there is little reason to expect these differences to vary much with the types of voting technology used. It is not the case that, within punch card counties, the oldest and most error-prone punch card devices are likely to be placed in the heavily-minority precincts: in most counties, the devices are stored in a central location between elections and are not earmarked for particular precincts, and they are assembled in a central location weeks prior to the election by a small number of elections administration staff (not by poll workers within the precinct). It is conceivable that African American voters are less likely than whites to request assistance from poll workers, or that poll workers in minority precincts are less able or willing to provide useful assistance. Although these studies control for educational level and voter experience to the extent allowed by the available data, they cannot control effectively for differences in education quality (as distinct from years of schooling completed), or for experience in undertaking unfamiliar administrative and bureaucratic tasks. In the absence of data to test such ideas, they must remain purely conjectural.

STEPHEN KNACK

REFERENCES

FEC (1982). *Voting System Standards: A Report to the Congress on the Development of Voluntary Engineering and Procedural Performance Standards for Voting Systems*. Washington, DC: The National Clearinghouse on Election Administration of the Federal Election Commission.

Caltech/MIT Voting Technology Project (2001). Residual votes attributable to technology: A preliminary assessment of the reliability of existing voting equipment (March 30 revision). Accessed at http://www.vote.caltech.edu.

Herron, M.C. and Sekhon, J.S. (2001). Overvoting and representation: An examination of overvoted presidential ballots in Broward and Miami-Dade counties. Unpublished manuscript.

Kimball, D.C., Owens, C., and McAndrew, K. (2001). "Who's afraid of an undervote?" Paper presented at the Southern Political Science Association annual meeting, Atlanta, GA, November 9.

Knack, S. and Kropf, M. (2002a). "Voided ballots in the 1996 presidential election: A county-level analysis." *Journal of Politics* (forthcoming).

Knack, S. and Kropf, M. (2002b). "Who uses inferior voting technology?" *PS: Political Science and Politics* (forthcoming, June).

Saltman, R.G. (1988). *Accuracy, Integrity and Security in Computerized Vote-Tallying*. National Bureau of Standards Special Publication 500-158.

Tomz, M. and Van Houweling, R. (2001). Who spoils their ballots? Voting equipment and race in the 2000 presidential election. Unpublished manuscript.

VOTING IN U.S. PRESIDENTIAL ELECTIONS

1. Introduction: The Electoral College

The United States elects its presidents through an indirect mechanism called the Electoral College, which has its roots in the U.S. Constitution (Article II, Section 1 and the 12th Amendment). There are various intricacies and details about the evolution and functioning of the Electoral College, but for present purposes, a short explanation will suffice.

Rather than allowing the popular vote to determine the winner of a presidential election, the U.S. Constitution set up an Electoral College wherein each state is given a number of Electors equal to the number of U.S. Senators (2) plus the number of its U.S. Representatives. The latter number changes after every Census (each 10 years) as the number of Representatives is reapportioned according to population. Rather than voting for a presidential candidate, voters cast their ballots for a slate of Electors representing their choice for president and vice-president. By the rules of the Electoral College, the candidate with the most votes in a state wins all of that state's electors. In other words, the system is a "winner-take-all" procedure (with some minor exceptions in Maine and Nebraska where two electors are chosen by statewide popular vote and the rest by popular vote in each Congressional district).

This is a sketch of how the Electoral College system generally works. It should be kept in mind that individual states and the electors have considerable discretion in this process. States can make their own rules about how many electors are allocated to each candidate. And, electors are technically free to vote for whomever they choose. For example, as noted below, one elector chose to abstain in the 2000 presidential election.

Ultimately, however, the Electors vote, and the candidate with the most electoral votes, provided it is more than one-half of the total, is declared president. The present magic number of electoral votes is 270. If no one obtains an absolute majority of electoral votes, the U.S. House of Representatives chooses the president from among the top three vote-getters in a process, with each state casting only one vote and an absolute majority of states being required to elect.

The current arithmetic of the Electoral College by state is listed in Table 1. Note that this will change in favor of states that gained population after the U.S. House districts are redrawn with respect to the results of the 2000 Census.

All of this, of course, is much better known and appreciated after the incredibly close and contested 2000 presidential election in the United States between Gore and Bush. Although Gore won more popular votes than Bush (500,000 plus), Bush ultimately won the hotly contested 25 electoral votes in Florida to achieve a victory in the Electoral College (271 to 266 with 1 abstention). Thus, a rare outcome was recorded when the popular vote winner lost in the Electoral College.

Much earlier, in 1824, Andrew Jackson won the popular vote and the electoral vote, but no candidate received a majority of electoral votes. Under the provisions of the 12th Amendment, the House voted for President (each state having one vote), and elected John Q. Adams. The 1876 election between Hayes and Tilden was also disputed with Tilden winning the popular vote, but Hayes was ultimately declared to have more electoral votes and to be president.

2. The U.S. Presidency from a Public Choice Perspective

With a few key exceptions covered below, public choice theory has not given much attention to the role of the executive branch in the determination of political outcomes. The bulk of public choice research has been on the legislative branch of government, with some attention also given to the judiciary by scholars in law and economics. This is unfortunate to say the least since the chief executive is a key political actor in a democratic setting. Nonetheless, confining attention to the United States, the presence of the

Table 1: Distribution of electoral votes total electoral vote: 538 needed to elect: 270

State	1991–2000
Alabama	9
Alaska	3
Arizona	8
Arkansas	6
California	54
Colorado	8
Connecticut	8
Delaware	3
D.C.	3
Florida	25
Georgia	13
Hawaii	4
Idaho	4
Illinois	22
Indiana	12
Iowa	7
Kansa	6
Kentucky	8
Louisiana	9
Maine	4
Maryland	10
Massachusetts	12
Michigan	18
Minnesota	10
Mississippi	7
Missouri	11
Montana	3
Nebraska	5
Nevada	4
New Hampshire	4
New Jersey	15
New Mexico	5
New York	33
North Carolina	14
North Dakota	3
Ohio	21
Oklahoma	8
Oregon	7
Pennsylvania	23
Rhode Island	4
South Carolina	8
South Dakota	3
Tennessee	11
Texas	32
Utah	5
Vermont	3
Virginia	13
Washington	11
West Virginia	5
Wisconsin	11
Wyoming	3

Electoral College, as outlined above, opens the door for a vote-maximizing theory of executive behavior.

Previous work on the U.S. presidency examined the president's formal and informal powers. Neustadt (1960) focused on the president's informal power and his ability to persuade or bargain with Congress in an institutional setting which places the two branches in conflict. The formal powers of the president (vetoes and appointments) have been examined using the structure induced-equilibrium (SIE) models introduced by Shepsle and Weingast (1981).

Although economists and political scientists have derived equilibrium results from the bargaining game and SIE models by including a presidential preference set, the content of this preference set remains a black box. Since these models do not specify the policies preferred by the president, few predictions can be made about the bills the president will veto, the budget he will propose, the people he will appoint, or the regulations he will promulgate and enforce.

The few works that have advanced positive theories of presidential behavior make the essential point that U. S. president is not a popular vote maximizer but an electoral vote maximizer. Wright (1974), in an important early paper, showed that New Deal spending in the 1930's could be explained as a function of a measure of electoral votes across states. Anderson and Tollison (1991a) found this same result while controlling for measures of congressional influence. Couch and Shughart (1998) provide a summary and extension of this work on New Deal Spending. The basic point of this research was to show that New Deal spending was not so much a public relief program as a political program designed to buy votes with the public purse. Electoral votes, not "need," drove the allocation of New Deal spending across states.

Building on Wright's approach. Anderson and Tollison (1991b) examine the allocation of Civil War causalities across the Northern states. Given that the Northern troops were organized by states and that President Lincoln sought to be reelected, these authors found that Northern causalities were partly determined by electoral votes in 1864. Troops from close states were much less likely to suffer causalities. In other words, dead men cannot vote.

A third application of the electoral vote model to presidential behavior concerns the use of the executive veto. Grier et al. (1995) argue that winner-take-all voting in states and the unequal distribution of electoral votes across states in presidential elections makes incumbent presidents rationally place more weight on the preference of voters in closely contested, larger states when making policy decisions. They tested this hypothesis by examining whether presidential veto decisions are influenced by the floor votes of Senators

from these electorally crucial states. In a pooled sample of 325 individual bills from 1970 through 1988, they found significant evidence of this behavior by incumbent presidents. That is, the more Senators from electorally important states oppose a bill, the more likely the president is to veto it, even when controlling for a wide variety of conditioning variables, including the overall vote on the bill.

Finally, Brams and Davis (1974) present a theoretical model of presidential campaign resource allocation that predicts candidates will spend resources in each state proportionally to the state's electoral votes raised to the 1.5 power, or the so-called 3/2's rule. Colantoni et al. (1975) confirmed the existence of a large state bias, but argued that the level of electoral competition (closeness) in states will also affect resource allocation. They also generally argued against the specific 3/2's rule. The evidence used in this debate was data on campaign appearances (by state) by presidential candidates in four elections (1964 through 1972).

2.1. Presidential Politics

Several basic points should be kept in mind here. First, the behavior of the executive branch of government is among the least studied parts of modern public choice analysis. This literature is in its infancy. Second, more so than other areas, this literature is tied exclusively to U.S. political institutions, namely, the Electoral College system of electing presidents. Third, the literature is rife with measurement issues. Some authors use electoral votes per capita, some use raw electoral votes (a proxy for population), and some use closeness weighted electoral votes (either per capita or raw).

Nonetheless, in keeping with the central tenet of public choice theory, presidential behavior in this approach is modeled as maximizing electoral votes subject to constraints. Essentially, the president is analyzed as a careful shopper for electoral votes in his effort to be elected or reelected. States in which the incumbent president or candidate expects to win or lose by a wide margin can safely be ignored in this process. States that are predicted to be close will be the recipients of presidential largesse and visits. The constraints on this activity include time, campaign resources, congressional influences over federal pork, and so on. Even where the president cannot run for reelection, this approach presumes that he behaves as if he were running. Such a model has thus far provided a strong predictive theory of presidential behavior in a variety of areas, as outlined above.

An economic model of presidential and presidential candidate behavior maps into this situation easily. When faced with a choice among states with respect, for example, to new funding initiatives, the president will estimate the probability that he will win the state times the number of electoral votes. States with higher expected values will receive the funding, following an equi—marginal rule of funding allocation. States that are not expected to be close (win or lose) or small states are left out in the cold in this calculation. Obviously, all forms of presidential behavior and not simply funding can be analyzed with this model. The relevant constraints on the president are the obvious ones — time and money.

3. Concluding Remarks

The electoral vote approach has been successfully employed, as noted above, to explain the allocation of New Deal spending across states, presidential vetoes, campaign stops by presidential candidates, and still other aspects of presidential decision making. Though still in its infancy, this approach, at least for the United States, has the potential to fill in the black box of presidential preferences and to offer a positive economic explanation of presidential behavior. It also clearly finds its roots in the basic economic methodology of maximizing expected value subject to constraints. Presidential aspirants, whether they know it or not, are rational economic actors when it comes to shopping for electoral votes.

ROBERT D. TOLLISON

REFERENCES

Anderson, G.M. and Tollison, R.D. (1991a). "Congressional influence and New Deal spending, 1933–1939." *Journal of Law and Economics* (April 1991): 161–175.

Anderson, G.M. and Tollison, R.D. (1991b). "Political influence on Civil War mortality rates: The electoral college as a battlefield." *Defence Economics*, 2(1991): 219–234.

Brams, S.J. and Davis, M.D. (1974). "The 3/2's rule in presidential campaigning." *American Political Science Review* (March 1974): 113–134.

Colantoni, C.S., Levesque, T.J., and Ordershook, P.C. (1975). "Campaign resource allocation under the college." *American Political Science Review* (March 1975): 141–160.

Couch, J.F. and Shughart, W.F. II (1998). *The Political Economy of the New Deal*. Northhampton, MA: Elgar.

Grier, K.B., MacDonald, M., and Tollison, R.D. (1995). "Electoral politics and the Presidential veto." *Economic Inquiry*, 33 (July 1995): 427–440.

Neustadt, R.E. (1960). *Presidential Power*. New York: Wiley.

Shepsle, K.A. and Weingast, B.R. (1981). "Structure-induced equilibrium and legislative choice." *Public Choice*, 37(3): 507–519.

Wright, G. (1974). "The political economy of New Deal spending." *Review of Economics and Statistics* (February): 30–38.

VOTING PARADOXES IN LIST SYSTEMS OF PROPORTIONAL REPRESENTATION

Social scientists have increasingly become aware of the possibility that individual preferences may not necessarily translate easily into meaningful collective choices, and that the methods by which the preferences are aggregated may exert significant influence upon the outcomes (Black, 1948; Black, [1958] 1998; Arrow, [1951] 1963; Riker, 1982, 1986). So far, the theoretical analysis has primarily dealt with Anglo-American electoral and parliamentary institutions and has only infrequently been applied to, e.g., proportional systems of representation such as found in the majority of electoral systems used in the world, and whereas the extent of formal social choice theorizing has been extensive, the examination of the possible empirical occurrence of voting paradoxes has been relatively modest (cf., e.g., Rasch, 1995; Van Deemen, 1998; Kurrild-Klitgaard, 2001).

Nonetheless, voting paradoxes may occur also in proportional systems and would seem to do so occasionally. The fundamental insight of social choice analysis is that whenever more than two persons are to choose between more than two issues certain paradoxical results may occur. The classical illustration is the so-called Condorcet Paradox, which depicts a situation of social choice where no unique majority winner exists, i.e., where no alternative is preferred more than all other alternatives when compared in pair wise contests. The paradox is usually illustrated by considering a hypothetical example with three voters contained in the nonempty and finite set $N = \{i_1, i_2, i_3\}$, who are faced with the three alternatives contained in the nonempty and finite set $M = \{x_1, x_2, x_3\}$, and where each voter $i \in N$ has a preference ordering, P_i, over the alternatives in M, which follows the standard formal assumptions about preferences (completeness, transitivity, asymmetry and irreflexivity). If we assume that the "relation" means "preferred at least as much as," "$x_1 \mathrel{_N} x_2$" means that x_1 is preferred at least as much as x_2 by N. We may hypothesize a situation, where the preferences are such, that they can be represented by a profile of individual preference orderings:

P_1: x_1 x_2 x_3

P_2: x_2 x_3 x_1

P_3: x_3 x_1 x_2

Given such preferences, and if the procedure for choosing is pair-wise comparisons, the collective preference ordering (or social ordering) of the group N may be said to be "cyclical":

$$P_N: x_1 \ x_2 \ x_3 \ x_1$$

In this case it is impossible to construct a transitive collective preference ordering, and there is no so-called "Condorcet winner," i.e., no stable equilibrium outcome exists that cannot be beaten by (at least) one other alternative. No matter what of the three alternatives is selected, another can beat it in a pair-wise comparison. One majority (i_1 and i_3) prefers x_1 to x_2, while another (i_1 and i_2) prefers x_2 to x_3, and a third (i_2 and i_3) prefers x_3 to x_1. This is a non-trivial paradox, because there would seem to be an obvious discrepancy between what is the actual observation and what would usually be the intuitive or common sense expectation: That if something is a democratic decision, it is reasonable to assume that one alternative would be preferred.

Traditionally social choice scholars have, in theoretical and empirical studies alike, tended to focus on choice-settings involving choices between, e.g., competing policies or candidates, and where the aggregation method is one of plurality. Paradoxes of social choice may, however, also occur in electoral systems with party lists and proportional representation, i.e., as found in most Western democracies. In such systems votes are not cast solely for individual candidates (as with the first-past-the-post systems of, e.g., the United Kingdom and the United States), but for candidates appearing on party lists and/or the party itself, and where the votes subsequently are converted into seats allocated to parties through the use of some vote-seat conversion method aiming at proportionality (e.g., the d'Hondt or Saint Lague formulas).

To see this, let us assume that we identify the voters as those contained in the nonempty and finite set N = $\{i_1, ..., i_n\}$, that these are confronted with the choice between political parties included in the nonempty and finite set M = $\{x_1, ..., x_m\}$. Furthermore let $s(x_i)$ be the number of seats s allocated in an electoral system to a political party i. We may identify the following paradoxes of voting, which may occur in democracies with list-systems of proportional representation (Van Deemen, 1993; Van Deemen and Vergunst, 1998: 239ff):

1. *The Condorcet Paradox*: Where a party x_1 is preferred to a party x_2 by a majority of the voters (x_1 N x_2), and where party x_2 in turn is preferred to a party x_3 by a majority (x_2 N x_3) by a majority, but where it is also the case that party x_3 is preferred to party x_1 (x_3 N x_1), i.e., that the social ordering is the intransitive ordering x_1 N x_2 N x_3 N x_1.

2. *The More-Preferred-Less-Seats Paradox*: Where a party x_1 is preferred to a party x_2 by a majority of the voters (x_1 N x_2), but where party x_1 receives less seats than party x_2, i.e., $s(x_1) < s(x_2)$.

3. *The Condorcet-Winner-Turns-Loser Paradox*: Where a party x_1 is the Condorcet winner and thus can beat any party in pair-wise comparisons (x_1 N ($x_2, ..., x_m$)), but where the party receives less seats than a party x_2, i.e., $s(x_1) < s(x_2)$, or even no seats at all.

4. *The Majority-Reversal Paradox*: Where a majority relation for an election (e.g., x_1 N x_2 N x_3) may be exactly the reversal of the ranking of the parties in correspondence with their number of seats as assigned by the system of proportional representation, i.e., $s(x_3) > s(x_2) > s(x_1)$.

It has been demonstrated that such paradoxes may in principle occur in proportional systems such as those used in a majority of democracies (Van Deemen, 1993) and that at least some of these paradoxes occur in practice (Van Deemen and Vergunst, 1998). In order to do the latter, it is necessary to have data from a relatively large number of voters and have information on their preference rankings. This may be done, e.g., if the analyst has access to "thermometer" evaluation, where respondents have been asked to assign points to alternatives on a scale ranging from the most positive to the most negative. In order to turn the "thermometer" values into Condorcet comparisons, we let $\Delta_i(x_1)$ stand for the points assigned by individual i to alternative x_1. We may thus assume that if a respondent assigns more points to x_1 than to x_2, then he strictly prefers x_1 to x_2, i.e., if $\Delta_i(x_1) > \Delta_i(x_2)$: x_1 $_i$ x_2, and that if an individual assigns the same number of points to x_1 and x_2, he is indifferent between the two, i.e., if $\Delta_i(x_1) = \Delta_i(x_2)$: $x_1 \sim_i x_2$. When the voter preferences over the alternatives have been constructed as such, these may be aggregated by majority rule, so that alternative x_1 is majority preferred to alternative x_2, if the number of voters who prefer x_1 to x_2 is larger than the number of voters who prefer x_2 to x_1. If we let N represent the group of voters in question, we may express this as if $N(x_1 \ _i \ x_2) > N(x_2 \ _i \ x_1)$: x_1 N x_2, and if $N(x_1 \ _i \ x_2) = N(x_2 \ _i \ x_1)$: $x_1 \sim_N x_2$. We may thus also say that an alternative x_1 is a Condorcet winner if and only if it is the case that for all other alternatives x it is the case that x_1 N x_2.

We may illustrate this with data derived from the Danish Election Survey Project (1973, 1994, 1998). Table 1 summarizes the results of the Condorcet comparisons for the three elections and contains the majority relation for the voters in each of the three elections (MR) as well as the order of the parties according to the number of seats allocated to them under proportional representation (PR).

Table 1: Social orderings and seats of political parties, Danish election surveys and parliamentary elections, 1973, 1994, 1998. Majority relations (MR) and seats according to proportional representation (PR)

Rank order	1973		1994		1998	
	MR	PR	MR	PR	MR	PR
1	A	A (46)	A	A (62)	A	A (63)
2	B	Z (28)	V	V (42)	V	V (42)
3	V	V (22)	C	C (27)	C	C (16)
4	Q	B (20)	B	F (13)	D	F (13)
5	M	C (16)	D	Z (11)	B	O (13)
6	C	M (14)	F	B (8)	F	D (8)
7	E	F (11)	Q	Ø (6)	Q	B (7)
8	Z	Q (7)	Z	D (5)	O	Ø (5)
9	F	K (6)	Ø	Indp (1)	Z	Q (4)
10	Y	E (5)		Q (0)	Ø	Z (4)
11	K	Y (0)			U	U (0)

Sources: Actual election results, with the number of seats received by the party given in brackets.

Abbreviations: MR: Majority Relation (i.e., ranking according to results of pair-wise Condorcet comparisons); PR: Proportional Representation (i.e., ranking according to proportions of votes in the election); A: Social Democratic Party; B: Radical Liberal Party; C: Conservative People's Party; D/M: Center-Democrats; E: Justice Party; F: Socialist People's Party; Indp: Jacob Haugaard, elected as an independent, was not included in the party survey; K: Danish Communist Party; Q: Christian People's Party; O: Danish People's Party; U: Democratic Renewal; V: Danish Liberal Party; Y: Left Socialists; Z: Progress Party; Ø: Socialist Unity List.

There were no examples in any of the three elections of the Condorcet Paradox (i.e., of a cycle involving all the alternatives) or of intransitivity more generally speaking (e.g., with a cycle among a sub-set of alternatives). Compared to the theoretical literature, these findings are somewhat surprising, i.e., much of social choice theory has predicted that intransitivity should be widespread in collective preferences. But compared to previous empirical findings, the present results are less surprising: With a few notable exceptions (Niemi, 1970; Kurrild-Klitgaard, 2001), social choice theorists have, so far, not been able to detect any examples of the full-fledged Condorcet Paradox in larger electorates and only relatively few examples of other forms of intransitivity. Specifically, the result is similar to a study of four Dutch election surveys, which found no examples of intransitivity in the preferences of voters over parties (Van Deemen and Vergunst, 1998).

Investigations such as these should, however, be accompanied by some reservations. First, since the election surveys are based on samples, it is impossible to be sure that the

collective preference orderings found necessarily can be generalized to be representative of all the voters. This has some specific consequences. In all three elections considered there are several pair-wise comparisons for which the most preferred alternative cannot be inferred with certainty if, e.g., a 99 pct. confidence interval is applied to the results of the pair-wise comparisons. For example, in the 1994 election this was the case with the differences between the Social Democrats and the Liberals, the Social Democrats and the Conservatives, the Liberals and the Conservatives, and the Socialist People's Party and the Center-Democrats, thus making it possible that there may in fact have been a cycle among the top-ranked alternatives.

In order to establish whether any of the other social choice paradoxes identified here were present in the preferences of the Danish voters, we must compare the social ordering according to the majority-relation with the actual results of the three elections. It is evident from the data in Table 1 that two of the paradoxes seem to be absent in the three elections. The Condorcet-Winner-Turns-Looser Paradox is not present in any of the elections; indeed the Condorcet winner is in all three elections also the party, which receives most seats, namely the Social Democrats. This is in contrast to the investigation of four Dutch election surveys, which found two examples of this paradox. This result would, due to the logical character of the paradox, stand for the sample as well as for the electorate as a whole; we can, however, not say at a 99 pct. confidence level that the Social Democrats in fact was the Condorcet winner for the electorate in 1994, and so the Condorcet-Winner-Turns-Loser Paradox may have been present in the preferences of the electorate as a whole. Given the absence of the Condorcet-Winner-Turns-Loser Paradox in the sample of voters, the Majority-Reversal Paradox is not present either. This was not found in the investigation of the four Dutch election surveys either. This result too would stand for the sample as well as for the electorate as a whole.

In contrast, the More-Preferred-Less-Seats Paradox is abundantly present in Danish elections, or at least all three elections considered here. It was present in the 1973 election, where only two of the eleven parties, the Social Democrats and the Liberals, had the same place in the social ordering and in terms of the allocation of seats. Most significantly, the Progress Party received more seats than no less than six other parties ranked higher in the social ordering. In the 1994 election the same three parties were top-ranked with the two different methods, but beyond this the orderings were quite different. For example, the Progress Party and the Socialist Unity List both received more seats than the Christian People's Party, which did not receive any seats at all despite beating both these parties in pair-wise comparisons. In 1998 a quite similar picture emerged as in 1994.

We can thus with some safety conclude that the More-Preferred-Less-Seats Paradox seems to occur quite frequently in list systems of proportional representation. But how 'much' does it occur? Van Deemen and Vergunst (1998: 484–485) calculated the robustness of the orderings by using Kendall's τ, which may be seen as a good indicator of the number of reversals; the smaller the difference between the rankings, the larger the Kendall's τ coefficient. For the four Dutch elections they found coefficients between 0.641 and 0.944 and with an average of 0.752. In the case of the Danish elections considered here, the coefficients were 1973: 0.491; 1994: 0.611; 1998: 0.745 and with an average of 0.615.

It is thus clear that a number of paradoxes of voting may and do occur not only in first-past-the-post systems but also in proportional representation systems. The analysis conducted so far suggests that one social choice paradox is present in virtually all elections using list-systems with proportional representation, albeit to different extents, namely the More-Preferred-Less-Seats Paradox. Two other paradoxes, the Condorcet-Winner-Turns-Loser Paradox and the Majority-Reversal Paradox, are occasionally, but rarely, present, while the fourth and most infamous, the Condorcet Paradox, is not found in any samples of voters, although its existence cannot be completely ruled out for the electorates.

The widespread presence of the More-Preferred-Less-Seats Paradox, i.e., that the proportional system entails a significant number of reversals vis-à-vis the majority relation, raises an interesting question, namely if the discrepancy between the two may be seen as an indication of a more fundamental instability in the political system, or perhaps as a cause of it? A preliminary analysis of the results suggests that it is relatively more "extremist" parties, which receive more seats under proportional representation than is consistent with their rank in the social ordering according to the majority-relation. In contrast, the "losers" to these parties would seem almost consistently to be small, centrist parties. More generally the presence of the paradox would seem to contradict a premise underlying much of contemporary democratic debate, namely that if more people

prefer one party than another, then it would be wrong for the latter party to receive more seats. Proportional representation obviously adds pluralism to a party system compared to, e.g., the first-past-the-post system, but it would also seem not only to do so by benefiting some parties at the cost of others but also to do so in direct opposition to the majority principle and thus to fly in the face of much of what underlies the general view of democracy.

PETER KURRILD-KLITGAARD

REFERENCES

Arrow, K.J. (1963 [1951]). *Social Choice and Individual Values*, Second Edition. New Haven: Yale University Press.

Black, D. (1948). "On the rationale of group decision making." *Journal of Political Economy*, 56: 23–34.

Black, D. (1998 [1958]). *The Theory of Committees and Elections*, Second Revised Edition. Dordrecht: Kluwer Academic Publishers.

Kurrild-Klitgaard, P. (2001). "An empirical example of the Condorcet paradox of voting in a large electorate." *Public Choice*, 107(1–2): 135–145.

Niemi, R.G. (1970). "The occurrence of the paradox of voting in university elections." *Public Choice*, 3: 91–100.

Rasch, B.E. (1995). "Parliamentary voting procedures," in H. Döring (ed.) *Parliaments and Majority Rule in Western Europe*, 488–527. Frankfurt: Campus Verlag.

Riker, W.H. (1982). *Liberalism Against Populism: A Confrontation Between the Theory of Democracy and the Theory of Social Choice*. San Francisco: W.H. Freeman.

Riker, W.H. (1986). *The Art of Political Manipulation*. New Haven: Yale University Press, Date of Copyright: 1986.

Van Deemen, A.M.A. (1993). "Paradoxes of voting in list systems of proportional representation." *Electoral Studies*, 12(3): 234–241.

Van Deemen, A.M.A. (1998). The Condorcet paradox: A review of research results. Paper presented at Workshop on Empirical Social Choice, 1998 ECPR Joint Sessions of Workshops, 23–28 March 1998, Warwick University.

Van Deemen, A.M.A. and Vergunst, N.P. (1998). "Empirical evidence of paradoxes of voting in Dutch elections." *Public Choice*, 97: 475–490.

W

THE WAR ON DRUGS

The first nation-wide shot in the "war on drugs" in the United States was the 1914 Harrison Narcotics Act. This war was escalated by the 1937 Marijuana Tax Act, which effectively outlawed cannabis and hashish. Since then, this war has waxed and waned repeatedly, although for the past thirty years it has largely accelerated.

By "war on drugs" I mean government's active prohibition of the production, distribution, possession, and use of certain mind- and mood-altering natural and chemical substances — a policy for which police, military, judicial, and penal forces all are employed toward the ostensible goal of minimizing the use of such substances in America. The "war," therefore, is more accurately described as a war on people who are either suppliers or buyers of outlawed drugs. It is, in short, a policy of prohibition. This policy is identical in all essential respects to the national prohibition of alcohol from 1920 to 1934. For the sake of accuracy, I will from here on in refer to the "war on drugs" as "drug prohibition."

Debate over the wisdom of drug prohibition typically focuses on its morality or its effectiveness. Neither of these issues turns principally on public-choice considerations. Nevertheless, drug prohibition has several public-choice aspects, although space permits only a handful to be reviewed here.

1. Bootleggers and Baptists

While the existence of rent-seeking special interest groups alone might often generate sufficient pressure on the legislature to enact statutes creating rents for these interest groups, Bruce Yandle (1983) argues that legislation benefiting a rent-seeking special interest group is more likely to be enacted if that legislation also is supported by a group whose motives are not (or not obviously) pecuniary. In Yandle's useful terminology and example, the legislature is more likely to outlaw alcohol if the "bootleggers" who stand to gain monetarily from this prohibition can rely upon the "Baptists" — people sincerely seeking to reduce alcohol consumption for religious reasons — to add pressure on the legislature and to take the lead in making the public case for prohibition.

Drug prohibition seems clearly to be a product of a "bootleggers and Baptists" phenomenon. The "Baptists" are the large number of Americans who are sincerely convinced that prohibition is in the public interest. But a conviction can be sincere without being deep or fundamental. Contrary to popular perception, the public's demand for drug prohibition seems not to originate with the public. Instead, it seems to be the product of interest-group efforts.

Bruce Benson and David Rasmussen (1997: 202–205) report evidence that public support for drug prohibition is, in large part, a *result* of a policy of prohibition. Building on the model of Breton and Wintrobe (1982) — in which regulators can release both true and false information and, thus, distort the public's perception of reality — Benson and Rasmussen (1997: 205) argue that such information distortion "has clearly been the case in the evolution of drug policy." (See also Twight, 2002: 19–53.) As an example, these scholars offer

> the bureaucratic campaigns leading up to the 1937 marijuana legislation [which] 'included remarkable distortions of the evidence of harm caused by marijuana, ignoring the findings of empirical inquiries' [Richards, 164]. The 'reefer madness' scare can be traced to the misinformation propagated by the Narcotics Bureau. Marijuana was alleged to cause insanity, to incite rape, and to trigger delirious rages in users making them irresponsible and prone to commit violent crimes. Factual distortions did not stop there, however. For instance, the bill was represented as one that was largely symbolic in that it would require no additional enforcement expenditures. (Benson and Rasmussen, 1997: 205)

Benson and Rasmussen (1997: 202–207) contend that the same process whereby rent-seeking interest groups — bootleggers — actively worked to create public hostility toward marijuana in 1937 was also at work throughout the entire U.S. experience with drug prohibition. In short, when it comes to illegal drugs, the bootleggers seem to play a prominent role in creating the Baptists.

2. Drugs and Crime

The most prominent justification for drug prohibition is its alleged promise to reduce crime rates (Miron, 1998: 648). Illegal drugs are thought to make their users more likely to commit crimes. Therefore, by raising the cost of drugs and, hence, reducing the quantity demanded, prohibition allegedly reduces crime rates.

Although not without some intuitive appeal, this argument suffers from several weaknesses. Most notably, while there is a connection between crime and the supply and use of currently illegal drugs, much of this crime is an artifact of prohibition.

First and most obviously, because the distribution, possession, and use of substances such as marijuana and cocaine are *defined* as criminal activities, crime statistics will show that sellers and users of these substances are criminals.

Second, because the illegal-drug trade necessarily takes place outside of the law, illegal-drug sellers and buyers have no access to formal institutions — such as courts, credit-rating agencies, and trade associations — that minimize conflict and help to settle disputes peaceably. In such a setting, violence enjoys a comparative advantage at dispute resolution.

Third and relatedly, the concern for reputation that plays a powerful role in promoting proper and honorable behavior (Klein, 1997) is enfeebled in those who deal in illegal drugs. One reason is that the more likely someone is to be guided by a concern to maintain a good reputation, the less likely he is to enter an enterprise popularly regarded as criminal, even if he himself finds nothing intrinsically wrong with it. Therefore, illegal activities — including the illegal-drug trade — will be dominated by people who are less apt than ordinary people to care about their good reputations. They are people who generally pay less heed to the counsel of Adam Smith's Impartial Spectator. Another reason is that, once a person is perceived as being a criminal, the marginal psychic cost to him of acting in ways that further diminish his reputation are low. He will, therefore, engage in more dishonorable activities. (That is, suppose someone keenly interested in his reputation nevertheless is attracted to the illegal-drug trade. Once in this trade, the big blow to his reputation has already been felt; his good reputation is already sacrificed. Once this good reputation is gone, concern for it is unlikely to restrain him from further acts of deceit, dishonesty, and, perhaps, even cruelty.)

Fourth, resources used to combat the distribution and use of illegal drugs are diverted from policing directly against crimes, such as murder and theft, that violate the rights of innocent people. Of course, it is an empirical question whether this diversion of criminal-justice resources from fighting crime directly to fighting it indirectly (by attempting to reduce drug use) increases, decreases, or leaves unchanged the rate of crime against innocent people and their property.

What evidence there is suggests that drug prohibition promotes rather than discourages crimes against persons and property. Again, much of the pioneering research on this question was done by Bruce Benson and his co-authors. Benson et al. (1995: 26) report that "[t]here is no evidence that increasing use of law enforcement resources to combat drugs has reduced other crime...Indeed, in sharp contrast to the political rhetoric, it seems that drug enforcement causes property crime." (See also Benson and Rasmussen, 1991.)

3. Asset Forfeiture

Many of the reasons that drug prohibition enhances rather than discourages non-drug crimes of the sort that people legitimately fear are revealed in an analysis of civil asset forfeiture. Asset forfeiture is now one of most widely used weapons of drug-prohibition enforcers, with the federal government seizing about $450 million annually and state governments seizing at least that much (Rising, 1999; Wollstein, 2001).

Asset-forfeiture statutes permit law-enforcement agents to seize and take title to property and cash reasonably suspected of being involved in illegal activities. Owners of the assets need not ever be convicted of, or even charged with, criminal wrongdoing. All that is needed by enforcement authorities is a reasonable suspicion that the assets have either been used to facilitate criminal behavior or are the proceeds of such behavior.

Some states and the federal government allow innocent-owner defenses: that is, if the owner is innocent of the wrongdoing, his property must be returned to him. However, such a defense is not constitutionally required — some states in some cases provide no innocent-owner defense — and oftentimes the property owner bears the burden of proving his innocence rather than enjoying a presumption of innocence. (This was the case under federal law until 2000, when Congress changed its forfeiture statutes to give owners of seized properties a presumption of innocence for purposes of the innocent-owner defense under federal asset-seizure law.)

Law-enforcement authorities justify asset forfeiture as a vital tool to fight drug distribution and use. Their argument is simple: civil forfeiture is a tax on the drug trade that simultaneously raises dealers' costs and increases the incentives of enforcement officials to hunt down and destroy illegal drugs.

But matters are not this straightforward. Consider a politician's choice between prohibition and taxation. Why would he ever vote to prohibit the possession and use of goods demanded by large numbers of people? The answer, of course, is that influential interest groups (likely bootleggers and Baptists) demand such prohibition. If prohibition succeeds, politicians gain votes by removing from the street goods intensely disliked by politically influential groups and/or a sufficiently large bloc of voters. But even if prohibition is ineffective, voters might still be swayed by the posturing of politicians stumbling over each other to display how tough they are on crime.

Political benefits, however, are never free. Prohibition prevents tax revenues from being collected on the outlawed substances. But asset forfeiture solves this problem for politicians. Because the government keeps the value of forfeited assets, forfeiture surreptitiously taxes prohibited substances.

As a form of taxation, though, asset forfeiture poses specific and troubling problems. They emerge from the following facts:

- Law-enforcement agencies keep part of the proceeds from forfeiture.

- Asset-forfeiture proceeds are collected only from a small and politically unorganized subgroup of the population.

- Constitutional protections against government abuses are often rejected by courts when asset forfeiture is used.

As a consequence of allowing law-enforcement officials to keep some of the proceeds from asset-forfeiture actions, these officials coalesce into an interest group supporting asset forfeiture. Empirical studies of the effect of asset forfeiture upon the size of enforcement-agencies' budgets indicate that forfeitures "have a significant positive impact on non-capital expenditures by police agencies" (Benson et al., 1995: 22). That is, asset forfeitures increase law-enforcement agencies' discretionary budgets.

Moreover, as a means of taxation, asset forfeiture is inequitable. Because of their civil-law (rather than criminal-law) nature, asset-forfeiture statutes permit government to confiscate assets without abiding by constitutional rules designed to guarantee a strong likelihood that persons convicted of criminal wrongdoing actually are guilty of criminal wrongdoing. Thus, government has a much easier time getting these assets than it has of convicting people of crimes. The wide discretionary scope that asset-forfeiture actions give to governments, therefore, almost surely results in too many innocent people losing their properties in asset-forfeiture actions, making a mockery of the claim that asset forfeiture is necessary in order to punish actual criminals.

In short, a large element of randomness mars asset-forfeiture actions (at least if the benchmark is the accuracy of actually convicting genuine criminals of their offenses). And random enforcement is unlikely to be effective enforcement. Also, the random manner in which asset-forfeiture taxes are levied hides from taxpayers a part of the cost of government operations. A disproportionate share of this cost is foisted upon owners whose properties are suspected of being used to commit drug offenses. This group — largely because of the randomness of the enforcement effort — is politically unorganized. Therefore, its members generally cannot adequately defend themselves in the political arena against the much more cohesive and self-aware law-enforcement officials who benefit materially from asset forfeiture.

The potential loss of property due to forfeiture is typically a one-time, low-probability event for each property owner. Thus, they have little incentive to form or to join lobbying groups pressing to rein in asset-forfeiture powers (Pritchard, 1991).

The perverse incentives created by asset forfeiture are even greater at the level of law-enforcement agencies that are able to keep all or part of the proceeds seized in forfeiture actions. To see why, consider briefly some basic economics of law enforcement.

The optimal level of deterrence for any particular crime — say, drug enforcement — is the level at which the marginal benefit of deterrence equals its marginal cost. If deterrence is less than that level, the benefit of spending an extra dollar on deterrence is greater than the cost of doing so. Deterrence efforts should be increased. If, in contrast, deterrence is at a super-optimal level, the value of spending an extra dollar on deterrence yields benefits less than the attendant costs. Deterrence efforts should be reduced.

A more precise way to make this point is to say that one necessary condition for the optimal level of deterrence is that the net benefit of spending a dollar of resources on deterrence of each of the several types of crime be equal. That is, if the last dollar spent investigating murder nets murder deterrence worth $15, while the last dollar spent investigating burglary nets burglary deterrence worth $25, resources should be shifted from murder investigations to burglary investigations until these net benefits are equal to each other.

The practice of asset forfeiture likely prevents the attainment of optimal levels of deterrence. The reason is that law-enforcement officials will adjust their enforcement efforts to maximize revenues from asset forfeitures rather than to achieve the optimal level of crime deterrence (Boudreaux and Pritchard, 1997: 352–355). And there is no reason to expect that the level of drug enforcement that yields maximum forfeiture revenues is also that enforcement level at which the marginal benefit of enforcement equals its marginal cost. Indeed, because the bulk of the cost of forfeitures is borne by people who are politically unorganized — and because the benefits of forfeiture actions are concentrated disproportionately on enforcement agencies — efforts to enforce drug prohibition using asset-forfeiture powers are likely to be excessive. Too many law-enforcement resources will be devoted to enforcing drug-prohibition statutes and, hence, too few resources will be devoted to enforcing laws against violence and theft.

This conclusion is strengthened by the recognition that forfeiture actions are generally less risky and more lucrative for law-enforcement agents than are efforts to hunt and capture violent criminals. Suppose that, from society's standpoint, extra man-hours and resources are better spent pursuing violent offenders rather than enforcing drug prohibitions. Unlike seeking out valuable properties whose owners fit a broad profile of drug trader or user, pursuing and capturing, say, murderers puts the agents' lives at some significant risk and, even if successful, probably does not pay to the law-enforcement agency a handsome monetary return.

The availability of asset forfeiture, therefore, likely tempts self-interested law-enforcement agencies to over-enforce drug prohibitions and under-enforce other criminal laws.

4. Conclusion

Other public-choice problems contaminate drug-prohibition efforts. For example, because there are seldom any victims to complain about drug transactions, enforcement authorities must often engage in sting operations that rely for their justification on the word of the enforcement agencies themselves. In addition, bribery of law-enforcement officials is an ever-present temptation, not only because of the large sums of money involved in the illegal-drug trade but also because the victimless nature of drug crimes means that fewer third-parties are available to detect evidence of bribery.

No evidence shows that drug prohibition works, and much evidence shows that drug prohibition has several perverse and unintended consequences. Regardless of the nobility of the notion of a nation free of drugs, prudence suggests that the best course of action is to end drug prohibition just as alcohol prohibition was ended seventy years ago. As with alcohol, the effects of ending the futile attempt to prevent people from enjoying intoxicants of their choosing likely will reduce crime and, at the same time, reduce the political pressures to ignore important provisions of the Constitution.

DONALD J. BOUDREAUX

REFERENCES

Benson, B.L. and Rasmussen, D.W. (1991). "The relationship between illicit drug enforcement policy and property crimes." *Contemporary Policy Issues*, 9(October): 106–115.

Benson, B.L., Rasmussen, D.W., and Sollars, D.L. (1995). "Police bureaucrats, their incentives, and the war on drugs." *Public Choice*, 83: 21–45.

Benson, B.L. and Rasmussen, D.W. (1997). "Predatory public finance and the origins of the war on drugs: 1984–1989," in W.F. Shughart (ed.) *Taxing Choice*. Oakland, CA: The Independent Institute, pp. 197–225.

Boudreaux, D.J. and Pritchard, A.C. (1997). "Civil forfeiture as a tax," in W.F. Shughart (ed.) *Taxing Choice*. Oakland, CA: The Independent Institute, pp. 347–367.

Breton, A. and Wintrobe, R. (1982). *The Logic of Bureaucratic Control*. Cambridge: Cambridge University Press.

Klein, D.R. (1997). *Reputation*. Ann Arbor, MI: University of Michigan Press.

Miron, J.A. (1998). "Drug Prohibition." in P. Newman (ed.) *The New Palgrave Dictionary of Economics and the Law*. London: Macmillan Reference Ltd, pp. 648–652.

Pritchard, A.C. (1991). "Government Promises and Due Process: An Economic Analysis of the 'New Property'." *Virginia Law Review*, 77: 1053–1090.

Rising, D. (1999). House Bill Would Put Limits on Asset Seizures. South Coast Today. Available on line at www.s-t.com/daily/08-99/08-08-99/a051o023.html.

Twight, C.A. (2002). *Dependent on D.C.* New York: Palgrave.

Wollstein, J. (2001). Government Property Seizures Out of Control. NewsMax.com. Available on line at www.asappain.com/Seizures_Out_Of_Control.html.

Yandle, B. (1983). "Bootleggers and Baptists: The Education of a Regulatory Economist." *Regulation*, 7(May–June): 12–16.

WELFARE ECONOMICS AND PUBLIC CHOICE

Welfare economics provides the basis for judging the achievements of markets and policy makers in allocating resources. Its most powerful conceptual tool is the utility possibility frontier. This defines the set of utility allocations that can be achieved in a society subject to the constraints of tastes and technologies. Any allocation on the frontier cannot be Pareto dominated and hence would satisfy a rather minimal condition for it to be socially desirable.

Distributional judgements about points on the Pareto frontier are typically embodied in a social welfare function. The social choice literature, beginning with Arrow (1951), has demonstrated the difficulties of *deriving* such a function from citizens' underlying preferences over social alternatives without making interpersonal comparisons of utility. By postulating a social welfare function for pedagogical purposes, the analyst is implicitly assuming that interpersonal comparisons of utility can be made and has adopted a position on how society should weigh such comparisons (Sen, 1977).

The analysis of competitive markets culminated in the fundamental theorems of welfare economics which elucidated the (restrictive) conditions under which resource allocation by markets would achieve Pareto efficiency. The first fundamental theorem says that all perfectly competitive equilibria with complete markets (to deal with externalities and uncertainty) are Pareto efficient. The second fundamental theorem says that any Pareto efficient allocation might be decentralized by suitable choice of lump-sum transfers.

Modern welfare economics builds on this by putting incentive constraints at centre stage. Among the seminal contributions are Mirrlees (1971) and Hammond (1979). This analysis dispenses with the assumption that lump-sum transfers are feasible because of the incentive problems that they create. The appropriate benchmark for government is second best Pareto efficiency, taking into account appropriate restrictions on policy instruments. A whole tradition of policy analysis in this vein has been developed (see, e.g., Atkinson and Stiglitz, 1980).

Welfare economic approaches to the policy process have been criticized by those operating in the public choice tradition, for failing to consider how actual policy choices are made. Thus, even if we were able to understand what optimal policies are, there is no guarantee that the kinds of decision making institutions that we observe in reality will bring them about. The *public choice critique of welfare economics* says that, by failing to model government, it provides a misleading view of the appropriate role for government. (See Buchanan, 1972) for a forceful plea for a level playing field.)

To see the logic of the critique, consider the argument that the government should intervene to fix a market failure, say by introducing a Pigouvian tax. Then, the welfare economist will select the tax, and other policy instruments, to maximize some social welfare objective. There is no reason at all to expect the political process to yield this outcome. Even if the tax is chosen to be second best Pareto efficient, the distributional outcome selected by the political process need not match that of the "social planner." While this may suggest that a public choice approach has to be more conservative, this is only true when equilibrium effects on other policy instruments are ignored. As argued in Besley and Coate (2003), it is possible for these other policy instruments to be changed in a welfare improving direction.

Many models in the public choice literature lead to efficient policies which fail to maximize social welfare. A good example is the Leviathan approach of Brennan and Buchanan (1980). In this case politicians extract resources for themselves at the expense of voters. Proponents of probabilistic voting models have sometimes suggested that particular social welfare functions are maximized in political equilibrium. (See Coughlin, 1992 for a discussion.)

However, they rest on strong assumptions and it appears unlikely that technological assumptions are at the heart of the distributional conflict implicit in political competition.

Some economists use the benchmark of social surplus to judge political outcomes. However, this is conceptually problematic and is even (misleadingly) labeled as an efficiency criterion. The notion of surplus is only defined under restrictive assumptions about preferences. Moreover, the criterion really only makes if (i) there are lump-sum transfers and (ii) social preferences weight a dollar in every citizen's hands equally. This would be fine if both the political process and the planner were able to use lump-sum transfers. However, even then, the exact allocation of transfers would enter the calculus of whether the intervention is justified unless (ii) also holds. But the latter is only one particular distributional preference and not an efficiency criterion.

Policies chosen by the political process may fail to be efficient using second-best efficiency as a benchmark. Besley and Coate (1998) define a welfare economic definition of *political failure* in this way. To motivate this, consider the textbook analysis of market efficiency. First, the set of efficient allocations is characterized (graphically, the utility possibility frontier). This is a purely technological notion of efficiency, since the frontier depends only on the tastes and technologies of the economy. The second step requires a model, such as that developed by Arrow-Debreu, to specify how markets allocate resources. The idea of market failure, then comes from observing that, under certain conditions, markets do not result in allocations that are on the frontier. The term "failure" is justified by the observation that, in principle, all citizens could be made better off. A parallel notion of political failure arises when resources used to determine policy fail to produce a selection from the second-best Pareto frontier so that, in principle, all citizens can be made better off.

This welfare economic notion of political failure should be contrasted with the standard approach to political failure rooted in the work of Wicksell. He argued that government intervention is legitimate only if government dominates a status quo point where government is absent. Then a political failure is defined when government fails to select a Pareto dominant point.

The welfare economic approach and Wicksellian approach are distinct. To see this, consider the comparison between the outcome attained from a political process to a policy vector x_0 which is the outcome that would prevail with no government intervention. A *Wicksellian political failure* is now defined as a situation in which the political process selects a policy outcome which does not Pareto dominate x_0 (See Figure 1). Let A denote the utility

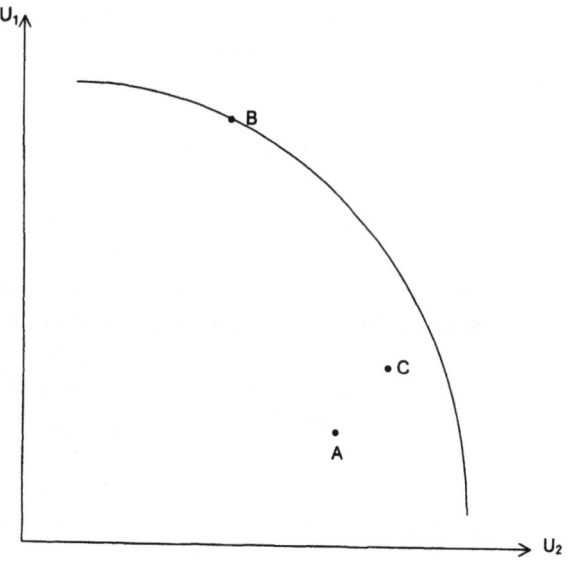

Figure 1

allocation associated with x_0. By fixing market failures, we suppose that (in-line with the welfare economic approach) the government can, in principle, shift out the Pareto frontier. Let x_0 be the new policy vector and consider possible utility outcomes associated with it. Point B which is on a higher Pareto frontier and hence is (second best) efficient. However, this point is not a Pareto improvement over point A. Hence, if chosen by government, it would constitute a Wicksellian political failure. However, it would not be a political failure according to the definition above as it is on the Pareto frontier and there is no scope for improving government efficiency. Now consider point C. According to the Wicksellian definition, it is not a political failure as it is a Pareto improvement relative to A. However, the definition based on second-best Pareto efficiency would regard it as a political failure. It is possible to make all citizens better off beginning from this point.

Wicksell's definition of political failure embodies an important distributional judgement which outlaws any pure redistribution of resources around point A except in so far as this is justified on citizens' underlying preferences for redistribution. A government can intervene efficiently in the welfare economic sense and yet still create a political failure. Moreover, the scope for political failure on this definition is vast, depending on the status quo point x_0 being posited.

Are there good reasons to believe that governments chose inefficient policies using second best Pareto efficiency as the criterion? In answering this, it is essential that the same set of instruments that a welfare economist would

allow the government to use should be available in the political process. Claims about the inefficiency of outcomes associated with the median voter often miss this point. Consider the claim that the median voter fails to provide public goods efficiently. While it is true that, in general, the Lindahl-Samuelson rule does not yield the same outcome as the median voter rule, this has nothing to do with political inefficiency. The Lindahl-Samuelson rule requires that lump-sum transfer are feasible while the median voter model usually works with a more restrictive tax system. The former achieves first best efficiency while the latter a very constrained form of second best efficiency.

Why then does this kind of claim persist? The difficulty lies in the need to make sufficient restrictions on the model of political resource allocation to get an equilibrium to exist. These often exclude the rich policy space studied in welfare economics. However, the failing is on the side of economists not governments — the latter struggling with a satisfactory theory of public choice. If the theory of market failure had proceeded in this way, it would have lead to many strange conclusions. Suppose that economists were limited in their ability to study multi-product pricing by firms. Then, we would conclude that there is always a market failure when the government can make these choices instead! This critique of the literature was raised in an important article by Wittman (1989).

In a static model of policy choice where rulers choose policy in their own interests (no matter how narrow), there is a presumption of second-best efficiency (Besley and Coate, 1997). A good example of this is the Leviathan model. There is no reason for Leviathan to extract resources from citizens in an inefficient way. However, there are potential sources of second-best Pareto inefficiency: the use of influence activities, legislative inefficiencies, coordination problems and strategic use of policies in a dynamic setting. We now discuss each of these briefly in turn.

There is a vast literature on why the policy process may be subject to influence activities — rent-seeking or lobbying. The literature on rent-seeking originating with Tullock (1967) and Krueger (1974) studied how private actions influence policy. Formal analysis has focused mostly on modelling competition among individuals or groups to obtain an indivisible policy favor, the aim being to characterize the aggregate expenditure on rent-seeking activities (see, e.g., Baye et al. (1994) and the references therein).

Whether this activity is inefficient depends critically on the form that it takes. Cash transfers, as modeled by Grossman and Helpman (1994) yield movements around the Pareto frontier. However, examples such as campaign finance as modeled in Grossman and Helpman (1996) yield real resource misallocation. For this to be second-best inefficient (i.e., a political failure), there must exist is a way of re-organizing the influence game so that all players (including those involved in the influence process) can be better off. An example along these lines is studied in Besley and Coate (2001). But why might political favors not be granted in the most efficient way? An intriguing answer is given in Coate and Morris (1995). If voters fail to re-elect politicians who engage in such behavior that disguised forms of transfer may be preferred to keep voters in the dark.

Political failure may also occur because of coordination difficulties among voters. Consider a world where there are both competent and incompetent candidates — the latter defined as candidates who (for fixed ideological preferences) can generate a potential Pareto improvement. Then, it is possible to construct a political equilibrium between two incompetent and one competent candidate of different ideologies where voters fail to coordinate on the competent candidate who therefore loses (Besley and Coate, 1997).

Legislative policy making is also a potential source of political failure — with important insights going back to the seminal work by Buchanan and Tullock (1957). However, for a legislature to pick a Pareto dominated point, it must be that there is some failure in the bargaining procedure used to make decisions — either limits on transfers or the credibility of promises.

In dynamic models, examples of political failure are created principally by the strategic use of policy. One of the earliest examples to illustrate this is the work of Persson and Svensson (1989) and Tabellini and Alesina (1990). They show that governments will have an incentive to run deficits to reduce the policy flexibility of future incumbents. Aghion and Bolton (1990) and Milesi-Ferretti and Spaolore (1994) show that strategic policy choice can also lead to changes in who is elected. This too may lead to policies being selected that are inefficient. Privatization decisions may be a key practical instance of this (Biais and Perrotti, 2002). Many governments underpriced privatizations to create a class of stakeholders committed to voting in favor of particular kinds of governments. This could explain privatization even without appealing to economic gains. Besley and Coate (1998) pulls this ideas together to give a unified definition of political failure in dynamic models where the criterion is second best Pareto efficiency.

So what do we learn from this pathology? In cases of true political failure, there should be unanimous consent that something should be done (provided that the failure results in a truly Pareto dominant outcome). In all the above cases, there are important and interesting questions about institutions can be redesigned to mitigate the political failure. This is similar in spirit to the notion, in traditional public choice writings, that there should be a focus on designing a fiscal and procedural constitution (Brennan and Buchanan, 1985). In practice, it is likely that progress will come from piece-meal analysis of specific institutional variations.

The juxtaposition of welfare economic and public choice approaches to the role of government is frequently overstated. There are as strong reasons for public choice economists to study welfare economics and optimal policy. Similarly, welfare economists need to understand public choice. Societies frequently have make choices about how to govern their affairs which have both efficiency and distributional implications. The role of welfare economics in a world of public choice is to provide an analysis of this.

TIMOTHY BESLEY

REFERENCES

Aghion, P. and Bolton, P. (1990). "Government debt and the risk of default: A politico-economic model of the strategic role of debt," in R. Dornbusch and M. Draghi (eds.) *Public Debt Management: Theory and History*. Cambridge: Cambridge University Press, England.

Arrow, K. (1951). *Social Choice and Individual Values*. New York: John Wiley (2nd Edition, 1963).

Atkinson, A.B. and Stiglitz, J.E. (1980). *Lectures on Public Economics*. New York: McGraw Hill.

Baye, M., Kovenock, D., and De Vries, C. (1994). "The solution to the tullock rent seeking game when $R > 2$: Mixed-strategy equilibria and mean dissipation rates." *Public Choice*, 81: 363–380.

Besley, T. and Coate, S. (1997). "An economic model of representative democracy." *Quarterly Journal of Economics*, 112(1): 85–114.

Besley, T. and Coate, S. (1998). "Sources of inefficiency in a representative democracy: A dynamic analysis." *American Economic Review* 88(1): 139–156.

Besley, T. and Coate, S. (2001). "Lobbying and welfare in a representative democracy." *Review of Economic Studies* 68(1): 67–82.

Besley, T. and Coate, S. (2003). "On the public choice critique of welfare economics." in *Public Choice*, 114: 253–273.

Biais, B. and Perotti, E. (2002). "Machiavellian Underpricing." in the *American Economic Review*, 92: 240–258.

Brennan, G. and Buchanan, J.M. (1980). *The Power to Tax: Analytical Foundations of a Fiscal Constitution*. Cambridge: Cambridge University Press.

Brennan, G. and Buchanan, J.M. (1985). *The Reason of Rules: Constitutional Political Economy*. Cambridge: Cambridge University Press.

Buchanan, J.M. (1972). "Toward an analysis of closed behavioral systems," chapter 2 in J. Buchanan and R. Tollison (eds.) *Theory of Public Choice*. Ann Arbor: University of Michigan Press.

Buchanan, J.M. and Tullock, G. (1962). *The Calculus of Consent: Logical Foundations of Constitutional Democracy*. Ann Arbor: University of Michigan Press.

Coate, S. and Morris, S. (1995). "On the form of transfers to special interests." *Journal of Political Economy*, 103: 1210–1235.

Coughlin, P. (1992). *Probabilistic Voting Theory*. New York: Cambridge University Press.

Grossman, G. and Helpman, E. (1994). "Protection for Sale." *American Economic Review*, 84: 833–850.

Grossman, G. and Helpman, E. (1996). "Electoral competition and special interest politics." *Review of Economic Studies*, 63(2): 265–286.

Hammond, P. (1979). "Straightforward incentive compatibility in large economies." *Review of Economic Studies*, 46: 263–282.

Krueger, A. (1974). "The Political Economy of the Rent-Seeking Society." *American Economic Review*, 64: 291–303.

Milesi-Ferretti, G.-M. and Spolaore, E. (1994). "How Cynical Can an Incumbent Be? Strategic Policy in a Model of Government Spending." *Journal of Public Economics*, 55: 121–140.

Mirrlees, J.A. (1971). "An exploration in the theory of optimum income taxation." *Review of Economic Studies*, 38: 175–208.

Persson, T. and Svensson, L. (1989). "Why a Stubborn Conservative Would Run a Deficit: Policy with Time-Inconsistent Preferences." *Quarterly Journal of Economics*, 104: 325–346.

Sen, A. (1977). "On weights and measures: informational constraints in social welfare analysis." *Econometrica*, 45: 1539–1572.

Tabellini, G. and Alesina, A. (1990). "Voting on the budget deficit." *American Economic Review*, 80: 37–49.

Tullock, G. (1967). "The welfare costs of tariffs, monopolies and theft." *Western Economic Journal*, 5: 224–232.

Wittman, D. (1989). "Why democracies produce efficient results." *Journal of Political Economy*, 97: 1395–1426.

WELFARE ECONOMICS AND THE THEORY OF THE STATE[1]

The most general attribute that distinguishes government from other organizations is its coercive role, circumscribing the activities of all of its citizens and the other inhabitants of its territories. Laws and their enforcement require members of the public to behave in certain way and preclude them from engaging in actions that some of them would otherwise undertake. Explicitly in a democracy and implicitly in any government that operates under some sort of social contract, this means that the governed must have chosen voluntarily to be subjected to coercion that prevents them from behaving as they would otherwise choose to do. Such a paradoxical arrangement nevertheless can constitute rational behavior on the part of the public. The theory of the state, in essence, entails resolution of this paradox. It will be shown that welfare economics deals with an entirely parallel issue. Indeed, the policy measures that welfare theory suggests are particular examples of coercive public sector acts that it would serve the interests of the public to support and accept voluntarily. The logic of the analysis applies to issues as varied as taxation, finance of national defense, counter-cyclical measures and programs to counteract congestion problems in road traffic and urban dwellings, among many others.

1. How Acceptance of Government Coercion can Serve the Interests of the Coerced

Acceptance of government coercion by the coerced can serve the self interest of the latter in only one of two circumstances: (1) where the coerced fear that they will not otherwise make decisions that really serve their best interests and (2) where acceptance by the individuals of rules circumscribing their own conduct is a prerequisite for adoption of rules coercing others. The first has been illustrated by Ulysses' request to be tied to the mast of his ship to prevent him from succumbing to the Sirens' song. Individuals may feel that they lack the strength of character to undertake an act that denies them an immediate pleasure but will be very beneficial to themselves later. Compulsory saving for retirement, as imposed by social security laws, are a clear example. This role of government, then, is recourse by citizens to the paternalism of government, with the latter assigned to make decisions for the individuals that are superior for their welfare than the decisions they would make themselves. Seat belt laws for automobile passengers, laws against consumption of narcotics or dangerous foods and taxes on cigarettes are all illustrations.

What is noteworthy here is that all of these are examples of a type of market failure that is usually omitted from the standard listings (see, e.g., Bator, 1958). In all of these cases, the reason the free market does not work is that individuals can sometimes be guided by transitory or illusory incentives to make decisions that do not really serve their interests and that, in many cases, even they themselves would concede to be self damaging. In such cases the market will sometimes compound the imperfection by offering rewards to those who tempt people to act self destructively, for example, via the profits that can be earned by the supply of tobacco products or drugs. But this brings us to a second category of coercive government acts that it may serve the self interest of the individual to accept.

This second category, which it will be convenient to divide further into two subcases, arguably encompasses the major tasks of government. These are cases in which the individual, A, would be better off if left free to make her own decisions, but in which no constraining rule will be applied to others unless it also holds for individual A as well. That is, the individual in principle is faced with three levels of welfare, $w_1 < w_2 < w_3$, with the last of these obtainable only if everyone else in the world is subject to some constraining rules but A is exempted from them. Welfare level w_2 is attainable if the rules are uniformly applied to everyone, while the absence of the constraining rules yields only welfare level w_1. As a practical matter, the w_3-yielding option is not really available, so the individual must choose between only the other two. In that case the reason for agreeing to be coerced is clear, at least in the abstract terms so far considered. It is convenient to refer to this situation as one that entails beneficial nondiscriminatory coercion.

The most widely recognized nondiscriminatory subcase entails protection of the individual from actions by others that damage the individual's interest. Laws against burglary, false advertising and monopolistic behavior are clear illustrations and other examples are easily cited. Most but not all[2] of these involve redistributive activities in which an agent seeks to benefit at the expense of others. Most often, this involves an attempt by the former to take away income, wealth or property of others, without compensation.

In many such cases it is not clear that the individual would benefit if that person alone were exempted from the constraining rules. Few of us would be likely to pursue the profits of bank robbery if the rules against this activity became inapplicable to us. But that is, arguably, because we live in a society in which it has become customary to deplore acts of violence and to take measures against them. History suggests, however, that in a society where there is little or no legal constraint upon violent behavior, it becomes not only acceptable but actually honorific, with status conferred upon those who are most successful in such activities. In any event, the point is that in these cases, at worst, the individual does not lose by being included among the universally coerced, and benefits to the extent that protection of private holdings against arbitrary takings is beneficial to all.

2. Generalized Externalities and the Theory of the State

The third and very significant category of circumstances in which self interest dictates acceptance of coercion is a generalization of the externalities phenomenon that plays a critical role in welfare economics (Pigou, 1932; Buchanan and Stubblebine, 1962). The issue arises when the individual's immediate self interest is served by a course of action that has more than offsetting effects upon others, so that if all individuals are left free to act in accord with their immediate interests there will be a net reduction in the product of the economy or the benefits of any sort available in the society, with the possibility that each and every person will end up worse off. This is not a matter of redistribution, as when a pickpocket obtains someone's wallet. Rather, it is a situation in which the entire inventory of benefits that is available for the members of the society to share is reduced by the self-interested actions of every individual.

What is critical here is the fact that such damaging actions do not constitute irrational behavior on the part of the individual. *In the absence of a rule that precludes everyone from the socially damaging behavior in question, the best course open to each and every individual is to behave in such a detrimental fashion.*

A standard example will make this clear. Consider the case of automotive emissions that are very harmful to health, and suppose that they can be avoided if an expensive suppression device, costing D dollars, is installed on every vehicle. In a city with 2 million autos the contribution of any one of them to deterioration of air quality is negligible. If no other person installs an emission suppressor, it would be a quixotic act of some one person to spend the D dollars to install the suppressor on his own vehicle, since this would make no discernable difference to air quality. Moreover, even if a law requiring suppressors on all vehicles were adopted and enforced, any one car owner could benefit by being granted a special and unique exemption, since his emissions would hardly affect the purity of the air. Yet, if the additional medical bills and cleaning cost resulting from failure to suppress everyone's emissions add up to more than D dollars per vehicle owner, failure to adopt the coercive suppressor installation law will clearly be damaging to all. There is no redistribution issue here. No one is in need of protection from the predation of others. Nor is any individual protected from inability to make rational decisions. Rather, it is only the community as a whole that effectively has the option of choosing between rational and irrational behavior, that is, behavior whose consequences the individual herself considers to be undesirable.

It is important to recognize, as is emphasized in the economic literature, that externalities can be as damaging to the interests of society when the affected activities are themselves beneficial as when they are detrimental. The example just discussed involves pollution emissions that are inherently damaging to others, and the problem is that, though some level of emissions is unavoidable, or further suppression beyond some low level is impractical, in the absence of rules individuals will end up emitting far more than is consistent with the public interest. The opposite result occurs where the externality-generating activity is beneficial. Here society's interests will be harmed because without coercion too little of such an activity will be undertaken.

A clear and important example is expenditure on the R&D that is plainly of crucial importance for economic growth. It has long been observed that much of the benefit from innovative activities goes to persons other than the inventors or those who invested in the process. This beneficial externality may, indeed, be far greater than generally recognized. If the bulk of the more than 10-fold rise in per capita GDP in the U.S. and much of Western Europe since the beginning of the industrial revolution is attributable to innovation, and one can estimate that less that 10 percent of GDP goes to persons who participate in the innovation process, it follows that the bulk of the beneficial externalities deriving from the efforts of the latter ultimately go to others. This means, and many studies confirm, that the incentives for innovative activity provided by the market are likely to be inadequate to induce a voluntary level of investment in innovation that is optimal in terms of the social interest.[3] This suggests that coercive collection of taxes by government to provide additional resources for innovation facilitating activities, such as basic research, can be beneficial to the entire community, particularly in the long run.

3. Size of the Community and Private Steps to Deal with Externality Issues

In a classic article, Ronald Coase (1960) shows, among other things, that where only a small number of decision makers is involved, a process of voluntary bargaining and compensatory payments by those affected by an externality may be able to provide an optimal result. In effect the "victim" of a detrimental externality can bribe its generator to cease and desist, or at least to cut back on the damaging activity to an optimal degree. Here, because only a few persons are involved, the need for governmental coercion patently is limited, and may even prove to be too much of a good thing.

That numbers make the difference for the rationality of voluntarily accepted coercion has long been recognized. For example, more than two centuries ago Hume, with his powerful insight wrote

> Two neighbors may agree to drain a meadow, which they possess in common; because it is easy for them to know each other's mind; and each must perceive that the immediate consequence of his failing in his part, is the abandonment of the whole project. But it is very difficult, and indeed impossible, that a thousand persons

should agree in any such action; it being difficult for them to concert so complicated a design and still more difficult for them to execute it; while each seeks a pretext to free himself of the trouble and expense, and would lay the whole burden on others. Political society easily remedies both these inconveniences...[4]

In these few words, Hume lays out much of the welfare economics that underlies the theory of the state, and brings out the importance of the presence of a substantial number of inhabitants for its rationale.

4. Government Activities that Fall into the Category of Externalities

Economic externalities are widespread, indeed arguably ubiquitous. The literature of welfare economics provides a profusion of illustrations. However, here it is more to the point to offer several examples in areas not usually cited in this arena. The illustrations are inflation, recession and unemployment and defense against terrorism.

Hyper inflation brings the point out most dramatically. When inflation proceeds at the fantastic rates experienced in Germany after the First Word War or, more recently, in Latin America and Israel, clearly money loses its value as it is being pocketed by the recipient. In such an economy, in the absence of governmental intervention, it is plainly in the interest of the recipient of any cash to spend it as quickly as it can be get rid of, before it becomes virtually worthless. But that is precisely the pattern of behavior most likely to exacerbate the inflation. And no one individual can afford to do otherwise or can achieve anything by doing so. Only strong and essentially coercive governmental action can bring the explosion of prices to an end, and has repeatedly done so in the past. This is clearly an example in which voluntary acceptance of coercion may be the only rational response by members of the public. Any one individual would be irrational to undertake unilaterally to curb hasty spending, yet it would be perfectly rational to vote for a government that coerces that person, along with everyone else, to do so.

The opposite argument clearly applies to an effort to counteract recession and unemployment. The enhanced risk of loss of jobs and investments in such circumstances provides a powerful incentive for the individual to curb spending and save as much as possible for the imminent rainy day. But, at least from the point of view of a Keynesian, this is the reverse of what the situation requires. By taking such defensive measures the individuals collectively do as much as they can to bring upon themselves the very problems against which they seek protection. Acting individually, they can do nothing to help bring the problem to an end. But if they vote support for a government that adopts appropriate and universally applied coercive measures they can achieve what unconstrained behavior makes impossible for them.

Finally, it is appropriate to end with an issue that is entirely removed from economics and that thereby underscores the broad pertinence of the externalities analysis. This is the issue of defense expenditure, in particular in its most recent form, defense against the threat of terrorism. Economists recognize the role of externalities here, and refer to such defense preparation as a public good, meaning that if it protects the society it protects all of its members, without an increase in cost resulting from an expansion in the number of recipients of its benefits. Once again, the individual is powerless to act effectively in this arena, and an isolated outlay by the individual for this purpose cannot be expected to achieve anything. Only by agreeing to use of the coercive powers of government to collect the required resources can the public obtain the benefit that it may value far higher than the cost.

5. Conclusion

The essential feature that defines a democratic government is voluntary agreement by the members of the public to subject themselves to its coercion. As is true of any paradox, despite its appearance there are good and logical reasons for them to do so. The logic of externalities analysis that is provided by the economics of welfare is a critical component of that explanation. Moreover, the phenomena to which this explanation applies are neither rare nor unimportant. Military defense, measures to counteract inflation and recession and the encouragement of innovation are hardly minor issues, and there are many more, including environmental protection, congestion in transportation and residences and a host of others. If this is not the full story of the logic of intervention by the state, it certainly is a good part of the tale.

WILLIAM J. BAUMOL

NOTES

1. On the general subject see (Baumol, 1952), (Downs, 1957), (Buchanan and Tullock, 1962) and (Olson, 1965).
2. Protection of the law against random and irrational violence is an example in which redistribution is not involved.
3. The market, however, does provide a higher share of the rewards to innovators than this suggests. A very substantial number of firms, many of them major enterprises, engage voluntarily in licensing and trading of their privately owned technology, thereby internalizing at least part of the externality. For example, newspaper reports suggest that in 2001

approximately 20 percent of IBM's net profits derived from technology license fees. On this subject see Baumol (2002 chapters 6 and 7).
4. (Hume, 1739). Olson (1965) also brings out the importance of the number of the governed.

REFERENCES

Bator, F.M. (1958). "The anatomy of market failure." *Quarterly Journal of Economics*, 47, 351–379.

Baumol, W.J. (1952). *Welfare Economics and the Theory of the State*. London: The London School of Economics and Political Science.

Baumol, W.J. (2002). *The Free-Market Innovation Machine: Analyzing the Growth Miracle of Capitalism*. Princeton: Princeton University Press.

Buchanan, J.M. and Stubblebine, W.C. (1962). "Externality," *Economica*, NS 29, November.

Buchanan, J.M. and Gordon Tullock (1962). *The Calculus of Consent*. Ann Arbor: University of Michigan Press.

Coase, R.H. (1960) "The problem of social cost." *Journal of Law and Economics*, 3: 1–44.

Downs, Anthony (1957). *An Economic Theory of Democracy*. New York: Harper.

Hume, David (1739). *A Treatise of Human Nature*. London: John Noon.

Olson, Mancur Jr. (1965). *The Logic of Collective Action*. Cambridge, MA: Harvard University Press.

Pigou, A.C. (4th edition 1932). *The Economics of Welfare*. London: Macmillan.

WHY GOVERNMENT SUCCEEDS

Government accomplishes some ambitious goals but fails miserably in meeting others. If government can send a man to the moon, why can it not eliminate poverty? If government can bomb the Taliban with deadly precision, why can it not control medical costs?

1. Special Interests

Most explanations for such differences focus on the explicitly political, highlighting two related themes:

(1) A policy succeeds only if government officials really want a program to attain its stated goals. Policy fails when the goals of politicians differ from those formally stated. The intent behind pork barrel projects, for example, may be to spend money in a legislative district, rather than to control floods or to protect the environment.

(2) Interest groups mold policy in ways that defeat the purpose of the program. Economic regulation is the classic example, but the deflection of goals by organized interests has also been claimed to undermine everything from social initiatives (Lowi, 1979) to economic growth (Olson, 1982).

This last idea has been extended in several ways. When voters are uncertain about who will lose and who will gain from a policy, a majority of voters may oppose a policy that, were it implemented, would benefit a majority (Fernandez and Rodrik, 1991; Glazer and Konrad, 1993). And even when voters unanimously prefer a policy over the status quo, the attempt by different groups to gain at the expense of others can lead them to delay adoption of the policy; such delay may be an effective way of showing that the benefits of the policy for that group are low and therefore that gaining its support requires giving it greater benefits (see Alesina and Drazen, 1991).

The influence of special interests is also a central element of the Transaction Costs explanation for government failure (Dixit, 1996, who views politics as constrained by asymmetric information and by limited commitment possibilities).

Implicit in these analyses is the belief that government could implement beneficial policies if politicians had the right incentives and if special interests were weaker.

2. Characteristics of Problems

But the features of the problems government addresses, and the innate characteristics of policy, may also explain some of the successes and failures. Some problems may be difficult to solve even for a government with the best intentions, because economic conditions and behavior create constraints which make policy ineffective in many areas.

Four elements appear to be prominent in explaining the success or failures of policies that are adopted (see Glazer and Rothenberg, 2001).

2.1. Credibility

Credibility requires officials to persuade others that government will follow through on the actions promised. Credibility will be especially important when the success of a policy requires government to induce firms and individuals to make costly, irreversible, investments. But an elected government can be thrown out of office and lacks many commitment methods (such as contracts enforceable by the courts) available to firms or consumers, making credibility problematic.

These constraints have been especially well studied in macroeconomics (for surveys see Persson, 1988; Persson and Tabellini, 1990; Cukierman, 1992; for a more political perspective, see Alesina and Rosenthal, 1995 and Keech, 1995). Dixit (1996) discusses the difficulty that government has in committing to future policies and the consequences of that difficulty. One way commitment problems are overcome is by an external agency: the IMF and the World Bank have played this role, although their motives and achievements are subject to controversy.

Sometimes public policies that are the least credible may be the most effective. For example, when future income is thought to be guaranteed, redistribution may be undermined by reduced work effort or savings by the beneficiaries. Redistributive policy may therefore be more effective if its continuance is in doubt.

2.2. Rational Expectations

Rational expectations refer to the collection of, and the sophisticated response to, information by decision makers. In general, policies readily anticipated and easily counteracted by economic agents are most likely to fail.

For example, rational consumers who foresee future taxes may increase savings if government increases its budget deficit, thereby negating the stumulative effects of fiscal policy (see Barro, 1989). Or rational workers who expect the central bank to stimulate the economy by expanding the money supply may anticipate inflation, demand higher wages, and thus negate the monetary stimulus. Similarly, offsetting behavior by consumers may negate the aims of regulations.

2.3. Crowding Out / Crowding In

Crowding out or, alternatively, crowding in, appears when the consumption or production of a good varies with the amount other firms or persons consume and produce. With crowding out, activity is reduced (e.g., when governmental subsidies to the arts, to medical research, or to universities, reduce private contributions). With crowding in, activity is increased (for instance, with fad behavior, where the participation by some in an activity makes it attractive to others). Depending upon whether the activity in question eases or obstructs the achievement of government goals, crowding out or crowding in may have different effects on what government can accomplish.

Regulation of personal behavior is especially constrained by crowding out. Consider the use of seatbelts in automobiles. The consensus is that offsetting behavior is substantial and that the increase in reckless driving has endangered pedestrians (Peltzman, 1975; Blomquist, 1988; Keeler, 1994). Similarly, some evidence suggests that air bags have reduced injuries less than hoped. The evidence, analogous to the findings for seat belts, shows that air bags cause more reckless driving (Peterson et al., 1995).

2.4. Multiple Equilibria

The idea of multiple equilibria refers to the theoretical and empirical possibility for different outcomes to be produced by the same circumstances. The important point is that on some issues government may determine which equilibrium is brought about. Thus, some government policy can be viewed as an attempt to nudge behavior towards a particular equilibrium. Though the existence of multiple equilibria does not guarantee the success of policy, it can provide opportunities for success, since government policy can induce a switch from chaos to a coordinated equilibrium, or from a bad to a good equilibrium.

Coordination problems are important instances where policy can be effective. Traffic laws (it is in my interest to stop at a red light because I expect the other drivers facing a green light to proceed), and daylight saving time are good examples of this.

But multiple equilibria are not limited to coordination problems. For example, policies aimed at reducing cigarette smoking appear to have been effective by inducing a shift from one equilibrium to another, where multiple equilibria can appear because an individual's propensity to smoke can vary with the number of other smokers.

2.5. Interaction of Features

The factors discussed above are inter-related. Often the beliefs of firms and consumers about what government will do, and the reactions of economic actors to the policies, are based on a rational analysis of what incentives or pressures government will face or what changes will occur (for example, through elections). Therefore, estimating the credibility of a policy often requires considering rational expectations of future policy. And to determine the effects of a credible policy it is also necessary to consider the behavior of economic actors in response to the policy, which can depend in part on what people expect the effects to be. Similarly, issues of crowding can be prominent, as when a change in the behavior of some people induces others to react in the same way (perhaps changing political pressures and expectations about policy along the way), thereby weakening or strengthening credibility. Under some, but not all, conditions

these updated expectations can reinforce the private behavior that government desires. Multiple equilibria can thus arise when one actor's behavior can affect the behavior of others, with the special characteristic that it allows a temporary policy to have permanent effects.

When the desired behavior by individuals or firms generates crowding in of that behavior, when people anticipate such crowding in, and when they believe that government is committed to pursuing the policy, they become yet more willing to engage in that behavior, thus making the policy self-sustaining. Crowding in may be sufficiently powerful to move the economy from one equilibrium to another, with individuals and firms continuing to behave in the manner that government desired even after government ends the policy. When some or all of these conditions are absent, a policy can be self-defeating, making success unlikely.

3. Example of Success

These features may explain the regulatory success in reducing chlorofluoro-carbon (CFC) production. The policies affected firms which produced inputs for firms in other industries and the actions of one set of firms undermined the ability of the other set of firms to hold out and violate regulatory standards.

Believing that the long-term prospects for the chemical's production were slim, manufacturers of products that used CFCs invested in technology to allow substitutes (Benedick, 1991). This undermined claims that firms using CFCs had no alternative. Given reduced demand for their product and an incentive to invest in goods that manufacturers wanted, CFC capacity and opposition to regulations also declined. Production of CFCs fell from about 1 million tons in 1986 to about 200,000 tons in 1995. Thus, one equilibrium may have had no investment in CFC substitutes and its continued production and use; the other equilibrium had investment in the production of less harmful chemicals and a drastic reduction in CFC use. The absence of vertical integration induced firms to invest, and allowed government to achieve its regulatory goals.

AMIHAI GLAZER

REFERENCES

Alesina, Alberto and Allan Drazen (1991). "Why are stabilizations delayed?" *American Economic Review*, 81(5): 1170–1189.

Alesina, Alberto and Howard Rosenthal (1995). *Partisan Politics, Divided Government, and the Economy*. Cambridge: Cambridge University Press.

Barro, Robert J. (1989). "The Ricardian approach to budget deficits." *Journal of Economic Perspectives*, 3: 37–54.

Benedick, Richard E. (1991). *Ozone Diplomacy: New Directions in Safeguarding the Planet*. Cambridge, MA: Harvard University Press.

Blomquist, Glenn C. (1988). *The Regulation of Motor Vehicle and Traffic Safety*. Boston, MA: Kluwer.

Cukierman, Alex (1992). *Central Bank Strategy, Credibility, and Independence: Theory and Evidence*. Cambridge, MA: MIT Press.

Dixit, Avinash (1996). *The Making of Economic Policy: A Transaction Cost Politics Perspective*. Cambridge, MA: MIT Press, 1996.

Fernandez, Raquel and Dani Rodrik (1991). "Resistance to reform: Status quo bias in the presence of individual-specific uncertainty." *American Economic Review*, 81(5): 1146–1155.

Glazer, Amihai and Kai Konrad (1993). "The evaluation of risky projects by voters." *Journal of Public Economics*, 52(3): 377–390.

Glazer, Amihai and Lawrence Rothenberg (2001). *Why Government Succeeds and Why it Fails*. Cambridge: Harvard University Press.

Keech, William R. (1995). *Economic Politics: The Costs of Democracy*. Cambridge: Cambridge University Press.

Keeler, Theodore E. (1994). "Highway safety, economic behavior, and driving environment." *American Economic Review*, 84: 684–693.

Lowi, Theodore J. (1979). *The End of Liberalism: The Second Republic of the United States*. Second edition. New York: W.W. Norton.

Olson, Mancur (1982). *The Rise and Decline of Nations: Economic Growth, Stagflation, and Social Rigidities*. New Haven: Yale University Press.

Peltzman, Sam (1975). "The effects of automobile safety regulation." *Journal of Political Economy*, 83: 677–725.

Persson, Torsten (1988). "Credibility of macroeconomic policy: An introduction and a broad survey." *European Economic Review*, 32: 519–532.

Persson, Torsten and Guido Tabellini (1990). *Macroeconomic Policy, Credibility, and Politics*. Chur: Harwood Academic Publishers.

Peterson, Steven, George Hoffer, and Edward Millner (1995). "Are drivers of air-bag-equipped cars more aggressive? A test of the offsetting behavior hypothesis." *Journal of Law and Economics*, 38: 251–264.

INDEX

Note: page numbers in **bold** type relate to individual articles